PRAISE FOR THE FIRST EDITIO

The *book on PowerShell, it has all the secrets.*

—James Truher, PowerShell I

If all it had going for it was the authoritative pedigree of the writer, it might be worth it, but it's also well-written, well-organized, and thorough, which I think makes it invaluable as both a learning tool and a reference.

—Slashdot.org

...an encyclopedic tome of PowerShell scripting bringing the reader through the basics with simple shell scripts through powerful and flexible scripts any Windows systems administrator will find immediately useful.

—ArsGeek.com

The nuances of PowerShell from the lead language designer himself! Excellent content and easy readability!

—Keith Hill, Software Architect

[It gives you] inside information, excellent examples, and a colorful writing style.

—Marc van Orsouw (MOW), PowerShell MVP

There's no better way to learn PowerShell than from someone on the core PowerShell team—and that's exactly what you get with this book.

—Joe Topjian, adminspotting.net

Where's the 6 stars option? I haven't enjoyed a software engineering book to the same extent for a long time.

—T. Kirby Green, Technical Architect, SunGard

Consider this book the definitive reference for PowerShell. As one of the designers of the PowerShell environment, the author knows all the ins and outs, back alleys, hidden rooms, and secret handshakes the language offers, and isn't afraid to grab you by the hand and drag you along (like it or not!) for the tour of your life.

—Jase T. Wolfe, Amazon reader

I love this book!

—Scott Hanselman ComputerZen.com

Windows PowerShell in Action, Second Edition

BRUCE PAYETTE

MANNING
Shelter Island

For online information and ordering of this and other Manning books, please visit www.manning.com. The publisher offers discounts on this book when ordered in quantity. For more information, please contact:

Special Sales Department
Manning Publications Co.
20 Baldwin Road
PO Box 261
Shelter Island, NY 11964
Email: orders@manning.com

Manning Publications Co.
20 Baldwin Road
PO Box 261
Shelter Island, NY 11964

Development Editor Cynthia Kane
Copyeditor: Liz Welch
Typesetter: Marija Tudor
Cover designer: Marija Tudor

ISBN 9781935182139
Printed in the United States of America
1 2 3 4 5 6 7 8 9 10 – MAL – 16 15 14 13 12 11

brief contents

contents

Part 2 Using PowerShell 661

16 Working with files, text, and XML 663

Appendixes are available for download from
www.manning.com/WindowsPowerShellinActionSecondEdition

preface

Well, it's been a wild ride since the first edition of this book was released. At that time, PowerShell had just shipped and had a fairly limited scope of influence. Things have changed a lot. PowerShell now ships in the box with Windows (at least Windows 7 and Server 2008 R2). The number of PowerShell users is now in the hundreds of thousands, if not millions (this is not a formal estimate—I just looked at some of the download counters for PowerShell-related tools and went from there).

One of the biggest events from my perspective was the release of PowerShell version 2 in July of 2009. Obviously it was time for a sequel to the book. I put together a short proposal and estimate of the amount of work needed to update the book. The initial estimate was for a few months of work—a couple of new chapters, a few updates here and there, and we're good to go. Wow, was I ever wrong about that! PowerShell v2 was a really big release.

When you are in the middle of something, working heads down, you tend to lose perspective of the overall project—that old forest/trees problem. It wasn't until I was preparing a talk for MMS (Microsoft Management Summit) that I realized just how BIG it was. In a one-hour talk, we barely had time to *list* all of the new stuff, much less describe it in detail. But describing it in detail was exactly what I needed to do and that's why this book took a great deal longer to write than anticipated. It's also much bigger than I had expected or wanted. At one point it was double the size of the first edition. So we cut some stuff that was no longer as relevant with PowerShell v2, moved some stuff into the online appendixes, and capped the book at about 1000 pages.

So why write the book in the first place? The answer is the same now as it was then—I wanted the PowerShell community to have a way to see "inside the box" and have a more intimate insight into the goals and motivations behind PowerShell. Although PowerShell draws heavily from existing technologies, it combines them in novel ways. This kind of novelty leads to misunderstandings which then turn into urban myths, like PowerShell does X because its designers were kitten-eating aliens. (Trust me—we're not.)

As we showed our work to the world I found that there were a number of questions that were being asked over and over again. These questions would usually arise as a result of some prior language experience that the user had. Typically a simple explanation was all it took to clear up the confusion. Unfortunately we couldn't keep answering these questions over and over on a one-by-one basis; that just couldn't scale. There needed to be a way to gather this information together in one place. The book was my attempt to address that problem, and the second edition continues on with this goal.

I continue to be amazed at just how much power comes out of the synergy of the various technologies underlying PowerShell. We see this in our own internal uses of PowerShell at Microsoft as well as in what the community has done with it. And so a second goal of this book was to try and foster that creativity by conveying just how capable PowerShell is.

And finally, this is the book I wanted to read. I love programming languages and the best books are the ones that explain not only *what* but also *why*. Look at the books that continue to sell year after year: Kernighan and Ritchie's *The C Programming Language,* Stroustrup's book on C++, and Ousterhout's book on TCL. The TCL book in particular describes a very early version of the TCL language, has never been updated, and yet it continues to sell. Why? Because these books give the reader something more than just technical detail. They convey a sense of the overall design and some element of the intent of the designer. (Let me know if I succeeded, okay?)

acknowledgments

First and foremost, this book is for my wife Tina. I could not have done it without her patience, support, and encouragement. She kept me fed and sane, and she even read early drafts of material about which she knows nothing. Now that's support! She also contributed the Gnome picture in chapter 21 and the bird-watching information and pictures in chapter 2. And I can now recognize the call of the California quail.

Thanks to my parents for their love and support over the years. Yes, I am finally done with the second edition!

Of course, there wouldn't be a PowerShell book without a PowerShell product in the first place and PowerShell wouldn't exist without the vision of its chief architect Jeffrey Snover. He was kind enough to do extensive reviews of both editions of the book. The book, like the product, has benefited greatly from his insight and suggestions.

PowerShell v2 would also not have been possible without the continued efforts on the part of Kenneth Hansen, lead Program Manager of the PowerShell team. Kenneth provided most of the day-to-day leadership during the Version 2/Windows 7 release cycle. He continues to be one of the strongest advocates for the customer that I've seen at Microsoft.

I'd like to thank the following PowerShell team members who took time to review specific chapters: Jason Shirk, who implemented most (all?) of the advanced function features in v2, reviewed chapters 7 and 8. Refaat Issa and Lucio Silveira, who were responsible for the design (Refaat) and implementation (Lucio) of the ISE, reviewed chapter 15 which covers the ISE.

To all of the MEAP readers and reviewers, many thanks for your feedback. I've incorporated as much of it as possible (boy, I make a lot of typos). In particular, I'd like to thank the following: Peter Johnson, Jonathan Medd, Sam Abraham, Andrew

Tearle, Keith Hill, Richard Siddaway, Paul Grebenc, Kirk Freiheit, Tony Niemann, Amos Bannister, Jeff Copeland, Marcus Baker, Massimo Perga, Tomas Restrepo, Jason Zions, Oisin Grehan, Kanwal Khipple, Brandon Shell, and Matthew Reynolds. Thanks to all of you for your patience. This book took way, way too long to complete.

Finally, special thanks to all of the people who piled on at the end of the project to finally get it done: Cynthia Kane, my development editor, who is still talking to me (I think), even after all of the missed deadlines; also Liz Welch, Mary Piergies, Tiffany Taylor, and everyone else at Manning who helped get this book out the door. All I can say is thanks, and thanks again.

And more super-special thanks to three of our wonderful PowerShell MVPs who helped enormously with the final reviews. Marco Shaw was the technical proofreader who read the chapters during production. Jeffrey Hicks, a fine author in his own right, helped with the last set of "author" reviews. And Aleksandar Nikolić went above and beyond the call, turning around reviewed chapters stunningly quickly, and then reviewing the reviews! Dude, you're a lifesaver!

about this book

Windows PowerShell is the next-generation scripting environment created by Microsoft. It's designed to provide a unified solution for Windows scripting and automation, able to access the wide range of technologies such as .NET, COM, and WMI through a single tool. Since its release in 2006, PowerShell has become the central component of any Windows management solution. In addition, due to PowerShell's comprehensive support for .NET, it also has broad application potential outside of the system administration space. PowerShell can be used for text processing, general scripting, build management, creating test frameworks, and so on.

This book was written by one of the principal creators of PowerShell to enable users to get the most out of the PowerShell environment. Using many examples, both small and large, this book illustrates the features of the language and environment and shows how to compose those features into solutions, quickly and effectively.

Note that, because of the broad scope of the PowerShell product, this book has a commensurately broad focus. It was not designed as a cookbook of pre-constructed management examples, like how to deal with Active Directory or how to script Exchange. Instead it provides information about the core of the PowerShell runtime and how to use it to compose solutions the "PowerShell Way." After reading this book, the PowerShell user should be able to take any example written in other languages like C# or Visual Basic and leverage those examples to build solutions in PowerShell.

Who should read this book?

This book is designed for anyone who wants to learn PowerShell and use it well. Rather than simply being a book of recipes to read and apply, this book tries to give the reader a deep knowledge about how PowerShell works and how to apply it. As a consequence, all users of PowerShell should read this book.

So, if you're a Windows sysadmin, this book is for you. If you're a developer and you need to get things done in a hurry, if you're interested in .NET, or just if you like to experiment with computers, PowerShell is for you and this book is for you.

Roadmap

The book is divided into two major parts plus four appendixes (which are available online from the publisher's website). The two parts of the book are "Learning PowerShell" and "Using PowerShell."

Part 1, "Learning PowerShell," is a comprehensive tour of the PowerShell language and runtime. The goal is to introduce new PowerShell users to the language as well as to provide experienced users with a deep insight into how and why things are the way they are.

In part 1, we look at all aspects of the PowerShell language including the syntax, the type system, and so on. Along the way we present examples showing how each feature works. Because the goal of the first part of the book is to focus on the individual features of the environment, most of the examples are quite small and are intended to be entered in an interactive session. The second part of this book focuses on larger examples that bring the individual features together to build larger applications.

Chapter 1 begins with some history and the rationale for why PowerShell was created in the first place. It then proceeds through a quick tour of the features of the environment. The remaining chapters in part 1 cover each element of the language, starting with basic PowerShell concepts in chapter 2.

Chapter 3 introduces the PowerShell type system and discusses its relationship to .NET. This chapter also presents the syntax for each of the PowerShell literal data types.

The discussion of operators and expressions (PowerShell has lots of these) begins in chapter 4 which covers the basic arithmetic, comparison, and assignment operators. It also covers the wildcard and regular expression pattern matching operators.

Chapter 5 continues the discussion of operators with the advanced operations for working with arrays (indexing, slicing) and objects (properties and methods). It also covers output redirection and the formatting operator, and introduces PowerShell variables.

Chapter 6 covers the PowerShell language constructs like `if` statements and loops.

Chapter 7 introduces programming in PowerShell and covers basic functions, variable scoping, and other programming-related topics.

Chapter 8 builds on the material in chapter 7, covering advanced function metadata, scripting, and how to create in-line documentation for scripts and functions.

Chapter 9 covers the basics of how to use PowerShell modules and how to create your own basic modules.

Chapter 10 looks at more advanced module features covering module manifests and how to use them to add information like a version number, dependences, and nested modules.

Chapter 11 builds on the material in chapters 7–10, introducing advanced programming techniques like object construction and extensions. It also covers first-class functions (scriptblocks) and shows how to extend the PowerShell language itself using these features.

Chapter 12 introduces PowerShell remoting, starting with basic configuration and setup. It then covers the various forms of remoting (interactive and non-interactive) and how to apply these techniques.

Chapter 13 explores remoting and the underlying protocols in more detail. Creation of custom remoting endpoints, including constrained endpoints, is included as well.

Chapter 14 covers the PowerShell Integrated Scripting Environment (ISE). This coverage includes basic editor operation and the debugger (graphics and command line), and looks briefly at the ISE extension model which allows you to do things like add custom menu items to the ISE.

Chapter 15 completes part 1, covering the various features available in PowerShell for handling errors and debugging scripts.

In part 2 of the book, "Using PowerShell," we shift our focus from individual features towards combining those features into larger examples. This part of the book looks at applying PowerShell in specific technology areas and problem domains.

We begin in chapter 16 looking at how PowerShell can be used to attack the kind of text processing tasks that have traditionally been the domain of languages like Perl. This chapter begins with basic string processing, then introduces file processing (including handling binary files), and finishes up with a section on working with XML documents.

Then, in chapter 17, we look at how we can explore and apply the vast capabilities of the .NET framework. We cover locating, exploring, and instantiating types in the .NET framework, including generic types. Then we look at a number of applications using these types, including network programming and graphical programming with WinForms and WPF.

In chapter 18 we look at how to work with COM objects. This includes using the application automation models to script applications like Microsoft Word with PowerShell.

Chapter 19 covers Windows Management Instrumentation (WMI) and Web Services for Management (WS-Man). We look at how to use WMI from the command line and in scripts to inspect, update, and manage a Windows system.

Chapter 20 looks at the asynchronous eventing subsystem in PowerShell. Eventing allows PowerShell scripts to respond to external events in real time—an important characteristic in systems automation.

Finally, in chapter 21, we introduce the security features in PowerShell along with a general discussion of security. This is a very important chapter to read. Like all powerful scripting tools (Perl, Python, and so on), PowerShell can be used to create malware-like virus and worm programs. The PowerShell runtime contains a number of features to allow you to deploy it in a manner that minimizes these risks.

In addition, there are four appendixes, available online from the publisher's website at www.manning.com/WindowsPowerShellinActionSecondEdition.

Appendix A compares and contrasts PowerShell with other languages that the reader may already know. This appendix tries to highlight similarities and the important differences with each of the languages.

Appendix B includes more examples showing how to apply PowerShell to solve problems. While it's by no means a complete management cookbook, it does show what can be done with PowerShell and how to do it.

Appendix C is a PowerShell quick reference that condenses much of the content of the book into a relatively short quick-reference document. Finally, appendix D contains information about a number of additional, less commonly used features and techniques in PowerShell.

Code conventions

Because PowerShell is an interactive environment, we show a lot of example commands as the user would type them, followed by the responses the system generates. Before the command text there is a prompt string that looks like this: `PS (2) >`. Following the prompt, the actual command is displayed. PowerShell's responses follow on the next few lines. Because PowerShell doesn't display anything in front of the output lines, you can distinguish output from commands by looking for the prompt string. These conventions are illustrated as follows:

```
PS (1) > get-date

Sunday, October 08, 2006 11:24:42 PM
```

Sometimes commands will span multiple lines. In this case subsequent lines of user input will be preceded by >> as shown:

```
PS (2) > 1..3 |
>> foreach {"+" * $_}
>>
+
++
+++
PS (4) >
```

Note that the actual prompt sequence you see in your PowerShell session will be somewhat different than what is shown in the book. The prompt display is user-controllable by redefining the "prompt" function (see appendix A section 1.8 for more information). For this book, a prompt sequence was chosen that includes command numbers to make it easier to follow the examples.

Code annotations accompany many of the listings, highlighting important concepts. In some cases, numbered bullets link to explanations that follow the listing.

Source code downloads

Source code for all working examples in this book is available for download from the publisher's website at www.manning.com/WindowsPowerShellinActionSecondEdition.

Author Online

Purchase of *Windows PowerShell in Action, Second Edition* includes free access to a private web forum run by Manning Publications where you can make comments about the book, ask technical questions, and receive help from the author and from other users. To access the forum and subscribe to it, point your web browser to www.manning.com/WindowsPowerShellinAction SecondEdition. This page provides information on how to get on the forum once you are registered, what kind of help is available, and the rules of conduct on the forum.

Manning's commitment to our readers is to provide a venue where a meaningful dialog between individual readers and between readers and the author can take place. It is not a commitment to any specific amount of participation on the part of the author, whose contribution to the AO remains voluntary (and unpaid). We suggest you try asking the author some challenging questions lest his interest stray!

The Author Online forum and the archives of previous discussions will be accessible from the publisher's website as long as the book is in print.

About the author

Bruce Payette is one of the founding members of the Windows PowerShell team. He is co-designer of the PowerShell language along with Jim Truher and the principal author of the language implementation. He joined Microsoft in 2001 working on Interix, the POSIX subsystem for Windows, then moved to help found the PowerShell project shortly after that. Prior to joining Microsoft, he worked at various companies including Softway (the creators of Interix) and MKS (producers of the MKS Toolkit) building UNIX tools for Windows. He lives in Bellevue, Washington, with his wife, many computers, and two extremely over-bonded codependent cats.

About the title

By combining introductions, overviews, and how-to examples, the *In Action* books are designed to help learning and remembering. According to research in cognitive science, the things people remember are things they discover during self-motivated exploration.

Although no one at Manning is a cognitive scientist, we are convinced that for learning to become permanent it must pass through stages of exploration, play, and, interestingly, retelling of what is being learned. People understand and remember new things, which is to say they master them, only after actively exploring them. Humans learn in action. An essential part of an *In Action* book is that it is example driven. It encourages the reader to try things out, to play with new code, and explore new ideas.

There is another, more mundane, reason for the title of this book: our readers are busy. They use books to do a job or solve a problem. They need books that allow them to jump in and jump out easily and learn just what they want just when they want it. They need books that aid them in action. The books in this series are designed for such readers.

about the cover illustration

The figure on the cover of *Windows PowerShell in Action, Second Edition* is a "Mufti," the chief of religion or the chief scholar who interpreted the religious law and whose pronouncements on matters both large and small were binding to the faithful. The illustration is taken from a collection of costumes of the Ottoman Empire published on January 1, 1802, by William Miller of Old Bond Street, London. The title page is missing from the collection and we have been unable to track it down to date. The book's table of contents identifies the figures in both English and French, and each illustration bears the names of two artists who worked on it, both of whom would no doubt be surprised to find their art gracing the front cover of a computer programming book...two hundred years later.

The collection was purchased by a Manning editor at an antiquarian flea market in the "Garage" on West 26th Street in Manhattan. The seller was an American based in Ankara, Turkey, and the transaction took place just as he was packing up his stand for the day. The Manning editor did not have on his person the substantial amount of cash that was required for the purchase and a credit card and check were both politely turned down. With the seller flying back to Ankara that evening the situation was getting hopeless. What was the solution? It turned out to be nothing more than an old-fashioned verbal agreement sealed with a handshake. The seller simply proposed that the money be transferred to him by wire and the editor walked out with the bank information on a piece of paper and the portfolio of images under his arm. Needless to say, we transferred the funds the next day, and we remain grateful and impressed by this unknown person's trust in one of us. It recalls something that might have happened a long time ago.

The pictures from the Ottoman collection, like the other illustrations that appear on our covers, bring to life the richness and variety of dress customs of two centuries ago. They recall the sense of isolation and distance of that period—and of every other historic period except our own hyperkinetic present.

Dress codes have changed since then and the diversity by region, so rich at the time, has faded away. It is now often hard to tell the inhabitant of one continent from another. Perhaps, trying to view it optimistically, we have traded a cultural and visual diversity for a more varied personal life. Or a more varied and interesting intellectual and technical life.

We at Manning celebrate the inventiveness, the initiative, and, yes, the fun of the computer business with book covers based on the rich diversity of regional life of two centuries ago—brought back to life by the pictures from this collection.

PART 1

Learning PowerShell

The first part of this book focuses primarily on the PowerShell language and its runtime environment. We'll cover the complete syntax for PowerShell in detail: the various kinds of conditional and loop statements, the operators, and the syntax for defining functions and modules. We'll look at how to configure and use PowerShell remoting to do remote access.

CHAPTER 1

Welcome to PowerShell

Space is big. Really big! You just won't believe how vastly hugely mind-bogglingly big it is. I mean you may think it's a long way down the road to the chemist, but that's just peanuts compared to space!

Don't Panic.

—Douglas Adams, *The Hitchhiker's Guide to the Galaxy*

Welcome to Windows PowerShell, the new command and scripting language from Microsoft. We begin this chapter with two quotes from *The Hitchhiker's Guide to the Galaxy.* What do they have to do with a new scripting language? In essence, where a program solves a particular problem or problems, a programming language can solve any problem, at least in theory. That's the "big, really big" part. The "Don't Panic" bit is, well—don't panic. Although PowerShell is new and different, it's been designed to leverage what you already know, making it easy to learn. It's also designed to allow you to learn it a bit at a time. Starting at the beginning, here's the traditional "Hello world" program in PowerShell:

```
"Hello world."
```

As you can see, no panic needed. But "Hello world" by itself isn't very interesting. Here's something a bit more complicated:

```
dir $env:windir\*.log | Select-String -List error |
Format-Table path,linenumber -AutoSize
```

Although this is more complex, you can probably still figure out what it does. It searches all the log files in the Windows directory, looking for the string "error", and then prints the full name of the matching file and the matching line number. "Useful, but not very special," you might think, because you can easily do this using `cmd.exe` on Windows or bash on UNIX. So what about the "big, really big" thing? Well, how about this example?

```
([xml](New-Object net.webclient).DownloadString(
"http://blogs.msdn.com/powershell/rss.aspx"
)).rss.channel.item | Format-Table title,link
```

Now we're getting somewhere. This script downloads the RSS feed from the PowerShell team blog and then displays the title and a link for each blog entry.

> **NOTE** RSS stands for Really Simple Syndication. This is a mechanism that allows programs to download blogs automatically so they can be read more conveniently than in the browser.

By the way, you weren't expected to figure out this example yet. If you did, you can move to the head of the class!

Finally, one last example:

```
[void][reflection.assembly]::LoadWithPartialName(
    "System.Windows.Forms")
$form = New-Object Windows.Forms.Form
$form.Text = "My First Form"
$button = New-Object Windows.Forms.Button
$button.text="Push Me!"
$button.Dock="fill"
$button.add_click({$form.close()})
$form.controls.add($button)
$form.Add_Shown({$form.Activate()})
$form.ShowDialog()
```

This script uses the Windows Forms library (WinForms) to build a graphical user interface (GUI) that has a single button displaying the text "Push Me!" The window this script creates is shown in figure 1.1.

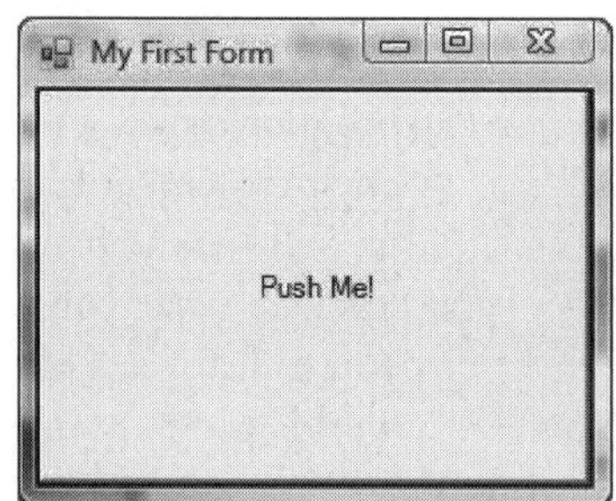

Figure 1.1 When you run the code from the example, this window will be displayed. If you don't see it, it may be hidden behind another window.

When you click the button, it closes the form and exits the script. With this you go from `"Hello world"` to a GUI application in less than two pages.

Now let's come back down to Earth for a minute. The intent of chapter 1 is to set the stage for understanding PowerShell—what it is, what it isn't, and, almost as important, why the PowerShell team made the decisions they made in designing the PowerShell language. Chapter 1 covers the goals of the project, along with some of the major issues the team faced in trying to achieve those goals. By the end of the chapter you should have a solid base from which to start learning and using PowerShell to solve real-world problems. All theory and no practice is boring, so the chapter concludes with a number of small examples to give you a feel for PowerShell. But first, a philosophical digression: while under development, from 2002 until just before the first public release in 2006, the codename for this project was Monad. The name Monad comes from *The Monadology* by Gottfried Wilhelm Leibniz, one of the inventors of calculus. Here's how Leibniz defined the Monad:

> *The Monad, of which we shall here speak, is nothing but a simple substance, which enters into compounds. By "simple" is meant "without parts."*
>
> —From *The Monadology* by Gottfried Wilhelm Leibniz (translated by Robert Latta)

In *The Monadology*, Leibniz described a world of irreducible components from which all things could be composed. This captures the spirit of the project: to create a toolkit of simple pieces that you compose to create complex solutions.

1.1 WHAT IS POWERSHELL?

What is PowerShell, and why was it created? PowerShell is the new command-line/scripting environment from Microsoft. The overall goal for this project was to provide the best shell scripting environment possible for Microsoft Windows. This statement has two parts, and they're equally important, because the goal wasn't just to produce a good generic shell environment but rather to produce one designed specifically for the Windows environment. Although drawing heavily from existing command-line shell and scripting languages, the PowerShell language and runtime were designed from scratch to be an optimal environment for the modern Windows operating system.

Historically, the Windows command line has been weak. This is mainly the result of Microsoft's early focus on computing for the average user, who is considered neither particularly technical nor particularly interested in computers. Most of the development effort for Windows was put into improving the graphical environment for the nontechnical user, rather than creating an environment for the computer professional. Although this was certainly an enormously successful commercial strategy for Microsoft, it has left some segments of the community underserved.

In the next couple of sections, I'll go over some of the other environmental forces that led to the creation of PowerShell. By *environmental forces*, I mean the various business pressures and practical requirements that needed to be satisfied. But first let's refine our definitions of shell and scripting.

1.1.1 Shells, command lines, and scripting languages

In the previous section, I called PowerShell a command-line shell. You may be asking, what's a shell? And how is that different from a command interpreter? What about scripting languages? If you can script in a shell language, doesn't that make it a scripting language? In answering these questions, let's start with shells.

Defining what a shell is can be a bit tricky, especially at Microsoft, because pretty much everything at Microsoft has something called a *shell.* Windows Explorer is a shell. Visual Studio has a component called the shell. Heck, even the Xbox has something they call a shell.

Historically, the term *shell* describes the piece of software that sits over an operating system's core functionality. This core functionality is known as the *operating system kernel* (shell...kernel...get it?). A shell is the piece of software that lets you access the functionality provided by the operating system. Windows Explorer is properly called a shell because it lets you access the functionality of a Windows system. For our purposes, though, we're more interested in the traditional text-based environment where the user types a command and receives a response. In other words, a shell is a command-line interpreter. The two terms can be used for the most part interchangeably.

Scripting languages vs. shells

If this is the case, then what is scripting and why are scripting languages not shells? To some extent, there's no difference. Many scripting languages have a mode in which they take commands from the user and then execute those commands to return results. This mode of operation is called a *Read-Evaluate-Print loop*, or REPL. Not all scripting languages have these interactive loops, but many do. In what way is a scripting language with a Read-Evaluate-Print loop not a shell? The difference is mainly in the user experience. A proper command-line shell is also a proper user interface. As such, a command line has to provide a number of features to make the user's experience pleasant and customizable. The features that improve the user's experience include aliases (shortcuts for hard-to-type commands), wildcard matching so you don't have to type out full names, and the ability to start other programs without having to do anything special such as calling a function to start the program. Finally, command-line shells provide mechanisms for examining, editing, and re-executing previously typed commands. These mechanisms are called *command history.*

If scripting languages can be shells, can shells be scripting languages? The answer is, emphatically, yes. With each generation, the UNIX shell languages have grown increasingly powerful. It's entirely possible to write substantial applications in a modern shell language, such as bash or zsh. Scripting languages characteristically have an advantage over shell languages, in that they provide mechanisms to help you develop larger scripts by letting you break a script into components, or *modules*. Scripting languages typically provide more sophisticated features for debugging your scripts. Next, scripting language runtimes are implemented in a way that makes their code execution more efficient, so that scripts written in these languages execute more quickly than they would in the corresponding shell script runtime. Finally, scripting language syntax is oriented more toward writing an application than toward interactively issuing commands.

In the end, there's no hard-and-fast distinction between a shell language and a scripting language. Some of the features that make a good scripting language result in a poor shell user experience. Conversely, some of the features that make for a good interactive shell experience can interfere with scripting. Because PowerShell's goal is to be both a good scripting language and a good interactive shell, balancing the tradeoffs between user experience and scripting authoring was one of the major language design challenges.

1.1.2 Why a new shell? Why now?

In the early 2000s, Microsoft commissioned a study to identify areas where it could improve its offerings in the server space. Server management, and particularly command-line management of Windows systems, was called out as a critical area for improvement. Some might say that this is like discovering that water is wet, but the important point is that people cared about the problem. When the survey team compared the command-line manageability of a Windows system to a UNIX system, Windows was found to be limited, and this was a genuine pain point with customers.

There are a couple of reasons for the historically weak Windows command line. First, as mentioned previously, limited effort had been put into improving the command line. The average desktop user doesn't care about the command line, so it wasn't considered important. Second, when writing GUIs, you need to access whatever you're managing through programmer-style interfaces called *application programming interfaces* (APIs). APIs are almost universally binary (especially on Windows), and binary interfaces aren't command-line friendly.

Managing Windows through objects

Another factor that drove the need for a new shell model is that, as Windows acquired more and more subsystems and features, the number of issues we had to think about when managing a system increased dramatically. To help us deal with this increase in complexity, the manageable elements were factored into structured data objects. This collection of *management objects* is known internally at Microsoft as the *Windows management surface*.

> **NOTE** Microsoft wasn't the only company that was running into issues due to increased complexity. Pretty much everyone in the industry was

having this problem. This led to the Distributed Management Task Force (dmtf.org), an industry organization, creating a standard for management objects called the Common Information Model (CIM). Microsoft's implementation of this standard is called the *Windows Management Instrumentation* (WMI). Chapter 19 covers PowerShell's support for WMI.

Although this factoring addressed overall complexity and worked well for graphical interfaces, it made it much harder to work with using a traditional text-based shell environment.

Finally, as the power of the PC increased, Windows began to move off the desktop and into the corporate datacenter. In the corporate datacenter, we had a large number of servers to manage, and the graphical point-and-click management approach that worked well for one machine didn't scale. All these elements combined to make it clear that Microsoft could no longer ignore the command line.

1.1.3 The last mile problem

Why should you care about command-line management and automation? Because it helps to solve the IT professional's version of the *last mile problem*. The last mile problem is a classical problem that comes from the telecommunications industry. It goes like this: The telecom industry can effectively amortize its infrastructure costs across all its customers until it gets to the last mile, where the service is finally run to an individual location. Installing service across this last mile can't be amortized because it serves only a single location. Also, what's involved in servicing any particular location can vary significantly. Servicing a rural farmhouse is different and significantly more expensive than running service to a house on a city street.

In the IT industry, the last mile problem is figuring out how to manage each IT installation effectively and economically. Even a small IT environment has a wide variety of equipment and applications. One approach to solving this is through consulting: IT vendors provide consultants who build custom last mile solutions for each end user. This, of course, has problems with recurring costs and scalability (it's great for the vendor, though). A better solution for end users is to empower them to solve their own last mile problems. We do this by providing a toolkit to enable end users to build their own custom solutions. This toolkit can't merely be the same tools used to build the overall infrastructure—the level of detail required is too great. Instead, we need a set of tools with a higher level of abstraction. This is where PowerShell comes in—its higher-level abstractions allow us to connect the various bits of your IT environment together more quickly and with less effort.

Now that you grasp the environmental forces that led to the creation of PowerShell—the need for command-line automation in a distributed object-based operating environment—let's look at the form the solution took.

1.2 SOUL OF A NEW LANGUAGE

The title of this section was adapted from Tracey Kidder's *Soul of a New Machine*, one of the best nontechnical technical books ever written. Kidder's book described how Data General developed a new 32-bit minicomputer, the Eclipse, in a single year. At that time, 32-bit minicomputers weren't just new computers; they represented a whole new class of computers. It was a bold, ambitious project; many considered it crazy. Likewise, the PowerShell project wasn't just about creating a new shell language. It required developing a new class of object-based shell languages—and we were told more than a few times that we were crazy.

In this section, I'll cover some of the technological forces that shaped the development of PowerShell.

1.2.1 Learning from history

In section 1.1.2, I described why Microsoft needed to improve the command line. Now let's talk about how the company decided to improve it. In particular, let's talk about why Microsoft created a new language. This is certainly one of the most common questions people ask about PowerShell (right after "What, are you guys nuts?"). People ask, "Why not just use one of the UNIX shells?" or "Why not extend the existing Windows command line?"

In practice, the team did start with an existing shell language. The original PowerShell grammar was based on the shell grammar for the POSIX standard shell defined in IEEE Specification 1003.2. The POSIX shell is a mature command-line environment available on a huge variety of platforms, including Microsoft Windows. It's based on a subset of the UNIX Korn shell, which is itself a superset of the original Bourne shell. Starting with the POSIX shell gave Microsoft a well-specified and stable base. Then we had to consider how to accommodate the differences that properly supporting the Windows environment would entail. The PowerShell team wanted to have a shell optimized for the Windows environment in the same way that the UNIX shells are optimized for this UNIX environment.

To begin with, traditional shells deal only with strings. Even numeric operations work by turning a string into a number, performing the operation, and then turning it back into a string. Given that a core goal for PowerShell was to preserve the structure of the Windows data types, the PowerShell team couldn't simply use the POSIX shell language as is. This factor impacted the language design more than any other. Next, the team wanted to support a more conventional scripting experience where, for example, expressions could be used as you'd normally use them in a scripting language such as VBScript, Perl, or Python. With a more natural expression syntax, it would be easier to work with the Windows management objects. Now the team just had to decide how to make those objects available to the shell.

1.2.2 Leveraging .NET

One of the biggest challenges in developing any computer language is deciding how to represent data in that language. For PowerShell, the key decision was to leverage the .NET object model. .NET is a unifying object representation that's being used across all the groups at Microsoft. It was a hugely ambitious project that took years to come to fruition. With this common data model, all the components in Windows can share and understand each other's data.

One of .NET's most interesting features for PowerShell is that the .NET object model is *self-describing*. By this, I mean that the object itself contains the information that describes the object's structure. This is important for an interactive environment, as you need to be able to look at an object and see what you can do with it. For example, if PowerShell receives an event object from the system event log, the user can inspect the object to see that it has a data stamp indicating when the event was generated.

Traditional text-based shells facilitate inspection because everything is text. Text is great—what you see is what you get. Unfortunately, what you see is *all* you get. You can't pull off many interesting tricks with text until you turn it into something else. For example, if you want to find out the total size of a set of files, you can get a directory listing, which looks something like the following:

```
02/26/2004  10:58 PM              45,452 Q810833.log
02/26/2004  10:59 PM              47,808 Q811493.log
02/26/2004  10:59 PM              48,256 Q811630.log
02/26/2004  11:00 PM              50,681 Q814033.log
```

You can see where the file size is in this text, but it isn't useful as is. You have to extract the sequence of characters starting at column 32 (or is it 33?) until column 39, remove the comma, and then turn those characters into numbers. Even removing the comma might be tricky, because the thousands separator can change depending on the current cultural settings on the computer. In other words, it may not be a comma—it may be a period. Or it may not be present at all.

It would be easier if you could just ask for the size of the files as a number in the first place. This is what .NET brings to PowerShell: self-describing data that can be easily inspected and manipulated without having to convert it to text until you need to.

Choosing to use the .NET object model also brings an additional benefit in that it allows PowerShell to directly use the extensive libraries that are part of the .NET Framework. This brings to PowerShell a breadth of coverage rarely found in a new language. Here's a simple example that shows the kinds of things .NET brings to the environment. Say you want to find out what day of the week December 13, 1974 was. You can do this in PowerShell as follows:

```
PS (1) > (Get-Date "December 13, 1974").DayOfWeek
Friday
```

In this example, the `Get-Date` command returns a .NET object, which has a property that will calculate the day of the week corresponding to that date. The PowerShell team didn't need to create a library of date and time manipulation routines for PowerShell—they got them for free by building on top of .NET. And the same `DateTime` objects are used throughout the system. For example, say you want to find out which of two files is newer. In a text-based shell, you'd have to get a string that contains the time each file was updated, convert those strings into numbers somehow, and then compare them. In PowerShell, you can simply do this:

```
PS (6) > (dir data.txt).lastwritetime -gt
>> (dir hello.ps1).lastwritetime
>>
True
```

You use the `dir` command to get the file information objects and then compare the last write time of each file. No string parsing is needed.

Now that you're sold on the wonders of objects and .NET, let's make sure we're all talking about the same thing when we use words like *object*, *member*, *method*, and *instance*. The next section discusses the basics of object-oriented programming.

1.3 BRUSHING UP ON OBJECTS

Because the PowerShell environment uses objects in almost everything it does, it's worth running through a quick refresher on objects and how they're used in programming. If you're comfortable with this material, feel free to skip most of this section, but do please read the section on objects and PowerShell.

There's no shortage of "learned debate" (also known as *bitter feuding*) about what objects are and what object-oriented programming is all about. For our purposes, we'll use the simplest definition. An *object* is a unit that contains both data (properties) and the information on how to use that data (methods). Let's look at a simple example. In this example, you're going to model a lightbulb as an object. This object would contain data describing its state—whether it's off or on. It would also contain the mechanisms or methods needed to change the on/off state. Non-object-oriented approaches to programming typically put the data in one place, perhaps a table of numbers where 0 is off and 1 is on, and then provide a separate library of routines to change this state. To change its state, the programmer would have to tell these routines where the value representing a particular `light bulb` was. This process could be complicated and is certainly error prone. With objects, because both the data and the methods are packaged as a whole, the user can work with objects in a more direct and therefore simpler manner, allowing many errors to be avoided.

1.3.1 Reviewing object-oriented programming

That's the basics of what objects are. Now, what's object-oriented programming? Well, it deals mainly with how you build objects. Where do the data elements come from? Where do the behaviors come from? Most object systems determine the object's capabilities through its type. In the lightbulb example, the type of the object is (surprise) `LightBulb`. The type of the object determines what properties the object has (for example, `IsOn`) and what methods it has (for example, `TurnOn` and `TurnOff`).

Essentially, an object's type is the blueprint for what an object looks like and how you use it. The type `LightBulb` would say that it has one data element—`IsOn`—and two methods—`TurnOn()` and `TurnOff()`. Types are frequently further divided into two subsets:

- Types that have an actual implementation of `TurnOn()` and `TurnOff()`. These are typically called *classes*.
- Types that only describe what the members of the type should look like but not how they work. These are called *interfaces*.

The pattern `IsOn/TurnOn()/TurnOff()` could be an interface implemented by a variety of classes such as `LightBulb`, `KitchenSinkTap`, or `Television`. All these objects have the same basic pattern for being turned on and off. From a programmer's perspective, if they all have the same interface (that is, the same mechanism for being turned on and off), once you know how to turn one of these objects on or off, you can use any type of object that has that interface.

Types are typically arranged in hierarchies with the idea that they should reflect logical taxonomies of objects. This taxonomy is made up of classes and subclasses. A sample taxonomy is shown in figure 1.2.

In this taxonomy, `Book` is the parent class, `Fiction` and `Non-fiction` are subclasses of `Book`, and so on. Although taxonomies organize data effectively, designing a good taxonomy is hard. Frequently, the best arrangement isn't immediately obvious. In figure 1.2, it might be better to organize by subject matter first, instead of the Novel/Short-Story Collection grouping. In the scientific world, people spend entire careers categorizing items. Because categorizing well isn't easy, people also arrange instances of objects into collections by containment instead of by type. A library contains books, but it isn't itself a book. A library also contains other things that aren't books, such as chairs and tables. If at some point you decide to re-categorize all of the books in a library, it doesn't affect what building people visit to get a book—it only

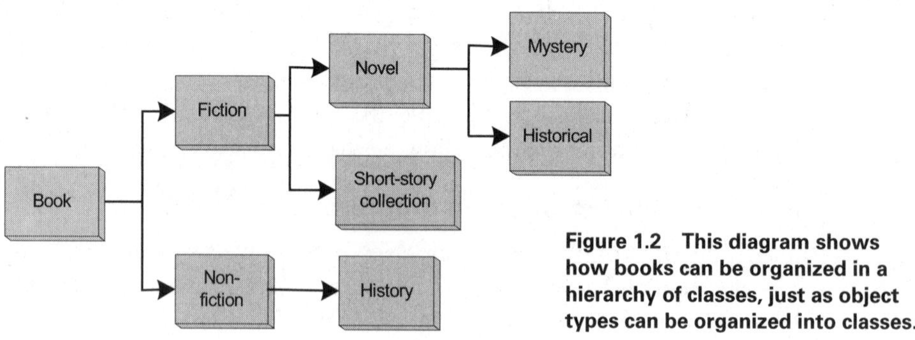

Figure 1.2 This diagram shows how books can be organized in a hierarchy of classes, just as object types can be organized into classes.

changes how you find a book once you reach that building. If the library moves to a new location, you have to learn where it is. Once inside the building, however, your method for looking up books hasn't changed. This is usually called a *has-a* relationship—a library *has-a* bunch of books. Now let's see how these concepts are used in the PowerShell environment.

1.3.2 Objects in PowerShell

Earlier I said that PowerShell is an object-based shell as opposed to an object-oriented language. What do I mean by object-based? In object-based scripting, you typically use objects somebody else has already defined for you. Although it's possible to build your own objects in PowerShell, it isn't something that you need to worry about—at least not for most basic PowerShell tasks.

Returning to the light bulb example, PowerShell would probably use the `LightBulb` class like this:

```
$lb = Get-LightBulb -Room bedroom
$lb.TurnOff()
```

Don't worry about the details of the syntax for now—we'll cover that later. The key point is that you usually get an object `foo` by saying

```
Get-Foo -Option1 -Option2 bar
```

rather than saying something like

```
new Foo()
```

as you would in an object-oriented language.

PowerShell commands, called *cmdlets*, use *verb-noun* pairs like `Get-Date`. The `Get-*` verb is used universally in the system to get at objects. Note that we didn't have to worry about whether `LightBulb` is a class or an interface, or care about where in the object hierarchy it comes from. You can get all the information about the member properties of an object through the `Get-Member` cmdlet (see the pattern?), which will tell you all about an object's properties.

But enough talk! By far the best way to understand PowerShell is to use it. In the next section, you'll get up and going with PowerShell, and we'll quickly tour through the basics of the environment.

1.4 Up and running with PowerShell

In this section, we'll look at the things you need to know to get going with PowerShell as quickly as possible. This is a brief introduction intended to provide a taste of what PowerShell can do and how it works. We'll begin with how to download and install PowerShell and how to start it once it's installed. Then we'll cover the basic format of commands, command-line editing, and how to use command completion with the Tab key to speed up command entry. Once you're up and running, you'll learn what you can do with PowerShell.

NOTE The PowerShell documentation package also includes a short Getting Started guide that will include up-to-date installation information and instructions. You may want to take a look at this as well.

1.4.1 PowerShell

How you get PowerShell depends on what operating system you're using. If you're using Windows 7 or Windows Server 2008 R2, you have nothing to do—it's already there. All Microsoft operating systems beginning with Windows 7 include PowerShell as part of the system. If you're using Windows Server 2008, PowerShell was included with this operating system but as an optional component that will need to be turned on before you can use it. For earlier Microsoft operating systems, you'll have to download and install the PowerShell package on your computer. For details about supported platforms, go to the PowerShell page on the Microsoft website: http://microsoft.com/powershell.

This page contains links to the appropriate installers as well as documentation packages and other relevant materials. Alternatively, you can go to Microsoft Update and search for the installer there. Once you've located the installer, follow the instructions to install the package.

1.4.2 Starting PowerShell

Now let's look at how you start PowerShell running. PowerShell follows a model found in many modern interactive environments. It's composed of two main parts:

- The PowerShell engine, which interprets the commands
- A host application that passes commands from the user to the engine

Although there's only one PowerShell engine, there can be many hosts, including hosts written by third parties. In PowerShell v1, Microsoft provided only one basic PowerShell host based on the old-fashioned Windows console. Version 2 introduced a much more modern host environment, called the PowerShell Integrated Scripting Environment (PowerShell ISE). We'll look at both of these hosts in the next few sections.

1.4.3 The PowerShell console host

To start an interactive PowerShell session using the console host, choose Start > All Programs > Accessories > Windows PowerShell > Windows PowerShell. PowerShell will start, and you'll see a screen like the one shown in figure 1.3.

This window looks a lot like the old Windows command window (except that it's blue and very pale yellow instead of black and white). Now type the first command most people type: `dir`. This produces a listing of the files on your system, as shown in figure 1.4.

Figure 1.3 When you start an interactive PowerShell session, the first thing you see is the PowerShell logo and then the prompt. As soon as you see the prompt, you can begin entering commands.

As you'd expect, the `dir` command prints a listing of the current directory to standard output.

> **NOTE** Let's stop for a second and talk about the conventions we're going to use in examples. Because PowerShell is an interactive environment, we'll show a lot of example commands as the user would type them, followed by the responses the system generates. Code font is used to distinguish examples from the rest of the text. Before the command text, there will be a prompt string that looks like `PS (2) >`. Following the prompt, the actual command will be displayed and then PowerShell's responses will follow on the next few lines. PowerShell doesn't display anything in front of the output lines, so you can distinguish output from commands by looking for the prompt string. These conventions are illustrated in figure 1.5.

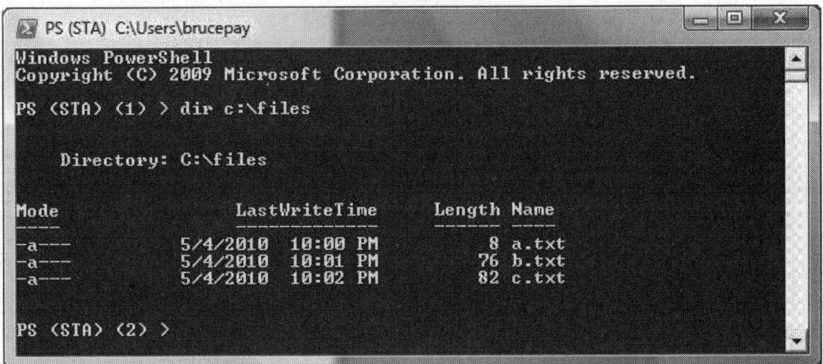

Figure 1.4 At the prompt, type `dir` and press Enter. PowerShell will then execute the `dir` command and display a list of files in the current directory.

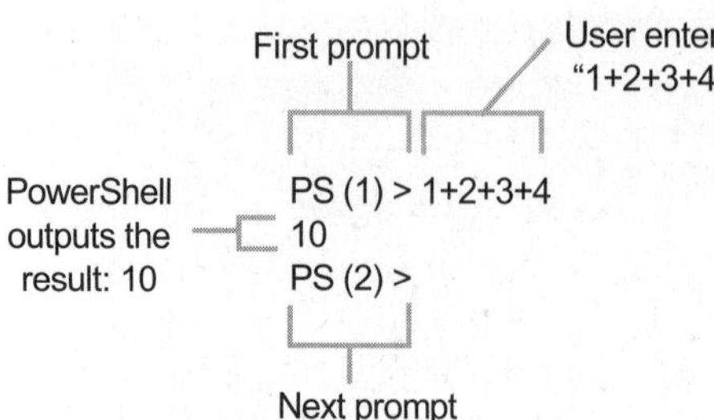

Figure 1.5 This diagram illustrates the conventions we're using for showing examples in this book. The code that the user enters appears to the right of the prompt. Any output generated by that command is shown on the following lines.

Command editing in the console

Typing in commands is all well and good, but you also want to be able to edit and rerun commands. Command-line editing works the same way in the PowerShell console window as it does for `cmd.exe`. The available editing features and keystrokes are listed in table 1.1.

Table 1.1 Command editing features

Keyboard sequence	Editing operation
Left/right arrows	Moves the editing cursor left and right through the current command line.
Ctrl-left arrow, Ctrl-right arrow	Holding the Ctrl key down while pressing the left and right arrow keys moves the editing cursor through the current command line one word at a time, instead of one character at a time.
Home	Moves the editing cursor to the beginning of the current command line.
End	Moves the editing cursor to the end of the current command line.
Up/down arrow	Moves up and down through the command history.
Insert key	Toggles between character insert and character overwrite modes.
Delete key	Deletes the character under the cursor.
Backspace key	Deletes the character to the left of the cursor.

These key sequences let you create and edit commands effectively at the command line. In fact, they're not part of PowerShell at all. These command-line editing features are part of the Windows console subsystem, so they're the same across all console applications.

Users of `cmd.exe` or any modern UNIX shell will also expect to be able to do command completion. Because this component is common to both host environments, we'll cover how it works in its own section.

Now let's leap into the 21st century and look at a modern shell environment: the PowerShell ISE.

1.4.4 The PowerShell Integrated Scripting Environment

Starting with v2, PowerShell includes a modern integrated environment for working with PowerShell: the Integrated Scripting Environment (ISE). To start the PowerShell ISE, choose Start > All Programs > Accessories > Windows PowerShell > Windows PowerShellISE. PowerShell will start, and you'll see a screen like that shown in figure 1.6.

You can see that, by default, the window is divided into three parts: the command entry area at the bottom, the output window in the middle, and an editor at the top. As you did in the console window, let's run the `dir` command. Type `dir` into the bottom pane, and press Enter. The command will disappear from the bottom pane and reappear in the middle pane, followed by the output of the command, as shown in figure 1.7.

Because the ISE is a real Windows application, it follows all of the Windows Common User Access (CUA) guidelines. The left and right arrows work as expected. The up and down arrows will move you through the history of commands that you've entered.

Something that requires special mention is how Ctrl-C works. By default, this is the key sequence for copying into the clipboard in Windows. It's also the way to interrupt a running command in most shells. As a result, the ISE has to treat Ctrl-C in a special way. When something is selected, Ctrl-C copies the selection. If there's a command running and there's no selection, then the running command will be interrupted.

There's also another way to interrupt a running command. You may have noticed the two buttons immediately above the command entry pane—the ones that look

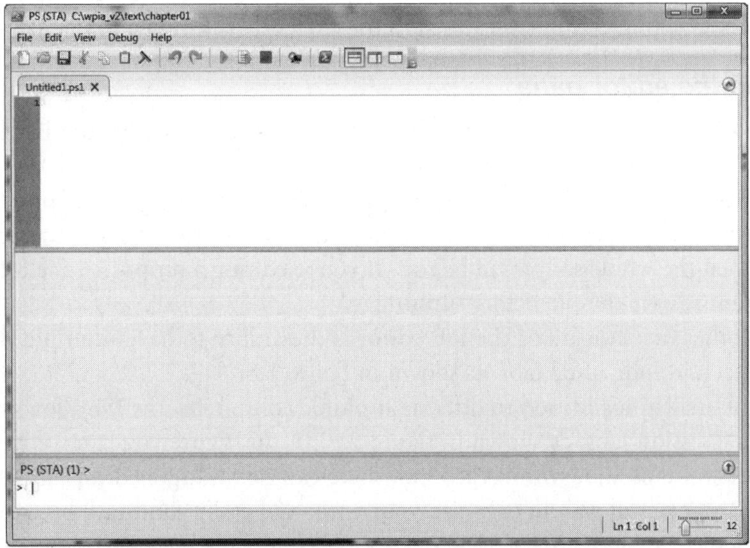

Figure 1.6 The PowerShell Integrated Scripting Environment

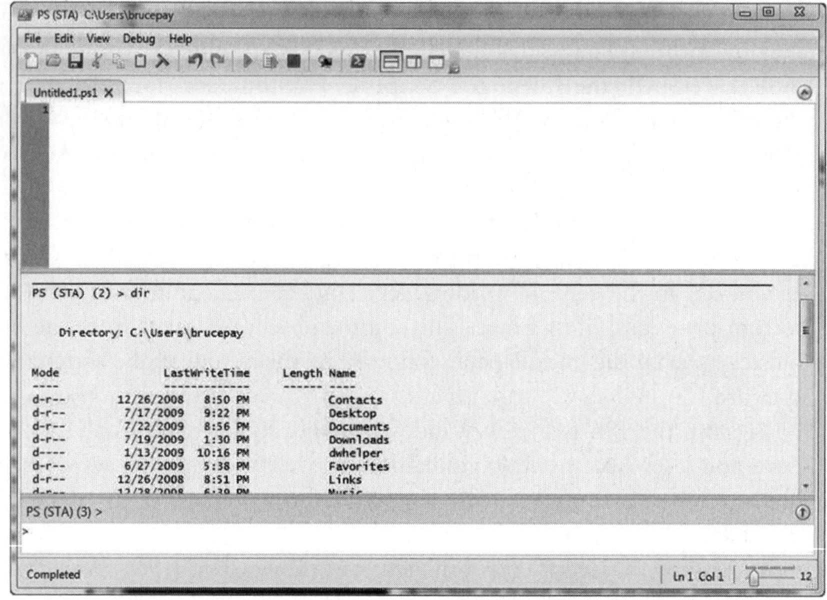

Figure 1.7 This figure shows running the `dir` command in the PowerShell ISE. The command is entered in the bottom pane and the result of the command is shown in the output pane in the middle.

like the play and stop buttons on a media player. As you might expect, the green "play" button will run a command just like if you press Enter. If there's a command running, the play button is disabled (grayed out) and the red "stop" button is enabled. Clicking this button will stop the currently running command.

Using the editor pane

The topmost pane in the ISE is a script editor that understands the PowerShell language. This editor will do syntax highlighting as you type in script text. It will also let you select a region and either press the play button above the pane or press the F8 key to execute the part of the script you want to test out. If nothing is selected in the window, then the whole script will be run. If you're editing a script file, the ISE will ask if you want to save the file before running it.

Another nice feature of the ISE editor is the ability to have multiple files open at once, each in individual tabs, as shown in figure 1.8.

And finally, in addition to offering multiple editor tabs, the ISE allows you to have multiple session tabs, as shown in figure 1.9. In this figure you can see that there are four session tabs and, within each tab, there can be multiple editor tabs. This makes the ISE a powerful way to organize your work and easily multitask between different activities.

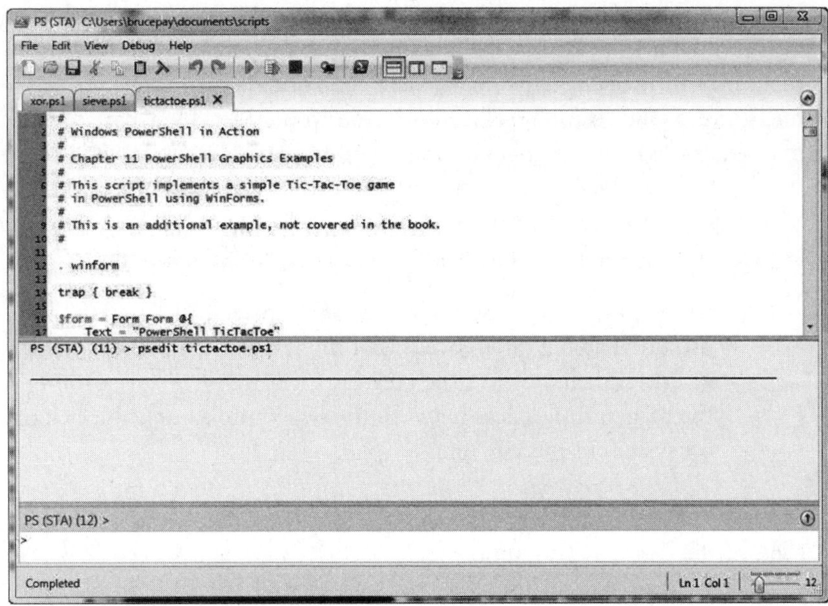

Figure 1.8 This figure shows using multiple tabs in the ISE editor. Each new file that's opened gets its own tab. Files can be opened from the File menu or by using the `psedit` command in the command window, as shown.

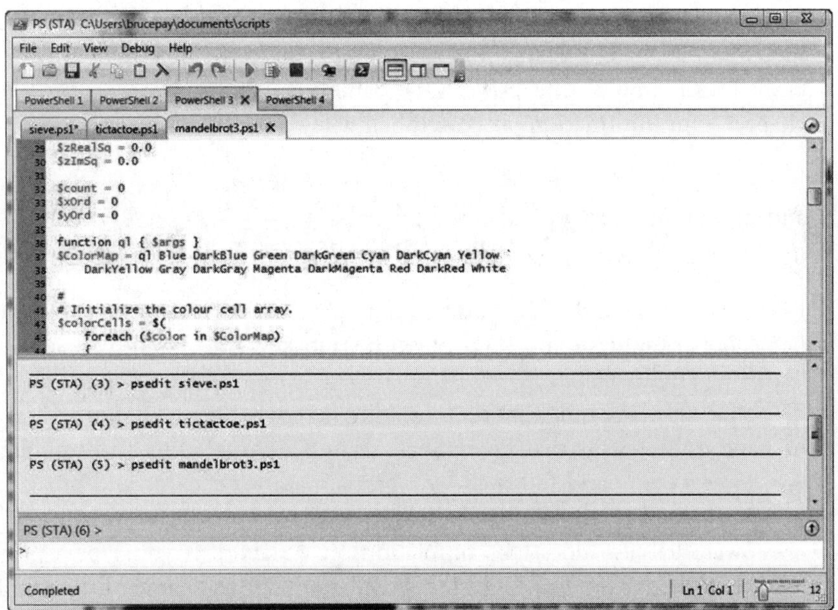

Figure 1.9 This figure shows how multiple session tabs are displayed in the ISE. Note that each session tab has its own set of editor tabs.

These are the basic concepts in the ISE. But the ISE isn't just a tool for writing, testing, and debugging PowerShell scripts. It's also *scriptable* by PowerShell. This means that you can use scripts to manipulate the contents of buffers, create new tabs and menu items, and so forth. This allows you to use the ISE as part of your application in much the same way that the Emacs editor was a component of custom applications. There are some limitations to this in the first version of the ISE—the PowerShell team didn't have time to do everything they wanted (there's never enough time), but the result is still powerful. You'll see more of this later on.

> **NOTE** Okay, so why is this an "ISE" instead of an "IDE" like Visual Studio? The big difference is that the ISE is intended for interactive use of PowerShell, not just the creation of PowerShell applications. One of the biggest differences between the two approaches is the lack of a project system in the ISE.

1.4.5 Command completion

One of the most useful editing features in PowerShell is *command completion*, also called *tab completion*. Although `cmd.exe` does have tab completion, PowerShell's implementation is significantly more powerful. Command completion allows you to partially enter a command, then press the Tab key, and have PowerShell try to fill in the rest of the command. By default, PowerShell will do tab completion against the file system, so if you type a partial filename and then press Tab, the system matches what you've typed against the files in the current directory and returns the first matching filename. Pressing Tab again takes you to the next match, and so on. PowerShell also supplies the powerful capability of tab completion on wildcards (see chapter 4 for information on PowerShell wildcards). This means that you can type

```
PS (1) > cd c:\pro*files<tab>
```

and the command is expanded to

```
PS (2) > cd 'C:\Program Files'
```

PowerShell will also do tab completion on partial cmdlet names. If you enter a cmdlet name up to the dash and then press the Tab key, the system will step through the matching cmdlet names.

So far, this isn't much more interesting than what `cmd.exe` provides. What's significantly different is that PowerShell also does completion on parameter names. If you enter a command followed by a partial parameter name and press Tab, the system will step through all of the possible parameters for that command.

PowerShell also does tab completion on variables. If you type a partial variable name and then press Tab, PowerShell will complete the name of the variable.

Finally, PowerShell does completion on properties in variables. If you've used the Microsoft Visual Studio development environment, you've probably seen the

IntelliSense feature. Property completion is kind of a limited IntelliSense capability at the command line. If you type something like

```
PS (1) > $a="abcde"
PS (2) > $a.len<tab>
```

the system expands the property name to

```
PS (2) > $a.Length
```

Again, the first Tab returns the first matching property or method. If the match is a method, an open parenthesis is displayed

```
PS (3) > $a.sub<tab>
```

which produces

```
PS (3) > $a.Substring(
```

Note that the system corrects the capitalization for the method or property name to match how it was actually defined. This doesn't impact how things work. PowerShell is case insensitive by default whenever it has to match against something. (There are operators that allow you to do case-sensitive matching, which are discussed in chapter 3.)

Version 2 of PowerShell introduced an additional tab completion feature (suggested by a PowerShell user, no less). PowerShell remembers each command you type. You can access previous commands using the arrow keys or show them using the `Get-History` command. A new feature was added to allow you to do tab completion against the command history. To recall the first command containing the string "abc", type the # sign, followed by the pattern of the command you want to find, and then press the Tab key:

```
PS (4) > #abc<tab>
```

This will expand the command line to

```
PS (4) > $a="abcde"
```

You can also select a command from the history by number. To do so, type the # sign, followed by the number of the command to run, and press Tab:

```
PS (5) > #2<tab>
```

And this should expand to

```
PS (5) > $a="abcde"
```

> **NOTE** The PowerShell tab completion mechanism is user extendable. Although the path completion mechanism is built into the executable, features such as parameter and property completion are implemented through a shell function that users can examine and modify. The name of this function is `TabExpansion`. Chapter 7 describes how to write and manipulate PowerShell functions.

1.5 DUDE! WHERE'S MY CODE?

Okay, enough talk, let's see some more example code! First, we'll revisit the `dir` example. This time, instead of simply displaying the directory listing, you'll save it into a file using output redirection just like in other shell environments. In the following example, you'll use `dir` to get information about a file named somefile.txt in the root of the C: drive. Using redirection, you direct the output into a new file, c:\foo.txt, and then use the `type` command to display what was saved. Here's what this looks like:

```
PS (2) > dir c:\somefile.txt > c:\foo.txt
PS (3) > type c:\foo.txt

    Directory: Microsoft.PowerShell.Core\FileSystem::C:\

Mode                LastWriteTime     Length Name
----                -------------     ------ ----
-a---        11/17/2004   3:32 AM          0 somefile.txt
PS (4) >
```

As you can see, commands work more or less as you'd expect.

> **NOTE** Okay, nobody has a file named somefile.txt in the root of their C: drive (except me). For the purpose of this example, just choose any file that does exist and the example will work fine, though obviously the output will be different.

Let's go over some other things that should be familiar to you.

1.5.1 Navigation and basic operations

The PowerShell commands for working with the file system should be pretty familiar to most users. You navigate around the file system with the `cd` command. Files are copied with the `copy` or `cp` commands, moved with the `move` and `mv` commands, and removed with the `del` or `rm` commands. Why two of each command, you might ask? One set of names is familiar to `cmd.exe`/DOS users and the other is familiar to UNIX users. In practice they're actually *aliases* for the same command, designed to make it easy for people to get going with PowerShell. One thing to keep in mind, however, is that although the commands are similar they're not exactly the same as either of the other two systems. You can use the `Get-Help` command to get help about these commands. Here's the output of `Get-Help` for the `dir` command:

```
PS (1) > Get-Help dir

NAME
    Get-ChildItem

SYNOPSIS
    Gets the items and child items in one or more specified locations.
```

```
SYNTAX
    Get-ChildItem [-Exclude <string[]>] [-Force] [-Include <string[]>]
    [-Name] [-Recurse] [[-Path] <string[]>] [[-Filter] <string>]
    [<CommonParameters>]

    Get-ChildItem [-Exclude <string[]>] [-Force] [-Include <string[]>]
   [-Name] [-Recurse] [[-Filter] <string>] [-LiteralPath] <string[]>
   [<CommonParameters>]


DETAILED DESCRIPTION
    The Get-Childitem cmdlet gets the items in one or more specified
    locations. If the item is a container, it gets the items inside the
    container, known as child items. You can use the Recurse parameter
    to get items in all child containers.

    A location can be a file system location, such as a directory,
    or a location exposed by another provider, such as a registry
    hive or a certificate store.


RELATED LINKS
    About_Providers
    Get-Item
    Get-Alias
    Get-Location
    Get-Process

REMARKS
    To see the examples, type: "get-help Get-ChildItem -examples".
    For more information, type: "get-help Get-ChildItem -detailed".
    For technical information, type: "get-help Get-ChildItem -full".
```

The PowerShell help subsystem contains information about all of the commands provided with the system and is a great way to explore what's available. You can even use wildcard characters to search through the help topics (v2 and later). Of course, this is the simple text output. The PowerShell ISE also includes help in the richer Windows format and will even let you select an item and then press F1 to view the help for the item. Finally, by using the `-Online` option to `Get-Help`, you can view the help text for a command or topic using a web browser.

> **NOTE** `Get-Help -Online` is the best way to get help because the online documentation is constantly being updated and corrected, whereas the local copies are not.

1.5.2 Basic expressions and variables

In addition to running commands, PowerShell can evaluate expressions. In effect, it operates as a kind of calculator. Let's evaluate a simple expression:

```
PS (4) > 2+2
4
```

Notice that as soon as you typed the expression, the result was calculated and displayed. It wasn't necessary to use any kind of print statement to display the result. It's important to remember that whenever an expression is evaluated, the result of the expression is output, not discarded. We'll explore the implications of this in later sections.

Here are a few more examples of PowerShell expressions:

```
PS (5) > (2+2)*3
12
PS (6) > (2+2)*6/2
12
PS (7) > 22/7
3.14285714285714
```

You can see from these examples that PowerShell supports most of the basic arithmetic operations you'd expect, including floating point.

> **NOTE** PowerShell supports single and double precision floating points, as well as the .NET decimal type. See chapter 3 for more details.

Because I've already shown you how to save the output of a command into a file using the redirection operator, let's do the same thing with expressions:

```
PS (8) > (2+2)*3/7
1.71428571428571
PS (9) > (2+2)*3/7 > c:\foo.txt
PS (10) > type c:\foo.txt
1.71428571428571
```

Saving expressions into files is useful; saving them in variables is more useful:

```
PS (11) > $n = (2+2)*3
PS (12) > $n
12
PS (13) > $n / 7
1.71428571428571
```

Variables can also be used to store the output of commands:

```
PS (14) > $files = dir
PS (15) > $files[1]
    Directory: Microsoft.PowerShell.Core\FileSystem::C:\Document
    s and Settings\brucepay

Mode                LastWriteTime     Length Name
----                -------------     ------ ----
d----         4/25/2006  10:32 PM            Desktop
```

In this example, you extracted the second element of the collection of file information objects returned by the `dir` command. You were able to do this because you saved the output of the `dir` command as an array of objects in the `$files` variable.

> **NOTE** Collections in PowerShell start at 0, not 1. This is a characteristic we've inherited from .NET. This is why `$files[1]` is extracting the second element, not the first.

Given that PowerShell is all about objects, the basic operators need to work on more than just numbers. So, for example, you can also use the plus sign (+) to add or concatenate strings as follows:

```
PS (16) > "hello" + " world"
hello world
```

In this case, the + operator adds the two strings together to produce a new, longer string. You can also mix and match argument types. You can add a number to a string and PowerShell will take care of turning the number into a string and then concatenating the two strings. Here's how this looks:

```
PS (17) > "a number: " + 123
a number: 123
```

The + operator also works with the object arrays we mentioned earlier. You can create an array of numbers simply by typing the numbers you want in the collection separated by a comma. You can then add these collections using the + operator as follows:

```
PS (18) > 1,2 + 3,4
1
2
3
4
```

As with strings, the + operator adds the two arguments together to produce a new, longer array. You can even add an array to a string:

```
PS (19) > "Numbers: " + 1,2,3,4
Numbers: 1 2 3 4
```

And again, PowerShell takes care of turning the array into a string and then appending it to the argument on the right-hand side. These examples only scratch the surface of what can be done with the PowerShell operators. Chapters 5 and 6 cover these features in detail.

1.5.3 Processing data

As you've seen in the preceding sections, you can run commands to get information, perform some basic operations on this information using the PowerShell operators, and then store the results in files and variables. Now let's look at some additional ways you can process this data. First you'll see how to sort objects and how to extract properties from those objects. Then we'll look at using the PowerShell flow-control statements to write scripts that use conditionals and loops to do more sophisticated processing.

Sorting objects

First let's sort the list of file information objects returned by `dir`. Because you're sorting objects, the command you'll use is `Sort-Object`. For convenience, you'll use the shorter alias sort in these examples. Start by looking at the default output, which shows the files sorted by name:

```
PS (16) > cd c:\files
PS (17) > dir
    Directory: Microsoft.PowerShell.Core\FileSystem::C:\files

Mode                LastWriteTime     Length Name
----                -------------     ------ ----
-a---         4/25/2006  10:55 PM         98 a.txt
-a---         4/25/2006  10:51 PM         42 b.txt
-a---         4/25/2006  10:56 PM        102 c.txt
-a---         4/25/2006  10:54 PM         66 d.txt
```

The output shows the basic properties on the file system objects sorted by the name of the file. Now, let's run it through sort:

```
PS (18) > dir | sort
    Directory: Microsoft.PowerShell.Core\FileSystem::C:\files

Mode                LastWriteTime     Length Name
----                -------------     ------ ----
-a---         4/25/2006  10:55 PM         98 a.txt
-a---         4/25/2006  10:51 PM         42 b.txt
-a---         4/25/2006  10:56 PM        102 c.txt
-a---         4/25/2006  10:54 PM         66 d.txt
```

Granted, it's not very interesting. Sorting an already sorted list by the same property gives you the same result. Let's do something a bit more interesting. Let's sort by name in descending order:

```
PS (19) > dir | sort -Descending
    Directory: Microsoft.PowerShell.Core\FileSystem::C:\files

Mode                LastWriteTime     Length Name
----                -------------     ------ ----
-a---         4/25/2006  10:54 PM         66 d.txt
-a---         4/25/2006  10:56 PM        102 c.txt
-a---         4/25/2006  10:51 PM         42 b.txt
-a---         4/25/2006  10:55 PM         98 a.txt
```

So there you have it—files sorted by name in reverse order. Now let's sort by something other than the name of the file: file length. You may remember from an earlier section how hard it would be to sort by file length if the output were just text.

Sort on UNIX

On a UNIX system, the sort command looks like

```
ls -l | sort -n -k 5
```

which, though pithy, is pretty opaque. Here's what it's doing. The -n option tells the sort function that you want to do a numeric sort. -k tells you which field you want to sort on.

(continued)

(The sort utility considers space-separated bits of text to be fields.) In the output of the `ls -l` command, the field containing the length of the file is at offset 5, as shown in the following:

```
-rw-r--r--  1 brucepay  brucepay  5754 Feb 19   2005 index.html
-rw-r--r--  1 brucepay  brucepay   204 Aug 19  12:50 page1.htm
```

You need to set things up this way because `ls` produces unstructured strings. You have to tell `sort` how to parse those strings before it can sort them.

In PowerShell, when you use the `Sort-Object` cmdlet, you don't have to tell it to sort numerically—it already knows the type of the field, and you can specify the sort key by property name instead of a numeric field offset. The result looks like this:

```
PS (20) > dir | sort -Property length
    Directory: Microsoft.PowerShell.Core\FileSystem::C:\files

Mode                LastWriteTime     Length Name
----                -------------     ------ ----
-a---         4/25/2006  10:51 PM         42 b.txt
-a---         4/25/2006  10:54 PM         66 d.txt
-a---         4/25/2006  10:55 PM         98 a.txt
-a---         4/25/2006  10:56 PM        102 c.txt
```

This illustrates what working with pipelines of objects gives you:

- You have the ability to access data elements by name instead of using substring indexes or field numbers.
- By having the original type of the element preserved, operations execute correctly without you having to provide additional information.

Now let's look at some other things you can do with objects.

Selecting properties from an object

In this section, we'll introduce another cmdlet for working with objects: `Select-Object`. This cmdlet allows you to select a subrange of the objects piped into it and to specify a subset of the properties on those objects.

Say you want to get the largest file in a directory and put it into a variable:

```
PS (21) > $a = dir | sort -Property length -Descending |
>> Select-Object -First 1
>>
PS (22) > $a
    Directory: Microsoft.PowerShell.Core\FileSystem::C:\files

Mode                LastWriteTime     Length Name
----                -------------     ------ ----
-a---         4/25/2006  10:56 PM        102 c.txt
```

From this you can see that the largest file is c.txt.

> **NOTE** You'll notice the secondary prompt >> in the previous example. The first line of the command ended in a pipe symbol. The PowerShell interpreter noticed this, saw that the command was incomplete, and prompted for additional text to complete the command. Once the command is complete, you type a second blank line to send the command to the interpreter. If you just want to cancel the command, you can press Ctrl-C at any time to return to the normal prompt.

Now say you want only the name of the directory containing the file and not all the other properties of the object. You can also do this with `Select-Object`. As with the `Sort-Object` cmdlet, `Select-Object` takes a `-Property` parameter (you'll see this frequently in the PowerShell environment—commands are consistent in their use of parameters):

```
PS (23) > $a = dir | sort -Property length -Descending |
>> Select-Object -First 1 -Property directory
>>
PS (24) > $a

Directory
---------
C:\files
```

You now have an object with a single property.

Processing with the ForEach-Object cmdlet

The final simplification is to get just the value itself. I'll introduce a new cmdlet that lets you do arbitrary processing on each object in a pipeline. The `ForEach-Object` cmdlet executes a block of statements for each object in the pipeline:

```
PS (25) > $a = dir | sort -Property length -Descending |
>> Select-Object -First 1 |
>> ForEach-Object { $_.DirectoryName }
>>
PS (26) > $a
C:\files
```

This shows that you can get an arbitrary property out of an object and then do arbitrary processing on that information using the `ForEach-Object` command. Combining those features, here's an example that adds up the lengths of all the objects in a directory:

```
PS (27) > $total = 0
PS (28) > dir | ForEach-Object {$total += $_.length }
PS (29) > $total
308
```

In this example, you initialize the variable `$total` to 0, and then add to it the length of each file returned by the `dir` command and finally display the total.

Processing other kinds of data

One of the great strengths of the PowerShell approach is that once you learn a pattern for solving a problem, you can use this same pattern over and over again. For example, say you want to find the largest three files in a directory. The command line might look like this:

```
PS (1) > dir | sort -Descending length | select -First 3
    Directory: Microsoft.PowerShell.Core\FileSystem::C:\files

Mode                LastWriteTime     Length Name
----                -------------     ------ ----
-a---         4/25/2006  10:56 PM        102 c.txt
-a---         4/25/2006  10:55 PM         98 a.txt
-a---         4/25/2006  10:54 PM         66 d.txt
```

Here, the `dir` command retrieved the list of file information objects, sorted them in descending order by length, and then selected the first three results to get the three largest files.

Now let's tackle a different problem. You want to find the three processes on the system with the largest working set size. Here's what this command line looks like:

```
PS (2) > Get-Process | sort -Descending ws | select -First 3
Handles  NPM(K)    PM(K)      WS(K) VM(M)   CPU(s)     Id ProcessName
-------  ------    -----      ----- -----   ------     -- -----------
   1294      43    51096      81776   367    11.48   3156 OUTLOOK
    893      25    55260      73340   196    79.33   5124 iexplore
   2092      64    42676      54080   214   187.23    988 svchost
```

This time you run `Get-Process` to get data about the processes on this computer and sort on the working set instead of the file size. Otherwise, the pattern is identical to the previous example. This command pattern can be applied over and over again. For example, to get the three largest mailboxes on an Exchange mail server, the command might look like this:

```
Get-MailboxStatistics | sort -descending TotalItemSize | select -First 3
```

Again the pattern is repeated except for the `Get-MailboxStatistics` command and the property to filter on.

Even when you don't have a specific command for the data you're looking for and have to use other facilities such as WMI, you can continue to apply the pattern. Say you want to find the three drives on the system that have the most free space. To do this you need to get some data from WMI. Not surprisingly, the command for this is `Get-WmiObject`. Here's how you'd use this command:

```
PS (4) > Get-WmiObject -Class Win32_LogicalDisk |
>> sort -Descending freespace | select -First 3 |
```

```
>> Format-Table -AutoSize deviceid, freespace
>>
deviceid   freespace
--------   ---------
C:        97778954240
T:        31173663232
D:          932118528
```

Once again, the pattern is almost identical. The `Get-WmiObject` command returns a set of objects from WMI. You pipe these objects into `sort` and sort on the `freespace` property, and then use `Select-Object` to extract the first three.

> **NOTE** Because of this ability to apply a command pattern over and over, most of the examples in this book are deliberately generic. The intent is to highlight the pattern of the solution rather than show a specific example. Once you understand the basic patterns, you can effectively adapt them to solve a multitude of other problems.

1.5.4 Flow-control statements

Pipelines are great, but sometimes you need more control over the flow of your script. PowerShell has the usual script flow-control statements found in most programming languages. These include the basic `if` statements, a powerful `switch` statement, and various loops like a `while` loop, `for` and `foreach` loops, and so on. Here's an example showing use of the `while` and `if` statements:

```
PS (1) > $i=0
PS (2) > while ($i++ -lt 10) { if ($i % 2) {"$i is odd"}}
1 is odd
3 is odd
5 is odd
7 is odd
9 is odd
PS (3) >
```

This example uses the `while` loop to count through a range of numbers, printing out only the odd numbers. In the body of the `while` loop is an `if` statement that tests to see whether the current number is odd, and then writes out a message if it is. You can do the same thing using the `foreach` statement and the range operator (`..`), but much more succinctly:

```
PS (3) > foreach ($i in 1..10) { if ($i % 2) {"$i is odd"}}
1 is odd
3 is odd
5 is odd
7 is odd
9 is odd
```

The `foreach` statement iterates over a collection of objects, and the range operator is a way to generate a sequence of numbers. The two combine to make looping over a sequence of numbers very clean.

Of course, because the range operator generates a sequence of numbers and numbers are objects like everything else in PowerShell, you can implement this using pipelines and the `ForEach-Object` cmdlet:

```
PS (5) > 1..10 | foreach { if ($_ % 2) {"$_ is odd"}}
1 is odd
3 is odd
5 is odd
7 is odd
9 is odd
```

These examples only scratch the surface of what you can do with the PowerShell flow-control statements (just wait until you see the `switch` statement!). The complete set of control structures is covered in detail in chapter 6 with lots of examples.

1.5.5 Scripts and functions

What good is a scripting language if you can't package commands into scripts? PowerShell lets you do this by simply putting your commands into a text file with a .ps1 extension and then running that command. You can even have parameters in your scripts. Put the following text into a file called hello.ps1:

```
param($name = "bub")
"Hello $name, how are you?"
```

Notice that the `param` keyword is used to define a parameter called `$name`. The parameter is given a default value of `"bub"`. Now you can run this script from the PowerShell prompt by typing the name as `.\hello`. You need the `.\` to tell PowerShell to get the command from the current directory (chapter 21 explains why this is needed).

> **NOTE** Before you can run scripts on a machine in the default configuration, you'll have to change the PowerShell execution policy to allow scripts to run. See `Get-Help -Online about_execution_policies` for detailed instructions.

The first time you run this script, you won't specify any arguments:

```
PS (1) > .\hello
Hello bub, how are you?
```

You see that the default value was used in the response. Run it again, but this time specify an argument:

```
PS (2) > .\hello Bruce
Hello Bruce, how are you?
```

Now the argument is in the output instead of the default value. Sometimes you just want to have subroutines in your code. PowerShell addresses this need through functions. Let's turn the hello script into a function. Here's what it looks like:

```
PS (3) > function hello {
>> param($name = "bub")
```

```
>> "Hello $name, how are you"
>> }
>>
```

The body of the function is exactly the same as the script. The only thing added is the `function` keyword, the name of the function, and braces around the body of the function. Now run it, first with no arguments as you did with the script:

```
PS (4) > hello
Hello bub, how are you
```

and then with an argument:

```
PS (5) > hello Bruce
Hello Bruce, how are you
```

Obviously the function operates in the same way as the script except that PowerShell didn't have to load it from a disk file so it's a bit faster to call. Scripts and functions are covered in detail in chapter 7.

1.5.6 Remoting and the Universal Execution Model

In the previous sections, you've seen the kinds of things you can do with PowerShell on a single computer. But the computing industry has long since moved beyond a one-computer world. Being able to manage groups of computers, without having to physically visit each one, is critical in the modern IT world. To address this, PowerShell v2 introduced built-in remote execution capabilities (remoting) and the *Universal Execution Model*—a fancy term that just means that if it works locally, then it should work remotely.

> **NOTE** At this point you should be asking "If this is so important why wasn't it in v1?" In fact it was planned from shortly *before* day one of the PowerShell project. But, to make something universal, secure, and simple is, in fact, very hard.

The core of PowerShell remoting is the `Invoke-Command` command, which, again for convenience, has a much shorter alias: `icm`. This command allows you to invoke a block of PowerShell script on the current computer, on a remote computer, or on a thousand remote computers. Let's see some of this in action. The example scenario will be to check the version of the Microsoft Management Console (MMC) host program installed on a computer. You might need to do this because you want to install an MMC extension (called a *snap-in)* on a set of machines and this snap-in requires a minimum version of the MMC host. You can do this locally by using the `Get-Command` command (`gcm`) to retrieve information about `mmc.exe`, the executable for the MMC host:

```
PS (1) > (gcm mmc.exe).FileVersionInfo.ProductVersion
6.1.7069.0
```

This is a simple one-line command, and it shows that version 6.1 of `mmc.exe` is installed on the local machine. Now let's run it on a remote machine. (We'll assume that your target machine names are stored in the variables $m1 and $m2.) Let's check the version on the first machine. Run the same command as before, but this time enclose it in braces as an argument to icm. Also give the icm command the name of the host to execute on:

```
PS (2) > icm $m1 {
>> (gcm mmc.exe).FileVersionInfo.ProductVersion
>> }
>>
6.0.6000.16386
```

Oops—this machine has an older version of mmc.exe. Okay, let's try machine 2. Run exactly the same command, but pass in the name of the second machine this time:

```
PS (3) > icm $m2 {
>> (gcm mmc.exe).FileVersionInfo.ProductVersion
>> }
>>
6.1.7069.0
```

This machine is up to date. At this point you've addressed the need to physically go to each machine but you're still executing the commands one at a time. Let's fix that too by putting the machines to check into a list. You'll use an array variable for this example, but this list could come from a file, an Excel spreadsheet, a database, or a web service. First, run the command with the machine list:

```
PS (4) > $mlist = $m1,$m2
PS (5) > icm $mlist {
>> (gcm mmc.exe).FileVersionInfo.ProductVersion
>> }
>>
6.0.6000.16386
6.1.7069.0
```

You get same the same results as last time but as a list instead of one at a time. In practice, most of your machines are probably up to date, so you really only care about the ones that don't have the correct version of the software. You can use the where command to filter out the machines you don't care about:

```
PS (6) > icm $mlist {
>> (gcm mmc.exe).FileVersionInfo.ProductVersion
>> } | where { $_ -notmatch '6\.1' }
>>
6.0.6000.16386
```

This returns the list of machines that have out-of-date mmc.exe versions. There's still a problem, though: you see the version number but not the computer's name. Obviously you'll need this too if you're going to update those machines. To address this, PowerShell remoting automatically adds the name of the originating computer to each received object using a special property called PSComputerName.

Now let's jump ahead a bit and see how much effort it'd be to produce a nice table of computer names and version numbers. You'll run the remote command again, use where to filter the results, extract the fields you want to display using the select command, and finally format the report using the Format-Table command. For the purpose of this example, you'll add the machine lists together so you know you'll get two records in your report. Here's what the command looks like:

```
PS (7) > icm ($mlist + $mlist) {
>>         (gcm mmc.exe).FileVersionInfo.ProductVersion } |
>>       where { $_ -notmatch '6\.1' } |
>>       select @{n="Computer"; e={$_.PSComputerName}},
>>           @{n="MMC Version"; e={$_}} |
>>       Format-Table -auto
>>

Computer       MMC Version
--------       -----------
brucepaydev07 6.0.6000.16386
brucepaydev07 6.0.6000.16386
```

Although the command may look a bit scary, you were able to produce your report with little effort. And the techniques you used for formatting the report can be used over and over again. This example shows how easily PowerShell remoting can be used to expand the reach of your scripts to cover one, hundreds, or thousands of computers all at once. But sometimes you just want to work with a single remote machine interactively. Let's see how to do that.

The Invoke-Command command is the way to programmatically execute PowerShell commands on a remote machine. When you want to connect to a machine so you can interact with it on a one-to-one basis, you use the Enter-PSSession command. This command allows you to start an interactive one-to-one session with a remote computer. Running Enter-PSSession looks like this:

```
PS (11) > Enter-PSSession server01

[server01]: PS > (gcm mmc.exe).FileVersionInfo.ProductVersion
6.0.6000.16386
[brucepaydev07]: PS > Get-Date

Sunday, May 03, 2009 7:40:08 PM

[server01]: PS > exit
PS (12) >
```

As shown here, when you connect to the remote computer, your prompt changes to indicate that you're working remotely. Otherwise, once connected, you can pretty much interact with the remote computer the same way you would with a local machine. When you're done, exit the remote session with the exit command, and this pops you back to the local session. This brief introduction covers some powerful techniques, but we've only begun to cover all the things remoting lets you do.

At this point, we'll end our "Cook's tour" of PowerShell. We've only breezed over the features and capabilities of the environment. There are many other areas of PowerShell that we haven't covered here, especially in v2, which introduced advanced functions and scripts, modules, eventing support, and many more features. In upcoming chapters, we'll explore each of the elements discussed here in detail and a whole lot more.

1.6 SUMMARY

This chapter covered what PowerShell is and, just as important, *why* it is. We also took a whirlwind tour through some simple examples of using PowerShell interactively. Here are the key points that we covered:

- PowerShell is the new command-line/scripting environment from Microsoft. Since its introduction with Windows Server 2008, PowerShell has rapidly moved to the center of Microsoft server and application management technologies. Many of the most important server products, including Exchange, Active Directory, and SQL Server, now use PowerShell as their management layer.
- The Microsoft Windows management model is primarily object based, through .NET, COM, and WMI. This required Microsoft to take a novel approach to command-line scripting, incorporating object-oriented concepts into a command-line shell. PowerShell uses the .NET object model as the base for its type system but can also access other object types like WMI.
- PowerShell is an interactive environment with two different host applications: the console host `PowerShell.exe` and the graphical host `powershell_ise.exe`. It can also be "hosted" in other applications to act as the scripting engine for those applications.
- Shell operations like navigation and file manipulation in PowerShell are similar to what you're used to in other shells.
- The way to get help about things in PowerShell is to use the `Get-Help` command (or by selecting text and pressing F1 in the ISE).
- PowerShell is sophisticated with a full range of calculation, scripting, and text processing capabilities.
- PowerShell v2 introduced a comprehensive set of remoting features to allow you to do scripted automation of large collections of computers.

In the following chapters, we'll look at each of the PowerShell features we showed you here in much more detail. Stay tuned!

CHAPTER 2

Foundations of PowerShell

"Begin at the beginning," the king said
"and then go on till you come to the end, then stop."

—Lewis Carroll, *Alice in Wonderland*

Vizzini: Inconceivable!

Inigo: You keep on using that word. I do not think it means what you think it means.

—William Goldman, *The Princess Bride*

This chapter introduces the foundational concepts underlying the PowerShell language and its environment. We'll cover language details that are specific to PowerShell and look at how the interpreter parses the commands we type. This chapter also covers the various types of commands you'll encounter along with the anatomy and operation of the pipeline itself. We'll look at the basic syntax for expressions and commands, including how to add comments to scripts and how arguments and parameters are handled. Finally, we'll close the chapter with a discussion of how the formatting and output subsystem works in PowerShell.

The chapter presents many examples that aren't completely explained. If you don't understand everything when you read the examples, don't worry—we'll revisit the material in later chapters. In this chapter, we just want to cover the core concepts—we'll focus on the details in subsequent chapters.

2.1 GETTING A SENSE OF THE POWERSHELL LANGUAGE

Before digging too deep into PowerShell concepts and terminology, let's capture some first impressions of the language: what does the PowerShell language look and feel like? Birdwatchers have to learn how to distinguish hundreds of species of fast-moving little brown birds (or LBBs, as they're known). To understand how they do this, I consulted with my wife, the "Master Birder." (The only bird I can identify is a chicken, preferably stuffed and roasted.) Birdwatchers use something called the *GISS* principle, which stands for General Impression, Size, and Shape. It's that set of characteristics that allow us to determine what we've seen even though we've had only a very brief or distant glance. Take a look at the silhouettes shown in figure 2.1. The figure shows the relative sizes of four birds and highlights the characteristic shape of each one. This is more than enough information to recognize each bird.

What does this have to do with computers (other than to prove we aren't the only ones who make up strange acronyms)? In essence, the GISS principle also works well with programming languages. The GISS of the PowerShell syntax is that it's like any of the C programming language descendents with specific differences such as the fact that variables are distinguished by a leading dollar ($) sign.

> **NOTE** PowerShell uses the at symbol (@) in a few places, has $_ as a default variable, and uses & as the function call operator. These elements lead people to say that PowerShell looks like Perl. In practice, at one point, we did use Perl as a root language, and these elements stem

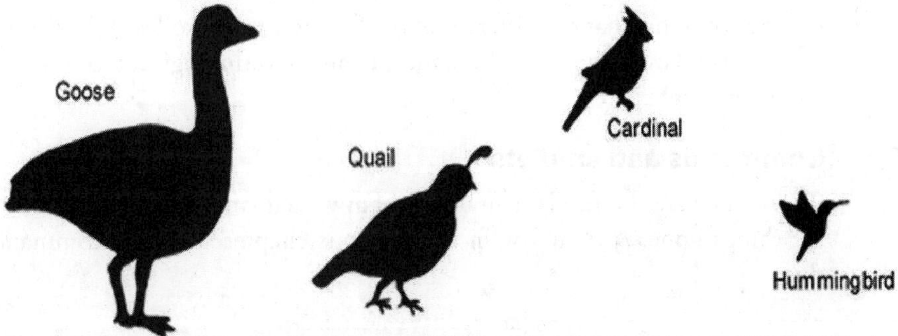

Figure 2.1 This figure illustrates the GISS principle—the general impression, size, and shape of some common birds. Even without any detail, the basic shape and size is enough for most people to identify these birds. This same principle can be applied when learning programming languages; a sense of the overall shape of the language allows you to identify common coding patterns in the language.

from that period. Later on, the syntax was changed to align more with C#, but we kept these elements because they worked well. In Perl terminology, they contributed significantly to the "whipupitude quotient" of the language. In fact, the language that PowerShell looks most like is PHP. (This wasn't deliberate. It's a case of parallel evolution—great minds thinking alike, and all that.) But don't let this fool you; semantically, PowerShell and PHP are quite different.

2.2 THE CORE CONCEPTS

The core PowerShell language is based on the IEEE standard POSIX 1003.2 grammar for the Korn shell. This standard was chosen because of its maturity and long history as a successful basis for modern shells like bash and zsh. The language design team (Jim Truher and I) deviated from this standard where necessary to address the specific needs of an object-based shell. We also deviated in areas where we wanted to make it easier to write sophisticated scripts. Originally, Perl idioms were appropriated for some of the advanced scripting concepts such as arrays and hash tables. As the project progressed, it became clear that aligning PowerShell syntax with C# was more appropriate. If nothing else, this would facilitate migrating code between PowerShell and C#. The major value this brings is that PowerShell code can be migrated to C# when necessary for performance improvements, and C# examples can be easily converted to PowerShell. This second point is important—the more examples you have in a new language, the better off you are.

2.2.1 Command concepts and terminology

As with any piece of new technology, PowerShell has its own terminology, although we've tried to stick to existing terms as much as we could. Consequently, much of the terminology used in PowerShell will be familiar if you've used other shells in the Linux or Windows world. But because PowerShell is a new kind of shell, there are a number of terms that are different and a few new terms to learn. In this section, we'll go over the PowerShell-specific concepts and terminology for command types and command syntax.

2.2.2 Commands and cmdlets

Commands are the fundamental part of any shell language; they're what you type to get things done. As you saw in the previous chapter, a simple command looks like this:

```
command -parameter1 -parameter2 argument1 argument2
```

A more detailed illustration of the anatomy of this command is shown in figure 2.2. This figure calls out all the individual elements of the command.

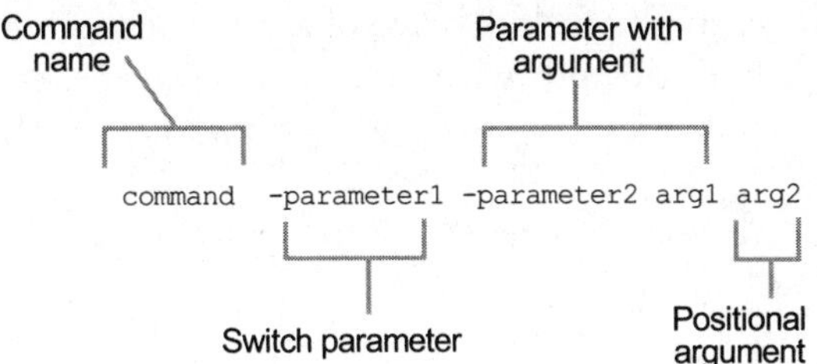

Figure 2.2 The anatomy of a basic command. It begins with the name of the command, followed by some number of parameters. These may be switch parameters that take no arguments, regular parameters that do take arguments, or positional parameters, where the matching parameter is inferred by the argument's position on the command line.

All commands are broken down into the command name, the parameters specified to the command, and the arguments to those parameters.

> **NOTE** The distinction between *parameter* and *argument* may seem a bit strange from a programmer's perspective. But if you're used to languages such as Python and Visual Basic that allow for keyword parameters, PowerShell parameters correspond to the keywords, and arguments correspond to the values.

The first element in the command is the name of the command to be executed. The PowerShell interpreter looks at this name and determines what has to be done. It must figure out not only which command to run but which *kind* of command to run. In PowerShell, there are four categories of commands: cmdlets, shell function commands, script commands, and native Windows commands. (We'll cover the different categories in detail in the following sections.) Following the command name come zero or more parameters and/or arguments. A parameter starts with a dash, followed by the name of the parameter. An argument, on the other hand, is the value that will be associated with, or *bound to*, a specific parameter. Let's look at an example:

```
PS (1) > Write-Output -InputObject Hello
Hello
```

In this example, the command is `Write-Output`, the parameter is `-InputObject`, and the argument is `Hello`.

What about the positional parameters mentioned in figure 2.1? When a PowerShell command is created, the author of that command specifies information that allows PowerShell to determine which parameter to bind an argument to, even if the parameter name itself is missing. For example, the `Write-Output` command has been defined so that the first parameter is `-InputObject`. This lets you write

```
PS (2) > Write-Output Hello
Hello
```

instead of having to specify `-InputObject`. The piece of the PowerShell interpreter that figures all of this out is called the *parameter binder*. The parameter binder is smart—it doesn't require that you specify the full name of a parameter as long as you specify enough for it to uniquely distinguish what you mean. This means you can write any of the following

```
PS (3) > Write-Output -input Hello
Hello
PS (4) > Write-Output -IN Hello
Hello
PS (5) > Write-Output -i Hello
Hello
```

and the parameter binder still does the right thing. (Notice that it doesn't matter whether you use uppercase or lowercase letters either.)

What else does the parameter binder do? It's in charge of determining how to match the types of arguments to the types of parameters. Remember that PowerShell is an object-based shell. Everything in PowerShell has a type. For this to work seamlessly, PowerShell has to use a fairly complex type-conversion system to correctly put things together, a subject that's covered in chapter 3. When you type a command at the command line, you're really typing strings. What happens if the command requires a different type of object? The parameter binder uses the type converter to try to convert that string into the correct type for the parameter.

Here's a simple example. Let's use the `Get-Process` command to get the process with the process ID 0. Instead of passing it the number 0, put the argument in quotes to force the argument to be a string. This means that the `-id` parameter, which requires a number, will be passed a string instead:

```
PS (7) > Get-Process -Id "0"

Handles  NPM(K)     PM(K)      WS(K) VM(M)   CPU(s)     Id ProcessName
-------  ------     -----      ----- -----   ------     -- -----------
      0       0         0         28     0               0 Idle
```

When you attempt to run this command, the parameter binder detects that `-id` needs a number, not a string, so it takes the string "0" and tries to convert it into a number. If this succeeds, the command continues, as you see in the example. What happens if it can't be converted? Let's try it:

```
PS (8) > Get-Process -Id abc
Get-Process : Cannot bind parameter 'Id'. Cannot convert value "abc"
to type "System.Int32". Error: "Input string was not in a correct
format."
At line:1 char:16
+ Get-Process -Id  <<<< abc
PS (9) >
```

You get an error message explaining that the type conversion failed. We'll discuss this in more detail in chapter 3 when we talk about types. Because we've introduced the use of quotation marks, let's see one more example. What happens if the argument you want to pass to the command starts with a dash? This is where the quotes come in. Let's use `Write-Output` to print out the string "-InputObject":

```
PS (1) > Write-Output -InputObject "-InputObject"
-InputObject
```

And it works as desired. Alternatively, you could type this:

```
PS (2) > Write-Output "-InputObject"
-InputObject
```

The quotes keep the parameter binder from treating the quoted string as a parameter.

Another, less frequently used way of doing this is by using the special "end-of-parameters" parameter, which is two hyphens back to back (`--`). Everything after this sequence will be treated as an argument, even if it looks like a parameter. For example, using `--` you can also write out the string `-InputObject` without using quotes:

```
PS (3) > Write-Output -- -InputObject
         -InputObject
```

The `--` sequence tells the parameter binder to treat everything after it as an argument, even if it looks like a parameter. This is a convention adopted from the UNIX shells and is standardized in the POSIX Shell and Utilities specification.

The final element of the basic command pattern is the *switch parameter*. These are parameters that don't require an argument. They're usually either present or absent (so obviously they can't be positional). A good example of this is the `-Recurse` parameter on the `dir` command. This switch tells the `dir` command to display files from a specified directory as well as all its subdirectories:

```
PS (1) > dir -Recurse -Filter c*d.exe c:\windows
    Directory: Microsoft.PowerShell.Core\FileSystem::C:\windows\
    system32

Mode                LastWriteTime     Length Name
----                -------------     ------ ----
-a---          8/10/2004  12:00 PM    102912 clipbrd.exe
-a---          8/10/2004  12:00 PM    388608 cmd.exe


PS (2) >
```

As you can see, the `-Recurse` switch takes no arguments.

> **NOTE** Although it's almost always the case that switch parameters don't take arguments, it's possible to specify arguments to them. We'll save discussion of when and why you might do this for section 7.2.6, which focuses on scripts (shell functions and scripts are the only time you need this particular feature, so we'll keep you in suspense for the time being).

Now that we've covered the basic anatomy of the command line, let's go over the types of commands that PowerShell supports.

2.2.3 Command categories

As we mentioned earlier, there are four categories of commands in PowerShell: cmdlets, functions, scripts, and native Win32 executables.

Cmdlets

The first category of command is a cmdlet (pronounced "command-let"). *Cmdlet* is a term that's specific to the PowerShell environment. A cmdlet is implemented by a .NET class that derives from the `Cmdlet` base class in the PowerShell Software Developers Kit (SDK).

> **NOTE** Building cmdlets is a developer task and requires the PowerShell SDK. This SDK is freely available for download from Microsoft and includes extensive documentation along with many code samples. Our goal is to coach you to effectively use and script in the PowerShell environment, so we're not going to do much more than mention the SDK in this book. We'll look at how to write inline cmdlets when we come to the `Add-Type` cmdlet in later chapters.

This category of command is compiled into a dynamic link library (DLL) and then loaded into the PowerShell process, usually when the shell starts up. Because the compiled code is loaded into the process, it's the most efficient category of command to execute.

Cmdlets always have names of the form `Verb-Noun`, where the verb specifies the action and the noun specifies the object to operate on. In traditional shells, cmdlets correspond most closely to what's usually called a *built-in command.* In PowerShell, though, anybody can add a cmdlet to the runtime, so there isn't any special class of built-in commands. Cmdlets have the most support in version 1 of PowerShell: full online help support, localization, and the best parameter binding support. (PowerShell v2 expands this support to fully include scripts and functions; see appendix D.)

In listing 2.1, you can see the C# source code for a simple cmdlet. This cmdlet just copies its input to its output. If `-Parameter1` is specified, its argument will be used as a prefix on the output string. We included this example to show you the basic structure of a cmdlet. There are a couple of important things to note in this listing. The first is the way the parameters are declared using the `Parameter` attribute. This information is used by the PowerShell runtime to automatically determine the parameters for the cmdlet. The cmdlet author doesn't have to write any code to do parameter parsing; the runtime takes care of all this work. Another thing to note is the `ValueFromPipeline=true` notation. This indicates that this parameter may be fulfilled by values coming from the pipeline. (We'll discuss what this means when we talk about pipelines later in this chapter.)

Listing 2.1 C# source code for a simple cmdlet

```
[Cmdlet("Write", "InputObject")]
public class MyWriteInputObjectCmdlet : Cmdlet          <-- Class declaration
{
    [Parameter]                                         <-- Marks parameter
    public string Parameter1;

    [Parameter(Mandatory = true, ValueFromPipeline=true)]   <-- Takes pipeline input
    public string InputObject;

    protected override void ProcessRecord()             <-- Process block
    {
        if (Parameter1 != null)
                WriteObject(Parameter1 + ":" + InputObject);
            else
                WriteObject(InputObject);
    }
}
```

If you aren't a programmer, this listing probably won't mean much to you. It's just here to show the basic pattern used by PowerShell commands. (When we get to advanced functions in chapter 8, you may want to come back and look at this example again.)

Functions

The next type of command is a *function*. This is a named piece of PowerShell script code that lives in memory while the interpreter is running and is discarded on exit. (See chapter 7 for more information on how you can load functions into your environment.) Functions consist of user-defined code that's parsed once when defined. This parsed representation is preserved so it doesn't have to be reparsed every time it's used.

Functions in PowerShell version 1 could have named parameters like cmdlets but were otherwise fairly limited. In version 2, this was fixed, and scripts and functions now have the full parameter specification capabilities of cmdlets. Notice, though, that the same basic structure is followed for both types of commands. The section in the script that begins with the `process` keyword (line 4 of listing 2.2) corresponds to the `ProcessRecord` method shown in listing 2.1. This allows functions and cmdlets to have the same streaming behavior. (See section 2.5.1 for more information on streaming.)

Listing 2.2 Source code for a simple shell function command

```
function Write-InputObject
{
    param($Parameter1)                    <-- Parameters
    process {                             <-- Process scriptblock
        if ($Parameter1)
```

```
        {
            "${Parameter1}:$_"
        } else {
            "$_"
        }
    }
}
```

Scripts

A *script command* is a piece of PowerShell code that lives in a text file with a .ps1 extension. These script files are loaded and parsed every time they're run, making them somewhat slower than functions to start (although once started, they run at the same speed). In terms of parameter capabilities, shell function commands and script commands are identical. An example of a script is shown in listing 2.3. The astute observer will notice that the only difference between this example and the previous function example is that the `function` keyword, the function name, and the braces enclosing the body are missing. This is because they aren't necessary anymore. A script takes its name from the name of the file and is delimited by the file itself, so no braces are needed.

Listing 2.3 Source code for the simple shell script command `my-script.ps1`

```
param($Parameter1)                              <-- Parameters
process {                       <-- Process scriptblock
    if ($Parameter1)
    {
        "${Parameter1}:$_"
    } else {
        "$_"
    }
}
```

Native commands (applications)

The last type of command is called a *native command*. These are external programs (typically executables) that can be executed by the operating system.

> **NOTE** Choosing names for things is always difficult, and the term *native command* does sound a bit strange. We had originally called external executables *legacy commands*, but the feedback was that *legacy* was perceived as being a negative term. On the other hand, simply calling them executables wasn't suitable, because this class of command also includes `cmd.exe` batch files. In the end, we settled on *native command* as sufficiently distinctive.

Because running a native command involves creating a whole new process for the command, native commands are the slowest of the command types. Also, native commands do their own parameter processing and so don't necessarily match the syntax of the other types of commands.

Native commands cover anything that can be run on a Windows computer, so you get a wide variety of behaviors. One of the biggest issues is when PowerShell waits for a command to finish but it just keeps on going. For example, say you're starting a text document at the command line:

```
PS (1) > .\foo.txt
PS (2) >
```

You get the prompt back more or less immediately, and your default text editor will pop up (probably `notepad.exe` because that's the default). The program to launch is determined by the file associations that are defined as part of the Windows environment.

> **NOTE** In PowerShell, unlike in `cmd.exe`, you have to prefix a command with `./` or `.\` if you want to run it out of the current directory. This is part of PowerShell's "Secure by Design" philosophy. This particular security feature was adopted to prevent Trojan horse attacks where the user is lured into a directory and then told to run an innocuous command such as `notepad.exe`. Instead of running the system `notepad.exe`, they end up running a hostile program that the attacker has placed in that directory and named `notepad.exe`. Chapter 21 covers the security features of the PowerShell environment in detail.

What about when you specify the editor explicitly?

```
PS (2) > notepad foo.txt
PS (3) >
```

The same thing happens—the command returns immediately. But what about when you run the command in the middle of a pipeline?

```
PS (3) > notepad foo.txt | sort-object
<exit notepad>
PS (4) >
```

Now PowerShell waits for the command to exit before giving you back the prompt. This can be handy when you want to insert something such as a graphical form editor in the middle of a script to do some processing. This is also the easiest way to make PowerShell wait for a process to exit.

Finally, let's run the `edit.com` program. This is the old console-based full screen editor included with MS-DOS and Windows since about DOS 4.0. (This also works with other console editors—vi, Emacs, and so forth.)

```
PS (6) > edit.com ./foo.txt
PS (7) >
```

As you'd expect, the editor starts up, taking over the console window. You can edit the file and then exit the editor and return to PowerShell. As you can see, the behavior of native commands depends on the type of native command, as well as where it appears in the pipeline.

A useful thing to remember is that the PowerShell interpreter itself is a native command: `powershell.exe`. This means you can call PowerShell from within PowerShell. When you do this, a second PowerShell process is created. In practice there's nothing unusual about this—that's basically how all shells work. PowerShell just doesn't have to do it very often, making it much faster than conventional shell languages.

The ability to run a child PowerShell process is particularly useful if you want to have isolation in portions of your script. A separate process means that the child script can't impact the caller's environment. This feature is useful enough that PowerShell has special handling for this case, allowing you to embed the script to run inline. If you want to run a fragment of script in a child process, you can do so by passing the block of script to the child process delimited by braces. Here's an example:

```
PS (1) > powershell { Get-Process *ss } | Format-Table name, handles

Name                                                         Handles
----                                                         -------
csrss                                                           1077
lsass                                                           1272
smss                                                              28
```

There are two things to note in this example. The script code in the braces can be any PowerShell code, and it will be passed through to the new PowerShell process. The special handling takes care of encoding the script in such a way that it's passed properly to the child process. The other thing to note is that, when PowerShell is executed this way, the output of the process is *serialized objects*—the basic structure of the output is preserved—and so can be passed into other commands. We'll look at this serialization in detail when we cover *remoting*—the ability to run PowerShell scripts on a remote computer—in chapter 12.

Now that we've covered all four PowerShell command types, let's get back to looking at the PowerShell syntax. Notice that a lot of what we've examined so far is a bit verbose. This makes it easy to read, which is great for script maintenance, but it looks like it would be a pain to type on the command line. PowerShell addresses these two conflicting goals—readability and writeability—with the concept of *elastic syntax*. Elastic syntax allows you to expand and collapse how much you need to type to suit your purpose. We'll see how this works in the next section.

2.3 ALIASES AND ELASTIC SYNTAX

We haven't talked about aliases yet or how they're used to achieve an elastic syntax in PowerShell. Because this concept is important in the PowerShell environment, we need to spend some time on it.

The cmdlet `Verb-Noun` syntax, while regular, is, as we noted, also verbose. You may have noticed that in most of the examples we're using commands such as `dir` and `type`. The trick behind all this is aliases. The `dir` command is really `Get-ChildItem`, and the `type` command is really `Get-Content`. You can see this by using the `Get-Command` command:

```
PS (1) > get-command dir
CommandType     Name                       Definition
-----------     ----                       ----------
Alias           dir                        Get-ChildItem
```

This tells you that the command is an alias for `Get-ChildItem`. To get information about the `Get-ChildItem` command, you then do this

```
PS (2) > get-command get-childitem
CommandType     Name                       Definition
-----------     ----                       ----------
Cmdlet          Get-ChildItem              Get-ChildItem [[-P...
```

which truncates the information at the width of the console window. To see all the information, pipe the output of `Get-Command` into `fl`:

```
PS (3) > get-command get-childitem | fl
Name             : Get-ChildItem
CommandType      : Cmdlet
Definition       : Get-ChildItem [[-Path] <String[]>] [[-Filter]
                    <String>] [-Include <String[]>] [-Exclude <S
                   tring[]>] [-Recurse] [-Force] [-Name] [-Verbo
                   se] [-Debug] [-ErrorAction <ActionPreference>
                   ] [-ErrorVariable <String>] [-OutVariable <St
                   ring>] [-OutBuffer <Int32>]
                   Get-ChildItem [-LiteralPath] <String[]> [[-Fi
                   lter] <String>] [-Include <String[]>] [-Exclu
                   de <String[]>] [-Recurse] [-Force] [-Name] [-
                   Verbose] [-Debug] [-ErrorAction <ActionPrefer
                   ence>] [-ErrorVariable <String>] [-OutVariabl
                   e <String>] [-OutBuffer <Int32>]

Path             :
AssemblyInfo     :
DLL              : C:\WINDOWS\assembly\GAC_MSIL\Microsoft.PowerS
                   hell.Commands.Management\1.0.0.0__31bf3856ad3
                   64e35\Microsoft.PowerShell.Commands.Managemen
                   t.dll
HelpFile         : Microsoft.PowerShell.Commands.Management.dll-
                   Help.xml
ParameterSets    : {Items, LiteralItems}
ImplementingType : Microsoft.PowerShell.Commands.GetChildItemCom
```

```
                      mand
Verb                : Get
Noun                : ChildItem
```

This shows you the full detailed information about this cmdlet. But wait—what's the `fl` command? Again you can use `Get-Command` to find out:

```
PS (4) > get-command fl
CommandType     Name                      Definition
-----------     ----                      ----------
Alias           fl                        Format-List
```

PowerShell comes with a large set of predefined aliases. There are two basic categories of aliases—*transitional aliases* and *convenience aliases*. By transitional aliases, we mean a set of aliases that map PowerShell commands to commands that people are accustomed to using in other shells, specifically `cmd.exe` and the UNIX shells. For the `cmd.exe` user, PowerShell defines `dir`, `type`, `copy`, and so on. For the UNIX user, PowerShell defines `ls`, `cat`, `cp`, and so forth. These aliases allow a basic level of functionality for new users right away.

The other set of aliases are the convenience aliases. These aliases are derived from the names of the cmdlets they map to. So `Get-Command` becomes `gcm`, `Get-ChildItem` becomes `gci`, `Invoke-Item` becomes `ii`, and so on. For a list of the defined aliases, type `Get-Alias` at the command line. You can use the `Set-Alias` command (whose alias is `sal`, by the way) to define your own aliases.

> **NOTE** Aliases in PowerShell are limited to aliasing the command name only. Unlike in other systems such as ksh, bash, and zsh, PowerShell aliases can't take parameters. If you need to do something more sophisticated than simple command-name translations, you'll have to use shell functions or scripts.

This is all well and good, but what does it have to do with elastics? Glad you asked! The idea is that PowerShell can be terse when needed and descriptive when appropriate. The syntax is concise for simple cases and can be stretched like an elastic band for larger problems. This is important in a language that is both a command-line tool and a scripting language. The vast majority of "scripts" that you'll write in PowerShell will be no more than a few lines long. In other words, they'll be a string of commands that you'll type on the command line and then never use again. To be effective in this environment, the syntax needs to be concise. This is where aliases like `fl` come in—they allow you to write concise command lines. When you're scripting, though, it's best to use the long name of the command. Sooner or later, you'll have to read the script you wrote (or—worse—someone else will). Would you rather read something that looks like this

```
gcm|?{$_.parametersets.Count -gt 3}|fl name
```

or this?

```
get-command |
  where-object {$_.parametersets.count -gt 3} |
    format-list name
```

I'd certainly rather read the latter. (As always, we'll cover the details of these examples later in the book.)

> **NOTE** PowerShell has two (or more) names for many of the same commands. Some people find this unsettling—they prefer having only one way of doing things. In fact, this "only one way to do it" principle is also true for PowerShell, but with a significant variation: we wanted to have one *best* way of doing something for each particular scenario or situation. Fundamentally this is what computers are all about; at their simplest, everything is just a bunch of bits. To be practical, you start from the simple bits and build solutions that are more appropriate for the problem you're trying to solve. Along the way, you create an intermediate-sized component that may be reused to solve other problems. PowerShell uses this same approach: a series of components at different levels of complexity intended to address a wide range of problem classes. Not every problem is a nail, so having more tools than a hammer is a good idea even if requires a bit more learning.

There's a second type of alias used in PowerShell: *parameter aliases*. Unlike command aliases, which can be created by end users, parameter aliases are created by the author of a cmdlet, script, or function. (You'll see how to do this when we look at advanced function creation in chapter 8.)

A parameter alias is just a shorter name for a parameter. But wait a second. Earlier we said that you just needed enough of the parameter name to distinguish it from other command parameters. Isn't this enough for convenience and elasticity? So why do you need parameter aliases? The reason you need these aliases has to do with *script versioning*. The easiest way to understand versioning is to look at an example.

Say you have a script that calls a cmdlet `Process-Message`. This cmdlet has a parameter `-Reply`. You write your script specifying just

```
Process-Message -Re
```

Run the script, and it works fine. A few months later, you install an enhanced version of the `Process-Message` command. This new version introduces a new parameter: `-receive`. Just specifying `-Re` is no longer sufficient. If you run the old script with the new cmdlet, it will fail with an ambiguous parameter message. In other words, the script is broken.

How do you fix this with parameter aliases? The first thing to know is that PowerShell always picks the parameter that exactly matches a parameter name or alias over a partial match. By providing parameter aliases, you can achieve pithiness without also making scripts subject to versioning issues. (We do recommend always using the full parameter name for production scripts or scripts you want to share. Readability is always more important in that scenario.)

Now that we've covered the core concepts of how commands are processed, let's step back a bit and look at PowerShell language processing overall. PowerShell has a small number of important syntactic rules that you should learn. When you understand these rules, your ability to read, write, and debug PowerShell scripts will increase tremendously.

2.4 PARSING AND POWERSHELL

In this section, we'll cover the details of how PowerShell scripts are parsed. Before the PowerShell interpreter can execute the commands you type, it first has to parse the command text and turn it into something the computer can execute, as shown in figure 2.3.

More formally, parsing is the process of turning human-readable source code into a form the computer understands. This is one area of computer science that deserves both of these words—*computer* and *science*. Science in this case means formal language theory, which is a branch of mathematics. And because it's mathematics, discussing it usually requires a collection of Greek letters. We'll keep things a bit simpler here. A piece of script text is broken up into tokens by the *tokenizer* (or *lexical analyzer*, if you want to be more technical). A token is a particular type of symbol in the programming language, such as a number, a keyword, or a variable. Once the raw text has been broken into a stream of tokens, these tokens are processed into structures in the language through syntactic analysis.

In syntactic analysis, the stream of tokens is processed according to the grammatical rules of the language. In normal programming languages, this process is straightforward—a token always has the same meaning. A sequence of digits is always a number; an expression is always an expression, and so on. For example, the sequence

```
3+2
```

would always be an addition expression, and "Hello world" would always be a constant string. Unfortunately, this isn't the case in shell languages. Sometimes you can't

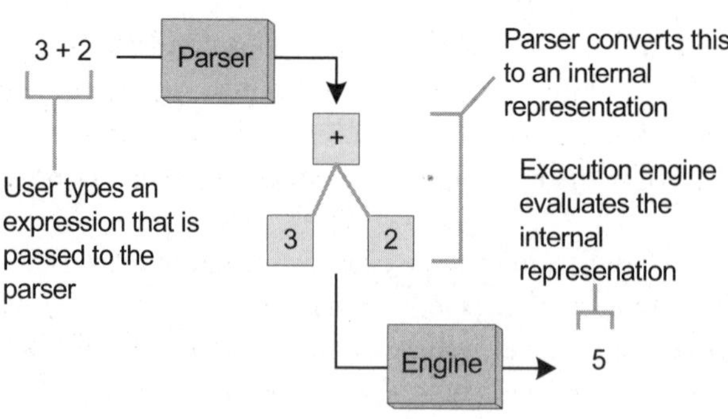

Figure 2.3 The flow of processing in the PowerShell interpreter, where an expression is transformed and then executed to produce a result

tell what a token is except through its context. In the next section, we go into more detail on why this is and how the PowerShell interpreter parses a script.

2.4.1 How PowerShell parses

For PowerShell to be successful as a shell, it can't require that everything be quoted. PowerShell would fail if it required people to continually type

```
cd ".."
```

or

```
copy "foo.txt" "bar.txt"
```

On the other hand, people have a strong idea of how expressions should work:

```
2
```

This is the number 2, not a string "2". Consequently, PowerShell has some rather complicated parsing rules. The next three sections will cover these rules. We'll discuss how quoting is handled, the two major parsing modes, and the special rules for newlines and statement termination.

2.4.2 Quoting

Quoting is the mechanism used to turn a token that has special meaning to the PowerShell interpreter into a simple string value. For example, the `Write-Output` cmdlet has a parameter `-InputObject`. But what if you want to actually use the string "-InputObject" as an argument, as mentioned earlier? To do this, you have to quote it; that is, you surround it with single or double quotes. The result looks like this:

```
PS (2) > Write-Output '-InputObject'
-inputobject
```

What would happen if you hadn't put the argument in quotes? Let's find out:

```
PS (3) > Write-Output -InputObject
Write-Output : Missing an argument for parameter 'InputObject'.
Specify a parameter of type 'System.Management.Automation.PSObject[]'and
          try again.
At line:1 char:25
+ Write-Output -inputobject <<<<
PS (4) >
```

As you can see, this produces an error message indicating that an argument to the parameter `-InputObject` is required.

PowerShell supports several forms of quoting, each with somewhat different meanings (or semantics). Putting single quotes around an entire sequence of characters causes them to be treated like a single string. This is how you deal with file paths that have spaces in them. For example, if you want to change to a directory whose path contains spaces, you type this:

```
PS (4) > cd 'c:\program files'
```

```
PS (5) > pwd
Path
----
C:\Program Files
```

What happens if you don't use the quotes?

```
PS (6) > cd c:\program files
Set-Location : A parameter cannot be found that matches paramete
r name 'files'.
At line:1 char:3
+ cd  <<<< c:\program files
```

When you don't use the quotes, you receive an error complaining about an unexpected parameter in the command because `"c:\program"` and `"files"` are treated as two separate tokens.

> **NOTE** Notice that the error message reports the name of the cmdlet, not the alias that was used. This way you know what is being executed. The position message shows you the text that was entered so you can see that an alias was used.

One problem with using matching quotes as we did in the previous examples is that you have to remember to start the token with an opening quote. This raises an issue when you want to quote a single character. You can use the backquote (`) character to do this (the backquote is usually the upper-leftmost key, below Esc):

```
PS (6) > cd c:\program` files
PS (7) > pwd
Path
----
C:\Program Files
```

The backquote, or *backtick*, as it tends to be called, has other uses that we'll explore later in this section. Now let's look at the other form of matching quote: double quotes. Once again, here's our favorite example:

```
PS (8) > cd "c:\program files"
PS (9) > pwd

Path
----
C:\Program Files
```

It looks pretty much like the example with single quotes, so what's the difference? In double quotes, variables are expanded. In other words, if the string contains a variable reference starting with a `$`, it will be replaced by the string representation of the value stored in the variable. Let's look at an example. First assign the string "files" to the variable `$v`:

```
PS (10) > $v = "files"
```

Now reference that variable in a string with double quotes:

```
PS (11) > cd "c:\program $v"
PS (12) > pwd

Path
----
C:\Program Files
```

The cd succeeded and the current directory was set as you expected. What happens if you try it with single quotes? Here you go:

```
PS (13) > cd 'c:\program $v'
set-location : Cannot find path 'C:\program $v' because it does
not exist.
At line:1 char:3
+ cd  <<<< 'c:\program $v'
PS (14) >
```

Because expansion is performed only in double quotes and not in single quotes, you get an error because the unexpanded path doesn't exist.

Take a look at another example:

```
PS (14) > '$v is $v'
$v is $v
PS (15) > "$v is $v"
files is files
```

In the single-quoted case, $v is never expanded; and in the double-quoted case, it's always expanded. But what if you really want to show what the value of $v is? To do this, you need to have expansion in one place but not in the other. This is one of those other uses we had for the backtick. It can be used to quote or escape the dollar sign in a double-quoted string to suppress expansion. Let's try it:

```
PS (16) > Write-Output "`$v is $v"
$v is files
```

Here's one final tweak to this example—if $v contained spaces, you'd want to make clear what part of the output was the value. Because single quotes can contain double quotes and double quotes can contain single quotes, this is straightforward:

```
PS (17) > Write-Output "`$v is '$v'"
$v is 'files'
PS (18) >
```

Now, suppose you want to display the value of $v on another line instead of in quotes. Here's another situation where you can use the backtick as an escape character. The sequence `n in a double-quoted string will be replaced by a newline character. You can write the example with the value of $v on a separate line as follows:

```
PS (19) > "The value of `$v is:`n$v"
The value of $v is:
Files
```

Table 2.1 lists the special characters that can be generated using backtick (also called *escape*) sequences.

Table 2.1 The PowerShell escape sequences

Escape sequence	Corresponding Special Character
`n	Newline
`t	Horizontal tab
`a	Alert
`b	Backspace
`'	Single quote
`"	Double quote
`0	The NULL character (in other words, 0)
``	A single backtick

Note that escape sequence processing, like variable expansion, is only done in double-quoted strings. In single-quoted strings, what you see is what you get. This is particularly important when writing a string to pass to a subsystem that does additional levels of quote processing.

If you've used another language such as C, C#, or Perl, you'll be accustomed to using the backslash instead of the backtick for escaping characters. Because PowerShell is a shell and has to deal with Windows' historical use of the backslash as a path separator, it isn't practical to use the backslash as the escape character. Too many applications expect backslash-separated paths, and that would require every path to be typed with the slashes doubled. Choosing a different escape character was a difficult decision that the PowerShell team had to make, but there wasn't any choice. It's one of the biggest cognitive bumps that experienced shell and script language users run into with PowerShell, but in the end, most people adapt without too much difficulty.

2.4.3 Expression-mode and command-mode parsing

As mentioned earlier, because PowerShell is a shell, it has to deal with some parsing issues not found in other languages. In practice, most shell languages are collections of mini-languages with many different parsing modes. PowerShell simplifies this considerably, trimming the number of modes down to two: expression mode and command mode.

In expression mode, the parsing is conventional: strings must be quoted, numbers are always numbers, and so on. In command mode, numbers are treated as numbers but all other arguments are treated as strings unless they start with `$`, `@`, `'`, `"`, or `(`. When an argument begins with one of these special characters, the rest of the argument is parsed as a value expression. (There's also special treatment for leading variable references in a string, which we'll discuss later.) Table 2.2 shows some examples that illustrate how items are parsed in each mode.

Table 2.2 Parsing mode examples

Example command line	Parsing mode and explanation
`2+2`	Expression mode; results in 4.
`Write-Output 2+2`	Command mode; results in 2+2.
`$a=2+2`	Expression mode; the variable `$a` is assigned the value 4.
`Write-Output (2+2)`	Expression mode; because of the parentheses, 2+2 is evaluated as an expression producing 4. This result is then passed as an argument to the `Write-Output` cmdlet.
`Write-Output $a`	Expression mode; produces 4. This is ambiguous—evaluating it in either mode produces the same result. The next example shows why the default is expression mode if the argument starts with a variable.
`Write-Output $a.Equals(4)`	Expression mode; `$a.Equals(4)` evaluates to true so `Write-Output` writes the Boolean value True. This is why a variable is evaluated in expression mode by default. You want simple method and property expressions to work without parentheses.
`Write-Output $a/foo.txt`	Command mode; `$a/foo.txt` expands to `4/foo.txt`. This is the opposite of the previous example. Here you want it to be evaluated as a string in command mode. The interpreter first parses in expression mode and sees that it's not a valid property expression, so it backs up and rescans the argument in command mode. As a result, it's treated as an expandable string.

Notice that in the `Write-Output (2+2)` case, the open parenthesis causes the interpreter to enter a new level of interpretation where the parsing mode is once again established by the first token. This means the sequence `2+2` is parsed in expression mode, not command mode, so the result of the expression (4) is emitted. Also, the last example in the table illustrates the exception mentioned previously for a leading variable reference in a string. A variable itself is treated as an expression, but a variable followed by arbitrary text is treated as though the whole thing were in double quotes. This is so you can write

```
cd $HOME/scripts
```

instead of

```
cd "$HOME/scripts"
```

As mentioned earlier, quoted and unquoted strings are recognized as different tokens by the parser. This is why

```
Invoke-MyCmdlet -Parm arg
```

treats `-Parm` as a parameter and

```
Invoke-MyCmdlet "-Parm" arg
```

treats "-Parm" as an argument. There's an additional wrinkle in the parameter binding. If an unquoted parameter like -NotAparameter isn't a parameter on Invoke-MyCmdlet, it will be treated as an argument. This lets you say

```
Write-Host  -this -is -a parameter
```

without requiring quoting.

This finishes our coverage of the basics of parsing modes, quoting, and commands. Commands can take arbitrary lists of arguments, so knowing when the statement ends is important. We'll cover this in the next section.

2.4.4 Statement termination

In PowerShell, there are two statement terminator characters: the semicolon (;) and (sometimes) the newline. Why is a newline a statement separator only *sometimes*? The rule is that if the previous text is a syntactically complete statement, a newline is considered to be a statement termination. If it isn't complete, the newline is simply treated like any other whitespace. This is how the interpreter can determine when a command or expression crosses multiple lines. For example, in the following

```
PS (1) > 2 +
>> 2
>>
4
PS (2) >
```

the sequence 2 + is incomplete, so the interpreter prompts you to enter more text. (This is indicated by the nest prompt characters, >>.) On the other hand, in the next sequence

```
PS (2) > 2
2
PS (3) > + 2
2
PS (4) >
```

the number 2 by itself is a complete expression, so the interpreter goes ahead and evaluates it. Likewise, + 2 is a complete expression and is also evaluated (+ in this case is treated as the unary plus operator). From this, you can see that if the newline comes after the + operator, the interpreter will treat the two lines as a single expression. If the newline comes before the + operator, it will treat the two lines as two individual expressions.

Most of the time, this mechanism works the way you expect, but sometimes you can receive some unanticipated results. Take a look at the following example:

```
PS (22) > $b = ( 2
>> + 2 )
>>
Missing closing ')' in expression.
```

```
At line:2 char:1
+ + <<<<  2 )
PS (23) >
```

This was a question raised by one of the PowerShell beta testers. They were surprised by this result and thought there was something wrong with the interpreter, but in fact, this is not a bug. Here's what's happening.

Consider the following text:

```
> $b = (2 +
> 2)
```

It's parsed as `$b = (2 + 2)` because a trailing + operator is only valid as part of a binary operator expression. Because the sequence `$b = ( 2 +` can't be a syntactically complete statement, the newline is treated as whitespace. On the other hand, consider the text

```
> $b = (2
> + 2)
```

In this case, `2` is a syntactically complete statement, so the newline is now treated as a line terminator. In effect, the sequence is parsed like `$b = (2 ; + 2 );` that is, two complete statements. Because the syntax for a parenthetical expression is

```
( <expr> )
```

you get a syntax error—the interpreter is looking for a closing parenthesis as soon as it has a complete expression. Contrast this with using a *subexpression* instead of just the parentheses:

```
>> $b = $(
>> 2
>> +2
>> )
>>
PS (24) > $b
2
2
```

Here the expression is valid because the syntax for subexpressions is

```
$( <statementList> )
```

But how do you deal with the case when you do need to extend a line that isn't extensible by itself? This is another place where you can use the backtick escape character. If the last character in the line is a backtick, then the newline will be treated as a simple breaking space instead of as a newline:

```
PS (1) > Write-Output `
>> -inputobject `
>> "Hello world"
>>
Hello world
PS (2) >
```

Finally, one thing that surprises some people is that strings aren't terminated by a newline character. Strings can carry over multiple lines until a matching, closing quote is encountered:

```
PS (1) > Write-Output "Hello
>> there
>> how are
>> you?"
>>
Hello
there
how are
you?
PS (2) >
```

In this example, you see a string that extended across multiple lines. When that string was displayed, the newlines were preserved in the string.

The handling of end-of-line characters in PowerShell is another of the trade-offs that had to be made for PowerShell to be useful as a shell. Although the handling of end-of-line characters is a bit strange compared to non-shell languages, the overall result is easy for most people to get used to.

2.4.5 Comment syntax in PowerShell

Every computer language has some mechanism for annotating code with expository comments. Like many other shells and scripting languages, PowerShell comments begin with a number sign (#) symbol and continue to the end of the line. The # character must be at the beginning of a token for it to start a comment. Here's an example that illustrates what this means:

```
PS (1) > echo hi#there
hi#there
```

In this example, the number sign is in the middle of the token `hi#there` and so isn't treated as the starting of a comment. In the next example, there's a space before the number sign:

```
PS (2) > echo hi #there
hi
```

Now the # is treated as starting a comment and the following text isn't displayed. It can be preceded by characters other than a space and still start a comment. It can be preceded by any statement-terminating or expression-terminating character like a bracket, brace, or semicolon, as shown in the next couple of examples:

```
PS (3) > (echo hi)#there
hi
PS (4) > echo hi;#there
hi
```

In both of these examples, the # symbol indicates the start of a comment.

Finally, you need to take into account whether you're in expression mode or command mode. In command mode, as shown in the next example, the + symbol is included in the token hi+#there:

```
PS (5) > echo hi+#there
hi+#there
```

But in expression mode, it's parsed as its own token. Now the # indicates the start of a comment, and the overall expression results in an error:

```
PS (6) > "hi"+#there
You must provide a value expression on the right-hand side of the '+'
operator.
At line:1 char:6
+ "hi"+ <<<< #there
```

The # symbol is also allowed in function names:

```
PS (3) > function hi#there { "Hi there" }
PS (4) > hi#there
Hi there
```

The reason for allowing the # in the middle of tokens was to make it easy to accommodate path providers that used # as part of their path names. People conventionally include a space before the beginning of a comment, so this doesn't appear to cause any difficulties.

Multiline Comments

In PowerShell version 2, a new type of *multiline* comment was introduced, primarily to allow you to embed inline help text in scripts and functions. A multiline comment begins with <# and ends with #>. Here's an example:

```
<#
 This is a comment
    that spans
 multiple lines
#>
```

This type of comment can be entered from the command line, which looks like this:

```
PS {1) > <#
>> this is a comment
>> that spans
>> multiple lines
>> #>
>>
PS {2) >
```

This type of comment need not span multiple lines, so you can use this notation to add a comment preceding some code:

```
PS {2) > <# a comment #> "Some code"
Some code
PS {3) >
```

In this example, the line is parsed, the comment is read and ignored, and the code after the comment is executed.

One of the things this type of comment allows you to do is easily embed chunks of preformatted text in functions and scripts. The PowerShell help system takes advantage of this feature to allow functions and scripts to contain *inline documentation* in the form of special comments. These comments are automatically extracted by the help system to generate documentation for the function or script. You'll learn how the comments are used by the help subsystem in chapter 8.

Now that you have a good understanding of the basic PowerShell syntax, let's look at how what you type gets executed by the PowerShell execution engine. We'll start with the pipeline.

2.5 HOW THE PIPELINE WORKS

At long last we get to the details of pipelines. We've been talking about them throughout this chapter, but here we discuss them in detail. A pipeline is a series of commands separated by the pipe operator (|), as shown in figure 2.4. In some ways, the term *production line* better describes pipelines in PowerShell. Each command in the pipeline receives an object from the previous command, performs some operation on it, and then passes it along to the next command in the pipeline.

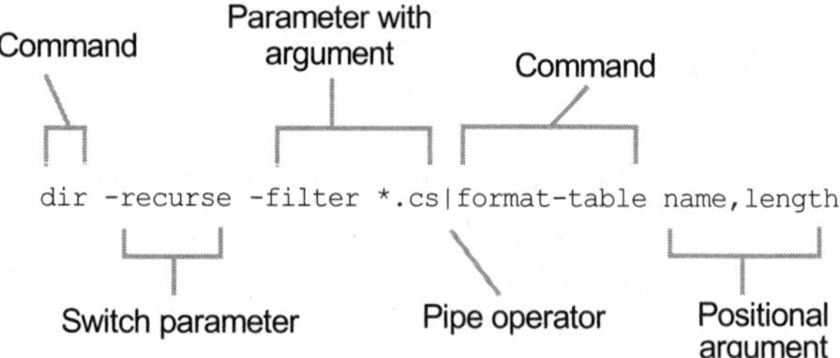

Figure 2.4 Anatomy of a pipeline

> **NOTE** This, by the way, is the great PowerShell Heresy. All previous shells passed strings only through the pipeline. Many people had difficulty with the notion of doing anything else. Like the character in *The Princess Bride*, they'd cry "Inconceivable!" And we'd respond, "I do not think that word means what you think it means."

All of the command categories take parameters and arguments. To review, a *parameter* is a special token that starts with a hyphen (-) and is used to control the behavior of the command. An *argument* is a data value consumed by the command. In the following example

```
get-childitem -filter *.dll -path c:\windows -recurse
```

`-filter` is a parameter that takes one argument, `*.dll`. The string "c:\windows" is the argument to the positional parameter `-path`.

Next we'll discuss the signature characteristic of pipelines—streaming behavior.

2.5.1 Pipelines and streaming behavior

Streaming behavior occurs when objects are processed one at a time in a pipeline. As mentioned, this is one of the characteristic behaviors of shell languages. In stream processing, objects are output from the pipeline as soon as they become available. In more traditional programming environments, the results are returned only when the entire result set has been generated—the first result and the last result are returned at the same time. In a pipelined shell, the first result is returned as soon as it's available and subsequent results return as they also become available. This flow is illustrated in figure 2.5.

At the top of figure 2.5 you see a PowerShell command pipeline containing four commands. This command pipeline is passed to the PowerShell parser, which does all the work of figuring out what the commands are, what the arguments and parameters are, and how they should be bound for each command. When the parsing is complete, the pipeline processor begins to sequence the commands. First it runs the `begin` clause of each of the commands, in sequence from first to last. After all the `begin` clauses have been run, it runs the `process` clause in the first command. If the command generates one or more objects, the pipeline processor passes these objects, one at a time, to the second command. If the second command also emits an object, this object is passed to the third command, and so on.

When processing reaches the end of the pipeline, any objects emitted are passed back to the PowerShell host. The host is then responsible for any further processing.

This aspect of streaming is important in an interactive shell environment, because you want to see objects as soon as they're available. The next example shows a simple pipeline that traverses through C:\Windows looking for all of the DLLs whose names start with the word "system":

```
PS (1) > dir -rec -fil *.dll | where {$_.name -match "system.*dll"}

    Directory: Microsoft.Management.Automation.Core\FileSystem::
[CA]C:\WINDOWS\assembly\[CA]GAC\System\1.0.3300.0__b77a5c561934e089
```

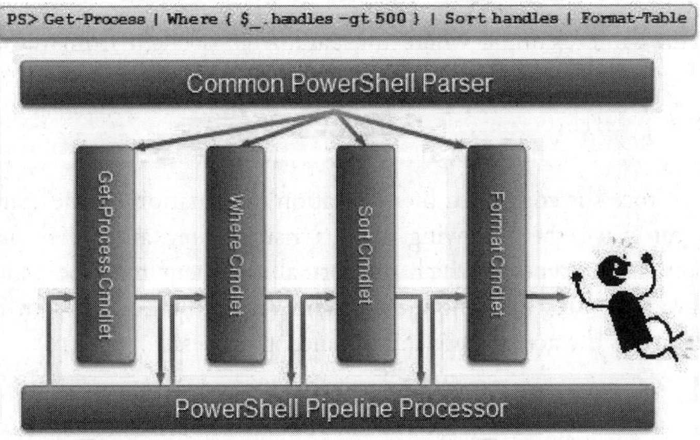

Figure 2.5 How objects flow through a pipeline one at a time. A common parser constructs each of the command objects and then starts the pipeline processor, stepping each object through all stages of the pipeline.

```
Mode                LastWriteTime     Length Name
----                -------------     ------ ----
-a---         2/26/2004   6:29 PM    1167360 System.dll

    Directory: Microsoft.Management.Automation.Core\FileSystem::
[CA]C:\WINDOWS\assembly
[CA]\GAC\System\1.0.5000.0__b77a5c561934e089

Mode                LastWriteTime     Length Name
----                -------------     ------ ----
-a---         2/26/2004   6:36 PM    1216512 System.dll
```

With streaming behavior, as soon as the first file is found, it's displayed. Without streaming, you'd have to wait until the entire directory structure has been searched before you'd start to see any results.

In most shell environments, streaming is accomplished by using separate processes for each element in the pipeline. In PowerShell, which only uses a single process (and a single thread as well), streaming is accomplished by splitting cmdlets into three clauses: `BeginProcessing`, `ProcessRecord`, and `EndProcessing`. In a pipeline, the `BeginProcessing` clause is run for all cmdlets in the pipeline. Then the `ProcessRecord` clause is run for the first cmdlet. If this clause produces an object, that object is passed to the `ProcessRecord` clause of the next cmdlet in the pipeline, and so on. Finally the `EndProcessing` clauses are all run. (We cover this sequencing again in more detail in chapter 7, which is about scripts and functions, because they can also have these clauses.)

2.5.2 Parameters and parameter binding

Now let's talk about more of the details involved in binding parameters for commands. *Parameter binding* is the process in which values are bound to the parameters on a command. These values can come from either the command line or the pipeline. Here's an example of a parameter argument being bound from the command line:

```
PS (1) > Write-Output 123
123
```

And here's the same example where the parameter is taken from the input object stream:

```
PS (2) > 123 | Write-Output
123
```

The binding process is controlled by declaration information on the command itself. Parameters can have the following characteristics: they are either mandatory or optional, they have a type to which the formal argument must be convertible, and they can have attributes that allow the parameters to be bound from the pipeline. Table 2.3 describes the actual steps in the binding process.

Table 2.3 Steps in the parameter binding process

Binding step	Description
1. Bind all named parameters.	Find all unquoted tokens on the command line that start with a dash. If the token ends with a colon, an argument is required. If there's no colon, look at the type of the parameter and see if an argument is required. Convert the type of actual argument to the type required by the parameter, and bind the parameter.
2. Bind all positional parameters.	If there are any arguments on the command line that haven't been used, look for unbound parameters that take positional parameters and try to bind them.
3. Bind from the pipeline by value with exact match.	If the command is not the first command in the pipeline and there are still unbound parameters that take pipeline input, try to bind to a parameter that matches the type exactly.
4. If not bound, then bind from the pipe by value with conversion.	If the previous step failed, try to bind using a type conversion.
5. If not bound, then bind from the pipeline by name with exact match.	If the previous step failed, look for a property on the input object that matches the name of the parameter. If the types exactly match, bind the parameter.
6. If not bound, then bind from the pipeline by name with conversion.	If the input object has a property whose name matches the name of a parameter, and the type of the property is convertible to the type of the parameter, bind the parameter.

As you can see, this binding process is quite involved. In practice, the parameter binder almost always does what you want—that's why a sophisticated algorithm is used. But there are times when you'll need to understand the binding algorithm to get a particular behavior. PowerShell has built-in facilities for debugging the parameter-binding process that can be accessed through the `Trace-Command` cmdlet. (`Trace-Command` is covered in detail in appendix D.) Here's an example showing how to use this cmdlet:

```
Trace-Command -Name ParameterBinding  -Option All `
-Expression { 123 | Write-Output } -PSHost
```

In this example, you're tracing the expression in the braces—that's the expression:

```
123 | Write-Output
```

This expression pipes the number 123 to the cmdlet `Write-Output`. The `Write-Output` cmdlet takes a single mandatory parameter `-InputObject`, which allows pipeline input by value. (The tracing output is long but fairly self-explanatory, so we haven't included it here. This is something you should experiment with to see how it can help you figure out what's going on in the parameter-binding process.)

And now for the final topic in this chapter: formatting and output. The formatting and output subsystem provides the magic that lets PowerShell figure out how to display the output of the commands you type.

2.6 FORMATTING AND OUTPUT

We've reached this point without discussing how PowerShell figures out how to display output. In general, we've just run commands and depended on the system to figure out how to display the results. Occasionally, we've used commands such as `Format-Table` and `Format-List` to give general guidance on the shape of the display but no specific details. Let's dig in now and see how this all works.

As always, because PowerShell is a type-based system, types are used to determine how things are displayed. But normal objects don't usually know how to display themselves. PowerShell deals with this by including a database of formatting information for various types of objects. This is part of the extended type system, which is an important component of the overall system. This extended type system allows PowerShell to add new behaviors to existing .NET objects. The default formatting database is stored in the PowerShell install directory, which you can get to by using the `$PSHOME` shell variable. Here's a list of the files that were included as of this writing:

```
PS (1) > dir $PSHOME/*format* | Format-Table name

Name
----
Certificate.format.ps1xml
Diagnostics.Format.ps1xml
DotNetTypes.format.ps1xml
FileSystem.format.ps1xml
Help.format.ps1xml
PowerShellCore.format.ps1xml
PowerShellTrace.format.ps1xml
Registry.format.ps1xml
WSMan.Format.ps1xml
```

You can more or less figure out what types of things each of these files contains descriptions for. (The others should become clear after reading the rest of this book.) These files are XML documents that contain descriptions of how each type of object should be displayed. These descriptions are fairly complex and somewhat difficult to write. It's possible for end users to add their own type descriptions, but that's beyond the scope of this chapter. The important thing to understand is how the formatting and outputting commands work together.

2.6.1 The formatting cmdlets

Display of information is controlled by the type of the objects being displayed, but the user can choose the "shape" of the display by using the `Format-*` commands:

```
PS (5) > Get-Command Format-* | Format-Table name

Name
----
Format-Custom
Format-List
Format-Table
Format-Wide
```

By *shape*, we mean things such as a table or a list. Here's how they work. The `Format-Table` cmdlet formats output as a series of columns displayed across your screen:

```
PS (1) > Get-Item c:\ | Format-Table

    Directory:

Mode                LastWriteTime     Length Name
----                -------------     ------ ----
d--hs          4/9/2006  10:04 PM            C:\
```

By default, it tries to use the maximum width of the display and guesses at how wide a particular field should be. This allows you to start seeing data as quickly as possible (streaming behavior) but doesn't always produce optimal results. You can achieve a better display by using the `-AutoSize` switch, but this requires the formatter to process every element before displaying any of them, and this prevents streaming. PowerShell has to do this to figure out the best width to use for each field. The result in this example looks like this:

```
PS (3) > Get-Item c:\ | Format-Table -AutoSize

    Directory:

Mode         LastWriteTime Length Name
----         ------------- ------ ----
d--hs   4/9/2006  10:04 PM        C:\
```

Okay—so it doesn't look much different: things are more compressed with less whitespace.

In practice, the default layout when streaming is pretty good and you don't need to use `-autosize`, but sometimes it can help make things more readable.

The `Format-List` command displays the elements of the objects as a list, one after the other:

```
PS (2) > Get-Item c:\ | Format-List

    Directory:

Name           : C:\
CreationTime   : 2/26/2001 3:38:39 PM
LastWriteTime  : 4/9/2006 10:04:38 PM
LastAccessTime : 4/11/2006 9:33:51 PM
```

If there's more than one object to display, they'll appear as a series of lists. Let's try it:

```
PS (3) > Get-Item c:\,d:\ | Format-List

    Directory:

Name           : C:\
CreationTime   : 2/26/2001 3:38:39 PM
LastWriteTime  : 6/21/2006 1:20:06 PM
LastAccessTime : 6/21/2006 9:14:46 PM
```

```
Name           : D:\
CreationTime   : 12/31/1979 11:00:00 PM
LastWriteTime  : 12/31/1979 11:00:00 PM
LastAccessTime : 12/31/1979 11:00:00 PM
```

This is usually the best way to display a large collection of fields that won't fit well across the screen. (Obviously the idea of an `-AutoSize` switch makes no sense for this type of formatter.)

The `Format-Wide` cmdlet is used when you want to display a single object property in a concise way. It'll treat the screen as a series of columns for displaying the same information. Here's an example:

```
PS (1) > Get-Process -Name s* | Format-Wide -Column 8 id

1372      640       516       1328      400       532       560       828
876       984       1060      1124      4
```

In this example, you want to display the process IDs of all processes whose names start with "s" in eight columns. This formatter allows for dense display of information.

The final formatter is `Format-Custom`, which displays objects while preserving the basic structure of the object. Because most objects have a structure that contains other objects, which in turn contain other objects, this can produce extremely verbose output. Here's a small part of the output from the `Get-Item` cmdlet, displayed using `Format-Custom`:

```
PS (10) > Get-Item c:\ | Format-Custom -Depth 1
v
class DirectoryInfo
{
  PSPath = Microsoft.PowerShell.Core\FileSystem::C:\
  PSParentPath =
  PSChildName = C:\
  PSDrive =
    class PSDriveInfo
    {
      CurrentLocation =
      Name = C
      Provider = Microsoft.PowerShell.Core\FileSystem
      Root = C:\
      Description = C_Drive
      Credential = System.Management.Automation.PSCredential
    }
```

The full output is considerably longer, and notice that we've told it to stop walking the object structure at a depth of 1. You can imagine how verbose this output can be! So why have this cmdlet? Mostly because it's a useful debugging tool, either when you're creating your own objects or for exploring the existing objects in the .NET class libraries. You can see that this is a tool to keep in your back pocket for when you're getting down and dirty with objects, but not something that you'll typically use on a day-to-day basis.

2.6.2 The outputter cmdlets

Now that you know how to format something, how do you output it? You don't have to worry because, by default, things are automatically sent to (can you guess?) `Out-Default`.

Note that the following three examples do exactly the same thing:

```
dir | Out-Default
dir | Format-Table
dir | Format-Table | Out-Default
```

This is because the formatter knows how to get the default outputter, the default outputter knows how to find the default formatter, and the system in general knows how to find the defaults for both. The Möbius strip of subsystems!

As with the formatters, there are several outputter cmdlets available in PowerShell out of the box. You can use the `Get-Command` command to find them:

```
PS (1) > Get-Command Out-* | Format-Table Name

Name
----
Out-Default
Out-File
Out-GridView
Out-Host
Out-Null
Out-Printer
Out-String
```

Here we have a somewhat broader range of choices. We've already talked about `Out-Default`. The next one we'll talk about is `Out-Null`. This is a simple outputter; anything sent to `Out-Null` is simply discarded. This is useful when you don't care about the output for a command; you want the side effect of running the command. For example, the `mkdir` command outputs a listing of the directory it just created:

```
PS (1) > mkdir foo

    Directory: Microsoft.PowerShell.Core\FileSystem::C:\Temp

Mode                LastWriteTime     Length Name
----                -------------     ------ ----
d----         6/25/2010   8:50 PM            foo
```

If you don't want to see this output, pipe it to `Out-Null`. First remove the directory you created, and then create the directory:

```
PS (2) > rmdir foo
PS (3) > mkdir foo | out-null
PS (4) > get-item foo

    Directory: Microsoft.PowerShell.Core\FileSystem::C:\Temp
```

```
Mode                LastWriteTime     Length Name
----                -------------     ------ ----
d----          6/25/2010   8:50 PM            foo
```

And finally, because you didn't get the message, you should verify that the directory was actually created.

Null redirect

For the I/O redirection fans in the audience; piping to `Out-Null` is essentially equivalent to doing redirecting to `$null`. So

```
mkdir foo | out-null
```

is equivalent to

```
mkdir foo > $null
```

Next we have `Out-File`. Instead of sending the output to the screen, this command sends it to a file. (This command is also used by I/O redirection when doing output to a file.) In addition to writing the formatted output, `Out-File` has several flags that control how the output is written. The flags include the ability to append to a file instead of replacing it, to force writing to read-only files, and to choose the output encodings for the file. This last item is the trickiest one. You can choose from a number of the text encodings supported by Windows. Here's a trick—enter the command with an encoding that you know doesn't exist:

```
PS (9) > out-file -encoding blah
Out-File : Cannot validate argument "blah" because it does
not belong to the set "unicode, utf7, utf8, utf32, ascii,
bigendianunicode, default, oem".
At line:1 char:19
+ out-file -encoding  <<<< blah
PS (10) >
```

You can see in the error message that all the valid encoding names are displayed. If you don't understand what these encodings are, don't worry about it, and let the system use its default value.

> **NOTE** Where you're likely to run into problems with output encoding (or input encoding for that matter) is when you're creating files that are going to be read by another program. These programs may have limitations on what encodings they can handle, especially older programs. To find out more about file encodings, search for "file encodings" on http://msdn.microsoft.com. MSDN contains a wealth of information on this topic. Chapter 5 also contains additional information about working with file encodings in PowerShell.

The `Out-Printer` cmdlet doesn't need much additional explanation; it routes its text-only output to the printer instead of to a file or to the screen.

The `Out-Host` cmdlet is a bit more interesting—it sends its output back to the host. This has to do with the separation in PowerShell between the interpreter or engine and the application that hosts that engine. In theory, the host could be any application. It could be Visual Studio, it could be one of the Microsoft Office applications, or it could be a custom third-party application. In each of those cases, the host application would have to implement a special set of interfaces so that `Out-Host` could render its output properly. (We see this used in version 2 of PowerShell, which includes two hosts: the console host and the ISE.)

> **NOTE** `Out-Default` delegates the actual work of outputting to the screen to `Out-Host`.

The last output cmdlet to discuss is `Out-String`. This one's a bit different. All the other cmdlets send the output off somewhere else and don't write anything to the pipeline. The `Out-String` cmdlet formats its input and sends it as a string to the next cmdlet in the pipeline. Note that we said *string*, not *strings*. By default, it sends the entire output as a single string. This is not always the most desirable behavior—a collection of lines is usually more useful—but at least once you have the string, you can manipulate it into the form you want. If you do want the output as a series of strings, use the `-Stream` switch parameter. When you specify this parameter, the output will be broken into lines and streamed one at a time.

Note that this cmdlet runs somewhat counter to the philosophy of PowerShell; once you've rendered the object to a string, you've lost its structure. The main reason for including this cmdlet is for interoperation with existing APIs and external commands that expect to deal with strings. So, if you find yourself using `Out-String` a lot in your scripts, stop and think if it's the best way to attack the problem.

PowerShell version 2 introduced one additional output command: `Out-GridView`. As you might guess from the name, this command displays the output in a grid, but rather than rendering the output in the current console window, a new window is opened with the output displayed using a sophisticated grid control (see figure 2.6).

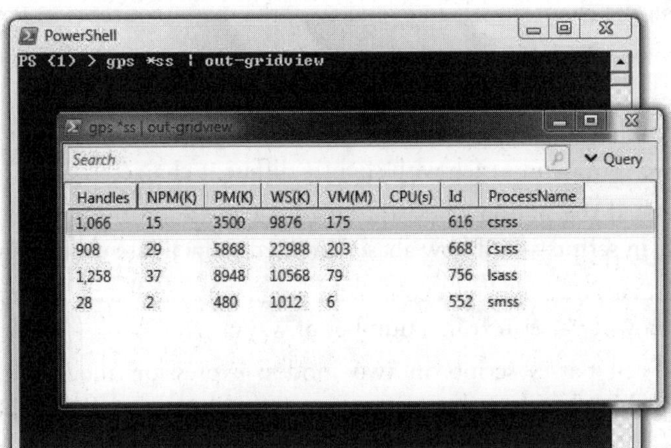

Figure 2.6 Displaying output with `Out-GridView`

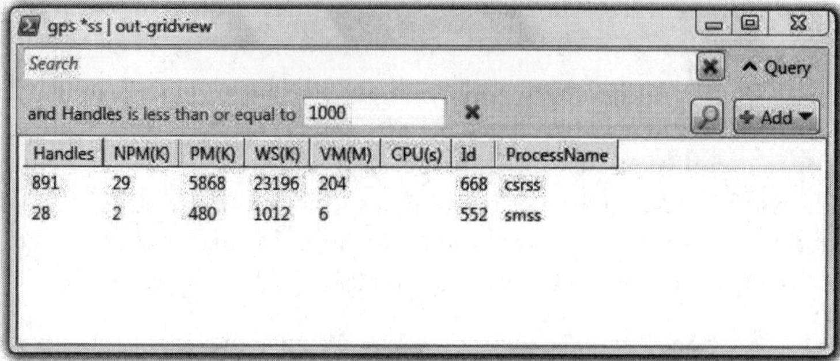

Figure 2.7 With the filtering features of control used by `Out-GridView`, you can drill into the dataset without having to regenerate the data.

The underlying grid control used by `Out-GridView` has all the features you'd expect from a modern Windows interface: columns can be reordered by dragging and dropping them, and the output can be sorted by clicking a column head. This control also introduces sophisticated filtering capabilities. This filtering allows you to drill into a dataset without having to rerun the command. Figure 2.7 shows an example of this filtering.

In figure 2.7, we've added a filter clause by clicking the Add button. This launches a dialog box that allows you to select a field to filter on as well as the criteria to use for the filter. In this case we've chosen to sort based on the Handles field, selecting rows where the number of handles is less than 1,000.

That's it for the basics: commands, parameters, pipelines, parsing, and presentation. You should now have a sufficient foundation to start moving on to more advanced topics in PowerShell.

2.7 SUMMARY

This chapter covered the basic structure of PowerShell commands, pipelines, and syntax:

- We began the chapter with an overview of the major concepts in PowerShell.
- We discussed the basic command and pipeline syntax and command parameter binding.
- PowerShell has four types of commands: cmdlets, functions, script commands, and native commands, each with slightly different characteristics.
- We discussed the notion of elastic syntax—concise on the command line and complete in scripts—and how aliases are used to facilitate elastic syntax.
- The fact that PowerShell is a command language as well as a scripting language impacts how it parses text in a number of ways:
  - PowerShell parses scripts in two modes: expression mode and command mode, which is a critical point to appreciate when using PowerShell.

  - The PowerShell escape character is a backtick (`), not a backslash.
  - PowerShell supports both double quotes and single quotes; variable and expression expansion is done in double quotes but not in single quotes.
  - Line termination is handled specially in PowerShell because it's a command language.
  - PowerShell has two types of comments: line comments that begin with # and block comments that start with <# and end with #>. The block comment notation was introduced in PowerShell version 2 with the intent of supporting inline documentation for scripts and functions.
- PowerShell uses a sophisticated formatting and outputting system to determine how to render objects without requiring detailed input from the user.

C H A P T E R 3

Working with types

"When I use a word," Humpty Dumpty said, in rather a scornful tone, "it means just what I choose it to mean—neither more nor less."

—Lewis Carroll, *Through the Looking Glass*

Most shell environments can only deal with strings, so the ability to use objects makes PowerShell different. Where you have objects, you also have object *types*. Much of the power of PowerShell comes from the innovative way it uses types. In this chapter, we'll look at the PowerShell type system, show how to take advantage of it, and examine some of the things you can accomplish with types in PowerShell.

3.1 TYPE MANAGEMENT IN THE WILD, WILD WEST

Shell languages are frequently called *typeless* languages. That characterization isn't really accurate because, fundamentally, programming is all about working with different types of objects. The more interesting question is how much implicit work the system does in handling types and how much work is required of you. This spectrum of effort is conventionally split into static and dynamic typing. In *statically typed* systems, much of the work is done for you as long as you stay within the domain of the types you're working on. Once you move outside that domain, it's up to the user to figure out how to move objects between those domains. The other cost of static typing is that you're required to declare the type of every variable, even when the compiler can figure it out for itself. Take the following C# statement, for example:

```
string myString = "hello world";
```

The variable `myString` is declared to be a string, even though it's obvious that it has to be a string. You're assigning a string to it, so what else could it be? It's this kind of redundancy that dynamic languages try to avoid. In *dynamically typed* languages, the user is rarely required to specify the type of a variable. Typically you don't even have to declare the variable at all.

> **NOTE** The statically typed language community recognizes that requiring the user to repeatedly specify type information is a problem. They address this, at least in part, through something called *type inferencing*. This is a mechanism where the language processor tries to figure out the type of each expression by looking at the types of each component of the expression. C# 3.0 is an example of a statically typed mainstream language that uses type inference for local variables and expressions.

3.1.1 PowerShell: a type-promiscuous language

The tendency is to characterize PowerShell as a dynamically typed language, but a better description is that PowerShell is a type-promiscuous language (sounds salacious, doesn't it?). By *type-promiscuous*, we mean that PowerShell will expend a tremendous amount of effort trying to turn what you have into what you need with as little work on your part as it can manage. When you ask for a property `Y`, PowerShell doesn't care if the object `foo` is a member of class `X`. It only cares whether `foo` has a property `Y`.

People who are used to strongly typed environments find this approach—well—disturbing. It sounds too much like "wild wild West" management. In practice, the interpreter is careful about making sure its transformations are reasonable and that no information is unexpectedly lost. This is particularly important when dealing with numeric calculations. In PowerShell, you can freely mix and match different types of numbers in expressions. You can even include strings in this mix. PowerShell converts everything as needed without specific guidance from the user, as long as there's no loss in precision. We'll use the remainder of this section to present a number of examples that illustrate this point. We'll look at operations where the conversions succeed and the type of the result of the operations. (For convenience, we'll use the .NET `GetType()` method to look at the base type of the results of the various expressions.) We'll also explore some examples where there's an error because the conversion causes some significant loss of information.

In our first example, you'll add an integer, a floating-point number, and a string that contains only digits:

```
PS (1) > 2 + 3.0 + "4"
9
PS (2) > (2 + 3.0 + "4").GetType().FullName
System.Double
```

As you can see from the result, everything was widened to a double-precision floating-point number. (*Widening* means converting to a representation that can handle larger or wider numbers: a `[long]` is wider than an `[int]`, and so forth.) Now let's be a bit trickier: put the floating-point number within quotes this time:

```
PS (3) > 2 + "3.0" + 4
9
PS (4) > (2 + "3.0" + 4).GetType().FullName
System.Double
```

Once again the system determines that the expression has to be done in floating point.

> **NOTE** The .NET single-precision floating-point representation isn't typically used unless you request it. In PowerShell, there usually isn't a performance benefit for using single precision, so there's no reason to use this less precise representation.

Now let's see a few simple examples that involve only integers. As you'd expect, all these operations result in integers as long as the result can be represented as an integer:

```
PS (5) > (3 + 4)
7
PS (6) > (3 + 4).GetType().FullName
System.Int32
PS (7) > (3 * 4).GetType().FullName
System.Int32
```

Try an example using the division operator:

```
PS (8) > 6/3
2
PS (9) > (6/3).GetType().FullName
System.Int32
```

Because 6 is divisible by 3, the result of this division is also an integer. But what happens if the divisor isn't a factor? Try it and see:

```
PS (10) > 6/4
1.5
PS (11) > (6/4).GetType().FullName
System.Double
```

The result is now a `[double]` type. The system noticed that there would be a loss of information if the operation were performed with integers, so it's executed using doubles instead.

Finally, try some examples using scientific notation. Add an integer to a large decimal:

```
PS (10) > 1e300
1E+300
PS (11) > 1e300 + 12
1E+300
```

The operation executed with the result being a double. In effect, adding an integer to a number of this magnitude means that the integer is ignored. This sort of loss is considered acceptable by the system. But there's another numeric type that's designed to be precise: `System.Decimal`. Normally you only use this type when you care about the precision of the result. Try the previous example, this time adding a decimal instead of an integer:

```
PS (12) > 1e300 + 12d
Cannot convert "1E+300" to "System.Decimal". Error: "Value was
either too large or too small for a
Decimal."
At line:1 char:8
+ 1e300 +  <<<< 12d
PS (13) >
```

This results in an error because when one of the operands involved is a `[decimal]` value, all operands are converted to decimal first and then the operation is performed. Because `1e300` is too large to be represented as a decimal, the operation will fail with an exception rather than lose precision.

From these examples, you can see that although the PowerShell type conversion system is aggressive in the types of conversions it performs, it's also careful about how it does things.

Now that you have a sense of the importance of types in PowerShell, let's look at how it all works.

3.1.2 The type system and type adaptation

Everything in PowerShell involves types in one way or another, so it's important to understand how the PowerShell type system works. That's what we're going to cover in this section. At the core of the PowerShell type system is the .NET type system. Little by little, the .NET Framework is expanding to encapsulate everything in the Windows world, but it hasn't swallowed everything yet. There are still several other object representations that Windows users, especially Windows system administrators, have to deal with. There's Common Object Model (COM) (essentially the precursor to .NET); Windows Management Instrumentation (WMI), which uses Management Object Format (MOF) definitions; ActiveX Data Objects (ADO) database objects; Active Directory Services Interface (ADSI) directory service objects; and so on (welcome to object alphabet soup). There's even everyone's favorite old/new (as in "everything old is new again") object representation: XML. And finally the .NET libraries, as well designed as they are, aren't always quite what you want them to be.

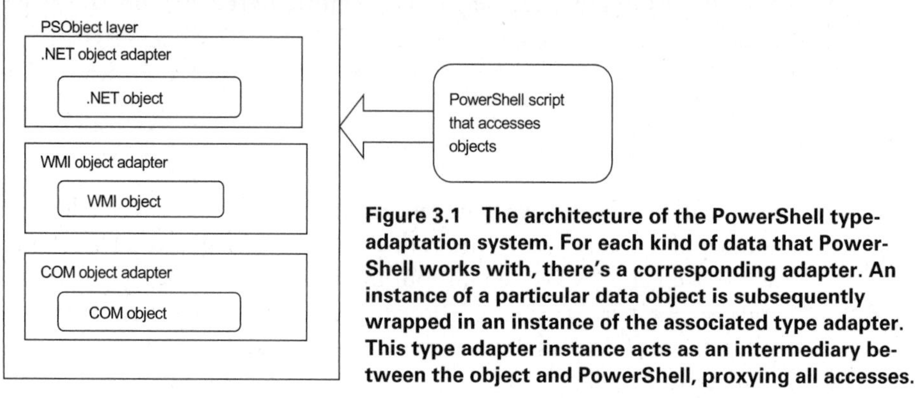

Figure 3.1 The architecture of the PowerShell type-adaptation system. For each kind of data that PowerShell works with, there's a corresponding adapter. An instance of a particular data object is subsequently wrapped in an instance of the associated type adapter. This type adapter instance acts as an intermediary between the object and PowerShell, proxying all accesses.

In an effort to bring harmony to this object soup and fix some of the shortcomings of the various object representations, PowerShell uses a *type-adaptation system* that masks all the details of these different objects' representations. A PowerShell script never directly accesses an object. It always goes through the type-adaptation layer—the `PSObject` (PowerShell Object) layer—that rationalizes the interfaces presented to the user. The `PSObject` layer allows for a uniquely consistent user experience when working with the different types of objects. This architecture is shown in figure 3.1.

When you see an expression like

```
$x.Count
```

you don't have to know or care about the type of object stored in `$x`. You only care that it has a property named `Count`. PowerShell never generates code to directly access the `Count` property on a particular type of object. Instead, it makes an indirect call through the `PSObject` layer, which figures out how a `Count` property for the object can be accessed. If `$x` contains a .NET object, it will return the value from that object's `Length` property. If `$x` contains an XML document, the XML adapter will look for a node called "count" on the top level of that XML document. The object in the variable might not even contain a `Count` property at all. With PowerShell, you can have a type system with a *synthetic property* (called a `PSMember`) defined by the type system itself, instead of on the object. Table 3.1 lists the set of available PowerShell object adapters.

Table 3.1 The basic set of object adapters available in PowerShell

Adapted object type	Description
`.NET Adapter`	This is the basic adapter for all .NET types. This adapter directly maps the properties on the .NET object and adds several new ones that start with a PS prefix.
COM Object Adapter	This adapter provides access to COM objects. Supported objects include the Windows Script Host classes and scriptable applications such as Microsoft Word or Internet Explorer.

Table 3.1 **The basic set of object adapters available in PowerShell *(continued)***

Adapted object type	Description
WMI Adapter	This adapts objects returned from a WMI provider.
ADO Adapter	This adapter allows you to treat the columns in ADO data tables as though they were properties.
Custom Object Adapter	This adapter manages objects for which there's no actual underlying object, only synthetic properties.
ADSI Object Adapter	This adapts objects returned from the Active Directory Service Interfaces.

Let's recap. In chapter 2, you saw how cmdlets produced various kinds of objects. These are the objects you have to manipulate to get your work done. In this section, we discussed how these manipulations work—how the adapter mechanism provides a uniform experience for the various types of objects. Now let's look at one more source of objects: the constants embedded in the script itself, which is accomplished through the various types of *literals*. All languages need to have some form of literal data for initializing variables, comparing against objects, and so on. To say, "Get me all the files smaller than 10 MB," you need a way to express *10 MB* in your script. You'll learn how this is done in the next section.

3.2 BASIC TYPES AND LITERALS

All programming languages have a set of basic or primitive types from which everything else is built. These primitive types usually have some form of corresponding syntactic literal. *Literal tokens* in the language are used to represent literal data objects in the program. In PowerShell there are the usual literals—strings, numbers, and arrays—but there are some other literals that aren't typically found outside of dynamic languages: dictionaries and hashtables. PowerShell also makes heavy use of *type literals* that correspond to type objects in the system. In this section, we'll go through each of the literals, illustrate how they're represented in script text, and explore the details of how they're implemented in the PowerShell runtime.

3.2.1 String literals

There are four kinds of string literals in PowerShell: single-quoted strings, double-quoted strings, single-quoted here-strings, and double-quoted here-strings. The underlying representation for all of these strings is the same.

String representation in PowerShell

In PowerShell, a string is a sequence of 16-bit Unicode characters and is directly implemented using the .NET `System.String` type. Because PowerShell strings use Unicode, they can effectively contain characters from every language in the world.

> **Encoding matters**
>
> The encoding used in strings is obviously important in international environments. If you're interested in the nitty-gritty details of the encoding used in `System.String`, here's what the Microsoft Developer's Network documentation has to say:
>
> > *Each Unicode character in a string is defined by a Unicode scalar value, also called a Unicode code point or the ordinal (numeric) value of the Unicode character. Each code point is encoded using UTF-16 encoding, and the numeric value of each element of the encoding is represented by a Char. The resulting collection of Char objects constitutes the String.*
> >
> > *A single Char usually represents a single code point; that is, the numeric value of the Char equals the code point. However, a code point might require more than one encoded element. For example, a Unicode supplementary code point (a surrogate pair) is encoded with two Char objects.*
>
> Refer to the Microsoft Developer Network (MSDN) documentation for additional details.

There are a couple of other characteristics that strings in PowerShell inherit from the underlying .NET strings. They can also be arbitrarily long and they're immutable—the contents of a string can be copied but can't be changed without creating an entirely new string.

Single- and double-quoted strings

Because of the expression mode/command mode parsing dichotomy described in chapter 2, strings can be represented in several ways. In expression mode, a string is denoted by a sequence of characters surrounded by matching quotes, as shown in the following example:

```
PS (1) > "This is a string in double quotes"
This is a string in double quotes
PS (2) > 'This is a string in single quotes'
This is a string in single quotes
PS (3) >
```

Literal strings can contain any character, including newlines, with the exception of an unquoted closing quote character. In double-quoted strings, to embed the closing quote character you have to either quote it with the backtick character or double it up. In other words, two adjacent quotes become a single literal quote in the string. In single-quoted strings, doubling up the quote is the only way to embed a literal quote in the string. This is one area where an important difference exists between single- and double-quoted strings: in single-quoted strings, the backtick isn't special. This means that it can't be used for embedding special characters such as newlines or escaping quotes.

Like the Unix shells, PowerShell supports variable substitutions. These variable substitutions or expansions are only done in double-quoted strings (which is why these are sometimes called *expandable* strings).

NOTE Arguments to commands are treated as though they were in double quotes, so variables will be expanded in that situation as well. You'll see examples of this later on.

Let's look at an example of string expansion:

```
PS (1) > $foo = "FOO"
PS (2) > "This is a string in double quotes: $foo"
This is a string in double quotes: FOO
PS (3) > 'This is a string in single quotes: $foo'
This is a string in single quotes: $foo
PS (4) >
```

In the preceding lines, you can see that `$foo` in the double-quoted string was replaced by the contents of the variable `FOO` but not in the single-quoted case.

Subexpression expansion in strings

Expandable strings can also include arbitrary expressions by using the *subexpression* notation. A subexpression is a fragment of PowerShell script code that's replaced by the value resulting from the evaluation of that code. Here are examples of subexpression expansion in strings:

```
PS (1) > "2+2 is $(2+2)"
2+2 is 4
PS (2) > $x=3
PS (3) > "$x * 2 is $($x * 2)"
3 * 2 is 6
PS (4) >
```

The expression in the `$( ... )` sequence in the string is replaced by the result of evaluating the expression. `$(2+2)` is replaced by `4`, and so on.

Using complex subexpressions in strings

So far, these examples show only simple embedded expressions. In fact, subexpressions allow statement lists—a series of PowerShell statements separated by semicolons—to be embedded. Here's an example where the subexpression contains three simple statements. First execute the three simple statements:

```
PS (1) > 1;2;3   # three statements
1
2
3
```

Now execute the same set of statements in a subexpression expansion:

```
PS (2) > "Expanding three statements in a string: $(1; 2; 3)"
Expanding three statements in a string: 1 2 3
PS (3) >
```

The result shows the output of the three statements concatenated together, space separated, and inserted into the result string. Here's another example of using a `for` statement in a subexpression expansion:

```
PS (1) > "Numbers 1 thru 10: $(for ($i=1; $i -le 10; $i++) { $i })."
Numbers 1 thru 10: 1 2 3 4 5 6 7 8 9 10.
PS (2) >
```

The output of all the iterations for the loop are gathered up, turned into a string with one value separated from the next by a space, and then substituted into the overall string. As you can see, this can be quite powerful. Using a subexpression in a string is one way to quickly generate formatted results when presenting data.

String expansion considerations

PowerShell expands strings when an assignment is executed. It doesn't reevaluate those strings when the variable is used later. This is an important point. Let's look at two examples that will make this clear. These examples use the postincrement operator `++`, which adds 1 to a variable, and the range operator, which expands to a sequence of numbers.

In the first example, initialize `$x` to 0 and then assign a string with an expansion that increments `$x` to a variable `$a`. Next output `$a` three times to see what happens to the value of `$x`:

```
PS (1) > $x=0
PS (2) > $a = "x is $($x++; $x)"
PS (4) > 1..3 | foreach {$a}
x is 1
x is 1
x is 1
```

As you can see, `$x` was incremented once when `$a` was assigned but didn't change on subsequent references. Now inline the string literal into the body of the loop and see what happens:

```
PS (5) > 1..3 | foreach {"x is $($x++; $x)"}
x is 1
x is 2
x is 3
```

This time around, you can see that `$x` is being incremented each time. To reiterate, string literal expansion is done only when the literal is assigned.

> **NOTE** There's a way to force a string to be expanded if you need to do it. You can do this by calling `$ExecutionContext.InvokeCommand.ExpandString( 'a is $a' )`. This method will return a new string with all the variables expanded.

Here-string literals

Getting back to the discussion of literal string notation, there's one more form of string literal, called a *here-string*. A here-string is used to embed large chunks of text inline in a script. This can be powerful when you're generating output for another program. Here's an example that assigns a here-string to the variable $a:

```
PS (1) > $a = @"
>> Line one
>> Line two
>> Line three
>> "@
>>
PS (2) > $a
Line one
Line two
Line three
```

> **NOTE** Here's a note for C# users. There's a lexical element in C# that looks a lot like PowerShell here-strings. In practice, the C# feature is most like PowerShell's single-quoted strings. In PowerShell, a here-string begins at the end of the line and the terminating sequence must be at the beginning of the line that terminates the here-string. In C#, the string terminates at the first closing quote that isn't doubled up.

When $a is displayed, it contains all the lines that were entered. Now you're probably saying, "Wait a minute—you told me I can do the same thing with a regular string. What makes here-strings so special?" It has to do with how quoting is handled. Here-strings have special quoting rules.

Here-strings start with `@<quote><newline>` and end with `<newline><quote>@`. The `<newlines>` are important because the here-string quote sequences won't be treated as quotes without them. The content of the here-string is all the lines between the beginning and ending quotes but not the lines the quotes are on. Because of the fancy opening and closing quote sequences, other special characters (such as quotes that would cause problems in regular strings) are fine here. This makes it easy to generate string data without having quoting errors. Here's a more elaborate example:

```
PS (1) > $a = @"
>> One is "1"
>> Two is '2'
>> Three is $(2+1)
>> The date is "$(get-date)"
>> "@ + "A trailing line"
>>
PS (2) > $a
One is "1"
Two is '2'
Three is 3
The date is "1/8/2006 9:59:16 PM"A trailing line
PS (3) >
```

On line 1, the here-string is assigned to the variable $a. The contents of the here-string start on line 2, which has a string containing double quotes. Line 3 has a string with single quotes. Line 4 has an embedded expression, and line 5 calls the Get-Date cmdlet in a subexpression to embed the current date into the string. Finally, line 6 appends some trailing text to the whole string. When you look at the output of the variable shown in lines 9–12, you see that the quotes are all preserved and the expansions are shown in place.

Here-strings come in single and double-quoted versions just like regular strings, with the significant difference being that variables and subexpressions aren't expanded in the single-quoted variant, as shown here:

```
PS (1) > $a=123
PS (2) > @"
>> a is $a
>> "@
>>
a is 123
```

In the double-quoted here-string, the variable `$a` is expanded, but in the single-quoted here-string

```
PS (3) > @'
>> a is $a
>> '@
>>
a is $a
PS (4) >
```

it isn't. The single-quoted version is best for embedding large blocks of literal text where you don't want to have to deal with individually quoting `$` everywhere. You'll see how useful this can be when we look at the `Add-Type` cmdlet in chapter 9.

That should be enough about strings for now. Let's move on to numbers and numeric literals. This will finally let us express that "10 MB" value we wanted to compare against earlier.

3.2.2 Numbers and numeric literals

As mentioned earlier, PowerShell supports all the basic .NET numeric types and performs conversions to and from the different types as needed. Table 3.2 lists these numeric types.

Table 3.2 Numeric literals

Example numeric literal	.NET full type name	Short type name
`1` `0x1FE4`	`System.Int32`	`[int]`
`10000000000` `101`	`System.Int64`	`[long]`
`1.1` `1e3`	`System.Double`	`[double]`

Table 3.2 Numeric literals *(continued)*

Example numeric literal	.NET full type name	Short type name
There is no single-precision numeric literal but you can use a cast: `[float] 1.3`	`System.Single`	`[single]` or `[float]`
`1d` `1.123d`	`System.Decimal`	`[decimal]`

Now that you know the basic numeric types, you need to understand how literals of each type are specified.

Specifying numeric literals

In general, you don't specify a literal having a particular type; the system will figure out the best way to represent the number. By default, an integer will be used. If the literal is too large for a 32-bit integer, a 64-bit integer will be used instead. If it's still too big or if it contains a decimal point, a `System.Double` will be used. (The `System.Single` single-precision floating point isn't used for numeric literals because it offers no advantages and just complicates the process.) The one case where you do want to tell the system that you're requesting a specific type is with the `System.Decimal` type. These are specified by placing the letter *d* at the end of the number with no intervening space, as shown:

```
PS (1) > ( 123 ).gettype().fullname
System.Int32
PS (2) > ( 123d ).gettype().fullname
System.Decimal
PS (3) > ( 123.456 ).gettype().fullname
System.Double
PS (4) > ( 123.456d ).gettype().fullname
System.Decimal
```

You can see that in each case where there's a trailing *d*, the literal results in a `[decimal]` value being created. (If there's a space between the number and the *d*, you'll get an error.)

The multiplier suffixes

Plain numbers are fine for most applications, but in the system administration world, there are many special values that you want to be able to conveniently represent, namely, those powers of two—kilobytes, megabytes, gigabytes, terabytes, and petabytes (terabyte and petabyte suffixes aren't available in PowerShell v1).

PowerShell provides a set of *multiplier suffixes* for common sizes to help with this, as listed in table 3.3. These suffixes allow you to easily express common very large numbers.

Table 3.3 The numeric multiplier suffixes supported in PowerShell. Suffixes marked v2 are only available in version 2 or PowerShell.

Multiplier suffix	Multiplication factor	Example	Equivalent value	.NET type
kb or KB	1024	1 KB	1024	`System.Int32`
kb or KB	1024	2.2 KB	2252.8	`System.Double`
mb or MB	1024*1024	1 MB	1048576	`System.Int32`
mb or MB	1024*1024	2.2 MB	2306867.2	`System.Double`
gb or GB	1024*1024*1024	1 GB	1073741824	`System.Int32`
gb or GB	1024*1024*1024	2.14 GB	2297807503.36	`System.Double`
tb or TB *(v2 only)*	1024*1024*1024*1024	1 TB	1099511627776	`System.Int64`
tb or TB *(v2 only)*	1024*1024*1024*1024	2.14 TB	2352954883440.64	`System.Double`
pb or PB *(v2 only)*	1024*1024*1024*1024*1024	1 PB	1125899906842624	`System.Int64`
pb or PB *(v2 only)*	1024*1024*1024*1024*1024	2.14 PB	2.40942580064322E+15	`System.Int64`

NOTE Yes, the PowerShell team is aware that these notations aren't consistent with the ISO/IEC recommendations (kilobyte, and so on). Because the point of this notation is convenience and most IT people are more comfortable with KB than with Ki, we choose to err on the side of comfort over conformance in this one case. This particular issue generated easily the second-most heated debate on the PowerShell internal and external beta tester lists. We'll cover the most heated debate later when we get to the comparison operators.

Hexadecimal literals

The last item we'll cover in this section is hexadecimal literals. When working with computers, it's obviously useful to be able to specify hex literals. PowerShell uses the same notation as C, C#, and so on—preceding the number with the sequence 0x and allowing the letters A–F as the extra digits. As always, the notation is case insensitive, as shown in the following examples:

```
PS (1) > 0x10
16
PS (2) > 0x55
85
PS (3) > 0x123456789abcdef
81985529216486895
PS (4) > 0xDeadBeef
-559038737
```

Now that we've covered the "basic" literals, strings, and numbers, let's move on to the more interesting and less common ones. This is one of the areas where the power of scripting languages shines. These literals let you express complex configuration data, inline in your script, in a clear and direct fashion. This, in turn, means that you don't have to use an external data language like XML or INI files to encode this configuration data. PowerShell lets you express this information in PowerShell itself.

3.3 COLLECTIONS: DICTIONARIES AND HASHTABLES

Perhaps the most flexible data type in PowerShell is the *hashtable*. This data type lets you map a set of keys to a set of values. For example, we may have a hashtable that maps "red" to 1, "green" to 2, and "yellow" to 4.

> **NOTE** A *dictionary* is the general term for a data structure that maps keys to values. In the .NET world, this takes the form of an interface (`System.Collections.IDictionary`) that describes how a collection should do this mapping. A *hashtable* is a specific implementation of that interface. Although the PowerShell hashtable literal syntax only creates instances of `System.Collections.Hashtable`, scripts that you write will work properly with any object that implements `IDictionary`.

3.3.1 Creating and inspecting hashtables

In PowerShell, you use hash literals to create a hashtable inline in a script. Here's a simple example:

```
PS (26) > $user = @{ FirstName = "John"; LastName = "Smith";
>> PhoneNumber = "555-1212" }
PS (27) > $user

Key                            Value
---                            -----
LastName                       Smith
FirstName                      John
PhoneNumber                    555-1212
```

This example created a hashtable that contains three key-value pairs. The hashtable starts with the token `@{` and ends with `}`. Inside the delimiters, you define a set of key-value pairs where the key and value are separated by an equals sign (=). Formally, the syntax for a hash literal is

```
<hashLiteral> = '@{' <keyExpression> '='  <pipeline> [ <separator>
            <keyExpression> '=' <pipeline> ] * '}'
```

Now that you've created a hashtable, let's see how you can use it. PowerShell allows you to access members in a hashtable in two ways—through property notation and through array notation. Here's what the property notation looks like:

```
PS (3) > $user.firstname
John
```

```
PS (4) > $user.lastname
Smith
```

This notation lets you treat a hashtable like an object. This access method is intended to facilitate the use of hashtables as a kind of lightweight data record. Now let's look at using the array notation:

```
PS (5) > $user["firstname"]
John
PS (6) > $user["firstname","lastname"]
John
Smith
```

Property notation works pretty much the way you'd expect; you specify a property name and get the corresponding value back. Array notation, on the other hand, is more interesting. In the second command in the example, you provided two keys and got two values back.

Here's an example that shows some additional features of the underlying hashtable object. The underlying object for PowerShell hashtables is the .NET type `System.Collections.Hashtable`. This type has a number of properties and methods that you can use. One of these properties is `keys`. This property will give you a list of all the keys in the hashtable:

```
PS (7) > $user.keys
LastName
FirstName
PhoneNumber
```

In the array access notation, you can use `keys` to get a list of all the values in the table:

```
PS (8) > $user[$user.keys]
Smith
John
555-1212
```

> **NOTE** A more efficient way to get all of the values from a hashtable is to use the `Values` property. The point of this example is to demonstrate how you can use multiple indexes to retrieve the values based on a subset of the keys.

You might have noticed that the `keys` property didn't return the keys in alphabetical order. This is because of the way hashtables work—keys are randomly distributed in the table to speed up access. If you do need to get the values in alphabetical order, here's how you can do it:

```
PS (10) > $user.keys | sort-object
FirstName
LastName
PhoneNumber
```

The `Sort-Object` (or just `sort`) cmdlet sorts the keys into alphabetical order and returns a list. Use this list to index the table:

```
PS (11) > $user[[string[]] ($user.keys | sort)]
John
Smith
555-1212
```

You'll notice something funny about the last example: we had to cast or convert the sorted list into an array of strings. This is because the hashtable keys mechanism expects strings, not objects, as keys. There's much more on casts later in this chapter.

A digression: sorting, enumerating, and hashtables

Let's digress for a second and address a question that comes up sometimes when people, especially .NET programmers, first encounter hashtables in PowerShell. The question is, "Are hashtables collections or scalar objects?" From the .NET perspective, they're enumerable collections just like arrays except they contain a collection of key-value pairs. However, and this is important, *PowerShell treats hashtables like scalar objects*. It does this because, in scripting languages, hashtables are commonly used as on-the-fly structures or data records. Using hashtables this way, you don't have to predefine the fields in a record; you just make them up as you go. If PowerShell treated hashtables as enumerable collections by default, this wouldn't be possible because every time you passed one of these "records" into a pipeline, it would be broken up into a stream of individual key-value pairs and the integrity of the original table would be lost.

This causes the most problems for people when they use hashtables in the `foreach` statement. In a .NET language like C#, the `foreach` statement iterates over all the pairs. In PowerShell, the `foreach` loop will run only once because the hashtable isn't considered an enumerable, at least not by default. So, if you do want to iterate over the pairs, you'll have to call the `GetEnumerator()` method yourself. This looks like

```
PS (12) >  $h = @{a=1; b=2; c=3}
PS (13) >  foreach ($pair in $h.GetEnumerator())
>>  {
>>      $pair.key + " is " + $pair.value
>>  }
>>
a is 1
b is 2
c is 3
```

In each iteration, the next pair is assigned to `$pair` and processing continues.

A significant part of the reason this behavior confuses people is that when PowerShell displays a hashtable, it uses enumeration to list the key-value pairs as part of the presentation. The result is that there's no visible difference between when you call

GetEnumerator() in the foreach loop and when you don't. Let's look at this. First, the no GetEnumerator() case:

```
PS (14) >  foreach ($pair in $h) { $pair }

Name                           Value
----                           -----
a                              1
b                              2
c                              3
```

Now call GetEnumerator() in the loop:

```
PS (15) >  foreach ($pair in $h.GetEnumerator()) { $pair }

Name                           Value
----                           -----
a                              1
b                              2
c                              3
```

As you can see, the output is identical in both cases. This is desirable in the sense that it's a good way to present a hashtable and doesn't require effort from the user to do this. On the other hand, it masks the details of what's really going on. As always, it's difficult to serve all audiences perfectly.

Another aspect of the hashtable collection question is that people want to be able to "sort" a hashtable the way you'd sort a list of numbers. In the case of a hashtable, this usually means that the user wants to be able to control the order in which keys will be retrieved from the hashtable. Unfortunately this can't work because the default hashtable object that PowerShell uses has no way to store any particular key ordering in the table. The keys are just stored in random order, as you saw earlier in this section. If you want to have an ordered dictionary, you'll have to use a different type of object, such as

```
[Collections.Generic.SortedDictionary[object,object]]
```

This is a sorted generic dictionary (we'll get to type literals and generics later in this chapter). And now, back to our regularly scheduled topic.

3.3.2 Modifying and manipulating hashtables

Next let's look at adding, changing, and removing elements in the hashtable. First let's add the date and the city where the user lives to the $user table.

```
PS (1) > $user.date = get-date
PS (2) > $user
Key                            Value
---                            -----
LastName                       Smith
date                           1/15/2006 12:01:10 PM
FirstName                      John
PhoneNumber                    555-1212
```

```
PS (3) > $user["city"] = "Seattle"
PS (4) > $user
Key                            Value
---                            -----
city                           Seattle
LastName                       Smith
date                           1/15/2006 12:01:10 PM
FirstName                      John
PhoneNumber                    555-1212
```

A simple assignment using either the property or array accessor notation allows you to add an element to a hashtable. Now let's say you got the city wrong—John really lives in Detroit. Let's fix that:

```
PS (5) > $user.city = "Detroit"
PS (6) > $user
Key                            Value
---                            -----
city                           Detroit
LastName                       Smith
date                           1/15/2006 12:01:10 PM
FirstName                      John
PhoneNumber                    555-1212
```

As this example shows, simple assignment is the way to update an element. Finally, you don't want this element, so remove it from the table with the `remove()` method:

```
PS (7) > $user.remove("city")
PS (8) > $user
Key                            Value
---                            -----
LastName                       Smith
date                           1/15/2006 12:01:10 PM
FirstName                      John
PhoneNumber                    555-1212
The hashtable no longer contains the element.
```

If you want to create an empty hashtable, use `@{ }` with no member specifications between the braces. This creates an empty table that you can then add members to incrementally:

```
PS (1) > $newHashTable = @{}
PS (2) > $newHashTable
PS (3) > $newHashTable.one =1
PS (4) > $newHashTable.two = 2
PS (5) > $newHashTable

Key                            Value
---                            -----
two                            2
one                            1
```

In the example, there were no members initially; you added two by making assignments. The members are created on assignment.

3.3.3 Hashtables as reference types

Hashtables are reference types, so if you create a hashtable, assign it to a variable `$foo`, and assign `$foo` to another variable, `$bar`, you'll have two variables that point to, or *reference*, the same object. Consequently, any changes that are made to one variable will affect the other, because they're pointing to the same object. Let's try this out. Create a new hashtable and assign it to `$foo`:

```
PS (2) > $foo = @{
>> a = 1
>> b = 2
>> c = 3
>> }
>>
PS (3) > $foo
Key                         Value
---                         -----
a                           1
b                           2
c                           3
```

Now assign `$foo` to `$bar` and verify that it matches `$foo` as you'd expect:

```
PS (4) > $bar = $foo
PS (5) > $bar
Key                         Value
---                         -----
a                           1
b                           2
c                           3
```

Next assign a new value to the element a in `$foo`:

```
PS (6) > $foo.a = "Hi there"
PS (7) > $foo.a
Hi there
```

And see what happened to `$bar`:

```
PS (8) > $bar.a
Hi there
PS (9) > $bar
Key                         Value
---                         -----
a                           Hi there
b                           2
c                           3
```

The change that was made to `$foo` has been reflected in `$bar`.

Now if you want to make a copy of the hashtable instead of just copying the reference, you can use the `Clone()` method on the object:

```
PS (1) > $foo=@{a=1; b=2; c=3}
PS (2) > $bar = $foo.Clone()
```

Change the a member in the table

```
PS (3) > $foo.a = "Hello"
```

and verify that the hashtable in `$foo` has changed

```
PS (4) > $foo.a
Hello
```

but the hashtable in `$bar` hasn't

```
PS (5) > $bar.a
1
```

because it's a copy, not a reference. This technique can be useful if you're creating a number of tables that are mostly the same. You can create a "template" table, make copies, and then change the pieces you need to.

There's still more to know about hashtables and how they work with operators, but we'll cover that in chapters 4 and 5. For now, let's move on to the next data type.

3.4 COLLECTIONS: ARRAYS AND SEQUENCES

In the previous section, we talked about hashtables and hash literals. Now let's talk about the PowerShell syntax for arrays and array literals. Most programming languages have some kind of array literal notation similar to the PowerShell hash literal notation, where there's a beginning character sequence followed by a list of values, followed by a closing character sequence. Here's how array literals are defined in PowerShell:

They're not. There's no array literal notation in PowerShell.

Yes, you read that correctly. There's no notation for an array literal in PowerShell. So how exactly does this work? How do you define an inline array in a PowerShell script? Here's the answer: instead of having array literals, there's a set of operations that create collections as needed. In fact, collections of objects are created and discarded transparently throughout PowerShell. If you need an array, one will be created for you. If you need a singleton (or scalar) value, the collection will be unwrapped as needed.

3.4.1 Collecting pipeline output as an array

The most common operation resulting in an array in PowerShell is collecting the output from a pipeline. When you run a pipeline that emits a sequence of objects and assign that output to a variable, it automatically collects the elements into an array, specifically into a .NET object of type `[object[]]`.

But what about building a simple array in an expression? The simplest way to do this is to use the comma operator (,). For example, at the command line, type

```
1,2,3
```

and you'll have created a sequence of numbers. (See chapter 5 for more information about using the comma operator.) When you assign that sequence to a variable, it's stored as an array. Assign these three numbers to a variable, `$a`, and look at the result type:

```
PS (1) > $a = 1,2,3
PS (2) > $a.gettype().fullname
System.Object[]
```

As in the pipeline case, the result is stored in an array of type `[object[]]`.

3.4.2 Array indexing

Let's explore some of the operations that can be performed on arrays. As is commonly the case, getting and setting elements of the array (array indexing) is done with square brackets. The length of an array can be retrieved with the `Length` property:

```
PS (3) > $a.length
3
PS (4) > $a[0]
1
```

Note that arrays in PowerShell are origin-zero; that is, the first element in the array is at index 0, not index 1. As the example showed, the first element of `$a` is in `$a[0]`.

As with hashtables, changes are made to an array by assigning new values to indexes in the array. The following example assigns new values to the first and third elements in `$a`:

```
PS (5) > $a[0] = 3.1415
PS (6) > $a
3.1415
2
3
PS (7) > $a[2] = "Hi there"
PS (8) > $a
3.1415
2
Hi there
PS (9) >
```

Looking at the output, you can see that elements of the array have been changed. Simple assignment updates the element at the specified index.

3.4.3 Polymorphism in arrays

Another important thing to note from the previous example is that arrays are *polymorphic* by default. By polymorphic we mean that you can store any type of object in an array. (A VBScript user would call these *variant arrays*.) When you created the array, you assigned only integers to it. In the subsequent examples, you assigned a floating-point number and a string. The original array was capable of storing any kind of object. In formal terms, PowerShell arrays are polymorphic by default (though it's possible to create type-constrained arrays).

Earlier you saw how to get the length of an array. What happens when you try to assign to an element past the end of the array? The next example illustrates this:

```
PS (9) > $a.length
3
PS (10) > $a[4] = 22
Array assignment failed because index '4' was out of range.
At line:1 char:4
+ $a[4 <<<< ] = 22
PS (11) >
```

Attempts to assign outside the bounds of an array will result in a range error. This is because PowerShell arrays are based on .NET arrays and their size is fixed. So how can you add more elements to a PowerShell array if the underlying objects are fixed in size? This is easily done through array concatenation using the plus (+) or plus-equals (+=) operators. Let's add two more elements to the array from the previous example:

```
PS (11) > $a += 22,33
PS (12) > $a.length
5
PS (13) > $a[4]
33
PS (14) >
```

So the length of the array in `$a` is now 5. The addition operation did add elements. Here's how this works:

1. PowerShell creates a new array large enough to hold the total number of elements.
2. It copies the contents of the original array into the new one.
3. It copies the new elements into the end of the array.

You didn't add any elements to the original array after all. Instead, you created a new, larger one.

3.4.4 Arrays as reference types

This copying behavior has some interesting consequences. You can explore this further by first creating a simple array and looking at the value. Let's use string expansion here so that the values in the variable are all displayed on one line:

```
PS (1) > $a=1,2,3
PS (2) > "$a"
1 2 3
```

Now assign `$a` to a new variable, `$b`, and check that `$a` and `$b` have the same elements:

```
PS (3) > $b = $a
PS (4) > "$b"
1 2 3
```

Next, change the first element in `$a`:

```
PS (5) > $a[0] = "Changed"
PS (6) > "$a"
Changed 2 3
```

Yes, the first element in $a was changed. But what about $b?

```
PS (7) > "$b"
Changed 2 3
```

It was also changed. As with hashtables, array assignment is done by reference. When you assigned $a to $b, you got a copy of the reference to the array instead of a copy of contents of the array. Add a new element to $b:

```
PS (8) > $b += 4
PS (9) > "$b"
Changed 2 3 4
```

$b is now four elements long. Because of the way array concatenation works, $b contains a copy of the contents of the array instead of a reference. If you change $a now, it won't affect $b. Let's verify that:

```
PS (10) > $a[0] = "Changed again"
PS (11) > "$a"
Changed again 2 3
PS (12) > "$b"
Changed 2 3 4
```

You see that $b wasn't changed. Conversely, changing $b should have no effect on $a:

```
PS (13) > $b[0] = 1
PS (14) > "$a"; "$b"
Changed again 2 3
1 2 3 4
PS (15) >
```

Again, there was no change.

To reiterate, arrays in PowerShell, like arrays in other .NET languages, are reference types, not value types. When you assign them to a variable, you get another reference to the array, not another copy of the array.

3.4.5 Singleton arrays and empty arrays

You saw how to use the comma operator to build up an array containing more than one element. You can also use the comma operator as a prefix operator to create an array containing only one element. The next example shows this:

```
PS (1) > , 1
1
PS (2) > (, 1).length
1
PS (3) >
```

This code creates an array containing a single element, 1.

How about empty arrays? The comma operator always takes an argument to work on. Even using `$null` as an argument to the comma operator will result in a one-element array containing the `$null` reference. Empty arrays are created through a special form of subexpression notation that uses the `@` symbol instead of the `$` sign to start the expression. Here's what it looks like:

```
PS (3) > @()
PS (4) > @().length
0
PS (5) >
```

In the preceding example, you created an array of length 0. This notation is more general—it takes the result of the expression it encloses and ensures that it's always returned as an array. If the expression returns `$null` or a scalar value, it will be wrapped in a one-element array. Given this behavior, the other solution to creating an array with one element is

```
PS (1) > @(1)
1
PS (2) > @(1).length
1
```

That is, you place the value you want in the array in `@( ... )` and you get an array back.

Use this notation when you don't know whether the command you're calling is going to return an array. By executing the command in this way, you're guaranteed to get an array back. Note that if what you're returning is already an array, it won't be wrapped in a new array. Compare this to the use of the comma operator:

```
PS (1) >  1,2,3
1
2
3
PS (2) > (1,2,3).Length
3
PS (3) > ( , (1,2,3) ).Length
1
PS (4) > ( @( 1,2,3 ) ).Length
3
```

Line 1 created a regular array; on line 5, you get the length and see that it's 3. Next, on line 7, you apply the prefix operator to the array and then get the length. The result now is only 1. This is because the unary comma operator always wraps its arguments in a new array. Finally, on line 9, you use the `@( ... )` notation and then get the length. This time it remains 3. The `@( ... )` sequence doesn't wrap unless the object isn't an array.

Now let's look at the last type of literal: the *type literal*. Because object types are so important in PowerShell, you need to be able to express types in a script. Remember with numbers, when you wanted to say, "Get me all the files larger than 10 MB," you needed numeric literals? The same concept applies to types. If you want to be able to say, "Get me all the objects of a particular type," you need to be able to express that type in the script.

3.5 TYPE LITERALS

In earlier sections, you saw a number of things that looked like `[type]`. These are the *type literals*. In PowerShell, you use type literals a variety of ways. You use them to specify a particular type. They can be used as operators in a *cast* (an operation that converts an object from one type to another), as part of a *type-constrained* variable declaration (see chapter 4), or as an object itself. Here's an example of a cast using a type literal:

```
$i = [int] "123"
```

In this example, you're casting or converting a string into a number, specifically an instance of primitive .NET type `System.Int32`. You could use the longer .NET type name to accomplish the same thing:

```
$i = [System.Int32] "123"
```

Now let's look at something a bit more sophisticated. If you wanted to make this into an array of integers, you'd do this:

```
$i = [int[]][object[]] "123"
```

In this example, you're not just casting the basic type, you're also changing it from a *scalar object* to an array. Notice that you had to do this in two steps. In the first step, you converted it into a collection but without changing the element type. In the second step, you converted the types of the individual elements. This follows the general type converter rule that no more than one conversion will be performed in a single step. This rule makes it much easier to predict what any given conversion will do.

> **NOTE** In this case, converting a scalar value into an array is so common that we added support for doing this directly in PowerShell v2. You can simply say `$i = [int[]] "123"`.

3.5.1 Type name aliases

Obviously, the shorter type name (or *type alias*, as it's known) is more convenient. Table 3.4 lists all the type aliases defined in PowerShell and the .NET types they correspond to. It also indicates which version of PowerShell the alias is available in. (Another change that was made in v2 is that there are no longer separate aliases for arrays of the base type. As a result, these aren't shown in the table as they were in the first version of the book.) Anything in the `System.Management.Automation` namespace is specific to PowerShell. The other types are core .NET types and are covered in the MSDN documentation.

Type resolution

When PowerShell resolves a type name, it first checks the type name alias table; then it checks to see whether a type exists whose full name matches the string specified. Finally it prepends the type with `system.` and checks to see whether a type exists that matches the new string. This means things that are in the `System` namespace look like they might be aliased.

For example, the type `System.IntPtr` can be referred to as `[intpr]` even though it's not in the alias table. For the most part, this referral is transparent. The one time it does matter is if, for some reason, a type was added to the system that lives in the top-level namespace. In this case, `[intptr]` would refer to the new type and you'd have to use `[system.intptr]` to refer to the system type. This should never happen because types should always be in namespaces.

Table 3.4 PowerShell type aliases and their corresponding .NET types

Type alias	Corresponding .NET type	Version
[int]	System.Int32	1, 2
[long]	System.Int64	1, 2
[string]	System.String	1, 2
[char]	System.Char	1, 2
[bool]	System.Boolean	1, 2
[byte]	System.Byte	1, 2
[double]	System.Double	1, 2
[decimal]	System.Decimal	1, 2
[float]	System.Single	1, 2
[single]	System.Single	1, 2
[regex]	System.Text.RegularExpressions.Regex	1, 2
[array]	System.Array	1, 2
[xml]	System.Xml.XmlDocument	1, 2
[scriptblock]	System.Management.Automation.ScriptBlock	1, 2
[switch]	System.Management.Automation.SwitchParameter	1, 2
[hashtable]	System.Collections.Hashtable	1, 2
[ref]	System.Management.Automation.PSReference	1, 2
[type]	System.Type	1, 2
[psobject]	System.Management.Automation.PSObject	1, 2
[pscustomobject]	System.Management.Automation.PSObject	2
[psmoduleinfo]	System.Management.Automation.PSModuleInfo	2

Table 3.4 **PowerShell type aliases and their corresponding .NET types *(continued)***

Type alias	Corresponding .NET type	Version
[powershell]	System.Management.Automation.PowerShell	2
[runspacefactory]	System.Management.Runspaces.RunspaceFactory	2
[runspace]	System.Management.Automation.Runspaces.Runspace	2
[ipaddress]	System.Net.IPAddress	2
[wmi]	System.Management.ManagementObject	1, 2
[wmisearcher]	System.Management.ManagementClass	1, 2
[wmiclass]	System.Management.ManagementClass	1, 2
[adsi]	System.DirectoryServices.DirectoryEntry	1, 2
[adsisearcher]	System.DirectoryServices.DirectorySearcher	1, 2

3.5.2 Generic type literals

There's a special kind of type in .NET called a *generic type*, which let you say something like "a list of strings" instead of just "a list." And although you could do this without generics, you'd have to create a specific type for the type of list. With generics, you create one generic list type (hence the name) and then *parameterize* it with the type it can contain.

> **NOTE** Generic type literal support was added in v2. In v1, it was possible to express a type literal, but it was a painful process. You'll learn how to do this later in the book.

This example shows the type literal for a generic list (`System.Collections.Generic.List`) of integers:

```
PS (1) > [system.collections.generic.list[int]] | ft -auto

IsPublic IsSerial Name   BaseType
-------- -------- ----   --------
True     True     List`1 System.Object
```

If you look at the type literal, it's easy to see how the collection element type is expressed: `[int]`. This is essentially a nested type literal where the type parameter is enclosed in nested square brackets. Create an instance of this type:

```
PS (2) > $l = new-object system.collections.generic.list[int]
```

Then add some elements to it:

```
PS (3) > $l.add(1)
PS (4) > $l.add(2)
```

Get the count of elements added and list the elements:

```
PS (5) > $l.count
2
```

```
PS (6) > $l
1
2
```

Try to add something that isn't an integer:

```
PS (7) > $l.add("hello")
Cannot convert argument "0", with value: "hello", for "Add" to
type "System.Int32": "Cannot convert value "hello" to type "System
.Int32". Error: "Input string was not in a correct format.""
at line:1 char:7
 $l.add <<<< ("hello")
   + CategoryInfo          : NotSpecified: (:) [], MethodExcep
  tion
   + FullyQualifiedErrorId : MethodArgumentConversionInvalidCa
  stArgument
```

This results in a type error because `"hello"` can't be converted into an integer. Now, if the string could be converted to a number, as in this example

```
PS (8) > $l.add("123")
PS (9) > $l.count
3
```

PowerShell would take care of the conversion and the operation could proceed without error.

Finally, let's look at a type that requires more than one type parameter. For example, a generic dictionary requires two type parameters: the type of the keys and the type of the values. Here's what this looks like:

```
PS (10) > [system.collections.generic.dictionary[string,int]] |
>> Format-List -auto

IsPublic IsSerial Name          BaseType
-------- -------- ----          --------
True     True     Dictionary`2 System.Object
```

The two type parameters are separated by a comma inside the square brackets.

Now let's take a trip into the "too-much-information" zone and look in detail at the process PowerShell uses to perform all of these type conversions. On first reading, you'll probably want to skim this section but read it in detail later when you're more comfortable with PowerShell. This is a "spinach" section—you may not like it, but it's good for you.

The primary uses for type literals are in performing type conversions and invoking *static methods*. We'll look at both of these uses in the next two sections.

3.5.3 Accessing static members with type literals

As mentioned, a common use for type literals is for accessing static methods on .NET classes. You can use the `Get-Member` cmdlet to look at the members on an object. To view the static members, use the `-Static` flag:

```
PS (1) > [string] | get-member -static

   TypeName: System.String

Name             MemberType Definition
----             ---------- ----------
Compare          Method     static System.Int32 Compare(String...
CompareOrdinal   Method     static System.Int32 CompareOrdinal...
Concat           Method     static System.String Concat(Object...
Copy             Method     static System.String Copy(String str)
Equals           Method     static System.Boolean Equals(Strin...
Format           Method     static System.String Format(String...
Intern           Method     static System.String Intern(String...
IsInterned       Method     static System.String IsInterned(St...
IsNullOrEmpty    Method     static System.Boolean IsNullOrEmpt...
Join             Method     static System.String Join(String s...
op_Equality      Method     static System.Boolean op_Equality(...
op_Inequality    Method     static System.Boolean op_Inequalit...
ReferenceEquals  Method     static System.Boolean ReferenceEqu...
Empty            Property   static System.String Empty {get;set;}
```

This code will dump out all the static members on the .NET `System.String` class. If you want to call one of these methods, you need to use the `::` operator. Let's use the join method to join an array of string. First create the array:

```
PS (2) > $s = "one","two","three"
```

Then use the join method to join all the pieces into a single string with plus signs in between:

```
PS (3) > [string]::Join(' + ', $s)
one + two + three
PS (4) >
```

Example: using advanced math functions

A good example of the power of static methods is the `[math]` class from the .NET Framework. This class—`[System.Math]`—is a pure static class. This means you can't create an instance of it—you can only use the static methods it provides. Again, let's use the `Get-Member` cmdlet to look at the methods. Here's a truncated listing of the output you'd see:

```
PS (1) > [math] | get-member -static

   TypeName: System.Math

Name             MemberType Definition
----             ---------- ----------
Abs              Method     static System.Single Abs(Single va...
Acos             Method     static System.Double Acos(Double d)
Asin             Method     static System.Double Asin(Double d)
Atan             Method     static System.Double Atan(Double d)
Atan2            Method     static System.Double Atan2(Double ...
      :
      :
```

```
Sqrt            Method     static System.Double Sqrt(Double d)
Tan             Method     static System.Double Tan(Double a)
Tanh            Method     static System.Double Tanh(Double v...
Truncate        Method     static System.Decimal Truncate(Dec...
E               Property   static System.Double E {get;}
PI              Property   static System.Double PI {get;}
```

As you can see, it contains a lot of useful methods and properties. For example, it contains useful constants like `Pi` and `e` as static properties:

```
PS (2) > [math]::Pi
3.14159265358979
PS (3) > [math]::e
2.71828182845905
PS (4) >
```

There are also all the trigonometric functions:

```
PS (4) > [math]::sin(22)
-0.00885130929040388
PS (5) > [math]::cos(22)
-0.999960826394637
PS (6) >
```

As we've said, types in PowerShell provide tremendous power and breadth of capabilities. In many cases, before rolling your own solution it's worth browsing the MSDN documentation on the .NET libraries to see if there's something you can use to solve your problems. Now that you've seen the types, let's look at how PowerShell does type conversions.

3.6 TYPE CONVERSIONS

In the previous section, we introduced type literals and the major data types used in PowerShell. But how do all these types work together? This is a critical question we had to address in designing PowerShell. In shell languages, there's usually only string data, so you never have to worry about things being of the wrong type. So how could the PowerShell team achieve this "typeless" behavior in PowerShell? The answer was a comprehensive system for handling type conversions automatically.

Automatic type conversion is the "secret sauce" that allows a strongly typed language like PowerShell to behave like a typeless command-line shell. Without a comprehensive type conversion system to map the output of one command to the input type required by another command, PowerShell would be nearly impossible to use as a shell.

In the next few sections, we'll go through an overview of how the type-conversion system works. Then we'll look at the conversion algorithm in detail. Finally, we'll explore special conversion rules that apply only when binding cmdlet parameters.

3.6.1 How type conversion works

Type conversions are used any time an attempt is made to use an object of one type in a context that requires another type (such as adding a string to a number). Here's a good example: In the previous chapter, we talked about how parameters are bound to cmdlets. The parameter binder uses the type conversion system heavily when trying to bind incoming objects to a particular parameter. If the user has supplied a string and the cmdlet requires a number, the system will quietly convert the source object to the destination type as long as it's not a destructive conversion. A destructive conversion is one where the sense of the original object has been lost or distorted in some significant way. With numbers, this typically means a loss of precision.

The type-conversion facility is also surfaced directly to the shell user through cast operations in the PowerShell language, as we mentioned in the previous section. In PowerShell, you use types to accomplish many things that you'd do with methods or functions in other languages. You use type literals as operators to convert (or cast) one type of object to another. Here's a simple example:

```
PS (1) > [int] "0x25"
37
PS (2) >
```

In this example, a string representing a hexadecimal number is converted into a number by using a cast operation. A token specifying the name of a type in square brackets can be used as a unary operator that will try to convert its argument into the desired type. These type cast operations can be composed—that is, several casts can be chained together. Here's an example of that type of composition. To get the ordinal value for a character, you can do this:

```
:
PS (2) > [int] [char]"a"
97
```

Notice that you first cast the string into a char and then into an int. This is necessary because the simple conversion would try to parse the entire string as a number. This only works for a string containing exactly one character, however. If you want to convert an entire string, you need to use array types. Here's what that looks like:

```
PS (3) > [int[]] [char[]] "Hello world"
72
101
108
108
111
32
119
111
114
108
100
```

The string was split into an array of characters, then that array of characters was converted into an array of integers and finally displayed as a list of decimal numbers. If you wanted to see those numbers in hex, you'd have to use the -f format operator and a format specifier string:

```
PS (4) > "0x{0:x}" -f [int] [char] "a"
0x61
```

And then, if you want to make a round trip, string to char to int to char to string, you can do this:

```
PS (6) > [string][char][int] ("0x{0:x}" -f [int] [char] "a")
a
```

Finally, here's a somewhat extreme example (for *2001: A Space Odyssey* fans). You'll take the string "HAL" and increment each of the characters in the string by 1:

```
PS (7) > $s = "HAL"
PS (8) > $OFS=""; [string] [char[]] ( [int[]] [char[]] $s |
>> foreach {$_+1} )
>>
IBM
```

Creepy, but cool (or just weird if you're not a *2001* fan)! Moving closer to home, we know that the Windows NT kernel was designed by the same person who designed the VMS operating system. Let's prove that Windows NT (WNT) is just VMS plus 1:

```
PS (9) > $s = "VMS"
PS (10) > $OFS=""; [string] [char[]] ( [int[]] [char[]] $s |
>> foreach {$_+1} )
>>
WNT
```

One final issue you may be wondering about: what is the $OFS (Output Field Separator) variable doing in the example? When PowerShell converts arrays to strings, it takes each array element, converts that element into a string, and then concatenates all the pieces together. Because this would be an unreadable mess, it inserts a separator between each element. That separator is specified using the $OFS variable. It can be set to anything you want, even the empty string. Here's an interesting example. Say you want to add the numbers from 1 to 10. Let's put the numbers into an array:

```
PS (1) > $data = 1,2,3,4,5,6,7,8,9,10
```

Now convert them to a string:

```
PS (2) > [string] $data
1 2 3 4 5 6 7 8 9 10
```

As an aside, variable expansion in strings goes through the same mechanism as the type converter, so you'll get the same result:

```
PS (3) > "$data"
1 2 3 4 5 6 7 8 9 10
```

Change $OFS to be the plus operator, and then display the data.

```
PS (4) > $OFS='+'
PS (5) > "$data"
1+2+3+4+5+6+7+8+9+10
```

Previously, the fields had been separated by spaces. Now they're separated by plus operators. This is almost what you need. You just have to find a way to execute this string. PowerShell provides that ability through the `Invoke-Expression` cmdlet. Here's how it works:

```
PS (6) > invoke-expression "$data"
55
PS (7) >
```

Ta-da! Note that this isn't an efficient way to add a bunch of numbers. The looping constructs in the language are a much better way of doing this.

3.6.2 PowerShell's type-conversion algorithm

In this section, we'll cover the steps in the conversion process in painful detail—much more than you'll generally need to know in your day-to-day work. But if you want to be an expert on PowerShell, this stuff's for you.

> **NOTE** Type conversion is one of the areas of the PowerShell project that grew "organically." In other words, we sat down, wrote a slew of specifications, threw them out, and ended up doing something completely different. This is one of the joys of this type of work. Nice, clean theory falls apart when you put it in front of real people. The type conversion algorithm as it exists today is the result of feedback from many of the early adopters both inside Microsoft as well as outside. The PowerShell community helped us tremendously in this area.

In general, the PowerShell type conversions are separated into two major buckets; a description follows.

PowerShell language standard conversions

These are built-in conversions performed by the engine itself. They're always processed first and consequently can't be overridden. This set of conversions is largely guided by the historical behavior of shell and scripting languages, and isn't part of the normal .NET type-conversion system.

.NET-based custom converters

This class of converters uses (and abuses in some cases) existing .NET mechanisms for doing type conversion.

Table 3.5 lists the set of built-in language conversions that PowerShell uses. The conversion process always starts with an object of a particular type and tries to produce a representation of that object in the requested target type. The conversions are applied in the order shown in table 3.5. Only one conversion is applied at a time. The PowerShell engine doesn't automatically chain conversions.

Table 3.5 The PowerShell language standard conversions

Converting from	To target type	Result description
`$null`	`[string]`	`""` (empty string)
	`[char]`	`'0'` (string containing a single character 0)
	Any kind of number	The object corresponding to 0 for the corresponding numeric type.
	`[bool]`	`$false`
	`[PSObject]`	`$null`
	Any other type of object	`$null`
Derived class	Base class	The original object is returned unchanged.
Anything	`[void]`	The object is discarded.
Anything	`[string]`	The PowerShell internal string converter is used.
Anything	`[xml]`	The original object is first converted into a string and then into an XML document object.
Array of type `[X]`	Array of type `[Y]`	PowerShell creates a new array of the target type, then copies and converts each element in the source array into an instance for the target array type.
Non-array (singleton) object	Array of type `[Y]`	Creates an array containing one element and then places the singleton object into the array, converting if necessary.
`System.Collections.IDictionary`	`[Hashtable]`	A new instance of `System.Collections.Hashtable` is created, and then the members of the source `IDictionary` are copied into the new object.
`[string]`	`[char[]]`	Converts the string to an array of characters.
`[string]`	`[regex]`	Constructs a new instance of a .NET regular expression object.
`[string]`	Number	Converts the string into a number using the smallest representation available that can accurately represent that number. If the string is not purely convertible (i.e., only contains numeric information), then an error is raised.
`[int]`	`System.Enum`	Converts the integer to the corresponding enumeration member if it exists. If it doesn't, a conversion error is generated.

If none of the built-in PowerShell language-specific conversions could be applied successfully, then the .NET custom converters are tried. Again, these converters are tried in order until a candidate is found that will produce the required target type. This candidate conversion is applied. If the candidate conversion throws an exception (that is, a matching converter is found but it fails during the conversion process), no further attempt to convert this object will be made and the overall conversion process will be considered to have failed.

> **NOTE** Developing an understanding of these conversions depends on a fair knowledge of the .NET type conversion mechanisms. You'll need to refer to additional documentation if you want to understand everything in table 3.6. On the other hand, with the .NET docs, you can see exactly what steps are being applied in the type-conversion process.

Custom converters are executed in the order described in table 3.6.

Table 3.6 Custom type conversions

Converter type	Description
`PSTypeConverter`	A `PSTypeConverter` can be associated with a particular type using the `TypeConverterAttribute` or the `<TypeConverter>` tag in the types.ps1xml file. If the value to convert has a `PSTypeConverter` that can convert to the target type, then it's called. If the target type has a `PSTypeConverter` that can convert from values to convert, then it's called. The `PSTypeConverter` allows a single type converter to work for a number of different classes. For example, an `enum` type converter can convert a string to any `enum` (there doesn't need to be separate type to convert each `enum`). Refer to the PowerShell SDK documentation from MSDN for complete details on this converter.
`TypeConverter`	This is a CLR defined type that can be associated with a particular type using the `TypeConverterAttribute` or the `<TypeConverter>` tag in the types file. If the value to convert has a `TypeConverter` that can convert to the target type, then it is called. If the target type has a `TypeConverter` that can convert from the source value, then it is called. The CLR `TypeConverter` doesn't allow a single type converter to work for a number of different classes. Refer to the PowerShell SDK documentation and the Microsoft .NET Framework documentation for details on the `TypeConverter` class.
`Parse()` method	If the value to convert is a string and the target type has a `Parse()` method, then that `Parse()` method is called. `Parse()` is a well-known method name in the CLR world and is commonly implemented to allow conversion of strings to other types.
Constructors	If the target type has a constructor that takes a single parameter matching the type of the value to convert; then this constructor is used to create a new object of the desired type.
Implicit cast operator	If the value to convert has an implicit cast operator that converts to the target type, then it's called. Conversely, if the target type has an implicit cast operator that converts from value to convert's type, then that's called.

Table 3.6 Custom type conversions *(continued)*

Converter type	Description
Explicit cast operator	If the value to convert has an explicit cast operator that converts to the target type, then it's called. Alternatively, if the target type has an explicit cast operator that converts from value to convert's type, then that's called.
`IConvertable`	`System.Convert.ChangeType` is then called.

This section covered the set of type conversions that PowerShell will apply in expressions. In the parameter binder are a few extra steps that are applied first.

3.6.3 Special type conversions in parameter binding

In this final section, we'll go over the extra type-conversion rules that are used in parameter binding that haven't already been covered. If these steps are tried and aren't successful, the parameter binder goes on to call the normal PowerShell type converter code.

> **NOTE** If at any time failure occurs during the type conversion, an exception will be thrown.

Here are the extra steps:

1. If there's no argument for the parameter, the parameter type must be either a `[bool]` or the special PowerShell type `SwitchParameter`; otherwise, a parameter binding exception is thrown. If the parameter type is a `[bool]`, it's set to true. If the parameter type is a `SwitchParameter`, it's set to `SwitchParameter.Present`.
2. If the argument value is null and the parameter type is `[bool]`, it's set to false. If the argument value is null and the parameter type is `SwitchParameter`, it's set to `SwitchParameter.Present`. Null can be bound to any other type, so it just passes through.
3. If the argument type is the same as the parameter type, the argument value is used without any type conversion.
4. If the parameter type is `[object]`, the current argument value is used without any coercion.
5. If the parameter type is a `[bool]`, use the PowerShell Boolean `IsTrue()` method to determine whether the argument value should set the parameter to true or false.
6. If the parameter type is a collection, the argument type must be encoded into the appropriate collection type. You'll encode a scalar argument type or a collection argument type to a target collection parameter type. You won't encode a collection argument type into a scalar parameter type (unless that type is `System.Object` or `PSObject`).

7 If the argument type is a scalar, create a collection of the parameter type (currently only arrays and `IList` are supported) of length 1 and set the argument value as the only value in the collection. If needed, the argument type is converted to the element type for the collection using the same type coercion process this section describes.

8 If the argument type is a collection, we create a collection of the parameter type with length equal to the number of values contained in the argument value. Each value is then coerced to the appropriate element type for the new collection using the recursive application of this algorithm.

9 If none of these steps worked, use the conversions in table 3.6. If those fail, then the overall parameter binding attempt fails.

Once again, this is a level of detail that you don't often need to consider, but it's useful to know it's available when you need it.

Scriptblock parameters

And finally, there's one last aspect of the parameter binder type converter to cover: a feature called *scriptblock parameters*.

First, a bit of a preview of things to come. PowerShell has something called a *scriptblock*. A scriptblock is a small fragment of code that you can pass around as an object itself. This is a powerful concept, and we'll cover scriptblocks in great detail in later chapters, but for now we're just going to look at them in the context of parameter binding.

Here's how scriptblock parameters work. Normally, when you pipe two cmdlets together, the second cmdlet receives values directly from the first cmdlet. Scriptblock parameters (you could also call them *computed parameters*) allow you to insert a piece of script to perform a calculation or transformation in the middle of the pipelined operation. This calculation can do pretty much anything you want since a scriptblock can contain any element of PowerShell script.

The following example shows how this works. You want to take a collection of XML files and rename them as text files. You could write a loop to do the processing, but scriptblock parameters greatly simplify this problem. To rename each file, use the `Rename-Item` cmdlet. This cmdlet takes two parameters: the current name of the file and the new name. Use a scriptblock parameter as an argument to the `-NewName` parameter to generate the new filename. This scriptblock will use the `-replace` operator to replace the .xml file extension with the desired .txt. Here's the command line that performs this task:

```
dir *.xml | Rename-Item -Path {$_.name} `
    -NewName {$_.name -replace '\.xml$', '.txt'} -whatif
```

The original path for `-Path` is just the current name of the file. The `-NewName` parameter is the filename with the extension replaced. The `-WhatIf` parameter will let you see what the command will do before actually moving anything. Once you're happy that the correct operations are being performed, just remove the `-WhatIf` and the renaming will proceed.

Scriptblock parameters can be used with any pipelined parameter as long as the type of that parameter is not `[object]` or `[scriptblock]`. In these cases, the scriptblock is passed as the actual parameter instead of using it to calculate a new value. You'll see why this is important when we look at the `Where-Object` and `ForEach-Object` cmdlets later on.

You now know everything you need to know about how types work on PowerShell. Well, not quite everything. In the next two chapters, we'll discuss how the PowerShell operators build on this basic type foundation. But for now, we're through!

3.7 SUMMARY

A solid understanding of the PowerShell type system will allow you to use PowerShell most effectively. By taking advantage of the built-in type system and conversions, you can accomplish startlingly complex tasks with little code. In this chapter, we covered the following topics:

- The PowerShell type system, how it works, and how you can use it
- The basic PowerShell types and how they are represented in PowerShell script (literals)
- Some of the more advanced types—hashtables and arrays
- The use of type literals in type casts and as a way to call static methods
- The added support in PowerShell version 2 for generic type literals that greatly simplify working with generic types
- The type conversion process for language conversions, the pre-conversion steps that are used by the parameter binder, and the relationship between the PowerShell types and the underlying .NET types
- Scriptblock parameters, which allow you to calculate new values for pipelined parameters instead of having to write a loop to do this (we'll look at scriptblocks in detail in chapter 9)

CHAPTER 4

Operators and expressions

Operators, Mr. Rico! Millions of them!

—Robert A. Heinlein, *Starship Troopers* (paraphrased)

So far, we've covered the basics, and we've covered the type system in considerable depth. Now let's look at how you can combine all this stuff and get some real work done. As in any language, objects are combined with operators to produce expressions. When these expressions are evaluated, the operators perform their operations on objects, giving you (hopefully) useful results. This chapter covers the set of basic operators in PowerShell and how they're used in expressions. The operators we're going to cover in this chapter are shown in figure 4.1.

As you can see, PowerShell has operators. Lots of operators—the full complement you'd expect in a conventional programming language and several more. In addition, PowerShell operators are typically more powerful than the corresponding operators in conventional languages such as C or C++. So, if you invest the time to learn what the PowerShell operators are and how they work, in a single line of code you'll be able to accomplish tasks that would normally take a significant amount of programming.

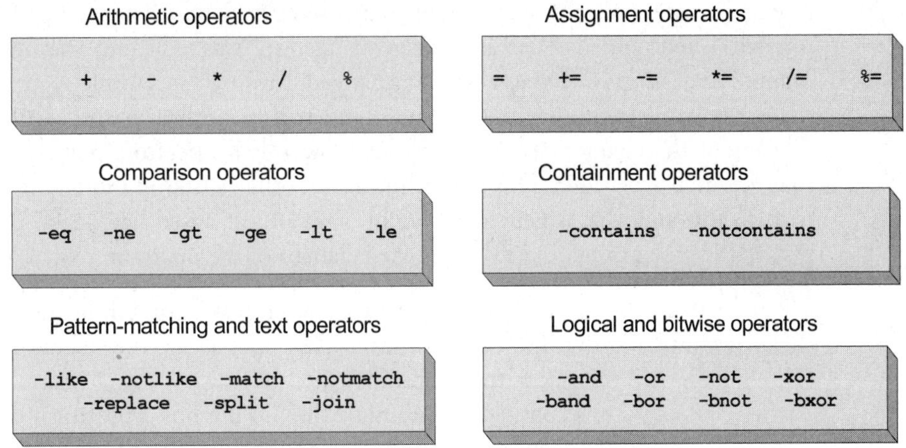

Figure 4.1 The broad groups of operators we'll cover in this chapter

Here's an example of the kind of thing that can be done using just the PowerShell operators. Say we have a file, old.txt, with the following text in it:

```
Hello there.
My car is red.  Your car is blue.
His car is orange and hers is gray.
Bob's car is blue too.
Goodbye.
```

Our task is to copy this content to a new file, making certain changes. In the new file, the word "is" should be replaced with "was," but only when it's in front of the word "red" or "blue." In most languages, this would require a fairly complex program. In PowerShell, it takes exactly one line. Here's the "script":

```
${c:old.txt} -replace 'is (red|blue)','was $1' > new.txt
```

It uses the `-replace` operator along with output redirection and variable namespaces. (The `-replace` operator is described later in this chapter.) Redirection and variable namespaces are features for working with files that are covered in chapter 5. After running this script, the content of new.txt looks like this:

```
Hello there.
My car was red.  Your car was blue.
His car is orange and hers is gray.
Bob's car was blue too.
Goodbye.
```

> **NOTE** For the impatient reader, the notation `${c:old.txt}` says, "Return the contents of the file old.txt from the current working directory on the C: drive." In contrast, `${c:\old.txt}` says, "Get the file old.txt from the root of the C: drive."

As you can see, only the second and fourth lines have been changed as desired. The phrases "is red" and "is blue" have been changed to "was red" and "was blue." The "is orange" and "is gray" phrases weren't changed. From this example, you can also see that it's possible to do quite a bit of work just with the operators.

One of the characteristics that makes PowerShell operators powerful is the fact that they're *polymorphic*. This simply means that they work on more than one type of object. Although this is generally true in other object-based languages, in those languages the type of the object defines the behavior of the operator.

> **NOTE** If you're a C# or Visual Basic user, here's something you might want to know. In "conventional" .NET languages, the operator symbols are mapped to a specific method name on a class called `op_<operatorName>`. For example, in C#, the plus operator (+) maps to the method `op_Addition()`. Although PowerShell is a .NET language, it takes a different approach that's more consistent with dynamic scripting languages, as you'll see in the following sections.

In PowerShell, the interpreter primarily defines the behavior of the operators, at least for common data types. Type-based polymorphic methods are only used as a backup. By common types, we mean strings, numbers, hashtables, and arrays. This allows PowerShell to provide more consistent behavior over this range of common objects and also to provide higher-level behaviors than are provided by the objects themselves, especially when dealing with collections. We'll cover these special behaviors in the sections for each class of operator. (The following sections have many examples, but the best way to learn is to try the examples in PowerShell yourself.) Now let's get going and start looking at the operators.

4.1 Arithmetic operators

First we'll cover the basic arithmetic operators shown in figure 4.2.

We touched on the polymorphic behavior of these operators briefly in chapter 3, where we discussed the various type conversions. The operators themselves are listed with examples in table 4.1.

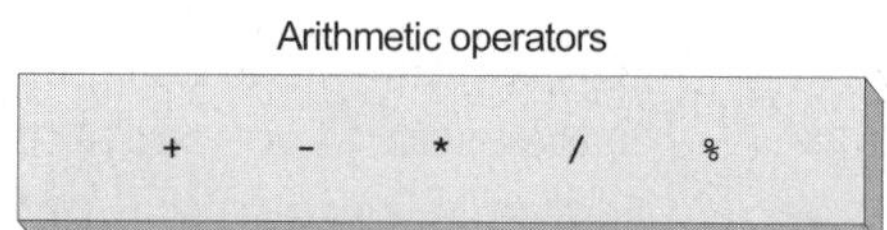

Figure 4.2 The arithmetic operators in PowerShell that will be covered in this section

Table 4.1 The basic arithmetic operators in PowerShell

Operator	Description	Example	Result
+	Add two values together.	`2+4`	`6`
		`"Hi " + "there"`	`"Hi there"`
		`1,2,3 + 4,5,6`	`1,2,3,4,5,6`

Table 4.1 The basic arithmetic operators in PowerShell *(continued)*

Operator	Description	Example	Result
*	Multiply two values.	`2 * 4`	`8`
		`"a" * 3`	`"aaa"`
		`1,2 * 2`	`1,2,1,2`
-	Subtract one value from another.	`6-2`	`4`
/	Divide two values.	`6/2`	`3`
		`7/4`	`1.75`
%	Return the remainder from a division operation.	`7%4`	`3`

In terms of behavior, the most interesting operators are + and *. We'll cover these operators in detail in the next two sections.

4.1.1 The addition operator

As mentioned earlier, PowerShell defines the behavior of the + and * operators for numbers, strings, arrays, and hashtables. Adding or multiplying two numbers produces a numeric result following the numeric widening rules. Adding two strings performs string concatenation, resulting in a new string, and adding two arrays joins the two arrays (array concatenation), producing a new array. Adding two hashtables creates a new hashtable with combined elements. The interesting part occurs when you mix operand types. In this situation, the type of the left operand determines how the operation will proceed. We'll look at how this works with addition first.

> **NOTE** The "left-hand" rule for arithmetic operators: the type of the left-hand operand determines the type of the overall operation. This is an important rule to remember.

If the left operand is a number, PowerShell will try to convert the right operand to a number. Here's an example. In the following expression, the operand on the left is a number and the operand on the right is the string "123":

```
PS (1) > 2 + "123"
125
```

Because the operand on the left is a number, according to the conversion rule the operand "123" must be converted into a number. Once the conversion is complete, the numeric addition operation proceeds and produces the result 125, as shown. Conversely, in the next example, when a string is on the left side

```
PS (2) > "2" + 123
2123
```

the operand on the right (the number 123) is converted to a string and appended to "2" to produce a new string, "2123".

If the right operand can't be converted into the type of the left operand, then a type-conversion error will be raised:

```
PS (3) > 2 + "abc"
Cannot convert "abc" to "System.Int32". Error: "Input string was not
 in a correct format."
At line:1 char:4
+ 2 +  <<<< "abc"
```

Because "abc" can't be converted into a number, you'll receive a type-conversion error. Now if this had been done using the hex notation as discussed in section 3.3.2, everything would be fine:

```
PS (4) > 2 + "0xabc"
2750
```

Because "a", "b", and "c" are valid hex digits, the string "0xabc" converts into the number 2748 and is then added to 2, yielding 2750.

The next PowerShell-defined polymorphic behavior for + involves arrays or collections. If the operand on the left is an array or collection, the operand on the right will be appended to that collection. If the right operand is a scalar value, it will be added to the array as is. If it's already an array (or any type of enumerable collection), it will be appended to the collection.

At this point, it's probably a good idea to reiterate how array catenation is done in PowerShell. Because the underlying .NET array objects are of fixed size (as discussed in chapter 3), catenation is accomplished by creating a new array of type `[object[]]` and copying the elements from the operands into this new array. In the process of creating the new array, any type constraint on the original arrays will be lost. For example, if the left operand is `[int[]]`—that is, an array of type `[int]`—and you add a non-numeric string to it, a new array will be created that will be of type `[object[]]`, which can hold any type of object. Let's look at an example. First create an integer array:

```
PS (1) > $a = [int[]] (1,2,3,4)
PS (2) > $a.GetType().FullName
System.Int32[]
```

Now let's do some assignments. First assign an integer:

```
PS (3) > $a[0] = 10
```

This works without error. Next try it with a string that can be converted into an integer. Use the hex string mentioned earlier:

```
PS (4) > $a[0] = "0xabc"
```

This also works fine. Finally, try assigning a non-numeric string to the array element:

```
PS (5) > $a[0] = "hello"
Array assignment to [0] failed: Cannot convert "hello" to
"System.Int32". Error: "Input string was not in a correct format.".
At line:1 char:4
+ $a[0 <<<< ] = "hello"
```

This fails, as you might expect. An array of type `[int[]]` can only hold integers. Because `"hello"` can't be converted into an integer, you get the type-conversion error shown. So far, so good. Now let's do an array concatenation:

```
PS (6) > $a = $a + "hello"
```

And now try the assignment that failed previously:

```
PS (7) > $a[0] = "hello"
PS (8) > $a
hello
2
3
4
hello
```

This time the assignment succeeds without error. What happened here? Let's look at the type of the array:

```
PS (9) > $a.GetType().FullName
System.Object[]
```

When the new, larger array was created to hold the combined elements, it was created as type `[object[]]`, which isn't type constrained. It can hold any type of object, so the assignment proceeded without error.

Finally, let's see how addition works with hashtables. Similar to arrays, addition of hashtables creates a new hashtable and copies the elements of the original tables into the new one. The left elements are copied first; then the elements from the right operand are copied. (This only works if both operands are hashtables.) If any collisions take place—that is, if the keys of any of the elements in the right operand match the keys of any element in the left operand—then an error will occur saying that the key already exists in the hashtable. (This was an implementation decision; the PowerShell team could've had the new element overwrite the old one, but the consensus was that generating an error message is usually the better thing to do.)

```
PS (1) > $left=@{a=1;b=2;c=3}
PS (2) > $right=@{d=4;e=5}
PS (3) > $new = $left + $right
PS (4) > $new

Key                            Value
---                            -----
d                              4
a                              1
b                              2
e                              5
c                              3
```

The new hashtable is of type `System.Collections.Hashtable`:

```
PS (5) > $new.GetType().FullName
System.Collections.Hashtable
```

The table is created in such a way that the strings that are used as keys are compared in a case-insensitive way.

This completes our discussion of the behavior of the addition operator. We covered how it works with numbers, strings, hashtables, and arrays. Now that we've finished with addition, let's move on to the multiplication operator.

4.1.2 The multiplication operator

As with addition, PowerShell defines multiplication behavior for numbers, strings, and arrays. (We don't do anything special for hashtables for multiplication.) Multiplying numbers works as expected and follows the widening rules discussed in chapter 3. In fact, the only legal right-hand operand for multiplication is a number. If the operand on the left is a string, then that string is repeated the number of times specified in the right operand. Let's try this out. Multiply the string "abc" by 1, 2, and then 3:

```
PS (1) > "abc" * 1
abc
PS (2) > "abc" * 2
abcabc
PS (3) > "abc" * 3
abcabcabc
```

The results are "abc", "abcabc", and "abcabcabc", respectively. What about multiplying by 0?

```
PS (4) > "abc" * 0
PS (5) >
```

The result appears to be nothing—but which "nothing"—spaces, empty string, or null? The way things are displayed, you can't tell by looking. Here's how to check. First check the type of the result:

```
PS (5) > ("abc" * 0).GetType().FullName
System.String
```

You see that it's a string, not `$null`. But it could still be spaces, so you need to check the length:

```
PS (6) > ("abc" * 0).Length
0
```

And, because the length is 0, you can tell that it is in fact an empty string.

Now let's look at how multiplication works with arrays. Because multiplication applied to a string repeats the string, logically you'd expect that multiplication applied to an array should repeat the array, which is exactly what it does. Let's look at some examples of this. First create an array with three elements:

```
PS (1) > $a=1,2,3
PS (2) > $a.Length
3
```

Now multiply it by 2:

```
PS (3) > $a = $a * 2
PS (4) > $a.Length
6
```

The length of the new array is 6. Looking at the contents of the array (using variable expansion in strings to save space), you see that it's "1 2 3 1 2 3"—the original array doubled.

```
PS (5) > "$a"
1 2 3 1 2 3
```

Multiply the new array by 3:

```
PS (6) > $a = $a * 3
```

And check that the length is now 18:

```
PS (7) > $a.Length
18
```

It is, so looking at the contents

```
PS (8) > "$a"
1 2 3 1 2 3 1 2 3 1 2 3 1 2 3 1 2 3
```

you see that it is six repetitions of the original three elements.

As with addition, first a new larger array is created during multiplication, and then the component elements are copied into it. This has the same issue that addition had, where the new array is created without type constraints. Even if the original array could only hold numbers, the new array can hold any type of object.

4.1.3 Subtraction, division, and the modulus operator

Addition and multiplication are the most interesting of the arithmetic operators in terms of polymorphic behavior, but let's go over the remaining operators. Subtraction, division, and the modulus (`%`) operators are only defined for numbers by PowerShell. (Modulus returns the remainder from a division operation.) Again, as with all numeric computations, the widening rules for numbers are obeyed. For the basic scalar types (such as strings and numbers), these operations are only defined for numbers, so if either operand is a number (not just the left-hand operand), an attempt will be made to convert the other operand into a number as well, as shown here:

```
PS (1) > "123" / 4
30.75
PS (2) > 123 / "4"
30.75
PS (3) >
```

In the first example, the string "123" is converted into a number. In the second example, the string "4" will be converted into a number.

NOTE Here's an important characteristic about how division works in PowerShell that you should keep in mind. Integer division underflows into floating point (technically `System.Double`). This means that 5 divided by 4 in PowerShell results in 1.25 instead of 1, as it would in C#. If you want to round the decimal part to the nearest integer, simply cast the result into `[int]`. You also need to be aware that PowerShell uses what's called "Banker's rounding" when converting floating point numbers into integers. Banker's rounding rounds .5 up sometimes and down sometimes. The convention is to round to the nearest even number, so that both 1.5 and 2.5 round to 2, and 3.5 and 4.5 both round to 4.

If neither operand is a number, the operation is undefined and you'll get an error:

```
PS (3) > "123" / "4"
Method invocation failed because [System.String] doesn't contain
a method named 'op_Division'.
At line:1 char:8
+ "123" /  <<<< "4"
PS (4) >
```

Take note of this particular error message, though. PowerShell has no built-in definition for this operation, so as a last step it looks to see whether the type of the left operand defines a method for performing the operation. In fact, PowerShell looks for the `op_<operation>` methods on the left operand if the operation isn't one of those defined by PowerShell itself. This allows the operators to work on types such as `System.Datetime` (the .NET representation of dates) even though there's no special support for these types in PowerShell.

Here's an example. Suppose you want to find the total number of days between January 1, 2006, and February 1, 2006. You can create objects representing these dates by casting strings into `DateTime` objects. Once you have these objects, you can convert them:

```
PS (1) > ([DateTime] "2006-2-1" - [DateTime]"2006-1-1").TotalDays
31
```

For those of you with children, here's a more useful example. Jeffrey Snover, the architect of PowerShell, tells a story about his daughter:

My daughter loves Christmas. She often asks me, "How long is it 'til Christmas?" The problem with that is that I'm one of those people who can barely remember what year it is, much less the date. Well, it's one thing to be a flawed person and it's another thing to disappoint your daughter. PowerShell to the rescue!

Here's a little date math routine I wrote to help me out:

```
function tillXmas ()
{
    $now = [DateTime]::Now
    [DateTime]( [string] $now.Year + "-12-25") - $Now
}
```

```
PS> tillxmas

Days              : 321
Hours             : 18
Minutes           : 8
Seconds           : 26
Milliseconds      : 171
Ticks             : 277997061718750
TotalDays         : 321.755858470775
TotalHours        : 7722.14060329861
TotalMinutes      : 463328.436197917
TotalSeconds      : 27799706.171875
TotalMilliseconds : 27799706171.875
```

Thanks to PowerShell, I can tell my daughter how many seconds to go until Christmas! Now if I can only get her to stop asking me in the car.

To take a look at the operator methods defined for `System.DateTime`, you can use the `GetMembers()` method. Here's a partial listing of the operator methods defined. This example uses the PowerShell `Select-String` cmdlet to limit what's displayed to only those methods whose names contain the string "op_":

```
PS (5) > [DateTime].GetMembers()| foreach{"$_"}| Select-String op_
System.DateTime op_Addition(System.DateTime, System.TimeSpan)
System.DateTime op_Subtraction(System.DateTime, System.TimeSpan)
System.TimeSpan op_Subtraction(System.DateTime, System.DateTime)
```

As you can see, not all the arithmetic operator methods are defined. In fact, no methods are defined for any operations other than addition and subtraction. If you try to divide a `DateTime` object by a number, you'll get the same error you saw when you tried to divide two strings:

```
PS (4) > [DateTime] "1/1/2006" / 22
Method invocation failed because [System.DateTime] doesn't contain
a method named 'op_Division'.
At line:1 char:24
+ [DateTime] "1/1/2006" /  <<<< 22
PS (5) >
```

The error occurred because PowerShell was looking for an `op_Division()` on the object on the left. It didn't find one, and therefore the operation failed.

Okay, now that you know all about arithmetic operators and operations in PowerShell, you need to have a way to save the results of these operations. Variable assignment is the answer, so we'll look at assignment and the assignment operators next.

4.2 THE ASSIGNMENT OPERATORS

In this section we'll cover the assignment operators, which are shown in figure 4.3 and listed with examples in table 4.2.

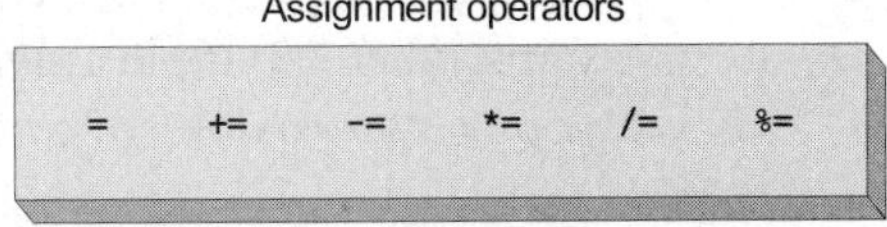

Figure 4.3 The PowerShell assignment operators

As you can see, along with simple assignment, PowerShell supports the compound operators that are found in

C-based languages. These compound operators retrieve, update, and reassign a variable's value all in one step. The result is a much more concise notation for expressing this type of operation.

In table 4.2, for each of the compound assignment operators, the third column shows the equivalent decomposed operation.

Table 4.2 PowerShell assignment operators

Operator	Example	Equivalent	Description
`=`	`$a= 3`		Sets the variable to the specified value
`+=`	`$a += 2`	`$a = $a + 2`	Performs the addition operation in the existing value, and then assigns the result back to the variable
`-=`	`$a -= 13`	`$a = $a - 13`	Performs the subtraction operation in the existing value, and then assigns the result back to the variable
`*=`	`$a *= 3`	`$a = $a * 3`	Multiplies the value of a variable by the specified value or appends to the existing value
`/=`	`$a /= 3`	`$a = $a / 3`	Divides the value of a variable by the specified value
`%=`	`$a %= 3`	`$a = $a % 3`	Divides the value of a variable by the specified value and assigns the remainder (modulus) to the variable

Of course, the arithmetic parts of the compound arithmetic/assignment operators follow all the rules for the arithmetic operators described in the previous section. The formal syntax for an assignment expression looks like this:

```
<lvalueList> <assignmentOperator> <pipeline>
<lvalueList> := <lvalue> [ , <lvalue> ] *
<lvalue> := <variable> | <propertyReference> | <arrayReference>
```

One interesting thing to note from this syntax is that multiple assignments are allowed. For example, the expression

```
$a,$b,$c = 1,2,3,4
```

is a perfectly legal statement. It says, "Assign 1 to $a, assign 2 to $b, and assign the remaining elements 3 and 4 of the list to $c." Multiple assignments can be used to greatly simplify certain types of operations, as you'll see in the next section.

4.2.1 Multiple assignments

Multiple assignment works only with the basic assignment operator. You can't use it with any of the compound operators. It can, however, be used with any type of assignable expression such as an array element or property reference. Here's a quick example where multiple assignment is particularly useful. The canonical pattern for swapping two variables in conventional languages is

```
$temp = $a
$a = $b
$b = $temp
```

This takes three lines of code and requires you to use a temporary variable. Here's how to do it using multiple assignments in PowerShell:

```
$a,$b = $b,$a
```

It's simple and clean—only one line of code with no temporary variables to worry about. Here's a more interesting example. The Fibonacci sequence is a sequence of numbers where each element is defined as the sum of the previous two numbers in the sequence. It looks like this:

```
1 1 2 3 5 8 13 21 …
```

> **NOTE** The Fibonacci sequence is an oddly popular bit of mathematics. It shows up in books, movies, and seashells. In the West, it was first studied by Leonardo of Pisa, a.k.a. Fibonacci. He used this sequence to describe how rabbits multiply. Rabbits aren't good at math, so it wasn't very accurate. The sequence also describes the progression of the spiral found in some shells. Mollusks are better at math than rabbits, apparently.

Here's how to generate this sequence in PowerShell using multiple assignments:

```
PS (53) > $c=$p=1; 1; while ($c -lt 100) { $c; $c,$p = ($c+$p),$c }
1
1
2
3
5
8
13
21
34
55
89
```

This example begins by initializing the two variables `$c` (current) and `$p` (previous) to 1. Then it loops while `$c` is less than 100. `$c` contains the current value in the sequence, so that value is emitted. Next comes the double assignment, where `$c` becomes the next element in the sequence and `$p` becomes the current (now previous) value in the sequence. So far, you've seen that using multiple assignments can simplify basic operations such as swapping values. But when combined with some of PowerShell's other features, it lets you do much more interesting things than that. You'll see this in the next section.

4.2.2 Multiple assignments with type qualifiers

This is all interesting, but let's look at a more practical example. Say you're given a text file containing some data that you want to parse into a form you can work with. First let's look at the data file:

```
quiet 0 25
normal 26 50
```

```
loud 51 75
noisy 75 100
```

This file contains a set of sound-level descriptions. The format is a string describing the level, followed by two numbers describing the upper and lower bounds for these levels out of a possible 100. You want to read this information into a data structure so you can use it to categorize a list of sounds later on. Here's the fragment of PowerShell code needed to do this:

```
PS (2) > $data = get-content data.txt | foreach {
>>     $e=@{}
>>     $e.level, [int] $e.lower, [int] $e.upper = -split $_
>>     $e
>> }
>>
```

You start by using the `Get-Content` cmdlet to write the data into a pipeline. Each line of the file is sent to the `ForEach-Object` cmdlet to be processed. The first thing you do in the body of the `foreach` cmdlet is initialize a hashtable in `$e` to hold the result. You take each line stored in the `$_` variable and apply the `-split` operator to it. This splits the string into an array at each space character in the string. (The `-split` operator is covered in detail later in this chapter.) For example, the string

```
"quiet 0 25"
```

becomes an array of three strings:

```
"quiet","0","25"
```

Then you assign the split string to three elements of the hashtable: `$e.level`, `$e.lower`, and `$e.upper`. But there's one more thing you want to do. The array being assigned is all strings. For the upper and lower bounds, you want numbers, not strings. To do this, add a cast before the assignable element. This causes the value being assigned to first be converted to the target type. The end result is that the upper and lower fields in the hashtable are assigned numbers instead of strings. Finally, note that the result of the pipeline is being assigned to the variable `$data`, so you can use it later on.

Let's look at the result of this execution. Because there were four lines in the file, there should be four elements in the target array:

```
PS (3) > $data.Length
4
```

You see that there are. Now let's see if the value stored in the first element of the array is what you expect: it should be the "quiet" level.

```
PS (4) > $data[0]
Key                            Value
---                            -----
upper                          25
level                          quiet
lower                          0
```

It is. Finally, let's verify that the types were properly converted:

```
PS (5) > $data[0].level
quiet
PS (6) > $data[0].lower
0
PS (7) > $data[0].upper
25
PS (8) > $data[0].level.GetType().FullName
System.String
PS (9) > $data[0].lower.GetType().FullName
System.Int32
PS (10) > $data[0].upper.GetType().FullName
System.Int32
```

Again you use the `GetType()` method to look at the types, and you can see that the level description field is a string and that the two bounds fields are integers, as expected.

In this last example, you've seen how array assignment can be used to perform sophisticated tasks in only a few lines of code. By now, you should have a good sense of the utility of assignments in processing data in PowerShell. There's one last point to cover about assignment expressions, which we'll discuss in the next section.

4.2.3 Assignment operations as value expressions

The last thing you need to know about assignment expressions is that they're expressions. This means that you can use them anywhere you'd use any other kind of expression. This lets you initialize multiple variables at once. Let's initialize `$a`, `$b`, and `$c` to the number 3:

```
PS (1) > $a = $b = $c = 3
```

Now verify that the assignments worked:

```
PS (2) > $a, $b, $c
3
3
3
```

Yes, they did. So what exactly happened? Well, it's the equivalent of the following expression:

```
PS (3) > $a = ( $b = ( $c = 3 ) )
```

That is, `$c` is assigned 3. The expression `($c = 3)` returns the value 3, which is in turn assigned to `$b`, and the result of that assignment (also 3) is finally assigned to `$a`, so once again, all three variables end up with the same value:

```
PS (4) > $a, $b, $c
3
3
3
```

Now, because you can "intercept" the expressions with parentheses, you can perform additional operations on the values returned from the assignment statements before this value is bound in the outer assignment. Here's an example that does this:

```
PS (5) > $a = ( $b = ( $c = 3 ) + 1 ) + 1
```

In this expression, `$c` gets the value 3. The result of this assignment is returned, and 1 is added to that value, yielding 4, which is then assigned to `$b`. The result of this second assignment also has 1 added to it, so `$a` is finally assigned 5, as shown in the output:

```
PS (6) > $a, $b, $c
5
4
3
```

Now you understand assignment and arithmetic operators. But a language isn't much good if you can't compare things, so let's move on to the comparison operators.

4.3 COMPARISON OPERATORS

In this section, we'll cover what the comparison operators are in PowerShell and how they work. These operators are shown in figure 4.4.

Comparison operators (case-insensitive)

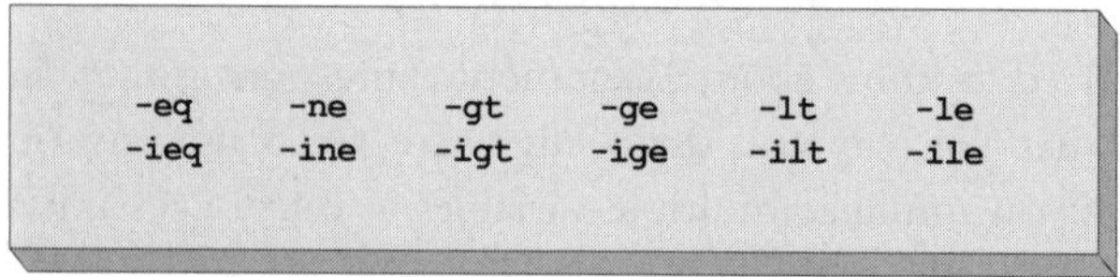

Comparison operators (case-sensitive)

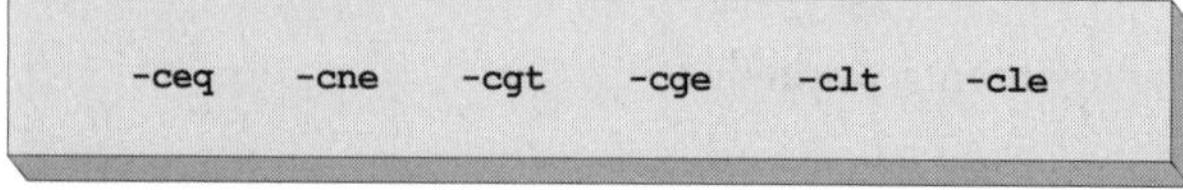

Figure 4.4 The comparison operators in PowerShell. Each operator has case-sensitive and case-insensitive versions.

We'll cover how case sensitivity factors into comparisons and how the operators work for scalar values and for collections of values. The ability of these operators to work on collections eliminates the need to write looping code in a lot of scenarios.

PowerShell has a sizable number of comparison operators, in large part because there are case-sensitive and case-insensitive versions of all the operators. These are listed with examples in table 4.3.

Table 4.3 PowerShell comparison operators

Operator	Description	Example	Result
`-eq, -ceq, -ieq`	Equals	`5 -eq 5`	`$true`
`-ne, -cne, -ine`	Not equals	`5 -ne 5`	`$false`

Table 4.3 **PowerShell comparison operators *(continued)***

Operator	Description	Example	Result
`-gt`, `-cgt`, `-igt`	Greater than	`5 -gt 3`	`$true`
`-ge`, `-cge`, `-ige`	Greater than or equal to	`5 -ge 3`	`$true`
`-lt`, `-clt`, `-ilt`	Less than	`5 -lt 3`	`$false`
`-le`, `-cle`, `-ile`	Less than or equal to	`5 -le 3`	`$false`

In table 4.3, you can see that for each operator there's a base or unqualified operator form, like `-eq` and its two variants, `-ceq` and `-ieq`. The "c" variant is case sensitive and the "i" variant is case insensitive. This raises the question, what's the behavior for the base operators with respect to case? The answer is that the unqualified operators are case insensitive. All three variants are provided to allow script authors to make their intention clear—that they meant a particular behavior rather than accepting the default.

Design decisions

Let's talk about the most contentious design decision in the PowerShell language. And the winner is: why the heck didn't we use the conventional symbols for comparison like >, >=, <, <=, ==, and !=? The answer is that the > and < characters are used for output redirection. Because PowerShell is a shell and all shell languages in the last 30 years have used > and < for I/O redirection, people expected that PowerShell should do the same. During the first public beta of PowerShell, this topic generated discussions that went on for months. We looked at a variety of alternatives, such as modal parsing where sometimes > meant greater-than and sometimes it meant redirection. We looked at alternative character sequences for the operators like :> or ->, either for redirection or comparison. We did usability tests and held focus groups, and in the end, settled on what we had started with.

The redirection operators are > and <, and the comparison operators are taken from the Unix `test(1)` command. We expect that, because these operators have a 30-year pedigree, they're adequate and appropriate to use in PowerShell. (We also expect that people will continue to complain about this decision, though hopefully not for 30 more years.)

Now that you're clear on the case-sensitivity issue, let's move on to discuss the semantics of the comparison operators. We'll begin in the next section by describing their operation on scalar data types; then in the subsequent section, we'll describe how they work with collections of objects.

4.3.1 Scalar comparisons

In this section, we'll explore how the comparison operators work with scalar objects. In particular, we'll cover their polymorphic behavior with the scalar data types.

Basic comparison rules

As with the assignment operators, the behavior of the comparison operators is significantly affected by the type of the left operand. If you're comparing a number and a string, the string will be converted into a number and a numerical comparison will be done. If the left operand is a string, the right operand will be converted to a string, and the results compared as strings. Let's look through some examples. First a simple numeric comparison:

```
PS (26) > 01 -eq 001
True
```

Because you're doing a numeric comparison, the leading zeros don't matter and the numbers compare as equal. Now let's try it when the right operand is a string:

```
PS (28) > 01 -eq "001"
True
```

Following the rule, the right operand is converted from a string into a number; then the two are compared and are found to be equal. Finally, try the comparison when the left operand is a string:

```
PS (27) > "01" -eq 001
False
```

In this example, the right operand is converted to a string, and consequently they no longer compare as equal. You can always use casts to force a particular behavior. In the next example, let's force the left operand to be a number:

```
PS (29) > [int] "01" -eq 001
True
```

And because you forced a numeric comparison, once again they're equal.

Type conversions and comparisons

As with any PowerShell operator that involves numbers, when comparisons are done in a numeric context, the widening rules are applied. This can produce somewhat unexpected results. Here's an example that illustrates this. In the first part of the example, you use a cast to convert the string "123" into a number. Once you're doing the conversion in a numeric context, the numbers get widened to double because the right operand is a double; and because 123.4 is larger than 123.0, the `-lt` operator returns true:

```
PS (37) > [int] "123" -lt 123.4
True
```

Now try it using a string as the right operand. The cast forces the left operand to be numeric, but the right operand is not yet numeric. It's converted to the numeric type of the left operand, which is [int], not [double]. This means that the value is truncated and the comparison now returns false:

```
PS (38) > [int] "123" -lt "123.4"
False
```

Finally, if you force the context to be [double] explicitly, the comparison again returns true:

```
PS (39) > [double] "123" -lt "123.4"
True
```

Although all these rules seem complicated (and, speaking as the guy who implemented them, they are), the results are generally what you'd intuitively expect. This satisfies the principle of least astonishment. So most of the time you don't need to worry about the specifics and can let the system take care of the conversions. It's only when things don't work as expected that you need to understand the details of the conversion process. To help you debug cases where this happens, PowerShell provides a type-conversion tracing mechanism to help you track down the problems. Chapter 7 describes how to use this debugging feature. Finally, you can always apply a set of casts to override the implicit behavior and force the results you want.

4.3.2 Comparisons and case sensitivity

Next let's look at the "i" and "c" versions of the comparison operators—the case-sensitive and case-insensitive versions. Obviously, case sensitivity only applies to strings. All the comparison operators have both versions. For example, the -eq operator has the following variants:

```
PS (1) > "abc" -eq "ABC"
True
PS (2) > "abc" -ieq "ABC"
True
PS (3) > "abc" -ceq "ABC"
False
```

The default case -eq is case insensitive, as is the explicitly case-insensitive operator -ieq, so in the example, "abc" and "ABC" compare as equal. The -ceq operator is case sensitive, so with this operator, "abc" and "ABC" compare as not equal.

The final item to discuss with scalar comparisons is how things that aren't strings and numbers are compared. In this case, the .NET comparison mechanisms are used. If the object implements the .NET IComparable interface, then that will be used. If not, and if the object on the left side has an .Equals() method that can take an object of the type of the right operand, this is used. If there's no direct mechanism for comparing the two, an attempt will be made to convert the right operand into an instance of the type of the left operand, and then PowerShell will try to compare the resulting objects. This lets you compare things such as [DateTime] objects, as shown here:

```
PS (4) > [DateTime] "1/1/2010" -gt [DateTime] "1/1/2009"
True
PS (5) > [DateTime] "1/1/2010" -gt [DateTime] "2/1/2010"
False
PS (6) >
```

Not all objects are directly comparable. For example, there's no direct way to compare a System.DateTime object to a System.Diagnostics.Process object:

```
PS (6) > [DateTime] "1/1/2010" -gt (Get-Process)[0]
The '-gt' operator failed: Cannot convert
"System.Diagnostics.Process (ALCXMNTR)" to "System.DateTime"..
At line:1 char:26
+ [] "1/1/2010" -gt  <<<< (Get-Process)[0]
PS (7) >
```

In this example, because there's no direct way to compare a DateTime object to a Process object, the next step is to try to convert the Process object into an instance of DateTime. This also failed, and as this is the last step in the comparison algorithm, an error message is produced explaining what happened. This is where a human has to intervene. The obvious field on a Process object to compare is the StartTime of the process. Use the property notation to do this:

```
PS (7) > [DateTime] "1/1/2010" -gt (Get-Process)[0].StartTime
False
PS (8) > [DateTime] "1/1/2011" -gt (Get-Process)[0].StartTime
True
```

In this expression, you're looking to see whether the first element in the list of Process objects had a start time greater than the beginning of this year (no) and whether it had a start time from before the beginning of next year (obviously true). You can use this approach to find all the processes on a computer that started today:

```
Get-Process | where {$_.starttime -ge [DateTime]::today}
```

The Get-Process cmdlet returns a list of all the processes on this computer, and the where cmdlet selects those processes where the StartTime property of the process is greater than or equal to today.

> **NOTE** The where used in the previous example is an alias for the Where-Object cmdlet, which is described in chapter 6.

This completes our discussion of the behavior of the comparison operators with scalar data. We paid a lot of attention to the role types play in comparisons, but so far we've avoided discussing collection types—lists, arrays, and so on. We'll get to that in the next section.

4.3.3 Using comparison operators with collections

In this section, we'll focus on the behavior of the comparison operators when they're used with collections of objects.

Basic comparison operations involving collections

Here's the basic behavior. If the left operand is an array or collection, the comparison operation will return the elements of that collection that match the right operand. Let's illustrate the rule with an example:

```
PS (1) > 1,2,3,1,2,3,4 -eq 2
2
2
```

This expression searches the list of numbers on the left side and returns those that match—the two "2"s. And this works with strings as well:

```
PS (2) > "one","two","three","two","one" -eq "two"
two
two
```

When processing the array, the scalar comparison rules are used to compare each element. In the next example, the left operand is an array containing a mix of numbers and strings, and the right operand is the string "2":

```
PS (3) > 1,"2",3,2,"1" -eq "2"
2
2
```

Again, it returns the two "2"s. Let's look at some more examples where you have leading zeros in the operands. In the first example

```
PS (4) > 1,"02",3,02,"1" -eq "2"
2
```

you only return the number 2 because 2 and "02" compare equally in a numeric context, but "2" and "02" are different in a string context. The same thing happens in the next example:

```
PS (5) > 1,"02",3,02,"1" -eq 2
2
```

When the elements are compared as numbers, they match. When compared as strings, they don't match because of the leading zero. Now one final example:

```
PS (6) > 1,"02",3,02,"1" -eq "02"
02
2
```

They both match. In a numeric context, the leading zeros don't matter; and in the string context, the strings match.

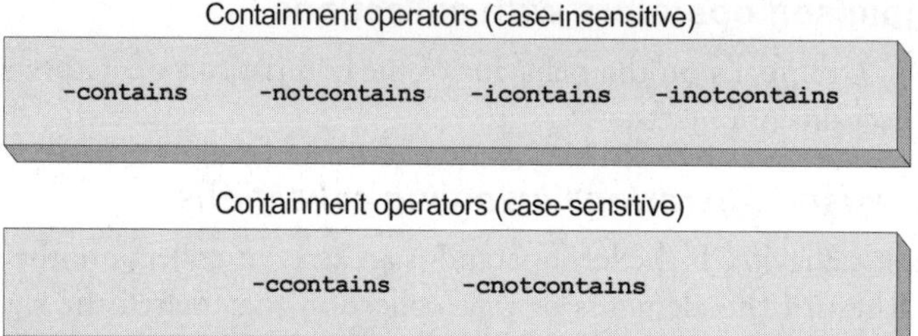

Figure 4.5 The PowerShell containment operators in case-insensitive and case-sensitive versions

The containment operators

All of the comparison operators we've discussed so far return the matching elements from the collection. Although this is extremely useful, there are times when you just want to find out whether or not an element is there. This is what the `-contains` and `-notcontains` operators, shown in figure 4.5, are for.

These operators return `$True` if the set contains the element you're looking for instead of returning the matching elements. They're listed in table 4.4 with examples.

Table 4.4 PowerShell containment operators

Operator	Description	Example	Result

`-contains`
`-ccontains`
`-icontains`
	The collection on the left side contains the value specified on the right side.	`1,2,3 -contains 2`	`$true`

`-notcontains`
`-cnotcontains`
`-inotcontains`
	The collection on the left side doesn't contain the value specified on the right side.	`1,2,3 -notcontains 2`	`$false`

Let's redo the example at the end of the previous section, but this time you'll use `-contains` instead of `-eq`:

```
PS (1) > 1,"02",3,02,"1" -contains "02"
True
PS (2) > 1,"02",3,02,"1" -notcontains "02"
False
```

Now, instead of returning 02 and 2, you just return a single Boolean value. Because all values in PowerShell can be converted into a Boolean value, this doesn't seem as if it would particularly matter, and usually it doesn't. The one case where it does matter is if the matching set of elements is something that's false. This even includes Booleans. The concept is easier to understand with an example:

```
PS (3) > $false,$true -eq $false
False
PS (4) > $false,$true -contains $false
True
```

In the first command, -eq searches the list for $false, finds it, and then returns the matching value. But because the matching value was literally $false, a successful match looks as if it failed. When you use the -contains operator in the expression, you get the result you'd expect, which is $true. The other way to work around this issue is to use the @(..) construction and the Count property:

```
PS (5) > @($false,$true -eq $false).count
1
```

The @(...) sequence forces the result to be an array and then takes the count of the results. If there are no matches the count will be zero, which is equivalent to $false. If there are matches the count will be nonzero, equivalent to $true. There can also be some performance advantages to -contains, because it stops looking on the first match instead of checking every element in the list.

> **NOTE** The @(..) construction is described in detail in chapter 5.

In this section, we covered all the basic comparison operators. We addressed the issue of case sensitivity in comparisons, and we covered the polymorphic behavior of these operations, first for scalar data types, then for collections. Now let's move on to look at PowerShell's operators for working with text. One of the hallmark features of dynamic languages is great support for text manipulation and pattern matching. In the next section, we'll cover how PowerShell incorporates these features into the language.

4.4 PATTERN MATCHING AND TEXT MANIPULATION

In this section, we explore the pattern-matching and text-manipulation operators in PowerShell (see figure 4.6).

Beyond the basic comparison operators, PowerShell has a number of pattern-matching operators. These operators work on strings, allowing you to search through text, extract pieces of it, and edit or create new strings. The other text-manipulation

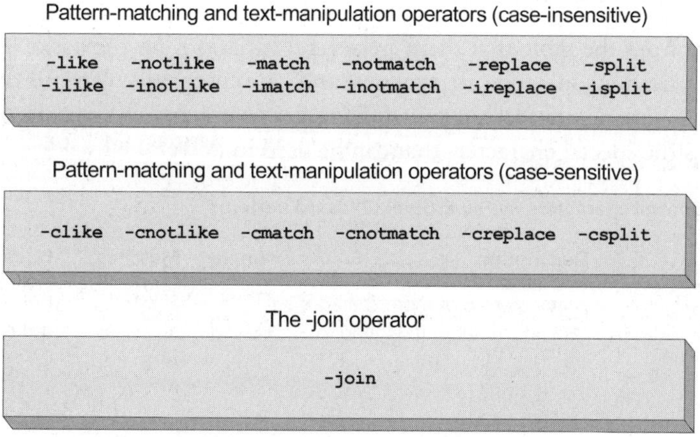

Pattern-matching and text-manipulation operators (case-insensitive)

-like	-notlike	-match	-notmatch	-replace	-split
-ilike	-inotlike	-imatch	-inotmatch	-ireplace	-isplit

Pattern-matching and text-manipulation operators (case-sensitive)

-clike	-cnotlike	-cmatch	-cnotmatch	-creplace	-csplit

The -join operator

-join

Figure 4.6 The pattern-matching and text-manipulation operators in PowerShell. All the operators that use patterns (everything except -join) have case-sensitive and case-insensitive forms.

operators allow you to break strings apart into pieces or add individual pieces back together into a single string.

We'll start with the pattern-matching operators. PowerShell supports two built-in types of patterns—*wildcard expressions* and *regular expressions*. Each of these pattern types is useful in distinct domains. We'll cover the operation and applications of both types of patterns along with the operators that use them.

4.4.1 Wildcard patterns and the -like operator

You usually find wildcard patterns in a shell for matching filenames. For example, the command

```
dir *.txt
```

finds all the files ending in .txt. Similarly

```
cp *.txt c:\backup
```

will copy all the text files into the directory c:\backup. In these examples, the * matches any sequence of characters. Wildcard patterns also allow you to specify character ranges. In the next example, the pattern

```
dir [st]*.txt
```

will return all the files that start with either the letter *s* or *t* that have a .txt extension. Finally, you can use the question mark (?) to match any single character.

The wildcard pattern-matching operators are listed in table 4.5. This table lists the operators and includes some simple examples of how each one works.

Table 4.5 PowerShell wildcard pattern-matching operators

Operator	Description	Example	Result
`-like`, `-clike`, `-ilike`	Do a wildcard pattern match.	`"one" -like "o*"`	`$true`
`-notlike`, `-cnotlike`, `-inotlike`	Do a wildcard pattern match; true if the pattern doesn't match.	`"one" -notlike "o*"`	`$false`

You can see from the table that there are several variations on the basic `-like` operator. These variations include case-sensitive and case-insensitive versions of the operator, as well as variants that return true if the target doesn't match the pattern. Table 4.6 summarizes the special characters that can be used in PowerShell wildcard patterns.

Table 4.6 Special characters in PowerShell wildcard patterns

Wildcard	Description	Example	Matches	Doesn't match

*	Matches zero or more characters anywhere in the string	`a*`	`a`
			`aa`
			`abc`
			`ab`
				`bc`
				`babc`

?	Matches any single character	`a?c`	`abc` `aXc`	`a~` `ab`

Table 4.6 Special characters in PowerShell wildcard patterns *(continued)*

Wildcard	Description	Example	Matches	Doesn't match

`[<char>-<char>]`	Matches a sequential range of characters	`a[b-d]c`	`abc`
			`acc`
			`adc`
				`aac`
				`aec`
				`afc`
				`abbc`

`[<char><char>...]`	Matches any one character from a set of characters	`a[bc]c`	`abc`
			`acc`
				`a`
				`ab`
				`Ac`
				`adc`

Although wildcard patterns are simple, their matching capabilities are limited, so PowerShell also provides a set of operators that use regular expressions.

4.4.2 Regular expressions

Regular expressions are conceptually (if not syntactically) a superset of wildcard expressions. By this, we mean that you can express the same patterns in regular expressions that you can in wildcard expressions, but with slightly different syntax.

> **NOTE** In fact, in versions 1 and 2 of PowerShell, wildcard patterns are translated internally into the corresponding regular expressions under the covers.

With regular expressions, instead of using `*` to match any sequence of characters as you would in wildcard patterns, you use `.*`—and, instead of using `?` to match any single character, you use the dot (`.`).

Why is the expression regular?

The name *regular expressions* comes from theoretical computer science, specifically the branches of automata theory (state machines) and formal languages. Ken Thompson, one of the creators of the Unix operating system, saw an opportunity to apply this theoretical aspect of computer science to solve a real-world problem—finding patterns in text in an editor—and the rest is history.

Most modern languages and environments that work with text now allow you to use regular expressions. This includes languages such as Perl, Python, and VBScript, and environments such as Emacs and Microsoft Visual Studio. The regular expressions in PowerShell are implemented using the .NET regular expression classes. The pattern language implemented by these classes is powerful, but it's also very large, so we can't completely cover it in this book. On the other hand, because PowerShell directly uses the .NET regular expression classes, any source of documentation for .NET regular expressions is also applicable to PowerShell. For example, the Microsoft Developer Network has extensive (if rather fragmented) online documentation on .NET regular expressions.

Although regular expressions are similar to wildcard patterns, they're much more powerful and allow you to do sophisticated text manipulation with small amounts of script. We'll look at the kinds of things you can do with these patterns in the next few sections.

4.4.3 The -match operator

The PowerShell version 1 operators that work with regular expressions are `-match` and `-replace`. These operators are shown in table 4.7 along with a description and some examples. PowerShell v2 introduced an additional `-split` operator, which we'll cover a bit later.

Table 4.7 PowerShell regular expression `-match` and `-replace` operators

Operator	Description	Example	Result

`-match`
`-cmatch`
`-imatch`
	Do a pattern match using regular expressions.	`"Hello" -match "[jkl]"`	`$true`

`-notmatch`
`-cnotmath`
`-inotmatch`
	Do a regex pattern match; return true if the pattern doesn't match.	`"Hello" -notmatch "[jkl]"`	`$false`

`-replace`
`-creplace`
`-ireplace`
	Do a regular expression substitution on the string on the left side and return the modified string.	`"Hello" -replace "ello","i"`	`"Hi"`

	Delete the portion of the string matching the regular expression.	`"abcde" -replace "bcd"`	`"ae"`

The `-match` operator is similar to the `-like` operator in that it matches a pattern and returns a result. Along with that result, though, it also sets the `$matches` variable. This variable contains the portions of the string that are matched by individual parts of the regular expressions. The only way to clearly explain this is with an example:

```
PS (1) > "abc" -match "(a)(b)(c)"
True
```

Here, the string on the left side of the `-match` operator is matched against the pattern on the right side. In the pattern string, you can see three sets of parentheses. Figure 4.7 shows this expression in more detail. You can see on the right side of the `-match` operator that each of the components in parentheses is a "submatch." We'll get to why this is important in the next section.

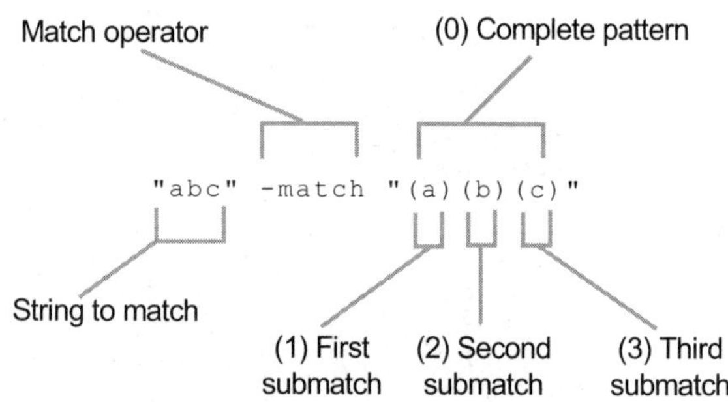

Figure 4.7 The anatomy of a regular expression match operation where the pattern contains submatches. Each of the bracketed elements of the pattern corresponds to a submatch pattern.

Figure 4.7 shows the anatomy of a regular expression match operation where the pattern contains submatches. Each of the bracketed elements of the pattern corresponds to a submatch pattern.

The result of this expression was true, which means that the match succeeded. It also means that `$matches` should be set, so let's look at what it contains:

```
PS (2) > $matches

Key                           Value
---                           -----
3                             c
2                             b
1                             a
0                             abc
```

`$matches` contains a hashtable where the keys of the hashtable are indexes that correspond to parts of the pattern that matched. The values are the substrings of the target string that matched. Note that even though you only specified three subpatterns, the hashtable contains four elements. This is because there's always a default element that represents the entire string that matched. Here's a more complex example that shows multiple nested matches:

```
PS (4) > "abcdef" -match "(a)(((b)(c))de)f"
True
PS (5) > $matches

Key                           Value
---                           -----
5                             c
4                             b
3                             bc
2                             bcde
1                             a
0                             abcdef
```

Now you have the outermost match in index 0, which matches the whole string. Next you have a top-level match at the beginning of the pattern that matches "a" at index 1. At index 2, you have the complete string matched by the next top-level part, which is "bcde". Index 3 is the first nested match in that top-level match, which is "bc". This match also has two nested matches: b at element 4 and c at element 5.

Matching using named captures

Calculating these indexes is fine if the pattern is simple. If it's complex, as in the previous example, it's hard to figure out what goes where—and even if you do, when you look at what you've written a month later, you'll have to figure it out all over again. The .NET regular expression library provides a way to solve this problem by using named captures. You specify a named capture by placing the sequence `?<name>` immediately inside the parentheses that indicate the match group. This allows you to reference the capture by name instead of by number, making complex expressions easier to deal with. Here's what this looks like:

```
PS (10) > "abcdef" -match "(?<o1>a)(?<o2>((?<e3>b)(?<e4>c))de)f"
True
PS (11) > $matches

Key                           Value
---                           -----
o1                            a
e3                            b
e4                            c
o2                            bcde
1                             bc
0                             abcdef
```

Now let's look at a more realistic example.

Parsing command output using regular expressions

Existing utilities for Windows produce text output, so you have to parse the text to extract information. (As you may remember, avoiding this kind of parsing was one of the reasons PowerShell was created. But it still needs to interoperate with the rest of the world.) For example, the `net.exe` utility can return some information about your computer configuration. The second line of this output contains the name of the computer. Your task is to extract the name and domain for this computer from that string. One way to do this is to calculate the offsets and then extract substrings from the output. This is tedious and error prone (since the offsets might change). Here's how to do it using the `$matches` variable. First let's look at the form of this string:

```
PS (1) > (net config workstation)[1]
Full Computer name            brucepay64.redmond.corp.microsoft.com
```

It begins with a well-known pattern, `Full Computer name`, so start by matching against that to make sure there are no errors. You'll see that there's a space before the name, and the name itself is separated by a period. You're pretty safe in ignoring the intervening characters, so here's the pattern you'll use:

```
PS (2) > $p='^Full Computer.* (?<computer>[^.]+)\.(?<domain>[^.]+)'
```

Figure 4.8 shows this pattern in more detail.

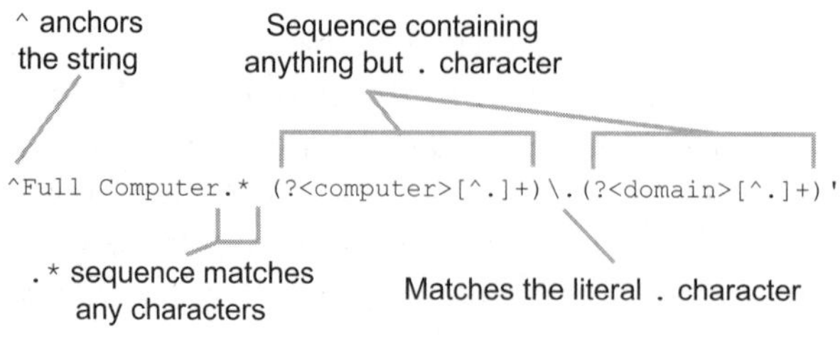

Figure 4.8 This is an example of a regular expression pattern that uses the named submatch capability. When this expression is used with the `-match` operator, instead of using simple numeric indexes in the `$matches` variable for the substrings, the names will be used.

You check the string at the beginning, and then allow any sequence of characters that ends with a space, followed by two fields that are terminated by a dot. Notice that you don't say that the fields can contain *any* character. Instead, you say that they can contain anything but a period. This is because regular expressions are greedy—that is, they match the longest possible pattern, and because the period is any character, the match won't stop at the period. Now let's apply this pattern:

```
PS (3) > (net config workstation)[1] -match $p
True
```

It matches, so you know that the output string was well formed. Now let's look at what you captured from the string:

```
PS (4) > $matches.computer
brucepay64
PS (5) > $matches.domain
redmond
```

You see that you've extracted the computer name and domain as desired. This approach is significantly more robust than using exact indexing for the following reasons. First, you checked with a guard string instead of assuming that the string at index 1 was correct. In fact, you could have written a loop that went through all the strings and stopped when the match succeeded. In that case, it wouldn't matter which line contained the information; you'd find it anyway. You also didn't care about where in the line the data actually appeared, only that it followed a basic well-formed pattern. With a pattern-based approach, output format can vary significantly, and this pattern would still retrieve the correct data. By using techniques like this, you can write more change-tolerant scripts than you would otherwise do.

The -match operator lets you match text; now let's look at how to go about making changes to text. This is what the -replace operator is for, so we'll explore that next.

4.4.4 The -replace operator

The -replace operator allows you to do regular expression–based text substitution on a string or collection of strings. The syntax for this operator is shown in figure 4.9.

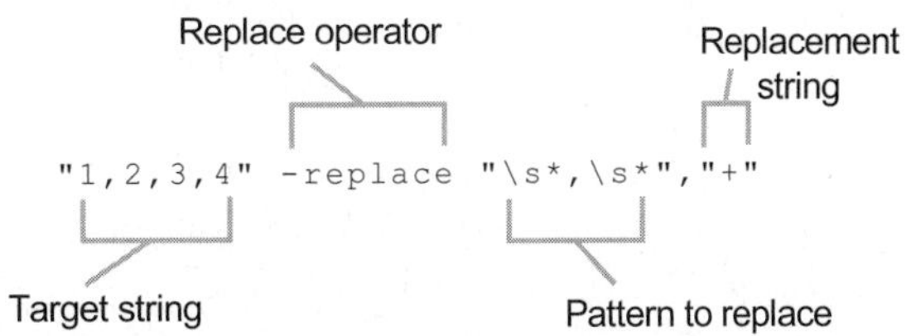

Figure 4.9 The syntax of the -replace operator

Let's run the example from the syntax diagram:

```
PS {1) > "1,2,3,4" -replace "\s*,\s*","+"
1+2+3+4
```

What this has done is replace every instance of a comma surrounded by zero or more spaces with a + sign. Now let's look at the example you saw at the beginning of this chapter:

```
${c:old.txt} -replace 'is (red|blue)','was $1' > new.txt
```

We can now discuss what the `-replace` operator is doing in this case. First look at the pattern to replace: `'is (red|blue)'`. From our earlier discussion about regular expressions with `-match`, you know that parentheses establish a submatch. Now look at the replacement string. It contains `'$1'`, which might be assumed to be a PowerShell variable. But because the string is in single quotes, it won't be expanded. Instead, the regular expression engine uses this notation to allow submatches to be referenced in the replacement expression. This allows PowerShell to intelligently replace `"is"` with `"was"`:

```
PS (2) > "The car is red" -replace 'is (red|blue)','was $1'
The car was red
PS (3) > "My boat is blue" -replace 'is (red|blue)','was $1'
My boat was blue
```

The pattern matches `"is red"` or `"is blue"` but you only want to replace `"is"`. These substitutions make this possible. The complete set of substitution character sequences is shown in table 4.8.

Finally, what happens if the pattern doesn't match? Let's try it:

```
PS (4) > "My bike is yellow" -replace 'is (red|blue)','was $1'
My bike is yellow
```

You see that if the pattern isn't matched, the string is returned as is.

Table 4.8 Character sequences for doing substitutions in the replacement pattern for the `-replace` operator

Character sequence	Description
`$number`	Substitutes the last submatch matched by group number
`${name}`	Substitutes the last submatch matched by a named capture of the form `(?<name> )`
`$$`	Substitutes a single `"$"` literal
`$&`	Substitutes a copy of the entire match itself
``$` ``	Substitutes all the text from the argument string before the matching portion
`$'`	Substitutes all the text of the argument string after the matching portion
`$+`	Substitutes the last submatch captured
`$_`	Substitutes the entire argument string

Sometimes you'll want to use regular expression substitutions and PowerShell variable expansion at the same time. You can do this by escaping the `'$'` before the substitution with a backtick (`` ` ``). The result looks like this:

```
PS (5) > $a = "really"
PS (6) > "The car is red" -replace 'is (red|blue)',"was $a `$1"
The car was really red
```

In the output string, the word "red" was preserved using the regular expression substitution mechanism and the word "really" was added by expanding the `$a` variable.

We've looked at lots of ways to substitute one thing for something else. But sometimes you don't want to substitute something—you want to substitute nothing. More simply, you just want to remove the matching parts. You can do this using `-replace` by omitting the replacement string:

```
PS (7) > "The quick brown fox" -replace 'quick'
The  brown fox
```

In this example, the word "quick" was removed from the sentence.

Here's one final point we should make clear. The `-replace` operator doesn't *change* strings—it returns a new string with the necessary edits applied. To illustrate this, put a string in a variable and then use it in a `-replace` expression:

```
PS (8) > $orig = "abc"
PS (9) > $orig -replace "b","B"
aBc
PS (10) > $orig
abc
PS (11) >
```

In the resulting output from the `-replace` expression, the lowercase *b* has been changed to an uppercase *B*. But when you look at the original string, you see that it's unchanged. The result string is a new string with the substitutions performed on it rather than on the original.

Up to this point, all the operations we've looked at have involved transformations on a single string. Now let's look at how to take strings apart and put them back together using two more string operators: `-split` and `-join`. This will complete your knowledge of the set of operators PowerShell provides for manipulating strings.

4.4.5 The -join operator

PowerShell version 2 introduced two new operators for working with collections and strings: `-split` and `-join`. These operators allow you to join the elements of a collection into a single string or split strings into a collection of substrings. We'll look at the `-join` operator first as it's the simpler of the two.

As we mentioned, the `-join` operator allows you to join collections of objects into a single string. This operator can be used both as a unary operator and a binary operator. The syntax for the unary form of the `-join` operator is shown in figure 4.10.

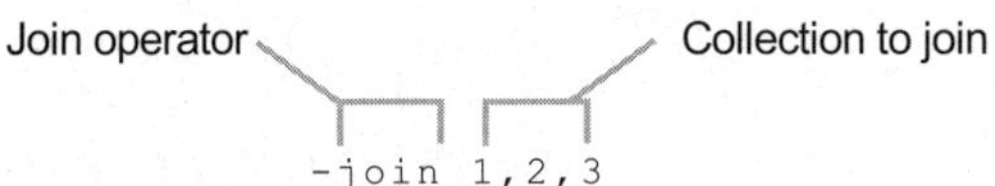

Figure 4.10 The unary join operator allows you to join a collection of objects into a single string with nothing between each element.

The unary form of the -join operator allows you to concatenate a collections of strings into a single string with no separator between each item in the resulting string. Here's a simple example. First assign an array of numbers to the variable $in:

```
PS (1) > $in = 1,2,3
```

Now check the type of the variable's value

```
PS (2) > $in.GetType().FullName
System.Object[]
```

and you see that it's an array of objects. (Remember that PowerShell arrays are always created as polymorphic arrays, regardless of the content of the arrays.) Now use the -join operator on this variable and assign the result to a new variable, $out:

```
PS (3) > $out = -join $in
```

Checking the type of the result

```
PS (4) > $out.GetType().FullName
System.String
```

you see that it's a string. The -join operator first converted each array element into a string and then joined the results into a single larger string. Let's look at the contents of $out to see what the result looks like:

```
PS (5) > $out
123
```

It's "123", as expected. Next, let's do something a bit more sophisticated. Say you want to reverse a string. Unfortunately the .NET [string] type has no built-in reverse operator, but the [array] type does have a static method for reversing arrays. This method takes an array as input and sorts it in place. To use this, you need to do two conversions: from a string to an array of characters and from an array of characters back to a string. From chapter 3, you know that you can use a cast to convert a string into a character array:

```
PS (6) > $ca = [char[]] "abcd"
```

Now that you have a character array, you can use the Reverse() method.

```
PS (7) > [array]::Reverse($ca)
```

This method reverses the contents of the array in-place so when you look at the result, you see that it's reversed as desired. But it's still an array of characters and you need a string:

```
PS (8) > $ca
d
c
b
a
```

This is where the unary -join comes into play. Use it to convert the character array back into a string:

```
PS (9) > $ra = -join $ca
```

And verify that the string has been created properly:

```
PS (10) > $ra
dcba
```

Yes, it has. Now let's look at one potential gotcha using the unary form of the operator. Let's redo the join of 1,2,3 again, but without using a variable to hold the value. Here's what that looks like:

```
PS (11) > -join 1,2,3
1
2
3
```

Surprise! Instead of joining the array members into a single string, it just returned the same array. This is because unary operators have higher precedence than binary operators and, in PowerShell, the comma is a binary operator. As a result, the expression is parsed like

```
PS (12) > (-join 1),2,3
1
2
3
```

So, to use the unary -join operator in a more complex expression, make sure you put parentheses around the argument expression:

```
PS (13) > -join (1,2,3)
123
```

When parentheses are used, the result of the expression is as expected. Next let's look at the (much more useful) binary form.

The binary form for the -join operator is shown in figure 4.11.

The obvious difference with this operator is that you can specify the string to use as an element separator instead of always using the default of nothing between the joined strings. Let's execute the example from the figure. Place the array to join into a variable called $numbers and put the joined result into a variable called $exp:

```
PS (1) > $numbers = 1,2,3
PS (2) > $exp = $numbers -join '+'
```

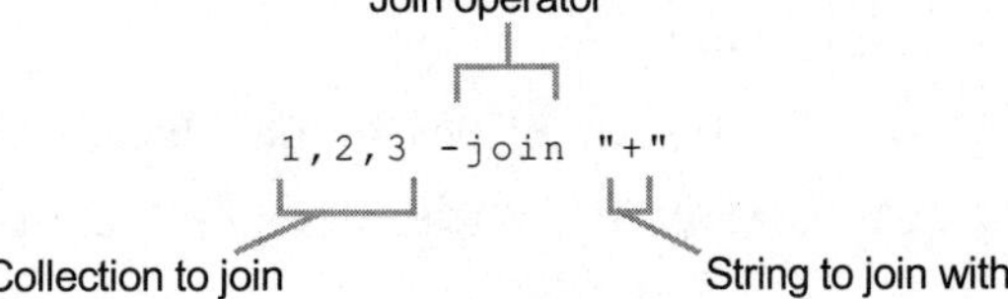

Figure 4.11 The binary form of the -join operator allows you to join a collection of objects into a single string using the specified join string.

Look at the contents of `$exp`:

```
PS (3) > $exp
1+2+3
```

It contains the numbers with a plus sign between each number. Because this is a valid PowerShell expression, you can pass the resulting string to the `Invoke-Expression` cmdlet for evaluation:

```
PS (4) > Invoke-Expression $exp
6
```

The result is 6. Of course, this works on any operator. Let's use the range operator (see chapter 5) and the multiply operator to calculate the factorial of 10. Here's what the code looks like:

```
PS (5) > $fact = Invoke-Expression (1..10 -join '*')
```

This code is evaluating `1*2*3` and so on up to 10, with the result

```
PS (6) > $fact
3628800
```

Although this is a simple way to calculate factorials, it's not efficient. Later on you'll see more efficient ways of writing this type of expression. For now, let's look at a more practical example and do some work with a file. Let's use a here-string to generate a test file on disk:

```
PS (7) > @'
>> line1
>> line2
>> line3
>> '@ > out.txt
>>
```

Now use the `Get-Content` cmdlet to read that file into a variable, `$text`:

```
PS (8) > $text = Get-Content out.txt
```

Use the `text` property to see how long the file was:

```
PS (9) > $text.Count
3
```

Clearly this isn't the number of characters in the file. It's actually the number of lines in the file. The `Get-Content` cmdlet returns the contents of a file as an array of strings. For example, to see the second line in the file, use this:

```
PS (10) > $text[1]
line2
```

To check the type of the value in `$text`, you can again use the `GetType()` method:

```
PS (11) > $text.GetType().FullName
System.Object[]
```

As you can see, it's an `[object]` array, which you should be used to by now. Although this is exactly what you want most of the time, sometimes you just want the entire file as a single string. The `Get-Content` cmdlet, as of PowerShell v2, has no parameter for doing this, so you'll have to take the array of strings and turn it back into a single string. You can do this with the binary `-join` operator if you specify the line separator as the string to use when joining the array elements. On Windows, the line separator is two characters: carriage return (`r) and a line feed (`n). In a single string, this is expressed as "`r`n". Now you can use this separator string in a `-join` expression:

```
PS (12) > $single = $text -join "`r`n"
PS (13) > $single.Length
19
```

That's more like it. And when you check index zero

```
PS (14) > $single[0]
1
```

you see that it's now a single character instead of a string.

Let's see one more example, which shows how to generate a string containing comma-separated values—a CSV string:

```
PS (16) > $csv = -join ('"',($numbers -join '","'), '"')
PS (17) > $csv
"1","2","3"
PS (18) >
```

You use `-join` to insert the sequence `","` between each element and then use string concatenation to add double quotes to either end. It's a very simple one-line CSV generator.

Now that you know how to put things together, we'll show you how to take them apart with `-split`.

4.4.6 The -split operator

The `-split` operator performs the opposite operation to `-join`: it splits strings into a collection of smaller strings. Again, this operator can be used in both binary and unary forms. The unary form of split is shown in figure 4.12.

In its unary form, this operator will split a string on *whitespace* boundaries, where whitespace is any number of spaces, tabs, or newlines. You saw this in an example earlier in this chapter.

The binary form of the operator is much more, ahem, sophisticated. It allows you to specify the pattern to match on, the type of matching to do, and the number of elements to return, as well as match

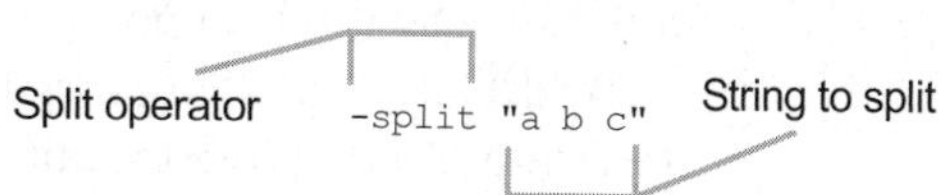

Figure 4.12 The unary `-split` operator allows you to split a string into a collection of smaller strings.

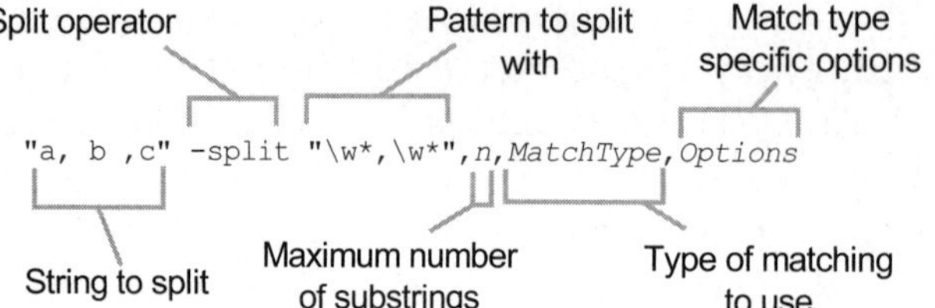

Figure 4.13 The `-split` operator allows you to split a string into a collection of smaller strings. It lets you specify a variety of arguments and options to control how the target string is split.

type-specific options. The full (and rather intimidating) syntax for this operator is shown in figure 4.13.

Although figure 4.13 looks intimidating, most of the time you just need to specify an argument string and split pattern and let the rest of the options use their default values. Let's take a look at the basic application of this operator. First, split a string on a character other than whitespace:

```
PS (11) > 'a:b:c:d:e' -split ':'
a
b
c
d
e
```

This is pretty straightforward. The string is split into five elements at the : character. But sometimes you don't want all the matches. The `-split` operator allows you to limit the number of elements to return. Do so by specifying an integer after the match pattern:

```
PS (12) > 'a:b:c:d:e' -split ':',3
a
b
c:d:e
```

In this case, you only asked for three elements to be returned. Notice that the third piece is the entire remaining string. If you specify a split count number less than or equal to 0, then all the splits take place:

```
PS (13) > 'a:b:c:d:e' -split ':',0
a
b
c
d
e
```

You'll see why this is important in a minute.

By default, `-split` uses regular expressions just like `-match` and `-replace`. But if the string you're trying to split contains one of the many characters that have special meaning in regular expressions, things become a bit more difficult because you'll have to escape these characters in the split pattern. This can be inconvenient and error prone, so -split allows you to choose *simple matching* through an option known as simplematch. When you specify simplematch, instead of treating the split pattern as a regular expression, it's handled as a simple literal string that must be matched. For example, say you want to split on *:

```
PS (14) > 'a*b*c' -split "*"
Bad argument to operator '-split': parsing "*" - Quantifier
 {x,y} following nothing..
At line:1 char:15
+ 'a*b*c' -split <<<<  "*"
    + CategoryInfo          : InvalidOperation: (:) [],
   RuntimeException
    + FullyQualifiedErrorId : BadOperatorArgument
```

This results in a regular expression parsing error. Now try it again with simplematch:

```
PS (15) > 'a*b*c' -split "*",0,"simplematch"
a
b
c
```

This time it worked properly. This option is particularly handy when you aren't using literal split strings but instead are getting them from a script argument or input file. In those cases, it's much simpler to use simplematch instead of escaping all the special regular expression characters.

-split operator options

The last element shown in the -split operator syntax diagram (figure 4.7) is the match options string. These options are shown in table 4.9. Multiple options can be specified in a string with commas between them, like RegexMatch,IgnoreCase,MultiLine or SimpleMatch,IgnoreCase.

Table 4.9 Match options for the -split operator

Option	Description	Applies to
IgnoreCase	Allows you to override default case-sensitive behavior when using the -csplit variant of the operator.	RegexMatch, SimpleMatch
CultureInvariant	Disables any culture-specific matching behavior (e.g., what constitutes uppercase) when matching the separator strings.	RegexMatch
IgnorePatternWhitespace	Ignores unescaped whitespace and comments embedded in the pattern. This allows for commenting complex patterns.	RegexMatch
MultiLine	Treat a string as though it's composed of multiple lines. A line begins at a newline character and will be matched by the ^ pattern.	RegexMatch

Table 4.9 Match options for the `-split` operator *(continued)*

Option	Description	Applies to
`SingleLine`	This option, which is the default, tells the pattern matcher to treat the entire string as a single line. Newlines in the string aren't considered the beginning of a line.	`RegexMatch`
`ExplicitCapture`	This option specifies that the only valid captures are explicitly named or numbered ones of the form `(?<name>...)`. This allows unnamed parentheses to act as noncapturing groups without the syntactic clumsiness of the expression `(?:...)`. See section 4.4.3 earlier in this chapter on how captures work.	`RegexMatch`

We won't cover all the options here. In practice, you aren't likely to need most of them, but we'll examine the ones that are typically useful, as well as some techniques for using them. The first one we'll look at is the `IgnoreCase` option. This option lets you change how case is handled when splitting the string. Normally this behavior is controlled by the name of the operator (case-sensitive for `-csplit` and case-insensitive for `-split` or `-isplit`). This is determined at parse time; then the script is transformed into an executable form. There are cases where you want to be able to override the parse time behavior at runtime. You can do this by using a variable to pass in the option instead of a constant string. Let's see how this works. Start with a `$opts` variable that contains an empty string:

```
PS (1) > $opts = ''
```

Now pass this in the options position for the operator:

```
PS (2) > 'axbXcxdXe' -csplit 'x',0, $opts
a
bXc
dXe
```

Because the option variable, `$opts`, was empty, you get the expected behavior: the split is done in the case-sensitive manner as determined by `-csplit`. Assign `ignorecase` to the variable, and try it again:

```
PS (3) > $opts = 'ignorecase'
PS (4) > 'axbXcxdXe' -csplit 'x',0, $opts
a
b
c
d
e
```

This time the string splits on all instances of `x` regardless of case, even though the `-csplit` operator was used. This shows how the parse-time defaults can be overridden at runtime.

The next option we want to look at is the `multiline` option. This option can only be used with regular expression matches and changes what the pattern matcher considers the beginning of the string. In regular expressions, you can match the beginning of a line with the ^ metacharacter. In the default `singleline` mode, the beginning of the line is the beginning of the string. Any newlines in the string aren't treated as the beginning of a line. When you use the `multiline` option, embedded newlines are treated as the beginning of a line. Here's an example. First you need some text to split—let's use a here-string to put this text into the `$text` variable:

```
PS (5) > $text = @'
>> 1
>> aaaaaaa
>> aaaaaaa
>> 2
>> bbbbbbb
>> 3
>> ccccccc
>> ccccccc
>> 4
>> ddddddd
>> '@
>>
```

In the example text, each section of the document is numbered. You want to split these "chapters" into elements in an array, so `$a[1]` is chapter 1, `$a[2]` is chapter 2, and so on. The pattern you're using (`^\d`) will match lines that begin with a number. Now use this pattern to split the document in `multiline` mode, assigning the result to `$a`:

```
PS (6) > $a = $text -split '^\d', 0, "multiline"
```

If all went as planned, `$a` should now contain four elements:

```
PS (7) > $a.Length
5
```

Wait a minute—the result is 5! But there were only four sections! There are actually five sections because the empty text before the 1 gets its own chapter. Now let's look at chapter 1, which should be in `$a[1]`

```
PS (8) > $a[1]

aaaaaaa
aaaaaaa
```

and chapter 2 in `$a[2]`:

```
PS (9) > $a[2]

bbbbbbb

PS (10) >
```

As you can see, the `multiline` option with regular expressions allows for some pretty slick text processing.

Using scriptblocks with the -split operator

As powerful as regular expressions are, sometimes you may need to split a string in a way that isn't convenient or easy to handle with regular expressions. To deal with these cases, PowerShell allows you to pass a scriptblock to the operator. The scriptblock is used as a *predicate function* that determines whether there's a match. Here's an example. First set up a string to split. This string contains a list of colors that you want to split into pairs, two colors per pair:

```
PS (17) > $colors = "Black,Brown,Red,Orange,Yellow," +
>> "Green,Blue,Violet,Gray,White'"
```

Next initialize a counter variable that will be used by the scriptblock. You're using an array here because you need to be able to modify the contents of this variable. Because the scriptblock is executed in its own scope, you must pass it an array so it can modify the value:

```
PS (18) > $count=@(0)
```

And now split the string. The scriptblock, in braces in the example, splits the string on every other comma:

```
PS (19) > $colors -split {$_ -eq "," -and ++$count[0] % 2 -eq 0 }
Black,Brown
Red,Orange
Yellow,Green
Blue,Violet
Gray,White'
```

This gives you the color pairs you were looking for.

Whew! So that's it for the pattern-matching and text-manipulation operators. In this section, we covered the two types of pattern-matching operators—wildcard patterns and regular expressions. Wildcard patterns are pretty simple, but learning to use regular expressions effectively requires more work. On the other hand, you'll find that the power of regular expressions is more than worth the effort invested to learn them. (We'll come back to these patterns again in chapter 6 when we discuss the `switch` statement.) We also looked at how to split strings into collections and join collections into strings. All very spiffy, but let's come back down to Earth now and cover the last of the basic operators in the PowerShell language. These are the logical operators (`-and`, `-or`, `-not`) and their bitwise equivalents (`-band`, `-bor`, `-bnot`).

4.5 LOGICAL AND BITWISE OPERATORS

Finally, PowerShell has logical operators `-and`, `-or`, `-xor`, and `-not` for combining simpler comparisons into more complex expressions. The logical operators convert their operands into Boolean values and then perform the logical operation.

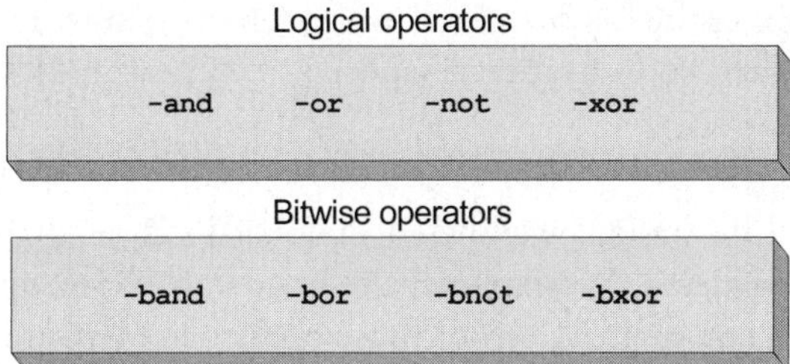

Figure 4.14 The logical and bitwise operators available in PowerShell

PowerShell also provides corresponding bitwise operators for doing binary operations on integer values. These operators can be used to test and mask bit fields. Both of these sets of operators are shown in figure 4.14.

Table 4.10 lists these operators with examples showing how each of these operators can be used.

Table 4.10 Logical and bitwise operators

Operator	Description	Example	Result
`-and`	Do a logical and of the left and right values.	`0xff -and $false`	`$false`
`-or`	Do a logical or of the left and right values.	`$false -or 0x55`	`$true`
`-xor`	Do a logical exclusive-or of the left and right values.	`$false -xor $true` `$true -xor $true`	`$true` `$false`
`-not`	Do the logical complement of the argument value.	`-not $true`	`$false`
`-band`	Do a binary and of the bits in the values on the left and right side.	`0xff -band 0x55`	`85 (0x55)`
`-bor`	Do a binary or of the bits in the values on the left and right side.	`0x55 -bor 0xaa`	`255 (0xff)`
`-bxor`	Do a binary exclusive-or of the left and right values.	`0x55 -bxor 0xaa` `0x55 -bxor 0xa5`	`255 (0xff)` `240 (0xf0)`
`-bnot`	Do the bitwise complement of the argument value.	`-bnot 0xff`	`-256` `(0x ffffff00)`

As with most languages based on C/C++, the PowerShell logical operators are *short-circuit* operators—they only do as much work as they need to. With the `-and` operator, if the left operand evaluates to `$false`, then the right operand expression isn't executed. With the `-or` operator, if the left operand evaluates to `$true`, then the right operand isn't evaluated.

> **NOTE** In PowerShell v1, the bitwise operators were limited in that they only supported 32-bit integers (`[int]`). In v2, support was added for 64-bit integers (`[long]`). If the arguments to the operators are

neither [int] nor [long], PowerShell will attempt to convert them into [long] and then perform the operation.

4.6 SUMMARY

That concludes our tour of the basic PowerShell operators. We covered a lot of information, much of it in great detail. We explored the basic PowerShell operators and expressions with semantics and applications of those operators. Here are the important points to remember:

- PowerShell operators are *polymorphic* with special behaviors defined by PowerShell for the basic types: numbers, strings, arrays, and hashtables. For other object types, the op_ methods are invoked.
- The behavior of most of the binary operators is determined by the type of the operand on the left.
- PowerShell uses widening when working with numeric types. For any arithmetic operation, the type of the result will be the narrowest .NET numeric type that can properly represent the result. Also note that integer division will underflow into floating point if the result of the operation isn't an integer. Casts can be used to force an integer result.
- There are two types of pattern matching operations in PowerShell: wildcard patterns (usually used for matching filenames) and regular expressions.
- Because the comparison and pattern-matching operators work on collections, in many cases you don't need a looping statement to search through collections.
- Regular expressions are powerful and can be used to do complex text manipulations with very little code. PowerShell uses the .NET regular expression classes to implement the regular expression operators in the language.
- PowerShell version 2 introduced two new operators for working with text: -split and -join. With the addition of these two, the set of text-manipulation operators is now complete.
- PowerShell has built-in operators for working with binary values: -band, -bor, -bxor, and -bnot.

But we're not done yet! In the next chapter, we'll finish our discussion of operators and expressions and also explain how variables are used. Stay tuned!

CHAPTER 5

Advanced operators and variables

The greatest challenge to any thinker is stating the problem in a way that will allow a solution.

—Bertrand Russell

The previous chapter covered the basic operators in PowerShell, and in this chapter we'll continue our discussion of operators by covering the advanced ones, which include things that some people don't think of as operators at all. We'll break the operators into related groups, as shown in figure 5.1.

In this chapter, we'll look at how to work with types, properties, and methods and how to use these operators to build complex data structures. The chapter concludes with a detailed discussion of how variables work in PowerShell and how you can use them with operators to accomplish significant tasks.

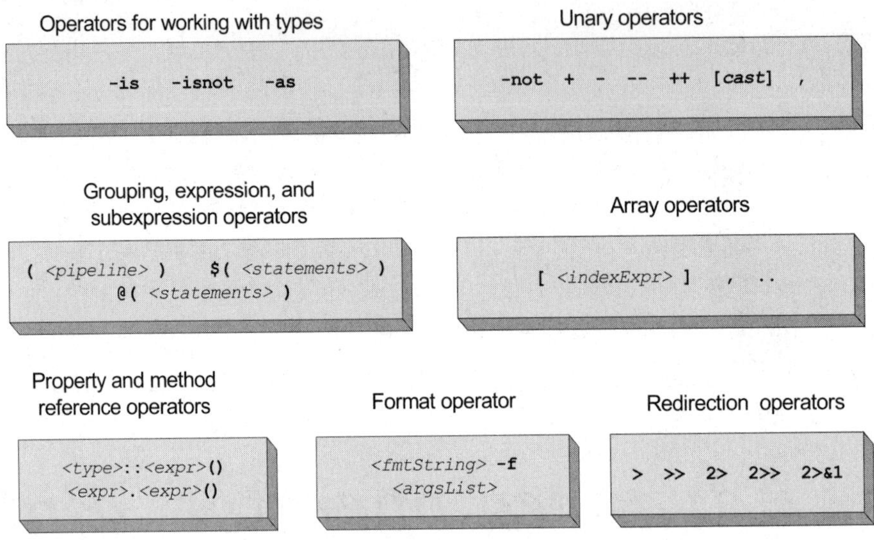

Figure 5.1 The broad groups of operators we'll cover in this chapter

5.1 OPERATORS FOR WORKING WITH TYPES

The type of an object is fundamental to determining the sorts of operations you can perform on that object. Up until now, you've allowed the type of the object to implicitly determine the operations that are performed. But sometimes you want to do this explicitly. PowerShell provides a set of operators that can work with types, as shown in figure 5.2. They're also listed in table 5.1 with examples and more description.

These operators let you test whether an object is of a particular type and enable you to convert an object to a new type. The `-is` operator returns true if the object on the left side is of the type specified on the right side. By "is," I mean that the left operator is either of the type specified on the right side or is derived from that type. (See section 1.3 in chapter 1 for an explanation of derivation.)

The `-isnot` operator returns true if the left side is not of the type specified on the right side. The right side of the operator must be represented as a type or a string that names a type. This means that you can use either a type literal such as `[int]` or the literal string "int". The `-as` operator will try to convert the left operand into the type

Operators for working with types

<value> **-is** <type>   <expr> **-isnot** <type>   <expr> **-as** <type>

Figure 5.2 The binary operators for working with types

specified by the right operand. Again, either a type literal can be used, or you can use a string naming a type.

> **NOTE** The PowerShell -is and -as operators are directly modeled on the corresponding operators in C#. But PowerShell's version of -as uses PowerShell's more aggressive approach to casting. For example, C# won't cast the string "123" into the number 123, whereas the PowerShell operator will do so. The PowerShell -as operator will also work on any type, and the C# operator is restricted to reference types.

You may be wondering why you need the -as operator when you can just use a cast. The reason is that the -as operator allows you to use a runtime expression to specify the type, whereas the cast is fixed at parse time. Here's an example showing how you can use this runtime behavior:

```
PS (1) > foreach ($t in [float],[int],[string]) {"0123.45" -as $t}
123.45
123
0123.45
```

This example loops over a list of type literals and converts the string into each of the types. This isn't possible when types are used as casts.

Finally, there's one additional difference between a regular cast and using the -as operator. In a cast, if the conversion doesn't succeed an error is generated. With the -as operator, if the cast fails, then the expression returns `$null` instead of generating an error.

```
PS (2) > [int] "abc" -eq $null
Cannot convert "abc" to "System.Int32". Error: "Input string was not
in a correct format."
At line:1 char:6
+ [int]  <<<< "abc" -eq $null
PS (3) > ("abc" -as [int]) -eq $null
True
PS (4) >
```

You can see this here. Casting "abc" to `[int]` generated an error, but the -as operator just returned `$null` instead. Table 5.1 provides several more examples of how to use the type operators PowerShell provides.

Table 5.1 PowerShell operators for working with types

Operator	Example	Results	Description
`-is`	`$true -is [bool]`	`$true`	True if the type of the left side matches the type of the object on the right side.
	`$true -is [object]`	`$true`	This is always true—everything is an object except `$null`.

Table 5.1 **PowerShell operators for working with types *(continued)***

Operator	Example	Results	Description
	`$true -is [ValueType]`	`$true`	The left side is an instance of a .NET value type such as an integer or floating-point number.
	`"hi" -is [ValueType]`	`$false`	A string is not a value type; it's a reference type so this expression returns `FALSE`.
	`"hi" -is [object]`	`$true`	A string is still an object.
	`12 -is [int]`	`$true`	12 is an integer.
	`12 -is "int"`	`$true`	The right side of the operator can be either a type literal or a string naming a type.
`-isnot`	`$true -isnot [string]`	`$true`	The object on the left side is not of the type specified on the right side.
	`$null -isnot [object]`	`$true`	The null value is the only thing that isn't an object.
`-as`	`"123" -as [int]`	`123`	Takes the left side and converts it to the type specified on the right side.
	`123 -as "string"`	`"123"`	Turns the left side into an instance of the type named by the string on the right.

In practice, most of the time the automatic type conversion mechanism will be all you need, and explicit casts will take care of the majority of the remaining cases. So why have these operators? They're mostly used in scripting. For example, if you want to have a script that behaves differently based on whether it's passed a string or a number, you'll need to use the `-is` operator to select which operation to perform. Obvious examples of this kind of functionality are the binary operators described in the previous chapter. The addition operator has different behavior depending on the type of its left argument. To write a script that did the same thing, you'd have to use `-is` to select the type of the operation to perform and `-as` to convert the right operand to the correct type.

5.2 THE UNARY OPERATORS

Now let's take a detailed look at the unary operators, which take only one argument. These operators are shown in figure 5.3 and listed with examples in table 5.2.

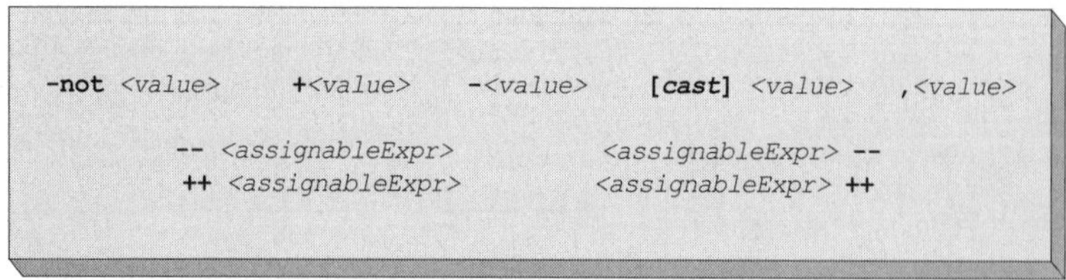

Figure 5.3 The binary various unary operators

You've seen most of these operators already in previous sections. The unary + and - operators do what you'd expect for numbers. Applying them to any other type results in an error.

The use of the type casts as unary operators was discussed at length in chapter 3, so we won't go into it again. The interesting operators in this section are the increment and decrement operators. They match the behavior of the equivalent operators in the C programming language with both the prefix and postfix forms of the operators.

These operators are special in that they take an *assignable expression* as an argument. An assignable expression is, well, anything that can be assigned to. This includes variables, array elements, and object properties. These operators retrieve the current value of the assignable expression, increment (add 1) or decrement (subtract 1) that value, and then assign it back to the assignable expression. For example, if you're using ++ with a variable, the value of the variable will be retrieved, incremented by 1, and then assigned back to the variable. As with the unary + and - operators, the increment (++) and decrement (--) operators are only defined for variables containing numbers. Applying them to a variable containing anything other than numbers results in an error.

Table 5.2 PowerShell unary operators

Operator	Example	Results	Description
-	- (2+2)	-4	Negation. Tries to convert its argument to a number, and then negates the result.
+	+ "123 "	123	Unary plus. Tries to converts its argument to a number and returns the result. This is effectively a cast to a number.
--	--$a ; $a--	Depends on the current value of the variable	Pre- and postdecrement operator. Converts the content of the variable to a number, and then tries to subtract one from that value. The prefix version returns the new value; the postfix version returns the original value.
++	++$a; $a++	Depends on the current value of the variable	Pre- and postincrement. Converts the variable to a number, and then adds 1 to the result. The prefix version returns the new value; the postfix version returns the original value.
[<type>]	[int] "0x123"	291	Type cast. Converts the argument into an instance of the type specified by the cast.
,	, (1+2)	One-element array containing the value of the expression	Unary comma operator. Creates a new one-element array of type [object[]] and stores the operand in it.

There's another thing that's special about these operators. The increment and decrement operators were almost not included in PowerShell because they introduced a problem. In languages such as C and C#, when you use one of these operators

```
$a++
```

as a statement, nothing is displayed. This is because statements in C and C# don't return values. In PowerShell, all statements return a value, which led to confusion. People would write scripts like this

```
$sum=0
$i=0
while ($i -lt 10) { $sum += $i; $i++ }
$sum
```

and be surprised to see the numbers 0 through 9 displayed. This was because `$a++` returned a value and PowerShell was displaying the results of every statement. This was so confusing that the language design team almost removed these operators from the language. Then we hit on the idea of a *voidable statement*. Basically, this means that certain types of expressions, when used as statements, aren't displayed. Voidable statements include assignment statements and the increment/decrement operators. When increment and decrement are used in an expression, they return a value, but when they're used as a stand-alone statement, they return no value. Again, this is one of those details that won't affect how you use PowerShell other than to make it work as you expect. Now, if you do want the value of the expression to be output, there's a trick you can use. If the expression is enclosed in parentheses, the result will be returned instead of discarded. This can be convenient sometimes, especially in string expansions. Let's try this. Your task is to print out a list of strings prefixed with the string number. Here's how:

```
PS {1) > $l=1
PS {2) > foreach ($s in "one","two","three")
>> { "$($l++): $s" }
>>
: one
: two
: three
```

The `foreach` statement loops over the strings and emits your output. The ++ in the subexpressions (which we'll get to next) causes the variable to be incremented. But because the expression is treated as a statement, there's no output in the string. Here's how you can fix it. You'll make one small change and add parentheses around the increment expression. Let's try it again:

```
PS {3) > $l=1
PS {4) > foreach ($s in "one","two","three")
>> { "$(($l++)): $s" }
>>
1: one
2: two
3: three
PS {5) >
```

This time it works properly—you see the numbers in the output strings.

> **NOTE** Only some statements are considered voidable. For other statement types, you'll have to explicitly discard the output of a statement.

In effect, you want to turn a regular statement into a voidable one. The way to do this through an explicit cast is to use `[void]`, as in `[void] (Write-Output "discard me")`. The statement whose value you want to discard is enclosed in parentheses, and the whole thing is cast to void. You'll see another way to accomplish the same effect using the redirection operators later in this chapter.

Having touched on subexpressions in our discussion of voidable statements, let's take a more formal look at them in the next section, where we'll cover all the grouping constructs in the language.

5.3 GROUPING AND SUBEXPRESSIONS

Grouping, expression, and subexpression operators

```
( <pipeline> )      $( <statementList> )      @( <statementList> )
```

Figure 5.4 The PowerShell operators for grouping expressions and statements

So far you've seen a variety of situations where collections of expressions or statements have been grouped together. You've even used these grouping constructs in string expansions. These operators are shown in figure 5.4.

Now let's look at them in more detail. Table 5.3 provides more details and some examples.

Table 5.3 Expression and statement grouping operators

Operator	Example	Results	Description
`( ... )`	`( 2 + 2 ) * 3` `(get-date).dayofweek`	12 Returns the current weekday	Parentheses group expression operations and may contain either a simple expression or a simple pipeline. They may not contain more than one statement or things like `while` loops.
`$( ... )`	`$($p = "a*";` `get-process $p )`	Returns the process objects for all processes starting with the letter *a*	Subexpressions group collections of statements as opposed to being limited to a single expression. If the contained statements return a single value, that value will be returned as a scalar. If the statements return more than one value, they will be accumulated in an array.

Table 5.3 Expression and statement grouping operators *(continued)*

Operator	Example	Results	Description
`@( ... )`	`@( dir c:\; dir d:\)`	Returns an array containing the `FileInfo` objects in the root of the C: and D: drives	The array subexpression operator groups collections of statements in the same manner as the regular subexpression operator, but with the additional behavior that the result will always be returned as an array.

The first grouping notation is the simple parenthetical notation. As in most languages, the conventional use for this notation is to control the order of operations, as shown by the following example:

```
PS (1) > 2+3*4
14
PS (2) > (2+3)*4
20
```

The parentheses in the second expression cause the addition operation to be performed first. In PowerShell, parentheses also have another use. Looking at the syntax specification shown in figure 5.4 for parenthetical expressions illustrates this:

(*<pipeline>*)

From the syntax, you can see that pipelines are allowed between simple parentheses. This allows you to use a command or pipeline as a value in an expression. For example, to obtain a count of the number of files in a directory, you can use the `dir` command in parentheses, then use the `Count` property to get the number of objects returned:

```
PS (1) > (dir).count
46
```

Using a pipeline in the parentheses lets you get a count of the number of files matching the wildcard pattern `*.doc`:

```
PS (2) > (dir | where {$_.name -like '*.doc'}).count
32
```

NOTE People familiar with other languages tend to assume that the expression `(1,2,3,4)` is an array literal in PowerShell. In fact, as you learned in chapter 3, this isn't the case. The comma operator, discussed in the next section, allows you to easily construct arrays in PowerShell, but there are no array literals as such in the language. All that the parentheses do is control the order of operations. Otherwise, there's nothing special about them. In fact, the precedence of the comma operator is such that you typically never need parentheses for this purpose. More on that later.

Now let's move on to the next set of grouping constructs—the subexpressions. There are two forms of the subexpression construct, as shown in the following:

```
$( <statementList> )
@( <statementList> )
```

5.3.1 Subexpressions $(...)

The syntactic difference between a subexpression (either form) and a simple parenthetical expression is that you can have any list of statements in a subexpression instead of being restricted to a single pipeline. This means that you can have any PowerShell language element in these grouping constructs, including loop statements. It also means that you can have several statements in the group. Let's look at an example. Earlier in this chapter, you saw a short piece of PowerShell code that calculates the numbers in the Fibonacci sequence below 100. At the time, you didn't count the number of elements in that sequence. You can do this easily using the subexpression grouping construct:

```
PS (1) > $($c=$p=1; while ($c -lt 100) {$c; $c,$p=($c+$p),$c}).count
10
```

By enclosing the statements in `$( ... )`, you can retrieve the result of the enclosed collection of statements as an array.

> **NOTE** Many languages have a special notation for generating collections of objects. For example, Python and functional languages such as Haskell have a feature called *list comprehensions* for doing this. PowerShell (and shell languages in general) don't need special syntax for this kind of operation. Collections occur naturally as a consequence of the shell pipeline model. If a set of statements used as a value returns multiple objects, they'll automatically be collected into an array.

Another difference between the subexpression construct and simple parentheses is how voidable statements are treated. We looked at this concept earlier with the increment and decrement operators. A voidable expression is one whose result is discarded when used directly as a statement. Here's an example that illustrates this. First initialize `$a` to 0; then use a postincrement expression in parentheses and assign it to the variable `$x`:

```
PS (1) > $a=0
PS (2) > $x=($a++)
```

Checking the value of `$x`, you see that it is 0, as expected, and that `$a` is now 1:

```
PS (3) > $x
0
PS (4) > $a
1
```

Now do a second assignment, this time with the expression in `$( ... )`:

```
PS (5) > $x=$($a++)
```

Checking the value, you see that it's actually `$null`:

```
PS (6) > $x
PS (7) > $x -eq $null
True
```

This is because the result of the postincrement operation was discarded, so the expression returned nothing. Try a more complex statement in the subexpression:

```
PS (8) > $x=$($a++;$a;$a++;$a)
PS (9) > $x
3
4
```

Notice that even though there are four statements in the subexpression, `$x` only received two values. Again, the results of the postincrement statements were discarded so they don't appear in the output.

Next, let's take a look at the difference between the array subexpression `@( ... )` and the regular subexpression.

5.3.2 Array subexpressions @(...)

The difference is that in the case of the array subexpression, the result is always returned as an array; this is a fairly small but useful difference. In effect, it's shorthand for

```
[object[]] $( ... )
```

This shorthand exists because in many cases you don't know if a pipeline operation is going to return a single element or a collection. Rather than writing complex checks, you can use this construction and be assured that the result will always be a collection. If the pipeline returns an array, no new array is created and the original value is returned as is. If the pipeline returns a scalar value, that value will be wrapped in a new one-element array. It's important to understand how this is different from the behavior of the comma operator, which *always* wraps its argument value in a new one-element array. Doing something like `@( @(1) )` doesn't give you a one-element array containing a second one-element array containing a number. These expressions

```
@(1)
@(@(1))
@(@(@(1)))
```

all return the same value. On the other hand,

```
,1
```

nests to one level,

```
,,1
```

nests to two levels, and so forth.

> **NOTE** How to figure out what the pipeline returns is the single hardest thing to explain in the PowerShell language. The problem is that

> people get confused; they see that `@(12)` returns a one-element array containing the number 12. Because of prior experience with other languages, they expect that `@(@(12))` should therefore produce a nested array, an array of one element containing an array of one element, which is the integer 12. As mentioned previously, this is *not* the case. `@(@(12))` returns exactly the same thing as `@(12)`. If you think of rewriting this expression as `[object[]]$([object[]] $( 12 ))`, then it's clear why this is the case—casting an array into an array of the same type has no effect; it's already the correct type, so you just get the original array.

Here's an example of where this feature is useful: a pipeline expression that sorts some strings, then returns the first element in the sorted collection. Start by sorting an array of three elements:

```
PS (1) > $("bbb","aaa","ccc" | sort )[0]
aaa
```

This returns "aaa," as you expect. Now do it with two elements:

```
PS (2) > $("bbb","aaa" | sort )[0]
aaa
```

Still "aaa," so everything makes sense. Now try it with one element:

```
PS (3) > $("aaa" | sort )[0]
a
```

Wait a minute—*what happened here*? Well, what happened is that you sorted one element, and in a pipeline, you can't tell if the commands in the pipeline mean to return a single object (a scalar) or an array containing a single object. The default behavior in PowerShell is to assume that if you return one element, you intended to return a scalar. In this case, the scalar is the string "aaa" and index 0 of this array is the letter *a*, which is what the example returns. This is where you use the array subexpression notation because it ensures that you always get what you want. you know you want the pipeline to return an array, and by using this notation, you can enforce the correct behavior. Here are the same three examples again, but this time using the array subexpression:

```
PS (4) > @("bbb","aaa","ccc" | sort )[0]
aaa
PS (5) > @("bbb","aaa" | sort )[0]
aaa
PS (6) > @("aaa" | sort )[0]
aaa
PS (7) >
```

This time, all three commands return "aaa" as intended. So why have this notation? Why not just use the casts? Well, here's what it looks like using the cast notation:

```
PS (7) > ( [object[]] ("aaa" | sort ))[0]
aaa
```

Because of the way precedence works, you need an extra set of parentheses to get the ordering right, which makes the whole expression harder to write. In the end, the array subexpression notation is easy to use, although it's a bit difficult to grasp at first. The advantage is that you only have to learn something once, but you have to use it over and over again.

Now let's move on to the other operations PowerShell provides for dealing with collections and arrays of objects. The ability to manipulate collections of objects effectively is the heart of any automation system. You can easily perform a single operation manually, but the problem is performing operations on a large set of objects. Let's see what PowerShell has to offer here.

5.4 ARRAY OPERATORS

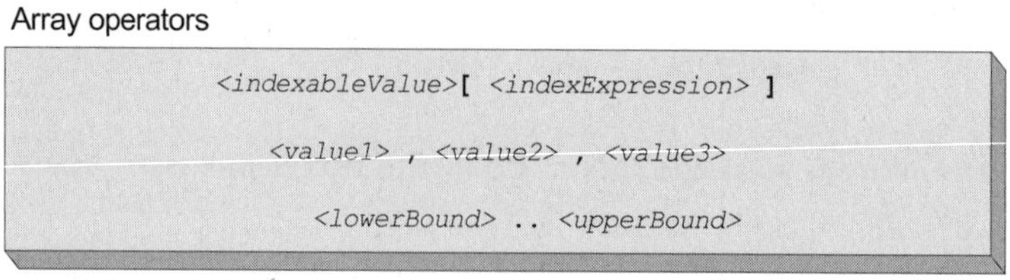

Array operators

```
<indexableValue>[ <indexExpression> ]

<value1> , <value2> , <value3>

<lowerBound> .. <upperBound>
```

Figure 5.5 The PowerShell array operators

Arrays or collections of objects occur naturally in many of the operations that you execute. An operation such as getting a directory listing in the file system results in a collection of objects. Getting the set of processes running on a machine or a list of services configured on a server both result in collections of objects. Not surprisingly, PowerShell has a set of operators and operations for working with arrays and collections. These operators are shown in figure 5.5.

We'll go over these operators in the following sections.

5.4.1 The comma operator

You've already seen many examples using the comma operator to build arrays. We covered this topic in some detail in chapter 3, but there are a couple of things we still need to cover. In terms of precedence, the comma operator has the highest precedence of any operator except for casts and property or array references. This means that when you're building an array with expressions, you need to wrap those expressions in parentheses. In the next example, you'll build an array containing the values 1, 2, and 3. You'll use addition to calculate the final value. Because the comma operator binds more strongly than the plus operator, you won't get what you want:

```
PS (1) > 1,2,1+2
1
2
1
2
```

The result is an array of the four elements 1,2,1,2 instead of 1,2,3. This is because the expression was parsed as (1,2,1)+2, building an array of three elements and then appending a fourth. You have to use parentheses to get the desired effect:

```
PS (2) > 1,2,(1+2)
1
2
3
```

Now you get the result you want.

> **NOTE** The comma operator has higher precedence than any other operator except type casts and property and array references. This is worth mentioning again because it's important to keep in mind when writing expressions. If you don't remember this, you'll produce some strange results.

The next thing we'll look at is nested arrays. Because a PowerShell array can hold any type of object, obviously it can also hold another array. You've already seen that using the array subexpression operation was *not* the way to build a nested array. Now let's talk about how you do it using assignments and the comma operator. Your task will be to build the tree structure shown in figure 5.6.

This data structure starts with an array of two elements. These two elements are also both arrays of two elements, and they, in turn, contain arrays of two numbers. Let's see how to go about constructing something like this.

There are a couple of ways you can approach this. First, you can build nested arrays one piece at a time using assignments. Alternatively, you can just nest the comma operator within parentheses. Starting with last things first, here's how to build a nested array structure using commas and parentheses. The result is concise:

```
PS (1) > $a = (((1,2),(3,4)),((5,6),(7,8)))
```

> **NOTE** LISP users should feel fairly comfortable with this expression if they ignore the commas. Everybody else is probably shuddering.

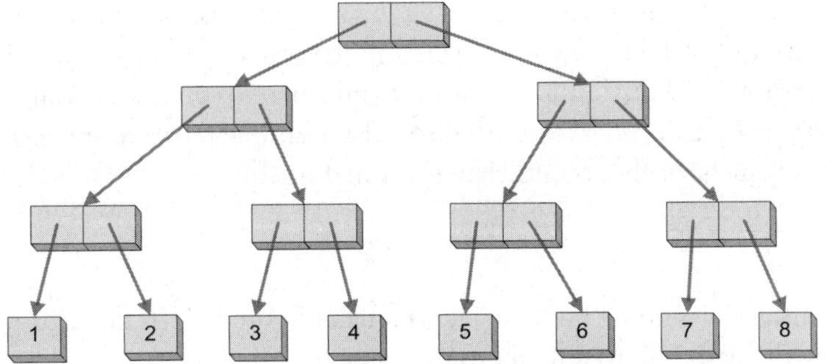

Figure 5.6 A binary tree (arrays of arrays of arrays)

And here's the same construction using intermediate variables and assignments. It's rather less concise but hopefully easier to understand.

```
$t1 = 1,2
$t2 = 3,4
$t3 = 5,6
$t4 = 7,8
$t1_1 = $t1,$t2
$t1_2 = $t3,$t4
$a = $t1_1, $t2_2
```

In either case, what you've done is build a data structure that looks like the tree shown in figure 5.6.

> **NOTE** For Perl and PHP users: in those languages, you have to do something special to get reference semantics with arrays. In PowerShell, arrays are always reference types, so no special notation is needed.

Let's verify the shape of this data structure. First, use the `length` property to verify that `$a` does hold an array of two elements:

```
PS (2) > $a.Length
2
```

Next, check the length of the array stored in the first element of that array:

```
PS (3) > $a[0].Length
2
```

It's also two elements long, as is the array stored in the second element:

```
PS (4) > $a[1].Length
2
```

Now let's look two levels down. This is done by indexing the result of an index as shown:

```
PS (5) > $a[1][0].Length
2
```

Note that `$a[0][0]` isn't the same as `$a[0,0]`, which is either a subset of the elements in the array called a *slice* if `$a` is one-dimensional, or a *single index* if the array is two-dimensional (see section 5.4.3 for more information on slices). You can compose index operations as deeply as you need to. This example retrieves the second element of the first element of the second element stored in `$a`:

```
PS (6) > $a[1][0][1]
6
```

To see exactly what's going on here, take a look at figure 5.7. In this figure, the dotted lines show the path followed to get to the value 6.

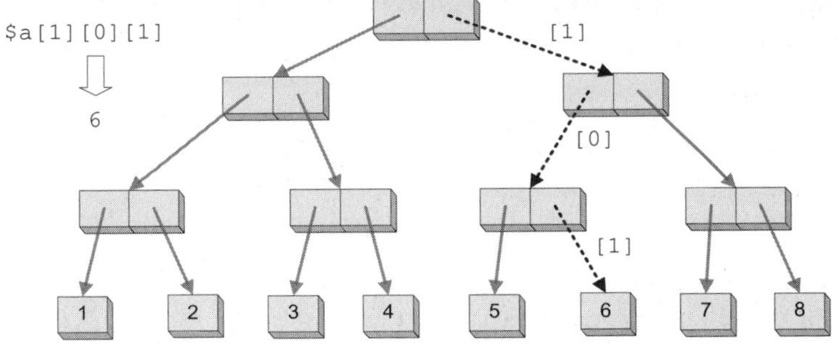

Figure 5.7 Indexing through a binary tree with the expression `$a[1][0][1]`

Here's another example. Index with `$a[0][0][0]`, which follows the leftmost edge of the tree, thus producing `1` (as shown in figure 5.8).

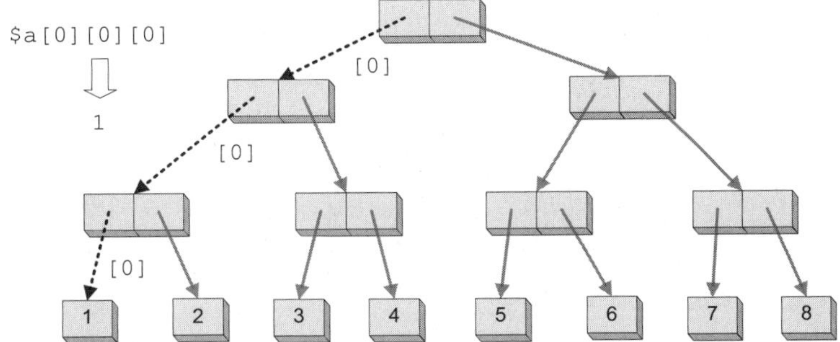

Figure 5.8 Indexing the leftmost edge of the same tree with `$a[0][0][0]`

These examples show how you can construct arbitrarily complex data structures in PowerShell. Although this isn't something you'll need to use frequently, the capability is there if you need it. In section 5.4.3, when we discuss array slices, you'll see an example using nested arrays to index multidimensional arrays.

5.4.2 The range operator

The next operator we'll discuss is the range operator (`..`). This operator is effectively a shortcut for generating a sequential array of numbers. For example, the expression

```
1..5
```

is equivalent to

```
1,2,3,4,5
```

although it's somewhat more efficient than using the commas. The syntax for the range operator is

```
<valueExpression> .. <valueExpression>
```

It has higher precedence than all the binary operators except for the comma operator. This means that expressions like

```
PS (1) > 1..3+4..6
1
2
3
4
5
6
```

work, but the following gives you a syntax error:

```
PS (2) > 1+3..4+6
Cannot convert "System.Object[]" to "System.Int32".
At line:1 char:3
+ 1+3 <<<< ..4+6
```

It's an error because the expression is being parsed like

```
1 + (3..4) + 6
```

This is because the range operator has higher precedence than the addition operator.

In a range operator expression, the left and right operands represent bounds, but either the left or the right can be the upper bound. If the left operand is greater than the right operand, a descending sequence is generated:

```
PS (3) > 5..1
5
4
3
2
1
```

The boundaries can also be negative:

```
PS (4) > -5..-1
-5
-4
-3
-2
-1
```

Finally, the upper and lower bounds must resolve to integers after applying the usual type conversions. A string that looks like a number will automatically be converted into a number and a floating-point value will automatically be converted to an integer using the banker's rounding algorithm described in chapter 4:

```
PS (5) > "1.1" .. 2.6
1
2
3
```

The range operator is most commonly used with the `foreach` loop because it allows you to easily loop a specific number of times or over a specific range of numbers. This is done so often that the PowerShell engine treats it in a special way. A range like

`1..10mb` doesn't generate a 10 MB array—it just treats the range endpoints as the lower and upper bounds of the loop, making it very efficient. (The `foreach` loop is described in detail in the next chapter.)

> **NOTE** In version 1 of PowerShell, the range operator was limited to an upper bound of 40 KB to avoid accidentally creating arrays that were too large. In practice this was never a problem, so this limit was removed in version 2 with one exception. In restricted language mode, this limit is still enforced. Restricted language mode is covered in appendix D on the book's website.

The other place where the range operator gets used frequently is with array slices, which you'll learn about next.

5.4.3 Array indexing and slicing

Most people don't think of indexing into an array as involving operators or that `[ ]` is an operator, but in fact, that's exactly what it is. It has a left operand and a right operand (the "right" operand is inside the square brackets). The syntax for an array indexing expression is

```
<valueExpression> [ <valueExpression> ]
```

There are a couple of things to note here. First, this is one of the few areas where you can't directly use a pipeline. That's because square brackets don't (and can't) delimit a pipeline. Square brackets are used in pipeline arguments as wildcard patterns, as shown in the following command:

```
dir [abc]*.txt | sort length
```

This pipeline returns all the text files in the current directory that start with a, b, or c, sorted by length. Now, if the square bracket ended the pipeline, you'd have to type this instead:

```
dir "[abc]*.txt" | sort length
```

So, if you do want to use a pipeline as an index expression, you have to use parentheses or the subexpression notation.

The second thing to note is that spaces aren't allowed between the last character of the expression being indexed and the opening square bracket. This is necessary to distinguish array expressions on the command line from wildcard patterns. Here's an example to illustrate why this is a problem. First assign an array of three elements to `$a`:

```
PS (14) > $a=1,2,3
```

Now write out the entire array along with the string "[0]" (remember, on the command line, strings don't need to be quoted):

```
PS (15) > write-host $a [0]
1 2 3 [0]
```

Next, just write out the first element of the array:

```
PS (16) > write-host $a[0]
1
```

You can see that the only difference between the first and second command lines is the presence of a space between the array variable and the opening square bracket. This is why spaces aren't permitted in array indexing operations. The square bracket is used for wildcard expressions, and we don't want those confused with array indexing on the command line.

From the syntax (and from previous examples), you can see that array indexing works on more than just variables; it can be applied to any expression that returns a value. Because the precedence of the square brackets is high (meaning that they get evaluated before most other operators), you usually have to put the expression in parentheses. If you don't, you'll get an error, as in the following example:

```
PS (1) > 1,2,3[0]
Unable to index into an object of type System.Int32.
At line:1 char:7
+ 1,2,3[0 <<<< ]
```

The error occurred because, due to precedence rules, you were in effect trying to index into the scalar quantity "3", which is not *indexable*. If you put the left value expression in parentheses, it works as desired:

```
PS (2) > (1,2,3)[0]
1
PS (3) >
```

In this example, you retrieved the first element in the collection, which is at index 0. (Like all .NET-based languages, indexes start at 0 in PowerShell.) PowerShell also supports negative indexes, which index from the end of the array. Let's try it out:

```
PS (3) > (1,2,3)[-1]
3
PS (4) > (1,2,3)[-2]
2
PS (5) > (1,2,3)[-3]
1
```

Specifying -1 retrieves the last element in the array, -2 retrieves the second-to-last element, and so on. In fact, negative indexes are exactly equivalent to taking the length of the array and subtracting the index from the array:

```
PS (7) > $a[$a.Length - 1]
3
PS (8) > $a[$a.Length - 2]
2
PS (9) > $a[$a.Length - 3]
1
```

In the example, `$a.Length - 1` retrieves the last element of the array just like -1 did. In effect, negative indexing is just a shorthand for `$array.Length - $index`.

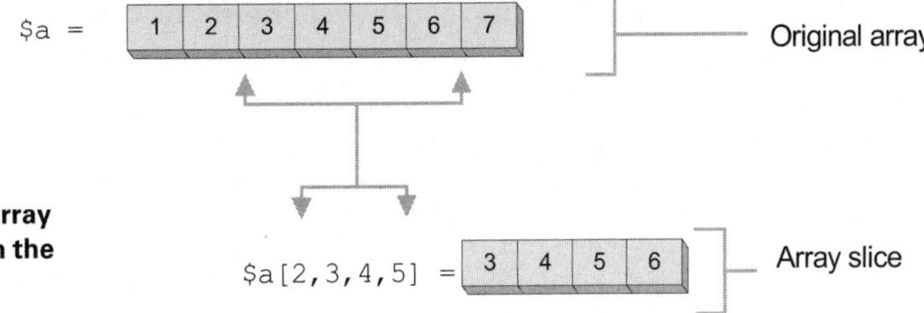

Figure 5.9 How an array slice is generated from the original array

Array slices

You've seen how to get individual elements out of an array. You can get sequences of elements out of arrays as well. Extracting these sequences is called *array slicing* and the results are *array slices*, as illustrated in figure 5.9.

Slicing is done by specifying an array of indexes instead of just a single index. The corresponding element for each index is extracted from the original array and returned as a new array that's a slice of the original. From the command line, this operation looks like this:

```
PS (1) > $a = 1,2,3,4,5,6,7
PS (2) > $a[2,3,4,5]
3
4
5
6
PS (3) >
```

This example used the array `2,3,4,5` to get the corresponding elements out of the array in `$a`. Here's a variation on this example:

```
PS (3) > $indexes = 2,3,4,5
PS (4) > $a[$indexes]
3
4
5
6
```

This time, the code stored the list of indexes in a variable, and then used the variable to perform the indexing. The effect was the same. Now let's process the values that are stored in the `$indexes` variable. You'll use the `Foreach-Object` cmdlet to process each element of the array and assign the results back to the array:

```
PS (5) > $indexes = 2,3,4,5 | foreach {$_-1}
```

You want to adjust for the fact that arrays start at index 0, so subtract 1 from each index element. Now when you do the indexing

```
:
PS (6) > $a[$indexes]
2
3
4
5
```

you get the elements that correspond to the original index value—2 returns 2, and so on. But do you need to use the intermediate variable? Let's try it:

```
PS (7) > $a[2,3,4,5 | foreach {$_-1}]
Missing ']' after array index expression.
At line:1 char:12
+ $a[2,3,4,5 | <<<<  foreach {$_-1}]
```

So you get a parsing error. This doesn't mean that you can't do it. It just means that you have to wrap the expression in brackets so it will be treated as a single value:

```
PS (8) > $a[(2,3,4,5 | foreach {$_-1})]
2
3
4
5
PS (9) >
```

This time there was no error, and you get the values you expected.

5.4.4 Using the range operator with arrays

There's one other tool in the indexing toolkit: the range operator discussed in the previous section. This operator is a convenient way to get slices of arrays. Say you have an array of 10 elements, 0 through 9. To get the first four elements of an array, you can use the range operator as follows:

```
PS (2) > $a[0..3]
0
1
2
3
```

By taking advantage of the way negative indexing works, you can get the last four elements of the array by doing this:

```
PS (3) > $a[-4..-1]
6
7
8
9
```

You can even use ranges to reverse an array. To do this, you need to know the length of the array, which you can get through the `length` property. You can see this in the following example, which casts the result of the expression to a string so it will be displayed on one line:

```
PS (6) > [string] $a[ ($a.Length-1) .. 0]
9 8 7 6 5 4 3 2 1 0
```

> **NOTE** This isn't an efficient way of reversing the array. Using the `Reverse` static member on the `[array]` class is more efficient. See section 5.4.4 for more information on how to use .NET methods in PowerShell.

In PowerShell, slicing works for retrieving elements of an array, but you can't use it for assignments. You get an error if you try. For example, try to replace the slice [2,3,4] with a single value 12:

```
PS (1) > $a = 1,2,3,4,5,6,7,8
PS (2) > $a[2,3,4] = 12
Array assignment to [2,3,4] failed because assignment to slices is
not supported.
At line:1 char:4
+ $a[2 <<<< ,3,4] = 12
```

As you can see, you get an error telling you that assignment to slices isn't supported. Here's what you have to do to get the desired transformation:

```
PS (3) > $a = $a[0,1] + 12 + $a[5 .. 7]
PS (4) > $a
1
2
12
6
7
8
```

Basically, you have to take the array slices before and after the desired values and then concatenate all three pieces together to produce a new array.

5.4.5 Working with multidimensional arrays

So far we've covered one-dimensional arrays as well as arrays of arrays (which are also called *jagged arrays*). The reason for the term "jagged" is shown in figure 5.10.

In figure 5.10, $a is an array of arrays as you've seen before, but each of the member arrays is a different length. So instead of having a regular structure, you have a jagged one because the counts are uneven.

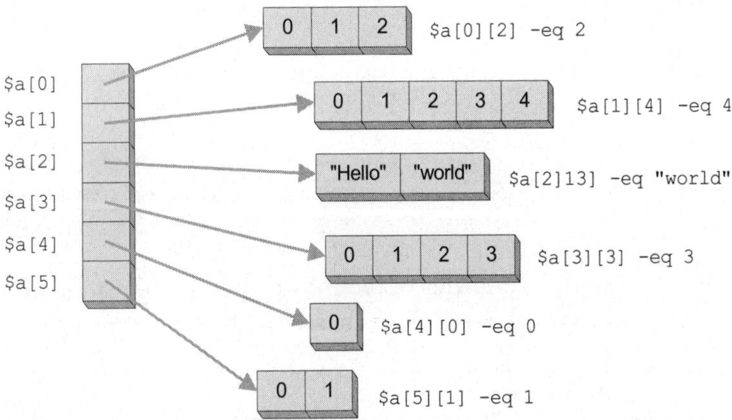

Figure 5.10 An example of a jagged array in the variable $a. Each member of $a is also an array but they are all of different lengths—hence the term "jagged."

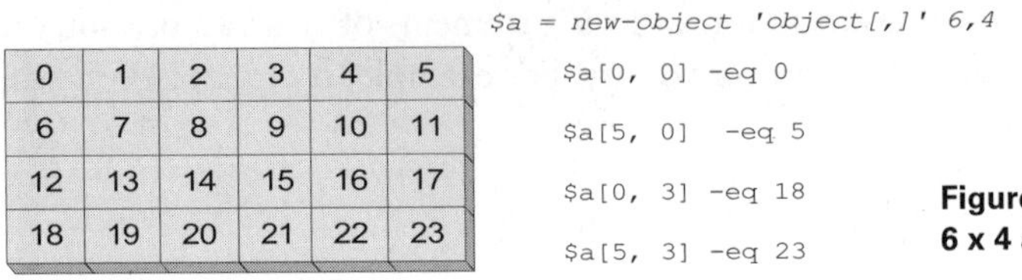

0	1	2	3	4	5
6	7	8	9	10	11
12	13	14	15	16	17
18	19	20	21	22	23

```
$a = new-object 'object[,]' 6,4
$a[0, 0] -eq 0
$a[5, 0]  -eq 5
$a[0, 3] -eq 18
$a[5, 3] -eq 23
```

Figure 5.11 A two-dimensional 6 x 4 array of numbers

Now that you understand what a jagged array is, we'll move on to multidimensional arrays. PowerShell needs to support multidimensional arrays because .NET allows for arrays to be multidimensional and PowerShell is built on top of .NET. Figure 5.11 shows a two-dimensional array.

As shown in figure 5.11, PowerShell indexes into multidimensional arrays by looking at the type of the array and mapping the set of indexes onto the number of dimensions or *rank* the array has. If you specify two indexes and the array is one-dimensional, you'll get two elements back. If the array is two-dimensional, you'll get one element back. Let's try this.

First, construct a multidimensional array using the `New-Object` cmdlet:

```
PS (1) > $2d = new-object 'object[,]' 2,2
```

This statement created a 2 x 2 array of objects. Look at the dimensions of the array by retrieving the `Rank` property from the object:

```
PS (2) > $2d.Rank
2
```

Now set the value in the array to particular values. Do this by indexing into the array:

```
PS (3) > $2d[0,0] = "a"
PS (4) > $2d[1,0] = 'b'
PS (5) > $2d[0,1] = 'c'
PS (6) > $2d[1,1] = 'd'
PS (7) > $2d[1,1]
d
```

This appears to imply that slices don't work in multidimensional arrays, but in fact they do when you use nested arrays of indexes and wrap the expression by using the comma operator in parentheses:

```
PS (8) > $2d[ (0,0) , (1,0) ]
a
b
```

This example retrieved the elements of the array at indexes (0,0) and (1,0). And, as in the case of one-dimensional arrays, you can use variables for indexing:

```
PS (9) > $one=0,0 ; $two=1,0
PS (10) > $2d [ $one, $two ]
Unexpected token ' $one, $two ' in expression or statement.
At line:1 char:18
+ $2d [ $one, $two ] <<<<
```

```
PS (11) > $2d[ $one, $two ]
a
b
```

And you can even use a variable containing a pair of index arrays:

```
PS (12) > $pair = $one,$two
PS (13) > $2d[ $pair ]
a
b
```

This covers pretty much everything we need to say about arrays. Now let's move on to properties and methods. As you'll remember from chapter 1, properties and methods are the attributes of an object that let you inspect and manipulate that object. Because PowerShell is an object-based shell, a good understanding of how properties and methods work is necessary if you want to master PowerShell. We're going to be spending a fair bit of time on these features, so let's get started.

5.5 PROPERTY AND METHOD OPERATORS

Property and method reference operators

```
<typeValue>::<memberNameExpr>        <typeValue>::<memberNameExpr>(<arguments>)

<value>.<memberNameExpr>             <value>.<memberNameExpr>(<arguments>)
```

Figure 5.12 The property and method operators in PowerShell

As you've seen in many examples so far, the property dereference operator in PowerShell is the dot (`.`). As was the case with array indexing, this is properly considered an operator in PowerShell with left and right operand expressions. This operator, along with the static member operator `::`, is shown in figure 5.12.

We'll get to what that means in a second.

> **NOTE** When we say *property* here, we're talking about any kind of data member on an object, regardless of the underlying Common Language Runtime representation (or implementation) of the member. If you don't know what this means, good—because it doesn't matter. But some people do like to know all the details of what's going on.

First let's look back at the basics. Everything in PowerShell is an object (even scripts and functions, as you'll see later on). As discussed in chapter 1, objects have properties (data) and methods (code). To get at both, you use the dot operator. To get the length of a string, you use the `length` property:

```
PS (1) > "Hello world!".Length
12
```

In a similar fashion, you can get the length of an array:

```
PS (3) > (1,2,3,4,5).Length
5
```

As was the case with the left square bracket in array indexing, spaces aren't permitted between the left operand and the dot:

```
PS (4) > (1,2,3,4,5) .count
Unexpected token '.count' in expression or statement.
At line:1 char:18
+ (1,2,3,4,5) .count <<<<
```

This is necessary to make sure that arguments to cmdlets aren't mistaken for property reference operations:

```
PS (5) > write-output (1,2,3,4,5) .count
1
2
3
4
5
.count
```

5.5.1 The dot operator

So much for the basics—now let's get back to this statement about the dot being an operator. What's special about it? Well, just as the left operand can be an expression, so can the right operand. The right operand is evaluated, which results in a value. That value is then used as the name of the property on the left operand to retrieve. This series of steps is illustrated in figure 5.13.

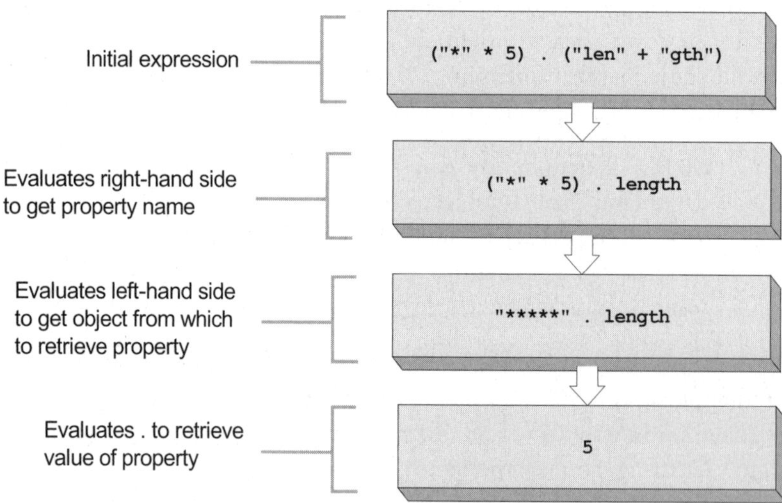

Figure 5.13 The steps performed to retrieve a calculated property from an object

Let's look at an example of how this process can be used with variables. First define a variable to hold the name of the property you want to retrieve:

```
PS (6) > $prop = "length"
```

Now, use that variable in an expression to retrieve the property:

```
PS (7) > "Hello world".$prop
11
```

This mechanism gives you that magic "one more level of indirection" computer science people are so fond of. Let's expand on this. To get a list of all the properties on an object, use the `Get-Member` (or `gm`) cmdlet on an object. This example uses `dir` to get a `FileInfo` object to work with:

```
PS (1) > @(dir c:\windows\*.dll)[0] | gm -type property

   TypeName: System.IO.FileInfo

Name              MemberType Definition
----              ---------- ----------
Attributes        Property   System.IO.FileAttributes Attributes ...
CreationTime      Property   System.DateTime CreationTime {get;s ...
CreationTimeUtc   Property   System.DateTime CreationTimeUtc {ge ...
Directory         Property   System.IO.DirectoryInfo Directory   ...
DirectoryName     Property   System.String DirectoryName {get;}
Exists            Property   System.Boolean Exists {get;}
Extension         Property   System.String Extension {get;}
FullName          Property   System.String FullName {get;}
IsReadOnly        Property   System.Boolean IsReadOnly {get;set;}
LastAccessTime    Property   System.DateTime LastAccessTime {get;s ...
LastAccessTimeUtc Property   System.DateTime LastAccessTimeUtc {ge ...
LastWriteTime     Property   System.DateTime LastWriteTime {get;se ...
LastWriteTimeUtc  Property   System.DateTime LastWriteTimeUtc {get ...
Length            Property   System.Int64 Length {get;}
Name              Property   System.String Name {get;}
```

This gives you a list of all the properties. Of course, you only need the name, so you can use the `Name` property on these objects:

```
PS (2) > @(dir c:\windows\*.dll)[0] | gm -type property |
>>> foreach {$_.name}
Attributes
CreationTime
CreationTimeUtc
Directory
DirectoryName
Exists
Extension
FullName
IsReadOnly
LastAccessTime
LastAccessTimeUtc
LastWriteTime
```

```
LastWriteTimeUtc
Length
Name
```

Next you'll use this list of names to get the corresponding values from the original object. First get the object into a variable:

```
PS (1) > $obj = @(dir c:\windows\*.dll)[0]
```

And get the list of names; for brevity's sake, just get the properties that start with the letter *l*:

```
PS (2) > $names = $obj | gm -type property l* | foreach {$_.name}
```

Finally, use the list of names to print out the value:

```
PS (3) > $names | foreach { "$_ = $($obj.$_)" }
LastAccessTime = 3/25/2006 2:18:50 AM
LastAccessTimeUtc = 3/25/2006 10:18:50 AM
LastWriteTime = 8/10/2004 12:00:00 PM
LastWriteTimeUtc = 8/10/2004 7:00:00 PM
Length = 94784
PS (4) >
```

Next let's look at using methods. The method call syntax is

```
<valueExpression> . <methodName> ( <argument> , <argument> , ... )
```

As always, spaces aren't allowed before or after the dot or before the opening parenthesis for the reasons discussed earlier. Here's a basic example:

```
PS (1) > "Hello world!".substring(0,5)
Hello
```

This example uses the `Substring` method to extract the first five characters from the left operand string. As you can see, the syntax for method invocations in PowerShell matches what you see in pretty much every other language that has methods. Contrast this with how commands are called. In method calls, arguments in the argument list are separated by commas and the whole list is enclosed in parentheses. With commands, the arguments are separated with spaces and the command ends at the end of line or at a command terminator, such as the semicolon or the pipe symbol.

This is another area where the language design team experimented with alternate syntaxes. One of the experiments we conducted resulted in a command-like method invocation syntax that looked something like

```
"Hello world!".(substring 0 5)
```

The team chose not to use this syntax for two reasons (which, by the way, means that you'll get an error if you try using it). First, it collided with the ability to perform indirect property name retrievals. The second (and more important) reason was that people also found it uncomfortably strange. Empirically, a programmer-style syntax for programmer-style activities like method invocations and a shell-style syntax for shell-style activities like command invocation seems to work best. This approach is not without some small issues. First, if you want to pass an expression to a method, you have to wrap that array in parentheses so the array comma operator isn't confused with the argument separator commas. Second, if you want to use the output of a command as an argument, you have to wrap the command in parentheses. Here's an example:

```
PS (1) > [string]::join('+',(1,2,3))
1+2+3
```

This example uses the `[string]::Join` method to create a string out of the array `1,2,3` with a plus sign between each one. Now let's do the same thing with the output of a command. Here's a command that returns the handle count for the `rundll` processes:

```
PS (1) > get-process rundll* | foreach{$_.handles}
58
109
```

Now join that output into a string, again separated with the plus sign (with spaces on either side this time):

```
PS (2) > [string]::join(" + ", (get-process rundll* |
>>> foreach{$_.handles}))
58 + 109
```

The observant reader will have noticed the use of the double-colon operator (::) in these examples. We briefly discussed this operator in chapter 3 as part of our discussion of types in PowerShell. In the next section, we'll look at it in more detail.

5.5.2 Static methods and the double-colon operator

The `::` operator is the static member accessor. Whereas the dot operator retrieved instance members, the double-colon operator accesses static members on a class, as is the case with the `join` method in the example at the end of the last section. The left operand to the static member accessor is required to be a type—either a type literal or an expression returning a type as you see here:

```
PS (1) > $t = [string]
PS (2) > $t::join('+',(1,2,3))
1+2+3
PS (3) >
```

The language design team chose to use a separate operator for accessing static methods because of the way static methods are accessed. Here's the problem. If you had a type `MyModule` with a static property called `Module`, then the expression

```
[MyModule].Module
```

is ambiguous. This is because there's also an instance member `Module` on the `System.Type` instance representing the type `MyModule`. Now you can't tell if the "Module" instance member on `System.Type` or the "Module" static member on `MyModule` should be retrieved. By using the double-colon operator, you remove this ambiguity.

> **NOTE** Other languages get around this ambiguity by using the `typeof()` operator. Using `typeof()` in this example, `typeof(MyModule).Module` retrieves the instance property on the `Type` object and `MyModule.Module` retrieves the static property implemented by the `MyModule` class.

5.5.3 Indirect method invocation

Earlier we talked about how you could do indirect property references by using a variable on the right side of the dot operator. You can do the same thing with methods, but it's a bit more complicated. The obvious approach

```
$x.$y(2)
```

doesn't work. What happens is that `$x.$y` returns an object that describes the method you want to invoke:

```
PS (1) > "abc".substring

MemberType           : Method
OverloadDefinitions  : {string Substring(int startIndex), st
                       ring Substring(int startIndex, int le
                       ngth)}
TypeNameOfValue      : System.Management.Automation.PSMethod
Value                : string Substring(int startIndex), str
                       ing Substring(int startIndex, int len
                       gth)
Name                 : Substring
IsInstance           : True
```

This turns out to be a handy way to get information about a method. Let's pick out the *overloads* for `Substring`—that is, the different forms of this method that you can use:

```
PS (2) > "abc".substring | foreach {
>> $_.OverloadDefinitions -split '\),' }
>>
string Substring(int startIndex)
string Substring(int startIndex, int length)
PS (3) >
```

Now you have this information object—what else can you do with it? The thing you most probably want to do is to invoke it. The way to do this is to use the `Invoke` method on the method information object:

```
PS (3) > "abc".substring.Invoke(1)
bc
```

In version 2 of PowerShell, this also works for static methods. First assign the name of the operation to invoke to a variable:

```
PS (4) > $method = "sin"
```

Look at the information about that method:

```
PS (5) > [math]::$method

MemberType          : Method
OverloadDefinitions : {static double Sin(double a)}
TypeNameOfValue     : System.Management.Automation.PSMethod
Value               : static double Sin(double a)
Name                : Sin
IsInstance          : True
```

And, finally, invoke it:

```
PS (6) > [math]::$method.invoke(3.14)
0.00159265291648683
```

Although it's an advanced technique, the ability to invoke properties and methods indirectly turns out to be powerful because it means that the behavior of your script can be configured at runtime. You'll learn how this can be used when we talk about scriptblocks in chapter 8.

This finishes our discussion of properties and methods. You may have noticed that in some of the examples so far, you've had to do some fairly complicated things to display the results in the way you want. Clearly, on occasion you'll need a better way to present output, and that's the purpose of the format operator, covered in the next section.

5.6 THE FORMAT OPERATOR

Most of the time, PowerShell's built-in formatting and output system will take care of presenting your results, but sometimes you need more explicit control over the formatting of your output. You may also want to format text strings in a specific way, like displaying numbers in hexadecimal format. PowerShell allows you to do these things with the format operator, shown in figure 5.14.

Format operator

```
<formatSpecificationString> -f <argumentList>
```

Figure 5.14 The format operator lets you control the formatting of your output.

The format operator (`-f`) is a binary operator that takes a format string as its left operand and an array of values to format as its right operand. Here's an example:

```
PS (1) > '{2} {1} {0}' -f 1,2,3
3 2 1
```

In the format string, the values enclosed in braces correspond to the index of the element in the right operand array. The element is converted into a string and then displayed. Along with reordering, when the elements are displayed, you can control how they're laid out.

NOTE For people familiar with the Python language, the PowerShell format operator is modeled on the Python `%` operator. But because PowerShell doesn't use the `%` character as part of its formatting directives, it didn't make mnemonic sense for the format operator in PowerShell to be `%`. Instead, the language design team chose `-f`.

Here are some more examples:

```
PS (3) > '|{0,10}| 0x{1:x}|{2,-10}|' -f 10,20,30
|        10| 0x14|30        |
```

Here, the first format specifier element (`,10`) tells the system to pad the text out to 10 characters. The next element is printed with the specifier `:x`, telling the system to display the number as a hexadecimal value. The final display specification has a field width specifier, but this time it's a negative value, indicating that the field should be padded to the right instead of to the left.

The `-f` operator is shorthand for calling the .NET `Format` method on the `System.String` class. The previous example can be rewritten as

```
PS (4) > [string]::Format('|{0,10}| 0x{1:x}|{2,-10}|',10,20,30)
|        10| 0x14|30        |
```

and you'll get exactly the same results. The key benefit of the `-f` operator is that it's a lot shorter to type. This is useful when you're typing on the command line. The underlying `Format()` method has a rich set of specifiers. The basic syntax of these specifiers is

```
{<index>[,<alignment>][:<formatString>]}
```

Some examples of using format specifiers are shown in table 5.4.

Table 5.4 Examples of using format specifiers

<table>
<tr><th>Format specifier</th><th>Description</th><th>Example</th><th>Output</th></tr>
<tr><td><code>{0}</code></td><td>Displays a particular element</td><td><code>"{0} {1}" -f "a","b"</code></td><td><code>a b</code></td></tr>
<tr><td><code>{0:x}</code></td><td>Displays a number in hexadecimal</td><td><code>"0x{0:x}" -f 181342</code></td><td><code>0x2c45e</code></td></tr>
<tr><td><code>{0:X}</code></td><td>Displays a number in hexadecimal with the letters in uppercase</td><td><code>"0x{0:X}" -f 181342</code></td><td><code>0x2C45E</code></td></tr>
<tr><td><code>{0:dn}</code></td><td>Displays a decimal number left-justified, padded with zeros</td><td><code>"{0:d8}" -f 3</code></td><td><code>00000003</code></td></tr>
<tr><td><code>{0:p}</code></td><td>Displays a number as a percentage</td><td><code>"{0:p}" -f .123</code></td><td><code>12.30 %</code></td></tr>
<tr><td><code>{0:C}</code></td><td>Display a number as currency</td><td><code>"{0:c}" -f 12.34</code></td><td><code>$12.34</code></td></tr>
<tr><td><code>{0,n}</code></td><td>Displays with field width <code>n</code>, left-aligned</td><td><code>"|{0,5}|" -f "hi"</code></td><td><code>| hi|</code></td></tr>
<tr><td><code>{0,-n)</code></td><td>Displays with field width <code>n</code>, right-aligned</td><td><code>"|{0,-5}|" -f "hi"</code></td><td><code>|hi |</code></td></tr>
</table>

Table 5.4 **Examples of using format specifiers *(continued)***

Format specifier	Description	Example	Output
{0:hh} {0:mm}	Displays the hours and minutes from a DateTime value	"{0:hh}:{0:mm}" -f (get-date)	01:34
{0:C}	Displays using the currency symbol for the current culture	"|{0,10:C}|" -f 12.4	| $12.40|

There are many more things you can do with formatting. Refer to the Microsoft MSDN documentation for the full details of the various options.

Now that you know how to format strings, let's look at how you can direct your output to files with the redirection operators.

5.7 REDIRECTION AND THE REDIRECTION OPERATORS

Redirection operators

```
<pipeline> > <outputFile>          <pipeline> >> <outputFile>
<pipeline> 2> <errorFile>          <pipeline> 2>> <errorFile>

                 <pipeline>  2>&1
```

Figure 5.15 The redirection operators that are available in PowerShell

All modern shell languages have input and output redirection operators, and PowerShell is no different. The redirection operators supported in PowerShell are shown in figure 5.15.

Table 5.5 presents the operators with examples and more details about their semantics.

Table 5.5 PowerShell redirection operators

Operator	Example	Results	Description
>	dir > out.txt	Contents of out.txt are replaced.	Redirect pipeline output to a file, overwriting the current contents.
>>	dir >> out.txt	Contents of out.txt are appended to.	Redirect pipeline output to a file, appending to the existing content.
2>	dir nosuchfile.txt 2> err.txt	Contents of err.txt are replaced by the error messages.	Redirect error output to a file, overwriting the current contents.
2>>	dir nosuchfile.txt 2>> err.txt	Contents of err.txt are appended with the error messages.	Redirect error output to a file, appending to the current contents.
2>&1	dir nosuchfile.txt 2>&1	The error message is written to the output.	The error messages are written to the output pipe instead of the error pipe.

Table 5.5 PowerShell redirection operators *(continued)*

Operator	Example	Results	Description
<	Not implemented in PowerShell v1.0 or v2.0		This operator is reserved for input redirection, which isn't implemented in v1.0 or v2.0 of PowerShell. Using this operator in an expression will result in a syntax error.

The redirection operators allow you to control where output and error objects are written (including discarding them if that's what you want to do). The following example saves the output of the `Get-Date` cmdlet to a file called out.txt:

```
PS (1) > get-date > out.txt
```

Now display the contents of this file:

```
PS (2) > type out.txt

Tuesday, January 31, 2006 9:56:25 PM
```

You can see that the object has been rendered to text using the same mechanism as you'd use when displaying on the console. Now let's see what happens when you redirect the error output from a cmdlet. You'll let the output be displayed normally:

```
PS (3) > dir out.txt,nosuchfile 2> err.txt

    Directory: Microsoft.Management.Automation.Core\FileSystem::C:\
    working

Mode                LastWriteTime     Length Name
----                -------------     ------ ----
-a---         1/31/2006   9:56 PM         40 out.txt
```

Obviously no error was displayed on the console. Let's see what was written to the error file:

```
PS (4) > type err.txt
get-childitem : Cannot find path 'C:\working\nosuchfile' because it
 does not exist.
At line:1 char:4
+ dir  <<<< out.txt,nosuchfile 2> err.txt
```

You see the full error message that would've been displayed on the console. Now try the append operator. Add another line to the output file you created earlier and display the contents of the file:

```
PS (5) > get-date >> out.txt
PS (6) > type out.txt

Tuesday, January 31, 2006 9:56:25 PM

Tuesday, January 31, 2006 9:57:33 PM
```

You see that there are now two records containing the current date. You can also append error records to a file using the `2>>` operator.

The next operator to discuss is the stream combiner, `2>&1`. This operator causes error objects to be routed into the output stream instead of going to the error stream. This allows you to capture error records along with your output. For example, if you want to get all the output and error records from a script to go to the same file, you'd just do

```
myScript > output.txt 2>&1
```

or

```
myScript 2>&1 > output.txt
```

The order doesn't matter. Now all the error records will appear inline with the output records in the file. This technique also works with assignment.

```
$a = myScript  2>&1
```

This code causes all the output and error objects from `myScript` to be placed in `$a`. You can then separate the errors by checking for their type with the `-is` operator, but it'd be easier to separate them up front. This is another place where you can use the grouping constructs. The following construction allows you to capture the output objects in `$output` and the error objects in `$error`:

```
$error = $( $output = myScript ) 2>&1
```

You'd use this idiom when you wanted to take some additional action on the error objects. For example, you might be deleting a set of files in a directory. Some of the deletions might fail. These will be recorded in `$error`, allowing you to take additional actions after the deletion operation has completed.

Sometimes you want to discard output or errors. In PowerShell, you do this by redirecting to `$null`. For example, if you don't care about the output from `myScript`, then you'd write

```
myScript > $null
```

and to discard the errors, you'd write

```
myScript 2> $null
```

The last thing to mention for I/O redirection is that, under the covers, redirection is done using the `Out-File` cmdlet. In fact,

```
myScript > file.txt
```

is just "syntactic sugar" for

```
myScript | out-file -path file.txt
```

In some cases, you'll want to use `Out-File` directly because it gives you more control over the way the output is written. The synopsis for `Out-File` is

```
Out-File [-FilePath] <String> [[-Encoding] <String>]
[-Append] [-Force] [-NoClobber] [-Width <Int32>]
[-InputObject <PSObject>]
[-Verbose] [-Debug] [-ErrorAction <ActionPreference>]
[-ErrorVariable <String>] [-OutVariable <String>]
[-OutBuffer <Int32>] [-WhatIf] [-Confirm]]
```

The interesting parameters are `-encoding`, which lets you specify the encoding (such as ASCII, Unicode, UTF8, and so on); `-append`, which appends to an existing file instead of overwriting it; `-noclobber`, which prevents you from overwriting (clobbering) an existing file; and `-width`, which tells the cmdlet how wide you want the output formatted. The full details for this cmdlet are available by running the command

```
get-help out-file
```

at the PowerShell command line.

Earlier in this section, we talked about assignment as being a kind of output redirection. This analogy is even more significant than we alluded to there. We'll go into details in the next section, when we finally cover variables themselves.

5.8 WORKING WITH VARIABLES

In many of the examples so far, you've used variables. Now let's look at the details of PowerShell variables. First, PowerShell variables aren't declared; they're just created as needed on first assignment. There also isn't any such thing as an uninitialized variable. If you reference a variable that doesn't yet exist, the system will return the value `$null` (although it won't create a variable):

```
PS (1) > $NoSuchVariable
PS (2) > $NoSuchVariable -eq $null
True
```

This example looks at a variable that doesn't exist and returns `$null`.

> **NOTE** `$null`, like `$true` and `$false`, is a special constant variable that's defined by the system. You can't change the value of these variables.

You can tell whether a variable exists by using the `Test-Path cmdlet`:

```
PS (3) > test-path variable:NoSuchVariable
False
```

This works because variables are part of the PowerShell unified namespaces. Just as files and the Registry are available through virtual drives, so are PowerShell variables. You can get a list of all of the variables that currently exist by using

```
dir variable:/
```

So how do you create a variable? Let's find out.

5.8.1 Creating variables

There are a number of variables that are defined by the system: `$true`, `$false`, and `$null` are the ones you've seen so far (we'll look at the others as we come to them). User variables are created on first assignment, as you can see here:

```
PS (3) > $var = 1
PS (4) > $var
1
PS (5) > $var = "Hi there"
PS (6) > $var
Hi there
PS (7) > $var = get-date
PS (8) > $var

Sunday, January 29, 2006 7:23:29 PM
```

In this example, first you assigned a number, then a string, then a `DateTime` object. This illustrates that PowerShell variables can hold any type of `object`. If you do want to add a type attribute to a variable, you use the cast notation on the left of the variable. Let's add a type attribute to the variable `$val`:

```
PS (1) > [int] $var = 2
```

Looking at the result, you see the number 2.

```
PS (2) > $var
2
```

That's fine. What happens if you try to assign a string to the variable?

```
PS (3) > $var = "0123"
PS (4) > $var
123
```

First, there was no error. Second, by looking at the output of the variable, you can see that the string "0123" was converted into the number `123`. This is why we say that the variable has a type attribute. Unlike strongly typed languages where a variable can only be assigned an object of the correct type, PowerShell will allow you to assign any object as long as it's convertible to the target type using the rules described in chapter 3. If the type isn't convertible, you'll get a runtime type-conversion error (as opposed to a "compile-time" error):

```
PS (5) > $var = "abc"
Cannot convert "abc" to "System.Int32". Error: "Input string was no
t in a correct format."
At line:1 char:5
+ $var  <<<< = "abc"
```

This code tried to assign "abc" to a variable with the type attribute `[int]`. Because "abc" can't be can't be converted to a number, you see a type-conversion error.

5.8.2 Variable name syntax

Now what about variable names? What characters are allowed in a variable name? The answer is, any character you want, with some caveats. There are two notations for variables. The simple notation starts with a dollar sign followed by a sequence of characters, which can include letters, numbers, the underscore, and the colon. The colon has a special meaning that we'll get to in a minute. The second notation allows you to use any character in a variable name. It looks like this:

```
${This is a variable name}
```

You can use any character you want in the braces. You can even use a close brace if you escape it, as you see here:

```
PS (7) > ${this is a variable name with a `} in it}
PS (8) > ${this is a variable name with a `} in it} = 13
PS (9) > ${this is a variable name with a `} in it}
13
```

Earlier, we said that the colon character was special in a variable name. This is used to delimit the *namespace* that the system uses to locate the variable. For example, to access PowerShell global variables, you use the global namespace:

```
PS (1) > $global:var = 13
PS (2) > $global:var
13
```

This example set the variable `var` in the global context to the value 13. You can also use the namespace notation to access variables at other scopes. This is called a *scope modifier*. Scopes will be covered in chapter 7, so we won't say anything more about that here.

Along with the scope modifiers, the namespace notation lets you get at any of the resources surfaced in PowerShell as drives. For example, to get at the environment variables, you use the `env` namespace:

```
PS (1) > $env:SystemRoot
C:\WINDOWS
```

In this example, you retrieved the contents of the `SystemRoot` environment variable. You can use these variables directly in paths. For example:

```
PS (3) > dir $env:systemroot\explorer.exe

    Directory: Microsoft.Management.Automation.Core\FileSystem::C:\
    WINDOWS

Mode                LastWriteTime     Length Name
----                -------------     ------ ----
-a---           8/10/2004  12:00 PM   1032192 explorer.exe
```

This expression retrieved the file system information for explorer.exe.

NOTE For `cmd.exe` or `command.com` users, the equivalent syntax would be `%systemroot%\explorer.exe`. There, the percent signs delimit the variable. In PowerShell, this is done with braces.

Many of the namespace providers are also available through the variable notation (but you usually have to wrap the path in braces). Let's look back at an example you saw at the beginning of chapter 4:

```
${c:old.txt} -replace 'is (red|blue)','was $1' > new.txt
```

The initial construct should now start to make sense. The sequence `${c:old.txt}` is a variable that references the file system provider through the C: drive and retrieves the contexts of the file named old.txt. With this simple notation, you read the contents of a file. No open/read/close—you treat the file itself as an atomic value.

NOTE Using variable notation to access a file can be startling at first, but it's a logical consequence of the unified data model in PowerShell. Because things like variables and functions are available as drives, things such as drives are also available using the variable notation. In effect, this is an application of the Model-View-Controller (MVC) pattern. Each type of data store (file system, variables, Registry, and so forth) is a "model." The PowerShell provider infrastructure acts as the controller, and there are (by default) two views: the "file system" navigation view and the variable view. The user is free to choose and use the view most suitable to the task at hand.

You can also write to a file using the namespace variable notation. Here's that example rewritten to use variable assignment instead of a redirection operator (remember, earlier we said that assignment can be considered a form of redirection in PowerShell):

```
${c:new.txt} = ${c:old.txt} -replace 'is (red|blue)','was $1'
```

You can even do an in-place update of a file by using the same variable on both sides of the assignment operator. To update the file old.txt instead of making a copy, use

```
${c:old.txt} = ${c:old.txt} -replace 'is (red|blue)','was $1'
```

All you did was change the name in the variable reference from new.txt to old.txt. This won't work if you use the redirection operator, because the output file is opened before the input file is read. This would have the unfortunate effect of truncating the previous contents of the output file. In the assignment case, the file is read atomically; that is, all at once, processed, then written atomically. This allows for "in-place" edits because the file is buffered entirely in memory instead of in a temporary file. To do this with redirection, you'd have to save the output to a temporary file and then rename the temporary file so it replaces the original. Now let's leverage this feature along with multiple assignments to swap two files, f1.txt and f2.txt. Earlier in this chapter you saw how to swap two variables. You can use the same technique to swap two files:

```
${c:f1.txt},${c:f2.txt} = ${c:f2.txt},${c:f1.txt}
```

> **NOTE** All of these examples using variables to read and write files cause the entire contents of files to be loaded into memory as a collection of strings. On modern computers it's possible to handle moderately large files this way, but doing it with large files is memory intensive and inefficient, and might even fail under some conditions. Keep this in mind when using these techniques.

When the file system provider reads the file, it returns the file as an array of strings.

> **NOTE** When accessing a file using the variable namespace notation, PowerShell assumes that it's working with a text file. Because the notation doesn't provide a mechanism for specifying the encoding, you can't use this technique on binary files. You'll have to use the `Get-Content` and `Set-Content` cmdlets instead.

This provides a simple way to get the length of a file:

```
${c:file.txt}.Length
```

The downside of this simple construct is that it requires reading the entire file into memory and then counting the result. It works fine for small files (a few megabytes), but it won't work on files that are gigabytes in size.

5.8.3 Working with the variable cmdlets

So far you've been using the PowerShell language features to access variables, but you can also work with variables using the variable cmdlets. These cmdlets let you do a couple of things you can't do directly from the language.

Indirectly setting a variable

Sometimes it's useful to be able to get or set a variable when you won't know the name of that variable until runtime. For example, you might want to initialize a set of variables from a CSV file. You can't do this using the variable syntax in the language because the name of the variable to set is resolved at parse time. Let's work through this example. First you need a CSV file:

```
PS (1) > cat variables.csv
"Name", "Value"
"srcHost",  "machine1"
"srcPath",  "c:\data\source\mailbox.pst"
"destHost", "machine2"
"destPath", "d:\backup"
```

As you can see, the CSV file is simply a text file with rows of values separated by commas, hence CSV or comma-separated values. Now you'll use the `Import-CSV` cmdlet to import this file as structured objects:

```
PS (2) > import-csv variables.csv

Name                           Value
----                           -----
srcHost                        machine1
srcPath                        c:\data\source\mailbox.pst
destHost                       machine2
destPath                       d:\backup
```

You can see the cmdlet has treated the first row in the table as the names of the properties to use on the objects and then added the name and value property to each object. The choice of `Name` and `Value` was deliberate because these are the names of the parameters on the `Set-Variable` cmdlet. This cmdlet takes input from the pipeline by property name so you can pipe the output of `Import-CSV` directly into `Set-Variable`

```
PS (3) > import-csv variables.csv | set-variable
```

and it's as simple as that. If you wanted to see the full details, you could specify the `-verbose` parameter to the cmdlet and it would display each variable as it was set. Now use the normal variable syntax to verify that you've set things up the way you planned:

```
PS (4) > $srcHost

Name                           Value
----                           -----
srcHost                        machine1
```

Okay, good. You can use the parameters on the cmdlet to directly set this variable

```
PS (5) > set-variable -name srcHost -value machine3
PS (6) > $srcHost
machine3
```

or use the (much) shorter alias `sv` to do it:

```
PS (7) > sv srcHost machine4
PS (8) > $srcHost
machine4
```

Now let's see what else you can do with the cmdlets.

Getting and setting variable options

If there's a cmdlet to set a variable, obviously there should also be a variable to get variables—the `Get-Variable` cmdlet:

```
PS (9) > get-variable -value srcHost
machine4
```

Notice that this example specified the -Value parameter. What happens if you don't do that?

```
PS (10) > get-variable srcHost | gm

   TypeName: System.Management.Automation.PSVariable

Name         MemberType Definition
----         ---------- ----------
Equals       Method     bool Equals(System.Object obj)
GetHashCode  Method     int GetHashCode()
GetType      Method     type GetType()
IsValidValue Method     bool IsValidValue(System.Object ...
ToString     Method     string ToString()
Attributes   Property   System.Collections.ObjectModel.C...
Description  Property   System.String Description {get;s...
Module       Property   System.Management.Automation.PSM...
ModuleName   Property   System.String ModuleName {get;}
Name         Property   System.String Name {get;}
Options      Property   System.Management.Automation.Sco...
Value        Property   System.Object Value {get;set;}
Visibility   Property   System.Management.Automation.Ses...
```

If a value for -Variable isn't specified, Get-Variable returns the PSVariable object that PowerShell uses to represent this object. You can see the Name and Value properties on this object, but there are a lot of other properties as well. Let's explore the Options property. This property allows us to set options on the variable including things like ReadOnly and Constant. The variables you've read from the CSV file are still changeable:

```
PS (11) > $srcHost = "machine9"
PS (12) > $srcHost
machine9
```

But, if you're using them to configure the environment, you may not want them to be. To address this, you can set the ReadOnly option using Set-Variable and the -Option parameter:

```
PS (13) > set-variable -option readonly srcHost machine1
PS (14) > $srcHost = "machine4"
Cannot overwrite variable srcHost because it is read-only o
r constant.
At line:1 char:9
+ $srcHost <<<<  = "machine4"
    + CategoryInfo          : WriteError: (srcHost:String)
    [], SessionStateUnauthorizedAccessException
    + FullyQualifiedErrorId : VariableNotWritable
```

Now when you try and change the value of this variable, you get an error. The variable is unchanged:

```
PS (15) > get-variable -value srcHost

Name                           Value
----                           -----
srcHost                        machine1
```

If you can't change it, how about removing it? Try just the `remove` command:

```
PS (16) > remove-variable srcHost
Remove-Variable : Cannot remove variable srcHost because it
 is constant or read-only. If the variable is read-only, tr
y the operation again specifying the Force option.
At line:1 char:16
+ remove-variable <<<<  srcHost
    + CategoryInfo          : WriteError: (srcHost:String)
    [Remove-Variable], SessionStateUnauthorizedAccessExce
  ption
    + FullyQualifiedErrorId : VariableNotRemovable,Microso
   ft.PowerShell.Commands.RemoveVariableCommand
```

This failed with the expected error. But you can still force the removal of a read-only variable by using the `-Force` parameter on `Remove-Variable`:

```
PS (17) > remove-variable -force srcHost
```

When you specify `-Force`, the variable is removed and there's no error. If you don't want the value to be changed, you can use the `Constant` option:

```
PS (18) > set-variable -option constant srcHost machine1
```

When this option is specified, even using `-Force` will fail:

```
PS (19) > remove-variable -force srcHost
Remove-Variable : Cannot remove variable srcHost because it
 is constant or read-only. If the variable is read-only, tr
y the operation again specifying the Force option.
At line:1 char:16
+ remove-variable <<<<  -force srcHost
    + CategoryInfo          : WriteError: (srcHost:String)
    [Remove-Variable], SessionStateUnauthorizedAccessExce
  ption
    + FullyQualifiedErrorId : VariableNotRemovable,Microso
   ft.PowerShell.Commands.RemoveVariableCommand
```

And now for one last trick. You've looked at how to use the name of a variable to access it indirectly. You can bypass the name-lookup process and use the variable reference directly. Let's see how this works.

Using PSVariable objects as references

To use a `PSVariable` object as a reference, first you have to get one. Earlier you saw how to do this with `Get-Variable` (or its alias `gv`):

```
PS (21) > $ref = gv destHost
```

Now that you have a reference, you can use the reference to get the variable's name

```
PS (22) > $ref.Name
destHost
```

or its value:

```
PS (23) > $ref.Value
machine2
```

Having the reference also allows you to set the variable's value:

```
PS (24) > $ref.Value = "machine12"
```

When you check the variable using the language syntax, you see the change.

```
PS (25) > $destHost
machine12
```

Variable names vs. variable values

Here's a tip to keep in mind if you're trying to do these tricks. You need to keep variable *name* and variable *value* firmly separated in your thinking. If you don't think about what you're doing closely enough, trying to use `$name` to get the value of the variable seems reasonable:

```
PS (26) > gv $srcPath
Get-Variable : Cannot find a variable with name '@{Name=src
Path; Value=c:\data\source\mailbox.pst}'.
At line:1 char:3
+ gv <<<<  $srcPath
    + CategoryInfo          : ObjectNotFound: (@{Name=srcP
   ath;...ce\mailbox.pst}:String) [Get-Variable], ItemNot
  FoundException
    + FullyQualifiedErrorId : VariableNotFound,Microsoft.P
   owerShell.Commands.GetVariableCommand
```

But it gives you a rather confusing error. This is because PowerShell resolved the token `$srcPath` and passed its *value* to the cmdlet, not the *name*. Even quoting it but still having the `$` sign in the string is wrong:

```
PS (27) > gv '$srcPath'
Get-Variable : Cannot find a variable with name '$srcPath'.
At line:1 char:3
+ gv <<<<  '$srcPath'
    + CategoryInfo          : ObjectNotFound: ($srcPath:St
   ring) [Get-Variable], ItemNotFoundException
    + FullyQualifiedErrorId : VariableNotFound,Microsoft.P
   owerShell.Commands.GetVariableCommand
```

This error seems bizarre because you know that there's such a variable. The reason it fails is because `$` isn't part of the variable's name. It's part of a token in the PowerShell language indicating that whatever follows the `$` is the name of a variable.

The correct way to do this is to use the variable name without the leading `$`.

```
PS (28) > gv srcPath

Name                           Value
----                           -----
srcPath                        @{Name=srcPath; Value=c:\...
```

Finally, here's why all of this works the way it does. Define a variable `$n` that has part of the path name:

```
PS (29) > $n = 'src'
```

Now combine that variable with another fragment using string expansion, and it works properly:

```
PS (30) > gv "${n}Path"

Name                           Value
----                           -----
srcPath                        @{Name=srcPath; Value=c:\...

PS (31) >
```

This gives you a great deal of flexibility when dealing with variable names. It can be complex but any situation where you need to do this is, by definition, complex. Having this facility doesn't complicate normal day-to-day activities but does make some more sophisticated scenarios possible. Now let's look at another set of potentially complex scenarios that can be solved by using variables in a special way.

5.8.4 Splatting a variable

The last topic that we're going to touch on in this chapter is something called *variable splatting*, which was added to PowerShell in version 2. This is a term taken from the Ruby scripting language and affects how argument variables are passed to commands.

Normally, when you have a variable containing an array or hashtable and you use this variable as a command argument, its value is passed as a single argument. Splatting turns each value in the collection into individual arguments. So, if you have an array with three elements in it, those elements will be passed as three individual arguments. If you have a hashtable, each name-value pair becomes a named parameter–argument pair for the command.

To do this is, when referencing the variable that you want to pass to the command, you use `@` instead of `$` as the prefix to the variable. Here's an example to show how this works. First you need a command to work with—you'll define a function (see chapter 7) that takes three arguments:

```
PS {1) > function s ($x, $y, $z) { "x=$x, y=$y, z=$z" }
```

This function uses string expansion to display the value of each of its parameters. Now create an array to pass into this command:

```
PS {2) > $list = 1,2,3
```

The variable `$list` contains three integers. Pass this using the normal variable notation:

```
PS (3) > s $list
x=1 2 3, y=, z=
```

From the output, you can see that all three values in the argument were assigned to the `$x` parameter. The other two parameters didn't get assigned anything. Next, splat the variable by calling the function with `@list` instead of `$list`:

```
PS (4) > s @list
x=1, y=2, z=3
```

This time the output shows that each parameter was assigned one member of the array in the variable. What happens if there are more elements than there are variables? Let's try it. First add some elements to your `$list` variable:

```
PS (5) > $list += 5,6,7
PS (6) > $list
1
2
3
5
6
7
```

Now the variable contains seven elements. Pass this to the function:

```
PS (7) > s @list
x=1, y=2, z=3
```

It appears that the last four arguments have vanished. In fact, what has happened is that they're assigned to the special variable `$args`. Let's redefine the function to show this:

```
PS (8) > function s ($x, $y, $z) { "$x,$y,$z args=$args" }
```

Print out the three formal arguments `$x`, `$`, and `$z` along with the special `$args` variable. When you run the new function

```
PS (9) > s @list
1,2,3 args=5 6 7
```

you see that the missing arguments have ended up in `$args`. The most important use for splatting is for enabling one command to effectively call another. You'll see how this can be used to wrap existing commands and either extend or restrict their behavior in later chapters. (Variable parameters and how they're bound is covered in much more detail in chapter 7.)

Now that you understand how an array of values can be splatted, let's look at how you work with named parameters. In the previous example, you could have used the explicit names of the parameters to pass things in instead of relying on position. For example, you can use the names to explicitly pass in values for `-x` and `-y`, in the reverse order

```
PS (10) > s -y first -x second
second,first, args=
```

and you see that second is in the first (x) position and first is in the second position. How can you use splatting to do this? Well, parameters and their values are name-value pairs, and in PowerShell, the way to work with name-value pairs is with hashtables. Let's try this out. First create a hashtable with the values you want:

```
PS (11) > $h = @{x='second'; y='first'}
```

Now splat the hashtable the same way you splatted the variable containing an array

```
PS (12) > s @h
second,first, args=
```

and, as before, the x parameter gets the value second and the y parameter gets the value first. The next question you should have is, what happens if you also want to explicitly pass in -z? Try it:

```
PS (13) > s -z third  @h 1 2 3
second,first,third args=1 2 3
```

It works exactly the way you want. If you specify the parameter both in the hashtable and explicitly on the command line, you'll get an error:

```
PS (14) > s -x boo  @h 1 2 3
s : Cannot bind parameter because parameter 'x' is specifie
d more than once. To provide multiple values to parameters
that can accept multiple values, use the array syntax. For
example, "-parameter value1,value2,value3".
At line:1 char:2
+ s <<<<  -x boo  @h 1 2 3
    + CategoryInfo          : InvalidArgument: (:) [s], Pa
   rameterBindingException
    + FullyQualifiedErrorId : ParameterAlreadyBound,s
```

Let's look at a practical example using this feature. The Write-Host cmdlet allows you to write strings to the screen specifying the foreground and background colors. This is great, but if you need to write a lot of strings or parameterize the colors that are used, repeatedly setting both parameters will get a bit tedious:

```
PS (16) > write-host -foreground black -background white Hi
Hi
```

Specifying the parameters takes up more space than the string you want to write! Using splatting, instead of passing in both parameters all the time, you can set up a hashtable once and pass that around instead:

```
PS (17) > $colors = @{foreground="black";background="white"}
PS (18) > write-host @colors "Hi there"
Hi there
```

This approach is more convenient and less error prone than having to explicitly pass both color parameters, making it an effective way to "style" your output using a single variable.

> **NOTE** By now I'm sure you're wondering why this technique is it called *splatting*. Here's the reasoning behind this term. Think of a rock hitting a car windshield. A rock is a solid object that remains intact after it bounces off your car. Next, think of a bug hitting the windshield instead of a rock. Splat! The contents of the bug are distributed over the windshield instead of remaining as a single object. This is what splatting does to a variable argument. It distributes the members of the argument collection as individual arguments instead of remaining a single intact argument. (The other rational behind this term is that, in Ruby, the operator is `*`, which is what the aforementioned insect looks like post-impact. PowerShell can't use `*` because it would be confused with the wildcard character. Instead it uses `@` because splatting involves arrays and PowerShell uses `@` for many array operations.) I submit that this is the most visceral mnemonic in the programming language field (at least that I'm aware of).

This is all we're going to say about variables here. In chapter 7, we'll return to variables and talk about how variables are defined in functions and how they're scoped in the PowerShell language. We'll also look at splatting again when we cover how commands can call other commands.

5.9 SUMMARY

In this chapter, we finished our coverage of PowerShell operators and expressions. We looked at how to build complex data structures in PowerShell and how to use the redirection operators to write output to files. We covered arrays, properties, and methods. Finally, we explored the basics of PowerShell variable semantics and variable namespaces. Here are the important points to remember:

- The type operators allow you to write scripts that have *polymorphic* behavior. By using these operators to examine the types of objects, you can decide how to process different types of objects. You can also use the operators to dynamically convert from one type of object to another.
- The prefix and postfix operators `++` and `--` are a convenient way of incrementing and decrementing variables.
- The subexpression operator `$( ... )` allows you to use arbitrary PowerShell script code anywhere that you can use a value expression. The array subexpression operator `@( ... )` also guarantees that the result of an expression will always be an array.

- PowerShell arrays support both *jagged* arrays—that is, arrays that contain or reference other arrays and multidimensional arrays. Array slicing is supported, both for one-dimensional and multidimensional arrays when retrieving values. It isn't supported when assigning to an array index.
- Use the comma operator (`,`)to build arrays and complex nested data structures such as jagged arrays.
- Use the dot operator (`.`) for accessing instance members and the double-colon (`::`) operator for accessing static members. We looked at how to indirectly invoke both properties and methods using these operators.
- The PowerShell redirection operators allow you to control where the output and error objects are written. They also allow you to easily discard these objects if so desired by redirecting to `$null`. The redirection operators are just "syntactic sugar" for the `Out-File` cmdlet. Using the cmdlet directly allows you to control things such as what file encoding will be used when writing to a file.
- The format operator `-f` can be used to perform complex formatting tasks when the default formatting doesn't produce the desired results. The formatting sequences are the same as the sequences used by the `System.String.Format()` method in the .NET Framework.
- PowerShell variable namespaces let you access a variety of Windows "data stores," including environment variables and the file system using the variable notation.
- It's possible to use the variable cmdlets to set options on variables and do indirect variable accesses using either the variable name or a `PSVariable` object.
- PowerShell version 2 introduced a new variable notation called *splatting* that allows you to take collections of values, either arrays or hashtables, and distribute the members of these collections as individual arguments to a command.

CHAPTER 6

Flow control in scripts

I may not have gone where I intended to go, but I think I have ended up where I needed to be.

—Douglas Adams, *The Long Dark Tea-Time of the Soul*

Previous chapters showed how you can solve surprisingly complex problems in PowerShell using only commands and operators. You can select, sort, edit,you and present all manner of data by composing these elements into pipelines and expressions. In fact, commands and operators were the only elements available in the earliest prototypes of PowerShell. Sooner or later, though, if you want to write significant programs or scripts, you must add custom looping or branch logic to your solution. This is what we're going to cover in this chapter: PowerShell's take on the traditional programming constructs that all languages possess.

The PowerShell flow-control statements and cmdlets are listed in figure 6.1, arranged in groups.

We'll go through each group in this chapter. As always, behavioral differences exist with the PowerShell flow-control statements that new users should be aware of.

Conditional statements

```
if ( <expr> ) { <statements> }
if ( <expr> ) { <statements> } else { <statements> }
if ( <expr> ) { <statements> } elseif ( <expr> ) { <statements> } else { <statements> }
```

Loop statements

```
while ( <expr> ) { <statements> }
do { <statements> } while ( <expr> )
do { <statements> } until ( <expr> )
for ( <expr> ; <expr> ; <expr> ) { <statements> }
foreach ( $var in <pipeline> ) { <statements> }
```

Break and continue statements

```
break                   break <label>
continue                continue <label>
```

The switch statement

```
switch ( <expr> ) { <pattern1> { <statements> } <pattern2> { <statements> } }
switch ( <expr> ) { <pattern1> { <statements> } default { <statements> } }
```

Flow-control cmdlets

```
... | ForEach-Object <scriptBlock>
... | ForEach-Object -Begin <scriptBlock> -Process <scriptBlock> -End <scriptBlock>
... | Where-Object <scriptBlock>
```

Figure 6.1 The PowerShell flow-control statements

The most obvious difference is that PowerShell typically allows the use of pipelines in places where other programming languages only allow simple expressions. An interesting implication of this pipeline usage is that the PowerShell `switch` statement is both a looping construct and a conditional statement—which is why it gets its own group.

This is also the first time we've dealt with *keywords* in PowerShell. Keywords are part of the core PowerShell language. This means that, unlike cmdlets, keywords can't be redefined or aliased. Keywords are also case insensitive so you can write `foreach`, `ForEach`, or `FOREACH` and they'll all be accepted by the interpreter. (By convention, though, keywords in PowerShell scripts are usually written in lowercase.) Keywords are also *context sensitive*, which means that they're only treated as keywords in a statement context—usually as the first word in a statement. This is important because it lets you have both a `foreach` loop statement and a `foreach` filter cmdlet, as you'll see later in this chapter. Let's begin our discussion with the conditional statement.

Conditional statements

```
if ( <expr> ) { <statements> }
if ( <expr> ) { <statements> } else { <statements> }
if ( <expr> ) { <statements> } elseif ( <expr> ) { <statements> } else { <statements> }
```

Figure 6.2 The syntax of the PowerShell conditional statements

6.1 THE CONDITIONAL STATEMENT

PowerShell has one main conditional statement: the `if` statement shown in figure 6.2.

This statement lets a script decide whether an action should be performed by evaluating a conditional expression, then selecting the path to follow based on the results of that evaluation. The PowerShell `if` statement is similar to the `if` statement found in most programming languages. The one thing that's a bit different syntactically is the use of `elseif` as a single keyword for subsequent clauses. Figure 6.3 shows the structure and syntax of this statement in detail.

Let's work through some examples that illustrate how the `if` statement works. You'll use all three of the elements—`if`, `elseif`, and `else`—in this example:

```
if ($x -gt 100)
{
    "It's greater than one hundred"
}
elseif ($x -gt 50)
{
    "It's greater than 50"
} else
{
    "It's not very big."
}
```

In this example, if the variable `$x` holds a value greater than 100, the string "It's greater than one hundred" will be emitted. If `$x` is greater than 50 but less than 100, it will emit "It's greater than 50"; otherwise, you'll get "It's not very big." Of course,

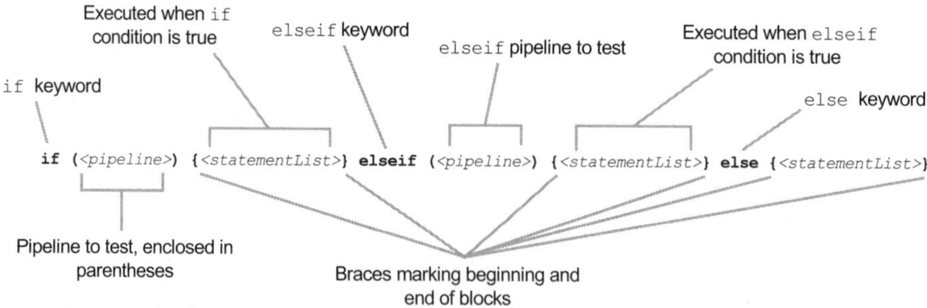

Figure 6.3 PowerShell's version of the `if` statement, which is the basic conditional statement found in all scripting and programming languages

you can have zero or more `elseif` clauses to test different things. The `elseif` and `else` parts are optional, as is the case in other languages.

As you might have noticed, the PowerShell `if` statement is modeled on the `if` statement found in C-derived languages, including C#, but a couple of differences exist. First, `elseif` is a single keyword with no spaces allowed between the words. Second, the braces are mandatory around the statement lists, even when you have only a single statement in the list (or no statements for that matter, in which case you would have to type `{}`). If you try to write something like

```
if ($x -gt 100) "It's greater than one hundred"
```

you'll get a syntax error:

```
PS (1) > if ($x -gt 100) "It's greater than one hundred"
Missing statement block after if ( condition ).
At line:1 char:17
+ if ($x -gt 100) " <<<< It's greater than one hundred"
PS (2) >
```

Grammar lessons

The PowerShell grammar technically could support the construction shown in the preceding example. In fact, we did enable this feature at one point, but when people tried it out, it resulted in a lot of errors. The problem is that a newline or a semicolon is required to terminate a command. This leads to the situation where you write something like

```
if ($x -gt 3) write x is $x while ($x--) $x
```

and discover that, because you've missed the semicolon before the `while` statement, it writes out the `while` statement instead of executing it. In the end, the cost of typing a couple of additional characters was more than offset by a decreased error rate. For this reason, the language design team decided to make the braces mandatory.

In general, the syntax of the `if` statement (and all the PowerShell flow-control statements) is freeform with respect to whitespace. In other words, you can lay out your code pretty much any way you want. You can write an `if` statement that looks like this

```
if($true){"true"}else{"false"}
```

with no whitespace whatsoever. Alternatively, you could also write it like this

```
if
(
$true
)
{
"true"
}
else
```

```
{
"false"
}
```

where each element is on a separate line.

There's one constraint on how you can format an `if` statement: when PowerShell is being used interactively, the `else` or `elseif` keyword has to be on the same line as the previous closing brace; otherwise, the interpreter will consider the statement complete and execute it immediately.

It's important to note that the PowerShell `if` statement allows a pipeline in the condition clause, not just a simple expression. This means it's possible to do the following:

```
if ( dir telly*.txt | select-string penguin )
{
    "There's a penguin on the telly."
}
```

In this example, the pipeline in the condition part of the `if` statement will scan all the text files whose names start with "telly" to see whether they contain the word "penguin." If at least one of the files contains this word, the statement block will be executed, printing out

```
There's a penguin on the telly.
```

Here's another example:

```
if (( dir *.txt | select-string -List spam ).Length -eq 3)
{
     "Spam! Spam! Spam!"
}
```

In this case, you search all the text files in the current directory looking for the word "spam." If exactly three files contain this word, then you print out

```
Spam! Spam! Spam!
```

> **NOTE** Yes, these are, in fact, Monty Python references. This is where the Python language got its name. If you're familiar with Python or Perl, you'll occasionally recognize cultural references from those languages in PowerShell examples here and elsewhere. Many of the PowerShell development team members had their first scripting experiences with those languages.

Because you can use pipelines and subexpressions in the conditional part of an `if` statement, you can write quite complex conditional expressions in PowerShell. With subexpressions, you can even use an `if` statement inside the condition part of another `if` statement. Here's what this looks like:

```
PS (2) > $x = 10
PS (3) > if ( $( if ($x -lt 5) { $false } else { $x } ) -gt
```

```
>>> 20) { $false } else {$true}
True
PS (4) > $x = 25
PS (5) > if ( $( if ($x -lt 5) { $false } else { $x } ) -gt
>>> 20) { $false } else {$true}
False
PS (6) > $x = 4
PS (7) > if ( $( if ($x -lt 5) { $false } else { $x } ) -gt
>>> 20) { $false } else {$true}
True
PS (8) >
```

If looking at this makes your head hurt, welcome to the club—it made mine hurt to write it. Let's dissect this statement and see what it's doing. Let's take the inner `if` statement first:

```
if ($x -lt 5) { $false } else { $x }
```

You can see that this statement is straightforward. If `$x` is less than the number 5, it returns false; otherwise, it returns the value of `$x`. Based on this, let's split the code into two separate statements:

```
$temp = $( if ($x -lt 5) { $false } else { $x } )
if ($temp -gt 20) { $false } else {$true}
```

What the outer `if` statement is doing is also pretty obvious: if the result of the first (formally inner) statement is greater than 20, return `$false`; otherwise return `$true`.

Now that you can do branching, let's move on to the looping statements.

6.2 Looping statements

Loop statements

```
while ( <expr> ) { <statements> }
do { <statements> } while ( <expr> )
do { <statements> } until ( <expr> )
for ( <expr> ; <expr> ; <expr> ) { <statements> }
foreach ( $var in <pipeline> ) { <statements> }
```

Figure 6.4 The PowerShell loop statements

Looping is the ability to repeat a set of actions some specific number of times, either based on a count or a condition expression. The PowerShell loop statements cover both of these cases and are shown in figure 6.4.

6.2.1 The while loop

In this section, we'll cover the basic looping statement in PowerShell: the `while` statement. The `while` statement (also known as a `while` *loop*) is the most basic PowerShell language construct for creating a loop. It executes the commands in the

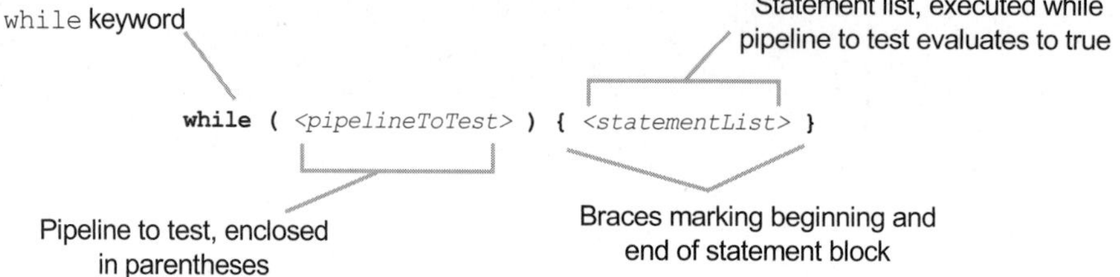

Figure 6.5 The PowerShell `while` loop statement syntax

statement list as long as a conditional test evaluates to true. Figure 6.5 shows the `while` statement syntax.

When you execute a `while` statement, PowerShell evaluates the `<pipeline>` section of the statement before entering the `<statementList>` section. The output from the pipeline is then converted to either true or false, following the rules for the Boolean interpretation of values described in chapter 3. As long as this result converts to true, PowerShell reruns the `<statementList>` section, executing each statement in the list.

For example, the following `while` statement displays the numbers 1 through 3:

```
$val = 0
while($val -ne 3)
{
    $val++
    write-host "The number is $val"
}
```

In this example, the condition (`$val` isn't equal to 3) is true while `$val` is 0, 1, and 2. Each time through the loop, `$val` is incremented by 1 using the unary ++ increment operator (`$val++`). The last time through the loop, `$val` is 3. When `$val` equals 3, the condition statement evaluates to false and the loop exits.

To more conveniently enter this command at the PowerShell command prompt, you can simply enter it all on one line:

```
$val=0; while ($val -ne 3){$val++; write-host "The number is $val"}
```

Notice that the semicolon separates the first command that adds 1 to `$val` from the second command, which writes the value of `$val` to the console.

You can accomplish all the basic iterative patterns just using the `while` loop, but PowerShell provides several other looping statements for common cases. Let's look at those next.

6.2.2 The do-while loop

The other `while` loop variant in PowerShell is the `do-while` loop. This is a *bottom-tested* variant of the `while` loop. In other words, it always executes the statement list

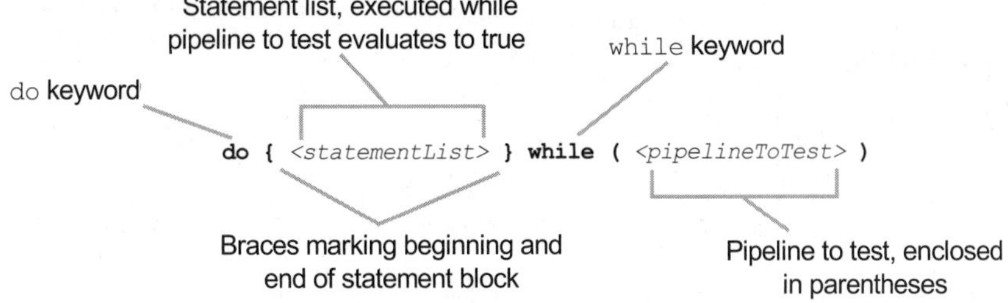

Figure 6.6 The PowerShell do-while loop statement syntax

at least once before checking the condition. The syntax of the `do-while` loop is shown in figure 6.6.

The `do-while` loop is effectively equivalent to

```
<statementList>
while ( <pipeLine> )
{
        <statementList>
}
```

where the two statement lists are identical. The final variation of the `while` loop is the `do/until` statement. It's identical to the `do/while` loop except that the sense of the test is inverted and the statement will loop *until* the condition is true instead of *while* it is true, as shown in this example:

```
PS (1) > $i=0
PS (2) > do { $i } until  ($i++ -gt 3)
0
1
2
3
4
```

In this case, the statement loops until `$i` is greater than 3.

Having covered the two variations of the `while` loop, we'll look at the `for` and `foreach` loops next.

6.2.3 The for loop

The `for` loop is the basic counting loop in PowerShell. It's typically used to step through a collection of objects. It's not used as often in PowerShell as in other languages because there are usually better ways for processing a collection, as you'll see with the `foreach` statement in the next section. But the `for` loop is useful when you need to know explicitly which element in the collection you're working with. Figure 6.7 shows the `for` loop syntax.

Notice that the three pipelines in the parentheses are just general pipelines. Conventionally, the initialization pipeline initializes the loop counter variable, the test

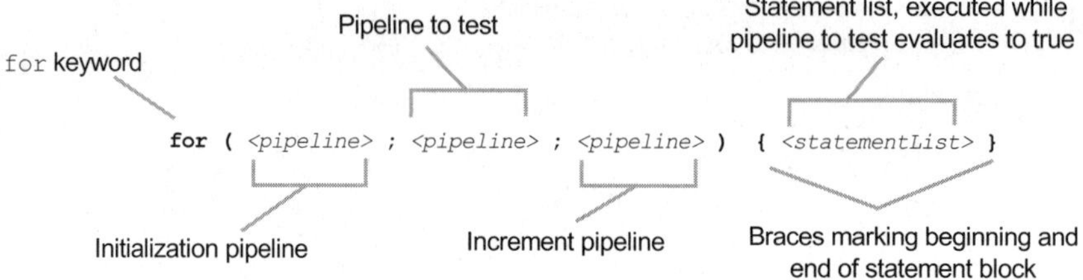

Figure 6.7 The PowerShell `for` loop statement syntax

pipeline tests this variable against some condition, and the increment pipeline increments the loop counter. The canonical example is

```
PS (1) > for ($i=0; $i -lt 5; $i++) { $i }
0
1
2
3
4
PS (2) >
```

But because these are arbitrary pipelines, they can do anything. (Note that if initialization and increment pipelines produce output, it's simply discarded by the interpreter.) Here's an example where the condition test is used to generate a side effect that's then used in the statement list body:

```
PS (2) > for ($i=0; $($y = $i*2; $i -lt 5); $i++) { $y }
0
2
4
6
8
PS (3) >
```

In this example, the pipeline to be tested is a subexpression that first sets `$y` to be twice the current value of `$i` and then compares `$i` to 5. In the loop body, you use the value in `$y` to emit the current loop counter times 2. A more practical example would be initializing two values in the initialization pipeline:

```
PS (3) > for ($($result=@(); $i=0); $i -lt 5; $i++) {$result += $i }
PS (4) > "$result"
0 1 2 3 4
```

Here you use a subexpression in the initialization pipeline to set `$result` to the empty array and the counter variable `$i` to 0. Then the loop counts up to 5, adding each value to the result array.

> **NOTE** It's a little funny to talk about the initialization and increment pipelines. You usually think of pipelines as producing some output. In the `for` statement, the output from these pipelines is discarded and the side effects of their execution are the interesting parts.

Now let's look at one more example using the `for` loop. Here you'll use it to sum up the number of handles used by the `svchost` processes. First you'll get a list of these processes:

```
PS (1) > $svchosts = get-process svchost
```

You'll loop through this list and add the handle count for the process to `$total`

```
PS (2) > for ($($total=0;$i=0); $i -lt $svchosts.count; $i++)
>> {$total+=$svchosts[$i].handles}
>>
```

and then print out the total:

```
PS (3) > $total
3457
```

So using the `for` loop is straightforward, but it's somewhat annoying to have to manage the loop counter. Wouldn't it be nice if you could just let the loop counter count take care of itself? That's exactly what the `foreach` loop does for you, so let's move on.

6.2.4 The foreach loop

Collections are important in any shell (or programming) environment. The whole point of using a scripting language for automation is so that you can operate on more than one object at a time. As you've seen in chapters 3 and 4, PowerShell provides many ways of operating on collections. Perhaps the most straightforward of these mechanisms is the `foreach` loop.

> **NOTE** Astute readers will remember that we mentioned a `foreach` cmdlet (which is an alias for the `ForEach-Object` cmdlet) as well as the `foreach` statement at the beginning of the chapter. To reiterate, when the word "foreach" is used at the beginning of a statement, it's recognized as the `foreach` keyword. When it appears in the middle of a pipeline, it's treated as the name of a command.

This statement is syntactically identical to the C# `foreach` loop with the exception that you don't have to declare the type of the loop variable (in fact, you can't do this). Figure 6.8 shows you the syntax for the `foreach` statement.

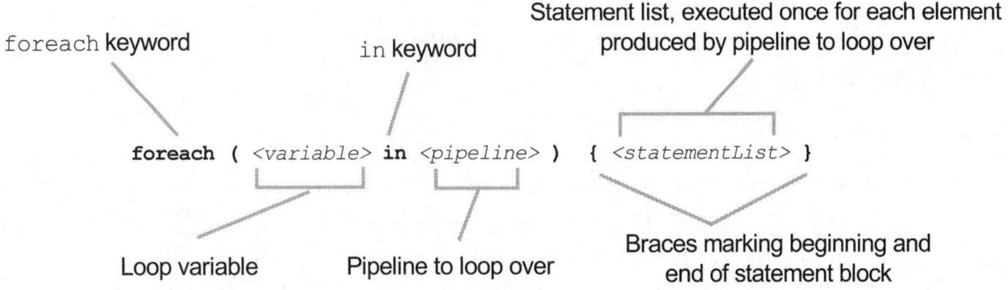

Figure 6.8 The PowerShell `foreach` loop statement syntax

Here's an example. This example loops over all the text files in the current directory, calculating the total size of all the files:

```
$l = 0; foreach ($f in dir *.txt) { $l += $f.length }
```

First you set the variable that will hold the total length to 0. Then, in the `foreach` loop, you use the `dir` command to get a list of the text files in the current directory (that is, files with the .txt extension). The `foreach` statement assigns elements from this list one at a time to the loop variable `$f` and then executes the statement list with this variable set. At the end of the statement, `$f` will retain the last value that was assigned to it, which is the last value in the list. Compare this example to the `for` loop example at the end of the previous section. Because you don't have to manually deal with the loop counter and explicit indexing, this example is significantly simpler.

> **NOTE** In C#, the `foreach` loop variable is local to the body of the loop and is undefined outside of the loop. This isn't the case in PowerShell; the loop variable is simply another variable in the current scope. After the loop has finished executing, the variable is still visible and accessible outside the loop and will be set to the last element in the list. If you do want to have a locally scoped variable, you can do this with scriptblocks, which are discussed in detail in chapter 8.

Now let's use a variation of a previous example. Say you want to find out the number of text files in the current directory and the total length of those files. First you'll initialize two variables: `$c` to hold the count of the files and `$l` to hold the total length:

```
PS (1) > $c=0
PS (2) > $l=0
```

Next run the `foreach` statement:

```
PS (3) > foreach ($f in dir *.txt) {$c += 1; $l += $f.length }
```

Finally display the results accumulated in the variables:

```
PS (4) > $c
5
PS (5) > $l
105
PS (6) >
```

Let's look at the actual `foreach` statement in detail now. The `<pipeline>` part in this example is

```
dir *.txt
```

This produces a collection of `System.IO.FileInfo` objects representing the files in the current directory. The `foreach` statement loops over this collection, binding each object to the variable `$f` and then executing the loop body.

Evaluation order in the foreach loop

It's important to note that this statement doesn't stream the results of the pipeline. The pipeline to loop over is run to completion and only then does the loop body begin executing. Let's take a second to compare this behavior with the way the `ForEach-Object` cmdlet works. Using the `ForEach-Object` cmdlet, this statement would look like

```
dir *.txt | foreach-object { $c += 1; $l += $_.length }
```

In the case of the `ForEach-Object`, the statement body is executed as soon as each object is produced. In the `foreach` statement, all the objects are collected before the loop body begins to execute. This has two implications.

First, because in the `foreach` statement case all the objects are gathered at once, you need to have enough memory to hold all these objects. In the `ForEach-Object` case, only one object is read at a time, so less storage is required. From this, you'd think that `ForEach-Object` should always be preferred. In the bulk-read case, though, there are some optimizations that the `foreach` statement does that allow it to perform significantly faster than the `ForEach-Object` cmdlet. The result is a classic speed versus space trade-off. In practice, you rarely need to consider these issues, so use whichever seems most appropriate to the solution at hand.

> **NOTE** The `ForEach-Object` cmdlet is covered later on in this chapter. For Ruby language fans, `ForEach-Object` is effectively equivalent to the `.map()` operator.

The second difference is that, in the `ForEach-Object` case, the execution of the pipeline element generating the object is interleaved with the execution of the `ForEach-Object` cmdlet. In other words, the command generates one object at a time and then passes it to `foreach` for processing before generating the next element. This means that the statement list can affect how subsequent pipeline input objects are generated.

> **NOTE** Unlike traditional shells where each command is run in a separate process and can therefore run at the same time, in PowerShell they're alternating—the command on the left side runs and produces an object, and then the command on the right side runs.

Using the $foreach loop enumerator in the foreach statement

Executing the `foreach` statement also defines a special variable for the duration of the loop. This is the `$foreach` variable, and it's bound to the *loop enumerator*. (An enumerator is a .NET object that captures the current position in a sequence of objects. The `foreach` statement keeps track of where it is in the collection through the loop enumerator.) By manipulating the loop enumerator, you can skip forward in the loop. Here's an example:

```
PS (1) > foreach ($i in 1..10)
>> { [void] $foreach.MoveNext(); $i + $foreach.current }
>>
3
7
11
15
19
PS (2) >
```

In this example, the `foreach` loop iterates over the collection of numbers from 1 to 10. In the body of the loop, the enumerator is used to advance the loop to the next element. It does this by calling the `$foreach.MoveNext()` method and then retrieving the next value using `$foreach.current`. This lets you sum up each pair of numbers—(1,2), (3,4), and so on as the loop iterates.

> **NOTE** The `foreach` statement can be used to iterate over anything PowerShell considers enumerable. This typically includes anything that implements the .NET `IEnumerable` interface, but PowerShell adapts that slightly. In particular, there are some classes that implement `IEnumerable` that PowerShell doesn't consider enumerable. This includes strings and dictionaries or hashtables. Because PowerShell unravels collections freely, you don't want a string to suddenly be turned into a stream of characters or a hashtable to be shredded into a sequence of key-value pairs. Hashtables in particular are commonly used as lightweight (that is, typeless) objects in the PowerShell environment, so you need to preserve their scalar nature.

The value stored in `$foreach` is an instance of an object that implements the `[System.Collections.IEnumerator]` interface. Here's a quick example that shows you how to look at the members that are available on this object:

```
PS (1) > [System.Collections.IEnumerator].Getmembers()|foreach{"$_"}
Boolean MoveNext()
System.Object get_Current()
Void Reset()
System.Object Current
PS (2) >
```

The output of this statement shows the `Current` and `MoveNext()` members you've used. There's also a `Reset()` member that will reset the enumerator back to the start of the collection.

One final thing you need to know about the `foreach` statement is how it treats scalar objects. Because of the way pipelines work, you don't know ahead of time if the pipeline will return a collection or a single scalar object. In particular, if the pipeline returns a single object, you can't tell if it's returning a scalar or a collection consisting of one object. You can use the `@( ... )` construction described in chapter 5 to force an array interpretation, but this ambiguity is common enough that the `foreach` statement takes care of this by itself. A scalar object in the `foreach` statement is automatically treated as a one-element collection:

```
PS (2) > foreach ($i in "hi") {$i }
hi
```

In this example, the value to iterate over is the scalar string "hi". The loop executes exactly once, printing `hi`. This works great most of the time, but there's one "corner case" that can cause some problems, as you'll see in the next section.

The foreach loop and $null

Now here's something that really surprises (and sometimes irritates) people. What happens if the value to iterate over is `$null`? Let's find out:

```
PS (3) > foreach ($i in $null) { "executing" }
Executing
```

So the loop executes. This illustrates that PowerShell treats `$null` as a scalar value. Now compare this with the empty array:

```
PS (4) > foreach ($i in @()) { "executing" }
PS (5) >
```

This time it doesn't execute. The empty array is unambiguously a collection with no elements, which is quite different from a collection having one member whose value is `$null`. In other words, `@()` and `@($null)` aren't the same thing. For programmers who are used to `$null` being nothing, this is a jarring notion. So why does PowerShell work this way? Let's look at some more examples. First we'll consider an example where you pass in an array of three nulls:

```
PS {6) > foreach ($i in $null, $null, $null) {"hi"}
hi
hi
hi
```

The statement prints `hi` three times because there were three elements in the array. Now use an array of two elements

```
PS {7) > foreach ($i in $null, $null) {"hi"}
hi
hi
```

and it prints `hi` twice. Logically, if there's only one `$null`, it should loop exactly once

```
PS {8) > foreach ($i in $null) {"hi"}
hi
```

which is exactly what it does. PowerShell is deeply consistent, even in this case. This is not, though, the expected or even desired behavior in a `foreach` loop in many cases, so here's how to work around it. You can use the `Write-Output` cmdlet (aliased to `write`) to preprocess the collection you want to iterate over. If the argument to `Write-Output` is `$null`, it doesn't write anything to the output pipe:

```
PS {9) > foreach ($i in write $null) {"hi"}
PS {10) >
```

And you see that the loop didn't execute. So let's run through the previous example with the arrays of nulls. First, with three nulls

```
PS {10) > foreach ($i in write $null,$null,$null) {"hi"}
hi
hi
hi
```

and you get three iterations. Now with two

```
PS {11) > foreach ($i in write $null,$null) {"hi"}
hi
hi
```

and you get two iterations. Finally, with one `$null`

```
PS {12) > foreach ($i in write $null) {"hi"}
PS {13) >
```

and this time the loop doesn't execute. Although this is inconsistent behavior, it matches user expectations and is a good trick to have in your toolkit.

> **NOTE** In the first edition of this book, I called this a *corner case* and suggested that most readers didn't need to know about this. I was wrong. It comes up on a surprisingly regular basis. In fact, the workaround using `Write-Output` was suggested by a user, not by the PowerShell team. Let's hear it for the community!

On that note, let's move on to a slightly different topic and talk about `break`, `continue`, and using labeled loops to exit out of nested loop statements.

6.3 LABELS, BREAK, AND CONTINUE

In this section, we'll discuss how to do nonstructured exits from the various looping statements using the `break` and `continue` statements shown in figure 6.9. We'll also cover *labeled loops* and how they work with `break` and `continue`. But first, some history.

In the dawn of computer languages, there was only one flow-control statement: `goto`. Although it was simple, it also resulted in programs that were hard to

The `break` and `continue` statements

```
break                    break <label>
continue                 continue <label>
```

Figure 6.9 The PowerShell `break` and `continue` statements, which may optionally take a label indicating which loop statement to break to

understand and maintain. Then along came structured programming. Structured programming introduced the idea of loops with single entry and exit points. This made programs much easier to understand and therefore maintain. Constructs such as `while` loops and `if/then/else` statements made it simpler to write programs that are easy to follow.

> **NOTE** For the academically inclined reader, Wikipedia.org has a nice discussion on the topic of structured programming.

So structured programming is great—that is, until you have to exit from a set of deeply nested `while` loops. That's when pure structured programming leads to pathologically convoluted logic because you have to litter your program with Boolean variables and conditionals trying to achieve the flow of control you need. This is when being a little "impure" and allowing the use of unstructured flow-control elements (including the infamous `goto` statement) is useful. Now, PowerShell doesn't actually have a `goto` statement. Instead, it has `break` and `continue` statements and *labeled loops*. Let's look at some simple examples. Here's a `while` loop that stops counting at 5:

```
PS (1) > $i=0; while ($true) { if ($i++ -ge 5) { break } $i }
1
2
3
4
5
PS (2) >
```

Notice in this example that the `while` loop condition is simply `$true`. Obviously, this loop would run forever were it not for the `break` statement. As soon as `$i` hits 5, the `break` statement is executed and the loop terminates. Now let's look at the `continue` statement. In this example, you have a `foreach` loop that loops over the numbers from 1 to 10:

```
PS (1) > foreach ($i in 1..10)
>> {
>>     if ($i % 2)
>>     {
>>         continue
>>     }
>>     $i
>> }
>>
2
4
6
8
10
PS (2) >
```

If the number isn't evenly divisible by 2, then the `continue` statement is executed. Where the `break` statement immediately terminates the loop, the `continue` statement causes the flow of execution to jump back to the beginning of the loop and move on to the next iteration. The end result is that only even numbers are emitted. The `continue` statement skips the line that would have printed the odd numbers.

So the basic `break` and `continue` statements can handle flow control in a single loop. But what about nested loops, which was the real problem you wanted to address? This is where *labels* come in. Before the initial keyword on any of PowerShell's loop statements, you can add a label naming that statement. Then you can use the `break` and `continue` keywords to jump to that statement. Here's a simple example:

```
:outer while (1)
{
    while(1)
    {
        break outer;
    }
}
```

In this example, without the `break` statement, the loop would repeat forever. Instead, the `break` will take you out of both the inner and outer loops.

> **NOTE** In PowerShell, labeled `break` and `continue` statements have one rather strange but occasionally useful characteristic: they'll continue to search up the calling stack until a matching label is found. This search will even cross script and function call boundaries. This means that a break inside a function inside a script can transfer control to an enclosing loop in the calling script. This allows for wide-ranging transfer of control. This will make more sense when you get to chapter 7, where functions are introduced.

One last thing to know about the `break` and `continue` statements—the name of the label to jump to is actually an expression, not a constant value. You could, for example, use a variable to name the target of the statement. Let's try this out. First set up a variable to hold the target name:

```
PS (1) > $target = "foo"
```

Now use it in a loop. In this loop, if the least significant bit in the value stored in `$i` is 1 (yet another way to test for odd numbers), you skip to the next iteration of the loop named by `$target`

```
PS (2) > :foo foreach ($i in 1..10) {
>> if ($i -band 1) { continue $target } $i
>> }
>>
2
4
6
8
10
PS (3) >
```

which produces a list of the even numbers in the range 1..10.

The switch statement

```
switch ( <expr> ) { <pattern1> { <statements> } <pattern2> { <statements> } }
switch ( <expr> ) { <pattern1> { <statements> } default { <statements> } }
```

Figure 6.10 The PowerShell `switch` statement syntax

At this point, we've covered all of the basic PowerShell flow-control statements, as well as using labels and `break`/`continue` to do nonlocal flow-control transfers. Now let's move on to the `switch` statement, which in PowerShell combines both looping and branching capabilities.

6.4 THE SWITCH STATEMENT

The `switch` statement, shown in figure 6.10, is the most powerful statement in the PowerShell language. This statement combines pattern matching, branching, and iteration all into a single control structure. This is why it gets its own section instead of being covered under either loops or conditionals.

At the most basic level, the `switch` statement in PowerShell is similar to the `switch` statement in many other languages—it's a way of selecting an action based on a particular value. But the PowerShell `switch` statement has a number of additional capabilities. It can be used as a looping construct where it processes a collection of objects instead of just a single object. It supports the advanced pattern matching features that you've seen with the `-match` and `-like` operators. (How the pattern is matched depends on the flags specified to the `switch` statement.) Finally, it can be used to efficiently process an entire file in a single statement.

6.4.1 Basic use of the switch statement

Let's begin by exploring the basic functions of the `switch` statement. See figure 6.11 for a look at its syntax in detail.

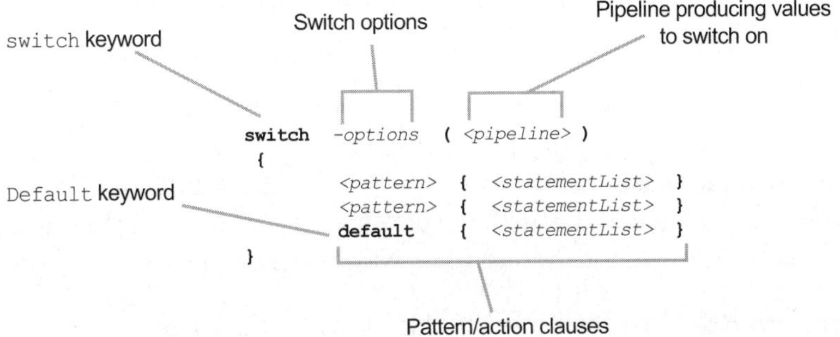

Figure 6.11 The PowerShell `switch` statement syntax. The switch options control how matching is done. These options are `-regex`, `-wildcard`, `-match`, and `-case`. The pipeline produces values to switch on; alternatively, you can specify the sequence `-file <expr>` instead of `( <pipeline> )`. All matching pattern/action clauses are executed; the default clause is executed only if there are no other matches.

This is a pretty complex construct, so let's start by looking at the simplest form of the statement. Here's the basic example:

```
PS (1) > switch (1) { 1 { "One" } 2 { "two" } }
One
```

The value to switch on is in the parentheses after the `switch` keyword. In this example, it's the number 1. That value is matched against the pattern in each clause and *all matching actions are taken*. You'll see how to change this in a second.

In this example, the switch value matches 1 so that clause emits the string "one". Of course, if you change the switch value to 2, you get

```
PS (2) > switch (2) { 1 { "One" } 2 { "two" } }
two
```

Now try a somewhat different example. In this case, you have two clauses that match the switch value:

```
PS (4) > switch (2) { 1 { "One" } 2 { "two" } 2 {"another 2"} }
two
another 2
```

You can see that both of these actions are executed. As we stated earlier, the `switch` statement executes all clauses that match the switch value. If you want to stop at the first match, you use the `break` statement:

```
PS (5) > switch (2) {1 {"One"} 2 {"two"; break} 2 {"another 2"}}
two
```

This causes the matching process to stop after the first matching statement was executed. But what happens if no statements match? Well, the statement quietly returns nothing:

```
PS (6) > switch (3) { 1 { "One" } 2 { "two"; break } 2 {"another 2"} }
PS (7) >
```

To specify a default action, you can use the `default` clause:

```
PS (7) > switch (3) { 1 { "One" } 2 { "two" } default {"default"} }
default
PS (8) > switch (2) { 1 { "One" } 2 { "two" } default {"default"} }
Two
```

In this example, when the switch value is 3, no clause matches and the default clause is run. But when there's a match, the default isn't run, as it's not considered a match. This covers the basic mode of operation. Now let's move on to more advanced features.

6.4.2 Using wildcard patterns with the switch statement

By default, the matching clauses make an equivalence comparison against the object in the clause. If the matching object is a string, the check is done in a case-insensitive way, as you see in the next example:

```
PS (1) > switch ('abc') {'abc' {"one"} 'ABC' {"two"}}
one
two
```

The switch value "abc" in this example was matched by both "abc" and "ABC". You can change this behavior by specifying the `-casesensitive` option:

```
PS (2) > switch -case ('abc') {'abc' {"one"} 'ABC' {"two"}}
one
```

Now the match occurs only when the case of the elements match.

> **NOTE** In this example, we only used the prefix `-case` instead of the full option string. In fact, only the first letter of the option is checked.

Next, let's discuss the next `switch` option, the `-wildcard` option. When `-wildcard` is specified, the switch value is converted into a string and the tests are conducted using the wildcard pattern. (Wildcard patterns were discussed in chapter 4 with the `-like` operator.) This is shown in the next example:

```
PS (4) > switch -wildcard ('abc') {a* {"astar"} *c {"starc"}}
astar
starc
```

In this example, the pattern `a*` matches anything that begins with the letter "a" and the pattern `*c` matches anything that ends with the letter "c." Again, all matching clauses are executed.

There's one more element to mention at this point. When a clause is matched, the element that matched is assigned to the variable `$_` before running the clause. This is always done, even in the simple examples we discussed earlier, but it wasn't interesting because you were doing exact comparisons so you already knew what matched. Once you introduce patterns, it's much more useful to be able to get at the object that matched. For example, if you're matching against filename extensions, you'd want to be able to get at the full filename to do any processing on that file. We'll look at some more practical uses for this feature in later sections. For now, here's a basic example that shows how this match works:

```
PS (5) > switch -wildcard ('abc') {a* {"a*: $_"} *c {"*c: $_"}}
a*: abc
*c: abc
```

In the result strings, you can see that `$_` was replaced by the full string of the actual switch value.

6.4.3 Using regular expressions with the switch statement

As we discussed in chapter 4, the wildcard patterns, while useful, have limited capabilities. For more sophisticated pattern matching, you used regular expressions.

Regular expressions are available in the switch statement through the -regex flag. Let's rewrite the previous example using regular expressions instead of wildcards:

```
PS (6) > switch -regex ('abc') {^a {"a*: $_"} 'c$' {"*c: $_"}}
a*: abc
*c: abc
```

As you see, $_ is still bound to the entire matching key. But one of the most powerful features of regular expressions is submatches. A submatch, or *capture*, is a portion of the regular expression that's enclosed in parentheses, as discussed in chapter 4 with the -match operator. With the -match operator, the submatches are made available through the $matches variable. This same variable is also used in the switch statement. The next example shows how this works:

```
PS (8) > switch -regex ('abc') {'(^a)(.*$)' {$matches}}

Key                            Value
---                            -----
2                              bc
1                              a
0                              abc
```

In the result shown here, $matches[0] is the overall key; $matches[1] is the first submatch, in this case the leading "a"; and $matches[2] is the remainder of the string. As always, matching is case insensitive by default, but you can specify the -case option to make it case sensitive, as shown here:

```
PS (9) > switch -regex ('abc') {'(^A)(.*$)' {$matches}}

Key                            Value
---                            -----
2                              bc
1                              a
0                              abc

PS (10) > switch -regex -case  ('abc') {'(^A)(.*$)' {$matches}}
```

In the first command, you changed the match pattern from a to A and the match still succeeded because case was ignored. In the second command, you added the -case flag and this time the match didn't succeed.

So far we've discussed three ways to control how matching against the switch value works—in other words, three matching modes (actually six, because the -case flag can be used with any of the previous three). But what if you need something a bit more sophisticated than a simple pattern match? The switch statement lets you handle this by specifying an expression in braces instead of a pattern. In the next example, you specify two expressions that check against the switch value. Again the switch value is made available through the variable $_:

```
PS (11) > switch (5) {
>> {$_ -gt 3} {"greater than three"}
>> {$_ -gt 7} {"greater than 7"}}
```

```
>>
greater than three
PS (12) > switch (8) {
>> {$_ -gt 3} {"greater than three"}
>> {$_ -gt 7} {"greater than 7"}}
>>
greater than three
greater than 7
PS (13) >
```

In the first statement, only the first clause was triggered because 5 is greater than 3 but less than 7. In the second statement, both clauses fired.

You can use these matching clauses with any of the other three matching modes:

```
PS (13) > switch (8) {
>> {$_ -gt 3} {"greater than three"}
>> 8 {"Was $_"}}
>>
greater than three
Was 8
```

The first expression, `{$_ -gt 3}`, evaluated to true so "greater than three" was printed, and the switch value matched 8 so "Was 8" also printed (where `$_` was replaced by the matching value).

Now you have exact matches, pattern matches, conditional matches, and the default clause. But what about the switch value itself? So far, all the examples have been simple scalar values. What happens if you specify a collection of values? This is where the `switch` statement acts like a form of loop.

> **NOTE** `switch` works like the other looping statements in that the expression in the parentheses is fully evaluated before it starts iterating over the individual values.

Let's look at another example where you specify an array of values:

```
PS (2) > switch(1,2,3,4,5,6) {
>> {$_ % 2} {"Odd $_"; continue}
>> 4 {"FOUR"}
>> default {"Even $_"}
>> }
>>
Odd 1
Even 2
Odd 3
FOUR
Odd 5
Even 6
```

In this example, the switch value is `1,2,3,4,5,6`. The `switch` statement loops over the collection, testing each element against all the clauses. The first clause returns "Odd `$_`" if the current switch element isn't evenly divisible by 2. The next clause prints out "FOUR" if the value is 4. The default clause prints out "Even $_" if the number is even. Note the use of continue in the first clause. This tells the switch statement to stop matching any further clauses and move on to the next element in the collection. In this instance, the switch statement is working in the same way that the continue statement works in the other loops. It skips the remainder of the body of the loop and continues on with the next loop iteration. What happens if you used break instead of continue?

```
PS (3) > switch(1,2,3,4,5,6) {
>> {$_ % 2} {"Odd $_"; break}
>> 4 {"FOUR"}
>> default {"Even $_"}
>> }
>>
Odd 1
```

As with the other loops, break doesn't just skip the remainder of the current iteration; it terminates the overall loop processing. (If you want to continue iterating, use continue instead. More on that later.)

Of course, iterating over a fixed collection isn't very interesting. In fact, you can use a pipeline in the switch value, as the next example shows. In this example, you want to count the number of DLLs, text files, and log files in the directory c:\windows. First you initialize the counter variables:

```
PS (1) > $dll=$txt=$log=0
```

Now you run the actual switch statement. This switch statement uses wildcard patterns to match the extensions on the filenames. The associated actions increment a variable for each extension type:

```
PS (2) > switch -wildcard (dir c:\windows)
>> {*.dll {$dll++} *.txt {$txt++} *.log {$log++}}
```

Once you have the totals, display them:

```
PS (3) > "dlls: $dll text files: $txt log files: $log"
dlls: 6 text files: 9 log files: 120
```

Note that in this example the pipeline element is being matched against every clause. Because a file can't have more than one extension, this doesn't affect the output, but it does affect performance somewhat. It's faster to include a continue statement after each clause so the matching process stops as soon as the first match succeeds.

Here's something else we glossed over earlier in our discussion of $_—it always contains the object that was matched against. This is important to understand when you're using the pattern matching modes of the switch statement. The pattern matches create a string representation of the object to match against, but $_ is still bound to the original object. Here's an example that illustrates this point. This is basically the same as the previous example, but this time, instead of counting the number of files, you want to calculate the total size of all the files having a particular extension. Here are the revised commands:

```
PS (1) > $dll=$txt=$log=0
PS (2) > switch -wildcard (dir) {
>> *.dll {$dll+= $_.length; continue}
>> *.txt {$txt+=$_.length; continue}
>> *.log {$log+=$_.length; continue}
>> }
>>
PS (3) > "dlls: $dll text files: $txt log files: $log"
dlls: 166913 text files: 1866711 log files: 6669437
PS (4) >
```

Notice how you're using `$_.length` to get the length of the matching file object. If `$_` were bound to the matching string, you'd be counting the lengths of the filenames instead of the lengths of the actual files.

6.4.4 Processing files with the switch statement

There's one last mode of operation for the `switch` statement to discuss: the `-file` option. Instead of specifying an expression to iterate over as the switch value, the `-file` option allows you to name a file to process. Here's an example that processes the Windows update log file. Again start by initializing the counter variables:

```
PS (1) > $au=$du=$su=0
```

Next use the `-regex` and `-file` options to access and scan the file WindowsUpdate.log, and check for update requests from Windows Update, Windows Defender, and SMS:

```
PS (2) > switch -regex -file c:\windows\windowsupdate.log {
>> 'START.*Finding updates.*AutomaticUpdates' {$au++}
>> 'START.*Finding updates.*Defender' {$du++}
>> 'START.*Finding updates.*SMS' {$su++}
>> }
>>
```

Print the results:

```
PS (3) > "Automatic:$au Defender:$du SMS:$su"
Automatic:195 Defender:10 SMS:34
```

Now it's possible to do basically the same thing by using `Get-Content` or even the file system name trick you learned in chapter 4:

```
PS (4) > $au=$du=$su=0
PS (5) > switch -regex (${c:windowsupdate.log}) {
>> 'START.*Finding updates.*AutomaticUpdates' {$au++}
>> 'START.*Finding updates.*Defender' {$du++}
>> 'START.*Finding updates.*SMS' {$su++}
>> }
>>
PS (6) > "Automatic:$au Defender:$du SMS:$su"
Automatic:195 Defender:10 SMS:34
```

This code uses `${c:windowsupdate.log}` to access the file content instead of `-file`. So why have the `-file` option? There are two reasons.

The -file operation reads one line at a time, so it uses less memory than the Get-Content cmdlet, which has to read the entire file into memory before processing. Also, because -file is part of the PowerShell language, the interpreter can do some optimizations, which gives -file performance advantages.

So, overall, the -file option can potentially give you both speed and space advantages in some cases (the space advantage typically being the more significant, and therefore the more important of the two). When your task involves processing a lot of text files, the -file switch can be a useful tool.

6.4.5 Using the $switch loop enumerator in the switch statement

One more point: just as the foreach loop used $foreach to hold the loop enumerator, the switch statement uses $switch to hold the switch loop enumerator. This is useful in a common pattern—processing a list of options. Say you have a list of options where the option -b takes an argument and -a, -c, and -d don't. You'll write a switch statement to process a list of these arguments. First set up a list of test options. For convenience, start with a string and then use the -split operator to break it into an array of elements:

```
PS (1) > $options= -split "-a -b Hello -c"
```

Next initialize the set of variables that will correspond to the flags:

```
PS (2) > $a=$c=$d=$false
PS (3) > $b=$null
```

Now you can write your switch statement. The interesting clause is the one that handles -b. This clause uses the enumerator stored in $switch to advance the item being processed to the next element in the list. Use a cast to [void] to discard the return value from the call to $switch.movenext()(more on that later). Then use $switch.current to retrieve the next value and store it in $b. The loop continues processing the remaining arguments in the list.

```
PS (4) > switch ($options)
>> {
>> '-a' { $a=$true }
>> '-b' { [void] $switch.movenext(); $b= $switch.current }
>> '-c' { $c=$true }
>> '-d' { $d=$true }
>> }
>>
```

The last step in this example is to print the arguments in the list to make sure they were all set properly:

```
PS (5) > "a=$a b=$b c=$c d=$d"
a=True b=Hello c=True d=False
PS (6) >
```

You see that $a and $c are true, $b contains the argument "Hello", and $d is still false because it wasn't in your list of test options. The option list has been processed correctly.

NOTE This isn't a robust example because it's missing all error handing. In a complete example, you'd have a default clause that generated errors for unexpected options. Also, in the clause that processes the argument for `-b`, rather than discarding the result of `MoveNext()` it should check the result and generate an error if it returns false. This would indicate that there are no more elements in the collection, so `-b` would be missing its mandatory argument.

This finishes the last of the flow-control statements in the PowerShell language, but as you saw at the beginning of this chapter, there's another way to do selection and iteration in PowerShell by using cmdlets. In the next section, we'll go over a couple of the cmdlets that are a standard part of the PowerShell distribution. These cmdlets let you control the flow of your script in a manner similar to the flow-control statements. (In later sections, we'll look at how you can create your own specialized flow-control elements in PowerShell.)

6.5 FLOW CONTROL USING CMDLETS

PowerShell's control statements are part of the language proper, but there are also some cmdlets, shown in figure 6.12, that can be used to accomplish similar kinds of things.

Flow-control cmdlets

```
... | ForEach-Object <scriptBlock>
... | ForEach-Object -Begin <scriptBlock> -Process <scriptBlock> -End <scriptBlock>
... | Where-Object <scriptBlock>
```

Figure 6.12 Flow-control cmdlets

These cmdlets use blocks of PowerShell script enclosed in braces to provide the "body" of the control statement. These pieces of script are called *scriptblocks* and are described in detail in chapter 8. The two most frequent flow-control cmdlets that you'll encounter are `ForEach-Object` and `Where-Object`.

6.5.1 The ForEach-Object cmdlet

The `ForEach-Object` cmdlet operates on each object in a pipeline in much the same way that the `foreach` statement operates on the set of values that are provided to it. For example, here's a `foreach` statement that prints the size of each text file in the current directory:

```
PS (1) > foreach ($f in dir *.txt) { $f.length }
48
889
23723
328
279164
```

Using the ForEach-Object cmdlet, the same task can be accomplished this way:

```
PS (2) > dir *.txt | foreach-object {$_.length}
48
889
23723
328
279164
```

The results are the same, so what's the difference? One obvious difference is that you don't have to create a new variable name to hold the loop value. The automatic variable $_ is used as the loop variable.

> **NOTE** Automatic variables are common in scripting languages. These variables aren't directly assigned to in scripts. Instead, they are set as the side effect of an operation. One of the earlier examples of this is in AWK. When a line is read in AWK, the text of the line is automatically assigned to $0. The line is also split into fields. The first field is placed in $1, the second is in $2, and so on. The Perl language is probably the most significant user of automatic variables. In fact, as mentioned previously, Perl inspired the use of $_ in PowerShell. Automatic variables can help reduce the size of a script, but they can also make a script hard to read and difficult to reuse because *your* use of automatics may collide with *mine*. From a design perspective, our approach with automatic variables follows the salt curve. A little salt makes everything taste better. Too much salt makes food inedible. The language design team tried to keep the use of automatics in PowerShell at the "just right" level. Of course, this is always a subjective judgment. Some people really like salt.

A more subtle difference, as discussed previously, is that the loop is processed one object at a time. In a normal foreach loop, the entire list of values is generated before a single value is processed. In the ForEach-Object pipeline, each object is generated and then passed to the cmdlet for processing.

The ForEach-Object cmdlet has an advantage over the foreach loop in the amount of space being used at a particular time. For example, if you're processing a large file, the foreach loop would have to load the entire file into memory before processing. When you use the ForEach-Object cmdlet, the file will be processed one line at a time. This significantly reduces the amount of memory needed to accomplish a task.

You'll end up using the ForEach-Object cmdlet a lot in command lines to perform simple transformations on objects (you've already used it in many examples so far). Given the frequency of use, there are two standard aliases for this cmdlet. The first one is (obviously) foreach. But wait a second—didn't we say earlier in this chapter that foreach is a keyword and keywords can't be aliased? This is true, but remember, keywords are only special when they're the first unquoted word in a statement (in other words, not a string). If they appear anywhere else (for example, as an argument or in the middle of a pipeline), they're just another command with no special meaning to the language. Here's another way to think about it: the first word in a statement is the key that the PowerShell interpreter uses to decide what kind of statement it's processing, hence the term "keyword."

This positional constraint is how the interpreter can distinguish between the keyword `foreach`

```
foreach ($i in 1..10) { $i }
```

and the aliased cmdlet `foreach`:

```
1..10 | foreach {$_}
```

When `foreach` is the first word in a statement, it's a keyword; otherwise it's the name of a command.

Now let's look at the second alias. Even though `foreach` is significantly shorter than `ForEach-Object`, there have still been times when users wanted it to be even shorter.

> **NOTE** Users wanted to get rid of this notation entirely and have `foreach` be implied by an open brace following the pipe symbol. This would have made about half of PowerShell users very happy. Unfortunately, the other half were adamant that the implied operation be `Where-Object` instead of `ForEach-Object`.

Where extreme brevity is required, there's a second built-in alias that's simply the percent sign (`%`). Now readers are saying, "You told us the percent sign is an operator!" Well, that's true, *but only when it's used as a binary operator*. If it appears as the first symbol in a statement, it has no special meaning, so you can use it as an alias for `ForEach-Object`. As with keywords, operators are also context sensitive.

The `%` alias you write results in very concise (but occasionally hard-to-read) statements such as the following, which prints the numbers from 1 to 5, times 2:

```
PS (1) > 1..5|%{$_*2}
2
4
6
8
10
PS (2) >
```

Clearly this construction is great for interactive use where brevity is important, but it probably shouldn't be used when writing scripts. The issue is that `ForEach-Object` is so useful that a single-character symbol for it, one that is easy to distinguish, is invaluable for experienced PowerShell users. But unlike the word `foreach`, `%` isn't immediately meaningful to new users. So this notation is great for "conversational"

PowerShell, but generally terrible for scripts that you want other people to be able to read and maintain.

The last thing to know about the ForEach-Object cmdlet is that it can take multiple scriptblocks. If three scriptblocks are specified, the first one is run before any objects are processed, the second is run once for each object, and the last is run after all objects have been processed. This is good for conducting accumulation-type operations. Here's another variation that sums the number of handles used by the service host svchost processes:

```
PS (3) > gps svchost |%{$t=0}{$t+=$_.handles}{$t}
3238
```

The standard alias for Get-Process is gps. This is used to get a list of processes where the process name matches svchost. These process objects are then piped into ForEach-Object, where the handle counts are summed up in $t and then emitted in the last scriptblock. This example uses the % alias to show how concise these expressions can be. In an interactive environment, brevity is important.

And here's something to keep in mind when using ForEach-Object. The ForEach-Object cmdlet works like all cmdlets: if the output object is a collection, it gets unraveled. One way to suppress this behavior is to use the unary comma operator. For example, in the following, you assign $a an array of two elements, the second of which is a nested array:

```
PS (1) > $a =  1,(2,3)
```

When you check the length, you see that it is 2 as expected

```
PS (2) > $a.length
2
```

and the second element is still an array:

```
PS (3) > $a[1]
2
3
```

But if you run it through ForEach-Object, you'll find that the length of the result is now 3, and the second element in the result is the number 2:

```
PS (4) > $b = $a | foreach { $_ }
PS (5) > $b.length
3
PS (6) > $b[2]
2
```

In effect, the result has been "flattened." But if you use the unary comma operator before the $_ variable, the result has the same structure as the original array:

```
PS (7) > $b = $a | foreach { , $_ }
PS (8) > $b.length
2
PS (9) > $b[1]
```

```
2
3
```

When chaining foreach cmdlets, you need to repeat the pattern at each stage:

```
PS (7) > $b = $a | foreach { , $_ } | foreach { , $_ }
PS (8) > $b.length
2
PS (9) > $b[1]
2
3
```

Why don't you just preserve the structure as you pass the elements through instead of unraveling by default? Well, both behaviors are, in fact, useful. Consider the following example, which returns a list of loaded module names:

```
Get-Process | %{$_.modules} | sort -u modulename
```

Here the unraveling is exactly what you want. When we were designing PowerShell, we considered both cases; and in applications, on average, unraveling by default was usually what we needed. Unfortunately, it does present something of a cognitive bump that surprises users learning to use PowerShell.

Using the return statement with ForEach-Object

Here's another tidbit of information about something that occasionally causes problems. Although the `ForEach-Object` cmdlet looks like a PowerShell statement, remember that it is in fact a command and the body of code it executes is a scriptblock, also known as an *anonymous function*. (By anonymous, we just mean that we haven't given it a name. Again, we cover this in detail in chapter 11.) The important thing to know is that the `return` statement (see chapter 7), when used in the scriptblock argument to `ForEach-Object`, only exits from the `ForEach-Object` scriptblock, not from the function or script that is calling `ForEach-Object`. So, if you do want to return out of a function or script in a `foreach` loop, either use the `foreach` statement where the `return` will work as desired, or use the nonlocal labeled `break` statement discussed earlier in this chapter.

How ForEach-Object processes its arguments

Let's talk for a moment about how the `ForEach-Object` cmdlet processes its argument scriptblocks. A reader of the first edition of this book observed what he thought was an inconsistency between how the cmdlet is documented and how the following example behaves:

```
$words | ForEach-Object {$h=@{}} {$h[$_] += 1}
```

The help text for the cmdlet (use `help ForEach-Object -Full` to see this text) says that the `-Process` parameter is the only positional parameter and that it's in position 1. Therefore, according to the help file, since the `-Begin` parameter isn't positional, the example shouldn't work. This led the reader to assume that either there was an error in the help file, or that he misunderstood the idea of positional parameters.

In fact the help file is correct (because the cmdlet information is extracted from the code) but the way it works is tricky.

If you look at the signature of the `-Process` parameter, you'll see that, yes, it is positional, but it also takes a collection of scriptblocks and receives all remaining unbound arguments. So, in the case of

```
dir | foreach {$sum=0} {$sum++} {$sum}
```

the `-Process` parameter is getting an array of three scriptblocks, whereas `-Begin` and `-End` are empty. Now here's the trick. If `-Begin` is empty and `-Process` has more than two scriptblocks in the collection, then the first one is treated as the `-Begin` scriptblock and the second one is treated as the `-Process` scriptblock. If `-Begin` is specified but `-End` is not and there are two scriptblocks, then the first one is treated as the `Process` clause and the second one is the `End` clause. Finally, if both `-Begin` and `-End` are specified, the remaining arguments will be treated as multiple `Process` clauses. This allows

```
dir | foreach {$sum=0} {$sum++} {$sum}
dir | foreach -begin {$sum=0} {$sum++} {$sum}
dir | foreach {$sum=0} {$sum++} -end {$sum}
dir | foreach -begin {$sum=0} {$sum++} -end {$sum}
```

and

```
dir | foreach -begin {$sum=0} -process {$sum++} -end {$sum}
```

to all work as expected.

On that note, we're finished with our discussion of `ForEach-Object`. We'll touch on it again in chapter 8 when we discuss scriptblocks, but for now, let's move on to the other flow-control cmdlet commonly used in PowerShell (which, by the way, also uses scriptblocks—you may detect a theme here).

6.5.2 The Where-Object cmdlet

The other common flow-control cmdlet is the `Where-Object cmdlet`. This cmdlet is used to select objects from a stream, kind of like a simple `switch` cmdlet. It takes each pipeline element it receives as input, executes its scriptblock (see!) argument, passing in the current pipeline element as `$_`, and then, if the scriptblock evaluates to true, the element is written to the pipeline. We'll show this with yet another way to select even numbers from a sequence of integers:

```
PS (4) > 1..10 | where {-not ($_ -band 1)}
2
4
6
8
10
```

The scriptblock enclosed in the braces receives each pipeline element, one after another. If the least significant bit in the element is 1, then the scriptblock returns the logical complement of that value (`$false`) and that element is discarded. If the least significant bit is 0, the logical complement of that is `$true` and the element is written to the output pipeline. Notice that the common alias for `Where-Object` is simply `where`. And, as with `ForEach-Object`, because this construction is so commonly used interactively, there's an additional alias, which is simply the question mark (`?`). This allows the previous example to be written as

```
PS (5) > 1..10|?{!($_-band 1)}
2
4
6
8
10
```

Again, this is brief, but it looks like the cat walked across the keyboard (trust me on this one). So, as before, although this is fine for interactive use, it isn't recommended in scripts because it's hard to understand and maintain. As another, more compelling example of "Software by Cats," here's a pathological example that combines elements from the last few chapters—type casts, operators, and the flow-control cmdlets—to generate a list of strings of even-numbered letters in the alphabet, where the length of the string matches the ordinal number in the alphabet ("A" is 1, "B" is 2, and so on):

```
PS (1) > 1..26|?{!($_-band 1)}|%{[string][char]([int][char]'A'+$_-1)*$_}
>>
BB
DDDD
FFFFFF
HHHHHHHH
JJJJJJJJJJ
LLLLLLLLLLLL
NNNNNNNNNNNNNN
PPPPPPPPPPPPPPPP
RRRRRRRRRRRRRRRRRR
TTTTTTTTTTTTTTTTTTTT
VVVVVVVVVVVVVVVVVVVVVV
XXXXXXXXXXXXXXXXXXXXXXXX
ZZZZZZZZZZZZZZZZZZZZZZZZZZ
PS (2) >
```

The output is fairly self-explanatory, but the code isn't. Figuring out how this works is left as an exercise to the reader and as a cautionary tale not to foist this sort of rubbish on unsuspecting coworkers. They know where you live.

Where-Object and Get-Content's -ReadCount Parameter

On occasion, a question comes up about the `Get-Content` cmdlet and how its `-ReadCount` parameter works. This can be an issue particularly when using this cmdlet and parameter with `Where-Object` to filter the output of `Get-Content`. The issue comes up when the read count is greater than 1. This causes PowerShell to act as if some of the objects returned from `Get-Content` are being skipped and affects both

ForEach-Object and Where-Object. After all, these cmdlets are supposed to process or filter the input one object at a time and this isn't what appears to be happening.

Here's what's going on. Unfortunately the -ReadCount parameter has a confusing name. From the PowerShell user's perspective, it has nothing to do with reading. What it does is control the number for records *written* to the next pipeline element, in this case Where-Object or ForEach-Object. The following examples illustrate how this works. In these examples, you'll use a simple text file named test.txt, which contains 10 lines of text and the ForEach-Object cmdlet (through its alias %) to count the length of each object being passed down the pipeline. You'll use the @(...) construct to guarantee that you're always treating $_ as an array. Here are the examples with -readcount varying from 1 to 4:

```
PS (119) > gc test.txt -ReadCount 1 | % { @($_).count } | select -fir 1
1
PS (120) > gc test.txt -ReadCount 2 | % { @($_).count } | select -fir 1
2
PS (121) > gc test.txt -ReadCount 3 | % { @($_).count } | select -fir 1
3
PS (122) > gc test.txt -ReadCount 4 | % { @($_).count } | select -fir 1
4
```

In each case where -ReadCount is greater than 1, the variable $_ is set to a *collection* of objects where the object count of that collection is equivalent to the value specified by -ReadCount. In another example, you'll use ForEach-Object to filter the pipeline:

```
PS (127) > gc test.txt -read 5 | ? {$_ -like '*'} | % { $_.count }
5
5
```

You can see that the filter result contains two collections of 5 objects each written to the pipeline for a total of 10 objects. Now use ForEach-Object and the if statement to filter the list:

```
PS (128) > (gc test.txt -read 10 | % {if ($_ -match '.') {$_}} |
>>> Measure-Object).count
>>>
10
```

This time you see a count of 10 because the value of $_ in the ForEach-Object cmdlet is unraveled when written to the output pipe. And now let's look at one final example using Where-Object:

```
PS (130) > (gc test.txt -read 4 | %{$_} | where {$_ -like '*a*'} |
>>> Measure-Object).count
>>>
10
```

Here you've inserted one more ForEach-Object command between the gc and the Where-Object, which simply unravels the collections in $_ and so you again see a count of 10.

NOTE Here's the annoying thing: from the `Get-Content` developer's perspective, it actually *is* doing a read of `-ReadCount` objects from the provider. `Get-Content` reads `-ReadCount` objects and then writes them as a single object to the pipeline instead of unraveling them. (I suspect that this is a bug that's turned into a feature.) Anyway, the name makes perfect sense to the developer and absolutely no sense to the user. This is why developers always have to be aware of the user's perspective even if it doesn't precisely match the implementation details.

In summary, whenever `-ReadCount` is set to a value greater than 1, usually for performance reasons, object collections are sent through the pipeline to `Where-Object` instead of individual objects. As a result, you have to take extra steps to deal with unraveling the batched collections of objects.

At this point we've covered the two main flow-control cmdlets in detail. We've discussed how they work, how they can be used, and some of the benefits (and pitfalls) you'll encounter when using them. An important point to note is that there's nothing special about these cmdlets—they can be implemented by anyone and require no special access to the inner workings of the PowerShell engine. This is a characteristic we'll explore in later chapters where you'll see how you can take advantage of it. In the meantime, let's look at one final feature of the PowerShell language: the ability to use all these statements we've been talking about as expressions that return values. Although not unique to PowerShell, this feature may seem a bit unusual to people who are used to working with languages like VBScript or C#. Let's take a look.

6.6 STATEMENTS AS VALUES

Let's return to something we discussed a bit earlier when we introduced subexpressions in chapter 5—namely, the difference between statements and expressions. In general, statements don't return values, but if they're used as part of a subexpression (or a function or script as you'll see later on), they do return a result. This is best illustrated with an example. Assume that you didn't have the range operator and wanted to generate an array of numbers from 1 to 10. Here's the traditional approach you might use in a language such as C#:

```
PS (1) > $result = new-object System.Collections.ArrayList
PS (2) > for ($i=1; $i -le 10; $i++) { $result.Append($i) }
PS (3) > "$($result.ToArray())"
1 2 3 4 5 6 7 8 9 10
```

First you create an instance of `System.Collections.ArrayList` to hold the result. Then you use a `for` loop to step through the numbers, adding each number to the result `ArrayList`. Finally you convert the `ArrayList` to an array and display the result. This is a straightforward approach to creating the array, but requires several steps. Using loops in subexpressions, you can simplify it quite a bit. Here's the rewritten example:

```
PS (4) > $result = $(for ($i=1; $i -le 10; $i++) {$i})
PS (5) > "$result"
1 2 3 4 5 6 7 8 9 10
```

Here you don't have to initialize the result or do explicit adds to the result collection. The output of the loop is captured and automatically saved as a collection by the interpreter. In fact, this is more efficient than the previous example, because the interpreter can optimize the management of the collection internally. This approach applies to any kind of statement. Let's look at an example where you want to conditionally assign a value to a variable if it doesn't currently have a value. First verify that the variable has no value:

```
PS (1) > $var
```

Now do the conditional assignment. This uses an `if` statement in a subexpression:

```
PS (2) > $var = $(if (! $var) { 12 } else {$var})
PS (3) > $var
12
```

From the output, you can see that the variable has been set. Change the variable, and rerun the conditional assignment:

```
PS (4) > $var="Hello there"
PS (5) > $var = $(if (! $var) { 12 } else {$var})
PS (6) > $var
Hello there
```

This time the variable isn't changed.

For PowerShell version 2, the ability to assign the output of a flow-control statement has been simplified so you can directly assign the output to a variable. Although this doesn't add any new capabilities, it does make things simpler and cleaner. For instance, the previous example can be simplified to

```
PS (7) > $var = if (! $var) { 12 } else {$var}
```

using this feature. And the `for` example you saw earlier can be simplified to

```
PS (4) > $result = for ($i=1; $i -le 10; $i++) {$i}
```

making it (somewhat) easier to read.

Used judiciously, the fact that statements can be used as value expressions can simplify your code in many circumstances. By eliminating temporary variables and extra initializations, creating collections is greatly simplified, as you saw with the `for` loop. On the other hand, it's entirely possible to use this statement-as-expression capability to produce scripts that are hard to read. (Remember the nested `if` statement example we looked at earlier in this chapter?) You should always keep that in mind when using these features in scripts. The other thing to keep in mind when you use statements is the performance of your scripts. Let's dig into this in a bit more detail.

6.7 A WORD ABOUT PERFORMANCE

Now that we've covered loops in PowerShell, this is a good time to talk about performance. PowerShell is an interpreted language, which has performance implications. Tasks with a lot of small repetitive actions can take a long time to execute. Anything with a loop statement can be a performance hotspot for this reason. Identifying these hotspots and rewriting them can have a huge impact on script performance. Let's take a look at a real example. I was writing a script to process a collection of events, extracting events having a specific name and ID and placing them into a new collection. The script looked something like this:

```
$results = @()
for ($i=0; $i -lt $EventList.length ; $i++)
{
   $name = [string] $Events[$i].ProviderName
   $id = [long] $Events[$i].Id

   if ($name -ne "My-Provider-Name")
   {
      continue
   }

   if ($id -ne 3005) {

      continue
   }

   $results += $Events[$i]
}
```

This script indexed through the collection of events using the `for` statement, and then used the `continue` statement to skip to the next event if the current event didn't match the desired criteria. If the event did match the criteria, it was appended to the result collection. Although this worked correctly, for large collections of events it was taking several minutes to execute. Let's look at some ways to speed it up and make it smaller.

First, consider how you're indexing through the collection. This requires a lot of index operations, variable retrievals and increments that aren't the most efficient operations in an interpreted language like PowerShell. Instead, PowerShell has a number of constructs that let you iterate through a collection automatically. Given that the task is to select events where some condition is true, the `Where-Object` cmdlet is an obvious choice. The second optimization is how the result list is built. The original code manually adds each element to the result array. If you remember our discussion on how array catenation works, this means that the array has to be copied each time an element is added. The alternative approach, as we discussed, is to simply let the pipeline do the collection for you. With these design changes, the new script looks like

```
$BranchCache3005Events = $events | where {
    $_.Id -eq 3005 -and $_.ProviderName -eq "My-Provider-Name"}
```

The revised script is both hundreds of times faster and significantly shorter and clearer.

So, the rule for writing efficient PowerShell scripts is to let the system do the work for you. Use `foreach` instead of explicit indexing with `for` if you can. If you ever find yourself doing catenation in a loop to build up a string or collection, look at using the pipeline instead. You can also take advantage of the fact that all PowerShell statements return values so an even faster (but less obvious or simple) way to do this is to use the `foreach` statement:

```
$BranchCache3005Events = @( foreach ($e in $events) {
   if ($e.Id -eq 3005 -or
      $e.ProviderName -eq "Microsoft-Windows-BranchCacheSMB") {$e}} )
```

The key here is still letting the system implicitly build the result array instead of constructing it manually with +=. Likewise for string catenation, this

```
$s = -join $(  foreach ($i in 1..40kb) { "a" } )
```

is faster than

```
$s = "";  foreach ($i in 1..40kb) { $s += "a" }
```

By following these guidelines, not only will your scripts be faster, they'll also end up being shorter and frequently simpler and clearer (though not always.)

6.8 SUMMARY

In chapter 6, we covered the branching and looping statements in the PowerShell language as summarized in the following list:

- PowerShell allows you to use pipelines where other languages only allow expressions. This means that, although the PowerShell flow-control statements appear to be similar to the corresponding statements in other languages, enough differences exist to make it useful for you to spend time experimenting with them.
- There are two ways of handling flow control in PowerShell. The first is to use the language flow-control statements such as `while` and `foreach`. But when performing pipelined operations, the alternative mechanism—the flow-control cmdlets `ForEach-Object` and `Where-Object`—can be more natural and efficient.
- When iterating over collections, you should keep in mind the trade-offs between the `foreach` statement and the `ForEach-Object` cmdlet.
- Any statement can be used as a value expression when nested in a subexpression. For example, you could use a `while` loop in a subexpression to generate a

collection of values. In PowerShell v2, for simple assignments, the subexpression notation is no longer needed and the output of a statement can be assigned directly to a variable. This mechanism can be a concise way of generating a collection, but keep in mind the potential complexity that this kind of nested statement can introduce.

- The PowerShell `switch` statement is a powerful tool. On the surface it looks like the `switch` statement in C# or the `select` statement in Visual Basic, but with powerful pattern matching capabilities, it goes well beyond what the statements in the other languages can do. And, along with the pattern matching, it can be used as a looping construct for selecting and processing objects from a collection or lines read from a file. In fact, much of its behavior was adapted from the AWK programming language.
- The choice of statements and how you use them can have a significant effect on the performance of your scripts. This is something to keep in mind, but remember, only worry about performance if it becomes a problem. Otherwise, try to focus on making things as clear as possible.

CHAPTER 7

PowerShell functions

Porcupine quills. We've always done it with porcupine quills.

—Dilbert

In this chapter, we'll begin looking at how to combine the features from the previous chapters into reusable commands. As you'll recall from chapter 2, there are four types of PowerShell commands: functions, cmdlets, scripts, and external commands. Functions and scripts are the two command types that can be written in the PowerShell language. We'll start with functions as they're the simpler of the two and are also easy to enter interactively in a session. In the next chapter we'll expand our discussion to include scripts as well as introduce advanced programming features available to both functions and scripts.

Before we dive in, there's one thing you need to be aware of if you have prior programming experience. This prior experience can be both a blessing and a curse when learning to program in PowerShell. Most of the time, what you already know makes it easier to program in PowerShell. The syntax and most of the concepts will probably be familiar. Unfortunately, *similar* isn't *identical*, and this is where prior experience can trip you up. You'll expect PowerShell to work like your favorite language, and it won't work quite the same way. We'll call out these issues as we encounter them. So, put away your porcupine quills and let's get started.

7.1 FUNDAMENTALS OF POWERSHELL FUNCTIONS

In this section we'll cover the basic concepts and features of PowerShell functions. Functions are the most lightweight form of PowerShell command. They only exist in memory for the duration of a session. When you exit the shell session, the functions are gone. They're also simple enough that you can create useful functions in a single line of code. We'll start by working through a number of examples showing you how to create simple functions. Let's take a look at our first example:

```
PS (1) > function hello { "Hello world" }
```

In this example, `hello` is pretty obviously a function because it's preceded by the `function` keyword. And, equally obvious, this function should emit the string "Hello world." Execute it to verify this:

```
PS (2) > hello; hello; hello
Hello world
Hello world
Hello world
```

Yes, it works exactly as expected. You've created your first command.

Okay, that was easy. Now you know how to write a simple PowerShell function. The syntax is shown in figure 7.1.

But a function that writes only "Hello world" isn't very useful. Let's see how to personalize this function by allowing an argument to be passed in.

7.1.1 Passing arguments using $args

The ability to pass values into a function is called *parameterizing* the function. In most languages, this means modifying the function to declare the parameters to process. For simple PowerShell functions, we don't have to do this because there's a default argument array that contains all the values passed to the function. This default array is available in the variable `$args`. Here's the previous `hello` example modified to use `$args` to receive arguments:

```
PS (3) > function hello { "Hello there $args, how are you?" }
PS (4) > hello Bob
Hello there Bob, how are you?
```

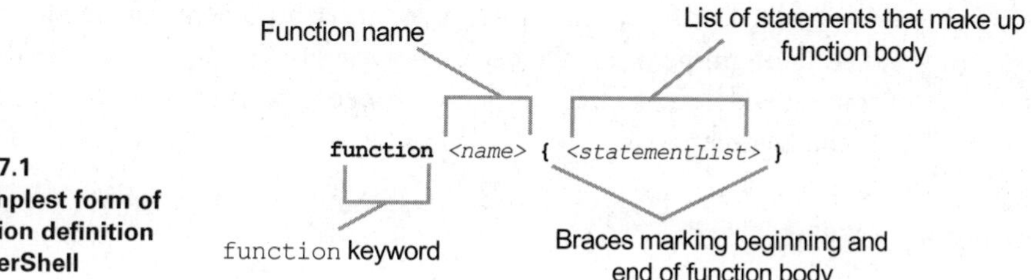

Figure 7.1 The simplest form of a function definition in PowerShell

This example uses string expansion to insert the value stored in `$args` into the string that is emitted from the `hello` function. Now let's see what happens with multiple arguments:

```
PS (5) > hello Bob Alice Ted Carol
Hello there Bob Alice Ted Carol, how are you?
```

Following the string expansion rules described in chapter 3, the values stored in `$args` get interpolated into the output string with each value separated by a space—or, more specifically, separated by whatever is stored in the `$OFS` variable. So let's take one last variation on this example. We'll set `$OFS` in the function body with the aim of producing a more palatable output. You can take advantage of the interactive nature of the PowerShell environment to enter this function over several lines:

```
PS (6) > function hello
>> {
>> $ofs=","
>> "Hello there $args and how are you?"
>> }
>>
PS (7) > hello Bob Carol Ted Alice
Hello there Bob,Carol,Ted,Alice and how are you?
```

That's better. Now at least you have commas between the names. Let's try it again, with commas between the arguments:

```
PS (8) > hello Bob,Carol,Ted,Alice
Hello there System.Object[] and how are you?
```

This isn't the result you were looking for! So what happened? Let's define a new function to clear up what happened:

```
PS (1) > function count-args {
>> "`$args.count=" + $args.count
>> "`$args[0].count=" + $args[0].count
>> }
>>
```

This function will display the number of arguments passed to it as well as the number of elements in the first argument. First you use it with three scalar arguments:

```
PS (2) > count-args 1 2 3
$args.count=3
$args[0].count=
```

As expected, it shows that you passed three arguments. It doesn't show anything for the `Count` property on `$args[0]` because `$args[0]` is a scalar (the number 1) and consequently doesn't have a `Count` property. Now try it with a comma between each of the arguments:

```
PS (3) > Count-Args 1,2,3
$args.count=1
$args[0].count=3
```

Now you see that the function received one argument, which is an array of three elements. And finally, try it with two sets of comma-separated numbers:

```
PS (4) > count-args 1,2,3 4,5,6,7
$args.count=2
$args[0].count=3
```

The results show that the function received two arguments, both of which are arrays. The first argument is an array of three elements and the second is an array with four elements. Hmm, you should be saying to yourself—this sounds familiar. And it is—the comma here works like the binary comma operator in expressions, as discussed in chapter 5.

Two values on the command line with a comma between them will be passed to the command as a single argument. The value of that argument is an array of those elements. This applies to any command, not just functions. If you want to copy three files, f1.txt, f2.txt, and f3.txt, to a directory, the command is

```
copy-item f1.txt,f2.txt,f3.txt target
```

The `Copy-Item` cmdlet receives two arguments: the first is an array of three filenames, and the second is a scalar element naming the target directory. Now let's look at a couple of examples where `$args` enables simple but powerful scenarios.

7.1.2 Example functions: ql and qs

The way `$args` works is straightforward, but it allows you to write some pretty slick commands. Here are two functions that aren't in the PowerShell base installation (although they may be in the future, but not in either v1 or v2 … sigh):

```
function ql { $args }
function qs { "$args" }
```

They may not look like much, but they can significantly streamline a number of tasks. The first function is `ql`, which stands for *quote list*. This is a Perl-ism. Here's what you can do with it. Say you want to build a list of the colors. To do this with the normal comma operator, you'd do the following,

```
$col = "black","brown","red","orange","yellow","green",
    "blue","violet","gray","white"
```

which requires lots of quotes and commas. With the `ql` function, you could write it this way:

```
$col = ql black brown red orange yellow green blue violet gray white
```

This is much shorter and requires less typing. Does it let you do anything you couldn't do before? No, but it lets you do something more efficiently when you have to. Remember that elastic syntax concept? When you're trying to fit a complex expression onto one line, things like `ql` can help. What about the other function, `qs`?

It does approximately the same thing but uses string concatenation to return its arguments as a single string instead of an array:

```
PS (1) > $string = qs This is a     string
PS (2) > $string
This is a string
PS (3) >
```

Note that the arguments are concatenated with a single space between them. The original spacing on the command line has been lost, but that usually doesn't matter.

7.1.3 Simplifying $args processing with multiple assignment

As handy as `$args` is, it can become awkward when trying to deal with parameters in a more complex way. Let's look at an example that illustrates this. You'll write a function that takes two arguments and adds them together. With what you've seen so far, you could use array indexing to get each element and then add them together. The result might look like this:

```
PS (1) > function Add-Two { $args[0] + $args[1] }
PS (2) > add-two 2 3
5
```

Notice that most of the work in this function is getting the arguments out of the array. This is where multiple assignment comes in. It allows you to extract the elements of the array in `$args` into name variables in a convenient way. Using this feature, the updated function looks like

```
PS (3) > function Add-Two {
>> $x,$y=$args
>> $x+$y
>> }
>>
PS (4) > add-two 1 2
3
```

In this example, the first statement in the function assigns the values passed in `$args` to the local variables `$x` and `$y`. Perl users will be familiar with this approach for dealing with function arguments, and, although it's a reasonable way to deal with parameters, it isn't the way most languages do it.

> **NOTE** The `$args` approach will be familiar to Perl 5 or earlier users. Perl 6 has a solution to the problem that's similar to what PowerShell does. I'd claim great minds think alike, but it's just the most obvious way to solve the problem.

For this reason, PowerShell provides other ways to declare the formal parameters. We'll cover those approaches in the next couple of sections.

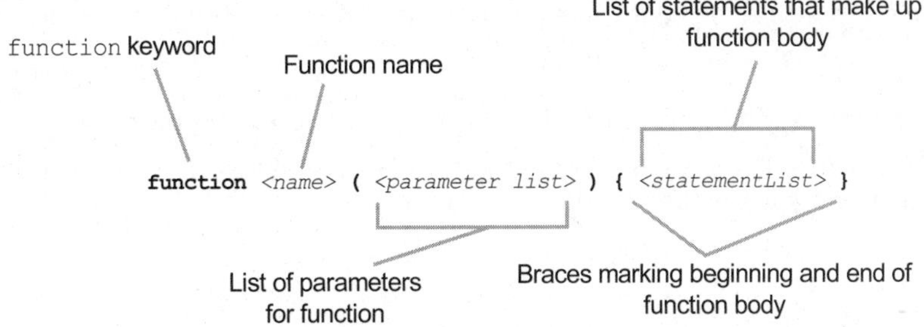

Figure 7.2 The syntax for defining a function with explicit parameters in PowerShell. The parameter list is optional: you can either have empty parentheses or omit them, as you saw in figure 7.1.

7.2 Declaring formal parameters for a function

With the fundamentals out of the way, we'll start to look at some of the more sophisticated features of PowerShell functions. We'll begin with a better way for declaring function parameters. Although the `$args` variable is a simple and automatic way of getting at the arguments to functions, it takes a fair amount of work to do anything with a level of sophistication, as you saw in the previous section. PowerShell provides a much more convenient (and probably more familiar to many people) way to declare parameters, which is shown in figure 7.2.

Here's a simple example of what this looks like in a real function:

```
function subtract ($from, $count) { $from - $count }
```

In this function definition, there are two formal parameters: `$from` and `$count`. When the function is called, each actual argument will be bound to the corresponding formal parameter, either by position or by name. What does that mean? Well, binding by position is obvious:

```
PS (1) > subtract 5 3
2
```

In this case, the first argument, `5`, is bound to the first formal parameter, `$x`, and the second argument is bound to the second parameter, `$y`. Now let's look at using the parameter names as keywords:

```
PS (2) > subtract -from 5 -count 2
3
PS (3) > subtract -from 4 -count 7
-3
```

What happens if you try and use the same parameter twice? You'll receive an error message that looks like this:

```
PS (4) > subtract -count 4 -count 7
subtract : Cannot bind parameter because parameter 'count' is
specified more than once. To provide multiple values to parameters that
can accept multiple values,  use the array syntax.  For example,
```

```
 "-parameter value1,value2,value3".
At line:1 char:25
+ subtract -count 4 -count  <<<< 7
```

As the message says, you can't specify a named parameter more than once. So you now know that there are two ways to match formal parameters with actual arguments. Can you mix and match? Let's try it:

```
PS (5) > subtract -from 5 6
-1
```

You see that it did work as you'd expect. `$from` is set to 5, `$count` is set to 6, and you know that 5 minus 6 is -1. Now change which parameter is named:

```
PS (6) > subtract -count 5 6
1
```

Now `$count` is set to 5 and `$from` is set to 6. This may seem a bit odd. Let's dig into the details of how it works next.

7.2.1 Mixing named and positional parameters

In this section, we'll explain the rules for how parameters are bound to named and positional parameters. Any named parameters are bound and then removed from the list of parameters that still need to be bound. These remaining parameters are then bound positionally. Now let's go back to the example function:

```
function subtract ($from, $count) { $from - $count }
```

When calling this function, if no named parameters are specified, then `$from` is position 0 and `$count` is position 1. If you specify `-from`, then `$from` is bound by name and removed from the list of things that need to be bound positionally. This means that `$count`, which is normally in position 2, is now in position 1. Got all that? Probably not, as I have a hard time following it myself. All you need to think about is whether you're using named parameters or positional ones. Try to avoid mixing and matching if possible. If you do want to mix and match, always put the parameters that you want to specify by name at the end of the parameter list. In other words, put them at the end of the `param` statement or the function argument list. That way, they don't affect the order of the parameters you want to bind by position. (In chapter 8, you'll learn a better way to control how parameters are processed.)

Functions as commands

The way functions are called in PowerShell tends to cause people with prior programming experience to make a common error. They see the word *function* and try to call a PowerShell function the way they would in whatever other language they're used to. So, instead of calling it like a command (which is what functions are), they try to call it by doing something like this:

```
subtract(1,2)
```

> ***(continued)***
>
> PowerShell will happily accept this because there's nothing syntactically wrong with it. The problem is that the statement is totally wrong semantically. Functions (as opposed to methods on objects) in PowerShell are commands like any other command. Arguments to commands are separated by spaces. If you want to provide multivalued arguments for a single command, then you separate those multiple values with commas (more on this later). Also, parentheses are only needed if you want the argument to be evaluated as an expression (see chapter 2 on parsing modes). So—what this "function call" is actually doing is passing a single argument, which is an array of two values. And that's just wrong. Consider yourself warned. Really. This has tripped up some very smart people. If you remember this discussion, then someday, somewhere, you'll be able to lord this bit of trivia over your coworkers, crushing their spirits like—oh—wait—sorry—it's that darned inner voice leaking out again…

So far, all your work has been with typeless parameters, and this has its advantages. It means that your functions can typically work with a wider variety of data types. But sometimes you want to make sure that the parameters are of a particular type (or at least convertible to that type). Although you could do this the hard way and write a bunch of type-checking code, PowerShell is all about making life easier for the user, so let's talk about a better way to do this by specifying typed parameters.

7.2.2 Adding type constraints to parameters

Scripting languages don't usually allow types to be specified for the parameters to a function and, as you've seen, you don't have to specify types for PowerShell function parameters either. But sometimes it can be quite useful because it allows you to catch type mismatches in function calls earlier and provide better error messages. Adding type constraints to parameters is what we'll cover in this section.

To type-constrain a parameter, you provide a type literal before the variable name in the parameter list. Figure 7.3 shows what this looks like.

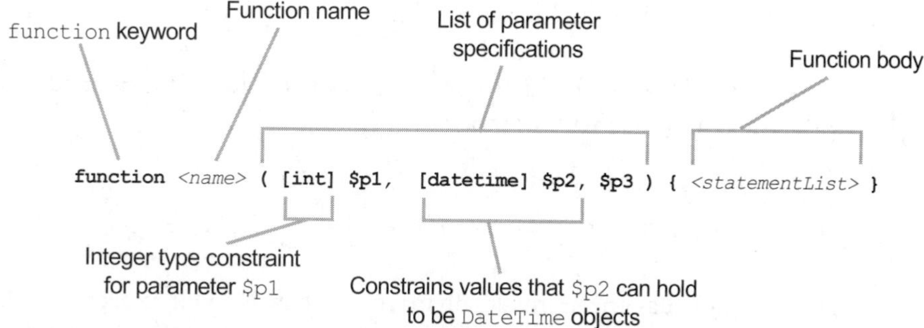

Figure 7.3 How type constraints are added to some of the parameters of a function. Type constraints aren't required for all parameters; in this case, $p3 is left unconstrained.

Let's work through an example. Define a function nadd that takes two parameters that you'll constrain to be integers:

```
PS (1) > function nadd ([int] $x, [int] $y) {$x + $y}
```

Now use this function to add two numbers:

```
PS (2) > nadd 1 2
3
```

Adding 1 and 2 gives 3. No surprise there. Now add two strings:

```
PS (3) > nadd "1" "2"
3
```

The answer is still 3. Because of the type constraints on the parameters, numeric addition is performed even though you passed in two strings. Now let's see what happens when you pass in something that can't be converted to a number:

```
PS (4) > nadd @{a=1;b=2}  "2"
nadd : Cannot convert "System.Collections.Hashtable" to "System.
Int32".
At line:1 char:5
+ nadd  <<<< @{a=1;b=2}  "2"
```

You get an error message mentioning where the function was used and why it failed. Now define another function that doesn't have the type constraints:

```
PS (5) > function add ($x, $y) {$x + $y}
```

Call this function with a hashtable argument:

```
PS (6) > add @{a=1;b=2}  "2"
You can add another hash table only to a hash table.
At line:1 char:28
+ function add ($x, $y) {$x +  <<<< $y}
```

You still get an error, but notice where the error message is reported. Because it happened in the body of the function, the error message is reported in the function itself, not where the function was called as it was in the previous function. It's much more useful for the user of the function to know where the call that failed was rather than knowing where in the function it failed.

Now let's look at the other two examples with the unconstrained function, first with strings and then with numbers:

```
PS (7) > add "1"  "2"
12
PS (8) > add 1 2
3
```

This function has the normal polymorphic behavior you expect from PowerShell. The type-constrained version only worked on numbers. Of course, if the arguments can be safely converted to numbers, then the operation will proceed. Let's try the type-constrained function with strings:

```
PS (9) > nadd "4" "2"
6
```

Because the strings "2" and "4" can be safely converted into numbers, they are, and the operation proceeds. If not, as in the following example,

```
PS (10) > nadd "4a" "222"
nadd : Cannot convert value "4a" to type "System.Int32". Error:
"Input string was not in a correct format."
At line:1 char:5
+ nadd  <<<< "4a" "222"
```

you'll get a type-conversion error. In effect, the type constraints on function parameters are really casts, and follow the type-conversion rules described in chapter 3.

> **PowerShell and overloading**
>
> If you're used to traditional object-oriented languages, you might expect to be able to create overloads for a particular function name by specifying different signatures, but overloading isn't supported in PowerShell. If you define a
>
> ```
> function a ([int] $b) { }
> ```
>
> and later define
>
> ```
> function a ([string] $b) { }
> ```
>
> the new definition will replace the old definition rather than adding a new overload.

When we started our discussion of parameters, you used `$args`, which was a bit awkward, but it let you specify a variable number of arguments to a function. In the next section, we'll see how you can do this even when you have a formal parameter list.

7.2.3 Handling variable numbers of arguments

Now that you know how to create explicit argument specifications, you're probably wondering if you can still handle variable numbers of arguments. The answer is, yes. By default, any remaining arguments that don't match formal arguments will be captured in `$args`. The following example function illustrates this:

```
PS (11) > function a ($x, $y) {
>> "x is $x"
>> "y is $y"
>> "args is $args"
>> }
>>
```

Now let's use it with a single argument:

```
PS (12) > a 1
x is 1
y is
args is
```

The single argument is bound to $x. $y is initialized to $null and $args has zero elements in it. Now try it with two arguments:

```
PS (13) > a 1 2
x is 1
y is 2
args is
```

This time $x and $y are bound but $args is still empty. Next try it with three arguments, and then with five:

```
PS (14) > a 1 2 3
x is 1
y is 2
args is 3
PS (15) > a 1 2 3 4 5
x is 1
y is 2
args is 3 4 5
```

Now you can see that the extra arguments end up in $args.

This automatic handling of excess arguments is useful behavior, but in a lot of cases, you prefer that extra arguments be treated as an error. One way to make sure that no extra arguments are passed to your function is to check whether the length of $args .length is 0 in the function body. If it's not 0, some arguments were passed. This is, however, a bit awkward. In chapter 8, we'll look at a much better way to handle this.

Earlier we mentioned that formal arguments that don't have corresponding actual arguments are initialized to $null. Although this is a handy default, it would be more useful to have a way of initializing the parameters to specific values instead of having to write a lot of extra code in the body of the function to handle this. We'll look at that next.

7.2.4 Initializing function parameters with default values

In this section, we'll show you how to initialize the values of function parameters. The syntax for this is shown in figure 7.4.

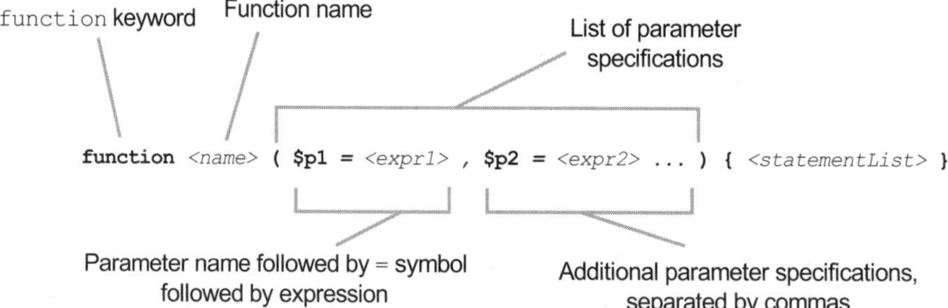

Figure 7.4 The more complex function definition syntax where initializer expressions are provided for each variable. Note that the initializers are constrained to be expressions, but, using the subexpression notation, you can put anything here.

Let's move right into an example:

```
PS (14) > function add ($x=1, $y=2) { $x + $y }
```

This function initializes the formal parameters `$x` to `1` and `$y` to `2` if no actual parameters are specified. So when you use it with no arguments

```
PS (15) > add
3
```

it returns 3. With one argument

```
PS (16) > add 5
7
```

it returns the argument plus 2, which in this case is 7. And finally with two actual arguments

```
PS (17) > add 5 5
10
```

it returns the result of adding them. From this example, it's obvious that you can initialize the variable to a constant value. What about something more complex? The initialization sequence as shown in figure 7.2 says that an initializer can be an expression. If you remember from chapter 5, an expression can be a subexpression and a subexpression can contain any PowerShell construct. In other words, an initializer can do anything: calculate a value, execute a pipeline, reformat your hard drive (not recommended), or send out for snacks from Tahiti by carrier pigeon (personally, I've not had much luck with this one).

Let's try this feature out. Define a function that returns the day of the week for a particular date:

```
PS (28) > function dow ([datetime] $d = $(get-date))
>> {
>> $d.dayofweek
>> }
>>
```

This function takes one argument, `$d`, that's constrained to be something that matches a date or time. If no argument is specified, it's initialized to the result of executing the `Get-Date` cmdlet (which returns today's date). Now let's try it out. First run it with no arguments,

```
PS (29) > dow
Tuesday
```

and it prints out what day today is. Then run it with a specific date

```
PS (30) > dow "jun 2, 2001"
Saturday
```

and you see that June 2, 2001, was a Saturday. This is a simple example of using a subexpression to initialize a variable.

7.2.5 Handling mandatory parameters, v1-style

There's one interesting scenario that we should still talk about. What happens if you don't want a default value? In other words, how can you require the user to specify this value? This is another thing you can use initializer expressions for, though it's a bit of a hack.

> **NOTE** This hack was the best way to handle mandatory parameters in PowerShell v1. It's not recommended for v2. A much better approach is to use parameter metadata and the `Mandatory` property, as described in chapter 8.

Here's how it works. Because the variable initializer expression can, by using a subexpression notation, be any piece of PowerShell code, you can use it to generate an error rather than initialize the variable. You'll do this using the `throw` statement (we'll cover the `throw` statement in detail in chapter 13). Here's how you can use the `throw` statement to generate the error. First define the function:

```
PS (31) > function zed ($x=$(throw "need x")) { "x is $x" }
```

Notice how the `throw` statement is used in the initializer subexpression for `$x`. Now run the function—first with a value to see whether it works properly,

```
PS (32) > zed 123
x is 123
```

and then without an argument:

```
PS (33) > zed
need x
At line:1 char:25
+ function zed ($x=$(throw  <<<< "need x")) { "x is $x" }
```

Without the argument, the initializer statement is executed and this results in an exception being thrown. This is how you make arguments mandatory in PowerShell v1.

Finally, there's one other thing we need to discuss with function parameters: how to define what are traditionally called *flags* or *switches* in shell languages. In most shell languages, you often provide just the name of a parameter with arguments to control a command's behavior. Let's see how this is handled in PowerShell.

7.2.6 Using switch parameters to define command switches

In this section, we're going to cover how to specify *switch parameters*, but before we do that, let's talk a bit more about parameter processing in general. In all shell environments, commands typically have three kinds of parameters, as shown in table 7.1.

Table 7.1 **Typical classifications of parameter types found in all command shells**

Parameter type	Description
Switches	Switches are present or absent, such as `Get-ChildItem -Recurse`.
Options	Options take an argument value, such as `Get-ChildItem -Filter *.cs`.
Arguments	These are positional and don't have a name associated with them.

This pattern holds true for most shells, including `cmd.exe`, the Korn Shell, and so on, although the specific details of the syntax may vary. In PowerShell we've canonicalized things a bit more. In other words, we've used formal terms for each of these, as shown in table 7.2.

Table 7.2 **Formal names for parameter types in PowerShell**

Parameter type	Formal name in PowerShell
Switches	Switch parameters
Options	Parameters
Arguments	Positional parameters

Arguments are positional parameters because they're always associated with a parameter name. But you can leave out the name and the interpreter will figure out what parameter it is from its position on the command line. For example, in the `dir` command, the `-path` parameter is a positional parameter whose position is 0. Therefore the command

```
dir c:\
```

is equivalent to

```
dir -path c:\
```

and the system infers that "c:\" should be associated with `-path`.

Switch parameters are just the opposite; you specify the parameter but the argument is left out. The interpreter assigns the parameter a value based on whether the parameter is present or absent. The `-recurse` parameter for `Get-ChildItem` is a good example. If it's present, then you'll get a recursive directory listing starting at the current directory:

```
dir -recurse
```

So how do you indicate that something should be a switch parameter? Because PowerShell characteristically uses types to control behavior, it makes sense to indicate that a parameter is a switch parameter by marking it with the type `[switch]`. This is illustrated in figure 7.5.

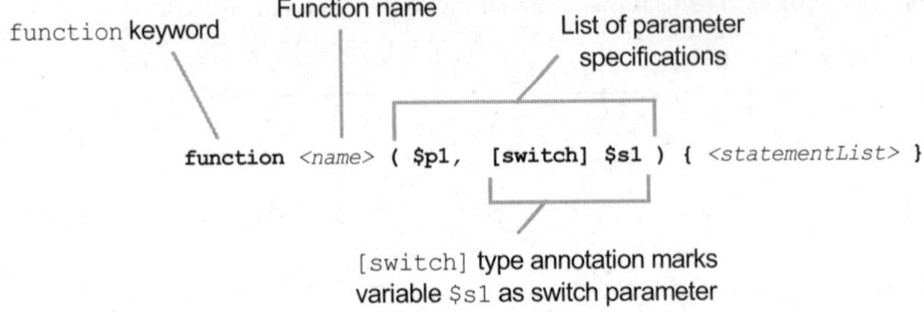

Figure 7.5 Marking a parameter as a switch or flag by adding the `[switch]` type constraint to it

Because the value of a switch is highly constrained, initializing switches is neither necessary nor recommended. Here's an example function that uses a switch parameter:

```
PS (1) > function get-soup (
>>     [switch] $please,
>>     [string] $soup= "chicken noodle"
>> )
>> {
>>     if ($please) {
>>         "Here's your $soup soup"
>>     }
>>     else
>>     {
>>         "No soup for you!"
>>     }
>> }
>>
```

Try out this function:

```
PS (2) > get-soup
No soup for you!
PS (3) > get-soup -please
Here's your chicken noodle soup
PS (4) > get-soup -please tomato
Here's your tomato soup
PS (5) >
```

So if you say, "please," you get soup. If not, no soup for you!

Soup or no soup, we're going to move on with our exploration of switch parameters and take a look at a feature that seems almost contradictory.

Specifying arguments to switch parameters

By definition, switch parameters don't take arguments. Nonetheless, PowerShell provides a way to do this. It sounds like a contradiction but it turns out that there's one very important scenario where you do need to do exactly this. The case in question happens when you need to pass the value of a switch parameter on one function to a switch parameter on another function. For example, consider a function foo that has a switch parameter -s. From function bar, you want to call

```
foo
```

sometimes and

```
foo -s
```

other times, and this will be controlled by a switch parameter on the bar function. You could use if statements to handle this, but even if there's only one parameter you need to pass through this way, you significantly complicate your code. And if there's more than one—well, let's just say it gets ugly very quickly. To avoid this, there's a feature in PowerShell designed with exactly this scenario in mind. Here's how it works. Although switch parameters don't require arguments, they *can* take one if you specify the parameter with a trailing colon:

```
dir -recurse: $true
```

Here's an example showing how the two functions mentioned previously would work. You'll define a bar function that passes its $x switch parameter to the -s switch parameter on function foo. First define the foo function:

```
PS (77) > function foo ([switch] $s) { "s is $s" }
PS (78) > foo -s
s is True
PS (79) > foo
s is False
```

Now define function bar, which will call foo as discussed previously:

```
PS (80) > function bar ([switch] $x) { "x is $x"; foo -s: $x }
```

Call bar without passing -x,

```
PS (81) > bar
x is False
s is False
```

and you see that $s emitted from foo is false. Now call bar again, but specify -x this time,

```
PS (82) > bar -x
x is True
s is True
```

and you see that specifying -x has caused -s to be set to true as well.

This functions-calling-functions pattern is pretty much the only time you should ever have to pass an argument to a switch function. As a corollary to this, a script author should *never* have to write a function, script, or cmdlet where a switch parameter is initialized to $true because it makes the commands very hard to use. Switch parameters are designed so that they need only be present or absent to get the desired effect. If you do have a situation where you're considering initializing a switch to $true, you probably should be using a Boolean parameter instead of a switch parameter. In the next section, we'll investigate how these two types of parameters are related.

7.2.7 Switch parameters vs. Boolean parameters

Having both Boolean and switch parameters in PowerShell may seem redundant—both types can only be true or false. But they're used to solve two quite different problems. To reiterate, the important difference between the two is that switch parameters don't require an argument and Booleans do. Simply specifying a switch parameter on the command line is sufficient for PowerShell to know that the parameter should be set to true:

```
PS (1) > function ts ([switch] $x) { [bool] $x }
PS (2) > ts
False
PS (3) > ts -x
True
```

With the `ts` function, if `-x` isn't present, the return value is `$false`. If it's present, then the return value is `$true`. For Boolean parameters (identified with the `[bool]` type accelerator), an argument must be specified each time the parameter is present. This is illustrated in the following example:

```
PS (4) > function tb ([bool] $x) { [bool] $x }
PS (5) > tb
False
PS (6) > tb -x
tb : Missing an argument for parameter 'x'. Specify a parameter of type
            'System.Boolean' and try again.
At line:1 char:6
+ tb -x <<<<
    + CategoryInfo          : InvalidArgument: (:) [tb],
ParameterBindingException
    + FullyQualifiedErrorId : MissingArgument,tb
PS (7) > tb -x $true
True
PS (8) > tb -x $false
False
```

With the `tb` function, if `-x` isn't present, the return value is `$false`. If it's present but no argument is specified, an error occurs. If it's present and a Boolean value is provided as the argument, then the return value is the same as the argument.

> **NOTE** There's a characteristic in how Boolean type conversions work for `[bool]` parameters that you need to be aware of. The argument to a `[bool]` parameter must either be an actual Boolean value (`$true`, `$false`, or the result of an expression that returns a Boolean) or a number where 0 is treated as `$false` and non-zero is treated as `$true`. This is a departure from how objects are converted to Boolean elsewhere in PowerShell. This inconsistency was introduced deliberately

because new PowerShell users would try commands like `Get-Something -boolParameter false` and be surprised when `-boolParameter` ended up being true, not false. (Remember, non-zero-length strings are considered true everywhere else in the system.) The cognitive dissonance resulting from having `"false"` evaluate to `$true` was a stumbling block for some new users. To mitigate this, PowerShell makes passing anything other than a number or a Boolean value an error condition. This seems to be the least inconsistent solution because the new behavior is a proper subset of normal type conversion.

The behavior of switch parameters is specifically designed for creating command switches. The scenario where you need Boolean parameters is quite different. You use Boolean parameters when you're writing a command to change the value of some of the properties on the object passing through the pipeline. This is part of the common Get/Update/Set pattern where you get an object from a store, change some properties on that object, and then pass it to an update command. In this pattern, you only want to change the value of the property if there's a corresponding parameter on the command line. This is where the `[bool]` parameter is useful—it's how you handle this pattern for Boolean properties. If the parameter is present, you want to set the property on the pipeline object to be the value passed to the parameter. If the parameter is absent, then you don't want to change it. We'll dig into this a bit more in the next section, but first we'll digress for a while to investigate a common configuration management pattern and how you deal with it in PowerShell.

A digression: the Get/Update/Set pattern

A lot of management data is contained in database-like remote stores. Microsoft Exchange and Active Directory are two examples of this kind of thing. The characteristic usage pattern for working with these stores is as follows:

1. Get a record from the remote store.
2. Modify some property or properties on this object.
3. Send the modified object back to the store where the changes are recorded.

For example, when managing Exchange mailboxes, the mailbox objects are retrieved from the server, modified, and then sent back to the server to update the database. This is the Get/Update/Set pattern in action. It's an important enough pattern that we're going to work through a somewhat extended example illustrating this approach in PowerShell. The following listing implements a simple database that contains information about familiar characters from the comic strips.

Listing 7.1 The `Get-Character` function

```
$characterData = @{
  "Linus" = @{ age = 8; human = $true}
  "Lucy" = @{ age = 8; human = $true}
```

Stores character data in hashtable of hashtables

```
  "Snoopy" = @{ age = 2; human = $true}
}

function Get-Character ($name = "*")
{
  foreach ($entry in $characterData.GetEnumerator() | Write-Output)
  {
    if ($entry.Key -like $name)
    {
        $properties = @{ "Name" = $entry.Key } +
          $entry.Value
        New-Object PSCustomObject -Property $properties
     }
  }
}

function Set-Character {
  process {
    $characterData[$_.name] =
      @{
        age = $_.age
        human = $_.human
      }
   }
}

function Update-Character (
  [string] $name = '*',
  [int] $age,
  [bool] $human
)
{
  begin
  {
    if ($PSBoundParameters."name")
    {
      $name = $PSBoundParameters.name
      [void] $PSBoundParameters.Remove("name")
    }
  }
  process
  {
    if ($_.name -like $name)
    {
      foreach ($p in $PSBoundParameters.GetEnumerator())
      {
        $_.($p.Key) = $p.value
      }
    }
    $_
  }
}
```

Gets data from table

Builds merged hashtable

Emits character record

Processes record; updates character entry

Updates properties on object

NOTE To make this example work, you need to use a few features that haven't been covered yet: the `process` keyword used in `Update-Character`, custom objects, and the `$PSBoundParameters` automatic variable. We'll cover the `process` keyword later in this chapter and the `$PSBoundParameters` is discussed in chapter 8. This variable is key to making this example work as it lets you see which parameters were specified on the command line. Creating custom objects using the `New-Object` command is explored in chapter 11. Of these features, only the `process` keyword is available in v1. The others are only available in v2.

In this example, the character data is stored in nested hashtables, making it easy to access by name. The `Get-Character` function retrieves characters from the table and emits custom objects for each character. The `Set-Character` data reverses this process and uses the inbound records to update the character table. The `Update-Character` function is where you see the use case for Boolean parameters mentioned in the previous section. Let's apply this code to manage your character database. First you'll get a listing of all the characters in the table:

```
PS (1) > Get-Character | Format-Table -auto

human Name   age
----- ----   ---
 True Snoopy   2
 True Lucy     8
 True Linus    8
```

You're passing the output of `Get-Character` through `Format-Table -auto` to get a nice, concise table showing the character data. Immediately you see that there's a problem with this data. It lists Snoopy as being human even though you know he's a dog (well, at least if you're a Peanuts fan). You'll need to use the `Update-Character` function to fix this:

```
PS (2) > Get-Character |
>>   Update-Character -name snoopy -human $false |
>>    Format-Table -auto
>>

human Name   age
----- ----   ---
False Snoopy   2
 True Lucy     8
 True Linus    8
```

Note that you haven't updated the table yet—you're just looking at how the updated table will look. You can verify the data hasn't changed by calling `Get-Character` again:

```
PS (3) > Get-Character | Format-Table -auto

human Name   age
----- ----   ---
 True Snoopy   2
 True Lucy     8
 True Linus    8
```

Now do the Set part of Get/Update/Set:

```
PS (4) > Get-Character |
>>   Update-Character -name snoopy -human $false |
>>   Set-Character
>>
```

Then, dump the table to verify that change:

```
PS (5) > Get-Character | Format-Table -auto

human Name   age
----- ----   ---
False Snoopy   2
 True Lucy     8
 True Linus    8
```

Now Snoopy is no longer marked as human. But there's also something else you want to check on. You'll dump the records that show the data for characters whose names begin with *L*:

```
PS (6) > Get-Character L* | Format-Table -auto

human Name  age
----- ----  ---
 True Lucy    8
 True Linus   8
```

And there's the problem: the table lists Lucy and Linus as being the same age. Because Linus is Lucy's younger brother, you know the current age property must be wrong. Again you'll use `Update-Character` piped to `Set-Character` to update the data, correcting the character's age:

```
PS (7) > Get-Character Linus |
>>   Update-Character -age 7 |
>>   Set-Character
>>
PS (8) > Get-Character | Format-Table -auto

human Name   age
----- ----   ---
False Snoopy   2
 True Lucy     8
 True Linus    7
```

Now the table is correct.

In this extended example, you looked at a common pattern for working with management data—Get/Update/Set—which you're likely to run into many times doing systems management. In the process, we demonstrated the reason for Boolean parameters being distinct from switch parameters: they address two quite different usage patterns.

By now, you've probably had enough discussion on how stuff gets passed into functions. Let's talk about how stuff comes out of functions instead. In the next section, we'll look at the various ways objects can be returned from functions.

7.3 RETURNING VALUES FROM FUNCTIONS

Now it's time to talk about returning values from functions. We've been doing this all along, but there's something we need to highlight. Because PowerShell is a shell, it doesn't return results—it writes output or *emits objects*. As you've seen, the result of any expression or pipeline is to emit the result object to the caller. At the command line, if you type three expressions separated by semicolons, the results of all three statements are output:

```
PS (1) > 2+2; 9/3; [math]::sqrt(27)
4
3
5.19615242270663
```

In this example, there are three statements in the list, so three numbers are displayed. Now let's put this into a function:

```
PS (2) > function numbers { 2+2; 9/3; [math]::sqrt(27) }
```

Now run that function:

```
PS (3) > numbers
4
3
5.19615242270663
```

Just as when you typed it on the command line, three numbers are output. Now run it and assign the results to a variable:

```
PS (4) > $result = numbers
```

Then, check the content of that variable:

```
PS (5) > $result.length
3
PS (6) > $result[0]
4
PS (7) > $result[1]
3
PS (8) > $result[2]
5.19615242270663
```

From the output, you can see that `$result` contains an array with three values in it. Here's what happened. As each statement in the function was executed, the result of that statement was captured in an array, and then that array was stored in `$result`. The easiest way to understand this is to imagine variable assignments working like redirection, except the result is stored in a variable instead of in a file.

Let's try something more complex. The goal here is twofold. First, you want to increase your understanding of how function output works. Second, you want to see how to take advantage of this feature to simplify your scripts and improve performance.

Let's redefine the function numbers to use a `while` loop that generates the numbers 1 to 10:

```
PS (11) > function numbers
>> {
>> $i=1
>> while ($i -le 10)
>> {
>> $i
>> $i++
>> }
>> }
>>
```

Now run it:

```
PS (12) > numbers
1
2
3
4
5
6
7
8
9
10
```

Capture the results in a variable:

```
PS (13) > $result = numbers
```

What ended up in the variable? First check the type

```
PS (14) > $result.gettype().fullname
System.Object[]
```

and the length:

```
PS (15) > $result.length
10
```

The output of the function ended up in an array of elements, even though you never mentioned an array anywhere. This should look familiar by now, because we talked about it extensively in chapter 5 in our discussion of arrays. The PowerShell runtime will spontaneously create a collection when needed. Compare this to the way you'd write this function in a traditional language. Let's rewrite this as a new function, `tradnum`. In the traditional approach, you have to initialize a result variable,

$result, to hold the array being produced, add each element to the array, and then emit the array:

```
PS (16) > function tradnum
>> {
>> $result = @()
>> $i=1
>> while ($i -le 10)
>> {
>>     $result += $i
>>     $i++
>> }
>> $result
>> }
>>
```

This code is significantly more complex: you have to manage two variables in the function now instead of one. If you were writing in a language that didn't automatically extend the size of the array, it would be even more complicated, as you'd have to add code to resize the array manually. And even though PowerShell will automatically resize the array, it's not efficient compared to capturing the streamed output. The point is to make you think about how you can use the facilities that PowerShell offers to improve your code. If you find yourself writing code that explicitly constructs arrays, consider looking at it to see if it can be rewritten to take advantage of streaming instead.

Of course, every silver lining has a cloud. As wonderful as all this automatic collecting of output is, there are some potential pitfalls. Sometimes you'll find things in the output collection that you didn't expect and have no idea how they got there. This can be hard (and frustrating) to figure out. In the next section we'll explore the reasons why this might happen and you'll learn how to go about debugging the problem if you encounter it.

7.3.1 Debugging problems in function output

When writing a function, there's something you need to keep in mind that's specific to shell environments. The result of all statements executed will appear in the output of the function. This means that if you add debug message statements that write to the output stream to your function, this debug output will be mixed into the actual output of the function.

> **NOTE** In text-based shells, the usual way to work around mixing debug information with output is to write the debug messages to the error stream (stderr). This works fine when the error stream is simple text; however, in PowerShell, the error stream is composed of error objects. All the extra information in these objects, while great for errors, makes them unpalatable for writing simple debug messages. There are better ways of handling this, as you'll see in chapter 9 when we talk about debugging.

Here's an example function where we've added a couple of debug statements:

```
PS (1) > function my-func ($x) {
>>     "Getting the date"
>>     $x = get-date
>>     "Date was $x, now getting the day"
>>     $day = $x.day
>>     "Returning the day"
>>     $day
>> }
>>
```

Let's run the function:

```
PS (2) > my-func
Getting the date
Date was 5/17/2006 10:39:39 PM, now getting the day
Returning the day
17
```

You see the debug output as well as the result. That's fine—that's the point of debugging messages. But now let's capture the output of the function into a variable:

```
PS (3) > $x = my-func
```

This time you see no output, which is expected, but neither do you see the debugging messages and that wasn't expected or desired. Take a look at what ended up in `$x`:

```
PS (4) > $x
Getting the date
Date was 5/17/2006 10:39:39 PM, now getting the day
Returning the day
17
```

You see that everything is there: output and debug, all mixed together. This is a trivial example and I'm sure it feels like we're beating the issue to death, but this is the kind of thing that leads to those head-slapping how-could-I-be-so-dumb moments in which you'll be writing a complex script and wonder why the output looks funny. Then you'll remember that debugging statement you forgot to take out. "Duh!" you cry, "How could I be so dumb!"

> **NOTE** This, of course, isn't exclusive to PowerShell. Back before the advent of good debuggers, people would do `printf`-debugging (named after the `printf` output function in C). It wasn't uncommon to see stray output in programs because of this. Now, with good debuggers, stray output is pretty infrequent. PowerShell provides debugging features (which we'll cover in chapters 14 and 15) that you can use instead of `printf` -debugging. In particular, the Integrated Scripting Environment (ISE) included with PowerShell v2 has a built-in graphical debugger for scripts.

Another thing to be careful about is operations that emit objects when you don't expect them to. This is particularly important to keep in mind if you use a lot of .NET methods in your scripts. The problem is that many of these methods return values that you don't need or care about. This isn't an issue with languages like C# because the default behavior in these languages is to discard the result of an expression. In PowerShell, though, the default is to always emit the result of an expression; consequently, these method results unexpectedly appear in your output. One of the most common times when people encounter this problem is when using the `System.Collections.ArrayList` class. The `Add()` method on this class helpfully returns the index of the object that was added by the call to `Add()` (I'm aware of no actual use for this feature—it probably seemed like a good idea at the time). This behavior looks like this:

```
PS (1) > $al = new-object system.collections.arraylist
PS (2) > $al.count
0
PS (3) > $al.add(1)
0
PS (4) > $al.add(2)
1
PS (5) > $al.add(3)
2
```

Every time you call `Add()`, a number displaying the index of the added element is emitted. Now say you write a function that copies its arguments into an `ArrayList`. This might look like

```
PS (6) > function addArgsToArrayList {
>> $al = new-object System.Collections.ArrayList
>> $args | foreach { $al.add($_) }
>> }
>>
```

It's a pretty simple function, but what happens when you run it? Take a look:

```
PS (7) > addArgsToArrayList a b c d
0
1
2
3
```

As you can see, every time you call `Add()`, a number gets returned. This isn't very helpful. To make it work properly, you need to discard this undesired output. Let's fix this. Here's the revised function definition:

```
PS (8) > function addArgsToArrayList {
>> $al = new-object System.Collections.ArrayList
>> $args | foreach { [void] $al.add($_) }
>> }
>>
```

It looks exactly like the previous one except for the cast to void in the third line. Now let's try it out:

```
PS (9) > addArgsToArrayList a b c d
PS (10) >
```

This time you don't see any output, as desired. This is a tip to keep in mind when working with .NET classes in functions.

7.3.2 The return statement

Now that you've got your output all debugged and cleaned up, let's talk about PowerShell's `return` statement. Yes, PowerShell does have a `return` statement, and yes, it's similar to the `return` statement in other languages. But remember—similar isn't the same.

Remember we talked about how functions in PowerShell are best described as writing output rather than returning results? So why, then, does PowerShell need a return statement? The answer is, *flow control.* Sometimes you want to exit a function early. Without a `return` statement, you'd have to write complex conditional statements to get the flow of control to reach the end. In effect, the `return` statement is like the break statement we covered in chapter 6—it "breaks" to the end of the function.

The next question is, is it possible to "return" a value from a function using the `return` statement? The answer is, yes. This looks like

```
return 2+2
```

which is really just shorthand for

```
Write-Output (2+2) ; return
```

The `return` statement is included in PowerShell because it's a common pattern that programmers expect to have. Unfortunately, it can sometimes lead to confusion for new users and nonprogrammers. They forget that, because PowerShell is a shell, every statement emits values into the output stream. Using the `return` statement can make this somewhat less obvious. Because of this potential for confusion, you should generally avoid using the `return` statement unless you need it to make your logic simpler. Even then, you should probably avoid using it to return a value. The one circumstance where it makes sense is in a "pure" function where you're only returning a single value. For example, look at this recursive definition of the factorial function:

```
PS (5) > function fact ($x) {
>> if ($x -lt 2) {return 1}
>> $x * (fact ($x-1))
>> }
>>
PS (6) > fact 3
6
```

This is a simple function that returns a single value with no side effects. In this case, it makes sense to use the return statement with a value.

> **Factorial facts**
>
> The factorial of a number x is the product of all positive numbers less than or equal to x. Therefore, the factorial of 6 is
>
> ```
> 6 * 5 * 4 * 3 * 2 * 1
> ```
>
> which is really
>
> ```
> 6 * (fact 5)
> ```
>
> which, in turn, is
>
> ```
> 6 * 5 * (fact 4)
> ```
>
> and so on down to 1.
>
> Factorials are useful in calculating permutations. Understanding permutations is useful if you're playing poker. This should not be construed as an endorsement for poker—it's just kind of cool. Bill Gates plays bridge.

7.4 USING SIMPLE FUNCTIONS IN A PIPELINE

So far, we've only talked about using functions as stand-alone statements. But what about using functions in pipelines? After all, PowerShell is all about pipelines, so shouldn't you be able to use functions in pipelines? Of course, the answer is, yes, with some considerations that need to be taken into account. The nature of a function is to take a set of inputs, process it, and produce a result. So how do you make the stream of objects from the pipeline available in a function? This is accomplished through the `$input` variable. When a function is used in a pipeline, a special variable, `$input`, is available that contains an enumerator that allows you to process through the input collection. Let's see how this works:

```
PS (1) > function sum {
>> $total=0;
>> foreach ($n in $input) { $total += $n }
>> $total
>> }
>>
```

A function `sum` is defined that takes no arguments but has one implied argument, which is `$input`. It will add each of the elements in `$input` to `$total` and then return `$total`. In other words, it will return the sum of all the input objects. Let's try this on a collection of numbers:

```
PS (2) > 1..5 | sum
15
```

Clearly it works as intended.

We said that `$input` is an *enumerator*. You may remember our discussion of enumerators from chapter 6 when we talked about the `$foreach` and `$switch` variables. The same principles apply here. You move the enumerator to the next element using the MoveNext() method and get the current element using the Current property. Here's the sum function rewritten using the enumerator members directly:

```
PS (3) > function sum2 {
>> $total=0
>> while ($input.movenext())
>> {
>> $total += $input.Current
>> }
>> $total
>> }
>>
```

Of course, it produces the same result:

```
PS (4) > 1..5 | sum2
15
```

Now write a variation of this that works with something other than numbers. This time you'll write a function that has a formal parameter and also processes input. The parameter will be the name of the property on the input object to sum up. Here's the function definition:

```
PS (7) > function sum3 ($p)
>> {
>> $total=0
>> while ($input.MoveNext())
>> {
>> $total += $input.current.$p
>> }
>> $total
>> }
>>
```

In line 6 of the function, you can see the expression $input.current.$p. This expression returns the value of the property named by $p on the current object in the enumeration. Use this function to sum the lengths of the files in the current directory:

```
PS (8) > dir | sum3 length
9111
```

You invoke the function passing in the string "length" as the name of the property to sum. The result is the total of the lengths of all of the files in the current directory.

This shows that it's pretty easy to write functions that you can use in a pipeline, but there's one thing we haven't touched on. Because functions run all at once, they can't do streaming processing. In the previous example, where you piped the output of dir into the function, what happened was that the dir cmdlet ran to completion and the accumulated results from that were passed as a collection to the function. So how can you use functions more effectively in a pipeline? That's what we'll cover next when we talk about the concept of filters.

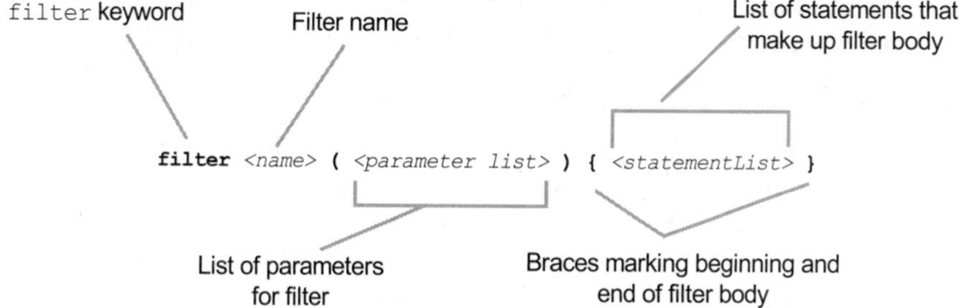

Figure 7.6 Defining a filter in PowerShell. The syntax is identical to the basic function definition except that it uses the `filter` keyword instead of the `function` keyword.

7.4.1 Filters and functions

In this section, we'll talk about filters and the `filter` keyword. Filters are a variation on the general concept of functions. Where a function in a pipeline runs once, a filter is run for each input object coming from the pipeline. The general form of a filter is shown in figure 7.6. PowerShell includes a `filter` keyword to make it easy to define this type of function.

As you can see, the only syntactic difference between a function and a filter is the keyword. The significant differences are all semantic. A function runs once and runs to completion. When used in a pipeline, it halts streaming—the previous element in the pipeline runs to completion; only then does the function begin to run. It also has a special variable `$input` defined when used as anything other than the first element of the pipeline. By contrast, a filter is run once and to completion for each element in the pipeline. Instead of the variable `$input`, it has a special variable, `$_`, that contains the current pipeline object.

At this point, we should look at an example to see what all this means. First, write a filter to double the value of all the input objects:

```
PS (1) > filter double {$_*2}
PS (2) > 1..5 | double
2
4
6
8
10
```

You should now be feeling a nagging sense of déjà vu. A little voice should be telling you, "I've seen this before." Remember the `ForEach-Object` cmdlet from chapter 6?

```
PS (3) > 1..5 | foreach {$_*2}
2
4
6
8
10
```

The ForEach-Object cmdlet is, in effect, a way of running an *anonymous filter*. By anonymous, we mean that you don't have to give it a name or predefine it. You just use it when you need it.

> **NOTE** When we first created PowerShell, we thought this shortcut way to create named filters would be useful. In fact, we were wrong and this keyword is rarely used. The foreach cmdlet and the process block in functions that you'll see in the next section pretty much eliminated the need for the keyword. Of course, we can't take it out because someone somewhere will have a script that uses it and we don't want to break existing scripts.

Functions in a pipeline run when all the input has been gathered. Filters run once for each element in the pipeline. In the next section, we'll talk about generalizing the role of a function so that it can be a first-class participant in a pipeline.

7.4.2 Functions with begin, process, and end blocks

You've seen how to write a function that sums up values in a pipeline but can't stream results. And you've seen how to write a filter to calculate the sum of values in a pipeline, but filters have problems with setting up initial values for variables or conducting processing after all the objects have been received. It would be nice if you could write user-defined cmdlets that can initialize some state at the beginning of the pipeline, process each object as it's received, then do cleanup work at the end of the pipeline. And of course you can. The full structure of a function cmdlet is shown in figure 7.7.

In figure 7.7 you see that you can define a clause for each phase of the cmdlet processing. This is exactly like the phases used in a compiled cmdlet, as mentioned in chapter 2. The begin keyword specifies the clause to run before the first pipeline

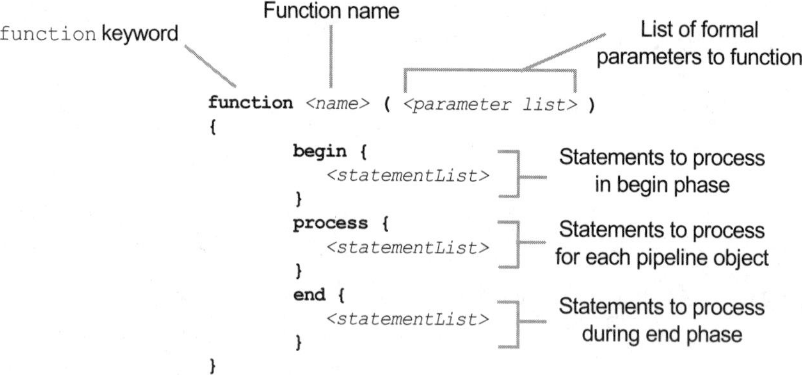

Figure 7.7 The complete function definition syntax for a function in PowerShell that will have cmdlet-like behavior

object is available. The process clause is executed once for each object in the pipeline, and the end clause is run once all the objects have been processed.

As with filters, the current pipeline object is available in the process clause in the special variable `$_`. As always, an example is the best way to illustrate this:

```
PS (1) > function my-cmdlet ($x) {
>> begin {$c=0; "In Begin, c is $c, x is $x"}
>> process {$c++; "In Process, c is $c, x is $x, `$_ is $_"}
>> end {"In End, c is $c, x is $x"}
>> }
>>
```

You define all three clauses in this function. Each clause reports what it is and then prints out the values of some variables. The variable `$x` comes from the command line; the variable `$c` is defined in the begin clause, incremented in the process clause, and displayed again in the end clause. The process clause also displays the value of the current pipeline object. Now let's run it. You'll pass the numbers 1 through 3 in through the pipeline and give it the argument 22 to use for `$x`. Here's what the output looks like:

```
PS (2) > 1,2,3 | my-cmdlet 22
In Begin, c is 0, x is 22
In Process, c is 1, x is 22, $_ is 1
In Process, c is 2, x is 22, $_ is 2
In Process, c is 3, x is 22, $_ is 3
In End, c is 3, x is 22
```

As you can see, the argument 22 is available in all three clauses and the value of `$c` is also maintained across all three clauses. What happens if there's no pipeline input? Let's try it:

```
PS (3) > my-cmdlet 33
In Begin, c is 0, x is 33
In Process, c is 1, x is 33, $_ is
In End, c is 1, x is 33
```

Even if there's no pipeline input, the process clause is still run exactly once. Of course, you don't have to specify all three of the clauses. If you specify only the process clause, you might as well just use the `filter` keyword, because the two are identical.

If you've been following along with the examples in this chapter, by now you'll have created quite a number of functions. Care to guess how to find out what you've defined?

7.5 MANAGING FUNCTION DEFINITIONS IN A SESSION

Because it's easy to create functions in PowerShell, it also needs to be easy to manage those functions. Rather than provide a custom set of commands (or worse yet, a set of keywords) to manage functions, you can take advantage of the namespace capabilities in PowerShell and provide a function drive. Because it's mapped as a drive, you can get a list of functions the same way you get a listing of the contents of any other drive. Let's use `dir` to find out about the `mkdir` function:

```
PS (7) > dir function:\mkdir

CommandType     Name                          Definition
-----------     ----                          ----------
Function        mkdir                         param([string[]]$pat...
```

By doing a `dir` of the path `function:\mkdir`, you can see `mkdir` exists and is a function. Wildcards can be used, so you could've just written `mk*` as shown:

```
PS (8) > dir function:\mk*

CommandType     Name                          Definition
-----------     ----                          ----------
Function        mkdir                         param([string[]]$pat...
```

And, if you just do `dir` on the function drive, you'll get a complete listing of all functions. Let's do this but just get a count of the number of functions:

```
PS (9) > (dir function:\).count
78
```

In my environment, I have 78 functions defined. Now let's create a new one,

```
PS (10) > function clippy { "I see you're writing a function." }
```

and check the count again:

```
PS (11) > (dir function:\).count
79
```

Yes—there's one more function than was there previously. Now check for the function itself:

```
PS (12) > dir function:\clippy

CommandType     Name                          Definition
-----------     ----                          ----------
Function        clippy                        "I see you're writin...
```

Running `dir` on `function:clippy` gives you the function definition entry for this function.

Now that you know how to add functions to your session, let's see how to remove them. You'll remove the `clippy` function you just created. Because you're removing an item from the function: drive, you'll remove the function the same way you'd remove a file from a file system drive with the `Remove-Item` command:

```
PS (13) > Remove-Item function:/clippy
```

And make sure that it's gone:

```
PS (14) > (dir function:/).count
78
```

```
PS (15) > dir function:clippy
Get-ChildItem : Cannot find path 'clippy' because it does not ex
ist.
At line:1 char:4
+ dir  <<<< function:clippie
```

Yes! You've removed `clippy` from the system.

> **NOTE** Longtime Microsoft Office users will no doubt be feeling an intense burst of satisfaction with this last example. We've all longed to eradicate that annoying paperclip "assistant," and at last we have the pleasure, if in name only. And, even more amusing: Microsoft Word doesn't even recognize "clippy"—it keeps trying to autocorrect to "clippie." Some unresolved issues, perhaps?

The techniques we've covered in this section allow you to manipulate the functions defined in your current session. As with any drive, you can list the functions, create new ones, delete them, and rename them. But regardless, all these functions will disappear when the session ends when you exit PowerShell. What about "permanent" functions? How can you define functions that are always available? This is where scripts come in, as you'll see in chapter 8. In the meantime, there's one more topic that impacts how functions work: variable scoping and lifetime. We've ignored it so far but we do need to cover it in some depth. So let's begin now.

7.6 VARIABLE SCOPING IN FUNCTIONS

In the final section of this chapter, we're going to cover the lifetime of variables. So far we've just ignored when variables are created, but there are specific rules that cover this. These rules govern when variables come into existence and where they're visible. The set or rules that cover variable lifetime and visibility are called the *scoping rules* of the language.

First, let's introduce some terminology for our discussion. In programming language design, there are two general approaches to scoping—*lexical* and *dynamic*. Most programming languages and many scripting languages are lexically scoped. In a lexically scoped language, it's *where* the name of something is defined that matters. Names are visible in the block they're defined in and in any nested blocks, but aren't visible outside the enclosing block unless they're explicitly exported in some way. Because where they're defined controls the visibility for the variable, this is determined at "compile" time and is therefore called *lexical* (or sometimes *static*) scoping.

On the other hand, dynamic scoping involves *when* the variable is defined. In other words, the visibility of the variable is controlled by the runtime or dynamic behavior of the program, not the compile-time or static behavior (hence the term *dynamic*).

> **NOTE** For the language folks in the audience, PowerShell actually uses a variation on traditional dynamic scoping: hygienic dynamic scoping. This has also been called *dynamic scoping with implicit let binding* (if you

care.) This significant difference is in how assignment is done. In traditional dynamic scoping, if a variable exists in an outer scope, then it will be assigned to the current scope. In PowerShell, even if there's an existing variable in an outer scope, a new local variable will be created on first assignment. This guarantees that a function, in the absence of scope modifiers, won't mess up the calling scopes (hence the term *hygienic*).

7.6.1 Declaring variables

Ignoring function parameters (which are a form of declaration), PowerShell has no variable declaration statement. In contrast to a language like Visual Basic, which uses `Dim` to declare a variable, in PowerShell a variable simply comes into existence on first assignment. We discussed this in chapter 5, but it's more important now. Figure 7.8 shows a diagram of how variable names are resolved in PowerShell.

Let's look at an example. First define two simple functions, `one` and `two`:

```
PS (1) > function one { "x is $x" }
PS (2) > function two { $x = 22; one }
```

Function `one` prints out a string displaying the value of `$x`. Function `two` sets the variable `$x` to a particular value, and then calls function `one`. Now let's try them out. Before you work with the functions, set `$x` to 7 interactively, to help illustrate how scoping works:

```
PS (3) > $x=7
```

Now call function `one`:

```
PS (4) > one
x is 7
```

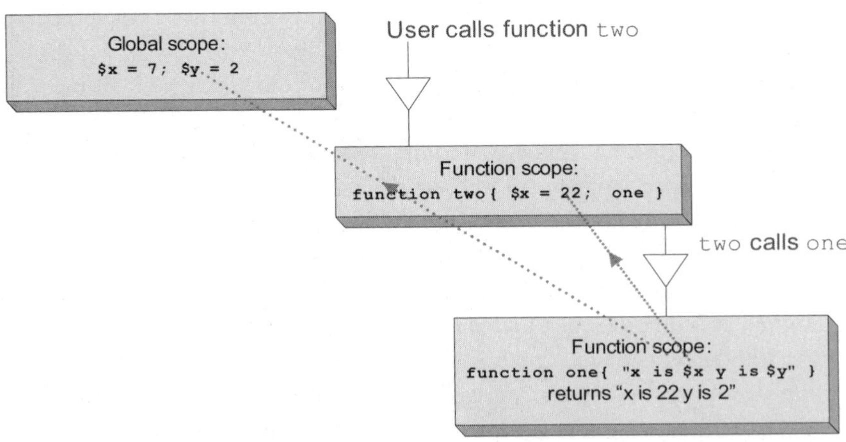

Figure 7.8 How variables are resolved across different scopes. They're resolved first in the local scope, then in the immediate caller's scope, and so on until the global scope is reached. In this case, lookup of $x resolves to 22 in the scope for function one. Lookup of $y resolves to 2 in the global scope, resulting in the output string "x is 22 y is 2".

As expected, it prints `x is 7`. Now call function `two`:

```
PS (5) > two
x is 22
```

Not surprisingly, because `two` sets `$x` to 22 before calling `one`, you see `x is 22` returned. So what happened to `$x`? Let's check:

```
PS (6) > $x
7
```

It's still 7! Now call `one` again:

```
PS (7) > one
x is 7
```

It prints `x is 7`. So what exactly happened here? When you first assigned 7 to `$x`, you created a new global variable, `$x`. When you called function `one` the first time, it looked for a variable `$x`, found the global definition, and used that to print the message. When you called function `two`, it defined a new local variable called `$x` before calling `one`. This variable is local—that is, it didn't change the value of the global `$x`, but it did put a new `$x` on the scope stack. When it called `one`, this function searched up the scope stack looking for `$x`, found the new variable created by function `two`, and used that to print `x is 22`. On return from function `two`, the scope containing its definition of `$x` was discarded. The next time you called function `one`, it found the top-level definition of `$x`. Now let's compare this to a language that's lexically scoped. I happen to have Python installed on my computer, so from PowerShell, I'll start the Python interpreter:

```
PS (1) > python
Python 2.2.3 (#42, May 30 2003, 18:12:08) [MSC 32 bit (Intel)] on
 win32
Type "help", "copyright", "credits" or "license" for more informa
tion.
```

Now let's set the global variable `x` to 7. (Note—even if you aren't familiar with Python, these examples are very simple, so you shouldn't have a problem following them.)

```
>>> x=7
```

Now print x to make sure it was properly set:

```
>>> print x
7
```

You see that it is, in fact, 7. Now let's define a Python function `one`:

```
>>> def one():
...     print "x is " + str(x)
...
```

And now define another function two that sets x to 22 and then calls one:

```
>>> def two():
...     x=22
...     one()
...
```

As with the PowerShell example, one prints x is 7.

```
>>> one()
x is 7
```

Now call two:

```
>>> two()
x is 7
```

Even though two defines x to be 22, when it calls one, one still prints 7. This is because the local variable x isn't lexically visible to one—it will always use the value of the global x, which you can see hasn't changed:

```
>>> print x
7
>>>
```

At this point, I hope you have a basic understanding of how variables are looked up in PowerShell. Sometimes, though, you want to be able to override the default lookup behavior. We'll discuss this in the next section.

> **NOTE** Unix shells used dynamic scoping because they didn't have a choice. Each script is executed in its own process and receives a copy of the parent's environment. Any environment variables that a script defines will then be inherited by any child scripts that it, in turn, calls. The process-based nature of the Unix shells predetermines how scoping can work. The interesting thing is that these semantics are pretty much what PowerShell uses, even though the PowerShell team wasn't limited by the process boundary. The team tried a number of different schemes and the only one that was satisfactory was the one that most closely mimicked traditional shell semantics. I suppose this shouldn't be a surprise—it's worked well for several decades now.

7.6.2 Using variable scope modifiers

We've now arrived at the subject of variable scope modifiers. In the previous section we discussed scope and the default PowerShell lookup algorithm. Now you'll see that you can override the default lookup by using a scope modifier. These modifiers look like the namespace qualifiers mentioned in chapter 6. To access a global variable $var, you'd write

```
$global:var
```

Let's revisit the functions from the previous section:

```
PS (1) > function one { "x is $global:x" }
```

This time, in the function one, you'll use the scope modifier to explicitly reference the global $x:

```
PS (2) > function two { $x = 22; one }
```

The definition of function two is unchanged. Now set the global $x to 7 (commands at the top level always set global variables, so you don't need to use the global modifier):

```
PS (3) > $x=7
```

Now run the functions:

```
PS (4) > one
x is 7
PS (5) > two
x is 7
```

This time, because you told one to bypass searching the scope change for $x and go directly to the global variable, calls to both one and two return the same result, x is 7.

When we look at scripts in chapter 8, you'll see that there are additional scoping rules and qualifiers, but for now, you have all you need to work with functions.

In the next chapter, you'll extend your PowerShell programming knowledge to include writing scripts. We'll also look at some of the advanced features in PowerShell, especially new features introduced with PowerShell v2 that you can use for your work.

7.7 SUMMARY

This chapter introduced the idea of programming in PowerShell. We covered a lot of material; here are the key points:

- PowerShell programming can be done either with functions or scripts, though in this chapter we focused only on functions.
- Functions are created using the `function` keyword.
- The simplest form of function uses `$args` to receive parameters automatically.
- More sophisticated parameter handling for functions requires the use of parameter declarations. This can be done by placing the parameter names in parentheses after the name of the function or in the body of the function using the `param` keyword.
- PowerShell uses dynamic scoping for variables. You can modify how a variable name is resolved by using the scope modifiers in the variable names.

- Functions stream their output. In other words, they return the results of every statement executed as though it were written to the output stream. This feature means that you almost never have to write your own code to accumulate results.
- Because of the differences between how functions work in PowerShell and how they work in more conventional languages, you may receive some unexpected results when creating your functions, so you picked up some tips on debugging these problems.
- Functions can be used as filters using the `filter` keyword or by specifying begin, process, and end blocks in the function body.
- The function: drive is used to manage the functions defined in your session. This means that you use the same commands you use for managing files to manage functions.

CHAPTER 8

Advanced functions and scripts

And now for something completely different…

—Monty Python

In chapter 7, we introduced the basic elements needed for programming in PowerShell when we looked at PowerShell functions. In this chapter we're going to expand our repertoire by introducing PowerShell scripts.

> **NOTE** If you skipped chapter 7, you should probably go back and read it before proceeding. Why? Because all the material we covered on functions also applies to scripts.

Once we're finished with the basics of scripts (which won't take long), we'll move on to the advanced production scripting features introduced in PowerShell v2. With these new features, it's possible to use the PowerShell language to write full-featured applications complete with proper documentation. By the end of this chapter, you should be well on your way to becoming an expert PowerShell programmer.

8.1 POWERSHELL SCRIPTS

In this section we're going to dig into scripts to see what behaviors they have in common with functions and what additional features you need to be aware of. We'll begin by looking at the execution policy that controls what scripts can be run. Then you'll see how parameters and the `exit` statement work in scripts. We'll also spend some time on the additional scoping rules that scripts introduce. Finally, you'll learn ways you can apply and manage the scripts you write.

Let's begin with defining what a script is. A PowerShell script is simply a file with a .ps1 extension that contains some PowerShell commands. Back in chapter 1, we talked about how PowerShell has the world's shortest "Hello world" program. The full text of that script was

```
"Hello world"
```

That's it—one line. Let's create this script now. You can do it from the command line using redirection to write the script text to a file called hello.ps1:

```
PS (2) > '"Hello world"' > hello.ps1
```

Note the double quotes in the example. You want the script to contain

```
"Hello world"
```

with the quotes intact, not

```
Hello world
```

Now execute the script:

```
PS (3) > ./hello.ps1
Hello world
```

You see that the file executed and returned the expected phrase.

> **NOTE** In this example, even though hello.ps1 is in the current directory, you had to put `./` in front of it to run it. This is because PowerShell doesn't execute commands out of the current directory by default. This prevents accidental execution of the wrong command. See chapter 13 on security for more information.

8.1.1 Script execution policy

Now there's a possibility that instead of getting the expected output, you received a nasty-looking error message that looked something like this:

```
PS (5) > ./hello.ps1
The file C:\Documents and Settings\brucepay\hello.ps1 cannot be
loaded. The file C:\Documents and Settings\brucepay\hello.ps1 is
 not digitally signed. The script will not execute on the system
. Please see "get-help about_signing" for more details.
At line:1 char:11
+ ./hello.ps1 <<<<
```

This is another security feature in PowerShell. When PowerShell is first installed, by default you can't run any scripts. This is controlled by a feature called the execution policy. The execution policy setting controls what kind of scripts can be run and is intended to prevent virus attacks like the "I-love-you" virus from a few years back. Users were being tricked into accidentally executing code mailed to them. The default execution policy for PowerShell prevents this type of attack.

A scripting tool is no good if you can't script, so there's a cmdlet called `Set-ExecutionPolicy` that can be used to change the execution policy. If you got the error when you tried to execute the script, you should run the following command as Administrator.

Running elevated

Running elevated is a term used on Windows Vista or later that has to do with the User Access Control (UAC) feature added in Vista. It essentially means that you're running with administrative privileges. This can only be done when starting a process. Interactively, you can start an elevated PowerShell session by right-clicking the PowerShell icon and selecting Run as Administrator. You then get the UAC prompt asking if you want to allow this action.

If you want to run a single command elevated in a script, you can do so with the `Start-Process` cmdlet and the `-Verb` parameter. For example, you can run `Set-ExecutionPolicy` in an elevated PowerShell session as follows:

```
Start-Process -Verb runas -FilePath powershell.exe
-ArgumentList 'Set-ExecutionPolicy -ExecutionPolicy RemoteSigned'
```

When this command is run, you're prompted to allow the action. If you say yes, a new console window appears, the command executes, and the newly created console window closes after the command is complete.

If you don't have administrator access, there's an alternative we'll get to in a second. Here's the command:

```
PS (6) > Set-ExecutionPolicy remotesigned
```

After the command has run successfully, you should be able to run hello.ps1:

```
PS (7) > ./hello.ps1
Hello world
```

> **NOTE** Running the cmdlet as shown will change the execution policy so that you can execute local scripts that you create yourself. PowerShell still won't execute scripts that come from remote sources such as email or a website unless they're signed. Of course, for this check to work, the mail tool or the web browser used to do the download must set the Zone Identifier Stream to indicate where the file came from. Internet Explorer and Microsoft Outlook set this properly. At a

minimum, I recommend you use the RemoteSigned policy. Chapter 17 covers all these security topics in detail.

Setting the execution policy for a single session

If you can't run Set-ExecutionPolicy with the necessary administrator privileges but you have PowerShell v2 installed, you can use the -Scope parameter on the cmdlet to just set the execution policy for the current session (the current process). This looks like

```
PS (1) > Set-ExecutionPolicy -Scope process remotesigned

Execution Policy Change
The execution policy helps protect you from scripts that
you do not trust. Changing the execution policy might
expose you to the security risks described in the
about_Execution_Policies help topic. Do you want to change
the execution policy?
[Y] Yes  [N] No  [S] Suspend  [?] Help (default is "Y"): y
PS (2) >
```

Note the prompt to confirm this operation. You reply y to tell the system to proceed to make the change. (You'll see more on confirmation of actions in section 8.2.2, where I show how to implement this feature in scripts.) Now when you try to run scripts, they'll work, but remember, you changed the execution policy only for this session. The next time you start PowerShell, you'll have to rerun the command.

Okay, now that you've got your basic script running, let's start adding functionality to this script.

8.1.2 Passing arguments to scripts

The first thing we'll look at is how you can pass arguments to a script. The answer is pretty much the same way you did it for basic functions. We'll start with the $args variable and look at a modified version of the basic script. Again, you can use redirection to create the script from the command line. In fact, this version overwrites the old version of the script:

```
PS (8) > '"Hello $args"' > hello.ps1
and run it with an argument:
PS (9) > ./hello Bruce
Hello Bruce
```

Great—hello PowerShell! But if you don't supply an argument

```
PS (10) > ./hello
Hello
```

you get a very impersonal greeting. (Notice, by the way, that I didn't have to specify the .ps1 extension when running the script. PowerShell adds this automatically when looking for a script file.)

Let's see what we can do to make the script a bit chattier. You can take advantage of a here-string to generate a slightly longer script:

```
PS (11) > @'
>> if ($args) { $name = "$args" } else { $name = "world" }
>> "Hello $name!"
>> '@ > hello.ps1
>>
```

This script has two lines. The first sets a local variable `$name` to the value of `$args` if it's defined. If it's not defined, it sets `$name` to `world`. If you run the script with no arguments, you get the generic greeting:

```
PS (12) > ./hello
Hello world!
```

If you run it with an argument, you get a specific greeting:

```
PS (13) > ./hello Bruce
Hello Bruce!
PS (14) >
```

These are the same basic things you did with functions, and, as was the case with functions, they have limitations. It would be much more useful to have named, typed parameters as was the case with functions. But there's a slight wrinkle: as you'll remember from chapter 7, the formal arguments to a function are defined outside the body of the function, or inside the body with the `param` statement. Obviously, the external definition isn't going to work with scripts because there's no "external." Consequently, there's only one way to define formal parameters for a script: through the `param` statement.

Using the param statement in scripts

As mentioned in the previous section, if you want to specify formal parameters for a script, you need to use the `param` statement. The `param` statement must be the first executable line in the script just as it must be the first executable line in a function. Only comments and empty lines may precede it. Let's visit the `hello` example one more time. Again you'll use a here-string and redirection to create the script. The here-string makes it easy to define a multiline script:

```
PS (14) > @'
>> param($name="world")
>> "Hello $name!"
>> '@ > hello.ps1
>>
```

Here you're adding a second line to the script to declare the script parameter. When you run the script, you find the expected results, first with no arguments

```
PS (15) > ./hello
Hello world!
```

and then with a name argument:

```
PS (16) > ./hello Bruce
Hello Bruce!
PS (17) >
```

The script could be written as a single line but splitting it across two lines makes it easier to read:

```
PS (17) > 'param($name="world") "Hello $name"' > hello.ps1
PS (18) > ./hello
Hello world
PS (19) > ./hello Bruce
Hello Bruce
```

The interesting thing that this example illustrates is that there's no need for any kind of separator after the param statement for the script to be valid. Because PowerShell lends itself to one-liner type solutions, this can be handy.

Obviously, scripts must have some additional characteristics that you don't find with functions. Let's explore those now.

8.1.3 Exiting scripts and the exit statement

You've seen that you can exit scripts (or functions) simply by getting to the end of the script. We've also looked at the return statement in our discussion of functions (section 7.3.2). The return statement lets you exit early from a function. It will also let you return early from a script but only if called from the "top" level of a script (not from a function called in the script). The interesting question is what happens when you return from a function defined inside a script. As discussed in chapter 7, what the return statement does is let you exit from the current scope. This remains true whether that scope was created by a function or a script. But what happens when you want to cause a script to exit from within a function defined in that script? PowerShell has the exit statement to do exactly this. So far, you've been using this statement to exit a PowerShell session. But when exit is used inside a script, it exits that script. This is true even when called from a function in that script. Here's what that looks like:

```
PS (1) > @'
>> function callExit { "calling exit from callExit"; exit}
>> CallExit
>> "Done my-script"
>> '@ > my-script.ps1
>>
```

The function CallExit defined in this script calls exit. Because the function is called before the line that emits

```
"Done my-script"
```

you shouldn't see this line emitted. Let's run it:

```
PS (2) > ./my-script.ps1
calling exit from CallExit
```

You see that the script was correctly terminated by the call to `exit` in the function `CallExit`.

The `exit` statement is also how you set the exit code for the PowerShell process when calling `PowerShell.exe` from another program. Here's an example that shows how this works. From within `cmd.exe`, run `PowerShell.exe`, passing it a string to execute. This "script" will emit the message "Hi there" and then call `exit` with an exit code of 17:

```
C:\>powershell "'Hi there'; exit 17"
Hi there
```

And now you're back at the `cmd.exe` prompt. `Cmd.exe` makes the exit code of a program it's run available in the variable `ERRORLEVEL`, so check that variable:

```
C:\>echo %ERRORLEVEL%
17
```

You see that it's 17 as expected. This shows how a script executed by PowerShell can return an exit code to the calling process.

Let's recap: so far in our discussion of scripts behaviors, we've covered execution policy, parameterization, and how to exit scripts. In the next section we'll look at another feature of scripts that you need to understand: variable scoping.

8.1.4 Scopes and scripts

In chapter 7, we covered the scoping rules for functions. These same general rules also apply to scripts:

- Variables are created when they're first assigned.
- They're always created in the current scope, so a variable with the same name in an outer (or global) scope isn't affected.
- In both scripts and functions, you can use the `$global:name` scope modifier to explicitly modify a global variable.

Now let's see what's added for scripts.

Scripts introduce a new named scope called the *script scope*, indicated by using the `$script:` scope modifier. This scope modifier is intended to allow functions defined in a script to affect the "global" state of the script without affecting the overall global state of the interpreter. This is shown in figure 8.1.

Let's look at an example. First, set a global variable `$x` to be 1:

```
PS (1) > $x = 1
```

Then, create a script called `my-script`. In this script, you'll create a function called `lfunc`. The `lfunc` function will define a function-scoped variable `$x` to be 100 and a script-scoped variable `$x` to be 10. The script itself will run this function and then

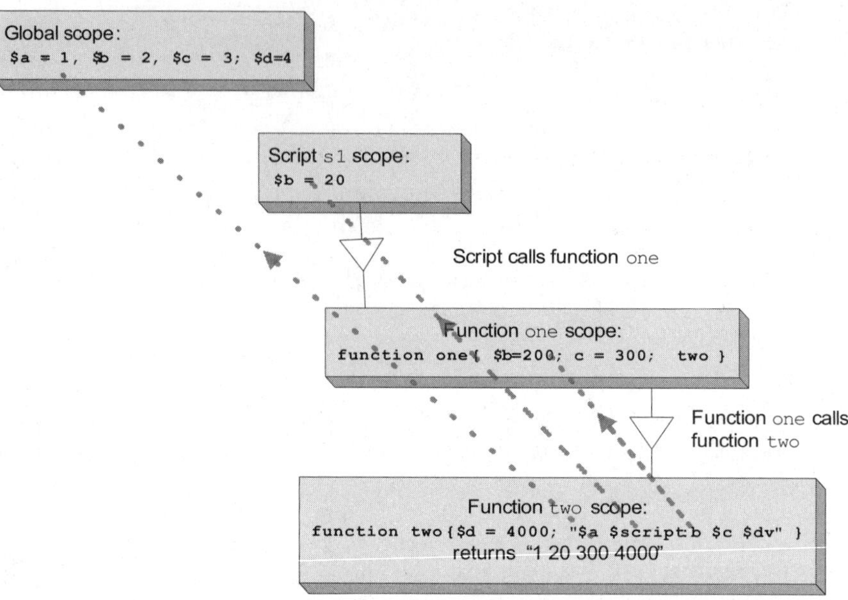

Figure 8.1 How variables are resolved across different scopes when scripts are involved. Variables prefixed with the `$script:` modifier resolve in the script scope. Variable references with no scope modifier resolve using the normal lookup rules. In this figure, the user calls script `s1`, which creates a new script scope. `s1` calls function `one`, which causes a new function scope to be created. `one` calls function `two`, creating a second function scope, and resulting in a total of four scopes in the scope chain. In function `two`, `$a` resolves in the global scope, `$script:b` resolves in the script scope (skipping the function `one` scope because of the `$script:` modifier), `$c` resolves in the function `one` scope, and `$d` resolves in the function `two` scope (`$d` is local to `two`).

print the script-scoped variable `$x`. Use a here-string and redirection to create the script interactively:

```
PS (2) > @'
>> function lfunc { $x = 100; $script:x = 10 ; "lfunc: x = $x"}
>> lfunc
>> "my-script:x = $x"
>> '@ > my-script.ps1
>>
```

Now run the script:

```
PS (3) > ./my-script.ps1
lfunc: x = 100
my-script:x = 10
```

You see that the function-scoped variable `$x` was 100; the script-scoped `$x` was 10

```
PS (4) > "global: x = $x"
global: x = 1
```

and the global `$x` is still 1.

Simple libraries: including one script from another

As you build libraries of useful functions, you need to have a mechanism to "include" one script inside another (or to run in the global environment) to make these library functions available. PowerShell allows you to do this through a feature called "dot-sourcing" a script or function.

> **NOTE** The dot-sourcing mechanism (sometimes called "dotting") is the only way to build libraries in PowerShell v1. In PowerShell v2, dot-sourcing is still used for configuration, but the modules feature (chapters 9 and 10) is the recommended way to create script libraries.

So far in our discussions, you've usually focused on the results of a function and wanted all the local variables when the script or function exits. This is why scripts and functions get their own scope. But sometimes you do care about all the intermediate by-products. This is typically the case when you want to create a library of functions or variable definitions. In this situation, you want the script to run in the current scope.

How cmd.exe works

This is how `cmd.exe` works by default, as this example shows. Say you have a CMD file, `foo.cmd`:

```
C:\files>type foo.cmd
set a=4
```

Set a variable to 1 and display it:

```
C:\files>set a=1
C:\files>echo %a%
1
```

Next run the CMD file

```
C:\files>foo
C:\files>set a=4
```

and you see that the variable has been changed:

```
C:\files>echo %a%
4
```

As a consequence of this behavior, it's common to have CMD files that do nothing but set a bunch of variables. To do this in PowerShell, you'd dot the script.

Dot-sourcing scripts and functions

So how do you "dot-source" a script? By putting a dot or period in front of the name when you execute it. Note that there has to be a space between the dot and the name; otherwise it will be considered part of the name. Let's look at an example. First create a script that sets $x to 22

```
PS (5) > @'
>> "Setting x to 22"
>> $x = 22
```

```
>> '@ > my-script.ps1
>>
```

and test it. Set $x to a known value

```
PS (6) > $x=3
PS (7) > $x
3
```

and then run the script as you would normally:

```
PS (8) > ./my-script
Setting x to 22
```

Checking $x, you see that it is (correctly) unchanged:

```
PS (9) > $x
3
```

Now dot the script:

```
PS (10) > . ./my-script
Setting x to 22
PS (11) > $x
22
```

This time, $x is changed. What follows the `.` isn't limited to a simple filename; it could be a variable or expression, as was the case with `&`:

```
PS (12) > $name = "./my-script"
PS (13) > . $name
Setting x to 22
```

The last thing to note is that dot-sourcing works for both scripts and functions. Define a function to show this:

```
PS (17) > function set-x ($x) {$x = $x}
PS (18) > . set-x 3
PS (19) > $x
3
```

In this example, you've defined the function `set-x` and dotted it, passing in the value 3. The result is that the global variable $x is set to 3. This covers how scoping works with scripts and functions. When we look at modules in chapter 9, you'll see another variation on scoping.

Now that you know how to build simple script libraries, we'll show you how to manage all these scripts you're writing.

8.1.5 Managing your scripts

Earlier we looked at managing functions using the function: drive. Because scripts live in the file system, there's no need to have a special drive for them—the file system drives are sufficient. But this does require that you understand how scripts are found in the file system. Like most shells, PowerShell uses the `PATH` environment variable to find scripts. You can look at the contents of this variable using the environment variable provider `$ENV:PATH`.

The other thing to know (and we've mentioned it previously but people still forget it) is that PowerShell doesn't run scripts out of the current directory (at least not by default). If you want to run a script out of the current directory, you can either add that directory to the path or prefix your command with `./` as in `./mycmd.ps1` or simply `./mycmd`. The script search algorithm will look for a command with the `.ps1` extension if there isn't one on the command. A common approach is to have a common scripts directory where all your personal scripts are placed and a share for sharing scripts between multiple users. Scripts are just text, so using a version control system like RCS or Subversion will work well for managing your scripts.

Now let's look at one more variation on scripting. So far, you've been running PowerShell scripts only from within PowerShell console. There are times when you need to run a PowerShell script from a non-PowerShell application like `cmd.exe`. For example, you may have an existing batch file that needs to call PowerShell for one specific task. To do this, you need to launch a PowerShell process to run the script or command. You also have to do this when creating shortcuts that launch PowerShell scripts because `PowerShell.exe` isn't the default file association for a .ps1 file (security strikes again—this prevents accidental execution of scripts).

8.1.6 Running PowerShell scripts from other applications

Let's look at what's involved in using `PowerShell.exe` to run a script and go over a few issues that exist.

Here's something that can trip people up when using `PowerShell.exe` to execute a script. The PowerShell v2 interpreter has two parameters that let you run PowerShell code when PowerShell is started. These parameters are `-Command` and `-File`, as shown in figure 8.2.

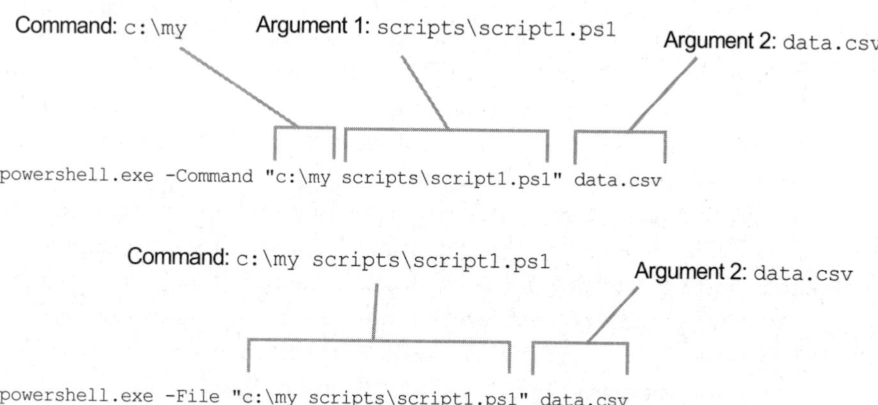

Figure 8.2 How the command line is processed when using the `-Command` parameter (top) versus the `-File` parameter (bottom). With `-Command`, the first argument is parsed into two tokens. With `-File`, the entire first argument is treated as the name of a script to run.

If you use the -Command parameter, the arguments to PowerShell.exe are accumulated and then treated as a script to execute. This is important to remember when you try to run a script using PowerShell from cmd.exe using this parameter. Here's the problem people run into: because the arguments to PowerShell.exe are a script to execute, not the name of a file to run, if the path to that script has a space in it, then because PowerShell treats the spaces as delimiters, you'll get an error. Consider a script called "my script.ps1". When you try to run this

```
powershell "./my script.ps1"
```

PowerShell will complain about my being an unrecognized command. It treats my as a command name and script.ps1 as an argument to that command. To execute a script with a space in the name, you need to do the same thing you'd do at the PowerShell command prompt: put the name in quotes and use the call (&) operator:

```
powershell.exe "& './my script.ps1'"
```

Now the script will be run properly. This is one of the areas where having two types of quotes comes in handy. Also note that you still have to use the relative path to find the script even if it's in the current directory.

To address this problem, in v2, PowerShell.exe now has a second parameter that makes this easier: the -File parameter. This parameter takes the first argument after the parameter as the name of the file to run and the remaining arguments are passed to the script. The example now simplifies to

```
powershell -File "my script.ps1"
```

This is clearly much simpler than the v1 example.

There's one more advantage to using -File. When you run a script using -Command, the exit keyword will exit the script but not the PowerShell session (though usually it looks like it did). This is because the arguments to -Command are treated the same way commands typed interactively into PowerShell work. You wouldn't want a script you're running to cause your session to exit accidentally. If you use -File instead of -Command, calling exit in the script will cause the PowerShell.exe process to exit. This is because -File treats the entire contents of the script as the command to execute instead of executing a command that names the script file.

Now let's see why this is important. It matters if you're depending on the exit code of the PowerShell process to decide some condition in the calling script. If you use -Command, the exit code of the script is set but the process will still exit with 0. If you use -File, PowerShell.exe will exit with the correct exit code. Let's try this. Create a script called exit33.ps1 that looks like this:

```
PS (1) > gc exit33.ps1
exit 33
```

This is a simple script—all it does is exit with the exit code 33. Now run it using `-Command` and check the exit code:

```
PS (2) > powershell.exe -Command ./exit33.ps1
PS (3) > $LASTEXITCODE
0
```

You see that the exit code of the `PowerShell.exe` process is 0, not 33, which is what you wanted. Let's take a closer look. Run the command again, but follow it with `$LASTEXITCODE` to emit the code returned from the script:

```
PS (6) > powershell.exe -Command `
>> './exit33.ps1 ; $LASTEXITCODE'
>>
33
```

You see that 33 was output because that was the last exit code of the script. But when you check the exit code of the process

```
PS (7) > $LASTEXITCODE
0
```

you see that it's still 0. (In fact, the piece of script that emits the exit code shouldn't even have run if the call to exit in the script had caused the process to exit.) In contrast, when you use `-File` or `-Command`

```
PS (4) > powershell.exe -File ./exit33.ps1
PS (5) > $LASTEXITCODE
33
```

you get the correct exit code because the `-File` option runs the specified command directly. This means that if the caller of `PowerShell.exe` depends on the exit code of the process, it will get the correct value.

This concludes our coverage of the basic information needed to run PowerShell scripts. If you've used other scripting languages, little of what you've seen so far should seem unfamiliar. In the next few sections we're going to look at things that are rather more advanced.

8.2 WRITING ADVANCED FUNCTIONS AND SCRIPTS

For the most part, all the features we've discussed so far were available in PowerShell v1. Although v1 scripts and functions were powerful, they didn't have all the features that compiled cmdlets did. In particular, there wasn't a good way to write production-quality scripts complete with integrated help, and so on. Version 2 introduced features that addressed these problems: commands written in the PowerShell language have all the capabilities available to cmdlets. In this section, we'll introduce these new features, and you'll learn how to use the create functions and scripts that have all the capabilities of cmdlets. We'll be using functions for all the examples just for simplicity's sake. Everything that applies to functions applies equally to scripts.

All these new features are enabled by adding *metadata* to the function or script parameters. Metadata is information about information, and you use it in PowerShell to declaratively control the behavior of functions and scripts. What this means is that you're telling PowerShell *what* you want to do but not *how* to do it. It's like telling a taxi driver where you want to go without having to tell them how to get there (although, it's always a good idea to make sure you're ending up where you want to be).

We're all ready to dive in now, but first, a warning. There's a lot of material here and some of it is a bit complex, so taking your time and experimenting with the features is recommended.

> **NOTE** This stuff is much more complex than the PowerShell team wanted. Could it have been simpler? Maybe, but the team hasn't figured out a way to do it yet. The upside of the way these features are implemented is that they match how things are done in compiled cmdlets. This way, the time invested in learning this material will be of benefit if you want to learn to write cmdlets at some point. And at the same time, if you know how to write cmdlets, then all this stuff will be pretty familiar.

8.2.1 Specifying script and function attributes

In this section, we'll look at the features you can control through metadata attributes on the function or script definition (as opposed to on parameters, which we'll get to in a minute). Figure 8.3 shows how the metadata attributes are used when defining a function, including attributes that affect the function as well as individual parameters on that function.

Notice that there are two places where the attributes can be added to functions: to the function itself and to the individual parameters. With scripts, the metadata attribute

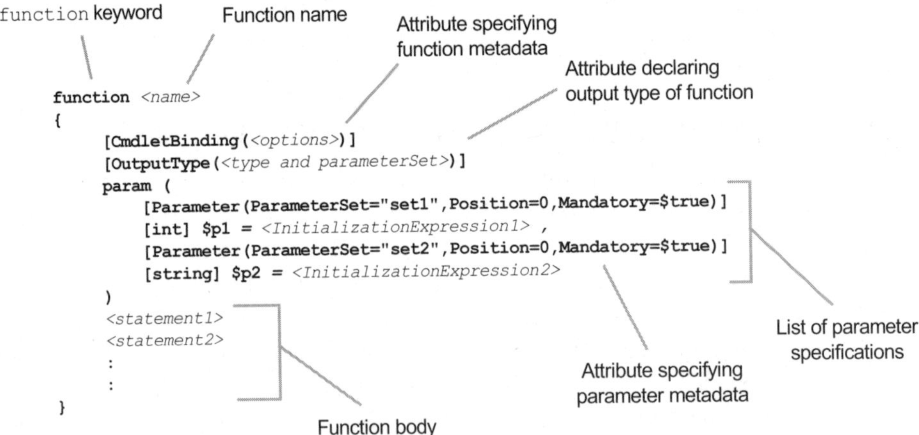

Figure 8.3 Attributes that apply to the entire function appear before the `param` statement, and attributes for an individual parameter appear before the parameter declaration.

has to appear before the param statement. (Earlier, I said param has to be the first noncomment line. This is still true because the metadata attributes are considered part of the param statement.)

The CmdletBinding attribute is used to add metadata to the function, specifying things like behaviors that apply to all parameters as well as things like the return type of the function. You should notice that the attribute syntax where the attribute names are enclosed in square brackets is similar to the way you specify types. This is because attributes are implemented using .NET types. The important distinction is that an attribute must have parentheses after the name. As you can see in figure 8.3, you can place properties on the attribute in the parentheses. But even if you're specifying no attributes, the parentheses must still be there so the interpreter can distinguish between a type literal and an attribute. Now let's look at the most important attribute: CmdletBinding.

8.2.2 The CmdletBinding attribute

The CmdletBinding attribute is used to specify properties that apply to the whole function or script. In fact, simply having the attribute in the definition changes how excess parameters are handled. If the function is defined without this attribute, the arguments for which there are no formal parameters are simply added to the $args variable, as shown in the next example. First, define a function that takes two formal parameters:

```
PS (1) > function x {param($a, $b) "a=$a b=$b args=$args"}
```

Now call that function with four arguments:

```
PS (2) > x 1 2 3 4
a=1 b=2 args=3 4
```

You see that the excess arguments end up in $args. As discussed earlier, although this can be useful, it's usually better to generate an error for this situation. You can check for this case and see if $args.Count is greater than 0, but it's easier to handle this declaratively by adding the metadata attribute, as shown here:

```
PS (3) > function x {[CmdletBinding()] param($a, $b)
>> "a=$a b=$b args=$args"}
>>
```

When you run the command with extra arguments

```
PS (4) > x 1 2 3 4
x : A positional parameter cannot be found that accepts argument '3'.
At line:1 char:2
+ x <<<<  1 2 3 4
    + CategoryInfo          : InvalidArgument: (:) [x],
          ParameterBindingException
    + FullyQualifiedErrorId : PositionalParameterNotFound,x
```

the system catches this and generates the error message for you. The fact that the system generates the error message instead of having to create the message yourself is a

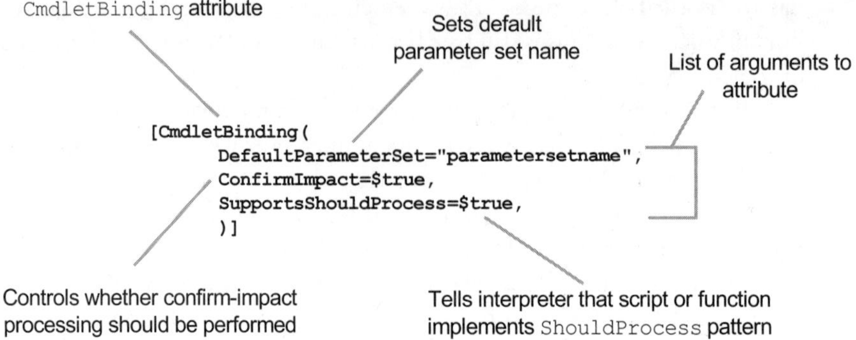
CmdletBinding attribute
Sets default parameter set name
List of arguments to attribute
[CmdletBinding(
DefaultParameterSet="parametersetname",
ConfirmImpact=$true,
SupportsShouldProcess=$true,
)]
Controls whether confirm-impact processing should be performed
Tells interpreter that script or function implements ShouldProcess pattern

Figure 8.4 All the properties that can be specified for the CmdletBinding attribute. These properties are used by the PowerShell runtime to control the execution of the associated function or script.

significant feature: it means that you get standard, complete, and consistent error messages that are already set up to display in many languages.

Now let's look at the properties that can be specified for the `CmdletBinding` attribute. These properties are shown in figure 8.4.

We'll describe what each of these properties does and how to use them in the next few subsections.

The SupportsShouldProcess property

When the `SupportsShouldProcess` property is set to true, it tells the runtime to enable the `-Confirm` and `-WhatIf` standard parameters because the function promises to make the necessary calls to the `ShouldProcess()` method on the object in the `$PSCmdlet` variable. The `ShouldProcess()` method is used to either ask the user for feedback before proceeding with the operation or to show what the operation might have done to the system. The `$PSCmdlet` variable is an automatic variable that provides the callback mechanisms that the function needs to make the expected calls. (We'll cover the `$PSCmdlet` variable in more detail at the end of this section.) Let's write an example function that shows how it all works. The purpose of this function is to allow the user to stop processes on the system. Because stopping the wrong process could have undesirable consequences, you want to be able to use `-Confirm` and `-WhatIf` parameters. The example code is shown in figure 8.5 with the necessary annotations highlighted.

This function uses the `Win32_Process` WMI class to get objects representing processes on the system (see chapter 19 for more information about WMI). You filter the set of processes using the `Where-Object` cmdlet and then call the `Terminate()` method on the process object. Obviously this is a potentially destructive operation, so you want to call the `ShouldProcess()` method before proceeding with the action (you saw this behavior with the `Set-ExecutionPolicy` cmdlet). You call this

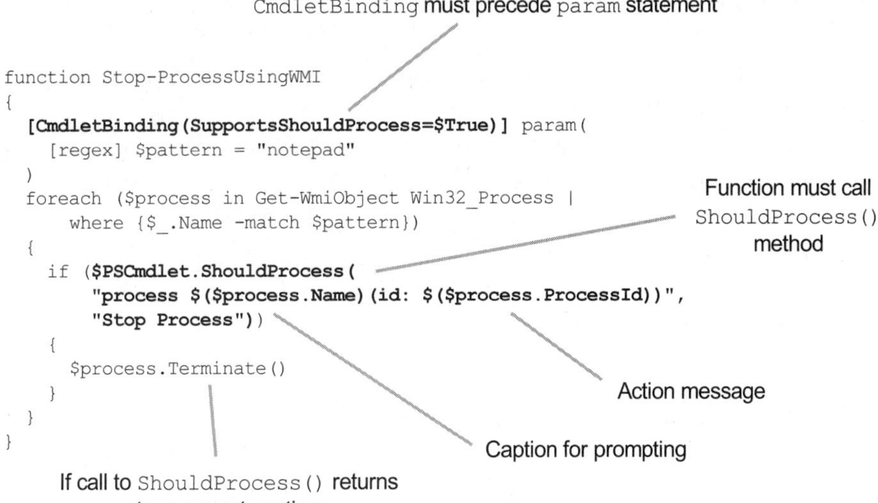

CmdletBinding must precede param statement
function Stop-ProcessUsingWMI
{
[CmdletBinding(SupportsShouldProcess=$True)] param(
[regex] $pattern = "notepad"
)
foreach ($process in Get-WmiObject Win32_Process |
where {$_.Name -match $pattern})
{
if ($PSCmdlet.ShouldProcess(
"process $($process.Name)(id: $($process.ProcessId))",
"Stop Process"))
{
$process.Terminate()
}
}
}
Function must call ShouldProcess() method
Action message
Caption for prompting
If call to ShouldProcess() returns true, execute action

Figure 8.5 The function annotations needed to enable `ShouldProcess` support. The `SupportsShouldProcess` property of the `CmdletBinding` attribute should be set to true, and there must be a call to the `ShouldProcess()` method in the body of the code.

method passing two `[string]` arguments. The first argument is used to tell the user what object you're going to operate on. The second argument describes the operation to be performed—essentially an operation caption. If this method returns true, you call `Terminate()` to end the process. Let's try it. First, define the function:

```
PS (1) > function Stop-ProcessUsingWMI
>> {
>>     [CmdletBinding(SupportsShouldProcess=$True)] param(
>>         [parameter(mandatory=$true)] [regex] $pattern
>>     )
>>     foreach ($process in Get-WmiObject Win32_Process |
>>         where { $_.Name -match $pattern })
>>     {
>>         if ($PSCmdlet.ShouldProcess(
>>             "process $($process.Name) " +
>>             " (id: $($process.ProcessId))" ,
>>             "Stop Process"))
>>         {
>>             $process.Terminate()
>>         }
>>     }
>> }
>>
```

Next, start a Notepad process:

```
PS (2) > notepad
```

Now call Stop-ProcessUsingWMI, specifying the -WhatIf parameter:

```
PS (3) > Stop-ProcessUsingWMI notepad -Whatif
What if: Performing operation "Stop Process" on Target "proc
ess notepad.exe  (id: 6748)".
```

You see a description of the operation that would be performed. The -WhatIf option was only supposed to show what it would have done but not actually do it, so you'll use Get-Process to verify that the command is still running:

```
PS (4) > Get-Process notepad | ft name,id -auto

Name     Id
----     --
notepad 6748
```

Let's perform the operation again but this time use the -Confirm flag. This requests that you be prompted for confirmation before executing the operation. When you get the prompt, you'll respond y to continue with the operation:

```
PS (5) > Stop-ProcessUsingWMI notepad -Confirm

Confirm
Are you sure you want to perform this action?
Performing operation "Stop Process" on Target "process
notepad.exe  (id: 6748)".
[Y] Yes  [A] Yes to All  [N] No  [L] No to All
[S] Suspend[?] Help (default is "Y"): y

__GENUS          : 2
__CLASS          : __PARAMETERS
__SUPERCLASS     :
__DYNASTY        : __PARAMETERS
__RELPATH        :
__PROPERTY_COUNT : 1
__DERIVATION     : {}
__SERVER         :
__NAMESPACE      :
__PATH           :
ReturnValue      : 0
```

And the operation was performed. Use Get-Process to confirm that the Notepad process no longer exists:

```
PS (6) > Get-Process notepad | ft name,id -auto
Get-Process : Cannot find a process with the name "notepad"
. Verify the process name and call the cmdlet again.
At line:1 char:12
+ get-process <<<<  notepad | ft name,id -auto
    + CategoryInfo          : ObjectNotFound: (notepad:Str
   ing) [Get-Process], ProcessCommandException
    + FullyQualifiedErrorId : NoProcessFoundForGivenName,M
   icrosoft.PowerShell.Commands.GetProcessCommand

PS (7) >
```

Using the ShouldProcess mechanism in your scripts and functions when they'll perform destructive operations is a scripting best practice. Although it requires a bit of effort on the script author's part, it adds tremendous value for the script user.

The $PSCmdlet variable

As mentioned earlier, the $PSCmdlet variable gives the script or function author the necessary callbacks and properties needed to be able to take advantage of all the advanced function features. As well as being able to call ShouldProcess(), this variable gives you access to the parameter set name through the $PSCmdlet.ParameterSetName property. It allows you to halt a pipeline containing this command by calling the $PSCmdlet.ThrowTerminatingError() method. It basically makes all the features available to compiled cmdlet writers available to script and function authors. Refer to the PowerShell SDK documentation to get complete details on the features available through $PSCmdlet. For now, we'll continue with our discussion of the properties on the CmdletBinding attribute.

The ConfirmImpact property

This is an extension on the idea of "should process." Not all commands have the same consequences, so you have a way to indicate this with this property. The ConfirmImpact property specifies when the action of the function should be confirmed by calling the ShouldProcess() method. The call to the ShouldProcess() method displays a confirmation prompt only when the ConfirmImpact argument is equal to or greater than the value of the $ConfirmPreference preference variable. (The default value of the argument is Medium.) Obviously this property should be used only when SupportsShouldProcess is also specified.

The DefaultParameterSetName property

The DefaultParameterSetName property specifies the name of the parameter set that the runtime will use if it can't figure out the parameter set from the specified parameters. We'll look at this a bit more when we cover the parameter metadata.

This completes our discussion of the CmdletBinding attribute and the properties that apply to the function or script as a whole. Next, we'll explore the other attribute that can be applied to function or script: OutputType.

8.2.3 The OutputType attribute

The OutputType attribute allows you to declare the expected return type of a function or script. Like the CmdletBinding attribute, this attribute applies to the whole function. In PowerShell v2, this attribute doesn't affect the output type and isn't checked by the runtime at any point. What it does do is allow you to document the expected return type in such a way that tools like editors can use it to do things like provide IntelliSense for the next cmdlet to add to a pipeline. In this scenario, the editor would show the list of cmdlets that take the previous output type as an input.

NOTE They could, but this feature was added late in the v2 ship cycle and Microsoft didn't have time to make use of it in either the ISE or the console host. Some of the third-party editors may be able to use it.

Specifying the return type sounds like it should be easy, but functions may return more than one type. In fact, some cmdlets like `Where-Object` can return any type because they just return what they were passed. A more common and manageable case occurs when you have different types of objects being returned when different parameters sets are used:

```
PS (1) > function Test-OutputType
>> {
>>   [CmdletBinding(DefaultParameterSetName = "1nt")]
>>   [OutputType("asInt", [int])]
>>   [OutputType("asString", [string])]
>>   [OutputType("asDouble", ([double], [single]))]
>>   [OutputType("lie", [int])]
>>   param (
>>     [parameter(ParameterSetName="asInt")] [switch] $asInt,
>>     [parameter(ParameterSetName="asString")] [switch] $asString,
>>     [parameter(ParameterSetName="asDouble")] [switch] $asDouble,
>>     [parameter(ParameterSetName="lie")] [switch] $lie
>>   )
>>   Write-Host "Parameter set: $($PSCmdlet.ParameterSetName)"
>>   switch ($PSCmdlet.ParameterSetName) {
>>       "asInt" { 1 ; break }
>>       "asString" { "1" ; break }
>>       "asDouble" { 1.0 ; break }
>>       "lie" { "Hello there"; break } }
>> }
>>
```

Now let's try out each of the different switches:

```
PS (2) > (Test-OutputType -asString).GetType().FullName
Parameter set: asString
System.String
PS (3) > (Test-OutputType -asInt).GetType().FullName
Parameter set: asInt
System.Int32
PS (4) > (Test-OutputType -asDouble).GetType().FullName
Parameter set: asDouble
System.Double
```

Okay—everything is as expected; in each case the correct type was returned. Now use the `-lie` parameter:

```
PS (5) > (Test-OutputType -lie).GetType().FullName
Parameter set: lie
System.String
```

Even though you specified the `OutputType` to be `[int]`, the function returned a string. As we said, the attribute is only documentation—it doesn't enforce the type.

So, if it's just documentation, then at least there must be an easy way to get at it, right? Well, unfortunately that's not the case either. This is another feature that was added right at the end of the ship cycle. As a consequence, there's no real interface to get this information. Instead, you have to look at the compiled attributes directly to see the values. For functions and scripts, you can retrieve this information from the scriptblock that defines the function body. This looks like

```
PS (6) > (Get-Command Test-OutputType).ScriptBlock.Attributes |
>>   Select-Object typeid, type |
>>   Format-List
>>

TypeId : System.Management.Automation.CmdletBindingAttribute
type   :

TypeId : System.Management.Automation.OutputTypeAttribute
Type   : {asInt, int}

TypeId : System.Management.Automation.OutputTypeAttribute
Type   : {asString, string}

TypeId : System.Management.Automation.OutputTypeAttribute
Type   : {asDouble, System.Double System.Single}

TypeId : System.Management.Automation.OutputTypeAttribute
Type   : {lie, int}
```

For cmdlets, it's even less friendly because you have to go through the .NET type that was used to define the cmdlet. Here's what that looks like:

```
PS (9) > $ct = (Get-Command Get-Command).ImplementingType
PS (10) > $ct.GetCustomAttributes($true) |
>>   Select-Object typeid, type |
>>   Format-List
>>

TypeId : System.Management.Automation.CmdletAttribute
type   :

TypeId : System.Management.Automation.OutputTypeAttribute
Type   : {System.Management.Automation.AliasInfo, System.Management.A
         utomation.ApplicationInfo, System.Management.Automation.Func
         tionInfo, System.Management.Automation.CmdletInfo...}
```

At this point, you might be saying, "Why bother to specify this?" The answer is that good scripts will last beyond any individual release of PowerShell. This information is somewhat useful now and will probably be much more useful in the future. As a best practice, it's strongly recommended that this information be included in scripts that you want to share with others.

Something we skipped over in the `OutputType` example was the `Parameter` attribute. We used it but didn't actually talk about what it does. We'll remedy this in the next section.

8.2.4 Specifying parameter attributes

We specify additional information on parameters using the `Parameter` attribute. This information is used to control how the parameter is processed. The attribute is placed before the parameter definition, as shown in figure 8.6.

As was the case with the `CmdletBinding` attribute, specific behaviors are controlled through a set of properties provided as "arguments" to the attribute. Although figure 8.6 shows all the properties that can be specified, you only have to provide the ones you want to set to something other than the default value. Let's look at an example first and then go through each of the properties.

The following example shows a parameter declaration that defines the `-Path` parameter. Say you want the parameter to have the following characteristics:

- It's mandatory—that is, the user must specify it or there's an error.
- It takes input from the pipeline.
- It requires its argument to be convertible to an array of strings.

The parameter declaration needed to do all of this looks like

```
param (
    [parameter(Mandatory=$true, ValueFromPipeline=$true)]
    [string[]] $Parameter
)
```

The result is fairly simple because you only need to specify the things you want to change. All other properties keep their default values. In the next few sections, we'll look at each of the possible properties, what it does, and how it can be used.

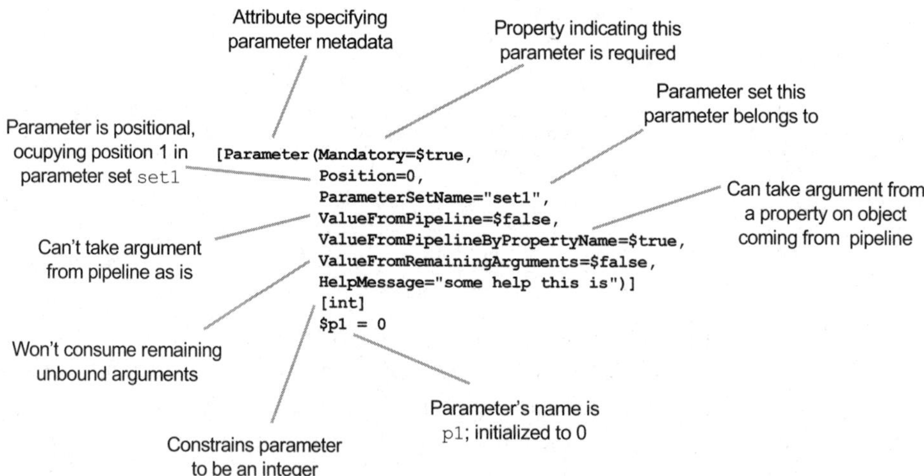

Figure 8.6 This figure shows how the `Parameter` attribute is used when declaring a variable. The attribute must appear before that variable name and its optional initializer expression. The figure includes all the properties that can be set on the parameter.

The Mandatory property

By default, all function and script parameters are optional, which means that the caller of the command doesn't have to specify them. If you want to require that the parameter be specified, set the `Mandatory` property in the `Parameter` attribute to `$true`; otherwise, if the property is absent or set to `$false`, the parameter is optional. The following example shows the declaration of a parameter that's required when the function is run:

```
PS (1) > function Test-Mandatory
>> {
>>     param ( [Parameter(Mandatory=$true)] $myParam)
>>     $myParam
>> }
>>
```

Now run this function without a parameter:

```
PS (2) > Test-Mandatory

cmdlet Test-Mandatory at command pipeline position 1
Supply values for the following parameters:
myParam: HELLO THERE
HELLO THERE
PS (3) >
```

The PowerShell runtime notices that a mandatory parameter wasn't specified on the command line, so it prompts the user to specify it, which we do. Now the function can run to completion.

The Position property

You saw earlier in this chapter that all parameters are both positional and named by default. When using advanced parameter specification metadata, either adding the `CmdletBinding` attribute to the whole function or specifying an individual `Parameter` attribute, parameters remain positional by default, until you specify a position for at least one of them. Once you start formally specifying positions, all parameters default to nonpositional unless the `Position` property for that parameter is set. The following example shows a function with two parameters, neither one having `Position` set:

```
PS (1) > function Test-Position
>> {
>>   param (
>>     [parameter()] $p1 = 'p1 unset',
>>     $p2 = 'p2 unset'
>>   )
>>   "p1 = '$p1' p2='$p2'"
>> }
>>
```

Now when you run it with positional parameters

```
PS (2) > Test-Position one two
p1 = 'one' p2='two'
```

the arguments are bound by position and there's no error. Add a position specification to one of the parameters, and now the function looks like

```
PS (3) > function Test-Position
>> {
>>     param (
>>         [parameter(Position=0)] $p1 = 'p1 unset',
>>         $p2 = 'p2 unset'
>>     )
>>     "p1 = '$p1' p2='$p2'"
>> }
>>
```

Run it again with two positional parameters:

```
PS (4) > Test-Position one two
Test-Position : A positional parameter cannot be found that
 accepts argument 'two'.
At line:1 char:14
+ Test-Position <<<<  one two
    + CategoryInfo          : InvalidArgument: (:) [Test-P
   osition], ParameterBindingException
    + FullyQualifiedErrorId : PositionalParameterNotFound,
   Test-Position
```

This time you get an error. Although there's a second parameter, it's no longer positional. If you run the function again specifying the second parameter by name,

```
PS (5) > Test-Position one  -p2 two
p1 = 'one' p2='two'
PS (6) >
```

it all works.

The ParameterSetName property

The `ParameterSetName` property allows you to specify the parameter set or sets that a parameter belongs to. If no parameter set is specified, the parameter belongs to all the parameter sets defined by the function. The following example shows the parameter declaration of two parameters that belong to two different parameter sets:

```
PS (1) > function Test-ParameterSets
>> {
>>   param (
>>      [parameter(ParameterSetName="s1")] $p1='p1 unset',
>>      [parameter(ParameterSetName="s2")] $p2='p2 unset',
>>      [parameter(ParameterSetName="s1")]
>>      [parameter(ParameterSetName="s2",Mandatory=$true)]
>>        $p3='p3 unset',
>>      $p4='p4 unset'
>>   )
>>   "Parameter set = " + $PSCmdlet.ParameterSetName
>>   "p1=$p1 p2=$p2 p3=$p3 p4=$p4"
>> }
>>
```

Let's try it. First call the function, specifying -p1 and -p4:

```
PS (2) > Test-ParameterSets -p1 one -p4 four
Parameter set = s1
p1=one p2= p3=p3 unset p4=four
```

The parameter binder resolves to parameter set s1, where the -p3 parameter isn't mandatory. Next specify -p1, -p3, and -p4:

```
PS (3) > Test-ParameterSets -p1 one -p3 three -p4 four
Parameter set = s1
p1=one p2= p3=three p4=four
```

You still resolve to parameter set s1 but this time -p3 is bound. Now let's look at the other parameter set. Because you're specifying -p2 instead of -p1, the second parameter set, s2, is used, as you can see in the output:

```
PS (4) > Test-ParameterSets -p2 two -p3 three
Parameter set = s2
p1= p2=two p3=three p4=p4 unset
```

Now in parameter set s2, the parameter -p3 is mandatory. Try running the function without specifying it:

```
PS (5) > Test-ParameterSets -p2 two

cmdlet Test-ParameterSets at command pipeline position 1
Supply values for the following parameters:
p3: THREE
Parameter set = s2
p1= p2=two p3=THREE p4=p4 unset
```

The runtime will prompt for the missing parameter. You provide the missing value at the prompt, and the function completes successfully.

Let's verify that the parameter -p4 is allowed in both parameter sets. You run the following command specifying -p4:

```
PS (6) > Test-ParameterSets -p2 two -p3 three -p4 four
Parameter set = s2
p1= p2=two p3=three p4=four
```

This works properly. Now try specifying all four of the parameters in the same command; this shouldn't work because -p1 and -p2 are in different parameter sets, so the parameter binder can't resolve to a single parameter set:

```
PS (7) > Test-ParameterSets -p1 one -p2 two -p3 three -p4 four
Test-ParameterSets : Parameter set cannot be resolved using
 the specified named parameters.
At line:1 char:19
+ Test-ParameterSets <<<<  -p1 one -p2 two -p3 three -p4 fo
ur
    + CategoryInfo          : InvalidArgument: (:) [Test-P
   arameterSets], ParameterBindingException
    + FullyQualifiedErrorId : AmbiguousParameterSet,Test-P
   arameterSets

PS (8) >
```

As expected, the system responds with an error. For more information about the parameter-binding process, see section 2.5.2.

The ValueFromPipeline property

You saw earlier how to use `$_` in the process block to handle pipeline objects. This approach works but makes it difficult to handle both pipeline and command-line bindings. The `ValueFromPipeline` property greatly simplifies this. In the following example you'll define a single parameter, `$x`, that can take values from the command line and the pipeline:

```
PS (1) > function Test-ValueFromPipeline
>> {
>>
>>     param([Parameter(ValueFromPipeline = $true)] $x)
>>     process { $x }
>> }
>>
```

Now try it with the command line

```
PS (2) > Test-ValueFromPipeline 123
123
```

and it works properly. Now try a pipelined value:

```
PS (3) > 123 | Test-ValueFromPipeline
123
```

This also works properly. And, because you're using the process block, you can handle a collection of values:

```
PS (4) > 1,2,3 | Test-ValueFromPipeline
1
2
3
PS (5) >
```

The `ValueFromPipeline` property allows you to tell the runtime to bind the entire object to the parameter. But sometimes you only want a property on the object. This is what the `ValueFromPipelineByPropertyName` attribute is for, as you'll see next.

The ValueFromPipelineByPropertyName property

Whereas `ValueFromPipeline` caused the entire pipeline object to be bound to the parameter, the `ValueFromPipelineByPropertyName` property tells the runtime to just use a property on the object instead of the whole object when binding the parameter. The name of the property to use comes from the parameter name. Let's modify the previous example to illustrate this:

```
PS (19) > function Test-ValueFromPipelineByPropertyName
>> {
>>   param(
```

```
>>    [Parameter(ValueFromPipelineByPropertyName=$true)]
>>    $DayOfWeek
>>  )
>>  process { $DayOfWeek }
>> }
>>
```

This function has one parameter, named `DayOfWeek`, that's bound from the pipeline by property name. Notice that you haven't added a type constraint to this property, so any type of value will work. Let's use the `Get-Date` cmdlet to emit an object with a `DayOfWeek` property:

```
PS (20) > Get-Date | Test-ValueFromPipelineByPropertyName
Tuesday
```

This returns `Tuesday`, so binding from the pipeline works fine. What happens when you bind from the command line?

```
PS (21) > Test-ValueFromPipelineByPropertyName (Get-Date)
Tuesday, June 30, 2009 12:27:56 AM
```

This time you get the entire `DateTime` object. Normal command-line binding isn't affected by the attribute. To get the same result, you have to extract the property yourself:

```
PS (22) > Test-ValueFromPipelineByPropertyName `
>>   ((Get-Date).DayOfWeek)
Tuesday
```

That takes care of the single-value case. Now let's look at the case where you have multiple values coming in:

```
PS (23) > $d = Get-Date
PS (24) > $d, $d.AddDays(1), $d.AddDays(2) |
>>       Test-ValueFromPipelineByPropertyName
>>
Tuesday
Wednesday
Thursday
PS (25) >
```

Each inbound pipeline object is bound to the parameter by property name one at a time. Next, we'll show how to handle variable numbers of arguments when using command metadata.

The ValueFromRemainingArguments property

You saw earlier that when you didn't use any of the metadata annotations, excess arguments ended up in the `$args` variable. But once you add the metadata, the presence of excess arguments results in an error. Because it's sometimes useful to allow a variable number of parameters, PowerShell provides the `ValueFromRemainingArguments` property, which tells the runtime to bind all excess arguments to this parameter. The following example shows a function with two parameters. The first argument goes into the -First parameter and the remaining arguments are bound to -Rest:

```
PS (1) > function vfraExample
>> {
>>   param (
>>     $First,
>>     [parameter(ValueFromRemainingArguments=$true)] $Rest
>>   )
>>   "First is $first rest is $rest"
>> }
>>
```

Let's run the function with four arguments:

```
PS (2) > vfraExample 1 2 3 4
First is 1 rest is 2 3 4
```

The first ends up in `$first` with the remaining placed in `$rest`. Now try using `-Rest` as a named parameter

```
PS (3) > vfraExample 1 -Rest 2 3 4
vfraExample : A positional parameter cannot be found that a
ccepts argument '3'.
At line:1 char:12
+ vfraExample <<<<  1 -Rest 2 3 4
    + CategoryInfo          : InvalidArgument: (:) [vfraEx
   ample], ParameterBindingException
    + FullyQualifiedErrorId : PositionalParameterNotFound,
   vfraExample
```

and this fails. When the parameter is specified by name, it won't receive the excess arguments and you'll get an error. If you use the parameter by name, you have to pass the remaining arguments explicitly as a list, as shown here:

```
PS (4) > vfraExample 1 -Rest 2,3,4
First is 1 rest is 2 3 4
PS (5) >
```

Now it works.

The HelpMessage property

The `HelpMessage` property allows you to attach a short help message to the parameter. This sounds like it should be useful but it isn't really. This message is displayed only when prompting for a missing mandatory parameter. We'll show you better ways to add help for your functions in section 8.4. Still, for completeness sake, let's work through an example.

First, you need a function that has a mandatory parameter so the runtime will prompt if you don't supply it. Also, make it an array so you can specify more than one object when prompted. Here's the function:

```
PS (1) > function helpMessageExample
>> {
```

```
>>    param (
>>      [parameter(Mandatory=$true,
>>          HelpMessage="An array of path names.")]
>>      [string[]]
>>      $Path
>>    )
>>    "Path: $path"
>> }
>>
```

Now run it with no arguments so the system will prompt for the missing value:

```
PS (2) > helpMessageExample

cmdlet helpMessageExample at command pipeline position 1
Supply values for the following parameters:
(Type !? for Help.)
Path[0]: !?
An array of path names.
Path[0]: fo
Path[1]: bar
Path[2]:
Path: fo bar
PS (3) >)
```

When prompted, you can enter `!?` to see the help message giving you more information about the type of thing you're supposed to enter.

And with that, we're finished with our discussion of the `Parameter` attribute and its properties. But we're not finished with parameter attributes quite yet. The next thing to look at is the `Alias` attribute. This is a pretty simple feature, but it has a couple of important uses.

8.2.5 Creating parameter aliases with the Alias attribute

The `Alias` attribute allows you to specify alternate names for a parameter. It's typically used to add a well-defined shortcut for that parameter. Here's why this is important. If you'll recall our parameter discussion in chapter 2, we said that you only have to specify enough of a parameter name to uniquely identify it. Unfortunately, there's a problem with that approach and that's *versioning* the command over time. By versioning we mean being able to add new capabilities to future versions of a command in such a way that older scripts using this command aren't broken. If you add a new parameter to a command that has the same prefix as an existing parameter, you now need a longer prefix to distinguish the name. Any scripts that used the old short prefix would fail because they'd be unable to distinguish which parameter to use. This is where the `Alias` attribute comes in. It can be used to add distinctive and mnemonic short forms for parameters.

Let's look at an example. The following function defines a single parameter: `-ComputerName`. You'll give this parameter an alias: `-CN`. Here's the function definition:

```
PS (1) > function Test-ParameterAlias
>> {
```

```
>>     param (
>>         [alias("CN")]
>>         $ComputerName
>>     )
>>     "The computer name is $ComputerName"
>> }
>>
```

When you run it using the full parameter name, it works as expected:

```
PS (2) > Test-ParameterAlias -ComputerName foo
The computer name is foo
```

And, of course, it also works with the alias:

```
PS (3) > Test-ParameterAlias -CN foo
The computer name is foo
```

Now try a prefix of the `-ComputerName` parameter:

```
PS (4) > Test-ParameterAlias -com foo
The computer name is foo
```

And it too works fine. Next, create a new version of the command. Add a new parameter: `-Compare`. Here's the new function definition:

```
PS (5) > function Test-ParameterAlias
>> {
>>     param (
>>         [alias("CN")]
>>         $ComputerName,
>>         [switch] $Compare
>>     )
>>     "The computer name is $ComputerName, compare=$compare
"
>> }
>>
```

Try running the command with the parameter prefix `-Com` again:

```
PS (6) > Test-ParameterAlias -Com foo
Test-ParameterAlias : Parameter cannot be processed because
 the parameter name 'Com' is ambiguous. Possible matches in
clude: -ComputerName -Compare.
At line:1 char:20
+ Test-ParameterAlias <<<<  -Com foo
    + CategoryInfo          : InvalidArgument: (:) [Test-P
   arameterAlias], ParameterBindingException
    + FullyQualifiedErrorId : AmbiguousParameter,Test-Para
   meterAlias
```

This time you get an error because `-com` could refer to either parameter. But if you use the `-CN` alias

```
PS (7) > Test-ParameterAlias -CN foo
The computer name is foo, compare=False
PS (8) >
```

it works.

Another scenario where you might add an alias is when you're also using the ValueFromPipelineByPropertyName property on the Parameter attribute. There are a number of places where the objects you're working with have similar parameters with different names. For example, the file system objects returned by dir have a Name property, whereas the objects returned by Get-Process have a ProcessName property. If you wanted to create a function that worked with both of these types, you could have a parameter named Name with an alias ProcessName. How about also working with services? The objects returned from Get-Service have a ServiceName property. No problem—just add another alias for ServiceName. In practice, there's no limit to the number of aliases that can be assigned to a parameter.

Now let's look at the last type of parameter metadata: the validation attributes that let you constrain the parameter values in much more interesting ways than just by type.

8.2.6 Parameter validation attributes

The last class of parameter attributes we'll cover are the parameter validation attributes. You already know how to add a type constraint to a parameter where you require that the argument be of a particular type. The parameter validation attributes allow you to specify additional constraints on the argument to a parameter. The available parameter validation attributes are shown in figure 8.7.

In many cases these constraints seem like trivial functions (and mostly they are), but they're valuable for a couple of reasons:

- They declare the parameter contract. This means that by inspecting the parameter declaration, you can see what constraints are present. This also means that other tools can work with this information as well to drive IntelliSense-like features.

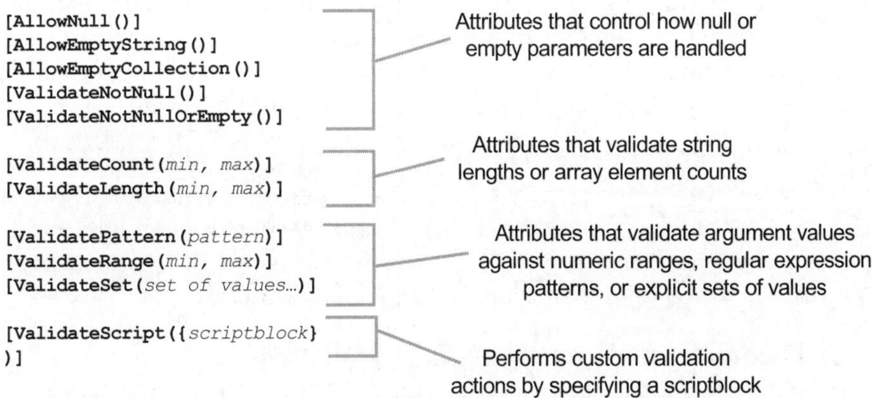

Figure 8.7 The validation attributes can be applied to script and function parameters to specify additional parameter checks to perform when binding arguments.

- You don't have to write any error-handling code. By specifying the attribute, you're declaring the constraint, and the runtime takes care of doing the work of checking the value for you. Because the PowerShell runtime does the check, it can generate standardized error messages, translated into whatever language the user's environment is configured for. It's a pretty nifty feature.

The other interesting thing is that the set of attributes isn't fixed; a .NET programmer can create new attributes by deriving from the existing base classes. Although this isn't possible in the PowerShell language yet, you do have `ValidateScript`, which lets you do similar things. We'll get to that once we cover the other attributes that are available.

Validation attribute: AllowNull

The `AllowNull` attribute should only makes sense if the associated parameter is marked as mandatory. This is because, by default, mandatory parameters don't allow you to pass `$null` to them. If this attribute is specified, the check is suppressed and `$null` can be passed to the parameter. The `AllowNullExample` function in the example shows how this might be used:

```
function allowNullExample
{
  param
  (
    [parameter(Mandatory=$true)]
    [AllowNull()]
    $objectToTest
  )
  $objectToTest -eq $null
)
```

Validation attribute: AllowEmptyString

The `AllowEmptyString` attribute is a variation on the `AllowNull` attribute. Mandatory parameters won't permit empty strings to be passed either. You should specify this attribute if, for some unknown reason, you want to allow your function or script to have to deal with empty strings in mandatory parameters.

> **NOTE** It's pretty hard to think of a good case where you want to allow `$null` or an empty argument to be passed to a function. If you do this but don't have correct code in your function or script implementation, your users may find themselves having to debug `NullReference` exceptions. Not a nice thing to do to your users.

Validation attribute: AllowEmptyCollection

This is the last variation on the attributes that are used with mandatory parameters to disable some of the default checks. The `AllowEmptyCollection` attribute allows an empty collection as the argument of a mandatory parameter.

Validation attribute: ValidateNotNull

The `ValidateNotNull` attribute is the opposite of `AllowNull`. This attribute turns on the check for `$null` if the parameter isn't mandatory. The following example shows the use of this attribute with a nonmandatory parameter:

```
function validateNotNullExample
{
  param
  (
    [ValidateNotNull()]
    $objectToTest
  )
  $objectToTest -eq $null
}
```

Validation attribute: ValidateNotNullOrEmpty

The `ValidateNotNullOrEmpty` attribute specifies that the argument of the parameter isn't permitted to be set to `$null`, an empty string, or an empty array.

Validation attribute: ValidateCount

The `ValidateCount` attribute specifies the minimum and maximum number of values that can be passed to an array parameter. The runtime generates an error if the number of elements in the argument is outside the range. In the following example, one parameter, `$pair`, requires exactly two values:

```
PS (1) > function validateCountExample
>> {
>>   param (
>>     [int[]] [ValidateCount(2,2)] $pair
>>   )
>>   "pair: $pair"
>> }
>>
```

Try the function with one argument:

```
PS (2) > validateCountExample 1
validateCountExample : Cannot validate argument on paramete
r 'pair'. The number of supplied arguments (1) is less than
 the minimum number of allowed arguments (2). Specify more
than 2 arguments and then try the command again.
At line:1 char:21
+ validateCountExample <<<<  1
    + CategoryInfo          : InvalidData: (:) [validateCo
   untExample], ParameterBindingValidationException
    + FullyQualifiedErrorId : ParameterArgumentValidationE
   rror,validateCountExample
```

You get the expected error. Next, pass in a pair of numbers:

```
PS (3) > validateCountExample 1,2
pair: 1 2
```

That works. Finally, pass in three numbers:

```
PS (4) > validateCountExample 1,2,3
validateCountExample : Cannot validate argument on paramete
r 'pair'. The number of supplied arguments (3) exceeds the
maximum number of allowed arguments (2). Specify less than
2 arguments and then try the command again.
At line:1 char:21
+ validateCountExample <<<<  1,2,3
    + CategoryInfo          : InvalidData: (:) [validateCo
   untExample], ParameterBindingValidationException
    + FullyQualifiedErrorId : ParameterArgumentValidationE
   rror,validateCountExample
```

Again, you get an error.

Validation attribute: ValidateLength

The `ValidateLength` attribute can only be used with strings or arrays of strings. It allows you to specify the minimum and maximum length of the argument strings. If the argument is an array of strings, each element of the array will be checked. In the following example, the specified computer names must have 1 to 10 characters:

```
function validateLengthExample
{
  param (
    [string][ValidateLength(8,10)] $username
  )
  $userName
}
```

Validation attribute: ValidatePattern

The `ValidatePattern` attribute allows you to specify a regular expression to use to validate the argument string. For example, the `$hostName` parameter in the following function must start with a letter from *a* to *z* followed by one to seven digits:

```
PS (1) > function validatePatternExample
>> {
>>   param (
>>     [ValidatePattern('^[a-z][0-9]{1,7}$')]
>>     [string] $hostName
>>   )
>>   $hostName
>> }
>>
```

Try it with a valid string:

```
PS (2) > validatePatternExample b123
b123
```

It returns the argument with no error. Now try an invalid argument that has too many numbers:

```
PS (3) > validatePatternExample c123456789
validatePatternExample : Cannot validate argument on parame
```

```
ter 'hostName'. The argument "c123456789" does not match th
e "^[a-z][0-9]{1,7}$" pattern. Supply an argument that matc
hes "^[a-z][0-9]{1,7}$" and try the command again.
At line:1 char:23
+ validatePatternExample <<<< c123456789
    + CategoryInfo          : InvalidData: (:) [validatePa
   tternExample], ParameterBindingValidationException
    + FullyQualifiedErrorId : ParameterArgumentValidationE
   rror,validatePatternExample
```

You get an error as expected. Unfortunately, the error message isn't helpful—all it reports is the pattern that failed but not why it failed or what the intent of the pattern was. This limits the usefulness of this attribute.

Validation attribute: ValidateRange

The `ValidateRange` attribute allows you to constrain the range of a numeric argument. This means that instead of just saying the argument must be an integer, you can say that it must be an integer in the range 1 through 10, as shown here:

```
PS (1) > function validateRangeExample
>> {
>>   param (
>>     [int[]][ValidateRange(1,10)] $count
>>   )
>>   $count
>> }
>>
```

As you saw with the `ValidateLength` attribute for strings, this attribute can be applied to a collection, in which case it will validate each member of the collection:

```
PS (2) > validateRangeExample 1
1
PS (3) > validateRangeExample 1,2,3
1
2
3
```

These two examples return no error because all the members are within range. Now try one with a member outside the range:

```
PS (4) > validateRangeExample 1,2,3,22,4
validateRangeExample : Cannot validate argument on paramete
r 'count'. The 22 argument is greater than the maximum allo
wed range of 10. Supply an argument that is less than 10 an
d then try the command again.
At line:1 char:21
+ validateRangeExample <<<< 1,2,3,22,4
    + CategoryInfo          : InvalidData: (:) [validateRa
   ngeExample], ParameterBindingValidationException
    + FullyQualifiedErrorId : ParameterArgumentValidationE
   rror,validateRangeExample

PS (5) >
```

It fails, indicating the value that couldn't be processed.

Validation attribute: ValidateSet

The ValidateSet attribute ensures that the argument is a member of the specific set of values passed to the attribute. In the following example, the argument to the $color parameter can contain only the values red, blue, or green:

```
PS (5) > function validateSetExample
>> {
>>   param (
>>     [ValidateSet("red", "blue", "green")]
>>     [ConsoleColor] $color
>>   )
>>   $color
>> }
>>
```

Try it with a valid argument

```
PS (6) > validateSetExample red
Red
```

and an invalid argument:

```
PS (7) > validateSetExample cyan
validateSetExample : Cannot validate argument on parameter
'color'. The argument "Cyan" does not belong to the set "re
d,blue,green" specified by the ValidateSet attribute. Suppl
y an argument that is in the set and then try the command a
gain.
At line:1 char:19
+ validateSetExample <<<<  cyan
    + CategoryInfo          : InvalidData: (:) [validateSe
   tExample], ParameterBindingValidationException
    + FullyQualifiedErrorId : ParameterArgumentValidationE
   rror,validateSetExample)
```

Note that the error message contains the list of valid values. Notice that you passed an array of arguments to the parameter, but the type of the parameter is [Console-Color], not [ConsoleColor[]]—that is, it's not an array parameter. This works because [ConsoleColor] is a .NET enum type where multiple values can be combined to produce a new value in the set. The PowerShell runtime understands that this and combines the arguments to produce a single result.

Validation attribute: ValidateScript

And now for the final validation attribute. As promised, we've saved the best (or at least the most powerful) for last. The ValidateScript attribute allows you to specify a chunk of PowerShell script to use to validate the argument. This means that it can do anything. The argument to test is passed in as $_to the code fragment, which should return $true or $false. In the following example, the attribute is used to verify that the argument is an even number:

```
PS (8) > function validateScriptExample
>> {
```

```
>>    param (
>>      [int] [ValidateScript({$_ % 2 -eq 0})] $number
>>    )
>>    $number
>> }
>>
```

This succeeds for 2

```
PS (9) > validateScriptExample 2
2
```

and fails for 3:

```
PS (10) > validateScriptExample 3
validateScriptExample : Cannot validate argument on paramet
er 'number'. The "$_ % 2 -eq 0" validation script for the a
rgument with value "3" did not return true. Determine why t
he validation script failed and then try the command again.
At line:1 char:22
+ validateScriptExample <<<<  3
    + CategoryInfo          : InvalidData: (:) [validateSc
   riptExample], ParameterBindingValidationException
    + FullyQualifiedErrorId : ParameterArgumentValidationE
   rror,validateScriptExample
```

As with the `ValidatePattern` attribute, the error message doesn't provide the best user experience, limiting the value of this attribute for validation. On the other hand, it can also be used for things like logging and tracing, counting the number of times the parameter was used, and so on simply by taking the appropriate action and then returning `$true`.

Now that we've covered all the things you can do with explicit parameters, we're going to investigate an alternate mechanism for parameter specification. This alternate mechanism allows you to do something that isn't possible with explicit parameter specification: write scripts and functions that can dynamically adapt their parameter signatures to the environment. We'll cover this topic in the next section.

8.3 Dynamic parameters and dynamicParam

Explicit or static parameters are defined as part of the source code for a script or function and are fixed when that script or function is compiled. But a script or function can also define parameters at *runtime*. These new parameters are added dynamically based on runtime conditions instead of statically at parse time. This allows you to write functions to *specialize* their interface (i.e., their parameters) based on ambient conditions. The best example of this is a cmdlet like `Set-Content`. When `Set-Content` is used in a file system drive, it lets you specify file-specific parameters like `-Encoding`. In other providers where this parameter doesn't make sense, it isn't present in the cmdlet signature. Because these parameters are defined dynamically, they're called (no surprise, I'm sure) *dynamic parameters*. Cmdlets have always had this capability, but PowerShell v2 makes the facility available for scripts and functions as well.

If you want your scripts and functions to have dynamic parameters, you have to use the `dynamicParam` keyword. The syntax for this keyword is

```
dynamicParam { <statement-list> }
```

Let's work through the steps needed to implement dynamic parameters. Warning: this isn't for the faint of heart, but it's a powerful technique that, when needed, allows you to deliver the best experience for the users of your scripts.

8.3.1 Steps for adding a dynamic parameter

In this section, we'll walk you through the steps necessary to define dynamic parameters in a function. First, you'll specify a `dynamicParam` block in your function. Then, in the body of the `dynamicParam` block, you'll use an `if` statement to specify the conditions under which the parameter is to be available. To define the actual parameters you want to expose, you need to use the `New-Object` cmdlet to create a instance of the type

```
System.Management.Automation.RuntimeDefinedParameter
```

You'll use this object to define your dynamic parameter and, at a minimum, you'll have to specify its name. If you need to apply some additional attributes, you'll have to use the `New-Object` command to create an instance of the type

```
System.Management.Automation.ParameterAttribute
```

which is used to include the `Mandatory`, `Position`, or `ValueFromPipeline` attributes you saw earlier in this chapter.

In the following example, you define a function with two static parameters—`Name` and `Path`—and an optional dynamic parameter named `dp1`. `dp1` is in the `set1` parameter set and has a type: `[int]`. The dynamic parameter is available only when the value of the `Path` parameter begins with `HKLM:`, indicating that it's being used in the Registry drive. The complete function is shown in figure 8.8.

This function will return the bound parameters in the end block of the function.

> **NOTE** The variable `$PSBoundParameters` is a new automatic variable introduced in PowerShell v2. This variable contains a hashtable with all the parameters that were bound when the command was invoked. You'll learn more about this variable when we cover proxy commands in chapter 11.

The presence of the `dynamicParam` block forces you to explicitly use the `end` keyword just like using the `begin` and `process` keywords would. Now run the function. Try the function in the C: drive:

```
PS (2) > dynamicParameterExample -dp1 13 -Path c:\
dynamicParameterExample : A parameter cannot be found that
matches parameter name 'dp1'.
At line:1 char:29
```

```
+ dynamicParameterExample -dp1 <<<<  13 -Path c:\
    + CategoryInfo          : InvalidArgument: (:) [dynami
   cParameterExample], ParameterBindingException
    + FullyQualifiedErrorId : NamedParameterNotFound,dynam
   icParameterExample
```

You get an error saying that no -dp1 parameter was found. Now try it with HKLM:

```
PS (3) > dynamicParameterExample -dp1 13 -Path HKLM:\

Key                            Value
---                            -----
Path                           HKLM:\
dp1                            13
```

This time, the function executes without error and shows you that the dynamic parameter was bound as desired.

```
function dynamicParameterExample
{
    [cmdletbinding()]
    param (
        [String]$name,
        [String]$path
    )

    dynamicparam
    {
        if ($path -match "^HKLM:")
        {
            $attributes = New-Object `
                System.Management.Automation.ParameterAttribute `
                -Property @{
                    ParameterSetName = "set1"
                    Mandatory = $false
                }

            $attributeCollection = New-Object `
                System.Collections.ObjectModel.Collection[System.Attribute]
            $attributeCollection.Add($attributes)

            $dynParam1 = New-Object `
                    System.Management.Automation.RuntimeDefinedParameter `
                    dp1,int, $attributeCollection

            $paramDictionary = New-Object `
                Management.Automation.RuntimeDefinedParameterDictionary
            $paramDictionary.Add("dp1", $dynParam1)

            $paramDictionary
        }
    }

    end {  $psboundparameters }
}
```

Static parameter definitions

Creates object that will provide parameter attributes

Returns parameter dictionary so runtime can use it for binding parameters

Creates parameter object and parameter dictionary to hold it

Returns bound parameters

Figure 8.8 A function that defines dynamic parameters. If the `-Path` parameter is set to something that starts with `HKML:` an additional parameter, `dp1`, will be defined for the function.

As you can see, using dynamic parameters is a fairly complex task. The task is basically the same in script or in a compiled language like C#. If you can follow this example, you're well on your way to understanding dynamic parameters in C#.

8.3.2 When should dynamic parameters be used?

So when would you use this technique? The most common case is something like the namespace providers mentioned earlier where most of the parameters are the same but certain parameters may only be present based on the path. This allows you to have one command to deal with many similar but slightly different scenarios. This reduces the number of commands a user has to learn. The other place where dynamic parameters might be used is when you want to base the parameters on some type of dynamic configuration, like the set of columns in a database table. You could write a single cmdlet, called something like `Update-DatabaseTable`, that uses the names and types of the columns to add dynamic parameters for the cmdlet.

This concludes our discussion of dynamic parameters and also completes the overall discussion of parameterization of scripts and functions. You now have all the necessary tools to define optimal interfaces or signatures for your scripts and functions. But knowing how to define the signature for a script is only half the battle—at least if you want someone other than yourself to use these scripts. No matter how good the interface is, production scripting still requires documentation for the scripts you're producing. In the next section, I'll explain how this is accomplished.

8.4 Documenting functions and scripts

In this section, we'll look at the various mechanisms you can use to provide documentation for your scripts. Unfortunately, in PowerShell v1, there was no good way to document functions and scripts. This was fixed in v2 by adding three new features:

- Automatic help information generated from the function or script definition
- A special way of processing comments to extract help information from them
- A mechanism for associating external help files with a function or script

The first of these mechanisms is the automatic generation of help text from a function or script definition. When you define a function, the PowerShell help system can generate some amount of help information for that function. To illustrate, define a simple function:

```
PS (1) > function abc ([int] $x, $y) { }
```

Now you can call `Get-Help` on this function

```
PS (2) > Get-Help abc
abc [[-x] <Int32>] [[-y] <Object>]
```

and you get the synopsis for the function. As you can see, the help subsystem tries to do as much work for you as it can automatically. In the next section we'll look at the fields that can be automatically generated.

8.4.1 Automatically generated help fields

A certain number of the help fields are generated automatically: name, syntax, parameter list, parameter attribute table, common parameters, and remarks. These elements are described in table 8.1.

Table 8.1 Automatically generated help fields

Help element	Description
`Name`	The `Name` section of the help topic for a function is taken from the name of the function. For a script, it's taken from the name of the script file.
`Syntax`	The `Syntax` section of the help topic is generated from the function or script syntax (in other words, the parameter definitions). If a parameter has a type attribute associated with it, that type will be displayed as part of the syntax. If you don't specify a parameter type, `Object` is inserted as the default value.
`Parameter` list	The `Parameter` list in the help topic is generated from the function or script syntax and from the descriptions that you add to the parameters. The function parameters appear in the "Parameters" section in the same order in which they appear in the function or script definition. The spelling and capitalization of parameter names is also taken from the definition.
Common parameters	The common parameters are added to the syntax and parameter list of the help topic, even if they have no effect.
Parameter attribute table	`Get-Help` generates the table of parameter attributes that appears when you use the `-Full` or `-Parameter` parameter of `Get-Help`. The value of the `Required`, `Position`, and `Default` properties is taken from the function or script definition.
Remarks	The `Remarks` section of the help topic is automatically generated from the function or script name.

The automatically generated help is minimal. You'll deliver a much better result by adding your own help content.

8.4.2 Creating manual help content

Although it's handy to know the command's syntax, knowing what the command does is more useful. This is where the manual documentation mechanisms come in. PowerShell provides two ways for documenting scripts and functions: in line with special documentation comments or externally in a help file.

Documentation comments (or *doc comments*) are a convention for using comments when writing scripts such that these comments can be automatically used to fill in help information. These comments must be placed in particular locations in scripts for them to be processed as doc comments and can contain a number of markup tags for structuring the help information. We'll cover these details in the next section. The final mechanism for providing function/script help uses external files.

External help files are XML files written in the Microsoft Assistance Markup Language (MAML) format. In PowerShell v1, this mechanism was available only for cmdlets. In v2, the help file facility can be used with functions and scripts as well. So why have these external files? Because they allow for the help content to be translated (localized) into many different languages whereas doc comments only allow help to be written in a single language. Doc comments also require the script file itself to be changed just to change a typo in the help documentation.

As you can see, the help mechanism scales from simple but incomplete up to a full production-level, localizable help system—one of the themes of PowerShell v2. We didn't need to say much about the automatic help facility (obviously), but the other two mechanisms require more explanation. We'll start with the doc comment mechanism.

8.4.3 Comment-based help

Comment-based help is the easiest way to add help for functions and scripts. It works by using special help comment tags in comments associated with a function definition or script. These comments are parsed by the PowerShell interpreter and used to create the help topics. Once this information is available, the `Get-Help` cmdlet returns help objects just like you get from the help files associated with cmdlets. When you specify the correct tags, doc comments can specify all the help views provided by `Get-Help`, such as `Detailed`, `Full`, `Example`, and `Online`, to display function and script help.

Comment-based help is written as a series of comments. These comments can either be single-line comments where there is a # before each line, or you can use the new block comment feature in PowerShell v2, where the comments are enclosed in <# and #> sequences. All of the lines in a doc comment topic must be contiguous. If a doc comment follows a comment that's not part of the help topic, there must be at least one blank line between the last non-help comment line and the beginning of the comment-based help.

For functions, the doc comments can be placed in one of three places:

- At the beginning of the function body, after the open brace.
- At the end of the function body.
- Before the function keyword. In this case, if the comment is to be processed as a doc comment, there can't be more than one blank line between the last line of the comment and the `function` keyword.

For scripts, the doc comments must be either at the beginning or the end of the script file. If they're at the beginning, there can only be non-doc comments or blank lines before the first doc comment. There's also one other little issue to consider: if the doc comments for a script are at the beginning of a script and the first thing a script contains is a function definition, then should the doc comment apply to the script or the function? This ambiguity is resolved by requiring that there be at least two blank lines between the end of the doc comment for the script and the beginning of the function.

Let's look at a basic example; you'll use single-line comments and the `.SYNOPSIS` tag to add a definition for the `abc` function you defined earlier. The definition now looks like

```
PS (1) > function abc ([int] $x, $y)
>> {
>> #.SYNOPSIS
>> #This is my abc function
>> }
>>
```

Run the `Get-Help` command again. The last time, you got a very basic synopsis. Let's see what you get this time:

```
PS (2) > Get-Help abc

NAME
    abc

SYNOPSIS
    This is my abc function

SYNTAX
    abc [[-x] <Int32>] [[-y] <Object>] [<CommonParameters>]

DESCRIPTION

RELATED LINKS

REMARKS
    To see the examples, type: "get-help abc -examples".
    For more information, type: "get-help abc -detailed".
    For technical information, type: "get-help abc -full".
```

Now you get much more output. Of course, much of it's empty—you haven't specified all the sections yet. You can guess pretty easily what some of the sections should be. Let's add a description for the function. This time you'll use the block comments notation—it's much easier to work with.

> **NOTE** PowerShell added block comments to make it easier to write doc comments. The sequences <# and #> were chosen in part because they look somewhat like XML, which is used for external help files.

Here's what the new function definition looks like:

```
PS (3) > function abc ([int] $x, $y)
>> {
>> <#
>> .SYNOPSIS
>> This is my abc function
```

```
>> .DESCRIPTION
>> This function is used to demonstrate writing doc
>> comments for a function.
>> #>
>> }
>>
```

When you run `Get-Help`, you see

```
PS (4) > Get-Help abc

NAME
    abc

SYNOPSIS
    This is my abc function

SYNTAX
    abc [[-x] <Int32>] [[-y] <Object>] [<CommonParameters>]

DESCRIPTION
    This function is used to demonstrate writing doc
    comments for a function.

RELATED LINKS

REMARKS
    To see the examples, type: "get-help abc -examples".
    For more information, type: "get-help abc -detailed".
    For technical information, type: "get-help abc -full".
```

with the description text in its proper place.

The basic pattern should be obvious by now. Each help section begins with a special tag of the form `.TAGNAME`, followed by the content for that section. The tag must appear on a line by itself to be recognized as a tag but can be preceded or followed by whitespace. The order in which tags appear doesn't matter. Tags are not case sensitive but by convention they're always written in uppercase. (This makes the structure of the comment easier to follow.)

For a comment block to be processed as a doc comment, it must contain at least one section tag. Most tags can be specified only once per function definition, but there are some exceptions. For instance, `.EXAMPLE` can appear many times in the same comment block. The help content for each tag begins on the line after the tag and can span multiple lines.

8.4.4 Tags used in documentation comments

A fairly large number of tags can be used when creating doc comments. These tags are shown in table 8.2. They're listed in the order in which they typically appear in output of `Get-Help`.

Table 8.2 Tags that can be used in doc comments

Tag name	Tag content
`.SYNOPSIS`	A brief description of the function or script. This tag can be used only once in each help topic.
`.DESCRIPTION`	A detailed description of the function or script.
`.PARAMETER`	The description of a parameter.
`.EXAMPLE`	An example showing how to use a command.
`.INPUTS`	The type of object that can be piped into a command.
`.OUTPUTS`	The types of objects that the command returns.
`.NOTES`	Additional information about the function or script.
`.LINK`	The name of a related topic.
`.COMPONENT`	The technology or feature that the command is associated with.
`.ROLE`	The user role for this command.
`.FUNCTIONALITY`	The intended use of the function.
`.FORWARDHELPTARGETNAME`	Redirects to the help topic for the specified command.
`.FORWARDHELPCATEGORY`	Specifies the help category of the item in the `.FORWARDHELPTARGETNAME` tag.
`.REMOTEHELPRUNSPACE`	Specifies the name of a variable containing the `PSSession` to use when looking up help for this function. This keyword is used by the `Export-PSSession` cmdlet to find the Help topics for the exported commands. (See section 12.4.2.)
`.EXTERNALHELP`	Specifies the path to an external help file for the command.

Some of these tags require a bit more explanation. This is addressed in the following sections.

.PARAMETER <Parameter-Name> help tag

This is where you add the description for a parameter. The parameter must be named in the argument to the tag. You can include a `.PARAMETER` tag for each parameter in the function or script, and the `.PARAMETER` tags can appear in any order in the comment block. The order in which things are presented is controlled by the parameter definition order, not the help tag order. If you want to change the display order, you have to change the order in which the parameters are defined.

Alternatively, you can specify a parameter description simply by placing a comment before the parameter definition on the body of the function or script. If you use both a syntax comment and a `.PARAMETER` tag, the description associated with the `.PARAMETER` tag is used, and the syntax comment is ignored.

.LINK help tag

The `.LINK` tag lets you specify the names of one or more related topics. Repeat this tag for each related topic. The resulting content appears in the Related Links section of the help topic. The `.LINK` tag argument can also include a Uniform Resource Identifier (URI) to an online version of the same help topic. The online version opens when you use the `-Online` parameter of `Get-Help`. The URI must begin with http or https.

.COMPONENT help tag

The `.COMPONENT` tag describes the technology or feature area that the function or script is associated with. For example, the component for `Get-Mailbox` would be `Exchange`.

.FORWARDHELPTARGETNAME <Command-Name> help tag

`.FORWARDHELPTARGETNAME` redirects to the help topic for the specified command. You can redirect users to any help topic, including help topics for a function, script, cmdlet, or provider.

.FORWARDHELPCATEGORY <Category> help tag

The `.FORWARDHELPCATEGORY` tag specifies the help category of the item in `Forward-HelpTargetName`. Valid values are `Alias`, `Cmdlet`, `HelpFile`, `Function`, `Provider`, `General`, `FAQ`, `Glossary`, `ScriptCommand`, `ExternalScript`, `Filter`, and `All`. You should use this tag to avoid conflicts when there are commands with the same name.

.REMOTEHELPRUNSPACE <PSSession-variable> help tag

The `.REMOTEHELPRUNSPACE` tag won't make sense to you until we cover remoting in chapter 11. It's used to specify a *session* that contains the help topic. The argument to the tag is the name of a variable that contains the `PSSession` to use. This tag is used by the `Export-PSSession` cmdlet to find the help topics for the exported commands.

.EXTERNALHELP <XML Help File Path>

The `.EXTERNALHELP` tag specifies the path to an XML-based help file for the script or function. In versions of Windows from Vista on, if the specified path to the XML file contains UI-culture-specific subdirectories, `Get-Help` searches the subdirectories recursively for an XML file with the name of the script or function in accordance with the language fallback standards for Windows Vista, just as it does for all other XML-based help topics. See appendix D for additional information about UI culture, message catalogs, and world-ready scripting.

And, at long last, we're finished with our journey through the advanced function and script features. You now know how to create, declare, constrain, and document your functions. At this point, you're well on your way to becoming a scripting expert.

8.5 SUMMARY

This chapter introduced scripting and programming in general in PowerShell. It also covered the advanced scripting features introduced in PowerShell v2. Here are the key points:

- PowerShell programming can be done either with functions or scripts. Scripts are pieces of PowerShell script text stored in a file with a .ps1 extension. In PowerShell, scripts and functions are closely related, and most of the same principles and techniques apply to both. There are a few exceptions. In scripts, for example, only the `param` keyword can be used to declare formal parameters.
- Scripts introduced a new kind of variable scope: the script command and the `$script:` scope modifier are used to reference variables at the script scope.
- PowerShell v2 introduced a sophisticated attribution system for annotating parameters. Using attributes, you can control a wide variety of argument binding behaviors. You can also specify alternate names for parameters using parameter aliases and additional constraints on the values that can be bound using validation attributes.
- PowerShell v2 also introduced comprehensive mechanisms for documenting your scripts and functions. You get simple documentation for free just by declaring a function. You can add inline documentation with your code using doc comments and provide external help files containing the documentation.

Even though we discussed a lot of material in this chapter, we've covered only part of the story of programming with PowerShell. In chapter 9, you'll learn about modules, which are new in PowerShell v2, and then in chapter 10, we'll dive into the plumbing underlying all of this when we cover scriptblocks, which are the objects underlying the infrastructure for scripts and functions.

CHAPTER 9

Using and authoring modules

The value of a telecommunications network is proportional to the square of the number of connected users of the system.

—Robert Metcalfe (Metcalfe's Law)

A popular meme in the software industry is that the best programmers are lazy. The idea is that, rather than writing new code to solve a problem, a good programmer will try to reuse existing code, thereby leveraging the work that others have already done to debug and document that code. Unfortunately, this kind of reuse happens less often than it should. The typical excuses for not doing this are overconfidence ("I can do a better job," also known as the "Not-Invented-Here" syndrome), underestimating ("It will only take me 10 minutes to do that"), and ignorance ("I didn't know somebody had already implemented that"). There's no excuse for this last point anymore. With modern search engines, it's easy to find things. But finding the code is only part of the solution because the code has to be in a form that can be reused. The most common way to facilitate code reuse is to package the code in a *module*. In this chapter, we're going to examine how PowerShell v2 facilitates code reuse with its module system. You'll learn how to find existing modules on your system and how to install new modules on the system. Then we'll look at how you can create modules and package your code so that others can use it.

> **NOTE** From user studies, we've verified that the most common reuse pattern in the IT professional community is copy and paste. This isn't surprising given that, for languages like VBScript and `cmd.exe`, it's pretty much the *only* reuse pattern. A user gets a script from "somewhere," copies it, and then modifies it, repeating these processes for each new application. Although this works to a degree and has a low barrier to entry, it doesn't scale very well.

9.1 THE ROLE OF A MODULE SYSTEM

In this section, we'll look at the intent behind PowerShell modules and the roles they play in our ecosystem. Before we get into the details of the way modules work in PowerShell, let's look at an example of just how successful a module system can be.

The preeminent example of a network of community-created modules is Perl's CPAN. CPAN stands for the Comprehensive Perl Archive Network and is an *enormous* collection of reusable scripts and modules created by the community that can be easily and effectively searched for existing solutions. This repository, which you can explore at http:/www.cpan.org, currently claims the following statistics:

- Online since October 1995
- 92,277 Perl modules
- Written by 8,890 authors
- Mirrored on 254 servers

This is an incredible (and enviable) resource for Perl developers. Clearly such a thing would be of tremendous value to the PowerShell community. With the introduction of modules in v2, we're taking the first important steps to get this going.

In the previous chapter, you organized your code into functions and scripts and used dot-sourcing to load libraries of reusable script code. This is the traditional shell-language approach to code reuse. PowerShell modules provide a more manageable, production-oriented way to package code. And, as is the usual case with PowerShell, modules build on features you've already learned. For example, a PowerShell script module is simply a PowerShell script with a special extension (.psm1) loaded in a special way. We'll cover all of these details in later sections, but first, you need to understand the problem domains that the PowerShell module system was designed to address.

9.1.1 Module roles in PowerShell

Modules serve three roles in PowerShell. These roles are listed in table 9.1.

Table 9.1 The roles modules play in PowerShell

Role	Description
Configuring the environment	The first role is configuration—packaging a set of functions to configure the environment. This is what you usually use dot-sourcing for, but modules allow you to do this in a more controlled way.
Code reuse	The second major role for modules is to facilitate the creation of reusable libraries. This is the traditional role of modules in a programming language.
Composing solutions	The final role is the most unusual one. Modules can be used to create solutions—essentially a domain-specific application. PowerShell modules have the unique characteristic of being nested. In most programming languages, when one module loads another, all of the loaded modules are globally visible. In PowerShell, modules nest. If the user loads module A and module A loads module B, then all the user sees is module A (at least by default). In fact, sometimes all you'll do in a module is import some other modules and republish a subset of those modules' members.

The concepts involved in the first role—configuration—were covered when we talked about dot-sourcing files. The second role—facilitating reuse—is, as we said, the traditional role for modules. The third role is unique to PowerShell. Let's look at this third role in a bit more detail.

9.1.2 Module mashups: composing an application

One of the features that PowerShell modules offer that's unique is the idea of a *composite management application*. This is conceptually similar to the idea of a web mashup, which takes an existing service and tweaks, or layers on top of it, to achieve some other more specific purpose. The notion of management mashups is important as we move into the era of "software+services" (or "clients+clouds" if you prefer). Low operating costs make hosted services attractive. The problem is how you manage all these services, especially when you need to delegate administration responsibility to a slice of the organization.

For example, you might have each department manage its own user resources: mailboxes, customer lists, web portals, and so forth. To do this, you need to slice the management interfaces and republish them as a single coherent management experience. Sounds like magic, doesn't it? Well, much of it still is, but PowerShell modules can help because they allow you to merge the interfaces of several modules and republish only those parts of the interfaces that need to be exposed. The individual modules that are being composed are hidden from the user so components can be swapped out as needed without necessarily impacting the end user. This magic is accomplished through module manifests and nested modules. We'll cover nested modules in this chapter but manifests are a large enough topic that they get their own chapter (chapter 10).

Now that you understand why you want modules, let's look at how you can use them in PowerShell.

9.2 Module basics

In this section, we'll cover the basic information needed to use PowerShell modules. The first thing to know is that the module features in PowerShell are exposed through cmdlets, not language keywords. For example, you can get a list of the module commands using the `Get-Command` command as follows:

```
PS (1) > Get-Command -type cmdlet *-*module* | select name

Name
----
Export-ModuleMember
Get-Module
Import-Module
New-Module
New-ModuleManifest
Remove-Module
Test-ModuleManifest
```

Note that in the command name pattern, you used wildcards because there are a couple of different types of module cmdlets. These cmdlets and their descriptions are shown in table 9.2.

Table 9.2 The cmdlets used for working with modules

Module cmdlet	Description
`Get-Module`	Gets a list of the modules currently loaded in memory
`Import-Module`	Loads a module into memory and imports the public commands from that module
`Remove-Module`	Removes a module from memory and removes the imported members
`Export-ModuleMember`	Used to specify the members of a module to export to the user of the module
`New-ModuleManifest`	Used to create a new metadata file for a module directory
`Test-ModuleManifest`	Runs a series of tests on a module manifest, validating its contents
`New-Module`	Creates a new dynamic module

You can also use the `Get-Help` command to search for a list of all the help topics for modules available in the built-in help:

```
PS (2) > Get-Help *module* | select name

Name
----
New-Module
Import-Module
Export-ModuleMember
Get-Module
Remove-Module
```

```
New-ModuleManifest
Test-ModuleManifest
about_modules
```

As expected, you see all the cmdlets listed but there's also an `about_modules` help topic that describes modules and how they work in PowerShell. You can use this built-in help as a quick reference when working in a PowerShell session.

9.2.1 Module terminology

Before we get too far into modules, there are a number of concepts and definitions we should cover. Along with the names of the cmdlets, table 9.2 introduced some new terms—*module member* and *module manifest*—and reintroduced a couple of familiar terms—*import* and *export*—used in the context of modules. These terms and their definitions are shown in table 9.3.

Table 9.3 A glossary of module terminology

Term	Description
Module member	A *module member* is any function, variable, or alias defined inside a script. Modules can control which members are visible outside the module by using the `Export-ModuleMember` cmdlet.
Module manifest	A *module manifest* is a PowerShell data file that contains information about the module and controls how the module gets loaded.
Module type	The type of module. Just as PowerShell commands can be implemented by different mechanisms like functions and cmdlets, so modules also have a variety of implementation types. PowerShell has three module types: *script*, *binary*, and *manifest* modules.
Nested module	One module can load another, either procedurally by calling `Import-Module` or by adding the desired module to the `NestedModules` element in the module manifest for that module.
Root module	The root module is the main module file loaded when a module is imported. It's called the root module because it may have associated nested modules.
Imported member	An imported module member is a function, variable, or alias imported from another module.
Exported member	An exported member is a module member that has been marked for export. In other words, it's marked to be visible to the caller when the module is imported. Of course, if module `foo` imports module `bar` as a nested member, the exported members of `bar` become the imported members in `foo`.

We'll talk more about these concepts in the rest of this chapter. Now let's introduce another core module concept.

9.2.2 Modules are single-instance objects

An important characteristic of modules is that there's only ever one instance of the module in memory. If a second request is make to load the module, the fact that the module is already loaded will be caught and the module won't be reprocessed (at least, as long as the module versions match; module versions are covered in chapter 10).

There are a couple of reasons for this behavior. Modules can depend on other modules, so an application may end up referencing a module multiple times and you don't want to be reloading all the time because it slows things down. The other reason is that you want to allow for private static resources—bits of data that are reused by the functions exported from a module and aren't discarded when those functions are, as is normally the case.

For example, say we have a module that establishes a connection to a remote computer when the module is loaded. This connection will be used by all the functions exported from that module. If the functions had to reestablish the connection every time they were called, the process would be extremely inefficient. When you store the connection in the module, it will persist across the function calls.

Let's recap: in this section, we looked at some module-specific terms; then we discussed how modules are single instance. In the next section you'll start using modules and the module cmdlets. You'll learn how to go about finding, loading, and using modules.

9.3 WORKING WITH MODULES

Let's start working with PowerShell modules. You'll begin by seeing which modules are loaded in your session and which modules are available for loading, learning how to load additional modules, and understanding how to unload them. (We'll leave *creating* a module until section 9.4.) Let's get started.

9.3.1 Finding modules on the system

The `Get-Module` cmdlet is used to find modules—either the modules that are currently loaded or the modules that are available to load. The signature for this cmdlet is shown in figure 9.1.

Run with no options, `Get-Module` lists all the top-level modules loaded in the current session. If `-All` is specified, both explicitly loaded and nested modules are shown. (We'll explain the difference between top-level and nested in a minute.) If `-ListAvailable` is specified, `Get-Module` lists all the modules available to be loaded based on the current `$ENV:ModulePath` setting. If both `-ListAvailable` and `-All` are specified, the contents of the module directories are shown, including subdirectories.

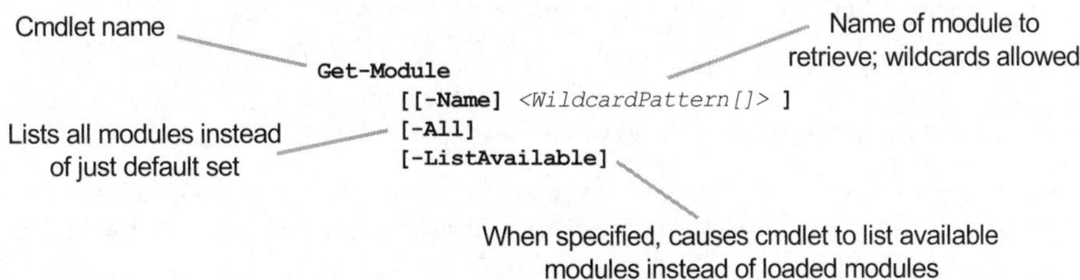

Figure 9.1 The syntax for the `Get-Module` cmdlet. This cmdlet is used to find modules, either in your session or available to be loaded.

Let's try this and see how it works. Begin by running `Get-Module` with no parameters:

```
PS (1) > Get-Module
PS (2) >
```

Okay, that wasn't very exciting. By default, PowerShell doesn't load any modules into a session. (Even in PowerShell v2, the system cmdlets are still loaded using the v1 snap-in commands for compatibility reasons—more on this later.)

Because you have nothing in memory to look at, let's see what's available for loading on the system. You can use the `-ListAvailable` parameter on `Get-Module` to find the system modules that are available. (In this example, the output is filtered using the `Where-Object` cmdlet so you don't pick up any nonsystem modules.)

```
PS (3) > Get-Module -list | where { $_.path -match "System32" }

ModuleType Name                      ExportedCommands
---------- ----                      ----------------
Manifest   FileTransfer              {}
Manifest   PSDiagnostics             {}

PS (4) >
```

And you see two modules listed.

> **NOTE** What you see listed will vary depending on which operating system you're running and which features are installed on the computer. On Server 2008R2, depending on what server roles are installed (such as Active Directory), you'll see additional modules in this output.

By default, the output only shows the module name, the module type, and the exported commands. Because PowerShell function definitions are created at runtime (more on this in section 11.1.3), the set of exported commands can't be known until the module has been loaded. This is why the list is empty—you haven't loaded them yet.

> **NOTE** Okay, sure, we could've implemented PowerShell modules so that you could statically determine the set of exported members. We thought about it, but we didn't have time. Next release, I hope.

In fact the set of properties for a module is much larger than what you saw in the default. Let's look at the full set of properties for the `PSDiagnostics` module:

```
PS (1) > Get-Module -list psdiag* | fl

Name              : PSDiagnostics
Path              : C:\Windows\system32\WindowsPowerShell\v1.0\
                    Modules\PSDiagnostics\PSDiagnostics.psd1
Description       : Windows PowerShell Diagnostic Utilities Mod
                    ule
ModuleType        : Manifest
Version           : 1.0.0.0
```

```
NestedModules      : {}
ExportedFunctions  : {}
ExportedCmdlets    : {}
ExportedVariables  : {}
ExportedAliases    : {}
```

In this output, you see the various types of module members that can be exported: functions, cmdlets, variables, and aliases. You also see the module type (`Manifest`), the module version, and a description. An important property to note is the `Path` property. This is the path to where the module file lives on disk.

In the next section, you'll see how PowerShell goes about finding modules on the system.

The $ENV:PSModulePath variable

As you saw in the output from `Get-Module`, loadable modules are identified by their path just like executables. They're loaded in much the same way as executables—a list of directories is searched until a matching module is found. There are a couple of differences, though. Instead of using `$ENV:PATH`, modules are loaded using a new environment: `$ENV:PSModulePath`. And, where the execution path is searched for files, the module path is searched for *subdirectories* containing module files. This arrangement allows a module to include more than one file. In the next section, you'll explore the search algorithm in detail.

The module search algorithm

The following algorithm, expressed in *pseudocode* (part code, part English description), is used for locating a module:

```
if (the module is an absolute path)
{
    if (the specified module name has a known extension)
    {
        join the path element and module name
        if (the composite path exists)
        {
            load the module and stop looking
        }
        else
        {
            continue with the next path element
        }
    }
    else
    {
        foreach ($extension in ".psd1",".psm1", ".dll"
        {
            join the path element, module name and extension
            if (the composite path exists)
            {
```

```
                load the module and stop looking
            }
            else
            {
                continue with the next path element
            }
        }
    }
}
foreach ($pathElement in $ENV:PSModulePath)
{
    if (the specified module name has a known extension)
    {
        Join the path element and module base name and name
        to create a new path
        if (the composite path exists)
        {
            load the module and stop looking
        }
        else
        {
            continue with the next path element
        }
    }
    else
    {
        foreach ($extension in ".psd1",".psm1", ".dll"
        {
            Join the path element and module base name, module name
            and extension.

            if (the composite path exists)
            {
                load the module and stop looking
            }
            else
            {
                continue with the next path element
            }
        }
    }
}
if (no module was found)
{
    generate an error
}
```

As you can see from the number of steps in the algorithm, the search mechanism used in loading a module is sophisticated but also a bit complicated. Later on we'll look at ways to get more information about what's being loaded.

Now that you know what modules are available, you need to be able to load them. You'll learn how next.

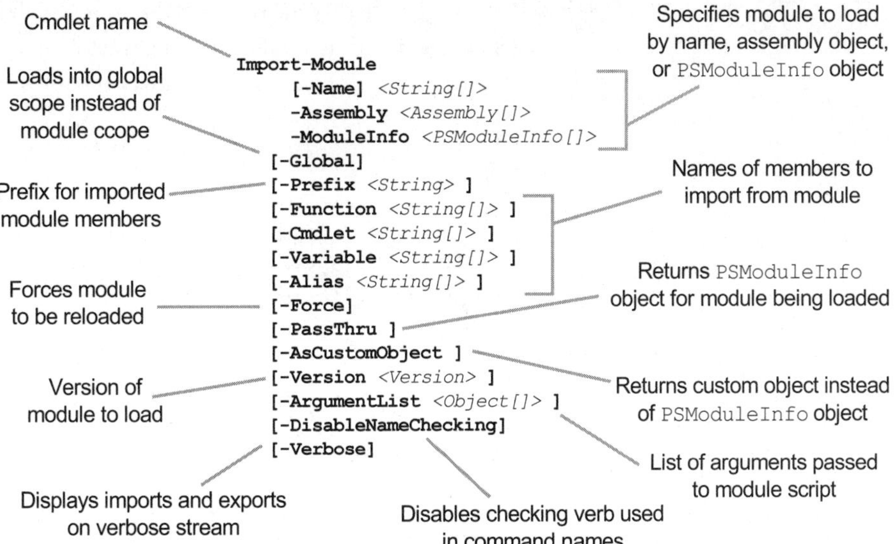

Figure 9.2 The syntax for the `Import-Module` cmdlet. This cmdlet is used to import modules into the current module context or the global context if `-Global` is specified.

9.3.2 Loading a module

Modules are loaded using the `Import-Module` cmdlet. The syntax for this cmdlet is shown in figure 9.2. As you can see, this cmdlet has a lot of parameters, allowing it to address a wide variety of scenarios. We'll look at the basic features of this cmdlet in this section and cover some obscure features in later sections of this chapter.

This cmdlet has a lot of parameters. We'll cover many of them in the next sections. Some of the more advanced parameters will be covered in chapters 10 and 11.

Loading a module by name

The most common way to load a module is to specify its name. You saw how to find modules using the `Get-Module` cmdlet in the previous section. One of the modules you discovered was `PSDiagnostics`. Let's use `Import-Module` to load this module now:

```
PS (1) > Import-Module psdiagnostics
```

By default, nothing is output when you load a module. This is as expected and desirable because when you're loading library modules in scripts or in your profile, you don't want chattiness. Unless there's an error, loading a module should be silent.

When you do want to see what was loaded, use `Get-Module`:

```
PS (2) > Get-Module

ModuleType Name                             ExportedCommands
---------- ----                             ----------------
Script     psdiagnostics                    {Enable-PSTrace, Enable-...
```

This shows that you have one module loaded named `PSDiagnostics`. This output is substantially abbreviated when displayed as a table, so let's use `Format-List` to see the details of the loaded modules just as you did when you were exploring the on-disk modules:

```
PS (3) > Get-Module | fl


Name              : psdiagnostics
Path              : C:\Windows\system32\WindowsPowerShell\v1.0\M
                    odules\psdiagnostics\PSDiagnostics.psm1
Description       :
ModuleType        : Script
Version           : 1.0.0.0
NestedModules     : {}
ExportedFunctions : {Disable-PSTrace, Disable-PSWSManCombinedTra
                    ce, Disable-WSManTrace, Enable-PSTrace...}
ExportedCmdlets   : {}
ExportedVariables : {}
ExportedAliases   : {}
```

Let's examine this output for a minute. The most obvious thing to notice is that the `ExportedFunctions` member in the output is no longer empty. When you load a module, you can finally see all the available exported members. The other thing to notice is that the module type has been changed from `Manifest` to `Script`. Again, the details of the implementation of the module aren't known until after the module has been loaded. We'll cover module manifests and the details on module types in chapter 10.

To see what commands were imported, you can use `Get-Command` with the `-Module` option:

```
PS (5) > Get-Command -Module psdiagnostics

CommandType     Name                        Definition
-----------     ----                        ----------
Function        Disable-PSTrace             ...
Function        Disable-PSWSManCombin...    ...
Function        Disable-WSManTrace          ...
Function        Enable-PSTrace              ...
Function        Enable-PSWSManCombine...    ...
Function        Enable-WSManTrace           ...
Function        Get-LogProperties           ...
Function        Set-LogProperties           ...
Function        Start-Trace                 ...
Function        Stop-Trace                  ...
```

This list matches the list of exports from the module, as you can see with `Get-Module`:

```
PS (6) > (Get-Module psdiag*).exportedfunctions

Key                                Value
---                                -----
Disable-PSTrace                    Disable-PSTrace
Disable-PSWSManCombinedTrace       Disable-PSWSManCombinedTrace
```

```
Disable-WSManTrace              Disable-WSManTrace
Enable-PSTrace                  Enable-PSTrace
Enable-PSWSManCombinedTrace     Enable-PSWSManCombinedTrace
Enable-WSManTrace               Enable-WSManTrace
Get-LogProperties               Get-LogProperties
Set-LogProperties               Set-LogProperties
Start-Trace                     Start-Trace
Stop-Trace                      Stop-Trace
```

Let's remove this module using the `Remove-Module` cmdlet and look at other ways you can specify which module to load:

```
PS (7) > Remove-Module PSDiagnostics
```

Again the command completes with no output.

In addition to loading a module by name, you can also load it by path, again paralleling the way executables work. Let's do this with the `PSDiagnostics` module. You saw the path in the output of the earlier example. We'll use this path to load the module. Because this is a system module, it's loaded from the PowerShell install directory. This means that you can use the built-in `$PSHOME` variable in the path:

```
PS (8) > Import-Module $PSHOME/modules/psdiagnostics/psdiagnostics
```

Call `Get-Module` verify that it has been loaded

```
PS (9) > Get-Module

ModuleType Name                         ExportedCommands
---------- ----                         ----------------
Script     psdiagnostics                {Enable-PSTrace, Enable-...
```

and there it is.

By loading a module using a full path, you know exactly which file will be processed. This can be useful when you're developing modules, as you'll see in section 9.4. Let's remove this module again as we move on to the next example:

```
PS (7) > Remove-Module PSDiagnostics
```

Tracing module loads with -Verbose

So far you've allowed the modules to be loaded without caring about the details of what's happening. This is fine as long as everything works, but remember how complex the module search algorithm was. When you get into more complex scenarios where you're loading multiple modules, it's useful to see what's happening. You can do this by specifying the `-Verbose` flag:

```
PS (15) > Import-Module psdiagnostics -Verbose
VERBOSE: Loading module from path
'C:\Windows\system32\WindowsPowerShell\v1.0\Modules\psdiagnostic
s\psdiagnostics.psd1'.
VERBOSE: Loading module from path
'C:\Windows\system32\WindowsPowerShell\v1.0\Modules\psdiagnostic
s\PSDiagnostics.psm1'.
```

```
VERBOSE: Importing function 'Disable-PSTrace'.
VERBOSE: Importing function 'Disable-PSWSManCombinedTrace'.
VERBOSE: Importing function 'Disable-WSManTrace'.
VERBOSE: Importing function 'Enable-PSTrace'.
VERBOSE: Importing function 'Enable-PSWSManCombinedTrace'.
VERBOSE: Importing function 'Enable-WSManTrace'.
VERBOSE: Importing function 'Get-LogProperties'.
VERBOSE: Importing function 'Set-LogProperties'.
VERBOSE: Importing function 'Start-Trace'.
VERBOSE: Importing function 'Stop-Trace'.
```

All of the output that begins with `VERBOSE:` is generated when the `-Verbose` flag is specified. It shows two things: the path to the module file and a list of all members (in this case, functions) being imported into your session. This is pretty straightforward with a simple scenario, but you'll see that it can become much more complicated when we get to nested modules in section 9.4.6.

Imports and Exports

So far, you've defaulted to loading everything that a module exports into your session. You don't have to do that—and there are cases where you don't *want* to do it. Importing too many commands clutters up your session and makes it hard to find what you're looking for. To avoid this, you can control what gets imported by using the `-Function`, `-Cmdlet`, `-Alias`, and `-Variable` parameters on `Import-Module`. As you'd expect, each of these parameters controls a particular type of import from the module. You've seen all the command types previously as well as PowerShell variables. The `PSDiagnostics` module only exports functions, so you can use that feature to restrict what gets loaded. Say you only wanted to load `Enable-PSTrace`. Here's what this would look like:

```
PS (12) > Import-Module  psdiagnostics -Verbose -Function Enable-
PSTrace
VERBOSE: Loading module from path
'C:\Windows\system32\WindowsPowerShell\v1.0\Modules\psdiagnostic
s\psdiagnostics.psd1'.
VERBOSE: Loading module from path
'C:\Windows\system32\WindowsPowerShell\v1.0\Modules\psdiagnostic
s\PSDiagnostics.psm1'.
VERBOSE: Importing function 'Enable-PSTrace'.
PS (13) > get-command -module psdiagnostics

CommandType     Name                        Definition
-----------     ----                        ----------
Function        Enable-PSTrace              ...
```

In the verbose output, you see that only `Enable-PSTrace` was imported into your session.

Now you know how to avoid creating clutter in your session. But what if it's too late and you already have too much stuff loaded? You'll learn how to fix that next.

9.3.3 Removing a loaded module

Because your PowerShell session can be long running, there may be times when you want to remove a module. As you saw earlier, you do this with the `Remove-Module` cmdlet.

> **NOTE** Typically, the only people who remove modules are those who are developing the module in question or those are working in an application environment that's encapsulating various stages in the process as modules. A typical user rarely needs to remove a module. The PowerShell team almost cut this feature because it turns out to be quite hard to do in a sensible way.

The syntax for `Remove-Module` is shown in figure 9.3.

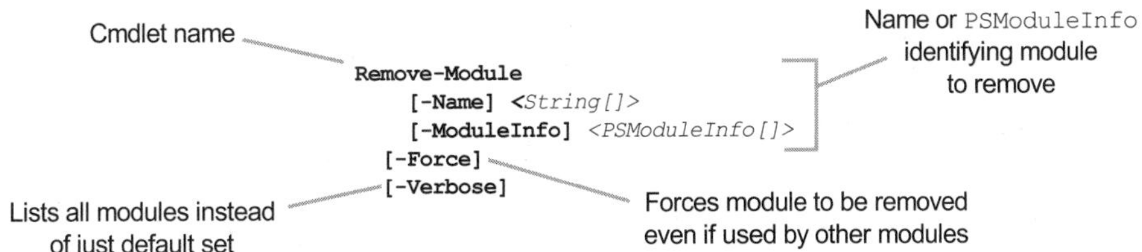

Figure 9.3 The syntax for `Remove-Module`. Note that this command doesn't take wildcards.

When a module is removed, all the modules it loaded as nested modules are also removed from the global module table. This happens *even if the module was explicitly loaded at the global level.* To illustrate how this works, let's take a look at how the module tables are organized in the environment. This organization is shown in figure 9.4.

First let's talk about the global module table. This is the master table that has references to all the modules that have been loaded either explicitly or implicitly by another module. Any time a module is loaded, this table is updated. An entry is also made in the environment of the caller. In figure 9.4, modules 1 and 3 are loaded

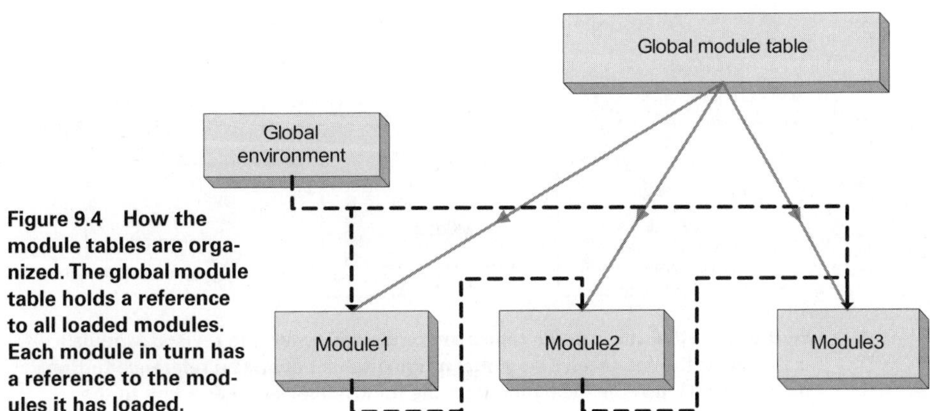

Figure 9.4 How the module tables are organized. The global module table holds a reference to all loaded modules. Each module in turn has a reference to the modules it has loaded.

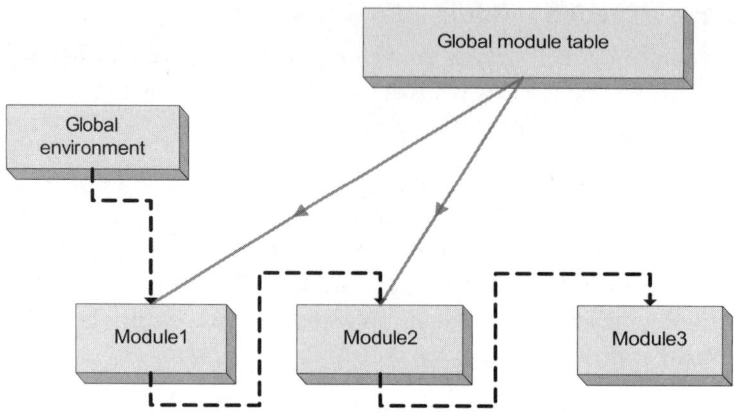

Figure 9.5 How the module tables are organized after Module3 is removed at the top level. The global module table no longer has a reference to Mo-dule3, but the local module table for Module2 still has a link to that object.

from the global module environment, so there are references from the top-level module table. Module1 loads Module2, causing a reference to be added the global module table and the private module table for Module1. Module2 loads Module3 as a nested module. Because Module1 has already been loaded from the global environment, no new entry is added to the global module table, but a private reference is added to the module table for Module2.

Now you'll remove Module3 from the global environment. The updated arrangement of modules is shown in figure 9.5.

Next, you'll update Module3 and reload it at the top level. The final arrangement of modules is shown in figure 9.6.

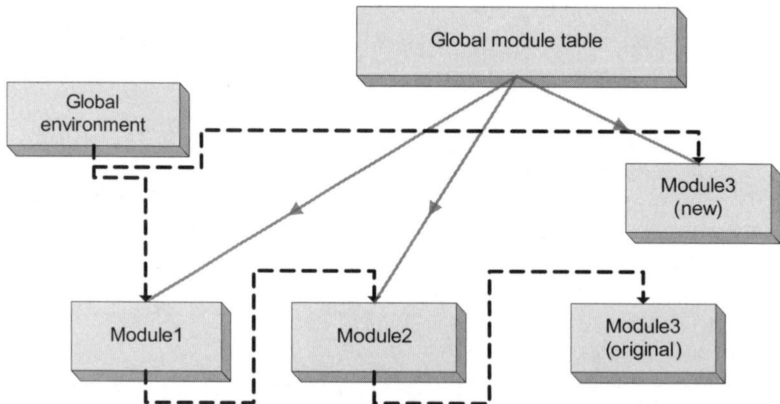

Figure 9.6 How the module tables are organized when the revised Module3 is loaded at the top level. The global module table now has a reference to the new Module3, but the local module table for Module2 still has a link to the original Module3.

In the final arrangement of modules in figure 9.6, there are two versions of Module3 loaded into the same session. Although this is extremely complicated, it permits multiple versions of a module to be loaded at the same time in the same session, allowing different modules that depend on different versions of a module to work at the same time. This is a pretty pathological scenario, but the real world isn't always tidy. Eventually you do have to deal with things you'd rather ignore, so it's good to know how.

How exported elements are removed

With an understanding of how modules are removed, you also need to know how the imported members are removed. There are two different flavors of member removal behavior depending on the type of member you're removing. Functions, aliases, and variables have one behavior. Cmdlets imported from binary modules have a slightly different behavior. This is an artifact of the way the members are implemented. Functions, aliases, and variables are data structures that are dynamically allocated and so can be replaced. Cmdlets are backed by .NET classes, which can't be unloaded from a session because .NET doesn't allow the assemblies containing these classes to be unloaded. Because of this, the implementation of the cmdlet table depends on hiding or *shadowing* a command when there's a name collision when importing a name from a module. For the other member types, the current definition of the member is replaced. So why does this matter? It doesn't matter at all until you try to remove a module.

If you remove a module that has imported cmdlets, causing existing cmdlets to be shadowed, when the module is removed the previously shadowed cmdlets become visible again. But when you remove a module importing colliding functions, aliases, or variables, because the old definitions were overridden instead of shadowed, the definitions are removed.

Okay, this has gotten a bit heavy. Let's move on to something more creative and exciting. In section 9.4, you'll finally start writing your own modules.

9.4 WRITING SCRIPT MODULES

In this section we'll start writing modules instead of just using them. For now, we'll limit our coverage to script modules. This is because script modules are written in the PowerShell language—something you're familiar with by now. In section 9.5, we'll expand our coverage to include binary modules, which requires dabbling with C#.

When showing you how to write script modules, we'll also explain how script modules work in more detail. Let's start by describing what a script module is. A script module is a file that contains PowerShell script text with a .psm1 extension instead of a .ps1 extension. In other words, a PowerShell script module is just a script with a different extension.

> **NOTE** Because a script module is a form of script, it obeys execution policy just like a script. So, before you can load a script module, you'll need to change the execution policy to be `RemoteSigned` as a minimum, as described in section 8.1.1.

Is it as simple as that? Well, almost. Let's walk through an example where you convert a script into a module and see what changes during the process.

9.4.1 A quick review of scripts

You're going to write a short script to work with in this conversion exercise. This script is indented to implement a simple counter. You get the next number from the counter by calling `Get-Count` and you reset the sequence using the `Reset-Count` command. Here's what the script looks like:

```
PS (STA) (27) > Get-Content counter.ps1
$script:count = 0
$script:increment = 1

function Get-Count
{
    return $script:count += $increment
}

function Reset-Count
{
    $script:count=0
    setIncrement 1
}

function setIncrement ($x)
{
    $script:increment = $x
}
```

As you can see, this script defines the two functions we mentioned, `Get-Count` and `Reset-Count`. But it also defines a number of other things that aren't part of the specification: a helper function, `setIncrement`, and two script-level variables, `$count` and `$increment`. These variables hold the state of the counter. Obviously just running the script won't be useful as the commands are defined at the script scope and are removed when the script exits. Instead, you'll dot-source the script to load the script members into your environment:

```
PS {2) > . .\counter.ps1
PS {3) >
```

This creates the elements without showing anything (which is what you want a library to do in most cases.) Now manually verify that you got what you intended:

```
PS {3) > Get-Command *-count

CommandType     Name                        Definition
-----------     ----                        ----------
Function        Get-Count                   ...
Function        Reset-Count                 ...
```

The functions are there so you can try them out. Start with `Get-Count`:

```
PS (4) >     Get-Count
1
PS (5) > Get-Count
2
```

Each call to `Get-Count` returns the next number in the sequence. Now use the `Reset-Count` command

```
PS (6) > Reset-Count
```

and call `Get-Count` to verify that the count has been reset:

```
PS (7) > Get-Count
1
```

Okay, great. But what about the other private members in the script? Using `Get-Command` you see that the `setIncrement` function is also visible:

```
PS (8) > Get-Command setIncrement

CommandType      Name                     Definition
-----------      ----                     ----------
Function         setIncrement             param($x)...
```

And you can even call it directly:

```
PS (9) > setIncrement 7
PS (10) > Get-Count
8
PS (11) > Get-Count
15
```

Because this function was supposed to be a private implementation detail, the fact that it's publicly visible isn't desirable. Likewise, you can also get at the state variables you created:

```
PS (12) > Get-Variable count, increment

Name                           Value
----                           -----
count                          15
increment                      7
```

The problem with this is clear: `$count` isn't a unique name so the chance of it colliding with a similarly named variable from another script is high. This lack of isolation between scripts makes using dot-sourcing a fragile way to build libraries.

Finally, let's try to remove this script, emulating what you've been doing with `Remove-Module`. This turns out to be quite complicated. You end up having to write a command that looks like this:

```
PS (13) > Remove-Item -Verbose  variable:count,
>>> variable:increment,function:Reset-Count,
```

```
>>> function:Get-Count,function:setIncrement
VERBOSE: Performing operation "Remove Item" on Target
"Item: count".
VERBOSE: Performing operation "Remove Item" on Target
"Item: increment".
VERBOSE: Performing operation "Remove Item" on Target
"Item: Reset-Count".
VERBOSE: Performing operation "Remove Item" on Target
"Item: Get-Count".
VERBOSE: Performing operation "Remove Item" on Target
"Item: setIncrement".
PS (14) >
```

This is necessary because there's no implicit grouping of all the members created by a script.

Finding function definitions

It's not true that there's no way to find out which functions came from a particular file. Another change in PowerShell v2 was to attach the path to the file where a function was defined to the scriptblock of the function. For the counter example we've been discussing, the path might look like

```
PS (23) > ${function:Get-Count}.File
C:\wpia_v2\text\chapter09\code\counter.ps1
PS (24) >
```

This `File` property makes it easier to figure out where things came from in your environment when you have to debug it. For example, all the functions that were defined in your profile will have the path to your profile in it, functions that were defined in the system profile will have the system profile path, and so on. (We discussed the set of profiles that PowerShell uses in chapter 2.) This only fixes part of the problem—managing functions—and doesn't deal with variables and aliases.

At this point, it's clear that, although it's possible to build libraries using dot-sourcing, there are a number of problems with this approach. Private implementation details leak into the public namespace, and the members of a dot-sourced script lose any sort of grouping that allows you to manage them as a whole. Let's turn this script into a module and see how that fixes the problem.

9.4.2 Turning a script into a module

Now let's turn the counter script into a module. Do this simply by changing the extension on the module from .ps1 to .psm1 (where the *m* stands for module):

```
PS (1) > copy .\counter.ps1 .\counter.psm1 -Force -Verbose
VERBOSE: Performing operation "Copy File" on Target "Item:
C:\wpia_v2\text\chapter09\code\counter.ps1 Destination:
C:\wpia_v2\text\chapter09\code\counter.psm1".
PS (2) >
```

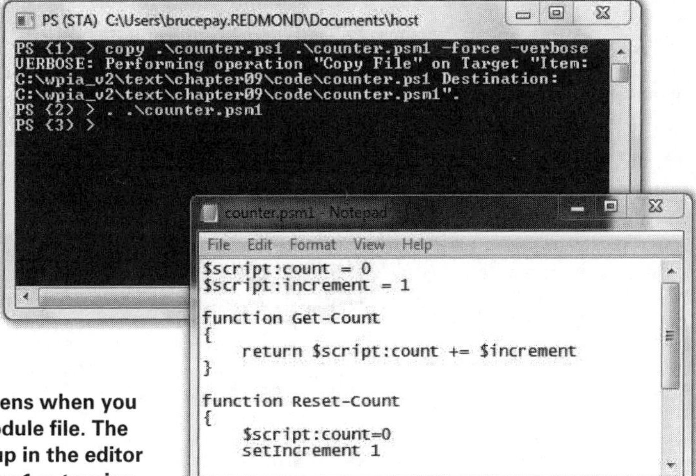

Figure 9.7 What happens when you try to directly run a module file. The module file is opened up in the editor associated with the .psm1 extension.

(You're using the `-Force` parameter here to make the example work all the time.) Try loading the renamed file. Figure 9.7 shows what you'll probably see when you do this.

The module wasn't run. The default action is to open the file in the editor associated with the extension. This is because module files aren't commands and can't just be run. Instead, you need to use the `Import-Module` command to load this module:

```
PS (3) > Import-Module .\counter.psm1
PS (4) >
```

Now that you've loaded a module, you can try the `Get-Module` command and see something useful:

```
PS (5) > Get-Module

ModuleType Name                        ExportedCommands
---------- ----                        ----------------
Script     counter                     {setIncrement, Get-Coun...
```

Again let's use the `Format-List` (alias: `fl`) cmdlet to see the object in more detail:

```
PS (6) > Get-Module | fl

Name              : counter
Path              : C:\wpia_v2\text\chapter09\code\counter.psm1
Description       :
ModuleType        : Script
Version           : 0.0
NestedModules     : {}
ExportedFunctions : {Get-Count, Reset-Count, setIncrement}
ExportedCmdlets   : {}
ExportedVariables : {}
ExportedAliases   : {}
```

An important thing to notice is that the Path property stores the full path to where the module was loaded from. The module type is script and the version is 0.0—the default for a script module. (When we look at manifests in chapter 10, you'll see how to change this.) The most important thing to notice are the export lists. You see that all the functions defined in the script module are being exported but no variables are. To verify this, use Get-Command to look for all the functions defined by the script:

```
PS {7) > Get-Command -Module counter

CommandType     Name                    Definition
-----------     ----                    ----------
Function        Get-Count               ...
Function        Reset-Count             ...
Function        setIncrement            param($x)...
```

You can immediately see one of the benefits of using modules: you can work with sets of related elements as a unit. (More on this in a bit.) Now that you've loaded the functions, you have to run them to make sure they work:

```
PS {8) > Get-Count
1
PS {9) > Get-Count
2
PS {10) > Get-Count
3
```

As before, you see that Get-Count returns the next element in the sequence. Now let's check on the variables used by Get-Count. These were a big problem when you dotted the script:

```
PS (14) > $count
PS (16) > $increment
```

Neither of them exist. Try assigning a value to $count and see whether it makes a difference:

```
PS (17) > $count = 100
PS (18) > Get-Count
4
```

As desired, it has no effect on Get-Count. Try Reset-Count and verify that it works:

```
PS (19) > Reset-Count
PS (20) > Get-Count
1
```

And it does. Now let's look at another issue you had to deal with when using script libraries: how to remove the imported elements. With modules, you can simply remove the module:

```
PS (21) > Remove-Module counter
```

This will remove the module from the session and remove all imported members, so if you try to run Get-Count now, you get an error:

```
PS (22) > Get-Count
The term 'Get-Count' is not recognized as the name of a cmdlet,
function, script file, or operable program. Check the spelling o
f the name, or if a path was included, verify that the path is c
orrect and try again.
At line:1 char:10
+ Get-Count <<<<
    + CategoryInfo          : ObjectNotFound: (Get-Count:String
   ) [], CommandNotFoundException
    + FullyQualifiedErrorId : CommandNotFoundException
```

In the next section, we'll look at ways to get more fine-grained control over the things that modules export.

9.4.3 Controlling member visibility with Export-ModuleMember

Let's recap what you saw in the last example. You converted a script to a module simply by changing the file extension. When you imported the module, all the functions you'd defined were visible by default but nothing else was. This is the default behavior in a module when you don't do anything to control member visibility. Because script libraries written for v1 typically depended on this behavior, simply renaming them with a .psm1 extension may be all that's needed to turn them into modules.

Although this approach is simple, it's not very flexible. For complex scenarios, you need to be able to control exactly what gets exported. You do this with the Export-ModuleMember cmdlet. This cmdlet lets you declare exactly which commands and variables are exported from the module. We'll start by reviewing how it works with functions.

Controlling which functions are exported

First we'll look at how you can hide the functions you want to be private in a module. Let's take a look at another variation of the counter module:

```
PS (1) > Get-Content .\counter1.psm1
$script:count = 0
$script:increment = 1

function Get-Count
{
    return $script:count += $increment
}

function Reset-Count
{
    $script:count=0
    setIncrement 1
}
```

```
function setIncrement ($x)
{
    $script:increment = $x
}

Export-ModuleMember *-Count
```

The only difference between this version and the previous one is the last line, which uses the `Export-ModuleMember` cmdlet. This line says "Export all functions matching the pattern *-Count." Now import the module:

```
PS (2) > Import-Module .\counter1.psm1
```

You verify that the count and reset commands are there:

```
PS (3) > Get-Command *-Count

CommandType     Name                            Definition
-----------     ----                            ----------
Function        Get-Count                       ...
Function        Reset-Count                     ...
```

But the `setIncrement` command isn't, because it wasn't explicitly exported:

```
PS (4) > Get-Command setIncrement
Get-Command : The term 'setIncrement' is not recognized as the n
ame of a cmdlet, function, script file, or operable program. Che
ck the spelling of the name, or if a path was included, verify t
hat the path is correct and try again.
At line:1 char:12
+ Get-Command <<<<  setIncrement
    + CategoryInfo          : ObjectNotFound: (setIncrement:Str
   ing) [Get-Command], CommandNotFoundException
    + FullyQualifiedErrorId : CommandNotFoundException,Microsof
   t.PowerShell.Commands.GetCommandCommand
```

Remove the module to clean up after yourself:

```
PS (5) > Remove-Module counter1
```

Here's the rule to remember: if there are no calls to `Export-ModuleMember` in a script module, all functions are exported by default and all other member types are private. If there's at least one call to `Export-ModuleMember`, whatever the cmdlet does overrides the default. This means that PowerShell doesn't know exactly what set of functions will be exported until the script has run to completion. We'll return to this concept in a minute but first let's finish up with variables and aliases.

Controlling what variables and aliases are exported

Although functions are exported by default, variables and aliases aren't. Again, to change the default set of exports, use the `Export-ModuleMember` cmdlet. Let's look at a third variation on the counter module:

```
PS (6) > Get-Content .\counter2.psm1
$script:count = 0
$script:increment = 1
```

```
function Get-Count { return $script:count += $increment }

function Reset-Count { $script:count=0;  setIncrement 1 }
New-Alias reset Reset-Count

function setIncrement ($x) {  $script:increment = $x }

Export-ModuleMember -Function *-Count -Variable increment -Alias reset
```

This time there are two changes to the script. First you're defining an alias for the `Reset-Count` function. Second, you're using the `Export-ModuleMember` to explicitly control all of the exports: functions, variables, and aliases. Now, if the member doesn't appear in a call to `Export-ModuleMember`, it won't be exported. Let's import the updated module

```
PS (7) > Import-Module .\counter2.psm1
```

and verify the contents. Are the `*-Count` commands loaded?

```
PS (8) > Get-Command *-Count

CommandType     Name                      Definition
-----------     ----                      ----------
Function        Get-Count                 ...
Function        Reset-Count               ...
```

Yes, they're all there. What about `setIncrement?` You were supposed to export it, so there should be an error when you try calling

```
PS (9) > setIncrement 10
The term 'setIncrement' is not recognized as the name of a cmdle
t, function, script file, or operable program. Check the spellin
g of the name, or if a path was included, verify that the path i
s correct and try again.
At line:1 char:13
+ setIncrement <<<<  10
    + CategoryInfo          : ObjectNotFound: (setIncrement:Str
   ing) [], CommandNotFoundException
    + FullyQualifiedErrorId : CommandNotFoundException
```

And there is. The function wasn't exported from the module so it can't be imported by the module loaded. Finally, check to see if your variables were exported properly by trying to display their contents:

```
PS (10) > $count
PS (11) > $increment
1
```

You can see that the `$count` variable wasn't exported because nothing was displayed. The `$increment` variable, on the other hand, was the value being output.

Next, check to see if the `reset` alias was exported. Run `Get-Count` a few times:

```
PS (12) > Get-Count
1
PS (13) > Get-Count
```

```
2
PS (14) > Get-Count
3
```

And call the `reset` command:

```
PS (15) > reset
```

You didn't get a "command not found error," meaning that the command exists—so check that the value was reset:

```
PS (16) > Get-Count
1
PS (17) > Get-Count
2
```

Once again, you can see from the output that it was.

When module exports are calculated

Now let's return to something we mentioned earlier: the set of module members to export is not known until runtime. In fact, the `Export-ModuleMember` cmdlet doesn't export the function; it adds it to a list of members to export. Once execution of the module body is completed, the PowerShell runtime looks at the accumulated lists of exports and exports those functions. The export algorithm is shown in figure 9.8.

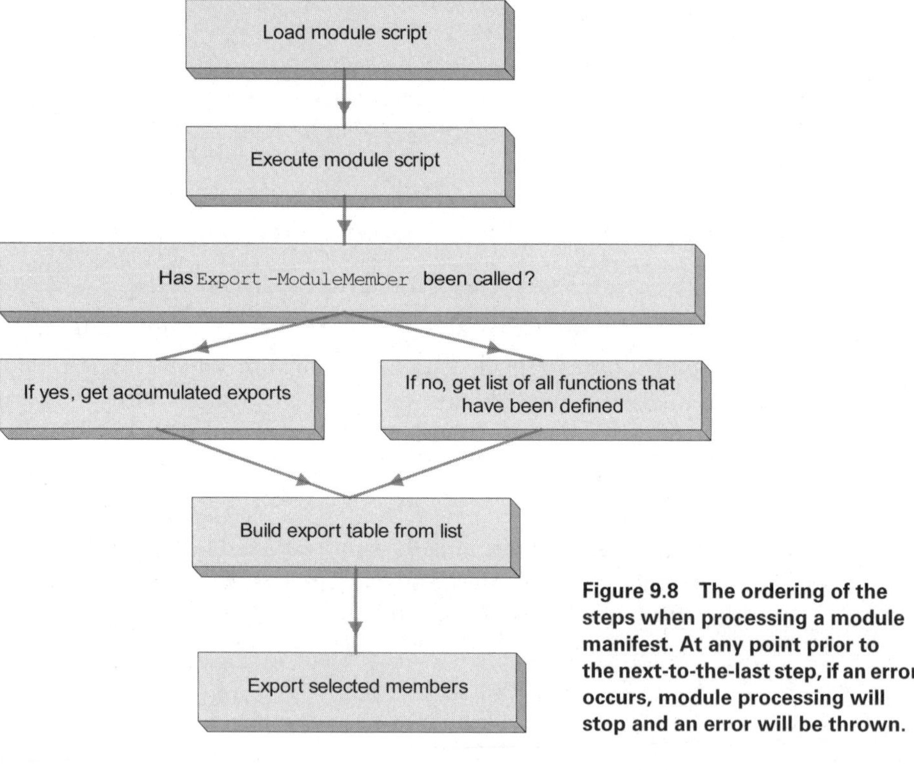

Figure 9.8 The ordering of the steps when processing a module manifest. At any point prior to the next-to-the-last step, if an error occurs, module processing will stop and an error will be thrown.

As shown in the figure, PowerShell loads and executes the module file. As execution proceeds, the module code defines functions and may or may not call `Export-ModuleMember`. If it does call `Export-ModuleMember`, then the specified members to export are added to the exports list. When execution has completed, control returns to the module loader, which checks to see if anything was put into the export list. If there were no calls to `Export-ModuleMember`, then this list is empty. In that case, the loader finds all the functions defined in the module's scope and exports them. If there was at least one call to `Export-ModuleMember`, then the module loader uses the export list to control what gets exported.

So far you've been loading the module using the path to the module file. This is a good approach for development, but eventually you need to put it into production. In the next section you'll learn how.

9.4.4 Installing a module

Once you have your module debugged and ready to put into production, you need to know how to install it. Fortunately, unlike with snap-ins, installation is simple. All you have to do is create a subdirectory of one of the directories in the module path—the proverbial "Xcopy install" that people like to talk about. Let's look at the first element of the module path:

```
PS (1) > ($ENV:PSModulePath -split ';')[0]
C:\Users\brucepay\Documents\WindowsPowerShell\Modules
```

The Modules directory in Documents\WindowsPowerShell is the user's personal module repository. You're going to install the counter module in it so you don't have to load it using the full path anymore. Let's get the repository path into a variable so it's easier to use:

```
PS (2) > $mm = ($ENV:PSModulePath -split ';')[0]
```

Next create the module directory:

```
PS (4) > mkdir $mm/Counter

    Directory: C:\Users\brucepay\Documents\WindowsPowerShell\Modules

Mode                LastWriteTime     Length Name
----                -------------     ------ ----
d----         1/31/2010   1:06 AM            Counter
```

Install the module by copying it into the directory just created:

```
PS (7) > copy .\counter.psm1 $mm/Counter
```

Now try it out. Use the `-List` option on `Get-Module` to see if the module lookup algorithm will find it:

```
PS (10) > Get-Module -List Counter | fl name, path

Name : Counter
Path : C:\Users\brucepay\Documents\WindowsPowerShell\Modules\Counter\
       Counter.psm1
```

And it does. This means you should be able to load it by name:

```
PS (12) > Import-Module -Verbose counter
VERBOSE: Loading module from path
'C:\Users\brucepay\Documents\WindowsPowerShell\Modules\counter\counte
r.psm1'.
VERBOSE: Exporting function 'Get-Count'.
VERBOSE: Exporting function 'Reset-Count'.
VERBOSE: Exporting function 'setIncrement'.
VERBOSE: Importing function 'Get-Count'.
VERBOSE: Importing function 'Reset-Count'.
VERBOSE: Importing function 'setIncrement'.
```

It works. Installing a module is as simple as copying a file. You may be wondering why you have to put in into a directory—it's just a single file. In chapter 10, you'll see that a production module is more than just a single .psm1 file. This is why modules are stored in a directory—it allows all the module resources to be gathered in one place, making it easy to distribute a multifile module. Just zip it up and send it out.

> **NOTE** Downloading and installing a zipped module on Windows 7 or Vista requires some extra steps because files downloaded using Internet Explorer are blocked by default. PowerShell honors this blocking attribute, so you won't be able to load the module until you unblock it. The most effective way to do this is to unblock the zip file before unzipping it. Then, when you unzip it, all the extracted files will also be unblocked. To unblock a file, right-click the file in Explorer, and select the Properties option. When the property dialog appears, if the file is blocked, you'll see a message saying that the file came from another computer. Beside the message text will be an Unblock button. Click this button to unblock the file, and then click OK to close the property dialog.

In all the exercises so far, you've depended on the module scoping semantics to make things work. Now is a good time to develop your understanding of exactly how these new scoping rules operate. In the next section, we'll at how function and variable names are resolved when using modules.

9.4.5 How scopes work in script modules

In section 8.4, we covered how scripts introduced script-specific scoping rules. As you've seen, modules also introduce some new scoping rules. The primary goal of these module-specific rules is to insulate modules from accidental contamination picked up from the caller's environment. This insulating property makes module behavior more predictable and that, in turn, makes modules more reusable.

To accomplish this isolation, each module gets its own scope chain. As with the default scope chain, the module scope chain eventually ends at the global scope (which means that module and default scope chains both share the same global variables). Walking up the module scope chain, right before you reach the global scope, you'll encounter a new distinguished scope: the *module scope*. This scope is somewhat similar to the script scope except it's only created once per loaded module and is used to share and preserve the state of that module. A diagram of all of these pieces is shown in figure 9.9.

Let's spend some time walking through figure 9.9. In the diagram, you see boxes indicating three functions. The two on the left (`one` and `two`) are defined in the default scope and will use the default scope chain to look up variables. The function shown on the right (`foo`) is defined inside a module and so uses the module scope chain. Now let's call function `one`. This function sets a local variable, `$y`, to 20 then calls function `two`.

In the body of `two`, you're adding `$x` and `$y` together. This means that you have to look up the variables to get their values. The smaller gray arrows in figure 9.9 show the order in which the scopes will be checked. Following the default scope path, the first instance of a variable named `$y` is found in the local scope of function `one` and has a value of 20. Next you follow the scope path to find `$x`, and you don't find it until you hit the global scope, where it resolves to 1. Now you can add them, yielding the value 21.

Function `two` then calls the module function `foo`. This function also adds `$x` and `$y`, but this time you'll use the module scope chain to look up the variables. You travel up the module chain and don't find the defined variable `$y` until you hit the global scope, where its value is 2. When you look up `$x`, you find that it was set to 10 in the module scope. You add 2 and 10 and get 12. This shows how local variables defined in the caller's scope can't have an impact on the module's behavior. The module's operations are insulated from the caller's environment.

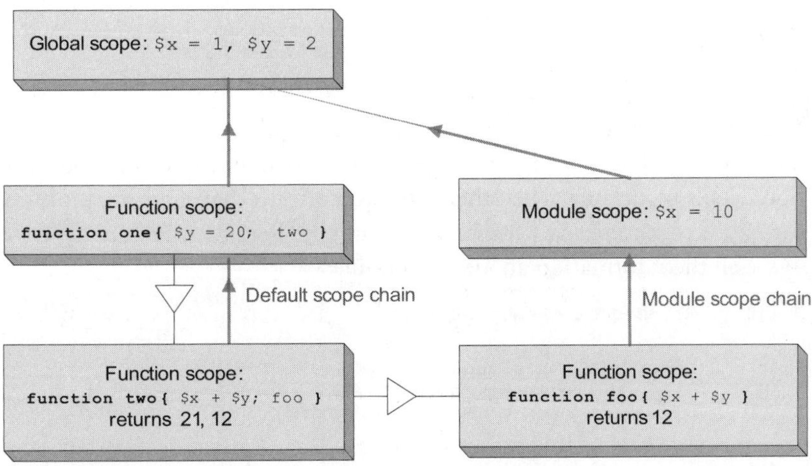

Figure 9.9 How variables are resolved in a module context. Function `one` calls `two`, and `two` calls the module function `foo`. Functions `one` and `two` look up variables in the default scope. The module function `foo` uses the module scope chain.

At this point, we've covered most of the important details of what happens when a module is loaded into the global environment. But modules can be loaded into other modules too. This is where reuse can really kick in—modules building on modules delivering more and more functionality. You'll see how this works in the next section when we introduce nested modules.

9.4.6 Nested modules

In this section, we'll cover what happens when modules import other modules. Because the `Import-Module` cmdlet is just a regular cmdlet, it can be called from anywhere. When it's called from inside another module, the result is a *nested module*. A nested module is only directly visible to the calling module. This is much easier to show than to explain. Let's look at a module called `usesCount.psm1`. Here are the contents of the module file:

```
PS (1) > Get-Content usesCount.psm1
Import-Module .\counter2.psm1

function CountUp ($x)
{
    while ($x-- -gt 0) { Get-Count }
}
```

This module imports the `counter2` module created earlier and then defines a single function, `countUp`. Import this module:

```
PS (2) > Import-Module .\usesCount.psm1
```

Now call `Get-Module` to see what's loaded:

```
PS (3) > Get-Module

ModuleType Name                          ExportedCommands
---------- ----                          ----------------
Script     usesCount                     {CountUp, Get-Count, Res...
```

The first thing to notice in this output is that the list of loaded modules doesn't show the nested module. This is by design—you don't want to expose module implementation details by default. The other thing to notice is that there are more commands in the `ExportedCommands` list than just `CountUp`. Let's use the `Format-List` (alias: `fl`) to see all the information about the module:

```
PS (4) > Get-Module usesCount | fl

Name              : usesCount
Path              : C:\wpia_v2\text\chapter09\code\usesCount.psm
                    1
Description       :
ModuleType        : Script
Version           : 0.0
NestedModules     : {counter2}
ExportedFunctions : {CountUp, Get-Count, Reset-Count}
```

```
ExportedCmdlets    : {}
ExportedVariables : {}
ExportedAliases    : {}
```

This shows you that three functions were exported from this module even though the module itself only defined one function. This is because the functions that are being imported from the nested module are exported from the root module, `usesCount`. Remember, by default all defined functions in a module are exported by default. This includes function definitions that were imported from a nested module as well as those defined in the module body.

Although nested modules are hidden by default, there's a way to see all the modules that are loaded, including nested modules. You use the `-All` flag on `Get-Module`:

```
PS (5) > Get-Module -All

ModuleType Name                          ExportedCommands
---------- ----                          ----------------
Script     counter2                      {Get-Count, Reset-Count}
Script     usesCount                     {CountUp, Get-Count, Res...
```

Using this flag you see both of the modules that are loaded.

Now let's look at some of the commands that were imported. First look at the function that came from the root module:

```
PS (6) > Get-Command CountUp | fl -Force *

HelpUri             :
ScriptBlock         : param($x)
                      while ($x-- -gt 0) { Get-Count }

CmdletBinding       : False
DefaultParameterSet :
Definition          : param($x)
                      while ($x-- -gt 0) { Get-Count }

Options             : None
Description         :
OutputType          : {}
Name                : CountUp
CommandType         : Function
Visibility          : Public
ModuleName          : usesCount
Module              : usesCount
Parameters          : {[x, System.Management.Automation.Paramete
                      rMetadata]}
ParameterSets       : {[[-x] <Object>]}
```

There's a lot of information here; the properties that are most interesting for this discussion are `ModuleName` and `Module`. `ModuleName` names the module that this function was exported from, whereas the `Module` property points to the module that *defined* this function. For top-level modules, the defining and exporting modules are the same; for nested modules, they aren't. From the ModuleName property, you see that this function was exported from module usesCount. Now let's look at one of the functions that was imported from the nested module and then re-exported:

```
PS (7) > Get-Command Get-Count | fl *

HelpUri             :
ScriptBlock         :
                          return $script:count += $increment

CmdletBinding       : False
DefaultParameterSet :
Definition          :
                          return $script:count += $increment

Options             : None
Description         :
OutputType          : {}
Name                : Get-Count
CommandType         : Function
Visibility          : Public
ModuleName          : usesCount
Module              : usesCount
Parameters          : {}
ParameterSets       : {}
```

From the output, you see that the module name for the function shows the top-level module name, not the name of the module where the function was defined. This makes sense because they're both exported from the same module. But they were defined in separate files. Knowing where a function is defined is critical to debugging, as you'll learn in chapter 15. The way to see where a function was defined is to look at the File property on the scriptblock that makes up the body of the function:

```
PS (8) > ${function:CountUp}.File
C:\wpia_v2\text\chapter09\code\usesCount.psm1
PS (9) > ${function:Get-Count}.File
C:\wpia_v2\text\chapter09\code\counter2.psm1
PS (10) >
```

This is a fairly easy way to see where the module came from, once you know how.

Import into the global environment with -Global

When one module loads another, by default it becomes a nested module. This is usually what you want, but perhaps you want to write a module that manipulates modules. In this scenario, you need to be able to import the module into a context other than your own. Although there isn't a way to import directly into an arbitrary context, the -Global flag on Import-Module allows you to import into the global context. Let's work on a variation of the usesCount module to see how this works. The modified script module looks like this:

```
PS (1) > Get-Content .\usesCount2.psm1
Import-Module -Global .\counter2.psm1
```

```
function CountUp ($x)
{
    while ($x-- -gt 0) { Get-Count }
}
```

The significant difference in this version is the use of the `-Global` parameter on `Import-Module`. First import the module

```
PS (2) > Import-Module .\usesCount2.psm1
```

and then look at the modules that are loaded:

```
PS (3) > Get-Module

ModuleType Name                        ExportedCommands
---------- ----                        ----------------
Script     counter2                    {Get-Count, Reset-Count}
Script     usesCount2                  CountUp
```

This time you see that both modules are loaded at the top level instead of one being nested inside another. Also, the `ExportedCommand` property for `usesCount2` doesn't report the functions defined in `counter2` as being exported from `usesCount2`. When you use `Get-Command` to look at functions from each of the modules:

```
PS (4) > Get-Command Get-Count | ft name,module

Name                              Module
----                              ------
Get-Count                         counter2
```

The functions defined in `counter2` are shown as being in the correct module, as is the case for the `CountUp` functions:

```
PS (5) > Get-Command CountUp | ft name,module

Name                              Module
----                              ------
CountUp                           usesCount2
```

In effect, you've written a module that manipulates modules.

This completes our coverage of script modules, which are the type of module most people are likely to write. The next type of module we'll look at are binary modules, which everyone uses but are usually created by programmers (because they're written in languages that must be compiled in an assembly or DLL file).

9.5 BINARY MODULES

This section explores how binary modules operate in PowerShell. Binary modules contain the classes that define cmdlets and providers. Unlike script modules, binary modules are written in compiled languages like C# or Visual Basic. They're used to deliver most of the packaged functionality in the PowerShell distribution. From a technical perspective, a binary module is simply a .NET assembly (a DLL) compiled against the PowerShell libraries.

Programming topics aren't the focus of the book, but we'll spend a bit of time looking at how binary modules are written and compiled. This implies that you'll have to do some C# programming to produce a module to work with. In the following sections, we'll look at how to create and load binary modules, how they interact with script modules, and any issues you need to be aware of when working with them.

9.5.1 Binary modules vs. snap-ins

Binary modules are the preferred way of packaging compiled cmdlets and providers in PowerShell v2. They essentially replace the snap-in concept used in PowerShell v1. Although the emphasis is now on modules, the snap-in mechanism is still present in v2, so we need to spend some time on it. (All the core assemblies in PowerShell v2 are still delivered as snap-ins to avoid accidentally breaking things.)

Like binary modules, snap-ins are just assemblies with a .dll extension. Unlike with modules, before you can load a snap-in into PowerShell, you have to *register* the snap-in. This registration model is based on a similar mechanism used by the Microsoft Management Console (MMC) and has the singular advantage that all modules on the system can be found by looking in the Registry. Unfortunately it also has a great many disadvantages.

First, registration is done using the `installutil.exe` program. This utility is installed in.NET Framework's installation directory, not in the normal command path, so you can't just call it. Instead, the first thing you have to do to register a snap-in is find `installutil.exe`. Fortunately you can create an alias to take care of this:

```
Set-Alias installutil `
    (Join-Path `
        (Split-Path ([object].Assembly.Location) -Parent) `
        installutil.exe)
```

This expression works by using the `Location` property on the assembly containing the `[object]` type to find the .NET Framework directory. It joins that path with the name of the command. Next, to be able to use this utility, you need to have local administrator capabilities. This is because you have to write to the system Registry as part of the registration process. Finally, all registered snap-ins are visible system-wide as soon as the registration completes. This means that there's no way to load and test changes to a snap-in without making those changes visible to all users of the system. All of these things combined make developing and testing snap-ins quite tedious.

Modules solve all of these problems: you don't need a separate tool to load modules; you don't need to be the admin on the machine; the module path allows public and private modules; and finally, to test a module, you can just use `Import-Module` and pass it the path to the file. There's nothing novel here—it works the same way for all types of modules. This consistency of experience is another benefit that modules provide.

Another difference between snap-ins and binary modules is the fact that the snap-in, besides containing the cmdlets and providers, also contains the snap-in metadata:

its name, author, version, and so on, as part of the snap-in assembly. The module mechanism handles this in a different way by specifying the metadata using a separate manifest file. This separation allows for a common representation of metadata independent of the type of module. (We'll spend a lot of time on module manifests in chapter 10.)

Now that you know the advantages provided by binary modules compared to snap-ins, you can begin working with them.

9.5.2 Creating a binary module

The first thing you'll need for our experiments is a module to work with, so in this section, you'll learn how to create that module. Remember that binary modules are written in a language like C#, so you'll do a bit of non-PowerShell programming. Fortunately, you should have some C# code handy from the example cmdlet you saw in chapter 2. Let's take this code and make a binary module out of it:

```
PS (1) > Get-Content ExampleModule.cs

using System.Management.Automation;

[Cmdlet("Write", "InputObject")]
public class MyWriteInputObjectCmdlet : Cmdlet
{
    [Parameter]
    public string Parameter1;

    [Parameter(Mandatory = true, ValueFromPipeline=true)]
    public string InputObject;

    protected override void ProcessRecord()
    {
        if (Parameter1 != null)
                WriteObject(Parameter1 +  ":" +  InputObject);
            else
                WriteObject(InputObject);
    }
}
```

If you were paying attention in the previous chapter, this should be pretty comprehensible. You should certainly recognize the `[Parameter()]` attributes from advanced functions. Before you can use this C# code as a module, you need to compile it. PowerShell v2 adds a handy, powerful new cmdlet called `Add-Type`. This cmdlet is designed to make this kind of thing easy. In this case, you'll use it to compile the source code from the path `.\ExampleModule.cs` into the output assembly `.\ExampleModule.dll`:

```
PS (2) > Add-Type -Path .\ExampleModule.cs `
>>     -OutputAssembly .\ExampleModule.dll
>>
```

Use the dir command to make sure that you got what you wanted:

```
PS (3) > dir examplemodule.dll

    Directory: C:\wpia_v2\text\chapter09\code

Mode                LastWriteTime     Length Name
----                -------------     ------ ----
-a---          8/31/2009   7:25 PM      3584 examplemodule.dll
```

There's your module: examplemodule.dll. Once the module DLL has been created, you can load it the same way you loaded a script module, using Import-Module:

```
PS (4) > Import-Module ./examplemodule.dll
```

As before, you'll use Get-Module to look at the module information object for ExampleModule:

```
PS (5) > Get-Module | Format-List

Name              : examplemodule
Path              : C:\wpia_v2\text\chapter09\code\examplemodule
                    .dll
Description       :
ModuleType        : Binary
Version           : 0.0.0.0
NestedModules     : {}
ExportedFunctions : {}
ExportedCmdlets   : Write-InputObject
ExportedVariables : {}
ExportedAliases   : {}
```

You see the name and path as expected. The module type is binary, and it's exporting a single cmdlet, Write-InputObject. Now try this new cmdlet:

```
PS (7) > 1,2,3 | Write-InputObject -Parameter1 "Number"
Number:1
Number:2
Number:3
```

It's all working fine.

So, other than the implementation of a binary module, there's not much difference in behavior when using it. Well, there's one major difference: binary modules are implemented as .NET assemblies and .NET assemblies can't be unloaded from a session (it's a .NET thing, not a PowerShell thing); therefore, binary modules can't be unloaded from a session. This means that you can't update a binary module once it's been loaded. You can't even update the assembly on disk because the file is locked when the assembly is loaded. If you rerun the Add-Type cmdlet you used to build the assembly earlier, you get a rather intimidating error message:

```
PS (8) > Add-Type -Path .\ExampleModule.cs `
>> -OutputAssembly .\ExampleModule.dll
>>
```

```
Add-Type : (0) : Could not write to output file 'c:\wpia_v2\text\chap
ter09\Code\ExampleModule.dll' -- 'The process cannot access the file
because it is being used by another process. '
At line:1 char:9
+ Add-Type <<<<  -Path .\ExampleModule.cs `
    + CategoryInfo          : InvalidData: (error CS0016: C...ther p
   rocess. ':CompilerError) [Add-Type], Exception
    + FullyQualifiedErrorId : SOURCE_CODE_ERROR,Microsoft.PowerShell
   .Commands.AddTypeCommand

Add-Type : Cannot add type. There were compilation errors.
At line:1 char:9
+ Add-Type <<<<  -Path .\ExampleModule.cs `
    + CategoryInfo          : InvalidData: (:) [Add-Type], InvalidOp
   erationException
    + FullyQualifiedErrorId : COMPILER_ERRORS,Microsoft.PowerShell.C
   ommands.AddTypeCommand
```

As we said, as long as the binary module is loaded into any PowerShell session, it can't be updated. This can be annoying when you're developing a binary module, but in a production environment it isn't likely to be a problem—at least until you need to service a binary module to fix a bug. This is one area where script modules do have an advantage: they're easier to update dynamically than binary modules.

A way to get aspects of both module types is to combine binary and script module files together in a single module directory. You'll learn how this all works next.

9.5.3 Nesting binary modules in script modules

In this section, we'll look at how binary and script modules can be used together. Back in section 9.4.6, we explored the idea of nested modules, where one script module is imported into another. This nesting concept also works with binary modules so script modules can import binary modules. One consequence is that it means that script modules may also export cmdlets even though they can't define them. The way nested modules work, the calling module can filter the exports of the nested module. This means you can use a script module to filter the members exported from a binary module. Let's see how this works. In the process of doing this, we'll introduce a couple of `Import-Module` features that you haven't seen so far.

For this example, you'll write a script module that loads the binary module created in the previous section. The text of this script module looks like this:

```
PS (1) > Get-Content .\WrapBinaryModule.psm1
param (
    [bool] $showCmdlet
)

Import-Module $PSScriptRoot\ExampleModule.dll -Verbose

function wof
{
    param ($o = "Hi there")
    Write-InputObject -InputObject $o
```

```
}

if ($showCmdlet)
{
    Export-ModuleMember -Cmdlet Write-InputObject
}
else
{
    Export-ModuleMember -Function wof
}
```

There are a number of interesting things to see in this module. Right at the beginning, you see a `param` statement defining a parameter for the module. As this implies, script modules can be parameterized. The values to bind to the module's parameters are passed using the `-ArgumentList` parameter on `Import-Module`. This parameter is used to pass a list of argument values, which means that module parameters can only be positional.

The other new feature can be seen in the call to `Import-Module`, where you're loading the binary module. The path to the binary module is specified using the `$PSScriptRoot` automatic variable. This variable was introduced in PowerShell v2 and contains the path to the directory from which the script module was loaded. In the script, the call to `Import-Module` specifies the `-Verbose` parameter so you can see this path.

> **NOTE** You'd think the correct name for this variable would be `$PSModuleRoot`, not `$PSScriptRoot`. As it happens, the original idea was that this variable would also be available in regular scripts, not just modules. Unfortunately that was never implemented, but the name wasn't changed either. And thus we have another question for the PowerShell trivia contest.

In the body of the module, you define a function, `wof`. This function uses the imported cmdlet to write an object to the output stream.

Finally, the module ends with an `if` statement that uses the `$showCmdlet` module parameter to decide whether the function or the cmdlet should be exported from the module. Let's load the module without specifying any arguments and see what happens:

```
PS (2) > Import-Module .\WrapBinaryModule.psm1
VERBOSE: Loading module from path
'C:\wpia_v2\text\chapter09\code\ExampleModule.dll'.
VERBOSE: Importing cmdlet 'Write-InputObject'.
```

From the `-Verbose` output, you can see that the binary module has been loaded and the location it has been loaded from. Now use `Get-Module` to get information about the loaded module:

```
PS (3) > Get-Module WrapBinaryModule |
>>     Format-List Name, ExportedFunctions, ExportedCmdlets
>>
```

```
Name              : WrapBinaryModule
ExportedFunctions : {[wof, wof]}
ExportedCmdlets   : {}
```

From the output, you see that the function was exported but no cmdlets were. Now try the function

```
PS (4) > wof 123
123
```

and it works, so everything is as intended. This is an important pattern to be aware of. Using this pattern, you can use a script module to wrap a cmdlet but leave the cmdlet itself hidden. This allows you to customize the command experience even though you may not be able to change the cmdlet itself.

Let's reverse the scenario. You'll reload the script module (using the `-Force` flag to make sure the script gets processed again), but this time, you'll pass in an argument to the script:

```
PS (5) > Import-Module .\WrapBinaryModule.psm1 -Force `
>>     -ArgumentList $true
>>
VERBOSE: Importing cmdlet 'Write-InputObject'.
```

Because the binary module is already loaded, you just see the importing message. Remember, you can't update a binary module in your session once it's been loaded. The point here is to use script modules to give you at least a partial workaround for this scenario—in this case, controlling the visibility of the cmdlet. Once again call `Get-Module` to see what was imported:

```
PS (6) > Get-Module WrapBinaryModule |
>>     Format-List Name, ExportedFunctions, ExportedCmdlets
>>

Name              : WrapBinaryModule
ExportedFunctions : {}
ExportedCmdlets   : {[Write-InputObject, Write-InputObject]}
```

This time you see the cmdlet but not the function as intended. Even though you couldn't change the binary module, you could still control what it exported.

> **NOTE** There are limits to this—you can't export more cmdlets; you can only filter the existing imports. You also can't rename the cmdlet itself, though you could proxy it through a function if you wanted to change its name. See section 11.5.2 for a description of how to create command proxies.

So far all of our work with modules has been pretty much ad hoc—we're just making stuff up as we go along. The modules have none of the metadata (description, author information, copyright, and so on.) needed in a production environment for figuring out things like which modules need to be patched. In the next chapter, we'll address this and see how module manifests are used to fill in the missing pieces.

9.6 SUMMARY

In this chapter, we introduced PowerShell modules, a new feature in PowerShell v2. Modules allow you to package collections of PowerShell resources into shareable, reusable units. Using this feature, you can start to build your library of reusable modules in a manageable way. Here are the important points to remember:

- Modules are manipulated, managed, and imported using cmdlets in PowerShell. Unlike many languages, no special syntax is needed. Modules are discovered, both in memory and on disk, using the `Get-Module` cmdlet. They're loaded with `Import-Module` and removed from memory with `Remove-Module`. These three cmdlets are all you need to know if you just want to use modules on your system.
- PowerShell uses the `$ENV:PSModulePath` environment variable to search the file system for modules to load when an unqualified module name is specified. Alternatively, a fully qualified path name can be used to load a module directly without going through the search process.
- There are two basic types of modules: script modules, which are written using the PowerShell language, and binary modules, which are written in a compiled language. Both types of modules are simply files on disk. No registration process is needed to make a module available for use—you just need to be able to read the file somehow.
- Because script modules are another form of script (with a .psm1 extension), they obey the Execution Policy setting just like regular scripts.
- Script modules execute in their own isolated environment, called the *module context*. A script module also has access to the global environment, which is shared across all modules.

In the next chapter we'll continue our exploration of modules. The focus in this chapter was on how to construct simple ad hoc modules. In the next chapter, we introduce module manifests—a mechanism to add production metadata to our modules as well as provide a way to deal with multifile modules.

CHAPTER 10

Module manifests and metadata

The world is my world: this is manifest in the fact that the limits of language (of that language which alone I understand) mean the limits of my world.

—Ludwig Wittgenstein, *Tractatus Logico-Philosophicus*

In chapter 9, we introduced PowerShell modules and covered the basics needed for using and writing modules. That chapter focused on simple ad hoc modules and ignored details like module descriptions and versioning. But it's these details that make the difference between ad hoc and production scripting. Because one of the goals for PowerShell v2 was to enable production-oriented scripting in PowerShell, there needed to be a way to attach production-oriented metadata to our modules. This is where module manifests come in. They allow you to annotate and organize the pieces in more complex, multifile modules.

Manifests are the subject of this chapter. We'll start with a discussion of the layout of a module's directory structure. Then we'll introduce the manifest and look at its contents. We'll explore the tools provided for authoring and testing manifests and walk through each manifest element, describing its purpose and how to use it. You'll learn advanced module techniques, including how to manipulate metadata from within a module, control the module access mode, and set up actions to take when a module is removed.

10.1 Module folder structure

Before we jump into manifests, let's spend a little time reviewing the way modules are organized on disk. A module in the module path (`$ENV:PSModulePath`) is a directory containing a collection of files. One of the files in the module directory is the module manifest. This file usually has the same name as the directory and has a .psd1 extension. You can see an example of this structure by looking at the contents of the system module directory. This directory contains modules that are with Windows and are visible in the directory $PSHome/Modules. The structure of some of the modules in this directory is shown in figure 10.1.

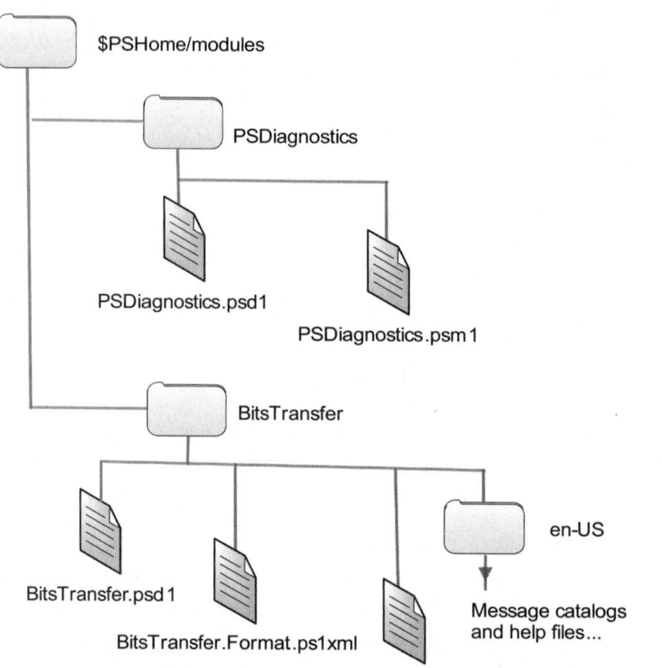

Figure 10.1 The layout of the modules that ship with Windows. Each module is stored in its own folder, with a .psd1 file containing the module manifest. The PSDiagnostics folder contains the PSDiagnostics module. And he BitsTransfer folder contains the BitsTransfer module.

In figure 10.1, you see that two modules are stored in the system module directory. These modules are just directories containing the files that make up the module contents. Each folder contains a .psd1 file that's the manifest for the module.

The first module is `PSDiagnostics`, which we looked at briefly in section 9.3.1 when we talked about finding modules on the system. The module directory contains two files: the manifest file and a script module that defines the commands for this module. Notice that the directory, manifest, and script file all have the same name.

The second module is the `BitsTransfer` module. The structure of this module folder is a little more complicated. In addition to the manifest, it includes a format file, an interop DLL, and a subdirectory, `en-US`. This subdirectory is used to hold the message catalogs that allow for localized messages. We'll go over how all these elements are used when we discuss the contents of module manifests in the next section.

10.2 MODULE MANIFEST STRUCTURE

As you saw in the previous section, a module manifest is stored in a file with a .psd1 extension. This extension indicates that it's a PowerShell data file, which is a type of script that's limited in the things it can contain. We'll talk about these restrictions in section 10.6, but for now, you just need to know that it's a text file containing some PowerShell script. This script code must return a hash table containing a predetermined set of keys when executed by the system. These keys define the manifest elements for the module. Because these manifest files are fairly long and somewhat complex, PowerShell provides a cmdlet, `New-ModuleManifest`, to help create a manifest. Go ahead and run this command so you'll have an example manifest to work with:

```
PS (1) > New-ModuleManifest testManifest.psd1

cmdlet New-ModuleManifest at command pipeline position 1
Supply values for the following parameters:
NestedModules[0]:
Author:
CompanyName:
Copyright:
ModuleToProcess:
Description:
TypesToProcess[0]:
FormatsToProcess[0]:
RequiredAssemblies[0]:
FileList[0]:
PS (2) >
```

The cmdlet takes advantage of the way PowerShell prompts for missing mandatory parameters. It will prompt for each of the values to assign to elements in the generated hash table. In this example, you're just pressing the Enter key and taking the default value. The generated file will also contain comments for each element, describing what the element is used for. Let's take a look at the file that was generated:

```
PS (3) > Get-Content testManifest.psd1
#
```

```
# Module manifest for module 'testManifest'
#
# Generated by: brucepay
#
# Generated on: 8/28/2009
#

@{

# Script module or binary module file associated with this manifest
ModuleToProcess = ''

# Version number of this module.
ModuleVersion = '1.0'

# ID used to uniquely identify this module
GUID = '586ce129-7e3b-4383-9c2c-b6e2e6920e21'

# Author of this module
Author = 'brucepay'

# Company or vendor of this module
CompanyName = 'Unknown'

# Copyright statement for this module
Copyright = '(c) 2011 brucepay. All rights reserved.'

# Description of the functionality provided by this module
Description = ''

# Minimum version of the Windows PowerShell engine required by this module
PowerShellVersion = ''

# Name of the Windows PowerShell host required by this module
PowerShellHostName = ''

# Minimum version of the Windows PowerShell host required by this module
PowerShellHostVersion = ''

# Minimum version of the .NET Framework required by this module
DotNetFrameworkVersion = ''

# Minimum version of the common language runtime (CLR) required
by this module
CLRVersion = ''

# Processor architecture (None, X86, Amd64, IA64) required by this module
ProcessorArchitecture = ''

# Modules that must be imported into the global environment prior to
             importing this module
RequiredModules = @()

# Assemblies that must be loaded prior to importing this module
RequiredAssemblies = @()
```

```
# Script files (.ps1) that are run in the caller's environment
prior to importing this module
ScriptsToProcess = @()

# Type files (.ps1xml) to be loaded when importing this module
TypesToProcess = @()

# Format files (.ps1xml) to be loaded when importing this module
FormatsToProcess = @()

# Modules to import as nested modules of the module specified in
 ModuleToProcess
NestedModules = @()

# Functions to export from this module
FunctionsToExport = '*'

# Cmdlets to export from this module
CmdletsToExport = '*'

# Variables to export from this module
VariablesToExport = '*'

# Aliases to export from this module
AliasesToExport = '*'

# List of all modules packaged with this module
ModuleList = @()

# List of all files packaged with this module
FileList = @()

# Private data to pass to the module specified in ModuleToProcess
PrivateData = ''

}
```

Remember that we said it was long and complex? In fact, it's complex enough that PowerShell also includes a cmdlet to test a manifest. This cmdlet is called (surprise) `Test-ModuleManifest`. You'll use it to test the manifest you've generated to make sure it's valid (though it would be surprising if it wasn't—after all, you just created it):

```
PS (4) > Test-ModuleManifest testManifest.psd1

ModuleType Name                          ExportedCommands
---------- ----                          ----------------
Manifest   testManifest                  {}
```

If the test is successful, the module information object is returned.

Now that you know it's valid, you can import it. Normally a module doesn't emit anything, but in this case, you want to see it immediately. So specify `-PassThru` (which will cause the module information object to be written to the output pipe),

```
PS (5) > Import-Module .\testManifest.psd1 -PassThru | Format-List

Name              : testManifest
Path              : C:\wpia_v2\text\chapter09\code\testManifest.
                    psd1
```

```
Description       :
ModuleType        : Manifest
Version           : 1.0
NestedModules     : {}
ExportedFunctions : {}
ExportedCmdlets   : {}
ExportedVariables : {}
ExportedAliases   : {}
```

and you see your essentially empty module.

The `New-ModuleManifest` cmdlet creates a manifest that contains all the allowed fields, but in fact most of the fields aren't required. The only field that's required is the module version. You can manually generate the minimal manifest by using redirection:

```
PS (4) > '@{ModuleVersion="1.0"}' > testManifest2.psd1
```

Now load the manifest and look at what was generated:

```
PS (5) > Import-Module .\testManifest2.psd1
PS (6) > Get-Module testManifest2 | fl

Name              : testManifest2
Path              : C:\wpia_v2\text\chapter09\code\testManifest2
                    .psd1
Description       :
ModuleType        : Manifest
Version           : 1.0
NestedModules     : {}
ExportedFunctions : {}
ExportedCmdlets   : {}
ExportedVariables : {}
ExportedAliases   : {}
```

This is identical to what you got from the more complicated default manifest.

In practice, it's always best to use `New-ModuleManifest` to generate a complete manifest for your modules even if you aren't going to use all the fields immediately. Once you've generated the manifest, you can easily add additional data to it over time using your favorite text editor.

In the next few sections, we'll go over the contents of the manifest. To make our exploration a bit more manageable, we've divided the manifest elements into three broad categories: production, construction, and content elements. We'll cover each of these areas and the elements they contain, starting with the production elements.

10.3 Production manifest elements

In this section we'll explore the elements that make up the production metadata. These elements are used to add things like copyright information and version numbers. The fields in the module for this are shown in table 10.1. The use of some of the elements is pretty obvious: `Author`, `CompanyName`, `Copyright`, and so forth. We won't cover them beyond the comments in the table. The remaining elements will be covered in the subsections that follow.

Table 10.1 The manifest elements in a module manifest file that contain production-oriented metadata

Manifest element	Type	Default value	Description
ModuleVersion	String	1.0	The version number of this module. This string must be in a form that can be converted into an instance of [System.Version].
GUID	String	Autogenerated	ID used to uniquely identify this module.
Author	String	None	The name of the module creator.
CompanyName	String	Unknown	The company, if any, that produced this module.
Copyright	String	(c) Year Author. All rights reserved.	The copyright declaration for this module with the copyright year and name of the copyright holder.
Description	String	''	The description of this module. Because this description may be used when searching for a module, it should be a reasonable description, mentioning the purpose of the module and technology area it relates to.
PowerShellVersion	String	''	Minimum version of the Windows PowerShell engine required by this module.
PowerShell-HostName	String	''	Name of the Windows PowerShell host required by this module
PowerShellHost-Version	String	''	Minimum version of the Windows PowerShell host required by this module.
DotNetFramework-Version	String	''	Minimum version of the .NET Framework required by this module.
CLRVersion	String	''	Minimum version of the common language runtime (CLR) required.
Processor-Architecture	String	''	The processor architecture this module requires. It may be '', None, X86, Amd64, or IA64.
RequiredModules	[object[]]	@()	Modules that must be imported into the global environment prior to importing this module.

In the next few sections, you'll see how the elements in this table are used to make modules more production worthy. We'll begin with a very important topic: *module identity*.

10.3.1 Module identity

For modules to be shared and serviced (that is, patched) effectively, there needs to be a strong notion of identity that allows you to uniquely identify a module. It can't just be the module name. The name of the module comes from the manifest filename and there's no guarantee somebody else won't give their module the same name as yours. To guarantee that you can always identify a module regardless of path changes, renames, and so on, the manifest contains a globally unique identifier (GUID). The algorithm used to generate GUIDs is guaranteed to produce a globally unique number. Once you know the GUID for a module, you can always identify it, even if the file gets renamed.

Another important aspect of module identity is the version number. Versioning is what allows you to determine if the module has been patched properly. The `ModuleVersion` element in the manifest is used to hold the module's version. This element uses the type `System.Version` to represent the version of a module internally. In the manifest file, the element should be assigned a string that can be converted into an instance of `System.Version`. This string must have the form of *#.#.#.#*, for example, 1.0.0.0. When you use the `-Version` parameter on `Import-Module`, it will search the path in `$ENV:PSModulePath`, looking for the first module whose name matches the requested name and whose module version is at least as large as the required version.

> **NOTE** Unfortunately, no mechanism has been provided for loading a module by specifying its GUID. This is a deficiency in the current implementation of `Import-Module`. The only place you can use the GUID to identify a module is when you specify module dependencies (as you'll see in the next section). As a workaround for this issue, a proxy function can be written that wraps `Import-Module` and adds this functionality.

10.3.2 Runtime dependencies

The remainder of the production elements in the manifest relate to identifying environmental dependencies—what needs to be in the environment for the module to work properly. For many script modules, most of these elements can be left in their default state. Let's go through these elements and what they're used for.

The `CLRVersion` and `DotNetFrameworkVersion` identify dependencies based on what version of the CLR (or .NET) is installed on the system. So why do you need two elements? Because the CLR runtime and the framework (all of the libraries) can and do vary independently. This is exactly what happened with CLR 3.0. In this version, the runtime version remained at 2.0, but there was a new framework version (3.0) where the LINQ technologies were introduced (we'll talk about LINQ in chapter 14). The framework version changed again with CLR 3.5. As before, the runtime remained at 2.0

but the framework moved to 3.5, where things like Windows Presentation Foundation (WPF) were added. The next version of the CLR, version 4.0, will update both the runtime and the framework. As a consequence of this pattern, it's necessary to be able to independently express the version requirements for each part.

When adding the dependencies to the manifest, you should specify the minimum highest version required. This depends on the higher revisions being backward compatible with earlier versions and is a fairly safe assumption for the CLR.

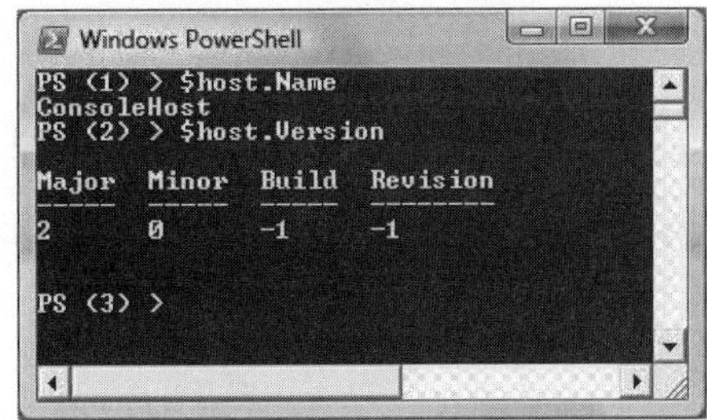

Figure 10.2 You can see the host name and version properties for the PowerShell console host.

Expressing a dependency on the processor architecture isn't likely to be common, but it's possible to have a module that uses .NET interoperation (chapter 17) or COM (chapter 18) and, as a consequence, have some processor architecture-specific dependency.

The next set of dependencies is on PowerShell itself. The `PowerShellVersion` is pretty straightforward. It specifies the minimum version of PowerShell needed by this module. The `PowerShellHostName` and `ModuleVersion` are only slightly more complex. They allow you to place a dependency on the application that's hosting the PowerShell runtime rather than on the runtime itself. For example, you can have a module that adds custom elements to the PowerShell ISE. This module clearly has a dependency on the name of the host. To find out the name of the string to place here, in the host, look at the `Name` property on the object in `$host`. Figure 10.2 shows how this looks in the PowerShell console host. Figure 10.3 shows the same information in the PowerShell ISE.

Once you know which host you're depending on, you also need the version number, which is available through the `Version` property on `$host`. This information for both the console host and ISE are also shown in figures 10.2 and 10.3.

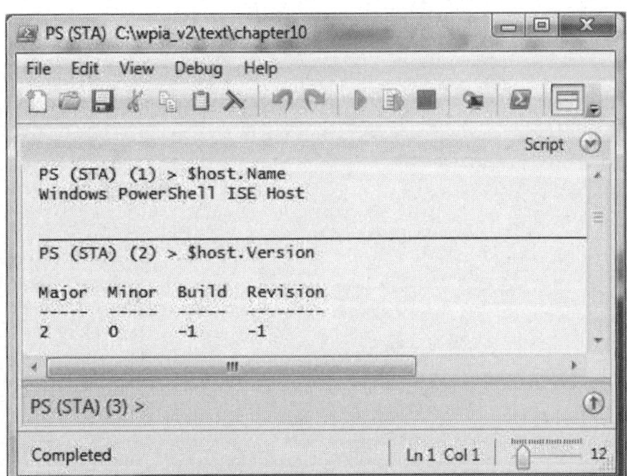

Figure 10.3 You can see the host name and version properties for the PowerShell ISE.

The final type of dependency is on the modules that are already loaded into the system. This is done through the `RequiredModules` manifest element. This element probably doesn't do what you'd expect. It doesn't load dependencies—it just checks to see if certain modules are loaded. This seems a bit useless but, perhaps the version of the required module currently loaded is too low and a newer module can't be loaded because there are other modules already using the loaded module. Whereas the other elements you've seen so far are either simple strings or strings that can be converted into a version number, this element can either take a module name string or a hash table containing two or three elements. These hash table elements allow you to precisely specify the module you're dependent on as they include the module name, the version number, and the GUID of the module that must be loaded (although the GUID is optional).

This covers all the production elements in the manifest. Now that you know you have the right module (Identity) and that it will work in your environment (Dependencies), let's look at the manifest elements that control what happens when the module is loaded. Load-time behavior is controlled by a set of manifest elements that contain entries that are used to construct the in-memory representation of the module.

10.4 CONSTRUCTION MANIFEST ELEMENTS

The construction metadata in this module are the fields that tell the engine what to load as part of this module. These fields are listed in table 10.2.

Table 10.2 The module manifest elements that contain data used in constructing the module

Manifest element	Type	Default value	Description
`ModuleToProcess`	`string`	`''`	Script module or binary module file associated with this manifest
`RequiredAssemblies`	`[string[]]`	`@()`	Assemblies that must be loaded prior to importing this module
`ScriptsToProcess`	`[string[]]`	`@()`	Script files (.ps1) that are run in the caller's environment prior to importing this module
`TypesToProcess`	`[string[]]`	`@()`	Type files (.ps1xml) to be loaded when importing this module
`FormatsToProcess`	`[string[]]`	`@()`	Format files (.ps1xml) to be loaded when importing this module
`NestedModules`	`[string[]]`	`@()`	Modules to import as nested modules of the module specified in `ModuleToProcess`
`FunctionsToExport`	`String`	`"*"`	Functions to export from this module
`CmdletsToExport`	`String`	`"*"`	Cmdlets to export from this module
`VariablesToExport`	`String`	`"*"`	Variables to export from this module
`AliasesToExport`	`String`	`"*"`	Aliases to export from this module

There are two subcategories in the construction elements: "things to load" and "things to export." We'll start with loading because you can't export anything until something has been loaded. As mentioned previously, none of the fields are required. If they aren't there, then PowerShell assumes the default value for each field, as shown in the table.

10.4.1 The loader manifest elements

The next few sections cover each of these manifest elements in the order that you're most likely to use them in when creating a manifest. This isn't the order that they're processed in when the module is loaded. We'll cover the load order as a separate topic (in section 10.4.2).

ModuleToProcess manifest element

The first loader element we'll discuss is `ModuleToProcess`. It's the most commonly used manifest element and identifies the main, or *root*, active module to load.

> **NOTE** So why isn't it called `RootModule`? Because the PowerShell team named (and renamed and renamed again) this field throughout the development process, but it wasn't until everything was done and we started to explain it to other people that the concept of a "root module" started spontaneously popping up conversations. Unfortunately, by then we were too far into the release process to be able to change it. Thus, `RootModule` became victim of the tyranny of the clock.

By *active*, I mean that the file defines executable elements, instead of just providing metadata definitions. The type of the module file specified in this member will determine the final module type. If no file is specified as the `ModuleToProcess`, then the type shown in the module information object will be `Manifest`. If it's a script or binary module, it will be the respective module type. Other types will raise errors. The various combinations are shown in table 10.3.

Table 10.3 Module types as determined by the `ModuleToProcess` member

Contents of `ModuleToProcess`	Final module type
empty	`Manifest`
Script module (.psm1)	`Script`
Binary module (.dll, .exe)	`Binary`
Module manifest (.psd1)	Error—not permitted
Script file	Error—not permitted

If a script or binary module is specified in the `ModuleToProcess` element, the type of the loaded module will be the same as the type of the module specified in the

`ModuleToProcess` element even though you're loading through a manifest. In other words, if the root module was binary, the `Type` property on the module information object shows `Binary`. If the root module was script module, the `Type` property returns `Script`. What it can't be, however, is another manifest module. It must be either a script or binary module (or be left empty). The reason for this constraint is that the job of a manifest is to add metadata to a script or binary module. If the main module is another manifest, you'd have to deal with colliding metadata. For example, one manifest may declare that the module is version 1.0.0.0 but the second module says it's version 1.2.0.0. There's no way to reconcile this type of collision so it's simply not allowed. As a result, PowerShell just won't look for a .psd1 file when searching for the module to process. As mentioned at the beginning of this subsection, it's expected that production modules will use `ModuleToProcess` to identify a single main module.

NestedModules manifest element

We'll review `NestedModules` next. `NestedModules` are loaded before the `ModuleToProcess` is loaded. Although the net effect is equivalent to having the main module call `Import-Module`, there are two advantages to this approach. First, it's easy to see what the module is going to load before loading the module. Second, if there's a problem with loading the nested modules, the main module won't have been loaded and won't have to deal with the load failures.

RequiredAssemblies manifest element

The `RequiredAssemblies` field sounds like it should have the same behavior as `RequiredModules` from the previous section. It doesn't. This field loads the assemblies listed in the element if they aren't already loaded. Figure 10.4 shows the set of steps taken when trying to find the module to load.

If one of the steps results in a successful load, PowerShell will proceed to the next step in loading a module. If it fails, the entire module loading process is considered a failure.

ScriptsToProcess manifest element

Now let's talk about `ScriptsToProcess` and scripts in general. Something we didn't discuss earlier is that `NestedModules` can also refer to script files. These script files are run in the root module's context—essentially equivalent to dot sourcing them into the root module script. The scripts listed in `ScriptToProcess` do something quite different. These scripts are run in the caller's environment, not the module environment, and are run before any of the modules are loaded. This allows for custom setup and environment validation logic. We talked about how version checks work—the first module with a version number equal to or greater than the requested

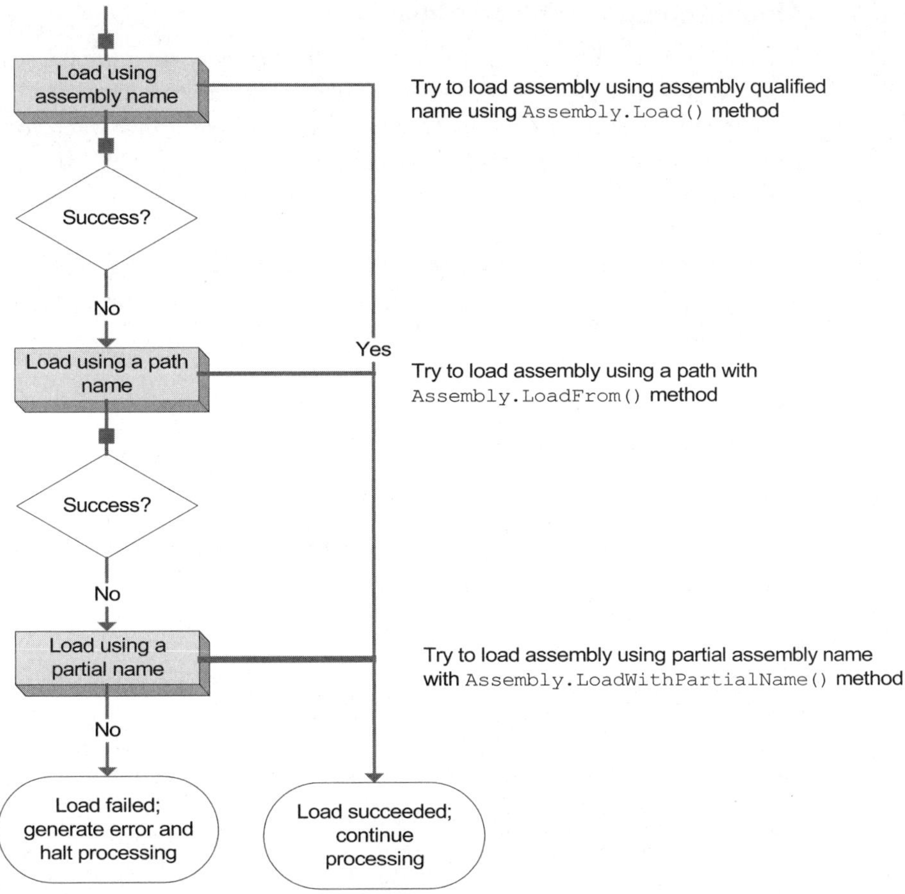

Figure 10.4 The steps taken when trying to load an assembly from the `RequiredAssemblies` module manifest field

version number will be loaded, assuming that things are backward compatible. In fact, this might not be true but there's no explicit support for this level of dependency checking currently. If you're in a situation where you have to do this, you can use a script referenced in `ScriptsToProcess`.

TypesToProcess and FormatsToProcess manifest elements

The last of the "loaded" manifest elements are `TypesToProcess` and `Formats-ToProcess`. These are files with a .ps1xml extension that contain formatting instructions and additional type metadata. (We'll delve more into the content of these files in chapter 16.)

10.4.2 Module component load order

Module components are loaded into the PowerShell environment using a fixed sequence of steps called the module load order. This load order is shown in figure 10.5.

The order that these steps are taken in can be of significance when you're trying to construct a module with a complex structure. In particular, there's an issue load order that causes problems when using binary modules with types and format files.

Because types and format files are loaded before `ModuleToProcess` is, if the types and format files contain references to any of the .NET types in the binary module, an error saying that the referenced types can't be found because the module's DLL hasn't been loaded yet will occur. To work around this, you need to make sure the DLL for

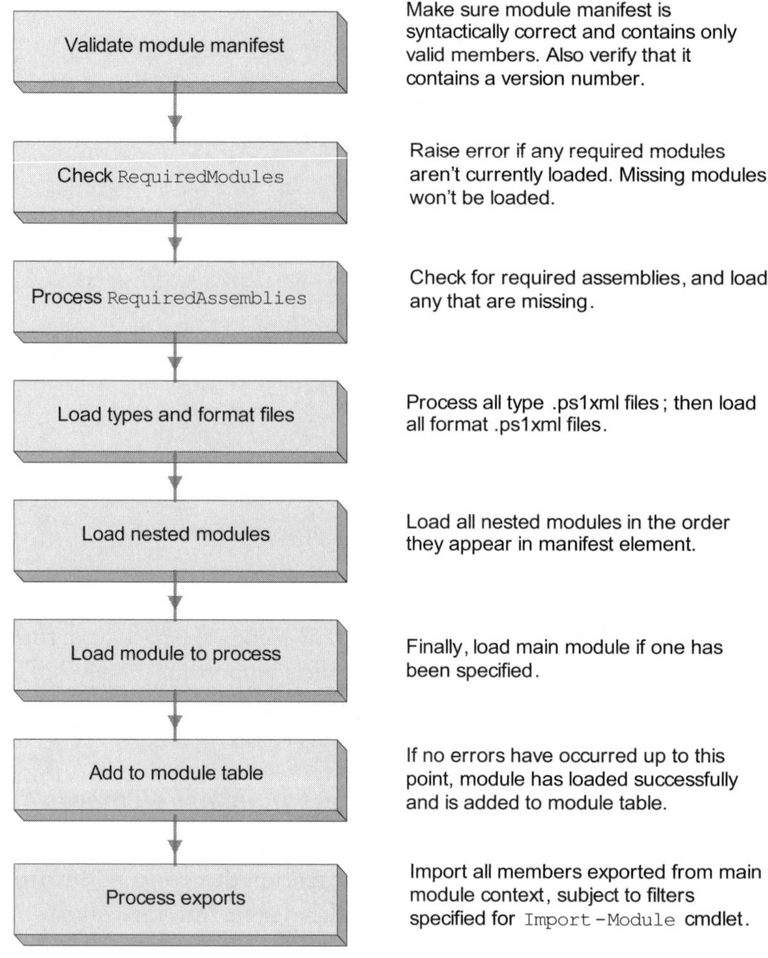
Validate module manifest
Make sure module manifest is syntactically correct and contains only valid members. Also verify that it contains a version number.
Check RequiredModules
Raise error if any required modules aren't currently loaded. Missing modules won't be loaded.
Process RequiredAssemblies
Check for required assemblies, and load any that are missing.
Load types and format files
Process all type .ps1xml files; then load all format .ps1xml files.
Load nested modules
Load all nested modules in the order they appear in manifest element.
Load module to process
Finally, load main module if one has been specified.
Add to module table
If no errors have occurred up to this point, module has loaded successfully and is added to module table.
Process exports
Import all members exported from main module context, subject to filters specified for Import-Module cmdlet.

Figure 10.5 The ordering of the steps when processing a module manifest. If an error occurs at any point prior to the next-to-last step, module processing will stop and an error will be thrown.

the binary module is loaded first. You do so by adding the DLL to the list of `RequiredAssemblies`. Because `RequiredAssemblies` is processed before the types and format file entries, there won't be a problem resolving the types. Then, when it's time to load the binary module, the DLL will already be loaded and will just need to be scanned to find the cmdlets and providers. This resolves the problem with effectively no performance impact and only a small increase of complexity for the module owner.

At this point, we've covered all the major module manifest topics. There are only a couple of things left to look at and then we'll be done.

10.5 CONTENT MANIFEST ELEMENTS

The content manifest elements are the component files that make up a module. There are two lists provided: a list of all loadable module files and a separate list for any other files (data files, icons, audio clips, and so on) that are part of the module. These elements are shown in table 10.4.

Table 10.4 Module manifest elements used to list the module's contents

Manifest element	Type	Default value	Description
`ModuleList`	`[string[]]`	`@()`	Non-normative list of all modules packaged with this module
`FileList`	`[string[]]`	`@()`	Non-normative list of all files packaged with this module
`PrivateData`	`[object]`	`''`	Private data to pass to the module specified in `ModuleToProcess`

Note that these "packing lists" are not *normative*. In other words, they aren't processed or enforced by PowerShell and filing them is entirely optional. As a best practice, though, it's recommended that they contain accurate data because external tools may be created to do the actual validation.

This last manifest element—`PrivateData`—provides a way for module writers to include custom data in manifests and make it available to modules when loaded. This element can contain any type of object permitted by the restricted language subset of PowerShell: strings, numbers, arrays, or hash tables. The system makes the data available to both script and binary modules, including to providers defined in binary modules. We'll look at how modules can access the data specified by this element in section 10.7.3.

At long last, we've covered all the manifest elements. We have one last thing to look at before we're done with manifest content. Back in section 10.2, we said that, although manifests are written in PowerShell, they use a restricted subset of the language. The restricted language is used to reduce the potential security risk associated with loading a script. This allows you to load a manifest file to access the metadata without being concerned that you'll execute malicious code. This also means that you need to know how to write these scripts properly. In the next section, you'll learn what you can do in a manifest file.

10.6 LANGUAGE RESTRICTIONS IN A MANIFEST

Because the manifest is a PowerShell data file, its contents are restricted to a small subset of PowerShell language features. This subset includes the basic PowerShell data types (numbers, strings, hash tables, and so on), the `if` statement, and the arithmetic and comparison operators. Things like assignment statements, function definitions, and loop statements aren't allowed. (See appendix D for full details on the language limitations.)

With only these elements, you'd be limited to using static values for element definitions. This means you wouldn't be able to accommodate for variations in system configuration—things like paths to system directories, software installation directories, and drive letters. To allow you to handle these situations, manifests are permitted to read (but not write) the `$ENV:` environment provider and can use the `Join-Path` cmdlet to construct paths at runtime. This allows manifest elements to be written in such a way that system differences can be handled.

Let's look at an example illustrating how these features can be used. In this example, imagine you have an application that uses PowerShell for management. This application installs its PowerShell modules in a directory in the module path, and then puts the rest of the application files in `Program Files`. Because the modules need access to some of the resources in the application directory, the application installer will set an environment variable, `$ENV:MYAPPDIR`, at install time that can be used by the manifest to find the necessary resources. A module entry using this environment variable would look like this:

```
RequiredAssemblies = (Join-Path $ENV:MYAPPDIR requiredAssembly.dll)
```

In the fragment, the `Join-Path` cmdlet is used to generate the absolute path to the required assembly using `$ENV:MYAPPDIR`. Now, to complicate things we'll say that this library is processor dependent, and you'll need to load a different DLL based on the setting of the system variable `$ENV:PROCESSOR_ARCHITECTURE`. This entry would look like

```
RequiredAssemblies = if ($ENV:PROCESSOR_ARCHITECTURE -eq "X86") {
                         Join-Path $ENV:MYAPPDIR requiredAssembly.dll
                     } else {
                         Join-Path $ENV:MYAPPDIR64 requiredAssembly.dll
                     }
```

This second example uses the `if` statement to select a different branch based on the processor architecture and then generates the system-specific path using `Join-Path`. These techniques allow modules to be flexible when dealing with system variations.

One thing missing from the module manifest story is the ability for scripts to read the manifest files without loading the module. This is unfortunate because it limits your ability to write scripts to explore the modules you have. The Test-ModuleManifest cmdlet does process the manifest but it doesn't return all the data in the manifest file. Because the language in the manifests is a subset of regular PowerShell, it's possible to load the module file contents into a string and then use Invoke-Expression to evaluate it. This will give you the data you want, but it means that the module is no longer running in restricted mode. As a workaround, you can use a hybrid approach. First, you'll validate the manifest with Test-ModuleManifest. This will verify that the manifest only contains elements that are permitted in the restricted language. Then you'll read and evaluate the module file to get the data. The following listing shows a function that can be used to do this.

Listing 10.1 The Read-ModuleManifest function

```
function Read-ModuleManifest ($manifestPath)
{
  trap { break }

  $fullpath = Resolve-Path $manifestPath -ErrorAction Stop
  if (Test-ModuleManifest $fullPath)
  {
    $PSScriptRoot = Split-Path -Parent $fullPath
    $content = (Get-Content $fullPath) -Join "`n"
    Invoke-Expression $content
  }
}
```

Load manifest text

Evaluate with Invoke-Expression

Let's use this function to load the BitsTransfer module manifest:

```
PS (1) > cd $pshome\modules\BitsTransfer
PS (2) > Read-ModuleManifest .\BitsTransfer.psd1

Name                           Value
----                           -----
ModuleVersion                  1.0.0.0
CLRVersion                     2.0
FormatsToProcess               BitsTransfer.Format.ps1xml
PowerShellVersion              2.0
GUID                           {8FA5064B-8479-4c5c-86EA-...
NestedModules                  Microsoft.BackgroundIntel...
Copyright                      c Microsoft Corporation. ...
CompanyName                    Microsoft Corporation
Author                         Microsoft Corporation
RequiredAssemblies             C:\Windows\System32\Windo...
```

The output of the function is the hash table defined in the manifest file.

And we're done with manifests! Like bookkeeping and inventory management, manifests are complicated and a bit boring but absolutely necessary when doing production scripting. In the next section, we'll explore features that are less tedious but (hopefully) more exciting.

10.7 ADVANCED MODULE OPERATIONS

In this section, you'll learn sophisticated things you can do with modules. These features are not intended for typical day-to-day use, but they allow for some sophisticated scripting. As always, if you aren't just scripting for yourself, have pity on the person who will have to maintain your code and avoid "stunt scripting."

10.7.1 The PSModuleInfo object

PowerShell modules, like everything in PowerShell, are objects you can work with directly. The type of the object used to reference modules is `System.Management.Automation.PSModuleInfo`.

You've been looking at these objects all along—this is what `Get-Module` returns—but you've only been using them to get basic information about a module. In practice, there are a lot of other things that can be done once you have a `PSModuleObject`. In this section, we'll look at what can be done (and try to explain why you'd do these things).

Invocation in the module context

In our discussion about module scopes, we introduced the concept of a module-level scope, which is used to isolate the private variables and functions. When you execute code where function and variable lookup is done in a module scope, we call this "executing in the module context." This is what happens anytime you execute a function that has been exported from a module. But you can also cause arbitrary code to be executed in the module context even though it wasn't defined in that context. In effect, you're *pushing* code into the module context. This is done with a `PSModuleInfo` object using the call operator `&`.

> **NOTE** Yes, this ability to inject code into a module context violates all the principles of isolation and information hiding. And from a language perspective, this is a bit terrifying, but people do it all the time when debugging. One of the nice things about dynamic languages is that you're effectively running the debugger attached all the time.

To try this out, you'll need a module object to play with. Let's load the `counter` module we looked at in section 9.4.1 again. First, let's quickly review the contents of the module—you'll use the `Select-Object` cmdlet to limit what gets output to the first eight lines, as that's all you're concerned with here:

```
PS (1) > Get-Content counter.psm1 | select -First 8
$script:count = 0
$script:increment = 1

function Get-Count
{
    return $script:count += $increment
}
```

This module has private state in the form of the two variables—`$count` and `$increment`—and one public function, `Get-Count`. Now import it

```
PS (2) > Import-Module .\counter.psm1
```

and use `Get-Module` to get the module reference:

```
PS (3) > $m = Get-Module counter
```

You could have done this in one step with the `-PassThru` parameter, as you saw earlier, but we're using two steps here to illustrate that these techniques can be done with any in-memory module. Now run the `Get-Count` function and it returns 1, as it should right after the module is first loaded:

```
PS (4) > Get-Count
1
```

Now set a global variable, `$count`, using the `Set-Variable` command (again, we're using the command instead of assignment to set the variable for illustration purposes):

```
PS (5) > Set-Variable count 33
```

When you run `Get-Count` again, it returns 2 because the `$count` variable it uses exists in the module context:

```
PS (6) > Get-Count
2
```

So far nothing much to see. Now let's do something a bit fancier. Let's see what the current value of `$count` in the module context is. You can do this by invoking `Get-Variable` in the module context with the call operator:

```
PS (7) > & $m Get-Variable count

Name                           Value
----                           -----
count                          2
```

You see the value is 2. Great—now you can inspect the private inner state of a module to see what's going on. Next, let's alter that state. You'll execute the same `Set-Variable` command as before, but inside the module this time:

```
PS (8) > & $m Set-Variable count 33
```

Call `Get-Count` to verify that you have made a change:

```
PS (9) > Get-Count
34
```

The call to `Get-Count` returned 34, so you've successfully changed the value of the variable it uses in its operation.

Okay, you know how to get and set state in the module, so let's try altering the code. First look at the body of the Get-Count function:

```
PS (10) > & $m Get-Item function:Get-Count

CommandType     Name                        Definition
-----------     ----                        ----------
Function        Get-Count                   ...
```

Now redefine the function in the module. Instead of simply adding the increment, add the increment times 2:

```
PS (11) > & $m {
>>     function script:Get-Count
>>     {
>>         return $script:count += $increment * 2
>>     }
>> }
>>
```

Although you've redefined the function in the module, you have to reimport the module in order to get the new definition into your function table:

```
PS (12) > Import-Module .\counter.psm1
```

Now you can call the function again to make sure you're getting what you expected:

```
PS (13) > Get-Count
36
PS (14) > Get-Count
38
```

Yes, Get-Count is now incrementing by 2 instead of 1.

All of these tweaks on the module only affect the module in memory. The module file on disk hasn't changed:

```
PS (15) > Get-Content counter.psm1 | select -First 8
$script:count = 0
$script:increment = 1

function Get-Count
{
    return $script:count += $increment
}
```

If you use the -Force parameter on Import-Module, you'll force the system to reload the file from disk, reinitializing everything to the way it was:

```
PS (16) > Import-Module .\counter.psm1 -Force
```

Verify this by running Get-Count:

```
PS (17) > Get-Count
1
PS (18) > Get-Count
2
```

```
PS (19) > Get-Count
3
```

Again this is one of the characteristics of dynamic languages: the ability of programs to modify themselves in a profound way at runtime and then restore the original state. In the next section we'll look at how to use properties on the `PSModuleInfo` to access the members of a module without importing them.

Accessing modules exports using the PSModuleInfo object

The exported members of a module are discoverable through properties on the `PSModuleInfo` object that represents the module. This gives you a way to look at the exported members without having to import them into your environment. For example, the list of exported functions is available in the `ExportedFunctions` member. These properties are hash tables, indexed by the name of the exported member. Let's look at some examples of what you can do using these properties.

As always, you need a module to work with. In this case, you'll use a dynamic module, which we'll cover in more detail in chapter 11. Dynamic modules don't require a file on disk, which makes them easy to use for experiments. You'll create a dynamic module and save the `PSModuleInfo` object in a variable called `$m`:

```
PS (1) > $m = New-Module {
>> function foo {"In foo x is $x"}
>> $x=2
>> Export-ModuleMember -func foo -var x }
>>
```

Now you can use the export lists on the `PSModuleInfo` to see what was exported:

```
PS (2) > $m | Format-List exported*

ExportedCommands     : {foo}
ExportedFunctions    : {[foo, foo]}
ExportedCmdlets      : {}
ExportedVariables    : {[x, System.Management.Automation.PSVariable]}
ExportedAliases      : {}
ExportedFormatFiles : {}
ExportedTypeFiles    : {}
```

In the output, you see that one function and one variable were exported. You also see the function turn up in the `ExportedCommands` member. Modules can export more than one type of command—functions, aliases, or cmdlets—and this property exists to provide a convenient way to see all commands regardless of type.

> **NOTE** By implementing the exported member properties as hash tables, you can access and manipulate the state of the module in a fairly convenient way. The downside is that the default output for the exported members is a bit strange, especially for functions where you see things like `[foo, foo]`. These tables map the name of a command

to the CommandInfo object for that command. When the contents of the table are displayed, both the key and the value are displayed as strings, and because the presentation of a CommandInfo object as a string is the name of the object, you see the name twice.

Let's use the ExportedFunctions property to see how the function foo is easier to write:

```
PS (3) > $m.ExportedFunctions.foo

CommandType     Name                       Definition
-----------     ----                       ----------
Function        foo                        "In foo x is $x"
```

The value returned from the expression is a CommandInfo object. This means that you can use the call operator, &, to invoke this function:

```
PS (4) > & $m.ExportedFunctions.foo
In foo x is 2
```

You can also use the PSModuleInfo object to change the value of the exported variable $x:

```
PS (5) > $m.ExportedVariables.x.value = 3
```

Call the function again to validate this change:

```
PS (6) > & $m.ExportedFunctions.foo
In foo x is 3
```

The return value from the call is the updated value as expected. Next, we'll look at some of the methods on PSModuleInfo objects.

10.7.2 Using the PSModuleInfo methods

The call operator isn't the only way to use the module information object. The object itself has a number of methods that can be useful. Take a look at some of these methods:

```
PS (20) > [psmoduleinfo].GetMethods() |
>>     Select-String -notmatch '(get_|set_)'
>>

System.Management.Automation.ScriptBlock NewBoundScriptBlock(
  System.Management.Automation.ScriptBlock)
System.Object Invoke(System.Management.Automation.ScriptBlock,
   System.Object[])
System.Management.Automation.PSObject AsCustomObject()
```

We'll cover the first two listed, Invoke() and NewBoundScriptBlock(), and save AsCustomObject() for chapter 11.

The Invoke() method

This method is essentially a .NET programmer way of doing what you did earlier with the call operator. Assuming you still have the counter module loaded, let's use this method to reset the count and change the increment to 5. First get the module information object:

```
PS (21) > $m = Get-Module counter
```

Now invoke a script block in the module context using this method:

```
PS (22) > $m.Invoke({$script:count = 0; $script:increment = 5})
```

The corresponding invocation using the call operator would be

```
& $m {$script:count = 0; $script:increment = 5}
```

This is scripter-friendly, but either way, let's try to verify the result:

```
PS (23) > Get-Count
5
PS (24) > Get-Count
10
PS (25) > Get-Count
15
PS (26) >
```

And the count was reset and `Get-Count` now increments by 5 instead of 1. Next let's look at a way to attach modules to a script block.

The NewBoundScriptBlock() method

In this topic, we're jumping ahead a bit as we won't cover script blocks in depth until chapter 11. Next we'll explore *module-bound script blocks.*

A module-bound script block is a piece of code—a script block—that has the module context to use attached to it. Normally an unbound script block is executed in the caller's context, but once a script block is bound to a module, it always executes in the module context. In fact, that's how exported functions work—they're implicitly bound to the module that defined them.

Let's use this mechanism to define a script block that will execute in the context of the `counter` module. First you need to get the module (again). You could use `Get-Module` as before, but now that you know that exported functions are bound to a module, you can just use the `Module` property on an exported command to get the module information object. Do so with `Get-Count`:

```
PS (26) > $gcc = Get-Command Get-Count
```

Now you can get the module for this command:

```
PS (27) > $gcc.module

ModuleType Name                            ExportedCommands
---------- ----                            ----------------
Script     counter                         {setIncrement, Get-Count...
```

Next you need to define the script block you're going to bind. Do this and place the script block into a variable:

```
PS (28) > $sb = {param($incr) $script:increment = $incr}
```

This script block takes a single parameter, which it uses to set the module-level `$increment` variable. Now you'll bind it to the target module. Note that this doesn't bind the module to the original script block; instead it creates a new script block with the module attached.

```
PS (29) > $setIncrement = $gcc.Module.NewBoundScriptblock( $sb )
```

Now test using the script block to set the increment. Invoke the script block with the call operator passing in an increment of 10:

```
PS (30) > & $setIncrement 10
```

And verify that the increment has been changed.

```
PS (31) > Get-Count
110
PS (32) > Get-Count
120
```

Okay, good. But if you want to use this mechanism frequently, it would be useful to have a named function. You can do this by assigning the scriptblock to `Set-Increment` in the function: drive:

```
PS (33) > ${function:Set-CountIncrement} = $setIncrement
```

Let's test the function:

```
PS (34) > Set-CountIncrement 100
PS (35) > Get-Count
220
PS (36) > Get-Count
320
```

And now the increment is 100 per the argument to the `Set-CountIncrement`. Now use `Get-Command` to look at the function you've defined:

```
PS (37) > Get-Command Set-CountIncrement | Format-Table name, module

Name                               Module
----                               ------
Set-CountIncrement                 counter
```

Similar to `Get-Count`, it's listed as being associated with the `counter` module. Now that you've introduced the idea of a function being dynamically attached to a module, you should learn about the context where a function gets evaluated—which we'll cover in the next section.

10.7.3 The defining module versus the calling module

In this section we'll go into greater detail about how the execution context for a module is established. We covered module scoping in section 9.4.4. By providing you with a deeper understanding of the details of how this works, we're setting the stage for some of the more advanced topics we'll cover in chapter 11.

Commands always have two module contexts: the context where they were defined and the context where they were called from. This is a somewhat subtle concept. Before PowerShell had modules, this wasn't terribly interesting except for getting filename and line number information for where the function was called and where it was defined. With modules, this distinction becomes more significant. Among other things, the module where the command was defined contains the module-specific resources like the manifest `PrivateData` element mentioned in section 10.5. For functions, the ability to access the two contexts allows the function to access the caller's variables instead of the module variables.

Accessing the defining module

The module that a function was defined in can be retrieved by using the expression `$MyInvocation.MyCommand.Module`. Similarly, the module a cmdlet was defined in is available through the instance property `this.MyInvocation.MyCommand.Module`. If the function is defined in the global scope (or top level), the module field will be `$null`. Let's try this. First define a function at the top level:

```
PS (1) > function Test-ModuleContext {
>>      $MyInvocation.MyCommand.Module
>> }
>>
```

Then run it, formatting the result as a list showing the module name and `PrivateData` fields:

```
PS (2) > Test-ModuleContext | fl name,privatedata
PS (3) >
```

Nothing was output because the defining module at the top level is always `$null`. Now let's define the function inside a module. Use a here-string to create a .psm1 file:

```
PS (4) > @'

>> function Test-ModuleContext {
>>      $MyInvocation.MyCommand.Module
>> }
>> '@ > TestModuleContext.psm1
>>
```

Now load the file and run the same test command as you did previously:

```
PS (5) > Import-Module ./TestModuleContext.psm1
PS (6) > Test-ModuleContext | fl name,privatedata

Name        : TestModuleContext
PrivateData :
```

This time the result of the function was not `$null`—you see the module name and, of course, the `PrivateData` field is empty because there was no module manifest to provide this data. You can remedy this by creating a module manifest to go along with the .psm1 file. This abbreviated manifest defines the minimum—the module version, the module to process, and a hash table for `PrivateData`:

```
PS (7) > @'
>> @{
>>     ModuleVersion = '1.0.0.0'
>>     ModuleToProcess = 'TestModuleContext.psm1'
>>     PrivateData = @{a = 1; b = 2 }
>> }
>> '@ > TestModuleContext.psd1
>>
```

Load the module using the manifest and `-Force` to make sure everything gets updated:

```
PS (8) > Import-Module -Force ./TestModuleContext.psd1
```

And run the test command:

```
PS (9) > Test-ModuleContext | fl name,privatedata

Name        : TestModuleContext
PrivateData : {a, b}
```

You see that the `PrivateData` field is now also filled in.

Accessing the calling module

The module that a function was called from can be retrieved by using the expression `$PSCmdlet.SessionState.Module`. Similarly, the module a cmdlet is called from is available through `this.SessionState.Module`. In either case, if the command is being invoked from the top level, this value will be `$null` because there is no "global module."

> **NOTE** It's unfortunate that we didn't get a chance to wrap the global session state in a module before we shipped. This means that this kind of code has to be special case for the module being `$null` some of the time.

Working with both contexts

Now let's look at a tricky scenario where you access both contexts at once. This is something that's rarely necessary but, when needed, is absolutely required.

In functions and script modules, accessing the module session is trivial since unqualified variables are resolved in the module context by default. To access the caller's context you need to use the caller's session state, which is available as a property on `$PSCmdlet`. Let's update the `Test-ModuleContext` module to access a variable, `$testv`, both in the caller's context and the module context. Here's the module definition:

```
PS (1) > @'
>> $testv = 123
>> function Test-ModuleContext {
>>     [CmdletBinding()] param()
```

```
>>     "module testv is $testv"
>>     $ctestv = $PSCmdlet.SessionState.PSVariable.Get("testv").Value;
>>     "caller's testv is $ctestv"
>> }
>> '@ > TestModuleContext.psm1
>>
```

This defines your test function, specifying that the cmdlet binding be used so you can access `$PSCmdlet`. The module body also defines a module-scoped variable, `$testv`. The test function will emit the value of this variable and then use the expression

```
$PSCmdlet.SessionState.PSVariable.Get("testv").Value
```

to get the value of the caller's `$testv` variable. Next load the module:

```
PS (2) > Import-Module -Force ./TestModuleContext.psm1
```

Now define a global `$testv`:

```
PS (3) > $testv = "456"
```

Next, run the command:

```
PS (4) > Test-ModuleContext
module testv is 123
caller's testv is 456
```

And you see the module `$testv` was correctly displayed as 123 and the caller's variable is the global value 456. Now wait a minute, you say, you could've done this much more easily by specifying `$global:testv`. This is true if you were only interested in accessing variables at the global level. But sometimes you want to get the local variable in the caller's dynamic scope. Let's try this. Define a new function, `nested`, that will set a local `$testv`:

```
PS (5) > function nested {
>>     $testv = "789"
>>     Test-ModuleContext
>> }
>>
```

This function-scoped `$testv` variable is the caller's variable you want to access so you should get 789 instead of the global value 456:

```
PS (6) > nested
module testv is 123
caller's testv is 789
```

It works. The module `$testv` was returned as 123 and the caller's `$testv` returned the value of the function-scoped variable instead of the global variable.

So when would you need this functionality? If you want to write a function that manipulates the caller's scope—say something like the `Set-Variable` cmdlet implemented as a function—then you'd need this capability. The other time you might need to do this is when you want to access the value of locally scoped configuration variables, such as `$OFS`.

10.7.4 Setting module properties from inside a script module

We've talked at length about how manifests are required to set metadata on a module, but there's a way for the script module to do some of this itself during the module load operation. To do this it needs to have access to its own `PSModuleInfo` object during the load. This can be retrieved using the rather awkward expression

```
$MyInvocation.MyCommand.ScriptBlock.Module
```

But once you have the `PSModuleInfo` object, the rest is easy. Try it out by setting the `Description` property on your own module.

Setting the module description

In this example, you'll set the `Description` property for a module from within the module itself. You'll create a module file in the current directory called setdescription.psm1. Here are the contents of this file:

```
PS (1) > Get-Content .\setdescription.psm1
$mInfo = $MyInvocation.MyCommand.ScriptBlock.Module
$mInfo.Description = "My Module's Description on $(Get-Date)"
```

On the first line of the module, you copy the reference to the `PSModuleInfo` object into a variable, `$mInfo`. On the second line, you assign a value to the `Description` property on that object. Import the module:

```
PS (2) > Import-Module .\setdescription.psm1
```

Then, call `Get-Module`, piping into `Format-List` so you can just see the module name and its description:

```
PS (3) > Get-Module setdescription |
>> Format-List name, description
>>

Name        : setdescription
Description : My Module's Description on 01/16/2010 21:33:13
```

And there you go. You've dynamically set the `Description` property on your module.

Along with being able to set this type of metadata entry on the `PSModuleInfo` object, there are a couple of behaviors you can control as well. You'll see how this works in the next two sections.

10.7.5 Controlling when modules can be unloaded

The module `AccessMode` feature allows you to restrict when a module can be unloaded. There are two flavors of restriction: *static* and *constant*. A *static module* is a module that can't be removed unless the `-Force` option is used on the `Remove-Module` cmdlet. A *constant module* can never be unloaded and will remain in memory until the session that loaded it ends. This model parallels the pattern for making variables and functions constant.

To make a module either static or constant, you need to set the AccessMode property on the module's PSModuleInfo object to the appropriate setting. Set it to ReadOnly for static modules and Constant for constant modules. Let's see how this is done. Here's an example script module called readonly.psm1 that makes itself ReadOnly:

```
PS (1) > Get-Content .\readonly.psm1
$mInfo = $MyInvocation.MyCommand.ScriptBlock.Module
$mInfo.AccessMode = "readonly"
```

The first line of the module is the same as the example in the previous section and retrieves the PSModuleInfo object. The next line sets the AccessMode to readonly. Now load this module and verify the behavior:

```
PS (2) > Import-Module .\readonly.psm1
PS (3) > Get-Module

ModuleType Name                          ExportedCommands
---------- ----                          ----------------
Script     readonly                      {}
```

You've verified that it's been loaded, so now try to remove it:

```
PS (5) > Remove-Module readonly
Remove-Module : Unable to remove module 'readonly' because it is
read-only. Use the -force flag to remove read-only modules.
At line:1 char:14
+ Remove-Module <<<<  readonly
   + CategoryInfo          : PermissionDenied: (readonly:PSModuleInfo)
   [Remove-Module], InvalidOperationException
   + FullyQualifiedErrorId :
   Modules_ModuleIsReadOnly,
   Microsoft.PowerShell.Commands.RemoveModuleCommand
```

When you try to remove the module, you get an error stating that -Force must be used to remove it. So do that:

```
PS (6) > Remove-Module readonly -Force
```

This time you don't get an error. You verify that the module has been removed by calling Get-Module:

```
PS (7) > Get-Module
PS (8) >
```

Nothing was returned, confirming that the module has been removed. The same approach is used to mark a module as constant.

And now, the final feature we're going to cover: how to run an action when a module is unloaded.

10.7.6 Running an action when a module is removed

Sometimes you need to do some cleanup when a module is unloaded. For example, if the module establishes a persistent connection to a server, when the module is unloaded you'll want that connection to be closed. You'll see an example of this pattern when we look at *implicit remoting* in chapter 13. The `PSModuleInfo` object provides a way to do this through its `OnRemove` property.

To set up an action to execute when a module is unloaded, assign a script block defining the action to the `OnRemove` property on the module's `PSModuleInfo` object. Here's an example that shows how this is done:

```
PS (1) > Get-Content .\onremove.psm1
$mInfo = $MyInvocation.MyCommand.ScriptBlock.Module
$mInfo.OnRemove = {
        Write-Host "I was removed on $(Get-Date)"
    }
```

You get the `PSModuleInfo` object in the first line, and then assign a script block that displays a message to the `OnRemove` property. (Note that you have to call `Write-Host` if you want to see the message because the output of the script block is simply ignored.) Let's try it out. Import the module:

```
PS (2) > Import-Module .\onremove.psm1
```

Then remove it:

```
PS (3) > Remove-Module onremove
I was removed on 01/16/2010 22:05:00
```

And the message from the script block was printed, confirming that the `OnRemove` action was executed.

And with that, we're done with modules...well, mostly done—there are a few even more advanced techniques that will be covered in chapter 11.

10.8 SUMMARY

In this chapter, you expanded your knowledge of PowerShell modules by exploring features provided to support production-oriented coding in PowerShell. We looked at module manifests and how they're used to add metadata to a module. Next we examined each of the manifest elements and their role in the process. Finally we investigated some advanced techniques using the module information object. Here are some important points about using modules with manifests:

- Production modules are stored in a directory containing the module manifest and content. The metadata or information about a module is contained in a .psd1 file usually with the same name as the module directory.
- The easiest way to create a module manifest is to use the `New-ModuleManifest` cmdlet. A second cmdlet, `Test-ModuleManifest`, is provided to test an existing module for issues.
- A manifest lets you define three types of information for your module: production, construction, and content. Production metadata defines things like version number and dependencies. Construction elements control how a module is

constructed, including specifying any nested modules. Content manifest elements deal with other types of content in the module.

In the latter part of this chapter, we looked in more detail at how modules are represented in memory and the kinds of operations you can perform once you have the module information object. Here are some of the key topics we covered:

- Modules in memory are represented by a `PSModuleInfo` object. This object allows you to perform a number of advanced scenarios with modules.
- The `PSModuleInfo` object for a module can be retrieved using `Get-Module`. Alternatively, the module object for a function can be retrieved using the `Module` property on a script block for that function.
- If you have access to the `PSModuleInfo` object for a module, you can inject code into the module, where it will be executed in the module context. This allows you to manipulate the state of a module without having to reload it. This feature is primarily intended for diagnostic and debugging purposes.
- From within a script module, you can use the `PSModuleInfo` object to directly set some metadata elements like the module description.
- `PSModuleInfo` object has an `AccessMode` field that controls the ability to update or remove a module from the session. This field is set to `ReadWrite` by default but can be set to `Static`, requiring the use of the `-Force` parameter (to update it) or `Constant` (which means it can't be removed from the session). A `Constant` module remains in the session until the session ends.
- To set up an action to be taken when a module is removed, you can assign a script block to the `OnRemove` property on the `PSModuleInfo` object for that module.

Let's stop for a minute and check where we are. With this chapter, we've now covered all the core topics necessary for understanding how to script in PowerShell. We discussed syntax, operators, and data types in chapters 2 through 6. In chapters 7 and 8, we covered functions and scripts, and finally, in chapters 9 and 10 we explored modules. In the next chapter, we'll look at some more advanced programming topics that build on what you've learned. These advanced topics will not only introduce some powerful new ways of using PowerShell, they'll also engender a deep understanding of how PowerShell works.

CHAPTER 11

Metaprogramming with scriptblocks and dynamic code

Philosophy have I digested, The whole of Law and Medicine, From each its secrets I have wrested, Theology, alas, thrown in. Poor fool, with all this sweated lore, I stand no wiser than I was before.

—Johann Wolfgang Goethe, *Faust*

Greek letters are cool...

—Not actually a quote from *Beavis and Butthead*

Chapters 7 and 8 covered the basic elements of programming in PowerShell: functions and scripts. Chapters 9 and 10 introduced modules as a way of aggregating your code into reusable pieces through modules. In this chapter, we'll take things to the next level and talk about *metaprogramming*. Metaprogramming is the term used to describe the activity of writing programs that create or manipulate other programs. If you're not already familiar with this concept, you may be asking why you should care. In chapter 1, we talked about designing classes and how hard it is to get those designs right. In most environments, if the designer makes a mistake, the user is stuck with the result. This isn't true in PowerShell. Metaprogramming lets you poke into the heart of the system and make things work the way you need them to. Here's an analogy that should give you the full picture.

Imagine buying a computer that was welded shut. There's still a lot you can do with it—run all the existing programs and even install new programs. But there are some things you can't do. If it doesn't have any USB ports, you can't add them. If it doesn't have any way to capture video, you can't add that either without opening the case. And even though most people buy a computer with the basic features they need and never add new hardware, a case that's welded shut doesn't allow for hardware tinkering.

Traditional programming languages are much like that welded computer. They have a basic set of features, and although you can extend what they do by adding libraries, you can't extend the core capabilities of the language. For example, you can't add a new type of looping statement. On the other hand, in a language that supports metaprogramming, you can undertake such activities as adding new control structures. This is how the `Where-Object` and `ForEach-Object` cmdlets are implemented. They use the metaprogramming features in PowerShell to add what appear to be new language elements. You can even create your own variations of these commands.

We'll begin our investigation with a detailed discussion of PowerShell scriptblocks, which are at the center of most of the metaprogramming techniques. This discussion takes up the first part of this chapter and lays the groundwork for the rest of what we'll discuss. With that material as context, we'll look at how and where scriptblocks are used in PowerShell. We'll look at the role scriptblocks play in the creation of custom objects and types, and how they can be used to extend the PowerShell language. We'll cover techniques like proxy functions, dynamic modules, and custom objects—all of which are examples of applied metaprogramming. Then we'll move on, and you'll see how you can use similar techniques with static languages like C# from within your scripts. Finally, we'll look at using events—a related technique that also involves scriptblocks. But first, you need to understand scriptblocks themselves.

11.1 SCRIPTBLOCK BASICS

In this section we'll talk about how to create and use scriptblocks. We'll begin by explaining how commands are invoked so you can understand all the ways to invoke scriptblocks. Next, we'll cover the syntax for scriptblock literals and the various types of scriptblocks you can create. This includes using scriptblocks as functions, as filters, and as cmdlets. Finally, we'll discuss how you can use scriptblocks to define new functions at runtime. Let's dive into the topic by starting with definitions.

In PowerShell, the key to metaprogramming (writing programs that write or manipulate other programs) is the scriptblock. This is a block of script code that exists as an object reference but doesn't require a name. The `Where-Object` and `ForEach-Object` cmdlets rely on scriptblocks for their implementation. In the example

```
1..10 | foreach { $_ * 2 }
```

the expression in braces—`{ $_ * 2 }`—is actually a scriptblock. It's a piece of code that's passed to the `ForEach-Object` cmdlet and is called by the cmdlet as needed.

So that's all a scriptblock is—a piece of script in braces—but it's the key to all the advanced programming features in PowerShell.

> **NOTE** What we call scriptblocks in PowerShell are called *anonymous functions* or sometimes lambda expressions in other languages. The term *lambda* comes from the lambda calculus developed by Alonzo Church and Stephen Cole Kleene in the 1930s. A number of languages, including Python and dialects of LISP, still use lambda as a language keyword. In designing the PowerShell language, the PowerShell team felt that calling a spade and spade (and a scriptblock a scriptblock) was more straightforward (the coolness of using Greek letters aside).

We've said that scriptblocks are anonymous functions, and of course functions are one of the four types of commands. But wait! You invoke a command by specifying its name. If scriptblocks are anonymous, they have no name—so how can you invoke them? This necessitates one more diversion before we really dig into scriptblocks. Let's talk about how commands can be executed.

11.1.1 Invoking commands

The way to execute a command is just to type its name followed by a set of arguments, but sometimes you can't type the command name as is. For example, you might have a command with a space in the name. You can't simply type the command because the space would cause part of the command name to be treated as an argument. And you can't put it in quotes, because this turns it into a string value. So you have to use the call operator, `&`. If, for instance, you have a command called `my command`, you'd invoke this command by typing the following:

```
& "my command"
```

The interpreter sees the call operator and uses the value of the next argument to look up the command to run. This process of looking up the command is called *command discovery*. The result of this command discovery operation is an object of type `System.Management.Automation.CommandInfo`, which tells the interpreter what command to execute. There are different subtypes of `CommandInfo` for each of the types of PowerShell commands. In the next section, you'll learn how to obtain these objects and how to use them.

Getting CommandInfo objects

You've used the `Get-Command` cmdlet before as a way to attain information about a command. For example, to get information about the `Get-ChildItem` cmdlet, you'd use the following:

```
PS (1) > Get-Command Get-ChildItem

CommandType     Name                    Definition
-----------     ----                    ----------
Cmdlet          Get-ChildItem           Get-ChildItem [[-Pat...
```

This shows you the information about a command: the name of the command, the type of command, and so on.

> **NOTE** In the previous `Get-Command` example, the command's definition was truncated to fit the book-formatting requirements. You can control how this information is described by using the `Format-List` and `Format-Table` commands.

This is useful as a kind of lightweight help, but in addition to displaying information, the object returned by `Get-Command` can be used with the call operator to invoke that command. This is significant. This extra degree of flexibility, invoking a command indirectly, is the first step on the road to metaprogramming.

Let's try this out—first get the `CommandInfo` object for the `Get-Date` command:

```
PS (1) > $d = Get-Command Get-Date
PS (2) > $d.CommandType
Cmdlet
PS (3) > $d.Name
Get-Date
```

As you can see from this example, the name `Get-Date` resolves to a cmdlet with the name `Get-Date`. Now run this command using the `CommandInfo` object with the call operator:

```
PS (4) > & $d

Sunday, May 21, 2006 7:29:47 PM
```

It's as simple as that. So why should you care about this? Because it's a way of getting a handle to a specific command in the environment. Say you defined a function `Get-Date`:

```
PS (1) > function Get-Date {"Hi there"}
PS (2) > Get-Date
Hi there
```

Your new `Get-Date` command outputs a string. Because PowerShell looks for functions before it looks for cmdlets, this new function definition hides the `Get-Date` cmdlet. Even using `&` with the string "Get-Date" still runs the function:

```
PS (3) > & "Get-Date"
Hi there
```

Because you created a second definition for Get-Date (the function), now if you use Get-Command you'll see two definitions. So how do you unambiguously select the cmdlet Get-Date?

```
PS (4) > Get-Command Get-Date

CommandType     Name                          Definition
-----------     ----                          ----------
Cmdlet          Get-Date                      Get-Date [[-Date] <D...
Function        Get-Date                      "Hi there"
```

One way is to select the CommandInfo object based on the type of the command:

```
PS (5) > Get-Command -CommandType cmdlet Get-Date

CommandType     Name                          Definition
-----------     ----                          ----------
Cmdlet          Get-Date                      Get-Date [[-Date] <D...
```

Now put the result of this command into a variable

```
PS (6) > $ci = Get-command -CommandType cmdlet Get-Date
```

and then run it using the call operator:

```
PS (7) > & $ci

Sunday, May 21, 2006 7:34:33 PM
```

The Get-Date cmdlet was run as expected. Another way to select which command to run, because Get-Command returns a collection of objects, is to index into the collection to get the right object:

```
PS (8) > &(Get-Command Get-Date)[0]

Sunday, May 21, 2006 7:41:28 PM
```

Here you used the result of the index operation directly with the call operator to run the desired command.

This is all interesting, but what does it have to do with scriptblocks? We've demonstrated that you can invoke a command through an object reference instead of by name. This was the problem we set out to work around. Scriptblocks are functions that don't have names; so, as you might expect, the way to call a scriptblock is to use the call operator. Here's what that looks like

```
PS (1) > & {param($x,$y) $x+$y} 2 5
7
```

In this example, the scriptblock is

```
{param($x,$y) $x+$y}
```

This example used the call operator to invoke it with two arguments, 2 and 5, so the call returns 7. This is how you can execute a function if it doesn't have a name. As long as you have access to the scriptblock, you can call it.

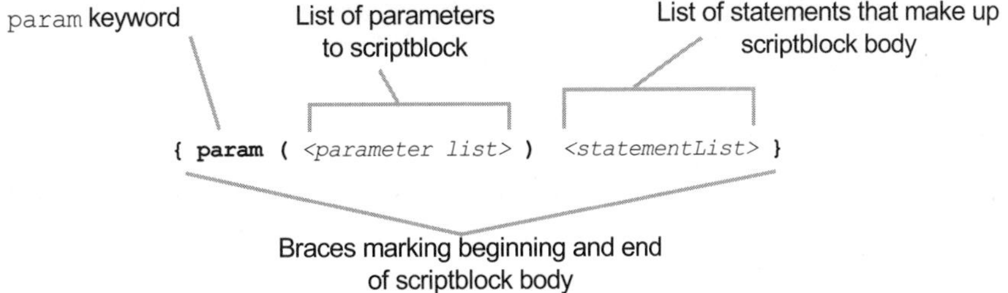

Figure 11.1 Defining a simple scriptblock. Note that the `param` statement is optional, so a minimal scriptblock only has the braces.

11.1.2 The scriptblock literal

Scriptblocks are the center of pretty much everything we do in this chapter. Because the most common form of scriptblock is the *scriptblock literal,* it's worth investing some time looking at them in detail. You'll learn how to specify a scriptblock literal that acts as a function, how to specify one that acts like a filter, and finally how to define a scriptblock cmdlet.

What you've been writing to create scriptblocks is called a scriptblock literal—in other words, a chunk of legitimate PowerShell script surrounded by braces. The syntax for this literal is shown in figure 11.1.

The definition of a scriptblock looks more or less like the definition of a function, except the `function` keyword and function name are missing. If the `param` statement isn't present, the scriptblock will get its arguments through `$args`, exactly as a function would.

> **Param vs. lambda**
>
> The `param` statement in PowerShell corresponds to the lambda keyword in other languages. For example, the PowerShell expression
>
> ```
> & {param($x,$y) $x+$y} 2 5
> ```
>
> is equivalent to the LISP expression
>
> ```
> (lambda (x y) (+ x y)) 2 5)
> ```
>
> or the Python expression
>
> ```
> (lambda x,y: x+y)(2,5)
> ```
>
> Also note that, unlike Python lambdas, PowerShell scriptblocks can contain any collection of legal PowerShell statements.

Scriptblocks, like regular functions or scripts, can also behave like cmdlets. In other words, they can have one or all of the `begin`, `process`, or `end` clauses that you can

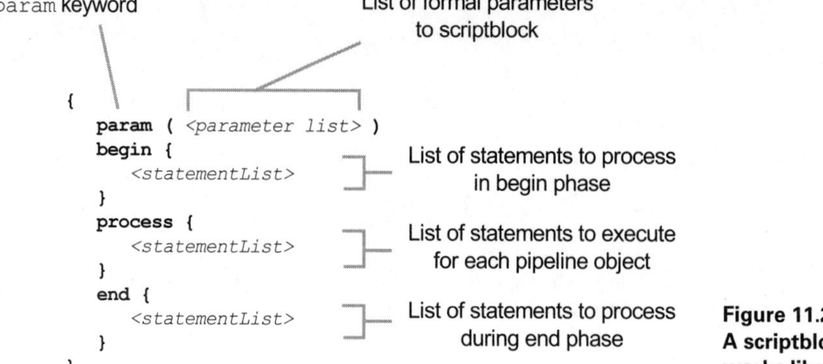

Figure 11.2 A scriptblock that works like a cmdlet

have in a function or script. Figure 11.2 shows the most general form of the scriptblock syntax, including all three clauses.

As was the case with a regular function, you don't have to define all the clauses. Here's an example that uses only the `process` clause:

```
PS (1) > 1..5 |&{process{$_ * 2}}
2
4
6
8
10
```

A scriptblock written this way works like the filters you saw in chapter 7. It also works like the `ForEach-Object` cmdlet, as shown here:

```
PS (2) > 1..5 |foreach {$_ * 2}
2
4
6
8
10
```

The `ForEach-Object` cmdlet is effectively a shortcut for the more complex scriptblock construction.

As we've been going along, we keep talking about how scriptblocks are anonymous functions. This is a good time to see how scriptblocks and named functions are related.

11.1.3 Defining functions at runtime

In earlier sections, we said that scriptblocks were functions without names. The converse is also true—functions are scriptblocks with names. So what exactly is the relationship between the two? In chapter 7, you learned how to manage the functions in your PowerShell session using the function: drive. To get a list of functions, you could do a `dir` of that drive:

```
dir function:/
```

You could also delete or rename functions. But we didn't cover the whole story. In fact, the function: drive is, in effect, a set of variables containing scriptblocks. Let's explore this further. First, let's define our favorite function, `foo`:

```
PS (1) > function foo {2+2}
PS (2) > foo
4
```

You can use the `dir` cmdlet to get the command information from the function provider:

```
PS (3) > dir function:foo

CommandType     Name                          Definition
-----------     ----                          ----------
Function        foo                           2+2
```

Now use `Get-Member` to get more information about the object that was returned:

```
PS (4) > dir function:foo | Get-Membersc*

   TypeName: System.Management.Automation.FunctionInfo

Name        MemberType Definition
----        ---------- ----------
ScriptBlock Property   System.Management.Automation.ScriptBlo...
```

The object that came back to you was a `FunctionInfo` object. This is the subclass of `CommandInfo` that's used to represent a function. As you see, one of the properties on the object is the scriptblock that makes up the body of the function. Retrieve that member:

```
PS (5) > (dir function:foo).ScriptBlock
2+2
```

The scriptblock, when displayed as a string, shows the source code for the scriptblock. Another, simpler way to get back the scriptblock that defines a function is to use the variable syntax:

```
PS (6) > $function:foo
2+2
PS (7) > $function:foo.GetType().Fullname
System.Management.Automation.ScriptBlock
```

Now here's the interesting part. Change the definition of this function by assigning a new scriptblock to the function:

```
PS (8) > $function:foo = {"Bye!"}
```

When you run the function again

```
PS (9) > foo
Bye!
```

you see that it's changed. The function keyword is, in effect, shorthand for assigning to a name in the function provider.

Now that you know how to manipulate scriptblocks and functions, let's take this one step further. As discussed in chapter 1, objects encapsulate data and code. We've spent a lot of time on data in the earlier chapters, and now we have a way of manipulating code too. This means that you're ready to take the next step and see how you can use data and scriptblocks to build your own objects.

11.2 BUILDING AND MANIPULATING OBJECTS

Let's kick our scripting up a notch and look at ways to build custom objects. Up to this point in the chapter we've been talking about scriptblocks as stand-alone functions. Now it's time to talk about how to use scriptblocks to build objects. At their core, as discussed in chapter 1, objects are a binding of data and behaviors. These behaviors are implemented by blocks of script. You needed to know how to build the blocks of code, scriptblocks, before we could talk about building objects. With a good understanding of scriptblocks, we can now discuss manipulating and building objects in PowerShell.

In chapter 2, we talked extensively about types. Now we're concerned with objects—that is, *instances* of types. A type is the pattern or template that describes an object, and an object is an instance of that pattern. In statically typed languages such as C#, once an object is instantiated, its interfaces can't be changed. With dynamic languages such as PowerShell (or Ruby or Python), this isn't true. Dynamic languages allow you to alter the set of members available at runtime.

> **NOTE** As of C# 4.0, the language is no longer strictly statically typed. C# 4.0 introduced a new "dynamic" keyword, allowing you to write programs that have dynamic types.

In the rest of this section, we'll explore manipulating objects and types in PowerShell. We'll start with a discussion of how to examine existing members, followed by a look at the types of members available on an object. Then we'll cover the various ways to add members to an object, and finally we'll look at the plumbing of the PowerShell type system to give you a sense of the flexibility of the overall system and how it facilitates your goal of writing programs to manipulate programs.

11.2.1 Looking at members

An object's interface is defined by the set of public members it exposes. Public members are the public fields, properties, and methods of the class. As always, the easiest way to look at those members is with the `Get-Member` cmdlet. For example, here are the members defined on an integer:

```
PS (1) > 12 | Get-Member

   TypeName: System.Int32

Name        MemberType Definition
----        ---------- ----------
CompareTo   Method     System.Int32 CompareTo(Int32 value), S...
Equals      Method     System.Boolean Equals(Object obj), Sys...
```

```
GetHashCode Method      System.Int32 GetHashCode()
GetType     Method      System.Type GetType()
GetTypeCode Method      System.TypeCode GetTypeCode()
ToString    Method      System.String ToString(), System.Strin...
```

Note that this doesn't show you all the members on an `[int]`. It only shows you the instance members. You can also use `Get-Member` to look at the static members:

```
PS (2) > 12 | Get-Member -Static

   TypeName: System.Int32

Name            MemberType Definition
----            ---------- ----------
Equals          Method     static System.Boolean Equals(Objec...
Parse           Method     static System.Int32 Parse(String s...
ReferenceEquals Method     static System.Boolean ReferenceEqu...
TryParse        Method     static System.Boolean TryParse(Str...
MaxValue        Property   static System.Int32 MaxValue {get;}
MinValue        Property   static System.Int32 MinValue {get;}
```

You'll use this mechanism to look at the members you'll be adding to objects in the next couple of sections.

Defining synthetic members

One of the most powerful features in the PowerShell environment is the ability to extend existing object types and instances. This allows PowerShell to perform adaptation across a wide variety of types of data. By *adaptation,* we mean overlaying a common set of interfaces onto existing data sources. This may be as simple as unifying the name of the property that counts a collection to be the string "count" across all countable objects or as complex as taking a string containing some XML data and being able to treat that string as an object with a set of properties and attributes.

This isn't the same as subclassing or creating derived types as you would in traditional object-oriented programming languages. In those languages, if you want to extend a new type, you can do so only by creating an entirely new type. In dynamic languages such as PowerShell, you can add members to existing types and objects. This sounds odd from the point of view of a conventional object-oriented language, because types and member definitions are so tightly tied together. In languages such as PowerShell, it's possible to have objects that don't have any type at all.

> **NOTE** If you're a JavaScript user, this won't be surprising. The object-oriented mechanisms in JavaScript use a mechanism called *prototypes.* Prototype-based systems don't have types as discrete objects. Instead, you use an object that has the set of members you want to use and use it as the prototype for your new object. Although PowerShell isn't strictly a prototype-based language, its type extension mechanisms can be used in much the same way.

Because the members you'll be adding to objects aren't natively part of the object's definition, they're called *synthetic members*. Synthetic members are used extensively throughout PowerShell for adaptation and extension. Let's look at an example. First, we'll examine the synthetic properties on an object returned by `dir` from the file system:

```
PS (6) > dir $profile | Get-Member ps*

   TypeName: System.IO.FileInfo

Name           MemberType   Definition
----           ----------   ----------
PSChildName    NoteProperty System.String PSChildName=Microsof...
PSDrive        NoteProperty System.Management.Automation.PSDri...
PSIsContainer  NoteProperty System.Boolean PSIsContainer=False
PSParentPath   NoteProperty System.String PSParentPath=Microso...
PSPath         NoteProperty System.String PSPath=Microsoft.Pow...
PSProvider     NoteProperty System.Management.Automation.Provi...
```

Now let's get the same information from the Registry:

```
PS (8) > dir hklm:\software | Get-Member ps*

   TypeName: Microsoft.Win32.RegistryKey

Name           MemberType   Definition
----           ----------   ----------
PSChildName    NoteProperty System.String PSChildName=Adobe
PSDrive        NoteProperty System.Management.Automation.PSDri...
PSIsContainer  NoteProperty System.Boolean PSIsContainer=True
PSParentPath   NoteProperty System.String PSParentPath=Microso...
PSPath         NoteProperty System.String PSPath=Microsoft.Pow...
PSProvider     NoteProperty System.Management.Automation.Provi...
```

You can see the same set of `PS*` properties with the PowerShell (PS) prefix on the object, even though they're completely different types. Take a look at these properties. They allow you to work with these two different objects in the same way. This means that you can always tell if an object might have children by looking at the `PSIsContainer` property, regardless of the type of the underlying object. And you can always get the path to the object through the `PSPath` property. We call this type of adaptation *object normalization*. By adding this set of synthetic properties to all objects returned from the provider infrastructure, you make it possible to write scripts that are independent of the type of object that the provider surfaces. This makes the scripts both simpler and more reusable. In the next section we'll start looking at ways to create synthetic members.

11.2.2 Using Add-Member to extend objects

The `Add-Member` cmdlet is the easiest way to add a new member to an object instance, either a static .NET object type or a custom synthetic object. It can be used to add any type of member supported by the PowerShell type system. The list of possible member types that can be added with `Add-Member` is shown in table 11.1.

You'll work through some examples showing how to use these members. You'll use an instance of the string "Hi there" to do this. For convenience, store it in a variable `$s` as shown:

```
PS (1) > $s = "Hi there"
```

Now let's go over how you add these member types to an object instance.

Table 11.1 Member types that can be added with `Add-Member`

Member type	Version	Description
`AliasProperty`	v1, v2	An alias property provides an alternate name for an existing property. For example, if there is an existing `Length` property, then you might alias this to `Count`.
`CodeProperty`	v1, v2	A property that maps to a static method on a .NET class.
`Property`	v1, v2	A native property on the object. In other words, a property that exists on the underlying object that is surfaced directly to the user. For example, there might be a native property `Length` that you choose to also make available through an extended alias member.
`NoteProperty`	v1, v2	A data-only member on the object (equivalent to a .NET field).
`ScriptProperty`	v1, v2	A property whose value is determined by a piece of PowerShell script.
`Properties`	v1, v2	The collection of properties exposed by this object.
`PropertySet`	v1, v2	A named group of properties.
`Method`	v1, v2	A native method on the underlying object. For example, the `SubString()` method on the class `System.String` shows up as a method.
`CodeMethod`	v1, v2	A method that is mapped to a static method on a .NET class.
`ScriptMethod`	v1, v2	A method implemented in PowerShell script.
`ParameterizedProperty`	v1, v2	A property that takes both arguments and a value to assign. This is typically used for things like indexers and might look like `$collection.item(2.3) = "hello"` This sets the element at 2,3 in the collection to the value `"hello"`.
`PSVariableProperty`	v2	A property that is backed by a variable. This type of member was introduced in version 2 along with modules. It has an advantage over note properties because it can be type-constrained.

Adding AliasProperty members

The first type of synthetic member you'll add is called an alias property. This property, whose name is (surprise) `AliasProperty`, allows you to provide a new name for an existing property. Let's work with the `Length` property on a string:

```
PS (2) > $s.Length
8
```

As you can see, this string has a length of 8. Let's say that you want to add an alias `size` for `Length` because you'll be working with a set of objects that all have a `size` property:

```
PS (3) > $s = Add-Member -PassThru -in $s AliasProperty size length
```

There are a couple things to note in this example. First (and most important) is that when you first add a synthetic member to an object, you're creating a new object (but not a new type). This new object wraps the original object in an instance of `System.Management.Automation.PSObject`. Just as `System.Object` is the root of the type system in .NET, `PSObject` is the root of the synthetic type system in PowerShell. For this reason, you assign the result of the `Add-Member` call back to the original variable. To do this, you have to add the `-PassThru` parameter to the command since, by default, the `Add-Member` cmdlet doesn't emit anything.

Let's look at the new member you've added using `gm` (the alias for `Get-Member`):

```
PS (4) > $s | gm size

   TypeName: System.String

Name MemberType    Definition
---- ----------    ----------
size AliasProperty size = length
```

Again, there are a couple of things to note. You can see that the `size` member is there and is an alias property that maps `size` to `Length`. Also, you need to note that the object's type is still `System.String`. The fact that it's wrapped in a `PSObject` is pretty much invisible from the script user's view, though you can test for it as shown in the next example. Using the `-is` operator, you can test to see whether or not the object you're dealing with is wrapped in a `PSObject`:

```
PS (5) > $s -is [PSObject]
True
PS (6) > "abc" -is [PSObject]
False
PS (7) > $s -is [string]
True
```

The result of the first command in the example shows that `$s` does contain a `PSObject`. The second command shows that the raw string doesn't, and the last line shows that the object in `$s` is still considered a string, even though it's also a `PSObject`.

The question now is, after all that explanation, did you actually create this aliased member? The answer is, yes:

```
PS (8) > $s.size
8
PS (9) > $s.Length
8
```

Both the `size` and `length` members return the value 8.

Adding NoteProperty members

Now let's add a note property. A note property is a way of attaching a new piece of data (a note) to an existing object, rather like putting a sticky note on your monitor. Again you'll use the same string in `$s`. Let's add a note property called `Description`. In this example, because you know that `$s` is already wrapped in a `PSObject`, you don't need to use `-PassThru` and do the assignment—you simply add the property to the existing object:

```
PS (10) > Add-Member -in $s NoteProperty description "A string"
PS (11) > $s.Description
A string
```

You've added a `Description` property to the object with the value "A string". And, to prove that this property isn't present on all strings:

```
PS (12) > "Hi there".Description
PS (13) >
```

You see that the property returned nothing.

Of course, the note property is a settable property, so you can change it with an assignment like any other settable property:

```
PS (14) > $s.Description = "A greeting"
PS (15) > $s.Description
A greeting
```

In this example, you changed the value in the note property to "A greeting". Note properties allow you to attach arbitrary data to an object. They aren't type constrained, so they can hold any type.

> **NOTE** Sooner or later, if you're working through all the examples in this chapter, something will fail because one example collides with another. If that happens, start a new PowerShell session and keep going. If you're using the ISE, you can switch to a new tab by pressing Ctrl-T. This will allow you to flip back and forth between sessions to compare things.

Next, set the `Description` property to a `[datetime]` object:

```
PS (16) > $s.Description = Get-Date
PS (17) > $s.Description

Sunday, May 28, 2006 4:24:50 PM
```

But the value stored in the object is still a [datetime] object, not a string. As such, you can get the DayOfWeek property out of the description property:

```
PS (18) > $s.Description.dayofweek
Sunday
PS (19) > $s.Description.GetType().FullName
System.DateTime
```

Adding ScriptMethod members

Both of the synthetic members you've added so far have been pure data properties; no code was involved. Now we'll look at adding members that execute code. We'll start with ScriptMethods, because they're easiest. You'll add a method that returns the string that it's associated with, reversed. First, let's find an easy way to reverse a string. If you examine [string], you'll see that there is (unfortunately) no reverse method on the string class. There is, though, a static reverse method on [array] that you can use:

```
PS (1) > [array] | Get-Member -Static reverse

   TypeName: System.Array

Name    MemberType Definition
----    ---------- ----------
Reverse Method     static System.Void Reverse(Array array), s...
```

This method takes an array and, because it's void, it must (obviously) reverse the array in place. This tells us two things: we need to turn the string into an array (of characters) and then save it in a variable so it can be reversed in place. Converting the string to an array of characters is simple—you can use a cast:

```
PS (19) > $s
Hi there
PS (20) > $a = [char[]] $s
```

Casting a string into the type [char[]] (array of characters) produces a new object that's the array of individual characters in the original string. Just to verify this:

```
PS (21) > $a.GetType().FullName
System.Char[]
PS (22) > "$a"
H i   t h e r e
```

You see that the type of the new object is [char[]] and it does contain the expected characters. Now reverse it using the [array]::reverse() static method:

```
PS (23) > [array]::reverse($a)
PS (24) > "$a"
e r e h t   i H
```

When you look at the contents of the array, you see that the array has been reversed. But it's still an array of characters. The final step is to turn this back into a string. To do this, you'll use the unary -join operator:

```
PS (25) > $ns = -join $a
PS (26) > $ns
```

```
ereht iH
PS (27) > $ns.GetType().FullName
System.String
```

At this point you have the reversed string in `$ns`. But the goal of this effort was to attach this as a method to the string object itself. To do so, you need to construct a scriptblock to use as the body of the `ScriptMethod`. This definition looks like

```
PS (28) > $sb = {
>>     $a = [char[]] $this
>>     [array]::reverse($a)
>>     -join $a
>> }
>>
```

This example introduces a new "magic" variable, which is defined only for scriptblocks that are used as methods or properties: the `$this` variable. `$this` holds the reference to the object that the `ScriptMethod` member was called from. Now let's bind this scriptblock to the object as a `ScriptMethod` using `Add-Member`:

```
PS (29) > Add-Member -in $s ScriptMethod Reverse $sb
```

Try it out:

```
PS (30) > $s.reverse()
ereht iH
```

You get the reversed string as desired.

Adding ScriptProperty members

The next type of member we'll look at is the `ScriptProperty`. A `ScriptProperty` has up to two methods associated with it—a getter and (optionally) a setter, just like a .NET property. These methods are expressed using two scriptblocks. As was the case with the `ScriptMethod`, the referenced object is available in the `$this` member. And, in the case of the setter, the value being assigned is available in `$args[0]`. Here's an example. You're going to add a `ScriptProperty` member, `desc`, to `$s` that will provide an alternate way to get at the description `NoteProperty` you added earlier, with one difference: you're only going to allow values to be assigned that are already strings. An attempt to assign something that isn't a string will result in an error.

Here's the definition of this property:

```
PS (31) > Add-Member -in $s ScriptProperty Desc `
>>   {$this.Description} `
>>   {
>>     $t = $args[0]
>>     if ($t -isnot [string]) {
>>       throw "this property only takes strings"
>>     }
>>     $this.Description = $t
>>   }
>>
```

The first scriptblock

```
{$this.Description}
```

is the code that will be executed when getting the property's value. All it does is return the value stored in the description `NoteProperty`. Because the setter needs to do some additional work, its scriptblock is more complex:

```
{
    $t = $args[0]
    if ($t -isnot [string])
    {
        throw "this property only takes strings"
    }
    $this.Description = $t
}
```

First, it saves the value to be assigned into a local variable, `$t`. Next, it checks whether this variable is of the correct type. If not, it throws an exception, failing the assignment.

Let's try out this property. First, directly set the note property to the string "Old description":

```
PS (32) > $s.Description = "Old description"
```

Now use the `ScriptProperty` getter to retrieve this value:

```
PS (33) > $s.Desc
Old description
```

You see that it's changed as expected. Next use the `ScriptProperty` to change the description:

```
PS (34) > $s.desc = "New description"
```

Verify the change by checking both the `NoteProperty` and the `ScriptProperty`:

```
PS (35) > $s.Description
New description
PS (36) > $s.desc
New description
PS (37) >
```

Yes, it's been changed. Now try assigning a `[datetime]` object to the property as you did with the description `NoteProperty` previously:

```
PS (37) > $s.desc = Get-Date
Exception setting "desc": "this property only takes strings"
At line:1 char:4
+ $s.d <<<< esc = Get-Date
```

The assignment failed. Using `ScriptProperty` members is a way to do validation and transformation in properties on objects.

> **NOTE** The idea of adding properties to synthetic objects may seem like an academic exercise, but it turns out to be useful. In particular,

it's incredibly useful when you need to adapt existing utilities so that they work effectively in the PowerShell environment. For example, section 11.7 shows how to adapt the output of the task scheduler utility `schtasks.exe` so that it can work effectively in the PowerShell environment. Another useful scenario for this technique is joining two collections of data properties into a single object, as illustrated in appendix B.

11.2.3 Adding note properties with New-Object

The most common case for adding members is when creating a synthetic object with a set of note properties. This is equivalent to creating records in other languages. In many cases, hashtables are sufficient for record-like scenarios, creating objects has some advantages—the formatting system treats objects in a more sophisticated way, and assigning to a member that doesn't exist is treated as an error, whereas assigning to a member that doesn't exist in a hashtable simply creates a new member. This is a common enough scenario that there's special support for this in PowerShell v2 with a new parameter on the `New-Object` cmdlet: `-Property`. This parameter takes a hashtable and sets each member on the object being created that corresponds to member in the hashtable. If the member doesn't exist, then a note property is added. If the object being created is a `PSObject`, then you end up with a pure synthetic object. Here's an example of how this works:

```
PS (1) > $obj = New-Object PSObject -Property @{a=1; b=2; c=3}
```

In this example, you created a new object with three properties: a, b, and c:

```
PS (2) > $obj | Format-Table -auto
a b c
- - -
1 2 3
```

Using `Get-Member` you can see that they are all of type `NoteProperty`:

```
PS (3) > $obj | Get-Member

   TypeName: System.Management.Automation.PSCustomObject

Name        MemberType   Definition
----        ----------   ----------
Equals      Method       bool Equals(System.Object obj)
GetHashCode Method       int GetHashCode()
GetType     Method       type GetType()
ToString    Method       string ToString()
a           NoteProperty System.Int32 a=1
b           NoteProperty System.Int32 b=2
c           NoteProperty System.Int32 c=3
```

Also notice that the type of the object returned is `System.Management.Automation.PSCustomObject`, which isn't a type you've seen before. This type of object is used as the base for all pure synthetic objects. Because the properties you added are note properties, you can change their values:

```
PS (4) > $obj.a = 5
PS (5) > $obj | Format-Table -auto
a b c
- - -
5 2 3
```

But if you try to assign to a nonexistent property

```
PS (6) > $obj.d = 10
Property 'd' cannot be found on this object; make sure it exists
 and is settable.
At line:1 char:6
+ $obj. <<<< d = 10
    + CategoryInfo          : InvalidOperation: (:) [], Runtime
   Exception
    + FullyQualifiedErrorId : PropertyAssignmentException
```

you get an error. This can help catch runtime bugs in your code and is one reason to favor synthetic objects over hashtables.

All `New-Object -Property` is doing is creating and attaching note properties in the cmdlet instead of requiring the user do it one at a time. There's another way to do this that's available in both v1 and v2 of PowerShell: the `Select-Object` cmdlet. Let's look at how this cmdlet lets you build custom objects.

11.3 USING THE SELECT-OBJECT CMDLET

Now that you know how to attach members using `Add-Member` and `New-Object`, let's explore some other ways to build synthetic objects. The `Select-Object` cmdlet, which is used to select a subset of properties on an object, creates a synthetic object to hold these properties.

The `Select-Object` cmdlet is also a way to select elements from a stream of objects. You can select a range of objects:

```
PS (1) > 1..10 | Select-Object -First 3
1
2
3
```

Here you've selected the first three elements. But, much more interesting for this discussion, it's a way to select fields from an object:

```
PS (1) > dir | Select-Object name,length

Name                                                      Length
----                                                      ------
a.txt                                                         98
b.txt                                                         42
c.txt                                                        102
d.txt                                                         66
```

At first this looks a lot like `Format-Table`. Let's use `Get-Member` to see how different it is:

```
PS (2) > dir | Select-Object name,length | Get-Member

   TypeName: System.Management.Automation.PSCustomObject

Name        MemberType   Definition
----        ----------   ----------
Equals      Method       System.Boolean Equals(Object obj)
GetHashCode Method       System.Int32 GetHashCode()
GetType     Method       System.Type GetType()
ToString    Method       System.String ToString()
Length      NoteProperty System.Int64 Length=98
Name        NoteProperty System.String Name=a.txt
```

As was the case with the objects returned from `New-Object -Property`, the type of the object is `System.Management.Automation.PSCustomObject`. As mentioned in the previous section, this is a PowerShell-specific type that's used as the base for pure synthetic objects. An object whose base is `PSCustomObject` has only synthetic members and is therefore called a synthetic object.

Even though it's a synthetic object, it's still a "first-class" citizen in the PowerShell environment. You can sort these objects

```
PS (3) > dir | Select-Object Name,Length | sort Length

Name                                                      Length
----                                                      ------
b.txt                                                         42
d.txt                                                         66
a.txt                                                         98
c.txt                                                        102
```

or do anything else that you can do with a regular object.

But there's more to using `Select-Object` than simply selecting from the existing set of members. For example, say you want to add a new field "minute" to these objects. This will be a calculated field as follows:

```
PS (9) > dir | foreach {$_.LastWriteTime.Minute}
5
51
56
54
```

In other words, it will be the minute at which the file was last written. You attach this field by passing a specially constructed hashtable describing the member to `Select-Object`. This hashtable has to have two members: name and expression (which can be shortened to "n" and "e" for brevity). The name is the name to call the property, and the expression is the scriptblock used to calculate the value of the field. The definition will look like this:

```
@{Name="minute";Expression={$_.LastWriteTime.Minute}}
```

Let's use it in the pipeline:

```
PS (11) > dir | Select-Object Name,Length,
>>  @{Name="Minute";Expression={$_.LastWriteTime.Minute}}
>>

Name                                    Length              minute
----                                    ------              ------
a.txt                                       98                  55
b.txt                                       42                  51
c.txt                                      102                  56
d.txt                                       66                  54
```

As intended, the result has three fields, including the synthetic `minute` property you specified with the hashtable. Use `Get-Member` to see what the object looks like:

```
PS (12) > dir | Select-Object  name,length,
>>  @{n="minute";e={$_.lastwritetime.minute}} | Get-Member
>>

   TypeName: System.Management.Automation.PSCustomObject

Name         MemberType   Definition
----         ----------   ----------
Equals       Method       System.Boolean Equals(Object obj)
GetHashCode  Method       System.Int32 GetHashCode()
GetType      Method       System.Type GetType()
ToString     Method       System.String ToString()
Length       NoteProperty System.Int64 Length=98
minute       NoteProperty System.Management.Automation.PSObjec...
Name         NoteProperty System.String Name=a.txt
```

You see that there are now three `NoteProperty` members on the objects that were output.

For the last few sections, we've been focusing on individual functions (scriptblocks) and object members. Let's switch gears a bit and look at how modules fit into all of this. In chapters 9 and 10, we talked only about modules that that were loaded from disk, but there's also a way to create modules dynamically.

11.4 Dynamic modules

Dynamic modules are modules created in memory at runtime rather than being loaded from disk. Dynamic modules relate to regular modules in much the same way as functions are related to scripts. In this section, we'll cover how to use dynamic modules to encapsulate local state in scripts, how they're used to implement a dynamic equivalent of the closure feature found in other languages, and finally, how they can be used to simplify the way you create custom objects.

11.4.1 Dynamic script modules

Just as there were two types of on-disk modules—script modules and binary modules (we can ignore manifest modules for this discussion)—there are also two types of dynamic modules. The first type is the dynamic script module. Let's create one and see what's involved.

To create a dynamic module, use the New-Module cmdlet. This cmdlet takes a scriptblock as an argument. This scriptblock is executed to define the modules contents. Here's what it looks like:

```
PS (1) > $dm = New-Module {
>>     $c=0
>>     function Get-NextCount
>>         { $script:c++; $script:c }}
>>
```

Other than how they're created, the content of the module looks pretty much like the on-disk modules you created in chapter 9. This is by design and means that all of the concepts you learned for on-disk modules also apply to dynamic modules. As we discussed in the previous chapter, if there's no call to Export-ModuleMember, all of the functions defined in the module are exported and the other types of module members aren't. Verify this by calling the function you defined

```
PS (2) > Get-NextCount
1
PS (3) > Get-NextCount
2
```

which works properly. And, because it wasn't exported, there's no variable $c:

```
PS (4) > $c
```

(Or at least not one related to this dynamic module.) Now try to use Get-Module to look at the module information

```
PS (5) > Get-Module
```

and you don't see anything. So what happened? Well, dynamic modules are objects like everything else in PowerShell. The New-Module cmdlet has created a new module object but hasn't added it to the module table. This is why you assigned the output of the cmdlet to a variable—so you'd have a reference to the module object. Let's look at that object:

```
PS (6) > $dm | fl

Name              : __DynamicModule_55b674b0-9c3c-4db0-94a3-a095
                    a4ac984e
Path              : 55b674b0-9c3c-4db0-94a3-a095a4ac984e
Description       :
ModuleType        : Script
Version           : 0.0
NestedModules     : {}
ExportedFunctions : Get-NextCount
ExportedCmdlets   : {}
ExportedVariables : {}
ExportedAliases   : {}
```

The interesting fields are the name and path fields. Because no file is associated with the module, you had to make up a unique "path" for that object. Likewise, you didn't specify a name, so the runtime made one up for you. So why did it do these things? It did this because, although a dynamic module isn't registered by default, it can be added to the module table by piping it to `Import-Module`. Let's give it a try:

```
PS (6) > $dm | Import-Module
```

Now check the module table:

```
PS (7) > Get-Module

ModuleType Name                        ExportedCommands
---------- ----                        ----------------
Script     __DynamicModule_b6dea7... Get-NextCount
```

There it is, ugly name and all. Now you can give a dynamic module a specific name using the `-Name` parameter on the `New-Module` cmdlet. First, clean up from the last example

```
PS (1) > Get-Module | Remove-Module
```

and define a new dynamic module, with the same body as last time:

```
PS (2) > New-Module -Name Dynamic1 {
>>     $c=0
>>     function Get-NextCount
>>         { $script:c++; $script:c }} |
>>             Import-Module
>>
```

Rather than saving the result to a variable, you're piping it directly to `Import-Module`. Now look at the result:

```
PS (3) > Get-Module

ModuleType Name                        ExportedCommands
---------- ----                        ----------------
Script     Dynamic1                    Get-NextCount
```

This time the module is registered in the table with a much more reasonable name.

So when would you use dynamic modules? When you need to create a function or functions that have persistent resources that you don't want to expose at the global level. This is basically the same scenario as the on-disk case, but this way you can package the module or modules to load into a single script file.

There's also another way the dynamic module feature is used: to implement the idea of closures in PowerShell. Let's move on and see how that works.

11.4.2 Closures in PowerShell

PowerShell uses dynamic modules to create dynamic *closures*. A closure in computer science terms (at least as defined in Wikipedia) is "a function that is evaluated in an environment containing one or more bound variables." A *bound variable* is, for our purposes, a variable that exists and has a value. The *environment* in our case is the dynamic module. Finally, the *function* is just a scriptblock. In effect, a closure is the inverse of an object, as discussed in chapter 1. An *object* is data with methods (functions) attached to that data. A *closure* is a function with data attached to that method.

The best way to understand what all this means is to look at an example. You'll use closures to create a set of counter functions, similar to what you did in chapter 9. The advantage closures give you over plain functions is that you can change what increment to use after the counter function has been defined. Here's the basic function:

```
function New-Counter ($increment=1)
{
    $count=0;
    {
        $script:count += $increment
        $count
    }.GetNewClosure()
}
```

There's nothing you haven't seen so far—you create a variable and then a scriptblock that increments that variable—except for returning the result of the call to the `GetNewClosure()` method. Let's try this function to see what it does. First, create a counter:

```
PS (1) > $c1 = New-Counter
PS (2) > $c1.GetType().FullName
System.Management.Automation.ScriptBlock
```

Looking at the type of the object returned, you see that it's a scriptblock, so you use the `&` operator to invoke it:

```
PS (3) > & $c1
1
PS (4) > & $c1
2
```

The scriptblock works as you'd expect a counter to work. Each invocation returns the next number in the sequence. Now, create a second counter, but this time set the increment to 2:

```
PS (5) > $c2 = New-Counter 2
```

Invoke the second counter scriptblock:

```
PS (6) > & $c2
2
PS (7) > & $c2
4
PS (8) > & $c2
6
```

It counts up by 2. But what about the first counter?

```
PS (9) > & $c1
3
```

```
PS (10) > & $c1
4
```

The first counter continues to increment by 1, unaffected by the second counter. So the key thing to notice is that each counter instance has its own copies of the `$count` and `$increment` variables. When a new closure is created, a new dynamic module is created, and then all the variables in the caller's scope are copied into this new module.

Here are some more examples of working with closures to give you an idea of how flexible the mechanism is. First, you'll create a new closure using a `param` block to set the bound variable `$x`. This is essentially the same as the previous example, except that you're using a scriptblock to establish the environment for the closure instead of a named function:

```
PS (11) > $c = & {param ($x) {$x+$x}.GetNewClosure()} 3.1415
```

Now evaluate the newly created closed scriptblock:

```
PS (12) > & $c
6.283
```

This evaluation returns the value of the parameter added to itself. Because closures are implemented using dynamic modules, you can use the same mechanisms you saw in chapter 9 for manipulating a modules state to manipulate the state of a closure. You can do this by accessing the module object attached to the scriptblock. You'll use this object to reset the module variable `$x` by evaluating `sv` (`Set-Variable`) in the closure's module context:

```
PS (13) > & $c.Module Set-Variable x "Abc"
```

Now evaluate the scriptblock to verify that it's been changed:

```
PS (14) > & $c
AbcAbc
```

Next, create another scriptblock closed over the same module as the first one. You can do this by using the `NewBoundScriptBlock()` method on the module to create a new scriptblock attached to the module associated with the original scriptblock:

```
PS (15) > $c2 = $c.Module.NewBoundScriptBlock({"x ia $x"})
```

Execute the new scriptblock to verify that it's using the same `$x`:

```
PS (16) > & $c2
x ia Abc
```

Now use `$c2.module` to update the shared variable:

```
PS (17) > & $c2.module sv x 123
PS (18) > & $c2
x ia 123
```

And verify that it's also changed for the original closed scriptblock:

```
PS (19) > & $c
246
```

Finally, create a named function from the scriptblock using the function provider

```
PS (20) > $function:myfunc = $c
```

and verify that calling the function by name works:

```
PS (21) > myfunc
246
```

Set the closed variable yet again, but use `$c2` to access the module this time:

```
PS (22) > & $c2.Module sv x 3
```

And verify that it's changed when you call the named function:

```
PS (23) > myfunc
6
```

These examples should give you an idea how all of these pieces—scriptblocks, modules, closures, and functions—are related. This is how modules work. When a module is loaded, the exported functions are closures bound to the module object that was created. These closures are assigned to the names for the functions to import. A fairly small set of types and concepts allows you to achieve advanced programming scenarios. In the next section, we'll go back to looking at objects and see how dynamic modules make it easier to create custom object instances.

11.4.3 Creating custom objects from modules

There's one more thing you can do with dynamic modules: provide a simpler way to build custom objects. This is a logical step because modules have private data and public members just like objects. As modules, they're intended to address a different type of problem than objects, but given the similarity between objects and modules, it would make sense to be able to construct an object from a dynamic module. This is done using the `-AsCustomObject` parameter on `New-Module`. You'll use this mechanism to create a "point" object from a module. Here's what this looks like:

```
PS (1) > function New-Point
>> {
>>     New-Module -ArgumentList $args -AsCustomObject {
>>         param (
>>             [int] $x = 0,
>>             [int] $y = 0
>>         )
>>         function ToString()
>>         {
>>             "($x, $y)"
>>         }
>>         Export-ModuleMember -Function ToString -Variable x,y
>>     }
>> }
>>
```

Now let's try it. Begin by defining two points, $p1 and $p2:

```
PS (2) > $p1 = New-Point 1 1
PS (3) > $p2 = New-Point 2 3
```

You'll use string expansion to display these objects, which will call the `ToString()` method you exported from the module:

```
PS (4) > "p1 is $p1"
p1 is (1, 1)
PS (5) > "p2 is $p2"
p2 is (2, 3)
```

Now try to assign a string to the X member on one of the points:

```
PS (6) > $p1.X = "Hi"
Cannot convert value "Hi" to type "System.Int32". Error: "Input
string was not in a correct format."
At line:1 char:5
+ $p1. <<<< X = "Hi"
    + CategoryInfo          : InvalidOperation: (:) [], Runtime
   Exception
    + FullyQualifiedErrorId : PropertyAssignmentException

PS (7) >
```

This results in an error because the exported variable is a special type of note property that is backed by the variable. Because it's backed by the variable, any constraints on the variable also apply to the note property, allowing you to create strongly typed members on a synthetic object.

So far we've covered scriptblocks, modules, and closures in PowerShell. Although these features are somewhat exotic, they're found in most modern (or modernized) languages, including Java, JavaScript, Visual Basic, C#, Python, and so on. In the next section, we're going to cover a related feature that's unique to PowerShell: *steppable pipelines*. Normally once a pipeline starts, it runs to completion. With a steppable pipeline, you can cause the pipeline to process one object at a time (with some limitations.) This is a concrete form of metaprogramming, where one script has precise control over the sequence of operations in another.

11.5 STEPPABLE PIPELINES

Steppable pipelines existed in PowerShell v1 but were not exposed to the end user. In v2 this feature was made available to the end user. The core use of this feature is to allow one command to wrap, or *proxy*, other commands. In this section, we'll begin with a look at how the feature works and then explore a useful example showing its value.

11.5.1 How steppable pipelines work

The central concept in PowerShell programs is the pipeline, which processes a sequence of objects, one at a time. In chapter 2, we illustrated this with a diagram of the pipeline processor. Let's take another look (see figure 11.3).

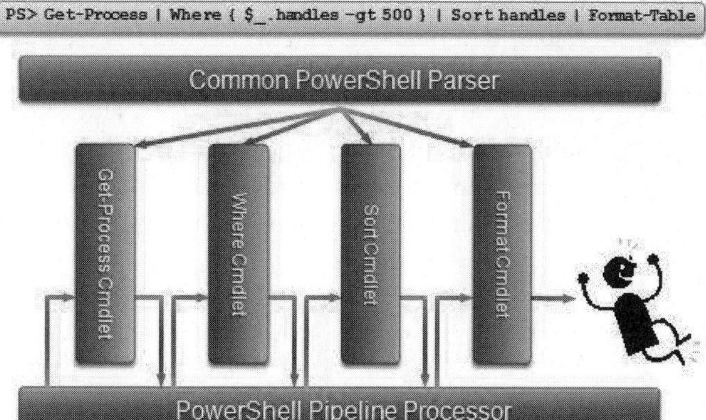

Figure 11.3 Objects flow through a pipeline one at a time. A common parser constructs each of the command objects and then starts the pipeline processor, stepping each object through all stages of the pipeline.

Each object is processed completely (ignoring things like sorting) before processing begins on the next one, but the pipeline itself has to process all objects in one go. There are times when it's useful to be able to start a pipeline and then feed it objects as needed. This is what a *steppable pipeline* lets you do. You can create a pipeline, start it (so all the `begin` clauses are executed), and then pass objects to it for processing one at a time. Let's see how to do this.

To get a steppable pipeline object, you need to have some object representation of a pipeline. The obvious way to do this is with a scriptblock object, and that's exactly how it works. First, create a scriptblock with exactly one pipeline in it:

```
PS (1) > $sb = { Select-Object name, length }
```

The "one pipeline" part is important—a steppable pipeline maps to a single pipeline, so the scriptblock used to create it must have only a single pipeline. Now get a steppable pipeline object:

```
PS (2) > $sp = $sb.GetSteppablePipeline()
```

Let's look at the type of object you got back and see what its members are:

```
PS (3) > $sp | Get-Member

   TypeName: System.Management.Automation.SteppablePipeline

Name        MemberType Definition
----        ---------- ----------
Begin       Method     System.Void Begin(bool expectInpu...
Dispose     Method     System.Void Dispose()
End         Method     array End()
Equals      Method     bool Equals(System.Object obj)
GetHashCode Method     int GetHashCode()
GetType     Method     type GetType()
Process     Method     array Process(System.Object input...
ToString    Method     string ToString()
```

In this list of members, you can see that there are methods that correspond to the clauses in a function: `Begin()`, `Process()`, and `End()`. These do what you'd expect: `Begin()` runs all the `begin` clauses in all of the commands in the pipeline, `Process()` runs all the `process` clauses, and `End()` runs all the `end` clauses. Let's try running this pipeline. When you call `Begin()` you have to pass a Boolean value telling the runtime whether to expect input. If there's no input, the pipeline will run to completion in a single step. You do want to pass input objects to the pipeline, so call `Begin()` with `$true`:

```
PS (4) > $sp.Begin($true)
```

You need to get some data objects to pass through the pipeline—you'll get a list of DLLs in the PowerShell install directory:

```
PS (5) > $dlls = dir $pshome -Filter *.dll
```

Now loop through this list, passing each element to the steppable pipeline:

```
PS (6) > foreach ($dll in $dlls) { $sp.Process($dll) }

Name                                                   Length
----                                                   ------
CompiledComposition.Micros...                          126976
PSEvents.dll                                            20480
pspluginwkr.dll                                        173056
pwrshmsg.dll                                             2048
pwrshsip.dll                                            28672
```

And you see that each element is processed through the pipeline. Finally, call the `End()`and `Dispose()` methods to clean up the pipeline:

```
PS (7) > $sp.End()

PS (8) > $sp.Dispose()
PS (9) >
```

What happens if you don't call them? If you don't call `End()`, you may not get all of the output from the pipeline. For example, if you're stepping a pipeline containing the `sort` cmdlet, it doesn't return its output until the end clause. And if you don't call `Dispose()`, then any resources held by cmdlets in the pipeline may not be cleaned up in a timely manner (for example, files may not be closed or other resources not released).

Now that you have an idea of how steppable pipelines work, let's look at how you can use them.

11.5.2 Creating a proxy command with steppable pipelines

In chapter 2, we discussed how the result of all of the things we type at the command line are streamed through `Out-Default` to display them on the screen. `Out-Default` uses steppable pipelines to run the formatter cmdlets to do its rendering and then calls `Out-Host` to display the formatted output. Let's see how you can add a frequently requested feature to the interactive experience using a proxy for `Out-Default`.

A commonly requested feature for interactive use is to capture the result of the last output object so it can be made available to the next pipeline. First, you enter a command that displays a result:

```
PS (1) > 2+2
4
```

You want to use that result in the next command you type, so it should be available in a variable called `$last`. This would let you do subsequent calculations like this:

```
PS (2) > $last+3
7
PS (3) > $last*7
49
```

This would be a nice feature, but it didn't make it into the product. Fortunately, with steppable pipelines and proxy functions, you can add this feature yourself. The trick is to wrap the `Out-Default` cmdlet in a proxy function. As mentioned in section 11.1.3, because functions are resolved before cmdlets, when the PowerShell host calls `Out-Default` to display output, it will call your function first. Now you could simply collect all of the output from the command the user typed and display it all at once, but that doesn't provide a good experience. Instead you'll create a steppable pipeline that runs the `Out-Default` cmdlet inside the `Out-Default` function. Every time the function receives an object, this object will be passed to the steppable pipeline to be rendered immediately. In the process of passing this object along, you can also assign it to the global `$LAST` variable. The function to do all of this is shown in the following listing.

Listing 11.1 Wrapper for the `Out-Default` cmdlet

```
function Out-Default
{
    [CmdletBinding(ConfirmImpact="Medium")]
    param(
        [Parameter(ValueFromPipeline=$true)] `
        [System.Management.Automation.PSObject] $InputObject
    )

    begin
    {

          $wrappedCmdlet = $ExecutionContext.InvokeCommand.GetCmdlet(
            "Out-Default")
          $sb = { & $wrappedCmdlet @PSBoundParameters }
          $__sp = $sb.GetSteppablePipeline()          <-- Create steppable
          $__sp.Begin($pscmdlet)                          pipeline wrapping
                                                          Out-Default
    }
    process
    {
            $do_process = $true
            if ($_ -is [System.Management.Automation.ErrorRecord])
            {
```

```
            if ($_.Exception -is
              [System.Management.Automation.CommandNotFoundException])
            {
                $__command = $_.Exception.CommandName
                if (Test-Path -Path $__command -PathType container)
                {
                    Set-Location $__command
                    $do_process = $false
                }
                elseif ($__command -match
                    '^http://|\.(com|org|net|edu)$')
                {
                    if ($matches[0] -ne "http://")
                    {
                        $__command = "HTTP://" + $__command
                    }
                    [System.Diagnostics.Process]::Start($__command)
                    $do_process = $false
                }
            }
        }
        if ($do_process)
        {
            $global:LAST = $_;
            $__sp.Process($_)
        }
    }
    end
    {
        $__sp.End()
    }
}
```

Check for command-not-found exceptions

If directory, cd there; if URL, open browser

Capture last output object

There are a couple of things to notice in this listing. First, when you start the steppable pipeline, rather than passing in a Boolean, you pass in the `$PSCmdlet` object (see chapter 8) for the function. This allows the steppable pipeline to write directly into the function's output and error streams so the function doesn't have to deal with any output from the pipeline. The next thing to notice is that this function does a couple of other useful things besides capturing the last output object. If the last command typed resulted in a "command not found" exception, then you check to see if the command was actually a path to a directory. If so, you set the current location to that directory. This allows you to type

```
c:\mydir\mysubdir
```

instead of

```
cd c:\mydir\mysubdir
```

The other thing you check is to see if the command looks like a URL. If it does, then try to open it in the browser. This lets you open a web page simply by typing the URL. Both of these are minor conveniences, but along with the `$LAST` variable, they make interactive use of PowerShell a more pleasant experience. This example should give you a sense of the flexibility that steppable pipelines provide.

We began this chapter with scriptblocks, moved from there to synthetic objects, then on to dynamic modules and closures, and finally to steppable pipelines. Now we're going to circle back to the type system and look at it in a bit more detail. We've covered the "nice" ways to add members to objects and build synthetic objects, so let's dig into the actual plumbing of the PowerShell type system. In the next section, we'll look at what's happening under the covers.

11.6 A CLOSER LOOK AT THE TYPE-SYSTEM PLUMBING

Earlier in this chapter, we said that the core of the PowerShell type system was the `PSObject` type. This type is used to wrap other objects, providing adaptation and inspection capabilities as well as a place to attach synthetic members. You've used `Get-Member` to explore objects and the `Add-Member`, `New-Object`, and `Select-Object` cmdlets to extend and create objects. In fact, you can do all of this directly by using the `PSObject` class itself. There's one thing you can't do without understanding `PSObject`: wrapping or shadowing an existing property. In this technique, the synthetic property calls the base property that it's hiding. (Don't worry; this is less esoteric than it sounds. A simple example will clarify what we're talking about here.)

> **NOTE** If you've done much object-oriented programming, this concept is similar to creating an override to a virtual method that calls the overridden method on the base class. The difference here is that it's all instance based; no new type is involved.

Let's look at `PSObject` in more detail. First, let's examine the properties on this object:

```
PS (1) > [psobject].getproperties() | %{$_.name}
Members
Properties
Methods
ImmediateBaseObject
BaseObject
TypeNames
```

From the list, you see some obvious candidates of interest. But how do you get at these members, given that the whole point of `PSObject` is to be invisible? The answer is that there's a special property attached to all objects in PowerShell called (surprise) `PSObject`. Let's look at this. First, you need a test object to work on. Use `Get-Item` to retrieve the `DirectoryInfo` object for the C: drive:

```
PS (2) > $f = Get-Item c:\
PS (3) > $f

    Directory:

Mode                LastWriteTime     Length Name
----                -------------     ------ ----
d--hs          5/29/2006   3:11 PM            C:\
```

Now let's look at the PSObject member attached to this object:

```
PS (4) > $f.psobject

Members             : {PSPath, PSParentPath, PSChildName, PSDriv
                      e...}
Properties          : {PSPath, PSParentPath, PSChildName, PSDriv
                      e...}
Methods             : {get_Name, get_Parent, CreateSubdirectory,
                       Create...}
ImmediateBaseObject : C:\
BaseObject          : C:\
TypeNames           : {System.IO.DirectoryInfo, System.IO.FileSy
                      stemInfo, System.MarshalByRefObject, Syste
                      m.Object}
```

Right away you see a wealth of information: all the properties you saw on the PSObject type, populated with all kinds of interesting data. First, let's look at the TypeNames member:

```
PS (6) > $f.psobject.typenames
System.IO.DirectoryInfo
System.IO.FileSystemInfo
System.MarshalByRefObject
System.Object
```

This member contains the names of all the types in the inheritance hierarchy for a DirectoryInfo object. (These types are all documented in the .NET class library documentation that's part of the Microsoft Developer Network [MSDN] collection. See http://msdn.microsoft.com for more information.)

We'll look at the Properties member next. This collection contains all the properties defined by this type. Let's get information about all the properties that contain the pattern "name":

```
PS (7) > $f.psobject.properties | where {$_.name -match "name"}

MemberType      : NoteProperty
IsSettable      : True
IsGettable      : True
Value           : C:\
TypeNameOfValue : System.String
Name            : PSChildName
IsInstance      : True

MemberType      : Property
Value           : C:\
IsSettable      : False
IsGettable      : True
TypeNameOfValue : System.String
Name            : Name
IsInstance      : True

MemberType      : Property
Value           : C:\
```

```
IsSettable       : False
IsGettable       : True
TypeNameOfValue : System.String
Name             : FullName
IsInstance       : True
```

This returned information on three properties, one NoteProperty PSPath and two base object properties, Name and FullName. You've seen these properties before; this is the same information that would be returned from Get-Member. This is exactly what Get-Member does—it uses the PSObject properties to get this information.

11.6.1 Adding a property

Now let's add a new member to this object. You could use Add-Member (and typically you would), but we're talking about the plumbing here, so we'll do it the hard way. First, you need to create the NoteProperty object that you want to add. Do this with the New-Object cmdlet:

```
PS (8) > $np = New-Object  `
>> System.Management.Automation.PSNoteProperty `
>> hi,"Hello there"
>>
```

Next, add it to the member collection:

```
PS (9) > $f.PSObject.Members.add($np)
```

And you're finished (so it wasn't really that hard after all). The hi member has been added to this object, so try it out:

```
PS (10) > $f.hi
Hello there
```

All of the normal members are still there:

```
PS (11) > $f.name
C:\
```

Now look at the member in the member collection:

```
PS (12) > $f.PSObject.Members | where {$_.name -match "^hi"}

MemberType       : NoteProperty
IsSettable       : True
IsGettable       : True
Value            : Hello there
TypeNameOfValue : System.String
Name             : hi
IsInstance       : True
```

Notice the Value member on the object. Because you can get at the member, you can also set the member

```
PS (13) > ($f.PSObject.Members | where {
>> $_.name -match "^hi"}).value = "Goodbye!"
```

```
>>
PS (14) > $f.hi
Goodbye!
```

which is equivalent to setting the property directly on `$f`:

```
PS (15) > $f.hi = "Hello again!"
PS (16) > $f.PSObject.Members | where {$_.name -match "^hi"}

MemberType      : NoteProperty
IsSettable      : True
IsGettable      : True
Value           : Hello again!
TypeNameOfValue : System.String
Name            : hi
IsInstance      : True
```

The `Value` member on the note property is "Hello again!"

In section 11.4.3 you saw a different type of note property used when constructing objects out of modules. This type of note property is backed by a variable. You can also create an instance of this type of property. But first you need a variable to use to back the property value:

```
PS (15) > [int] $VariableProperty = 0
```

Now create the `PSVariableProperty` object, passing in the variable to bind:

```
PS (16) > $vp = New-Object `
>>     System.Management.Automation.PSVariableProperty `
>>     (Get-Variable VariableProperty)
>>
```

Note that the name of the property and the name of the variable will be the same. Add the property

```
PS (17) > $f.psobject.members.add($vp)
```

and verify that it can be read and written:

```
PS (18) > $f.VariableProperty
0
PS (19) > $f.VariableProperty = 7
PS (20) > $f.VariableProperty
7
```

So you can read and write integers, but the backing variable was constrained to be an integer. Let's verify that the constraint was preserved by trying to assign a string to it:

```
PS (21) > $f.VariableProperty = "Hi"
Cannot convert value "Hi" to type "System.Int32". Error: "Input
string was not in a correct format."
At line:1 char:4
+ $f. <<<< VariableProperty = "Hi"
    + CategoryInfo          : InvalidOperation: (:) [], Runtime
   Exception
    + FullyQualifiedErrorId : PropertyAssignmentException
```

You get the error just like you saw in section 11.4.3 when you exported a constrained variable from a module as a property.

11.6.2 Shadowing an existing property

There's one last item to cover in our discussion of the plumbing: the mechanism that allows you to bypass the adapted members and lets you get at the raw object underneath. This is accomplished through another special member on `PSObject` called `PSBase`. This member allows you to get at the object directly, bypassing all the synthetic member lookup. It also makes it possible to create a synthetic member to adapt an existing member. We can clarify this with an example. Say you want to change the `name` property on a `DirectoryInfo` object to always return the name in uppercase. Here's what it looks like unadapted:

```
PS (18) > $f = Get-Item c:\windows
PS (19) > $f.name
windows
```

To do this, create a new `PSProperty` object called `Name` that will "shadow" the existing property:

```
PS (20) > $n=New-Object Management.Automation.PSScriptProperty `
>>     name,{$this.psbase.name.ToUpper()}
>>
```

In the body of the scriptblock for this `PSProperty`, you'll use `$this.psbase` to get at the `name` property on the base object (if you just accessed the `name` property directly, you'd be calling yourself). You apply the `ToUpper()` method on the string returned by name to acquire the desired result. Now add the member to the object's member collection

```
PS (21) > $f.psobject.members.add($n)
```

and try it out:

```
PS (22) > $f.name
WINDOWS
```

When you access the `name` property on this object, the synthetic member you created gets called instead of the base member, so the name is returned in uppercase. The base object's `name` property is unchanged and can be retrieved through `psbase.name`:

```
PS (23) > $f.psbase.name
windows
PS (24) >
```

Although this isn't a technique that you'll typically use on a regular basis, it allows you to do some pretty sophisticated work. You could use it to add validation logic, for example, and prevent a property from being set to an undesired value. You could also use it to log accesses to a property to gather information about how your script or application is being used.

With a solid understanding of the plumbing, you're ready to use everything you've learned and do some applied metaprogramming. In the next section, you'll learn how to write a domain-specific extension to PowerShell.

11.7 EXTENDING THE POWERSHELL LANGUAGE

In the previous section, you learned how to add members to existing objects one at a time, but sometimes you'll want to construct new types rather than extend the existing types. In this section, we'll explain how to do that and also how to use scripting techniques to "add" the ability to create objects to the PowerShell language.

11.7.1 Little languages

The idea of *little languages*—small, domain-specific languages—has been around for a long time. This was one of the powerful ideas that made the UNIX environment so attractive. Many of the tools that were the roots for today's dynamic languages came from this environment.

In effect, all programs are essentially an exercise in building their own languages. You create the nouns (objects) and verbs (methods or functions) in this language. These patterns are true for all languages that support data abstraction. Dynamic languages go further because they allow you to extend how the nouns, verbs, and modifiers are composed in the language. For example, in a language such as C#, it'd be difficult to add a new looping construct. In PowerShell, this is minor. To illustrate how easy it is, let's define a new looping keyword called *loop*. This construct will repeat the body of the loop for the number of times the first argument specifies. You can add this keyword by defining a function that takes a number and scriptblock. Here's the definition:

```
PS (1) > function loop ([int] $i, [scriptblock] $b) {
>> while ($i-- -gt 0) { . $b }
>> }
>>
```

Try it out:

```
PS (2) > loop 3 { "Hello world" }
Hello world
Hello world
Hello world
PS (3) >
```

In a few lines of code, you've added a new flow-control statement to the PowerShell language that looks pretty much like any of the existing flow-control statements.

You can apply this technique to creating language elements that allow you to define your own custom types. Let's add some "class" to PowerShell!

11.7.2 Adding a CustomClass keyword to PowerShell

Next you'll use the technique from the previous section to extend the PowerShell language to allow you to define your own custom classes. First, let's gather the requirements. You want the syntax for defining a class to look fairly natural (at least for PowerShell). Here's what you want a class definition to look like:

```
CustomClass point {
    note x 0
    note y 0
    method ToString { "($($this.x), $($this.y))"}
    method scale {
        $this.x *= $args[0]
        $this.y *= $args[0]
    }
}
```

Once you've defined this custom class, you want to be able to use it as follows. First, create a new instance of the `point` class:

```
$p = new point
```

> **NOTE** The `new` command here is not an alias for the `New-Object` cmdlet. The cmdlet creates new instances of .NET or COM objects. It doesn't know anything about the "classes" we're defining here. Instead, it's a custom function that we'll get to in a minute.

Then, set the `x` and `y` members on this instance to particular values:

```
$p.x=2
$p.y=3
```

Finally, call the `ToString()` method to display the class:

```
$p.ToString()
```

This will give you a natural way to define a class in PowerShell. Now let's look at implementing these requirements.

> **NOTE** In section 11.4.3 you saw how you could do this with dynamic modules. The focus here is to see how you can directly implement this type of facility. In practical circumstances, this dynamic module approach is certainly easier.

We'll put the code for this script in a file called class.ps1. Let's go over the contents of that script a piece at a time. (The complete script is included in the book's source code.)

First, you need a place to store the types you're defining. You need to use a global variable for this, because you want it to persist for the duration of the session. Give it a name that's unlikely to collide with other variables (you'll put two underscores at each end to help ensure this) and initialize it to an empty hashtable:

```
$global:__ClassTable__ = @{}
```

Next, define the function needed to create an instance of one of the classes you'll create. This function will take only one argument: the scriptblock that creates an instance of this class. This function will invoke the scriptblock provided to it. This scriptblock is expected to return a collection of synthetic member objects. The function will then take these members and attach them to the object being created. This is a helper function that also has to be global, so again you'll give it a name that's unlikely to collide with other global functions:

```
function global:__new_instance ([scriptblock] $definition)
{
```

At this point you define some local functions to use in the body of the `__new_instance` function. First, define a helper method for generating error messages:

```
    function elementSyntax ($msg)
    {
        throw "class element syntax: $msg"
    }
```

In the example, you had keywords for each of the member types you could add. You'll implement this by defining functions that implement these keywords. Because of the way dynamic scoping works (see chapter 7), these functions will be visible to the scriptblock when it's invoked, because they're defined in the enclosing dynamic scope.

First, define the function for creating a note element in the class. This implements the note keyword in the class definition. It takes the name of the note and the value to assign to it and returns a `PSNoteProperty` object to the caller:

```
     function note ([string]$name, $value)
    {
        if (! $name) {
            elementSyntax "note name <value>"
        }
        New-Object Management.Automation.PSNoteProperty `
            $name,$value
    }
```

Next, define the function that implements the method keyword. This function takes the method name and scriptblock that will be the body of the method and returns a `PSScriptMethod` object:

```
    function method ([string]$name, [scriptblock] $script)
    {
        if (! $name) {
            elementSyntax "method name <value>"
        }
        New-Object Management.Automation.PSScriptMethod `
            $name,$script
    }
```

You could continue to define keyword functions for all the other member types, but to keep it simple, stick with just these two.

Having defined your keyword functions, you can look at the code that actually builds the object. First, create an empty `PSObject` with no methods or properties:

```
    $object = New-Object Management.Automation.PSObject
```

Next, execute the scriptblock that defines the body of this class. As mentioned previously, the result of that execution will be the set of members to attach to the new object you're creating:

```
    $members = &$definition
```

Finally, attach the members to the object:

```
    foreach ($member in $members) {
        if (! $member) {
            Write-Error "bad member $member"
        } else {
                $object.psobject.members.Add($member)
        }
    }
```

The last thing to do is return the constructed object:

```
    $object
}
```

As mentioned, the _new_instance function was a worker function; the user never calls it directly. Now define the function that the user employs to define a new class. Again, this has to be a global function, but this time, because the user calls it, you'll give it a conventional name:

```
function global:CustomClass
{
```

This function takes the name of the class and the scriptblock to execute to produce the members that will be attached to that class:

```
    param ([string] $type, [scriptblock] $definition)
```

If there's already a class defined by the name that the user passed, throw an error:

```
    if ($global:__ClassTable__[$type]) {
        throw "type $type is already defined"
    }
```

At this point, you'll execute the scriptblock to build an instance of the type that will be discarded. You do this to catch any errors in the definition at the time the class is defined, instead of the first time the class is used. It's not strictly necessary to do this, but it will help you catch any errors sooner rather than later:

```
    __new_instance $definition > $null
```

Finally, add the class to the hashtable of class definitions

```
    $global:__ClassTable__[$type] = $definition
}
```

and you're finished implementing the class keyword. Next you have to define the new keyword. This turns out to be a simple function. The new keyword takes the name of the class you want to create an instance of, looks up the scriptblock to execute, and calls `__new_instance` to build the object:

```
function global:new ([string] $type)
{
    $definition = $__ClassTable__[$type]
    if (! $definition) {
        throw "$type is undefined"
    }
    __new_instance $definition
}
```

Finally, add one last helper function that will allow you to remove a class definition from the hashtable:

```
function remove-class ([string] $type)
{
    $__ClassTable__.remove($type)
}
```

This, then, is the end of the class.ps1 script. You should try it out with the point example you saw at the beginning of this section. First run the script containing the code to set up all the definitions. (Because you explicitly defined things to be global in the script, there's no need to "dot" this script.)

```
PS (1) > ./class
```

Now define the point class:

```
PS (2) > CustomClass point {
>>     note x 0
>>     note y 0
>>     method ToString { "($($this.x), $($this.y))"}
>>     method scale {
>>         $this.x *= $args[0]
>>         $this.y *= $args[0]
>>     }
>> }
>>
```

Next, create an instance of this class:

```
PS (3) > $p = new point
```

Use `Get-Member` to look at the members on the object that was created:

```
PS (4) > $p | Get-Member

   TypeName: System.Management.Automation.PSCustomObject

Name        MemberType   Definition
----        ----------   ----------
Equals      Method       System.Boolean Equals(Object obj)
GetHashCode Method       System.Int32 GetHashCode()
GetType     Method       System.Type GetType()
```

```
x          NoteProperty System.Int32 x=0
y          NoteProperty System.Int32 y=0
scale      ScriptMethod System.Object scale();
ToString   ScriptMethod System.Object ToString();
```

You see the actual type of the object is `PSCustomType`—the type that PowerShell uses for pure synthetic objects. You can also see the members you defined in the class definition: the two note properties, `x` and `y`, and the two methods, `scale()` and `ToString()`. To try them out, first call `ToString()`:

```
PS (5) > $p.tostring()
(0, 0)
```

You see the default values for the note members, formatted as intended. Next, set the note members to new values:

```
PS (6) > $p.x=2
PS (7) > $p.y=3
```

Verify that they've been set:

```
PS (8) > $p.tostring()
(2, 3)
```

Now call the `scale()` method to multiply each note member by a scale value:

```
PS (9) > $p.scale(3)
```

And again, verify the values of the note members with `ToString()`:

```
PS (10) > $p.tostring()
(6, 9)
```

The values have been scaled.

Finally, to see how well this all works, use this object with the format operator, and you'll see that your `ToString()` method is properly called:

```
PS (11) > "The point p is {0}" -f $p
The point p is (6, 9)
```

So, in less than 100 lines of PowerShell script, you've added a new keyword that lets you define you own classes in PowerShell. Obviously, this isn't a full-featured type definition system; it doesn't have any form of inheritance, for example. But it does illustrate how you can use scriptblocks along with dynamic scoping to build new language features in PowerShell in a sophisticated way.

Now let's change gears a bit to talk about types.

11.7.3 Type extension

You might have noticed that all the examples we've looked at so far involve adding members to instances. But what about adding members to types? Having to explicitly add members to every object you encounter would be pretty tedious, no matter how clever you are. You need some way to extend types. Of course, PowerShell also lets you do this. In this section, we'll introduce the mechanisms that PowerShell provides that let you extend types.

Type extension is performed in PowerShell through a set of XML configuration files. These files are usually loaded at startup time, but they can be extended after the shell has started. In this section, you'll learn how to take advantage of these features.

Let's look at an example. Consider an array of numbers. It's fairly common to sum up a collection of numbers; unfortunately, there's no `Sum()` method on the `Array` class:

```
PS (1) > (1,2,3,4).sum()
Method invocation failed because [System.Object[]] doesn't conta
in a method named 'sum'.
At line:1 char:14
+ (1,2,3,4).sum( <<<< )
```

Using the techniques we've discussed, you could add such a method to this array:

```
PS (3) > $a = Add-Member -PassThru -in $a scriptmethod sum {
>> $r=0
>> foreach ($e in $this) {$r += $e}
>> $r
>> }
>>
```

And finally use it:

```
PS (4) > $a.sum()
10
```

But this would be painful to do for every instance of an array. What you need is a way to attach new members to a type, rather than through an instance. PowerShell does this through type configuration files. These configuration files are stored in the installation directory for PowerShell and loaded at startup. The installation directory path for PowerShell is stored in the `$PSHome` variable, so it's easy to find these files. They have the word *type* in their names and have an extension of .ps1xml:

```
PS (5) > dir $pshome/*type*.ps1xml

    Directory: Microsoft.PowerShell.Core\FileSystem::C:\Program
    Files\Windows PowerShell\v1.0


Mode                LastWriteTime     Length Name
----                -------------     ------ ----
-a---         4/19/2006   4:12 PM      50998 DotNetTypes.Format.
                                             ps1xml
-a---         4/19/2006   4:12 PM     117064 types.ps1xml
```

You don't want to update the default installed types files because when you install updates for PowerShell, they'll likely be overwritten and your changes will be lost. Instead, create your own custom types file containing the specification of the new member for `System.Array`. Once you've created the file, you can use the

Update-TypeData cmdlet to load it. Here's the definition for the Sum() method extension you want to add to System.Array:

```
<Types>
   <Type>
        <Name>System.Array</Name>
        <Members>
            <ScriptMethod>
                <Name>Sum</Name>
                <Script>
                    $r=$null
                    foreach ($e in $this) {$r += $e}
                    $r
                </Script>
            </ScriptMethod>
        </Members>
    </Type>
</Types>
```

This definition is saved to a file called SumMethod.ps1xml. Now load the file and update the type system definitions:

```
PS (9) > Update-TypeData SumMethod.ps1xml
```

If the file loads successfully, you won't see any output. You can now try out the sum() function:

```
PS (10) > (1,2,3,4,5).sum()
15
```

It worked. And, because of the way the script was written, it will work on any type that can be added. So let's add some strings:

```
PS (11) > ("abc","def","ghi").Sum()
abcdefghi
```

You can even use it to add hashtables:

```
PS (12) > (@{a=1},@{b=2},@{c=3}).sum()

Name                           Value
----                           -----
a                              1
b                              2
c                              3
```

You can see that the result is the composition of all three of the original hashtables. You can even use it to put a string back together. Here's the "hal" to "ibm" example from chapter 3, this time using the Sum() method:

```
PS (13) > ([char[]] "hal" | %{[char]([int]$_+1)}).sum()
ibm
```

Here you break the original string into an array of characters, add 1 to each character, and then use the Sum() method to add them all back into a string.

You should take some time to examine the set of type configuration files that are part of the default PowerShell installation. Examining these files is a good way to see what you can accomplish using these tools.

We've covered an enormous amount of material so far in this chapter, introducing ideas that are pretty new to a lot of users. If you've hung on to this point, congratulations! There are only a few more topics to complete your knowledge of metaprogramming with PowerShell. Scriptblocks, dynamic modules, and closures can be passed around, invoked, and assigned at runtime, but the body of these blocks is still defined at compile time. In the next section we'll expand our repertoire of techniques by looking at ways to dynamically create code.

11.8 BUILDING SCRIPT CODE AT RUNTIME

This final section presents the mechanisms that PowerShell provides for compiling script code and creating new scriptblocks at runtime. To saying that you're "compiling" when PowerShell is an interpreted language may sound a odd, but that's essentially what creating a scriptblock is: a piece of script text is compiled into an executable object. In addition, PowerShell provides mechanisms for directly executing a string, bypassing the need to first build a scriptblock. In the next few sections we'll look at how each of these features works.

11.8.1 The Invoke-Expression cmdlet

The `Invoke-Expression` cmdlet is a way to execute an arbitrary string as a piece of code. It takes the string, compiles it, and then immediately executes it in the current scope. Here's an example:

```
PS (1) > Invoke-Expression '$a=2+2; $a'
4
```

In this example, the script passed to the cmdlet assigned the result of `2+2` to `$a` and wrote `$a` to the output stream. Because this expression was evaluated in the current context, it should also have affected the value of `$a` in the global scope:

```
PS (2) > $a
4
```

You see that it did. Now invoke another expression:

```
PS (3) > Invoke-Expression '$a++'
PS (4) > $a
5
```

Evaluating this expression changes the value of `$a` to 5.

There are no limits on what you can evaluate with `Invoke-Expression`. It can take any arbitrary piece of script code. Here's an example where you build a string with several statements in it and execute it:

```
PS (5) > $expr = '$a=10;'
PS (6) > $expr += 'while ($a--) { $a }'
```

```
PS (7) > $expr += '"A is now $a"'
PS (8) > [string](Invoke-Expression $expr)
9 8 7 6 5 4 3 2 1 0 A is now -1
```

The first three commands in this example build a string to execute. The first line initializes the variable `$a`, the second adds a `while` loop that decrements and outputs `$a`, and the third line outputs a string telling you the final value of `$a`. Note the double quoting in the last script fragment. Without the nested double quotes, it would try to execute the first word in the string instead of emitting the whole string.

11.8.2 The ExecutionContext variable

One of the predefined variables (also called automatic variables) provided by the PowerShell engine is `$ExecutionContext`. This variable is another way to get at various facilities provided by the PowerShell engine. It's intended to mimic the interfaces available to the cmdlet author. The services that matter most to us in this chapter are those provided through the `InvokeCommand` member. Let's look at the methods this member provides:

```
PS (1) > $ExecutionContext.InvokeCommand | Get-Member

   TypeName: System.Management.Automation.CommandInvocationIntri
nsics

Name            MemberType Definition
----            ---------- ----------
Equals          Method     System.Boolean Equals(Object obj)
ExpandString    Method     System.String ExpandString(String s...
GetHashCode     Method     System.Int32 GetHashCode()
GetType         Method     System.Type GetType()
InvokeScript    Method     System.Collections.ObjectModel.Coll...
NewScriptBlock  Method     System.Management.Automation.Script...
ToString        Method     System.String ToString()
```

The interesting methods in this list are `ExpandString()`, `InvokeScript()`, and `NewScriptBlock()`. These methods are covered in the next few sections.

11.8.3 The ExpandString() method

The `ExpandString()` method lets you perform the same kind of variable interpolation that the PowerShell runtime does in scripts. Here's an example. First, set `$a` to a known quantity:

```
PS (2) > $a = 13
```

Next, create a variable `$str` that will display the value of `$a`:

```
PS (3) > $str='a is $a'
```

Because the variable was assigned using single quotes, no string expansion took place. You can verify this by displaying the string:

```
PS (4) > $str
a is $a
```

Now call the ExpandString() method, passing in $str:

```
PS (5) > $ExecutionContext.InvokeCommand.ExpandString($str)
a is 13
```

It returns the string with the variable expanded into its value.

11.8.4 The InvokeScript() method

The next method to look at is InvokeScript(). This method does the same thing that the Invoke-Expression cmdlet does (in fact, the cmdlet just calls the method). It takes its argument and evaluates it like a script. Call this method passing in the string "2+2"

```
PS (7) > $ExecutionContext.InvokeCommand.InvokeScript("2+2")
4
```

and it will return 4.

11.8.5 Mechanisms for creating scriptblocks

The final method is the NewScriptBlock() method. Like InvokeScript(), this method takes a string, but instead of executing it, it returns a scriptblock object that represents the compiled script. Let's use this method to turn the string '1..4 | foreach {$_ * 2}' into a scriptblock:

```
PS (8) > $sb = $ExecutionContext.InvokeCommand.NewScriptBlock(
>> '1..4 | foreach {$_ * 2}')
>>
```

You saved this scriptblock into a variable, so let's look at it. Because the ToString() on a scriptblock is the code of the scriptblock, you just see the code that makes up the body of the scriptblock:

```
PS (9) > $sb
1..4 | foreach {$_ * 2}
```

Now execute the scriptblock using the & call operator:

```
PS (10) > & $sb
2
4
6
8
```

The scriptblock executed, printing out the even numbers from 2 to 8.

PowerShell v2 introduced a simpler way of doing this by using a static method on the ScriptBlock class. Here's how to use this static factory class:

```
PS (11) > $sb = [scriptblock]::Create('1..4 | foreach {$_ * 2}')
PS (12) > & $sb
2
4
6
```

```
8
PS (13) >
```

Using the [scriptblock] type accelerator, the newer mechanism is significantly simpler than the rather long expression in the earlier example.

> **NOTE** Many people have asked why we (the PowerShell team) don't allow you to cast a string to a scriptblock. The reason is that we want to make the system resilient against code injection attacks. We want to minimize the number of places where executable code can be injected into the system, and we particularly want code creation to be an explicit act. Casts are more easily hidden, leading to accidental code injections, especially when the system may prompt for a string. We don't want those user-provided strings to be converted into code without some kind of check. See chapter 18 for more extensive discussions about security.

11.8.6 Creating functions using the function: drive

The final way to create a scriptblock is a side effect of creating elements in the function: drive. Earlier you saw that it's possible to create a named function by assigning a scriptblock to a name in the function: drive:

```
PS (1) > $function:foo = {"Hello there"}
PS (2) > foo
Hello there
```

You could also use the Set-Item or New-Item cmdlet to do this. For example:

```
PS (3) > New-Item function:foo -value {"Hi!"}
New-Item : The item at path 'foo' already exists.
At line:1 char:9
+ New-Item  <<<< function:foo -value {"Hi!"}
```

You received an error because the function already exists, so use the -Force parameter to overwrite the existing definition:

```
PS (4) > New-Item function:foo -value {"Hi!"} -Force

CommandType      Name                      Definition
-----------      ----                      ----------
Function         foo                       "Hi!"
```

New-Item returns the item created, so you can see that the function has been changed. But that's using scriptblocks. What happens if you pass in strings? The interpreter will compile these strings into scriptblocks and then assign the scriptblock to the name. Here's an example where the body of the function is determined by the expanded string:

```
PS (5) > $x=5
PS (6) > $y=6
PS (7) > $function:foo = "$x*$y"
```

```
PS (8) > foo
30
PS (9) > $function:foo
5*6
```

The variables `$x` and `$y` expanded into the numbers 5 and 6 in the string, so the resulting scriptblock was

```
{5*6}
```

Now define another function using `foo`, but add some more text to the function:

```
PS (10) > New-Item function:bar -Value "$function:foo*3"

CommandType     Name                          Definition
-----------     ----                          ----------
Function        bar                           5*6*3

PS (11) > bar
90
```

In the expanded string, `$function:foo` expanded into "5*6", so the new function bar was assigned a scriptblock `{5*6*3}`.

This finishes our discussion of the techniques PowerShell provides for compiling script code at runtime. In the next section we'll look at how to embed static languages like C# and Visual Basic in your scripts. This ability to embed fragments of C# or Visual Basic vastly increases what can be done directly with scripts but at the cost of some increase in complexity.

11.9 COMPILING CODE WITH ADD-TYPE

In the previous section, we covered techniques for compiling script code at runtime. In this section, you'll learn how to inline code written in static languages into your scripts. The key to doing this is the `Add-Type` cmdlet, introduced in PowerShell v2.

With the `Add-Type` cmdlet, you can embed code fragments written in compiled languages like C# or Visual Basic in your scripts and then compile that code when the scripts are loaded. A particularly interesting application of this technique is that you can create dynamic binary modules. This combines some of the best aspects of script modules with binary modules.

`Add-Type` fills in another other hole in the PowerShell v1 functionality: you can use it to dynamically load existing assemblies at runtime. Finally, this cmdlet can be used to simplify writing scripts that compile static language code into libraries or executables.

11.9.1 Defining a new .NET class: C#

Let's jump into an example where you'll dynamically add a new .NET class at runtime. You'll write the code for this class using C#. It's a simple class, so even if you aren't a C# programmer, you should be able to follow along. The fragment looks like this:

```
Add-Type @'
using System;

public static class Example1
{
    public static string Reverse(string s)
    {
        Char[] sc = s.ToCharArray();
        Array.Reverse(sc);
        return new string(sc);
    }
}
'@
```

Now run this code:

```
PS (7) > Add-Type @'
>> using System;
>>
>> public static class Example1
>> {
>>     public static string Reverse(string s)
>>     {
>>         Char[] sc = s.ToCharArray();
>>         Array.Reverse(sc);
>>         return new string(sc);
>>     }
>> }
>> '@
>>
```

This command should have run with no errors. Once it's run, use the new type that you've added:

```
PS(8) > [example1]::Reverse("hello there")
ereht olleh
PS (STA) (9) >
```

And there you go. You now have a new method for reversing strings. You could also have saved the file externally and then loaded it at runtime. Put the C# code into a file example1.cs, which looks like this:

```
PS (9) > Get-Content example1.cs
using System;

public static class Example1
{
    public static string Reverse(string s)
    {
        Char[] sc = s.ToCharArray();
        Array.Reverse(sc);
        return new string(sc);
    }
}
```

And now you can add this to your session:

```
PS (MTA) (15) > Add-Type -Path example1.cs
```

11.9.2 Defining a new enum at runtime

An enum type in .NET is a way of creating a fixed set of name-value constants. The ability to define these types is missing from PowerShell, but you can work around this by using Add-Type. You'll define an enum that can be used to specify a coffee order. You'll constrain the types of coffee orders you'll allow to Latte, Mocha, Americano, Cappuccino, or Espresso. First, set a variable to the list of drink types:

```
PS (1) > $beverages = "Latte, Mocha, Americano, Cappuccino, Espresso"
```

Pass a string to Add-Type that contains the fragment of C# needed to define an enum type:

```
PS (2) > Add-Type "public enum BeverageType { $beverages }"
```

It should be easy to see what's going on. You're defining a public type called BeverageType using the list of drinks in $beverages. Now that you have the type defined, you can use it in a function to create new drink orders:

```
PS (3) > function New-DrinkOrder ([BeverageType] $beverage)
>> {
>>     "A $beverage was ordered"
>> }
>>
```

This function uses the enum to constrain the type of the argument to the function and then return a string showing what was ordered. Use the function to order a latte:

```
PS (4) > New-DrinkOrder latte
A Latte was ordered
```

And the order goes through. Notice that casing of the drink name matches what was in the DrinkOrder enum definition, not what was in the argument. This is because the argument contains an instance of the DrinkOrder type and not the original string. Let's try to order something other than a coffee and see what happens:

```
PS (5) > New-DrinkOrder coke
New-DrinkOrder : Cannot process argument transformation on parameter
'beverage'. Cannot convert value "coke" to type "BeverageType" due to
invalid enumeration values. Specify one of the following enumeration
values and try again. The possible enumeration values are "Latte, Mocha,
Americano, Cappuccino, Espresso".
At line:1 char:10
+ New-DrinkOrder <<<<  coke
    + CategoryInfo          : InvalidData: (:) [New-Order],
    ParameterBindin...mationException
    + FullyQualifiedErrorId : ParameterArgumentTransformationError,
    New-Order
```

This results in a somewhat verbose but helpful error message telling you why the order failed and what the valid drink types are. That's all well and good, but the customer really wants a Coke. So modify the enum definition to include Coke in the list of beverages:

```
PS (6) > $beverages += ", Coke"
```

And call Add-Type again:

```
PS (7) > Add-Type "public enum BeverageType { $beverages }"
Add-Type : Cannot add type. The type name 'BeverageType' already exis
ts.
At line:1 char:9
+ Add-Type <<<<  "public enum BeverageType { $beverages }"
    + CategoryInfo          : InvalidOperation: (BeverageType:String
   ) [Add-Type], Exception
    + FullyQualifiedErrorId : TYPE_ALREADY_EXISTS,Microsoft.PowerShe
   ll.Commands.AddTypeCommand
```

This time it fails. Remember what we said about static types: once they're defined, they can't be changed. This is something to consider when using Add-Type to inline static code in a script. Static type definitions mean that the script isn't as easy to update as a normal PowerShell-only script. Now let's look at how Add-Type can be combined with dynamic modules.

11.9.3 Dynamic binary modules

Like dynamic script modules, a dynamic binary module is constructed in memory rather than loaded from disk. This is where Add-Type comes in. The content of a binary module is defined by a compiled assembly, not script text, and Add-Type lets you build these in-memory assemblies. Look at the following example script that constructs a binary module. This script packages the C# code for a cmdlet into a here-string. It then uses Add-Type to produce the required in-memory assembly, which it passes to Import-Module.

Listing 11.2 The ExampleModuleScript

```
$code = @'                                        <-- Contains cmdlet code
using System.Management.Automation;

[Cmdlet("Write", "InputObject")]
public class MyWriteInputObjectCmdlet : Cmdlet
{
    [Parameter]
    public string Parameter1;

    [Parameter(Mandatory = true, ValueFromPipeline=true)]
    public string InputObject;

    protected override void ProcessRecord()
    {
```

```
        if (Parameter1 != null)
            WriteObject(Parameter1 + ":" + InputObject);
        else
            WriteObject(InputObject);
    }
}
'@
$bin = Add-Type $code -PassThru        # Compile code in memory
$bin.Assembly | Import-Module          # Get assembly ref from type
```

The one wrinkle in this approach is the fact that `Add-Type` returns type objects, not assemblies. Fortunately, this is easy to work around: the type object makes its containing assembly available through the `Assembly` property. Let's try out the script. First load it:

```
PS (2) > ./ExampleModuleScript
```

Then check to see if the module has been created:

```
PS (3) > Get-Module

ModuleType Name                      ExportedCommands
---------- ----                      ----------------
Binary     dynamic_code_module_1t... Write-InputObject
```

And there it is. Next, get the `CommandInfo` object for the new cmdlet:

```
PS (4) > $cmd = Get-Command Write-InputObject
PS (5) > $cmd | fl

Name             : Write-InputObject
CommandType      : Cmdlet
Definition       : Write-InputObject [-Parameter1 <String>] -Inp
                   utObject <String> [-Verbose] [-Debug] [-Error
                   Action <ActionPreference>] [-WarningAction <A
                   ctionPreference>] [-ErrorVariable <String>] [
                   -WarningVariable <String>] [-OutVariable <Str
                   ing>] [-OutBuffer <Int32>]


Path             :
AssemblyInfo     :
DLL              :
HelpFile         : -Help.xml
ParameterSets    : {[-Parameter1 <String>] -InputObject <String>
                    [-Verbose] [-Debug] [-ErrorAction <ActionPre
                   ference>] [-WarningAction <ActionPreference>]
                    [-ErrorVariable <String>] [-WarningVariable
                   <String>] [-OutVariable <String>] [-OutBuffer
                    <Int32>]}
ImplementingType : MyWriteInputObjectCmdlet
Verb             : Write
Noun             : InputObject
```

Notice that the `Path`, `DLL`, and `AssemblyInfo` fields for this command are empty. Because the assembly for a dynamic binary module is in-memory only, these items are empty. They need an assembly that was loaded from disk in order to be defined.

Dynamic binary modules make it possible to get the advantages of a script module (being able to read the script) along with the advantages of compiled code (speed and static type checking). The only disadvantage to the user compared with regular binary modules is that the load time may be a bit longer.

11.10 SUMMARY

In this chapter, we covered advanced topics in programming and metaprogramming with PowerShell. Although many of the techniques covered in the chapter are quite advanced, used appropriately they can significantly improve your productivity as a scripter. You'll also see in later chapters how language elements such as scriptblocks make graphical programming in PowerShell easy and elegant. In this chapter we covered the following topics:

- Metaprogramming is a set of powerful techniques that essentially "crack open" the PowerShell runtime. They allow you to extend the runtime with new keywords and control structures. You can directly add properties and methods to objects in PowerShell; this is useful because it lets you adapt or extend objects logically in specific problem domains.
- The fundamental unit of PowerShell code, including the content of all functions, scripts, and modules, is actually scriptblocks. Scriptblocks also let you define methods that can be added to objects as script methods. Scriptblocks don't necessarily need to be named, and they can be used in many situations, including as the content of variables. Although scriptblocks are the key to all of the metaprogramming features in PowerShell, they're also an "everyday" feature that users work with all the time when they use the `ForEach-Object` and `Where-Object` cmdlets.
- The call operator `&` allows you to invoke commands indirectly, that is, by reference rather than by name (a scriptblock is just a reference). This also works with the `CommandInfo` objects returned from `Get-Command`.
- When using the `Update-TypeData` cmdlet, you can load type configuration files that allow you to extend a type instead of a single instance of that type.
- PowerShell supports the use of "little language," or domain-specific language techniques, to extend the core language. This allows you to more naturally specify solutions for problems in a particular domain.
- There are a variety of techniques for compiling and executing code at runtime. You can use the `Invoke-Expression` cmdlet, engine invocation intrinsics on

the `$ExecutionContext` variable, or the `CreateScriptBlock()` static method on the `[scriptblock]` type.

- Dynamic modules allow you to do local isolation in a script. They also underlie the implementation of closures in PowerShell and provide a simpler way to create custom objects.
- The `Add-Type` cmdlet lets you work with compiled languages from within PowerShell. It also provides a means to embed code in these languages directly in your scripts. This ability adds significant power to the environment at some cost in complexity.
- `Add-Type` also makes it possible to create dynamic binary modules, allowing you to combine some of the benefits of both static and dynamic coding techniques.

CHAPTER 12

Remoting and background jobs

In a day when you don't come across any problems, you can be sure that you are traveling in the wrong path.

—Swami Vivekananda

A tool intended for enterprise management that can't actually manage distributed systems isn't useful. Unfortunately, in PowerShell v1 very little support for remote management was built into PowerShell. This issue was fixed in PowerShell v2 by adding a comprehensive built-in remoting subsystem. This facility allows you to handle most remoting tasks in any kind of remoting configuration you might encounter.

Another related feature that v2 introduced was built-in support for *background jobs*. Background jobs allow multiple tasks to be executed within a single session, including mechanisms for starting, stopping, and querying these tasks. Again, this is an important feature in the enterprise environment, where you frequently have to deal with more than one task at a time.

In this chapter we're going to cover the various features of remoting and how you can apply them. We'll use an extended example showing how to combine the various features to solve a nontrivial problem. Then we'll look at background jobs and how to apply them to create concurrent solutions. We'll end the chapter by looking at some of the configuration considerations you need to be aware of when using PowerShell remoting.

12.1 GETTING STARTED WITH REMOTING

In this section, we'll go through the basic concepts and terminology used by PowerShell remoting. The ultimate goal for remoting is to be able to execute a command on a remote computer. There are two ways to approach this. First, you could have each command do its own remoting. In this scenario, the command is still executed locally but uses some system-level networking capabilities like DCOM to perform remote operations. There are a number of commands that do this, which we'll cover in the next section. The negative aspect of this approach is that each command has to implement and manage its own remoting mechanisms. As a result, PowerShell includes a more general solution, allowing you to send the command (or pipeline of commands or even a script) to the target machine for execution and then retrieve the results. With this approach, you only have to implement the remoting mechanism once and then it can be used with any command. This second solution is the one we'll spend most of our time discussing. But first, let's look at the commands that do implement their own remoting.

12.1.1 Commands with built-in remoting

A number of commands in PowerShell v2 have a `-ComputerName` parameter, which allows you to specify the target machine to access. This list is shown in table 12.1.

Table 12.1 The PowerShell v2 commands with built-in remoting

Name	Synopsis
`Clear-EventLog`	Deletes all entries from specified event logs on the local or remote computers
`Get-Counter`	Gets performance counter data from a group of computers
`Get-EventLog`	Gets the events in an event log, or a list of the event logs, on the local or remote computers
`Get-HotFix`	Gets the hotfixes that have been applied to a computer
`Get-Process`	Gets the processes that are running on a computer
`Get-Service`	Gets information about the services configured on one or more computers
`Get-WinEvent`	Gets event information from either the traditional event logs or the Event Tracing for Windows (ETW) trace log facility introduced with Windows Vista
`Limit-EventLog`	Sets the event log properties that limit the size of the event log and the age of its entries
`New-EventLog`	Creates a new event log and a new event source on a local or remote computer

Table 12.1 The PowerShell v2 commands with built-in remoting *(continued)*

Name	Synopsis
`Remove-EventLog`	Deletes an event log or unregisters an event source
`Restart-Computer`	Restarts ("reboots") the operating system on local and remote computers
`Set-Service`	Starts, stops, and suspends a service, and changes its properties
`Show-EventLog`	Displays the event logs of the local or a remote computer in Event Viewer
`Stop-Computer`	Stops (shuts down) local and remote computers
`Test-Connection`	Sends ICMP echo request packets ("pings") to one or more computers
`Write-EventLog`	Writes an event to an event log

These commands do their own remoting either because the underlying infrastructure already supports remoting or they address scenarios that are of particular importance to system management.

There are also two sets of "self-remoting" commands that weren't mentioned in this table. These are the `WMI` and `WSMan` commands. These commands allow you to access a wide range of management information using standards-based techniques and are important enough to get their own chapter (chapter 19).

Obviously, the set of commands that do self-remoting is quite small, so the remaining commands must rely on the PowerShell remoting subsystem to access remote computers. This is what we'll start looking at in the next section.

12.1.2 The PowerShell remoting subsystem

Way back in chapter 1, you saw a few brief examples of how remoting works. You may remember that all those examples used the same basic cmdlet: `Invoke-Command`. This cmdlet allows you to remotely invoke a scriptblock on another computer and is the building block for most of the features in remoting. The syntax for this command is shown in figure 12.1.

```
Invoke-Command
      [[-ComputerName] <string[]>] [-JobName <string>]
      [-ScriptBlock] <scriptblock>
      [-Credential <PSCredential>]
      [-ArgumentList <Object[]>] [-InputObject <psobject>]
      [-ThrottleLimit <int>]  [-AsJob]
      [-Port <int>] [-UseSSL] [-CertificateThumbprint <string>]
      [-ApplicationName <string>]
      [-Authentication <authenticationMethod>]
      [-ConfigurationName <string>]
      [-HideComputerName]
      [-SessionOption <PSSessionOption>]
```

Figure 12.1 The syntax for the `Invoke-Command` cmdlet, which is the core of PowerShell's remoting capabilities. This cmdlet is used to execute commands and scripts on one or more computers. It can be used synchronously or asynchronously as a job.

The `Invoke-Command` cmdlet is used to invoke a scriptblock on one or more computers. You do so by specifying a computer name (or list of names) for the machines on which you want to execute the command. For each name in the list, the remoting subsystem will take care of all the details needed to open the connection to that computer, execute the command, retrieve the results, and then shut down the connection. If you're going to run the command on a large set of computers, `Invoke-Command` will also take care of all resource management details, such as limiting the number of concurrent remote connections.

This is a simple but powerful model if you only need to execute a single command or script on the target machine. But if you want to execute a series of commands on the target, the overhead of setting up and taking down a connection for each command becomes expensive. PowerShell remoting addresses this situation by allowing you to create a persistent connection to the remote computer called a *session*. You do so by using the `New-PSSession` cmdlet.

Both of the scenarios we've discussed so far involve what is called *noninteractive remoting* because you're just sending commands to the remote machines and then waiting for the results. You don't interact with the remote commands while they're executing.

Another standard pattern in remoting occurs when you want to set up an *interactive session* where every command you type is sent transparently to the remote computer. This is the style of remoting implemented by tools like Remote Desktop, telnet, or ssh (Secure Shell). PowerShell allows you to start an interactive session using the `Enter-PSSession` cmdlet. Once you've entered a remote session, you can suspend the session without closing the remote connection by using `Exit-PSSession`. Because the connection isn't closed, you can later reenter the session with all session data preserved by using `Enter-PSSession` again.

These cmdlets—`Invoke-Command`, `New-PSSession`, and `Enter-PSSession`—are the basic remoting tools you'll be using. But before you can use them, you need to make sure remoting is enabled, so we'll look at that next.

12.1.3 Enabling remoting

To satisfy the "secure by default" principle, before you can use PowerShell remoting to access a remote computer, the remoting service on that computer has to be explicitly enabled. You do so using the `Enable-PSRemoting` cmdlet. To run this command, you have to have Administrator privileges on the machine you're going to enable. From a PowerShell session that's running with Administrator privileges, when you run the `Enable-PSRemoting` command, the resulting sequence of interactions will look something like this:

```
PS C:\Windows\system32> Enable-PSRemoting
WinRM Quick Configuration
```

```
Running command "Set-WSManQuickConfig" to enable this machine
for remote management through WinRM service.
 This includes:
    1. Starting or restarting (if already started) the WinRM service
    2. Setting the WinRM service type to auto start
    3. Creating a listener to accept requests on any IP address
    4. Enabling firewall exception for WS-Management traffic
       (for http only).
Do you want to continue?
[Y] Yes  [A] Yes to All  [N] No  [L] No to All  [S] Suspend
[?] Help (default is "Y"): y
WinRM has been updated to receive requests.
WinRM service type changed successfully.
WinRM service started.
Configured LocalAccountTokenFilterPolicy to grant administrative
rights remotely to local users.
WinRM has been updated for remote management.
Created a WinRM listener on HTTP://* to accept WS-Man requests to
any IP on this machine.
WinRM firewall exception enabled.
PS C:\Windows\system32>
```

At various points in the process, you'll be prompted to confirm each step. It's worth spending a few minutes understanding what each step is doing because these operations have security implications for that computer. Click y (yes) to all these steps to make sure everything is enabled properly. (Once you're comfortable with what's being done, you can use the `-Force` parameter to skip all the questions and just get it done.) The `Enable-PSRemoting` command performs all the configuration steps needed to allow users with local Administrator privileges to remote to this computer in a domain environment. In a nondomain or workgroup environment, as well as for nonadmin users, some additional steps are required for remoting to work.

12.1.4 Additional setup steps for workgroup environments

If you're working in a workgroup environment (e.g., at home), you must take a few additional steps before you can connect to a remote machine. With no domain controller available to handle the various aspects of security and identity, you have to manually configure the names of the computers you trust. For example, if you want to connect to the computer `computerItrust`, then you have to add it to the list of trusted computers (or *trusted hosts list*). You can do this via the WSMan: drive, as shown in table 12.2. Note that you need to be running as administrator to be able to use the WSMan: provider.

Once you've completed these steps, you're ready to start playing with some examples.

Table 12.2 Additional steps needed to enable remote access to a computer in a workgroup environment

Step	Command	Description
1	`cd wsman:\localhost \client`	`Cd`'ing into the client configuration node in the WSMan: drive allows you to access the WSMan configuration for this computer using the provider cmdlets.
2	`$old = (Get-Item .\TrustedHosts).Value`	You want to update the current value of the `TrustedHosts` item, so you get it and save the value in a variable.
3	`$old += ',computerItrust'`	The value of `TrustedHosts` is a string containing a comma-separated list of the computers considered trustworthy. You add the new computer name to the end of this list, prefixed with a comma. (If you're comfortable with implicitly trusting any host, then set this string to `*`, which matches any hostname.)
4	`Set-Item .\TrustedHosts $old`	Once you've verified that the updated contents of the variable are correct, you assign it back to the `TrustedHosts` item, which updates the configuration.

A note on security

The computers in the `TrustedHosts` list are implicitly trusted by adding their names to this list. The identity of these computers won't be authenticated when you connect to them. Because the connection process requires sending *credential information* to these machines, you need to be sure that you can trust these computers. Also be aware that the `TrustedHosts` list on a machine applies to everyone who uses that computer, not just the user who changed the setting.

That said, unless you allow random people to install computers on your internal network, this shouldn't introduce substantial risk most of the time. If you're comfortable with knowing which machines you'll be connecting to, you can put `*` in the `TrustedHosts` list, indicating that you're implicitly trusting any computer you might be connecting to. As always, security is a principle tempered with pragmatics.

12.1.5 Enabling remoting in the enterprise

As you saw in the previous section, you enable PowerShell remoting on a single computer using the `Enable-PSRemoting` cmdlet. In the enterprise scenario, enabling machines one by one isn't a great solution because you may be dealing with tens, hundreds, or thousands of machines. Obviously, you can't use PowerShell remoting to turn on remoting, so you need another way to push configuration out to a collection of machines. This is exactly what Group Policy is designed for. You can use Group Policy to enable and configure remoting as part of the machine policy that gets pushed out.

PowerShell depends on the WinRM (Windows Remote Management) service for its operation. To enable the WinRM listener on all computers in a domain, enable the Allow Automatic Configuration of Listeners policy in the following Group Policy path:

```
Computer Configuration\Administrative Templates\Windows Components\
Windows Remote Management (WinRM)\WinRM service
```

This policy allows WinRM to accept remoting requests. To enable a firewall exception for all computers in a domain, enable the Windows Firewall: Allow Local Port Exceptions policy in the following Group Policy path:

```
Computer Configuration\Administrative Templates\Network\
Network Connections\Windows Firewall\Domain Profile
```

This policy allows members of the Administrators group on the computer to use Windows Firewall in Control Panel to create a firewall exception for the WinRM service.

You also need to ensure that the WinRM service is running on all machines you want to access. On server operating systems like Windows Server 2003, Windows Server 2008, and Windows Server 2008 R2, the startup type of the WinRM service is set to Automatic by default, so nothing needs to be done for these environments. (This makes sense because the whole point of PowerShell is server management.) But on client operating systems (Windows XP, Windows Vista, and Windows 7), the WinRM service startup type is Disabled by default, so you need to start the service or change the startup type to Automatic before remote commands can be sent to these machines.

> **NOTE** Even if WinRM isn't started, you can still remote *from* the machine—outbound connections don't go through the WinRM service. If you're using a client machine and only want to connect from the client to the server, it makes sense to leave WinRM disabled on this machine.

To change the startup type of a service on a remote computer, you can use the `Set-Service` cmdlet. This cmdlet can change the state of a service on a remote machine and doesn't depend on the WinRM service so it can be used to "bootstrap" remoting. Here's an example showing how you'd do this for a set of computers. First, you need a list of the names of the computers on which to change the state. In this example, you'll get the names from a text file:

```
PS (1) > $names = Get-Content MachineNames.txt
```

Now you can pass this list of names to the `Set-Service` cmdlet to change the startup type of the WinRM to Automatic:

```
PS (2) > Set-Service -Name WinRM -ComputerName $names `
>>> -Startuptype Automatic
```

To confirm the change, use the following command to display the `StartMode` for the service (see section 19.2.2 for information on the `Get-WmiObject` cmdlet):

```
PS (1) >  Get-WmiObject Win32_Service |
>> where { $_.name -match "winrm" } |
```

```
>> Format-List displayname, startmode
>>

displayname : Windows Remote Management (WS-Management)
startmode   : Auto
```

At this point, you've done everything necessary to enable remoting on the target machines, and you can get on with using the remoting feature to solve your remote management problems.

12.2 APPLYING POWERSHELL REMOTING

With remoting services enabled, you can start to use them to get your work done. In this section, we're going to look at some of the ways you can apply remoting to solve management problems. We'll start with some simple remoting examples. Next, we'll work with some more complex examples where we introduce concurrent operations. Then you'll apply the principles you've learned to solve a specific problem: how to implement a multimachine configuration monitor. You'll work through this problem in a series of steps, adding more capabilities to your solution and resulting in a simple but fairly complete configuration monitor. Let's start with the most basic examples.

12.2.1 Basic remoting examples

In chapter 1, you saw the most basic examples of remoting:

```
Invoke-Command Servername {"hello world"}
```

The first thing to notice is that `Invoke-Command` takes a scriptblock to specify the actions. This pattern should be familiar by now—you've seen it with `ForEach-Object` and `Where-Object` many times. The `Invoke-Command` does operate a bit differently, though. It's designed to make remote execution as transparent as possible. For example, if you want to sort objects, the local command looks like this:

```
PS (1) > 1..3 | Sort -Descending
3
2
1
```

Now if you want to do the sorting on the remote machine, you'd do this:

```
PS (2) > 1..3 | Invoke-Command localhost { Sort -Descending }
3
2
1
```

You're essentially splitting the pipeline across local and remote parts, and the scriptblock is used to demarcate which part of the pipeline should be executed remotely. This works the other way as well:

```
PS (3) > Invoke-Command localhost { 1..3 } | sort -Descending
3
2
1
```

Here you're generating the numbers on the remote computer and sorting them locally. Of course, scriptblocks can contain more than one statement. This implies that the semantics need to change a bit. Whereas in the simple pipeline case, streaming input into the remote command was transparent, when the remote command contains more than one statement, you have to be explicit and use the `$input` variable to indicate where you want the input to go. This looks like the following:

```
PS (4) > 1..3 | Invoke-Command localhost {
>> "First"
>> $input | sort -Descending
>> "Last"
>> }
>>
First
3
2
1
Last
```

The scriptblock argument to `Invoke-Command` in this case contains three statements. The first statement emits the string "First", the second statement does the sort on the input, and the third statement emits the string "Last". What happens if you don't specify input? Let's take a look:

```
PS (5) > 1..3 | Invoke-Command localhost {
>> "First"
>> Sort -Descending
>> "Last"
>> }
>>
First
Last
```

Nothing was emitted between "First" and "Last". Because `$input` wasn't specified, the input objects were never processed. You'll need to keep this in mind when you start to build a monitoring solution. Now let's look at how concurrency—multiple operations occurring at the same time—impacts your scripts.

12.2.2 Adding concurrency to the examples

In chapter 2, we talked about how each object passed completely through all states of a pipeline, one by one. This behavior changes with remoting because the local and remote commands run in separate processes that are executing concurrently. This means that you now have two threads of execution—local and remote—and this can have an effect on the order in which things are executed. Consider the following statement:

```
PS (12) > 1..3 | foreach { Write-Host $_; $_; Start-Sleep 5 } |
>> Write-Host
>>
1
```

```
1
2
2
3
3
```

This statement sends a series of numbers down the pipeline. In the body of the foreach scriptblock, the value of the current pipeline object is written to the screen and then passed to the next state in the pipeline. This last stage also writes the object to the screen. Given that you know each object is processed completely by all stages of the pipeline, the order of the output is as expected. The first number is passed to the foreach, where it's displayed and then passed to Write-Output, where it's displayed again, so you see the sequence 1, 1, 2, 2, 3, 3. Now let's run this command again using Invoke-Command in the final stage:

```
PS (10) > 1..3 | foreach {
>>   Write-Host -ForegroundColor cyan  $_
>>     $_; Start-Sleep 5 } |
>>       Invoke-Command localhost  { Write-Host }
>>
1
2
1
3
2
3
```

Now the order has changed—you see 1 and 2 from the local process in cyan on a color display, then you see 1 from the remote process, and so on. The local and remote pipelines are executing at the same time, which is what's causing the changes to the ordering. Predicting the order of the output is made more complicated by the use of buffering and timeouts in the remoting protocol, the details of which we'll cover in chapter 13.

You used the Start-Sleep command in these examples to force these visible differences. If you take out this command, you get a different pattern:

```
PS (13) > 1..3 | foreach { Write-Host $_; $_ } |
>> Invoke-Command localhost { Write-Host }
>>
1
2
3
1
2
3
```

This time, all the local objects are displayed and then passed to the remoting layer, where they're buffered until they can be delivered to the remote connection. This way, the local side can process all objects before the remote side starts to operate. Concurrent operation and buffering make it appear a bit unpredictable, but if you didn't have the Write-Hosts in place, it'd be essentially unnoticeable. The important thing to understand is that objects being sent to the remote end will be processed concurrently with the local execution. This means that the remoting infrastructure doesn't have to buffer everything sent from the local end before starting execution.

Up to now, you've only been passing simple commands to the remote end. But because `Invoke-Command` takes a scriptblock, you can, in practice, send pretty much any valid PowerShell script. You'll take advantage of this fact in the next section when you start to build your multimachine monitor.

> **NOTE** So why does remoting require scriptblocks? There are a couple of reasons. First, scriptblocks are always compiled locally so you'll catch syntax errors as soon as the script is loaded. Second, using scriptblocks limits vulnerability to code injection attacks by validating the script before sending it.

12.2.3 Solving a real problem: multimachine monitoring

In this section, you're going to build a solution for a real management problem: multimachine monitoring. With this solution, you're going to gather some basic health information from the remote host. The goal is to use this information to determine when a server may have problems such as out of memory, out of disk, or reduced performance due to a high faulting rate. You'll gather the data on the remote host and return it as a hashtable so you can look at it locally.

Monitoring a single machine

To simplify things, you'll start by writing a script that can work against a single host. The following listing shows this script.

Listing 12.1 Defining the data acquisition scriptblock

```
$gatherInformation ={
    @{
        Date = Get-Date
        FreeSpace = (Get-PSDrive c).Free
        PageFaults = (Get-WmiObject `
            Win32_PerfRawData_PerfOS_Memory).PageFaultsPersec
        TopCPU = Get-Process | sort CPU -desc | select -First 5
        TopWS = Get-Process | sort -desc WS | select -First 5
    }
}
Invoke-Command servername $gatherInformation
```

This script uses a number of mechanisms to get the required data and returns the result as a hashtable. This hashtable contains the following pieces of performance-related information:

- The amount of free space on the C: drive from the `Get-PSDrive` command
- The page fault rate retrieved using WMI (see chapter 19)

- The processes consuming the most CPU from `Get-Process` with a pipeline
- The processes that have the largest working set, also from `Get-Process`

You write the information-gathering scriptblock in exactly the same way you'd write it for the local host—the fact that it's being executed on another computer is entirely transparent. All you had to do was wrap the code in an extra set of braces and pass it to `Invoke-Command`.

Monitoring multiple machines

Working against one machine was simple, but your goal was *multimachine* monitoring. So you need to change the script to run against a list of computers. You don't want to hardcode the list of computers in the script—that interferes with reuse—so you'll design it to get the data from a file called servers.txt. The content of this file is a list of hostnames, one per line, which might look like this:

```
Server-sql-01
Server-sql-02
Server-sql-03
Server-Exchange-01
Server-SharePoint-Markerting-01
Server-Sharepoint-Development-01
```

Adding this functionality requires only a small, one-line change to the call to `Invoke-Command`. This revised command looks like this:

```
Invoke-Command (Get-Content servers.txt) $gatherInformation
```

You could make this more complex—say you only wanted to scan certain computers on certain days. You'll update the servers.txt file to be a CSV file:

```
Name, Day
Server-sql-01,Monday
Server-sql-02,Tuesday
Server-sql-03,Wednesday
Server-Exchange-01, Monday
Server-SharePoint-Markerting-01, Wednesday
Server-Sharepoint-Development-01, Friday
```

Now when you load the servers, you'll do some processing on this list, which looks like this:

```
$servers = Import-CSV servers.csv |
    where { $_.Day -eq (Get-Date).DayOfWeek } |
    foreach { $_.Name }
Invoke-Command $servers $gatherInformation
```

There are still no changes required in the actual data-gathering code. Let's move on to the next refinement.

Resource management using throttling

In a larger organization, this list of servers is likely to be quite large, perhaps hundreds or even thousands of servers. Obviously it isn't possible to establish this many concurrent connections—doing so would exhaust the system resources. To manage the amount of resources consumed, you can use *throttling*. In general, throttling allows you to limit the amount of resources that an activity can consume at one time. In this case, you're limiting the number of connections that command makes at one time. There's a built-in throttle limit to prevent accidental resource exhaustion. By default, `Invoke-Command` will limit the number of concurrent connections to 32. To override this, use the `-ThrottleLimit` parameter on `Invoke-Command` to limit the number of connections. In this example you're going to limit the number of concurrent connections to 10:

```
$servers = Import-CSV -Path servers.csv |
    where { $_.Day -eq (Get-Date).DayOfWeek } |
    foreach { $_.Name }
Invoke-Command -ThrottleLimit 10 -ComputerName $servers `
 -ScriptBlock $gatherInformation
```

At this point, you'll consolidate the incremental changes you've made and look at the updated script as a whole, as shown in the next listing.

Listing 12.2 Data acquisition script using servers.csv file

```
$gatherInformation ={
    @{
        Date = Get-Date
        FreeSpace = (Get-PSDrive c).Free
        PageFaults = (Get-WmiObject `
            Win32_PerfRawData_PerfOS_Memory).PageFaultsPersec
        TopCPU = Get-Process | sort CPU -desc | select -First 5
        TopWS = Get-Process | sort -desc WS | select -First 5
    }
}
$servers = Import-CSV -Path servers.csv |
    where { $_.Day -eq (Get-Date).DayOfWeek } |
    foreach { $_.Name }
Invoke-Command -Throttle 10 -ComputerName $servers `
  -ScriptBlock $gatherInformation
```

This has become a pretty capable script: it gathers a useful set of information from a network of servers in a manageable, scalable way. It'd be nice if you could generalize it a bit more so you could use different lists of servers or change the throttle limits.

Parameterizing the solution

You can increase the flexibility of this tool by adding some parameters to it. Here are the parameters you want to add:

```
param (
    [Parameter()]
       [string] $ServerList = "servers.txt",
    [Parameter()]
       [int] $ThrottleLimit = 10,
   [Parameter()]
```

```
        [int] $NumProcesses = 5
)
```

The first two are obvious: `$ServerList` is the name of the file containing the list of servers to check, and `$ThrottleLimit` is the the throttle limit. Both of these parameters have reasonable defaults. The third one, `$NumProcesses`, is less obvious. This parameter controls the number of process objects to include in the `TopCPU` and `TopWS` entries in the table returned from the remote host. Although you could, in theory, trim the list that gets returned locally, you can't add to it, so you need to evaluate this parameter on the remote end to get full control. That means it has to be a parameter to the remote command. This is another reason scriptblocks are useful. You can add parameters to the scriptblock that's executed on the remote end. You're finally modifying the data collection scriptblock; the modified scriptblock looks like this:

```
$gatherInformation ={
    param ($procLimit = 5)
    @{
        Date = Get-Date
        FreeSpace = (Get-PSDrive c).Free
        PageFaults = (Get-WmiObject `
            Win32_PerfRawData_PerfOS_Memory).PageFaultsPersec
        TopCPU = Get-Process | sort CPU -desc | select -First $procLimit
        TopWS = Get-Process | sort -desc WS | select -First $procLimit
    }
}
```

And the updated call to `Invoke-Command` looks like this:

```
Invoke-Command -Throttle 10 -ComputerName $servers `
       -ScriptBlock $gatherInformation `
       -ArgumentList $numProcesses
```

Once again, let's look at the complete updated script, shown in the following listing.

Listing 12.3 Parameterized data acquisition script

```
param (
    [parameter]
       [string] $serverFile = "servers.txt",
    [parameter]
       [int] $throttleLimit = 10,
   [parameter]
       [int] $numProcesses = 5
)

$gatherInformation ={
    param ([int] $procLimit = 5)
    @{
        Date = Get-Date
        FreeSpace = (Get-PSDrive c).Free
        PageFaults = (Get-WmiObject `
            Win32_PerfRawData_PerfOS_Memory).PageFaultsPersec
        TopCPU = Get-Process | sort CPU -desc | select -First $procLimit
```

```
        TopWS = Get-Process | sort -desc WS | select -First $procLimit
    }
}

$servers = Import-CSV servers.csv |
    where { $_.Day -eq (Get-Date).DayOfWeek } |
    foreach { $_.Name }

Invoke-Command -Throttle 10 -ComputerName $servers `
       -ScriptBlock $gatherInformation `
       -ArgumentList $numProcesses
```

This script is starting to become a bit complex. At this point, it's a good idea to separate the script code in `$gatherInformation` that *gathers* the remote information from the "infrastructure" script that *orchestrates* the information gathering. You'll put this information-gathering part into its own script. Call this new script BasicHealthModel.ps1 (shown in the following listing) because it gathers some basic information about the state of a machine.

Listing 12.4 Basic Health Model script

```
param ($procLimit = 5)
@{
    Date = Get-Date
    FreeSpace = (Get-PSDrive c).Free
    PageFaults = (Get-WmiObject `
        Win32_PerfRawData_PerfOS_Memory).PageFaultsPersec
    TopCPU = Get-Process | sort CPU -desc | select -First $procLimit
    TopWS = Get-Process | sort -desc WS | select -First $procLimit
}
```

The orchestration code has to be changed to invoke this script. This step turns out to be easy—you can just use the `-FilePath` option on `Invoke-Command`:

```
Invoke-Command -Throttle 10 -ComputerName $servers `
       -FilePath BasicHealthModel.ps1 `
       -ArgumentList $numProcesses
```

You'll put the final revised orchestration script into a file called Get-HealthData.ps1, shown in the next listing.

Listing 12.5 Data acquisition driver script

```
param (
    [parameter]
       [string] $serverFile = "servers.txt",
    [parameter]
       [int] $throttleLimit = 10,
   [parameter]
       [int] $numProcesses = 5
   [parameter]
       [string] $model = "BasicHealthModel.ps1"
)
```

```
$servers = Import-CSV servers.csv |
    where { $_.Day -eq (Get-Date).DayOfWeek } |
    foreach { $_.Name }

Invoke-Command -Throttle 10 -ComputerName $servers `
      -FilePath $model `
      -ArgumentList $numProcesses
```

This separation of concerns allows you to add a parameter for specifying alternative health models.

The result is that, with a small amount of code, you've created a flexible framework for an "agentless" distributed health monitoring system. With this system, you can run this health model on *any* machine without having to worry about whether the script is installed on that machine or whether the machine has the correct version of the script. It's always "available" and always the right version because the infrastructure is pushing it out to the target machines.

> **NOTE** What we're doing here isn't what most people would call monitoring. Monitoring usually implies a continual semi-real-time mechanism for noticing a problem and then generating an alert. This system is certainly not real-time and it's a pull model, not a push. This solution is more appropriate for configuration analysis. The Microsoft Baseline Configuration Analyzer has a similar (though much more sophisticated) architecture.

You now have an idea of how to use remoting to execute a command on a remote server. This is a powerful mechanism, but sometimes you need to send more than one command to a server—for example, you might want to run multiple data-gathering scripts, one after the other on the same machine. Because there's a significant overhead in setting up each remote connection, you don't want to create a new connection for every script you execute. Instead, you want to be able to establish a persistent connection to a machine, run all the scripts, and then shut down the connection. In the next section you'll learn how this is accomplished with sessions.

12.3 SESSIONS AND PERSISTENT CONNECTIONS

In the previous section, you learned how to run individual scriptblocks on remote machines. For each scriptblock you sent, a new connection was set up that involved authentication and version checks, an instance of PowerShell was created, the scriptblock was executed, the results were serialized and returned to the caller, and finally, the PowerShell instance was discarded and the connection was torn down. From the user's point of view, the `Invoke-Command` operation is simple, but under the covers a lot of work has to be done by the system, which makes creating a new connection each time a costly proposition. A new connection for each operation also means that you can't maintain any state on the remote host—things like variable settings or function definitions. To address these issues, in this section we'll show you how to create persistent connections called *sessions* that will give you much better performance when you want to perform a series of interactions with the remote host as well as allow you to maintain remote state.

In simplest terms, a session is the environment where PowerShell commands are executed. This is true even when you run the console host: `PowerShell.exe`. The console host program creates a local session that it uses to execute the commands you type. This session remains alive until you exit the program.

When you use remoting to connect to another computer, you're also creating one remote session for every local session you remote from, as shown in figure 12.2.

As mentioned earlier, each session contains all the things you work with in PowerShell—all the variables, all the functions that are defined, and the history of the commands you typed—and each session is independent of any other session. If you want to work with these sessions, then you need a way to manipulate them. You do this in the "usual way": through objects and cmdlets. PowerShell represents sessions as objects that are of type `PSSession`.

These `PSSession` objects play an important role in remote computing: they hold the state on the remote computer. By default, every time you connect to a remote computer by name with `Invoke-Command`, a new `PSSession` object is created to represent the connection to that remote machine. For example, when you run the command

```
Invoke-Command mycomputer { "hello world" }
```

PowerShell connects to the remote machine, creates a `PSSession` on that computer, executes the command, and then discards the session. This process is inefficient and will be quite slow because setting up a connection and then creating and configuring a session object is a lot of work. This pattern of operations is shown in figure 12.3.

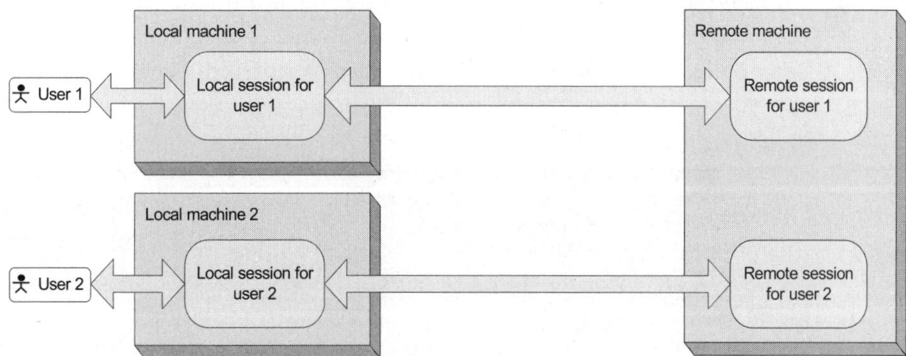

Figure 12.2 Each local session that connects to a remote target requires a corresponding session on the target machine. This session may be transient and go away at the end of the command, or it may remain open until explicitly closed.

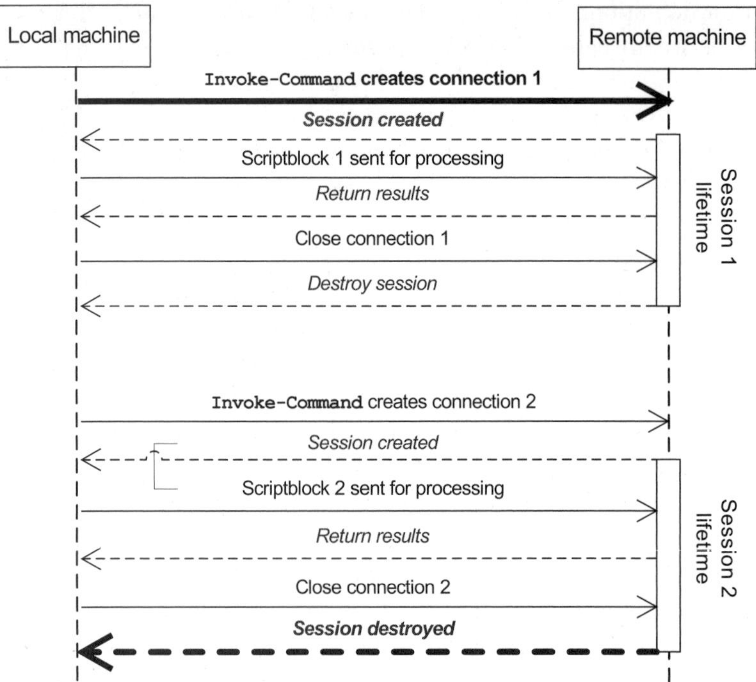

Figure 12.3 The sequences of operations between the local and remote machines when the name of the computer is specified for each command instead of using a `PSSession` object. Each command sent from the local machine to the remote machine results in a new session being created on the remote machine. Solid lines show messages from the local machine to the remote machine, and dashed lines are responses sent from the remote machine.

In this figure, you see the local machine setting up and then tearing down a session for each call to `Invoke-Command`. If you're going to run more than one command on a computer, you need a way to create persistent connections to that computer. You can do this with `New-PSSession`; the syntax for this cmdlet is shown in figure 12.4.

```
New-PSSession
    [[-ComputerName] <String[]>] [-Port <Int32>]
    [-Credential <PSCredential>] [-UseSSL]
    [-Authentication <AuthenticationMechanism>]
    [-CertificateThumbprint <String>]
    [-Name <String[]>]
    [-ConfigurationName <String>] [-ApplicationName <String>]
    [-ThrottleLimit <Int32>]
    [-SessionOption <PSSessionOption>]
```

Figure 12.4 The syntax for the `New-PSSession` cmdlet. This cmdlet is used to create persistent connections to a remote computer.

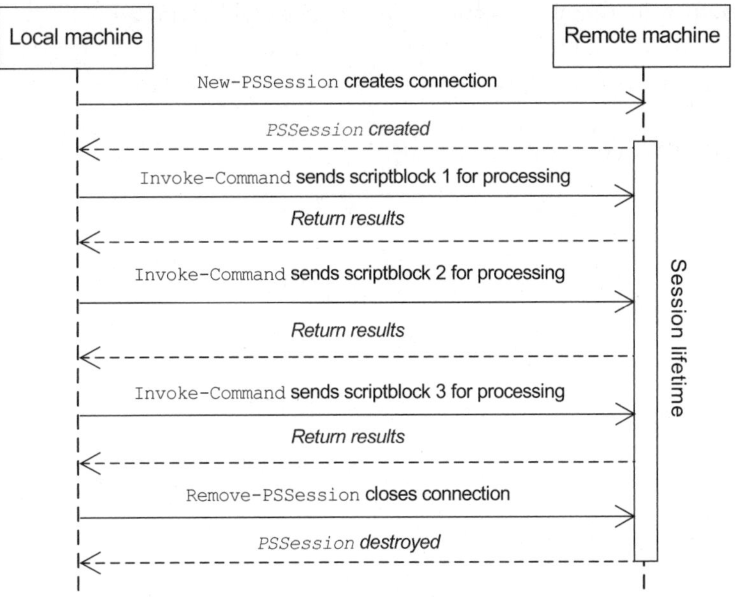

Figure 12.5 The sequence of operations between the local and remote machines when a `New-PSSession` is used to create a persistent session. When `New-PSSession` is used, multiple commands are processed before the session is removed with `Remove-PSSession`.

This command has many of the same parameters that you saw in `Invoke-Command`. The difference is that, for `New-PSSession`, these parameters are used to configure the persistent session instead of the transient sessions you saw being created by `Invoke-Command`. The `PSSession` object returned from `New-PSSession` can then be used to specify the destination for the remote command instead of the computer name. When you use a `PSSession` object with `Invoke-Command`, you see the pattern of operations shown in figure 12.5.

In contrast to the pattern shown in figure 12.3, in this figure the lifetime of the session begins with the call to `New-PSSession` and persists until it's explicitly destroyed by the call to `Remove-PSSession`. Let's look at an example that illustrates just how much of a performance difference sessions can make. You'll run `Get-Date` five times using `Invoke-Command` and see how long it takes using `Measure-Command` (which measures command execution time). First, execute the test without sessions:

```
PS (1) > Measure-Command { 1..5 |
>> foreach { Invoke-Command brucepayx61 {Get-Date} } } |
>> Format-Table -AutoSize TotalSeconds
>>

TotalSeconds
------------
   5.5867397
```

The result from `Measure-Command` shows that each operation appears to be taking about 1 second. Modify the example to create a session at the beginning, and then reuse it in each call to `Invoke-Command`:

```
PS (2) > Measure-Command {
>>   $s = New-PSSession brucepayx61
>>   1..5 |
>>     foreach { Invoke-Command $s {Get-Date} }
>>   Remove-PSSession $s
>> } |
>> Format-Table -AutoSize TotalSeconds
>>

TotalSeconds
------------
    1.138609
```

This output shows that it's taking about one-fifth the time as the first command. As a further experiment, you'll change the number of remote invocations from 5 to 50:

```
PS (3) > Measure-Command {
>>   $s = New-PSSession brucepayx61
>>   1..50 |
>>     foreach { Invoke-Command $s {Get-Date} }
>>   Remove-PSSession $s
>> } |
>> Format-Table -AutoSize TotalSeconds
>>

TotalSeconds
------------
    1.608232
```

The result shows that there's barely any increase in execution time. Clearly, for this simple example the time to set up and break down the connection totally dominates the execution time. Other factors affect real scenarios, such as network performance, the size of the script, and the amount of information being transmitted. Still, it's quite obvious that in a situation where multiple interactions are required, using a session will result in substantially better performance.

As you've seen in this section, the basic patterns of operation with `PSSessions` are straightforward and can have substantial performance benefits. There are still a few additional details to explore, as you'll see in the next section.

12.3.1 Additional session attributes

This section describes some `PSSession` attributes that you should be aware of. These attributes can have an impact on the way you write your scripts.

Technically, a session is an environment or *execution context* where PowerShell executes commands. Each PowerShell session includes an instance of the PowerShell engine and is associated with a *host program*, which manages the interactions between PowerShell and the end user. These interactions include how text is displayed, how prompting is done, and so on. The host services are made available to scripts through the $host variable, which also has a Name property used to determine what host the script is running under. Two client host applications are included with PowerShell v2—the PowerShell console host

```
PS (1) > $host.Name
ConsoleHost
```

and the PowerShell ISE:

```
PS (1) > $host.Name
Windows PowerShell ISE Host
```

Also included is a server host used by the remoting layer:

```
PS (2) > Invoke-Command localhost { $host.Name }
ServerRemoteHost
```

NOTE An impressive number of third-party client hosts are also available. As of this writing, these third-party hosts include *PowerShell Plus* from Idera Software, *PowerGUI* from Quest Software, *PowerWF* from Devfarm Software Corporation, and *Citrix Workflow Studio* from Citrix. In addition, Sapien Technologies offers the *PrimalScript* IDE for doing script development in PowerShell. These products present a wide variety of approaches to hosting the PowerShell engine. In addition, a number of open source PowerShell host projects are available on www.codeplex.com that you may choose to explore.

Sessions and hosts

The host application running your scripts can impact the portability of your scripts if you become dependent on specific features of that host. (This is why PowerShell module manifests include the PowerShellHostName and PowerShellHostVersion elements.) Dependency on specific host functionality is a consideration with remote execution because the remote host implementation is used instead of the normal interactive host. This is necessary to manage the extra characteristics of the remote or job environments. This host shows up as a process named wsmprovhost corresponding to the executable wsmprovhost.exe. This host only supports a subset of the features available in the normal interactive PowerShell hosts.

Session isolation

Another point is the fact that each session is configured independently when it's created, and once it's constructed, it has its own copy of the engine properties, execution policy, function definitions, and so on. This independent session environment exists for the duration of the session and isn't affected by changes made in other sessions. This principle is called *isolation*—each session is isolated from, and therefore not affected by, any other session.

Only one command runs at a time

A final characteristic of a session instance is that you can run only one command (or command pipeline) in a session at one time. If you try to run more than one command at a time, a "session busy" error will be raised. But there's some limited command queuing: if there's a request to run a second command synchronously (one at a time), the command will wait up to 4 minutes for the first command to be completed before generating the "session busy" error. But if a second command is requested to run asynchronously—that is, without waiting—the busy error will be generated immediately.

With some knowledge of the characteristics and limitations of PowerShell sessions, you can start to look at how to use them.

12.3.2 Using the New-PSSession cmdlet

In this section, you'll learn how to use the `New-PSSession` cmdlet. Let's start with an example. First, you'll create a `PSSession` on the local machine by specifying `localhost` as the target computer:

```
PS (1) > $s = New-PSSession localhost
```

> **NOTE** By default on Windows Vista, Windows Server 2008 R2, and above, a user must be running with elevated privileges to create a session on the local machine. Section 13.1.4 explains why this is the case and describes how to change the default setting. (Earlier platforms like XP don't require the user to be elevated.)

You now have a `PSSession` object in the `$s` variable that you can use to execute "remote" commands. Earlier we said each session runs in its own process. You can confirm this by using the `$PID` session variable to see what the process ID of the session process is. First, run this code in the remote session:

```
PS (2) > Invoke-Command $s { $PID }
7352
```

And you see that the process ID is 7352. When you get the value in the local session by typing `$PID` at the command line, as shown here

```
PS (3) > $PID
5076
```

you see that the local process ID is 5076. Now define a variable in the remote session:

```
PS (4) > Invoke-Command $s {$x=1234}
```

With this command, you've set the variable `$x` in the remote session to 1234. Now invoke another command to retrieve the value:

```
PS (5) > Invoke-Command $s { $x }
1234
```

You get the expected value back. If you had done this without using the session, you wouldn't have gotten the correct value back because the value of $x would have been lost when the remote session was closed down. Next, define a function hi:

```
PS (6) > Invoke-Command $s { function hi { "Hello there" } }
```

And then use Invoke-Command to call it:

```
PS (7) > Invoke-Command $s { hi }
Hello there
```

This works in much the same way as it does in the local case—changes to the remote environment are persisted across the invocations. You can redefine the function and make it reference the $x variable you defined earlier:

```
PS (8) > Invoke-Command $s { function hi { "Hello there, x is $x" } }
PS (9) > Invoke-Command $s { hi }
Hello there, x is 1234
```

You get the preserved value.

> **NOTE** We've had people ask if other users on the computer can see the sessions we're creating. As mentioned earlier, this isn't the case. Users have access only to the remote sessions they create and only from the sessions they were created from. In other words, there's no way for one session to connect to another session that it didn't itself create. The only aspect of a session that may be visible to another user is the existence of the wsmprovhost process hosting the session.

As you've seen, remote execution is just like the local case...well, almost. You have to type Invoke-Command every time. If you're executing a lot of interactive commands on a specific machine, this task becomes annoying quickly. PowerShell provides a much better way to accomplish this type of task, as you'll see in the next section.

12.3.3 Interactive sessions

In the previous sections, you learned how to issue commands to remote machines using Invoke-Command. This approach is effective but gets annoying for more interactive types of work. To make this scenario easier, you can start an *interactive session* using the Enter-PSSession cmdlet. Once you're in an interactive session, the commands that you type are automatically passed to the remote computer and executed without having to use Invoke-Command. Let's try this out. You'll reuse the session you created in the previous section. In that session, you defined the variable $x and the function hi. To enter interactive mode during this session, you'll call Enter-PSSession, passing in the session object:

```
PS (10) > Enter-PSSession $s
[localhost]: PS C:\Users\brucepay\Documents>
```

As soon as you enter interactive mode, you see that the prompt changes: it now displays the name of the machine you're connected to and the current directory.

> **NOTE** The default prompt can be changed in the remote session in the same way it can be changed in the local session. If you have a prompt definition in your profile, you may be wondering why that wasn't used. We'll get to that later in section 12.6.2, when we look at some of the things you need to keep in mind when using remoting.

Now let's check out the value of `$x`:

```
[localhost]: PS C:\Users\brucepay\Documents> $x
1234
```

It's 1234, which is the last value you set it to using `Invoke-Command` in the previous section. The remote session state has been preserved and is now available to you interactively. Let's try running the `hi` function you defined:

```
[localhost]: PS C:\Users\brucepay\Documents> hi
Hello there, x is 1234
```

It also works. In addition to examining the state of things, you can change them. Change the value of `$x`, and then rerun the `hi` function, which uses `$x` in its output:

```
[localhost]: PS C:\Users\brucepay\Documents> $x=6
[localhost]: PS C:\Users\brucepay\Documents> hi
Hello there, x is 6
```

The changed value is displayed in the output. You can exit an interactive remote session either by using the `exit` keyword or by using the `Exit-PSSession` cmdlet (section 13.2.6 explains why there are two ways to do this):

```
[localhost]: PS C:\Users\brucepay\Documents> exit
```

You see that the prompt changed back, and when you try to run the `hi` function

```
PS (11) > hi
The term 'hi' is not recognized as the name of a cmdlet, function,
script file, or operable program. Check the spelling of the name,
or if a path was included, verify that the path is correct
and try again.
At line:1 char:3
+ hi <<<<
    + CategoryInfo          : ObjectNotFound: (hi:String) [],
CommandNotFoundException
    + FullyQualifiedErrorId : CommandNotFoundException
```

you get an error because the function was only defined in the remote environment. Now try to reenter the session:

```
PS (12) > Enter-PSSession $s
[localhost]: PS C:\Users\brucepay\Documents> $x
6
```

When you reenter the session, the environment is exactly as you left it. You can run the `hi` function

```
[localhost]: PS C:\Users\brucepay\Documents> hi
Hello there, x is 6
```

and it works. Now you can exit it again

```
[localhost]: PS C:\Users\brucepay\Documents> exit
PS (13) >
```

and you're back in your local environment. You can enter and exit a session as often as you need to as long as it's not removed in the interim.

Another useful feature to consider is the fact that you can have more than one session open at a time. This means that you can pop back and forth between multiple computers as needed. In chapter 15, you'll see how the PowerShell ISE takes advantage of this capability, allowing you to have different sessions open in different tabs. The ability to have multiple concurrent sessions makes dealing with multiple machines very convenient.

Additional differences exist between the pattern where you used `Invoke-Command` for each command and the interactive mode. In the noninteractive `Invoke-Command` case, the remote commands send objects back, where they're formatted on the local machine. In the interactive remoting case, the objects are formatted on the *remote* machine and simple strings are sent to the local machine to be displayed. This process is illustrated in figure 12.6.

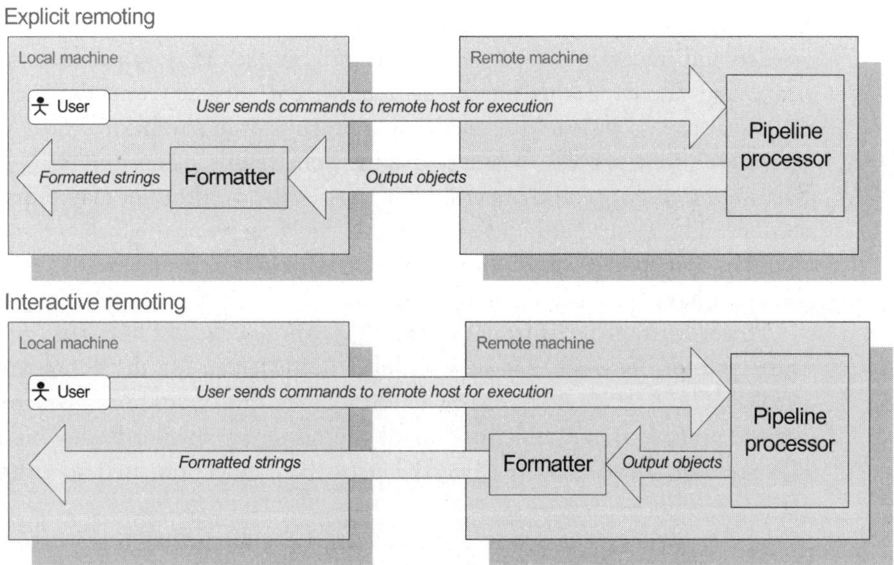

Figure 12.6 When using explicit remoting (top), objects are returned from the remote host and formatted locally. With interactive remoting (bottom), the objects are formatted on the remote machine and the formatted strings are sent back to the local machine.

The differences in behavior this process may cause are somewhat subtle. Most of the time the process is invisible. Situations where you might experience some consequences are when the local session and the remote session are in different *locales*—that is, the sessions have different language and cultural settings. In this case, things like dates will be displayed differently in the local and remote cases. The other scenario where there could be a visible difference is when there's formatting information for the objects you're working with that's different (or missing) on one end or the other.

Finally, as with the noninteractive remoting case, you can run an interactive session in a temporary session by passing the name of the computer instead of an existing `PSSession`. Using the `PSSession` has the advantage that you can enter and exit the remote session and have the remote state preserved between activities. If the name of the computer is passed in, the connection will be torn down when you exit the session. Because a remote session involved creating a remote host process, forgetting to close your sessions can lead to wasting resources. At any point, you can use the `Get-PSSession` to get a list of the open sessions you currently have and use `Remove-PSSession` to close them as appropriate.

By now, you should be comfortable with creating and using persistent remote sessions. What we haven't spent much time on is how to manage all these connections you're creating. We'll expand our discussion to include these topics in the next section.

12.3.4 Managing PowerShell sessions

Each `PSSession` is associated with an underlying `Windows` process. As such, it consumes significant resources even when no commands are being executed in it. To limit the load on the remote system, you should delete `PSSessions` that are no longer needed and maintain only the ones currently in use. This step reduces the memory usage and similar drains on the remote system. At the same time, creating new `PSSessions` also puts a load on the system, consuming additional CPU resources to create each new process. When managing your resource consumption, you need to balance the cost of creating new sessions against the overhead of maintaining multiple sessions. There's no hard-and-fast rule for deciding what this balance should be. In the end, you should decide on an application-by-application basis. Let's review the tools you have for session management.

To get a list of the existing `PSSessions`, you use the `Get-PSSession` command, and to remove sessions that are no longer needed, you use the `Remove-PSSession` cmdlet. The `Remove-PSSession` cmdlet closes the `PSSession`, which causes the remote process to exit and frees up all the resources it held. Removing the session also frees up local resources like the network connection used to connect to the remote session.

So far, the focus of our resource management discussion has been on managing connections from the client end. On the client end, if you don't explicitly remove the sessions or set timeouts, local sessions will remain open until you end your PowerShell session. But what happens if the client fails for some reason without closing its sessions? If these sessions are allowed to persist without some mechanism for closing them, eventually the remote server's resources could become exhausted. In this scenario you can't rely on being able to reconnect to the remote machine, which means you need a mechanism to allow it to do its own cleanup.

To address this problem, the PowerShell remoting infrastructure uses a "heartbeat" pulse sent between the local and remote machines to make sure that the connection between the machines is still valid. The heartbeat pulse is sent every 3 minutes to validate the connection. If the client computer doesn't respond to the pulse within 4 minutes, the `PSSession` associated with that connection will be closed automatically. This allows the remote machine to prevent "orphaned" processes that are no longer being used by the client from eventually exhausting its resource.

At this point, let's review what we've covered. We've looked at the basic remoting concepts. We've examined the use of transient and persistent sessions in noninteractive and interactive scenarios. In the next section, we'll explore another feature that lets you merge local and remote operations in an almost seamless way.

12.4 IMPLICIT REMOTING

When doing noninteractive remoting, you have to call `Invoke-Command` every time you want to execute a remote operation. You can avoid this task by using `Enter-PSSession` to set up a remote interactive session. This approach makes remote execution easy but at the cost of making local operations difficult. In this section, we'll look at a mechanism that makes both local and remote command execution easy. This mechanism is called *implicit remoting*.

> **NOTE** For implicit remoting to work, the execution policy on the client machine has to be configured to allow scripts to run, typically by setting it to `RemoteSigned`. This is necessary because implicit remoting generates a temporary module, and PowerShell must be allowed to execute scripts in order to load this module. If execution policy is set to `Restricted` or `AllSigned`, it won't be able to do this. This requirement only applies to the local client machine. A remote server can still use a more restrictive policy. See section 21.3.2 for more information about execution policy.

The goal of implicit remoting is to make the fact that remote operations are occurring invisible to the user and to have all operations look as much like local operations as possible. You can accomplish this goal by generating *local proxy functions* that run the remote commands under the covers. The user calls the local proxy, which takes care of the details involved in making the remote command invocation, as shown in figure 12.7.

The net effect is that everything looks like a local operation because everything *is* a local operation. In the next section, you'll see how to use this facility.

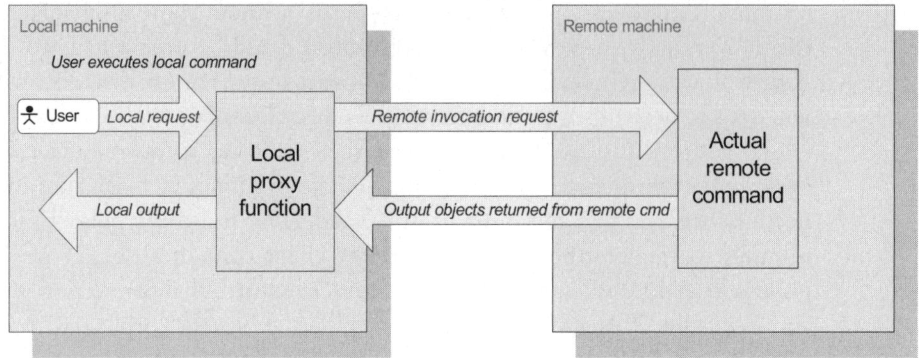

Figure 12.7 With implicit remoting, the user calls a local proxy command. This command takes care of making the remote invocation. The user need not be concerned with the details of the remote invocation.

12.4.1 Using implicit remoting

To set up the remote proxy functions mentioned in the previous section, use the `Import-PSSession` cmdlet. The syntax for this cmdlet is shown in figure 12.8.

Let's explore how this cmdlet works by walking through an example. You'll create a `PSSession` and then define a function in that session. The goal is to be able to execute this remote function as though it was defined locally. In other words, you want to implicitly remote the function. To accomplish this, you call `Import-PSSession`, which generates a function that you can call locally. This local function does the remote call on your behalf—it acts as your *proxy*. The steps in this process are shown in figure 12.9.

You'll begin by creating the connection to a remote machine. To do this, you may need to get credentials for the remote host.

```
Import-PSSession
    [-Session] <PSSession>
    [[-CommandName] <String[]>]
    [[-FormatTypeName] <String[]>]
    [-Prefix <String>]
    [-DisableNameChecking]
    [-AllowClobber] [-ArgumentList <Object[]>]
    [-CommandType <CommandTypes>]
    [-Module <String[]>]
```

Figure 12.8 The syntax for the `Import-PSSession` cmdlet. This cmdlet is used to create local proxy commands that invoke the corresponding remote command on the target computer.

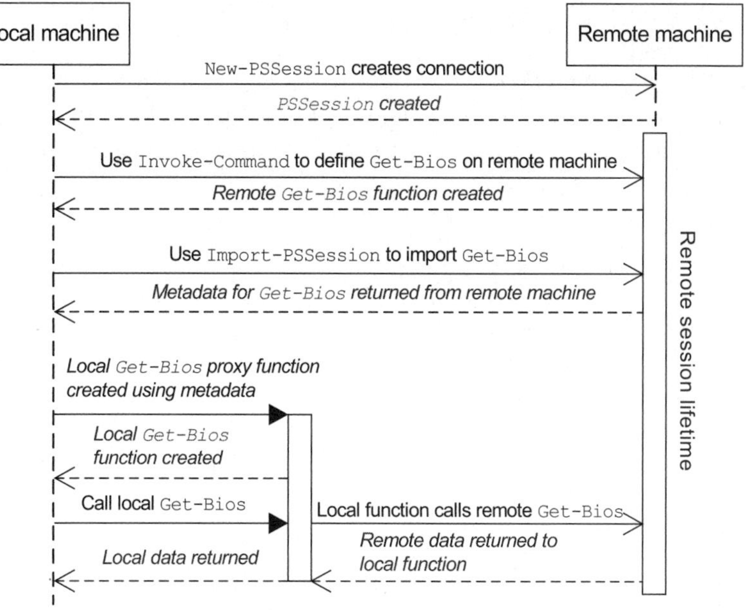

Figure 12.9 The sequence of steps needed to create a session, define a new remote command in that session, use `Import-PSSession` to import that command, and finally call the imported command. When you use `Import-PSSession` to import a command, metadata describing the remote command is retrieved from the target machine and used to create a local proxy command. When this proxy command is called, it implicitly calls the remote command to perform the operation on the remote machine.

> **NOTE** In a domain environment, this step is unnecessary as long as your user account has sufficient privileges to access the remote end point. But if you want to log on as a different used, credentials will be required.

The `Get-Credential` cmdlet will prompt you for your username and password:

```
PS (1) > $cred = Get-Credential

cmdlet Get-Credential at command pipeline position 1
Supply values for the following parameters:
Credential
```

Now that you have the credential object in `$cred`, you can establish a session on the remote machine:

```
PS (2) > $s = New-PSSession brucepay64h -Credential $cred
```

Next, you'll use `Invoke-Command` to define a new function on the remote machine. This is the command you'll import:

```
PS (3) > Invoke-Command $s {
>> function Get-Bios { Get-WmiObject Win32_Bios }
```

```
>> }
>>
```

The new remote function is called `Get-Bios` and uses WMI (chapter 19) to retrieve information about the BIOS on the remote machine. Invoke this function through explicit remoting using `Invoke-Command` so you can see what it does:

```
PS (4) > Invoke-Command $s {Get-Bios}

SMBIOSBIOSVersion : 3.34
Manufacturer      : Phoenix Technologies, LTD
Name              : Phoenix - Award BIOS v6.00PG
SerialNumber      : MXK5380BK3 NA580
Version           : HP-CPC - 42302e31
PSComputerName    : brucepay64h
```

It returns a set of information about the BIOS on the remote machine. Now you're set up to use `Import-PSSession` to create a local proxy for this command:

```
PS (5) > Import-PSSession -Session $s -CommandName Get-Bios

ModuleType Name                      ExportedCommands
---------- ----                      ----------------
Script     tmp_00288002-bcec-43fd... Get-Bios
```

You might recognize the output from this command—it's the same thing you see when you do `Import-Module`. We'll discuss what that means in a minute, but first let's see if you now have a local `Get-Bios` command by running it:

```
PS (6) > Get-Bios

SMBIOSBIOSVersion : 3.34
Manufacturer      : Phoenix Technologies, LTD
Name              : Phoenix - Award BIOS v6.00PG
SerialNumber      : MXK5380BK3 NA580
Version           : HP-CPC - 42302e31
```

You get the same result you saw when you did the explicit remote invocation, but without having to do any extra work to access the remote machine. The proxy command did that for you. This is the goal of implicit remoting: to make the fact that the command is being executed remotely invisible. In the next section, you'll learn how it all works.

12.4.2 How implicit remoting works

Now that you've seen implicit remoting in action, let's look at how it's implemented. The sequence of operations performed by the implicit remoting mechanism is shown in figure 12.10.

When the user requests that a command be imported, a message is sent to the remote computer for processing. The import request processor looks up the command and retrieves the metadata (i.e., the `CommandInfo` object) for that command. That metadata is processed to simplify it, removing things like complex type attributes. Only the core

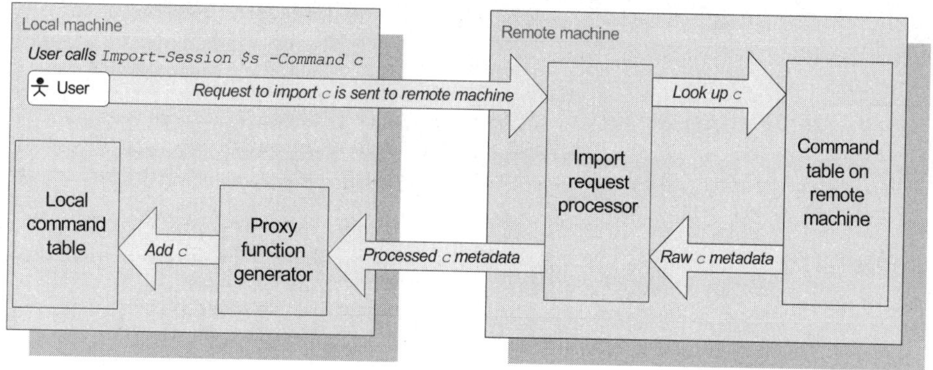

Figure 12.10 How remote commands are imported by the implicit remoting mechanism. `Import-PSSession` works by sending a message to the remote computer to retrieve the metadata for the requested command. This metadata is processed and returned to the local machine, where a proxy advanced function is generated.

remoting types are passed along. This metadata is received by the local machine's proxy function generator. It uses this metadata to generate a function that will implicitly call the remote command. Let's take closer look at what the generated proxy looks like. You can look at the imported `Get-Bios` command using `Get-Command`:

```
PS (7) > Get-Command Get-Bios

CommandType     Name                    Definition
-----------     ----                    ----------
Function        Get-Bios                ...
```

The output shows that you have a local function called `Get-Bios`. You can look at the definition of that function by using the `Definition` property on the `CommandInfo` object returned by `Get-Command`:

```
PS (8) > Get-Command Get-Bios | % { $_.Definition }
    param(
    [Switch]
    ${AsJob})
begin {
    try {
       $positionalArguments = & $script:NewObject collections.arraylist
       foreach ($parameterName in $PSBoundParameters.BoundPositionally)
       {
           $null = $positionalArguments.Add(
                   $PSBoundParameters[$parameterName] )
           $null = $PSBoundParameters.Remove($parameterName)
       }
       $positionalArguments.AddRange($args)
       $clientSideParameters = Get-PSImplicitRemotingClientSideParameters `
           $PSBoundParameters $False
       $scriptCmd = { & $script:InvokeCommand `
```

```
                    @clientSideParameters `
                    -HideComputerName `
                    -Session (Get-PSImplicitRemotingSession `
                        -CommandName 'Get-Bios') `
                    -Arg ('Get-Bios', $PSBoundParameters,
                         $positionalArguments) `
                    -Script { param($name, $boundParams,
                                 $unboundParams)
                              & $name @boundParams @unboundParams}}

        $steppablePipeline = $scriptCmd.GetSteppablePipeline(
                                $myInvocation.CommandOrigin)
        $steppablePipeline.Begin($myInvocation.ExpectingInput,
                                  $ExecutionContext)
    } catch {
        throw
    }
}
process {
    try {
        $steppablePipeline.Process($_)
    } catch {
        throw
    }
}
end {
    try {
        $steppablePipeline.End()
    } catch {
        throw
    }
}
```

Even though this output has been reformatted a bit to make it more readable, it's a pretty complex function and uses many of the more sophisticated features we've covered in previous chapters. It uses advanced functions, splatting, scriptblocks, and steppable pipelines. Fortunately, you never have to write these functions yourself.

> **NOTE** You don't have to create proxy functions for this particular scenario, but back in section 11.5.2 you saw how this technique can be very powerful in extending the PowerShell environment.

The `Import-PSSession` cmdlet does this for you. It will create a proxy function for each command it's importing, which could lead to a lot of commands. Managing a lot of new commands in your environment could be a problem, so let's go back to looking at exactly what the output from `Import-PSSession` was. We commented at the time that it looked like the output from `Import-Module`, and this is exactly what it is. As well as generating proxy functions on your behalf, `Import-PSSession` creates a module to contain these functions. You'll use `Get-Module` to verify this and format the output as a list to see all the details:

```
PS (9) > Get-Module | Format-List *

ExportedCommands      : {Get-Bios}
Name                  : tmp_00288002-bcec-43fd-853f-8059edfd2430_y
                        hv1i4f4.ogw
Path                  : C:\Users\brucepay\AppData\Local\Temp\tmp_0
                        0288002-bcec-43fd-853f-8059edfd2430_yhv1i4
                        f4.ogw\tmp_00288002-bcec-43fd-853f-8059edf
                        d2430_yhv1i4f4.ogw.psm1
Description           : Implicit remoting for http://brucepay64h/w
                        sman
Guid                  : 00288002-bcec-43fd-853f-8059edfd2430
ModuleBase            : C:\Users\brucepay\AppData\Local\Temp\tmp_0
                        0288002-bcec-43fd-853f-8059edfd2430_yhv1i4
                        f4.ogw
PrivateData           : {ImplicitRemoting}
Version               : 1.0
ModuleType            : Script
AccessMode            : ReadWrite
ExportedFunctions     : {[Get-Bios, Get-Bios]}
ExportedCmdlets       : {}
NestedModules         : {}
RequiredModules       : {}
ExportedVariables     : {}
ExportedAliases       : {}
SessionState          : System.Management.Automation.SessionState
OnRemove              :
                        $sourceIdentifier =
                        [system.management.automation.wildcardpattern]::
                            Escape(
                             $eventSubscriber.SourceIdentifier)
                        Unregister-Event -SourceIdentifier `
                           $sourceIdentifier -Force -ErrorAction `
                           SilentlyContinue

                        if ($previousScript -ne $null)
                        {
                            & $previousScript $args
                        }

ExportedFormatFiles : {C:\Users\brucepay\AppData\Local\Temp\tmp_
                        00288002-bcec-43fd-853f-8059edfd2430_yhv1i
                        4f4.ogw\tmp_00288002-bcec-43fd-853f-8059ed
                        fd2430_yhv1i4f4.ogw.format.ps1xml}
ExportedTypeFiles     : {}

PS (10) >
```

Things to notice in this output (again reformatted for readability) include the fact that the module name and path are temporary generated names. This module also defines an `OnRemove` handler (see chapter 10) to clean up when the module is removed. To see the contents of the module, you can look at the temporary file that was created by opening it in an editor using the module's `Path` property. For example, to open the module file in PowerShell ISE, use this code:

```
PS (14) > powershell_ise (Get-Command Get-Bios).Module.Path
```

Alternatively, you can save the session to an explicitly named module for reuse with `Export-PSSession`. You'll save this session as a module called `bios`:

```
PS (15) > Export-PSSession -OutputModule bios -Session $s `
>> -type function -CommandName Get-Bios -AllowClobber
>>

    Directory: C:\Users\brucepay\Documents\WindowsPowerShell\Mod
    ules\bios

Mode                LastWriteTime     Length Name
----                -------------     ------ ----
-a---        11/29/2009   1:05 PM      10359 bios.psm1
-a---        11/29/2009   1:05 PM         99 bios.format.ps1xml
-a---        11/29/2009   1:05 PM        532 bios.psd1
```

Executing this command created a new module in your user module directory. It created the script module file (.psm1), the module manifest (.psd1), and a file containing formatting information for the command. You used the `-AllowClobber` parameter because the export is using the remote session to gather the data. If it finds a command being exported that already exists in the caller's environment, this would be an error. Because `Get-Bios` already exists, you had to use `-AllowClobber`. Now you'll try out the new module. First, you need to clean the existing module and session:

```
PS (32) > Get-Module | Remove-Module
PS (33) > Remove-PSSession $s
```

Import the module

```
PS (34) > Import-Module bios
```

and it returns right away. It can do this because it hasn't actually set up the remote connection yet. This will happen the first time you access one of the functions in the module. Run `Get-Bios`:

```
PS (35) > Get-Bios
Creating a new session for implicit remoting of "Get-Bios"
command...
The term 'Get-Bios' is not recognized as the name of a cmdlet,
function, script file, or operable program. Check the spelling of
 the name, or if a path was included, verify that the path is
```

```
correct and try again.
    + CategoryInfo          : ObjectNotFound: (Get-Bios:String)
    [], CommandNotFoundException
    + FullyQualifiedErrorId : CommandNotFoundException
```

When you ran this command, you saw a message indicating that a new connection was being created, and then the credential prompt popped up. This is pretty much as expected. But then you got an error saying the command `Get-Bios` wasn't found. This is because you dynamically added the function to the remote session. When you established a new session, because you didn't add the function, it wasn't there. In the next section, we'll describe how to create remote endpoints that always contain your custom functions.

Let's briefly review where we are. You've seen how PowerShell remoting allows you to execute commands on a remote machine. You know how to use explicit remoting to send scriptblocks to the remote computer to be executed. We explored interactive remoting where every command is sent to the remote machine, making it look as if you're working directly on that machine. Finally, we looked at implicit remoting, which makes it appear that all your commands are being run locally. This greatly simplifies remoting for the casual user. It allows you to do things like manage an Exchange mail server without having to install any code locally: you can use implicit remoting to generate a proxy module for the Exchange management module residing on another.

One thing that's been constant across all of these remoting experiences is that you always had to wait for the remote commands to complete before issuing the next command. But early on in our discussion of remoting, we noted that because there are two (or more) processes involved, things actually do happen concurrently. In the next section, you'll see how this characteristic is used to implement background jobs in PowerShell.

12.5 Background jobs in PowerShell

In the previous section, you saw that although remote PowerShell sessions run in separate processes, the user is still prevented from running new commands until the remote command completes. If you change things so that the caller doesn't block, then other commands can run in parallel. This is how PowerShell background jobs work. With background jobs, the arrangement of executing commands and processes is shown in figure 12.11.

> **NOTE** In section 12.1.1, you saw that some commands have built-in remoting capabilities. In a similar fashion, there are also commands that have built-in job support. For example, the WMI commands have an `-AsJob` parameter that allows one or more WMI operations to execute in the background. This type of job doesn't rely on the background

execution mechanism we're describing in this section. Instead, they use their own implementation of background execution. In the case of WMI jobs, they run in process but on a separate thread. The PowerShell job infrastructure was explicitly designed to support this kind of extension. If third parties expose their job abstractions as subclasses of the PowerShell `Job` type, these extension jobs can be managed using the built-in job cmdlets just like native PowerShell jobs.

There's more to background jobs than simply executing multiple things at the same time. Background jobs are designed to be commands that run asynchronously while you continue to do other things at the console. This means that there needs to be a way to manage these background jobs—starting and stopping them as well as retrieving the output in a controlled way.

> **NOTE** Background jobs are implemented using processes that are children of your interactive PowerShell process. This means that if you end your PowerShell session, causing the process to exit, this will also cause all the background jobs to be terminated, because child processes are terminated when the parent process exits.

In this section we'll cover the cmdlets that are used to accomplish these tasks. We'll look at starting, stopping, and waiting for jobs. We'll explore the `Job` objects used to represent a running job. Finally, you'll learn how to combine remoting with jobs to run jobs on remote machines.

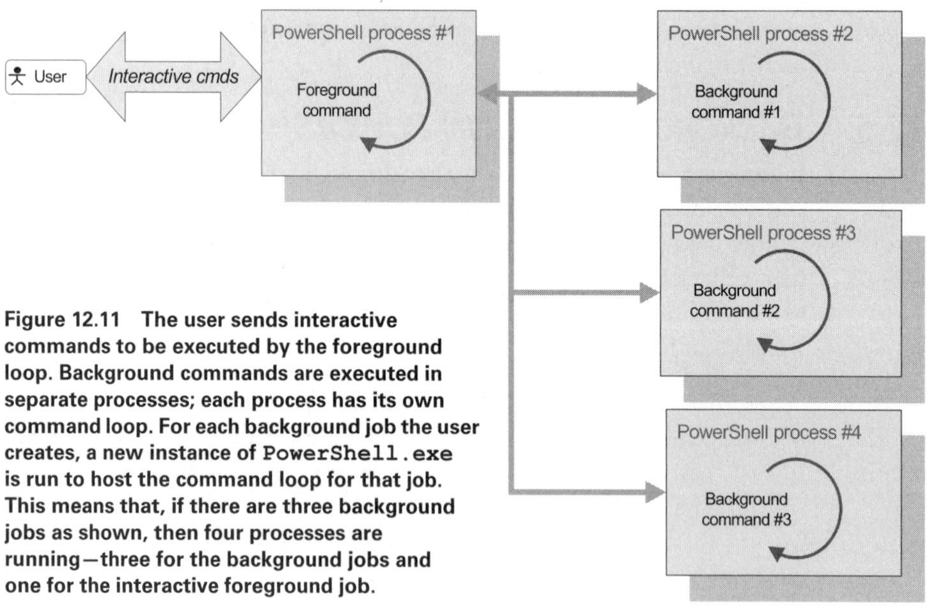

Figure 12.11 The user sends interactive commands to be executed by the foreground loop. Background commands are executed in separate processes; each process has its own command loop. For each background job the user creates, a new instance of `PowerShell.exe` is run to host the command loop for that job. This means that, if there are three background jobs as shown, then four processes are running—three for the background jobs and one for the interactive foreground job.

12.5.1 The job commands

As with remoting, jobs are managed with a set of cmdlets. These cmdlets are shown in table 12.3.

Table 12.3 The cmdlets for working with PowerShell jobs

Cmdlet	Description
`Start-Job`	Used to start background jobs. It takes a scriptblock as the argument representing the job to execute.
`Stop-Job`	Stops a job based on the `JobID`.
`Get-Job`	Returns a list of currently executing jobs associated with the current session.
`Wait-Job`	Waits for one or more jobs to complete.
`Receive-Job`	Gets the results for a specific job.
`Remove-Job`	Removes a job from the job table so the resources can be released.

A background job runs commands asynchronously. They're used to execute long-running commands in a way that the interactive session isn't blocked until that command completes.

When a synchronous command runs, PowerShell waits until that command has completed before accepting any new commands. When a command is run in the background, instead of blocking, the command returns immediately, emitting an object that represents the new background job.

Although you get back control immediately (a new prompt) with the `Job` object, you obviously won't get the results of that job even if the job runs quickly. Instead, you use a separate command to get the job's results. You also have commands to stop the job, to wait for the job to be completed, and finally to delete the job. Let's see how these commands are used.

12.5.2 Working with the job cmdlets

You use the `Start-Job` command to start a background job on a local computer. Let's try this with a simple example. You'll start a job and then pipe the resulting `Job` object through `Format-List` so you can see of the members on the object:

```
PS (1) > Start-Job { "Hi" } | Format-List

HasMoreData   : True
StatusMessage :
Location      : localhost
Command       :  "Hi"
JobStateInfo  : Running
Finished      : System.Threading.ManualResetEvent
InstanceId    : fefc87f6-b5a7-4319-9145-616317ac8fcb
Id            : 1
Name          : Job1
ChildJobs     : {Job2}
```

```
Output        : {}
Error         : {}
Progress      : {}
Verbose       : {}
Debug         : {}
Warning       : {}
State         : Running
```

As with the remoting cmdlets, the command to execute is specified by a scriptblock. When the command runs, you see that an object is returned, containing a wealth of information about the job. We'll look at this object in a detail later on. For now, we'll keep looking at the cmdlets. Now that you've started a job, you can use the `Get-Job` cmdlet to get information about that job:

```
PS (3) > Get-Job | fl

HasMoreData   : True
StatusMessage :
Location      : localhost
Command       :  "Hi"
JobStateInfo  : Completed
Finished      : System.Threading.ManualResetEvent
InstanceId    : fefc87f6-b5a7-4319-9145-616317ac8fcb
Id            : 1
Name          : Job1
ChildJobs     : {Job2}
Output        : {}
Error         : {}
Progress      : {}
Verbose       : {}
Debug         : {}
Warning       : {}
State         : Completed
```

This cmdlet returned the same `Job` object that you saw returned from `Start-Job`. (You can tell it's the same object by looking at the `InstanceId`, which is a `GUID` and is guaranteed to be unique for each job.) There's one significant different in this output: if you look at the `State` property, you see that it has changed from `Running` to `Completed`. So the first thing to note is that a job remains in the job table even after it has completed and will remain there until it's explicitly removed using the `Remove-Job` cmdlet. To get the results of the job, you can use another cmdlet: `Receive-Job`. This cmdlet will return the results of the command that was executed:

```
PS (5) > Receive-Job 1
Hi
```

This returns the string that was emitted by the scriptblock passed to `Start-Job`. This isn't a very interesting example. Let's try something that will take a bit longer to run. First, define the scriptblock you want to run in the `$jsb` variable:

```
PS (9) > $jsb = {
>> foreach ($i in 1..10) { Start-Sleep 1; "i is $i" }
```

```
>> }
>>
```

Now start the job running. Let the `Job` object that was returned use the default formatting, which complains if the screen is too narrow for all the columns to be displayed. The compressed output doesn't matter because the only thing you want at this point is the job's ID:

```
PS (10) > Start-Job $jsb

WARNING: column "Command" does not fit into the display and was
removed.

Id              Name            State      HasMoreData     Locat
                                                           ion
--              ----            -----      -----------     -----
5               Job5            Running    True            lo...
```

Start calling `Receive-Job` with the job's ID:

```
PS (11) > Receive-Job 5
i is 1
i is 2
```

The first call returned the first two items out of the 10 you're expecting. Call it again

```
PS (12) > Receive-Job 5
i is 3
i is 4
```

and you get another two items. Call it again quickly

```
PS (13) > Receive-Job 5
i is 5
```

and you get one additional item. Keep calling it until you get all the items:

```
PS (14) > Receive-Job 5
i is 6
i is 7
PS (15) > Receive-Job 5
i is 8
PS (16) > Receive-Job 5
i is 9
PS (17) > Receive-Job 5
i is 10
PS (18) > Receive-Job 5
```

This last call didn't return anything because the job has completed and all items have already been returned. You can verify this by calling `Get-Job`

```
PS (19) > Get-Job 5

WARNING: column "Command" does not fit into the display and was
removed.
```

```
Id              Name            State       HasMoreData     Locat
                                                            ion
--              ----            -----       -----------     -----
5               Job5            Completed   False           lo...
```

and you see that its state is Completed. Because the job is running asynchronously, the number of items that are returned depends on when you call Receive-Job.

Waiting for jobs to complete

So how do you wait until the job has completed? You could write a loop to keep checking the State property, but that would be annoying and inefficient. Instead, you can use the Wait-Job cmdlet:

```
PS (21) > $jb = Start-Job $jsb; Wait-Job $jb ; Receive-Job $jb

Id              Name            State       HasMoreData     Locat
                                                            ion
--              ----            -----       -----------     -----
9               Job9            Completed   True            lo...
i is 1
i is 2
i is 3
i is 4
i is 5
i is 6
i is 7
i is 8
i is 9
i is 10
```

In this example, you're capturing the job object emitted by Start-Job in the $jb variable so you can use it in the subsequent Wait-Job and Receive-Job commands. Because of the Wait-Job, when you call Receive-Job you get all the input.

Notice that Wait-Job returns the object representing the job that has finished. You can use this to simplify the example a bit:

```
PS (22) > Start-Job $jsb | Wait-Job | Receive-Job
i is 1
i is 2
i is 3
i is 4
i is 5
i is 6
i is 7
i is 8
i is 9
i is 10
```

In this example, Start-Job passes the Job object to Wait-Job. When the job completes, Wait-Job passes the Job object to Receive-Job to get the results. This eliminates the need for an intermediate variable.

Removing jobs

So far, you've been creating jobs but haven't removed any. This means that when you call `Get-Job`, you'll see that there are a number of jobs still in the job table:

```
PS (23) > Get-Job

WARNING: column "Command" does not fit into the display and was
removed.

Id              Name            State       HasMoreData     Locat
                                                            ion
--              ----            -----       -----------     -----
1               Job1            Completed   False           lo...
3               Job3            Completed   False           lo...
5               Job5            Completed   False           lo...
7               Job7            Completed   True            lo...
9               Job9            Completed   False           lo...
```

Each time you start a job, it gets added to the job table. You can clean things up using the `Remove-Job` cmdlet. To empty the table, use `Remove-Job` with a wildcard:

```
PS (24) > Remove-Job *
```

Now when you call `Get-Job`, nothing is returned:

```
PS (25) > Get-Job
PS (26) >
```

This is probably not the best way to clean things up. A better solution would be to look for jobs that have completed and have no more data. This would look like the following:

```
function Clear-CompletedJobs {
    Get-Job | where { $_.State -eq "Completed" -and
                            -not $_.HasMoreData } | Remove-Job
}
```

This function calls `Get-Job` to get the list of all jobs, filters that list based on the `State` and `HasMoreData` properties, and then pipes the filtered list into `Remove-Job`. By doing this, only completed jobs for which all data has been received will be removed. This allows you to clean up the job table without worrying about losing information or getting errors. If you do want to kill all of the jobs immediately, you can use the `-Force` parameter on `Remove-Job`.

In the next section, we'll look at ways you can apply concurrent jobs to solve problems.

12.5.3 Working with multiple jobs

So far we've looked at simple patterns working with one job at a time, but you can run a number of jobs at the same time. Doing so complicates things—you have to be able to handle the output from multiple jobs. Let's look at how to do this. The following listing shows how to wait for a set of jobs and then receive the results.

Listing 12.6 Example of running multiple jobs

```
1..5| foreach {
    Start-Job -name "job$_" -ScriptBlock {
        param($number)
        $waitTime = Get-Random -min 4 -max 10
        Start-Sleep -Seconds $waitTime
        "Job $number is complete; waited $waitTime"
        } -ArgumentList $_ > $null }

Wait-Job job* | Receive-Job
```

This example starts a number of jobs that will run concurrently, waits for all of them to complete, and then gets all the results. Run this code and see what happens:

```
PS (1) > 1..5| foreach {
>>     Start-Job -name "job$_" -ScriptBlock {
>>         param($number)
>>         $waitTime = Get-Random -min 4 -max 10
>>         Start-Sleep -Seconds $waitTime
>>         "Job $number is complete; waited $waitTime"
>>         } -ArgumentList $_ > $null }
>>
PS (2) > wait-Job job* | Receive-Job
Job 1 is complete; waited 4
Job 2 is complete; waited 4
Job 3 is complete; waited 8
Job 4 is complete; waited 5
Job 5 is complete; waited 7
```

As you can see, all the results are captured, ordered by the job name. Now let's look at a more useful application of this pattern. The following listing shows a function that searches multiple directories in parallel looking for a specific pattern.

Listing 12.7 A function that searches a collection of folders in parallel

```
function Search-FilesInParallel
{
    param (
        [parameter(mandatory=$true, position=0)]
            $Pattern,
        [parameter(mandatory=$true, position=1)]
        [string[]]
            $Path,
        [parameter(mandatory=$false)]
            $Filter = "*.txt",
        [parameter(mandatory=$false)]
        [switch]
            $Any
    )
```

```
    $jobid = [guid]::NewGuid().ToString()          <-- Generate GUID to use for job ID
    $jobs = foreach ($element in $path)
    {
        Start-Job -name "$Srch{jobid}" -scriptblock {      <-- Start search job for each path
            param($pattern, $path, $filter, $any)
            Get-ChildItem -Path $path -Recurse -Filter $filter |
                Select-String -list:$any $pattern          <-- Pass -any switch to Select-String
        } -ArgumentList $pattern,$element,$filter,$any
    }

    Wait-Job -any:$any $jobs | Receive-Job            <-- Wait for any or all jobs
    Remove-Job -force $jobs
}
```

This function takes a list of folder paths to search, along with a pattern to search for. By default, the function will only search TXT files. It also has a switch, `-any`, that controls how the search is performed. If the switch isn't specified, all matches from all folders will be returned. If it's specified, only the first match will be returned and the remaining incomplete jobs will be canceled.

This function seems like a useful tool. Unfortunately, jobs are implemented by creating new processes for each job, and this is an expensive operation—so expensive, in fact, that generally it's much slower than simply searching all the files serially. In practice, PowerShell jobs are a way of dealing with latency (the time it takes for an operation to return a result) and not throughput (the amount of data that gets processed). This is a good trade-off for remote management tasks when you're talking to many machines more or less at once. The amount of data, as you saw in the monitoring example in section 12.2, is frequently not large, and the overall execution time is dominated by the time it takes to connect to a remote machine. With that in mind, let's look at how remoting and jobs work together.

12.5.4 Starting jobs on remote computers

Because the job infrastructure is based on the remoting framework, it follows that we can also create and manage jobs on remote computers.

> **NOTE** To work with remote jobs, remoting must be enabled on the remote machine. For local jobs, remoting doesn't have to be enabled because a different communication channel (anonymous pipes) is used between the parent session and the child jobs.

The easiest way to do this is to use the `-AsJob` parameter on `Invoke-Command`. Alternatively, the scriptblock passed to `Invoke-Command` can call `Start-Job` explicitly. Let's see how this works.

Child jobs and nesting

So far we've talked about `Job` objects as atomic—one `Job` object per job. In practice it's a bit more sophisticated than that. There are scenarios when you need to be able to aggregate collections of jobs under a single master, or *executive*, job. We'll get to those situations in a minute. For now, just know that background jobs always consist of a parent job and one or more child jobs.

For jobs started using `Start-Job` or the `-AsJob` parameter on `Invoke-Command`, the parent job is the executive. It doesn't run any commands or return any results.

> **NOTE** The executive does no actual work—it just supervises. All the work is done by the subordinates. That sounds familiar somehow….

This collection of child jobs is stored in the `ChildJobs` property of the parent `Job` object. The child `Job` objects have a name, ID, and instance ID that differ from the parent job so that you can manage the parent and each child job individually or as a single unit.

To see the parent and all the children in a `Job`, use the `Get-Job` cmdlet to get the parent `Job` object, and then pipe it to `Format-List`, which displays the `Name` and `ChildJobs` as properties of the objects. Here's what this looks like:

```
PS (1) > Get-Job | Format-List -Property Name, ChildJobs
Name            : Job1
ChildJobs       : {Job2}
```

You can also use a `Get-Job` command on the child job, as shown in the following command

```
PS (2) > Get-Job job2

Id     Name   State      HasMoreData  Location    Command
--     ----   -----      -----------  --------    -------
2      Job2   Completed  True         localhost   Get-Process
```

and so on until you get to a `Job` that has no children.

Child jobs with Invoke-Command

Let's look at the scenario where you need to have more than one child job. When `Start-Job` is used to start a job on a local computer, the job always consists of the executive parent job and a single child job that runs the command. When you use the `-AsJob` parameter on `Invoke-Command` to start a job on multiple computers, you have the situation where the job consists of an executive parent job and one child job for each command running on a remote server, as shown in figure 12.12.

When you use `Invoke-Command` to explicitly run `Start-Job` on the remote machines, the result is the same as a local command run on each remote computer. The command returns a job object for each computer. The `Job` object consists of an executive parent job and one child job that runs the command.

The parent job represents all the child jobs. When you manage a parent job, you also manage the associated child jobs. For example, if you stop a parent job, all child

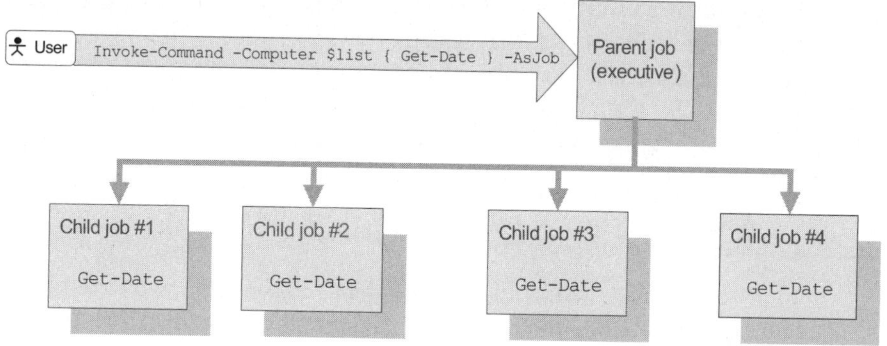

Figure 12.12 The relationship between the executive job and the nested jobs created when `Invoke-Command -AsJob` is used to run commands on multiple remote computers. The user calls `Invoke-Command` to start a job with multiple nested jobs, one for each target node in `$list`.

jobs are also stopped. Similarly, when you get the results of a parent job, you're also getting the results of all child jobs.

Most of the time, you don't need to be concerned with the fact that there are parent and child jobs; but it's possible to manage the child jobs individually. This approach is typically only used when you want to investigate a problem with a job or get the results of only one of a number of child jobs started by using the `-AsJob` parameter of `Invoke-Command`.

The following command uses `Invoke-Command` with `-AsJob` to start background jobs on the local computer and two remote computers. The command saves the job in the `$j` variable:

```
PS (1) > $j = Invoke-Command -ComputerName localhost, Server01, Server02 `
    -Command {Get-Date} -AsJob
```

When you display the `Name` and `ChildJob` properties of the object in `$j`, it shows that the command returned a `Job` object with three child jobs, one for each computer:

```
PS (2) > $j | Format-List name, childjobs

Name      : Job3
ChildJobs : {Job4, Job5, Job6}
```

When you display the parent job, it shows that the overall job was considered to have failed:

```
PS (3) > $j

Id   Name    State   HasMoreData     Location              Command
--   ----    -----   -----------     --------              -------
 1    Job3    Failed  True            localhost,server... Get-Date
```

But on further investigation, when you run Get-Job on each of the child jobs, you find that only one of them has failed:

```
PS (4) > Get-Job job4, job5, job6

Id    Name    State        HasMoreData      Location             Command
--    ----    -----        -----------      --------             -------
4     Job4    Completed    True             localhost            get-date
5     Job5    Failed       False            Server01             get-date
6     Job6    Completed    True             Server02             get-date
```

To get the results of all child jobs, use the Receive-Job cmdlet to obtain the results of the parent job. But you can also get the results of a particular child job, as shown in the following command:

```
PS (5) > Receive-Job -Job 6 -Keep |
>> Format-Table ComputerName,DateTime -AutoSize

ComputerName DateTime
------------ --------
Server02     Thursday, March 13, 2008 4:16:03 PM
```

In this example, you're using the -Keep parameter, which allows you to read, but not remove, output from a job. When you use -Keep, the output from the job is retained in the output buffer for that job. You're using it here so that when you do a Receive-Job on the executive job, you'll get the output of all jobs in a single collection. In effect, this is a way of "peeking" at the output of one of the child jobs. By using child jobs, you have much more granular control over the set of activities you have running.

The way you've been working with jobs so far has been much like when you were using Invoke-Command and specifying the name of a computer. Each time you contacted the computer, Invoke-Command created a new session. You're doing much the same thing when you use Start-Job. With Invoke-Command, you were able to improve your efficiency by creating sessions. In the next section you'll see how sessions work with jobs.

12.5.5 Running jobs in existing sessions

Each background job runs in its own PowerShell session, paralleling the way each remote command is also executed in its own session. As was the case with remoting, this session can be a temporary one that exists only for the duration of the background job, or it can be run in an existing PSSession. But the way to do this isn't obvious because the Start-Job cmdlet doesn't have a -Session parameter. Instead you have to use Invoke-Command with the -Session and -AsJob parameters. Here's what that looks like. First, create a PSSession object:

```
PS (1) > $s = New-PSSession
```

Now pass that session object to Invoke-Command with -AsJob specified:

```
PS (2) > $j = Invoke-Command -Session $s -AsJob {$PID}
```

The scriptblock that you're passing in returns the process ID of the session. Use `Receive-Job` to retrieve it:

```
PS (3) > Receive-Job $j
10808
```

You can call `Invoke-Command` without `-AsJob` with the same session object and scriptblock:

```
PS (4) > Invoke-Command -Session $s {$PID}
10808
```

You get the same process ID back, which is expected because the session is persistently associated with the same process.

Start-Job and sessions

So why is there no `-Session` parameter on `Start-Job`? This parameter did exist at one point in the development of PowerShell v2. At that time, jobs and remoting used the same message *transport*, not just the same basic infrastructure. Using the same transport was found to be problematic for a number of reasons:

- It was inefficient for communication with local jobs.
- It required that the remoting service be enabled on the local machine, which has security implications.
- It required users to be running with admin privileges to be able to use the job feature.

To resolve these issues, the existing WSMan-based transport used by jobs was replaced with anonymous pipes. This change solved these problems, but it had the unfortunate side effect that jobs could no longer be directly run with in `PSSession` instances because the `PSSession` object was tied to WSMan remoting.

Keep in mind that when a job is run in an existing `PSSession`, that session can't be used to run additional tasks until the job has completed. This means that you have to create multiple `PSSession` objects if you need to run multiple background tasks but want to avoid the overhead of creating new processes for each job. As always, it's up to the script author to decide how best to manage resources for their script.

12.6 CONSIDERATIONS WHEN RUNNING COMMANDS REMOTELY

When you run commands on multiple computers, you need to be aware, at least to some extent, of how the execution environment can differ on the target machines. For example, the target machine may be running a different version of the operating system, or it may have a different processor. There may also be differences in which applications are installed, how files are arranged, or where things are placed in the Registry. In this section, we'll look at a number of these issues.

12.6.1 Remote session startup directory

When a user connects to a remote computer, the system sets the startup directory for the remote session to a specific value. This value will change depending on the version of the operating system on the target machine:

- If the machine is running Windows Vista, Windows Server 2003 R2, or later, the default starting location for the session is the user's home directory, which is typically C:\Users\<UserName>.
- On Windows Server 2003, the user's home directory is also used but resolves to a slightly different path: C:\Documents and Settings\<UserName>.
- On Windows XP, the default user's home directory is used instead of the connecting user's. This typically resolves to C:\Documents and Settings\Default User.

The default starting location can be obtained from either the `$ENV:HOMEPATH` environment or the PowerShell `$HOME` variable. By using these variables instead of hardcoded paths in your scripts, you can avoid problems related to these differences. Next, we'll examine issues related to startup and profiles.

12.6.2 Profiles and remoting

Most PowerShell users eventually create a custom startup script or profile that they use to customize their environment. These customizations typically include defining convenience functions and aliases. Although profiles are a great feature for customizing local interactive sessions, if the convenience commands they define are used in scripts that you want to run remotely, you'll encounter problems. This is because your profiles aren't run automatically in remote sessions, and that means the convenience commands defined in the profile aren't available in the remote session. In fact, the `$PROFILE` variable, which points to the profile file, isn't even populated for remote sessions.

As a best practice, for production scripting you should make sure your scripts never become contaminated with elements defined by your profiles. One way to test this is to run the script from `PowerShell.exe` with the `-NoProfile` option, which looks like this:

```
powershell -NoProfile -File myscript.ps1
```

This command will run the script without loading your profile. If the script depends on anything defined in the profile, it will generate errors.

But for remote interactive sessions, it'd be nice to have the same environment everywhere. You can accomplish this by using `Invoke-Command` with the `-FilePath` parameter to send your profile file to the remote machine and execute it there. The set of commands you need to accomplish this are as follows:

```
$c = Get-Credential
$s = New-PSSession -Credential $ -ComputerName targetComputer
Invoke-Command -Session $s -FilePath $PROFILE
Enter-PSSession $s
```

First, you get the credential for the target machine (this typically won't be needed in the domain environment). Next, you create a persistent session to the remote computer. Then you use -FilePath on Invoke-Command to execute the profile file in the remote session. Finally, with the session properly configured, you can call Enter-PSSession to start your remote interactive session with all of your normal customizations.

Alternatively, sometimes you may want to run a profile on the remote machine instead of your local profile. Because $PROFILE isn't populated in your remote session, you'll need to be clever to make this work. The key is that, although $PROFILE isn't set, $HOME is. You can use this to compose a path to your profile on the remote computer. The revised list of commands looks like this:

```
$c = Get-Credential
$s = New-PSSession -Credential $ -ComputerName targetComputer

Invoke-Command -Session $s {
  . "$home\Documents\WindowsPowerShell\profile.ps1" }
Enter-PSSession $s
```

This command dot-sources (see section 8.1.4) the profile file in the user's directory on the remote machine into the session. Note that this script won't work on XP or Windows Server 2003 because the document directory on those versions of Windows is Documents and Settings instead of Documents. For those operating systems, the set of steps would look like this:

```
$c = Get-Credential
$s = New-PSSession -Credential $ -ComputerName targetComputer

Invoke-Command -Session $s {
  . "$home\Documents and Setting\WindowsPowerShell\profile.ps1" }
Enter-PSSession $s
```

In this section you learned how to cause your profile to be used to configure the remote session environment. At the end of the section, we revisited the idea that some system paths will vary depending on the operating system version. In the next section, we'll examine another area where these variations can cause problems.

12.6.3 Issues running executables remotely

PowerShell remoting allows you to execute the same types of commands remotely as you can locally, including external applications or executables. The ability to remotely execute commands like shutdown to restart a remote host or ipconfig to get network settings is critical for system management.

For the most part, console-based commands will work properly because they read and write only to the standard input, output, and error pipes. Commands that won't work are ones that directly call the Windows Console APIs, like console-based editors or text-based menu programs. The reason is that no console object is available in the remote session. Because these applications are rarely used anymore, this fact typically won't have a big impact. But there are some surprises. For example, the net command will work fine most of the time, but if you do something like this (which prompts for a password)

```
PS (1) > net use p: '\\machine1\c$'  /user:machine1\user1 *
Type the password for \\machine1\c$:
```

in a remote session you'll get an error:

```
[machine1]: > net use p: '\\machine1\c$'  /user:machine1\user1 *
net.exe : System error 86 has occurred.
    + CategoryInfo          : NotSpecified: (System error 86 has
       occurred.:String) [], RemoteException
    + FullyQualifiedErrorId : NativeCommandError

The specified network password is not correct.
Type the password for \\machine1\c$:
[machine1]: >
```

This command prompted for a password and returned an empty string.

The other kind of program that won't work properly are commands that try to open a user interface (also known as "try to pop GUI") on the remote computer.

If the remote command starts a program that has a GUI interface, the program starts but no window will appear. If the command eventually completes, control will be returned to the caller and things will be more or less fine. But if the process is blocked waiting for the user to provide some input to the invisible GUI, the command will hang and you must stop it manually by pressing Ctrl-C. If the keypress doesn't work, you'll have to use some other mechanism to terminate the process.

For example, if you use Invoke-Command to start Notepad on a remote machine, the process will start on the remote computer but the Notepad window will never appear. At this point, the command will appear to be "hung" and you'll have to press Ctrl-C to stop the command and regain control.

Now let's look at more areas where accessing the console can cause problems and how to avoid these problems.

12.6.4 Reading and writing to the console

As you saw in the previous section, executables that read and write directly to the console won't work properly. The same considerations apply to scripts that do things like call the System.Console APIs directly themselves. For example, call the [Console]::WriteLine() and [Console]::ReadLine() APIs in a remote session:

```
[machine1]: > [Console]::WriteLine("hi")
[machine1]: >
[machine1]: > [Console]::ReadLine()
[machine1]: >
```

Neither of these calls worked properly. When you called the [Console]::WriteLine() API, nothing was displayed, and when you called the [Console]::ReadLine() API, it returned immediately instead of waiting for input.

It's still possible to write interactive scripts, but you have to use the PowerShell host cmdlets and APIs:

```
[machine1]: > Write-Host Hi
Hi
[machine1]: >
[machine1]: > Read-Host "Input"
Input: some input
some input
```

If you use these cmdlets as shown in the example, you can read and write to and from the host, and the remoting subsystem will take care of making everything work.

> **TIP** To ensure that scripts will work in remote environments, don't call the console APIs directly. Use the PowerShell host APIs and cmdlets instead.

With console and GUI issues out of the way, let's explore how remoting affects the objects you're passing back and forth.

12.6.5 Remote output vs. local output

Much of the power in PowerShell comes from the fact that it passes objects around instead of strings. In this section you'll learn how remoting affects these objects.

When PowerShell commands are run locally, you're working directly with the "live" .NET objects, which means that you can use the properties and methods on these objects to manipulate the underlying system state. The same isn't true when you're working with remote objects. Remote objects are *serialized*—converted into a form that can be passed over the remote connection—when they're transmitted between the client and the server. Although a small number of types are transmitted in such a way that they can be fully re-created by the receiving end, the majority of the types of objects you work with aren't. Instead, when they're deserialized, they're turned into *property bags*—collections of data properties with the same names as the original properties. This property bag has a special property, `TypeNames`, which records the name of the original type. This difference in operation is illustrated in figure 12.13.

Typically, you can use deserialized objects just as you'd use live objects, but you must be aware of their limitations. Another thing to be aware of is that the objects that are returned through remoting will have had properties added that allow you to determine the origin of the command.

PowerShell serialization

Because you can't guarantee that every computer has the same set of types, the PowerShell team chose to limit the number of types that serialize with *fidelity*, where the remote type is the same type as the local type. To address the restrictions of a bounded set of types, types that aren't serialized with fidelity are serialized as collections of properties, also called *property bags*. The serialization code takes each object

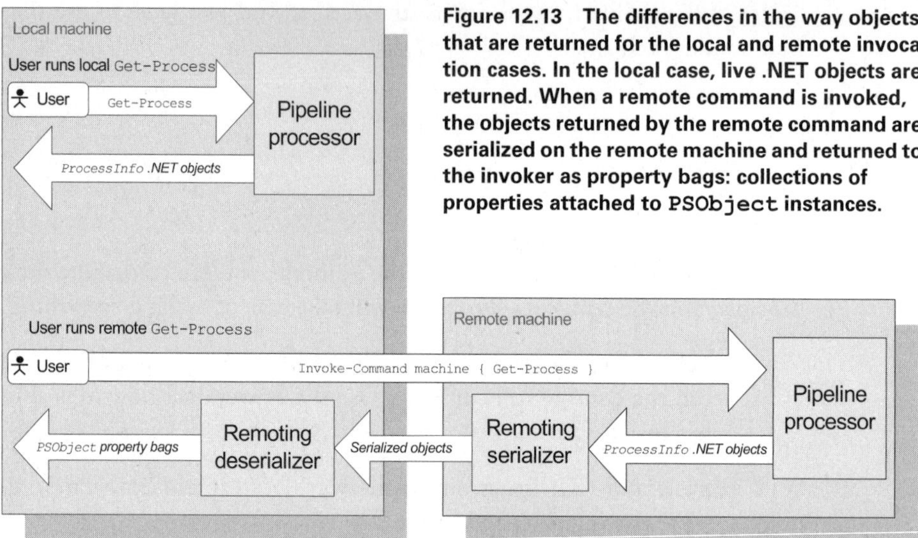

Figure 12.13 The differences in the way objects that are returned for the local and remote invocation cases. In the local case, live .NET objects are returned. When a remote command is invoked, the objects returned by the remote command are serialized on the remote machine and returned to the invoker as property bags: collections of properties attached to `PSObject` instances.

and adds all its properties to the property bag. Recursively, it looks at values of each the members. If the member value isn't one of the ones supported with fidelity, a new property bag is created, and the members of the member's values are added to the new property bag, and so on. This approach preserves structure if not the actual type and allows remoting to work uniformly everywhere.

Default serialization depth

The approach we just described allows any object to be encoded and transferred to another system. But there's another thing to consider: objects have members that contain objects that contain members, and so on. The full tree of objects and members can be complex. Transferring all the data makes the system unmanageably slow. This is addressed by introducing the idea of serialization depth. The recursive encoding of members stops when this serialization depth is reached. The default for objects is 1.

The final source of issues when writing portable, remotable scripts has to do with processor architectures and the operating system differences they entail. We'll work through this final set of issues in the next (and last) section of this chapter.

12.6.6 Processor architecture issues

We've looked at a number of aspects of the remote execution environment that may cause problems: operating system differences and issues with session initialization, GUIs, and console interactions. The last potential source of problems that we'll explore is the fact that the target machine may be running on a different processor architecture (i.e., 64-bit vs. 32-bit) than the local machine. If the remote computer is running a 64-bit version of Windows and the remote command is targeting a 32-bit session configuration, such as Microsoft.PowerShell32, the remoting infrastructure loads a Windows 32-bit on a Windows 64-bit (WOW64) process, and Windows automatically redirects all references to the $ENV:Windir\System32 directory to the $ENV:WINDIR\SysWOW64 directory. For the most part, everything will still work (that's the point of the redirection), unless you try to invoke an executable in the System32 directory that doesn't have a corresponding equivalent in the SysWOW64 directory. Let's see what this looks like. First, run defrag on a 64-bit OS targeting the 32-bit configuration. This results in the following output:

```
PS (1) > Invoke-Command -ConfigurationName Microsoft.PowerShell32 `
>> -ComputerName localhost -command { defrag.exe /? }
>>
The term 'defrag.exe' is not recognized as the name of a cmdlet,
 function, script file, or operable program. Check the spelling
of the name, or if a path was included, verify that the path is
correct and try again.
    + CategoryInfo          : ObjectNotFound: (defrag.exe:Strin
   g) [], CommandNotFoundException
    + FullyQualifiedErrorId : CommandNotFoundException
```

Because there was no corresponding `defrag.exe` in the SysWoW64 directory, the command wasn't found. Now target the 32-bit configuration:

```
PS (2) > Invoke-Command -ConfigurationName microsoft.powershell `
>> -ComputerName localhost -command { defrag.exe /? }
>>
Description:  Locates and consolidates fragmented files on local
 volumes to improve system performance.

Syntax:  Defrag.exe <volume> -a [-v]
         Defrag.exe <volume> [{-r | -w}] [-f] [-v]
         Defrag.exe       -c [{-r | -w}] [-f] [-v]
:
:
```

And everything works properly.

> **NOTE** Depending on how your system is configured and the version/SKU of Windows you're using (e.g., Vista vs. Windows 7, Enterprise vs. Ultimate), this technique may work in both cases.

To find the processor architecture for the session, you can check the value of the `$ENV:PROCESSOR_ARCHITECTURE` variable. The following command finds the processor architecture of the session in the `$s` variable. Try this, first with the 32-bit configuration:

```
PS (10) > Invoke-Command -ConfigurationName microsoft.powershell32 `
>> -ComputerName localhost { $ENV:PROCESSOR_ARCHITECTURE }
>>
x86
```

You get the expected x86 result, indicating a 32-bit session, and on the 64-bit configuration

```
PS (11) > Invoke-Command -ConfigurationName microsoft.powershell `
>> -ComputerName localhost { $ENV:PROCESSOR_ARCHITECTURE }
>>
AMD64
```

you get AMD64, indicating a 64-bit configuration.

This is the last remoting consideration we're going to look at in this chapter. Don't let these issues scare you—they're mostly edge cases. With some attention to detail, the typical script should have no problems working as well remotely as it does locally. The PowerShell remoting system goes to great lengths to facilitate a seamless remote execution experience. But it's always better to have a heads up on some of the issues so you'll know where to start looking if you run into a problem. In chapters 14 and 15, we'll dig further into the whole PowerShell diagnostic and debugging story.

12.7 SUMMARY

In this chapter we introduced PowerShell remoting and the kinds of things you can do with it. We covered these topics:

- The basic concepts and terminology used in PowerShell remoting
- How to enable remoting in both domain-joined and private workgroup environments using the `Enable-PSRemoting` cmdlet
- How to apply remoting to build a multimachine monitoring solution
- How to create and manage persistent connections to remote machines using the `New-PSSession` cmdlet
- How to establish an interactive session using `Enter-PSSession`

Then we moved on to look at PowerShell jobs, which allow you to run tasks in the background. In this part of the chapter, we explored the following:

- The basic concepts behind jobs and the commands that you can use to create and manage jobs using the `Start-Job`, `Stop-Job`, `Receive-Job`, and `Remove-Job` cmdlets
- How to create jobs on remote machines
- How to apply the job concept to implement concurrent solutions for problems you might encounter

We closed this chapter by looking into some of the issues you might encounter when using remoting to solve management problems:

- Differences in startup directories
- The fact that user profiles aren't run by default in a remote session
- Some issues using external applications or executables in a remote session

- Differences in behavior due to the fact that remote objects are always serialized before returning them to the caller
- Differences that occur due to different processor architectures being used on the remote end

The information we covered in this chapter is sufficient to apply PowerShell remoting effectively for most distributed management tasks. That said, our focus in the chapter has been confined to the "remoting client" user perspective. There are some additional advanced application and service scenarios that we didn't cover here. In chapter 13, we'll introduce a new role where you switch from being the user of existing remoting configurations to authoring your own custom applications and services. We'll show you how to create custom configurations and how to use these configurations to build solutions for delegated administration tasks.

CHAPTER 13

Remoting: configuring applications and services

He who is outside his door already has a hard part of his journey behind him.

—Dutch proverb

In chapter 12, we explained how you can use PowerShell's remoting capabilities to monitor and manage remote computers. Now we're going to switch from service consumer to remote service/application creator. Our goal is that, by the end of this chapter, you'll be able to build your own custom remoting services with PowerShell. But before you can start building those services, we need to look at some additional background material.

Our first topic is how PowerShell remoting works. We'll pay special attention to Web Services for Management (WSMan) and see how it fits into this infrastructure. You'll learn how to manage the Windows WSMan implementation using cmdlets and the WSMan provider. This material will help you to understand and debug issues in the infrastructure.

If you want your services to be usable, among other aspects you need to be sure that they're secure and reliable. Among the factors related to security that you must take into account are authentication (who's connecting to the service) and authorization (what they're allowed to do).

The other aspect—reliability—entails managing and controlling resource consumption. We looked at resource consumption from the user perspective when we discussed command-level throttling in chapter 12. In this chapter, we'll look at how to control resource consumption from the application end.

Once we're done with the background material, we'll show you how to construct services by building custom named remoting configurations that users can connect to. We'll explain how to create these configurations and how to define the set of commands these configurations expose. We'll look at configurations with extended command sets where commands are added to the default set PowerShell that exposes and, more important, how to restrict the set of commands that can be accessed through an endpoint configuration. This second scenario is important because it allows you to securely create applications like self-service kiosks. Let's start with the infrastructure investigation and see how you can achieve these goals.

13.1 Remoting infrastructure in depth

Before you start building services and applications with PowerShell remoting, you must develop a good understanding for how everything works. Understanding how things work will help you design and deploy your services more effectively. You'll have the knowledge to make sure your services are available to the service consumer, and you'll be able to effectively debug what's gone wrong when something doesn't work the way it's expected.

We'll begin our infrastructure exploration by looking at the *protocol stack*—the layers of networking technology used to enable PowerShell remoting. Because basic connectivity for PowerShell remoting is provided by the WSMan layer, the next thing we'll explore are the cmdlets that you can use to configure and manage WSMan.

Then we'll describe how authentication is handled, both from the client and from the servers' perspective. We'll look at how targets are addressed and the concerns that you need to be aware of in this area. Finally, we'll end this section by looking at managing connection-related issues such as resource consumption. These topics will help you build your services in such a way that your end user can depend on them. Let's begin by looking at the protocol stack.

13.1.1 The PowerShell remoting protocol stack

Most networked applications are built on top of multiple layers of software, and PowerShell remoting is no different. In this section, we'll describe the various components used by PowerShell remoting.

For remoting to work, there must be layers of software to provide the transport mechanism for sending messages between the client and the server. These layers are

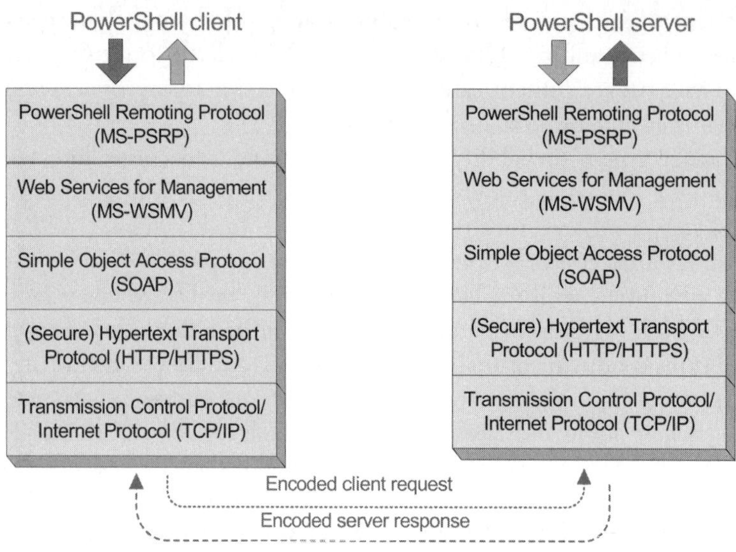

Figure 13.1 The PowerShell remoting protocol stack. The PowerShell Remoting Protocol (MS-PSRP) is based on industry-standard "firewall friendly" protocols simplifying deployment in an enterprise environment.

called the *protocol layers*, which are organized in a protocol stack. Within this stack, higher layers build on the services provided by the lower layers. For PowerShell remoting, there are five layers to the stack. The top layer is MS-PSRP, the PowerShell Remoting Protocol. MS-PSRP is built on top of WSMan. WSMan is, in turn, built on top of the Simple Object Access Protocol (SOAP). SOAP is built on top of the Hypertext Transport Protocol (HTTP), or more precisely, Secure HTTP (HTTPS), and finally the hypertext transfer protocols are in turn based on TCP/IP. The complete stack of protocols is shown in figure 13.1.

The PowerShell Remoting Protocol uses Microsoft's implementation of the WSMan protocol, designated Web Services Management Protocol Extensions for Windows Vista (MS-WSMV) to establish a connection and transfer data between the client and the server. MS-WSMV is built on top of the standard protocols shown in table 13.1.

Table 13.1 The standard protocols used by PowerShell remoting

Protocol	Standards body	Specification
SOAP (Version 1.2)	World Wide Web Consortium (W3C)	SOAP 1.2/1
Hypertext Transfer Protocol (HTTP/1.1)	Internet Engineering Task Force (IETF)	RFC 2616
HTTP over TLS	IETF	RFC 2818
Transmission Control Protocol	IETF	RFC 793
Internet Protocol	IETF	RFC 791

Although MS-PSRP is a proprietary protocol, it's fully documented and this documentation is freely available. The complete specification for the PowerShell remoting-protocol is available at http://mng.bz/b4eo.

Likewise, the complete documentation for the specific implementation of the WSMan protocol that PowerShell uses for MS-WSMV is available at http://mng.bz/92fo.

> **NOTE** These protocols are made available under the Microsoft Communications Protocol Program. The goal of this program is to facilitate to interoperation and communications natively with Windows Server operating systems.

Protocol operation

When the user passes a PowerShell scriptblock to the remoting cmdlets for execution, the scriptblock will first be encoded by the remoting layers as structured XML text. (The structure, or *schema*, for this XML is documented in MS-PSRP.) The encoded text is then sent to the target computer where it's decoded or rehydrated into a pipeline that can be executed on the remote machine.

Along with the commands in the pipeline, the encoded pipeline needs to include any arguments to the commands. Although encoding the commands is relatively easy, encoding the arguments is more difficult because they can be any arbitrary type. Here's the issue you'll run into: as mentioned in chapter 12, serializing an object so you can get the same type of object at the destination requires that the type metadata for that object be present on both ends of the connection. If the original type description doesn't exist at the receiver, then the object can't be completely rehydrated because there's no concrete type definition to rehydrate to. In the systems management world, this situation is quite common because servers tend to be assigned to different roles. For example, an Exchange server will have a different set of types than a database server, and the client that's managing both of these servers may not have any of these types. To mitigate this problem, PowerShell takes a different approach to sharing objects among different computers.

> **NOTE** We say *mitigate* here because there really isn't a perfect solution with an unbounded set of types. If you restrict the types, you lose functionality, and if you require all types everywhere, systems become unmanageably complex. By the way, you'll see the term *mitigate* again in chapter 21 when we discuss another problem that can't be completely resolved: security.

Representing objects and types in the protocol

Instead of trying to accommodate all possible types, PowerShell defines a core set of types that are required to be on both ends of the connection. Any object that's one of these types will be rehydrated into the correct type. For any types that aren't in this core set, a different approach is used. These objects are "shredded" into property bags of type PSObject. (We discussed PSObject at length in chapter 11.) The algorithm for doing this is described in detail in section 2.2.5 of MS-PSRP. The types that are serialized with fidelity are shown in table 13.2.

Table 13.2 The types that are serialized with fidelity by the PowerShell remoting protocol

MS-PSRP	Protocol element	Corresponding PowerShell/.NET type
2.2.5.1.1	String	`[string]`
2.2.5.1.2	Character	`[char]`
2.2.5.1.3	Boolean	`[bool]`
2.2.5.1.4	Date/Time	`[DateTime]`
2.2.5.1.5	Duration	`[TimeSpan]`
2.2.5.1.6	Unsigned Byte	`[byte]`
2.2.5.1.7	Signed Byte	`[sbyte]`
2.2.5.1.8	Unsigned Short	`[uint16]`
2.2.5.1.9	Signed Short	`[int16]`
2.2.5.1.10	Unsigned Int	`[uint32]`
2.2.5.1.11	Signed Int	`[int32]`
2.2.5.1.12	Unsigned Long	`[int64]`
2.2.5.1.13	Signed Long	`[uint64]`
2.2.5.1.14	Float	`[float]` or `[single]`
2.2.5.1.15	Double	`[double]`
2.2.5.1.16	Decimal	`[decimal]`
2.2.5.1.17	Array of Bytes	`[byte[]]`
2.2.5.1.18	GUID	`[Guid]`
2.2.5.1.19	URI	`[Uri]`
2.2.5.1.20	Null Value	`$null`
2.2.5.1.21	Version	`[Version]`
2.2.5.1.22	XML Document	`[xml]`
2.2.5.1.23	ScriptBlock	`[ScriptBlock]`
2.2.5.1.24	Secure String	`[System.Security.SecureString]`
2.2.5.1.25	Progress Record	`[System.Management.Automation.ProgressRecord]`
2.2.5.2.7	Enums	`[int32]`

There are also some types of collections that are serialized with some level of fidelity. These types are listed in table 13.3.

Table 13.3 **Collection types handled by the serializer**

Protocol type	Encoded type	Decoded type
Stack	[System.Collections.Stack]	[System.Collections.Stack]
Queue	[System.Collections.Queue]	[System.Collections.Queue]
List	[System.Collections.IList]	[System.Collections.ArrayList]
Dictionaries	[System.Collections.IDictionary]	[hashtable]

Note that table 13.3 lists different types for encoding and decoding in two cases: `List` and `Dictionary`. In case you're wondering what that means, here's an explanation. On the sender's side, any object that implements the `IList` interface will be encoded as `List` when serialized. On the receiver's side, PowerShell will always decode the collection into an instance of type `System.Collections.ArrayList`. For example:

```
PS (1) > $r = Invoke-Command localhost {
>>     ,(1,2,3)
>>     }
>>
```

In this example, you're sending a collection of integers through the remoting layer.

> **NOTE** The leading comma in this example is not a typo. The unary comma operator (see section 5.2) wraps its argument in a one-element array. This is necessary to make sure the array is passed as a single array object instead of as a sequence of numbers.

Let's look at the type of object the receiver actually gets:

```
PS (2) > $r.GetType().FullName
System.Collections.ArrayList
```

Even though you send a simple array of numbers, the remoting layer decoded it into an `ArrayList`. This behavior applies to more complex list types as well. In the next example, you're sending a generic collection of integers. This collection also comes back as `System.Collections.ArrayList` on the receiving end:

```
PS (3) > $r = Invoke-Command localhost {
>>     $l = New-Object System.Collections.Generic.List[int]
>>     1..10 | %{ $l.Add($_) }
>>     ,$l
>>     }
>>
PS (4) > $r.GetType().FullName
System.Collections.ArrayList
```

Similarly, any .NET type that implements the interface `System.Collections.IDictionary` will be encoded as `Dictionary` and decoded into `[hashtable]`.

When you're sending an object that isn't in the known type pool, you get a property bag back instead of an instance of the original type. For example, let's return a `Process` object through the remoting channel:

```
PS (1) > $r = Invoke-Command localhost { (Get-Process csrss)[0] }
```

Now look at the output:

```
PS (2) > $r | fl

Id             : 568
Handles        : 956
CPU            : 39.0626504
Name           : csrss
PSComputerName : localhost
```

It appears to return the same set of members as a real `Process` object would, but there are some differences. For example, look at the `VM` property:

```
PS (3) > $r | Get-Member vm

   TypeName: Deserialized.System.Diagnostics.Process

Name MemberType   Definition
---- ----------   ----------
VM   NoteProperty System.Int32 VM=77340672
```

Now compare this output to a real `Process` object:

```
PS (4) > Get-Process | Get-Member vm

   TypeName: System.Diagnostics.Process

Name MemberType    Definition
---- ----------    ----------
VM   AliasProperty VM = VirtualMemorySize
```

In the deserialized case, the type of the object is shown prefixed with `Deserialized` and the `VM` property is a `NoteProperty` containing a fixed integer value. On the live `Process` object, you see that the `VM` property is an alias that points to the `VirtualMemorySize` property on the object. Another difference is that the deserialized object has fewer members on it:

```
PS (5) > ($r | Get-Member).count
66
PS (6) > (Get-Process csrss | Get-Member).count
90
```

In particular, the deserialized object has only one method in it, `ToString()`

```
PS (7) > @($r | Get-Member -type method).count
1
```

as opposed to the live object, which has the full set of methods defined for the type:

```
PS (8) > @(Get-Process csrss | Get-Member -type method).count
19
```

Because the object isn't live (meaning that there's no connection to the `Process` object, it was derived from on the remote machine), propagating the methods makes no sense. And, for performance reasons, not all the properties are included and, if an included property is itself a complex type, the deserialized version may only contain the `ToString()` of the value of the live property. This compression of properties is done to reduce the amount of information transmitted, thereby improving performance in the remoting layer.

This approach works well in that it allows for easy operation between the various clients and servers but with the downside that a certain amount of information is lost. But because of the way PowerShell parameter binding works, this "lossy serialization" isn't usually a problem. PowerShell functions and cmdlets don't care what type the object is as long as the required properties are there.

Now that you have a good grasp of how the PowerShell protocol layer works, let's move down the protocol stack to the WSMan layer. We won't be digging into the details of the protocol itself—that's beyond the scope of this chapter. What you really need to know is how the WSMan layer is managed, so that's what we'll focus on.

13.1.2 Using the WSMan cmdlets and providers

Because PowerShell remoting is built on top of Microsoft's implementation of WSMan, in this section we'll look at configuring and managing the WSMan service on a computer. The management interface for WSMan is exposed through cmdlets and through the WSMan provider, which implements the WSMan: drive. The WSMan cmdlets are listed in table 13.4.

Table 13.4 Cmdlets for working with WSMan

Cmdlet name	Description
`Test-WSMan`	Submits an identification request that determines whether the WinRM service is running on a local or remote computer. If the tested computer is running the service, the cmdlet displays the WSMan identity schema, protocol version, product vendor, and the product version of the tested service.
`Connect-WSMan` `Disconnect-WSMan`	The `Connect-WSMan` cmdlet establishes a persistent connection to the WinRM service on a remote computer. Once the connection is established, the remote computer will appear as a subdirectory of the root directory of the WSMan: drive. Use the `Disconnect-WSMan` cmdlet to terminate the connection to the remote computer.

`Get-WSManCredSSP`
`Enable-WSManCredSSP`
`Disable-WSManCredSSP`
	The `Get-WSManCredSPP` cmdlet gets the Credential Security Service Provider (CredSSP) status for the machine on which it is run. The output shows the machines status for both the client role (will or won't forward credentials) and the server role (will or won't accept forwarded credentials). Use the `Enable-WSManCredSSP` cmdlet to enable the `CredSSP` delegation on either the client or server. Use the `Disable-WSManCredSSP` to disable CredSSP on a server.

`New-WSManSession-Option`	Creates a WSMan session option hashtable, which can be passed into WSMan cmdlets, including `Connect-WSMan`.

You'll how to use these cmdlets in the next few sections.

Testing WSMan connections

You can use the `Test-WSMan` cmdlet to see if the WSMan connection to your target host is working:

```
PS (1) > Test-WSMan brucepay64h

wsmid           : http://schemas.dmtf.org/wbem/wsman/identity/1/
                  wsmanidentity.xsd
ProtocolVersion : http://schemas.dmtf.org/wbem/wsman/1/wsman.xsd
ProductVendor   : Microsoft Corporation
ProductVersion  : OS: 0.0.0 SP: 0.0 Stack: 2.0
```

In the output of the command, you see that the WSMan service is running and available on the target machine.

Establishing a remote WSMan connection

Once you've verified that the service is available, you can use the `Connect-WSMan` cmdlet to connect to the target service. Run the following:

```
PS (2) > Connect-WSMan brucepay64h
```

The prompt returns immediately without displaying any information. So how can you check to see if the connection was created? This is where the WSMan: drive comes into the picture. This drive lets you examine and manipulate the WSMan service using the normal provider cmdlets. Start by looking at the contents of that drive using the `dir` command:

```
PS (3) > dir wsman:\

   WSManConfig:

ComputerName                                         Type
------------                                         ----
brucepay64h                                          Container
localhost                                            Container
```

Here you see the connection you just created. Now get more details about the connected computer:

```
PS (5) > dir wsman:\brucepay64h | ft -auto

   WSManConfig: Microsoft.WSMan.Management\WSMan::brucepay64h

Name                  Value      Type
----                  -----      ----
MaxEnvelopeSizekb     150        System.String
MaxTimeoutms          60000      System.String
MaxBatchItems         32000      System.String
MaxProviderRequests 4294967295 System.String
Client                           Container
```

```
Service                          Container
Shell                            Container
Listener                         Container
Plugin                           Container
ClientCertificate                Container
```

Digging further, you can obtain information about the `Shell` container:

```
PS (6) > dir wsman:\brucepay64h\shell | ft -auto

  WSManConfig: Microsoft.WSMan.Management\WSMan::brucepay64h\Shell

Name                   Value      Type
----                   -----      ----
AllowRemoteShellAccess true       System.String
IdleTimeout            180000     System.String
MaxConcurrentUsers     5          System.String
MaxShellRunTime        2147483647 System.String
MaxProcessesPerShell   15         System.String
MaxMemoryPerShellMB    150        System.String
MaxShellsPerUser       5          System.String
```

A WSMan shell, though not identical to a PowerShell session, encapsulates each PowerShell session when a user connects—one shell per connection, so `MaxShellsPerUser` controls how many remote connects a user may have to a machine. It's worth spending some time exploring the WSMan: drive as we'll be returning to it a number of times throughout the rest of this section. Our next topic is authentication; you'll see how both the target computer and connecting user are verified.

13.1.3 Authenticating the target computer

When you're performing remote operations on a machine, these operations may involve transmitting sensitive information to the target computer. As a consequence, you need to ensure that the machine you're connecting to is the one you think it is. In this section, we'll show you how to manage verifying server identity when working in a nondomain environment.

In a domain environment, you've already established a trust relationship with the domain controller you're connected to. If the target computer is also connected to the same domain controller (that is, it has verified its identity to the domain controller), then you can rely on the domain controller to ensure that you're connecting to the correct machine. But if you're either not working in a domain environment or the target computer isn't connected to the same domain controller, then you need an alternate mechanism for establishing trust. We'll look at two mechanisms for addressing this problem: using HTTPS and using the `TrustedHosts` WSMan configuration item. First, though, you need to make sure that passwords are set up on the machines you're connecting to. The system won't allow you to connect to an account without a password.

Once you have the account password, authenticating to the server is easy—you just use the `-Credential` parameter and send your credentials to the target server. In this case, it's extremely important to know what system you're connecting to as you certainly don't want to send passwords to the wrong machine. The first mechanism we'll look at involves using HTTPS and certificates.

Using HTTPS to establish server identity

One way of validating the identity of the target computer is to use HTTPS when connecting to that computer. This works because, in order to establish an HTTPS connection, the target server must have a valid certificate installed where the name in the certificate matches the server name. As long as the certificate is signed by a trusted certificate authority, you know that the server is the one it claims to be. Unfortunately, this process does require that you have a valid certificate, issued either by a commercial or local certificate authority. This is an entirely reasonable requirement in an enterprise environment but may not always be practical in smaller or informal environments.

If you aren't able to obtain a valid certificate, then you'll have to use a different mechanism for letting the remoting service know that you trust the target computer. This involves manually adding the target computer to the `TrustedHosts` list on the client. We'll review how to do that in the next section.

Using the TrustedHosts list

The `TrustedHosts` list is a WSMan configuration item that lists the names of target computers you trust. We looked at `TrustedHosts` briefly in chapter 12 (section 12.1.4). To review, the `TrustedHosts` list is a string containing a comma-separated list of computer names, IP addresses, and fully qualified domain names. Wildcards are permitted to make it easy to specify groups of computers you want to trust.

We'll repeat the steps used in chapter 12, but this time we'll explain things in more detail. The easiest way to view or change the `TrustedHosts` list is to use the WSMan: drive. The `TrustedHosts` configuration item for a machine is in the WSMan:\<*machine name*>\Client node. For the local machine this is WSMan:\localhost\Client. To view the current `TrustedHosts` list, use the `Get-Item` cmdlet:

```
PS (1) > Get-Item wsman:\localhost\Client\TrustedHosts | Format-Table -auto

   WSManConfig: Microsoft.WSMan.Management\WSMan::localhost\Client

Name         Value                     Type
----         -----                     ----
TrustedHosts brucepayx61,brucepay64h System.String
```

To set this item to a new value, use the `Set-Item` cmdlet:

```
PS (2) > Set-Item wsman:localhost\client\trustedhosts brucepay64h

WinRM Security Configuration.
This command modifies the TrustedHosts list for the WinRM
client. The computers in the TrustedHosts list might not be
```

```
authenticated. The client might send credential information to
these computers. Are you sure that you want to modify this list?
[Y] Yes  [N] No  [S] Suspend  [?] Help (default is "Y"): y
```

Because this operation affects the state of the system in a significant way (it has security implications), you're prompted to confirm this action. If you didn't want this prompt, you'd use the `-Force` parameter. Now use `Get-Item` to confirm the change:

```
PS (3) > Get-Item wsman:\localhost\Client\TrustedHosts | Format-Table -auto

   WSManConfig: Microsoft.WSMan.Management\WSMan::localhost\Client

Name         Value       Type
----         -----       ----
TrustedHosts brucepay64h System.String
```

The old list was completely replaced by the new one. This may not be what you want—you may want to just edit or append to the list. To do this, first retrieve the current value:

```
PS (5) > $cv = Get-Item wsman:\localhost\Client\TrustedHosts
PS (6) > $cv.Value
brucepay64h
```

It's what you set it to previously. Now add some additional hostnames to the list in the `Value` key:

```
PS (7) > $cv.Value = $cv.Value + ', brucepayx61 , 192.168.1.13,bp3'
PS (8) > $cv.Value
brucepay64h,brucepayx61, 192.168.1.13,bp3
```

As mentioned earlier, both machine names and IP addresses are allowed in the list. Now use `Set-Item` to assign the updated value:

```
PS (9) > Set-Item wsman:localhost\client\trustedhosts $cv.value `
>> -Force
```

Finally, verify the result:

```
>> Get-Item wsman:\localhost\Client\TrustedHosts | ft -auto
>>

   WSManConfig: Microsoft.WSMan.Management\WSMan::localhost\Client

Name         Value                                     Type
----         -----                                     ----
TrustedHosts brucepay64h,brucepayx61,192.168.1.13,bp3 System.String
```

> **NOTE** There's a somewhat easier way to add items to the `TrustedHosts` list. The WSMan provider implements a `-Concatenate` dynamic parameter on the `Set-Item` cmdlet that allows you to add a new host by using `Set-Item -Concatenate.\TrustedHosts newHost`. Although this technique works, it's unique to the WSMan provider and inconsistent with the normal PowerShell command pattern, so it

doesn't get mentioned very often. Supporting `Set-Content` and `Add-Content` for this property would've been a better, more consistent approach.

If you want to add all the computers in a particular domain, you can specify a wildcard (*) in the name you're adding to the list. For example, the following command sets the configuration element to a value that will trust all servers in the yourdomain.com domain:

```
Set-Item wsman:localhost\client\trustedhosts *.yourdomain.com -WhatIf
```

If you want to trust all computers, set the `TrustedHosts` configuration element to `*`, which matches all computers in all domains. This approach isn't generally recommended for security reasons.

You can also use this technique to add a computer to the `TrustedHosts` list on a remote computer. You can use the `Connect-WSMan` cmdlet to add a node for the remote computer to the WSMan: drive on the local computer. Then use a `Set-Item` command to update that machine's `TrustedHosts` configuration element.

Now you know how you should set things up so that your users can be confident that they're connecting to the correct service provider. The service provider is also extremely interested in verifying the identity of the connecting users before allowing them to access any services. That's the topic of the next section.

13.1.4 Authenticating the connecting user

In the previous section, you saw how the client verifies the identity of the target computer. Now we'll explore the converse of this—how the target computer verifies the identity of the connecting user. PowerShell remoting supports a wide variety of ways of authenticating a user, including NTLM and Kerberos. Each of these mechanisms has its advantages and disadvantages. The authentication mechanism also has an important impact on how data is transmitted between the client and the server. Depending on how you authenticate to the server, the data passed between the client and server may or may not be encrypted. Encryption is extremely important in that it protects the contents of your communications with the server against tampering and preserves privacy. If encryption isn't being used, you need to ensure the physical security of your network. No untrusted access to the network can be permitted in this scenario. The possible types of authentication are shown in table 13.5.

Table 13.5 The possible types of authentication available for PowerShell remoting

Auth type	Description	Encrypted payload
Default	Use the authentication method specified by the WS-Management protocol.	Depends on what was specified.
Basic	Use Basic Authentication, part of HTTP, where the username and password are sent unencrypted to the target server or proxy.	No, use HTTPS to encrypt the connection.

Table 13.5 The possible types of authentication available for PowerShell remoting *(continued)*

Auth type	Description	Encrypted payload
Digest	Use Digest Authentication, which is also part of HTTP. This mechanism supersedes Basic authentication and encrypts the credentials.	Yes.
Kerberos	The client computer and the server mutually authenticate using the Kerberos network authentication protocol.	Yes.
Negotiate	Negotiate is a challenge-response scheme that negotiates with the server or proxy to determine the scheme to use for authentication. For example, negotiation is used to determine whether the Kerberos protocol or NTLM is used.	Yes.
CredSSP	Use Credential Security Service Provider (CredSSP) authentication, which allows the user to delegate credentials. This mechanism, introduced with Windows Vista, is designed to support the second-hop scenario, where commands that run on one remote computer need to hop to another computer to do something.	Yes.

For all of the authentication types except Basic, the payload of the messages you send is encrypted directly by the remoting protocol. If Basic authentication is chosen, you have to use encryption at a lower layer, for example by using HTTPS instead of HTTP.

In simple network configurations, you only have to worry about connecting directly to the target machine and authenticating to that computer. There's a fairly common configuration where things are more complicated and you have to go through an intermediate machine before you can connect to the final target. This configuration is the so-called "second-hop" scenario. We'll look at how authentication is handled in this configuration next.

Forwarding credentials in multihop environments

In a domain environment, when a user connects from one computer to another, identity is validated by the domain controller. If the validation process completes successfully, a *network token* is created for those users, allowing them to operate as themselves on the target machine.

This arrangement works perfectly when the user can connect directly to the target computer, but that's not always the case in an enterprise environment. Sometimes, for security or performance reasons, you have to go through a gateway or bastion server to get to your final target. In this scenario, you run into a problem with the normal remote-access authentication mechanism. Because you only have a *network token* on the second computer, you can't directly connect to another computer. This is a deliberate restriction in the domain architecture designed to limit the amount of damage an attacker can inflict on the enterprise. An *interactive token*—what you get when you sit down in front of a PC and log on "on the glass"—is required to automatically connect to another computer, and to create an interactive token, the user's credentials are needed. This means that you have to get the user's credentials to the second computer, a process that's called *credential forwarding*.

To accomplish this credential forwarding magic, PowerShell uses a mechanism introduced with Windows Vista called CredSSP (Credential Security Service Provider). This mechanism was originally designed for Windows Terminal Server to facilitate single sign-on. Since then, it has been expanded to work with web services as well, so PowerShell, through WSMan, can take advantage of it. The CredSSP mechanism enables you to securely pass your credentials to a target machine via a trusted intermediary. This process is shown in figure 13.2.

> **NOTE** CredSSP is another of the protocols that are publicly documented through the Microsoft Communications Protocol Program. The specification for CredSSP, designated MS-CSSP, is available at http://mng.bz/q6Qo.

In the upper part of the figure, you see what happens when a user remotely connects to the first-hop computer. A network token is created for the user, allowing local access; but when they try to connect to the second machine, the connection fails. In the lower sequence, CredSSP is enabled and the user has provided credentials to the first-hop computer, allowing it to create an interactive token. With an interactive token, the user can successfully connect to the second-hop computer.

For this delegation process to work, both the client and the server have to be enabled to allow it. To do so, use the `Enable-WSManCredSSP` cmdlet. To enable the client side, execute the following command on the client:

```
Enable-WSManCredSSP -Role client -DelegateComputer computername
```

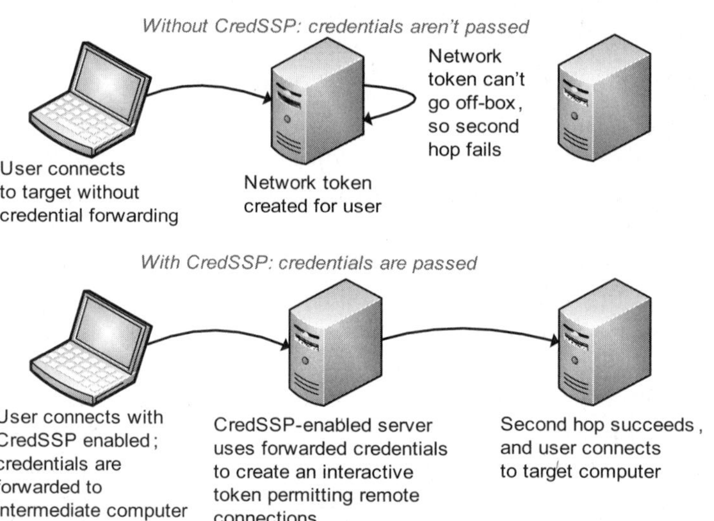

Figure 13.2 How second-hop authentication changes when CredSSP is used. Without credential forwarding, the second hop fails because the user is operating with a network token. When CredSSP is enabled, the intermediate computer uses the forwarded credentials to create an interactive token, allowing it to create remote connections.

This command enables you to pass credentials from the client to the delegate computer for authentication. To enable the server side, run the following command on the server:

```
Enable-WSManCredSSP -Role server
```

As you might expect, you have to run these commands from an elevated PowerShell session.

Be aware that there are some security concerns with this mechanism. It requires that the credentials be stored on the intermediate machine, even if only temporarily. If that machine is compromised, these stored credentials are at risk. The more machines that store credentials, the greater the potential risk of having credentials stolen becomes. In a bastion server scenario, this may represent a serious concern and so care must be taken in choosing when and where to use this feature.

There's one more variation in our discussion of user authentication that we have to cover before we move on: handling administrator privileges in cross-domain scenarios.

Enabling remoting for administrators in other domains

In a large enterprise with more than one domain, an administrator in one domain may have to perform administrative tasks cross-domain and may encounter a problem with the way remoting works. Even when a user in another domain is a member of the Administrators group on the local computer, the user can't connect to the target computer remotely with Administrator privileges. The reason is that, with the default settings, remote connections from other domains run with only standard user privilege tokens. To enable what you want, you can use the `LocalAccountTokenFilterPolicy` Registry entry to change the default behavior and allow remote users who are members of the Administrators group to run with Administrator privileges.

> **NOTE** Allowing remote users who are members of the Administrators group to run with Administrator privileges isn't the default because making this change has a specific security concern. Setting the `LocalAccountTokenFilterPolicy` entry will disable User Account Control (UAC) remote restrictions for all users on all affected computers. Make sure you've considered the consequences of this change before proceeding with it.

To change the policy you must define a new value at a specific place in the Registry. You'll use the provider commands and the Registry provider to make this change, setting the value of the `LocalAccountTokenFilterPolicy` Registry entry to 1. The command to do this looks like this:

```
C:\PS> New-ItemProperty -Path `
 HKLM:\SOFTWARE\Microsoft\Windows\CurrentVersion\Policies\System `
 -Name LocalAccountTokenFilterPolicy `
 -PropertyType DWord -Value 1
```

This code will create the new LocalAccountTokenFilterPolicy value in the Registry at the path

```
HKLM:\SOFTWARE\Microsoft\Windows\CurrentVersion\Policies\System
```

Once this change has been made, administrators from another domain will be able to remotely access this computer through PowerShell.

At this point, you're able to set things up so that the server can verify the identity of the connecting user and the user can verify that they're connected to the correct server. Next you'll learn the various ways you can address the target computer.

13.1.5 Addressing the remoting target

In this section we'll look at how to specify the address of the target remoting service that you want to connect to. With TCP/IP-based protocols, there are two parts to a service address: the IP address of the computer and the network *port* number that service is operating on. We'll examine both of these elements and also show how proxy servers fit into the overall scheme.

DNS names and IP addresses

The typical way to address a computer is to use its name. This name is resolved through the Domain Name Service (DNS) into an IP address. But sometimes it's necessary to specify the IP address of a computer explicitly instead of going through DNS. To permit this, the New-PSSession, Enter-PSSession, and Invoke-Command cmdlets can also take the IP address of the computer. But because Kerberos authentication doesn't support IP addresses, NTLM authentication is used by default whenever you specify an IP address. In other words, you're looking at the same issues you encountered earlier when working in a nondomain environment. The IP addresses for these machines must be added to the TrustedHosts list. See section 13.1.2 for details on how to do this.

Connecting to nondefault ports

By default, PowerShell connects to port 5985 for inbound remoting over HTTP and to port 5986 for connections over HTTPS. This information can also be retrieved directly from the WSMan: drive using the following command:

```
PS (1) > dir WSMan:\localhost\Service\DefaultPorts |
>> Format-Table -AutoSize name,value
Name   Value
----   -----
HTTP   5985
HTTPS  5986
```

On the client end, when you need to connect to a nondefault port, use the -Port parameter as follows:

```
Invoke-Command -ComputerName localhost -Port 5985 -ScriptBlock {hostname}
```

On the server side, you can change the default port that the service listens on using the WSMan: drive.

> **NOTE** If you change the default port, you may also be required to add a new firewall exception for that port.

You use the `Set-Item` cmdlet to change the `Port` value in the path WSMan:\localhost\Listener\<*listener*>\Port. For example, the following command changes the default port to 8080:

```
Set-Item WSMan:\localhost\Listener\Listener_641507880\Port -Value 8080
```

You can verify the change using the `dir` command on the path WSMan:\localhost\Listener\Listener_641507880\Port.

Addressing using a URI

Given all this talk about HTTP, IP addresses, and ports, you might expect that a machine can be addressed using a URI (or URL) just like a web server and this is, in fact, the case. In the following example, you'll use a URI to connect to the default service on machine1:

```
PS (1) > Invoke-Command `
>>   -ConnectionUri http://machine1:5985/WSMAN `
>>  -Credential $c -ScriptBlock { hostname }
>>
machine1
PS (2) >
```

This URI tells `Invoke-Command` the protocol to use (HTTP), the machine name (machine1), and the port (5985) to connect to, all in a single string.

Specifying default session options

It should be apparent by now that the number of options you can specify for a connection is quite large. Specifying this option collection eventually becomes cumbersome, so PowerShell provides a mechanism for predefining the options to use via the `New-PSSession-Option` cmdlet. This cmdlet will create an object that contains the default values to use. If this object is then stored in the variable `$PSSessionOption`, it'll be used to set the defaults for subsequent connection. You'll see an example of this in a minute.

The other approach for managing sets of options is to assign them to a hashtable and then use splatting to parameterize the command. Splatting was covered in section 5.8.4.

That covers the basic addressing mechanisms. Now we'll look at how proxy servers come into all of this.

Working with proxy servers

Because PowerShell remoting is built on top of the HTTP protocol, it can take advantage of HTTP proxy servers. For this to work, you have to specify proxy setting options for the remote command. Three settings are available: `ProxyAccessType`, `ProxyAuthentication`, and `ProxyCredential`. They can be specified either as explicit parameters to `New-PSSession` when you create a session, or can be configured in a `SessionOption` object and passed via the `-SessionOption` parameter of the `New-PSSession`, `Enter-PSSession`, or `Invoke-Command` cmdlet. The settings object can also be stored in the `$PSSessionOption` preference variable. If this variable is defined, the cmdlets will use these settings as the default (explicit settings will always override this, of course).

In the following example, you'll create a session option object with proxy session options and then use that object to create a remote session. First, create the session object:

```
PS (1) > $PSSessionOption = New-PSSessionOption `
>> -ProxyAccessType IEConfig `
>> -ProxyAuthentication Negotiate `
>> -ProxyCredential Domain01\User01
>>
PS (2) >
```

When you run this command, it'll prompt you to enter the credentials for the user `Domain01\User01`. Because this object now has the credentials needed to connect, you won't have to enter them again. Now you establish a connection to the remote server:

```
PS (3) > New-PSSession -ConnectionURI https://www.myserver.com
PS (4) >
```

It connects without any problems.

We've now covered the identification, authentication, and addressing issues that impact establishing a remote connection. Now we'll explore additional issues that you might need to address depending on what versions of the Windows operation system you're running on the target computers.

13.1.6 Windows version-specific connection issues

When connecting to older client operating systems through remoting, you must consider a couple of additional issues.

> **NOTE** These settings affect all users on the system and can make the system more vulnerable to a malicious attack. Use caution when making these changes.

Windows XP with SP3

Windows XP SP3 is the oldest client operating system that PowerShell remoting is supported on. For remote access to work properly on a machine running this version of Windows, you have to change the default setting for the Network Access: Sharing and Security Model for Local Accounts security policy. On non-domain joined machines, this change is necessary to allow remote logons using local account credentials to authenticate using those credentials. To make this change, use the Local Security Policy MMC snap-in.

> **NOTE** Just to be clear, we're talking about a Microsoft Management Console (MMC) snap-in, not a PowerShell v1 snap-in.

To start this snap-in, run secpol.msc. You can do so from the PowerShell command line or by choosing Start > Run to launch MMC with this snap-in, as shown in figure 13.3.

In the left-hand pane of the MMC window, navigate to the path Security Settings\Local Policies\Security Options to see the list of local security settings. From that list, double-click Network Access: Sharing and Security Model for Local Accounts. In the resulting property dialog box, change the setting to Classic - Local Users Authenticate as Themselves, as shown in figure 13.3.

Windows Vista

To enable remote access on Windows Vista clients, you need to set the Local Account Token Filter policy—which requires setting the `LocalAccountTokenFilterPolicy` Registry entry in

```
HKLM\SOFTWARE\Microsoft\Windows\CurrentVersion\Policies\System
```

to 1. You can use PowerShell to do this. Run the following command to create the entry:

```
New-ItemProperty `
 -Path HKLM:\SOFTWARE\Microsoft\Windows\CurrentVersion\Policies\System `
 -Name LocalAccountTokenFilterPolicy -PropertyType DWord -Value 1
```

With this change, it becomes possible to connect to a computer running Vista through PowerShell remoting.

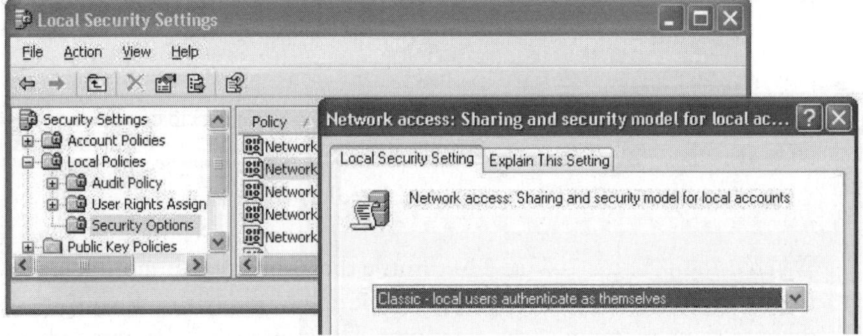

Figure 13.3 You can use the secpol.msc MMC snap-in on Windows XP SP3 to enable PowerShell remoting to access this machine. The displayed policy item must be set to Classic for remoting to work.

At this point, you're able to reliably connect your clients to your servers, but there's one more consideration you need to address if you want to ensure the reliability of your network: resource consumption. In the next section, we'll describe the various options available to you for resource management.

13.1.7 Managing resource consumption

In chapter 12, we talked about throttling at the command level using the `-ThrottleLimit` parameter. The remoting cmdlets allow you to connect to many computers at once and send commands to all of those computers concurrently. It's also possible for many people to connect to the same machine at the same time. Allowing an arbitrary number of connections requires an arbitrarily large number of resources, so to prevent overloading either the client or the server, the remoting infrastructure supports throttling on both the client and server ends. Throttling allows you to limit the number of concurrent connections, either outbound or inbound. We'll look at the outbound case first.

To help you manage the resources on the local computer, PowerShell includes a feature that lets you limit the number of concurrent remote connections that are established for each command that's executed. The default is 32 concurrent connections, but you can use the `-ThrottleLimit` parameter to change the default throttle setting for a particular command. The commands that support `-ThrottleLimit` are shown in table 13.6.

Table 13.6 PowerShell cmdlets supporting the `-ThrottleLimit` parameter

Name	Synopsis
`Invoke-Command`	Runs commands on local and remote computers
`New-PSSession`	Creates a persistent connection to a local or remote computer
`Get-WmiObject`	Gets instances of Windows Management Instrumentation (WMI) classes or information about the available classes
`Invoke-WmiMethod`	Calls WMI methods
`Remove-WmiObject`	Deletes an instance of an existing WMI class
`Set-WmiInstance`	Creates or updates an instance of an existing WMI class
`Test-Connection`	Sends ICMP echo request packets (pings) to one or more computers
`Restart-Computer`	Restarts (reboots) the operating system on local and remote computers
`Stop-Computer`	Stops (shuts down) local and remote computers

When using `-ThrottleLimit` to throttle the number of connections, remember that it only applies to the current command. It doesn't apply to subsequent commands or other sessions running on the computer. This means that if commands are being run concurrently in multiple sessions, the number of active connections on the client computer is the sum of the concurrent connections in all the sessions.

Controlling resource consumption with quotas

Controlling the number of connections is one way to limit resource consumption on the client. But even when the number of connections is restricted, a single connection can still consume a large amount of resources if a lot of data is being transferred. To manage this, you can use quota settings to restrict the amount of data that gets transferred. These settings can be made at several different levels.

> **Managing resource consumption**
>
> The idea of constraining resource consumption in a session isn't unique to remoting. This principle has been applied throughout the system starting with PowerShell v1. PowerShell provides mechanisms to limit resource consumption in a number of areas using a set of constraint variables. For example, the maximum number of variables that can be created is constrained using the `$MaximumVariableCount` variable. (To see all of the constraint variables, execute `dir variable:max*`.)
>
> The PowerShell team's philosophy on this point was to try to provide a safe environment by understanding what problems might occur, and then defining reasonable limits with healthy margins in each area. Users can then adjust these limits up or down as appropriate for their environment or application.

On a per-session level, you can protect the local computer by using the `MaximumReceivedDataSizePerCommandMB` and `MaximumReceivedObjectSizeMB` parameters of the `New-PSSessionOption` cmdlet and the `$PSSessionOption` preference variable.

Alternatively, on the host end you can add restrictions to the endpoint configuration through the `MaximumReceivedDataSizePerCommandMB` and `MaximumReceivedObjectSizeMB` parameters of the `Register-PSSessionConfiguration` cmdlet.

Finally, at the WSMan layer, there are a number of settings you can use to protect the computer. The `MaxEnvelopeSizeKB` and `MaxProviderRequests` settings let you limit the amount of data that can be sent in a single message and specify the total number of messages that can be sent. These settings are available under the *<ComputerName>* node in the root of the WSMan: drive. You can use the `Max*` settings in the WSMan:*<ComputerName>*\Service node to control the maximum number of connections, and concurrent operations on a global and current basis. The following command shows these settings for the local host:

```
PS (1) > dir wsman:\localhost\service\maxc* | fl name,value

Name  : MaxConcurrentOperations
Value : 4294967295

Name  : MaxConcurrentOperationsPerUser
Value : 15
```

```
Name  : MaxConnections
Value : 25
```

This output shows that the user is limited to 15 concurrent operations, and a maximum of 25 connections is allowed.

When these quotas are exceeded, an error will be generated. At that point, you need to take a look at what you (or someone else) are trying to do. If the operation is legitimate, it makes sense to increase the quotas.

For example, the following command increases the object size quota in the `Microsoft.PowerShell` session configuration on the remote computer from 10 MB (the default value) to 11 MB:

```
Set-PSSessionConfiguration -Name microsoft.powershell `
    -MaximumReceivedObjectSizeMB 11 -Force
```

Again, this configuration is based on the type of activity that you need to perform.

Another kind of resource that you need to manage is the open connections to a target machine. We'll show you how to manage them using timeouts.

Setting timeouts on operations

We've looked at managing the number of connections and controlling the amount of data that can be sent or received. The last mechanism for managing resource consumption is to limit the amount of processor time that an operation is permitted to consume. You can do so by setting timeouts on operations. If an operation exceeds the timeout value, then an error will occur and the operation will be terminated. Note that timeouts can be set at both the client and server ends of the connection. The shortest timeout of the two settings always takes precedence.

Through the WSMan: drive, you have access to both client-side and server-side timeout settings. To protect the client, you can change the `MaxTimeoutms` setting in the node in the WSMan: drive that corresponds to the computer in question. To look at these settings for the local machine, first `cd` into the appropriate node:

```
PS (1) > cd wsman:\localhost
```

Use `Get-ChildItem` to see the settings:

```
PS (2) > Get-ChildItem | Format-Table -auto

   WSManConfig: Microsoft.WSMan.Management\WSMan::localhost

Name                Value      Type
----                -----      ----
MaxEnvelopeSizekb   150        System.String
MaxTimeoutms        60000      System.String
MaxBatchItems       32000      System.String
MaxProviderRequests 4294967295 System.String
Client                         Container
Service                        Container
Shell                          Container
```

```
Listener                        Container
Plugin                          Container
ClientCertificate               Container
```

On the server side, you need to be connected to remote machine via WSMan, so use the `Connect-WSMan` command with the appropriate credentials to connect:

```
PS (1) > Connect-WSMan -ComputerName brucepay64h `
>> -Credential (Get-Credential)
>>

cmdlet Get-Credential at command pipeline position 1
Supply values for the following parameters:
Credential
```

The remote machine will now be visible as a node under the WSMan: drive:

```
PS (2) > cd wsman:\
PS (3) > Get-ChildItem

   WSManConfig:

ComputerName                                 Type
------------                                 ----
localhost                                    Container
brucepay64h                                  Container
```

Set your current directory to the Service subnode of the remote machine

```
PS (4) > cd brucepay64h\service
```

and look at the contents:

```
PS (5) > Get-ChildItem | Format-Table -auto
WSManConfig: Microsoft.WSMan.Management\WSMan::brucepay64h\Service

Name                              Value
----                              -----
RootSDDL                          O:NSG:BAD:P(A;;GA;;;BA)S:P(A...
MaxConcurrentOperations           4294967295
MaxConcurrentOperationsPerUser    15
EnumerationTimeoutms              60000
MaxConnections                    25
MaxPacketRetrievalTimeSeconds     120
AllowUnencrypted                  false
Auth
DefaultPorts
IPv4Filter                        *
IPv6Filter                        *
EnableCompatibilityHttpListener   false
EnableCompatibilityHttpsListener  false
CertificateThumbprint
```

You can see the `EnumerationTimeoutms` and the `MaxPacketRetrievalTime-Seconds` timeout settings.

Alternatively, you can protect the local computer by setting the various timeouts on the session when you create it. You can do so by creating a session option object using the New-PSSessionOption cmdlet with the -CancelTimeout, -IdleTimeout, -OpenTimeout, and -OperationTimeout parameters. Once you've created this object, you can explicitly pass it to New-PSSession using the -SessionOption parameter (or implicitly by assigning it to the $PSSessionOption preference variable).

One problem with timeouts is that it's hard to tell if the operation timed out because there was a problem or because it just needed more time to complete the operation. If the timeout expires, the remoting infrastructure will simply terminate the operation and generate an error.

It's up to you to investigate why the timeout occurred and either change the command to complete within the timeout interval or determine the source of the timeout (client or server) and increase the timeout interval to allow the command to complete.

In this example, you'll use the New-PSSessionOption cmdlet to create a session option object with a -OperationTimeout value of 10 seconds. This parameter takes its value in milliseconds so you'll provide the value accordingly:

```
PS (1) > $pso = New-PSSessionOption -OperationTimeout (10*1000)
```

Now use the session option object to create a remote session:

```
PS (2) > $s = New-PSSession -ComputerName brucepay64h `
>>> -SessionOption $pso
```

Now try running a command in this session that takes longer than 10 seconds. Use the foreach cmdlet along with Start-Sleep to slowly emit strings of stars. Here's what happens:

```
PS (3) > Invoke-Command $s `
>> { 1..10 | foreach {"$_" + ('*' * $_) ; Start-Sleep 1}}
1*
2**
3***
4****
Processing data from remote server failed with the
following error message: The WinRM client cannot complete
the operation within the time specified. Check if the machine
name is valid and is reachable over the network and firewall
exception for Windows Remote Management service is enabled.
For  more information, see the about_Remote_Troubleshooting
Help topic.
    + CategoryInfo          : OperationStopped:
(System.Manageme...pressionSyncJob:PSInvokeExpressionSyncJob) []
  , PSRemotingTransportException
    + FullyQualifiedErrorId : JobFailure
```

When the timeout occurs, you get an error message explaining that the operation was terminated due to the timeout and suggesting some remedial actions or a way to get more information.

This completes our in-depth coverage of the remoting infrastructure. At this point, you have all the background needed to be able to set up and manage the remoting infrastructure so you can effectively deploy services. Now let's move on to the fun stuff! In the next section, we'll look at how to create custom remoting services. Using the mechanisms provided by PowerShell, you can address a variety of sophisticated scenarios that normally require lots of hardcore programming. In PowerShell, this work reduces to a few lines of script code.

13.2 BUILDING CUSTOM REMOTING SERVICES

In chapter 12, we looked at remoting from the service consumer perspective. It's time for you to take on the role of service creator instead. In this section, you'll learn how to create and configure custom services instead of just using the default PowerShell remoting service. You'll see how to configure your services to limit the operations a client can perform through these endpoints in a very precise way.

13.2.1 Remote service connection patterns

We'll start with a short discussion about service architecture. There are two connection patterns used in remoting: fan-in and fan-out. What you saw in chapter 12 were primarily fan-out patterns. When you create custom remoting services, you'll also be using the fan-in pattern, so we'll briefly describe these two patterns in this section.

Fan-out remoting

The most common remoting scenario for administrators is the one-to-many configuration, in which one client computer connects to a number of remote machines in order to execute remote commands on those machines. This is called the *fan-out* scenario because the connections fan out from a single point, as shown in figure 13.4.

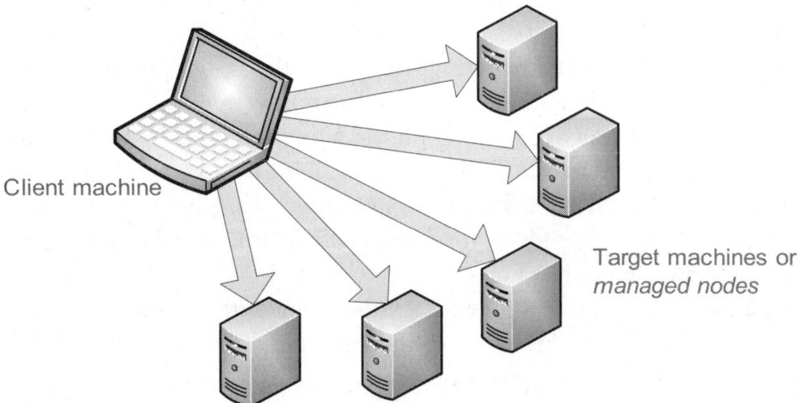

Figure 13.4 In fan-out remoting, a single client fans out connections to manage multiple servers.

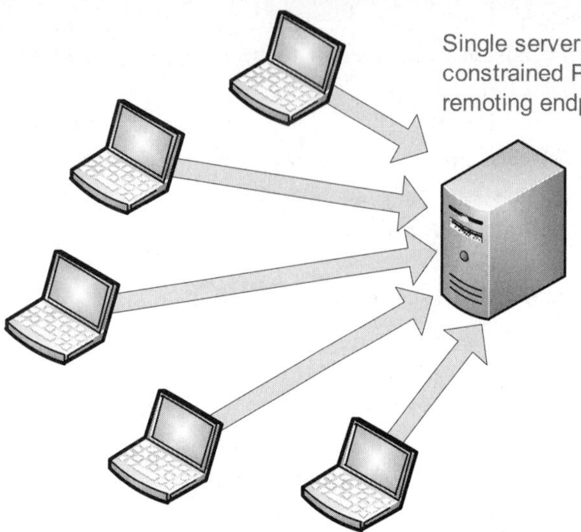

Figure 13.5 In the fan-in arrangement, multiple client computers connect to a single server. This is usually a delegated administration scenario in which a constrained endpoint is used to provide access to controlled services to a variety of clients. This model is used by Outlook.com.

In this figure, you see a single client with concurrent connections to a number of servers that it wants to manage, usually as part of a group of operations. Custom services fit into the fan-out model when you want to restrict the access that the client has. For example, you may want to define a service that only exposes the health data from the monitoring example in section 12.2.3. In this type of scenario, there will typically only be a single client connecting to your service.

Fan-in remoting

In enterprises and hosted solution scenarios, you'll find the opposite configuration where many client computers connect to a single remote computer, such as a file server or a kiosk. This many-to-one is known as the *fan-in* configuration, shown in figure 13.5.

Windows PowerShell remoting supports both fan-out and fan-in configurations. In the fan-out configuration, PowerShell remoting connects to the remote machine using the WinRM service running on the target machine. When the client connects to the remote computer, the WSMan protocol is used to establish a connection to the WinRM service. The WinRM service then launches a new process (`wsmprovhost.exe`) that loads a plug-in that hosts the PowerShell engine. This arrangement is shown in figure 13.6.

Creating a new process for each session is fine if there aren't many users connecting to the service. But if several connections are expected, as is the case for a high-volume service, the one-process-per-user model won't scale very well. To address this issue, an alternate hosting model, targeted at developers, is available for building custom fan-in applications on top of PowerShell remoting. Instead of using the WinRM service to host WSMan and the PowerShell plug-in, Internet Information

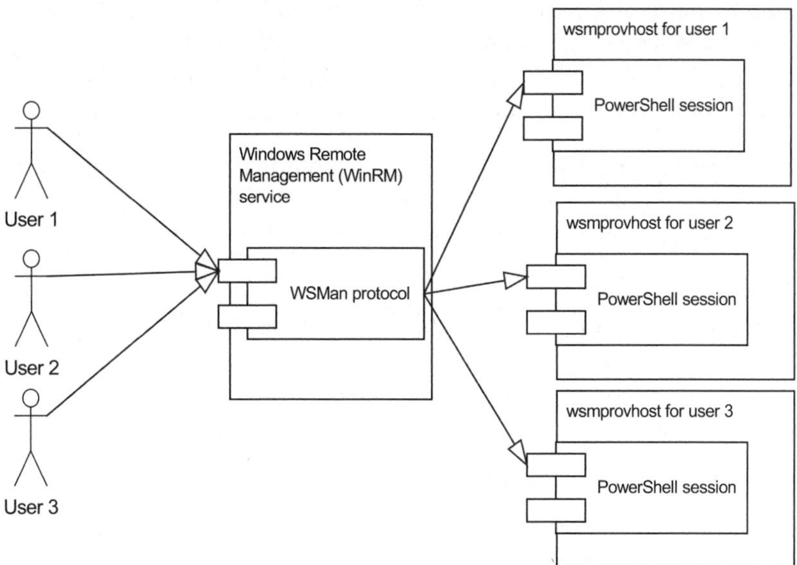

Figure 13.6 When multiple users connect to the WinRM service, a new `wsmprovhost` process is created to host the PowerShell session for that user. Even when the same user connects multiple times, a new process is still created for each connection.

Services (IIS) is used instead. In this model, instead of starting each user session in a separate process, all the PowerShell sessions are run in the same process along with the WSMan protocol engine. This configuration is shown in figure 13.7.

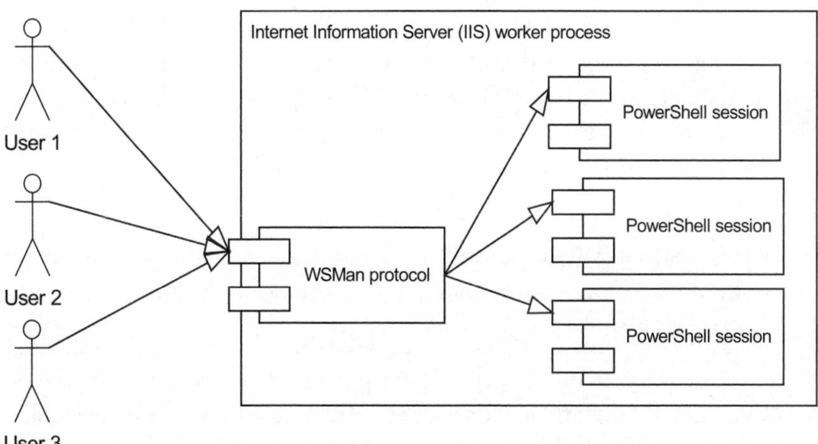

Figure 13.7 When IIS hosting is used for fan-in, each user still gets their own session but only one process is used to host all the sessions. This is much more efficient because you aren't creating a process per user.

Another feature of this hosting model is that the authentication mechanism is pluggable, which allows for alternate authentication services like LiveID to be used. A guide for setting up remoting is available on MSDN as part of the WinRM documentation under the topic "IIS Host Plug-in Configuration" (but be aware that this isn't a simple process).

> **NOTE** IIS hosting and fan-in remote management aren't supported on Windows XP or Windows Server 2003. They require Windows Vista or above when using a nonserver operating system and Windows Server 2008 or later for a server OS.

Having all the sessions running in the same process has certain implications. Because PowerShell lets you get at pretty much everything in a process, multiple users running unrestricted in the same process could interfere with one another. On the other hand, because the host process persists across multiple connections, it's possible to share process-wide resources like database connections between sessions.

Given the lack of session isolation, this approach isn't intended for full-featured general-purpose PowerShell remoting. Instead, it's designed for use with constrained, special-purpose applications using PowerShell remoting. To build these applications, you need two things:

- A way to create a constrained application environment
- A way to connect to PowerShell remoting so the user gets the environment you've created instead of the default PowerShell configuration

We'll start with the second one first and look at how you specify custom remoting endpoints in the next section.

13.2.2 Working with custom configurations

In section 13.1.6, we talked about connecting to a computer by name (and optionally by port number) when using PowerShell remoting. The remoting infrastructure will always connect to the default PowerShell remoting service. In the nondefault connection case, you also have to specify the *configuration* on the target computer to connect to. A configuration is made up of three elements:

- The name you use to connect to the endpoint
- A script that will be run to configure the sessions that will run in the endpoint
- An ACL used to control who has access to the endpoint

When using the `Invoke-Command`, `New-PSSession`, or `Enter-PSSession` cmdlet, you can use the `-ConfigurationName` parameter to specify the name of the session configuration you want to connect to. Alternatively, you can override the normal default configuration by setting the `$PSSessionConfigurationName` preference variable to the name of the endpoint you want to connect to.

When you connect to the named endpoint, a PowerShell session will be created and then the configuration script associated with the endpoint will be executed. This configuration script should define the set of capabilities available when connecting to that endpoint. For example, there may be different endpoints for different types of management tasks—managing a mail server, managing a database server, or managing a web server. For each task, a specific endpoint would be configured to expose the appropriate commands (and constraints) required for performing that task. In the next section, you'll see how to create your own custom endpoints.

13.2.3 Creating a custom configuration

Following on our theme of remote monitoring from chapter 12, you're going to create a configuration that exposes a single custom command, `Get-PageFaultRate`. This command will return the page fault rate from the target computer.

Session configuration

Every remoting connection will use one of the named configurations on the remote computer. These configurations set up the environment for the session and determine the set of commands visible to users of that session.

When remoting is initially enabled using the `Enable-PSRemoting` cmdlet, a default configuration is created on the system called `Microsoft.PowerShell` (on 64-bit operating systems, there's also the `Microsoft.PowerShell32` endpoint). This endpoint is configured to load the default PowerShell configuration with all commands enabled. The `Enable-PSRemoting` cmdlet also sets the security descriptor for this configuration so that only members of the local Administrators group can access the endpoint.

You can use the session configuration cmdlets to modify these default session configurations, to create new session configurations, and to change the security descriptors of all the session configurations. These cmdlets are shown in table 13.7.

Table 13.7 The cmdlets for managing the remoting endpoint configurations

Cmdlet	Description
`Disable-PSSessionConfiguration`	Denies access to the specified session configuration on the local computer by adding an "Everyone AccessDenied" entry to the access control list (ACL) on the configuration
`Enable-PSSessionConfiguration`	Enables existing session configurations on the local computer to be accessed remotely
`Get-PSSessionConfiguration`	Gets a list of the existing, registered session configurations on the computer
`Register-PSSessionConfiguration`	Creates and registers a new session configuration
`Set-PSSessionConfiguration`	Changes the properties of an existing session configuration
`Unregister-PSSessionConfiguration`	Deletes the specified registered session configurations from the computer

In the next section, we'll look at using these cmdlets to create and manage a custom endpoint.

Registering the endpoint configuration

Endpoints are created using the `Register-PSSessionConfiguration` cmdlet and are customized by registering a startup script. In this example, you'll use a simple startup script that defines a single function, `Get-PageFaultRate`. The script looks like this:

```
PS (1) > @'
>> function Get-PageFaultRate {
>>    (Get-WmiObject Win32_PerfRawData_PerfOS_Memory).PageFaultsPersec
>> }
>> '@ > Initialize-HMConfiguration.ps1
>>
```

Before you can use this function, you need to register the configuration, specifying the full path to the startup script. Call this new configuration `wpia1`. From an elevated PowerShell session, run the following command to create the endpoint:

```
PS (2) > Register-PSSessionConfiguration -Name wpia1 `
>>    -StartupScript $pwd/Initialize-HMConfiguration.ps1 -Force
>>

   WSManConfig: Microsoft.WSMan.Management\WSMan::localhost\Plugin

Name                      Type                 Keys
----                      ----                 ----
wpia1                     Container            {Name=wpia1}
```

The output of the command shows that you've created an endpoint in the WSMan plug-in folder. To confirm this, `cd` into that folder and run the `dir` command:

```
PS (3) > cd  wsman:\localhost\plugin
PS (4) > dir

   WSManConfig: Microsoft.WSMan.Management\WSMan::localhost\Plugin

Name                      Type                 Keys
----                      ----                 ----
Event Forwarding Plugin   Container            {Name=Event Fo...
microsoft.powershell      Container            {Name=microsof...
Microsoft.PowerShell32    Container            {Name=Microsof...
WMI Provider              Container            {Name=WMI Prov...
wpia1                     Container            {Name=wpia1}
```

This shows a list of all the existing endpoints, including the one you just created, `wpia1`. Now test this endpoint with the `Invoke-Command` command and run the function defined by the startup script:

```
PS (5) > Invoke-Command localhost -ConfigurationName wpia1 {
>>  Get-PageFaultRate }
58709002
```

This code verifies that the endpoint exists and is properly configured. Now clean up by unregistering the endpoint:

```
PS (6) > Unregister-PSSessionConfiguration -Name wpia1 -Force
PS (7) >
```

Next, verify that the endpoint has been removed:

```
PS (8) > dir

   WSManConfig: Microsoft.WSMan.Management\WSMan::localhost\Plugin

Name                      Type                 Keys
----                      ----                 ----
Event Forwarding Plugin   Container            {Name=Event Fo...
microsoft.powershell      Container            {Name=microsof...
Microsoft.PowerShell32    Container            {Name=Microsof...
WMI Provider              Container            {Name=WMI Prov...
```

This covers the basic tasks needed to create a custom PowerShell remoting endpoint using a configuration script to *add* additional functionality to the session defaults. Our ultimate goal, though, was to create a custom endpoint with *reduced* functionality, exposing a restricted set of commands to qualified users, so clearly you aren't done yet. There are two remaining pieces to look at: controlling individual command visibility, which we'll get to in section 13.2.5, and controlling overall access to the endpoint, our next topic.

13.2.4 Access controls and endpoints

By default, only members of the Administrators group on a computer have permission to use the default session configurations. To allow users who aren't part of the Administrators group to connect to the local computer, you have to give those users Execute permissions on the session configurations for the desired endpoint on the target computer. For example, if you want to enable nonadministrators to connect to the default remoting `Microsoft.PowerShell` endpoint, you can do so by running the following command:

```
Set-PSSessionConfiguration Microsoft.PowerShell -ShowSecurityDescriptorUI
```

This code launches the dialog box shown in figure 13.8.

You add the name of a user or a group you want to enable to the list, then select the Execute (Invoke) check box. Then dismiss the dialog box by clicking OK. At this point, you'll get a prompt telling you that you need to restart the WinRM service for the change to take effect. Do so by running `Restart-Service winrm` as shown:

```
PS (1) > Restart-Service winrm
PS (2) >
```

Once the service is restarted, the user or group you've enabled can connect to the machine using remoting.

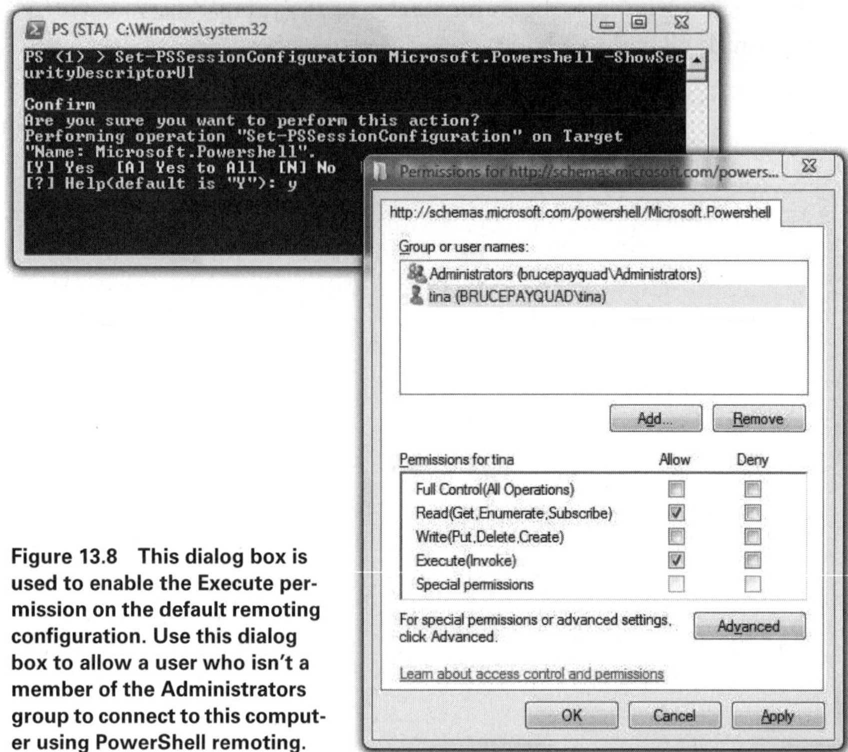

Figure 13.8 This dialog box is used to enable the Execute permission on the default remoting configuration. Use this dialog box to allow a user who isn't a member of the Administrators group to connect to this computer using PowerShell remoting.

Setting security descriptors on configurations

When `Enable-PSRemoting` creates the default session configuration, it doesn't create explicit security descriptors for the configurations. Instead, the configurations inherit the security descriptor of the `RootSDDL`. The `RootSDDL` is the security descriptor that controls remote access to the listener, which is secure by default. To see the `RootSDDL` security descriptor, run the `Get-Item` command as shown:

```
PS (1) > Get-Item wsman:\localhost\Service\RootSDDL

   WSManConfig: Microsoft.WSMan.Management\WSMan::localhost\Service

WARNING: column "Type" does not fit into the display and was removed.

Name                       Value
----                       -----
RootSDDL                   O:NSG:BAD:P(A;;GA;;;BA)S:P(AU;FA;GA;;;WD...
```

The string format shown in the `Value` output in the example uses the syntax defined by the Security Descriptor Definition Language (SDDL), which is documented in the Windows Data Types specification MS-DTYP in section 2.5.1.

To change the `RootSDDL`, use the `Set-Item` cmdlet in the WSMan: drive. To change the security descriptor for an existing session configuration, use the `Set-PSSessionConfiguration` cmdlet with the `-SecurityDescriptorSDDL` or `-ShowSecurityDescriptorUI` parameter.

At this point, you know how to create and configure an endpoint and how to control who has access to that endpoint. But in your configuration all you've done is add new commands to the set of commands you got by default. You haven't addressed the requirement to *constrain* the environment. The next section introduces the mechanisms used to restrict which commands are visible to the remote user.

13.2.5 Constraining a PowerShell session

You first need to know how to constrain a local session. In a constrained environment, you want to limit the variables and commands available to the user of the session. You accomplish this by controlling command and variable *visibility*. Let's look at command visibility first.

Command and variable visibility is conceptually similar to exporting functions from a module, but it uses a different implementation. When a command is exported from a module, it's registered in the caller's command table. In the remoting scenario with `Invoke-Command`, there's no "table" to copy the commands into and so you need a different mechanism to control visibility of the command.

> **NOTE** The same is true of explicit remoting and interactive remoting. With implicit remoting, you do copy commands into the caller's command table, but they're local proxy commands instead of local references to exported commands.

Another more important consideration is security. Module exports are designed to prevent namespace collisions but don't prevent you from accessing the content of the module. In other words, it's not a security boundary, as shown in figure 13.9.

In figure 13.9, the user can't call `Get-Count` directly because it hasn't been exported from the module. But by using the call operator `&` and the `PSModuleInfo` object for that module, users can still indirectly invoke the command with a scriptblock, illustrating that a module boundary doesn't constitute a security boundary.

In a constrained session, you need to establish a boundary and explicitly prevent access to the state of the session other than through the public or visible commands. Now that you've defined the boundary, let's look at controlling which commands are exposed.

> **NOTE** In local sessions, where the user operates in the same process as the session, the session boundary isn't sufficient to provide a true security. Only when you combine a constrained session with remote (and therefore out-of-process) access do you actually get a security boundary.

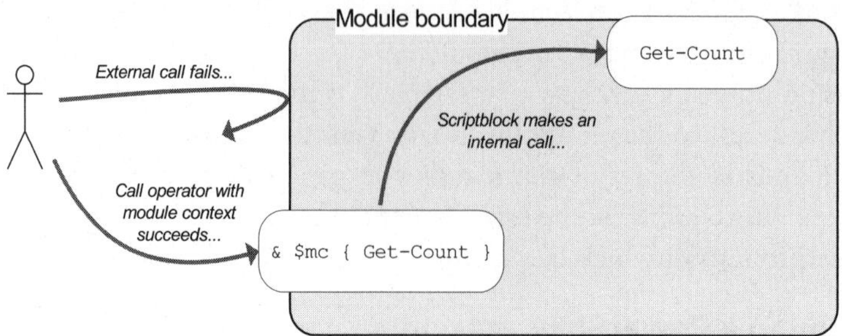

Figure 13.9 Even though the `Get-Count` command isn't exported, by using the call operator and the `PSModuleInfo` object for that module, the user can still *indirectly* call the private function. The module boundary only facilitates organizing command namespaces and doesn't constitute a security boundary.

Controlling command visibility

The mechanism used to control command visibility is the `Visibility` property on the `CommandInfo` object for that command. This mechanism isn't restricted to remoting, by the way—you can use this mechanism in the normal interactive PowerShell session. In fact, it's a good way of testing your configuration without creating an endpoint.

To make a command invisible or private, first use `Get-Command` to get the `CommandInfo` object, then set the `Visibility` property on that object to `Private`. You'll modify your current session to make the `Get-Date` command private. This is a good place to start playing with visibility because hiding `Get-Date` (typically) won't break anything (more on that later). First, run the command as you might conventionally do:

```
PS (1) > Get-Date

Saturday, April 16, 2011 9:04:20 PM
```

This returns today's date—nothing unexpected here. Now use `Get-Command` to retrieve the `CommandInfo` object for `Get-Date`:

```
PS (2) > $gd = Get-Command Get-Date
```

Let's look at the current setting of the `Visibility` property:

```
PS (3) > $gd.Visibility
Public
```

It returns `Public`, meaning it can be seen and therefore executed from outside the session. Change this to `Private`:

```
PS (4) > $gd.Visibility = "Private"
```

Verify the change:

```
PS (5) > $gd.Visibility
Private
```

Now try calling the cmdlet again:

```
PS (6) > Get-Date
The term 'Get-Date' is not recognized as the name of a cmdlet,
function, script file, or operable program. Check the spelling of
the name, or if a path was included, verify that the path is
correct and try again.
At line:1 char:9
+ Get-Date <<<<
    + CategoryInfo          : ObjectNotFound: (Get-Date:String)
    [], CommandNotFoundException
    + FullyQualifiedErrorId : CommandNotFoundException
```

You got an error complaining that the command doesn't exist.

> **NOTE** Notice that this is the same error you'd get if the command really didn't exist. Obscuring the error message this way prevents attacks that probe for hidden commands. We'll talk more about this type of attack in chapter 21 when we discuss security.

Just to be sure, try calling it another way using the call (`&`) operator:

```
PS (7) > & "Get-Date"
The term 'Get-Date' is not recognized as the name of a cmdlet,
function, script file, or operable program. Check the spelling of
the name, or if a path was included, verify that the path is
correct and try again.
At line:1 char:2
+ & <<<<  "Get-Date"
    + CategoryInfo          : ObjectNotFound: (Get-Date:String)
    [], CommandNotFoundException
    + FullyQualifiedErrorId : CommandNotFoundException
```

And of course it still fails. But, because you're a sophisticated PowerShell user, you'll try one more technique: using a scriptblock with the call operator to invoke the command:

```
PS (8) > & {Get-Date}

Saturday, April 16, 2011 9:04:20 PM
```

This time it worked! So what's going on here? The difference in this case is that the external user didn't call the command directly. Instead, you called a visible function—the scriptblock—defined inside the session and, because it was calling from inside, it was able to call the private function. This is shown in figure 13.10.

This is a very important point to understand because it's the key to creating a restricted special-purpose endpoint: an *external* call can only access visible commands; but these commands, because they're defined as part of the configuration, can

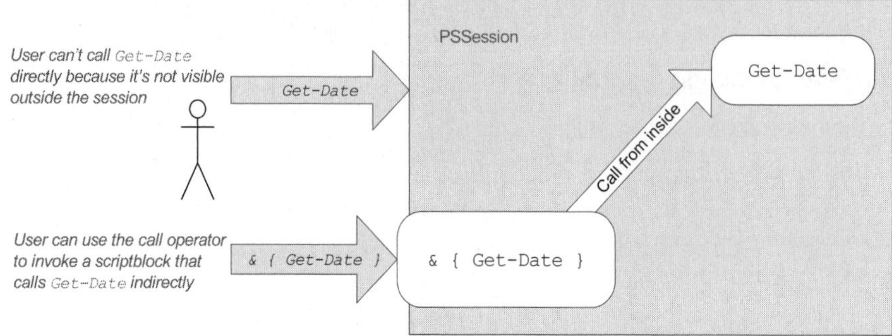
Internal vs. external command access in a session
PSSession
User can't call Get-Date directly because it's not visible outside the session
Get-Date
Get-Date
Call from inside
User can use the call operator to invoke a scriptblock that calls Get-Date indirectly
& { Get-Date }
& { Get-Date }

Figure 13.10 If the command isn't visible across the session boundary, the user can't call it. If the user can call a visible command, that visible command can call the private internal command.

see all the other commands in the configuration. This means that an externally visible command can call any internal commands in the session. So, if the user makes an external call to a visible command, that visible command is able to call the private commands.

These calling conventions are very similar to the way methods on classes or exported functions work. The external caller of the session/class/module can only call the public/exported commands (at least directly) but the private commands have implicit access to the private state of the session/class/module. This means you can create a public wrapper function that calls the private function. For example, you can create a function `MyGetDate` that calls `Get-Date` and then converts the result into a string and returns that string. Here's what that looks like:

```
PS (9) > function MyGetDate { [string] (Get-Date) }
```

When you call it, you get the default string representation of the date:

```
PS (10) > MyGetDate

11/17/2009 22:11:39
```

Now you've officially constrained the session because the `MyGetDate` wrapper function has less functionality than the private `Get-Date` function. There are a couple of additional things you need to do to get a truly constrained environment. But first let's make `Get-Date` visible again. You can do this by setting the `Visibility` property back to `Public`:

```
PS (11) > $gd.Visibility = "public"
PS (12) > Get-Date

Tuesday, November 17, 2009 9:05:59 PM
```

And everything is back to normal.

It's not much of a security mechanism if you can just use the properties on the command objects to control the visibility of commands. Clearly there needs to be more to the story, so in the next section we'll revisit the restricted language we mentioned in section 10.6 when we discussed module manifests and the data language.

Setting the language mode

In the previous section, you learned how to make a command private and then call it through a public function. Obviously if you allow external users to create their own functions, this won't be very secure. So the next thing you need to do is constrain what PowerShell language features the user has access to. You accomplish this through the `$ExecutionContext` variable. As you saw in chapter 11, `$ExecutionContext` captures—well—the execution context of the session. The property of interest in this case is `SessionState`. Let's see what that property exposes:

```
PS (1) > $ExecutionContext.SessionState

Drive                          : System.Management.Automation.Dri
                                 veManagementIntrinsics
Provider                       : System.Management.Automation.Cmd
                                 letProviderManagementIntrinsics
Path                           : System.Management.Automation.Pat
                                 hIntrinsics
PSVariable                     : System.Management.Automation.PSV
                                 ariableIntrinsics
LanguageMode                   : FullLanguage
UseFullLanguageModeInDebugger : False
Scripts                        : {*}
Applications                   : {*}
Module                         :
InvokeProvider                 : System.Management.Automation.Pro
                                 viderIntrinsics
InvokeCommand                  : System.Management.Automation.Com
                                 mandInvocationIntrinsics
```

And you see a lot of interesting things. Of particular interest are three properties: `LanguageMode`, `Scripts`, and `Applications`.

When we looked at constrain commands in the previous section, you used the `Visibility` property on the `CommandInfo` object to make `Get-Date` private. This approach works for commands that exist in memory, but scripts and executables are loaded from disk each time, which means that a new `CommandInfo` object is returned each time. Setting the `Visibility` property won't be very useful if you're returning a new object each time. Another mechanism is needed for this, and this mechanism is a list of permitted commands and scripts. The default setting for these properties is a single element, `*`, which means that any external command or script may be executed. If this element is deleted so that the list is empty, it means that no commands of this type may be executed. To permit only specific commands to be called, add the full path to the command or script to this list.

NOTE You might logically assume that wildcards would be permitted in this list. They aren't. The only pattern that has a special significance is when the list contains a single `*`. Pattern matching may be added in future releases, but although it was considered, it wasn't implemented in PowerShell v2.

Let's work through an example showing how these lists work. First, you'll get the absolute path to the `ipconfig` command using the `Definition` property on its `CommandInfo` object:

```
PS (1) > $ipp = (Get-Command ipconfig.exe).Definition
```

This is an easy way of getting the full path to the command, regardless of which operating system you're on. Once you have that, you'll clear the Applications list. (You had to get the `CommandInfo` for `ipconfig` before you cleared the list because after you cleared the list `Get-Command` would no longer be able to find the command.)

```
PS (2) > $ExecutionContext.SessionState.Applications.Clear()
```

Now add the path you saved in `$ipp` to the command to the list:

```
PS (3) > $ExecutionContext.SessionState.Applications.Add($ipp)
```

And now try to run the command:

```
PS (4) > ipconfig | Select-String ipv4

   IPv4 Address. . . . . . . . . . . : 192.168.1.15
   IPv4 Address. . . . . . . . . . . : 192.168.1.5
```

The command works as intended—this was the point of adding its path to the list, after all. Now let's try a command that isn't on the list:

```
PS (5) > expand /? | Select-String expand
The term 'expand.exe' is not recognized as the name of a cmdlet,
 function, script file, or operable program. Check the spelling
of the name, or if a path was included, verify that the path is
correct and try again.
At line:1 char:7
+ expand <<<<  /? | Select-String expand
    + CategoryInfo          : ObjectNotFound:
(expand.exe:String) [], CommandNotFoundException
    + FullyQualifiedErrorId : CommandNotFoundException
```

You get a "command not found" error. Notice that this error doesn't say that the command is private—the system behaves as though the command doesn't exist. It does so for security purposes. Now let's attempt something that will seem a bit strange. Try calling the hidden command from inside a scriptblock:

```
PS (6) > & { expand /? | Select-String expand }

Expands one or more compressed files.
EXPAND [-r] Source Destination
```

```
EXPAND -r Source [Destination]
EXPAND -D Source.cab [-F:Files]
EXPAND Source.cab -F:Files Destination
  -r        Rename expanded files.
  -F:Files    Name of files to expand from a .CAB.
```

And the command was found! So what's going on here? Well, this is part of the constrained session model. Private commands are hidden from *external commands*—that is, commands that come across the session boundary, in this case, between the console host and the PowerShell interpreter. Scripts and functions (including scriptblocks) are considered *internal commands* and so they can see all functions. This is similar to the way modules work. Only public/exported members are visible outside the session/module boundary. The one big difference is that there's a way to see inside the module (for debugging purposes) but there's no way to see inside the session once restrictions are in place. Now let's reset the Applications list:

```
PS (7) > $ExecutionContext.SessionState.Applications.Clear()
PS (8) > $ExecutionContext.SessionState.Applications.Add('*')
PS (9) >
```

You now know how to use the Applications list to constrain the set of external commands that may be run. This is intended to be a security measure, but as you saw earlier, if you can create a scriptblock, that scriptblock can "bypass" the security boundary. You'll also need to limit the ability to create functions and scriptblocks. You can do so using the `LanguageMode` property on `SessionState`. Here's the default setting:

```
PS (2) > $ExecutionContext.SessionState.LanguageMode
FullLanguage
```

The default setting is to allow all aspects of the PowerShell language to be used when sending commands to the engine. You'll change this setting in a minute, but first you need to set up a way to undo what you're doing. Once you've constrained the language in a session, there won't be a way to unconstrain it for that session.

> **NOTE** All the settings we're looking at in this section are transient and only apply to the current session you're working with. Other sessions aren't affected, nor are any new sessions that are created. So if you do find that you've broken your session by doing something out of order, simply exit and start a new session.

First, create a function to restore the `LanguageMode` to `FullLanguage`:

```
PS (3) > function Restore-FullLanguageMode {
>>     $ExecutionContext.SessionState.LanguageMode = "FullLanguage"
>> }
>>
```

When you run this function, it'll reset `LanguageMode` to `FullLanguage`.

Now change LanguageMode to RestrictedLanguage. RestrictedLanguage is the subset of the PowerShell language that's used in PowerShell data files. We talked about this when we covered module manifests in chapter 10 (section 10.6):

```
PS (4) > $ExecutionContext.SessionState.LanguageMode =
>> "RestrictedLanguage"
>>
```

Now see how your session has been affected. First, you can't set variables:

```
PS (5) > $a=123
Assignment statements are not allowed in restricted language
mode or a Data section.
At line:1 char:4
+ $a= <<<< 123
    + CategoryInfo          : ParserError: (=:OperatorToken) []
   , ParentContainsErrorRecordException
    + FullyQualifiedErrorId : AssignmentStatementNotSupportedIn
   DataSection
```

You also can't create functions of any kind:

```
PS (6) > function foo {}
Function declarations are not allowed in restricted language
mode or a Data section.
At line:1 char:13
+ function foo <<<<  {}
    + CategoryInfo          : ParserError: (foo:Token) [],
ParentContainsErrorRecordException
    + FullyQualifiedErrorId : FunctionDeclarationNotSupportedIn
   DataSection
```

You can try to be clever and use the Set-Item cmdlet as you saw in chapter 11 in section 11.8.6:

```
PS (7) > Set-Item function:foo {}
Scriptblock literals are not allowed in restricted language
mode or a Data section.
At line:1 char:25
+ set-item function:foo {} <<<<
    + CategoryInfo          : ParserError: (:) [],
ParentContai   nsErrorRecordException
    + FullyQualifiedErrorId :
ScriptBlockNotSupportedInDataSection
```

Because you can't perform assignments, obviously you can't use assignment to reset the language:

```
PS (8) > $ExecutionContext.SessionState.LanguageMode = "FullLanguage"
Assignment statements are not allowed in restricted language
mode or a Data section.
At line:1 char:46
+ $ExecutionContext.SessionState.LanguageMode = <<<<
"FullLanguage"
    + CategoryInfo          : ParserError: (=:OperatorToken) []
```

```
, ParentContainsErrorRecordException
 + FullyQualifiedErrorId : AssignmentStatementNotSupportedIn
DataSection
```

Use the restore function you defined before you switched over to `Restricted-Language` mode:

```
PS (9) > Restore-FullLanguageMode
```

And everything works again:

```
PS (10) > $a=123
PS (11) >
```

Now that you know how to constrain a session, you're halfway to your goal of being able to create constrained custom endpoints. In the next section, we'll look at the second piece: creating a custom remoting endpoint.

13.2.6 Creating a constrained execution environment

The idea behind a constrained endpoint is that it allows you to provide controlled access to services on a server in a secure manner. This is the mechanism that the hosted Exchange product Outlook.com uses to constrain who gets to manage which sets of mailboxes.

As mentioned earlier, for the environment to be secure, there needs to be both access restriction and a boundary. Remoting allows a boundary to be established as long as the only way to access the remote end is through the remoting layer. The restrictions can be established by controlling command visibility and restricting the language. You combine these into a custom remoting endpoint configured with a script that sets the configuration so that only a small subset of things is visible through the remoting layer. The code to accomplish this is shown in the following listing.

Listing 13.1 Initialize-ConstrainedHMConfiguration.ps1

```
foreach ($cmd in Get-Command)                          <- Hide all commands in session
{
    $cmd.Visibility = "private"
}
foreach ($var in Get-Variable)           <- Hide all variables in session
{
    $var.Visibility = "private"
}

$ExecutionContext.SessionState.Applications.Clear()   | Hide all external
$ExecutionContext.SessionState.Scripts.Clear()        | programs, scripts
$ExecutionContext.SessionState.LanguageMode = "NoLanguage"   <- Set to NoLanguage mode

function Get-HealthModel        <- Define public Get-HealthModel
{
    @{
        Date = Get-Date
```

```
        FreeSpace = (Get-PSDrive c).Free
        PageFaults = (Get-WmiObject `
            Win32_PerfRawData_PerfOS_Memory).PageFaultsPersec
        TopCPU = Get-Process | sort -Descending CPU  | select -First 5
        TopWS = Get-Process | sort -Descending WS | select -First 5
    }
}
```

The first part of this script is generic and reusable. It can be used as a preamble to any constrained endpoint configuration script. Any function defined after the line setting the session to `NoLanguage` mode will be publicly visible and represents the services this endpoint provides.

> **NOTE** When some people first looked at the example in listing 13.1 they thought there was a bug because some statements are executed *after* the language mode is set. This isn't the case for two reasons: First, because this is an endpoint configuration script, it's executed inside the session boundary where the restrictions don't apply. Second, a PowerShell script is completely parsed before execution begins so all language processing for this script was completed before the language mode change was made, and language mode checks are only done during parse time.

In this example, you're adapting the health model function you saw in chapter 12, section 12.2.3, to be run in this endpoint. Try this script. From an elevated PowerShell session, run the following commands:

```
PS (1) > Unregister-PSSessionConfiguration -Name wpia1 -Force
PS (2) > Register-PSSessionConfiguration -Name wpia1 `
>>     -StartupScript $pwd/Initialize-ConstrainedHMConfiguration.ps1 `
>>     -Force
>>

   WSManConfig: Microsoft.WSMan.Management\WSMan::localhost\Plugin

Name                      Type                 Keys
----                      ----                 ----
wpia1                     Container            {Name=wpia1}
```

The first command removes the existing endpoint definition in case it may be left from an earlier operation. The second line creates the new endpoint with the script from listing 13.1. With the endpoint installed, you can try it. Run the `Get-HealthModel` command:

```
PS (3) > icm localhost -ConfigurationName wpia1 {Get-HealthModel}

Name                           Value
----                           -----
Date                           2/24/2010 11:32:49 PM
TopWS                          {System.Diagnostics.Process (svchos...
PageFaults                     63217485
```

```
TopCPU                          {System.Diagnostics.Process (svchos...
FreeSpace                       362546515968
```

It executes properly. Try another command:

```
PS (4) > Invoke-Command localhost -ConfigurationName wpia1 {Get-Date}
The term 'Get-Date' is not recognized as the name of a cmdlet,
function, script file, or operable program. Check the spelling of the name,
 or if a path was included, verify that the path is correct and try
again.
    + CategoryInfo          : ObjectNotFound: (Get-Date:String) [],
   CommandNotFoundException
    + FullyQualifiedErrorId : CommandNotFoundException
```

This code fails with the expected error. Try using `Get-Command` to see the list of the things you can execute:

```
PS (5) > Invoke-Command localhost -ConfigurationName wpia1 {Get-Command}
The term 'Get-Command' is not recognized as the name of a cmdlet,
function, script file, or operable program. Check the spelling of the
name, or if a path was included, verify that the path is correct and
try again.
    + CategoryInfo          : ObjectNotFound: (Get-Command:String) [
   ], CommandNotFoundException
    + FullyQualifiedErrorId : CommandNotFoundException
```

This code also fails—not unexpected, but it'd be nice to see what's exposed. Try interactive remoting:

```
PS (6) > Enter-PSSession localhost -ConfigurationName wpia1
Enter-PSSession : The term 'Get-Command' is not recognized as the
name of a cmdlet, function, script file, or operable program. Check the
spelling of the name, or if a path was included, verify that the path
 is correct and try again.
At line:1 char:16
+ Enter-PSSession <<<<  localhost -ConfigurationName wpia1
    + CategoryInfo          : ObjectNotFound: (Get-Command:String) [
   Enter-PSSession], CommandNotFoundException
    + FullyQualifiedErrorId : CommandNotFoundException
```

This code also fails because an interactive session requires certain commands to be available on the remote end, like the default outputter commands we discussed earlier. Let's move on to implicit remoting. Where interactive remoting isn't likely to be very interesting with only one command, the constrained endpoint is the ideal scenario for implicit remoting:

```
PS (8) > $s = New-PSSession localhost -ConfigurationName wpia1
PS (9) > Import-PSSession $s -Verbose
Import-PSSession : Import-PSSession cmdlet needs the following
commands in the remote session: Get-Command, Get-FormatData, Select-Object.
  The following commands are used, but optional: Get-Help,
Measure-Object.  Please make sure the remote session includes the required
            commands and try again.
At line:1 char:17
+ Import-PSSession <<<< $s -Verbose
```

```
    + CategoryInfo          : ObjectNotFound: (:) [Import-PSSession]
   , RuntimeException
    + FullyQualifiedErrorId : ErrorRequiredRemoteCommandNotFound,Mic
   rosoft.PowerShell.Commands.ImportPSSessionCommand
PS (10) >
```

This code also fails for the same reason. For implicit remoting to work, it needs to be able to get the information about the commands in the remote session. From the error message for the `Import-PSSession` case, you can see the list of commands that need to be present. You could create a script to handle this, but there's a feature in the PowerShell API that was specifically designed to address this case. There's a .NET class that's part of the PowerShell software development kit (SDK) that's intended to be used by programmers who are writing custom hosts for the PowerShell engine. This class is used to create the initial settings for a session used in different applications. This class is called `InitialSessionState` and you can use it as follows:

```
$iss = [Management.Automation.Runspaces.InitialSessionState]::
            CreateRestricted(
"remoteserver")
```

This creates an object that contains the settings needed for building a constrained environment intended for a `remoteserver` application. You don't need all the settings that this object contains, but it does have something very useful in it: a set of function definitions that fulfill the needs of both interactive and implicit remoting. You can see this list by running this code:

```
PS (1) > $iss =
>> [Management.Automation.Runspaces.InitialSessionState]::CreateRestricted(
>> "RemoteServer")
>>
PS (2) > $iss.Commands | where { $_.Visibility -eq "Public" } |
>> Format-Table name
>>

Name
----
Get-Command
Get-FormatData
Select-Object
Get-Help
Measure-Object
Exit-PSSession
Out-Default
```

The bodies of these functions are similar to the proxy functions used for implicit remoting that you saw in chapter 12, section 12.4.2.

> **NOTE** When you look at this list of commands, you may wonder why some of them are included. For example, `Measure-Object` seems like a strange thing to have on the list. The reason these commands are included is that they're needed to implement some of the elements of

the PowerShell remoting protocol. In particular, they're used to help with the command-discovery component described in MS-PSRP section 3.1.4.5, "Getting Command Metadata."

The goal here is a bit different because they're used to provide public facades for private commands. If you're interested in how these functions are defined, look at the `Definition` property on the objects returned by `Commands` by using the following code:

```
PS (3) > $p = $iss.Commands | where { $_.Visibility -eq "Public" }
PS (4) > $p[0] | Format-List name,definition
Name       : Get-Command
Definition : [CmdletBinding()]
             param(
                 [ValidateLength(0, 1000)]
                 [ValidateCount(0, 1000)]
                 [System.String[]]
                 ${Name},

                 [ValidateLength(0, 1000)]
                 [ValidateCount(0, 100)]
                 [System.String[]]
                 ${Module},
:
:
```

The output is truncated here because it's quite long. (Again, be happy you don't have to write these functions—you're welcome to explore them at your leisure but we're not going to spend any more time looking at them.) Once you have this object, you can copy these functions into your session:

```
foreach ($cmd in $iss.Commands | where { $_.Visibility -eq "Public"})
{
    $needsAlias = Get-Command -CommandType Cmdlet `
       -ErrorAction SilentlyContinue $cmd.Name
    if ($needsAlias)
    {
        $a = Set-Alias $cmd.Name "$($needsAlias.ModuleName)\$($cmd.Name)" `
            -PassThru
        $a.Visibility = "Private"
    }
    Set-Item "function:global:$($cmd.Name)" $cmd.Definition
}
```

This code fragment loops through the set of command definitions, looking for the public definitions, and then uses the function provider to define new public functions in the session. It also defines some new private aliases that are used to bypass the proxies for internal calls. This step is necessary because some of the public functions you want to write may use the some of the cmdlets you've just proxied. Because the proxies don't implement all the features of the wrapped cmdlets, not being able to

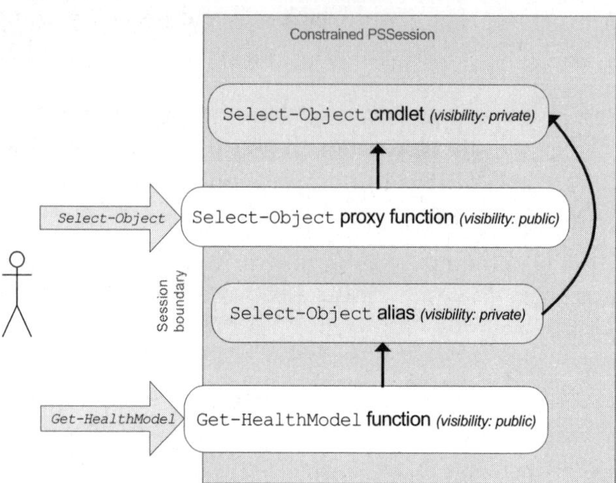

Figure 13.11 The call flow from the public constrained `Select-Object` proxy function to the private unconstrained `Select-Object` cmdlet. When the user calls the public `Get-HealthModel` and it calls `Select-Object`, the call resolves to the private `Select-Object` alias. This alias is hard-coded to bypass the constrained proxy function and call the cmdlet directly giving unconstrained access internally.

access to the un-proxied commands could interfere with the operation of any new commands you want to write.

Using aliases to bypass the proxies works because of the way command resolution operates. Remember that, when you're looking for a command, you look for aliases first, then functions, and then cmdlets. This order is always followed when the call is coming from inside the session. If the call is coming from outside the session, the lookup order doesn't change, but if one of the things it finds is private, that definition is skipped and the lookup moves on to the next type of command. So, if you define an alias that uses the module-qualified name of a cmdlet, internal lookups will resolve to the alias. This alias uses module-qualified name for the cmdlet, thereby skipping the function and going directly to the cmdlet. External lookups, on the other hand, won't see the alias because it's private. They can only see the public constrained proxy function. These lookup patterns are shown in figure 13.11.

Now let's see how all this looks when you add these code fragments to your configuration script. The following listing shows the updated configuration script.

Listing 13.2 Initialize-ComplexConstrainedHMConfiguration.ps1

```
foreach ($cmd in Get-Command)
{
    $cmd.Visibility = "private"
}
foreach ($var in Get-Variable)
{
    $var.Visibility = "private"
}
$ExecutionContext.SessionState.Applications.Clear()
$ExecutionContext.SessionState.Scripts.Clear()
```

Hide existing commands

```
ExecutionContext.SessionState.LanguageMode =                    <-- Set NoLanguage mode
    "NoLanguage"
$iss =                                      <-- Get list of required proxies
  [Management.Automation.Runspaces.InitialSessionState]::CreateRestricted(
    "remoteserver")
foreach ($proxy in $iss.Commands | where { $_.Visibility -eq "Public"}) <-- Bind private alias and proxy function
{
    $cmd = Get-Command -type cmdlet -ea silentlycontinue $proxy.name
    if ($cmd)
    {
        $a = Set-Alias "$($proxy.name)" `
            "$($cmd.ModuleName)\$($cmd.Name)" -PassThru
        $a.Visibility = "Private"
    }
    Set-Item "function:global:$($proxy.Name)" `
        $proxy.Definition
}
function Get-HealthModel                          <-- Define public content
{
    @{
        Date = Get-Date
        FreeSpace = (Get-PSDrive c).Free
        PageFaults = (Get-WmiObject `
            Win32_PerfRawData_PerfOS_Memory).PageFaultsPersec
        TopCPU = Get-Process | sort -Descending CPU | select -First 5
        TopWS = Get-Process | sort -Descending WS | select -First 5
    }
}
```

This script is identical to the earlier script with the exception that it has the additional lines needed to define the proxy functions. Let's test this out. First, re-create the endpoint using the new configuration script:

```
PS (1) > Unregister-PSSessionConfiguration -Name wpia1 -Force
PS (2) > Register-PSSessionConfiguration -Name wpia1 -StartupScript `
>> $pwd/Initialize-ComplexConstrainedHMConfiguration.ps1.ps1 -Force
>>

   WSManConfig: Microsoft.WSMan.Management\WSMan::localhost\Plugin

Name                      Type                 Keys
----                      ----                 ----
wpia1                     Container            {Name=wpia1}
```

> **NOTE** In practice, you wouldn't normally bother to re-create the endpoint because the script is actually loaded and run each time a session starts. It's sufficient to simply edit the script and then start a new connection to test your changes (existing connections will remain unaffected).

Start an interactive remoting session with this new configuration:

```
PS (3) > Enter-PSSession localhost -ConfigurationName wpia1
```

This time it succeeds without any problems. You can run Get-Command to get the list of available commands in the session:

```
[localhost]: PS>Get-Command

CommandType     Name                           Definition
-----------     ----                           ----------
Function        Exit-PSSession                 [CmdletBinding()]...
Function        Get-Command                    [CmdletBinding()]...
Function        Get-FormatData                 [CmdletBinding()]...
Function        Get-HealthModel                ...
Function        Get-Help                       [CmdletBinding()]...
Function        Measure-Object                 [CmdletBinding()]...
Function        Out-Default                    [CmdletBinding()]...
Function        Select-Object                  [CmdletBinding()]...
```

Now try running the Get-HealthModel function:

```
[localhost]: PS>Get-HealthModel

Name                           Value
----                           -----
FreeSpace                      359284412416
PageFaults                     215576420
Date                           2/26/2010 10:05:30 PM
TopWS                          {System.Diagnostics.Process (svchos...
TopCPU                         {System.Diagnostics.Process (sqlser...
```

It works as expected. Now exit the session by calling exit:

```
[localhost]: PS>exit
The syntax is not supported by this runspace. This might be because
it is in no-language mode.
    + CategoryInfo          :
    + FullyQualifiedErrorId : ScriptsNotAllowed
```

You get an error. This error occurs because you're in NoLanguage mode and exit is a keyword. You haven't seen this before because you haven't done interactive remoting with a constrained session before. The solution to this is to use the Exit-PSSession function that was defined as part of the standard set of proxy functions:

```
[localhost]: PS>Exit-PSsession
```

Now import this session:

```
PS (6) > $s = New-PSSession localhost -ConfigurationName wpia1
PS (9) > Import-PSSession $s

ModuleType Name                      ExportedCommands
---------- ----                      ----------------
Script     tmp_9bed4009-478e-4e91... Get-HealthModel
```

The import worked, so you can call `Get-HealthModel`:

```
PS (10) > Get-HealthModel

Name                           Value
----                           -----
Date                           2/26/2010 10:52:36 PM
TopWS                          {System.Diagnostics.Process (svchos...
PageFaults                     217681970
TopCPU                         {System.Diagnostics.Process (sqlser...
FreeSpace                      360739450880
```

It works just like a local command. The details of remoting are hidden.

Let's step back and think about what you've accomplished here. With about 40 lines of script, you've defined a secure remote service. And of these 40 lines, most of them are a boilerplate preamble. Just paste them at the beginning of the configuration script and then add the additional functions to define the services you want to expose.

From the users' perspective, by using `Import-PSSession` they're able to install the necessary client software to use this service *simply by connecting to the service.*

Constrained sessions combined with implicit remoting results in an extremely flexible system, allowing you to create precise service boundaries with very little server-side code and *no* client code. Consider how much code would be required to create an equivalent service using alternate technologies!

And with this, we've come to end of our coverage of the remoting features in PowerShell.

13.3 SUMMARY

In this chapter, we looked at a PowerShell remoting from the service or application creator's point of view. The goal of the chapter was to show you how to create a custom service using the remoting capabilities.

To make sure you have the necessary background and context for building this service, we explored how PowerShell remoting works. Topics included the following:

- Describing the PowerShell remoting protocol stack, which includes HTTP and WSMan
- Managing WSMan using cmdlets and the WSMan: drive
- Authenticating both the target computer and the incoming user connecting to the service
- Understanding various issues related to addressing the target computer
- Ensuring the reliability of your services by managing resource consumption

Next, you started to build your service. You began by looking at the fan-in and fan-out service architectures. Then we covered the following:

- Creating custom configurations and remoting endpoints
- Configuring an endpoint with a startup script
- Controlling who has access to the endpoint using ACLs
- Constraining a session by controlling the set of commands visible to users connecting to the endpoint
- Controlling the flavor of PowerShell that's available to the endpoint user
- Using a startup script in a custom configuration that sets up the necessary constraints for the application
- Configuring the session so that implicit remoting can be used with the endpoint

PowerShell remoting and the underlying technologies are both broad and deep areas. In this chapter and the previous one, we've covered most of the features of the technologies and how they can be applied. The next chapter explores errors and exceptions.

CHAPTER 14

Errors and exceptions

Progress, far from consisting in change, depends on retentiveness. Those who cannot remember the past are condemned to repeat it.

—George Santayana, *The Life of Reason*

It's always useful to keep in mind that PowerShell isn't "just" a shell or scripting language. Its primary purpose is to be an automation tool and perform critical management tasks on a server, such as send software updates, inspect log files, or provision user accounts. You need to be sure that either the task is completed properly or the reason for failure is appropriately recorded.

In this chapter, we'll focus on the latter topic: how PowerShell reports, records, and manages error conditions. Handling of error conditions is one of the areas where PowerShell shines compared to other scripting tools. The support for diagnostic tracing and logging is practically unprecedented in traditional scripting languages. Unfortunately, these features don't come entirely free—there are costs in terms of complexity and execution overhead that aren't there in other environments. All these capabilities are very much a part of PowerShell as a management tool; Microsoft set a higher bar for PowerShell than has been set for most other language environments.

We'll begin the chapter by looking at the error processing subsystem. Errors in PowerShell aren't simply error codes, strings, or even exceptions as found in languages such as C# and VB.NET. They're rich objects that include just about everything you could think of that might be useful in debugging a problem.

> **NOTE** Some people dislike (okay, despise) the use of the word *rich* in this context. But given the wealth of information that PowerShell error objects contain, *rich* really is the right word.

We'll examine these `ErrorRecord` objects in detail, along with how they're used by the various PowerShell mechanisms to manage error conditions. We'll also look at the other mechanisms that are available for solving script execution problems, including tracing and script debugging. PowerShell v1 had fairly weak debugging tools. We'll look at how this was addressed by the new features in v2.

14.1 ERROR HANDLING

Error handling in PowerShell is very structured. PowerShell errors aren't simply bits of text written to the screen—they're rich objects that contain a wealth of information about where the error occurred and why. There's one aspect to error handling in PowerShell that's unique: the notion of *terminating* versus *nonterminating* errors. This aspect aligns with the streaming model that PowerShell uses to process objects.

Here's a simple example that will help you understand this concept. Think about how removing a list of files from your system should work. You stream this list of files to the cmdlet that will delete the files. Imagine that you can't delete all the files on the list for various reasons. Do you want the command to stop processing as soon as it hits the first element in the list? The answer is probably, no. You'd like the cmdlet to do as much work as it can but capture any errors so that you can look at them later. This is the concept of a *nonterminating* error—the error is recorded and the operation continues. On the other hand, there are times when you do want an operation to stop on the first error. These are called *terminating* errors. Sometimes you want an error to be terminating in one situation and nonterminating in another, and PowerShell provides mechanisms that allow you to do this.

Because the architecture supports multiple nonterminating errors being generated by a pipeline, it can't just throw or return an error. Here's where streaming comes into play: nonterminating errors are simply written to the error stream. By default, these errors are displayed, but there are a number of other ways of working with them. In the next few sections, we'll look at those mechanisms. But first we need to take at look at the error records themselves.

14.1.1 ErrorRecords and the error stream

As we delve into the topic of error handling, we'll first take a look at capturing error records in a file using redirection, and then you'll learn how to capture error messages in a variable. By capturing these errors instead of just displaying them, you can go back at a later time to analyze and hopefully fix what went wrong.

First, let's review the normal behavior of objects in the pipeline. Output objects flow from cmdlet to cmdlet but error records are written directly to the default output processor. By default, this is the `Out-Default` cmdlet and the error records are displayed:

```
PS (1) > dir nosuchfile
Get-ChildItem : Cannot find path 'C:\files\nosuchfile' because
it does not exist.
At line:1 char:4
+ dir  <<<< nosuchfile
```

These flows are shown in figure 14.1.

In the figure, you see the output objects go from A to B to C and finally to `Out-Default`. But the error record streams are all merged and go directly to `Out-Default`.

When you use the redirection operators discussed in chapter 5, you can change flow. For example, you can redirect the error messages to a file:

```
PS (2) > dir nosuchfile 2> err.txt
```

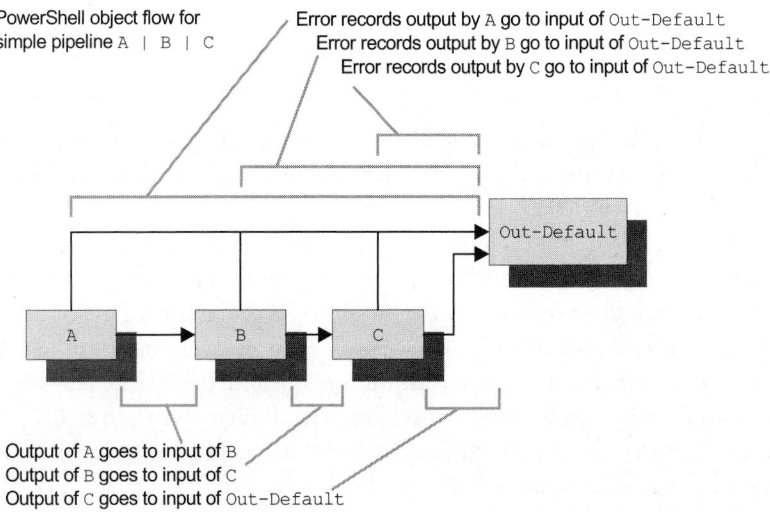
PowerShell object flow for
simple pipeline A | B | C
Error records output by A go to input of Out-Default
Error records output by B go to input of Out-Default
Error records output by C go to input of Out-Default
Out-Default
A
B
C
Output of A goes to input of B
Output of B goes to input of C
Output of C goes to input of Out-Default

Figure 14.1 This diagram shows the output object and error record routing; then, the simple pipeline `A | B | C` is run from a PowerShell host process like `PowerShell.exe` or `PowerShell_ISE.exe`. Output objects go to the next command in the pipeline and error objects go directly to `Out-Default`.

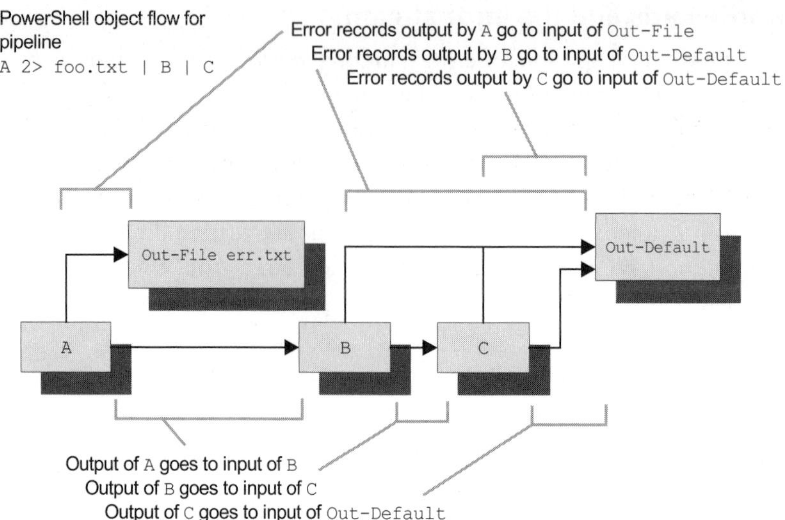
PowerShell object flow for pipeline
A 2> foo.txt | B | C
Error records output by A go to input of Out-File
Error records output by B go to input of Out-Default
Error records output by C go to input of Out-Default
Out-File err.txt
Out-Default
A
B
C
Output of A goes to input of B
Output of B goes to input of C
Output of C goes to input of Out-Default

Figure 14.2 Revised pipeline including the use of redirection operators

This changes the diagram to look like what's shown in figure 14.2.

But this approach has the downside that the error message is rendered to displayable text before writing it to the file. When that happens, you lose all the extra information in the objects. Take a look at what was saved to the file:

```
PS (3) > Get-Content err.txt
Get-ChildItem : Cannot find path 'C:\files\nosuchfile' because
it does not exist.
At line:1 char:4
+ dir  <<<< nosuchfile 2> err.txt
```

The error text is there as it would've been displayed on the console, but you've lost all of the elements of the object that haven't been displayed. And this lost information may be critical to diagnosing the problem. You need a better way to capture this information. The first mechanism we'll look at is capturing the error records by using the stream merge operator `2>&1`, and then assigning the result to a variable.

When you add error stream merging into the picture, the flow of objects changes. With stream merging, instead of having all error records going to the default output stream, they're routed into the output stream and the combined set of objects is passed to the input of the next command. This flow is shown in figure 14.3.

Let's see how this works. First use the stream merge operator to capture the error stream in a variable by using assignment:

```
PS (4) > $err = dir nosuchfile 2>&1
```

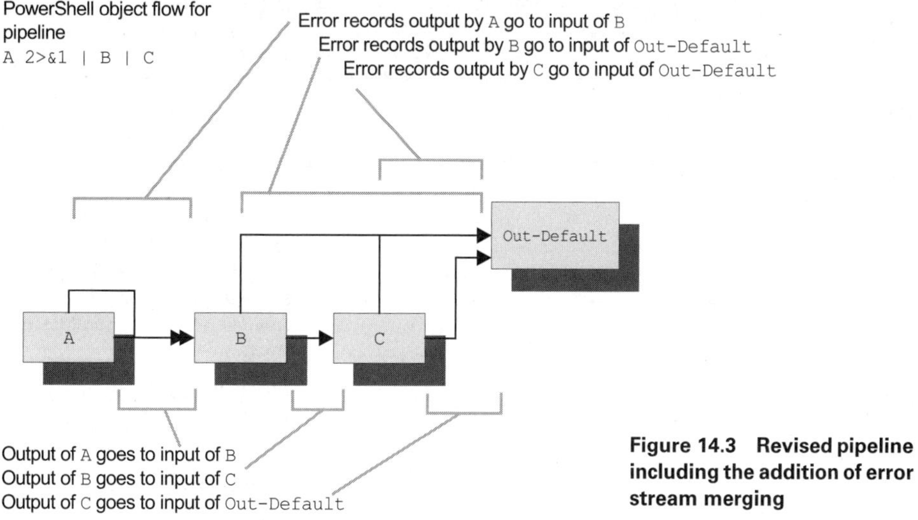
PowerShell object flow for pipeline
A 2>&1 | B | C
Error records output by A go to input of B
Error records output by B go to input of Out-Default
Error records output by C go to input of Out-Default
Out-Default
A
B
C
Output of A goes to input of B
Output of B goes to input of C
Output of C goes to input of Out-Default

Figure 14.3 Revised pipeline including the addition of error stream merging

Now use `Get-Member` to display the properties on the object. Use the `-Type` parameter on `Get-Member` to filter the display and only show the properties:

```
PS (5) > $err | Get-Member -Type property

   TypeName: System.Management.Automation.ErrorRecord

Name                  MemberType Definition
----                  ---------- ----------
CategoryInfo          Property   System.Management.Automation...
ErrorDetails          Property   System.Management.Automation...
Exception             Property   System.Exception Exception {...
FullyQualifiedErrorId Property   System.String FullyQualified...
InvocationInfo        Property   System.Management.Automation...
TargetObject          Property   System.Object TargetObject {...
```

Although this shows you all the properties and their definitions, some of the property names are a little tricky to figure out, so further explanation is in order. Table 14.1 lists all the properties, their types, and a description of each property.

Table 14.1 `ErrorRecord` properties and their descriptions

Property name	Property type	Description
`CategoryInfo`	`ErrorCategoryInfo`	This string breaks errors into a number of broad categories.
`ErrorDetails`	`ErrorDetails`	This may be null. If present, `ErrorDetails` can specify additional information, most importantly `ErrorDetails.Message`, which (if present) is a more exact description and should be displayed instead of `Exception.Message`.

Table 14.1 `ErrorRecord` properties and their descriptions *(continued)*

Property name	Property type	Description
`Exception`	`System.Exception`	This is the underlying .NET exception corresponding to the error that occurred.
`FullyQualifiedErrorId`	`System.String`	This identifies the error condition more specifically than either the `ErrorCategory` or the `Exception`. Use `FullyQualifiedErrorId` to filter highly specific error conditions. Note that this is a nonlocalized field, so performing string matches against it will continue to work regardless of language settings.
`InvocationInfo`	`InvocationInfo`	This is an object that contains information about where the error occurred—typically the script name and line number.
`TargetObject`	`System.Object`	This is the object that was being operated on when the error occurred. It may be null, as not all errors will set this field.

You can look at the values of an error record's properties by piping the error object into `Format-List`. To see all the properties, you must specify `-Property *` along with `-Force`. This command tells the formatting subsystem to skip the default presentation and show all properties. The result looks like this:

```
PS (10) > $err | Format-List -Property * -Force

Exception             : System.Management.Automation.ItemNotFoun
                        dException: Cannot find path 'C:\files\n
                        osuchfile' because it does not exist.
                           at System.Management.Automation.Sessi
                        onStateInternal.GetChildItems(String pat
                        h, Boolean recurse, CmdletProviderContex
                        t context)
                           at System.Management.Automation.Child
                        ItemCmdletProviderIntrinsics.Get(String
                        path, Boolean recurse, CmdletProviderCon
                        text context)
                           at Microsoft.PowerShell.Commands.GetC
                        hildItemCommand.ProcessRecord()
TargetObject          : C:\files\nosuchfile
CategoryInfo          : ObjectNotFound: (C:\files\nosuchfile:Str
                        ing) [Get-ChildItem], ItemNotFoundExcept
                        ion
FullyQualifiedErrorId : PathNotFound,Microsoft.PowerShell.Comman
                        ds.GetChildItemCommand
ErrorDetails          :
InvocationInfo        : System.Management.Automation.InvocationI
                        Nfo
```

In this output, you can see the exception that caused the error was `ItemNotFound-Exception`. The `TargetObject` property contains the full path the cmdlet used to locate the item. This overall error is placed in the broader category of ObjectNotFound. There are no additional error details for this object.

Let's take a closer look at the InvocationInfo property. This member provides information about where the error occurred. Here's what it looks like:

```
PS (6) > $err.InvocationInfo

MyCommand        : Get-ChildItem
ScriptLineNumber : 1
OffsetInLine     : 11
ScriptName       :
Line             : $err = dir nosuchfile 2>&1
PositionMessage  :
                   At line:1 char:11
                   + $err = dir  <<<< nosuchfile 2>&1
InvocationName   : dir
PipelineLength   : 1
PipelinePosition : 1
```

Because you entered this command on the command line, the script name is empty and the script line is 1. OffsetInLine is the offset in the script line where the error occurred. Other information is also available, such as the number of commands in the pipeline that caused an error, as well as the index of this command in the pipeline. This message also includes the line of script text where the error occurred. Finally, there's the PositionMessage property. This property takes all the other information and formats it into what you see in PowerShell errors.

Extracting all of the detailed information from an error record is a fairly common occurrence when debugging scripts, so it's worth writing a small helper function to make it easier. Listing 14.1 shows a function that will dump out all the properties of an error object and then iterate through any InnerException properties on the error record exception to show all the underlying errors that occurred.

Listing 14.1 The Show-ErrorDetails function

```
function Show-ErrorDetails
{
    param(
        $ErrorRecord = $Error[0]
    )

    $ErrorRecord | Format-List * -Force
    $ErrorRecord.InvocationInfo | Format-List *
    $Exception = $ErrorRecord.Exception
    for ($depth = 0; $Exception -ne $null; $depth++)      ❶ Show depth of nested exception
    {   "$depth" * 80
        $Exception |Format-List -Force *                    ❷ Show exception properties
        $Exception = $Exception.InnerException             ❸ Link to nest exceptions
    }
}
```

This function takes a single parameter, which holds the error record to display. By default, it shows the most recent error recorded in $error. It begins by showing all the properties in the record followed by the invocation information for the faulting command. Then it loops, tracing through any nested exceptions ❸, showing each one ❷ proceeded by a separator ❶ line showing the nesting depth of the displayed exception.

There's a lot of information in these objects that can help you figure out where and why an error occurred. The trick is to make sure that you have the right error objects available at the right time. It simply isn't possible to record every error that occurs—it'd take up too much space and be impossible to manage. If you limit the set of error objects that are preserved, you want to make sure that you keep those you care about. Obviously, having the wrong error objects doesn't help. Sometimes you're interested only in certain types of errors or only in errors from specific parts of a script. To address these requirements, PowerShell provides a rich set of tools for capturing and managing errors. The next few sections cover these tools and the techniques for using them.

14.1.2 The $error variable and –ErrorVariable parameter

The point of rich error objects is that you can examine them after the error has occurred and possibly take remedial action. Of course, to do this you have to capture them first. In the previous section, I showed you how to redirect the error stream, but the problem with this approach is that you have to think of it beforehand. Because you don't know when errors occur, in practice you'd have to do it all the time. Fortunately, PowerShell performs some of this work for you and automatically "remembers the past," at least as far as errors go. There's a special variable `$error` that contains a collection of the errors that occurred while the engine has been running. This collection is maintained as a circular bounded buffer. As new errors occur, old ones are discarded, as shown in figure 14.4.

The number of errors that are retained is controlled by the `$MaximumErrorCount` variable, which can be set to a number from 256 (the default setting) to 32768. The collection in `$error` is an array (technically an instance of `System.Collections.ArrayList`) that buffers errors as they occur. The most recent error is always stored in `$error[0]`.

> **NOTE** Although it's tempting to think that you could just set `$MaximumErrorCount` to some very large value (32768 is the largest allowed) and never have to worry about capturing errors, in practice this strategy isn't a good idea. Rich error objects also imply fairly large error objects. If you set `$MaximumErrorCount` to too large a value, you won't have any memory left. In practice, there's usually no reason to set it to anything larger than the default, though you may set it to something smaller if you want to make more space available for other things. Also, even if you only have a few objects, these objects may be very large. If you find that this is the case for a particular script, you can change the maximum error count to something small. As an alternative, you could clean out all the entries in `$error` by calling `$error.Clear()`.

Let's explore using the $error variable. You'll start with the same error as before:

```
PS (1) > dir nosuchfile
Get-ChildItem : Cannot find path 'C:\working\book\nosuchfile' be
cause it does not exist.
At line:1 char:4
+ dir  <<<< nosuchfile
```

You didn't explicitly capture it, but it's available in $error[0]

```
PS (2) > $error[0]
Get-ChildItem : Cannot find path 'C:\working\book\nosuchfile'
because it does not exist.
At line:1 char:4
+ dir  <<<< nosuchfile
```

with all of the error properties. For example, here's the exception object:

```
PS (3) > $error[0].exception
Cannot find path 'C:\working\book\nosuchfile' because it does
not exist.
```

And here's the target object that caused the error:

```
PS (4) > $error[0].targetobject
C:\working\book\nosuchfile
```

Now let's do something that will cause a second error:

```
PS (5) > 1/$null
Attempted to divide by zero.
At line:1 char:3
+ 1/$ <<<< null
```

Here you have a division-by-zero error.

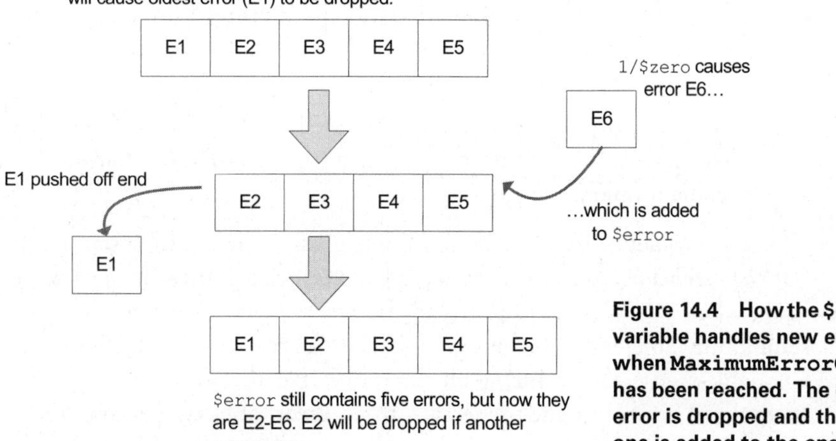
$error currently contains five errors E1-E5. $MaximumErrorCount is set to limit $error to five elements, so next error to be generated will cause oldest error (E1) to be dropped.
E1
E2
E3
E4
E5
1/$zero causes error E6...
E6
E1 pushed off end
E2
E3
E4
E5
...which is added to $error
E1
E1
E2
E3
E4
E5
$error still contains five errors, but now they are E2-E6. E2 will be dropped if another error occurs.

Figure 14.4 How the $error variable handles new errors when MaximumErrorCount has been reached. The oldest error is dropped and the new one is added to the end.

NOTE The example here uses `1/$null`. The reason for doing this instead of simply 1/0 is because the PowerShell interpreter does something called *constant expression folding*. It looks at expressions that contain only constant values. When it sees one, it evaluates that expression once at compile time so it doesn't have to waste time doing it again at runtime. This means that impossible expressions, such as division by zero, are caught and treated as parsing errors. Parsing errors can't be caught and don't get logged when they're entered interactively, so they don't make for a good example. (If one script calls another script and that script has one of these errors, the calling script can catch it, but the script being parsed can't.)

Let's verify that the second error is in `$error[0]`. Look at the exception member:

```
PS (6) > $error[0].exception
Attempted to divide by zero.
```

Yes, it is. You'll also verify that the previous error, "file not found," is now in position 1:

```
PS (7) > $error[1].exception
Cannot find path 'C:\working\book\nosuchfile' because it does no
t exist.
```

Again, yes, it is. As you can see, each new error shuffles the previous error down one element in the array.

TIP The key lesson to take away from this is that when you're going to try to diagnose an error, you should copy it to a "working" variable so it doesn't get accidentally shifted out from under you because you made a mistake in one of the commands you're using to examine the error.

The `$error` variable is a convenient way to capture errors automatically, but there are two problems with it:

- First, as we discussed earlier, `$error` only captures a limited number of errors so important information may fall off the end of the buffer.
- Second, `$error` contains all the errors that occur, regardless of where they came from or what command generated them, all mixed together in a single collection. You'll find it hard to locate the information you need to diagnose a specific problem.

The first problem can be worked around using redirection to capture all the errors, but that still doesn't address mixing all the errors together. To deal with this second issue, when you want to capture all the errors from a specific command you use a standard parameter on all commands called `-ErrorVariable`. This parameter names a variable to use for capturing all the errors that the command generates. Here's an example. This command generates three error objects, because the files nofuss, nomuss, and nobother don't exist:

```
PS (1) > dir nofuss,nomuss,nobother -ErrorVariable errs
Get-ChildItem : Cannot find path 'C:\Documents and Settings\bruc
epay\nofuss' because it does not exist.
At line:1 char:4
+ dir  <<<< nofuss,nomuss,nobother -ErrorVariable errs
Get-ChildItem : Cannot find path 'C:\Documents and Settings\bruc
epay\nomuss' because it does not exist.
At line:1 char:4
+ dir  <<<< nofuss,nomuss,nobother -ErrorVariable errs
Get-ChildItem : Cannot find path 'C:\Documents and Settings\bruc
epay\nobother' because it does not exist.
At line:1 char:4
+ dir  <<<< nofuss,nomuss,nobother -ErrorVariable errs
```

In the command, you specified the name of the error variable to place these records into: `errs`.

> **NOTE** The argument to `-ErrorVariable` is the name of the variable with no leading `$`. If `errs` had been written as `$errs`, then the errors would've been stored in the variable named by the value in `$errs`, not `$errs` itself. Also note that the `-ErrorVariable` parameter works like a tee—that is, the objects are captured in the variable, but they're also streamed to the error output.

Let's verify that the errors were actually captured. First, the number of elements in `$err` should be 3:

```
PS (2) > $errs.count
3
```

It is. Now dump the errors themselves:

```
PS (3) > $errs
Get-ChildItem : Cannot find path 'C:\Documents and Settings\bruc
epay\nofuss' because it does not exist.
At line:1 char:4
+ dir  <<<< nofuss,nomuss,nobother -ErrorVariable errs
Get-ChildItem : Cannot find path 'C:\Documents and Settings\bruc
epay\nomuss' because it does not exist.
At line:1 char:4
+ dir  <<<< nofuss,nomuss,nobother -ErrorVariable errs
Get-ChildItem : Cannot find path 'C:\Documents and Settings\bruc
epay\nobother' because it does not exist.
At line:1 char:4
+ dir  <<<< nofuss,nomuss,nobother -ErrorVariable errs
```

They do, in fact, match the original error output.

> **NOTE** The errors should match the original output because they're actually the same error objects. The `-ErrorVariable` parameter (alias -ev) captures references to each object written to the error stream. In effect, the same object is in two places at once—well, three if you count the default `$error` variable.

Because there's no need to see the object twice, you can use redirection to discard the written objects and save only the references stored in the specified variable. Let's rerun the example this way:

```
PS (4) > dir nofuss,nomuss,nobother -ErrorVariable errs 2>$null
```

This time nothing was displayed; verify the error count:

```
PS (5) > $errs.count
3
```

It's 3 again, as intended. Let's just check the `TargetObject` member of the last error object to verify that it's the filename nobother:

```
PS (6) > $errs[2].TargetObject
C:\Documents and Settings\brucepay\nobother
PS (7) >
```

Yes, it is. This example illustrates a more sophisticated way of capturing error objects than merely displaying them. In section 14.1.5, you'll see an even more flexible way to control how errors are redirected.

All of these mechanisms provide useful tools for handling collections of error objects, but sometimes all you care about is that an error occurred at all. A couple of additional status variables, `$?` and `$LASTEXITCODE`, enable you to determine whether an error occurred.

14.1.3 Determining if a command had an error

Displaying errors is very useful; it lets the user know what happened. But scripts also need to know when an error has occurred so they can react properly. For example, a script shouldn't try to remove a file if the `cd` into the directory containing the file failed. PowerShell makes this easy by providing two error variables that capture the command status. First, to see if an error occurred when executing a command, a script can check the status of the variable `$?`, a simple Boolean variable that holds the execution status of the last variable.

> **NOTE** The use of the `$?` variable is borrowed from the UNIX shells.

The `$?` variable will be true if the entire operation succeeded, and false otherwise. For example, if any of the operations wrote an error object, then `$?` will be set to false even if the error was discarded using redirection. This is an important point: it means that a script can determine whether an error occurred even if the error isn't displayed. Here are some examples showing the use of `$?`. First you call `Get-Item`, passing in two item names that you know exist and one you know doesn't exist:

```
PS (1) > Get-Item c:,nosuchfile,c:

    Directory:

Mode                LastWriteTime     Length Name
----                -------------     ------ ----
d--hs          6/13/2006  10:12 PM           C:\
```

```
Get-Item : Cannot find path 'C:\nosuchfile' because it does not
exist.
At line:1 char:9
+ Get-Item  <<<< c:,nosuchfile,c:
d--hs          6/13/2006  10:12 PM            C:\
```

You get the expected error.

```
PS (2) > $?
False
```

And `$?` is false. Now try the same command, but this time specify only the names of items that exist:

```
PS (3) > Get-Item c:,c:

    Directory:

Mode                LastWriteTime     Length Name
----                -------------     ------ ----
d--hs          6/13/2006  10:12 PM           C:\
d--hs          6/13/2006  10:12 PM           C:\

PS (4) > $?
True
```

This time, there are no errors and `$?` is true.

Whereas the `$?` variable only indicates success or failure, `$LASTEXITCODE` contains the exit code of the last command run. But this applies only to two types of commands: native or external commands and PowerShell scripts (but not functions).

> **NOTE** On Windows, when a process exits it can return a single integer as its exit code. This integer is used to encode a variety of conditions, but the only one we're interested in is whether it's zero or non-zero. This convention is used by almost all programs. If they were successful, then their exit code is zero. If they encountered an error, then the exit code is non-zero.

PowerShell captures the exit code from a script or executable in `$LASTEXITCODE`, and if that value is non-zero, it sets `$?` to false. Let's use `cmd.exe` to demonstrate this. You can tell `cmd` to execute a single command by passing it the `/c` option along with the text of the command. In this example, the command you want to run is `exit`, which takes a value to use as the exit code for the command:

```
PS (1) > cmd /c exit 0
```

You told `cmd` to exit with code 0. Verify this by checking the values of `$LASTEXIT-CODE` and `$?`, respectively:

```
PS (2) > $LASTEXITCODE
0
PS (3) > $?
True
```

As expected, the exit code was zero, and consequently `$?` is true. Next try it with a non-zero value:

```
PS (4) > cmd /c exit 1
PS (5) > $LASTEXITCODE
1
PS (6) > $?
False
```

This time, the exit code is 1, so `$?` is set to false. You can do the same exercises with scripts. First create a script that exits with a zero exit code:

```
PS (7) > "exit 0" > invoke-exit.ps1
PS (8) > ./invoke-exit
PS (9) > $LASTEXITCODE
0
PS (10) > $?
True
$LASTEXITCODE is 0 and $? is true. Now try it with a non-zero value.
PS (11) > "exit 25" > invoke-exit.ps1
PS (12) > ./invoke-exit
PS (13) > $LASTEXITCODE
25
PS (14) > $?
False
```

Now `$LASTEXITCODE` contains the value the script exited with, which is 25, and `$?` is set to false.

So far, we've looked at how to capture errors and how to detect when they occur. Next we'll explore some of the methods PowerShell provides to control what happens when an error is generated.

14.1.4 Controlling the actions taken on an error

Earlier, we talked about the differences between terminating and nonterminating errors. Sometimes you want to be able to turn nonterminating errors into terminating ones because the operation you're performing is too critical to tolerate nonterminating errors. For example, imagine you're setting up a website for a user. You want to reuse a directory that had been previously used for someone else. First you want to remove all the old files and then install the new user's files. Obviously, you can't start installing the new files until all the old ones are deleted. In this situation, the failure to delete a file, which is normally a nonterminating error, must now be treated as a terminating error. The next step in the process can't begin until the current step is 100% complete.

The way to control whether errors are terminating or nonterminating is by setting the error action policy, which you do by setting the error action preference. This is a mechanism that allows you to control the behavior of the system when an error occurs. There are four possible settings for this preference: `Continue`, `Silently-Continue`, `Stop`, and `Inquire`. These preferences are described in table 14.2.

Table 14.2 **The supported identifiers and numeric equivalents for `ErrorActionPreference`**

Identifier	Numeric value	Descriptions
`Continue`	2	This is the default preference setting. The error object is written to the output pipe and added to `$error`, and `$?` is set to false. Execution then continues at the next script line.
`SilentlyContinue`	0	When this action preference is set, the error message isn't written to the output pipe before continuing execution. Note that it's still added to `$error`, and `$?` is still set to false. Again, execution continues at the next line.
`Stop`	1	This error action preference changes an error from a nonterminating error to a terminating error. The error object is thrown as an exception instead of being written to the output pipe. `$error` and `$?` are still updated. Execution does not continue.
`Inquire`	3	Prompts the user requesting confirmation before continuing on with the operation. At the prompt, the user can choose to continue, stop, or suspend the operation.

There are two ways to set the error action preference: by setting the `$ErrorActionPreference` variable as in

```
$ErrorActionPreference = "SilentlyContinue"
```

or by using the `-ErrorAction` (or `-ea`) parameter that's available on all cmdlets, advanced functions, and advanced scripts.

> **TIP** When setting any of the preferences, you can use either the identifier string (such as `"Stop"`) or its numeric equivalent (such as `1`). The numeric value is more convenient for interactive use. If you do need to set a preference in a script for some reason, using the identifier string is preferred.

Let's see some examples of these preferences in action. Here's a simple one. First run a command that has some nonterminating errors. You'll use the `Get-Item` cmdlet to get two items that exist and two items that don't exist:

```
PS (1) > Get-Item c:\,nosuchfile,c:\,nosuchfile

    Directory:

Mode                LastWriteTime     Length Name
----                -------------     ------ ----
d--hs         6/13/2006  10:12 PM            C:\
Get-Item : Cannot find path 'C:\Documents and Settings\brucepay\
nosuchfile' because it does not exist.
At line:1 char:9
+ Get-Item  <<<< c:\,nosuchfile,c:\,nosuchfile
```

```
d--hs         6/13/2006  10:12 PM            C:\
Get-Item : Cannot find path 'C:\Documents and Settings\brucepay\
nosuchfile' because it does not exist.
At line:1 char:9
+ Get-Item  <<<< c:\,nosuchfile,c:\,nosuchfile
```

If you look at the output, you can see that there are two output objects and two error messages. You can use redirection to discard the error messages, making the code easier to read:

```
PS (2) > Get-Item c:\,nosuchfile,c:\,nosuchfile 2> $null

    Directory:

Mode                LastWriteTime     Length Name
----                -------------     ------ ----
d--hs         6/13/2006  10:12 PM            C:\
d--hs         6/13/2006  10:12 PM            C:\
```

Now you just see the output objects because you've sent the error objects to `$null`. You can use the `-ErrorAction` parameter to do the same:

```
PS (3) > Get-Item c:\,nosuchfile,c:\,nosuchfile `
>> -ea SilentlyContinue
>>

    Directory:

Mode                LastWriteTime     Length Name
----                -------------     ------ ----
d--hs         6/13/2006  10:12 PM            C:\
d--hs         6/13/2006  10:12 PM            C:\
```

Again, the error messages aren't displayed, but this time it's because they aren't being written at all instead of written and discarded. Finally, let's try the "Stop" preference:

```
PS (4) > Get-Item c:\,nosuchfile,c:\,nosuchfile `
>> -ea Stop
>>
    Directory:

Mode                LastWriteTime     Length Name
----                -------------     ------ ----
d--hs         6/13/2006  10:12 PM            C:\
Get-Item : Command execution stopped because the shell variable
"ErrorActionPreference" is set to Stop: Cannot find path
'C:\Documents and Settings\brucepay\nosuchfile' because it does not
exist.
At line:1 char:9
+ Get-Item  <<<< c:\,nosuchfile,c:\,nosuchfile `
```

This time, you see only one output message and one error message—the first one. This is because the error is treated as a terminating error and execution stops. Note that the error message contains additional text explaining that execution stopped because of the error action preference setting.

Of course, the `-ErrorAction` parameter controls the error behavior for exactly one cmdlet. If you want to change the behavior for an entire script or even a whole session, you can do so by setting the `$ErrorActionPreference` variable. Let's redo the last example but use the variable instead of the parameter:

```
PS (5) > & {
>> $ErrorActionPreference="Stop"
>> Get-Item c:\,nosuchfile,c:\,nosuchfile
>> }
>>

    Directory:

Mode                LastWriteTime     Length Name
----                -------------     ------ ----
d--hs         6/13/2006  10:12 PM            C:\
Get-Item : Command execution stopped because the shell variable
"ErrorActionPreference" is set to Stop: Cannot find path
'C:\Documents and Settings\brucepay\nosuchfile' because it does not
exist.
At line:3 char:9
+ Get-Item  <<<< c:\,nosuchfile,c:\,nosuchfile
```

Again, the cmdlet stops at the first error instead of continuing.

> **NOTE** In this example, note the use of the call operator `&` with a scriptblock containing the scope for the preference setting. Using the pattern `& { ...script text... }`, you can execute fragments of script code so that any variables set in the enclosed script text are discarded at the end of the scriptblock. Because setting `$ErrorActionPreference` has such a profound effect on the execution of the script, we're using this technique to isolate the preference setting.

Through the `-ErrorActionPreference` parameter and the `$ErrorActionPreference` variable, the script author has good control over when errors are written and when they're terminating. Nonterminating errors can be displayed or discarded at will. But what about terminating errors? How does the script author deal with them? Sometimes you only want an error to terminate part of an operation. For example, you might have a script move a set of files using a series of steps for each move. If one of the steps fails, you want the overall move operation to terminate for that file, but you want to continue processing the rest of the files. To do this, you need a way to trap these terminating errors or exceptions, and that's what we'll discuss next.

14.2 Dealing with errors that terminate execution

This section will deal with the ways that PowerShell processes errors that terminate the current flow of execution, also called *terminating errors*. Here we'll cover the language elements for dealing with terminating errors and how you can apply these features. If you have a programming background, you're probably more familiar with terminating errors when they're called by their more conventional name—exceptions. So call them what you will; we're going to delve into catching these terminating errors. We'll look at ways to trap or catch these errors and take some action as a consequence. In some cases, these may be remedial actions (such as trying to fix the problem) or simply recording that the errors occurred. PowerShell provides two statements for dealing with terminating errors: the `trap` statement, which is somewhat similar to the `on error` statement in Visual Basic or VBScript, and the `try/catch` statement, modeled after the `try/catch` statement in C#.

14.2.1 The trap statement

The only way for exceptions to be caught in PowerShell v1 was by using the `trap` statement. This feature is also present in PowerShell v2 and has some unique characteristics that we'll cover in this section. The `trap` statement syntax is shown in figure 14.5.

The `trap` statement can appear anywhere in a block of code. This means that it may be specified after a statement that generates an error and still handle that error. When an exception (terminating error) occurs that isn't otherwise handled, control will be transferred to the body of the `trap` statement and the statements in the body are then executed.

You can optionally specify the type of exception to catch, such as division by zero. If no exception is specified, then it will trap all exceptions. Here's an example:

```
PS (1) > trap { "Got it!"  } 1/$null
Got it!
Attempted to divide by zero.
At line:1 char:30
+ trap { "Got it!" ; break } 1/$ <<<< zero
```

In this example, the statement

```
1/$null
```

was executed. `$null` is treated like zero in integer expressions, causing a division-by-zero exception to occur. When this happens, control transfers to the statement list in the body of the `trap` statement. In this case, it just writes "Got it!" which you see in

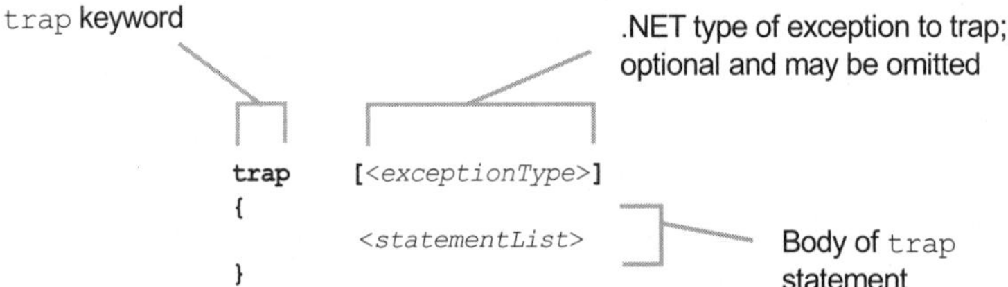

Figure 14.5 The syntax of the `trap` statement. The body of the statement will be executed when an exception with matching type is caught. If no exception type is specified, all exceptions will be caught.

the output. You also see that the error message is still displayed, even though you trapped this exception. This is a significant point. What happens after a trap handler execution has completed depends on how the block finishes. If the body of the trap handler block finishes normally, an error object will be written to the error stream, and, depending on the setting of $ErrorActionPreference, either the exception will be rethrown or execution will continue at the statement after the statement that caused the exception. This is what you saw in the previous example. To make this point clearer, let's add another statement after the one that caused the error:

```
PS (2) > trap { "Got it!" } 1/$zero; "LAST"
Got it!
Attempted to divide by zero.
At line:1 char:22
+ trap { "Got it!" } 1/$ <<<< zero; "LAST"
LAST
```

You see the error message—but following it, you see output from the last statement.

The interpreter's behavior after you leave the trap handler can be controlled by the break and continue keywords. (See chapter 6 for other uses of these keywords.) Let's look at break first. Here's the example again, but this time you'll terminate the trap block with break:

```
PS (3) > trap { "Got it!"; break  } 1/$zero; "LAST"
Got it!
Attempted to divide by zero.
At line:1 char:30
+ trap { "Got it!"; break  } 1/$ <<<< zero; "LAST"
```

You see the error record, but you don't see the output "LAST" because after the trap block exited, the error was rethrown as a terminating error instead of resuming execution. This flow of control is shown in figure 14.6.

The other modification to the trap flow control is to use the continue statement:

```
PS (4) > trap { "Got it!"; continue  } 1/$zero; "LAST"
Got it!
LAST
```

This time, you see the output from the trap block and from the "LAST" statement, but no error record. Exiting a trap block is somewhat equivalent to the error action preference

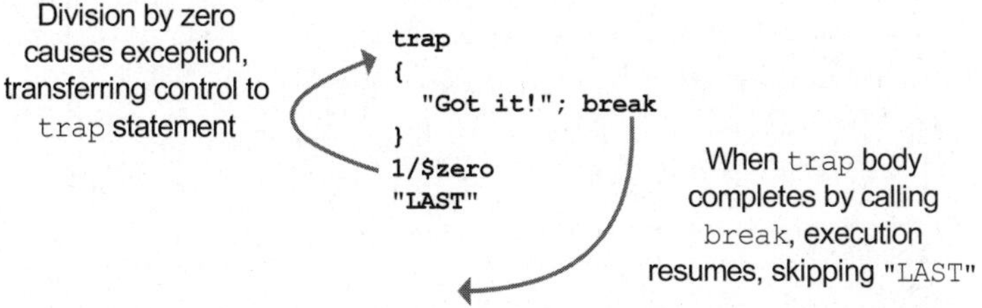
Division by zero causes exception, transferring control to trap statement
trap
{
"Got it!"; break
}
1/$zero
"LAST"
When trap body completes by calling break, execution resumes, skipping "LAST"

Figure 14.6 The flow of control when break is used in a trap statement. When the division-by-zero exception occurs, control jumps to the trap block and then breaks out of the script.

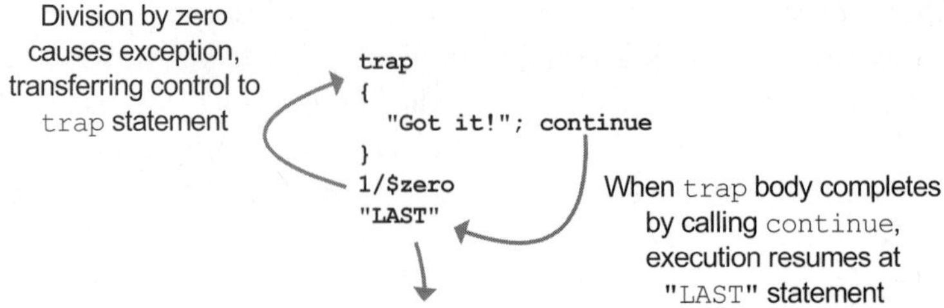
Division by zero causes exception, transferring control to trap statement
trap
{
"Got it!"; continue
}
1/$zero
"LAST"
When trap body completes by calling continue, execution resumes at "LAST" statement

Figure 14.7 The flow of control when `continue` is used in a `trap` statement instead of `break`. When the division-by-zero exception occurs, control jumps to the `trap` block and then resumes at the `"LAST"` statement before exiting the script.

`SilentlyContinue`. This works in a similar manner to the VBScript `On Error Resume Next` statement. Figure 14.7 shows the control flow when `continue` is used.

There's one other feature available in the `trap` block itself. The exception that was trapped is available in the `trap` block in the `$_` variable. Here's the example, but with the output of the `trap` statement showing the value in `$_` as a string:

```
PS (5) > trap { "Got it: $_"; continue  } 1/$zero;
Got it: Attempted to divide by zero.
```

In this case, the output is the `ToString()` of the exception. But `$_` isn't an exception; it's an error record, so the `trap` handler has full access to all the information in the error handler. Let's verify the type of this object:

```
PS (6) > trap { "Got it: " + $_.gettype(); continue  } 1/$zero;
Got it: System.Management.Automation.ErrorRecord
```

In the `trap` block in this example, you're displaying the type of the value in `$_`. How all this works is shown in figure 14.8.

There are some paths through the figure that we haven't talked about yet, so let's work through a few more examples. We said earlier that control transfers to the next statement after the one that caused the exception. Actually it's a bit more complicated than that. It transfers to the next statement in the same scope as the `trap` statement. This flow of control is illustrated in figure 14.9.

And now an example. You'll use scriptblocks to create the two scopes. The code looks like this:

```
&{
    trap {"TRAP"}
    &{
        "one"
        "two"
        1/$null
        "three"
        "four"
    }
    "OUTERBLOCK"
}
```

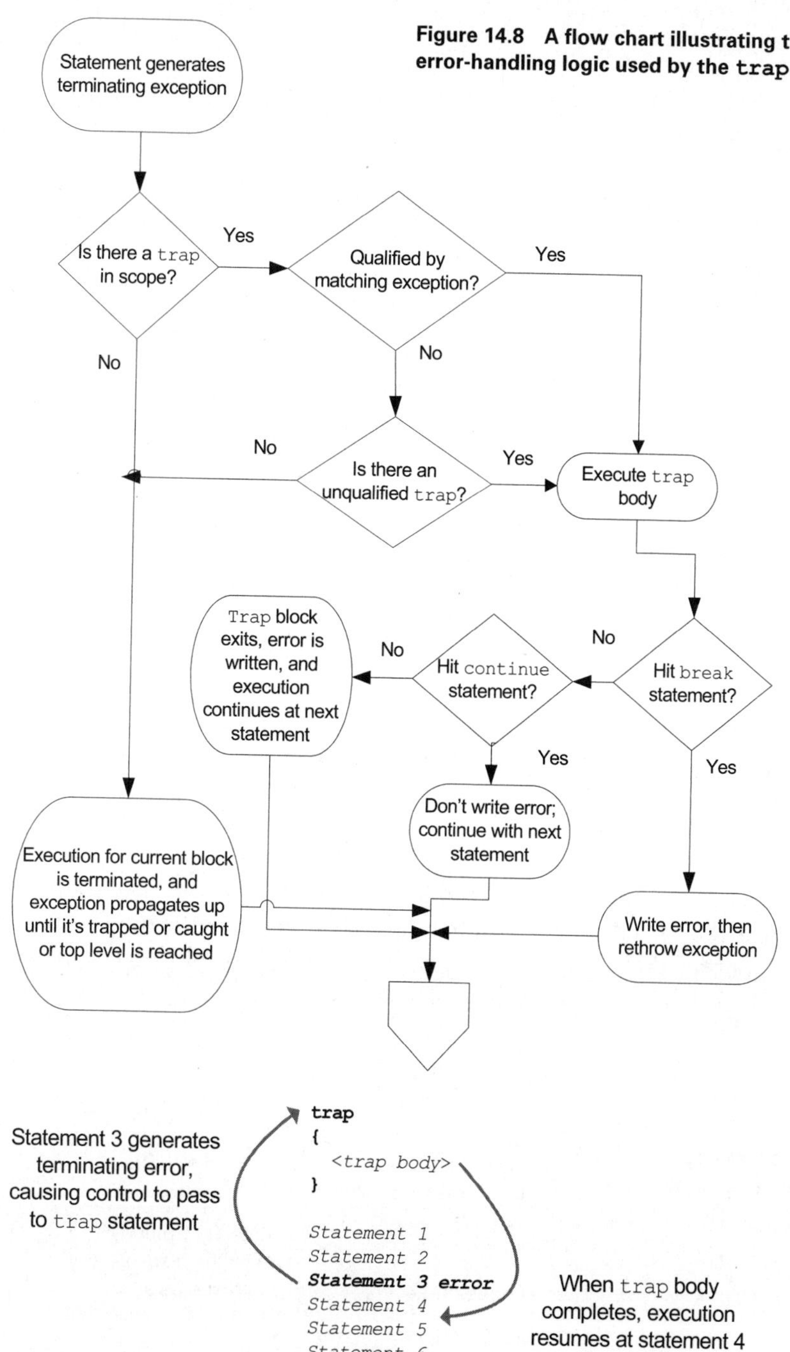
Statement generates terminating exception
Is there a trap in scope?
Yes
No
Qualified by matching exception?
Yes
No
Is there an unqualified trap?
No
Yes
Execute trap body
Hit break statement?
No
Yes
Hit continue statement?
No
Yes
Trap block exits, error is written, and execution continues at next statement
Don't write error; continue with next statement
Write error, then rethrow exception
Execution for current block is terminated, and exception propagates up until it's trapped or caught or top level is reached
Statement 3 generates terminating error, causing control to pass to trap statement
trap
{
<trap body>
}
Statement 1
Statement 2
Statement 3 error
Statement 4
Statement 5
Statement 6
When trap body completes, execution resumes at statement 4

Figure 14.8 A flow chart illustrating the complete error-handling logic used by the `trap` statement

Figure 14.9 The flow of control when a `trap` statement is used. If there's a `trap` statement in scope, control transfers to the body of the `trap` statement where the error is processed.

The trap statement in the outer block writes out the string "TRAP" so you'll know it was executed:

```
PS (7) > & {
>> trap {"TRAP"}
>> &{
```

Now create an inner scope that will emit a number of strings:

```
.
>> "one"
>> "two"
>> 1/$null
```

Part of the way through, throw an exception:

```
>> "three"
>> "four"
>> }
>> "OUTERBLOCK"
```

At the end of the output block, write out the string "OUTERBLOCK" so you'll know where you are:

```
>> }
>>
one
two
TRAP
Attempted to divide by zero.
At line:6 char:3
+ 1/$ <<<< null
OUTERBLOCK
```

Look at the output that was produced. You can see the first couple of numbers printed and then the exception, but look where execution resumed—at the first statement outside the block. This pattern allows you to skip entire sections of code instead of a single line, as shown in figure 14.10.

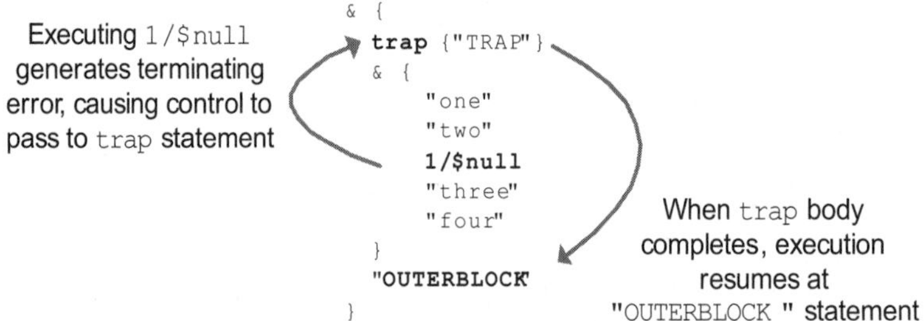

& {
trap {"TRAP"}
& {
"one"
"two"
1/$null
"three"
"four"
}
"OUTERBLOCK"
}
Executing 1/$null generates terminating error, causing control to pass to trap statement
When trap body completes, execution resumes at "OUTERBLOCK " statement

Figure 14.10 The flow of control when a trap statement is used with nested blocks. When the error occurs, control transfers to the trap body. When the trap body completes, execution resumes at the first statement after the nested scriptblock.

It essentially mimics the way the `try/catch` statement found in other languages such as C# works and was the only way to accomplish this in version 1. In fact, the `try/catch` (or `try/catch/finally`) pattern is so common that it was added to PowerShell in v2. We'll look at how this statement can be used to simplify your scripts in the next section.

14.2.2 The try/catch/finally statement

The `trap` statement, while powerful and flexible, ended up being hard to use for a lot of the traditional script/programming error-handling patterns. To address this, v2 introduced the more familiar `try/catch/finally` statement found in other languages. As is the case with all of the other PowerShell flow-control statements, this statement adopts the syntax from C#. This syntax is shown in figure 14.11.

The figure shows that there are three parts to this statement: the `try` block, the `catch` block, and the `finally` block. The `try` block is always required along with at least one of the `catch` or `finally` clauses. If an error occurs in the code in the `try` block resulting in an exception, PowerShell checks to see if there is a `catch` block specified. If there is a `catch` block, then it checks to see if specific exception types are to be caught. If there is and at least one of the specified types matches, then the `catch` block is executed. If not, then the search continues looking for another `catch` block that might match.

> **NOTE** This is one place where the PowerShell `try/catch` statement has some advantages over its C# cousin. In C#, only one exception can be specified per catch clause so it's more complicated to take the same action for multiple exceptions that don't have a common base class.

If there's a `catch` block with no exception types specified, this clause will be executed (which tends to be the most common case). And if there's a `finally` block, the code

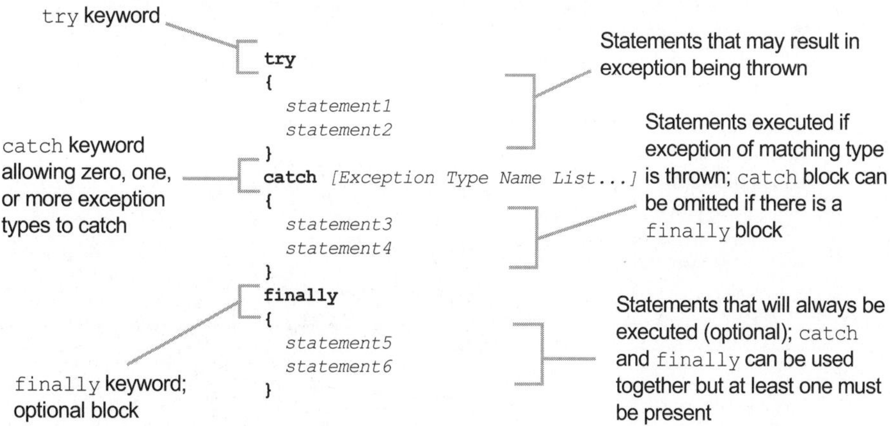

Figure 14.11 The syntax of the `try/catch/finally` statement. This statement allows exceptions to be processed in a structured way.

in the finally block runs. (Actually the finally block always runs whether there was an exception or not.) Here's an example using a catch statement with no exception type specified:

```
PS (1) > try
>> {
>>     1
>>     2
>>     3/$null
>>     4
>>     5
>> }
>> catch
>> {
>>     "ERROR: $_"
>> }
>> finally
>> {
>>     "ALL DONE"
>> }
>>
1
2
ERROR: Attempted to divide by zero.
ALL DONE
PS (2) >
```

In this example, the third statement in the try block causes a terminating error. This error is caught and control transfers to the catch block. Then, when the catch block is complete, the finally block is executed. This flow of control is shown in figure 14.12.

The complete processing logic for the try/catch/finally statement is shown in the flowchart in figure 14.13.

Which should you use in your scripts? In general, the flow of control with try/catch/finally is almost always easier to understand than the trap statement

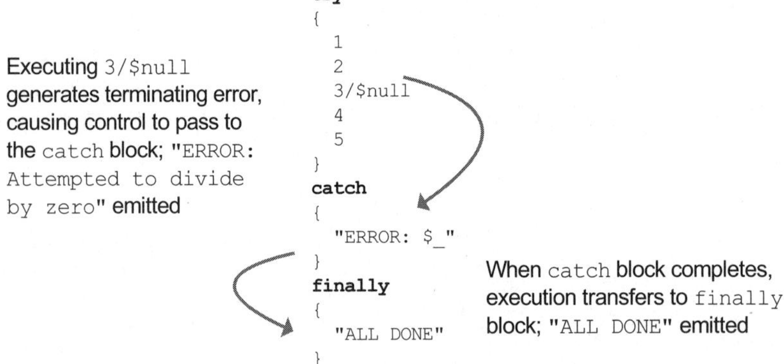

Figure 14.12 The flow of control in a try/catch/finally statement. When an exception occurs, control transfers to the catch block and then the finally block.

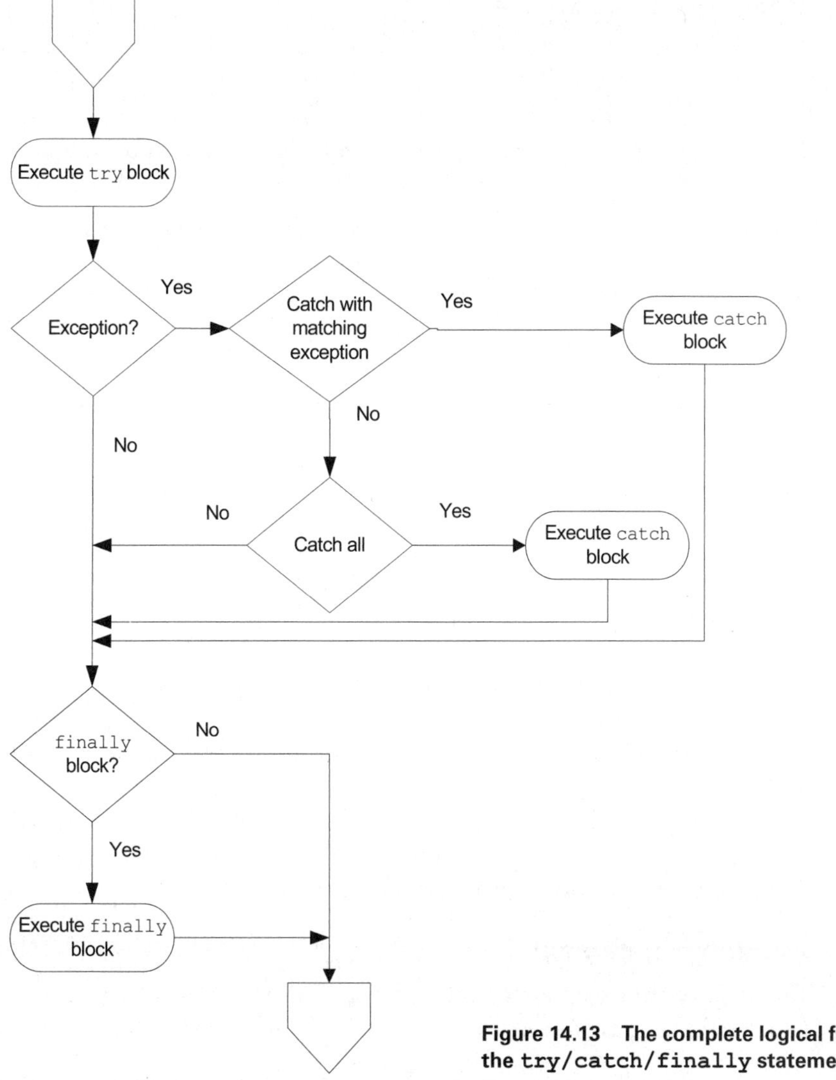

Figure 14.13 The complete logical flow in the `try/catch/finally` statement

except in some very simple cases. For example, in a function or script, you may want to have a general "catch all" exception that generates an error and then exits the function or script. You can do so simply by putting a `trap` statement at the top of the script rather than wrapping the body of the script in a `try/catch`. There are also some exception handling patterns that can be expressed with `trap` that are hard to handle with `try/catch`. That said, if you encounter something like this, think hard about what you're doing. The `trap` statement is like the infamous `goto` statement: you can express any flow of control, but patterns that can't be expressed with a structure statement tend to be hard to understand, debug, and maintain.

Using try/catch in expressions

An interesting application of the try/catch statement when used in combination with PowerShell's expression-oriented syntax is that it makes it fairly easy to write functions that provide default values if an expression throws an exception. Let's look at using try/catch in a custom div function. We want a function that never throws an exception even when dividing by zero. The function might look like this:

```
function div ([int] $x, [int] $y) {try { $x/$y } catch {[int]::MaxValue}}
```

Give it a try

```
PS (2) > div 1 0
2147483647
```

and you get the maximum integer value instead of the error you normally get when you divide by zero:

```
PS (3) > 1/0
Attempted to divide by zero.
At line:1 char:3
+ 1/ <<<< 0
    + CategoryInfo          : NotSpecified: (:) [], ParentConta
   insErrorRecordException
    + FullyQualifiedErrorId : RuntimeException
```

We'll take a look at another application of this technique later in section 14.3.3 when we talk about handling nonexistent property errors.

Clearly exceptions are a powerful error-handling mechanism. With this mechanism, errors are never missed because you forgot to check for a return code. In fact, you have to do the opposite and take action to suppress them instead. Having mastered catching other people's exceptions, let's look at how you can leverage this feature in your own scripts with the throw statement.

14.2.3 The throw statement

To complete the exception handling topic, you need a way to generate terminating errors or exceptions. You can accomplish this by using the throw statement.

> **NOTE** In the original design, throw was supposed to be a cmdlet rather than a keyword in the language. But having a cmdlet throw the exception meant that the thrown exception was subject to the cmdlet's error action policy, and the whole point of throw was to bypass this policy and always generate an exception. It wasn't so much a case of the tail wagging the dog as it was staple-gunning the poor beast to the floor. And so, learning from past mistakes, Microsoft made it into a keyword.

The syntax of the throw statement is shown in figure 14.14.

Figure 14.14 The syntax of the throw statement

The simplest example is to throw nothing:

```
PS (8) > throw
ScriptHalted
At line:1 char:5
+ throw <<<<
```

This approach is convenient for casual scripting. You don't need to create an error object or exception object—the `throw` statement takes care of all of this. Unfortunately, the message you get isn't very informative. If you want to include a meaningful message, you can easily provide your own:

```
PS (9) > throw "My Message!"
My Message!
At line:1 char:6
+ throw  <<<< "My Message!"
```

You see the message in the output. It's also possible to use `throw` to throw `ErrorRecord` objects or .NET exceptions if you want to use more detailed error handling. Instead of passing a string, you pass these objects.

Now let's revisit the multiscope `catch` and use `throw` this time instead of dividing by `$null`:

```
PS (10) > &{
>> trap {"$_" ; continue}
>> &{
>> "one"
>> "two"
>> throw "CATCH"
>> "three"
>> }
>> "ALL DONE"
>> }
>>
one
two
CATCH
ALL DONE
```

The pattern is the same as in the previous case, except that now you throw a specific message that appears in the output. This is followed by the output from the next statement in the outer scope.

There are other important applications of the throw statement in function definitions—for instance, times when you want to make a function parameter mandatory. The throw statement provides an efficient way to do this. Take a look at the following function definition:

```
PS (11) > function hi ($name=$(throw '$name is required'))
>> { "Hi $name" }
>>
```

In this example, you're using the throw statement in a subexpression as the initializer for $name. As you'll recall from chapter 7, the initializer expression is executed if no value was provided on the command line. Try this function out, first with a value for name:

```
PS (12) > hi Bob
Hi Bob
```

You receive the expected greeting. Next try it without a value:

```
PS (13) > hi
$name is required
At line:1 char:27
+ function hi ($name=$(throw  <<<< '$name is required'))
PS (14) >
```

You get a terminating error telling you that you have to provide a value for $name. This is a simple pattern that can be used to enforce mandatory parameters on functions and scripts. And speaking of functions and scripts, all these error features are great for letting you know something is wrong, but how do you go about fixing the problem? This is our cue to segue into our next section: debugging.

14.3 Debugging with the host APIs

The most basic form of debugging a script is to put statements in your script that display information about the execution of the script. Because you don't want your debugging output mixed into the rest of the output, you need mechanisms to display output directly on the console. You do this either by using the Write-Host cmdlet or by using what are called the *host APIs*. These APIs are available through the $host variable. This object has the following members:

```
PS (1) > $host

Name             : ConsoleHost
Version          : 1.0.10568.0
InstanceId       : 5c685c70-c950-4ce5-9aae-78331e4091a7
UI               : System.Management.Automation.Internal.Host.In
                   ternalHostUserInterface
CurrentCulture   : en-US
CurrentUICulture : en-US
PrivateData      :
```

The information available from `$host` includes the name of the host, its version, and so forth. The member that you're most interested in is the `UI` member. This member surfaces a number of methods that can be used to write messages directly to the host instead of the error stream. The ones you're most interested in are the `read` and `write` methods:

```
PS (2) > $host.ui | Get-Member [rw]*line*

   TypeName: System.Management.Automation.Internal.Host.Internal
HostUserInterface

Name                    MemberType Definition
----                    ---------- ----------
ReadLine                Method     System.String ReadLine()
ReadLineAsSecureString Method     System.Security.SecureStrin...
WriteDebugLine          Method     System.Void WriteDebugLine(...
WriteErrorLine          Method     System.Void WriteErrorLine(...
WriteLine               Method     System.Void WriteLine(), Sy...
WriteVerboseLine        Method     System.Void WriteVerboseLin...
WriteWarningLine        Method     System.Void WriteWarningLin...
```

For example, if you want to write out a text message, you can use

```
PS (3) > $host.ui.writeline("Hi there")
Hi there
```

to print out a simple string. Or you can use a more complex form of this method

```
PS (4) > $host.ui.writeline("red","green", "Hi there")
Hi there
```

to print out a string in color. You can also get input from the user. To read a line from the console, use the `ReadLine()` method:

```
PS (6) > $host.ui.readline()
Hi
Hi
```

There's a second level of host `UI` available called `RawUI`. This provides even more low-level functions for accessing the console. For example, to read a single key from the console, you can use

```
PS (7) > $host.ui.rawui.readkey()
g
  VirtualKeyCode        Character ControlKeyState          KeyDown
  --------------        --------- ---------------          -------
              71                g               0             True
```

This returns information about the key code and other attributes of the keypress instead of simply the character.

The other way to access the host interfaces is through the `Read-Host` and `Write-Host` cmdlets. These cmdlets do approximately the same thing as the host methods but can be a bit easier to use. In particular, the `Read-Host` cmdlet allows you to specify a prompt when reading:

```
PS (8) > Read-Host "Enter some text"
Enter some text: some text
some text
```

It even inserts a colon after your text when prompting.

Using the features described in this section, you can instrument your scripts in order to debug their behavior. Although this is a tried and true way of debugging, it requires you to make changes to your scripts to see what going on. PowerShell provides other mechanisms to find problems in your scripts. One of these features is "strict mode," which is our next topic.

14.3.1 Catching errors with strict mode

PowerShell provides some built-in static and runtime checks to help you catch errors in your scripts. Static checks are performed at script load/compile time, and runtime checks are dynamic checks done at runtime.

> **NOTE** These features are similar to Option Explicit in Visual Basic or strict mode in PERL and are named after the PERL feature.

PowerShell v1 offered a limited set of checks, enabled through the `Set-PSDebug` cmdlet. PowerShell v2 introduced a new cmdlet—`Set-StrictMode`—which enables a much more comprehensive set of checks. In the next two sections we'll look at what these checks are and how they can help you catch bugs in your code.

Using the v1 strict mode

In this section, we'll cover the v1 strict mode checks. These checks are enabled using the `Set-PSDebug` cmdlet with the `-Strict` parameter. The syntax for this command is shown in figure 14.15.

This cmdlet allows you to turn on *tracing* and *stepping*, which act to provide a rudimentary debugger feature. We're going to cover debugging in chapter 15 so we won't discuss `-Trace` or `-Step` further at this point. The `-Off` parameter turns off all features enabled through `Set-PSDebug`. Let's look at the set of checks performed in strict mode v1.

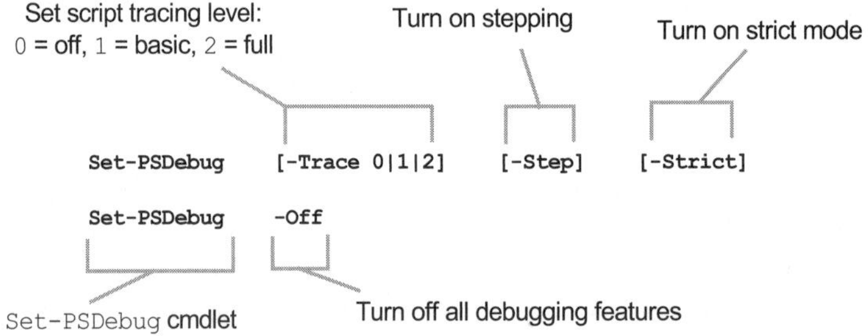

Figure 14.15 The `Set-PSDebug` cmdlet parameters. Among other things, this cmdlet is used to turn the v1 strict mode features on and off.

Catching undefined variables with strict mode

A common source of errors in scripts is the use of undefined or uninitialized variables, usually because you misspelled the variable's name. As in many other scripting languages, in PowerShell if a variable is undefined, it's treated as though it was defined and set to the value `$null`. You can test this behavior with a simple expression:

```
PS (1) > 2 * $nosuchvariable
0
```

In this expression, `$nosuchvariable` isn't defined. This means that it's treated as though it were `$null`. Because `$null` in a numeric expression is treated as zero, the whole expression evaluates to zero. You should note that the variable is only *treated* as though it were `$null`. This doesn't mean that a variable named `$nosuchvariable` is actually created as a side effect. You can verify this using `dir` with the variable provider to see if the variable is defined:

```
PS (2) > dir variable:\nosuchvariable
Get-ChildItem : Cannot find path 'nosuchvariable' because it doe
s not exist.
At line:1 char:4
+ dir  <<<< variable:\nosuchvariable
```

Now that you've seen the default behavior for variables that don't exist, let's turn on strict mode and try it again. First enable v1 strict mode:

```
PS (3) > Set-PSDebug -Strict
```

Try evaluating the same expression:

```
PS (4) > 2 * $nosuchvariable
The variable $nosuchvariable cannot be retrieved because it has
not been set yet.
At line:1 char:19
+ 2 * $nosuchvariable <<<<
```

This time, you get an error telling you that the variable hasn't been defined. So, define it

```
PS (5) > $nosuchvariable=13
```

and run the command again:

```
PS (6) > 2 * $nosuchvariable
26
```

Now you get the expected result. If you delete the variable using the provider

```
PS (7) > del variable:\nosuchvariable
```

and run the expression for a third time

```
PS (8) > 2 * $nosuchvariable
The variable $nosuchvariable cannot be retrieved because it has
not been set yet.
At line:1 char:19
+ 2 * $nosuchvariable <<<<
```

you're back to the error message. This mechanism is quite helpful in finding bugs in scripts. Unfortunately, the way it's implemented, it will only catch these errors if the problematic statement is actually executed.

There's also one type of uninitialized variable use that won't be caught even at runtime with v1 strict mode, and that is the use of uninitialized variables when double-quoted strings are expanded. This means that, even if you're catching things like this

```
$result = 2 + $nosuchvariable
```

no error will be raised for

```
$result = "the variable is $nosuchvariable"
```

so you may still have hidden bugs in this type of construct.

Some of the shortcomings of strict mode in v1 were addressed in PowerShell v2 by adding some additional types of checks. Let's see what was added.

14.3.2 The Set-StrictMode cmdlet in PowerShell v2

The v1 strict mode feature enabled through `Set-PSDebug -Strict` is useful, but the set of checks is limited to undefined variables. PowerShell v2 introduced a new version of strict mode and a new cmdlet, `Set-StrictMode`, to enable additional checks. The syntax for this cmdlet is shown in figure 14.16.

The `-Version` parameter takes either 1 or 2 as an argument controlling whether v1 or v2 checks are enabled. Version 2 strict mode includes the undefined variable check from v1 and adds some additional checks. In the next few sections, we'll look at what these new checks do.

Catching uninitialized variable use in string expansions

As mentioned earlier, strict mode in v1 only caught references to uninitialized variables in script text. It didn't catch the use of uninitialized variables in string expansions. Strict mode v2 fixes this and the use of uninitialized variables is caught everywhere. Let's look at an example. To refresh, in nonstrict mode, when you reference a nonexistent variable it's treated as being equivalent to `$null`:

```
PS (1) > $nosuchvariable
PS (2) >
```

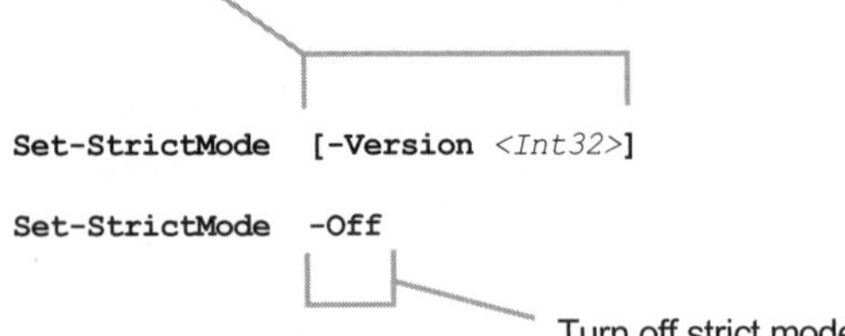
Turn on strict mode, optionally specifying version 1 or version 2 checks; use string "latest" to select newest set of checks
Set-StrictMode [-Version <Int32>]
Set-StrictMode -Off
Turn off strict mode

Figure 14.16 The `Set-StrictMode` cmdlet and its parameters. This is a new cmdlet in version 2 that enables additional compile-time and runtime checks processing a script.

Now turn on strict mode v1 and reference the variable again

```
PS (2) > Set-PSDebug -Strict
PS (3) > $nosuchvariable
The variable '$nosuchvariable' cannot be retrieved because it
has not been set.
At line:1 char:16
+ $nosuchvariable <<<<
    + CategoryInfo          : InvalidOperation: (nosuchvariable
   :Token) [], RuntimeException
    + FullyQualifiedErrorId : VariableIsUndefined
```

and you get the uninitialized variable message as expected. Now put the string in quotes

```
PS (4) > "$nosuchvariable"

PS (5) >
```

and it expands the string with no errors. Turn on strict mode v2 and try the string expansion

```
PS (5) > Set-StrictMode -Version 2
PS (6) > "$nosuchvariable"
The variable '$nosuchvariable' cannot be retrieved because it
has not been set.
At line:1 char:16
+ "$nosuchvariabl <<<< e"
    + CategoryInfo          : InvalidOperation: (nosuchvariable
   :Token) [], RuntimeException
    + FullyQualifiedErrorId : VariableIsUndefined
```

and you also get the uninitialized variable error in the string expansion case. Next we'll look at some of the new strict mode v2 features.

Catching attempts to read nonexistent properties

To have appropriately shell-like behavior, by default PowerShell allows you to try dereferencing nonexistent properties. That means you can do things like display a mixed collection of `[System.IO.FileInfo]` and `[System.IO.DirectoryInfo]` objects, including a reference to the `Length` property that doesn't exist for `[System.IO.DirectoryInfo]` objects. Imagine how annoying it'd be to type `dir` and get a lot of "property not found" errors. Try running

```
dir | foreach { $_.name + " " + $_.length }
```

in your home directory with strict mode v2 turned on and you'll see what I mean.

> **NOTE** This only applies to explicit property references in script text. Cmdlets still ignore missing properties even when strict mode v2 is turned on. The interactive environment is pretty much unusable otherwise.

Try a simple example. First turn strict mode off, then get a `[DateTime]` object into the variable `$date`:

```
PS (1) > Set-StrictMode -Off
PS (2) > $date = Get-Date
```

Now reference a nonexistent property

```
PS (3) > $date.nosuchproperty
PS (4) >
```

and no error is raised. You can verify that this will not be caught with strict mode v1:

```
PS (4) > Set-StrictMode -Version 1
PS (5) > $date.nosuchproperty
PS (5) >
```

You get no error, as before. Now turn on strict mode v2 and try accessing the property:

```
PS (6) > Set-StrictMode -Version 2
PS (7) > $date.nosuchproperty
Property 'nosuchproperty' cannot be found on this object. Make
sure that it exists.
At line:1 char:7
+ $date. <<<< nosuchproperty
    + CategoryInfo          : InvalidOperation:
(.:OperatorToken) [], RuntimeException
    + FullyQualifiedErrorId : PropertyNotFoundStrict
```

This time you get an error. As with the variable check, property checks will help catch typos in your script. It would be better if you could catch them at compile time, but then you'd need to know the types of all the expressions. Because PowerShell is dynamically typed, that isn't really possible.

> **NOTE** But what about checking against the type-constraints on variables, you might ask? Strict mode could include this kind of check, but it can't do a complete check because PowerShell allows extensions on instances as well as types. For example, when you look at a file entry in PowerShell, you see a `Mode` property. The underlying .NET type `[System.IO.FileInfo]` doesn't have a property with this name. The `Mode` property is one of the properties added by the PowerShell runtime. Because these properties can be added at runtime, even for a type-constrained variable, the most you could say is that the member probably won't exist by the time the statement is executed. Only the runtime check is guaranteed to be correct.

Checking for functions called like methods

An extremely common source of errors for experienced programmers is to call functions in the same way you would in other languages, or in the same way methods are called in PowerShell. Let's see this in action. Turn off strict mode (or set it to v1):

```
PS (1) > Set-StrictMode -Off
```

Then define a function that looks like this:

```
PS (2) > function divide ($x,$y) { $x / $y }
```

This function takes two arguments, divides the first by the second, and returns the result. Now let's call it like a method with parentheses around a function. This is how you'd call a function in a language like C#:

```
PS (3) > divide(9, 3)
Method invocation failed because [System.Object[]] doesn't
contain a method named 'op_Division'.
At line:1 char:31
+ function divide ($x,$y) { $x / <<<<  $y }
    + CategoryInfo          : InvalidOperation:
(op_Division:String) [], RuntimeException
    + FullyQualifiedErrorId : MethodNotFound
```

What happens is that you get a very surprising error. You know that numbers can be divided, so why did this fail? By putting the two arguments in parentheses, you're telling the system to pass a single argument, which is an array of two numbers. We talked about this problem in section 7.2.1. Now turn on strict mode v2, and try it again:

```
PS (4) > Set-StrictMode -Version 2
PS (5) > divide(9, 3)
The function or command was called as if it were a method.
Parameters should be separated by spaces. For information
about parameters, see the about_Parameters Help topic.
At line:1 char:7
+ divide <<<< (9, 3)
    + CategoryInfo          : InvalidOperation: (:) [], Runtime
   Exception
    + FullyQualifiedErrorId : StrictModeFunctionCallWithParens
```

Now you get a very prescriptive error message explaining exactly what's gone wrong. Follow the instructions, rewriting the function call, removing the parameters, and separating it with spaces instead of a comma; then try running it again:

```
PS (6) > divide 9 3
3
PS (7) >
```

This time it works.

This technique may seem like a trivial, almost silly check, but this issue has caused a lot of problems for a lot of people, including members of the PowerShell team.

Checking for empty variable references in strings

The final check is another corner-case check, this time for empty delimited variables. A delimited variable is something like `${a variable}`, which allows you to have characters in a variable name that are normally not allowed. For example:

```
PS (1) > Set-StrictMode -off
PS (2) > ${a variable} = "foo"
```

The other important use for delimited variables is in string expansion, where the variable name being expanded could be confused with the rest of the string:

```
PS (3) > $prefix = "foo"; "The word is ${prefix}bar"
The word is foobar
```

Here the variable `${prefix}` is expanded properly. Without the braces, the runtime would've tried to expand `$prefixbar` and failed. Now let's move on to the problematic scenario. Normally, outside of a string, if no names are specified between the braces, an error will occur, strict mode or not:

```
PS (4) > ${}
Empty ${} variable reference, there should be a name between the
 braces.
At line:1 char:1
+  <<<< ${}
    + CategoryInfo          : ParserError: (:) [],
ParentContainsErrorRecordException
    + FullyQualifiedErrorId : EmptyVariableReference
```

But in string expansions, it expands into `$`, as in

```
PS (5) > "The word is ${}bar"
The word is $bar
```

A minor error to be sure, but it's one you can detect at compile time (at least in PowerShell v2), so you check for it. Turn on v2 strict mode and rerun the command

```
PS (6) > Set-StrictMode -Version 2
PS (7) > "The word is ${}bar"
Braced variable name cannot be empty.
At line:1 char:21
+ "The word is ${}bar" <<<<
    + CategoryInfo          : InvalidOperation: (:) [], Runtime
   Exception
    + FullyQualifiedErrorId : EmptyBracedVariableName
```

and now you get the error.

Applying strict mode v2 to scripts

You now know what the new checks are—let's talk about when to apply them. In general, it's recommended that new code be written to be strict mode v2 "clean." In other words, the code should produce no errors when strict mode v2 is turned on. The temptation is to leave it on all the time. Unfortunately, this approach can break a lot of script code. Many scripts are written to take advantage of the default property dereference behavior. This means that a lot of fixing may need to be done. There are also cases where rewriting the code to not depend on this behavior can be very messy—the code would have to either explicitly check for the existence of a property before trying to access it, or explicitly trap the exception and ignore it. Consider the example at the beginning of the section that addressed catching references to nonexistent properties:

```
dir | foreach { $_.name + " " + $_.length }
```

This code results in an error every time dir returns a directory object. To make this work in strict mode v2, you'd have to do something like this

```
dir | foreach { $_.name + " " + $(try { $_.length } catch { $null })}
```

where the try/catch statement is used to process the error. In this code, if there's no exception, then the value of the property is returned. If there is an exception, the catch block returns $null. (At least the expression-oriented nature of the PowerShell language simplifies this example instead of requiring intermediate variables and an if statement.)

14.3.3 Static analysis of scripts

Most of the checks performed in strict mode are only applied at runtime, but there are some other checks you can do statically before you ever run the script. This was made possible in PowerShell v2 by the introduction of the PowerShell tokenizer API, a .NET class that takes the text of a PowerShell script and breaks it down into pieces called *tokens*. Tokens correspond to the types of elements found in the PowerShell language, which include things like keywords, operators, and so on—basically all the things we talked about in chapters 2 through 8. Unfortunately, this mechanism isn't packaged in a convenient way for scripting. It was designed for the PowerShell ISE, as you'll see in the next chapter. But, with a little work, it's still usable from a script. First we'll discuss how to use the API. We'll start by tokenizing a small piece of script text. (If you have strict mode turned on, you'll have to turn it off for these examples.) Put the text you want to tokenize into a variable:

```
PS (2) > $script = "function abc ($x) {dir; $x + 1}"
```

The tokenizer returns two things: the tokens that make up the script and a collection of any errors encountered while parsing the script. Because the API is designed for use from languages that can't return multiple values, you also need to create a variable to hold these errors:

```
PS (3) > $parse_errs = $null
```

Now you're ready to tokenize the script. Do so by calling the static method Tokenize() on the PSParser class as follows:

```
PS (4) > $tokens = [System.Management.Automation.PSParser]::Tokenize(
>>    $script,
>>    [ref] $parse_errs)
```

This code will put the list of tokens in the $tokens variable and any parse errors will be placed into a collection in $parse_errs. Now dump these two variables—$parse _errs—to the error stream and $tokens to the output stream:

```
>> $parse_errs | Write-Error
>> $tokens | Format-Table -auto type,content,startline,startcolumn
>>
```

```
                Type Content   StartLine StartColumn
                ---- -------   --------- -----------
             Keyword function          1           1
     CommandArgument abc               1          10
          GroupStart (                 1          14
            GroupEnd )                 1          15
          GroupStart {                 1          17
             Command dir               1          18
  StatementSeparator ;                 1          21
            Operator +                 1          24
              Number 1                 1          26
            GroupEnd }                 1          27
```

Because the text being tokenized is valid PowerShell script, no errors are generated. You do get a list of all the tokens in the text displayed on the screen. You can see that each token includes the type of the token, the content or text that makes up the token, as well as the start line and column number of the token. You'll now wrap this code up into a function to make it easier to call; name the function `Test-Script`:

```
PS (5) > function Test-Script ($script)
>> {
>>   $parse_errs = $null
>>   $tokens = [system.management.automation.psparser]::Tokenize(
>>   $script,
>>     [ref] $parse_errs)
>>   $parse_errs | Write-Error
>>   $tokens
>> }
>>
```

Try it on a chunk of invalid script text:

```
PS (6) > Test-Script "function ($x) {$x + }" |
>> ft -auto type,content,startline, startcolumn
>>
Test-Script : System.Management.Automation.PSParseError
At line:1 char:12
+ Test-Script <<<<  "function ($x) {$x + }" |
    + CategoryInfo          : NotSpecified: (:) [Write-Error], Write
   ErrorException
    + FullyQualifiedErrorId : Microsoft.PowerShell.Commands.WriteErr
   orException,Test-Script

Test-Script : System.Management.Automation.PSParseError
At line:1 char:12
+ Test-Script <<<<  "function ($x) {$x + }" |
    + CategoryInfo          : NotSpecified: (:) [Write-Error], Write
   ErrorException
    + FullyQualifiedErrorId : Microsoft.PowerShell.Commands.WriteErr
   orException,Test-Script

Test-Script : System.Management.Automation.PSParseError
At line:1 char:12
+ Test-Script <<<<  "function ($x) {$x + }" |
```

```
   + CategoryInfo          : NotSpecified: (:) [Write-Error], Write
  ErrorException
   + FullyQualifiedErrorId : Microsoft.PowerShell.Commands.WriteErr
  orException,Test-Script

      Type Content  StartLine StartColumn
      ---- -------  --------- -----------
   Keyword function         1           1
GroupStart (                1          10
  GroupEnd )                1          11
GroupStart {                1          13
  Operator +                1          15
  GroupEnd }                1          17
```

Now you see a number of errors. When you run a script that has syntax errors, you get just one error before the parsing continues. With the tokenizer API, the parser tries to reset itself and continue. This means that you may be able to deal with more errors at one time, but the reset process doesn't always work and sometimes you get incorrect errors. The other thing to notice is that, in the list of tokens being displayed, some of the actual tokens in the script, such as the variables, aren't output. Again, this is because when the parser attempts to recover, it can get confused and miss some tokens. (This is why, when you just run a script you only get one error—you know the first error is correct but aren't sure about the rest. It's simpler [if not more efficient] to deal with one correct error at a time rather than a collection of possible incorrect errors.)

Let's rewrite the test function. You're going to do a little work to clean up the errors, but you'll also add a new static check. Because the tokenizer output tells you what tokens are commands, you can use `Get-Command` to see if there are any references to commands that don't exist. This won't always be an error—a script may load a module defining the missing command at runtime—so you need to consider it to be a warning to investigate instead of an actual error. Here's what the new script looks like:

```
PS (7) > function Test-Script ($script)
>> {
>>   $parse_errs = $null
>>   $tokens = [system.management.automation.psparser]::Tokenize(
>>     $script,
>>     [ref] $parse_errs)
>>   foreach ($err in $parse_errs)
>>   {
>>     "ERROR on line " +
>>       $err.Token.StartLine +
>>       ": " + $err.Message +
>>       "`n"
>>   }
>>   foreach ($token in $tokens)
>>   {
>>     if ($token.Type -eq "Command")
>>     {
>>       $gcmerr = Get-Command $token.Content 2>&1
```

```
>>         if (! $? )
>>         {
>>           "WARNING on line " +
>>             $gcmerr.InvocationInfo.ScriptLineNumber +
>>             ": " + $gcmerr.Exception.Message +
>>             "`n"
>>         }
>>       }
>>     }
>> }
>>
```

The first part of the script hasn't changed much—you tokenize the string and then display any errors, though in a more compact form. Then you loop through all of the tokens looking for code commands. If you find a command, you check to see if it exists. If not, you display a warning. Let's try it out. First, define the test script with expected errors and an undefined command:

```
PS (8) > $badScript = @'
>> for ($a1 in nosuchcommand)
>> {
>>     while ( )
>>     $a2*3
>> }
>> '@
>>
```

Now run the test and see what you get:

```
PS (9) > Test-Script $badScript
ERROR on line 1: Unexpected token 'in' in expression or statement.

ERROR on line 1: Unexpected token 'nosuchcommand' in expression or
statement.

ERROR on line 3: Missing expression after 'while' in loop.

ERROR on line 4: Missing statement body in while loop.

WARNING on line 18: The term 'nosuchcommand' is not recognized as
the name of a cmdlet, function, script file, or operable program. Check
the spelling of the name, or if a path was included, verify that the
path is correct and try again.
```

In the output you see the expected syntax errors, but you also get a warning for the undefined command. There are a lot of things you could do to improve this checker. For example, you could look for variables that are used only once. By using these analysis techniques on the script text, you can find potential problems much sooner than you would if you waited to hit them at runtime.

So far we've looked at a number of tools and approaches that you can use to learn what's wrong with your scripts. But how do you figure out what's going on when other people are running your (or other people's) scripts in a different environment, possibly at a remote location? To help with this, the PowerShell console host includes a *session transcript* mechanism. You'll learn how this works in the next section.

14.4 CAPTURING SESSION OUTPUT

When trying to debug what's wrong with someone's script at a remote location, you'll find extremely helpful the ability to see the output and execution traces from a script run. The PowerShell console host allows you to do this via a mechanism that captures console output in transcript files. This transcript capability is exposed through the `Start-Transcript` and `Stop-Transcript` cmdlets, shown in figure 14.17.

> **NOTE** Unfortunately, the implementation of these cmdlets is a feature of the console host (`PowerShell.exe`) and so is not available in other hosts, including the PowerShell ISE. But all is not lost—there's a way to effectively achieve the equivalent with the ISE, as you'll see in the next chapter. Other host applications may have similar mechanisms.

14.4.1 Starting the transcript

To start a transcript, run `Start-Transcript` as shown in the next example. Let's begin the example by running a command before starting the transcript so you can see what is and is not recorded. Run `Get-Date` to get the current date

```
PS (1) > Get-Date

Thursday, April 15, 2011 10:10:12 PM
```

and now start the transcript:

```
PS (2) > Start-Transcript
Transcript started, output file is C:\Users\brucepay\Documents\
PowerShell_transcript.20100415221017.txt
```

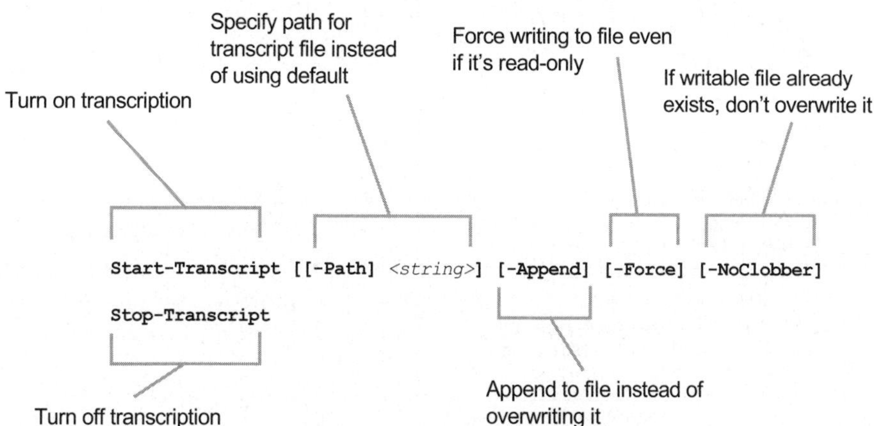

Figure 14.17 The cmdlets to start and stop console transcription. When transcription is turned on, all output to the console is written to the transcript file.

Because you didn't specify a filename for the transcript file, one will be automatically generated for you in your Documents directory. Now run a couple of additional commands:

```
PS (3) > 2+2
4
PS (4) > $psversiontable

Name                           Value
----                           -----
CLRVersion                     2.0.50727.4200
BuildVersion                   6.0.6002.18111
PSVersion                      2.0
WSManStackVersion              2.0
PSCompatibleVersions           {1.0, 2.0}
SerializationVersion           1.1.0.1
PSRemotingProtocolVersion      2.1
```

Stop the transcript. Again, it conveniently tells you the name of the file containing the transcript:

```
PS (5) > Stop-Transcript
Transcript stopped, output file is C:\Users\brucepay\Documents\
PowerShell_transcript.20100415221017.txt
```

Now let's see what was captured:

```
PS (6) > Get-Content C:\Users\brucepay\Documents\PowerShell_transcript
.20100415221017.txt
**********************
Windows PowerShell Transcript Start
Start time: 20100415221017
Username  : brucepayquad\brucepay
Machine   : BRUCEPAYQUAD (Microsoft Windows NT 6.0.6002 Service Pack
2)
**********************
Transcript started, output file is C:\Users\brucepay\Documents\
PowerShell_transcript.20100415221017.txt
PS (3) > 2+2
4
PS (4) > $psversiontable

Name                           Value
----                           -----
CLRVersion                     2.0.50727.4200
BuildVersion                   6.0.6002.18111
PSVersion                      2.0
WSManStackVersion              2.0
PSCompatibleVersions           {1.0, 2.0}
SerializationVersion           1.1.0.1
PSRemotingProtocolVersion      2.1

PS (5) > Stop-Transcript
**********************
Windows PowerShell Transcript End
End time: 20100415221038
**********************
```

The transcript file includes a header showing you the start time, the name of the user running the script, and the name and OS information about the computer on which the command is run.

You see the filename yet again because it was written out after transcription was turned on and so is captured in the transcript.

After that, you see the output of the commands you ran (including `Stop-Transcript`) and then finally a trailer showing the time the transcript stopped.

14.4.2 What gets captured in the transcript

It seems obvious that everything should get captured in the transcript file, but that isn't the case. As mentioned earlier, the transcript captures everything written through the host APIs that were described in section 14.3. What *doesn't* get captured is anything that bypasses these APIs and writes directly to the console. This missing information is most significant when you're running applications like `ipconfig.exe`. If these commands aren't redirected within PowerShell, then their output goes directly to the console and bypasses the host APIs. Let's see how this looks. Start a new transcript that writes to a different file (a new filename is generated each time):

```
PS (1) > Start-Transcript
Transcript started, output file is C:\Users\brucepay\Documents\PowerS
hell_transcript.20100415222650.txt
```

Run two commands, one of which uses `cmd` to echo something directly to the console:

```
PS (2) > cmd /c echo THIS WONT BE CAPTURED
THIS WONT BE CAPTURED
PS (3) > "This will"
This will
```

Now, stop the transcript and look at the output:

```
PS (4) > Stop-Transcript
Transcript stopped, output file is C:\Users\brucepay\Documents\
PowerShell_transcript.20100415222650.txt
PS (5) > Get-Content C:\Users\brucepay\Documents\PowerShell_transcript
.20100415222650.txt
**********************
Windows PowerShell Transcript Start
Start time: 20100415222650
Username  : brucepayquad\brucepay
Machine   : BRUCEPAYQUAD (Microsoft Windows NT 6.0.6002 Service Pack
2)
**********************
Transcript started, output file is C:\Users\brucepay\Documents\
PowerShell_transcript.20100415222650.txt
PS (2) > cmd /c echo THIS WONT BE CAPTURED
PS (3) > "This will"
This will
PS (4) > Stop-Transcript
**********************
```

```
Windows PowerShell Transcript End
End time: 20100415222708
**********************
```

You see the same headers and trailers as before, but notice that the `cmd` command is run but there's no output for it. Because `cmd` wrote directly to the console buffer, the transcript mechanism didn't capture it. The way to make sure that you do capture the output of this kind of command is to pipe it through `Write-Host`, forcing it to go through the host APIs. Here's what that looks like:

```
PS (7) > Start-Transcript
Transcript started, output file is C:\Users\brucepay\Documents\
PowerShell_transcript.20100415223336.txt
PS (8) > cmd /c echo THIS WILL BE CAPTURED 2>&1 | Write-Host
THIS WILL BE CAPTURED
PS (9) > Stop-Transcript
Transcript stopped, output file is C:\Users\brucepay\Documents\
PowerShell_transcript.20100415223336.txt
PS (10) > Get-Content  C:\Users\brucepay\Documents\
PowerShell_transcript.20100415223336.txt
**********************
Windows PowerShell Transcript Start
Start time: 20100415223336
Username  : brucepayquad\brucepay
Machine   : BRUCEPAYQUAD (Microsoft Windows NT 6.0.6002 Service Pack
2)
**********************
Transcript started, output file is C:\Users\brucepay\Documents\
PowerShell_transcript.20100415223336.txt
PS (8) > cmd /c echo THIS WILL BE CAPTURED 2>&1 | write-host
THIS WILL BE CAPTURED
PS (9) > Stop-Transcript
**********************
Windows PowerShell Transcript End
End time: 20100415223410
**********************
```

This time, when you look at the transcript, you can see that the output of command 8 was captured in the transcript.

Using the transcript cmdlets, it's easy to have the remote user capture the output of their session. Simply have the remote user call `Start-Transcript`, run their script, and then call `Stop-Transcript`. This process will produce a transcript file that the user can send to you for examination.

Session transcripts are a handy way to capture what's going on with a script, but they require someone to actively call them to get the transcript. There's another place where activity is recorded continuously, including for PowerShell: the event log. The event log is the central store for log messages from the system as well as from all the applications, services, and drivers running on that machine. It's a one-stop shop for diagnostic information. We'll see how to access this diagnostic treasure trove using PowerShell in the final section in this chapter.

14.5 POWERSHELL AND THE EVENT LOG

And now, the final topic in this chapter: exploring the Windows event log using PowerShell.

The Windows event log provides a central place where applications and operating system components can record events like the starting and stopping of an operation, progress, and especially system and application errors. For system administration, having access to the event log is critical. Obviously, as an admin tool, PowerShell support for the event log is very important so that's what we're going to look at in this section.

14.5.1 The EventLog cmdlets

PowerShell v1 had only a single, fairly limited command (`Get-EventLog`) for working with the event log. More sophisticated operations required using the underlying .NET classes. PowerShell v2 fills in this gap and provides a comprehensive set of cmdlets for working with the event log, as shown in table 14.3.

Table 14.3 The PowerShell `EventLog` cmdlets

Cmdlet name	PowerShell version	Description
`Get-EventLog`	v1, enhanced in v2	Gets the events in an event log, or a list of the event logs, on the local or remote computers
`Clear-EventLog`	v2	Deletes all entries from specified event logs on the local or remote computers
`Write-EventLog`	v2	Writes a new event log entry to the specified event log on the local or remote computer
`Limit-EventLog`	v2	Sets the event log properties that limit the size of the event log and the age of its entries
`Show-EventLog`	v2	Displays the event logs of the local or a remote computer using the event viewer MMC console
`New-EventLog`	v2	Creates a new event log and a new event source on a local or remote computer
`Remove-EventLog`	v2	Deletes an event log or unregisters an event source

Show-EventLog

You might be wondering why PowerShell includes this cmdlet—all it does is launch the event log viewer. The answer is simple: usability. PowerShell is a command-line shell, so you should be able to launch GUI applications from the command line. You can, of course, but there's a small problem: most of the commands you want to run, especially GUI commands, have names that aren't obvious. For example, to launch the control panel applet for adding and removing software, you run appwiz.cpl. To

(continued)
change the display settings, run desk.cpl. These command names, though related to their function, are certainly not obvious to a user. Similarly, the command to start the event viewer is eventvwr.msc. In contrast, the `Show-EventLog` cmdlet, which follows the PowerShell naming guidelines, can easily be intuited once you know the rules. The next question is, why provide a cmdlet instead of an alias? Because, as well as command naming, a cmdlet provides standard parameter handling, which allows for things like tab completion. So by providing a "shim" cmdlet for the existing application, one more small bump is removed from the command-line user's experience.

The `Get-EventLog` cmdlet is what we'll focus our attention on here. This cmdlet allows you to retrieve a list of the available application and system event logs and then look at the content of each of the logs. To get a list of the available logs, run `Get-EventLog -List`. The output will look something like this:

```
PS (1) > Get-EventLog -List

  Max(K) Retain OverflowAction        Entries Log
  ------ ------ --------------        ------- ---
  20,480      0 OverwriteAsNeeded      42,627 Application
  15,168      0 OverwriteAsNeeded           0 DFS Replication
  20,480      0 OverwriteAsNeeded           0 HardwareEvents
     512      7 OverwriteOlder              0 Internet Explorer
  20,480      0 OverwriteAsNeeded           0 Key Management Service
   8,192      0 OverwriteAsNeeded      11,695 Media Center
  16,384      0 OverwriteAsNeeded          80 ODiag
  15,360      0 OverwriteAsNeeded         101 Operations Manager
  16,384      0 OverwriteAsNeeded         790 OSession
  20,480      0 OverwriteAsNeeded      34,798 Security
  20,480      0 OverwriteAsNeeded      47,875 System
  15,360      0 OverwriteAsNeeded      11,988 Windows PowerShell
```

In addition to the names of the various logs, you can see the configuration settings for each log, such as the amount of space the log might take and what happens when the log fills up. You can use the `Limit-EventLog` cmdlet to change these limits for a log:

```
PS (4) > Limit-EventLog -LogName Application -MaximumSize 256kb
```

Then verify that the limit has been changed:

```
PS (6) > Get-EventLog -List | where {$_.Log -match "application"}

  Max(K) Retain OverflowAction        Entries Log
  ------ ------ --------------        ------- ---
     256      0 OverwriteAsNeeded      42,627 Application
```

As well as listing the available logs, `Get-EventLog` lets you see the events in any log. Because the event logs can be very large, the cmdlet supports a variety of options to control the amount of data returned. The parameters to `Get-EventLog` are shown in figure 14.18.

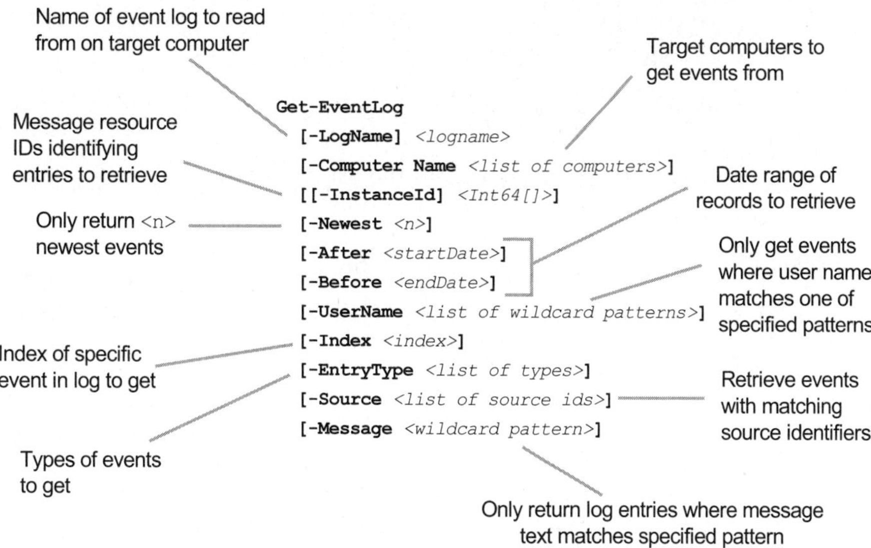
Name of event log to read from on target computer
Target computers to get events from
Message resource IDs identifying entries to retrieve
Get-EventLog
[-LogName] <logname>
[-Computer Name <list of computers>]
[[-InstanceId] <Int64[]>]
[-Newest <n>]
[-After <startDate>]
[-Before <endDate>]
[-UserName <list of wildcard patterns>]
[-Index <index>]
[-EntryType <list of types>]
[-Source <list of source ids>]
[-Message <wildcard pattern>]
Date range of records to retrieve
Only return <n> newest events
Only get events where user name matches one of specified patterns
Index of specific event in log to get
Retrieve events with matching source identifiers
Types of events to get
Only return log entries where message text matches specified pattern

Figure 14.18 The `Get-EventLog` cmdlet has a large number of parameters that allow you to control where the events are retrieved from and which events are to be retrieved. You can use event type, number, and date range to control the number of events retrieved and filter those events by username or strings in the event message.

Table 14.4 describes the various `Get-EventLog` filter parameters in more detail.

Table 14.4 The types of filters provided by the `Get-EventLog` cmdlet

Filter	Description
`Source`	The `-Source` parameter allows you to filter log entries based on the name used to register the event source. This name is usually the name of the application logging the events, but for larger applications, it may be the name of a subcomponent within that application.
`Message`	The `-Message` parameter allows the retrieved entries to be filtered based on the event's message text. The specified filter strings may contain wildcard patterns. (Note that because the text of a message is usually translated, the use of the `-Message` filter may not be portable to different locations.)
`InstanceID`	The `InstanceId` for an entry is the message resource identifier for the event. This identifier is used to retrieve the localized text for a message from the resource file for the registered event source. Because this identifier isn't localized, the `-InstanceID` parameter provides a way to filter events by message that's portable across locales because the message text is localized but the resource ID is always the same value.
`EntryType`	The entry type (or severity level) is a way of classifying events based on the potential impact of the corresponding event on the system's behavior. The entry types are `Information`, `Warning`, `Error`, and `Critical`. Two additional event types can occur in the security log: `Success Audit` and `Failure Audit`.
`User`	The `-User` parameter filters based on the name of the user on whose behalf the event occurred. Wildcards patterns can be used in arguments to this parameter.

Let's see how these parameters are used by working through a few examples. We'll look at the Operations Manager log.

> **NOTE** This log may not be present on your system—it requires that you use Microsoft Operations Manager (MOM). If you don't use MOM, just pick a log from the list you saw earlier (such as System) to work with instead.

Start by listing the newest 10 events in this log:

```
PS (1) > Get-EventLog -LogName 'Operations Manager' -Newest 10

   Index Time          EntryType   Source                 InstanceID
   ----- ----          ---------   ------                 ----------
     101 Apr 14 03:28  Information HealthService          1073743827
     100 Apr 14 03:28  Error       HealthService          3221227482
      99 Apr 14 03:28  Information Health Service ES...          102
      98 Mar 31 03:20  Information HealthService          1073743827
      97 Mar 31 03:20  Error       HealthService          3221227482
      96 Mar 31 03:20  Information Health Service ES...          102
      95 Mar 10 03:30  Information HealthService          1073743827
      94 Mar 10 03:30  Error       HealthService          3221227482
      93 Mar 10 03:30  Information Health Service ES...          302
      92 Mar 10 03:30  Information Health Service ES...          301
```

The `-Index` parameter lets you retrieve a specific entry from the log. Save this entry in a variable and then use `Format-List` to display additional properties of the entry:

```
PS (2) > $e = Get-EventLog -LogName 'Operations Manager' -Index 99
PS (3) > $e | Format-List

Index              : 99
EntryType          : Information
InstanceId         : 102
Message            : HealthService (2264) Health Service Store: The d
                     atabase engine (6.00.6002.0000) started a new in
                     stance (0).
Category           : General
CategoryNumber     : 1
ReplacementStrings : {HealthService, 2264, Health Service Store: , 0.
                     ..}
Source             : Health Service ESE Store
TimeGenerated      : 4/14/2010 3:28:02 AM
TimeWritten        : 4/14/2010 3:28:02 AM
UserName           :
```

Using `Format-List` shows you, among other things, the `InstanceID` and text of the event message. Now retrieve all the events using this message `InstanceID`:

```
PS (4) > Get-EventLog -LogName 'Operations Manager' -Newest 10 `
>> -InstanceId 102
>>
```

```
Index Time          EntryType   Source                  InstanceID
----- ----          ---------   ------                  ----------
   99 Apr 14 03:28  Information Health Service ES...           102
   96 Mar 31 03:20  Information Health Service ES...           102
   90 Mar 10 03:29  Information Health Service ES...           102
   84 Feb 24 03:23  Information Health Service ES...           102
   81 Feb 14 17:55  Information Health Service ES...           102
   78 Feb 10 03:28  Information Health Service ES...           102
   72 Jan 23 03:21  Information Health Service ES...           102
   66 Jan 13 03:25  Information Health Service ES...           102
   60 Dec 10 03:27  Information Health Service ES...           102
   57 Nov 25 03:21  Information Health Service ES...           102
```

You can use `-Before` and `-After` to retrieve messages around a specific date (and time if desired):

```
PS (5) > Get-EventLog -LogName 'Operations Manager' `
>> -After 'Oct 15/2009' -Before "Oct 28/2009"
>>

Index Time          EntryType   Source                  InstanceID
----- ----          ---------   ------                  ----------
   28 Oct 27 23:08  Information HealthService           1073743827
   27 Oct 27 23:08  Error       HealthService           3221227482
   26 Oct 27 23:07  Information Health Service ES...           102
   25 Oct 27 21:41  Information HealthService           1073743827
   24 Oct 27 21:41  Error       HealthService           3221227482
   23 Oct 27 21:40  Information Health Service ES...           102
   22 Oct 27 20:58  Information HealthService           1073743827
   21 Oct 27 20:58  Error       HealthService           3221227482
   20 Oct 27 20:58  Information Health Service ES...           102
   19 Oct 18 11:24  Information HealthService           1073743827
   18 Oct 18 11:24  Error       HealthService           3221227482
   17 Oct 18 11:23  Information Health Service ES...           102
   16 Oct 15 03:10  Information HealthService           1073743827
   15 Oct 15 03:10  Error       HealthService           3221227482
   14 Oct 15 03:09  Information Health Service ES...           102
```

Here you've retrieved all the messages between October 15 and October 28 in 2009. You can combine `-Before` and `-Newest` to get a specific number of messages before a particular date:

```
PS (7) > Get-EventLog -LogName 'Operations Manager' `
>> -Before 'Oct 15/2009' -Newest 10
>>

Index Time          EntryType   Source                  InstanceID
----- ----          ---------   ------                  ----------
   13 Oct 11 03:09  Information HealthService           1073743827
   12 Oct 11 03:09  Error       HealthService           3221227482
   11 Oct 11 03:08  Information Health Service ES...           102
   10 Oct 10 08:48  Information HealthService           1073743827
    9 Oct 10 08:48  Error       HealthService           3221227482
    8 Oct 10 08:48  Information Health Service ES...           302
    7 Oct 10 08:46  Information Health Service ES...           301
```

```
     6 Oct 10 08:46  Information Health Service ES...          300
     5 Oct 10 08:46  Information Health Service ES...          102
     4 Sep 17 15:18  Information HealthService          1073743827
```

And finally, you can use `-Message` and `-After` to find all messages matching a specific pattern that occurred after a specific date. For this example, just use the month and day numbers and let the year default to the current year:

```
PS (9) > Get-EventLog -LogName 'Operations Manager' `
>> -Message "*Data*6.0*" -After '4/1' |
>> Format-List Name,Time,EntryType,Message
>>

EntryType : Information
Message   : HealthService (2264) Health Service Store: The database
engine (6.00.6002.0000) started a new instance (0).
```

This command returns a single entry indicating that the database engine started a new instance.

So why is all this useful? Imagine you see a critical error in an application. This error shows up in the Application log. You suspect that it might be related to either a hardware issue or a bad device driver. Rather than manually poring over hundreds of log entries, you can use the date from the Application log entry to retrieve the events in the System log that occurred shortly before the application.

Digging through the entries, you identify the problem that led to the failure. From this, you get the `Source` and `InstanceID` identifying the problematic entry. You quickly write a script to remediate the problem on this machine but realize that there may be other machines in the organization with similar issues. You put together a list of potentially at-risk machines and pass this list to `Get-EventLog` using the `-ComputerName` parameter. You also specify the `-Source` and `-InstanceID` parameters of the problematic message. This command will search the event logs of all the at-risk machines, returning a list of event log entries matching the criteria. From this set of events, you can get the names of all the computers that need to be fixed. Finally, you can use PowerShell remoting to run the remediation script on all the machines with the problem.

> **NOTE** Although you need PowerShell remoting to run the remediation script on the target machines, PowerShell remoting isn't used when you use `Get-EventLog` to access a remote computer. `Get-EventLog` uses its own remoting protocol, as mentioned in chapter 12. This means `Get-EventLog` can be used to examine the logs of the target computer to help diagnose what went wrong using its own built-in remoting to connect to that computer. It's not dependent on PowerShell remoting.

The `Get-EventLog` filtering capabilities make this kind of "forensic" analysis very easy. One of the things you might want to analyze is PowerShell itself.

14.5.2 Examining the PowerShell event log

When PowerShell is installed, the installation process creates a new event log called Windows PowerShell. As PowerShell executes, it writes a variety of information to this log, which you can see using the `Get-EventLog` cmdlet. Let's use the cmdlet to get the last few records from the PowerShell event log. As always, you can use the tools PowerShell provides to filter and scope the data you want to look at. You'll use an array slice to get the last five records from the log:

```
PS (2) > (Get-EventLog 'windows powershell')[-5..-1]

WARNING: column "Message" does not fit into the display and was
removed.

   Index Time          EntryType   Source                 InstanceID
   ----- ----          ---------   ------                 ----------
       5 Dec 27 17:25  Information PowerShell                    600
       4 Dec 27 17:25  Information PowerShell                    600
       3 Dec 27 17:25  Information PowerShell                    600
       2 Dec 27 17:25  Information PowerShell                    600
       1 Dec 27 17:25  Information PowerShell                    600
```

The default presentation of the event records doesn't show much information. Let's look at one event in detail and see what it contains:

```
PS (3) > (Get-EventLog "windows powershell")[0] | Format-List *
```

First, you get some basic event log elements common to all event log entries:

```
EventID            : 400
MachineName        : brucepayquad
Data               : {}
Index              : 8915
```

Next, you see the event category. This isn't the same as the error category discussed earlier. PowerShell event log entries are grouped into several large categories:

```
Category           : Engine Lifecycle
CategoryNumber     : 4
```

Next is the entry type and a message describing the entry. This is followed by a collection of detail elements, which include things such as the state transition for the engine, as well as some of the versioning information you saw on the `$host` object earlier. This is included in case you have multiple hosts for a particular engine:

```
EntryType          : Information
Message            : Engine state is changed from None to Available.
                     Details:
                       NewEngineState=Available
                       PreviousEngineState=None
                       SequenceNumber=9
                       HostName=ConsoleHost
                       HostVersion=2.0
                       HostId=29f2d25c-551c-4e8b-9c15-3cd2103c4a70
                       EngineVersion=2.0
```

```
                    RunspaceId=ffff212a-7e81-4344-aecd-c6bcab05b
                    715

                    PipelineId=
                    CommandName=
                    CommandType=
                    ScriptName=
                    CommandPath=
                    CommandLine=
Source            : PowerShell
```

The following fields specify the replacement strings that are available. These strings are substituted into the log message text:

```
ReplacementStrings : {Available, None,      NewEngineState=Available
                     PreviousEngineState=None
                     SequenceNumber=9
                     HostName=ConsoleHost
                     HostVersion=2.0
                     HostId=29f2d25c-551c-4e8b-9c15-3cd2103c4a70
                     EngineVersion=2.0
                RunspaceId=ffff212a-7e81-4344-aecd-c6bcab05b715
                     PipelineId=
                     CommandName=
                     CommandType=
                     ScriptName=
                     CommandPath=
                     CommandLine=}
```

Finally, some additional information for identifying the event log entry and when it occurred:

```
InstanceId        : 400
TimeGenerated     : 1/10/2010 6:02:19 PM
TimeWritten       : 1/10/2010 6:02:19 PM
UserName          :
Site              :
Container         :
```

Granted, the output isn't all that interesting, but when you're trying to figure out what went wrong on your systems, being able to see when the PowerShell interpreter was started or stopped could be useful. There are also certain types of internal errors (also known as *bugs*) that may cause a PowerShell session to terminate. These errors also will be logged in the PowerShell event log.

That's all we're going to cover on event logs in this chapter. From these examples, you can see that the event logs provide a lot of information, much of which can help you manage and maintain your systems. The trick is being able to extract and correlate the information across the various logs, and this is where PowerShell can be very useful.

14.6 SUMMARY

This chapter focused on the diagnostic features of PowerShell: the error-handling mechanisms and the various debugging, tracing, analysis, and logging features. And, although this is a fairly long chapter, it still can't claim to be an exhaustive discussion of all of these features. Let's summarize the areas that we did cover. We started with basic error handling:

- The two types of errors in PowerShell: *terminating* and *nonterminating*
- The `ErrorRecord` object and the error stream
- The `$error` variable and `-ErrorVariable` parameter
- The `$?` and `$LASTEXITCODE` variables
- `$ErrorActionPreference` and the `-ErrorAction` parameter

Next, we showed you how to work with terminating errors and exceptions:

- The `trap` statement and how to use it
- The `try/catch/finally` statements in PowerShell v2
- Using the `throw` statement to generate your own terminating exceptions

And then we discussed some of the tools and techniques for finding static and runtime errors in scripts:

- Using the host APIs to do `printf`-style debugging
- Catching errors with strict mode, both v1 and v2 versions
- Using the PowerShell tokenizer API to do static analysis of a script to catch problems before they happen

Finally, we looked at some techniques for examining the behavior of script that other people may be running by using the transcript feature in `PowerShell.exe` and by looking at the event log using the `Get-EventLog` cmdlet.

This chapter looked at ways to deal with errors in PowerShell scripts after they have occurred (sometimes long after, in the event log case). In chapter 15, we'll look at ways of preventing errors in your scripts by using the PowerShell ISE and the built-in debugger.

CHAPTER 15

The PowerShell ISE and debugger

Big Julie: "I had the numbers taken off for luck, but I remember where the spots formerly were."

—*Guys and Dolls,* words and music by Frank Loesser

In the previous chapter, you learned how PowerShell deals with errors and how those features help you find bugs in your scripts. In this chapter, we're going to look at more tools that help you create correct, reliable scripts. We'll cover the graphical Integrated Scripting Environment (ISE) as well as the debugger, both of which were introduced with PowerShell v2. First, we'll begin by covering the basic operation and usage patterns of the ISE. Next, we'll look at customizing and extending the ISE using the object model provided for that purpose. Then, we'll review how the debugger works within the ISE and from the command line.

15.1 THE POWERSHELL ISE

PowerShell v2 significantly improved the PowerShell scripting experience with the introduction of the ISE. This new PowerShell host application adds many of the features expected in a modern scripting environment:

- Syntax highlighting in the editor and command panes
- Multiple concurrent sessions
- Multiple editor tabs within a session
- Full globalization support
- An extension mechanism that allows you to add your own functionality to the environment

The goal of the first part of this chapter is to learn to use the ISE effectively and adapt it to the individual's working style and environment. We'll begin with examining the layout and major features of the ISE.

15.1.1 Controlling the ISE pane layout

The basic layout of the ISE consists of three resizable panes: the editor, output, and command panes. The layout is shown in figure 15.1.

As you'd expect, the Editor pane holds all the current files being edited, and the output pane is where the output of executed commands is displayed. The last pane is the command pane and is intended for command entry. This arrangement is a bit different than most shells. Typically, shells interleave user commands with the output text all in the same pane. The ISE does display the commands as they're executed in context with the output, but the commands themselves are entered into a separate

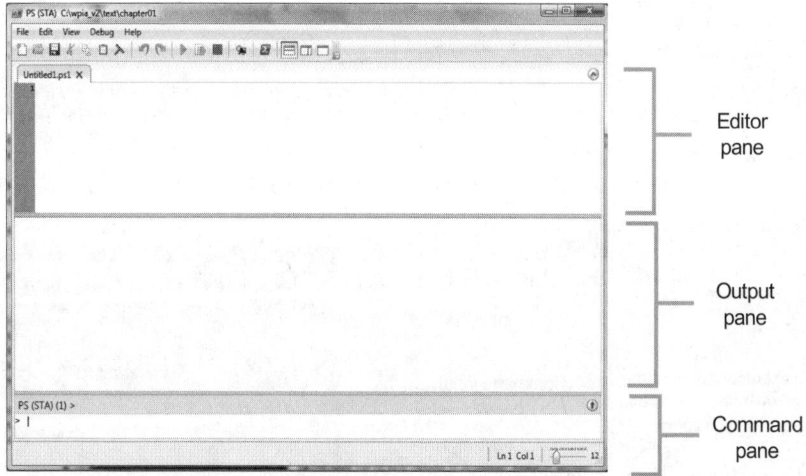

Figure 15.1 The basic layout of the PowerShell ISE. The user interface is broken into three panes: editor, output, and command input.

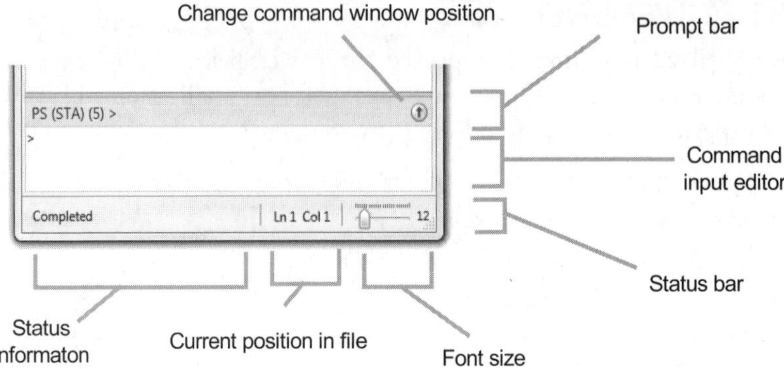

Figure 15.2 The ISE command pane includes the prompt line, the command input editor and the status line, as well as controls to change the font size and command pane position.

pane. This arrangement makes it possible to edit complex commands interactively while preserving the critical aspects of the traditional shell experience. Let's take a closer look at the elements in the command pane.

The command pane

The command pane is composed of three separate pieces: the command input editor, the prompt line, and the status line, as shown in figure 15.2. In figure 15.2, you can see that there are two elements in the prompt line: the text of the prompt and a control for changing the position of the command pane relative to the editor pane. As is

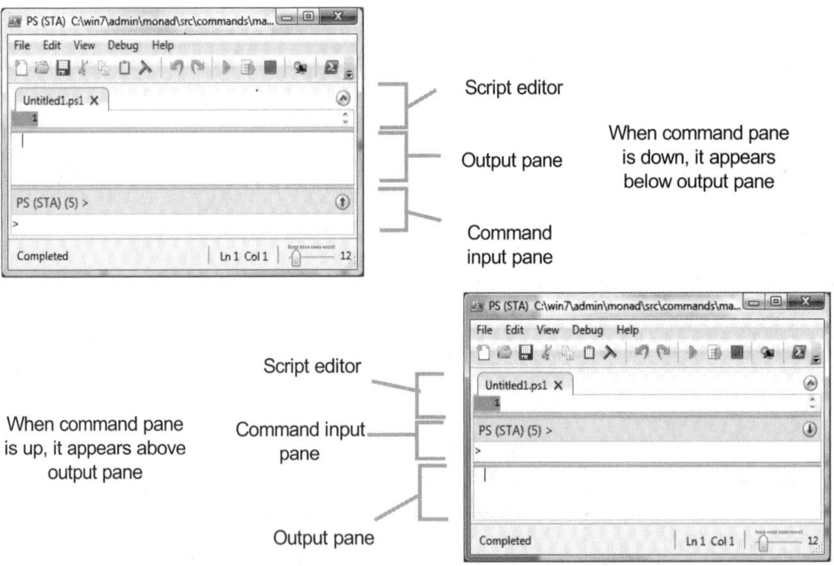

Figure 15.3 The command pane can be above or below the output pane.

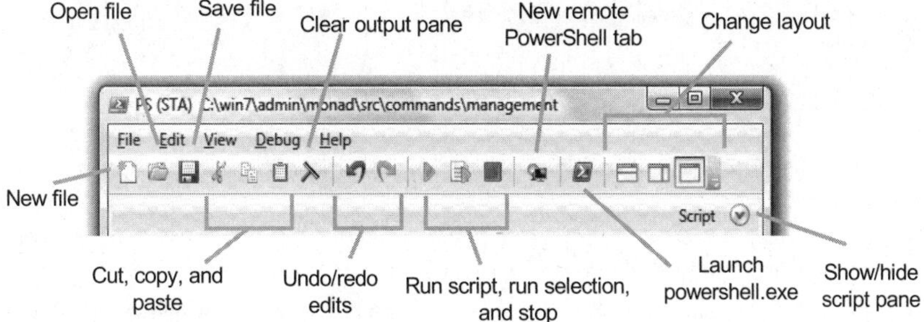

Figure 15.4 The ISE toolbar provides controls to create, open, and save files; run scripts; and control the layout of the ISE. It also allows the user to start a remote PowerShell session in a new tab as well as launch the console host `PowerShell.exe`.

the case with the console host, the prompt text is set by the user-definable `prompt` function. The position control is used to exchange the relative positions of the output and command panes, as shown in figure 15.3.

When the position icon (an up arrow) is clicked, the command pane moves from below the output pane to above it and the icon changes to a down arrow, as shown in figure 15.3. When the position icon is clicked again, the original positions are restored.

The ISE toolbar

Moving on in our coverage of the basic ISE elements, let's look at the toolbar. The toolbar gives you quick access to common features (such as cut, copy, and paste) but some PowerShell-specific features are also included. The toolbar is shown in figure 15.4.

In the ISE toolbar, along with the standard items are ISE-specific controls for running scripts, for creating remote tabs, and for launching the console host `PowerShell.exe`. We'll cover remote tabs later in section 15.2.2. The toolbar also contains controls that allow additional layout options for the ISE. You can see one of these alternate layouts in figure 15.5.

The side-by-side layout in figure 15.5 is most effective on a large monitor, allowing you to have full-sized execution and editor panes beside each other.

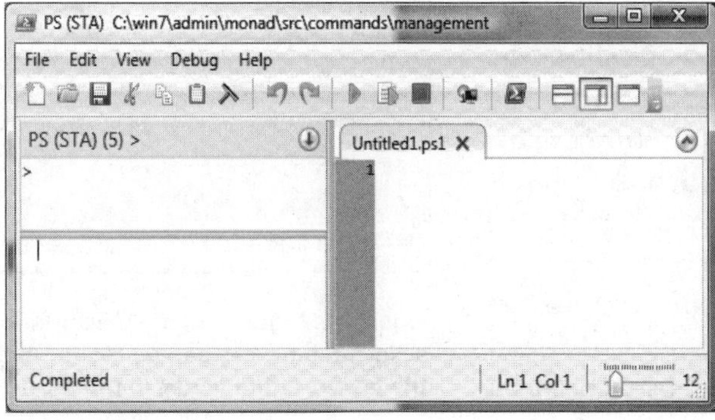

Figure 15.5 The layout of the PowerShell ISE with the editor pane on the side. The organization of the three major panes in the ISE can be controlled to a large extent by user settings.

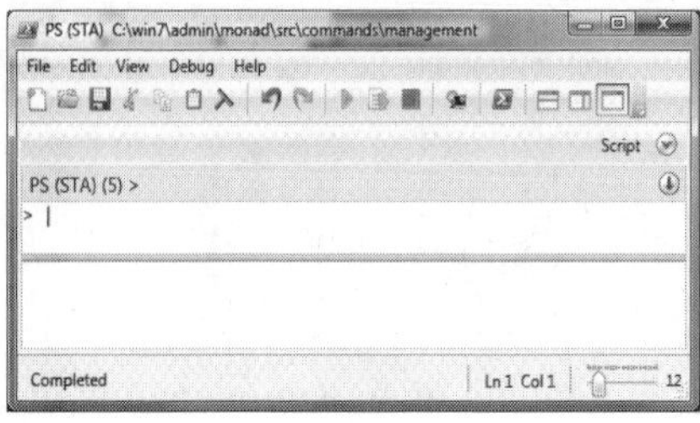

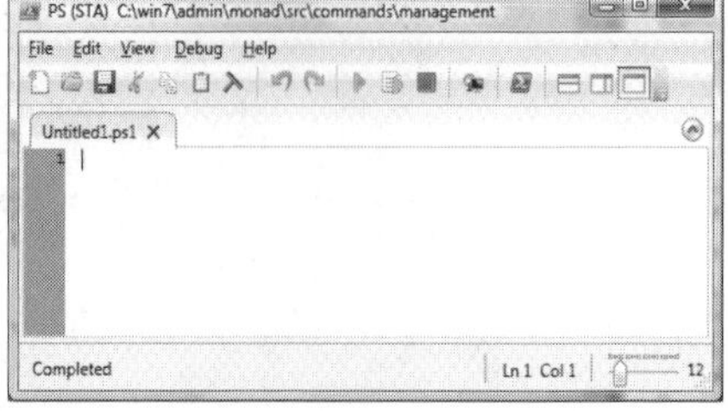

Editor pane hidden　　　　Editor pane mazimized

Figure 15.6 On the left side of this figure, the editor pane has been hidden and the full space used for the command and output panes. On the right side, the editor pane has been maximized, hiding the other panes. These modes can also be toggled by pressing Ctrl-R.

There are two other layout modes with the editor pane either hidden or maximized. These modes are shown in figure 15.6.

Whereas the side-by-side mode is ideal if there's a lot of screen real estate, the mode in figure 15.6 allows the ISE to be used effectively on smaller screen devices like netbooks or tablets. All of these modes can be set from the menus. The other thing you can do is use hotkey sequences to switch configurations. The View menu in figure 15.7 shows a number of these hotkeys.

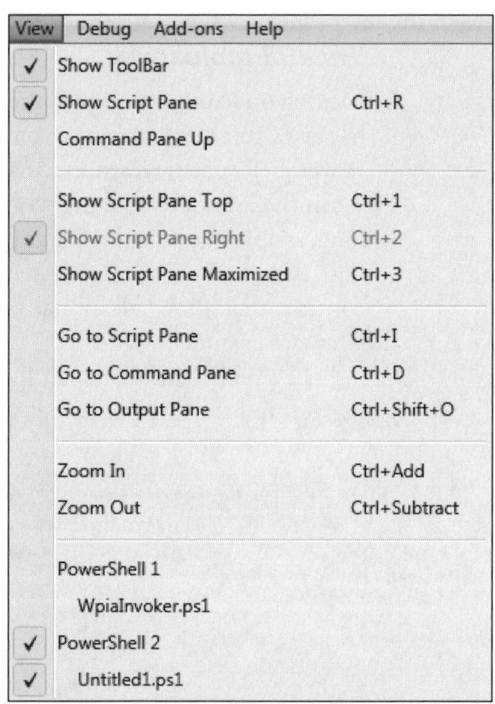

Figure 15.7 Items in the View menu and their associated hotkey sequences for managing the layout of the panes in the ISE

Now that you know how to use the layout settings to choose the best layout for your work, let's see what benefits the ISE editor brings to the PowerShell user.

15.1.2 Using the ISE editor

The PowerShell ISE editor is built on the same editor control used in recent versions of Microsoft Visual Studio and the Expression Blend designer tool. As such, it follows the key-binding sequences used by these tools and they, in turn, follow the Windows Common User Access (CUA) bindings. Because the same control is used everywhere, the CUA guidelines apply everywhere, and you can finally use Ctrl-C and Ctrl-V to copy and paste between panes, including the command pane. The more interesting key bindings are shown in table 15.1. Where there are special behaviors associated with the keys in the ISE, they're marked as ISE in the left column.

Table 15.1 The PowerShell ISE editor key bindings

	Key	Description
	F1	Open the PowerShell help viewer. This launches the hypertext help viewer, which allows the contents of the PowerShell help system to be searched and navigated much more easily than the command-line version of help.
ISE	Ctrl-F	Search forward in the current editor pane from the current cursor position. This doesn't wrap and thus won't find occurrences earlier in the text.
	F3	Search forward in the current editor pane to find the next occurrence of the pattern specified to Ctrl-F.
ISE	Shift-F3	Search backward in the current editor pane to find earlier occurrences. As with the forward search, this won't wrap around and continue searching from the end of the file once the start has been reached.
ISE	Ctrl-H	Replace strings in the current editor pane.
ISE	Ctrl-G	Go to a specific line number in the current file.
ISE	F5	Execute the contents of the file in the current editor pane. The file will be saved to disk before execution. Note: The file will be as though it were dot-sourced, modifying the global environment.
ISE	F8	Dot-source the currently selected text.
ISE	Ctrl-Shift-P	Start an instance of `PowerShell.exe`. This is useful for commands that require the console window environment.
	Ctrl-F4	Close the current editor pane, prompting to save if the buffer hasn't been saved.
	Alt-F4	Exit the ISE. If there are no unsaved files, this will cause the ISE to immediately exit without prompting.
ISE	Ctrl-N	Open a new editor tab.
	Ctrl-S	Save the current editor tab.
ISE	Ctrl-R	Toggle visibility of the script pane.
ISE	Ctrl-1	Show the editor pane above the command pane.
ISE	Ctrl-2	Show the editor pane on the right
ISE	Ctrl-3	Show the editor pane maximized.
	Ctrl-O	Open an existing file.
ISE	Ctrl-T	Start a new PowerShell session tab.
ISE	Ctrl-W	Close the current PowerShell session tab.
ISE	Ctrl-Shift-R	Open a new remote PowerShell session tab.

Table 15.1 The PowerShell ISE editor key bindings *(continued)*

	Key	Description
	Ctrl-A	Select everything in the current pane. This works in command and output panes as well as the editor pane.
ISE	Tab	If nothing is selected, move to next tab stop. The ISE will insert four spaces by default. It doesn't insert tab characters. If more than one line is selected, then it will shift all the selected lines one tab stop right.
ISE	Shift-Tab	If more than one line is currently selected in the editor pane, the text will be shifted one tab stop (four spaces by default) left.
ISE	Ctrl-Tab	Cycle through the editor buffers in the current PowerShell tab.
	Home, End	Move the cursor to the beginning or end of the line. The first time the Home key is pressed, it moves the cursor to the first nonblank character in the line. Pressing it again will move to the cursor to the first character in the line.
ISE	Enter	In the command pane, execute the command. In the editor pane, insert a new line. Tab offset is maintained for the new lists.
	Shift-Down arrow, Shift-Up arrow	Extend the text selection up to the next or previous line.
	Shift-Left arrow	Add the next item/character to the selection.
	Shift-Right arrow	Add the previous item/character to the selection.
	Shift-F10	Display the context menu for current pane (similar to right-clicking).
	Ctrl-Home, Ctrl-End	Go to the beginning or end of the current editor panes.

In the table are a couple of items that we'll explore in detail later in the chapter, such as the new remote PowerShell tab (section 15.2.2). We'll also look at the key bindings used by the debugger. But for now, we'll finish our discussion of the basic operation of the editor.

Opening a file

In table 15.1, you saw that one way to open a file is to select File > Open or just press Ctrl-O. This is what you'd expect from an editor. From a shell, though, you expect to do things with commands—and you can. A command is available in the ISE called `psEdit` that will allow you to open files from the command line. It takes wildcards, so you can use it to open multiple files at once. This command is actually a function, and the default definition looks like:

```
PS (STA) (2) > Get-Content function:psedit
param([Parameter(Mandatory=$true)]$filenames)
foreach ($filename in $filenames)
    {
        dir $filename | where {!$_.PSIsContainer} | %{
            $psISE.CurrentPowerShellTab.Files.Add($_.FullName) > $null
        }
    }
```

The thing to notice in this function definition is the `$psISE` variable. This variable is the root of the ISE object model and lets you script against the ISE itself. We'll cover this topic in detail later in this chapter.

Creating a new file

Opening existing files is fine, but the goal of the ISE is to help you create new scripts. Again, you can choose File > New or press Ctrl-N, but there's an annoyance here: the Windows file browser dialog box has its own idea of what the current directory should be and it's not the same as the current directory you see in the command pane.

If you want to create a file in the current directory, you'll have to do it from the command line. Unfortunately, `psEdit` will just complain if you tell it to open a file that doesn't exist. Instead, you have to create the file yourself with the `New-Item` cmdlet or with

```
PS (STA) (4) > "" > newfile.ps1
```

This code will create a file with one empty line in it. You verify that it was created:

```
PS (STA) (5) > dir .\newfile.ps1

    Directory: C:\Users\brucepay

Mode                LastWriteTime     Length Name
----                -------------     ------ ----
-a---          5/6/2010  10:02 PM          6 newfile.ps1
```

Then, open it:

```
PS (STA) (6) > psEdit .\newfile.ps1
```

Why are there six characters in a one line file?

You might have noticed something funny in the output when you looked at the file using `dir`:. It was supposed to be a single empty line, which implies two characters (CR and LF), not six. The other four characters are the Unicode Byte order mark, or BOM, indicating that this is a Unicode text file.

Tab expansion in the editor pane

One of the most useful tools for learning and working with PowerShell is the tab completion feature. This feature is available in the console host, but it really shines in the ISE because it works in the editor and the command panes. It also doesn't suffer from the limitation that the console shell has where pressing Tab is treated as the end of line and everything after it is deleted. In the ISE, tab completion can be used anywhere in the editor panes.

When the tab completion function executes, it operates against the state of the live shell session in the current tab. This means that if you have a variable defined in your session, the editor will tab-complete against the existing definition of the variable, even if it's used in a different way in the script you're editing. Likewise, it will resolve command parameters against existing commands, not the commands that are defined in a particular file. At times, this behavior can be confusing. The fact that the ISE dot-sources scripts when run with F5 mitigates this confusion to some extent because the script variables become global variables. Now let's look at the other significant feature that the ISE offers for writing scripts.

Syntax highlighting in the ISE panes

Another useful feature of the ISE is that it does syntax highlighting in both the editor and command panes. As text is entered in either of these panes, the ISE will color the content of the buffer based on the syntax of what you've typed. If there's an error at some point in what you type, then the highlighting will stop. This is a way to catch syntax errors while you're entering your code. Note that syntax highlighting is limited to PowerShell script files with .ps1, .psm1, and .psd1 extensions.

> **NOTE** The syntax highlighting is done using the tokenizer API introduced in chapter 14. The PowerShell team made this a public API to make it easier for other editor environments hosting PowerShell to support syntax highlighting.

At this point, let's switch from talking about using the ISE to creating code and looking at what it brings to the table as far as running code is concerned.

15.1.3 Executing commands in the ISE

Because this is an integrated scripting environment, you want to be able to run your scripts as well as create them. As with the console host, you can run a script simply by typing the name of the script and pressing Enter. But the ISE offers additional ways to run scripts, as you'll see in the next few sections.

Running current editor pane contents

To run the contents of the current editor pane, you press F5. This is consistent with most other Microsoft products that have an execution capability, like Visual Studio and PowerPoint. There's one significant difference between running from the command pane and running by pressing F5: how the script is run. When run from the command pane, a script runs in its own scope, as described in chapter 9. But when it's run using F5, it runs in the current scope. In other words, it *dot-sources* the script into the environment.

> **WARNING** This point is important enough to be repeated. When you use F5 to run a script, the script is executed in the global environment of the current session tab. Keeping these variables around means that any scripts or variables defined in the script will persist after the script

has exited. Keeping these variables around is good for tab completion and debugging but can also be confusing as more things are added to the global environment. When testing a script in the ISE, you should do the testing in a separate PowerShell tab using the command line to launch the script rather than pressing F5.

Dot-sourcing has significant consequences, both positive and negative. On the positive side, because the script is dot-sourced, you can examine the state of variables and functions it defined because they're still available in the global session state. On the negative side, all of these things that are being defined clutter up the global state and may possibly overwrite existing variables or functions.

Executing selected text

As well as executing the contents of the current editor, you can execute selected regions of script. Simply select the region of text and then press F8 (see figure 15.8). The figure shows selecting some lines in a file snippets.ps1 and then executing that text. As was the case with F5, fragments executed with F8 are run in the global scope.

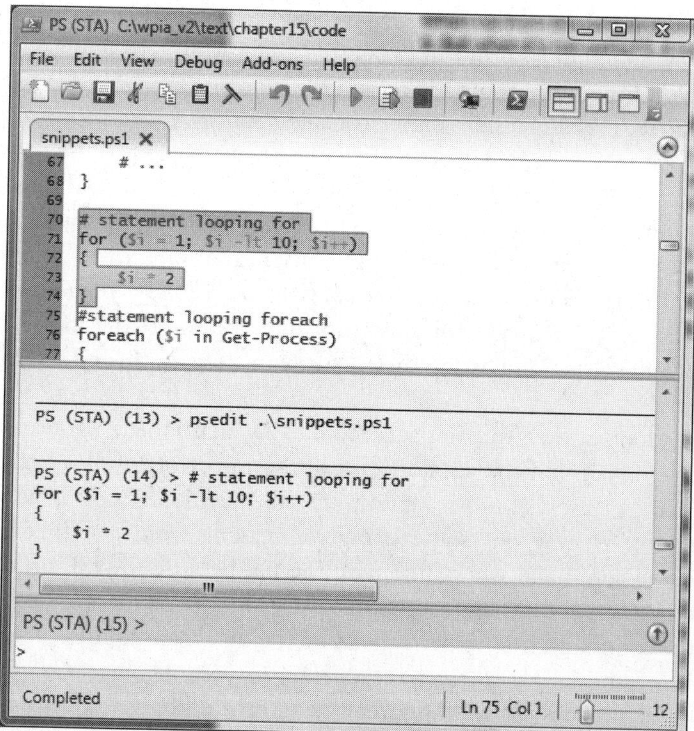

Figure 15.8 Fragments of code can be executed by selecting the text and pressing F8. Doing so allows you to test fragments of a script as it's being developed.

This makes sense with fragments—you want to be able to execute incrementally and then examine the effects at each step.

> **NOTE** You may wonder why the key to execute the selected region is F8. Originally, it was F6. It changed when a very senior person (who will remain nameless) was doing a demonstration and accidentally hit F5 (execute the entire script) instead of F6 (execute the selection). The results were decidedly nonoptimal. So "execute selected" was moved from F6 to F8.

15.1.4 Considerations when running scripts in the ISE

Up until now, we've focused on how to use the ISE and what you can do with it. But there are also a few things to be aware of that can lead to different behaviors between the ISE and the console host. In this section, we're going to investigate a couple of these issues. Both of these concerns involve aspects of how the Windows operating system executes programs. Let's take a look.

Issues with native commands

The things that are most likely to cause problems with the ISE are external executables, or native commands compiled as console applications. To understand the possible issues, we'll begin with some background.

In Windows, executables are either console applications or Win32 applications. Windows itself treats the two types differently when they're executed, automatically allocating *console objects* for console applications. Although this feature was intended to simplify things, in practice it can make things more complicated. If a console application is launched from a Win32 application, the system will allocate a console window for the application, *even if that application will never use that window*. As a result, the user sees a console window suddenly appear. If the user is unaware of where the window is coming from, they're likely to close it, causing the console application to exit.

Now let's look at how this impacts the ISE. As mentioned, a console application has a console object that the application can use to perform full-screen interactions with the user. For most console applications, all they need to do is perform simple interactions like writing out some strings or reading from a redirected input. In these cases, the command works fine with the ISE because the ISE properly handles redirection.

But if the command tries to perform an interaction that requires calling one of the console APIs—especially if it tries to read from the console object (as opposed to the standard input stream)—it will appear to hang in the ISE. Of course, it's not really hung and can still be stopped by pressing Ctrl-C or Ctrl-Break, but it's generally better to prevent the hang in the first place. To address this, the ISE maintains a list of applications that are known not to work properly. For example, the full-screen editor edit.com doesn't work in the ISE, and trying to run it will result in the error message displayed in figure 15.9.

The list of applications that are blocked by the ISE is stored in a preference variable, `$psUnsupportedConsoleApplications`, and can be updated or edited by the user. The default list is as follows:

```
PS (STA) (5) > $psUnsupportedConsoleApplications
cmd
cmd.exe
diskpart
diskpart.exe
edit.com
netsh
netsh.exe
nslookup
nslookup.exe
powershell
powershell.exe
```

You might be surprised to see PowerShell on this list, but it uses the console object to read commands from the user so that tab completion and editing can work. So, if `PowerShell.exe` is just run as a command, reading and writing to pipes or with input redirected, it's allowed to run from the ISE. But if you try to run it interactively (which is determined by the fact that it's at the end of the pipeline), then it will be blocked.

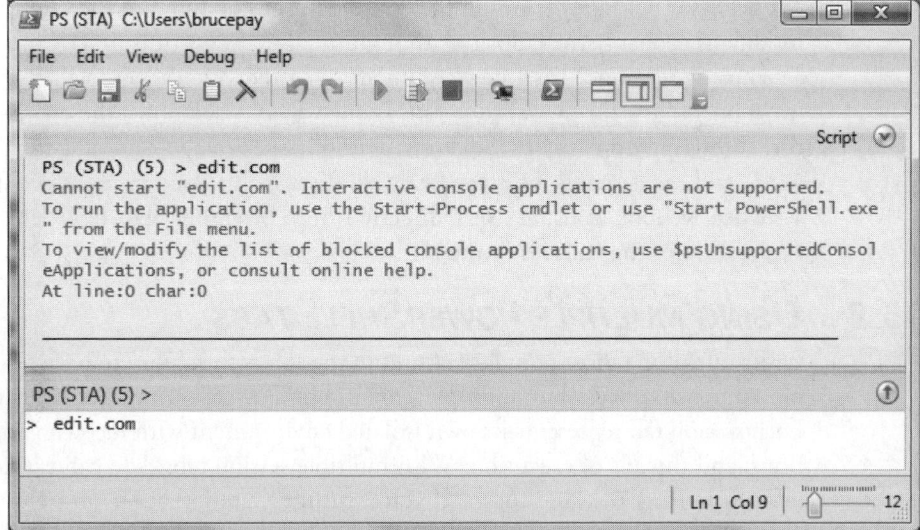

Figure 15.9 Interactive console applications that try to read from the console object aren't supported in the ISE and result in an error.

Threading differences between the console and the ISE

Another difference between the console host environment and the ISE is the default *threading apartment model*. The threading model primarily affects applications using COM (see chapter 18).

> **What is the apartment threading model?**
>
> In simplest terms, the threading apartment model controls the number of threads of execution in any single object at any given time. In the multithreaded apartment (MTA), multiple threads can be accessing an object at the same time, so if the object hasn't been carefully designed, it could suffer from race conditions. For example, two threads may be trying to update the same property at the same time, and it becomes a race to see whose change takes effect. These race conditions lead to very hard-to-track-down bugs.
>
> In the single-threaded apartment (STA), the system guarantees that only one thread is updating an object at a time, making everything much simpler. So why have MTA at all? Because for a lot of objects, multiple threads in the object may be fine—for example, they may only be reading data but not changing state. This type of concurrent access, in turn, leads to better performance characteristics, especially in this day of multicore processors.

The console host runs MTA by default but the ISE runs STA. This difference in threading model is where you may see occasional behavioral differences between the two environments when using COM. If you run into a situation where you see different behavior if a script is run in the console host as opposed to the ISE, the threading module is probably the culprit. Although the ISE always runs in STA mode, the console host in version 2 has a new argument `-Sta` that allows you to change the threading model to use for the session. This is one way to track down these COM problems: run the script from the console host without specifying `-Sta` and then again with `-Sta`, and see if there's a difference. We'll discuss this issue in more detail in chapter 17 when we look at using .NET directly from PowerShell. For now, let's resume our exploration of the features in the ISE.

15.2 USING MULTIPLE POWERSHELL TABS

Easily one of the most popular features in the ISE is the ability to have not just multiple editor instances, but multiple concurrent PowerShell *sessions* available as tabs. Each session tab represents its own isolated environment with its own variables, functions, and threads of execution. With multiple session tabs, you can execute multiple tasks from the same ISE process. If you're running a task that's taking a long time, you can simply start an additional tab in the ISE by pressing Ctrl-T. In fact, there are two types of session tabs, as you'll see in the next two sections: local and remote tabs.

15.2.1 Local in-memory session tabs

For the most part, sessions in separate tabs are isolated, but they are all executing in the same process. Given what you've seen with remoting and jobs, this might seem somewhat surprising. Up until now, we've pretty much implied there's one PowerShell session per process. In fact, it's possible to have an arbitrary number of session-like objects called *runspaces* in a single process, limited only by system resources.

> **What's a runspace?**
>
> You may (or may not) have heard the term *runspace* before. It shows up in discussions periodically but is usually not mentioned in the end-user documentation. Simply put, a runspace is a space where PowerShell commands can be run. This sounds pretty similar to how we described a PowerShell session in our discussion of remoting. In fact, each session contains an instance of a runspace object, visible as a property on the session object.
>
> So how did we end up with two terms? Here's what happened. Originally, there was only the runspace. Then we did some usability testing on remoting and discovered that the term really seemed to confuse users, with the common response being "so a runspace is just like a session—right?" Eventually, to minimize confusion, we added the `PSSession` object for end users and kept the *runspace* term for developers. (We also had to keep *runspace* because it's part of the PowerShell API.)

The runspace feature is primarily targeted at programmers and isn't normally exposed to the end user. In fact, the only place you're likely to encounter a runspace is with tabs in the ISE and even there it's pretty much invisible.

You don't need to care about this much except when you're doing things that affect the ISE's environment at the process level. In fact, the most obvious instances of a process-wide resource are environment variables and `$ENV`:. Because there's only one environment table per process, changes to the `$ENV:` in one tab will affect the other tabs.

Although this in-process tab model is efficient, to get real isolation between your sessions, you need to create additional processes. As you'll see in the next section, you can do so through remoting.

15.2.2 Remote session tabs in PowerShell ISE

In the previous section, we looked at how in-memory sessions work. The ISE also supports interactive remoting from within a tab (incidentally giving you process isolation between tabs). This means that a session tab can be connected to a remote computer. A remote session tab is effectively equivalent to calling the `Enter-PSSession` cmdlet in a local session tab, but rather than force you to start a local session and then create a remote session, the ISE treats this as a first-class experience, allowing you to create a remote tab directly.

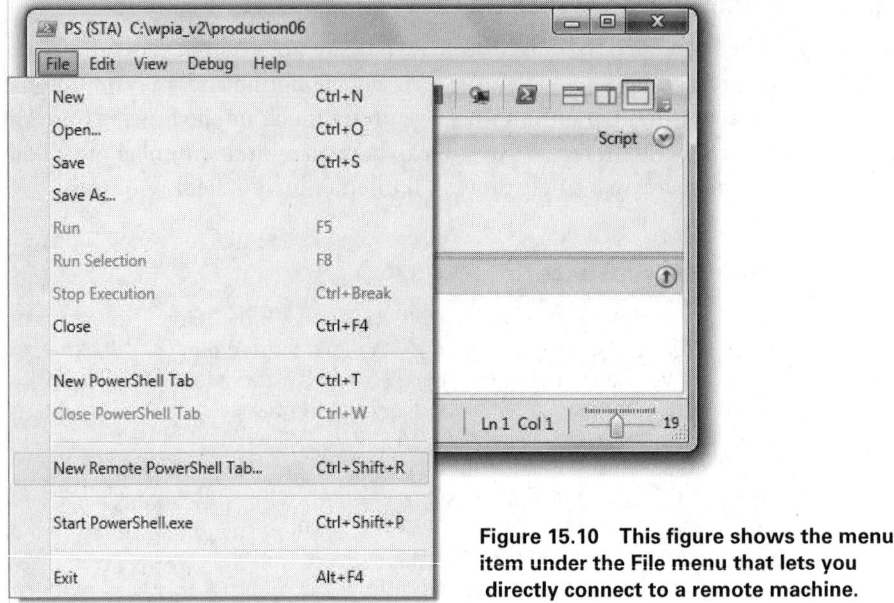

Figure 15.10 This figure shows the menu item under the File menu that lets you directly connect to a remote machine.

To start a remote connection, from the File menu select New Remote PowerShell Tab, as shown in figure 15.10.

Clicking this item will pop up a dialog (see figure 15.11) asking for the name of the target computer and who to connect as when connecting to that computer.

Figure 15.11 When using the ISE to connect to a remote computer, you will be prompted to enter the name of the computer to connect to and the username to use when connecting.

Fill in the name of the computer and the user to connect as, and then click Connect. At this point, a second credential dialog will be displayed, asking for the password for the specified user account.

> **NOTE** So why are there two dialogs? The credential dialog is a system dialog that provides for enhanced security and, as a result, has to be displayed separately.

Once you're connected to the remote endpoint, you'll see a new tab in the ISE that displays the name of the computer you're connected to. Figure 15.12 shows what this looks like.

Notice the content of the output pane: it shows the actual commands that were run to establish the remote connection. The `Enter-PSSession` is nothing new, but the line

```
if ($?) {$psISE.CurrentPowerShellTab.DisplayName = 'brucepayquad'}
```

is something you haven't seen so far.

If the `Enter-PSSession` command succeeds and a remote connection is established, then the value of the variable `$?` will be `$true`. When that happens, the PowerShell ISE *object model* is used to change the display name of the tab to the name of the remote computer. The object stored in `$psISE` is a .NET object that lets scripts manipulate the ISE itself. We'll look at using this object model in the next section.

In chapter 12, we discussed how interactive remoting works in the case where you're just using the console host. This is a relatively simple situation because the console host is effectively limited to one interactive session at a time. With the ISE,

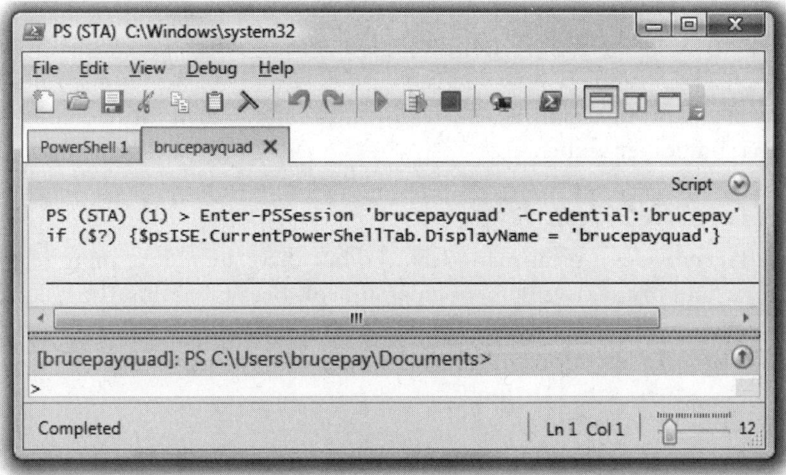

Figure 15.12 The PowerShell ISE allows you to have multiple sessions running at the same time. These sessions can be either local or remote. In this figure, the first tab is a local session and the second tab is a remote session connected to another computer.

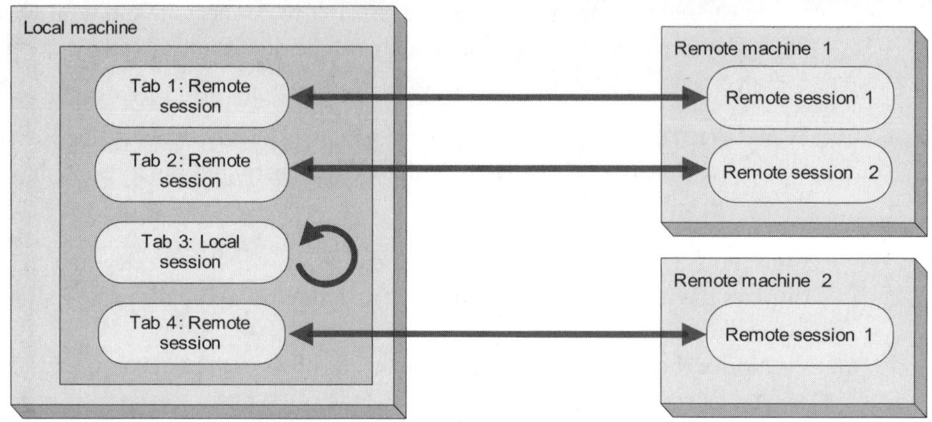

Figure 15.13 In the PowerShell ISE, the user may have multiple tabs open. Each tab has a session. Local tabs have local sessions, and remote tabs have remote sessions.

things are more sophisticated and therefore somewhat more complex. A graphical environment allows you to work with multiple sessions, including multiple local and remote sessions, where each session has its own tab in the interface. Figure 15.13 shows the arrangement of connections that you can set up with the ISE.

In this figure, you see that the ISE running on the local machine has three tabs open: two tabs connected to one remote machine, and one local table and one remote tab connected to machine 2. This illustrates the flexibility that the ISE provides, allowing you to easily work with multiple machines from a single ISE instance.

At this point, you should have a pretty good understanding of the ISE from a user perspective. In the next section, we'll look at the *object model*, mentioned earlier in section 15.2.2, and see how you can customize and extend the environment through scripting. This mechanism will allow you to bind your favorite commands to menu items and hotkey sequences.

15.3 EXTENDING THE ISE

The ISE provides a great many features, but there are always more features or tools you can add to any development environment. Because of this, the ISE provides a surprisingly easy-to-use (at least compared to a lot of other IDEs!) extension model that allows you to add your own features to the environment.

15.3.1 The $psISE variable

All extensibility points are available through the `$psISE` variable. This makes the object model easy to discover because you can use tab completion to navigate and

Get-Member to explore the objects. Here's what the output of Get-Member looks like for this object:

```
PS (STA) (3) > $psISE | Get-Member -MemberType Property |
>>Format-List name,definition

Name       : CurrentFile
Definition : Microsoft.PowerShell.Host.ISE.ISEFile CurrentFile {get;}

Name       : CurrentPowerShellTab
Definition : Microsoft.PowerShell.Host.ISE.PowerShellTab
CurrentPowerShellTab {get;}

Name       : Options
Definition : Microsoft.PowerShell.Host.ISE.ISEOptions Options {get;}

Name       : PowerShellTabs
Definition : Microsoft.PowerShell.Host.ISE.PowerShellTabCollection
PowerShellTabs {get;}
```

Table 15.2 shows each of these properties and provides a brief description of their purpose.

Table 15.2 The top-level properties in the ISE object model

Name	Description
CurrentFile	This object represents the file shown in the current editor pane. With this property, you can access the text in the buffer, save the file, and so on.
CurrentPowerShellTab	This gives you access to the tab currently in use—in other words, the one where you're typing your commands. Through this member, you can access file objects for all the files open in this table, add custom menu items, and so on.
Options	We looked at some of the various options that can be set for the ISE earlier in this chapter. Through the Options property, you can set additional options as well as perform the customization you saw earlier from a script.
PowerShellTabs	This gives a list of all the tabs in the session. You can perform the same operations from these tabs as you can for the current tab, but work with all the tabs in the process.

In the next few sections, we'll walk through these members and explore the kinds of things you can do with them. To help you orient your discovery, figure 15.14 provides a map showing the hierarchy of objects in the object model.

As we mentioned earlier, the most effective way to explore the contents of the object model is to start with $psISE and use tab completion to step through the properties. Let's begin our exploration with the Options property.

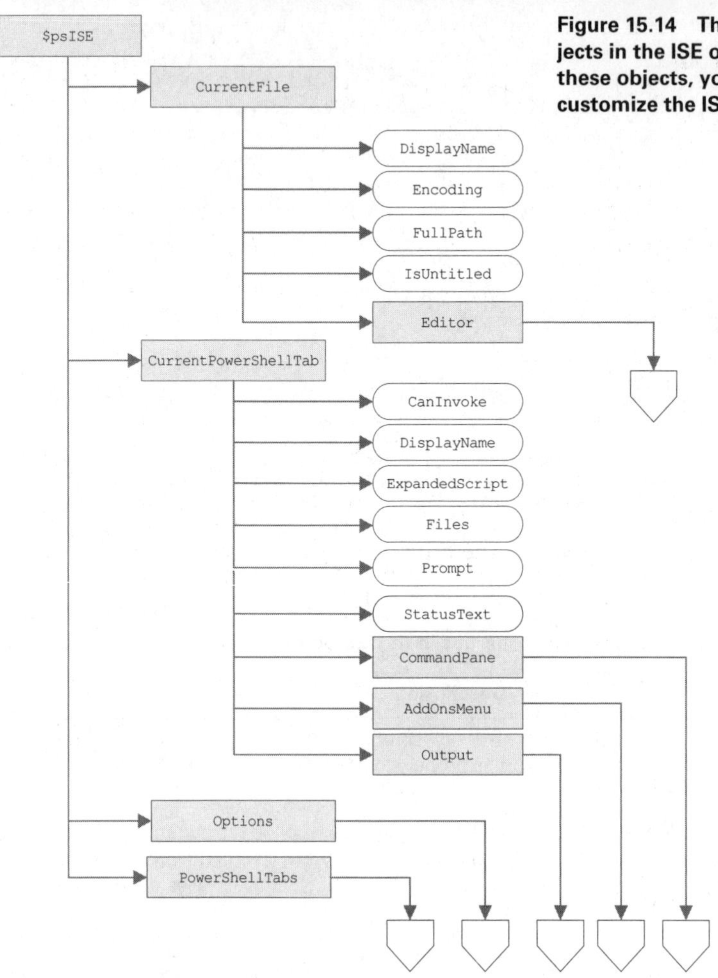

Figure 15.14 The hierarchy of objects in the ISE object model. Using these objects, you can extend and customize the ISE environment.

15.3.2 Using the Options property

The `Options` property lets you set a number of ISE options that aren't directly accessible from the menus. Let's use `Get-Member` to display the contents of this property:

```
PS (STA) (6) > $psISE.Options
SelectedScriptPaneState        : Top
ShowToolBar                    : True
TokenColors                    : {[Attribute, #FFADD8E6],
[Command, #FF0000FF], [CommandArgument, #FF8A2B
                                 E2], [CommandParameter, #FF000080]...}
DefaultOptions                 : Microsoft.PowerShell.Host.ISE.ISEOptions
FontSize                       : 12
FontName                       : Lucida Console
ErrorForegroundColor           : #FFFF0000
ErrorBackgroundColor           : #00FFFFFF
WarningForegroundColor         : #FFFF8C00
WarningBackgroundColor         : #00FFFFFF
```

```
VerboseForegroundColor         : #FF0000FF
VerboseBackgroundColor         : #00FFFFFF
DebugForegroundColor           : #FF0000FF
DebugBackgroundColor           : #00FFFFFF
OutputPaneBackgroundColor      : #FFF0F8FF
OutputPaneTextBackgroundColor  : #FFF0F8FF
OutputPaneForegroundColor      : #FF000000
CommandPaneBackgroundColor     : #FFFFFFFF
ScriptPaneBackgroundColor      : #FFFFFFFF
ScriptPaneForegroundColor      : #FF000000
ShowWarningForDuplicateFiles   : True
ShowWarningBeforeSavingOnRun   : False
UseLocalHelp                   : True
CommandPaneUp                  : False
```

You can see that a number of options correspond to the toolbar and menu items: `CommandPaneUp`, `ShowToolBar`, and so on. There are also a number of new options that let you set the colors of the various elements in the interface. You can control the foreground and background colors of each of the panes, as well as change the colors used to display tokens by assigning color values to these properties.

> **TIP** Although the output from the `Options` property shows numeric values for the color settings, you don't have to use them when assigning a value to the properties. You can use color names like red or blue in assignments and the type converter will do the necessary work to convert the string to the corresponding color value.

Through the `Options` property, you can write scripts that can automatically configure the ISE the way you want. This stuff is pretty obvious, so we'll move on to something a bit more exotic (and useful!).

15.3.3 Managing tabs and files

The top-level objects in the ISE are tabs, which in turn contain editor instances. To get a list of the tabs, use the `PowerShellTabs` property. You can do this interactively from the command pane. We'll try setting up an ISE instance with the arrangement of tabs as shown in figure 15.15.

Open the ISE, and press Ctrl-T to create a second session tab. Then, in the command pane, run the following command:

```
PS (STA) (13) > $psise.PowerShellTabs

DisplayName    : PowerShell 1
AddOnsMenu     : Microsoft.PowerShell.Host.ISE.ISEMenuItem
StatusText     : Running script / selection.  Press Ctrl+Break to stop.
ExpandedScript : True
Prompt         : PS (STA) (13) >
CommandPane    : Microsoft.Windows.PowerShell.Gui.Internal.CommandEditor
Output         : Microsoft.Windows.PowerShell.Gui.Internal.OutputEditor
Files          : {Untitled1.ps1*}
CanInvoke      : False
```

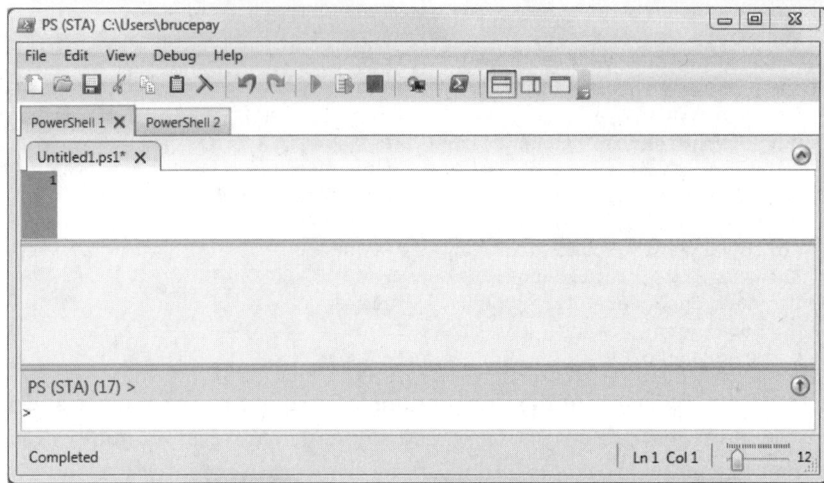

Figure 15.15 This is the arrangement of panes in the ISE we'll use in our examples. In this case, the ISE has two tabs open and the current tab is labeled PowerShell 1.

```
DisplayName     : PowerShell 2
AddOnsMenu      : Microsoft.PowerShell.Host.ISE.ISEMenuItem
StatusText      :
ExpandedScript  : False
Prompt          : PS (STA) (1) >
CommandPane     : Microsoft.Windows.PowerShell.Gui.Internal.CommandEditor
Output          : Microsoft.Windows.PowerShell.Gui.Internal.OutputEditor
Files           : {}
CanInvoke       : True
```

In the output from this command, you see the list of the tabs currently open in the ISE. This output shows you the `DisplayName` of the tab, the current prompt value, the text in the status line, and so on. In the PowerShell 1 session tab, where the command ran, you see the status of this tab is "running a script," which, of course is the command you just typed. Because it's running a command, you also see that the `CanInvoke` property is false, indicating that this tab is busy executing a command. If you look at the output for PowerShell 2, the status text is blank and the `CanInvoke` property is true, indicating that there's no command running in that tab.

Now let's look at the methods on this session tab object. Because the output from the previous command returned a collection, we'll look at the second item (representing the tab you're not currently using) with `Get-Member`:

```
PS (STA) (17) > $psISE.PowerShellTabs[1] | Get-Member -type method

   TypeName: Microsoft.PowerShell.Host.ISE.PowerShellTab

Name        MemberType Definition
----        ---------- ----------
Equals      Method     bool Equals(System.Object obj)
GetHashCode Method     int GetHashCode()
GetType     Method     type GetType()
```

```
Invoke       Method     System.Void Invoke(scriptblock script)
ToString     Method     string ToString()
```

Notice that this object has an `Invoke()` method, which will invoke a command in that tab. Let's try it out. It takes a scriptblock as an argument, so use the `Create()` method on `[ScriptBlock]` to compile the code you want to run:

```
PS (STA) (27) > $sb =[ScriptBlock]::Create('1..20 | %{sleep 1; Get-Date} ')
```

The scriptblock contains a number of calls to `sleep` (the alias for `Start-Sleep`) to make sure it's running long enough to see what's going on. Let's verify that you can invoke your scriptblock in the other tab:

```
PS (STA) (28) > $psISE.PowerShellTabs[1].CanInvoke
True
```

Checking the `CanInvoke` property for that tab confirms that you can execute, so call `Invoke()` on your scriptblock:

```
PS (STA) (30) > $psISE.PowerShellTabs[1].Invoke($sb)
```

The call to `Invoke()` starts the scriptblock executing in the other tab, then returns immediately rather than waiting until the command finishes execution. Let's check the `CanInvoke` property again to verify that the command is running. This time you expect the property to return false, and it does:

```
PS (STA) (31) > $psISE.PowerShellTabs[1].CanInvoke
False
```

Now switch to the PowerShell 2 tab and look at the output (figure 15.16).

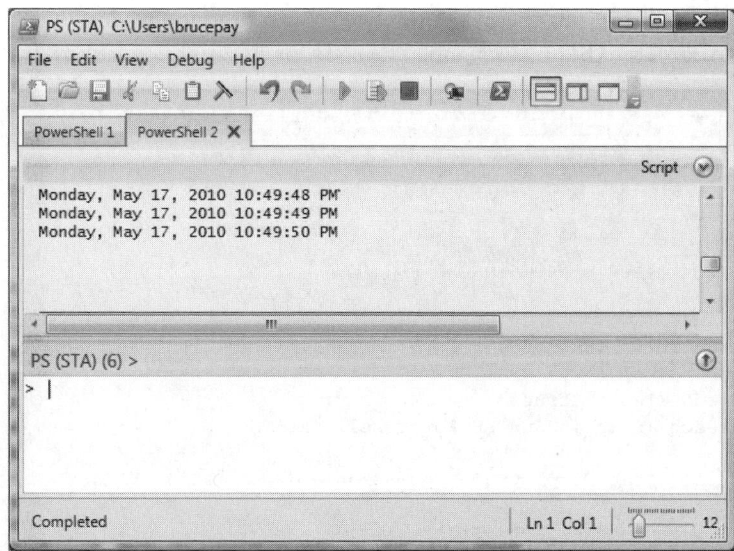

Figure 15.16 This tab shows the output of our script. Although you started the script in the first tab, it's actually run in the second tab with the output displayed in that tab.

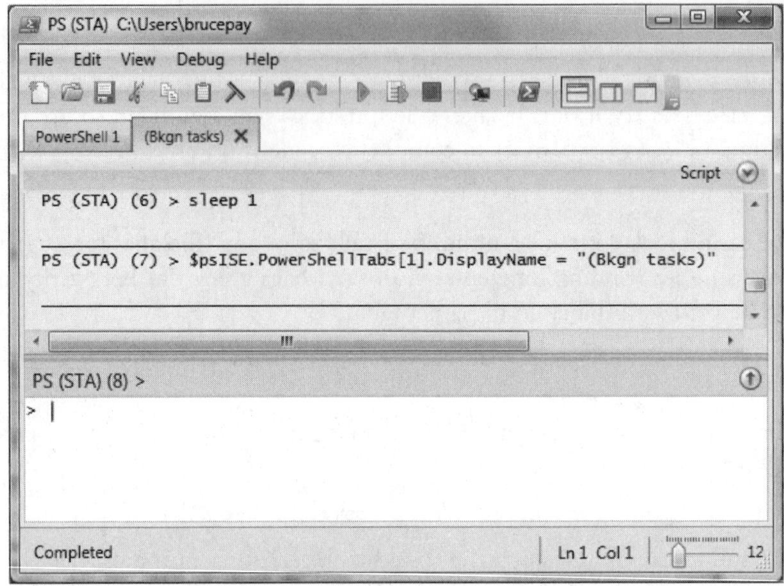

Figure 15.17 Changing the display name of the current tab to (Bkgn tasks)

In the output pane of the PowerShell 2 tab, you see the results of the command you ran. In effect, you're using the second tab to do background processing. It'd be nice if you could have a better name for this tab. You can use the `DisplayName` property on the tab object to change it, as shown in figure 15.17.

Finally, you can put the pieces together into a function to automatically invoke a scriptblock on the (Bkgn tasks) tab. The code for this function is shown in this listing.

Listing 15.1 The `Invoke-InBackgroundTab` function

```
function Invoke-InBackgroundTab
{
    param (
        [parameter(mandatory=$true)]
            $ScriptBlockToInvoke
    )

    $bkgnTab = '(Bkgn tasks)'
    $tab = $null
    $needNewTab = $true
    foreach ($tab in $psISE.PowerShellTabs)
    {
        if ($tab.DisplayName -eq $bkgnTab)
        {
            $needNewTab = $false
            break
        }
    }
```

```
    if ($needNewTab)
    {
        $tab = $psISE.PowerShellTabs.Add()
        $tab.DisplayName = $bkgnTab
        do {
            Start-Sleep -Milliseconds 200
        }
        while (-not $tab.CanInvoke)
    }
    if (! $tab.CanInvoke)
    {
        Write-Error `
         "Background tab is currently busy. Try again later"
    }
    $tab.Invoke($ScriptBlockToInvoke)
}
Set-Alias ibg Invoke-InBackgroundTab
```

Creates background tab if necessary

Runs only one background task

Invokes scriptblock

First, this function searches for the target tab and, if it doesn't exist, it creates a new tab. When it finds the tab, if it's not already busy, the scriptblock is invoked and the output is shown in the target tab's output pane.

This relatively simple example gives you an idea of how you can work with tabs. You can perform sophisticated operations with very little code. In the next section, we're going to look at how to work with the elements inside a tab: the editor and output panes.

15.3.4 Working with text panes

During script creation, you spend most of your time in the command and editor panes and the results of executing commands are shown in the output pane. As was the case with tabs, the ISE object model allows you to manipulate the contents of these panes using scripts. Using this capability, you can add custom tools to extend the built-in set of editor functions. Let's start by exploring what you can do with the output pane.

Saving the output pane contents

In chapter 14, we discussed how you can use the transcript facility in the console host to capture the output of your commands for later examination. The ISE doesn't have a corresponding transcript mechanism, but you can still copy the contents of the output pane to a file. As before, you start with the `$psISE` variable to access the contents of the output pane. Let's use `Get-Member` to see what this looks like:

```
PS (STA) (94) > $psISE.CurrentPowerShellTab.Output |
  Get-Member -MemberType method,property

   TypeName: Microsoft.Windows.PowerShell.Gui.Internal.OutputEditor

Name               MemberType Definition
----               ---------- ----------
Clear              Method     System.Void Clear()
EnsureVisible      Method     System.Void EnsureVisible(int lineNumber)
```

```
Equals            Method     bool Equals(System.Object obj)
Focus             Method     System.Void Focus()
GetHashCode       Method     int GetHashCode()
GetLineLength     Method     int GetLineLength(int lineNumber)
GetType           Method     type GetType()
InsertText        Method     System.Void InsertText(string text)
Select            Method     System.Void Select(int startLine, int
startColumn, int endLine, int endColumn)
SetCaretPosition Method      System.Void SetCaretPosition(int lineNumber,
int columnNumber)
ToString          Method     string ToString()
CaretColumn       Property   System.Int32 CaretColumn {get;}
CaretLine         Property   System.Int32 CaretLine {get;}
LineCount         Property   System.Int32 LineCount {get;}
SelectedText      Property   System.String SelectedText {get;}
Text              Property   System.String Text {get;set;}
```

Looking at the members on this object, you see that there are members available to select text in the pane, insert text, and so on. You're looking for one specific member: the `Text` property itself. This property gives you access to the full text in the output pane, which you can save to a file by using redirection:

```
PS (STA) (22) > $psISE.CurrentPowerShellTab.Output.Text > output.txt
```

This command copies the contents of the output pane to a file called output.txt. You can then use Notepad to look at this file:

```
PS (STA) (23) > notepad output.txt
```

The results of this command are shown in figure 15.18.

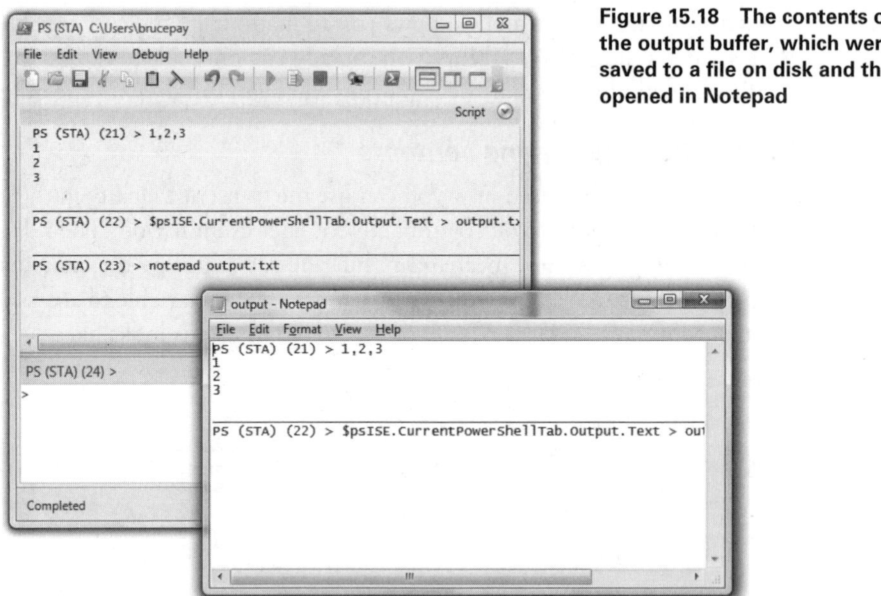

Figure 15.18 The contents of the output buffer, which were saved to a file on disk and then opened in Notepad

We used Notepad to display this output rather than use the ISE so you can see both the output and the contents of the saved file at the same time. Next, we'll look at the object model for the editor pane and see what you can do with that.

Making changes in the editor pane

You've seen how to save the contents of the output pane to a file, but you're limited in what you can do in this pane because it's read-only. With the editor pane, you're also able to change the contents of the `Text` property. Let's see how to do this by working through an example where you'll rename a variable in the editor buffer. Your task will be to replace the `$tab` variable name in listing 15.1 with the more descriptive `$currentTab`.

Assuming the listing is loaded in the current editor pane, let's see how lines of the function reference this variable. You can do so with the following command:

```
PS (STA) (110) > $psISE.CurrentFile.Editor.Text -split "`n" -match '\$tab'
    $tab = $null
    foreach ($tab in $psISE.PowerShellTabs)
        if ($tab.DisplayName -eq $bkgnTab)
        $tab = $psISE.PowerShellTabs.Add()
        $tab.DisplayName = $bkgnTab
        while (-not $tab.CanInvoke)
    if (-not $tab.CanInvoke)
    $tab.Invoke($ScriptBlockToInvoke)
```

In this command, because the text in the editor buffer is returned as a single file, you use the `-split` operator to split the text at newline characters and then use the `-match` operator to see the lines containing the pattern. To get a simple count, just use this:

```
PS (STA) (111) > ($psISE.CurrentFile.Editor.Text -split "`n" `
>> -match '\$tab').Count
8
```

We'll look at modifying the text in the editor using the object model next. However, before we do that, let's copy the text to another editor buffer. Direct updates to the contents of the editor panes aren't tracked by the normal undo mechanism, but by making a copy, you're providing your own "undo" mechanism in case something goes wrong. First, get a reference to the current tab:

```
$curFile = $psISE.CurrentFile
```

You'll use this to get at the contents of the editor. Create a new file tab and save the result in the `$newFile` variable:

```
$newFile = $psISE.CurrentPowerShellTab.Files.Add()
```

When you run this command, the tab you just created will become the currently displayed file tab. Now you can use the reference to the original file tab to get the text source text. Using the -replace operator, you can make the replacement and assign the result to the Text property on the editor object in the new file tab:

```
$newFile.Editor.Text = $curFile.Editor.Text -replace '\$tab', '$currentTab'
```

This command will also set the new buffer to be the current buffer so you can see the results of your operation.

Finally, if you want to set current file back to the original file, use this:

```
$psISE.CurrentPowerShellTab.Files.SetSelectedFile($curFile)
```

which changes the current file tab back to the original.

In the next section, we'll look at an example where you work with both tabs and editor panes to save the state of the ISE.

Saving the list of open files

With the ability to have multiple session tabs with multiple files open, you can end up with a lot of files open, working on different parts of a project. Unfortunately, the ISE doesn't have a project mechanism to keep track of all these files. But now that you know how to work with both session tabs and file tabs, you can write your own tool to save a list of the files you're working with. A function to do this is shown in the following listing.

Listing 15.2 A function that saves the list of currently open files in the ISE

```
$PathToSavedISEState =
    "~/documents/WindowsPowerShell/SavedISEState.ps1xml"     <-- Save list of files
function Save-ISEState
{
    $state = foreach ($tab in $psISE.PowerShellTabs)
    {
        foreach ($file in $tab.Files)                <-- Loop through each file in tab
        {
            if ($file.FullPath)
            {
                @{
                    Tab = $tab.DisplayName             <-- Use hashtable for data
                    DisplayName = $file.DisplayName
                    FullPath = $file.FullPath
                }
            }
        }
    }
    $state | Export-Clixml $PathToSavedISEState
}
```

This function loops through all of the ISE tabs and then the files in each tab. For the file tabs that have been saved (and therefore have a file path), the code builds a hashtable containing the information you need to restore the tabs. This data is saved to the target file using the CliXML format (essentially equivalent to the way remoting serialization works).

Now you need a way to read the data back. This task turns out to be quite simple, as shown by the following function:

```
function Get-SavedISEState
{
    Import-Clixml $PathToSavedISEState
}
```

Using the `Import-Clixml` cmdlet, you can re-create the collection of hashtables you saved.

Reading the data isn't as interesting as reloading the files, so the following listing shows a function that does this as well.

Listing 15.3 A function that restores the file tabs

```
function Restore-ISEState
{
    $tab = ""
    Import-Clixml $PathToSavedISEState |        <-- Reload saved hashtables
        foreach {
            if ($_.Tab -ne $tab)
            {
                $targetTab = $psise.PowerShellTabs.Add()
                $tab = $_.Tab
            }
            $targetTab.Files.Add($_.FullPath)      <-- Add file to current tab
        }
}
```

This function loads the data and then loops through the hashtables. If the name of the target tab in the hashtable doesn't match the current tab name, a new tab is created and the file is added to the new tab. This isn't a perfect solution—it always creates new tabs—but it shows how this type of operation can be performed.

So far, all of our ISE object model examples have required that you type commands in the command pane to do things. In the next section, you'll learn how to speed things up by adding menu items and hotkeys to execute your extensions.

15.3.5 Adding a custom menu

In this section, you'll see how to add custom menu items and hotkeys to the ISE. You do so by accessing the `AddOnsMenu` property on the tab object:

```
$psise.CurrentPowerShellTab.AddOnsMenu
```

> **NOTE** This property is associated with a specific tab. This means it isn't possible to add a custom menu item to all tabs through a single API call. On the other hand, it means that different tabs can have different custom menus, allowing for task-specialized tabs. Of course, if you do want to add a menu item automatically to each tab, you can put the code into your profile, which is run every time a new tab is created.

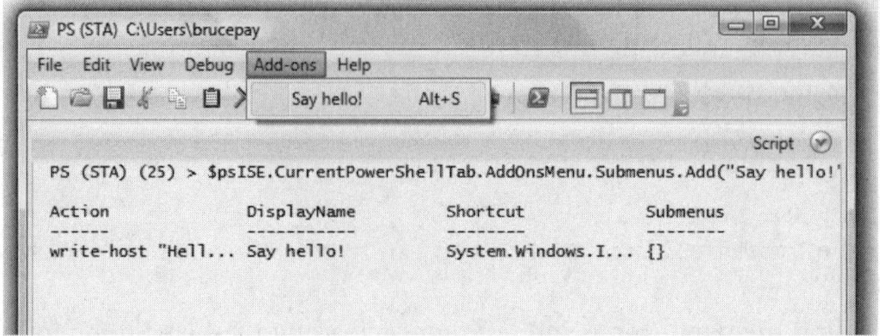

Figure 15.19 When you add a custom menu item, it always appears under the Add-ons menu. The first time a custom item is added, the Add-ons item appears on the menu bar.

Custom menu items are always added as submenus of the Add-ons menu. By default, the Add-ons menu isn't displayed until the first custom menu item is added. When this happens, the menu will appear. Start by adding a simple menu item that just prints some text to the output pane. The command to do this is

```
$psISE.CurrentPowerShellTab.AddOnsMenu.Submenus.Add("Say hello!",
    {Write-Host "Hello there"}, "Alt+s")
```

This command adds a submenu item with the name Say hello!, a scriptblock that defines the action to take, and a hotkey sequence to invoke the item from the keyboard. Figure 15.19 shows what the added menu item looks like.

In this figure, you can see that executing this command returns the object representing this menu item. If you try to add another item with the same hotkey sequence, you'll get an error:

```
PS (STA) (26) > $psISE.CurrentPowerShellTab.AddOnsMenu.Submenus.Add(
    "Say hello!", {Write-Host "Hello there"}, "Alt+s")
Exception calling "Add" with "3" argument(s): "The menu 'Say hello!'
uses shortcut 'Alt+S', which is already
in use by the menu or editor functionality."
At line:1 char:52
+ $psISE.CurrentPowerShellTab.AddOnsMenu.Submenus.Add <<<<
("Say hello!", {Write-Host "Hello there"}, "Alt+s"
)
    + CategoryInfo          : NotSpecified: (:) [],
MethodInvocationException
    + FullyQualifiedErrorId : DotNetMethodTargetInvocation
```

But you can add a second item with the same name as long as there's no colliding hotkey sequence associated with it:

```
PS (STA) (29) > $psISE.CurrentPowerShellTab.AddOnsMenu.Submenus.Add(
"Say hello!", {Write-Host "Hello there"}, $null)

Action                     DisplayName       Shortcut       Submenus
------                     -----------       --------       --------
Write-Host "Hello there" Say hello!                               {}
```

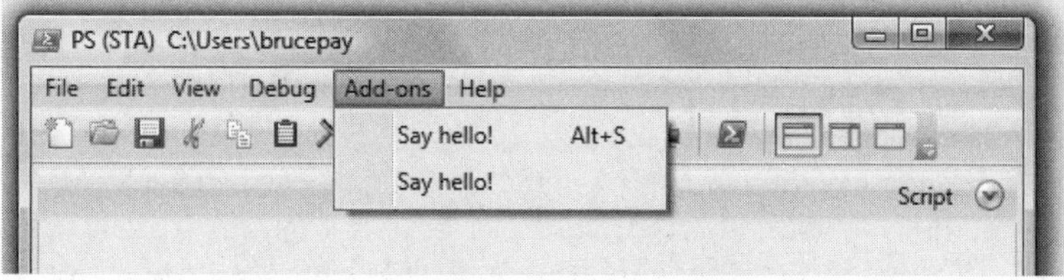

Figure 15.20 The Add-ons menu can have more than one item with the name caption. If you add a second item with the same caption, two items with the same caption will be displayed, but you can't have two items with the same shortcut key.

Adding this second item adds another item to the menu instead of replacing the existing one, as you can see in figure 15.20.

Although you can't modify an existing item, you can remove it and add a new item to replace it. Items in the submenu collection can be accessed like an array:

```
PS (STA) (33) > $psISE.CurrentPowerShellTab.AddOnsMenu.Submenus[0]

Action               DisplayName          Shortcut             Submenus
------               -----------          --------             --------
Write-Host "Hello... Say hello!           System.Windows.I... {}
```

This code returns the corresponding menu item, which you'll need in order to remove the item:

```
PS (STA) (36) > $mi = $psISE.CurrentPowerShellTab.AddOnsMenu.Submenus[0]
PS (STA) (37) > $psISE.CurrentPowerShellTab.AddOnsMenu.Submenus.Remove($mi)
True
```

In this example, first you retrieve the menu item and then pass that object to the `Remove()` method. If you check the Add-ons menu item, you'll see that the item has been removed. If you want to remove all the items, run the following code:

```
foreach ($item in @($psISE.CurrentPowerShellTab.AddOnsMenu.Submenus))
{
  $psISE.CurrentPowerShellTab.AddOnsMenu.Submenus.Remove($item)
}
```

This code gathers the collection of menu items to remove and then loops over the collection, removing them one at a time.

Modifying collections

There's a trick in this example that's useful to know. You'd normally expect to be able to use the `Submenus` collection directly in the `foreach` loop. A problem arises, though, when you remove items from the collection you're cycling through. This occurs because the `foreach` statement uses a .NET enumerator to keep track of where you are in the collection. If you remove an item from the collection, the enu-

> ***(continued)***
>
> merator won't match the collection anymore. To avoid problems with inconsistency in the collection, an error is raised.
>
> To get around this problem, you need to create an intermediate collection of the submenu items. In PowerShell, doing so is easy: simply use the `@(...expression...)` operator. This operator evaluates the expression it contains and returns a new collection containing the results of that evaluation. Because the new collection is a snapshot of the collection you're changing, the problem goes away.

A simpler way to remove all menu items is to call the `Clear()` method on the `Submenus` collection:

```
$psISE.CurrentPowerShellTab.AddOnsMenu.Submenus.Clear()
```

But the looping solution is more general in that you can selectively remove menu items by adding conditions to the body of the `foreach` statement.

Let's make our example a little more sophisticated. Add some code to prompt the user for a name to display. You can use the host object's prompt function to do this:

```
$sb = {
  $name = Read-Host "Enter the name of the person to say hi to"
  Write-Host "Hello name!"
}
$psISE.CurrentPowerShellTab.AddOnsMenu.Submenus.Add("Say hello!",
$sb, $null)
```

This code will cause a message box to be displayed, as you can see in figure 15.21.

The ability to prompt the user for input significantly increases what you can do with your extensions. For example, you can add a search tool that wraps around when it reaches the end of the editor buffer. But you can try that on your own. Right now, we'll move on to something else that's also quite useful.

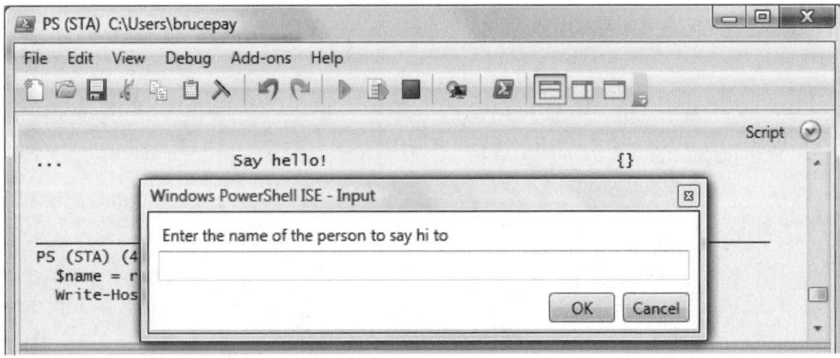

Figure 15.21 The prompt from the example menu item looks like this.

Adding a file checker menu item

Let's look at a more useful example. In chapter 14, you learned how to use the PowerShell tokenizer API to check a script for certain kinds of errors. This ability is pretty handy in the ISE, so let's add it as a menu item. The code for this appears in the following listing.

Listing 15.4 Script code that adds a syntax checker to the ISE

```
function Test-Buffer
{
    $text = $psISE.CurrentFile.Editor.Text
    $out=$null
    $tokens = [management.automation.psparser]::Tokenize($text, [ref] $out)
    $out | fl message, @{
        n="line";
        e = {
            "{0} char: {1}" -f $_.Token.StartLine, $_.Token.StartColumn
        }
    }
}
$psISE.CurrentPowerShellTab.AddOnsMenu.Submenus.Add("Test Buffer",
  {Test-Buffer}, "Control+F5")
```

The code in listing 15.4 adds a custom menu item that will run the script-checking code when you press Ctrl-F5 (as opposed to pressing F5, which actually runs the script). This turns out to be a surprisingly handy feature. Although the ISE does syntax highlighting, when there's an error, it just stops the highlighting without showing you the error. Using the extension you just added, you can find the syntax errors without having to run the script.

A submenu for snippets

We'll look at one final example where you create a custom nested menu. In this example, you want to create a Snippets menu showing various PowerShell examples. Because there are multiple items, you'll add this as a submenu of the Add-ons menu. The next listing shows the necessary code.

Listing 15.5 Adding a Snippets menu

```
$snippetText = @'                                          <- Define snippets
if ($true) { "if-Part" } elseif { "elseif-Part" } else { "else-Part" }
while ($true) { Write-Host "in while loop" }
foreach ($i in 1..10) { $i; Write-Host "i is $i" }
for ($i=1; $i -lt 20; $i++) { $i }
function basicFunc ($p1, $p2) { $p1 + $p2 }
'@ -split "`n"                                   <- Split on newlines

$addOns = $psISE.CurrentPowerShellTab.AddOnsMenu
$snippets = $addOns.Submenus.Add("snippets", $null, $null)   <- Add top-level Snippets menu
```

```
foreach ($snip in $snippetText )
{
    [void] $snippets.SubMenus.Add($snip, {
            $psise.CurrentFile.Editor.InsertText($snip)
        }.GetNewClosure(),
        $null)
}
```

Add each line as submenu

Use closure to capture text

Most of this function is straightforward. You use a here-string to define the snippets and then split it into individual lines with the `-split` operator. Then you define a top-level Snippets menu that has no action and add each line as a submenu of the top-level menu. The one somewhat unusual thing is the use of a *closure* (see chapter 11) and then defining the action. This closure captures the value of the `$snip` variable so the code to insert the text is very simple.

In the first part of this chapter, we introduced the ISE and spent a fair amount of time on how to customize the ISE using the object model. Having a more modern environment like the ISE makes scripting in PowerShell much easier, but the biggest advantage is the integrated debugger. Through the remainder of this chapter, we'll look at how to use the debugging feature built into the ISE to debug your scripts. You'll also see how to use the debugger from the command line and the additional features it has to offer. Combined, the ISE and debugger provide powerful tools for debugging scripts in a variety of environments.

15.4 POWERSHELL SCRIPT DEBUGGING FEATURES

This section covers the various tools and techniques for debugging PowerShell scripts. PowerShell v1 didn't include a debugger but did have some limited tracing capabilities. Version 2 introduced a much more comprehensive debugger along with graphical debugging support in the ISE. We'll start by looking at the limited (but still useful) tracing features carried over from v1. Then you'll learn how to debug from the ISE. Finally, you'll see the command-line debugger and the additional capabilities it has to offer.

15.4.1 The Set-PSDebug cmdlet

In chapter 14, we introduced the `Set-PSDebug` cmdlet and talked about using it to set the PowerShell v1 strict mode. In this section, we'll cover the remaining features, tracing and stepping through scripts, that this cmdlet offers. The syntax for this command is shown in figure 15.22.

The details of each of these features are covered in the following sections.

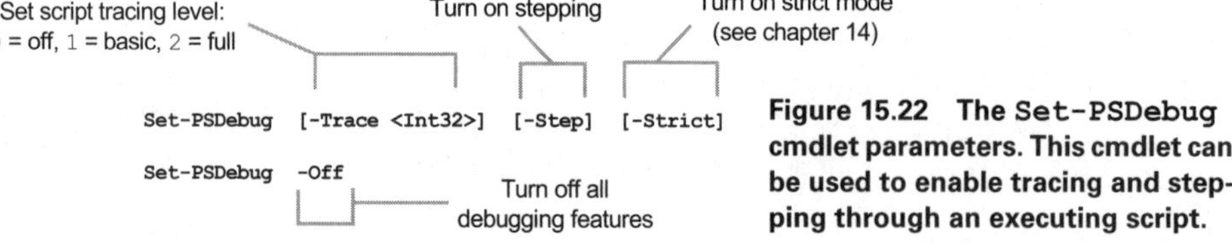

Figure 15.22 The `Set-PSDebug` cmdlet parameters. This cmdlet can be used to enable tracing and stepping through an executing script.

Tracing statement execution

You turn on basic script tracing as follows:

```
PS (1) > Set-PSDebug -Trace 1
```

In this trace mode, each statement executed by the interpreter will be displayed on the console as shown:

```
PS (2) > 2+2
DEBUG:    1+ 2+2
4
PS (3) > $a=3
DEBUG:    1+ $a=3
PS (4) > pwd
DEBUG:    1+ pwd

Path
----
C:\files
```

The debugging output is prefixed with the `DEBUG:` tag and is typically shown in a different color than normal text. Note that the entire script line is displayed. This means that if you have a loop all on one line, you'll see the line repeated:

```
PS (5) > foreach ($i in 1..3) {"i is $i"}
DEBUG:    1+ foreach ($i in 1..3) {"i is $i"}
DEBUG:    1+ foreach ($i in 1..3) {"i is $i"}
i is 1
DEBUG:    1+ foreach ($i in 1..3) {"i is $i"}
i is 2
DEBUG:    1+ foreach ($i in 1..3) {"i is $i"}
i is 3
```

In this example, you see the line repeated four times: once for evaluating the expression `1..3` in the `foreach` loop and then once for each iteration of the loop, for a total of four times. This is a good reason, even though PowerShell doesn't require it, to write scripts with one statement per line: it can help with debugging, both when tracing and when using the debugger to set breakpoints.

Basic tracing doesn't show you any function calls or scripts you're executing. First, define a function `foo`:

```
PS (6) > function foo {"`$args is " + $args}
DEBUG:    1+ function foo {"`$args is " + $args}
```

And run it in a loop:

```
PS (7) > foreach ($i in 1..3) {foo $i}
DEBUG:    1+ foreach ($i in 1..3) {foo $i}
DEBUG:    1+ foreach ($i in 1..3) {foo $i}
DEBUG:    1+ function foo {"`$args is " + $args}
$args is 1
DEBUG:    1+ foreach ($i in 1..3) {foo $i}
DEBUG:    1+ function foo {"`$args is " + $args}
```

```
$args is 2
DEBUG:    1+ foreach ($i in 1..3) {foo $i}
DEBUG:    1+ function foo {"`$args is " + $args}
$args is 3
```

In this output, you can only see the line that's being executed. You don't see when you enter the actual function. To get this extra information, you need to turn on full tracing:

```
PS (8) > Set-PSDebug -Trace 2
DEBUG:    1+ Set-PSDebug -Trace 2
```

In this mode, you also see the function calls:

```
PS (9) > foreach ($i in 1..3) {foo $i}
DEBUG:    1+ foreach ($i in 1..3) {foo $i}
DEBUG:    1+ foreach ($i in 1..3) {foo $i}
DEBUG:     ! CALL function 'foo'
DEBUG:    1+ function foo {"`$args is " + $args}
$args is 1
DEBUG:    1+ foreach ($i in 1..3) {foo $i}
DEBUG:     ! CALL function 'foo'
DEBUG:    1+ function foo {"`$args is " + $args}
$args is 2
DEBUG:    1+ foreach ($i in 1..3) {foo $i}
DEBUG:     ! CALL function 'foo'
DEBUG:    1+ function foo {"`$args is " + $args}
$args is 3
```

In addition to function calls, full tracing adds to the display by showing variable assignments. Let's redefine the function so that it performs a variable assignment. We'll split it across multiple lines so the trace is a bit clearer:

```
PS (10) > function foo {
>> $x = $args[0]
>> "x is $x"
>> }
>>
DEBUG:    1+ function foo {
```

And run it again:

```
PS (11) > foreach ($i in 1..3) {foo $i}
DEBUG:    1+ foreach ($i in 1..3) {foo $i}
DEBUG:    1+ foreach ($i in 1..3) {foo $i}
DEBUG:     ! CALL function 'foo'
DEBUG:    2+ $x = $args[0]
DEBUG:     ! SET $x = '1'.
DEBUG:    3+ "x is $x"
}
x is 1
DEBUG:    1+ foreach ($i in 1..3) {foo $i}
DEBUG:     ! CALL function 'foo'
DEBUG:    2+ $x = $args[0]
DEBUG:     ! SET $x = '2'.
DEBUG:    3+ "x is $x"
```

```
}
x is 2
DEBUG:     1+ foreach ($i in 1..3) {foo $i}
DEBUG:      ! CALL function 'foo'
DEBUG:     2+ $x = $args[0]
DEBUG:      ! SET $x = '3'.
DEBUG:     3+ "x is $x"
}
x is 3
```

You can see that for each iteration in the loop, tracing shows the following:

- Loop iteration
- Function call
- Statement doing the assignment
- Actual assignment to `$x`, including the value assigned
- Statement that emits the value

The value displayed is the string representation of the object being assigned, truncated to fit in the display. It depends on the `ToString()` method defined for that object to decide what to display. This isn't always as useful as you'd like. For example, with the hashtable

```
PS (12) > $a = @{x=1; y=2}
DEBUG:     1+ $a = @{x=1; y=2}
DEBUG:      ! SET $a = 'System.Collections.Hashtable'.
```

it shows you the type of the object, but nothing about its actual value. For arrays and other collections, it shows you a truncated representation of the elements of the list. So, for an array of 100 numbers, you see this:

```
PS (13) > $a = 1..100
DEBUG:     1+ $a = 1..100
DEBUG:      ! SET $a = '1 2 3 4 5 6 7 8 9 10 11 12 13 14 15 16 17
 18 19 20 21 22 23...'.
```

Overall, script tracing is pretty effective, but sometimes you still need to add calls to `Write-Host` to your script to help with debugging, as we mentioned in chapter 14.

Debugging scripts run by other people

The other thing we mentioned in chapter 14 was the transcript capability. Transcripts combined with tracing provide a valuable tool to help with debugging scripts that are being run by other people in your organization. By capturing the trace output in a transcript file, you can get a much better idea of what a script is doing in the other user's environment.

Tracing is also valuable in debugging remote scripts where you can't use the ISE debugger, as you'll see later in this chapter.

Stepping through statement execution

The next debugging feature we'll look at is the mechanism that PowerShell provides for stepping through a script.

> **NOTE** Like the tracing mechanism, this stepping feature is also a carryover from PowerShell v1. It's largely subsumed by the ISE debugger, but there are some advanced scenarios, such as debugging dynamically generated code, where it's still very useful. For example, if you use `[ScriptBlock]::Create()` to dynamically generate a scriptblock, you can't set a breakpoint because you don't have a line number in a file to use to set the breakpoint. More on this later.

You turn stepping on by calling the `Set-PSDebug` cmdlet with the `-Step` parameter:

```
PS (14) > Set-PSDebug -Step
DEBUG:    1+ Set-PSDebug -Step
```

Rerun the `foreach` loop and take a look at the prompt that's displayed:

```
PS (15) > foreach ($i in 1..3) {foo $i}

Continue with this operation?
   1+ foreach ($i in 1..3) {foo $i}
[Y] Yes  [A] Yes to All  [N] No  [L] No to All  [S] Suspend
[?] Help(default is "Y"): y
DEBUG:    1+ foreach ($i in 1..3) {foo $i}

Continue with this operation?
   1+ foreach ($i in 1..3) {foo $i}
[Y] Yes  [A] Yes to All  [N] No  [L] No to All  [S] Suspend
[?] Help(default is "Y"): y
DEBUG:    1+ foreach ($i in 1..3) {foo $i}
DEBUG:     ! CALL function 'foo'

Continue with this operation?
```

The interpreter displays the line to be executed, then asks the user to select Yes, Yes to All, No, or No to All. The default is Yes.

If you answer Yes, that line will be executed and you'll be prompted as to whether you want to execute the next line. If you answer Yes to All, then step mode will be turned off and execution will continue normally. If you answer either No or No to All, the current execution will be stopped and you'll be returned to the command prompt. There's no difference in the behavior between No and No to All. The following shows the message you'll see if you enter No:

```
Continue with this operation?
   2+ $x = $args[0]
[Y] Yes  [A] Yes to All  [N] No  [L] No to All  [S] Suspend
[?] Help(default is "Y"): y
DEBUG:    2+ $x = $args[0]
```

```
DEBUG:      ! SET $x = '2'.
Continue with this operation?
   3+ "x is $x"
}
[Y] Yes  [A] Yes to All  [N] No  [L] No to All  [S] Suspend
[?] Help(default is "Y"): l
WriteDebug stopped because the DebugPreference was 'Stop'.
At line:1 char:23
+ foreach ($i in 1..3) {f <<<< oo $i}
PS (16) >
```

There's one more option in the stepping list that we haven't talked about yet: Suspend. This option is interesting enough to cover in its own section.

15.4.2 Nested prompts and the Suspend operation

One of the most interesting aspects of dynamic language environments is that a script can recursively call the interpreter. You've already seen this with the `Invoke-Expression` cmdlet in chapter 11. A variation is to recursively call the interpreter *interactively*. This means that you are, in effect, suspending the currently running command and starting a new nested session. This sequence of events is illustrated in figure 15.23.

In the figure, you see that the user makes a call to the engine using the interfaces provided by the host application. In this case, instead of returning to the caller, the engine calls back to the host indicating that it should enter a nested-prompt mode. While in nested-prompt mode, because the original command pipeline is still active (the engine never returned to the host), the host must now use *nested pipelines* to execute commands. This continues until the engine calls the `Exit()` API, usually in response to a request from the user, and the host can resume the original pipeline.

The net effect of all this is that you can suspend the currently executing PowerShell pipeline and interact with PowerShell at the nested prompt. Why is this interesting?

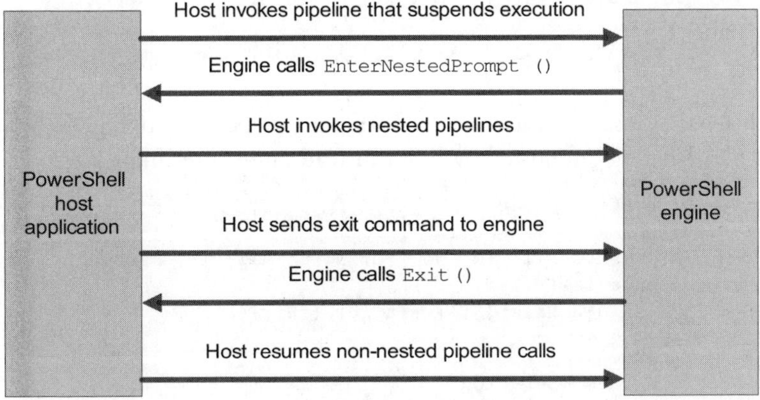

Figure 15.23 Suspending execution and entering a nested prompt requires operations on both the host and engine sides of the session.

Because this allows you to examine and modify the state of the suspended session simply by using the regular PowerShell commands you're used to. Instead of creating a whole new language just for debugger operations, you use the same language you're debugging. This feature is the core of all of the debugging capabilities in PowerShell.

There are a couple ways to enter a nested-prompt session, as you'll see in the next two sections.

Suspending a script while in step mode

Creating a nested interactive session is what the Suspend operation prompt shown during stepping does. Let's try it out. First, turn on stepping:

```
PS (1) > Set-PSDebug -Step
```

Then run a statement that should loop 10 times, printing out the numbers from 1 to 10:

```
PS (2) > $i=0; while ($i++ -lt 10) { $i }

Continue with this operation?
   1+ $i=0; while ($i++ -lt 10) { $i }
[Y] Yes  [A] Yes to All  [N] No  [L] No to All  [S] Suspend
[?] Help(default is "Y"):
DEBUG:     1+ $i=0; while ($i++ -lt 10) { $i }
```

You'll see all of the intermediate blather. Keep stepping until the first number is displayed:

```
Continue with this operation?
   1+ $i=0; while ($i++ -lt 10) { $i }
[Y] Yes  [A] Yes to All  [N] No  [L] No to All  [S] Suspend
[?] Help(default is "Y"):
DEBUG:     1+ $i=0; while ($i++ -lt 10) { $i }

Continue with this operation?
   1+ $i=0; while ($i++ -lt 10) { $i }
[Y] Yes  [A] Yes to All  [N] No  [L] No to All  [S] Suspend
[?] Help(default is "Y"):
DEBUG:     1+ $i=0; while ($i++ -lt 10) { $i }
1
```

At this point, use the Suspend operation to suspend stepping. When prompted, respond by typing s followed by Enter instead of just pressing Enter:

```
Continue with this operation?
   1+ $i=0; while ($i++ -lt 10) { $i }
[Y] Yes  [A] Yes to All  [N] No  [L] No to All  [S] Suspend
[?] Help(default is "Y"): y
DEBUG:     1+ $i=0; while ($i++ -lt 10) { $i }
1

Continue with this operation?
   1+ $i=0; while ($i++ -lt 10) { $i }
[Y] Yes  [A] Yes to All  [N] No  [L] No to All  [S] Suspend
[?] Help(default is "Y"): s
1>> PS (3) >
```

You immediately receive a new prompt. Notice that the prompt has changed to indicate that you're now working in a nested prompt, or *subshell.*

> **NOTE** The way to tell when you're in nested-prompt mode is to check the `$NestedPromptLevel` variable. If you're in a nested prompt, this variable will be greater than 0.

In this nested prompt, you can do anything you'd normally do in PowerShell. In this case, you want to inspect the state of the system. For example, let's check to see what the variable `$i` is set to. Because the last statement executed was `$i++` and the printed value for `$i` was 1, the value should be 2:

```
1>> PS (4) > $i
2
```

In fact, it is. But you're not limited to inspecting the state of the system: you can change it. In this case, let's make the loop end early by setting the value to something larger than the terminating condition. Set it to 100:

```
1>> PS (5) > $i=100
1>> PS (6) > $i
100
```

Now exit the nested-prompt session with the normal `exit` statement. This returns you to the previous level in the interpreter where, because you're stepping, you're prompted to continue. Respond by typing a followed by Enter for `[A] Yes to All` to get out of step mode:

```
1>> PS (7) > exit

Continue with this operation?
   1+ $i=0; while ($i++ -lt 10) { $i }
[Y] Yes  [A] Yes to All  [N] No  [L] No to All  [S] Suspend
[?] Help(default is "Y"): a
DEBUG:    1+ $i=0; while ($i++ -lt 10) { $i }
100
```

There are two things to notice here: the loop terminates, printing only one number, and that value is the value you set `$i` to, which is 100. Check one more time to verify that `$i` is 100:

```
PS (8) >  $i
100
```

Using the Suspend feature, you can stop a script at any point and examine or modify the state of the interpreter. You can even redefine functions in the middle of execution (although you can't change the function that's currently executing). This makes for a powerful debugging technique, but it can be annoying to use stepping all the time. This is where having a real debugger makes all the difference. But before we get to that, there's one more thing you need to look at: the mechanics of how a breakpoint works.

Creating a breakpoint command

In section 14.3.1, we looked at the `$host` variable and talked about how you can use it to write your debugging messages. The `$host` variable has another method that can be used for debugging called `EnterNestedPrompt()`. This is the method we mentioned earlier when we looked at the stepping feature on `Set-PSDebug`. Using this method, you can start a nested session at any point you want, and that point can be used approximately like a breakpoint. (Don't worry, there are real breakpoints—we'll get there.) To cause your script to break, you insert a call to `EnterNestedPrompt()` at the desired location and, when it's hit, a new interactive session starts. Let's try it out. You'll execute a loop that counts from 0 to 9. In this loop, when the loop counted is equal to 4, you'll call `EnterNestedPrompt()`:

```
PS (1) > for ($i=0; $i -lt 10; $i++)
>> {
>>     "i is $i"
>>     if ($i -eq 4) {
```

When execution gets to this point, you'll output the string "*break*" and then enter a nested-prompt level:

```
>>         "*break*"
>>         $host.EnterNestedPrompt()
>>     }
>> }
>>
i is 0
i is 1
i is 2
i is 3
i is 4
```

Now `$i` is equal to 4, so you hit the breakpoint code. As in the stepping case, you can examine and change the state of the interpreter

```
*break*
1>> PS (2) > $i
4
1>> PS (3) > $i=8
```

and use `exit` to resume the top-level execution thread:

```
1>> PS (4) > exit
i is 9
PS (6) >
```

Let's see how you can use this feature to create a `breakpoint` command. Once again, you'll take advantage of scriptblocks to add a way to trigger the breakpoint based on a particular condition:

```
PS (1) > function bp ([scriptblock] $condition)
>> {
>>     if ($condition)
>>     {
```

```
>>          if (. $condition)
>>          {
```

If the $condition parameter to bp is not null, evaluate it. If it evaluates to $true, then execute the breakpoint and enter a nested-shell level:

```
>>              $host.UI.WriteLine("*break*")
>>              $host.EnterNestedPrompt()
>>          }
>>      } else {
>>          $host.UI.WriteLine("*break*")
>>          $host.EnterNestedPrompt()
>>      }
>> }
>>
PS (2) > for ($i=0; $i -lt 10; $i++)
>> {
>>      . bp {$i -eq 5}
```

Here you're inserting a breakpoint that will cause execution to break when $i is equal to 5. Note that you're dot-sourcing the bp function. This is because you want it to be executed in the current scope, allowing you to change the state of the loop variable:

```
>>      "`$i is $i"
>> }
>>
$i is 0
$i is 1
$i is 2
$i is 3
$i is 4
*break*
```

You hit the breakpoint. Increment the loop variable so that 5 is never displayed, and exit the nested-prompt level and resume execution:

```
1>> PS (3) > $i++
1>> PS (4) > exit
$i is 6
$i is 7
$i is 8
$i is 9
PS (5) >
```

The loop exits, never having printed 5.

Now that you have a basic idea of how the debugging environment works, let's move on to the main event and look at debugging from the ISE.

15.5 THE POWERSHELL V2 DEBUGGER

With PowerShell v2, a powerful new debugger was added to the product. In this section, we'll start with how to use the debugger from the ISE and then move on to what you can do with command-line debugging.

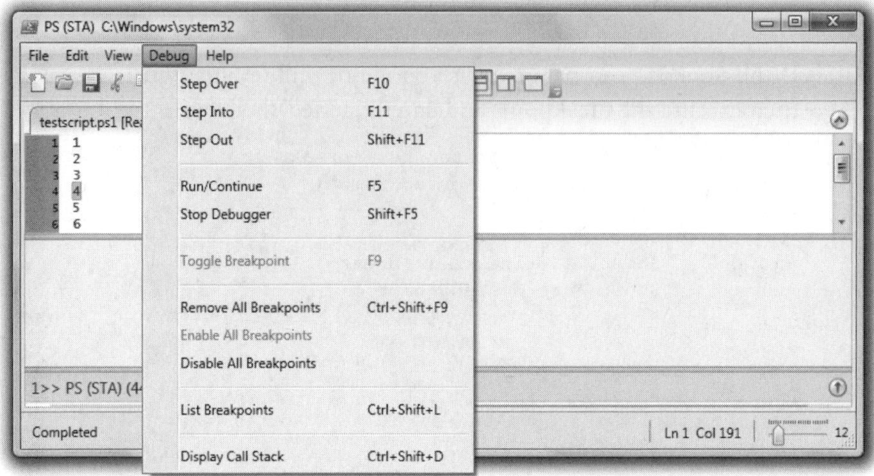

Figure 15.24 The debug menu options allow you to set breakpoints and step through your script, line by line.

15.5.1 The graphical debugger

As you've seen, the ISE provides an integrated environment for editing and running scripts. It's also the easiest and frequently most effective way to debug scripts. This is because the integrated debugger makes it easy to see where you are and what's going on in your scripts. The major debugging features can be found in the Debug menu, shown in figure 15.24.

If you've used Microsoft Visual Studio, you should notice that the keyboard shortcuts are the same as the Visual Studio debugger. A description for each of these menu items is shown in table 15.3.

Table 15.3 Menu items in the ISE Debug menu

Menu item	Key	Command equivalent	Description
Step Over	F10	`V (Step-Over)`	Step over the current function call rather than stepping into the function.
Step Into	F11	`S (Step-Into)`	Step the script, stepping into functions and scripts as they're encountered.
Step Out	Shift-F11	`O (Step-Out)`	Execute script lines until the end of the current function has been reached.
Run/Continue	F5	`C (Continue)`	If no command is running, the contents of the current editor buffer are executed. If the interpreter is paused at a breakpoint, execution will resume.
Stop Debugger	F5	`Q (Stop)`	Stop debugging session and the script being debugged.

Table 15.3 Menu items in the ISE Debug menu *(continued)*

Menu item	Key	Command equivalent	Description
Toggle Breakpoint	F9	`Set-PSBreakpoint`, `Remove-PSBreakpoint`	If there's no breakpoint on the current line, then one will be added. If there's a breakpoint, then it will be removed.
Remove All Breakpoints	Ctrl-Shift-F9	`Remove-PSBreakpoint`	All breakpoints that are set in the current session (current tab) will be deleted. Breakpoints in other tabs are unaffected.
Enable All Breakpoints	*n/a*	`Enable-PSBreakpoint`	All breakpoints in the current session (tab) are enabled. If a breakpoint is currently enabled, it will remain active. If a breakpoint is disabled, it will be enabled.
Disable All Breakpoints	*n/a*	`Disable-PSBreakpoint`	All existing breakpoints in the current session (tab) are left in place but disabled. They may be re-enabled at a later time.
List-Breakpoints	Ctrl-Shift-L	`Get-PSBreakpoint`	List all defined breakpoints in the current session (tab).
Display Call Stack	Ctrl-Shift-D	`Get-PSCallStack`	After a breakpoint has been hit, this command will let you see all the functions or scripts that were called to get you to where you are.

Table 15.3 shows the menu item name, the keyboard shortcut if one's available, and the description of the corresponding functionality. What's a bit unusual for a graphical debugger is that the table also lists command-line equivalents to the menu functionality. In fact, there are two types of command equivalents: an actual cmdlet that can be called at any time and special single-character shortcut commands that can only be used while debugging a script. We'll walk through an example to see how this all works.

Debugging a script

In this example, you're debugging a trivial script that just outputs numbers. You want to put a breakpoint on line 4, so you move the cursor to line 4 and press F9. The line will be highlighted in red, indicating that there's a breakpoint set on that line. Remember that the debugger only works on scripts so you have to save the buffer to a file first. Once that's done, press F5 to begin (if the script had been modified since the last save, you'd also be prompted to save it before execution begins). Execution proceeds, outputting numbers until line 4 in the script is hit and the breakpoint triggers. At this point, the line where the breakpoint was hit is highlighted in yellow and the command pane displays the debugging prompt, as shown in figure 15.25.

When the debugging prompt is displayed, that means the special debug mode–only commands are now available.

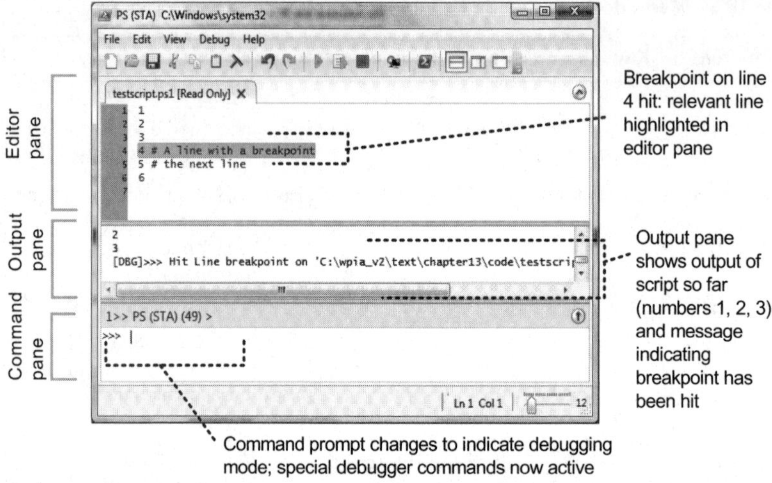

Figure 15.25 The command pane changes once a breakpoint has been hit. The prompt is prefixed with >> to indicate that you're debugging and the debugger commands are enabled.

> **NOTE** Earlier we said that because of the way debugging works in PowerShell, you don't need a new language. This is definitely true—but you do need some convenience aliases; otherwise, things are too verbose to use easily. That's what you're seeing here.

For example, to step the next line, you could either type the command `s` or `Step-Over` or use the Debug > Step Over menu item. Regardless of how you enter the command, the line where you'd hit the breakpoint is executed and then breaks at the next line in the script. This line is now highlighted in yellow. The previous line is highlighted in red because it has an actual breakpoint on it, as you can see in figure 15.26.

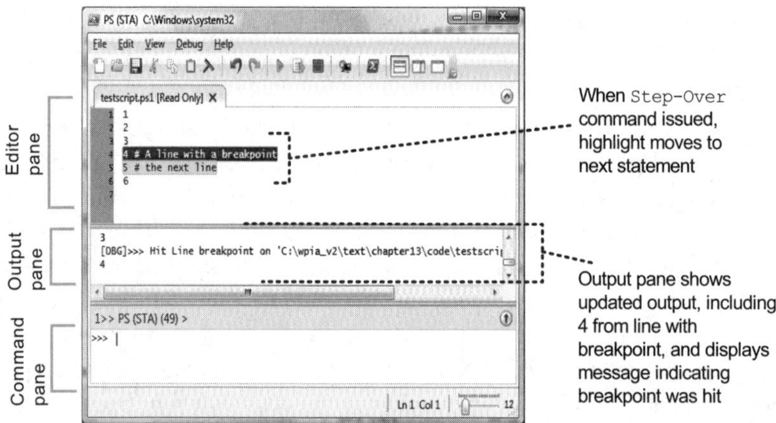

Figure 15.26 The command pane changes once a breakpoint has been hit. The prompt is prefixed with >> to indicate that you're debugging and the debugger commands are enabled.

The full set of debugger shortcut commands is shown in table 15.4.

Table 15.4 The special commands that are available in debug mode

Command	Full name	Description
`v`	`Step-Over`	Step over the current function call rather than stepping into the function.
`s`	`Step-Into`	Step through the script, stepping into functions and scripts as they're encountered.
`o`	`Step-Out`	Execute script lines until the end of the current function has been reached.
`c`	`Continue`	If no command is running, the contents of the current editor buffer are executed. If the interpreter is paused at a breakpoint, execution will resume.
`L [<m> [<n>]]`	`List`	List the portion of the script around the line where you're currently stopped. By default, the current line is displayed, preceded by the 5 previous lines, and then followed by the 10 subsequent lines. To continue listing the script, press the Enter key. The `List` command can be optionally followed by a number specifying the number of lines to display before and after the current line. If two numbers are specified, the first number is the number of preceding lines and the second is the number of following lines.
`Q`	`Stop`	Stop execution, which also stops the debugger.
`K`	`Get-PSCallStack`	Display up to the current execution point. This command isn't specific to debug mode and may be used anywhere.
`<Enter>`		Pressing the Enter key on an empty line repeats the last `S`, `V`, or `L` command entered. This makes it easy to continue stepping or to list the script.
`?, h`		Display all the special debugger commands in the output pane.

Executing other commands in debug mode

If you look at the various tables so far, there's clearly something missing. Knowing where you are is great, but you need more for effective debugging. You need to be able to examine variables, change their values, look at functions, and so on. The solution turns out to be simple: for the most part, you can just use the same cmdlets you've used all along. To see a variable, use `Get-Variable`; to change a variable, use assignment or the `Set-Variable` command. Debug mode just adds some new commands to the environment; all of the existing commands are still available so you have the full power of PowerShell available in this environment.

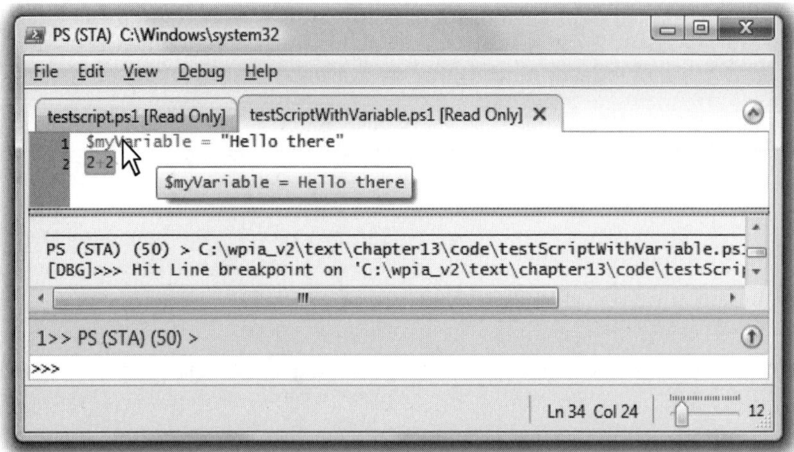

Figure 15.27 When the mouse pointer is placed over the variable, the variable's value is displayed in a tooltip.

Hovering over variables to see their values

Some users don't want to type a command to look at variables, so like Visual Studio, the ISE allows you to hover the mouse pointer over a variable to see its value. Simply place the mouse pointer over the variable you want to see in the editor and its value will be displayed. Figure 15.27 shows what this looks like.

Note that there is one caveat: if the script isn't running, then the variable won't have a value. Or, more confusingly, if there's another variable in an active scope with the same name, you'll see that value rather than the one you were expecting. This is one of the tricky aspects of dynamically scoped environments.

> **NOTE** By now you may have noticed that you aren't passing parameters to the scripts you're running. In fact, when you run a script by pressing F5 or using the menu, you have no way to specify parameters to the script you're about to run. The workaround is to run the script from the ISE command line where you can specify parameters.

Because PowerShell is a shell, you also have to be able to debug directly from the command line, which is our next topic.

15.6 COMMAND-LINE DEBUGGING

Given the nature of the PowerShell environment, you need to support debugging in a variety of environments. The most effective way to do this is to enable debugging scripts from the command line. This makes it possible to use the debugger from the console host as well. As always, these debugging features are surfaced through a set of cmdlets. The cmdlets are listed in table 15.5.

Table 15.5 **The PowerShell debugger cmdlets**

Cmdlet	Description
`Get-PSCallStack`	Gets the current call stack
`Enable-PSBreakPoint`	Enables an existing breakpoint
`Disable-PSBreakPoint`	Disables a breakpoint without removing it
`Set-PSBreakPoint`	Sets a breakpoint
`Get-PSBreakPoint`	Gets the list of breakpoints
`Remove-PSBreakPoint`	Removes an existing breakpoint

Command-line debugging is also important for another reason: there are many more things you can do using these cmdlets, including writing scripts to debug scripts. In other words, all of the features you've seen in the GUI debugger are available from the command line, but not all of the command-line features are available from the GUI.

> **NOTE** There is, of course, no deep technical reason why this is so. Using the ISE object model, it's possible to backfill many of the missing features.

In fact, the GUI debugger only surfaces a portion of the functionality of what can be done with the PowerShell debugger. In the next few sections, we'll dig into these capabilities.

15.6.1 Working with breakpoint objects

Let's begin our discussion by taking a detailed look how breakpoints are implemented. So far you've seen a fairly conventional debugger experience, but the introspective nature of PowerShell allows you to do much more when working with breakpoints. As with most everything else, breakpoints in PowerShell are objects that you can script against. As always, you'll use `Get-Member` to examine these objects:

```
PS (STA) (42) > Get-PSBreakPoint | Get-Member

   TypeName: System.Management.Automation.LineBreakpoint

Name        MemberType Definition
----        ---------- ----------
Equals      Method     bool Equals(System.Object obj)
GetHashCode Method     int GetHashCode()
GetType     Method     type GetType()
ToString    Method     string ToString()
Action      Property   System.Management.Automation.ScriptBlock Action
            {get;}
Column      Property   System.Int32 Column {get;}
Enabled     Property   System.Boolean Enabled {get;}
HitCount    Property   System.Int32 HitCount {get;}
Id          Property   System.Int32 Id {get;}
Line        Property   System.Int32 Line {get;}
Script      Property   System.String Script {get;}
```

In this output, you see some familiar bits of information: the breakpoint ID and the line and script where it applies. Much more interesting are things like `HitCount` and especially the `Action` property.

The `HitCount` property records the number of times a breakpoint has been hit—not terribly interesting but useful sometimes. The really interesting property is `Action`, which holds instances of our old friend the scriptblock. By specifying actions in scriptblocks, breakpoints can do much more than simply interrupting execution when the breakpoint is hit. Using scriptblocks allows you to perform arbitrary actions controlling when or even if the breakpoint fires. Let's see how this works with a simple test script:

```
PS (1) > Get-Content testscript2.ps1
"Starting"
$sum = 0
foreach ($i in 1..10)
{
    $sum += $i
}
"The sum is $sum"
```

This script loops over the numbers from 1 to 10, summing them up and then printing the result. Now define a breakpoint for this script using the `Set-PSBreakPoint` command:

```
PS (2) > $firstBP = Set-PSBreakpoint -Script testscript2.ps1 -Line 5 `
>> -Action {
>>     if ($i -gt 3 -and $i -lt 7)
>>     {
>>         Write-Host ">>> DEBUG ACTION: i = $i, sum = $sum"
>>     }
>> }
>>
```

This command specifies that a scriptblock will be executed every time you hit line 5 in the test script. In the body of the scriptblock, you're checking to see if the value of `$i` is greater than 3 and less than 7. If so, you'll display a message. You have to use `Write-Host` to display this message because the results of the scriptblock aren't displayed. The `Set-PSBreakpoint` command returns an instance of a breakpoint object. Let's display it as a list so you can see its members:

```
PS (3) > $firstBP  | Format-List

Id       : 1
Script   : C:\wpia_v2\text\chapter15\code\testscript2.ps1
Line     : 5
Column   : 0
Enabled  : True
HitCount : 0
Action   :
               if ($i -gt 3 -and $i -lt 7)
               {
```

```
            Write-Host ">>> DEBUG ACTION: i = $i, sum = $sum"
        }
```

This code shows the full path to the script and the line in the script that will trigger the action as well as the action itself. Run the test script to see how it works:

```
PS (4) > ./testscript2.ps1
Starting
>>> DEBUG ACTION: i = 4, sum = 6
>>> DEBUG ACTION: i = 5, sum = 10
>>> DEBUG ACTION: i = 6, sum = 15
The sum is 55
```

The output shows the value of `$i` and `$sum` as long as `$i` is between 3 and 7 as intended.

Before we move on to the next example, remove all of the breakpoints so they don't confuse the results in the example:

```
PS (5) > Get-PSBreakpoint | Remove-PSBreakpoint
```

This time, instead of just displaying a message, you're going to use the `break` keyword to break the script under specific conditions. Here's the command to define the new breakpoint:

```
PS (6) > $firstBP = Set-PSBreakpoint -Script testscript2.ps1 -Line 5 -
Action {
>>      if ($i -eq 4)
>>      {
>>          Write-Host ">>> DEBUG ACTION: i = $i, sum = $sum"
>>          break
>>      }
>> }
>>
```

For this breakpoint, you'll only fire the action on line 5 of the test script. In the scriptblock body, you display the message as before and then call `break`, which will break the execution of the script:

```
PS (7) > ./testscript2.ps1
Starting
>>> DEBUG ACTION: i = 4, sum = 6
Entering debug mode. Use h or ? for help.

Hit Line breakpoint on
'C:\wpia_v2\text\chapter15\code\testscript2.ps1:5'

testscript2.ps1:5       $sum += $i
```

As was the case in the graphical debugger, you have the same set of options available at the break prompt:

```
PS (8) > ?
 s, stepInto      Single step (step into functions, scripts, etc.)
 v, stepOver      Step to next statement (step over functions, scri
```

```
pts, etc.)
 o, stepOut       Step out of the current function, script, etc.
 c, continue      Continue execution
 q, quit          Stop execution and exit the debugger

 k, Get-PSCallStack Display call stack

 l, list    List source code for the current script.
            Use "list" to start from the current line, "list <m>"
            to start from line <m>, and "list <m> <n>" to list <n>
            lines starting from line <m>
 <enter>    Repeat last command if it was stepInto, stepOver or list
 ?, h                 Displays this help message

For instructions about how to customize your debugger prompt, type
"help about_prompt".
```

You'll use the c command to continue execution:

```
PS (9) > c
The sum is 55
```

The completed script displays the sum. And, as before, clean up the breakpoint:

```
PS (10) > Get-PSBreakpoint | Remove-PSBreakpoint
```

Now, let's move on to the next example.

15.6.2 Setting breakpoints on commands

The most common scenario using the debugger involves setting breakpoints on lines in a file, but it's also possible to break on a specific command. Define a simple function

```
PS (15) > function hello { "Hello world!" }
```

and set a breakpoint on that function:

```
PS (16) > Set-PSBreakpoint -Command hello

  ID Script           Line Command          Variable         Action
  -- ------           ---- -------          --------         ------
   0                       hello
```

This time you won't associate an action and you'll allow the default behavior—causing a break in execution—to occur. Execute the function:

```
PS (17) > hello
Entering debug mode. Use h or ? for help.

Hit Command breakpoint on 'hello'

hello
```

When the command is run, you immediately hit the breakpoint. Enter c and allow the function to complete:

```
PS (18) > c
Hello world!
```

Among other things, the ability to set breakpoints on commands as opposed to specific lines in a script allows you to debug interactively entered functions. Now let's move on to the final example in this section: setting breakpoints on variables.

15.6.3 Setting breakpoints on variable assignment

In the previous examples, the breakpoints were triggered when execution reached a certain line in the script or you entered a command. You can also cause a break when variables are read or written. In the following command, you'll specify an action to take when the `$sum` variable is written:

```
PS (12) > $thirdBP = Set-PSBreakpoint -Variable sum -Mode Write `
>> -Action {
>>      if ($sum -gt 10)
>>      {
>>          Write-Host ">>> VARIABLE sum was set to $sum"
>>      }
>> }
>>
```

For this breakpoint, you're using `-Mode Write` to specify that the breakpoint should only trigger when the variable is written. In practice, this could have been omitted because `Write` is the default mode (the other modes are `Read` and `ReadWrite`). Then in the action scriptblock, you'll use `Write-Host` as before to display the value of `$sum`, but only when it's greater than 10. Let's see what this breakpoint looks like:

```
PS (13) > $ thirdBP | Format-List


Id         : 3
Variable   : sum
AccessMode : Write
Enabled    : True
HitCount   : 0
Action     :
                  if ($sum -gt 10)
                  {
                      Write-Host ">>> VARIABLE sum was set to $sum"
                  }
```

You see the line, variable, and access mode that will trigger the action and the scriptblock to execute when triggered. Run the test script:

```
PS (14) > ./testscript2.ps1
Starting
>>> VARIABLE sum was set to 15
>>> VARIABLE sum was set to 21
>>> VARIABLE sum was set to 28
>>> VARIABLE sum was set to 36
>>> VARIABLE sum was set to 45
The sum is 55
```

You see the output messages from the action scriptblock. One of the nice things is that a variable-based breakpoint isn't tied to a specific line number in the script so it will continue to work even when you edit the script.

Although these examples are by no means exhaustive, they give you a sense of the capabilities of the PowerShell command-line debugger. You're able to do much more sophisticated debugging from the command line. But even for the command line, there are a number of limitations to the debugging capabilities. We'll look at these limitations in the final section in this chapter.

15.6.4 Debugger limitations and issues

The PowerShell debugger, though powerful, does suffer from a number of limitations. Probably the biggest limitation is that remote debugging isn't currently supported. Even in an interactive remoting session, the debugger won't work:

```
[localhost]: PS (1) > Set-PSBreakpoint -Script `
>> testfile2.ps1 -Line 5
Debugging is not supported on remote sessions.
    + CategoryInfo          :
    + FullyQualifiedErrorId : SetPSBreakpoint:RemoteDebuggerNotSuppo
   rted,Microsoft.PowerShell.Commands.SetPSBreakpointCommand
```

This is, in part, because the remote host environment doesn't support the required `EnterNestedPrompt()` function you saw earlier:

```
[localhost]: PS (2) > $host.EnterNestedPrompt()
Exception calling "EnterNestedPrompt" with "0" argument(s): "Remote
host method get_Runspace is not implemented."
At line:1 char:24
+ $host.EnterNestedPrompt <<<< ()
    + CategoryInfo          : NotSpecified: (:) [], MethodInvocation
   Exception
    + FullyQualifiedErrorId : DotNetMethodException
```

A corollary to this is that you can't attach to a running PowerShell instance to debug it. In fact, of all of the debugging tools we've looked at, the only one available in the remoting environment is tracing using the `Set-PSDebug` command.

There are some other issues to be aware of as well. The dynamic nature of the PowerShell language means that code can be created at any time and you aren't always able to set breakpoints on this code. This is where the techniques you saw earlier in the chapter can help. The example breakpoint function can be inserted into dynamic or anonymous code, allowing you to effectively set a breakpoint in that code.

Finally, because variables are never declared, it's not possible to specify an instance of a variable via its declaration; you can only select the target variable by name. Scoping a breakpoint to a particular file or command helps with correctly targeting the desired variable.

In practice, the only one of these limitations that's likely to impact day-to-day scripting is the limitation on remote debugging. In those scenarios, if tracing is insufficient you'll need to replicate the remote environment locally to do the debugging.

At this point, we'll wrap up our discussion of the PowerShell debugging capabilities. We started with tracing and simulating breakpoints, then looked at using the integrated debugger in the ISE, and finally spent some time looking at how to use the command-line debugger. With these simple examples, we've only scratched the surface of what can be done with the debugger. The ability to associate actions with breakpoints allows you to create arbitrarily sophisticated criteria for triggering breakpoints, including having breakpoints create other breakpoints dynamically. At the same time, the nature of PowerShell as a highly dynamic environment can make debugging some scenarios quite challenging. As always, with PowerShell debugging, the most effective way to learn it is to use and experiment with its capabilities.

This completes our coverage of the PowerShell ISE and debugger. We said at the beginning of the chapter that this is a very large topic, so congratulations for making it all the way through. This also completes our coverage of the PowerShell features. In the next chapter, we switch from looking at PowerShell on a feature-by-feature basis and take a holistic approach to applying the things that you've learned.

15.7 SUMMARY

This chapter introduced the PowerShell ISE and debugger. We began the chapter by covering the basic operations and features of the ISE:

- Controlling and customizing ISE pane layout
- Running scripts with F5 and portions of scripts with F8
- Working with the editor
- Working with multiple tabs, including remote PowerShell tabs

Next we looked at how to extend the ISE environment using the ISE object model. We started with an overview of the types in the object model, then looked at working with the following:

- Adding and renaming tabs
- Invoking commands in another tab
- Accessing the contents of the output and editor panes

Then we explored adding custom menus to the environment. You followed examples where you added menu items to insert snippets of code into the editor buffer and a command to run a syntax check on the current editor buffer.

In the second part of the chapter, we looked at the PowerShell debugger. We described the tracing and stepping features that were carried over from the first release of PowerShell. When these features are largely subsumed by the newer debugger, there are still scenarios like debugging remote scripts where they're useful.

In our work with the debugger, we started by looking at how the debugger is integrated into the ISE and uses the same command-key bindings as the Visual Studio debugger. You saw how to set breakpoints, look at variables, and step through code.

Finally we ended the chapter by covering the command-line debugger. It offers a superset of the graphical debugger features, including the ability to have conditional breakpoints and breakpoints on variables where they're read or set. We also explained some of the limitations in the debugger as shipped in v2.

This chapter concludes the first part of book. In part 1 of *Windows PowerShell in Action*, our focus was on exploring the features of the PowerShell language and runtime largely in isolation. In the second part of the book, we look at applying this knowledge in various technology domains to solve broader problems. The technology areas that are covered are files, paths, and text (chapter 16), .NET (chapter 17), COM (chapter 18), WMI and WSMan (chapter 19), and event handling (chapter 20). The last chapter in the book is devoted to security, covering topics that are extremely important for PowerShell users who need to be able to write secure scripts.

PART 2

Using PowerShell

In the second part of the book, we look at applying your PowerShell knowledge in various technology domains to solve broader problems. The technology areas that are covered are files, paths, and text (chapter 16); .NET (chapter 17); COM (chapter 18); WMI and WSMan (chapter 19); and event handling in chapter 20. The last chapter (chapter 21) in the book is devoted to security, covering topics that are extremely important for PowerShell users who need to be able to write secure scripts.

CHAPTER 16

Working with files, text, and XML

Where is human nature so weak as in the bookstore?

—Henry Ward Beecher

Outside of a dog, a book is man's best friend. Inside of a dog, it's too dark to read.

—Groucho Marx

In this chapter, we're going to cover PowerShell's features for processing text and files. We'll look at how PowerShell deals with file paths and concepts behind the provider model. We'll revisit regular expressions and take another look at the language features and cmdlets that are provided for dealing with text. This chapter also covers the features that PowerShell offers for dealing with a special kind of text—XML—as strings and in files. In the process, you'll see how to use the .NET classes to accomplish tasks when the native PowerShell language features may not be sufficient.

16.1 POWERSHELL AND PATHS

In this section we'll explore the basic concepts underlying PowerShell's path processing. PowerShell does a lot of work to promote a consistent user experience when navigating through hierarchical namespaces. This consistency allows you to use the same commands to work with the file system, the Registry, and other stores. The core mechanism that PowerShell uses to accomplish this is the PowerShell *provider model*. A PowerShell provider is a software component, loaded through modules or snapins, that's used to produce a file system–like experience for other data stores, such as the Registry.

16.1.1 Providers and the core cmdlets

A PowerShell *provider* is an installable component usually packaged as part of a PowerShell module or snap-in. So far, there's no way to write a provider in PowerShell—they have to be written in a compiled language like C#. That said, the basic architecture of the provider module aligns with what are called the *core cmdlets*. These cmdlets provide the common (or core) activities and are grouped by noun: `Item`, `ChildItem`, `Content`, and `ItemProperty`. The `Item` cmdlets work with an item in the store. For example, using `Get-Item` on a file will return information about that file. The `ChildItem` cmdlets provide a way to work with items that are children of a particular item. Using `Get-ChildItem` on a directory in the file system will return the files in that directory. If the target is a file, then `Get-Content` will return the content of the file. Finally, the `ItemProperty` cmdlets allow properties on an item to be manipulated. Once you learn these patterns, you can apply them to any store surfaced as a provider.

This may seem like an overly complex arrangement, but it allows the core cmdlets to work with a wide variety of types of stores, including the Registry and Active Directory. It's even possible to write a provider for an XML document (though PowerShell doesn't include one at this time). Many of these stores are more complex than the file system and may allow structures like data elements with both content and children. (This isn't possible in the Windows file system, but it does happen in the Registry.) By learning these core patterns, PowerShell users will have a mental model that will allow them to use new providers as they're encountered.

You can get a list of the providers installed in your session by using the `Get-PSProvider` cmdlet:

```
PS (1) > Get-PSProvider

Name                 Capabilities                 Drives
----                 ------------                 ------
WSMan                Credentials                  {WSMan}
Alias                ShouldProcess                {Alias}
Environment          ShouldProcess                {Env}
FileSystem           Filter, ShouldProcess        {C, D, L, M...}
Function             ShouldProcess                {Function}
Registry             ShouldProcess, Transa...     {HKLM, HKCU}
Variable             ShouldProcess                {Variable}
Certificate          ShouldProcess                {cert}
```

You've worked with most of these providers already. In section 16.1.6 you'll work with a Registry provider, and in chapter 21 (section 21.4.3) you'll use the certificate provider when you learn script signing.

Providers are the heart of the namespace mechanism, but you don't usually work directly with them. Instead, you work through named *drives* that allow you access to the provider's capabilities.

16.1.2 Working with PSDrives

PowerShell providers are typically accessed through named drives. This means that each provider must have at least one drive associated with it for it to be usable. The drives that a provider exports needn't correspond to things like system disk drives (though the file system provider usually has one drive name exported for each physical drive on the computer). Their names can also be longer than the single character permitted in drive letters. You saw an example of both of these things when you used the WSMan: drive to manage PowerShell remoting in section 13.1.2.

To keep people from mixing up the PowerShell drives with the system drives, Microsoft calls them *PSDrives.* Similarly, a path that contains a PSDrive is called a *PSPath,* and a path that contains a physical drive is called a *provider-specific path.* A PSPath must be translated to the provider-specific path form before it can be processed by the system, as you'll see in the next example.

Another useful feature supported by many providers is the ability to create your own drive names. That means you can, for example, create a PSDrive as a shortcut to a common resource. For example, it might be convenient to have a docs: drive that points to your document directory. You can create this drive using the `New-PSDrive` cmdlet:

```
PS (1) > New-PSDrive -Name docs -PSProvider filesystem `
>>  -Root (Resolve-Path ~/*documents)
>>

Name        Provider      Root                              Current
                                                            Location
----        --------      ----                              --------
docs        FileSystem    C:\Documents and Settings\brucep
```

Notice the path used as the argument to the `-Root` parameter. The string "~/documents" is passed to the `Resolve-Path` command. In this string, ~ means the home drive for this provide. The call to `Resolve-Path` converts the PSPath to an absolute provider path.

Once the drive has been created, you can `cd` into it

```
PS (2) > cd docs:
```

and then use `Get-Location` (to see where you are):

```
PS (3) > Get-Location

Path
----
docs:\
```

You are, at least according to PowerShell, in the docs: drive. Create a file here:

```
PS (4) > "Hello there!" > junk.txt
```

Next, try to use `cmd.exe` to display it (we'll get to why you're doing this in a second):

```
PS (5) > cmd /c type junk.txt
Hello there!
```

This code displays the context of the file with no problems. Next, display it using `Get-Content` with the fully qualified path, including the docs: drive:

```
PS (6) > Get-Content docs:/junk.txt
Hello there!
```

This code also works as expected. But when you try to use the full path with `cmd.exe`

```
PS (7) > cmd /c type docs:/junk.txt
The syntax of the command is incorrect.
```

it fails. This is because non-PowerShell applications don't understand the PowerShell drive fiction and can't process PSPaths. But when you "`cd`'ed" to the location first, you were able to use `cmd.exe` to display the file. This worked because when you're "in" that drive, the system automatically sets the current directory properly on the child process object to the provider-specific path before starting the process. This is why using relative paths from `cmd.exe` worked. But if you pass in PSPath as an argument, it fails. To mitigate this issue, use the `Resolve-Path` cmdlet to get the provider-specific path. This cmdlet takes the PSPath and translates it into the provider's native path representation. Use this cmdlet to pass the translated path to `cmd.exe`:

```
PS (7) > cmd /c type (Resolve-Path docs:/junk.txt).ProviderPath
Hello there!
```

This time, it works. You need to be somewhat careful when dealing with this concept and think about how things should work with non-PowerShell applications. If you wanted to open a file with Notepad in the doc: directory, you'd have to do the same thing you did for `cmd.exe` and resolve the path first:

```
notepad (Resolve-Path docs:/junk.txt).ProviderPath
```

If you frequently use Notepad in PSPaths, then you can create a function in your profile:

```
function notepad
{
     $args | foreach { notepad.exe (Resolve-Path $_).ProviderPath }
}
```

You could even create a function to launch an arbitrary executable:

```
function Start-Program
{
    $cmd, $files = $args
    $cmd = @(Get-Command -type Application $cmd)[0].Definition
    $files | foreach { & $cmd  (Resolve-Path $_).ProviderPath }
}
```

This function uses PowerShell's multiple-assignment feature to split the list of arguments into two parts: the command name and the list of files. It then uses `Get-Command` to limit the type of command to run to external applications and resolves the names of the argument files.

Each provider has a home directory

Another feature supported by the PowerShell path mechanism is a shortcut notation that allows you to easily access the default, or home, directory for that provider. Start the path with the tilde (~) character, and the remaining path components will be resolved relative to the provider's home directory. In the file system, this directory will be the user's home directory, giving you easy access to the subdirectories off your home directory. For example, to `cd` to the desktop folder, you just have to use this:

```
cd ~/desktop
```

This code makes accessing these directories very convenient.

Remember, though, the ~ always refers to the home directory for the current drive's associated provider. Consequently, if your current location is somewhere in the Registry provider, using `cd ~/desktop` won't work because the ~ will resolve to the home directory of the Registry provider, not the file system provider.

While we're on the topic of paths, let's look at some additional features PowerShell provides for working with paths.

16.1.3 Working with paths that contain wildcards

Another great feature of the PowerShell provider infrastructure is universal support for wildcards (see chapter 4 for details on wildcard patterns). You can use wildcards any place you can navigate to, even in places such as the alias: drive. For example, say you want to find all the aliases that begin with `gc`. You can do this with wildcards in the Alias provider:

```
PS (1) > dir alias:gc*

CommandType     Name                  Definition
-----------     ----                  ----------
Alias           gc                    Get-Content
Alias           gci                   Get-ChildItem
Alias           gcm                   Get-Command
```

As you can see, there are three of them.

We might all agree that this is a great feature, but there's a downside. Suppose you want to access a path that contains one of the wildcard metacharacters: ?, *, [, and]. In the Windows file system, * and ? aren't a problem because you can't use these characters in a file or directory name. But you can use [and]. Working with files whose names contain [or] can be quite a challenge because of the way wildcards and quoting (see chapter 3) work. Square brackets are used a lot in filenames in browser caches to avoid collisions by numbering the files. Let's run some experiments on some of the files in the Internet Explorer (IE) cache.

Dealing with hidden files

By default, the `Get-ChildItem` cmdlet (and its alias `dir`) won't show hidden files. To see the hidden files, use the `-Force` parameter. For example, to find the Application Data directory in your home directory, you might try

```
PS (1) > dir ~/app*
```

but nothing is returned. That's because this directory is hidden. To see the directory, use `-Force` as in:

```
PS (2) > dir ~/app* -Force
Directory:Microsoft.PowerShell.Core\FileSystem::C:\Docum
                 ents and Settings\brucepay
Mode                LastWriteTime     Length Name
----                -------------     ------ ----
d-rh-        12/14/2006   9:13 PM            Application Data
```

Now the directory is visible. You'll need to use `-Force` to get into the directory containing the temporary Internet files.

16.1.4 Suppressing wildcard processing in paths

In one of the directories used to cache temporary Internet files, say you want to find all of the files that begin with "thumb*". It's easy enough:

```
PS (2) > dir thumb*

    Directory: Microsoft.PowerShell.Core\FileSystem::C:\Doc
    uments and Settings\brucepay\Local Settings\Temporary I
    nternet Files\Content.IE5\MYNBM9OJ

Mode                LastWriteTime     Length Name
----                -------------     ------ ----
-a---          9/7/2006  10:34 PM       4201 ThumbnailServe
                                             r[1].jpg
-a---          9/7/2006  10:35 PM       3223 ThumbnailServe
                                             r[2].jpg
-a---          7/8/2006   7:58 PM       2066 thumb[1].jpg
-a---         9/11/2006   2:48 PM      12476 thumb[2].txt
-a---         9/11/2006   2:48 PM      11933 thumb[3].txt
```

You get five files. Now you want to limit the set of files to things that match "thumb[". Try this directly using a wildcard pattern:

```
PS (3) > dir thumb[*
Get-ChildItem : Cannot retrieve the dynamic parameters for
the cmdlet. The specified wildcard pattern is not valid:
thumb[*
At line:1 char:3
+ ls  <<<< thumb[*
```

Of course, it fails because the [is being treated as part of a wildcard pattern. Clearly you need to suppress treating [as a wildcard by quoting it. The obvious first step, as you'll recall from chapter 4, is to try a single backtick:

```
PS (4) > dir thumb`[*
Get-ChildItem : Cannot retrieve the dynamic parameters for
the cmdlet. The specified wildcard pattern is not valid:
thumb\[*
At line:1 char:3
+ ls  <<<< thumb`[*
```

This code fails because the single backtick is discarded in the parsing process. In fact, it takes four backticks to cause the square bracket to be treated as a regular character:

```
PS (5) > dir thumb````[*

    Directory: Microsoft.PowerShell.Core\FileSystem::C:\
    Documents and Settings\brucepay\Local Settings\Temporary
    Internet Files\Content.IE5\MYNBM9OJ

Mode                LastWriteTime     Length Name
----                -------------     ------ ----
-a---          7/8/2006   7:58 PM       2066 thumb[1].jpg
-a---         9/11/2006   2:48 PM      12476 thumb[2].txt
-a---         9/11/2006   2:48 PM      11933 thumb[3].txt
```

The reason is that one set of backticks is removed by the interpreter and a second set is removed by the provider itself. (This second round of backtick removal is so you can use escaping to represent filenames that contain literal quotes.) Putting single quotes around the pattern keeps the interpreter from performing quote processing in the string, simplifying this to needing only two backticks:

```
PS (8) > ls 'thumb``[*'

    Directory: Microsoft.PowerShell.Core\FileSystem::C:\Doc
    uments and Settings\brucepay\Local Settings\Temporary I
    nternet Files\Content.IE5\MYNBM9OJ

Mode                LastWriteTime     Length Name
----                -------------     ------ ----
-a---          7/8/2006   7:58 PM       2066 thumb[1].jpg
-a---         9/11/2006   2:48 PM      12476 thumb[2].txt
-a---         9/11/2006   2:48 PM      11933 thumb[3].txt
```

In this particular example, much of the complication arises because you want some of the metacharacters to be treated as literal characters, whereas the rest still do pattern matching. Trial and error is usually the only way to get this right.

> **NOTE** As we've said before, this stuff is hard. It's hard to understand and it's hard to get right. Unfortunately, no one has come up with a better mechanism yet. This problem occurs in any language that supports pattern matching. Patience, practice, and experimentation are the only ways to figure it out.

16.1.5 The -LiteralPath parameter

You don't have to turn to trial and error when you know the name of the file and want to suppress all pattern-matching behavior. You can accomplish this by using the -LiteralPath parameter available on most core cmdlets. Say you want to copy a file from the previous example. If you use the regular path mechanism in Copy-Item

```
PS (11) > Copy-Item thumb[1].jpg c:\temp\junk.jpg
PS (12) > Get-ChildItem c:\temp\junk.jpg
Get-ChildItem : Cannot find path 'C:\temp\junk.jpg' because
 it does not exist.
At line:1 char:4
+ dir  <<<< c:\temp\junk.jpg
```

the copy fails because the square brackets were treated as pattern-matching metacharacters. Now try it using -LiteralPath:

```
PS (13) > Copy-Item -literalpath thumb[1].jpg c:\temp\junk.jpg
PS (14) > Get-ChildItem c:\temp\junk.jpg

    Directory: Microsoft.PowerShell.Core\FileSystem::C:\temp

Mode                LastWriteTime     Length Name
----                -------------     ------ ----
-a---          7/8/2006   7:58 PM       2066 junk.jpg
```

This time it works properly. When you pipe the output of a cmdlet such as Get-ChildItem into another cmdlet like Remove-Item, the -LiteralPath parameter is used to couple the cmdlets so that metacharacters in the paths returned by dir don't cause problems for Remove-Item. If you want to delete the files we were looking at earlier, you can use Get-ChildItem to see them:

```
PS (16) > Get-ChildItem thumb````[*

    Directory: Microsoft.PowerShell.Core\FileSystem::C:\Doc
    uments and Settings\brucepay\Local Settings\Temporary
    Internet Files\Content.IE5\MYNBM9OJ

Mode                LastWriteTime     Length Name
----                -------------     ------ ----
-a---          7/8/2006   7:58 PM       2066 thumb[1].jpg
-a---         9/11/2006   2:48 PM      12476 thumb[2].txt
-a---         9/11/2006   2:48 PM      11933 thumb[3].txt
```

Now pipe the output of Get-ChildItem into Remove-Item

```
PS (17) > Get-ChildItem thumb````[* | Remove-Item
```

and verify that they've been deleted:

```
PS (18) > Get-ChildItem thumb````[*
```

No files are found, so the deletion was successful.

This essentially covers the issues around working with file paths. From here we can move on to working with the file contents.

16.1.6 The Registry provider

PowerShell uses paths to access many types of hierarchical information on a Windows computer. One of the most important (okay, maybe *the* most important) types of hierarchical information is the Registry. The Registry is a store of hierarchical configuration information, much like the file system. But there's one significant difference: in the Registry, a container has two axes: children and properties or, as you're more used to calling them from hashtables, keys and values. This is one of the more complex scenarios that the provider model addresses.

In the Registry provider, it's no longer sufficient to just have the path; you also need to know whether you're accessing a name or a property. Let's take a look. Start by `cd`'ing to the PowerShell hive in the Registry:

```
PS (1) > cd hklm:\software\microsoft\powershell
```

Use `dir` to see what's there:

```
PS (2) > dir

    Hive: HKEY_LOCAL_MACHINE\software\microsoft\powershell

SKC  VC Name                           Property
---  -- ----                           --------
  4   2 1                              {Install, PID}
```

Unfortunately, the default display for a Registry entry is a bit cryptic. We'll `Format-List` to make it a bit more comprehensible:

```
PS (3) > dir | Format-List

Name        : 1
ValueCount  : 2
Property    : {Install, PID}
SubKeyCount : 4
```

This code is quite a bit clearer. In this path you find a single item named 1. This item has two properties, or values, associated with it and four children, or subkeys. Now `cd` into the container and run `Get-ChildItem` again:

```
PS (4) > cd ./1
PS (5) > Get-ChildItem
    Hive: HKEY_LOCAL_MACHINE\software\microsoft\powershell\1

SKC  VC Name                           Property
---  -- ----                           --------
  0   1 0409                           {Install}
  0   7 PowerShellEngine               {ApplicationBase, PSCompati...
  1   0 PSConfigurationProviders       {}
  2   0 ShellIds                       {}
```

You see information about the subkeys. But what about accessing the properties? You do this using the `Get-ItemProperty` cmdlet. To get the value of the PowerShell Product ID property, use the following:

```
PS (6) > Get-ItemProperty -Path . -Name PID

PSPath       : Microsoft.PowerShell.Core\Registry::HKEY_LOCAL_MACHINE
               \software\microsoft\powershell\1
PSParentPath : Microsoft.PowerShell.Core\Registry::HKEY_LOCAL_MACHINE
               \software\microsoft\powershell
PSChildName  : 1
PSDrive      : HKLM
PSProvider   : Microsoft.PowerShell.Core\Registry
PID          : 89383-100-0001260-04309
```

Notice that you need to specify both the path and the name of the property to retrieve. Properties are always relative to a path. By specifying `.` as the path, the property is relative to the current directory. There's another somewhat annoying thing about how `Get-ItemProperty` works. It doesn't return the value of the property; it returns a new object that has the property value as a member. So, before you can do anything with this value, you need to extract it from the containing object:

```
PS (9) > (Get-ItemProperty -Path . -Name PID).PID
89383-100-0001260-04309
```

By using the `.` operator to extract the member's value, you can get just the value.

> **NOTE** This is another one of those design trade-offs the PowerShell team encountered as we developed this environment. If we returned just the value, we'd lose the context for the value (where it came from, and so on.) And so, in order to preserve this information, the team ended up forcing people to write what appears to be redundant code. A better way to handle this might've been to return the value with the context attached as synthetic properties.

16.2 FILE PROCESSING

Let's recap and see where we are. You know that PowerShell has a *provider* abstraction allowing users to work with system data stores as though they were drives. A provider is an installable software component that surfaces a data store in a form that can be mounted as a "drive." These drives are a PowerShell fiction; that is, they have meaning only to PowerShell as opposed to system drives that have meaning everywhere. Also, unlike the system drives, PowerShell drive names can be longer than one character.

You've already seen some examples of non-file-system providers in earlier chapters, where we worked with the variable: and function: drives. These providers let you use the `New-Item` and `Remove-Item` cmdlets to add and remove variables or functions just as if they were files.

A key piece to making this provider abstraction is the set of core cmdlets listed in table 16.1. These cmdlets are the core set of commands for manipulating the system and correspond to commands found in other shell environments. Because these commands are used so frequently, short aliases—the canonical aliases—are provided for the commands. By canonical, we mean that they follow a standard form: usually the first letter or two of the verb followed by the first letter or two of the noun. Two additional sets of "user portability" aliases are provided to help new users work with the system. There's one set for `cmd.exe` users and one set for UNIX shell users. Note that these aliases map only the name; they don't provide exact functional correspondence to either the `cmd.exe` or UNIX commands.

Table 16.1 List of core cmdlets, aliases, and equivalents in other shells

Cmdlet name	Canonical	Cmd.exe	UNIX sh	Description
`Get-Location`	`gl`	`cd`	`pwd`	Get the current directory.
`Set-Location`	`sl`	`cd, chdir`	`cd, chdir`	Change the current directory.
`Copy-Item`	`cpi`	`copy`	`cp`	Copy files.
`Remove-Item`	`ri`	`del, rd`	`rm, rmdir`	Remove a file or directory. PowerShell has no separate command for removing directories as opposed to files.
`Move-Item`	`mi`	`move`	`mv`	Move a file.
`Rename-Item`	`rni`	`ren`	`mv`	Rename a file.
`Set-Item`	`si`			Set the contents of a file.
`Clear-Item`	`cli`			Clear the contents of a file.
`New-Item`	`ni`			Create a new empty file or directory. The type of object is controlled by the `-ItemType` parameter.
`MkDir`		`md`	`mkdir`	`MkDir` is implemented as a function in PowerShell so that users can create directories without having to specify `-Type directory`.
`Get-Content`	`gc`	`type`	`cat`	Send the contents of a file to the output stream.
`Set-Content`	`sc`			Set the contents of a file. UNIX and `cmd.exe` have no equivalent. Redirection is used instead. The difference between `Set-Content` and `Out-File` is discussed later in this chapter.

Online help is available for all of these commands; type

```
help cmdlet-name
```

and you'll receive detailed help on the cmdlets, their parameters, and some simple examples showing how to use them.

NOTE The `help` command (which is a wrapper function for `Get-Help`) also supports an `-Online` parameter. This parameter will cause help information retrieved from Microsoft TechNet to be displayed using the default web browser rather than on the console. The online information is constantly being updated and corrected, so this is the best solution for getting help on PowerShell topics.

In the next few sections, we'll look at some more sophisticated applications of these cmdlets, including how to deal with binary data. In traditional shell environments, binary data either required specialized commands or forced you to create new executables in a language such as C, because the basic shell model couldn't cope with binary data. You'll see how PowerShell can work directly with binary data. But first, let's take a minute to look at the PowerShell drive abstraction to simplify working with paths.

16.2.1 Reading and writing files

In PowerShell, files are read using the `Get-Content` cmdlet. This cmdlet allows you to work with text files using a variety of character encodings. It also lets you work efficiently with binary files, as you'll see in a minute. Writing files is a bit more complex, because you have to choose between `Set-Content` and `Out-File`. The difference here is whether the output goes through the formatting subsystem. We'll also explain this later on in this section. It's important to point out that there are no separate `open/read/close` or `open/write/close` steps to working with files. The pipeline model allows you to process data, and never have to worry about closing file handles—the system takes care of this for you.

Reading files with the Get-Content cmdlet

The `Get-Content` cmdlet is the primary way to read files in PowerShell. Actually, it's the primary way to read any content available through PowerShell drives. Figure 16.1 shows a subset of the parameters available on the cmdlet.

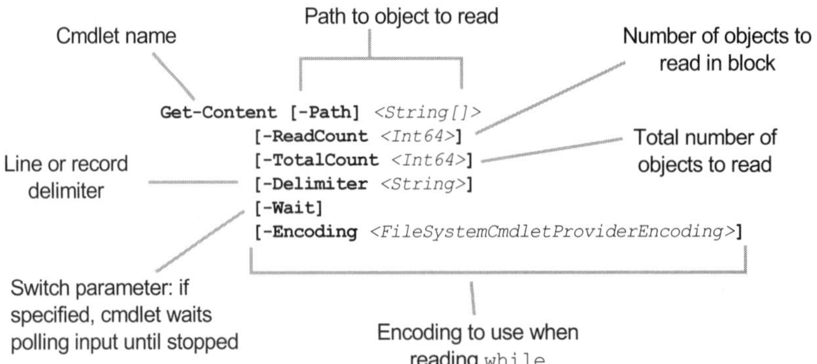

Figure 16.1 The `Get-Content` cmdlet parameters. This cmdlet is used to read content from a content provider's store.

Reading text files is simple. The command

```
Get-Content myfile.txt
```

will send the contents of myfile.txt to the output stream. Notice that the command signature for `-Path` allows for an array of path names. This is how you concatenate a collection of files together. Let's try this. First, create a collection of files:

```
PS (1) > 1..3 | foreach { "This is file $_" > "file$_.txt"}
PS (2) > dir

    Directory: Microsoft.PowerShell.Core\FileSystem::C:\Temp\fil
    es

Mode                LastWriteTime     Length Name
----                -------------     ------ ----
-a---          7/6/2006   8:33 PM         34 file1.txt
-a---          7/6/2006   8:33 PM         34 file2.txt
-a---          7/6/2006   8:33 PM         34 file3.txt
```

And now display their contents:

```
PS (3) > Get-Content file1.txt,file2.txt,file3.txt
This is file 1
This is file 2
This is file 3
```

or simply

```
PS (4) > Get-Content *.txt
This is file 1
This is file 2
This is file 3
```

In this example, the contents of file1.txt, file2.txt, and file3.txt are sent to the output stream in order. For `cmd.exe` users, this is equivalent to

```
copy file1.txt+file2.txt+file3.txt con
```

Let's try this in `cmd.exe`:

```
C:\Temp\files>copy file1.txt+file2.txt+file3.txt con
file1.txt
 T h i s   i s   f i l e   1
 file2.txt
  h i s   i s   f i l e   2
 file2.txt
  h i s   i s   f i l e   3
         1 file(s) copied.
```

The output looks funny because the files were written in Unicode. You need to tell the copy command to write in ASCII, and try it again:

```
C:\Temp\files>copy /a file1.txt+file2.txt+file3.txt con
file1.txt
This is file 1
```

```
file2.txt
This is file 2
file2.txt
This is file 3
        1 file(s) copied.
```

By default, PowerShell uses Unicode for text, but you can override this. You'll see how to do this in the section on writing files. In the meantime, let's see how to work with binary files.

Example: the Get-HexDump function

Let's look at an example that uses some of these features to deal with nontext files. You're going to write a function that can be used to dump out a binary file. You'll call this function `Get-HexDump`. It takes the name of the file to display, the number of bytes to display per line, and the total number of bytes as parameters. You want the output of this function to look like the following:

```
PS (130) > Get-HexDump "$env:windir/Soap Bubbles.bmp" -w 12 -t 100
42 4d ba 01 01 00 00 00 00 00 ba 01 BM ....... .
00 00 28 00 00 00 00 01 00 00 00 01 ...........
00 00 01 00 08 00 00 00 00 00 00 00 ...........
01 00 12 0b 00 00 12 0b 00 00 61 00 ..........a.
00 00 61 00 00 00 6b 10 10 00 73 10 ..a...k...s.
10 00 73 18 18 00 7b 21 21 00 84 29 ..s.........
29 00 84 31 31 00 6b 08 08 00 8c 39 ...11.k....9
31 00 84 31 29 00 8c 31 31 00 7b 18 1..1...11...
18 00 8c 39 ...9
```

In this example, you're using `Get-HexDump` to dump out the contents of one of the bitmap files in the Windows installation directory. You've specified that it display 12 bytes per line and stop after the first 100 bytes. The first part of the display is the value of the byte in hexadecimal, and the portion on the right side is the character equivalent. Only values that correspond to letters or numbers are displayed. Nonprintable characters are shown as dots. The following listing shows the code for this function.

Listing 16.1 Get-HexDump

```
function Get-HexDump ($path = $(throw "path must be specified"),
$width=10, $total=-1)
{
    $OFS=""
    Get-Content -Encoding byte $path -ReadCount $width `
        -TotalCount $total | %{
        $record = $_
        if (($record -eq 0).count -ne $width)
        {
            $hex = $record | %{
                " " + ("{0:x}" -f $_).PadLeft(2,"0")}
            $char = $record | %{
                if ([char]::IsLetterOrDigit($_))
                    { [char] $_ } else { "." }}
```

❶ Set $OFS to empty

❷ Skip record if length is zero

❸ Format data

```
            "$hex $char"
        }
    }
}
```

As required, the function takes a mandatory path parameter and optional parameters for the number of bytes per line and the total number of bytes to display. You're going to be converting arrays to strings and you don't want any spaces added, so you'll set the output field separator character ❶ to be empty.

The `Get-Content` cmdlet does all of the hard work. It reads the file in binary mode (indicated by setting encoding to byte), reads up to a maximum of `-TotalCount` bytes, and writes them into the pipeline in records of length specified by `-ReadCount`. The first thing you do in the `foreach` scriptblock is save the record that was passed in, because you'll be using nested scriptblocks that will cause `$_` to be overwritten.

If the record is all zeros ❷, you're not going to bother displaying it. It might be a better design to make this optional, but we'll leave it as is for this example. For display purposes, you're converting the record of bytes ❸ into two-digit hexadecimal numbers. You use the format operator to format the string in hexadecimal and then the `PadLeft()` method on strings to pad it out to two characters. Finally, you prefix the whole thing with a space. The variable `$hex` ends up with a collection of these formatted strings.

Now you need to build the character equivalent of the record. You'll use the methods on the `[char]` class to decide whether you should display the character or a dot (.). Notice that even when you're displaying the character, you're still casting it into a `[char]`. This is necessary because the record contains a byte value, which, if directly converted into a string, will be formatted as a number instead of as a character. Finally, you'll output the completed record, taking advantage of string expansion to build the output string (which is why you set `$OFS` to `""`).

This example illustrates the basic technique for getting at the binary data in a file. The technique has a variety of applications beyond simply displaying binary data, of course. Once you reach the data, you can determine a variety of characteristics about the content of that file. In the next section, we'll look at an example and examine the content of a binary file to double-check on the type of that file.

Example: the Get-MagicNumber function

If you looked closely at the output from the BMP file earlier, you might have noticed that the first two characters in the file were BP. In fact, the first few bytes in a file are often used as a "magic number" that identifies the type of the file. You'll write a short function called `Get-MagicNumber` that displays the first four bytes of a file so you can investigate these magic numbers. Here's what you want the output to look like. First, try this on a BMP file:

```
PS (1) > Get-MagicNumber $env:windir/Zapotec.bmp
424d 3225 'BM2.'
```

and then on an EXE:

```
PS (2) > Get-MagicNumber $env:windir/explorer.exe
4d5a 9000 'MZ..'
```

This utility dumps the header bytes of the executable. The first two bytes identify this file as an MS-DOS executable.

> **NOTE** As you can see, the ASCII representation of the header bytes (0x5A4D) is MZ. These are the initials of Mark Zbikowski, one of the original architects of MS-DOS.

The code for `Get-MagicNumber` is shown in the following listing.

Listing 16.2 Get-MagicNumber

```
function Get-MagicNumber ($path)
{
    $OFS=""
    $mn = Get-Content -Encoding byte $path -read 4 -total 4
    $hex1 = ("{0:x}" -f ($mn[0]*256+$mn[1])).PadLeft(4, "0")
    $hex2 = ("{0:x}" -f ($mn[2]*256+$mn[3])).PadLeft(4, "0")
    [string] $chars = $mn| %{ if ([char]::IsLetterOrDigit($_))
                { [char] $_ } else { "." }}
    "{0} {1} '{2}'" -f  $hex1, $hex2, $chars
}
```

There's not much that's new in this function. Again, you set the output field separator string to be empty. You extract the first four bytes as two pairs of numbers formatted in hex and also as characters if they correspond to printable characters. Finally, you format the output as desired.

From these examples, you see that `Get-Content` allows you to explore any type of file on a system, not just text files. For now, though, let's return to text files and look at another parameter on `Get-Content: -Delimiter`. When reading a text file, the default line delimiter is the newline character.

> **NOTE** The end-of-line sequence on Windows is generally a two-character sequence: carriage return followed by newline. The .NET I/O routines hide this detail and let us just pretend it's a newline. In fact, the runtime will treat newline by itself, carriage return by itself, and the carriage return/newline sequence all as end-of-line sequences.

This parameter lets you change that. With this new knowledge, let's return to the word-counting problem from earlier. If you set the delimiter to be the space character instead of a newline, you can split the file as you read it. Let's use this in an example that operates on one of the About help files included with PowerShell. Here's the command:

```
Get-Content $pshome/en-us/about_Assignment_Operators.help.txt `
    -Delimiter " " |
    foreach { $_ -replace "[^\w]+"} |
    where { $_ -notmatch "^[ `t]*`$"} |
```

```
group |
sort -Descending count |
select -First 10 |
ft -auto name, count
```

The -Delimiter parameter is used to split the file on space boundaries instead of newlines. You're using the same group, sort, and format operations as before, but this time you're sorting in descending order so you can use the Select-Object cmdlet instead of array indexing to extract the top 10 words. You're also doing more sophisticated filtering. You're using a foreach filter to get rid of the characters that aren't legal in a word. This is accomplished with the -replace operator and the regular expression "[^\w]+". The \w pattern is a metacharacter that matches any legal character in a word. Putting it in the square brackets prefixed with the caret says it should match any character that isn't valid in a word. The where filter is used to discard any empty lines that may be in the text or that may have been created by the foreach filter.

At this point, you should have a pretty good handle on reading files and processing their contents. It's time to look at the various ways to write files.

16.2.2 Writing files

There are two major ways to write files in PowerShell—by setting file content with the Set-Content cmdlet and by writing files using the Out-File cmdlet. The big difference is that Out-File, like all the output cmdlets, tries to format the output. Set-Content, on the other hand, simply writes the output. If its input objects aren't already strings, it will convert them to strings by calling the ToString() method. This isn't usually what you want for objects, but it's exactly what you want if your data is already formatted or if you're working with binary data.

The other thing you need to be concerned with is how the files are encoded when they're written. In an earlier example, you saw that, by default, text files are written in Unicode. Let's rerun this example, changing the encoding to ASCII instead:

```
PS (48) > 1..3 | %{ "This is file $_" |
>> Set-Content -Encoding ascii file$_.txt }
>>
```

The -Encoding parameter is used to set how the files will be written. In this example, the files are written using ASCII encoding. Now let's rerun the cmd.exe copy example that didn't work earlier:

```
PS (49) > cmd /c copy file1.txt+file2.txt+file3.txt con
file1.txt
This is file 1
file2.txt
This is file 2
file3.txt
This is file 3
        1 file(s) copied.
```

This time it works fine, because the encoding matches what cmd.exe expected. In the next section, we'll look at using -Encoding to write binary files.

16.2.3 All together now—reading and writing

Our next topic involves combining reading and writing operations with binary files. First, you'll set up paths to two files: a source bitmap file

```
$src = "$env:windir/Soap Bubbles.bmp"
```

and a destination in a temporary file:

```
$dest = "$env:temp/new_bitmap.bmp"
```

Next, copy the contents from one file to the other:

```
Get-Content -Encoding byte -read 10kb $src |
    Set-Content -Encoding byte $dest
```

Now let's define a (not very good) checksum function that simply adds up all the bytes in the file:

```
function Get-CheckSum ($path)
{
    $sum=0
    Get-Content -Encoding byte -read 10kb $path | %{
        foreach ($byte in $_) { $sum += $byte }
    }
    $sum
}
```

Use this function to verify that the file you copied is the same as the original file (note that this is a fairly slow function and takes awhile to run):

```
PS (5) > Get-CheckSum $src
268589
PS (6) > Get-CheckSum $dest
268589
```

The numbers come out the same, so you have some confidence that the copied file matches the original.

16.2.4 Performance caveats with Get-Content

PowerShell makes file processing easy, but the pipeline processor (at least as of version 2) is rather slow and this makes certain types of processing on large files problematic. For example, a user at Microsoft had a script that processed a large file to remove the first three lines from the file. This was done by using the following series of steps:

```
$lines = Get-Content $file -ReadCount 0
$lines = $lines | select -Skip 3
$lines | Set-Content temp.txt
move temp.txt $file -Force
```

This script read in all the lines the file, used `select` to skip the first three lines, wrote the result to a temporary file, and then did a forced rename to replace the original file. On the target file, this simple process was taking well over a minute due to pipeline processor overhead, and it had to be run on a very large number of files. Although there wasn't much that could be done in the pipeline to speed things up, a workaround was available: use the raw .NET I/O classes. The workaround looked something like this:

```
function Skip3 ($file, $encoding = [System.Text.Encoding]::Unicode)
{
    $input = Resolve-Path $file
    $output = Join-Path (Split-Path -Parent $input) out.txt

    [io.file]::WriteAllLines( $output,
        [io.file]::ReadAllLines($input)[3..$text.length], $encoding)
}
```

In this function, the .NET methods are used to read and write the file, and array indexing is used to strip of the first three lines. This script ran in less than a second for each file, making the intended task feasible. This type of workaround should be the exception rather than the rule. PowerShell is fast enough for most typical applications. It is nice, however, to know that faster techniques are available directly from PowerShell (at the cost of some complexity) instead of having to switch to a different tool.

This wraps up our coverage of the file system provider. In the next section we'll look another useful provider: the Registry provider.

16.3 PROCESSING UNSTRUCTURED TEXT

Although PowerShell is an object-based shell, it still has to deal with text. In chapter 4, we covered the operators (`-match`, `-replace`, `-like`, `-split`, `-join`) that PowerShell provides for working with text. We showed you how to concatenate two strings together using the plus operator. In this section, we'll cover some of the more advanced string processing operations. We'll discuss techniques for splitting and joining strings using the `[string]` and `[regex]` members and using filters to extract statistical information from a body of text.

16.3.1 Using System.String to work with text

One common scenario for scripting is processing log files. This requires breaking the log strings into pieces to extract relevant bits of information. PowerShell v2 address this by using the `-split` operator, but in PowerShell v1, if you needed to split a string into pieces, you had to use the `Split()` method on the `[string]` class. This is still fairly simple to do:

```
PS (1) > "Hello there world".Split()
Hello
there
world
```

The `Split()` method with no arguments splits on spaces. In this example, it produces an array of three elements.

```
PS (2) > "Hello there world".Split().length
3
```

You can verify this with the `Length` property. In fact, it splits on any of the characters that fall into the `WhiteSpace` character class. This includes tabs, so it works properly on a string containing both tabs and spaces:

```
PS (3) > "Hello`there world".Split()
Hello
there
world
```

In the revised example, you still get three fields, even though space is used in one place and tab in another.

And while the default is to split on a whitespace character, you can specify a string of characters to use split fields:

```
PS (4) > "First,Second;Third".Split(',;')
First
Second
Third
```

Here you specified the comma and the semicolon as valid characters to split the field.

There is, however, an issue; the default behavior for "split this" isn't necessarily what you want. The reason why is that it splits on each separator character. This means that if you have multiple spaces between words in a string, you'll get multiple empty elements in the result array. For example:

```
PS (5) > "Hello there    world".Split().length
6
```

In this example, you end up with six elements in the array because there are three spaces between "there" and "world." Now let's continue on paralleling the features of the `-split` operator.

Using SplitStringOptions

The `-split` operator allows you to specify a number of options that are used to control the splitting process. Let's see how you can do the same thing using the `Split()` method. You can get a list of all of the method overloads by using the `OverloadDefinitions` member on the `PSMethod` object for `Split`:

```
PS (6) > "hello".split.OverloadDefinitions
string[] Split(Params char[] separator)
string[] Split(char[] separator, int count)
string[] Split(char[] separator, System.StringSplitOptions options)
string[] Split(char[] separator, int count, System.StringSplitOptions
 options)
string[] Split(string[] separator, System.StringSplitOptions options)
string[] Split(string[] separator, int count, System.StringSplitOptio
ns options)
```

The methods that take the `options` argument look promising. Let's see what the `SplitStringOptions` are. Do so by trying to cast a string into these options:

```
PS (8) > [StringSplitOptions] "abc"
Cannot convert value "abc" to type "System.StringSplitOptions"
due to invalid enumeration values. Specify one of the following
enumeration values and try again. The possible enumeration values
 are "None, RemoveEmptyEntries".
At line:1 char:21
+ [StringSplitOptions]  <<<< "abc"
```

The error message tells you the legitimate values for the enumeration. If you look up this class in the online documentation on MSDN, you'll see that this option tells the `Split()` method to discard empty array elements. This sounds just like what you need, so let's try it:

```
PS (9) > "Hello there    world".split(" ",
>> [StringSplitOptions]::RemoveEmptyEntries)
>>
Hello
there
world
```

It works as desired. Next you can apply this technique to a larger problem.

Analyzing word use in a document

Given a body of text, say you want to find the number of words in the text as well as the number of unique words and then display the 10 most common words in the text. For our purposes, we'll use one of the PowerShell help text files: about_Assignment_operators.help.txt. This isn't a particularly large file (about 17 KB) so you can load it into memory using the `Get-Content` (`gc`) cmdlet:

```
PS (10) > $s = gc $PSHOME/en-US/about_Assignment_operators.help.txt
PS (11) > $s.length
747
```

The variable `$s` now contains the text of the file as a collection of lines (747 lines, to be exact). This is usually what you want, because it lets you process a file one line at time. But, in this example, you actually want to process this file as a single string. To do so, you could use the `-join` operator, but let's use the `String.Join()` method instead. You'll join all of the lines, adding an additional space between each line:

```
PS (12) > $s = [string]::join(" ", $s)
PS (13) > $s.length
22010
```

Now `$s` contains a single string containing the whole text of the file. You verify this by checking the length rather than displaying it. Next, split it into an array of words:

```
PS (14) > $words = $s.Split(" `t",
>> [stringsplitoptions]::RemoveEmptyEntries)
>>
PS (15) > $words.length
3316
```

So the text of the file has 3,316 words in it. You need to find out how many unique words there are. You have a couple ways of doing this. The easiest approach is to use the `Sort-Object` cmdlet with the `-Unique` parameter. This code will sort the list of words and then remove all the duplicates:

```
PS (16) > $uniq = $words | sort -Unique
PS (17) > $uniq.count
604
```

The help topic contains 604 unique words. Using the `Sort-Object` cmdlet is fast and simple, but it doesn't cover everything you wanted to do, because it doesn't give the frequency of use. Let's look at another approach: using the `ForEach-Object` cmdlet and a hash table.

16.3.2 Using hashtables to count unique words

In the previous example, you used the `-Unique` parameter on `Sort-Object` to generate a list of unique words. Now you'll take advantage of the set-like behavior of hashtables to do the same thing, but in addition you'll be able to count the number of occurrences of each word.

> **NOTE** In mathematics, a set is a collection of unique elements. This is how the keys work in a hashtable. Each key in a hashtable occurs exactly once. Attempting to add a key more than once will result in an error. In PowerShell, assigning a new value to an existing key replaces the old value associated with that key. The key itself remains unique. This turns out to be a powerful technique, because it's a way of building index tables for collections of objects based on arbitrary property values. These index tables let you run database-like operations on object collections. See appendix B for an example of how you can use this technique to implement a SQL-like join operation on two collections of objects.

Once again, you split the document into a stream of words. Each word in the stream will be used as the hashtable key, and you'll keep the count of the words in the value. Here's the script:

```
PS (18) > $words | % {$h=@{}} {$h[$_] += 1}
```

It's not much longer than the previous example. The code uses the `%` alias for `ForEach-Object` to keep it short. In the `begin` clause in `ForEach-Object`, you're initializing the variable `$h` to hold the resulting hashtable. Then, in the process scriptblock, you increment the hashtable entry indexed by the word. You're taking advantage of the way arithmetic works in PowerShell. If the key doesn't exist yet, the hashtable returns `$null`. When `$null` is added to a number, it's treated as 0. This allows the expression

```
$h[$_] += 1
```

to work. Initially, the hashtable member for a given key doesn't exist. The += operator retrieves `$null` from the table, converts it to 0, adds 1, and then assigns the value back to the hashtable entry.

Let's verify that the script produces the same answer for the number of words as you found with the `Sort-Object -Unique` solution:

```
PS (19) > $h.keys.count
604
```

You have 604, the same as before.

Now you have a hashtable containing the unique words and the number of times each word is used. But hashtables aren't stored in any particular order, so you need to sort it. You'll use a scriptblock parameter to specify the sorting criteria. Tell it to sort the list of keys based on the frequency stored in the hashtable entry for that key:

```
PS (20) > $frequency = $h.keys | sort {$h[$_]}
```

The words in the sorted list are ordered from least frequent to most frequent. This means that `$frequency[0]` contains the least frequently used word:

```
PS (21) > $frequency[0]
avoid
```

The last entry in frequency contains the most commonly used word. If you remember from chapter 3, you can use negative indexing to get the last element of the list:

```
PS (22) > $frequency[-1]
the
```

It comes as no surprise that the most frequent word is "the," and it's used 344 times:

```
PS (23) > $h["The"]
344
```

The next most frequent word is "to," which is used 138 times:

```
PS (24) > $h[$frequency[-2]]
138
PS (25) > $frequency[-2]
to
```

Here are the top 10 most frequently used words in the `about_Assignment_operators` help text:

```
PS (26) > -1..-10 | %{ $frequency[$_]+" "+$h[$frequency[$_]]}
the 344
to 138
a 124
$a 116
value 102
C:\PS> 85
of 80
```

```
= 74
variable 57
Operator 53
```

PowerShell includes a cmdlet that's also useful for this kind of task: `Group-Object`. This cmdlet groups its input objects into collections sorted by the specified property. This means that you can achieve the same type of ordering with the following:

```
PS (27) > $grouped = $words | group | sort count
```

Once again, you see that the most frequently used word is "the":

```
PS (28) > $grouped[-1]

Count Name                      Group
----- ----                      -----
  344 the                       {the, the, the, the...}
```

You can display the 10 most frequent words with this:

```
PS (29) > $grouped[-1..-10]

Count Name                      Group
----- ----                      -----
  344 the                       {the, the, the, the...}
  138 to                        {to, to, to, to...}
  124 a                         {a, a, a, a...}
  116 $a                        {$a, $a, $a, $a...}
  102 value                     {value, value, value, value...}
   85 C:\PS>                    {C:\PS>, C:\PS>, C:\PS>, C:\PS>...}
   80 of                        {of, of, of, of...}
   74 =                         {=, =, =, =...}
   57 variable                  {variable, variable, variable, var...
   53 Operator                  {Operator, operator, operator, ope...
```

The code creates a nicely formatted display courtesy of the formatting and output subsystem built into PowerShell.

In this section, you learned how to split strings using the methods on the `[string]` class. You even saw how to split strings on a sequence of characters. But in the world of unstructured text, you'll quickly run into examples where simple splits aren't enough. As is so often the case, regular expressions come to the rescue. In the next couple of sections, you'll see how you can do more sophisticated string processing using the `[regex]` class.

16.3.3 Using regular expressions to manipulate text

In the previous section, we looked at basic string processing using members on the `[string]` class. Although this class offers a lot of potential, there are times when you need to use more powerful tools. This is where regular expressions come in. As we discussed in chapter 4, regular expressions are a domain-specific language (DSL) for matching and manipulating text. We covered a number of examples using regular expressions with the -match and -replace operators. This time, you're going to work with the regular expression class itself.

Splitting strings with regular expressions

As mentioned in chapter 3, there's a type accelerator, [regex], for the regular expression type. The [regex] type also has a Split() method, but it's much more powerful because it uses a regular expression to decide where to split strings instead of a single character:

```
PS (1) > $s = "Hello-1-there-22-World!"
PS (2) > [regex]::split($s,'-[0-9]+-')
Hello
there
World!
PS (3) > [regex]::split($s,'-[0-9]+-').count
3
```

In this example, the fields are separated by a sequence of digits bound on either side by a dash. This pattern couldn't be specified with simple character-based split operations.

When working with the .NET regular expression library, the [regex] class isn't the only class that you'll run into. You'll see this in the next example, when we look at using regular expressions to tokenize a string.

Tokenizing text with regular expressions

Tokenization, or the process of breaking a body of text into a stream of individual symbols, is a common activity in text processing. In chapter 2 we talked a lot about how the PowerShell interpreter has to tokenize a script before it can be executed, and you saw this in action in chapters 14 and 15. In the next example, we're going to look at how you can write a simple tokenizer for basic arithmetic expressions you might find in a programming language. First, you need to define the valid tokens in these expressions. You want to allow numbers made up of one or more digits; allow numbers made up of any of the operators +, -, *, or /; and also allow sequences of spaces. Here's what the regular expression to match these elements looks like:

```
PS (4) > $pat = [regex] "[0-9]+|\+|\-|\*|/| +"
```

This is a pretty simple pattern using only the alternation operator | and the quantifier +, which matches one or more instances. Because you used the [regex] cast in the assignment, $pat contains a regular expression object. You can use this object directly against an input string by calling its Match() method:

```
PS (5) > $m = $pat.match("11+2 * 35 -4")
```

The Match() method returns a Match object (the full type name is System.Text.RegularExpressions.Match). You can use the Get-Member cmdlet to explore the full set of members on this object at your leisure, but for now we're interested in only three members. The first member is the `Success` property. This will be true if the pattern matched. The second interesting member is the `Value` property, which will contain the matched value. The final member we're interested in is the `NextMatch()` method. Calling this method will step the regular expression engine to the next match in the string, and is the key to tokenizing an entire expression. You can use this method in a `while` loop to extract the tokens from the source string one at a time. In the example, you keep looping as long the `Match` object's `Success` property is true. Then you display the `Value` property and call `NextMatch()` to step to the next token:

```
PS (6) > while ($m.Success)
>> {
>>     $m.value
>>     $m = $m.NextMatch()
>> }
>>
11
+
2

*

35

-
4
```

In the output, you see each token, one per line in the order in which they appeared in the original string.

You now have a powerful collection of techniques for processing strings. The next step is to apply these techniques to processing files. Of course, you also need to spend some time finding, reading, writing, and copying files. In the next section, we'll review the basic file abstractions in PowerShell and then look at file processing.

16.3.4 Searching files with the Select-String cmdlet

You encountered the `Select-String` cmdlet earlier, but we haven't looked at it in great detail. We'll fix that in this section.

The `Select-String` cmdlet allows you to search through collections of strings or collections of files. It's similar to the `grep` command on UNIX-derived systems and the `findstr` command on Windows. Figure 16.2 shows the parameters on this cmdlet.

You might ask why this cmdlet is needed—doesn't the base language do everything it does? The answer is yes, but searching through files is such a common operation that having a cmdlet optimized for this purpose makes sense. Let's look at some

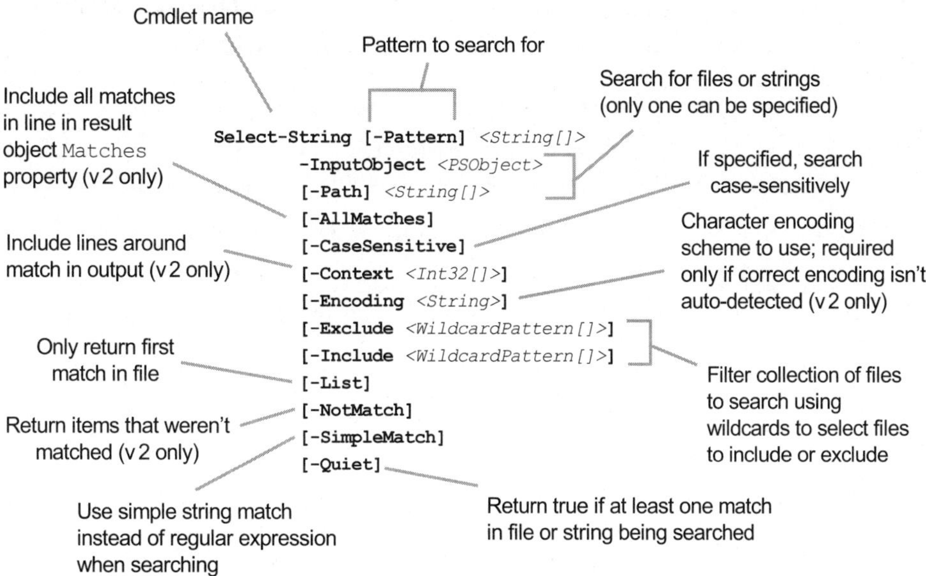

Figure 16.2 The `Select-String` cmdlet is a powerful tool for extracting information from unstructured text. Parameters marked "v2 only" were introduced in PowerShell v2.

examples. First, you'll search through all of the "about_*" topics in the PowerShell installation directory to see if the phrase "wildcard description" is there:

```
PS (1) > Select-String "wildcard description" $pshome/en-US/about*.txt

C:\Windows\System32\WindowsPowerShell\v1.0\en-US\about_wildcards.help
.txt:42:        Wildcard Description        Example  Match
  No match
```

You see that there's exactly one match, but notice the uppercase letters in the matching string. Now rerun the search using the `-CaseSensitive` parameter:

```
PS (2) > Select-String -case "wildcard description" `
>> $pshome/en-US/about*.txt
>>
```

This time nothing was found. If you alter the case in the pattern to match the target string, then it works again:

```
PS (3) > Select-String -case "Wildcard Description" `
>> $pshome/en-US/about*.txt
>>

C:\Windows\System32\WindowsPowerShell\v1.0\en-US\about_wildcards.help
.txt:42:        Wildcard Description        Example  Match
  No match
```

Searching through files this way can sometimes produce more results than you really need. We'll show you how to control what's returned next.

Using the -List and -Quiet parameters

Now let's try out the `-List` parameter. Normally `Select-String` will find all matches in a file. The `-List` switch limits the search to only the first match in a file:

```
PS (4) > Select-String -List wildcard $pshome/en-US/about*.txt

C:\Windows\System32\WindowsPowerShell\v1.0\en-
            US\about_aliases.help.txt:147:     Property parameter of
            Format-List with
a wildcard character (*) to display
C:\Windows\System32\WindowsPowerShell\v1.0\en-
            US\about_Comment_Based_Help.help.txt:377:      Accept wildcard
characters?
C:\Windows\System32\WindowsPowerShell\v1.0\en-
US\about_Comparison_Operators.help.txt:90:      Description: Match using
the wildcard character (*).
C:\Windows\System32\WindowsPowerShell\v1.0\en-
US\about_Language_Keywords.help.txt:339:          switch
[-regex|-wildcard|-exact][-casesensitive] ( pipeline )
C:\Windows\System32\WindowsPowerShell\v1.0\en-
US\about_operators.help.txt:47:      the like operators
(-like, -notlike), which find patterns using wildcard
C:\Windows\System32\WindowsPowerShell\v1.0\en-
US\about_parameters.help.txt:53:    wildcard character (*) with
the Parameter parameter to find information
C:\Windows\System32\WindowsPowerShell\v1.0\en-
US\about_pipelines.help.txt:272:          Accept wildcard characters?
true
C:\Windows\System32\WindowsPowerShell\v1.0\en-
US\about_properties.help.txt:112:     more properties and their values.
Or, you can use the wildcard
C:\Windows\System32\WindowsPowerShell\v1.0\en-
US\about_remote_troubleshooting.help.txt:140:    Enable the policy and
specify the IPv4 and IPv6 filters. Wildcards (*) are
C:\Windows\System32\WindowsPowerShell\v1.0\en-US\about_Switch.help.txt:65:
switch [-regex|-wildcard|-exact][-casesensitive] ( pipeline )
C:\Windows\System32\WindowsPowerShell\v1.0\en-
US\about_wildcards.help.txt:2:    about_Wildcards
```

In the result, you see exactly one match per file. Try using the `-Quiet` switch:

```
PS (5) > Select-String -Quiet wildcard $pshome/en-US/about*.txt
True
```

This switch returns `$true` if any of the files contained a match and `$false` if none of them did. You can also combine the two switches so that the cmdlet returns the first match in the set of files:

```
PS (6) > Select-String -Quiet -List wildcard $pshome/en-US/about*.txt

C:\Windows\System32\WindowsPowerShell\v1.0\en-
            US\about_aliases.help.txt:147:     Property parameter of
            Format-List with
 a wildcard character (*) to display
```

Searching a tree of files

If you want to search a more complex set of files, you can pipe the output of `Get-ChildItem` into the cmdlet and it will search all of these files. Let's search all the log files in the `system32` subdirectory:

```
PS (7) > Get-ChildItem -rec -Filter *.log $env:windir\system32 |
>> Select-String -List fail | Format-Table path
>>

Path
----
C:\WINDOWS\system32\CCM\Logs\ScanWrapper.LOG
C:\WINDOWS\system32\CCM\Logs\UpdateScan.log
C:\WINDOWS\system32\CCM\Logs\packages\RMSSP1_Client_RTW.log
C:\WINDOWS\system32\CCM\Logs\packages\RMSSP1_Client_RTW_BC_In...
C:\WINDOWS\system32\wbem\Logs\wbemcore.log
C:\WINDOWS\system32\wbem\Logs\wbemess.log
C:\WINDOWS\system32\wbem\Logs\wmiadap.log
C:\WINDOWS\system32\wbem\Logs\wmiprov.log
```

Notice that you're only displaying the path. The output of `Select-String` is objects, as shown:

```
PS (3) > Select-String wildcard $PSHOME/en-US/about*.txt |
>> Get-Member -type property
>>

   TypeName: Microsoft.PowerShell.Commands.MatchInfo

Name       MemberType Definition
----       ---------- ----------
Context    Property   Microsoft.PowerShell.Commands.MatchInfo...
Filename   Property   System.String Filename {get;}
IgnoreCase Property   System.Boolean IgnoreCase {get;set;}
Line       Property   System.String Line {get;set;}
LineNumber Property   System.Int32 LineNumber {get;set;}
Matches    Property   System.Text.RegularExpressions.Match[] ...
Path       Property   System.String Path {get;set;}
Pattern    Property   System.String Pattern {get;set;}
```

With these fields, there are many things you can do by selecting specific members. For example, the filename can be used to open the file in an editor and the `Line` number can be used to set the line in the file to the matching item. In the next section, we'll look at some of the more exotic properties on the `MatchInfo` object.

Searching with contexts

In the output from Get-Member, you can see that there's a context property. This property allows you to have Select-String include the lines before and after the matching line:

```
PS (1) > Get-Help Select-String |
>> Out-String -Stream |
>> Select-String syntax -Context 3
>>

      Finds text in strings and files.

> SYNTAX
      Select-String [-Path] <string[]> [-Pattern] <string[]> [-All
      Matches] [-CaseSensitive] [-Context <Int32[]>] [-Encoding
<string>] [-Exclude <string[]>] [-Include <string[]>] [-List]
]
```

This code gets the lines you want but it also gets the lines before the target that you don't want. You can solve this issue by specifying two numbers to the parameter. The first number is the length of the prefix context and the second is the suffix context. So to get what you want, you just have to specify a prefix context of 0. The result looks like this:

```
PS (2) > Get-Help Select-String |
>> Out-String -Stream |
>> Select-String syntax -Context 0,3
>>

> SYNTAX
      Select-String [-Path] <string[]> [-Pattern] <string[]>
     [-All Matches] [-CaseSensitive] [-Context <Int32[]>]
     [-Encoding <string>] [-Exclude <string[]>]
     [-Include <string[]>] [-List]
```

Getting all matches in the line

Another property on the MatchInfo object is the Matches property. This property is used when the -AllMatches switch is specified to the cmdlet. It causes all matches in the line to be returned instead of just the first match. You'll use this switch to perform the same type of tokenization that you did with regular expressions in section 16.2.2. You'll pipe the expression string into Select-String with the -AllMatches switch and the same regular expression you used earlier:

```
PS (12) > "1 + 2 *3" |
>>     Select-String -AllMatches "[0-9]+|\+|\-|\*|/| +" |
>>     foreach { $_.Matches } | Format-Table -AutoSize
>>
```

```
Groups Success Captures Index Length Value
------ ------- -------- ----- ------ -----
{1}       True {1}          0      1 1
{ }       True { }          1      1
{+}       True {+}          2      1 +
{ }       True { }          3      1
{2}       True {2}          4      1 2
{ }       True { }          5      1
{*}       True {*}          6      1 *
{3}       True {3}          7      1 3
```

You used the `foreach` cmdlet to isolate the `Matches` property and then formatted the output as a table. You can see each of the extracted tokens in the `Value` field in the `Matches` object. Using this mechanism, you can effectively and efficiently process things like large log files where the output is essentially formatted as a table.

So far in this chapter, we've looked at manipulating text with PowerShell operators, .NET methods, and finally the `Select-String` cmdlet. All of this text has been *unstructured text* where there's no rigorously defined layout for that text. As a consequence, you've had to work fairly hard to extract the information you want out of this text. There are, however, large bodies of structured text, where the format is well defined in the form of XML documents. In the next section, we'll show you how to work with XML in PowerShell.

16.4 XML STRUCTURED TEXT PROCESSING

XML (Extensible Markup Language) is becoming increasingly important in the computing world. XML is being used for everything from configuration files to log files to databases. PowerShell uses XML for its type and configuration files as well as for the help files. For PowerShell to be effective, it has to be able to process XML documents effectively. Let's look at how XML is used and supported in PowerShell.

> **NOTE** This section assumes you possess some basic knowledge of XML markup.

We'll look at the XML object type, as well as the mechanism that .NET provides for searching XML documents.

16.4.1 Using XML as objects

PowerShell supports XML documents as a core data type. This means that you can access the elements of an XML document as though they were properties on an object. For example, let's create a simple XML object. Start with a string that defines a top-level node called `top`. This node contains three descendants: `a`, `b`, and `c`, each of which has a value. Let's turn this string into an object:

```
PS (1) > $d = [xml] "<top><a>one</a><b>two</b><c>3</c></top>"
```

The [xml] cast takes the string and converts it into an XML object of type System.XML.XmlDocument. This object is then adapted by PowerShell so you can treat it like a regular object. Let's try this out. First, display the object:

```
PS (2) > $d

top
---
top
```

As you expect, the object displays one top-level property corresponding to the top-level node in the document. Now let's see what properties this node contains:

```
PS (4) > $d.top

a                    b                    c
-                    -                    -
one                  two                  3
```

There are three properties that correspond to the descendants of top. You can use conventional property notation to look at the value of an individual member:

```
PS (5) > $d.top.a
One
```

Modifying this node is as simple as assigning a new value to the node. Let's assign the string "Four" to the node a:

```
PS (6) > $d.top.a = "Four"
PS (7) > $d.top.a
Four
```

You can see that it's been changed. But there's a limitation: you can only use an actual string as the node value. The XML object adapter won't automatically convert nonstring objects to strings in an assignment, so you get an error when you try it, as seen here:

```
PS (8) > $d.top.a = 4
Cannot set "a" because only strings can be used as values to
set XmlNode properties.
At line:1 char:8
+ $d.top.a <<<<  = 4
```

All of the normal type conversions apply, of course. The node c contains a string value that's a number:

```
PS (8) > $d.top.c.gettype().FullName
System.String
```

You can add this field to an integer, which will cause it to be converted into an integer:

```
PS (9) > 2 + $d.top.c
5
```

Because you can't simply assign to elements in an XML document, we'll dig a little deeper into the [xml] object and show how you can add elements.

16.4.2 Adding elements to an XML object

Let's add an element `d` to this document. To do so, you need to use the methods on the XML document object. First, you have to create the new element:

```
PS (10) > $el= $d.CreateElement("d")
```

In text, what you've created looks like <d></d>. The tags are there, but they're empty. Let's set the element text, the "inner text," to a value and then show the element:

```
PS (11) > $el.set_InnerText("Hello")

#text
-----
Hello
```

Notice that you're using the property setter method here. This is because the XML adapter hides the basic properties on the `XmlNode` object. The other way to set this would be to use the `PSBase` member as you did with the hashtable example earlier in this chapter:

```
PS (12) > $ne = $d.CreateElement("e")
PS (13) > $ne.InnerText = "World"
PS (14) > $d.top.AppendChild($ne)

#text
-----
World
```

Take a look at the revised object:

```
PS (15) > $d.top

a : one
b : two
c : 3
d : Hello
e : World
```

The document now has five members instead of the original three. But what does the string look like? It'd be great if you could simply cast the document back to a string and see what it looks like:

```
PS (16) > [string] $d
System.Xml.XmlDocument
```

Unfortunately, as you can see, it isn't that simple. Instead, save the document as a file and display it:

```
PS (17) > $d.save("c:\temp\new.xml")
PS (18) > type c:\temp\new.xml
<top>
  <a>one</a>
  <b>two</b>
  <c>3</c>
```

```
  <d>Hello</d>
  <e>World</e>
</top>
```

The result is a nicely readable text file. Now that you know how to add children to a node, how can you add attributes? The pattern is basically the same as with elements. First, create an attribute object:

```
PS (19) > $attr = $d.CreateAttribute("BuiltBy")
```

Next, set the value of the text for that object:

```
PS (20) > $attr.Value = "Windows PowerShell"
```

And finally add it to the top-level document:

```
PS (21) > $d.DocumentElement.SetAttributeNode($attr)

#text
-----
Windows PowerShell
```

Let's look at the top node once again:

```
PS (22) > $d.top

BuiltBy : Windows PowerShell
a       : one
b       : two
c       : 3
d       : Hello
e       : World
```

The attribute has been added.

> **XML and formatting**
>
> Although PowerShell's XML support is good, there are some issues. The PowerShell formatting code has a bug: trying to display an XML node that has multiple children with the same name causes an error to be generated by the formatter. For example, the statement
>
> ```
> [xml] $x =
>    "<root><item>1</item><item>2</item></root>";  $x.Root
> ```
>
> will result in an error. This can be annoying when you're trying to explore a document. By accessing the `Item` property on the `Root` node as follows
>
> ```
> [xml] $x =
>    "<root><item>1</item><item>2</item></root>" ; $x.Root.Item
> ```
>
> you'll be able to see the elements without error. Also, for experienced .NET XML and XPath users, there are times when the XML adapter hides properties on an `Xml-`

(continued)

Document or XmlNode object that the .NET programmer expects to find. In these scenarios, the PSBase property is the workaround that lets you access the raw .NET object.

Finally, some XPath users may get confused by PowerShell's use of the property operator . to navigate an XML document. XPath uses / instead. Despite these issues, for the nonexpert user or for "quick and dirty" scenarios, the XML adapter provides significant benefit in terms of reducing the complexity of working with XML.

It's time to save the document:

```
PS (23) > $d.save("c:\temp\new.xml")
```

Then retrieve the file. You can see how the attribute has been added to the top node in the document:

```
PS (24) > type c:\temp\new.xml
<top BuiltBy="Windows PowerShell">
  <a>one</a>
  <b>two</b>
  <c>3</c>
  <d>Hello</d>
</top>
```

You've constructed, edited, and saved XML documents, but you haven't loaded an existing document yet, so that's the next step.

16.4.3 Loading and saving XML files

At the end of the previous section, you saved an XML document to a file:

```
PS (1) > $nd = [xml] (Get-Content -Read 10kb c:\temp\new.xml)
```

Here's what you're doing with this code. You use the Get-Content cmdlet to read the file using a large read-count size. When you have the text, you cast the whole thing into an XML document.

> **TIP** By default, Get-Content reads one record at a time. This process can be quite slow. When processing large files, you should use the -ReadCount parameter to specify a block size of –1. Doing so will cause the entire file to be loaded and processed at once, which is much faster. Alternatively, here's another way to load an XML document using the .NET methods:
>
> ```
> $nd = [xml]"<root></root>" ).Load("C:\temp\new.xml")
> ```
>
> Note that this does require that the full path to the file be specified.

Let's verify that the document was read properly by dumping out the top-level node and then the child nodes:

```
PS (2) > $nd

top
---
top

PS (3) > $nd.top

BuiltBy : Windows PowerShell
a       : one
b       : two
c       : 3
d       : Hello
```

All is as it should be. Even the attribute is there.

Although this is a simple approach and the one you'll probably use most often, it's not necessarily the most efficient approach because it requires loading the entire document into memory. For very large documents or collections of many documents, loading all the text into memory may become a problem. In the next section, we'll look at some alternative approaches that, though more complex, are more memory efficient.

Using the XmlReader class

Our previously discussed method for loading an XML file is simple but not especially efficient. It requires that you load the file into memory, make a copy of the file while turning it into a single string, and create an XML document representing the entire file using the XML Document Object Model (DOM) representation. The DOM is what allows you to treat an XML document as a hierarchy of objects, but to do so it consumes a lot of memory. A much more space-efficient way to process XML documents is to use the `System.Xml.XmlReader` class. This class streams through the document one element at a time instead of loading the whole thing into memory. You'll write a function that will use the XML reader to stream through a document and output it properly indented—an XML pretty-printer, if you will. Here's what you want the output of this function to look like when it dumps its built-in default document:

```
PS (1) > Format-XmlDocument
<top BuiltBy = "Windows PowerShell">
    <a>
        one
    </a>
    <b>
        two
    </b>
    <c>
        3
    </c>
    <d>
```

```
        Hello
    </d>
</top>
```

Now let's test our function on a more complex document where there are more attributes and more nesting. The following listing shows how to create this document.

Listing 16.3 Creating the text XML document

```
@'
<top BuiltBy = "Windows PowerShell">
    <a pronounced="eh">
        one
    </a>
    <b pronounced="bee">
        two
    </b>
    <c one="1" two="2" three="3">
        <one>
            1
        </one>
        <two>
            2
        </two>
        <three>
            3
        </three>
    </c>
    <d>
        Hello there world
    </d>
</top>
'@ > c:\temp\fancy.xml
```

When you run the function in listing 16.3, you see

```
PS (2) > Format-XmlDocument  c:\temp\fancy.xml
<top BuiltBy = "Windows PowerShell">
    <a pronounced = "eh">
        one
    </a>
    <b pronounced = "bee">
        two
    </b>
    <c one = "1"two = "2"three = "3">
        <one>
            1
        </one>
        <two>
            2
        </two>
        <three>
            3
        </three>
    </c>
```

```
    <d>
        Hello there world
    </d>
</top>
```

which is close to the original document. The code for the `Format-XmlDocument` function is shown in the next listing.

Listing 16.4 The `Format-XmlDocument` function

```
function global:Format-XmlDocument ($doc="$PWD\fancy.xml")
{
  $settings = New-Object System.Xml.XmlReaderSettings        # 1 Create settings object
  $doc = (Resolve-Path $doc).ProviderPath
  $reader = [System.Xml.XmlReader]::create($doc, $settings)
  $indent=0
  function indent ($s) { "  "*$indent+$s }                 # 2 Define formatting function
  while ($reader.Read())
  {
    if ($reader.NodeType -eq [Xml.XmlNodeType]::Element)      # 3 Process element nodes
    {
      $close = $(if ($reader.IsEmptyElement) { "/>" } else { ">" })
      if ($reader.HasAttributes)
      {
        $s = indent "<$($reader.Name) "
        [void] $reader.MoveToFirstAttribute()
        do
        {
          $s += "$($reader.Name) = `"$($reader.Value)`" "
        }
        while ($reader.MoveToNextAttribute())
        "$s$close"
      }
      else
      {
        indent "<$($reader.Name)$close"
      }
      if ($close -ne '/>') {$indent++}                        # 4 Increase indent level
    }
    elseif ($reader.NodeType -eq [Xml.XmlNodeType]::EndElement )
    {
      $indent--
      indent "</$($reader.Name)>"
    }
    elseif ($reader.NodeType -eq [Xml.XmlNodeType]::Text)
    {
      indent $reader.Value                                    # 5 Format text element
    }
  }
  $reader.close()
}
```

`Format-XmlDocument` is a complex function, so it's worthwhile to take it one piece at a time. Let's start with the basic function declaration, where it takes an optional argument that names a file. Next you create the settings object ❶ you need to pass in when you create the XML reader object. You also need to resolve the path to the document, because the XML reader object requires an absolute path (see chapter 17 for an explanation of why this is). Now you can create the `XmlReader` object itself. The XML reader will stream through the document, reading only as much as it needs, as opposed to reading the entire document into memory.

You want to display the levels of the document indented, so you initialize an indent level counter and a local function ❷ to display the indented string. Now you'll read through all of the nodes in the document. You'll choose different behavior based on the type of the node. An element node ❸ is the beginning of an XML element. If the element has attributes, then you'll add them to the string to display. You'll use the `MoveToFirstAttribute()` and `MoveToNextAttribute()` methods to move through the attributes. (Note that this pattern parallels the enumerator pattern you saw in chapter 5 with the `$foreach` and `$switch` enumerators.) If there are no attributes, just display the element name. At each new element, increase ❹ the indent level if it's not an empty element tag. If it's the end of an element, decrease the indent level and display the closing tag. If it's a text element, just display the value of the element ❺. Finally, close the reader. You always want to close a handle received from a .NET method. It'll eventually be discarded during garbage collection, but it's possible to run out of handles before you run out of memory.

This example illustrates the basic techniques for using an XML reader object to walk through an arbitrary document.

But where are the pipelines, you ask? Neither of these last two examples has taken advantage of PowerShell's pipelining capability. In the next section, we'll remedy this omission.

16.4.4 Processing XML documents in a pipeline

Pipelining is one of the signature characteristics of shell environments in general and PowerShell in particular. Because the previous examples didn't take advantage of this feature, we'll look at how it can be applied. You're going to write a function that scans all the PowerShell help files, both the text about topics and the XML files.

> **NOTE** PowerShell v1 didn't have a way to search help, so this example is useful as well as illustrative. In PowerShell v2, the `Get-Help` cmdlet was enhanced to search all help using wildcards.

For example, let's search for all the help topics that mention the word "scriptblock":

```
PS (1) > Search-Help scriptblock
about_Display
about_Types
Get-Process
Group-Object
Measure-Command
Select-Object
```

```
Trace-Command
ForEach-Object
Where-Object
```

This tool provides a simple, fast way to search for all the help topics that contain a particular pattern. The source for the function is shown in this listing.

Listing 16,5 Search-Help

```
function Search-Help
{
    param ($pattern = $(throw "you must specify a pattern"))

    Select-String -List $pattern $PSHome\about*.txt |
        %{$_.filename -replace '\..*$'}

    dir $PShome\*dll-help.*xml |
        foreach { [xml] (get-content -read -1 $_) } |
        foreach{$_.helpitems.command} |
        where {$_.get_Innertext() -match $pattern} |
        foreach {$_.details.name.trim()}
}
```

The `Search-Help` function takes one parameter to use as the pattern for which you're searching. Listing 16.5 uses the `throw` keyword described in chapter 14 to generate an error if the parameter wasn't provided.

First, you search all the text files in the PowerShell installation directory and return one line for each matching file. Then you pipe this line into `ForEach-Object` (or, more commonly, its alias `foreach`) to extract the base name of the file using the `-replace` operator and a regular expression. This operation will list the filenames in a form that you can type back into `Get-Help`.

Next, you get a list of the XML help files and turn each file into an XML object. You specify a read count of -1 so the whole file is read at once. You extract the command elements from the XML document and then see if the text of the command contains the pattern you're looking for. If it does, then you emit the name of the command, trimming off unnecessary spaces.

As well as being a handy way to search help, this function is a nice illustration of using the divide-and-conquer strategy when writing scripts in PowerShell. Each step in the pipeline brings you incrementally closer to the final solution.

Now that you know how to manually navigate through an XML document, let's look at some of the .NET Framework's features that make navigation a bit easier and more efficient.

16.4.5 Processing XML with XPath

The support for XML in the .NET Framework is extensive so we can't possibly cover all of it in this book. There is, however, one more useful thing that we want to cover:

the XML Path Language, also known as XPath. This is a *path-based pattern language*, which means it's like the collision between paths, wildcards, and regular expressions. It's useful because it gives you a fast, concise way to select pieces of information from an XML document.

In PowerShell v1, you had to work with the raw .NET classes to be able to use XPath. PowerShell v2 introduced a new cmdlet, `Select-Xml`, that makes XPath much more accessible. In this section, we'll look at how XPath expressions work and use them to extract information from documents. We'll start with a short overview of the XPath fundamentals.

XPath basics

XPath is another domain-specific language, this time for specifying patterns that allow you to concisely extract information from XML documents. You've already seen patterns for working with hierarchies in the file system in the form of file path and wildcards. You've worked with text-oriented pattern languages like regular expressions. XPath combines these two concepts into a single mechanism for accessing data in an XML document. An XPath expression can be used to extract nodes, content, or attributes from a document. It also allows calculations to be used in the expressions to get even greater flexibility. Table 16.2 shows the basic patterns in this language and the corresponding commands you'd use in the file system.

Table 16.2 Examples of basic XPath patterns

XPath expression	Description	Equivalent file operation
`/`	Gets all of the nodes under the document root	`dir /`
`.`	Selects the current node	`Get-Item .`
`..`	Selects the parent node	`Get-Item ..`
`A`	Selects all of the children under node a	`dir a`
`/a/b/c`	Gets all nodes under path /a/b/c	`dir /a/b/c`
`//b`	Gets all elements with the name b anywhere in the document	`dir -rec -Filter b`

Things get a bit more complex because XML allows for multiple nodes with the same name and allows attributes on nodes. Next, we'll set up a test document and explore these more complex patterns.

Setting up the test document

You'll work through a couple of examples using XPath, but first you need a document to process. The following script fragment creates a string you'll use for the examples. It's a fragment of a bookstore inventory database. Each record in the database has the name of the author, the book title, and the number of books in stock. Save this string in a variable called `$inventory`, as shown in this listing.

Listing 16.6 Creating the bookstore inventory

```
$inventory = @"
  <bookstore>
    <book genre="Autobiography">
      <title>The Autobiography of Benjamin Franklin</title>
      <author>
        <first-name>Benjamin</first-name>
        <last-name>Franklin</last-name>
      </author>
      <price>8.99</price>
      <stock>3</stock>
    </book>
    <book genre="Novel">
      <title>Moby Dick</title>
      <author>
        <first-name>Herman</first-name>
        <last-name>Melville</last-name>
      </author>
      <price>11.99</price>
      <stock>10</stock>
    </book>
    <book genre="Philosophy">
      <title>Discourse on Method</title>
      <author>
        <first-name>Rene</first-name>
        <last-name>Descartes</last-name>
      </author>
      <price>9.99</price>
      <stock>1</stock>
    </book>
    <book genre="Computers">
      <title>Windows PowerShell in Action</title>
      <author>
        <first-name>Bruce</first-name>
        <last-name>Payette</last-name>
      </author>
      <price>39.99</price>
      <stock>5</stock>
    </book>
  </bookstore>
"@
```

Now that you've created your test document, let's see what you can do with it.

The Select-Xml cmdlet

PowerShell v2 introduced the `Select-Xml` cmdlet, which allows you to do XPath queries without resorting to the raw .NET Framework. The syntax for this cmdlet is shown in figure 16.3.

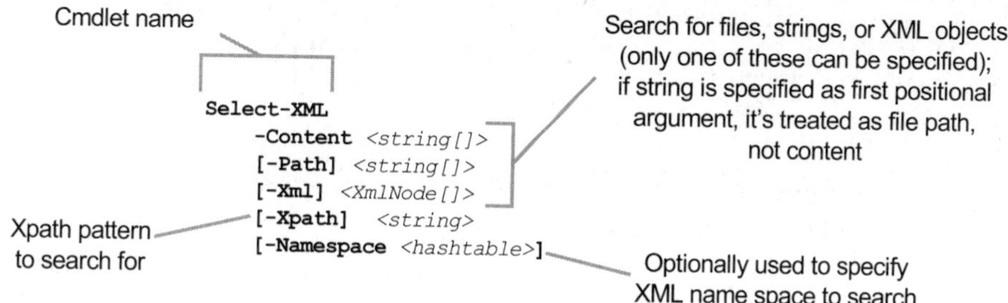
Cmdlet name
Select-XML
-Content <string[]>
[-Path] <string[]>
[-Xml] <XmlNode[]>
[-Xpath] <string>
[-Namespace <hashtable>]
Search for files, strings, or XML objects (only one of these can be specified); if string is specified as first positional argument, it's treated as file path, not content
Xpath pattern to search for
Optionally used to specify XML name space to search

Figure 16.3 The `Select-Xml` cmdlet parameters. This cmdlet allows you to perform XPath queries on XML documents stored in files or strings.

You're going to use this cmdlet in most of the examples in this section. Let's start with something very simple, getting the bookstore node at the root of the document:

```
PS (1) > Select-Xml -Content $inventory -XPath /bookstore

Node                    Path                    Pattern
----                    ----                    -------
bookstore               InputStream             /bookstore
```

Unfortunately, the output doesn't look very promising. The node object you're after is mixed in with the context of the query: where the processed text came from and what the query was. To extract the node object, you just have to reference it as a property:

```
PS (2) > (Select-Xml -Content $inventory -XPath /bookstore).Node

book
----
{book, book, book, book}
```

This output shows that there are four child nodes under bookstore. So extend your query to get these child items in a similar manner to how you could get the contents of a directory in the file system:

```
PS (3) > Select-Xml -Content $inventory -XPath /bookstore/book

Node                    Path                    Pattern
----                    ----                    -------
book                    InputStream             /bookstore/book
book                    InputStream             /bookstore/book
book                    InputStream             /bookstore/book
book                    InputStream             /bookstore/book
```

And here's the nested-node issue again. Again you have to use the . operator to retrieve the actual content. This works for one node

```
PS (4) > (Select-Xml -Content $inventory `
>>   -XPath /bookstore/book)[0].Node
>>
```

```
genre  : Autobiography
title  : The Autobiography of Benjamin Franklin
author : author
price  : 8.99
stock  : 3
```

but it won't work for the entire collection. For each of the nodes, you need to extract the Node property, and so you apply the `foreach` cmdlet:

```
PS (5) > Select-Xml -Content $inventory -XPath /bookstore/book |
>> foreach { $_.node }
>>

genre  : Autobiography
title  : The Autobiography of Benjamin Franklin
author : author
price  : 8.99
stock  : 3

genre  : Novel
title  : Moby Dick
author : author
price  : 11.99
stock  : 10

genre  : Philosophy
title  : Discourse on Method
author : author
price  : 9.99
stock  : 1

genre  : Computers
title  : Windows PowerShell in Action
author : author
price  : 39.99
stock  : 5
```

This time you see the properties of all four nodes. If you want to extract just the title nodes, add `title` to the end of the path:

```
PS (6) > Select-Xml -Content $inventory -XPath /bookstore/book |
>> foreach { $_.node.title }
>>
The Autobiography of Benjamin Franklin
Moby Dick
Discourse on Method
Windows PowerShell in Action
PS (7) > Select-Xml -Content $inventory `
>> -XPath /bookstore/book/title |
>> foreach { $_.node }
>>

#text
-----
The Autobiography of Benjamin Franklin
```

```
Moby Dick
Discourse on Method
Windows PowerShell in Action
```

At this point, using foreach all the time is getting tedious, so let's define a filter to simplify this:

```
PS (8) > filter node { $_.node }
```

This filter will make the examples a little less messy.

Now let's look at some more advanced examples. So far, you've returned the entire set of nodes, but when querying for some information, you usually just want to get part of that information. You can do this quite easily with the Where-Object cmdlet:

```
PS (9) > Select-Xml -Content $inventory -XPath /bookstore/book |
>> node | where { [double] ($_.price) -lt 10}
>>

genre  : Autobiography
title  : The Autobiography of Benjamin Franklin
author : author
price  : 8.99
stock  : 3

genre  : Philosophy
title  : Discourse on Method
author : author
price  : 9.99
stock  : 1
```

This example retrieves all the books priced less than $10. XPath has built-in functionality that's similar to the Where-Object cmdlet: *predicate expressions*. These expressions appear in the path surrounded by square brackets and can contain simple logical expression. Nodes where the expression evaluates to true are returned. Here's an example that uses a predicate expression in the XPath path to do the same thing you did with the Where-Object cmdlet:

```
PS (10) > Select-Xml -Content $inventory `
>> -XPath '/bookstore/book[price < 10]' |
>> node
>>

genre  : Autobiography
title  : The Autobiography of Benjamin Franklin
author : author
price  : 8.99
stock  : 3

genre  : Philosophy
title  : Discourse on Method
author : author
price  : 9.99
stock  : 1
```

You get the same result in both cases. Notice that in the predicate expression you were able to reference price directly as opposed to [double] ($_.price) the way you did in the switch case. Because the expression is being executed by the XPath engine, it can make these optimizations, simplifying the reference to the price item and treating it as a number automatically.

In the previous example, the price item was actually a path relative to the current node. You can use things like .. to reference the parent node. Let's write our expression so that it returns only the titles of the books whose price is less than $10:

```
PS (11) > Select-Xml -Content $inventory `
>> -XPath '/bookstore/book/title[../price < 10]' |
>> node
>>

#text
-----
The Autobiography of Benjamin Franklin
Discourse on Method
```

The path selects the title node but filters on the path ../price, which is a sibling to the title node.

As we discussed earlier, elements are all that an XML document can contain. Another major item is the attribute. XPath allows an attribute to be referenced instead of an element by prefixing the name with @, as you see here:

```
PS (12) > Select-Xml -Content $inventory -XPath '//@genre' | node

#text
-----
Autobiography
Novel
Philosophy
Computers
```

This example shows the genre attribute for each of the book nodes. You can also use attributes in predicate expressions in the path:

```
PS (13) > Select-Xml -Content $inventory `
>> -XPath '//book[@genre = "Novel"]' |
>> node
>>

genre  : Novel
title  : Moby Dick
author : author
price  : 11.99
stock  : 10
```

This example uses the @genre attribute in the node to only return books in the Novel genre. Note that, unlike the PowerShell relational operators, XPath operators are case sensitive. If you specify novel for the genre instead of Novel

```
PS (14) > Select-Xml -Content $inventory `
>> -XPath '//book[@genre = "novel"]' |
```

```
>> node
>>
```

nothing is retrieved, whereas doing the same thing with the `Where-Object` cmdlet works just fine:

```
PS (15) > Select-Xml -Content $inventory `
>> -XPath '//book' | node |
>> where {$_.genre -eq 'novel' }
>>

genre  : Novel
title  : Moby Dick
author : author
price  : 11.99
stock  : 10
```

This should make it clear that XPath is its own language and doesn't necessarily behave the same way as the equivalent expression in PowerShell.

Now let's do some processing on the data in the document instead of just retrieving the node. In this example, you'll calculate the total value of the inventory, which is the sum of the product of multiplying the `price` node and the `stock` node:

```
PS (16) > Select-Xml -Content $inventory `
>> -XPath '//book' | node |
>> foreach {[double] $_.price * $_.stock } |
>> Measure-Object -Sum | foreach { $_.sum }
>>
356.81
```

This code uses XPath to extract the relevant nodes and then uses PowerShell to perform the calculations.

The examples in this section illustrate the basic mechanism for using XPath to extract data from documents. They're far from comprehensive, though. There's a lot more to learn about the details of the XPath language—the functions it supports, how to do calculations, and so forth—but this level of detail is probably not needed for most scenarios because PowerShell can do all of these things in a much more flexible way.

In this section, we introduced XPath as a well-known, standard way of accessing documents. It's an effective tool, but it involves learning an entirely separate language for expression queries. Microsoft addressed this multilanguage issue (for SQL as well as XML) by introducing a .NET feature called the Language Integrated Query (LINQ). The flavor of LINQ for XML is called XLinq and is a new API for working with XML. We'll briefly touch on this in the next section.

16.4.6 A hint of XLinq

XPath is a domain-specific language (DSL) for querying XML documents—which means that you must learn new syntax and semantics to use it. With XLinq, you just have to learn a few new methods and not a new syntax.

Because the XLinq library isn't automatically loaded when PowerShell starts, you'll use Add-Type to add the necessary assemblies:

```
PS (17) > Add-Type -AssemblyName System.Core
PS (18) > Add-Type -AssemblyName System.Xml.Linq
```

You're ready to try out a query. Let's re-implement the previous example where you calculated the value of the inventory using XLinq. First, you have to create an instance of an XDocument document, which is the class that XLinq uses to represent a document instead of the XmlDocument, which is what the built-in XML support uses. Even so, as is the case with [xml], you can just cast your inventory string into an XDocument instance:

```
PS (19) > $xldoc = [System.Xml.Linq.XDocument] $inventory
```

Now that you have the document, you can run the query. As before, you need to retrieve all of the book elements that are descendants of the root node. To do so, all you have to do is call the Descendants() method on the document and pass in the name of the elements you want to retrieve. Then you have to extract the properties from the nodes that are returned. XLinq isn't natively supported in PowerShell, so you can't use the simple property references as you did in the XPath case. Instead, you have to call the Element() method on the node, passing in the name of the element to retrieve:

```
PS (20) > $xldoc.Descendants("book") |
>> foreach {
>>     [double] $_.Element("price").value *
>>         $_.Element("stock").value } |
>> Measure-Object -Sum | foreach { $_sum }
>>
356.81
```

Once you have the elements, the rest is basically the same: you cast the element strings into numbers, multiply them, and then use Measure-Object to sum the results.

We've looked at how to use the XML facilities in the .NET Framework to create and process XML documents. As the XML format is used more frequently in the computer industry, these features will become critical. We've only scratched the surface of what's available in the .NET Framework. We've covered some of the XML classes and a little of the XPath query language. We haven't discussed how to use the Extensible Stylesheet Language Transformations (XSLT) language, XML schemas, or any of a number of XML-related standards and tools. That said, most of these tools are directly available from within the PowerShell environment. The interactive nature of the PowerShell environment makes it an ideal place to explore, experiment, and learn more about XML. In the next section, we'll show you how to generate XML documents from PowerShell objects automatically by using the built-in cmdlets.

16.4.7 Rendering objects as XML

Up to this point, you've been working with XML as objects. Now you're going to switch it around and render objects into XML using cmdlets. PowerShell provides two cmdlets for rendering objects as XML, each with slightly different purposes. The `ConvertTo-Xml` renders objects with relatively simple but verbose format. This cmdlet is useful for interoperating between PowerShell and other environments. Conversions using `Export-Clixml` are much more complex but also more compact and are intended for efficiently passing data between instances of PowerShell. We'll start with the simpler of the two: `ConvertTo-Xml`.

The ConvertTo-Xml cmdlet

The `ConvertTo-Xml` cmdlet does a fairly simple and direct rendering of PowerShell objects into XML. Its primary value is to facilitate interoperability between PowerShell and other environments (including non-Windows environments). Because the encoding used is simple, it can be easily consumed by other applications. The signature for this command is shown in figure 16.4.

As you see in the figure, the cmdlet takes an object as an argument or (more commonly) as pipeline input and generates an XML document from it. Let's use it to produce XML from a list of Windows services. You'll get the list using the `Get-Service` cmdlet, but you'll limit the number of services you'll work with to three for brevity's sake:

```
PS (1) > (Get-Service)[0..2]

Status   Name               DisplayName
------   ----               -----------
Stopped  AdtAgent           Operations Manager Audit Forwarding...
Running  AeLookupSvc        Application Experience
Stopped  ALG                Application Layer Gateway Service
```

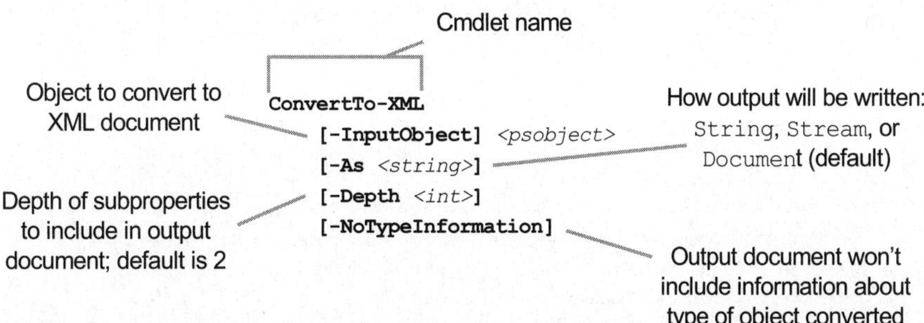

Figure 16.4 The `ConvertTo-Xml` cmdlet parameters. This cmdlet facilitates interoperation between PowerShell and other applications by using a simple XML encoding.

In this output, you see the normal PowerShell presentation for `ServiceController` objects. Convert them into XML:

```
PS (2) > $doc = (Get-Service)[0..2] | ConvertTo-Xml
```

Look at the resulting XML document:

```
PS (3) > $doc

xml                                  Objects
---                                  -------
version="1.0"                        Objects
```

The collection of objects is rendered into an XML document with the top node `Object`, which, in turn, contains a collection of `Object` elements as shown:

```
PS (4) > $doc.Objects.Object

Type                                 Property
----                                 --------
System.ServiceProcess.ServiceCo... {Name, RequiredServices, CanPau...
System.ServiceProcess.ServiceCo... {Name, RequiredServices, CanPau...
System.ServiceProcess.ServiceCo... {Name, RequiredServices, CanPau...
```

Here you see that each `Object` element has the type and properties of the source object included in the output document. But this representation doesn't show the document format effectively, so use the `-As` parameter to display the document as a single string:

```
PS (5) > $services[0] | ConvertTo-Xml -As string
<?xml version="1.0"?>
<Objects>
 <Object Type="System.ServiceProcess.ServiceController">
  <Property Name="Name" Type="System.String">AdtAgent</Property>
  <Property Name="RequiredServices"
    Type="System.ServiceProcess.ServiceController[]">
      <Property Type="System.ServiceProcess.ServiceController">
        System.ServiceProcess.ServiceController</Property>
      <Property Type="System.ServiceProcess.ServiceController">
        System.ServiceProcess.ServiceController</Property>
  </Property>
  <Property Name="CanPauseAndContinue" Type="System.Boolean">
    False</Property>
  <Property Name="CanShutdown" Type="System.Boolean">
    False</Property>
  <Property Name="CanStop" Type="System.Boolean">False</Property>
  <Property Name="DisplayName" Type="System.String">
    Operations Manager Audit Forwarding Service</Property>
  <Property Name="DependentServices"
    Type="System.ServiceProcess.ServiceController[]" />
      <Property Name="MachineName" Type="System.String">.</Property>
      <Property Name="ServiceName" Type="System.String">
        AdtAgent</Property>
  <Property Name="ServicesDependedOn"
    Type="System.ServiceProcess.ServiceController[]">
      <Property Type="System.ServiceProcess.ServiceController">
```

```
System.ServiceProcess.ServiceController</Property>
      <Property Type="System.ServiceProcess.ServiceController">
        System.ServiceProcess.ServiceController</Property>
  </Property>
  <Property Name="ServiceHandle"
    Type="System.Runtime.InteropServices.SafeHandle" />
  <Property Name="Status"
    Type="System.ServiceProcess.ServiceControllerStatus">
      Stopped</Property>
  <Property Name="ServiceType"
    Type="System.ServiceProcess.ServiceType">
      Win32OwnProcess</Property>
  <Property Name="Site" Type="System.ComponentModel.ISite" />
  <Property Name="Container" Type="System.ComponentModel.IContainer" />
</Object>
```

Now the structure of the saved data is much clearer. The type name of the original object is included as an attribute on the `Object` tab. The child elements of `Object` are a collection of `Property` objects with the property name and type as attributes and the value as the element content.

One thing we didn't mention yet was the "serialization" depth. The default depth is 2. You see this in the `RequiredServices` property, whose content is two additional nested properties. You can override the default depth using the `-Depth` parameter on the cmdlet.

> **NOTE** You might be tempted to set the depth to a larger value to preserve more information, but be aware that the size of the document can explode with deep nesting. For example, saving the process table with the default depth of 2 produces a 700 KB file, which is already quite large. Increasing the depth to 3 explodes the file to 7 MB—a tenfold increase in size!

The other parameter on the cmdlet that we haven't talked about is `-NoTypeInformation`. When you specify this parameter, no type information is included in the generated document. Let's see how the resulting document looks without the type information by rerunning the example with `-NoTypeInformation`:

```
PS (6) > $services[0] | ConvertTo-Xml -NoTypeInformation -As string
<?xml version="1.0"?>
<Objects>
  <Object>
    <Property Name="Name">AdtAgent</Property>
    <Property Name="RequiredServices">
      <Property>System.ServiceProcess.ServiceController</Property>
      <Property>System.ServiceProcess.ServiceController</Property>
    </Property>
    <Property Name="CanPauseAndContinue">False</Property>
    <Property Name="CanShutdown">False</Property>
    <Property Name="CanStop">False</Property>
    <Property Name="DisplayName">Operations Manager Audit Forwarding
```

```
Service</Property>
    <Property Name="DependentServices" />
    <Property Name="MachineName">.</Property>
    <Property Name="ServiceName">AdtAgent</Property>
    <Property Name="ServicesDependedOn">
      <Property>System.ServiceProcess.ServiceController</Property>
      <Property>System.ServiceProcess.ServiceController</Property>
    </Property>
    <Property Name="ServiceHandle" />
    <Property Name="Status">Stopped</Property>
    <Property Name="ServiceType">Win32OwnProcess</Property>
    <Property Name="Site" />
    <Property Name="Container" />
  </Object>
</Objects>
PS (7) >
```

This simplifies the output even further. It makes sense if the target consumer for the generated document isn't a .NET-based application and therefore wouldn't be able to do much with the type names.

The `ConvertTo-XML` cmdlet is useful for interoperation with non-PowerShell applications, but for PowerShell-to-PowerShell communication, too much information is lost. For the PowerShell-to-PowerShell scenario, a much better solution is to use the `Export-Clixml` and `Import-Clixml` cmdlets. We'll cover these next.

The Import-Clixml and Export-Clixml cmdlets

The next two cmdlets we're going to cover are `Import-Clixml` and `Export-Clixml`. These cmdlets provide a way to save and restore collections of objects from the PowerShell environment with higher fidelity (less data loss) than the `ConvertTo-Xml` cmdlet. The signature for `Export-Clixml` is shown in figure 16.5.

The encoding these cmdlets use is essentially what PowerShell remoting uses to send objects between hosts, as discussed in chapter 12 (section 12.6.5).

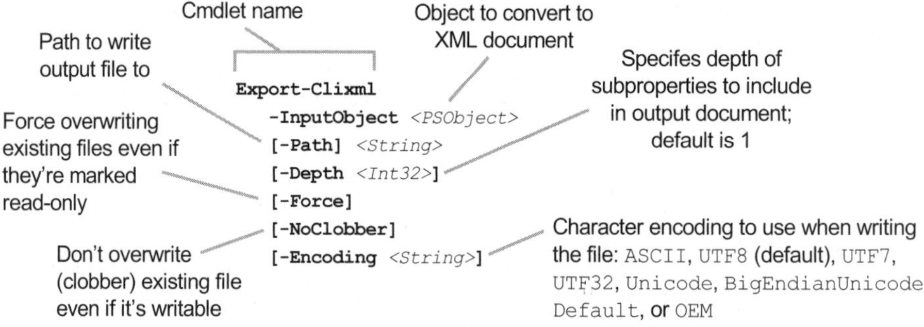

Figure 16.5 The `Export-Clixml` cmdlet is used to export or serialize PowerShell objects to a file using an encoding similar to the remoting protocol object encoding.

To recap our discussion, we mentioned that there's only a small set of types that serialize with fidelity and that other types are shredded into property bags. With the *-`Clixml` cmdlets, you can see what the encoding looks like. Let's try this out. First, create a collection of objects: a hashtable, a string, and some numbers:

```
PS (1) > $data = @{a=1;b=2;c=3},"Hi there", 3.5
```

Now serialize them to a file using the Export-Clixml cmdlet:

```
PS (2) > $data | Export-Clixml out.xml
```

Let's see what the file looks like:

```
PS (3) > type out.xml
<Objs Version="1.1.0.1"
  xmlns="http://schemas.microsoft.com/powershell/2004/04">
  <Obj RefId="0">
    <TN RefId="0">
      <T>System.Collections.Hashtable</T>
      <T>System.Object</T>
    </TN>
    <DCT>
      <En>
        <S N="Key">a</S>
        <I32 N="Value">1</I32>
      </En>
      <En>
        <S N="Key">b</S>
        <I32 N="Value">2</I32>
      </En>
      <En>
        <S N="Key">c</S>
        <I32 N="Value">3</I32>
      </En>
    </DCT>
  </Obj>
  <S>Hi there</S>
  <Db>3.5</Db>
</Objs>
```

This first part identifies the schema for the `CLIXML` object representation:

```
<Objs Version="1.1.0.1"
  xmlns="http://schemas.microsoft.com/powershell/2004/04">
  <Obj RefId="0">
   <TN RefId="0">
    <T>System.Collections.Hashtable</T>
    <T>System.Object</T>
   </TN>
   <DCT>
```

Here are the key-value pair encodings:

```
    <En>
        <S N="Key">a</S>
```

```
    <I32 N="Value">1</I32>
  </En>
  <En>
    <S N="Key">b</S>
    <I32 N="Value">2</I32>
  </En>
  <En>
    <S N="Key">c</S>
    <I32 N="Value">3</I32>
  </En>
```

Now encode the string element

```
<S>Hi there</S>
```

and the double-precision number:

```
<Db>3.5</Db>
```

Import these objects back into the session using `Import-Clixml`

```
PS (5) > $new_data = Import-Clixml out.xml
```

and compare the old and new collections:

```
PS (6) > $new_data

Name                                   Value
----                                   -----
a                                      1
b                                      2
c                                      3
Hi there
3.5

PS (7) > $data

Name                                   Value
----                                   -----
a                                      1
b                                      2
c                                      3
Hi there
3.5
```

They match, member for member.

These cmdlets provide a simple way to save and restore collections of objects, but they have limitations. They can only load and save a fixed number of primitive types. Any other type is "shredded," which means it's broken apart into a property bag composed of these primitive types. This allows any type to be serialized but with some loss of fidelity. In other words, objects can't be restored to exactly the same type they were originally. This approach is necessary because there can be an infinite number of object types, not all of which may be available when the file is read back. Sometimes you don't have the original type definition. Other times, there's no way to re-create the original object, even with the type information, because the type doesn't support this operation. By restricting the set of types that are serialized with fidelity, the `Clixml` format can always recover objects regardless of the availability of the original type information.

There's also another limitation on how objects are serialized. An object has properties. Those properties are also objects that have their own properties, and so on. This chain of properties that have properties is called the *serialization depth*. For some of the complex objects in the system, such as the `Process` object, serializing through all the levels of the object results in a huge XML file. To constrain this, the serializer only traverses to a certain depth. The default depth is 2. You can override this default either on the command line using the `-Depth` parameter or by placing a `<SerializationDepth>` element in the type's description file. If you look at `$PSHome/types.ps1xml`, you can see some examples of where this has been done.

16.5 SUMMARY

In this chapter, we covered the kind of tasks that are the traditional domain of scripting languages and shells: paths, files and text processing. You learned about the following:

- Basic text processing—how to split and join strings using the `[string]::Split()` and `[string]::Join()` methods to augment the `-split` and `-join` operators.
- More advanced text processing with the `[regex]` class. You saw how to use this class to conduct more advanced text operations such as tokenizing a string.
- The core cmdlets and how they correspond to the commands in other shell environments.
- How to set up shortcuts to long or specialized paths in the file system using `New-PSDrive`. For example

  ```
  New-PSDrive AppData FileSystem "$Home\Application Data"
  ```

  creates a drive named AppData mapped to the root of the current user's Application Data directory.
- How to read and write files in PowerShell using `Get-Content` and `Set-Content`, and how to deal with character encodings in text files.
- How to work with binary files. You wrote a of couple handy utility functions in the process.
- Using the `Select-String` cmdlet to efficiently search through collections of files.
- The basic support in PowerShell for XML documents in the form of the XML object adapter. PowerShell provides a shortcut for creating an XML document

with the [xml] type accelerator. For example: [$xml]"<docroot>...</docroot>".

- How to construct XML documents by adding elements to an existing document using the CreateElement() method.
- Using the XmlReader class to search XML documents without loading the whole document into memory.
- Building utility functions for searching and formatting XML documents.
- Examples of processing XML documents using PowerShell pipelines.
- Extracting content from XML documents using the XPath language.
- How to save and restore collections of objects using ConvertTo-Xml, Import-Clixml, and Export-Clixml.

In this chapter, in working with paths, files, and text, you used a number of the .NET Framework features do your work. In the next chapter, we'll build on this knowledge. The main focus of chapter 17 is how to use more of the .NET Framework to do some of the things that aren't built into PowerShell as cmdlets, including how to write a graphical front end to your scripts.

CHAPTER 17

Extending your reach with .NET

I love it when a plan comes together!

—Col. John "Hannibal" Smith, *The A-Team*

When we started the design work on PowerShell, our focus was almost exclusively on cmdlets. The plan was to have lots of cmdlets and everything would be done through them. Unfortunately, as Robert Burns observed, "The best laid plans of mice and men often go awry," and we found that we didn't have the resources to get all the required cmdlets completed in time. Without these cmdlets, we wouldn't have adequate coverage for all of our core scenarios. How to solve this, we asked? "Let's just depend on .NET," was the answer. We decided to make it easier to work directly with the .NET Framework. That way, although it might not be as easy to do everything the way we wanted, at least it would be possible.

In retrospect, this may have been one of the best things to happen to PowerShell. Not only did we backfill our original scenarios, but the set of problem domains (such as creating graphical user interfaces) in which we found PowerShell to be applicable greatly exceeded our original expectations.

In this chapter, we'll show you how to effectively apply the .NET Framework to extend the reach of your scripts. We'll also look at some considerations in PowerShell's support for .NET and how they might lead to problems.

17.1 USING .NET FROM POWERSHELL

As we discussed in chapter 1, everything in .NET is encapsulated in types: as classes, interfaces, structures, or primitive types such as integers. Consequently, solving problems using the .NET Framework requires finding the right types to build the solution. We've covered a number of commonly used types in previous chapters, but there are many more useful types available to PowerShell users.

In this section, we'll show you how to find and inspect the types that are loaded into PowerShell by default. We'll also look at how to make additional types available by loading .NET libraries or assemblies, extending what you can do even further. Along the way, you'll build some handy tools for exploring the framework and its types. We'll explain how to create instances of the types you discover, and address some of the potentially problematic areas in .NET.

17.1.1 .NET basics

Let's start with a review of the .NET type system. The basic arrangement of entities in .NET is as follows: members (properties, methods, and so on) are contained in types (classes, structs, and interfaces). These types are, in turn, grouped into namespaces.

> **NOTE** Keep in mind that the .NET type system was designed to allow programmers to construct arbitrarily sophisticated applications. As a consequence, it's fairly complex. But the designers of this system did an excellent job of not requiring you to know everything in order to do anything. The type system, like PowerShell, was designed to support progressive discovery where what you need to know scales with the complexity of what you're trying to do. Simple things remain simple and the level of complexity scales reasonably with the complexity of the application. As a side note, PowerShell is an excellent way to learn and explore the .NET Framework.

Let's see how this exploration works by looking at one specific type: `System.Collections.ArrayList`. This type has an `Add()` method that exists on instances of the class `ArrayList`. This class lives in the namespace `System.Collections`. Another example is the `IEnumerable` interface, which is also in `System.Collections`. This interface defines, but doesn't implement, a single method, `GetEnumerator()`.

The arrangement of types into class and namespaces is called *logical type* containment. You also need to understand *physical type* containment. In other words, where do these collections of types live on a computer? This organization is done through the *assemblies* we mentioned earlier. An assembly is just a file stored somewhere so that the program loader can find them when needed. Each *assembly* contains the definitions for one or more types. Because a set of types is contained in an assembly, clearly the set of assemblies that are loaded determines the complete set of types available to you. PowerShell loads most of the assemblies you'll need for day-to-day work by default when it starts, but sometimes (like when you want to do GUI programming) you'll have to load additional assemblies.

17.1.2 Working with assemblies

As we mentioned, the physical partitioning of the .NET Framework is based on individual assemblies. Assemblies are a refinement of the dynamic link library (DLL) facility that has been part of Microsoft Windows from the beginning. (In Unix, the equivalent concept is called *shared libraries.*) Let's review the benefits and liabilities of dynamic linking.

The pros and cons of dynamic linking

The DLL mechanism allows the system to dynamically load required DLLs when the program starts up (and sometimes while it's running). This feature works because each executable has a list of the necessary DLLs compiled into it. The traditional purpose of this feature was to cut down on the size of programs—instead of "statically" linking a library to an executable, all executables could share one copy of that code. The ability to share makes the executables smaller and also allows them to be serviced. By *serviced*, we mean that a bug in the DLL could be fixed for all programs that used that DLL simply by replacing one file. But all is not sweetness and light, as they say. A fix intended to address a specific problem in one program could unintentionally cause another program to fail. Another problem is our old friend from section 10.3.1: *versioning*. How can you manage change over time? If you add new things to a DLL, you may break existing programs. To avoid this risk, the traditional approach involves introducing a new version of the DLL. But now this forces the developer to decide which version of the DLL to use. Should they use the latest version? What if it isn't on all machines yet? And what if someone installs a malicious copy of the DLL to introduce a virus?

Versioning and assemblies

With .NET, Microsoft tried to solve some of these problems with assemblies. In effect, an assembly is just a DLL with additional metadata in the form of an *assembly manifest.*

> **NOTE** This isn't the same manifest we talked about in chapter 10 when we covered module manifests, though the goal is similar. In both cases, version information is added. A PowerShell module manifest adds

another layer of versioning information on top of the assembly. This extra layer allows a group of assemblies to be versioned as a unit even though the component assemblies have their own version numbers.

This assembly manifest lists the contents of the DLL as well as the name of the DLL. The full (or *strong*) name for an assembly is a complex beast and warrants some discussion. To try to solve some of the identity and versioning problems we mentioned, .NET introduced the idea of a *strong name*. As well as the assembly filename, a strong name uses public key cryptography to add information that will allow you to validate the identity of the DLL author. When a .NET program is linked against a strong-named assembly, it will run only if *exactly the same assembly* it was linked against is present. Simply replacing the file won't work, because the strong name will be wrong.

One more thing that's included in the strong name is the version number. The result is that when the DLL is loaded, the correct version must always be loaded even if later versions are available. But it also means that to service the assembly to fix bugs, you can't change the version number of the assembly because the version number is part of the strong name. So you end up with two versions of an assembly with the same version number. The net effect of all of this is that .NET didn't really solve the versioning problem; it just moved things around a bit.

The default PowerShell assemblies

Now let's talk about how PowerShell finds types and assemblies. All compiled programs contain a list of assemblies needed for the program to execute. This list (the manifest mentioned earlier) is created as part of the linking phase when the program is compiled. When the program executes, the referenced assemblies are loaded automatically as needed. When the system tries to locate a required assembly, the loader performs a process called *probing* to find that assembly. It looks in a number of places automatically; the most important one is the global assembly cache (GAC). If an assembly has been installed in the GAC, you don't have to care where it actually is—the system will find it for you as long as you know its name.

Because the PowerShell interpreter is a compiled program, it also contains a list of required assemblies. Through the automatic loading mechanism, all of these assemblies and the types they contain are available to PowerShell scripts by default. Section 17.1.3 shows you how to view this default list.

Dynamic assembly loading

Automatic loading only applies to compiled programs like `Notepad.exe` or `PowerShell.exe` because it depends on the required assembly list contained in the executable. PowerShell scripts are interpreted and have no compile or "static" link phase, so if you want to make sure that an assembly you need is loaded, you have to explicitly load it. In chapter 10, you saw how to do this with module manifests; you add the list of required assemblies to the `RequiredAssemblies` manifest element. In effect,

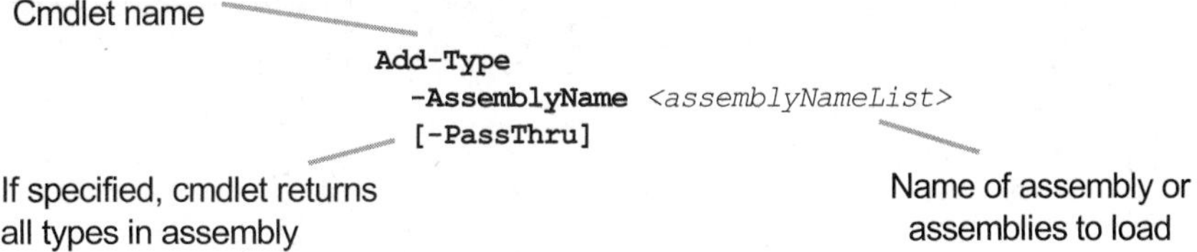

Figure 17.1 The Add-Type parameters allow you to load new assemblies into the PowerShell process at runtime.

module manifests are the dynamic equivalent to the static manifest found in an assembly. But with simple scripts you don't have a manifest, so in this case you'll use the `Add-Type` cmdlet—the "Swiss Army cmdlet" for dealing with assemblies and compiled code. Given the versatility of this cmdlet, we'll discuss it in pieces. The syntax for the first `Add-Type` feature we're going to cover is shown in figure 17.1.

When used with this parameter set, `Add-Type` lets you dynamically load assemblies by name. You can even use wildcards in the assembly name (but an error is generated if more than one assembly filename matches the pattern). For example, to load the Windows Forms assembly (`winforms`) that's in `System.Windows.Forms`, instead of the full name, you can use the following:

```
Add-Type -AssemblyName System*forms
```

This works because `Add-Type` has a fixed list of short names that correspond to specific versions of the .NET Framework assemblies. `Add-Type` will only allow you to use the short name for assemblies that are on this list. If it's not on the list, you have to use the strong name for the assembly. For `winforms`, the strong name looks like this,

```
"System.Windows.Forms, Version=2.0.0.0, Culture=neutral,
          PublicKeyToken=b77a5c561934e089"
```

which is a little bit unwieldy. Still, as long as you stick to the assemblies Microsoft ships with Windows, you can use the short names and wildcard. If you choose a non-Windows assembly, you have to use the full name.

Loading assemblies the hard way

Because `Add-Type` wasn't part of PowerShell v1, users had to come up with an alternate way to load assemblies. This technique involved using .NET methods directly. Remember that whole "not easy but possible" discussion from the introduction to this chapter? This is an example of the not-quite-so-easy part.

To load new assemblies without `Add-Type`, you'll have to use methods from the `System.Reflection.Assembly` class. Here's an example:

```
PS (2) > [system.reflection.assembly]::LoadWithPartialName(
>> "System.Windows.Forms") | fl
>>
```

```
CodeBase                  : file:///C:/WINDOWS/assembly/GAC_MSIL/Sy
                            stem.Windows.Forms/2.0.0.0__b77a5c56193
                            4e089/System.Windows.Forms.dll
EntryPoint                :
EscapedCodeBase           : file:///C:/WINDOWS/assembly/GAC_MSIL/Sy
                            stem.Windows.Forms/2.0.0.0__b77a5c56193
                            4e089/System.Windows.Forms.dll
FullName                  : System.Windows.Forms, Version=2.0.0.0,
                            Culture=neutral, PublicKeyToken=b77a5c5
                            61934e089
GlobalAssemblyCache       : True
HostContext               : 0
ImageFileMachine          :
ImageRuntimeVersion       : v2.0.50727
Location                  : C:\WINDOWS\assembly\GAC_MSIL\System.Win
                            dows.Forms\2.0.0.0__b77a5c561934e089\Sy
                            stem.Windows.Forms.dll
ManifestModule            : System.Windows.Forms.dll
MetadataToken             :
PortableExecutableKind    :
ReflectionOnly            : False
```

This not only loads the assembly, it also returns an instance of `System.Reflection.Assembly` that has a great deal of information about the assembly. Take a look at the `FullName` property. You load the assembly using its partial name. The `FullName` property shows the strong name for this assembly:

```
System.Windows.Forms, Version=2.0.0.0, Culture=neutral,
            PublicKeyToken=b77a5c561934e089
```

As we discussed earlier, the strong name includes the namespace of the assembly, the version number, the culture for this assembly, and the public key used to sign the assembly. You can load a specific version of an assembly with the full name:

```
PS (5) > [System.Reflection.Assembly]::Load (
>> "System.Windows.Forms, Version=2.0.0.0, Culture=neutral," +
>> "PublicKeyToken=b77a5c561934e089")
>>

GAC    Version        Location
---    -------        --------
True   v2.0.50727     C:\WINDOWS\assembly\GAC_MSIL\System.Win...
```

Keep in mind that you didn't load the assembly again. Once an assembly has been loaded into a process, it can't be unloaded, so all this did was verify that the assembly was loaded.

For assemblies that have been added to the GAC, you don't need the path to the assembly. But if the assembly you're loading *hasn't* been added to the GAC, you'll need the full path to the DLL. If you look at the output from the `Load()` method, you can see where this file is stored. Let's "load" it one more time using the filename:

```
PS (6) > $name = "C:\WINDOWS\assembly\GAC_MSIL\" +
>> "System.Windows.Forms\2.0.0.0__b77a5c561934e089\" +
```

```
>> "System.Windows.Forms.dll"
>>
PS (7) > [System.Reflection.Assembly]::LoadFrom($name)

GAC    Version        Location
---    -------        --------
True   v2.0.50727     C:\WINDOWS\assembly\GAC_MSIL\System.Win...
```

At this point, we've covered the most important aspects of assembly loading as they apply to PowerShell.

> **NOTE** This is another "tip of the iceberg" topic where we've only covered the minimum necessary. For more details read the Microsoft Developer Network documentation at http://msdn.microsoft.com.

You should now have a good understanding of how to find and load assemblies, but your ultimate goal is to use the *types* these assemblies contain to solve problems. Our next step toward helping you achieve this goal is to demonstrate how you can view the contents of an assembly.

17.1.3 Finding types

There are a lot of types with a lot of members loaded into the PowerShell process. Fortunately, to get the list of what's available, you simply ask the system to tell you. To start, you need to get a list of all the assemblies that are loaded. The following function provides a convenient way to do this:

```
function Get-Assembly
{
    [System.AppDomain]::CurrentDomain.GetAssemblies()
}
```

The `AppDomain` class used in this function is .NET's way of encapsulating an isolated execution environment. It's similar in some ways to PowerShell sessions but even more isolated. For example, each `AppDomain` can have its own set of assemblies whereas `PSSessions` all share the same assemblies. The static `CurrentDomain` property lets you access the domain you're executing in and `GetAssemblies()` gives you the list of assemblies currently loaded into the `AppDomain`.

> **NOTE** At times it might seem like you're building the software equivalent of a *matryoshka*, the famous Russian nesting dolls. The operating system contains processes, processes contain `AppDomains`, `AppDomains` contain `PSSessions`, and so on. Each layer provides its own set of features and boundaries.

Once you have the list of assemblies, you can use the `GetTypes()` and `GetExported-Types()` methods on each assembly object to get all the types in that assembly. The `GetExportedTypes()` method gives you all the public types, which is usually what you want. `GetTypes()` returns both public and private types, which is primarily useful for exploring how things are organized below the public façade. We'll wrap `GetExportedTypes()` in a function as well:

```
function Get-Type ($Pattern=".")
{
    Get-Assembly | foreach{ $_.GetExportedTypes() } |
        where {$_ -match $Pattern}
}
```

This function will get the full names of all of the public types in each assembly and match them against the pattern provided in the function argument (which defaults to matching everything). Let's use this function to find all the types that have the namespace prefix `System.Timers`:

```
PS (1) > Get-Type ^system\.timers | %{ $_.FullName }
System.Timers.ElapsedEventArgs
System.Timers.ElapsedEventHandler
System.Timers.Timer
System.Timers.TimersDescriptionAttribute
```

In this example, you searched through all the assemblies and found the four types that matched the regular expression you specified. (There are enough types loaded in PowerShell that this might take a while to run.)

Once you know how to get all the types, we'll explore the members of those types. You want to see all the methods defined on all the types in the `System.Timers` namespace that have the word "begin" in their name. To make this task easier, you'll define a couple of filters. Here's what you want the output to look like:

```
PS (1) > Get-Type ^system\.timers | Select-Member begin |
>> Show-Member -method
>>
[System.Timers.ElapsedEventHandler]:: System.IAsyncResult
BeginInvoke(System.Object, System.Timers.ElapsedEventArgs,
System.AsyncCallback, System.Object)
[System.Timers.Timer]:: Void BeginInit()
```

In the output, you see that two methods match your requirements—the `BeginInvoke()` method on `System.Timers.ElapsedEventHandler` and `BeginInit()` on `System.Timers.Timer`.

Let's look at the filters you used in this example. The first is a filter that will dump all the members whose names match a regular expression. The code for this filter is as follows:

```
filter Select-Member ($Pattern = ".")
{
    $_.GetMembers() | where {$_ -match $Pattern }
}
```

Remembering that the body of a filter is applied once to each inbound pipeline object, you can see that this code gets the list of members on each type and filters them according to the provided pattern.

Here, a second filter deals with the presentation of the results, because the default presentation for the member information isn't all that it might be:

```
filter Show-Member ([switch] $Method)
{
    if (!$Method -or $_.MemberType -match "method")
    {
        "[{0}]:: {1}" -f $_.declaringtype, $_
    }
}
```

Again, the operation of this filter is straightforward. If `-Method` is specified, only methods will be displayed. The member to be displayed will be formatted into a string displaying the type containing the method and the name of the method.

Now you can load assemblies and find out what types are in those assemblies. The next step (and our next topic) is to create instances of those types so you can finally start applying what you've learned to getting this done.

17.1.4 Creating instances of types

Now that you can find types, you generally need to create instances of these types to use their properties and methods (although there are some types such as `[System.Math]` that only have static members and so don't require instantiation). For example, before you can search using the `[regex]` type, you need to create an instance of that type from a pattern string. As you saw in earlier chapters, you can use the `New-Object` cmdlet to create instances of types in PowerShell. Figure 17.2 shows the signature for this cmdlet.

This cmdlet takes the name of the type to create, a list of parameters to pass to the type's constructor, and a hashtable of property name/values to set on the object once it has been constructed.

The New-Object -Property parameter

Version 2 of PowerShell added the `-Property` parameter, which allows individual properties to be set on the object after it has been constructed. In many cases, doing

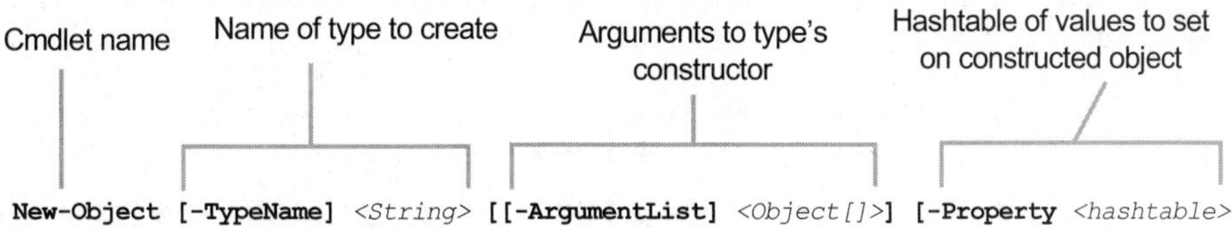

Figure 17.2 The `New-Object` cmdlet parameters

so can greatly simplify the code needed to completely initialize an object. For a simple example, let's create a `Timer` object:

```
PS (1) > New-Object System.Timers.Timer -Property @{
>> AutoReset = $true
>> Interval = 500
>> Enabled = $true
>> }
>>

AutoReset           : True
Enabled             : True
Interval            : 500
Site                :
SynchronizingObject :
Container           :
```

In this example, you're creating the object and then setting three properties—`AutoReset`, `Interval`, and `Enabled`—in a single statement. Without `-Property`, you'd have to create an intermediate variable and use four statements. You'll see more interesting uses for this technique when we look at building graphical user interfaces in section 17.3. But first, some more cautions...

A word of caution about using New-Object

Although the signature for the `New-Object` cmdlet is pretty simple, it can be more difficult to use than you might think. People who are accustomed to programming in languages such as C# have a tendency to use this cmdlet like the `new` operator in those languages. As a consequence, they tend to write expressions like this:

```
New-Object string($x,1,3)
```

Unfortunately, writing the expression this way obscures the fact that it's a cmdlet, making things confusing. It'll work fine, but it looks too much like a function call in other programming languages, and that leads people to misinterpret what's happening. As you saw in figure 17.2, the syntax for `New-Object` is

```
New-Object [-TypeName] <String> [[-ArgumentList] <Object[]>]
```

so the previous example could be written like this:

```
New-Object -TypeName string -ArgumentList $x,1,3
```

The comma notation indicates an argument that's passed as an array. This is equivalent to

```
$constructor_arguments= $x,1,3
New-Object string $constructor_arguments
```

Note that you're not wrapping `$constructor_arguments` in yet another array. If you want to pass an array as a single value, you need to do it yourself and write it in parentheses with the unary comma operator, as discussed in chapter 3.

New-Object cmdlet examples

Let's work through a couple of examples using `New-Object`. In the first example, you're going to construct a new string object from a portion of a `char` array. You need to specify the offset into the source array and the number of characters to copy. Doing so looks like

```
PS (1) > New-Object string ([char[]] "Hello"),1,4
ello
```

In this example, the type to instantiate was `string` and you passed three arguments to the `string` constructor: the source array, the start index, and the length to copy. This code created a new string object starting from the second character (remember, origin 0 for array indexing) and copied four characters. This example may seem a bit silly, but it illustrates how complex the punctuation can get even in simple examples. If you put the `char` array into a variable first, the resulting command becomes simpler:

```
PS (2) > $str = [char[]] "Hello"
PS (3) > New-Object string $str,1,4
ello
```

A much trickier example is the one where you want to pass the `char` array as the only argument to the constructor. In this situation, you need to wrap the `char` array in a nested array using the unary comma operator:

```
PS (4) > New-Object string (,$str)
Hello
```

In this example, you've created a string by copying all the characters from the `char` array, starting from the beginning.

You now know how to discover existing types and created instances of those types, but you haven't created any new .NET types of your own. (Chapter 11, section 11.4.3 showed how to create objects with `New-Module` but that's quite a different thing.) There are some situations where you do need to create your own types, usually to facilitate interoperation with existing .NET classes or the operating system. In the next section, you'll see how to do this using the `Add-Type` cmdlet.

17.1.5 Defining new types with Add-Type

PowerShell is a ".NET language" in that it works with and consumes the types. But it (still, even in v2!) has no native way to create new types. There are no "class" or "type" keywords in the language to create a new type. This is where the `Add-Type` cmdlet comes in.

> **NOTE** A common question is why the PowerShell team didn't add some sort of native mechanism to create .NET types in v2. It's because a) we were incredibly busy and b) we didn't want to screw up. With the Dynamic Language Runtime (DLR) on the verge of becoming part of .NET (and it is as of .NET 4.0) the way to create types was in flux.

Because we had to ship well before .NET 4 was out, we decided to wait one more release and let the dust settle. We're keeping our fingers crossed that we'll finally get native type definition capabilities into v3 (actually fingers, toes, eyes, and any other anatomical protuberances that come to mind).

In addition to providing a mechanism for loading assemblies, the `Add-Type` cmdlet provides a workaround of sorts for this inability to create new types. In fact `Add-Type` offers a variety of ways to create types. We'll cover each mechanism in the following subsections.

Creating singleton member definitions

The first approach for creating types with the `Add-Type` cmdlet is to define a single member, typically a method. The signature for this use is shown in figure 17.3.

With this signature, you're creating a member whose name is specified by the `-Name` parameter and whose source code is specified by the `-MemberDefinition` parameter. Because the member definition is just a string, you also have to specify the language used to define the member. You can do so with the `-Language` parameter, which supports four languages in v2, selected by passing in one of the following strings: "CSharp", "CSharpVersion3", "VisualBasic", or "JScript". These are the four base languages shipped by Microsoft with .NET. If nothing is specified, v2 defaults to C#.

Because types in .NET are organized by namespaces, you can use the `-Namespace` parameter to put the member into a specific namespace.

Next, you have to specify what the member definition depends on. The point of this variant is that you only need to write a fragment of a source file, so you can't specify the dependencies in the source. Instead, you do it through the `-Using-Namespace` parameter.

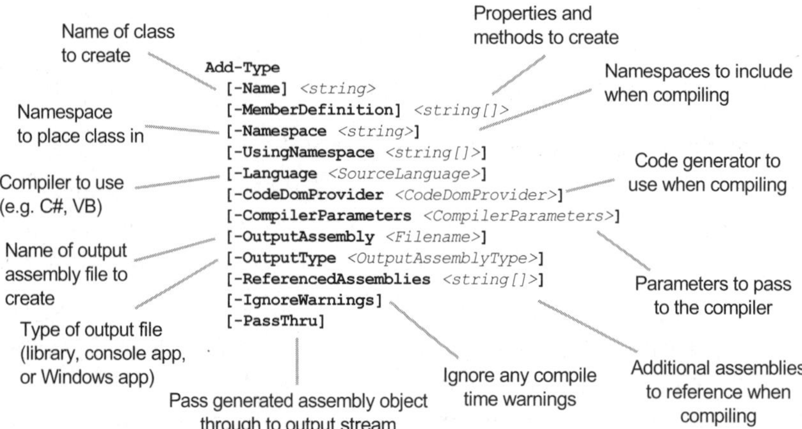

Figure 17.3 This signature for the `Add-Type` cmdlet allows you to create type members without having to include all the other details needed to build the containing class.

The remaining parameters are common across all the variations of the cmdlet and allow you to specify additional assemblies that the member depends on (all of the PowerShell assemblies are included by default so they never need to be explicitly added). You can also choose to ignore any compiler warnings using the `-IgnoreWarnings` parameter.

Let's try out what you've learned so far. First, you need a method definition. The following string defines a C# method that takes an array of integers as its argument, sums them up, and then returns the result:

```
PS (1) > $sumMethod = @'
>>   static public int Sum(int[] na)
>>   {
>>       int result = 0;
>>       if (na == null || na.Length == 0)
>>       {
>>         return 0;
>>       }
>>       foreach (int n in na)
>>       {
>>         result += n;
>>       }
>>       return result;
>>   }
>> '@
>>
```

Let's use Add-Type to compile this method as part of the class Utils:

```
PS (2) > Add-Type -Name Utils -MemberDefinition $sumMethod
```

Try to run it:

```
PS (3) > [utils]::Sum((1..10))
Unable to find type [utils]: make sure that the assembly containing
this type is loaded.
At line:1 char:8
+ [utils] <<<< ::Sum((1..10))
    + CategoryInfo          : InvalidOperation: (utils:String) [],
RuntimeException
    + FullyQualifiedErrorId : TypeNotFound
```

You get an error! So what happened here? Why did you not find the type? Well, as it turns out, -Namespace has a somewhat unwieldy default value, resulting in the type name:

```
'Microsoft.PowerShell.Commands.AddType.AutoGeneratedTypes'
```

By properly specifying this full type name, you're able to call the new method:

```
PS (4) > `
[Microsoft.PowerShell.Commands.AddType.AutoGeneratedTypes.Utils]::Sum(
(1..10))
55
```

Note that the preceding command is a one-line expression but it wraps here. Even so, this approach is a bit awkward. Fix this by recompiling the member, specifying `WPIA` as the namespace for the class:

```
PS (5) > Add-Type -Name Utils -MemberDefinition $sumMethod `
>>    -Namespace WPIA
>>
```

Now it's much easier to run:

```
PS (6) > [WPIA.Utils]::Sum((1..100))
5050
```

As an experiment, let's try this method on floating-point numbers:

```
PS (7) > [WPIA.Utils]::Sum((3.14,2,33.6))
39
```

Note that, even though the arguments are floating-point numbers, you still got an integer back. Because there's no overload for floating-point arguments, the array was coerced to integers and passed to the integer `Sum()` function. To fix this, you can create a new overload that takes doubles. In fact, you can just use the `-replace` operator to change `'int'` to `'double'` in the original code and then recompile:

```
PS (8) > $fsumMethod = $sumMethod -replace 'int','double'
```

Now let's compile the new overload:

```
PS (9) > Add-Type -Name Utils -MemberDefinition $fsumMethod `
>>    -Namespace WPIA
>>
Add-Type : Cannot add type. The type name 'WPIA.Utils' already exists
.
At line:1 char:9
+ Add-Type <<<<  -Name Utils -MemberDefinition $fsumMethod `
    + CategoryInfo          : InvalidOperation: (WPIA.Utils:String)
   [Add-Type], Exception
    + FullyQualifiedErrorId : TYPE_ALREADY_EXISTS,Microsoft.
PowerShell.Commands.AddTypeCommand
```

This resulted in an error because once a type is defined, .NET doesn't allow new methods to be added to that type. (This is one of the reasons the PowerShell extended type system exists: to support this scenario.) So to add this new method, change the class name from `Utils` to `Utils2` and rerun the command:

```
PS (10) > Add-Type -Name Utils2 -MemberDefinition $fsumMethod `
>>    -Namespace WPIA
>>
PS (11) > [WPIA.Utils2]::Sum((3.14,2,33.6))
38.74
```

This time the compile was successful and you were able to run the method. Try rerunning the command that compiled the original integer method:

```
PS (12) > Add-Type -Name Utils -MemberDefinition $sumMethod
PS (13) >
```

And, somewhat unexpectedly, it compiles without error. The reason is that Add-Type records the code that defined the method originally. If it sees the same source code again, it knows not to recompile and just exits with success. But if you change the method definition even slightly

```
PS (14) > $sumMethod = @'
>>   static public int Sum(int[] na)
>>   {
>>       int result = 0;
>>         if (na != null && na.Length > 0)
>>         {
>>         foreach (int n in na)
>>         {
>>           result += n;
>>         }
>>       }
>>       return result;
>>   }
>> '@
>>
```

and try to compile it again

```
PS (15) > Add-Type -Name Utils -MemberDefinition $sumMethod
Add-Type : Cannot add type. The type name 'Microsoft.PowerShell.
Commands.AddType.AutoGeneratedTypes.Utils' already exists.
At line:1 char:9
+ Add-Type <<<<  -Name Utils -MemberDefinition $sumMethod
    + CategoryInfo          : InvalidOperation: (Microsoft.Power...a
   tedTypes.Utils:String) [Add-Type], Exception
    + FullyQualifiedErrorId : TYPE_ALREADY_EXISTS,
         Microsoft.PowerShe ll.Commands.AddTypeCommand
```

you get the same error as when you tried to add the floating-point version. In .NET, once a method has been defined, it can't be redefined or removed.

From this example, it would seem that this is a pretty awkward way to define a type. In practice, this variant is primarily intended to address Platform Invoke (P/Invoke) scenarios. P/Invoke is the powerful mechanism that .NET uses to interoperate with the native Windows system calls.

> **NOTE** At this point, we're crossing into programmer territory. This kind of stuff is great for enabling complex scenarios in PowerShell scripts but is definitely not something most programmers (let alone IT pros) will do every day. But at least you should be aware that the capability exists. If you find that you do need to do this kind of thing, there are a number of excellent resources, including the P/Invoke wiki at http://pinvoke.net/, which provides a list of the P/Invoke signatures for each API.

Let's take a look at an example showing what you can do with P/Invoke.

Being able to run scripts in a hidden window is a fairly standard automation requirement. This is because it keeps users from inadvertently stopping a script by closing the console window before the script can finish. Out of the box, neither PowerShell nor the .NET `[System.Console]` class has built-in ways of minimizing, maximizing, or hiding a console window.

> **NOTE** Yes, Microsoft added the `-WindowStyle` parameter to `PowerShell.exe` for the purpose of using hidden windows. The `Start-Process` cmdlet also has a `-WindowStyle` parameter allowing new processes to be launched with hidden windows. But these features don't allow a script to show the console, read input from a user, and then hide it again after the information has been received and the processing can start.

Interoperation using Add-Type and P/Invoke

Let's see how you can use `Add-Type` and P/Invoke to add these features to your session. First you need to know what functions to import. In this case you need `GetConsoleWindow()` to get the console handle and `ShowWindow()` to change the state of the window. Here are the commands to add these functions to your session:

```
PS (1) > Add-Type -Name ConsoleUtils -Namespace WPIA `
>>  -MemberDefinition @'
>>     [DllImport("Kernel32.dll")]
>>     public static extern IntPtr GetConsoleWindow();
>>     [DllImport("user32.dll")]
>>     public static extern bool ShowWindow(IntPtr hWnd, Int32 nCmdShow);
>> '@
>>
```

This code is importing the two functions—`GetConsoleWindow()` from Kernel32.dll and `ShowWindow()` from user32.dll—into a class called `[WPIA.ConsoleUtils]`.

Next, you need to know what values you should pass to `ShowWindow()` to accomplish what you want. You'll define a hashtable to hold these values for convenience:

```
PS (2) > $ConsoleMode = @{
>>     HIDDEN = 0;
>>     NORMAL = 1;
>>     MINIMIZED = 2;
>>     MAXIMIZED = 3;
>>     SHOW = 5
>>     RESTORE = 9
>> }
>>
```

Now you're ready to call your APIs. Use `GetConsoleWindow()` to get the console window handle

```
PS (3) > $hWnd = [WPIA.ConsoleUtils]::GetConsoleWindow()
```

and display the value you get back:

```
PS (4) > $hWnd
22877126
```

Let's maximize the console with `ShowWindow()`, passing in the value from the `$ConsoleMode` needed to do this:

```
PS (5) > [WPIA.ConsoleUtils]::ShowWindow($hWnd, $ConsoleMode.MAXIMIZED)
True
```

The method call should succeed and return true, and the console window will be maximized. With the following lines, you step through each option in sequence, waiting 2 seconds between each call:

```
PS (6) > Start-Sleep 2
PS (7) > [WPIA.ConsoleUtils]::ShowWindow($hWnd, $ConsoleMode.NORMAL)
True
PS (8) > Start-Sleep 2
PS (9) > [WPIA.ConsoleUtils]::ShowWindow($hWnd, $ConsoleMode.MINIMIZED)
True
PS (10) > Start-Sleep 2
PS (11) > [WPIA.ConsoleUtils]::ShowWindow($hWnd, $ConsoleMode.RESTORE)
True
PS (12) > Start-Sleep 2
PS (13) > [WPIA.ConsoleUtils]::ShowWindow($hWnd, $ConsoleMode.HIDDEN)
True
PS (14) > Start-Sleep 2
PS (15) > [WPIA.ConsoleUtils]::ShowWindow($hWnd, $ConsoleMode.SHOW)
False
PS (16) >
```

This sequence will cause the console to be restored to normal, then minimized, restored, hidden, and then shown again. (This sequence is more fun to run than describe—trust me.)

> **CAUTION** These examples work with the *console* APIs—which means that they're only appropriate to run from a console application like `PowerShell.exe`. Running them in a graphical application like the ISE may produce unexpected results up to and including causing the application to crash. Using P/Invoke means that you're poking holes in the .NET safety layer and interacting directly with the Win32 layer. This is powerful stuff, but it requires working without a safety net. The worst-case scenario involves crashing or hanging your process, so when playing with P/Invoke, save early and save often.

Now that we've got member definitions out of the way, we'll look at the `-TypeDefinition` variant next.

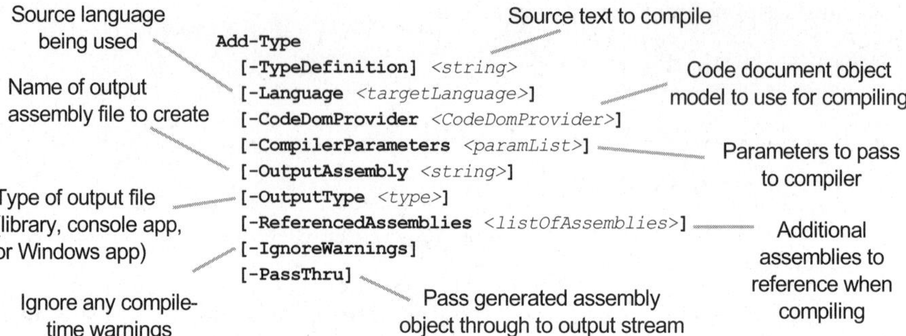

Figure 17.4 The Add-Type type definition parameter set allows you to define a complete class or classes.

The -TypeDefinition parameter set

This parameter set is designed to allow for larger pieces of inline code than just a couple of member definitions. Looking at the parameter set in figure 17.4, this time you have the `-TypeDefinition` parameter instead of the `-Name`, `-MemberDefinition`, `-Namespace`, and `-UsingNamespace` parameters.

With this variation, you have to provide the full definition of the class, including the namespace and any `using` statements that are required. You'll rewrite the previous examples for use with `-TypeDefinition`. The code to do so looks like the following:

```
PS (1) > $utils = @'
>> using System;
>> using System.Runtime.InteropServices;
>>
>> namespace WPIA {
>>   public static class Utils
>>   {
>>     static public int Sum(int[] na)
>>     {
>>       int result = 0;
>>       if (na == null || na.Length == 0)
>>         return 0;
>>       foreach (int n in na)
>>       {
>>         result += n;
>>       }
>>       return result;
>>     }
>>
>>     static public double Sum(double[] na)
>>     {
>>       double result = 0;
>>       if (na == null || na.Length == 0)
>>         return 0;
>>       foreach (double n in na)
```

```
>>         {
>>           result += n;
>>         }
>>         return result;
>>     }
>>   }
>>
>>   public static class ConsoleUtils
>>   {
>>      [DllImport("Kernel32.dll")]
>>      public static extern IntPtr GetConsoleWindow();
>>      [DllImport("user32.dll")]
>>      public static extern bool ShowWindow(
>>          IntPtr hWnd, Int32 nCmdShow);
>>   }
>> }
>> '@
>>
```

This source text defines the two classes you created previously: `WPIA.Utils` and `WPIA.ConsoleUtils`. Now you can compile everything with a single command:

```
PS (14) > Add-Type -TypeDefinition $utils
```

In fact, because this is the default parameter set, it simply becomes

```
PS (15) > Add-Type $utils
PS (16) >
```

Next, let's look at the final parameter set for `Add-Type` with the `-Path` parameter.

The -Path parameter set

The last parameter set for `Add-Type` is the `-Path` parameter set. This parameter set is much like `-TypeDefinition` except that instead of including the code to compile inline in the script, you'll load the file specified by `-Path`. This parameter set is shown in figure 17.5.

This parameter set is even simpler than the one for `-TypeDefinition`. Because you're reading the code from a file, you can use the file's extension to determine what

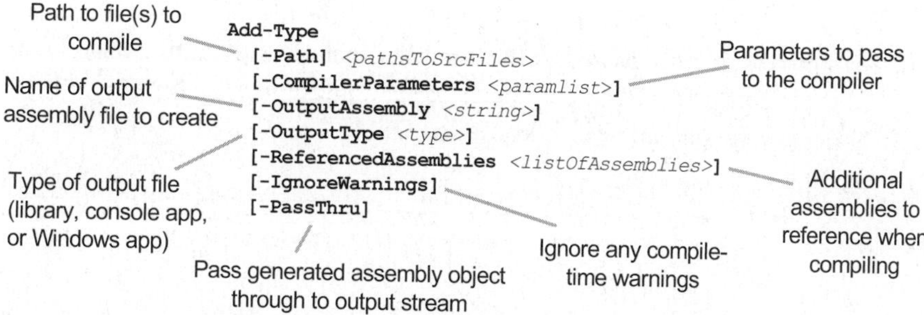

Figure 17.5 The `Add-Type -Path` parameter set reads the input source from a file. It uses the file extension to select the source language.

language to expect. If you write the code you saved in the `$utils` variable earlier to a file, you can try using `-Path`:

```
PS (4) > $utils > wpia.utils.cs
PS (5) > Add-Type -Path wpia.utils.cs
Add-Type : Cannot add type. The type name 'WPIA.Utils' already exists
.
At line:1 char:9
+ Add-Type <<<<  -Path wpia.utils.cs
    + CategoryInfo          : InvalidOperation: (WPIA.Utils:String)
   [Add-Type], Exception
    + FullyQualifiedErrorId : TYPE_ALREADY_EXISTS,Microsoft.PowerShe
   ll.Commands.AddTypeCommand
```

You get an error because, although the text is the same, it comes from a different source, resulting in a "type already exists" error. You can, however, load it into a new PowerShell process:

```
PS (7) > powershell 'Add-Type -Path wpia.utils.cs; [WPIA.Utils]::Sum(
>> (1..10))'
55
```

The other thing you can do is have the file compiled into an assembly on disk instead of in memory. You do this with the `-OutputAssembly` parameter:

```
PS (8) > Add-Type -Path wpiautils.cs -OutputAssembly wpiautils.dll `
>> -OutputType library
```

This time you didn't get the error because the assembly wasn't being loaded. You can use the `dir` command to see what was produced:

```
PS (9) > dir wpiautils.*

    Directory: C:\Users\brucepay

Mode                LastWriteTime     Length Name
----                -------------     ------ ----
-a---          8/1/2010   6:50 PM       1564 wpiautils.cs
-a---          8/1/2010   6:50 PM       3584 wpiautils.dll
-a---          8/1/2010   6:50 PM      13824 wpiautils.pdb
```

Notice that, as well as the wpiautils.dll file, you also have the file wpiautils.pdb, which contains debugging information. This file is created because the default parameters that are passed to the compiler include the `/debug` flag.

You used the `-Path` parameter to load and compile the source file but you can also use it to load an already compiled DLL:

```
PS (10) > powershell '
>>    Add-Type -Path $PWD\wpiautils.dll
>>    [WPIA.Utils]::Sum((1..10))
>> '
>>
55
PS (11) >
```

Again you did it in a child process to avoid getting the type-collision error. The DLL loads, the Sum() method is called, and you see the sum 55 displayed on the console.

> **TIP** In section 17.1.2, you used -AssemblyName to load assemblies into the process. You might expect that you'd also use this parameter to load assemblies by path. But that assumptions isn't correct. You have to use -Path to load an assembly by path (or Import-Module). Remembering this may save you some frustration.

To recap, you've loaded assemblies, found and instantiated existing types, and used Add-Type to define new ones. There's one last piece you need to look at to complete our picture of types: *generic types*. Because generic types are used frequently in the .NET Framework, you'll need to know something about them.

17.1.6 Working with generic types

With version 2.0 of .NET, a feature was added to the CLR type system called *generic types* (or simply *generics*). Generics introduce the idea of a *type parameter*. Instead of passing objects as arguments when creating an instance of type, generics also require you to pass in *type parameters* that are used to determine the final types of some part of the object. This concept is rather confusing if you haven't encountered it before. As usual, an example should make things clearer.

Generics are easiest to understand when you talk about creating collections. Before the introduction of generics, if you wanted to create a collection class either you had to write a new version of the class for each type of object you wanted it to store or you had to allow it to hold any type of object, which meant that you had to do your own error checking. With generics, you can write a collection that can be constrained to only contain integers or strings or hashtables.

In PowerShell v1, though it was reasonably easy to work with existing instances of generic types, it was difficult to express generic type names or create new instances of these types. This issue was fixed in PowerShell v2, and you can now create generic types naturally. Let's look at some examples.

Creating instances of generic types

We'll start by creating a list, specifically a list of integers. To do this, you need to know the base type of the collection and the type parameter you need to pass when creating an instance of the collection. The base type you're going to use is System.Collections.Generic.List, which takes a single type argument. To create an instance of the collection, you pass the "closed" type name to New-Object. By *closed*, I mean that a concrete type has been specified as the type parameter. For a collection of integer, this looks like

```
$ilist = New-Object System.Collections.Generic.List[int]
```

where the name in the square brackets is the type parameter. You can use other types as well. To create a list of strings, you'd write

```
$slist = New-Object System.Collections.Generic.List[string]
```

You can even use generics in the type parameter:

```
$nlist = New-Object `
System.Collections.Generic.List[System.Collections.Generic.List[int]]
```

This example defines a list of lists of integers. In general, nested generic types are discouraged as they quickly become difficult to understand.

So far, we've only dealt with a single type parameter, but generics can take as many type parameters as are needed. For example, a generic `Dictionary`, which is similar to our old friend the hashtable, takes two type parameters: the type of the key and the type of the value. This looks like

```
$stoi = New-Object 'System.Collections.Generic.Dictionary[string,int]'
```

Notice that this time we had to put quotes around the type name; otherwise the comma between the two type parameters would cause the type name to be treated as two separate parameters.

With all this time we've spent playing the .NET trivia challenge game, we're sure heads are buzzing and coffee is being desperately sought. In the remainder of this chapter, we'll look at how you can apply some of the things you've learned to build more interesting applications.

17.2 POWERSHELL AND THE INTERNET

In this section, we're going to put the network back into .NET. As you'd expect from a modern programming environment, .NET (and consequently PowerShell) has a comprehensive set of types for doing network programming.

> **NOTE** The .NET Framework has good networking capabilities, but I suspect that the name came out of the marketing frenzy during the first internet bubble: .NET 1.0 was released in 2001. At that time, people were calling everything dot-something.

In this section, we'll look at a couple of useful examples of network programming with the .NET networking classes.

17.2.1 Retrieving a web page

The most common networking task in the internet age is to download a web page. Here's how to do that in PowerShell using the `[System.Net.WebClient]` type. This is a type that provides common methods for sending data to and receiving data from websites (or anything else that can be addressed with a URL). In this example, you'll

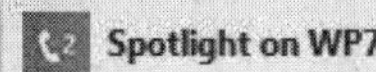
Spotlight on WP7
The Windows Phone Developer Tools Beta is now available. Start building great games and applications for Windows Phone 7.
Search > Windows Phone 7

Figure 17.6 This is a fragment of the MSDN blog home page. You're going to use PowerShell to identify and capture this text.

use this type to download data from the MSDN blog home page. Figure 17.6 shows the chunk of HTML you're targeting.

First you need to create an instance of `System.Net.WebClient`:

```
PS (1) > $wc = New-Object System.Net.WebClient
```

And you're ready to go. Let's take a look at what's happening on the MSDN blog site. Download the page into a variable:

```
PS (2) > $page = $wc.DownloadString("http://blogs.msdn.com")
PS (3) > $page.Length
46757
```

Checking the length, it's a bit long to look at as text. Let's simplify things and get rid of the HTML tags:

```
PS (4) > $page = $page -replace "\<[^<]*\>"
PS (5) > $page.Length
10930
```

You used a regular expression to remove anything enclosed in < and >. Doing so has shortened things a lot, but it's still a bit long. Let's get rid of unnecessary spaces:

```
PS (6) > $page = $page -replace " +", " "
PS (7) > $page.Length
7816
```

Split it into a collection of lines, getting rid of empty lines:

```
PS (8) > $lines = $page -split "`n" | where {$_ -match '[a-z]'}
427
```

Now you have something pretty short. Let's use the `Select-String` cmdlet with the `-Context` option to extract the text you're interested in:

```
PS (10) > $lines | Select-String -Context 0,2 'Spotlight.*WP7'

> Spotlight on WP7
  The Windows Phone Developer Tools Beta is now available. Start
building great games and applications for Windows Phone 7.
  Search &gt; Windows Phone 7
```

And there you go—a readable chunk of text. Note that the only new part was using the `WebClient` class. Everything else was just basic application of PowerShell operators and cmdlets.

NOTE There are much better ways to scrape text out of an HTML page. For example, the HTML Agility pack on CodePlex (http://htmlagilitypack.codeplex.com/) is a managed code library that provides an HTML processing experience similar to the way you handled XML in chapter 16.

Now let's see what else you can do with the `WebClient` class.

17.2.2 Processing an RSS feed

Let's explore RSS feeds. These are feeds that let you see the most recent postings in a blog formatted in XML. As you saw in the previous chapter, XML is easy to work with in PowerShell. The following example shows a function that downloads an RSS feed and prints out the feed titles and links:

```
function Get-RSS ($url)
{
    $wc = New-Object System.Net.WebClient
    $xml = [xml]$wc.DownloadString($url)
    $xml.rss.channel.item | Select-Object title,link
}
```

Let's use it to read the PowerShell team blog's RSS feed:

```
PS (2) > Get-RSS http://blogs.msdn.com/powershell/rss.aspx |
>>  Select-Object -First 3
>>

title                                link
-----                                ----
Intel vPro PowerShell Module         http://blogs.msdn.com/b/powersh...
PowerShell V2.0 Book Available ...  http://blogs.msdn.com/b/powersh...
Improving Parameter Set Design       http://blogs.msdn.com/b/powersh...
```

You downloaded the feed, then displayed the title and links for the first three items.

Let's use this function in something a bit more useful. Listing 17.1 shows a new function that will display a menu of the most recent articles in an RSS feed. You can select an item from the menu and it will be displayed using the default browser.

Listing 17.1 The `Get-RSSMenu()` function

```
function Get-RSSMenu (
    $url="http://blogs.msdn.com/powershell/rss.aspx",
    $number=3
)
{
    $entries = Get-RSS $url | Select-Object -First $number    <-- Download the RSS data
    $links = @()
    $entries | foreach {$i=0} {
        "$i - " + $_.title
        $links += $_.link
```

```
        $i++
    }
    while (1)
    {
        $val = Read-Host "Enter a number [0-$($i-1)] or q to quit"
        if ($val -eq "q") { return }
        $val = [int] $val
        if ($val -ge 0 -and $val -le $i)
        {
            $link = $links[$val]
            "Opening $link`n"
            Start-Process $link
        }
    }
}
```

Prompt user for link number

Open the link with default browser

By default, this function downloads the RSS feed for the PowerShell blog and shows a menu of entries and links containing the three most recent entries. (You can override both the blog and the number of items to show.) Here's what the function looks like when you run it:

```
PS (1) > Get-RSSMenu
0 - Kudos to NetApp for Data ONTAP PowerShell ToolKit
1 - Export and Import PowerShell ISE Opened Files
2 - Save All PowerShell ISE files
Enter a number [0-2] or q to quit: 0
Opening http://blogs.msdn.com/b/powershell/archive/2010/06/16/kudos-t
o-netapp-for-data-ontap-powershell-toolkit.aspx

Enter a number [0-2] or q to quit: q
PS (2) >
```

The menu shows the three most recent items from the blog. When you select an item number and press Enter, the `Start-Process` cmdlet is used to launch the URL using the current default browser.

With this example, we've begun to move into the area of user interface creation. We'll continue on this path and show you how to build "real" graphical interfaces for your scripts.

17.3 PowerShell and graphical user interfaces

The full name of the PowerShell package is *Windows PowerShell.* In this section, we'll look at the *Windows* part of the name. (PowerShell is part of the Windows product group. But you can do GUI programming with PowerShell, as you'll see in this section.)

One of the earliest successful scripting environments was something called *Tool Command Language/Tool Kit* (TCL/TK). TCL was intended to be a standard scripting language that could be used to automate systems. (This sounds familiar!) Its biggest success was TK, which was (and still is) a toolkit for building graphical applications with scripts. The ability to write a basic graphical application with a few dozen lines of code was wildly popular. The same kind of thing can be done in PowerShell using the .NET Windows Forms (WinForms) library or Windows Presentation Foundation (WPF).

> **NOTE** We're going to look at both WinForms and WPF in this chapter because the framework used in a particular scenario will depend on a number of criteria. First and foremost, WPF can't be used with PowerShell v1 because v1 doesn't support the STA threading model. If you need to write a UI that works in both versions, WinForms is your only choice. Second, the tools you have available will influence your choice. There are now GUI designers that support using WinForms with PowerShell. This may make WinForms the better, easier, and faster way to do things. WPF, on the other hand, makes it much easier to create rich, modern UIs. It also supports clean separation of business logic and presentation, allowing the look of the application to be changed without requiring changes to the underlying scripts. You'll see more of these details as we look at each framework. Finally, WinForms has been part of .NET since the beginning, whereas WPF was added with .NET 3.0. If you need your GUI to run on a .NET 2.0–only system, then you should look at using WinForms.

Each of these libraries provides a framework and collection of utility classes for building graphical application user interfaces. Let's see what you can do with these libraries. We'll begin by looking at WinForms.

17.3.1 PowerShell and WinForms

The core concepts in WinForms are controls, containers, properties, and events. A *control* is an element in a user interface—buttons, list boxes, and so on. Most controls, like buttons, are visible controls that you interact with directly, but there are some controls, such as timers, that aren't visible but still play a role in the overall user experience. Controls have to be laid out and organized to present a GUI. This is where containers come in. *Containers* include things such as top-level forms, panels, splitter panels, tabbed panels, and so on. Within a container, you can also specify a layout manager. The layout manager determines how the controls are laid out within the panel. (In TCL/TK, these were called *geometry managers.*) *Properties* are just regular properties, except that they're used to set the visual appearance of a control. You use them to set things such as the foreground and background colors or the font of a control.

The final piece in the WinForms architecture is the event. *Events* are used to define the behavior of a control both for specific actions, such as when a user clicks on the Do It button, as well as when the container is moved or resized and the control has to take some action. Like everything else in .NET (and PowerShell), events are represented as objects. For WinForms, the most common type of event is `System.EventHandler`. For PowerShell, anywhere an instance of `System.EventHandler` is required, you can use a scriptblock. (There is a lot more to handling events than we'll cover here. Chapter 20 is devoted to this topic.) If you want a particular action to occur when a button is clicked, you attach a scriptblock to the button click event.

EventHandler arguments

For an event handler to do its job, it requires information about the event that caused it to be invoked. You saw a similar pattern with `ForEach-Object` and `Where-Object`, where the value that the scriptblock operated on was passed using the automatic variable `$_`. The `EventHandler` integration in PowerShell follows the same basic pattern. In .NET, when an `EventHandler` is invoked, it's passed two arguments: the object that fired the event and any arguments that are specific to that event. The signature of the method that's used to invoke an event handler looks like this:

```
void Invoke(System.Object, System.EventArgs)
```

These values are made available to the scriptblock handling the event using the automatic variables `$this` and `$_`. The variable `$this` contains a reference to the object that generated the event, and `$_` holds any event-specific arguments that might have been passed. In practice, you don't need these variables most of the time because of the way variables in PowerShell work. With global, script, and module scopes, you can usually access the objects directly. Still, it's good to be aware of them in case you need them. (See appendix B for an example showing their use.)

These concepts are best illustrated through an example.

"Hello world" for winforms

We'll now look at the simplest WinForms example. This is the example you saw in chapter 1:

```
Add-Type -AssemblyName System.Windows.Forms
$form = New-Object System.Windows.Forms.Form
$form.Text = "My First Form"
$button = New-Object System.Windows.Forms.Button
$button.Text="Push Me!"
$button.Dock="fill"
$button.add_Click({ $form.close()})
$form.controls.add($button)
$form.Add_Shown({ $form.Activate()})
$form.ShowDialog()
```

Because it's short enough to type at the command line, let's go through the code interactively. First you have to load the `winforms` assembly—it's not loaded into PowerShell by default:

```
PS (1) > Add-Type -AssemblyName System.Windows.Forms
```

All applications have to have a top-level form, so you'll create one and save it in the variable `$form`:

```
PS (2) > $form = New-Object System.Windows.Forms.Form
```

Set the Text property on the form so that the title bar will display "My First Form":

```
PS (3) > $form.Text = "My First Form"
```

Next create a button and set the text to display in the button to "Push Me!":

```
PS (4) > $button = New-Object System.Windows.Forms.Button
PS (5) > $button.text="Push Me!"
```

You'll use the Dock property on the button control to tell the form layout manager that you want the button to fill the entire form.

```
PS (6) > $button.Dock="fill"
```

Now you need to add a behavior to the button. When you click the button, you want the form to close. You add this behavior by binding a scriptblock to the Click event on the button. Events are bound using special methods that take the form add_<eventName>:

```
PS (7) > $button.add_Click({$form.close()})
```

Be careful to match up all the parentheses and braces. In the scriptblock you're adding, you'll call the Close() method on the form, which will "end" the application.

> **NOTE** If you've programmed with WinForms in other languages such as C# or Visual Basic, you may be curious about how the event binding works. (If not, feel free to skip this note.) The add_Click() function corresponds to the Click event described in the MSDN documentation. PowerShell doesn't support the "+=" notation for adding events so you have to use the raw add_Click() method. In general, events require an instance of System.Delegate. The Click event in particular requires a subclass of System.Delegate called System.EventHandler. Although scriptblocks aren't derived from that type, PowerShell knows how to automatically convert a scriptblock into an EventHandler object so it all works seamlessly. We'll talk about other event types later in this chapter.

Now you need to add your button to the form. Do so by calling the Add() method on the Controls member of the form:

```
PS (8) > $form.Controls.add($button)
```

When the form is first displayed, you want to make it the active form. That's what the next line does; it sets up an event handler that will activate the form when it's first shown:

```
PS (9) > $form.Add_Shown({$form.Activate()})
```

You want to show the form you've built. There are two methods you could call. The first—Show()—displays the form and returns immediately. Unfortunately, this means that the form closes immediately as well. This is because the form is running on the same thread as the command. When the command ends, so does the form.The way to get around this issue is to use the `ShowDialog()` method. This method shows the form and then waits until the form is closed—which is what you want to do here. You call this method and PowerShell will seem to freeze:

```
PS (9) > $form.ShowDialog()
```

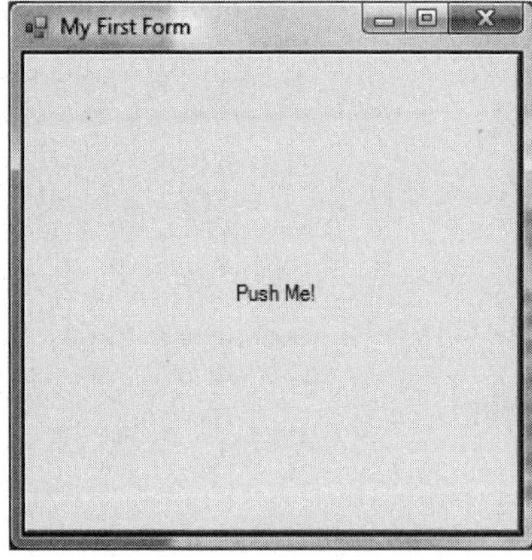

Figure 17.7 This is what the My First Form Windows Form looks like. It consists of a single button control that fills the form when it's resized.

Then, on the desktop, a form that looks like figure 17.7 will appear.

When you locate the window, you can resize it and move it around and everything works fine. Finally, click the "Push Me!" button, causing the form to disappear, and control will return to the PowerShell session. You'll see something like

```
Cancel
PS (10) >
```

The word *Cancel* is the return value from the `ShowDialog()` methods. Dialogs usually return a result such as *Cancel* or *OK*. Because you called `ShowDialog()`, you get a dialog reply.

Building a simple dialog box

Now let's look at something a bit more sophisticated. Because you're displaying the form like a dialog box, let's make it look more like a normal Windows dialog box. To do so, you'll build a form with three elements this time—a label and two buttons, OK and Cancel. The form will look like the image shown in figure 17.8.

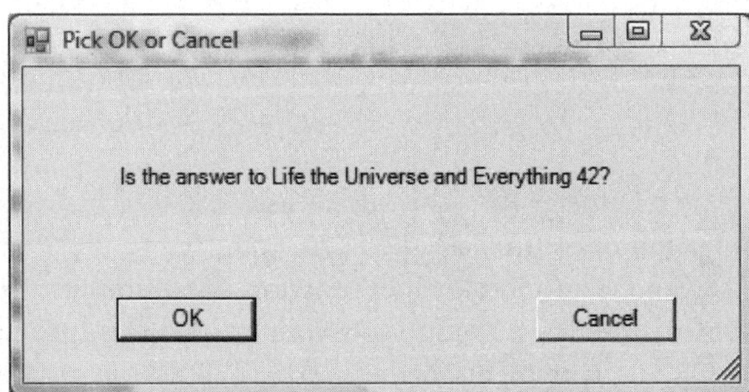

Figure 17.8 The dialog box created by the `Get-OkCancel()` function displays a simple message and two buttons.

The code for this function is shown in the following listing.

Listing 17.2 The `Get-OkCancel()` WinForms example

```
function Get-OkCancel
{
  [CmdletBinding()] param ($question=
   "Is the answer to Life the Universe and Everything 42?")

  function New-Point ($x,$y)
    {New-Object System.Drawing.Point $x,$y}

  Add-Type -AssemblyName System.Drawing,System.Windows.Forms

  $form = New-Object Windows.Forms.Form
  $form.Text = "Pick OK or Cancel"
  $form.Size = New-Point 400 200

  $label = New-Object Windows.Forms.Label
  $label.Text = $question
  $label.Location = New-Point 50 50
  $label.Size = New-Point 350 50
  $label.Anchor="top"

  $ok = New-Object Windows.Forms.Button
  $ok.text="OK"
  $ok.Location = New-Point 50 120
  $ok.Anchor="bottom,left"
  $ok.add_click({
      $form.DialogResult = "OK"
      $form.close()
  })

  $cancel = New-Object Windows.Forms.Button
  $cancel.text="Cancel"
  $cancel.Location = New-Point 275 120
  $cancel.Anchor="bottom,right"
  $cancel.add_click({
    $form.DialogResult = "Cancel"
    $form.close()
  })

  $form.controls.addRange(($label,$ok,$cancel))
  $form.Add_Shown({$form.Activate()})
  $form.ShowDialog()
}
```

❶ Define parameters

❷ Point helper function

❸ Load the required assemblies

❹ Create form and controls

❺ Add controls

This function takes one parameter ❶—the question to ask—with a default. When setting the size and location of controls on the form, you need to use `System.Drawing.Point` objects, so you create a local helper function ❷ to simplify things.

In addition to `System.Windows.Forms`, you need to load the `System.Drawing` assembly ❸ to get the `Point` type mentioned earlier.

NOTE In the PowerShell ISE, all of these assemblies are loaded by default. This is hardly surprising because the ISE is a graphical user interface. You may, however, wonder why you don't just load everything into the console host by default. The issue has to do with size and startup time. The more assemblies you load by default, the longer it takes to start `PowerShell.exe`. Having more assemblies also means that each running instance of `PowerShell.exe` becomes substantially larger. Finally, when a process on Windows is allowed to go idle (i.e., isn't used for a period of time) the image is paged to disk and the memory it was using is freed for other programs. This is why when you return to that process it takes a long time to respond, and the bigger it is, the longer it takes to page back in.

Once you have the prerequisites out of the way, you create the top-level `Form` ❹ and set the `Caption` and `Size` of this form.

Next you create a `Label`, setting the size of the control and the `Location` where it should be placed on the parent form. You also set the `Anchor` property to `Top`; this tells the layout manager to keep the label control "anchored" to the top of the form. No matter what the size of the form is, the label will always stay the same distance from the top of the form.

Then you create the OK button, setting the caption and location. Again, you're using the `Anchor` property to tell the layout manager to maintain the button's position relative to the bottom and left edges of the form when resizing the form. You also defined the click handler scriptblock. Doing so sets the `DialogResult` property to `OK`. When the form is closed, this is the value that will be returned from the call to `ShowDialog()`.

Finally, you define the `Cancel` button, this time anchoring it to the lower right of the form and adding a click handler that will cause `ShowDialog()` to return Cancel when the form is closed.

The last step is to add all the controls to the form and call `ShowDialog()` ❺. As before, the window may be hidden on your desktop when it appears.

There are a couple of things to note about this example. The first is that figuring out the size and location for each control is annoying. Calculation or a lot of trial and error is needed to get it right.

NOTE The forms editor in an IDE such as Visual Studio makes these types of chores much easier. If you look at the kind of code produced by a forms editor, you'll see it generates something that looks a lot like our example: object instantiations and a lot of property assignments.

The second thing to notice is that a lot of the code is almost identical. The definition for each of the buttons is the same except for the label and the anchor position.

Fortunately, you have a high-level scripting language you can use to build a library of functions to simplify this.

We'll also look at using smarter layout managers that try to get rid of a lot of the manual positioning. In the next section, we'll introduce a `winforms` module called `WPIAForms` that addresses these issues.

17.3.2 Creating a winforms module

There are a lot of elements in building a Windows Forms application that are repeated over and over. If you're working in an environment such as Visual Studio, the environment takes care of generating the boilerplate code. But if you're building a form using Notepad, you need to be a bit more clever to avoid unnecessary work. Let's build a module containing a number of convenience functions that make it easier to work with WinForms. We'll call this module `WPIAForms`. If this module is placed somewhere in your module path, then you can use it by including the line

```
Import-Module WPIAForms
```

at the beginning of your script. The code for this module is shown in the following listing.

Listing 17.3 The `WPIAForms.psm1` module

```
Add-Type -Assembly System.Drawing, System.Windows.Forms    # 1 Load required assemblies

function New-Size                                          # 2 Create Size objects
{
  param (
    [Parameter(mandatory=$true)] $x,
    [Parameter(mandatory=$true)] $y
  )
  New-Object System.Drawing.Size $x,$y
}

function New-Control                                       # 3 Create controls
{
  param (
    [Parameter(mandatory=$true)]
    [string]
      $ControlName,
    [hashtable] $Properties = @{}
  )

  $private:events = @{}
  $private:controls = $null

  foreach ($pn in "Events", "Controls")                    # 4 Extract events, controls from hashtable
  {
    if ($v = $Properties.$pn)
    {
      Set-Variable private:$pn $v
```

```
      $Properties.Remove($pn)
    }
  }
                                                              ❺ Construct
  $private:control = if ($Properties.Count) {          <--      control object
    New-Object "System.Windows.Forms.$ControlName" `
      -Property $Properties }
        else {
          New-Object "System.Windows.Forms.$ControlName" }

  if ($controls) {                                        <--   Add child
    [void] $control.Controls.AddRange(@(& $controls)) }      ❻ controls

  foreach ($private:en in $events.keys)             <--   Bind event
  {                                                     ❼ handlers
    $method = "add_$en"
    $control.$method.Invoke($events[$en])
  }
                                                   ❽ Ensure form
  if ($control -eq "form") {               <--      is visible
    $c.add_Shown({ $this.Activate() }) }
                                                    ❾ Return configured
  $control                                     <--    control
}
```

The first thing a `winforms` module should do is make sure that the necessary assemblies are loaded ❶. (Remember that trying to load an assembly multiple times is harmless.)

Next you define a convenience function ❷ for creating `Size` objects. Like many helper functions, it simply hides the long type names used to construct the objects.

Then you come to the heart of the module: the `New-Control` function ❸. This function is used to construct all the controls for your user interface. It takes as arguments the name of the `winforms` control class to instantiate and a hashtable containing three types of entries:

- Simple properties to set on the control
- An Events hashtable specifying which control events you want to handle
- A scriptblock used to create the child controls for this form

The function iterates over the keys in the hashtable ❹), looking to extract the `Controls` and `Events` members because they aren't simple properties on the object you're creating. The scriptblock in the `Controls` member will be evaluated and any control objects it returns will be added as children of the current control. The `Events` member requires more complex processing. It's also a hashtable but, in this case, the keys are the names of control events and the values are the scriptblocks to bind to those events.

Once the two special members have been extracted, the function passes the cleaned-up hashtable to the `-Property` parameter on `New-Object` ❺ to initialize the control. Unfortunately there's an annoying limitation on `-Property`: if the value

```
PS (STA) (50) > $form = New-Control form @{
  Text = "Hi"
  Size = New-Size 100 60
  Controls = {
    New-Control button @{
      Text = "Push Me"
      Dock = "fill"
      Events = @{
        Click = { $form.Close() }
      }
    }
  }
}
$form.ShowDialog()
```

Push Me

Figure 17.9 An example using the `WPIAForms` module. Both the code and the resulting window are shown here.

passed to `New-Object` is either `$null` or empty, it will error out. This necessitates wrapping the call to `New-Object` in an `if` statement so `-Property` only gets used when the hashtable is *not* empty.

Now that the control object exists, add any child controls that were extracted ❻ and bind any event handlers that were specified ❼. One additional event handler is added to ensure that the window is visible ❽. Finally, the completely configured control object is returned ❾.

Although there doesn't seem to be much to this library, it can significantly clarify the structure of the application you're building. Try it out by re-implementing the one-button example and see what it looks like. The result is shown in figure 17.9.

The resulting code isn't actually shorter but the hierarchical structure of the form is much more obvious. The top-level form is created using `New-Control` and sets the title to "Hi" and the size of the form to 100 x 60. The `Controls` member scriptblock creates the child controls for the form. In this case you're adding a `Button` object and again you use `New-Control` to create the object, set the `Text` and `Dock` properties, and define the `Click` event handler. Notice that at no point did you have to write any conditional loops—instead of describing how to build the form, you've simply declared what you want. In effect, you've created a simple domain-specific language (DSL) for defining WinForms-based user interfaces.

> **NOTE** When PowerShell v1 was released, the only way to build a GUI with PowerShell was through script code. There were no GUI builder tools available with support for the PowerShell language at that time. Things have changed considerably as PowerShell has become more popular. By the time v2 was released, there were a number of GUI builders on the market that supported building WinForms UIs in PowerShell, including SAPIEN Technologies PrimalForms and iTripoli's Admin Script Editor (which has an integrated PowerShell forms designer). Both of these tools provide sophisticated PowerShell authoring environments as well as (or with) the forms designer. GUI builders eliminate most of the manual layout and UI construction code.

Let's see where you've ended up. In the previous example, you invented a rather limited DSL for building GUIs in a declarative way. Clearly the ability to separate user interface *structure* from the implementation logic is compelling, so it would be nice if, rather than inventing your own language, you could use an existing GUI definition language. In practice, this is exactly what the Windows Presentation Foundation (WPF) is. Therefore, we're going to spend some time seeing how WPF can simplify building UIs in PowerShell.

17.3.3 PowerShell and Windows Presentation Foundation

In this section, you'll learn how to use WPF from PowerShell to construct GUIs. WPF is a modern, markup-based approach to declaratively constructing a user interface, much more in tune with the web than the older code-based WinForms approach.

WPF takes a different approach to constructing a GUI compared to WinForms. With WPF the UI is written *declaratively* using an XML-based markup language called XAML (Extensible Application Markup Language). The approach used in WPF is similar to the DSL you wrote as well as to the way HTML works: you describe the basic components and the framework handles all of the construction details. An important aspect of the design of WPF is that the UI description is *decoupled* from the UI logic. This separation of appearance and behavior aligns with well-established best practices for UI design (such as coders write code and design specialists do design).

> **NOTE** If you want to see what happens when this rule is broken, take a look at some of the very early websites that were created. These stand as excellent testaments to the fact that, with very few exceptions, programmers aren't designers.

In the next section, you'll see how this all works by building a simple GUI front end to some PowerShell commands. We'll only cover a fraction of the features of WPF—just enough to accomplish our goal of quickly building a simple UI. First you'll have to satisfy a few prerequisites before you can use WPF from PowerShell.

WPF preconditions

Although WPF has been around as long as PowerShell, in PowerShell v1, you weren't able to use WPF without a lot of tricks. This is because WPF can only be called from an STA-mode thread (yes, here it is again.) With PowerShell v2 and the `-sta` parameter, this limitation ceases to be an impediment. (And in the ISE, which is a WPF application, you always run in STA mode so, by default, everything will just work.)

The other thing you need to do to use WPF in your scripts is to load the WPF assemblies, `PresentationCore` and `PresentationFramework`, using `Add-Type`. With these prerequisites out of the way, you can start working on our example project.

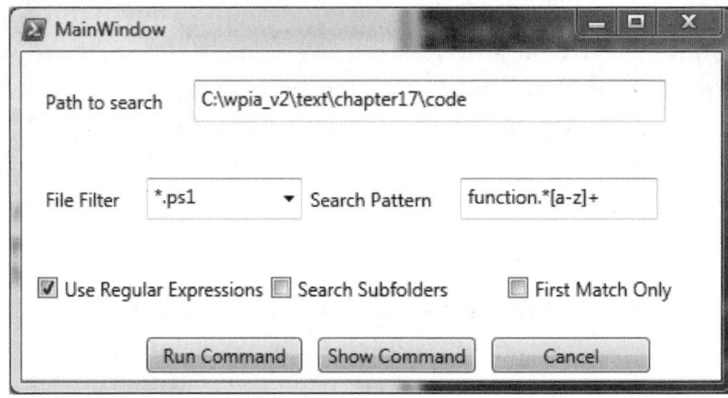

Figure 17.10 A dialog box that front-ends the PowerShell `Get-ChildItem` and `Select-String` cmdlets, allowing users to search with PowerShell even if they don't know the language

Building a file search tool

The goal of this exercise is to create a GUI front end to the `Get-ChildItem` and `Select-String` cmdlets using WPF. You want novice users to be able to execute a file search without having to be experts in PowerShell. A screen shot of the desired UI is shown in figure 17.10.

In this form, the user can specify the path to search (defaulting to the current directory), the extension of the files to search, and the pattern to use when searching the file text. By default, regular expressions will be used in the text search, but an option is provided to suppress this. There are also options to indicate that subfolders should be searched as well and that only the first match in each file may be returned. At the bottom of the dialog box, there are buttons to run or cancel the search. There's also a button that will display the command to be run before executing it—a very useful mechanism for learning PowerShell.

Although this is a very simple dialog box, it would be annoying to implement with WinForms due to all the manual control layout required. In the next section, you'll learn how easily you can describe this form with XAML.

Defining the search form's appearance

In this section, we're going to jump right into the user interface markup for the form. The XAML text for the interface is shown in the following listing.

Listing 17.4 The search.xaml file declaring the file search interface

```
<Window
  xmlns="http://schemas.microsoft.com/winfx/2006/xaml/presentation"
   xmlns:x="http://schemas.microsoft.com/winfx/2006/xaml"
    Title="PowerSearch: Search Files for String"
     SizeToContent="WidthAndHeight" >                          Create top-level window
  <DockPanel>
    <StackPanel HorizontalAlignment="Left" Orientation="Horizontal"      Create StackPanel to hold controls
      Width="425" DockPanel.Dock="Top" Margin="10,17,10,17">
       <Label Width="100" >Path to search</Label>              Add Label to StackPanel
```

```
<TextBox Name="Path" Width="300" >Add Row</TextBox>
    </StackPanel>
    <StackPanel HorizontalAlignment="Left" Orientation="Horizontal"
      Width="425" DockPanel.Dock="Top" Margin="10,17,10,17">
        <Label Width="70" >File Filter</Label>
        <ComboBox Name="FileFilter" Width="100" IsEditable="True">
          *.ps1
        </ComboBox>
        <Label Width="100" >Search Pattern</Label>
        <TextBox Name="TextPattern" Width="125" >
           function.*[a-z]+
        </TextBox>
    </StackPanel>
    <StackPanel HorizontalAlignment="Left" Orientation="Horizontal"
      Width="425" DockPanel.Dock="Top" Margin="10,17,10,17">
        <CheckBox Name="UseRegex" Width="150" >
           Use Regular Expressions
        </CheckBox>
        <CheckBox Name="Recurse" Width="150" >
          Search Subfolders
        </CheckBox>
        <CheckBox Name="FirstOnly" Width="150" >
            First Match Only
        </CheckBox>
    </StackPanel>
    <StackPanel HorizontalAlignment="Left" Orientation="Horizontal"
      DockPanel.Dock="Top" Margin="75,5,5,5">
        <Button Width="100" Name="Run" Margin="5,0,5,0" >
         Run Command
        </Button>
        <Button Width="100" Name="Show" Margin="5,0,5,0" >
         Show Command
        </Button>
        <Button Width="100" Name="Cancel" Margin="5,0,5,0" >
         Cancel
        </Button>
    </StackPanel>
  </DockPanel>
</Window>
```

Add named TextBox to StackPanel

Create another StackPanel for next row

Add ComboBox for file filter

Add dialog buttons to bottom

Looking through the XAML code, you see a lot of things that are familiar from the WinForms examples: `Label` controls, `TextBox`es, `Button`s, and so on. This means that you don't have to learn a lot of new concepts, just a new way to describe how they should be put together. In this UI description, the dialog box is constructed as a set of rows of controls. A `StackPanel` layout control is used to arrange the elements in each row and a `DockPanel` holds all the rows. Let's look at one of the control declarations in detail. The XAML that declares the Run button looks like this:

```
<Button Width="100" Name="Run" Margin="5,0,5,0" >
  Run Command
</Button>
```

Simply by inspecting the text, you can see that you're creating a `Button` control, setting the `Width` property on that control to 100, and setting the control `Margin` property with values for left, top, right and bottom margins. Of particular importance is the Name property that lets you associate a unique name string with the control. You'll need this information later when you're binding actions to the controls.

This XAML document describes what our form will look like but it doesn't say anything about how it behaves.

> **NOTE** At this point, the XAML experts in the audience will be shouting that there are, in fact, many elements in XAML that *do* let you describe behaviors (animations, triggers, and such). These features are beyond the scope of this exercise, but you're encouraged explore all the things that can be done with XAML. It's amazing how much you can accomplish just using markup.

In the next section, we'll introduce a PowerShell script that will "light up" your user interface.

Specifying the form's behavior

In the previous section, you described your form's appearance using XAML markup. In this section you'll learn how to attach your business logic to this markup.

To display your form, you must load the XAML into the session and use it to create an instance of System.Windows.Window. The WPF framework includes utility classes to do most of the heavy lifting for this task. Once you have the UI object, you just have to attach PowerShell actions to the controls. The following listing shows the script that does both of these things for you.

Listing 17.5 search.ps1: defining the file search behavior

```
Add-Type -Assembly PresentationCore,PresentationFrameWork    <-- Load WPF assemblies

trap { break }

$mode = [System.Threading.Thread]::CurrentThread.ApartmentState
if ($mode -ne "STA")
{
  $m = "This script can only be run when powershell is " +
   "started with the -sta switch."
  throw $m
}

function Add-PSScriptRoot ($file)                       <-- Compute path to XAML file
{
  $caller = Get-Variable -Value -Scope 1 MyInvocation
  $caller.MyCommand.Definition |
    Split-Path -Parent |
      Join-Path -Resolve -ChildPath $file
}

$xamlPath = Add-PSScriptRoot search.xaml
```

```
$stream = [System.IO.StreamReader] $xamlpath
$form = [System.Windows.Markup.XamlReader]::Load(
      $stream.BaseStream)
$stream.Close()

$Path = $form.FindName("Path")
$Path.Text = $PWD

$FileFilter = $form.FindName("FileFilter")
$FileFilter.Text = "*.ps1"

$TextPattern = $form.FindName("TextPattern")
$Recurse = $form.FindName("Recurse")

$UseRegex = $form.FindName("UseRegex")
$UseRegex.IsChecked = $true

$FirstOnly = $form.FindName("FirstOnly")

$Run = $form.FindName("Run")
$Run.add_Click({
    $form.DialogResult = $true
    $form.Close()
  })

$Show = $form.FindName("Show")
$Show.add_Click({Write-Host (Get-CommandString)})

$Cancel = $form.FindName("Cancel")
$Cancel.add_Click({$form.Close()})

function Get-CommandString
{
  function fixBool ($val) { '$' + $val }
  "Get-ChildItem $($Path.Text) ``
    -Recurse: $(fixBool $Recurse.IsChecked) ``
    -Filter '$($FileFilter.Text)' |
      Select-String -SimpleMatch: (! $(fixBool $UseRegex.IsChecked)) ``
        -Pattern '$($TextPattern.Text)' ``
        -List: $(fixBool $FirstOnly.IsChecked)"
}

if ($form.ShowDialog())
{
  $cmd = Get-CommandString
  Invoke-Expression $cmd
}
```

Load XAML that constructs UI

Find and set Path control to $PWD

Set default file filter extension

Set up CheckBox controls

Bind button Click actions

Build command string

Format Booleans so "True" becomes $true

Show form and wait

As was the case with the contents of the XAML file, there are many elements in this script that should be familiar from the WinForms examples. To add an action to a button, you use the `add_Click()` event method just like you did with WinForms. You use the `Text` property on `TextBox` controls to get and set the contents of those controls. Check boxes have an `IsChecked` property, as was the case with WinForms.

The biggest difference here is that, instead of binding actions as you construct the form, the XAML loader does all the construction and returns the completed object. You then have to find the controls by name to be able to access them. In practice, this turns out to be pretty simple. Once you've located the control objects, everything else is much the same as it was with WinForms. The `Get-CommandString` function is used to generate a string containing the PowerShell command that will perform the actual search. This function uses the retrieved control objects along with string expansion to produce a complete command.

Advantages of using WPF

The biggest advantage of using WPF is the separation of UI description from UI behavior. By not mixing code and markup, each piece becomes simpler and can be modified fairly independently. For example, because you're identifying the controls by name, it doesn't matter where they get moved around in the form; you'll still get the correct control when you ask for it by name.

The other big advantage to this separation of concerns is that you can now use all the WPF XAML GUI builders with PowerShell. Unlike WinForms, where the tools needed to know PowerShell to work, XAML is XAML so the actual programming language (for the most part) doesn't matter and the UI can be designed independently, decoupled from any code. This also means that the UI can be designed by an expert UI designer and the code added by an expert scripter. Finally, the higher-level nature of the WPF framework means that more effective PowerShell GUI frameworks can be created.

PowerShell frameworks for WPF

Inspired by possibilities that arise from the combination of PowerShell and WPF/XAML, the PowerShell community has created a number of higher-level libraries for building WPF GUIs in PowerShell. As of this writing there are two good libraries available free for download:

- The `WPK` library written by James Brundage, who was a member of the PowerShell team. This library is available at http://code.msdn.microsoft.com/PowerShellPack.
- The `PowerBoots` library, originally written and coordinated by Joel "Jaykul" Bennett, who is a PowerShell MVP. PowerBoots is available on CodePlex at http://powerboots.codeplex.com/.

Both of these libraries are packaged as PowerShell modules and provide a multitude of useful features. And with that, we've finished our tour of .NET and what you can do with it.

17.4 SUMMARY

We introduced a number of areas where PowerShell can be applied thanks to its ability to access classes in the .NET Framework. When a particular application domain may not have adequate coverage through cmdlets, if there's a .NET API for that area, the odds are good that PowerShell can be used to script it.

The first part of this chapter focused on expanding our knowledge of .NET. We covered a variety of areas:

- Basic concepts in .NET and the common language runtime
- How to load assemblies into the PowerShell session using the `Add-Type` cmdlet with the `-AssemblyName` parameter
- How to represent type names, including generic types, in the PowerShell language and how to create instances of these types using the `New-Object` cmdlet
- Using the `Add-Type` cmdlet to create new .NET types dynamically in a PowerShell session

The next section of the chapter looked at some of the application domains supported by .NET. These examples included network programming in PowerShell. We looked at

- Retrieving a simple web page in a script using the `System.Net.WebClient` class
- How to address more complex scenarios with the `WebClient` class such as using PowerShell's built-in XML support to process an RSS feed
- How to build graphical interfaces for PowerShell using Windows Forms and WPF

In the next chapter we'll continue with our exploration of Windows technologies and look at COM and how it expands what you can do with PowerShell.

CHAPTER 18

Working with COM

A horse! A horse! My kingdom for a horse!

—King Richard in William Shakespeare's *The Life and Death of King Richard III*

At the end of Shakespeare's *Richard III*, King Richard stands upon a plain, surrounded by foes, crying out for the one thing that he needs to continue on. Sort of like the noble sysadmin: "A tool! A tool! My kingdom for a tool!" Okay, perhaps not exactly like that, but at times, we do feel set upon from all sides, crying out desperately for something to help us solve our problems. Fortunately, we in the PowerShell world do get our horse: a framework called the Component Object Model (COM), which can help us win our battles by giving us access to the necessary facilities.

In this chapter, we'll cover the important details of working with COM from PowerShell. We'll look at a number of examples that illustrate how COM objects work and the sorts of tasks that can be accomplished. You'll also learn how to leverage earlier Windows scripting technologies in PowerShell scripts.

18.1 WORKING WITH COM IN POWERSHELL

COM is an interface specification describing how to write libraries that can be used from multiple languages or environments. Prior to technologies like COM, each programming language required its own set of libraries: Basic could only use libraries written for Basic, C could only use libraries written for C, and so on. The COM specification allowed the creation libraries of *components* that could be accessed from multiple languages. But beyond simply sharing library code, COM allowed running applications to expose automation interfaces that external programs could use to remotely control them. In this section, we'll introduce COM and see how to leverage COM classes using PowerShell. COM provides easy (and in some cases trivial) access to many Windows features. We'll work through a number of examples in a variety of application scenarios such as scheduling a task using the Windows task scheduler. Finally, we'll complete our COM coverage by examining some of the issues and limitations the PowerShell scripter may encounter.

18.1.1 Creating COM objects

The first thing you need to know if you want to work with COM (or any other object system for that matter) is how to create instances of COM objects. As with .NET objects, you use the `New-Object` cmdlet, but for COM objects, you have to specify the `-ComObject` parameter. This signature is shown in figure 18.1.

Notice that, unlike .NET objects, COM doesn't have a way to pass arguments to the object's constructor, making it hard to initialize the object. As a workaround for this, in PowerShell v2 (and later), you use the `-Property` parameter to initialize properties on the constructed object before returning it.

Unique to the COM parameter set is the `-Strict` switch. This switch tells the cmdlet to generate an error if a .NET/COM `Interop` library is loaded. Explaining what this means and why it's important is a bit complicated, so we'll go through it in pieces in the next section.

COM and Interop assemblies

In chapter 3, we talked about how the PowerShell type system uses *adaptation* to give the user a consistent experience with different kinds of objects. COM objects are one of these adapted types, but the way the PowerShell adapter works is affected by the

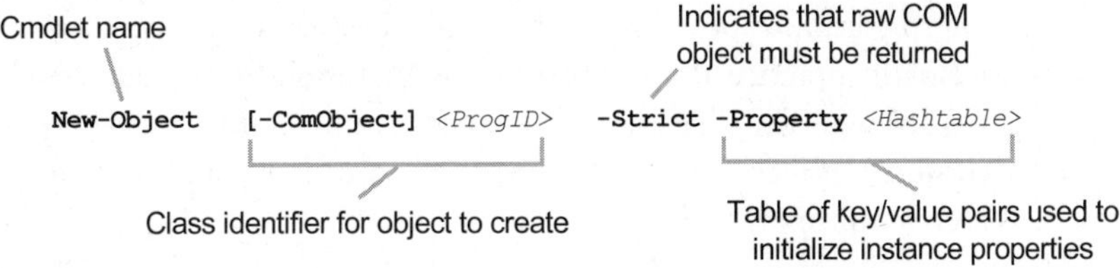

Figure 18.1 The `New-Object` parameter set for creating COM objects

presence or absence of a COM `Interop` library. In effect, this `Interop` library is .NET's own adaptation layer for COM. The net effect is that the PowerShell COM adapter will project a different view of a COM object if an `Interop` library is loaded versus when there's no `Interop` library. This becomes a problem because, for any given COM class on any given machine, there may or may not be an `Interop` library, so you may or may not get the doubly adapted COM object. If you want to be able to write scripts that behave consistently everywhere, you need a way to control how the adaptation is done. The `-Strict` parameter allows you to detect this when an `Interop` library is loaded. Once you know what's happening, you can decide whether you want to fail or continue but along a different code path. This kind of portability issue is something to keep in mind when you're writing a script using COM that you plan to deploy on other machines. But for now, let's move on to our next topic and see how to find out which COM classes are available.

18.1.2 Identifying and locating COM classes

In this section, you'll learn how to identify or name a COM class and find out what classes are available on a machine. Officially, all COM classes are identified by a globally unique ID (GUID). The following example uses the .NET `System.GUID` class to show you what a GUID looks like:

```
PS (1) > [System.Guid]::NewGuid()
Guid
----
aaae24e3-14ea-4f70-9234-dfc3cbce9fb8
```

This isn't a particularly friendly way to identify—well, anything really. So, as far as PowerShell is concerned, COM objects are identified by a much more usable name called the *ProgID*. This is a string alias that's provided when the class is registered on the system. Using the ProgID is the most human-friendly way of identifying the object. By convention, the ProgID has the form

```
<Program>.<Component>.<Version>
```

which (at least according to the MSDN documentation) should be fewer than 39 characters in length.

> **NOTE** Although this format is the recommended way to create a ProgID, there's no real way to enforce it, resulting in some interesting interpretations for what each of the elements means. Generally, it seems in practice that *<Program>* is the application suite, toolset, or vendor who installed it; *<component>* is the COM classname; and the version number is normally not used in calls, though it may exist in even a multipart form.

COM objects are registered in (where else?) the Registry. This means that you can use the Registry provider to search for ProgIDs from PowerShell. Here's a function we'll call `Get-ProgID` that will do it:

```
function Get-ProgID
{
    param ($filter = '.')

    $ClsIdPath = "REGISTRY::HKey_Classes_Root\clsid\*\progid"
    dir $ClsIdPath |
        foreach {if ($_.name -match '\\ProgID$') { $_.GetValue("") }} |
            where {$_ -match $filter}
}
```

This searches through the Registry starting at the root of the classes hierarchy, where COM objects are registered for keys whose paths end in "ProgID." From the keys, you retrieve the default property, which contains the name string of the ProgID. You check this string against the filter and, if it matches, write it to the output stream. Let's try it out. You want to find the ProgID for Internet Explorer:

```
PS (1) > Get-ProgID internetexplorer
InternetExplorer.Application.1
```

And there it is: `InternetExplorer.Application.1`. This ProgID follows the recommended format: the program is `InternetExplorer` and the component in this case is the actual Internet Explorer application. You can use this same pattern to find the *automation interfaces* for other applications. Let's look for Microsoft Word:

```
PS (2) > Get-ProgID word.*applica
Word.Application.11
```

You find the ProgID for Microsoft Word 11. This function works for non-Microsoft applications as well. Let's pick an application that you may have installed on your computer—say, Apple's iTunes media player:

```
PS (3) > Get-ProgID itunes.*application
iTunes.Application.1
```

Again, it follows the naming convention.

Now let's look at another way to find ProgIDs: through WMI (which is the subject of the next chapter). Here's an alternate function that uses WMI:

```
function Get-ProgID
{
    param ($filter = '.')

    Get-WmiObject Win32_ProgIDSpecification |
        where {$_.ProgId -match $filter} |
            Select-Object ProgID,Description
}
```

Not only is this script simpler, it also provides additional information: a description of the class. Let's look up Microsoft Word again to see this in action:

```
PS (6) > (Get-ProgID word.application) | select-object -First 1

ProgID                          Description
------                          -----------
Word.Application.11             Microsoft Word Application
```

This time you get the ProgID and its description. The downside to this mechanism is that it only locates a subset of the registered ProgIDs, so the Registry-based script is usually the best approach.

Once you have the ProgID, you can use it with `New-Object` to create instances of these objects. Starting the next section, you'll see some of the things you can do using COM.

18.2 AUTOMATING WINDOWS WITH COM

The first area where you'll apply COM will be working with and automating basic features and services built into Windows itself. Table 18.1 lists a number of the classes that are useful in this area. Note that not all classes are available on all versions of Microsoft Windows

For the rest of section 18.2, we'll focus on the `Shell.Application` class and look at a number of examples demonstrating how to apply this class. The examples

Table 18.1 COM classes for accessing Windows features

Class ProgID	Description
`Shell.Application`	Provides access to Windows Explorer and its capabilities. Allows automation of many shell tasks like opening file browser windows; launching documents or the help system; finding printers, computers, or files; and so on.
`SAPI.SpVoice`	Provides access to the Microsoft Speech API. Allows text-to-speech with the `Speak("string")` method.
`WMPlayer.OCX`	Manipulates the Windows Media Player.
`MMC20.Application`	Manipulates the Microsoft Management Console application.
`Agent.Control`	Interface to the Windows Animated Agents framework. Allows animated characters to be displayed.
`Microsoft.Update.Session`	Provides access to the Windows Update Agent (WUA), allowing you to scan, download, and install updates.
`Schedule.Service`	Allows you to create and schedule tasks, get a list of running tasks, and delete task definitions (see section 18.6 for examples).
`WScript.Shell`	Provides access to system information and environment variables; lets you create shortcuts and work with the Registry (see section 18.3 for examples).

start with automating Windows Explorer; then we'll explore activating a Control Panel applet and automating an application by sending keystrokes to it.

18.2.1 Exploring with the Shell.Application class

In this section, you'll learn how to automate the Windows file browser using the `Shell.Application` COM class. Through this class, Windows Explorer provides an automation model that allows you to automate a significant number of tasks.

> **NOTE** Automation model in this sense means that there's a COM object interface that lets an external program manipulate some aspects of an application.

The first thing you need to do is create an instance of this class:

```
PS (3) > $shell = New-Object -ComObject Shell.Application
```

As always in PowerShell, COM objects, like any other object type, can be examined using `Get-Member`. Let's look at the members on the object you just created:

```
PS (4) > $shell | Get-Member

   TypeName: System.__ComObject#{efd84b2d-4bcf-4298-be25-eb542a5
9fbda}

Name                 MemberType Definition
----                 ---------- ----------
AddToRecent          Method     void AddToRecent (Variant, st...
BrowseForFolder      Method     Folder BrowseForFolder (int, ...
CanStartStopService  Method     Variant CanStartStopService (...
CascadeWindows       Method     void CascadeWindows ()
ControlPanelItem     Method     void ControlPanelItem (string)
EjectPC              Method     void EjectPC ()
Explore              Method     void Explore (Variant)
ExplorerPolicy       Method     Variant ExplorerPolicy (string)
FileRun              Method     void FileRun ()
FindComputer         Method     void FindComputer ()
FindFiles            Method     void FindFiles ()
FindPrinter          Method     void FindPrinter (string, str...
GetSetting           Method     bool GetSetting (int)
GetSystemInformation Method     Variant GetSystemInformation ...
Help                 Method     void Help ()
IsRestricted         Method     int IsRestricted (string, str...
IsServiceRunning     Method     Variant IsServiceRunning (str...
MinimizeAll          Method     void MinimizeAll ()
NameSpace            Method     Folder NameSpace (Variant)
Open                 Method     void Open (Variant)
RefreshMenu          Method     void RefreshMenu ()
ServiceStart         Method     Variant ServiceStart (string,...
ServiceStop          Method     Variant ServiceStop (string, ...
SetTime              Method     void SetTime ()
ShellExecute         Method     void ShellExecute (string, Va...
ShowBrowserBar       Method     Variant ShowBrowserBar (strin...
```

```
ShutdownWindows      Method     void ShutdownWindows ()
Suspend              Method     void Suspend ()
TileHorizontally     Method     void TileHorizontally ()
TileVertically       Method     void TileVertically ()
ToggleDesktop        Method     void ToggleDesktop ()
TrayProperties       Method     void TrayProperties ()
UndoMinimizeALL      Method     void UndoMinimizeALL ()
Windows              Method     IDispatch Windows ()
WindowsSecurity      Method     void WindowsSecurity ()
Application          Property   IDispatch Application () {get}
Parent               Property   IDispatch Parent () {get}
```

Woo-hoo! Jackpot! Look at all that stuff! Let's try it out. Start with the `Explore()` method, which will launch an Explorer window on the path specified:

```
PS (10) > $shell.Explore("c:\")
```

At this point, you should see something like figure 18.2. This method call opened an Explorer window at the root of the C: drive.

Here's a handy function for laptop users who move around a lot. Many laptops have docking stations that allow you to easily connect multiple peripherals. This is great except that you need to undock the laptop before heading to a meeting. Depending on the laptop, this can be annoying, so here's a quick one-line function to undock a laptop:

```
function eject { ( New-Object -ComObject Shell.Application ).EjectPC() }
```

This function gets an instance of the `Shell.Application` object and then calls the `EjectPC()` method to undock the laptop.

NOTE I love this function. I go to way too many meetings.

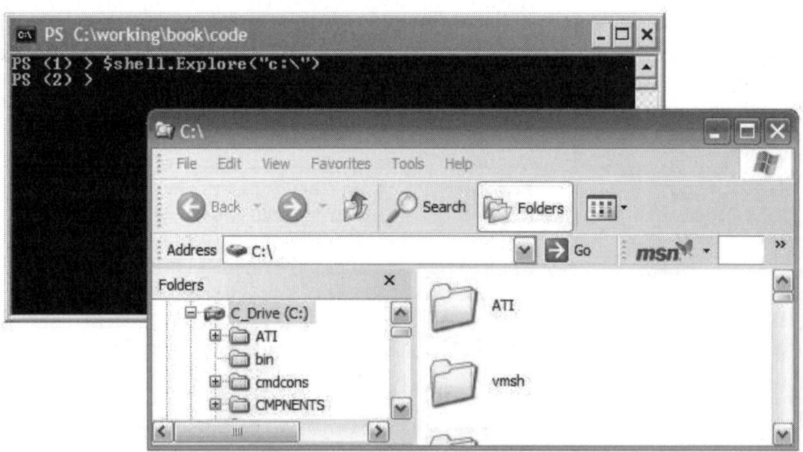

Figure 18.2 Launching the Windows Explorer on C:

18.2.2 Managing browser windows using COM

Now let's look at some examples where you actually work with the windows in Windows. The `Windows()` method on `Shell.Application` allows you to get a list of the Explorer and Internet Explorer windows that are currently open:

```
PS (16) > ($shell.Windows()).count
47
```

So there are 47 windows open in the current session. Let's see what these `Window` objects look like:

```
PS (17) > $shell.Windows() | Get-Member | Format-Wide Definition

void ClientToWindow (int, int)      void ExecWB (OLECMDID, OLECMDEX...
Variant GetProperty (string)        void GoBack ()
void GoForward ()                   void GoHome ()
void GoSearch ()                    void Navigate (string, Variant,...
void Navigate2 (Variant, Varian... void PutProperty (string, Variant)
OLECMDF QueryStatusWB (OLECMDID)    void Quit ()
void Refresh ()                     void Refresh2 (Variant)
void ShowBrowserBar (Variant, V... void Stop ()
bool AddressBar () {get} {set}      IDispatch Application () {get}
bool Busy () {get}                  IDispatch Container () {get}
IDispatch Document () {get}         string FullName () {get}
bool FullScreen () {get} {set}      int Height () {get} {set}
int HWND () {get}                   int Left () {get} {set}
string LocationName () {get}        string LocationURL () {get}
bool MenuBar () {get} {set}         string Name () {get}
bool Offline () {get} {set}         IDispatch Parent () {get}
string Path () {get}                tagREADYSTATE ReadyState () {get}
bool RegisterAsBrowser () {get}... bool RegisterAsDropTarget () {g...
bool Resizable () {get} {set}       bool Silent () {get} {set}
bool StatusBar () {get} {set}       string StatusText () {get} {set}
bool TheaterMode () {get} {set}     int ToolBar () {get} {set}
int Top () {get} {set}              bool TopLevelContainer () {get}
string Type () {get}                bool Visible () {get} {set}
int Width () {get} {set}
```

Again, you see lots of tantalizing things to play with. Let's try looking at the first item in the collection that was returned:

```
PS (21) > $shell.Windows()[0]
Unable to index into an object of type System.__ComObject.
At line:1 char:18
+ $shell.Windows()[0 <<<< ]
```

Hmm... you got an error. So what happened here? If you look at the type of the object returned by the method, you see that it's of type `System.__ComObject`, which is the .NET wrapper mechanism for accessing COM objects. PowerShell, in turn, adapts the wrapped objects. Unfortunately, the adaptation mechanism isn't perfect and this is one of the places where these imperfections show through. The PowerShell interpreter doesn't know how to automatically index on these collections. This doesn't mean that you can't do it; you just have to work a bit harder. Instead of normal indexing syntax, you have to use the `Item()` *parameterized property*. Parameterized properties are similar to methods in that they can take arguments like a method, but they can also be assigned to like a property, hence parameterized properties. In this case, the `Item()` property is used for indexing a collection.

Let's try it again:

```
PS (18) > $shell.Windows().Item(0)

Application            : System.__ComObject
Parent                 : System.__ComObject
Container              :
Document               : mshtml.HTMLDocumentClass
TopLevelContainer      : True
Type                   : HTML Document
Left                   : 354
Top                    : 80
Width                  : 838
Height                 : 489
LocationName           : WinRM and WSMAN - Vista Forums
LocationURL            : http://www.vistax64.com/network-shar
                         ing/187197-winrm-wsman.html
Busy                   : False
Name                   : Windows Internet Explorer
HWND                   : 591430
FullName               : C:\Program Files\Internet Explorer\i
                         explore.exe
Path                   : C:\Program Files\Internet Explorer\
Visible                : True
StatusBar              : True
StatusText             :
ToolBar                : 1
MenuBar                : True
FullScreen             : False
ReadyState             : 4
Offline                : False
Silent                 : False
RegisterAsBrowser      : False
RegisterAsDropTarget   : True
TheaterMode            : False
AddressBar             : True
Resizable              : True
```

This output shows you lots of information about this window. You can see that it's an Internet Explorer window along with the title and URL of the page that's being displayed in it. Let's select just the name and URL properties:

```
PS (19) > $shell.Windows() |
>> Select-Object -First 1 locationname,locationurl | Format-List
>>

LocationName : WinRM and WSMAN - Vista Forums
LocationURL  : http://www.vistax64.com/network-sharing/187197-winrm-w
               sman.html
```

Figure 18.3 This figure shows a browser window where the menu bar is visible. Remember where the menu bar shows up, as you'll hide it next.

This is a browser page pointing at a forum with a question about WSMan.

Okay, what else can you do with this object besides look at its properties? Well, for one thing, you can change a lot of those properties. For example, let's turn off all the extra widgets that clutter up our browser windows to maximize our screen real estate. First, let's get rid of the menu bar. Examine the current state of the menu bar by using

```
PS (10) > $shell.Windows().Item(0).MenuBar
True
```

A browser window with the menu bar turned on is shown in figure 18.3.

You can turn it off by setting the `MenuBar` property to `$false`:

```
PS (19) > $shell.Windows().Item(0).MenuBar = $false
```

Figure 18.4 shows what the window looks like now. The menu bar is gone and you've reclaimed that space to view your web pages.

Figure 18.4 This is how the browser window looks after running a PowerShell command to hide the menu bar. Compare this to the previous figure to verify that the menu bar is indeed gone.

In the next section, you'll take what you've learned about these objects and build a module for managing all the browser windows.

18.2.3 A browser window management module

In this section, you'll build a COM-based tool to help manage the inevitable clutter of browser windows you (or at least I) always end up with. You'll call this function `Get-BrowserWindow` and it will be exported from a module you'll call `COMtools.psm1`. You'll also define an alias, `gbw`, for this function. The functional specification for this command is as follows:

1. Calling this function with no arguments lists the names of open Internet Explorer windows.
2. If a string argument is passed to this function, this argument will be used as a regular expression pattern to match against the names of the open windows.
3. The function will allow the following actions to be performed on the selected browser windows:
   - Make the window visible on the desktop
   - Minimize the window
   - Close the window

The user experience should look like the following. First, you load the module:

```
PS (1) > Import-Module .\COMtools.psm1
```

This module imports the `Get-BrowserWindow` function and its alias `gbw`. To get a list of all of the open windows, you call the function with no arguments:

```
PS (2) > (Get-BrowserWindow).Count
33
```

Using the `Count` property on the collection returned by the command, you can see that there are 33 browser windows open. Let's see how many search windows are being used:

```
PS (3) > Get-BrowserWindow bing
powershell and COM - Bing
powershell xaml - Bing
powershell blogs - Bing
```

You currently have three Bing windows open. You decide that you don't need the blogs search window, so close it:

```
PS (4) > Get-BrowserWindow blogs.*bing -close
```

Then verify that it was closed by rerunning the search command:

```
PS (7) > Get-BrowserWindow bing
powershell and COM - Bing
powershell xaml - Bing
```

Now let's turn this specification into working code. You know how to get the list of windows and filter them based on the window title. You'll apply this knowledge (and a bit of programmer pixie dust) to write your module. The following listing shows the resulting source.

Listing 18.1 The `COMtools.psm1` module

```
$Shell = New-Object -com Shell.Application

Add-Type -Namespace WPIA -Name WindowUtils
    -MemberDefinition @'
      [DllImport("user32.dll")]
      public static extern bool ShowWindow(
        IntPtr hWnd, Int32 nCmdShow);
'@

function Show-Window
{
  [CmdletBinding()] param (
    [Parameter(ValueFromPipeline=$true)]
      $window,
    [switch] $Minimize
  )

  if (-not $window) { return }
  try
  {
    $hwnd = $window.HWND
    [void] [WPIA.WindowUtils]::ShowWindow($hwnd,6)
    if ($Minimize) { return }
    [void] [WPIA.WindowUtils]::ShowWindow($hwnd, 9)
    [void] [WPIA.WindowUtils]::ShowWindow($hwnd, 1)
  } catch { }
}

function windows ($pattern)
{
  $shell.Windows() | where {
    $_.Name -match 'Internet' -and
         $_.LocationName -match $pattern
    }
}


function Get-BrowserWindow
{
  [CmdletBinding(DefaultParameterSetName="full")]
  param (
   [Parameter(Position=0)]
     $Pattern = ".",
   [Parameter(ParameterSetName="full")]
     [switch] $Full,
   [Parameter(ParameterSetName="show")]
```

❶ **Create COM object in module scope**

❷ **Define ShowWindow interop class**

❸ **Define number of functions**

```
    [switch] $Show,
   [Parameter(ParameterSetName="minimize")]
    [switch] $Minimize,
   [Parameter(ParameterSetName="close")]
    [switch] $Close  )

  foreach ($window in windows $Pattern)
  {
    if ($Show) { Show-Window $window }
    elseif ($Minimize) { Show-Window -Minimize $window }
    elseif ($Close) { $window.Quit() }
    else
    {
      if ($Full) { $window }
      else { $window.LocationName }
    }
  }
}
Set-Alias gbw Get-BrowserWindow
Export-ModuleMember -Function Get-BrowserWindow -Alias gbw
```

Let's quickly walk through some interesting elements in this code and see how they track against the functional specification. As always, you begin by creating the COM object you'll be using ❶. You also need to use P/Invoke (see section 17.1.5) to access the APIs needed to show and hide windows ❷. You define a function to wrap the API calls ❸. Because the APIs may throw exceptions, you enclose the calls inside a `try/catch` statement. To guarantee that the target window is visible and on the top, you make a series of calls to the `ShowWindow()` API to minimize, restore, and ensure visibility. You use the `Windows()` method on the `Shell.Application` object to get the list of windows. This collection includes both Explorer and Internet Explorer windows but our spec says you only want the IE windows. To satisfy this, you create a `windows` helper function that filters out non-IE windows by checking the `WindowName` property. This function also does the work of filtering the window collection by title. It uses the `-match` operator to match the `$Pattern` parameter against the `LocationName` property.

The main interface for this module is the `Get-BrowserWindow` function. This is an advanced function (see section 8.2) that uses parameter sets to mark mutually exclusive parameters. This function loops over the matched windows and shows, minimizes, closes, or lists the window information on the console. Finally, you define a short alias to make it more convenient to use the function and then export both the alias and the function.

Let's try using this module. Our first task will be to see if there are any open pages with the word "Seattle" in the title. Call `Get-BrowserWindow` with `Seattle` as the pattern argument:

```
PS (1) > Get-BrowserWindow Seattle
The Seattle Times | Seattle Times Newspaper
```

This call returned one page. You can make that page visible by adding the -Show switch to the command:

```
PS (2) > Get-BrowserWindow Seattle -Show
```

The browser window should now be visible (although it may not be the selected tab in that window). Once you're done with the page, you can close it, so you replace -Show in the command with -Close:

```
PS (3) > Get-BrowserWindow Seattle -Close
```

Once the command has completed, either the tab containing the page will vanish or the browser window will close.

The ability to find, view, or close browser windows is particularly handy when you're investigating a topic that ends up using dozens of browser windows for all the different pages discussing the topic. But you can make it even more useful by adding a -Gui option to the function as you'll do in the next section.

Adding a graphical front end

The ability to list and manipulate browser windows from the command line is effective, but sometimes it's difficult to isolate a specific window just using patterns. In these situations, it'd be helpful to display the matches in a list and then select the items to operate on from there. In this section, you'll see how to do exactly this. You'll add a new -Gui switch to the Get-BrowserWindow function that tells it to display the matches in a list box. The resulting display is shown in figure 18.5.

To do this, you'll need to make a few small changes to the original function. You need to add the -Gui parameter definition to the param block. The new parameter definition is as follows:

```
[Parameter(ParameterSetName="gui")]
  [switch] $Gui
```

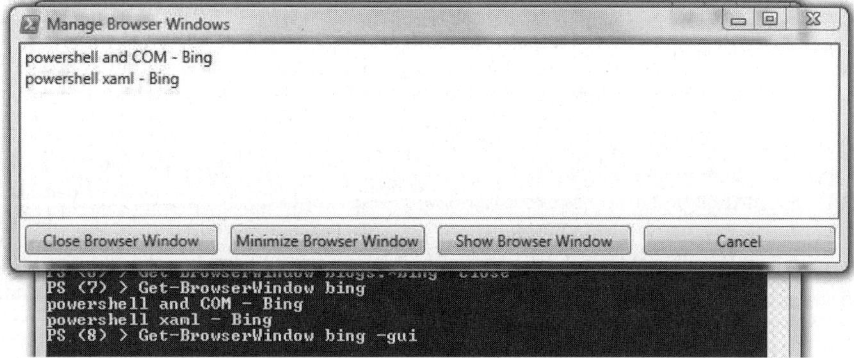

Figure 18.5 This figure shows the GUI interface for the `Get-BrowserWindow` function. When `-Gui` is passed to the command, the dialog box will appear showing the filtered list of browser windows, which can then be shown, closed, or minimized.

To implement the processing for this new switch, you'll add an `if` statement right after the `param` block that looks like this:

```
if ($Gui)
{
  Invoke-Gui $Pattern
  return
}
```

Now you're done. If the `-Gui` flag is specified, the function will call `Invoke-Gui`, passing in the pattern to match and then return. Next, you have to write the `Invoke-Gui` piece. In practice, writing this GUI turns out to be fairly easy to do.

Defining the GUI in XAML

In chapter 17, you saw how to build GUIs in PowerShell using WPF and XAML. You'll reuse what you learned as well as some of the code from section 17.3.3 to build your GUI.

First, you'll define the XAML text that describes the user interface you want to display. You can leverage some of the markup code that was shown in listing 17.9 to make this easy. The markup for the new browser management form is shown in the following listing.

Listing 18.2 The XAML markup describing the Browser Window GUI

```
$uiXaml = @'                                    <-- (1) Define module-level variable to hold XAML
 <Window Title="Manage Browser Windows"
  xmlns="http://schemas.microsoft.com/winfx/2006/xaml/presentation"
  xmlns:x="http://schemas.microsoft.com/winfx/2006/xaml"
   Height="250" MinHeight="200" Width="700" MinWidth="650">         <-- (2)
  <DockPanel>                                                        <-- (3)
   <StackPanel Orientation="Horizontal" DockPanel.Dock="Bottom"      <-- (4)
    HorizontalAlignment="Center">
    <Button Width="150" Name="cw" Margin="5"          Define stack panel (4)
     Content="Close Browser Window"/>
    <Button Width="150" Name="mw" Margin="5"          Define dock panel (3)
     Content="Minimize Browser Window"/>
    <Button Width="150" Name="sw" Margin="5"          Define form size (2)
     Content="Show Browser Window"/>
    <Button Width="150" Name="cancel" Margin="5"
     Content="Cancel"/>
   </StackPanel>
   <ListBox Name="BrowserWindows" HorizontalAlignment="Stretch"      <-- (5)
    DockPanel.Dock="Bottom" SelectionMode="Extended"/>
  </DockPanel>                                        Specify list
</Window>                                             box to hold
'@                                                    window titles (5)
```

Begin by assigning the here-string to a variable (1). In code, you're defining a form (2) with a `ListBox` and four `Button` controls. A `DockPanel` (3) is used to hold the entire form and manage the positions of the controls. The four button controls—close, minimize, show, and cancel are laid out horizontally in a `StackPanel` ❹, which is docked at the bottom of the form. The `ListBox` ❺ is declared last to take advantage of the fact that the `DockPanel` control "fills" the form with the last control added so you don't have to do anything to get reasonable resizing behavior.

Defining the control actions

Now that you've defined the form, you need to run some PowerShell commands to the control actions and then display the form (see the following listing).

Listing 18.3 The PowerShell code for the Browser Window GUI

```
function Invoke-Gui ($pattern = '.')                          Check for STA- ❶
{                                                            mode PowerShell
  $mode = [System.Threading.Thread]::CurrentThread.ApartmentState   <-
  if ($mode -ne "STA") {
    Write-Error ("The -Gui option can only be used when PowerShell " +
      "is started using the -sta option")
    return
  }
                                                                ❷ Load WPF
  Add-Type -Assembly PresentationCore,PresentationFrameWork  <-   assemblies

  $xmlStream = [System.Xml.XmlReader]::Create(           <-   Convert XAML
    [System.IO.StringReader] $uiXaml )                     ❸ text to window
  $form = [System.Windows.Markup.XamlReader]::Load(
    $xmlStream)
  $xmlStream.Close()

  $listBox = $form.FindName("BrowserWindows")

  $windowMap = @{}
  function setupListBox                <-   Initialize
  {                                       ❹ ListBox
    $windowMap.Clear()
    $listBox.Items.Clear()
    $count = 0
    foreach ($w in windows $pattern)
    {
      $name = "(" + $count++ + ") " + $w.LocationName
      $windowMap[$name] = $w
      [void] $listBox.Items.Add($name)
    }
  }
  setUpListBox
                                                   ❺ Specify FindName()
  $form.FindName("cw").add_Click(               <-   method
  {
    foreach ($sw in $listBox.SelectedItems | Write-Output)
    {
      try
      {
        $windowMap[$sw].Quit()
```

```
      }
      catch { }
    }
    setupListBox
  })

  $form.FindName("mw").add_Click(
  {
     foreach ($sw in $listBox.SelectedItems)
     {
       Show-Window -Minimize $windowMap[$sw]
     }
  })

  $form.FindName("sw").add_Click(
  {
     foreach ($sw in $listBox.SelectedItems)
     {
       Show-Window $windowMap[$sw]
     }
  })

  $form.FindName("cancel").add_Click({ [void] $form.Close() })

  [void] $form.ShowDialog()                    <-6 Show form as dialog
}
```

This listing follows the same basic pattern you saw in chapter 17. First, you check to see if you're running in STA mode ❶ because that's required to use WPF. If you're running STA, then you load the WPF assemblies ❷ and generate the GUI window from the XAML definition ❸. Once you have the GUI object, you find the desired controls by name and define the control actions using a scriptblock. You define a hashtable to map the index to the window object and a function ❹ to set up the map and `ListBox` contents. You use the `FindName()` method to find each of the button controls ❺. Finally you call `ShowDialog()` to display the form ❻.

Loading XAML from a here-string

One thing that's a bit different from the example you saw in chapter 17 is how the XAML is stored and loaded. In this example, instead of using a file, the XAML text is embedded in the module as a here-string, stored in a module-level variable. When it comes time to generate the UI object, you cast the XAML text into an instance of `System.IO.StringReader`, which essentially allows you to read from a string the same way you'd read from a file. Then you create an `XmlReader` class out of that stream and finally use the static `Create()` method on the `XamlReader` class to build the form from the `XmlReader`.

The other slightly complicated piece of code results from the fact that `ListBox` only contains the titles of the windows and you need to get the actual object back to be able to operate on it. You accomplish this by using a hashtable where the keys are the browser window's name and the values are the objects. Also, because it's possible for multiple windows to have the same title, you prefix the title with an index so that all the strings are guaranteed to be unique. The final detail to consider is that, after you've loaded `ListBox`, one of the windows listed may have been closed some other way, which could lead to errors. You have `try/catch` statements around the elements that might throw an error to address this case.

Moving right along, let's look at what you can do with some of the other COM classes. In the next section, you'll learn how to use the Windows Script Host shell object (`WScript.Shell`) from PowerShell.

18.3 Working with the WScript.Shell class

The `WScript.Shell` class will be familiar to any VBScript user writing Windows management scripts. It contains a collection of useful methods for writing scripts on Windows. As always, you'll explore this object first. You'll create an instance to work with and put it into the `$wshell` variable:

```
PS (1) > $wshell = New-Object -com WScript.Shell
```

Now let's see what it can do using `Get-Member`:

```
PS (2) > $wshell | Get-Member

   TypeName: System.__ComObject#{41904400-be18-11d3-a28b-00104bd
35090}

Name                        MemberType            Definition
----                        ----------            ----------
AppActivate                 Method                bool AppActiva...
CreateShortcut              Method                IDispatch Crea...
Exec                        Method                IWshExec Exec ...
ExpandEnvironmentStrings    Method                string ExpandE...
LogEvent                    Method                bool LogEvent ...
Popup                       Method                int Popup (str...
RegDelete                   Method                void RegDelete...
RegRead                     Method                Variant RegRea...
RegWrite                    Method                void RegWrite ...
Run                         Method                int Run (strin...
SendKeys                    Method                void SendKeys ...
Environment                 ParameterizedProperty IWshEnvironmen...
CurrentDirectory            Property              string Current...
SpecialFolders              Property              IWshCollection...
```

The purpose of many of these methods is fairly obvious just by looking at the name. For example, to pop up a message box you use the `Popup()` method. From the command line, enter the following command

```
$wshell.Popup("Hi there")
```

and up pops a message box, as shown in figure 18.6.

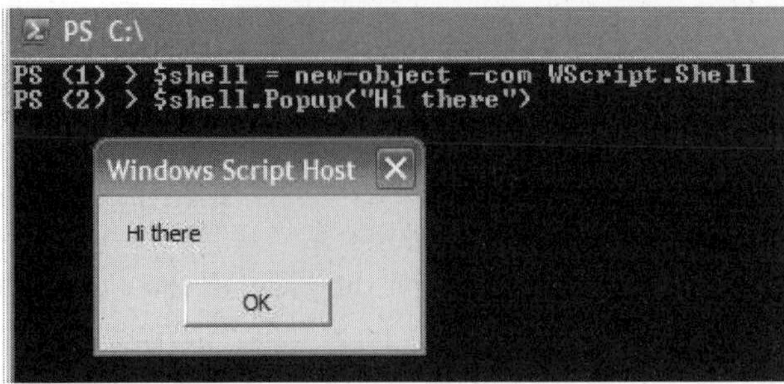

Figure 18.6 When you use the `WScript.Shell` object to pop up a message box, it will look like this.

Let's look at something a bit more focused on automating Windows (and windows). One of the methods on the `WScript.Shell` class is `SendKeys()`. This method allows you to send keys to an application just as if the user was typing them at the keyboard. Let's look at how you can use this feature to automate a Windows GUI application. You'll work with the Windows calculator (`calc.exe` or `calc`) in this example. First, you need to get an instance of the `WScript.Shell` class:

```
$wshell = New-Object -Com WScript.Shell
```

Next, you'll start a calculator process. Because PowerShell is a shell, you could just run `calc` from the command line, but because this section is all about COM, use the `Run()` method on the `WScript.Shell` instead:

```
[void] $wshell.Run("calc")
```

After you give the application a second to start, use the `AppActivate()` method to set the focus on the calculator window. When you're sure the window is active, send a sequence of keys to the application, waiting for a second between each operation:

```
Start-Sleep 1
if ($wshell.AppActivate("Calculator"))
{
    "Calculator activated..."
    Start-Sleep 1
    $wshell.SendKeys("10{+}")
    Start-Sleep 1
    $wshell.SendKeys("22")
    Start-Sleep 1
    $wshell.SendKeys("~")
    Start-Sleep 1
    $wshell.SendKeys("*3")
    Start-Sleep 1
    $wshell.SendKeys("~")
    Start-Sleep 1
    $wshell.SendKeys("%{F4}")
}
```

If you ran this script, you'd see "10" appear in the result window, followed by "22" shortly thereafter; then the two are added to give "32," and so on. Finally, you send the sequence `<alt><f4>` to tell the application to close. (This is why you made sure that the calculator process is active; otherwise, you might have sent the keystrokes to the wrong application. Closing the wrong window is…well, bad.)

Up to now, you've only been working with Windows on the desktop. Let's expand our COM exploration to additional areas and applications.

18.4 Using COM to manage applications

In this section, we'll explore some COM networking classes and then look at examples of how to automate applications like Microsoft Word. You'll start with the Internet Explorer class.

18.4.1 Looking up a word using Internet Explorer

In this example, you're going to use Internet Explorer to access a web page through its COM automation object.

> **NOTE** Accessing a website is not the main point of this example. You've already seen an efficient way to do this using .NET classes in section 17.2.1. The intention here is to see how to automate *applications* using a PowerShell script.

The goal here is to use the Wiktionary website to look up the definition of a word. Our script will take two parameters: the word to look up and an optional switch to tell the script that you want to make the browser window visible and leave it open during the search. As before, the programmer pixie dust is sprinkled and the complete function magically appears.

> **NOTE** Although the notion of "programmer pixie dust" is rather silly, there are many, many online resources that are almost as magical. Here are just a few of the sites available: http://technet.microsoft.com, http://microsoft.com/powershell, http://poshcode.org, http://codeplex.org, and http://powershellcommunity.org. Remember: Good programmers write good code; great programmers steal great code.

The code for the `Get-WordDefinition` function is shown in the following listing.

Listing 18.4 The `Get-WordDefinition` function

```
param(
    $word = $(throw "You must specify a word to look up."),
    [switch] $visible
)

Add-Type -AssemblyName System.Web                    # (1) Load System.Web

$ie = New-Object -ComObject InternetExplorer.Application
$ie.Visible = $visible
```

```
$ie.Navigate2("http://en.wiktionary.org/wiki/" +
    [Web.HttpUtility]::UrlEncode($word))

while($ie.ReadyState -ne 4)
{
     start-sleep 1
}

$bodyContent = $ie.Document.getElementById("bodyContent").innerHtml

$showText=$false
$lastWasBlank = $true
$gotResult = $false

switch -regex ($bodyContent.Split("`n"))
{
'^\<DIV class=infl-table' {
        $showText = $true
        continue
    }
'^\<DIV|\<hr' {
        $showText = $false
    }
'\[.*edit.*\].*Translations' {
        $showText = $false
    }
{$showText} {
        $line = $_ -replace '\<[^>]+\>', ' '
        $line = ($line -replace '[ \t]{2,}', ' ').Trim()

        if ($line.Length)
        {
            $line
            $gotResult = $true
            $lineWasBlank = $false
        }
        else
        {
            if (! $lineWasBlank)
            {
                $line
                $lineWasBlank = $true
            }
        }
    }
}

if (! $gotResult)
{
    "No Answer Found for: $word"
}

if (! $visible)
{
    $ie.Quit()
}
```

❷ Navigate to Wiktionary

❸ Wait until ready

❹ Extract data

❺ Process data

❻ Close IE

You're going to load an additional .NET assembly ❶ because you need to encode your word into a URL to send it to the Wiktionary site. Next, you get an instance of the Internet Explorer object. You tell IE to navigate to the Wiktionary website and look up the word ❷. This may take a while, so you loop, waiting for the document to be loaded ❸. When the document is ready, you use the Internet Explorer Document Object Model to extract the information you want out of the document ❹. Even after you've extracted the document, the information you're after still requires a significant amount of work to locate and extract. You do this using the `switch` statement ❺. If there was an answer, you display it; if not, you give the user an error message.

And finally, if the `visible` flag hasn't been specified, close the browser window ❻. Let's try looking something up:

```
PS (1) > ./Get-WordDefinition.ps1 factorial

Singular factorial

Plural factorials
factorial ( plural factorials )

( mathematics ) The result of multiplying a given number of
 consecutive integers from 1 to the given number. In
equations, it is symbolized by an exclamation mark (!). For
example, 5! = 1 * 2 * 3 * 4 * 5 = 120.

[ edit ] Usage notes
" n !" is read as "factorial of n ."

PS (2) >
```

And there you go—a world of crucial knowledge at our fingertips!

> **NOTE** In practice, this type of script, which is dependent on a website that you don't control, is very fragile. It's extremely dependent on the structure of pages generated by the target website, and these are subject to change at any time. (In fact, this example had to be revised during the production of the book because Encarta, the original target website, changed its format.) If the page structure changes, your script will be broken. (A well-structured data source such as the RSS feed, as you'll see in the next example, allows for much more reliable scripts.)

18.4.2 Using Microsoft Word to do spell checking

Wouldn't it be great if every environment you worked in had spell checking like word processors do? With PowerShell and COM, you can get at least part of the way there. You're going to write a script that will use Microsoft Word to spell-check the contents of the clipboard and then paste them back. You'll call this script `Get-Spelling.ps1`.

Let's see how it's used. First, you start Notepad and type some text with errors into it:

```
PS (1) > notepad
```

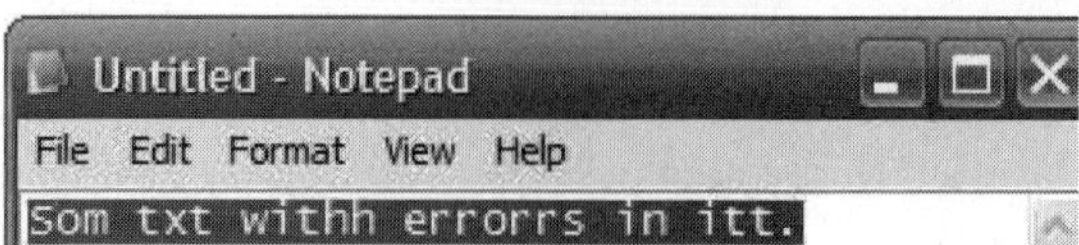

Figure 18.7 This Notepad window shows the misspelled text that you will be fixing using the Get-Spelling script.

Next, select the text and copy it to the clipboard. This is shown in figure 18.7.

Now run the script:

```
PS (2) > Get-Spelling
```

You'll see the Word Spelling dialog box pop up, as shown in figure 18.8.

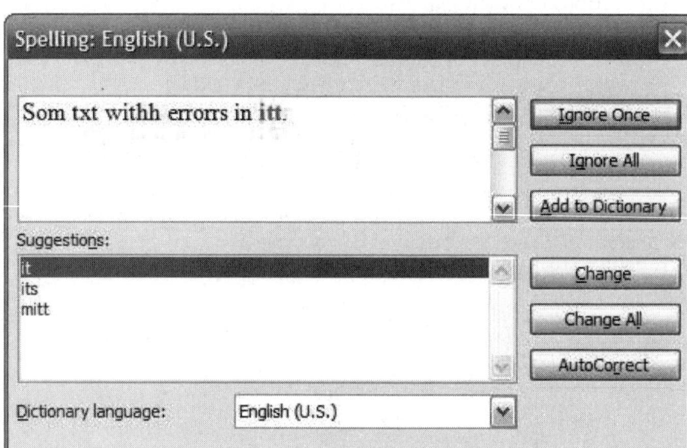

Figure 18.8 The Microsoft Word spell checker launched by the Get-Spelling script shows the misspelled text that was copied from the clipboard.

You go through all of the spelling errors and fix them as appropriate. Once all the errors are fixed, the dialog box will disappear and the pop-up box will be displayed, indicating that the revised text is available in the clipboard. Switch back to the Notepad window and paste the revised text into the window as shown in figure 18.9.

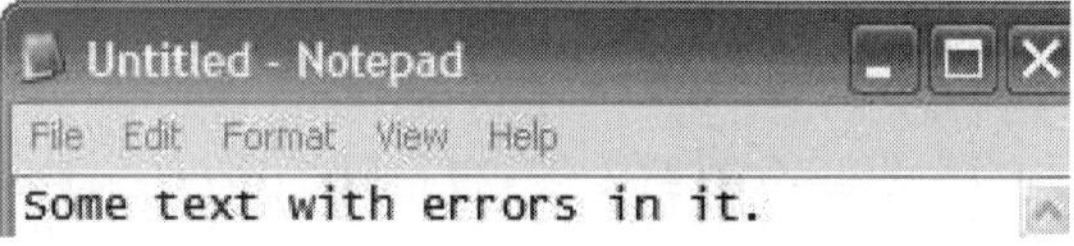

Figure 18.9 The Notepad window showing the corrected text

And you're done. The text in the Notepad window is correctly spelled. Now that you know how to use this script, let's take a look at the actual code, which is shown in the following listing.

Listing 18.5 The Get-Spelling script

```
$wshell = New-Object -com WScript.Shell
$word = New-Object -com Word.Application
$word.Visible = $false
```

```
$doc = $word.Documents.Add()
$word.Selection.Paste()

if ($word.ActiveDocument.SpellingErrors.Count -gt 0)
{
    $word.ActiveDocument.CheckSpelling()
    $word.Visible = $false
    $word.Selection.WholeStory()
    $word.Selection.Copy()
    $wshell.PopUp( "The spell check is complete, " +
        "the clipboard holds the corrected text." )
}
else
{
    [void] $wshell.Popup("No Spelling Errors were detected.")
}

$x = [ref] 0
$word.ActiveDocument.Close($x)
$word.Quit()
```

The first thing you do is create the object instances you're going to use. You need an instance of `WScript.Shell` to pop up a message box and the `Word.Application` object for the bulk of the work. Once you have the `Word.Application` object, you'll make the Word window invisible, and then add an empty document to hold the text you want to spell-check. Next, you copy the contents from the clipboard to the Word document you created and see if you need to spell-check the text. If you do, you present the Spelling dialog box. When the spell check is complete, you select all the text and copy it back to the clipboard so you can paste it into the original document and inform the user that the corrected text is available. If there were no spelling errors, you'll display a message box confirming this. The last step is to discard the document you created and close the application. With this script, you can add spell-checking capabilities to any application that lets you select and copy text.

> **NOTE** Obviously, if Microsoft Word is not your word processor of choice, it should be simple to modify the script to work with any word processor that exports a similar automation model.

So far, we've focused on using COM to manipulate applications, but it can also be used to access other features in Windows. Let's see how COM can be used to bridge between PowerShell and older Active Scripting–based languages like VBScript.

18.5 The WSH ScriptControl class

In this section, we'll show how to use the `ScriptControl` class from PowerShell. This object will allow PowerShell to evaluate fragments of VBScript (or JavaScript or any other language that has an `ActiveScript` engine) embedded inline in a PowerShell script. This allows you to reuse existing VBScript code simply by copying the code into a PowerShell script.

NOTE There's another reason that this example is important. Some COM objects work in COM automation languages such as VBScript, but not in .NET environments such as PowerShell. Using this example, you can package any required fragments of VBScript into the overall PowerShell script.

18.5.1 Embedding VBScript code in a PowerShell script

You start by using the `ScriptControl` class to build a VBScript `CodeObject`. Be aware that this class is not available on all versions of Microsoft Windows. This object makes the VBScript functions defined in the script available to the caller as methods on this code object. The function shown in the following listing returns a code object with two of these methods on it: `GetLength()`, which returns the length of a string, and `Add()`, which adds two objects together.

Listing 18.6 The `Call-VBScript` function

```
function Call-VBScript
{
    $sc = New-Object -ComObject ScriptControl
    $sc.Language = 'VBScript'
    $sc.AddCode('
      Function GetLength(ByVal s)
          GetLength = Len(s)
      End Function
      Function Add(ByVal x, ByVal y)
          Add = x + y
      End Function
    ')
    $sc.CodeObject
}
```

Let's use the function to mix and match some PowerShell with VBScript:

```
PS (1) > $vb = Call-VBScript
```

Calling the function gives you an object with the VBScript functions available as methods. First use the `GetLength()` method to get the length of a string:

```
PS (2) > "Length of 'abcd' is " + $vb.getlength("abcd")
Length of 'abcd' is 4
```

Now use the `Add()` method, but use it inside a string expansion to illustrate how seamless this all is:

```
PS (3) > "2 + 5 is $($vb.add(2,5))"
2 + 5 is 7
PS (4) >
```

In the string expansion, the VBScript function is called to add the two numbers and return the result. The result is converted to a string and included in the expanded result string.

18.5.2 Embedding JScript code in a PowerShell script

The script control also supports JScript, Microsoft's implementation of ECMAScript (JavaScript). This listing shows the same example but using JScript.

Listing 18.7 The `Call-JScript` function

```
function Call-JScript
{
    $sc = New-Object -ComObject ScriptControl
    $sc.Language = 'JScript'                          ❶ Specify JScript
    $sc.AddCode('
      function getLength(s)                           ❷ Add code
        {
          return s.length
      }
      function Add(x, y)
        {
          return x + y
      }
    ')
    $sc.CodeObject                                    ❸ Return CodeObject
}
```

First, you create the script control, this time specifying that the language is JScript ❶.

Then you add the code to define your functions ❷ and finally return the object ❸ containing your functions. You call this function to get the code object back:

```
PS (4) > $js = Call-JScript
```

When you run the functions on this object, you get the same results you did in the VBScript example:

```
PS (5) > "Length of 'abcd' is " + $js.getlength("abcd")
Length of 'abcd' is 4
PS (6) > "2 + 5 is $($js.add(2,5))"
2 + 5 is 7
```

This time, the JScript functions are called to return the results to PowerShell for display.

Our last example with the `ScriptControl` mixes everything together. In a one-line script (command line), you can mix PowerShell, VBScript, and JScript. In fact, you can have three languages all in one expression:

```
PS (7) > "The answer is " +
>> $js.add($vb.getlength("hello"),2) * 6
>>
The answer is 42
PS (8) >
```

This example illustrates the basics of how to use the script control from PowerShell. Although we could continue to explore this type of embedding for quite some time, there's one final, important COM example we need to cover. A common requirement for many management operations is the ability to schedule tasks to be run either on a reoccurring schedule or when a particular event occurs. For example, backup and housekeeping activities are usually scheduled to run late at night. In the next section, you'll see how to do this kind of scheduling using PowerShell.

18.6 WORKING WITH THE WINDOWS TASK SCHEDULER

In this section, you'll learn how to use PowerShell to create, list, and manage Windows Task Scheduler tasks.

> **NOTE** These examples will only work on Windows Vista/Server 2008 or above. Starting with those releases, the Windows Task Scheduler was significantly enhanced, adding many new features.

The COM class you need to work with the Task Scheduler is `Schedule.Service`. This class allows you to create and schedule tasks, get a list of running tasks, and delete task definitions. In this example, our goal is to schedule a task that will start a `PowerShell.exe` process in 30 seconds from the time the task is created. This PowerShell command will open a console window and then execute some script code that will slowly count up from 1 to 10. Once it reaches 10, it'll wait for quite a long time so the Task Scheduler will be forced to shut that task down. Let's walk through the commands to do this.

18.6.1 Getting started with the Schedule.Service class

First, you need to use `New-Object` to get an instance of the `Schedule.Service` object. Using `Get-Member` as always, you look to see what this class can do for you:

```
PS (2) > $ts = New-Object -ComObject Schedule.Service
PS (3) > $ts | Get-Member

   TypeName: System.__ComObject#{2faba4c7-4da9-4013-9697-20cc3fd40f85}

Name              MemberType Definition
----              ---------- ----------
Connect           Method     void Connect (Variant, Variant, Variant...
GetFolder         Method     ITaskFolder GetFolder (string)
GetRunningTasks   Method     IRunningTaskCollection GetRunningTasks ...
NewTask           Method     ITaskDefinition NewTask (uint)
Connected         Property   bool Connected () {get}
ConnectedDomain   Property   string ConnectedDomain () {get}
ConnectedUser     Property   string ConnectedUser () {get}
HighestVersion    Property   uint HighestVersion () {get}
TargetServer      Property   string TargetServer () {get}
```

The method names provide a reasonably clear description of the basic operations you can perform. More detailed descriptions are shown in table 18.2.

Table 18.2 The list of basic methods for the Windows Task Scheduler COM object

Schedule.Service method	Description
`Connect()`	Connect to the local or remote computer. Calling the method with no arguments connects to the local service.
`GetRunningTasks()`	Get a list of the currently running tasks (which is not the same as the currently defined tasks). Not all definitions may be running at any given time.
`NewTask()`	Create a new task definition.

18.6.2 Listing running tasks

Let's connect to the Task Scheduler on the local machine and list the running tasks:

```
PS (4) > $ts.Connect()
PS (5) > $ts.GetRunningTasks(0)

Name          : UserTask
InstanceGuid  : {115A7A03-36B5-4937-8E23-E08B6E974488}
Path          : \Microsoft\Windows\CertificateServicesClient\UserTask
State         : 4
CurrentAction : Certificate Services Client Task Handler
EnginePID     : 4784

Name          : TMM
InstanceGuid  : {6433D865-3D03-4F62-B70D-D8E314799EBB}
Path          : \Microsoft\Windows\MobilePC\TMM
State         : 4
CurrentAction : Transient Multi-Monitor Manager
EnginePID     : 4784

Name          : SystemSoundsService
InstanceGuid  : {266F6DD9-8A1F-4C00-B62A-8CF0A47D4359}
Path          : \Microsoft\Windows\Multimedia\SystemSoundsService
State         : 4
CurrentAction : Microsoft PlaySoundService Class
EnginePID     : 4784
```

You can see that there are three tasks running currently: `UserTask`, `TMM`, and `System-SoundsService`. Because there may be more than one instance of a task running at any given time, each task instance is uniquely identified by the `InstanceGUID` field. You'll get to the path field in a minute, but the other interesting field to notice is the `CurrentAction` field. Each task has one or more *triggers* (events that start the task) and one or more *actions* (operations performed by the task when it's triggered). Let's see how to build a new task definition using the `Schedule.Service` object.

18.6.3 Creating a new scheduled task

To create a new task definition, you start by calling the `NewTask()` method:

```
PS (8) > $nt = $ts.NewTask(0)
```

> **NOTE** People often ask what the 0 passed to `NewTask()` stands for. The answer currently is nothing. This method argument is reserved for future use, and all current scripts and programs should always pass 0.

Once you have the task object, you can begin to configure it starting with information that will be used to identify the task once it's registered. To set up this information, you need to get the registration object returned by the `RegistrationInfo` property on the new task object:

```
PS (9) > $ri = $nt.RegistrationInfo
```

With this object, you can set the `Description` and `Author` fields to help identify this task definition:

```
PS (10) > $ri.Description = "Count to 10"
PS (11) > $ri.Author = "Bruce Payette"
```

Next, you have to establish the circumstances under which the task will be run. Because you want to see the window displayed on the screen, you're going to set the `LogonType` to be 3 (interactive):

```
PS (12) > $principal = $nt.Principal
PS (13) > $principal.LogonType = 3
```

Now you need to establish when the task will be run by creating some triggers. The numeric argument that's passed in indicates the type of trigger to create. In this case, you want to create a `TimeTrigger`, which is specified by passing 1 to the API:

```
PS (14) > $trigger = $nt.Triggers.Create(1)
```

To set the start and stop times for this task, you'll have to write a small function to convert a .NET time string into the format required by the Task Scheduler. This format is almost the same as .NET's string representation of the UTC time except that there's a space in the .NET string where the Task Scheduler expects the letter T. To fix this, you can use the `-replace` operator to substitute `T` for `' '`:

```
PS (15) > function XmlTime ([datetime] $d)
>> {
>>   $d.ToUniversalTime().ToString("u") -replace " ","T"
>> }
>>
```

Set the start and end boundary times to run the task:

```
PS (16) > $trigger.StartBoundary = XmlTime ((Get-Date).AddSeconds(30))
PS (17) > $trigger.EndBoundary = XmlTime ((Get-Date).AddMinutes(5))
```

These settings mean that the task will trigger 30 seconds from now, but it must start before the EndBoundary time is reached.

You want to limit how long the task can run by using the ExecutionTimeLimit property. Limit the execution time to one minute:

```
PS (18) > $trigger.ExecutionTimeLimit = "PT1M"     # One minute
```

Set the trigger Id string to identify the trigger. Remember that there may be more than one trigger, in which case this field helps you to tell them apart:

```
PS (19) > $trigger.Id = "Trigger in 30 seconds"
```

Finally you enable the trigger:

```
PS (20) > $trigger.Enabled = $true
```

In order for the task to do anything when it triggers, you'll also need to define an action object for the task. Do so with the Actions.Create() method:

```
PS (21) > $action = $nt.Actions.Create(0)
```

As with the NewTask() call, the argument to this function is reserved for future use and currently must always be 0. Next you'll set up the action to take and any arguments to that action:

```
PS (22) > $action.Path = @(Get-Command powershell.exe)[0].Definition
PS (23) > $action.Arguments = @'
>>   foreach ($i in 1..10) { $i; sleep 1 }; sleep 1000
>> '@
>>
```

These commands specify the executable to run (PowerShell.exe) and the arguments to pass to it when the process is launched.

Now you come to the Folder object. This object is used to control where the task is stored. Task Scheduler definitions are organized in a hierarchy of folders like the file system. This allows you to organize related sets of tasks in their own folder. The following command retrieves an object that represents the root of the task folder hierarchy:

```
PS (24) > $tsFolder = $ts.GetFolder("\")
```

Once you have this object, you can use it to navigate the task tree and create new folders in that tree. But to keep the current example simple, just create the task in the root of the task definition tree.

18.6.4 Credentials and scheduled tasks

The final thing you need before you can register this task is to specify the credentials to use when running the task. These credentials are passed to the API used to register a task RegisterTaskDefinition(), which will store them for later use when the task is created. You'll use the Get-Credential cmdlet to get the user credentials in the PSCredential object:

```
PS (25) > $cred = Get-Credential

cmdlet Get-Credential at command pipeline position 1
Supply values for the following parameters:
Credential
```

At this point, you've run into a bit of a problem. The RegisterTaskDefinition() method doesn't understand PSCredential objects. It requires a name and a password, which means that you'll have to extract these fields from the credential object. Getting the user name is trivial: UserName is a string-valued property on the credential object. Getting the password, however, is less obvious. The Password field on the credential object is a SecureString (see section 21.5.4), which the task registration API also doesn't understand. It requires the password to be a simple clear-text string. Fortunately this scenario is covered and you can use the GetNetworkCredential() method on the PSCredential object to get the necessary clear-text password.

Finally, you can put all of the pieces together and register your task with the Task Scheduler. When you register the task, give it the name PowerShellTimeTrigger-Test to make it easy to find later. Here's the command to register the task:

```
PS (26) > $tsFolder.RegisterTaskDefinition(
>>    "PowerShellTimeTriggerTest", $nt, 6,
>>      $cred.UserName,
>>        $cred.GetNetworkCredential().Password, 3)
>>
Name                 : PowerShellTimeTriggerTest
Path                 : PowerShellTimeTriggerTest
State                : 3
Enabled              : True
LastRunTime          : 12/30/1899 12:00:00 AM
LastTaskResult       : 1
NumberOfMissedRuns   : 0
NextRunTime          : 8/19/2010 11:23:40 PM
Definition           : System.__ComObject
Xml                  : ...
```

This call returns a task registration object that includes all the task information you passed. Of particular interest is the Xml property. This property contains the task registration information registered as an XML document. The content of this document is shown in listing 18.8. In this listing, you can see elements corresponding to each of the object you created: RegistrationInfo, Triggers, Actions, and Principal. There's also a section for the Settings element that contains additional information about how the task is to be run.

Listing 18.8 The XML representation of the new task

```
<?xml version="1.0" encoding="UTF-16"?>
<Task version="1.2" xmlns=
    "http://schemas.microsoft.com/windows/2004/02/mit/task">
 <RegistrationInfo>
   <Author>Bruce Payette</Author>
   <Description>Count to 10</Description>
 </RegistrationInfo>
 <Triggers>
   <TimeTrigger id="Trigger in 30 seconds">
     <StartBoundary>2010-08-20T06:23:40Z</StartBoundary>
     <EndBoundary>2010-08-20T06:28:10Z</EndBoundary>
     <ExecutionTimeLimit>PT1M</ExecutionTimeLimit>
     <Enabled>true</Enabled>
   </TimeTrigger>
 </Triggers>
 <Settings>
   <IdleSettings>
     <Duration>PT10M</Duration>
     <WaitTimeout>PT1H</WaitTimeout>
     <StopOnIdleEnd>true</StopOnIdleEnd>
     <RestartOnIdle>false</RestartOnIdle>
   </IdleSettings>
   <MultipleInstancesPolicy>IgnoreNew</MultipleInstancesPolicy>
   <DisallowStartIfOnBatteries>true</DisallowStartIfOnBatteries>
   <StopIfGoingOnBatteries>true</StopIfGoingOnBatteries>
   <AllowHardTerminate>true</AllowHardTerminate>
   <StartWhenAvailable>false</StartWhenAvailable>
   <RunOnlyIfNetworkAvailable>false</RunOnlyIfNetworkAvailable>
   <AllowStartOnDemand>true</AllowStartOnDemand>
   <Enabled>true</Enabled>
   <Hidden>false</Hidden>
   <RunOnlyIfIdle>false</RunOnlyIfIdle>
   <WakeToRun>false</WakeToRun>
   <ExecutionTimeLimit>PT72H</ExecutionTimeLimit>
   <Priority>7</Priority>
 </Settings>
 <Actions Context="Author">
   <Exec>
     <Command>
       C:\Windows\System32\WindowsPowerShell\v1.0\powershell.exe
     </Command>
     <Arguments>
       foreach ($i in 1..10) { $i; sleep 1 }; sleep 1000
     </Arguments>
   </Exec>
 </Actions>
 <Principals>
   <Principal id="Author">
   <UserId>\brucepay</UserId>
   <LogonType>InteractiveToken</LogonType>
  </Principal>
 </Principals>
</Task>
```

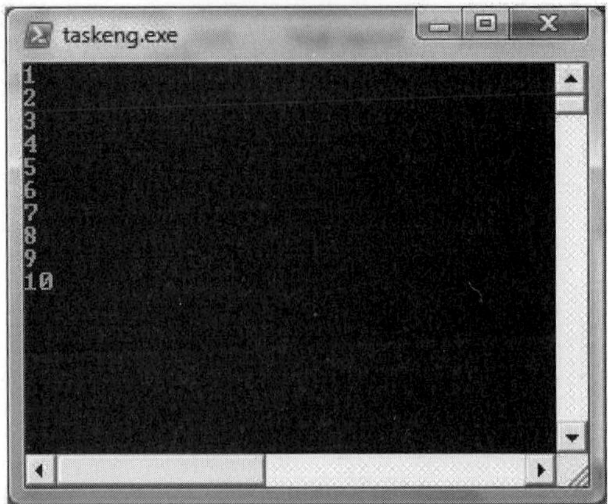

Figure 18.10 This is the window you'll see when the scheduled task you created is triggered and executes. The window shows the output of the PowerShell commands that were passed as arguments to the task executable.

Once this `RegisterTaskDefinition()` method has been run, your task is active and scheduled. So 30 seconds after calling the method, you'll see a window pop up on your desktop displaying the numbers from 1 to 10, as shown in figure 18.10.

This window will continue to be displayed until the task duration timeout occurs, at which point the Task Scheduler service terminates the triggered process.

18.6.5 Viewing the life cycle of a task

To see all of the events in the task life cycle, you can use the Task Scheduler tool to see the task's history. To start this tool, run `taskschd.msc` at the command line. Figure 18.11 shows the Task Scheduler window displaying the events in the task's History tab.

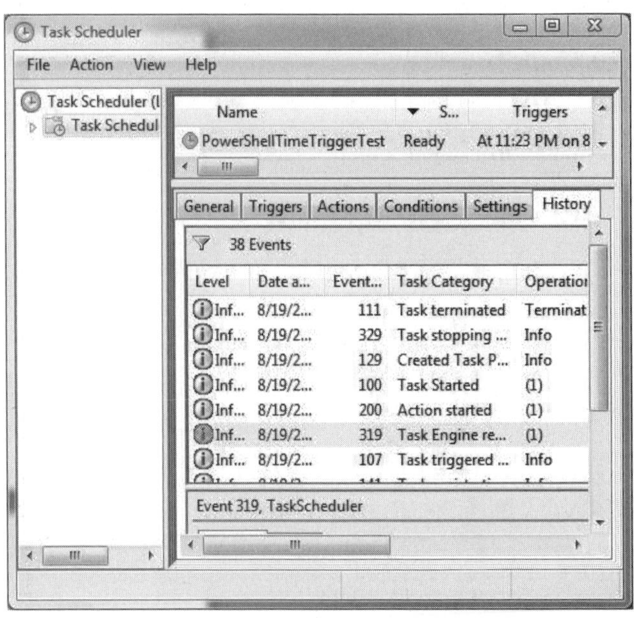

Figure 18.11 This figure shows the event history for the task you created using PowerShell. It shows the task triggering, starting execution and finally being terminated because it exceeded the maximum execution time for the task.

In this history, you see each step in the execution of the task: the trigger, starting the task action execution, launching the task process, and finally stopping and terminating the task.

Using COM in PowerShell lets you do amazing things—automating applications, mixing and matching languages, and so on. But there are also issues with COM support, which we'll cover in the next section.

18.7 ISSUES WITH COM

Support for COM in PowerShell is very good but not perfect. In part, this is due to the fact that PowerShell depends on .NET, and .NET's support for COM is also not perfect. In this section, we'll explore a few problems that you may run into when using COM from PowerShell, including more information on the `Interop` assembly issue mentioned in section 18.1.1.

18.7.1 64-bit vs. 32-bit issues

One problem that arises is that some COM objects are only available to 32-bit applications. On 64-bit systems, the 64-bit PowerShell binaries are run by default, so if you need to use a 32 bit–only COM object, you'll have to explicitly start the 32-bit version of PowerShell. This can also be an issue when using remoting because the default remoting configuration on 64-bit systems is 64 bit as well. To remotely run a script that requires a 32-bit COM object, you'll have to connect to the 32-bit configuration on the remote machine, regardless of whether the local system is 32 or 64 bit. (Section 12.6.6 in chapter 12 covers the details on how to target a specific remoting configuration.)

18.7.2 Threading model problems

By default `PowerShell.exe` runs in multithreaded apartment (MTA) mode. A significant number of COM objects require the caller to be in single-threaded apartment (STA) mode. Most of the time this will be transparent to you because the PowerShell COM type adapter does a bunch of magic under the covers, and most of the time it works fine. Occasionally, though, you'll encounter something that doesn't work. The solution is to restart `PowerShell.exe` with the `-sta` switch and try it again. The `-sta` switch starts PowerShell in STA mode instead of the default MTA mode, and this is usually sufficient to get things working.

> **NOTE** Remember that, although the default mode for `PowerShell.exe` is MTA, the default (and only) mode for the PowerShell ISE is STA. This difference can occasionally cause the same script to behave differently in the two environments.

18.7.3 Interop assemblies, wrappers, and typelibs

As mentioned in 18.1.1, another thing that can potentially cause problems has to do with the way the COM object has been wrapped or adapted. There are three possible categories of COM object you may encounter: a COM object that has a .NET Interop library, a COM object that has a type library (commonly called a typelib) but no Interop assembly, and a COM object that has neither.

In the first category, you get a COM object that has been wrapped in a .NET interop wrapper. This wrapper may introduce changes in the object's interface or behavior that affects how you work with that object compared to the raw COM object. For this reason, the New-Object cmdlet's ComObject parameter set has an additional parameter, -Strict, that causes a nonterminating error to be written if an Interop assembly is loaded. Let's look at some examples. Start by creating an instance of the Word.Application object you used earlier:

```
PS (23) > $word = New-Object -Com word.application
```

Now try it again but with the -Strict parameter:

```
PS (24) > $word = New-Object -Com word.application -Strict
New-Object : The object written to the pipeline is an instance of the type
             "Microsoft.Office.Interop.Word.ApplicationClass" from the
             component's primary interop assembly. If this type exposes
             different members than the IDispatch members, scripts written
             to work with this object might not work if the primary interop
             assembly is not installed.
At line:1 char:19
+ $word = New-Object  <<<< -Com word.application -Strict
```

You get a detailed error message explaining that the object that was loaded is a wrapped object. Note that this is a nonterminating error message, so the object is still returned and execution proceeds. Here's how to use this feature to write a script that can adapt its behavior appropriately.

First, you don't want the error message to appear in the output of your script, so redirect it to $null. But even when you do this, the $? variable, which indicates whether the last command executed was successful, is still set to $false so you know that an error occurred:

```
PS (26) > $word = New-Object -com Word.Application `
>>  -strict 2> $null
>>
PS (27) > $?
False
```

A script should check this variable and take an alternate action for the wrapped and nonwrapped cases. Investigating further, let's take a look at what was returned by the call to New-Object:

```
PS (28) > $word.gettype().fullname
Microsoft.Office.Interop.Word.ApplicationClass
```

The output shows that the object is an instance of the Interop assembly mentioned earlier.

Next, take a look at an object for which there's no Interop assembly and see how that behaves differently. Create an instance of the Shell.Application class you worked with earlier:

```
PS (43) > $shell = New-Object -ComObject Shell.Application
PS (44) > $shell | Get-Member

   TypeName: System.__ComObject#{efd84b2d-4bcf-4298-be25-eb
542a59fbda}

Name                 MemberType Definition
----                 ---------- ----------
AddToRecent          Method     void AddToRecent (Varian...
BrowseForFolder      Method     Folder BrowseForFolder (...
:
```

In this situation, you see that the type of the object is System.__ComObject followed by the GUID of the registered type library. This type library is what allows you to see the members on the object but doesn't affect the object's behavior.

18.8 SUMMARY

This chapter introduced Windows' native object model, the COM framework, and we showed you how to use it with PowerShell. COM objects and automation interfaces are the core mechanism used by older, unmanaged scripting languages such as VBScript and JScript. And, although the .NET Framework and managed code continues to grow in functionality, having direct access to these unmanaged scripting interfaces still offers substantial value.

In this chapter, we covered the following points:

- We introduced the basic elements of COM, how to identify a COM object using ProgIDs, and how to get a list of these ProgIDs.
- You saw that the Get-Member cmdlet is a powerful tool for learning about and examining COM objects.

This chapter included many examples of how to use COM:

- Writing scripts that manipulate browser and shell windows using the Shell.Application class
- Using the WScript.Shell object to pop up message boxes or send keystroke sequences to automate a Windows application
- Using the browser to look up a word in an online resource with the InternetExplorer.Application class
- Using COM automation to control applications like Microsoft Word to perform scripted tasks via the Word.Application class

- Using the `ScriptControl` to allow a PowerShell script to call functions written in VBScript or JScript
- Creating scheduled tasks for the Windows Task Scheduler using the `Scheduler.Service` class

We also covered some of the issues you might run into using COM from PowerShell such as STA versus MTA threading issues and 32-bit versus 64-bit controls.

You are now comfortable with .NET and COM objects, but these are general-purpose technologies. In the next chapter we'll look at an object framework and set of technologies (CIM, WMI, and WSMan) that are specifically targeted at management tasks. These technologies are based on industry standards with the goal of providing broad cross-platform support for datacenter management.

CHAPTER 19

Management objects: WMI and WS-MAN

A horse is a horse, of course, of course. And no one can talk to a horse, of course. That is, of course, unless the horse is the famous Mister Ed!

—Theme song from the *Mister Ed* television show

In the previous chapter, we explored the kinds of things you can do with COM, the Windows "native" object framework. Although COM and .NET can be used for many management tasks, management isn't their primary purpose. In this chapter we'll look at an object system that's specifically designed to address the needs of systems management: Windows Management Instrumentation (WMI). WMI is Microsoft's implementation of the industry-standard Common Information Model (CIM).

In this chapter, you'll learn what WMI is, how to access it from PowerShell, and what you can do with WMI once you have this access. You'll work through a number of examples to see how things work, exploring the sorts of tasks that can be accomplished. The second part of the chapter looks at Web Services for Management (WS-Man). WS-Man is another standard related to CIM. We introduced WS-Man in chapter 13 in the context of PowerShell remoting, but in this chapter, you'll see how to use it to access the CIM objects and why that matters.

19.1 WORKING WITH WMI IN POWERSHELL

WMI is Microsoft's implementation of the Common Information Model. CIM is an industry standard (a set of related standards) created by Microsoft, HP, IBM, and many other computer companies with the goal of defining a common set of management abstractions. By creating interoperable *common models* for managed elements like services, processes, or CPUs, we can start to build management tools and processes that can be applied universally.

In addition, as environments become increasingly more interconnected and devices like power supplies and air conditioners are networked right alongside desktop PCs, servers, and cell phones, the need for a common way to transmit management data becomes critical. This requirement is driving work on new management-oriented protocols like WS-Man that build on top of established, standard Internet protocols.

Collectively, these common models and protocols lay the groundwork for creating effective cross-platform management solutions for the modern, heterogeneous, distributed IT infrastructure.

> **NOTE** At one point in the early 2000s, it looked like there was a movement away from standard management technologies like WMI. People were going around saying things like "WMI is dead." In fact, this turns out not to be the case at all, and we're seeing increasing interest in CIM and related standards. WS-Man is a major factor in this because it provides a tractable, nonproprietary transport mechanism for the CIM APIs.

For example, the vPro technologies available in some Intel motherboards allow remote management of computer features, independent of the installed OS.

Now that you have an understanding of why standard management technologies like WMI and WS-Man are important, let's see how all this works.

19.1.1 Exploring WMI

If you're a Windows system administrator or Windows Server applications developer, WMI should already be familiar to you. If you're not a Windows administrator, chances are good (at least until recently) that you've never heard of it, which is too bad. WMI is one of the best not-so-secret technologies that the industry has to offer, both for users and for developers. But if it's so wonderful, why don't you hear more about it? Well, in part, because it has historically suffered from the "one-telephone" syndrome: there's no point in owning a telephone if there's no one to call. For example, prior to PowerShell, the only way you could use WMI was to write a program in

C++, write a script in VBScript, or use the WMI command-line tool (WMIC, a sort of limited precursor to PowerShell). Unfortunately, all of these solutions made even the simplest use of WMI fairly complex for a nonprogrammer. With the advent of things like PowerShell, WMI becomes a convenient command-line tool for everyday users, as you'll see.

Let's talk about what WMI actually is. To quickly refresh your acronym knowledge, WMI stands for Windows Management Instrumentation, which is Microsoft's implementation of the Distributed Management Task Force (DMTF) CIM. CIM is, in turn, an industry standard for an object model used to encapsulate the managed elements in a system. The DMTF website (www.dmtf.org) describes CIM in the following way:

> *CIM provides a common definition of management information for systems, networks, applications, and services, and allows for vendor extensions. CIM's common definitions enable vendors to exchange semantically rich management information between systems throughout the network.*

That's a very erudite if somewhat abstract definition. What it really means is that there are "standard" ways of wrapping up bits of management data in a well-defined standard package so you can work with this data across different vendors and environments in a consistent, standard way. For example, CIM defines a "class" called `CIM_Process` that abstracts out the details of what a process looks like on any given system. This means that, when encapsulated using this `CIM_Process` class or model, a process object on Windows, Solaris, Linux, or even a smartphone OS has the same basic set of properties and methods. Thus if you need to find out the ID of a process, `CIM_Process` defines a standard property `ProcessID` for accessing this information. Similarly, if you need to stop this process, you can call the `CIM_Process.Terminate()` method, and the underlying CIM implementation will map (or adapt) this call into the necessary system-specific API call.

To support environment-specific extensions, CIM also allows vendors to create derived classes of the CIM base classes that can surface nonstandard features as a set of extensions while still preserving the common base characteristics of the model. The goal of all of this is to make it easier to create system administration tools (and, by corollary, system administrators) that can work effectively in heterogeneous environments. In the next section, we'll look at how the CIM/WMI infrastructure facilitates these goals.

19.1.2 The WMI infrastructure

The core of WMI is a Windows service that hosts the components of the WMI infrastructure. These components include the WMI/CIM Object Manager, commonly called a CIMOM, a repository for CIM/WMI object instances, and a set of *providers* that provide the adaptation layer between concrete system resources the standard

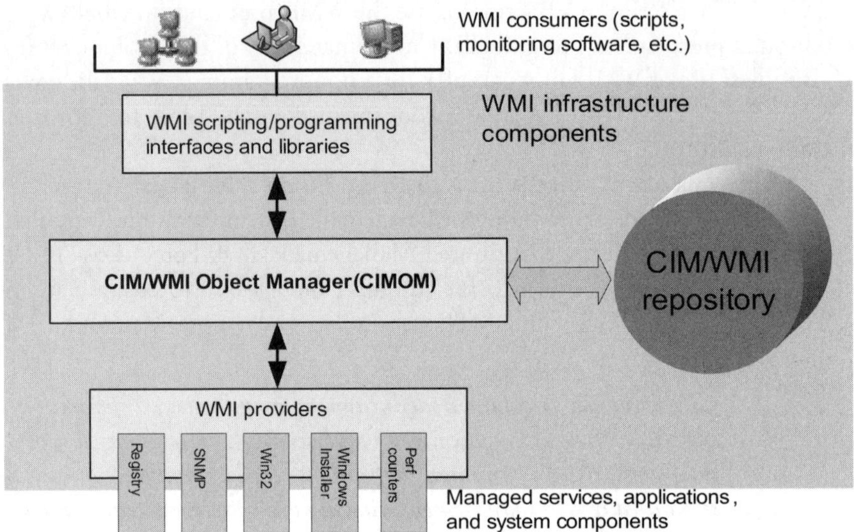

Figure 19.1 The WMI implementation architecture. WMI providers surface managed elements to the Object Manager. The WMI repository stores instances of active objects.

CIM classes use to manage those resources. Figure 19.1 shows how these components are organized.

The classes surfaced by the providers are logically arranged into a hierarchy of namespaces. Within each namespace are related (at least in theory) classes or types that represent (or *model*) management elements. In addition to classes, namespaces can contain nested namespaces.

> **NOTE** None of this should be new to anyone who's paid attention so far; we discussed at length how .NET does logical and physical type organization in section 17.1. CIM has the same basic arrangement of provider (physical) and namespace (logical) groupings.

Notice that there is no one-to-one mapping between namespaces and providers. More than one provider can surface types with a namespace. In fact, a lot of the Windows core providers expose (dump) all of their classes in the `root\cimv2` namespace, as you'll see later.

> **NOTE** The astute reader may be wondering how WMI providers might relate to the *namespace providers* that PowerShell uses for accessing stores such as the file system and the Registry. WMI providers and PowerShell providers are completely independent technologies (although conceptually they're both ways of accessing objects).

Table 19.1 includes a partial list of the WMI namespaces that are configured on Windows.

Table 19.1 Partial list of the standard WMI providers

Provider	Namespace	Description
Active Directory	`root\directory\ldap`	Provides access to Active Directory objects
Event log	`root\cimv2`	Provides classes to manage Windows event logs
Performance counter	`root\cimv2`	Provides access to raw performance data counters
Registry	`root\default`	Provides access to the Registry, for reading, writing, enumerating, monitoring, creating, and deleting Registry keys and values
SNMP	`root\snmp`	Provides access to SNMP MIB data and traps from SNMP-managed devices
WDM	`root\wmi`	Provides access to information about Windows device drivers
Win32	`root\cimv2`	Provides a broad array of classes for managing a computer, including information about the computer, disks, peripheral devices, networking components, operating system, printers, processes, and so on
Windows Installer	`root\cimv2`	Provides access to information about software installed on this computer

In the next section, we'll (finally) leave the theoretical discussions (mostly) behind and start talking about more practical applications of this technology when we introduce the PowerShell cmdlets for accessing and manipulating WMI objects.

19.2 THE WMI CMDLETS

PowerShell has four cmdlets for working with WMI. These cmdlets are shown in table 19.2. This table has the name and description as well as which versions of PowerShell each cmdlet is available in.

Table 19.2 The cmdlets for working with WMI

Cmdlet	Description	Availability
`Get-WmiObject`	Retrieves objects from WMI	v1 and v2
`Set-WmiInstance`	Sets the properties on a WMI class or object	v2
`Invoke-WmiMethod`	Invokes a method on a WMI class or instance	v2
`Remove-WmiObject`	Removes an object instance from the repository	v2

In the next few sections, we'll look at each of the WMI cmdlets in detail; but first, let's examine the (rather large) set of parameters that are common to all the cmdlets. Rather than repeating them for each cmdlet, we'll look at them all at once.

19.2.1 The WMI cmdlet common parameters

In this section, we'll describe the parameters that are common to all the WMI cmdlets. These common parameters are shown in figure 19.2

In this figure, you see many parameters that are related to communications, like `-ComputerName`, `-Authority`, and `-Authentication`. Because WMI is a *distributed object model*, these parameters are obviously important. On Windows, WMI uses the DCOM protocol as the basic transport layer for all of its communications.

> **NOTE** Whenever we talk about protocols, we find ourselves in Acronym Land (like Disneyland, but boring.) In this case, DCOM is Distributed COM, which is an extension of the Component Object Model you saw in chapter 18. DCOM extends COM so that an object's implementation doesn't have to be on the same server as the object's consumer. DCOM uses the MSRPC (Microsoft Remote Procedure Call) facility, and MSRPC is an extension of the DCE/RPC (Distributed Computing Environment/Remote Procedure Call) standard. Do you really need to care about this? To some extent, the answer is yes because communication issues will interfere with your ability to use WMI remotely. For example, this arrangement of protocols is why you sometimes see errors like "RPC server not available" coming from WMI.

Note that some of the parameters are similar to the parameters you saw on the remoting cmdlets in chapters 12 and 13: `-Credential`, `-ComputerName`, `-ThrottleLimit`, and `-AsJob`. Others have the same name but are slightly different because WMI uses DCOM and PowerShell remoting uses WS-Man as the transport layer. For

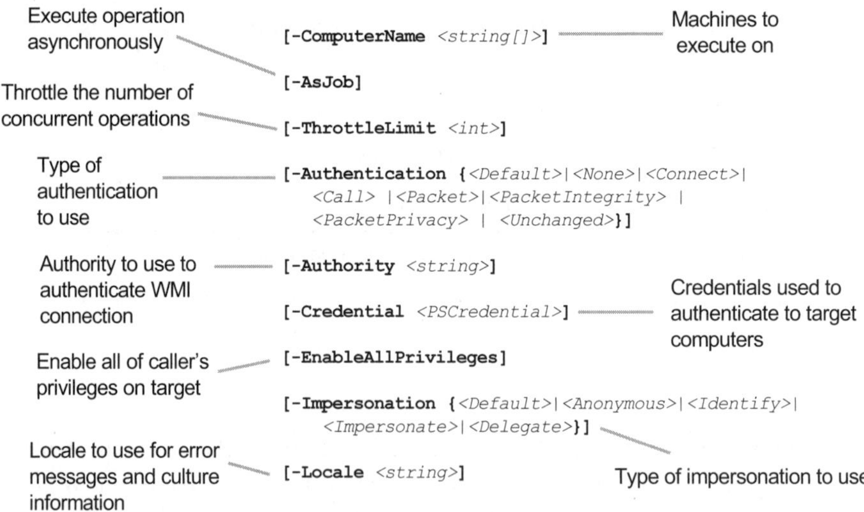

Figure 19.2 The common parameters available on all of the WMI cmdlets. These parameters primarily deal with remote connection issues but also include the `-AsJob` parameter.

instance, in both cases you have the `-Authentication` parameter but the meanings aren't the same because of the different protocol requirements.

Finally, there are a few parameters that are specific to the WMI rather than DCOM. The `-Locale` parameter allows you to tell the target computer what language to use when it returns error messages. The `-Impersonation` parameter allows you to control how your user token is created on the target computer.

> **NOTE** There's one significant architectural difference between PowerShell remoting and WMI that has to do with object methods and "live versus dead objects." In PowerShell remoting, the objects that are returned are always "dead" objects—essentially, snapshots of the state of the object when it was transmitted over the remoting channel. Because these objects are just copies, decoupled from the original object, changing them doesn't affect the remote system. WMI uses a very different approach. WMI objects are "live" and maintain state that's used for communicating changes back to the original object. In the WMI case, changing the local copy will affect the remote system. This is why WMI objects have methods but PowerShell remoting objects don't. There are pros and cons to maintaining the association between the local and remote in terms of performance and consistency, as you'll see.

Jobs and throttling

A major enhancement added to the WMI cmdlets in PowerShell v2 is the `-AsJob` and `-ThrottleLimit` parameters. The cmdlets can take a list of computer names to execute against, and this list can be very large. In PowerShell v1, there was no way for the user to control the number of concurrent connections and therefore the resources consumed when using `Get-WmiObject` against a lot of computers. Version 2 fixes this by adding `-ThrottleLimit`, which, as was the case for the PowerShell remoting cmdlets, limits the number of concurrent connections and uses a "sliding window," where as soon as one operation completes and that connection is closed, the next target is pulled from a queue and a new connection is initiated.

The second major enhancement was the addition of the `-AsJob` parameter. This conceptually works in the same way as `-AsJob` parameter on `Invoke-Command` or the `Start-Job` cmdlet, but the implementation is quite different. Whereas the `Start-Job` cmdlet created a new process for each job, the WMI jobs run in process but on another thread. This means that WMI jobs don't go through a serialization boundary like PowerShell jobs and consume far fewer resources than PowerShell jobs. But the abstractions are maintained and, although WMI jobs are started using the WMI cmdlets, these jobs are managed using the same `Get-Job`/`Receive-Job`/`Stop-Job` cmdlets that you saw in section 12.5.1.

And now (at last) we're ready to move on to the cmdlets themselves, starting with the most important one: `Get-WmiObject`.

19.2.2 The Get-WmiObject cmdlet

In this section, you'll see how to use the `Get-WmiObject` cmdlet to do two things: explore the WMI namespaces and classes available on a computer and retrieve instances of those classes from a computer.

As we observed earlier, the overall WMI architecture is rather like a database in that you connect to the WMI service on a particular computer, optionally providing additional connection information, and then retrieve the objects using a query. `Get-WmiObject` is the cmdlet you use to perform these queries. Its signature is shown in figure 19.3.

As always, the best way to see how something works is to use it in examples. To kick things off, here's a quick little PowerShell "script" that will return information about the BIOS on the local computer:

```
PS (1) > Get-WmiObject -Class Win32_BIOS
>>

SMBIOSBIOSVersion : 5.30
Manufacturer      : American Megatrends Inc.
Name              : BIOS Date: 09/05/08 10:24:25 Ver: 5.30
SerialNumber      : MXX84000D8
Version           : HPQOEM - 20080905
```

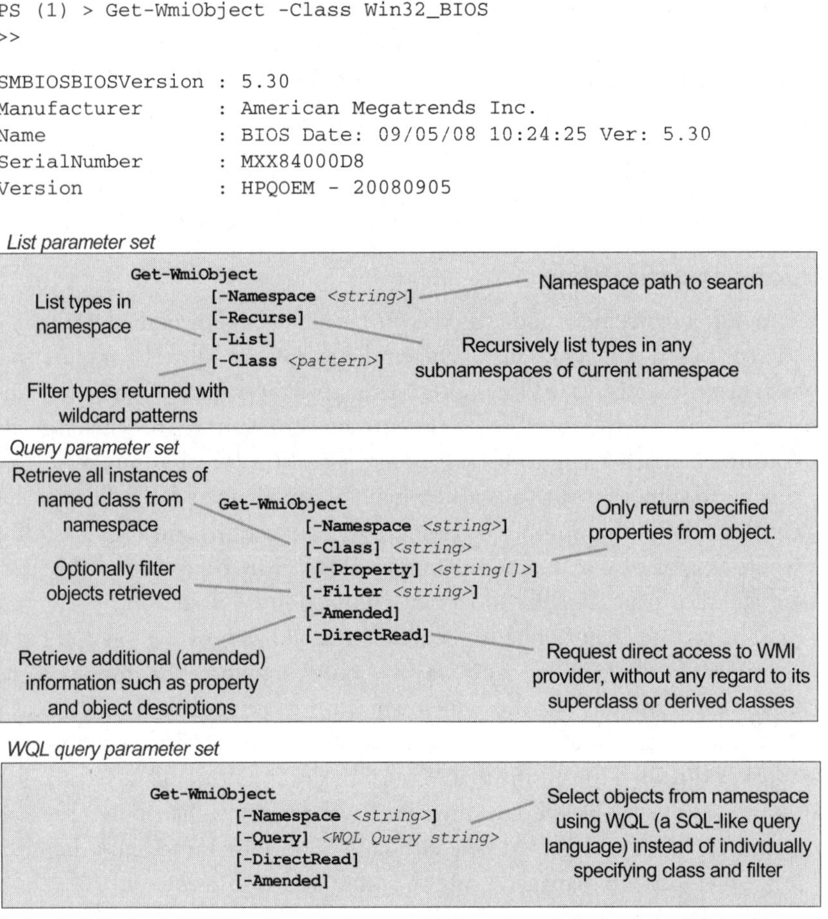

Figure 19.3 The signature for the `Get-WmiObject` cmdlet. This cmdlet has three parameter sets and allows you to explore WMI using the `-List` parameter and to retrieve objects from the repository with the `-Class` and `-Query` parameters.

To run this same command against a remote computer, you just have to add the -ComputerName parameter to the command. You get this:

```
PS (4) > Get-WmiObject -ComputerName brucepayx61 `
>>     -Class Win32_BIOS `
>>     -Credential redmond\brucepay
>>

SMBIOSBIOSVersion : 7SET33WW (1.19 )
Manufacturer      : LENOVO
Name              : Ver 1.00PARTTBL
SerialNumber      : LVB7KY3
Version           : LENOVO - 1190
```

In this second example, you also have to specify credentials to access the target machine because this was being done in a non-domain-joined environment. Now let's look at another, somewhat more complicated example. You need to get information about some of the network adapters on a computer. You want a list of all the adapters using DHCP to get their IP address and then print out the description and IP address for the machines as well as see when the DHCP lease will expire. Managing network adapters is exactly the kind of task that WMI was designed for, so as you expect, there's a WMI class that will give you this information: Win32_NetworkAdapterConfiguration. There's a property called DHCPEnabled on this class that you'll use to filter for the adapters with DHCP enabled. The IP address assigned to that adapter is available through another property, IPAddress. Finally, the description of the adapter is available through the Description property. (You'll see how you learn all this in the next section.)

```
PS (3) > Get-WmiObject Win32_NetworkAdapterConfiguration |
>>   where { $_.DHCPEnabled } |
>>     Format-List Description, IPAddress, DHCPLeaseExpires
>>

Description      : Realtek RTL8168C(P)/8111C(P) Family PCI-E GBE NIC
IPAddress        : {192.168.0.101, fe80::ec97:2ed7:3203:b22d}
DHCPLeaseExpires : 20100908002817.000000-420

Description      : 802.11n Wireless PCI Express Card LAN Adapter
IPAddress        : {192.168.0.105, fe80::c128:dbf3:3b1:76e0}
DHCPLeaseExpires : 20100908002819.000000-420
```

In this example, you used the Where-Object (where) cmdlet to filter the objects returned and then formatted the desired properties with Format-List. There's one small issue with this output, however: the times aren't exactly human readable. Fortunately, PowerShell adds a script method that can be used to fix this formatting problem. You can have a *calculated property* (see section 11.3) in the list of properties that will convert this value into a more readable DateTime object. The revised command looks like this:

```
PS (4) > Get-WmiObject Win32_NetworkAdapterConfiguration |
>>   where { $_.DHCPEnabled } |
```

```
>>     Format-List Description, IPAddress,
>>      @{
>>        name = "DHCPLeaseExpires"
>>        expression = {$_.ConvertToDateTime($_.DHCPLeaseExpires)}}
>>

Description      : Realtek RTL8168C(P)/8111C(P) Family PCI-E GBE NIC
IPAddress        : {192.168.0.101, fe80::ec97:2ed7:3203:b22d}
DHCPLeaseExpires : 9/8/2010 12:28:17 AM

Description      : 802.11n Wireless PCI Express Card LAN Adapter
IPAddress        : {192.168.0.105, fe80::c128:dbf3:3b1:76e0}
DHCPLeaseExpires : 9/8/2010 12:28:19 AM
```

The hashtable defining the calculated property in this example sets the name to be the same as the original property but sets the expression to generate the value (`expression` in the hashtable) to use this method to convert the value. The net result is that you get the information you need with a single line of script.

Even though we've only looked at a couple of examples so far, it's clear that WMI is an extremely valuable source of management information—if only you knew how to find that information. This is exactly what we'll show you in the next section.

Using Get-WmiObject to find WMI classes

The key element you need to get information from WMI is the name of the class you want to access such as `Win32_BIOS` or `Win32_NetworkAdapterConfiguration`. Using the class name, `Get-WmiObject` sends a request to the remote CIMOM asking it to retrieve the object or objects identified by this class name. Then the CIMOM looks up the class name in its tables and retrieves the associated data if the class exists.

Because the CIMOM knows all about the classes that are defined, it'd make sense to be able to ask CIMOM to tell you what's there. In fact, this operation is explicitly covered by the CIM specification. CIM is *self-describing* technology, which means it provides ways for a client application to ask the object manager on the target system what's available. PowerShell leverages these mechanisms to provide you with the `-List` parameter on `Get-WmiObject`, which will return a list of the available classes. For example, to see all of the classes with `BIOS` in their name, use this:

```
PS (1) > Get-WmiObject -List *bios*

   NameSpace: ROOT\cimv2

Name                                Methods              Properties
----                                -------              ----------
CIM_VideoBIOSFeature                {}                   {Caption,...
CIM_BIOSFeature                     {}                   {Caption,...
Win32_SMBIOSMemory                  {SetPowerState, R... {Access, ...
CIM_BIOSElement                     {}                   {BuildNum...
Win32_BIOS                          {}                   {BiosChar...
CIM_VideoBIOSElement                {}                   {BuildNum...
```

```
Win32_SystemBIOS                    {}                  {GroupCom...
CIM_VideoBIOSFeatureVideoBIOSEle... {}                  {GroupCom...
CIM_BIOSFeatureBIOSElements         {}                  {GroupCom...
CIM_BIOSLoadedInNV                  {}                  {Antecede...
```

This output shows each of the available class names along with the methods and properties defined by those classes. As you saw with .NET, the amount of information returned from the commands is frequently enough for your purposes, but all of the standard classes that Microsoft includes with Windows are well documented on MSDN:

```
http://mng.bz/4X76
```

This documentation includes many examples showing how to use classes, which is terrific. (Not so terrific is that these examples are still mostly written in VBScript, although this is becoming less true over time.)

Going back to the output from the previous example, there's one piece of information that we need to elaborate on. In section 19.1.2, we mentioned that WMI classes are arranged in namespaces. In this output, you saw

```
NameSpace: ROOT\cimv2
```

indicating that the classes listed were located in this namespace. Because this is the default namespace, you haven't needed to use the `-Namespace` parameter yet. In the next section, we'll look at how you work with CIM namespaces from PowerShell.

Navigating CIM namespaces

Returning to the first example in this chapter, you ran the command

```
Get-WmiObject -Class Win32_Bios
```

to get your data. The more complete way to write this command is to explicitly specify the namespace containing the class as well as the class name. The revised command would look like this:

```
Get-WmiObject -Namespace root\cimv2 -Class Win32_Bios
```

All classes are identified by a path of the form:

```
\\<computer>\<namespace>\<namespace>:<class>
```

You can see this path for any object returned using `Get-WmiObject` by looking at the `__PATH` property on the object.

> **NOTE** The vast majority of WMI classes that you'll use on a regular basis live in the `root\cimv2` namespace, which is why you don't force the use of the `-Namespace` parameter. Because the `-Class` parameter is positional, many WMI commands can simply be written as `Get-WmiObject Win32_Bios`.

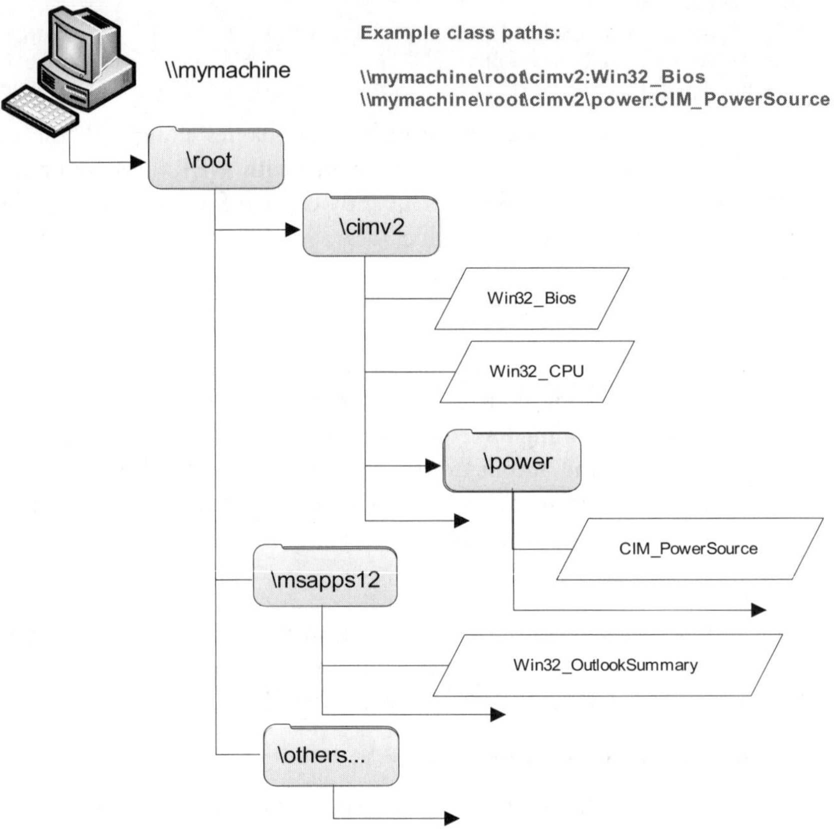

Figure 19.4 A portion of the WMI/CIM namespace hierarchy. The full path to a class begins with the name through the root namespace and eventually to a specific class.

Figure 19.4 shows the basic structure of a portion of the WMI/CIM namespace.

In figure 19.4, you can see that namespaces contain both classes as well as nested namespaces. The `-List` option on `Get-WmiObject` provides you with a list of classes, but it doesn't list the nested namespaces. So how do you discover the nested namespaces? As it turns out, there's a special class called `__NAMESPACE` that you can query to get the list of namespaces in a namespace (remember that CIM is self-describing). To get a list of the namespaces under `root\cimv2`, you use the following command:

```
PS (2) > Get-WmiObject -Namespace root\cimv2 -Class __NAMESPACE |
>> Format-List name
>>

name : Security
name : SMS
name : ms_409
name : Applications
```

To find out what's contained in the nested namespaces, you'd have to run a similar command against each one, repeating this pattern for each level of nesting. Doing this kind of manual navigation of namespaces is annoying if you're trying to search for a class name and aren't sure what namespace it's in. To simplify things, `Get-WmiObject` also includes a `-Recurse` parameter that will cause `-List` to recursively search all of the nested namespaces. Let's try it in another example. The following command will search the WMI repository starting at the root, looking for all classes with the string "power" in them:

```
PS (3) > Get-WmiObject -Namespace root -Recurse -List `
>>  -Class *power* | Format-Table __PATH
>>
__PATH
------
\\BRUCEPAYQUAD\ROOT\CIMV2:Win32_PowerManagementEvent
\\BRUCEPAYQUAD\ROOT\CIMV2:CIM_PowerSupply
\\BRUCEPAYQUAD\ROOT\CIMV2:CIM_UninterruptiblePowerSupply
\\BRUCEPAYQUAD\ROOT\WMI:MSNdis_StatusDevicePowerOn
\\BRUCEPAYQUAD\ROOT\WMI:MSNdis_StatusDevicePowerOff
\\BRUCEPAYQUAD\ROOT\WMI:MSPower
\\BRUCEPAYQUAD\ROOT\WMI:MSPower_DeviceWakeEnable
\\BRUCEPAYQUAD\ROOT\WMI:MSPower_DeviceEnable
\\BRUCEPAYQUAD\ROOT\WMI:MSNdis_80211_TransmitPowerLevel
\\BRUCEPAYQUAD\ROOT\WMI:MSNdis_80211_PowerMode
\\BRUCEPAYQUAD\ROOT\WMI:SystemConfig_V1_Power
\\BRUCEPAYQUAD\ROOT\WMI:SystemConfig_Power
\\BRUCEPAYQUAD\ROOT\WMI:SystemConfig_V0_Power
\\BRUCEPAYQUAD\ROOT\MSAPPS12:Win32_PowerPoint12Tables
\\BRUCEPAYQUAD\ROOT\MSAPPS12:Win32_PowerPointSummary
\\BRUCEPAYQUAD\ROOT\MSAPPS12:Win32_PowerPointActivePresentation
\\BRUCEPAYQUAD\ROOT\MSAPPS12:Win32_PowerPoint12Table
:
:
```

This output displays the path for each class. Notice that the output includes classes from a number of different namespaces.

> **NOTE** The set of WMI classes available on a machine depends on what's installed on that machine (both applications and operating system). For example, in the output from the previous command, a number of Microsoft PowerPoint classes are listed. If the machine on which the command is being run doesn't have PowerPoint installed on it, you wouldn't see these classes. As a consequence, if you do try some of these examples, don't be surprised if you get results that are different from what's shown here.

At this point, you have a good idea how to get information out of WMI. You know how to get a list of the classes available on a remote computer and how to use those classes to get information. Something we haven't touched on yet is the type of information received for a specific class. The classes we've looked at so far returned only a small amount of data. There are, however, many classes that return potentially very large datasets. You could filter them using the `Select-Object` and `Where-Object` cmdlets as you've been doing all along, but remember, you may be executing the operation on a remote computer. For remote operations, retrieving a lot of data can have serious performance implications. To mitigate this, WMI has a built-in way to filter the data being returned at the source instead of at the receiver's end. This mechanism is available to the PowerShell user through the `-Filter` and `-Query` parameter sets. In the next section, you'll see how to use these parameters to manage the amount of data you have to deal with.

Selecting WMI object instances using filters and queries

The syntax for `Get-WmiObject` in figure 19.2 mentioned two parameters that we haven't talked about yet: `-Filter` and `-Query`. These parameters allow you to leverage the intrinsic filtering capabilities built into WMI, allowing you to control how much data is returned from the target.

As part of the overall CIM infrastructure, the environment includes a native query language called WQL (WMI Query Language). This is a SQL-like language (remember that database hint earlier?) that's used to select data from a WMI class or enumeration. The `-Filter` and `-Query` parameters both make use of this query language, although in slightly different ways. Let's look at the `-Filter` parameter first.

The -Filter parameter

The `-Filter` parameter takes a string as an argument that contains a *predicate expression* defined using a subset of the overall WQL language. By predicate expression, we mean an expression that has things like comparisons and logical operators (ANDs, ORs). Whether or not a value is returned from the collection is predicated on this expression returning `TRUE` (hence, predicate expression). The WQL operators that can be used in these expressions are shown in table 19.3.

Table 19.3 The WQL operators that can be used in the `-Filter` parameter

WQL operator	PowerShell operator	Operator description
`=`	`-eq`	Equal to.
`<`	`-lt`	Less than.
`>`	`-gt`	Greater than.
`<=`	`-le`	Less than or equal to.
`>=`	`-ge`	Greater than or equal to.
`!=` or `<>`	`-ne`	Not equal to.
AND	`-and`	"ANDs" two Boolean expressions and returns `TRUE` when both expressions are true, equivalent to `-and` in PowerShell.

Table 19.3 The WQL operators that can be used in the `-Filter` parameter *(continued)*

WQL operator	PowerShell operator	Operator description
`OR`	`-or`	"`ORs`" two Boolean expressions and returns `TRUE` if either expression is true, equivalent to `-or` in PowerShell. When more than one logical operator is used in a statement, the `OR` operators are evaluated after the `AND` operators.
`TRUE`	`$true`	Boolean operator that evaluates to –1.
`FALSE`	`$false`	Boolean operator that evaluates to 0.
`NULL`	`$null`	Indicates an object doesn't have an explicitly assigned value. `NULL` isn't equivalent to 0 or blank.
`ISA`	`-as`	Operator that applies a query to the subclasses of a specified class.
`IS`	`n/a`	Comparison operator used with `NOT` and `NULL`. The syntax for this statement is the following: `IS [NOT] NULL` (where `NOT` is optional).
`LIKE`	`-like`	Similar to the PowerShell-like operator that does wildcard matches except that the wildcard characters are different: `%` (any string), _ (any single character), `[ab=z]` (match character range, ^ (don't match range).
`NOT`	`not`	Comparison operator that use in a WQL `SELECT` query.
`__CLASS`	`n/a`	References the class of the object in a query.

Let's look at an example of filter expressions. You'll rework the `Win32_NetworkAdapterConfiguration` but this time use the `-Filter` parameter instead of the `Where-Object` cmdlet to do the filtering:

```
PS (1) > Get-WmiObject Win32_NetworkAdapterConfiguration `
>>   -Filter  'DHCPEnabled = TRUE' |
>>     Format-List Description, IPAddress
>>

Description : Realtek RTL8168C(P)/8111C(P) Family PCI-E GBE NIC
IPAddress   : {192.168.0.101, fe80::ec97:2ed7:3203:b22d}

Description : 802.11n Wireless PCI Express Card LAN Adapter
IPAddress   : {192.168.0.105, fe80::c128:dbf3:3b1:76e0}
```

In the next example, you'll use the `LIKE` operator to match against the `Description` string:

```
PS (2) > Get-WmiObject Win32_NetworkAdapterConfiguration `
>>   -Filter 'DHCPEnabled = TRUE AND Description LIKE "%wire%"' |
>>     Format-List Description, IPAddress
>>

Description : 802.11n Wireless PCI Express Card LAN Adapter
IPAddress   : {192.168.0.105, fe80::c128:dbf3:3b1:76e0}
```

Add the NOT operator to select the nonwireless adapters:

```
PS (3) > Get-WmiObject Win32_NetworkAdapterConfiguration `
>>    -Filter 'DHCPEnabled = TRUE AND NOT (Description LIKE "%wire%")' |
>>      Format-List Description, IPAddress
>>
Description : Realtek RTL8168C(P)/8111C(P) Family PCI-E GBE NIC
IPAddress   : {192.168.0.101, fe80::ec97:2ed7:3203:b22d}
```

At this point, compare the last LIKE WQL example to the PowerShell equivalent:

```
PS (4) > Get-WmiObject Win32_NetworkAdapterConfiguration |
>>  where {$_.DHCPEnabled -eq $true -and -not
>>    ($_.Description -like "*wire*")} |
>>      Format-List Description, IPAddress
>>

Description : Realtek RTL8168C(P)/8111C(P) Family PCI-E GBE NIC
IPAddress   : {192.168.0.101, fe80::ec97:2ed7:3203:b22d}
```

This last example showed you the corresponding PowerShell predicate. This predicate can be created from the WQL expression, working element by element to get the PowerShell predicate. The resulting PowerShell predicate expression is slightly longer than the WQL filter, but if you take advantage of some of the PowerShell features to shorten the expression, it turns into

```
PS (5) > Get-WmiObject Win32_NetworkAdapterConfiguration |
>>  where {$_.DHCPEnabled -and ($_.Description -notlike "*wire*")} |
>>      Format-List Description, IPAddress
>>

Description : Realtek RTL8168C(P)/8111C(P) Family PCI-E GBE NIC
IPAddress   : {192.168.0.101, fe80::ec97:2ed7:3203:b22d}}
```

Now for a direct comparison of the predicate expressions:

```
WQL:           DHCPEnabled = TRUE AND NOT (Description LIKE "%wire%")
PowerShell: $_.DHCPEnabled -and ($_.Description -notlike "*wire*")
```

This makes the correspondence very clear. Next, you'll see how -Query works and build on top of this.

Selecting WMI objects using -Query

The -Query parameter takes a complete WQL query instead of just the predicate expression. The basic syntax for the WQL SELECT statement is

```
SELECT <propertyList> FROM <class> WHERE <predicateExpression>
```

which is patterned after SQL's select operation. In this query, the predicate expression is what you were passing through the -Filter parameter. Using the predicate from the previous example, you can write the equivalent WQL query as follows:

```
SELECT Description,IPAddress
FROM Win32_NetworkAdapterConfiguration
WHERE DHCPEnabled = TRUE AND NOT (Description LIKE "%wire%")
```

Now execute this query with Get-WmiObject:

```
PS (5) > Get-WmiObject -ComputerName brucepaydev01 -Query @'
>>    SELECT Description,IPAddress
>>    FROM Win32_NetworkAdapterConfiguration
>>    WHERE DHCPEnabled = TRUE AND NOT (Description LIKE "%wire%")
>> '@
>>

__GENUS          : 2
__CLASS          : Win32_NetworkAdapterConfiguration
__SUPERCLASS     :
__DYNASTY        :
__RELPATH        :
__PROPERTY_COUNT : 2
__DERIVATION     : {}
__SERVER         :
__NAMESPACE      :
__PATH           :
Description      : Intel(R) 82566DM-2 Gigabit Network
                   Connection
IPAddress        : {157.59.86.40,
                   fe80::653f:2770:d4e:4ac8,
                   2001:4898:2b:3:8901:6b57:2cf8:5cb,
                   2001:4898:2b:3:653f:2770:d4e:4ac8}
```

This command sends the WQL query to the CIMOM on the remote server, where it's executed and the results returned. The resulting object contains the properties you requested along with all of the WMI metaproperties. The fact that the query is executed on the remote server is significant. Rather than transferring a large amount of data and then filtering it locally, by filtering on the target you can greatly reduce the amount of data that must be transmitted.

By now, you should be reasonably comfortable using Get-WmiObject to discover WMI classes and retrieve WMI objects, both locally and remotely. You know how to filter the set of objects returned using the -Filter and -Query parameters. These parameters allow you to efficiently retrieve a lot of information about the target system. This is great for monitoring but not much good for maintenance. To manage and maintain a system, you need a way to effect changes on the target system. In the next section, you'll see how to do so using the Set-WmiInstance cmdlet.

19.2.3 The Set-WmiInstance cmdlet

In this section you'll learn how to update the properties on a WMI object using the Set-WmiInstance cmdlet, shown in figure 19.5.

This cmdlet has the parameters common to all of the WMI cmdlets, such as the -Class and -Namespace parameters you saw on Get-WmiObject. The purpose of the remaining properties should be fairly easy to intuit. As you'd expect from a PowerShell cmdlet, the -InputObject parameter allows you to update objects coming from the input pipe. This technique allows the output of Get-WmiObject to be piped to Set-WmiInstance. The -Arguments parameter is a hashtable containing

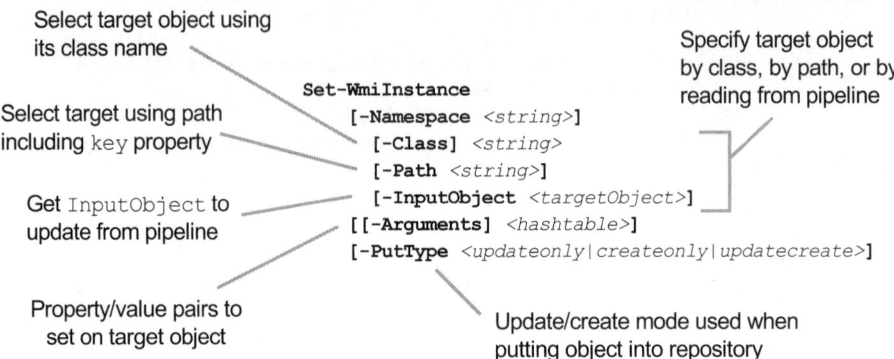

Figure 19.5 The `Set-WmiInstance` cmdlet allows the user to change the properties on an instance of a WMI class.

the names of the properties to update and the new values to use. The `-PutType` parameter allows you to specify that you only want to create a new object, only want to update an existing object, or want to create a new object if there isn't one and otherwise update the existing instance.

The `-Path` parameter is a bit more interesting. It allows you to identify not just the class but the actual object you want to update. Earlier in the chapter, we talked about how WMI classes are arranged in a hierarchy, like files and directories in the file system, and like files in the file system, classes in the WMI namespace hierarchy can be addressed through a path specification. The interesting thing about WMI paths is that you can also target *instances* of a class. In the next section you'll see how to do this.

Using WMI paths to target instances

When you retrieve objects from WMI, you expect to get one or more objects depending on the way you wrote your query. But for updating an object, you need to know exactly which instance to update. When you work with singleton objects, where there's only a single instance, the class name and namespace are enough to uniquely identify the target. But for collections (or *enumerations)* of objects, to do a set operation you have to identify a *specific instance* in the collection as the target.

CIM/WMI solves this problem in an interesting way: each object instance in the collection has a unique path. These paths look like

```
\\<computer>\<namespace>:<class>.<keyproperty>="<value>"
```

where *<keyproperty>* is a property that uniquely identifies the instance. In the database world, this would be called the *primary key*. WMI allows you to see the "instance path" for any object returned using `Get-WmiObject` through the `__PATH` property on that object. Let's try this with the `Win32_Service` class. The following command will give you the path for the Remote Desktop service instance:

```
PS (1) > Get-WmiObject -Class Win32_Service `
>>  -Filter 'Name = "TermService"' |
```

```
>>     foreach { $_.__PATH }
>>
\\BRUCEPAYX61\root\cimv2:Win32_TerminalService.Name="TermService"
```

The path string shown in the output from this command includes the computer name, namespace, and class. The portion of the path following the dot (.) is the *key property* for this object. For services, this is the `Name` property. For processes, it's the process ID (or `Handle`) property.

The key properties for an object are identified by *qualifiers* on those properties. To find the key properties for a class, you use the `Get-WmiObject` cmdlet to get the metadata for a class:

```
PS (1) > $class = Get-WmiObject -list Win32_Process
```

Then, from the metadata, you can look at the `Handle` property on the object:

```
PS (2) > $p = $class.Properties | where { $_.Name -eq "Handle" }
PS (3) > $p
Name        : Handle
Value       :
Type        : String
IsLocal     : False
IsArray     : False
Origin      : CIM_Process
Qualifiers : {CIMTYPE, key, MaxLen, read}
```

In this output, you see that the property has a `Qualifiers` attribute. This attribute is a dictionary of key-value pairs. Let's look at the `key` qualifier for this property:

```
PS (5) > $p.Qualifiers["key"] | Format-List Name,Value
Name                    : key
Value                   : True
```

From this, you can see that the key *properties* on an object have the `key` *qualifier* set to `TRUE`. This allows you to identify the key properties for a class by running the following command:

```
PS (6) > $class.Properties |
>>   where { $_.Qualifiers["key"]} |
>>     Format-Table -AutoSize name, type
>>

Name     Type
----     ----
Handle String
```

It's also possible for a class to require more than a single property to identify a specific instance. For example, the `Win32_Environment` class has two key properties, as shown in the following:

```
PS (7) > (Get-WmiObject -List Win32_Environment).Properties |
>>   where { $_.Qualifiers["key"]} |
>>     Format-Table -AutoSize name, type
>>
```

```
Name     Type
----     ----
Name     String
UserName String
```

In the next section, you'll see how to work with objects that have multiple key properties when you look at setting environment variables using the Win32_Environment class.

Setting the instance properties

In this section, you'll apply what you've learned about WMI paths to start setting object properties. For your experiments, you'll use the Win32_Environment class that allows you to get and set the values in the Registry used to initialize a process's environment table. These settings are stored in the Registry as properties of the key at the following path:

```
PS (1) > $path = 'HKLM:\System\CurrentControlSet\Control\Session
Manager\Environment'
```

Before we jump into the WMI examples, you'll use Set-ItemProperty to create a new environment variable property that you can experiment with safely:

```
PS (2) > Set-ItemProperty -Path $path `
>>   -Name 'TestProperty' -Value '3.14'
>>
```

Validate that the property was set by calling Get-ItemProperty to retrieve the value:

```
PS (3) > Get-ItemProperty -Path $path -Name TestProperty

PSPath       : Microsoft.PowerShell.Core\Registry::HKEY_LOCAL_MA
               CHINE\System\CurrentControlSet\Control\Session Ma
               nager\Environment
PSParentPath : Microsoft.PowerShell.Core\Registry::HKEY_LOCAL_MA
               CHINE\System\CurrentControlSet\Control\Session Ma
               nager
PSChildName  : Environment
PSDrive      : HKLM
PSProvider   : Microsoft.PowerShell.Core\Registry
TestProperty : 3.14
```

The output confirms that you've created the property with the name TestProperty and value 3.14. You're ready to begin your WMI experiments.

The first thing you're going to do is use the Win32_Environment WMI class to retrieve this property. You'll use a filter expression to restrict what's returned to the single property you're interested in:

```
PS (4) > Get-WmiObject -Class Win32_Environment `
>>   -Filter 'Name = "TestProperty"' |
>>     Format-List Name,VariableValue,__PATH
>>
```

```
Name          : TestProperty
VariableValue : 3.14
__PATH        : \\BRUCEPAYX61\root\cimv2:Win32_Environment.Name=
                "TestProperty",UserName="<SYSTEM>"
```

By doing this, you can discover the WMI path needed to access this object. Notice that, in this particular case, the path includes two key fields. Because each user can have his or her own instance of a variable `foo`, you need two keys: the variable name and the username, to uniquely identify an environment variable. In the previous output, you can see that you're targeting a systemwide environment variable.

Save this path in `$vPath` so you can use it later but with one small modification. Instead of having the actual computer name at the top level, use . instead. This indicates that the path applies to the current computer (i.e., localhost):

```
PS (5) > $vPath =
>> '\\.\root\cimv2:Win32_Environment.Name="TestProperty",UserName
="<SYSTEM>"'
>>
```

You can use this instance path to update the object. The following command will set the `VariableValue` property of the targeted environment variable to a new value:

```
PS (6) > Set-WmiInstance -Path $vPath `
>>   -Arguments @{VariableValue = "Hello"}
>>

VariableValue          Name                   UserName
-------------          ----                   --------
Hello                  TestProperty           <SYSTEM>
```

The output returned by the command shows the result of the operation. Just to be extra careful, also confirm that the operation succeeded by using `Get-WmiObject`, filtering by name:

```
PS (7) > Get-WmiObject -Class Win32_Environment `
>>   -Filter 'Name = "TestProperty"' |
>>     Format-List Name,VariableValue,__PATH
>>

Name          : TestProperty
VariableValue : Hello
__PATH        : \\BRUCEPAYX61\root\cimv2:Win32_Environment.Name=
                "TestProperty",UserName="<SYSTEM>"
```

And you see that the change was, indeed, made.

You can also use `Set-WmiInstance` to create a new environment variable by including the `Name` and `UserName` properties in the arguments hashtable. You'll try this initially by targeting the `TestProperty` variable you've been working with. Because you're attempting to create a new instance, you only need to specify the machine, namespace, and the class. To shorten the example command a bit, use the

-Class parameter and allow the target machine and namespace to default to localhost and cimv2, respectively. Give it a try:

```
PS (8) > Set-WmiInstance -Class win32_environment `
>>   -Arguments @{
>>     Name="TestProperty"
>>     VariableValue="Bye!"
>>     UserName="<SYSTEM>"
>>   }
>>
Set-WmiInstance : Object or property already exists
At line:1 char:16
+ Set-WmiInstance <<<<  -Class win32_environment `
    + CategoryInfo          : InvalidOperation: (:) [Set-WmiIns
   tance], ManagementException
    + FullyQualifiedErrorId : SetWMIManagementException,Microso
   ft.PowerShell.Commands.SetWmiInstance
```

This command failed because the target object already existed. Change the name of the instance to create to TestProperty2 and try it again:

```
PS (9) > Set-WmiInstance -Class win32_environment `
>>   -Arguments @{
>>     Name="TestProperty2"
>>     VariableValue="Bye!"
>>     UserName="<SYSTEM>"
>>   } | Format-List Name,VariableValue,__PATH
>>

Name          : TestProperty2
VariableValue : Bye!
__PATH        : \\BRUCEPAYX61\root\cimv2:Win32_Environment.Name=
                "TestProperty2",UserName="<SYSTEM>"
```

This time the command succeeded in creating the new object.

Because of the predictable nature of environment variable names, you can easily figure out what the WMI instance path for any environment variable will be. Given that you can specify the path for a variable even if it doesn't exist yet, you might think that you could use this path with Set-WmiInstance to create the target instance. Let's try it. The following would be the path to an environment variable named tp2:

```
PS (10) > $v2Path =
>> '\\.\root\cimv2:Win32_Environment.Name="tp2",UserName="<SYSTEM>"'
>>
```

Pass this path to Set-WmiInstance and see what happens:

```
PS (11) > Set-WmiInstance -Path $v2Path `
>>   -Arguments @{VariableValue = "Hello"}
>>
Set-WmiInstance : Invalid parameter
At line:1 char:16
+ Set-WmiInstance <<<<  -Path $v2Path `
    + CategoryInfo          : InvalidOperation: (:) [Set-WmiIns
   tance], ManagementException
```

```
+ FullyQualifiedErrorId : SetWMIManagementException,Microso
ft.PowerShell.Commands.SetWmiInstance
```

The command failed: clearly you can't use this mechanism to create instances even though you have all the information you need. In practice, this makes sense when you look at WMI as a whole. For most object types (such as processes), you aren't able to figure out what the instance path will be ahead of time. This means that the set of classes where it could work is quite limited.

With `Get-WmiObject` you've seen how to discover classes and retrieve instance. With `Set-WmiInstance`, you know how to update existing objects and create new instances. Our next topic is method invocation. Like .NET and COM objects, WMI objects have methods. You'll see how to invoke these methods in the next section.

19.2.4 The Invoke-WmiMethod cmdlet

In this section you'll learn how to invoke methods on WMI classes and instances by using the `Invoke-WmiMethod` cmdlet. In addition to the common WMI cmdlet parameters, the parameters specific to this command are shown in figure 19.6.

Like .NET classes (see section 5.5), WMI classes can have both static or *class members* and object or *instance members*. Static methods are the easier of the two types to call because you just need the class name, method name, and arguments to call. Instance methods are more complex because you need to specify additional information to identify which instance of the target class to invoke the method on. (This is the same issue you had when using `Set-WmiInstance`.)

Calling a static method

As our test case for static methods, let's use the static `Create()` method on the `Win32_Process` class to create an instance of (i.e., start) a process—in this case, `calc.exe`. The command to do this looks like this:

```
PS (1) > $result = Invoke-WmiMethod Win32_Process `
>>   -Name Create -ArgumentList calc
>>
```

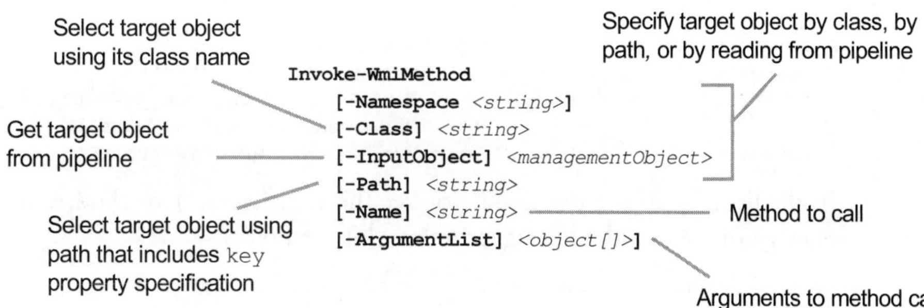

Figure 19.6 The `Invoke-WmiMethod` cmdlet allows the user to invoke a method on WMI objects.

Let's take a second and examine the type of object that was returned from this command:

```
PS (2) > $result.GetType().FullName
System.Management.ManagementBaseObject
```

This isn't an instance of the Win32_Process class. Instead, it's a ManagementBaseObject, which rather, like the PowerShell PSCustomObject, just serves as a base for other object types. It has two interesting properties that give you the result of the operation, ProcessID and ReturnValue:

```
PS (3) > $result | Format-Table ProcessId, ReturnValue

ProcessId           ReturnValue
---------           -----------
9376                0
```

If the method call was successful, then the ReturnValue will be 0, indicating this success, and the ProcessID will contain the process ID or handle of the new process. It's 0 here, so a new instance of the calculator applet should have appeared on the desktop. You can also use a WQL query to confirm this:

```
PS (4) > $proc = Get-WmiObject -Query @"
>> SELECT __PATH, Handle
>> FROM Win32_PROCESS
>> WHERE ProcessId = $($result.ProcessID)
>> "@
>>
```

The result of this query is a Win32_Process object instance representing the calc process, which you can confirm using Get-Member. In this case, you're going to limit the output from Get-Member to include only the methods on the object:

```
PS (6) > $proc | Get-Member -MemberType Method

   TypeName: System.Management.ManagementObject#root\cimv2\Win32
_Process

Name            MemberType Definition
----            ---------- ----------
AttachDebugger Method      System.Management.ManagementBaseObj...
GetOwner        Method     System.Management.ManagementBaseObj...
GetOwnerSid     Method     System.Management.ManagementBaseObj...
SetPriority     Method     System.Management.ManagementBaseObj...
Terminate       Method     System.Management.ManagementBaseObj...
```

In the list of methods displayed, you see the Terminate() method. On a wider display, you'd see that the full signature for this method is

```
System.Management.ManagementBaseObject Terminate(System.UInt32 Reason)
```

This is the method you need to terminate (i.e., stop) a running process. The method takes a single argument that encodes the reason for terminating this process. You're going to pass 0 for this value. Now let's look at the __PATH property on the object:

```
PS (7) > $proc | Format-List __PATH

__PATH : \\BRUCEPAYX61\root\cimv2:Win32_Process.Handle="9376"
```

This property allows you to target this specific object using Invoke-WmiMethod's -Path parameter. Let's run the command. You'll use the __PATH member on the object in $proc to identify the process object you're going to terminate, set the method name to be Terminate using -Name, and pass it the value 0 using -Argument:

```
PS (9) > Invoke-WmiMethod -Path $proc.__PATH `
>>   -Name Terminate -Argument 0
>>
Invoke-WmiMethod : Unable to cast object of type 'System.
Management.Automation.PSObject' to type 'System.IConvertible'.
At line:1 char:17
+ Invoke-WmiMethod <<<<  -Path $proc.__PATH `
    + CategoryInfo          : NotSpecified: (:)
    [Invoke-WmiMeth   od], InvalidCastException
    + FullyQualifiedErrorId : System.InvalidCastException,
    Micro   soft.PowerShell.Commands.InvokeWmiMethod
```

And it fails! What did you do wrong? As it turns out, absolutely nothing. What you wrote is correct, but there's a bug in the Set-WmiInstance cmdlet that's causing it to fail. You'll encounter this bug anytime a numeric literal is passed directly as an argument to the method.

The Invoke-WmiMethod bug details

For those who are interested, here are the nitty-gritty details behind this bug. When the PowerShell parser encounters a command-line argument that "looks" like a number, it compiles that token as a number, but just in case you really wanted a string, it then wraps this number in a PSObject and adds the original text of the string as a note on this PSObject. This is done because you're doing this at parse time and won't know the actual type of the argument until runtime when you look up the actual command. The reason you need to preserve the original token string is that there were a lot of people using arguments like 0001 for filenames. PowerShell was taking these tokens and turning them into numbers. The argument 0001 becomes 1 as a number. As a result, the file was named 1 instead of 0001.

To fix this, you can add a wrapper that retains the original string. So why does this cause Invoke-WmiMethod to fail? The reason is that the cmdlet is just taking its arguments and passing them directly through to the WMI client layer. Because this layer doesn't understand the PSObject type, it fails. By using an expression like (1) instead of a simple number 1, you can force the runtime to pass an unwrapped number.

To avoid this error and work around the bug, you need to use a literal *expression* instead of a simple numeric token as the argument. To do so, you just have to put parentheses around the number. Let's run the command updated to do this:

```
PS (10) > Invoke-WmiMethod -Path $proc.__PATH `
>>   -Name Terminate -Argument (0) |
>>      select -First 1 -Property '[a-z]*'
>>

ReturnValue      : 0
Properties       : {ReturnValue}
SystemProperties : {__GENUS, __CLASS, __SUPERCLASS, __DYNASTY...
                   }
Qualifiers       : {}
ClassPath        : __PARAMETERS
Site             :
Container        :
```

The return value is 0, indicating that the call was successful. At this point, the `calc` process will have vanished from the desktop. To confirm that the process has been terminated, call the `Get-Process` cmdlet:

```
PS (11) > Get-Process calc
Get-Process : Cannot find a process with the name "calc". Verify
 the process name and call the cmdlet again.
At line:1 char:12
+ Get-Process <<<<  calc
    + CategoryInfo          : ObjectNotFound: (calc:String)
   [Ge   t-Process], ProcessCommandException
    + FullyQualifiedErrorId : NoProcessFoundForGivenName,
    Micros    oft.PowerShell.Commands.GetProcessCommand
```

No process with the name `calc` was found, confirming that it has been terminated (assuming, of course, that there aren't other `calc` processes still running from earlier examples).

Now, let's look at the last of the WMI cmdlets, which will let you remove objects from the system or the CIM repository.

19.2.5 The Remove-WmiObject cmdlet

The final WMI cmdlet to cover is `Remove-WmiObject`, which is shown in figure 19.7.

By now, you should have a good handle on these parameters, so let's jump right into the example. You'll start another `calc` process, and then use a WQL query to get the path to this process instance:

```
PS (1) > calc
PS (2) > $proc = Get-WmiObject -Query @"
>> SELECT __PATH
>> FROM Win32_PROCESS
>> WHERE Name='calc.exe'
>> "@
>>
```

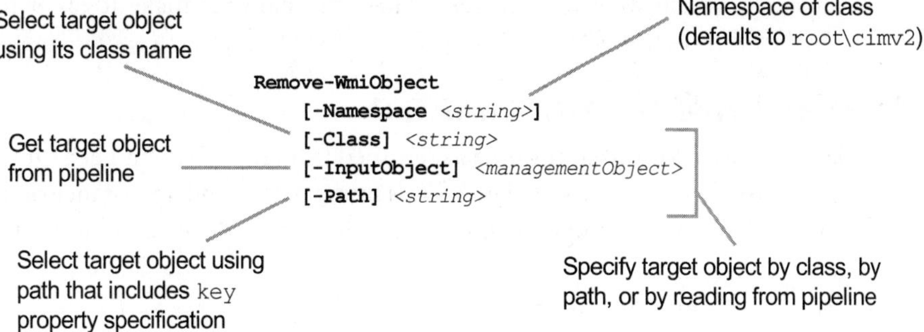

Figure 19.7 The `Remove-WmiObject` cmdlet allows you to remove objects from the system using WMI.

When you have the path, you can call `Remove-WmiObject`:

```
PS (3) > Remove-WmiObject -Path $proc.__PATH
PS (4) >
```

This code will cause the process to be terminated, just as if you'd called the `Terminate()` method. You can also use this cmdlet to remove the environment variable you created earlier. First, verify that it still exists:

```
PS (5) > Get-WmiObject -Class Win32_Environment `
>>   -Filter 'Name = "TestProperty"' |
>>     Format-List Name,VariableValue,__PATH
>>

Name          : TestProperty
VariableValue : Hello
__PATH        : \\BRUCEPAYX61\root\cimv2:Win32_Environment.Name=
                "TestProperty",UserName="<SYSTEM>"
```

To remove this variable, pipe the output of `Get-WmiObject` into the **`Remove-WmiObject`** cmdlet:

```
PS (6) > Get-WmiObject -Class Win32_Environment `
>>   -Filter 'Name = "TestProperty"' |
>>     Remove-WmiObject
>>
```

And finally, verify that it's been removed:

```
PS (7) > Get-WmiObject -Class Win32_Environment `
>>  -Filter 'Name = "TestProperty"' |
>>    Format-List Name,VariableValue,__PATH
>>
PS (8) >
```

Nothing is returned from the query, confirming that the variable has been removed.

This covers all of the cmdlets that PowerShell includes for working with WMI, but there's one more thing to cover: the WMI object adapter and the WMI type shortcuts, which we'll look at next. These mechanisms make it easier to work with WMI from PowerShell.

19.3 THE WMI OBJECT ADAPTER

Let's take a closer look at the objects returned from the WMI cmdlets. Once again, we'll look at the `Win32_Process` class for this investigation and an instance of the calculator applet. You start the program and then get the `Win32_Process` object for that process:

```
PS (1) > calc
PS (2) > $g=Get-WmiObject Win32_process `
>> -filter 'Name = "calc.exe"'
>>
```

Use `Get-Member` to examine the methods and properties on the object that was returned:

```
PS (3) > $g |gm -membertype "Method,Property"

TypeName: System.Management.ManagementObject#root\cimv2\Win32_Process

Name                      MemberType Definition
----                      ---------- ----------
AttachDebugger            Method     System.Management....
GetOwner                  Method     System.Management....
GetOwnerSid               Method     System.Management....
SetPriority               Method     System.Management....
Terminate                 Method     System.Management....
__CLASS                   Property   System.String __CL...
__DERIVATION              Property   System.String[] __...
__DYNASTY                 Property   System.String __DY...
__GENUS                   Property   System.Int32 __GEN...
__NAMESPACE               Property   System.String __NA...
__PATH                    Property   System.String __PA...
__PROPERTY_COUNT          Property   System.Int32 __PRO...
__RELPATH                 Property   System.String __RE...
```

What you see here are the *adapted* WMI methods for that process object, not the methods and properties on the .NET type `System.Management.ManagementObject`. To get at the method of the base .NET object, you need to use the `PSBase` property. From chapter 11 (section 11.6.2), you know that `PSBase` is the way to bypass the type adapter and get at the native capabilities of an object. Let's see what this gives you:

```
PS (7) > $g.PSBase | Get-Member -MemberType Method

   TypeName: System.Management.Automation.PSMemberSet

Name                      MemberType Definition
----                      ---------- ----------
add_Disposed              Method     System.Void add_Dis...
Clone                     Method     System.Object Clone()
CompareTo                 Method     System.Boolean Comp...
```

```
CopyTo                      Method      System.Management.M...
CreateObjRef                Method      System.Runtime.Remo...
Delete                      Method      System.Void Delete(...
Dispose                     Method      System.Void Dispose()
Equals                      Method      System.Boolean Equa...
Get                         Method      System.Void Get(), ...
get_ClassPath               Method      System.Management.M...
```

Notice the `Delete()` method that the base object exposes. This is what `Remove-WmiObject` calls in order to delete an object instance. Also notice in the earlier output that there was no `Delete()` method on the adapted object. This is because the Delete operation is supported by the infrastructure rather than a specific class. This illustrates why you may occasionally have to use the raw object—sometimes the adapted type hides something that you need.

Another feature that makes it easy to use WMI from PowerShell is the WMI shortcuts, which we'll explore in the next section.

19.3.1 The WMI type accelerators

PowerShell provides three type aliases or *accelerators* for working with WMI: `[WMI]`, `[WMICLASS]`, and `[WMISEARCHER]`. Let's look at each of these accelerated types.

The [WMISEARCHER] type accelerator

The `[WMISEARCHER]` alias is a type accelerator for

```
[System.Management.ManagementObjectSearcher]
```

This type accelerator allows the user to directly cast a string containing a WQL query into a *searcher* object. Once you have this searcher object, you just have to call its `GET()` method to retrieve the corresponding data:

```
PS (1) > $qs = 'Select * from Win32_Process ' +
>> 'where Handlecount > 1000'
>>
PS (2) > $s = [WmiSearcher] $qs
PS (3) > $s.Get() | sort handlecount |
>> fl handlecount,__path,name
>>

handlecount : 1124
__PATH      : \\BRUCEPAY64H\root\cimv2:Win32_Process.Handle
              ="3144"
name        : iexplore.exe

handlecount : 1341
__PATH      : \\BRUCEPAY64H\root\cimv2:Win32_Process.Handle
              ="3380"
name        : OUTLOOK.EXE

handlecount : 1487
__PATH      : \\BRUCEPAY64H\root\cimv2:Win32_Process.Handle
              ="2460"
name        : powershell.exe
```

```
handlecount : 1946
__PATH      : \\BRUCEPAY64H\root\cimv2:Win32_Process.Handle
              ="988"
name        : svchost.exe
```

The [WMI] type accelerator

The `[WMI]` alias is a type accelerator or shortcut for the type

```
[System.Management.ManagementObject]
```

which, as you know from our earlier experiments, is how .NET wraps a WMI object instance.

You can use this accelerator to cast a string containing a WMI instance path (see section 19.2) into the corresponding WMI object instance. You'll use this accelerator in an example where you use the calculator app again. Let's start the target process:

```
PS (1) > calc
```

Then, create a `WmiSearcher` instance, which you'll use to get the process object's WMI path:

```
PS (2) > $s = [WmiSearcher] `
>> 'Select * from Win32_Process where Name = "calc.exe"'
>>
```

You'll call `Get()` on the searcher instance to retrieve the object, but you're going to need a trick to get the actual object. This is because the output of the call to `Get()` is always a collection, even if the query matched only a single object. To complicate matters, this collection can't be indexed, like an array. Instead it's an *enumeration*, so to get at the objects in the collection, you need to enumerate that collection. Fortunately, PowerShell enumerates by default, making this process easy to do: just use the collection as input to a pipeline. To do so with no additional processing, you pipe into the `Write-Output` cmdlet and it will stream the enumeration.

> **NOTE** The approach just described is probably the only real practical use for `Write-Output`. It's the easiest way to transform an enumeration into a collection that can be indexed with no additional processing. Another pedagogical application for some people is to use the cmdlet to make explicit the fact that output is being done. They use the command `Write-Output $foo` instead of simply `$foo` to make the write operation explicit. This approach is largely a matter of personal preference.

Let's stream the enumeration to get our target object:

```
PS (3) > $proc = $s.Get() | Write-Output
```

When you have the object, you can get the path to the object using the `_PATH` property as you saw earlier:

```
PS (4) > $proc = [WMI] $so.__PATH
```

This code yields an instance of the process object. Now that you have this instance, you can examine the process's properties:

```
PS (4) > $proc.Name
calc.exe
PS (5) > $proc.HandleCount
49
```

You can update properties (which we won't show here) and you can call methods. For example, you can terminate the process by calling the `Terminate()` method:

```
PS (6) > $proc.Terminate()

__GENUS          : 2
__CLASS          : __PARAMETERS
__SUPERCLASS     :
__DYNASTY        : __PARAMETERS
__RELPATH        :
__PROPERTY_COUNT : 1
__DERIVATION     : {}
__SERVER         :
__NAMESPACE      :
__PATH           :
ReturnValue      : 0
```

This code performs the same operation as when you called the `Terminate()` method using `Invoke-WmiMethod`.

Whereas the `[WMI]` accelerator allows you to cast a path to an instance, the `[WMICLASS]` accelerator casts a path into a class, as you'll see next.

The [WMICLASS] type accelerator

The `[WMICLASS]` alias is a type accelerator for the

```
[System.Management.ManagementClass]
```

class. This accelerator can be used to cast a WMI class path into a WMI class object as follows:

```
PS (7) > $c = [WMICLASS]"Win32_Process"
```

When you use `Get-Member` to look at the methods on this class

```
PS (8) > $c | Get-Member -MemberType method | Format-List

TypeName   : System.Management.ManagementClass#ROOT\cimv2\Win32_
             Process
Name       : Create
MemberType : Method
Definition : System.Management.ManagementBaseObject Create(Syste
             m.String CommandLine, System.String CurrentDirector
             y, System.Management.ManagementObject#Win32_Process
             Startup ProcessStartupInformation)
```

you see that there's one method, `Create()`, for creating processes. Let's use it to start a Notepad process:

```
PS (9) > $c.Create("notepad.exe") |
>>   Format-Table ReturnValue, ProcessId
>>

                    ReturnValue                           ProcessId
                    -----------                           ---------
                              0                                8588
```

Verify the process creation with `Get-WmiObject`:

```
PS (10) > Get-WmiObject Win32_Process `
>>   -Filter 'Name = "notepad.exe"' |
>>     Format-Table Name, Handle
>>

Name                             Handle
----                             ------
notepad.exe                      8588
```

This mimics what you did with the `Create()` method and `Invoke-WmiMethod`.

There's still one more detail about the WMI object adapter that we need to cover in the last part of this section: writing data to the repository.

19.3.2 Putting modified WMI objects back

We need to cover one last, very important topic about using the WMI type accelerators. So far, we've looked at getting data, and we've looked at calling methods. Now, let's look at putting data back. In other words, how do you go about saving changes you've made to a WMI object back to the repository?

Why is this even a topic, you ask? After all, you don't have to do this with any of the other object types, right? The reason is that because the underlying store for a WMI object may be on a remote computer, incrementally flushing a set of changes over a remote connection is too inefficient to use on a large scale. As a consequence, the PowerShell WMI object adapter has a `Put()` method that must be called before property changes made to the local copy of an object are reflected back to the underlying store. Let's look at an example to see how this works. In this example, you're going to use WMI to change the volume name of the C: drive. First, get the WMI object for the logical C: drive:

```
PS (9) > $disks = Get-WmiObject Win32_LogicalDisk
```

On this system, the C: drive is the first logical disk:

```
PS (10) > $disks[0]

DeviceID     : C:
DriveType    : 3
ProviderName :
FreeSpace    : 95329701888
```

```
Size         : 241447768064
VolumeName   : C_Drive
```

It currently has the boring name of `C_Drive`. Let's give it a rather more dramatic name:

```
PS (11) > $disks[0].VolumeName = "PowerShellRocks"
```

Verify that the property in the object has been changed:

```
PS (12) > $disks[0]

DeviceID     : C:
DriveType    : 3
ProviderName :
FreeSpace    : 95329701888
Size         : 241447768064
VolumeName   : PowerShellRocks
```

And it has. But has this information been updated in the system yet? You can check on this by querying the repository again, thereby getting a new instance, independent of the one you modified:

```
PS (13) > (Get-WmiObject Win32_LogicalDisk)[0]

DeviceID     : C:
DriveType    : 3
ProviderName :
FreeSpace    : 95329603584
Size         : 241447768064
VolumeName   : C_Drive
```

As you can see, the underlying system object hasn't been updated. The change so far applies only to the object you modified. Now call the `Put()` method on the object to flush the changes back to the system:

```
PS (14) >  $result = $disks[0].Put()
```

Notice that you've saved the result of the `Put()` call. We'll get to that in a second. First, let's make sure that the system was properly updated:

```
PS (15) > (Get-WmiObject WIN32_LogicalDisk)[0]

DeviceID     : C:
DriveType    : 3
ProviderName :
FreeSpace    : 95329579008
Size         : 241447768064
VolumeName   : PowerShellRocks
```

This time you see that the system has been updated. Next, let's look at what you got back from the `Put()` call. Let's look at the type first:

```
PS (16) > $result.GetType().FullName
System.Management.ManagementPath
PS (17) > "$result"
\\localhost\root\cimv2:Win32_LogicalDisk.DeviceID="C:"
```

It's a [System.Management.ManagementPath] object, which you can then cast back into the corresponding drive instance object, per the earlier discussion of the WMI type accelerators:

```
PS (18) > $d = [wmi] "$result"
PS (19) > $d

DeviceID      : C:
DriveType     : 3
ProviderName  :
FreeSpace     : 95328575488
Size          : 241447768064
VolumeName    : PowerShellRocks
```

Now you have a new instance of the logical disk object.

This example illustrates the basic approach for using PowerShell to modify system settings through the WMI object adapter. First, you retrieve the object, then make the necessary updates, and finally use Put() to put it back. Because this is an unfortunate but necessary departure from the behavior of the other types of objects, it's important to be aware of it. It's also important to note that Set-WmiInstance doesn't suffer from this limitation. A set of properties is specified at once using the hashtable, so there's no need for a separate Put() operation.

This completes our coverage of using WMI from PowerShell. With this foundation, it should be possible for you to adapt existing WMI samples and resources in your work with PowerShell. That said, WMI is rich and deep and there's no way to cover all the details in a single chapter, so additional exploration is recommended to truly master the technology. You can find a great deal of information about WMI available online at http://technet.microsoft.com; it's a good place to start growing your knowledge.

In the next section, we'll investigate a related technology, WS-Man, that builds on what you know about CIM and WMI objects. WS-Man allows you to perform the same types of operations that you did through WMI using standard internet and web protocols instead of DCOM. The use of more broadly supported protocols greatly expands the reach of the CIM model.

19.4 EXPLORING WS-MAN

In chapter 13 we introduced WS-Man (Web Services for Management) in the context of PowerShell remoting, where it's used as a transport layer for PowerShell commands. What it also does (among other things) is provide an alternative transport layer for CIM/WMI. A major limiting factor for WMI as far as interoperability goes is that, whereas the object model is platform agnostic, the communications layer used to talk to the object manager is not because WMI uses the Microsoft-proprietary DCOM protocol.

NOTE In practice, there are a number of non-Microsoft implementations of DCOM. For example, the Open Group (the merger of X/Open and OSF) has an open source implementation of DCOM called COMSource. These implementations haven't seen significant uptake in the industry, though.

Obviously, a single-vendor protocol isn't very useful if the goal is to foster interoperability between different systems. To address this, in 2004 the DMTF released a new standard, "Document DSP0226: Web Services for Management (WS-Management) Specification," which was created through the joint efforts of AMD, Dell, Intel, Microsoft, and Sun Microsystems. (Since then, many additional companies, including Oracle, Symantec, BEA, and Hitachi, have joined this effort.) This protocol was based on widely adopted standards like web services and HTTP, giving it a much higher chance for success. Although it's still early in the adoption cycle, it does seem to be getting the necessary traction to succeed.

Staring with Windows Vista and Windows Server 2008, Microsoft began including an implementation of WS-Man with the operating system. In the Windows 7/Server 2008 R2 operating system releases, the implementation was substantially updated and support for WS-Man was added to PowerShell to allow access to CIM over WS-Man. In the next section, we'll examine the cmdlets that were added to enable this access.

NOTE Given the limitations of the WS-Man implementation as released with PowerShell v2, it should probably not be your default choice when trying to solve a problem. In almost all cases, WMI is still the better (i.e., faster and easier) choice. The key scenarios where you'd need WS-Man are either when the target doesn't support WMI (most non-Windows systems) or when network/firewall issues exist that you need to deal with. This is because WS-Man builds on top of HTTP, and it's more "firewall friendly" than WMI/DCOM.

19.4.1 The WS-Man cmdlets

The cmdlets included with PowerShell for managing a system through WS-Man are shown in table 19.4. Although the names of these cmdlets parallel the names of the WMI cmdlets quite closely, as shown in the table, there are some annoying differences in their behavior. These differences will be pointed out as we encounter them.

Table 19.4 The WS-Man cmdlets

WS-Man cmdlet	Description	WMI equivalent
`Get-WSManInstance`	Retrieves an instance of an object through the WS-Man service on the target machine.	`Get-WmiObject`
`Set-WSManInstance`	Creates an object using the specified WS-Man resource.	`Set-WmiInstance`

Table 19.4 **The WS-Man cmdlets *(continued)***

WS-Man cmdlet	Description	WMI equivalent
`Invoke-WSManAction`	Invokes a method on the object on the target machine.	`Invoke-WmiMethod`
`Remove-WSManInstance`	Removes an object using the specified WS-Man resource.	`Remove-WmiObject`
`New-WSManInstance`	Creates a new WS-Man resource. Note: Although the client side of the protocol is complete, the Windows 7 release of the WS-Man server component doesn't support instance creation except for managing some aspects of the WS-Man service itself. This cmdlet will, however, allow instances to be created in non-Windows WS-Man implementations if the operation is supported.	None

In the following sections we'll go over each of these cmdlets, introducing WS-Man concepts as we go as well as contrasting how these cmdlets work with the WMI cmdlets.

19.4.2 Using Get-WSManInstance to retrieve management data

The first cmdlet we'll work with is `Get-WSManInstance`. The signature for this cmdlet is shown in figure 19.8.

In figure 19.8, you see that there are a large number of parameters related to connections. These are basically the same parameters that you saw on the PowerShell remoting commands in section 13.1.5. This should be no surprise because remoting is built on top of WS-Man.

Let's look at using `Get-WSManInstance` to retrieve a WMI class. We'll do the parallel operation using the WMI cmdlets to highlight the similarities (and differences) between the two. We'll start with a WMI example and then see what the equivalent WS-Man cmdlet looks like. Our example query will be to retrieve information about the target machine's operating system using the `Win32_OperatingSystem` class. We'll limit the amount of information displayed by passing a list of properties to display to the `Format-List` cmdlet.

Start by putting these property names into a variable so you can reuse them later:

```
PS (1) > $properties = "Caption", "OSArchitecture","Version",
>>   "WindowsDirectory"
>>
```

Now, call the `Get-WmiObject` cmdlet and the specified properties as a list:

```
PS (2) > Get-WmiObject Win32_OperatingSystem |
>>       Format-List $properties
>>
Caption          : Microsoftr Windows VistaT Home Premium
OSArchitecture   : 64-bit
```

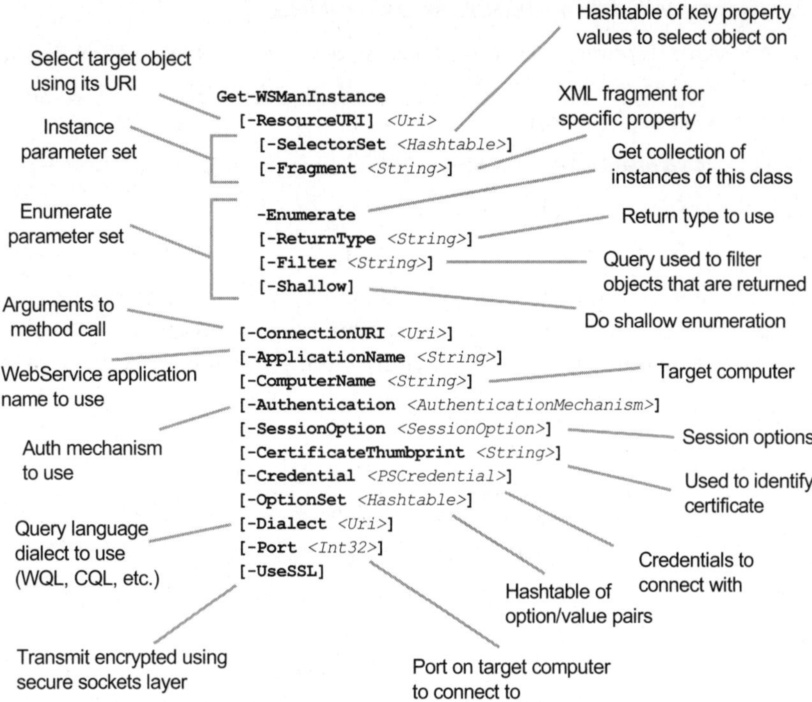

Figure 19.8 The `Get-WSManInstance` cmdlet is used to retrieve management object instances from the target computer. It can either retrieve a specific instance of a class or enumerate all instances of that class with optional filtering.

```
Version           : 6.0.6002
WindowsDirectory : C:\Windows
```

This output shows that the target computer is running Windows Vista 64-bit version 6.0.6002, installed in C:\Windows. In this command, you relied on positional parameters and the default namespace to shorten the command. Write it with the parameter names included and the namespace explicitly spelled out:

```
PS (3) > Get-WmiObject -Namespace root\cimv2 `
>>   -Class Win32_OperatingSystem |
>>     Format-List $properties
>>
Caption           : Microsoftr Windows VistaT Home Premium
OSArchitecture    : 64-bit
Version           : 6.0.6002
WindowsDirectory : C:\Windows
```

It's a bit longer to write, but the results are the same. In the next section, you'll convert the WMI command to a WS-Man command. The first change you need to make is that, instead of specifying the namespace and class name separately, you using a single resource URI that includes both parts.

Targeting WS-Man resources using URIs

In WS-Man, resources (classes) are accessed using a URI (Uniform Resource Identifier) that corresponds to the WMI path for the equivalent resource. If the path for a class in WMI is of the form

```
\\root\<namespace>\<class>
```

then the corresponding URI for a resource in WS-Man is

```
http://schemas.microsoft.com/wbem/wsman/1/wmi/root/<namespace>/<class>
```

As a concession to usability, the WS-Man cmdlets allow you to use URI aliases instead of returning the full resource URI every time. The supported WS-Man aliases and corresponding resource URIs they substitute for are shown in table 19.5.

Table 19.5 The WS-Man URI aliases

WS-Man alias	Resource URI
`Wmi`	http://schemas.microsoft.com/wbem/wsman/1/wmi
`wmicimv2`	http://schemas.microsoft.com/wbem/wsman/1/wmi/root/cimv2
`cmv2`	http://schemas.dmtf.org/wbem/wscim/1/cim-schema/2
`Winrm`	http://schemas.microsoft.com/wbem/wsman/1
`Wsman`	http://schemas.microsoft.com/wbem/wsman/1
`Shell`	http://schemas.microsoft.com/wbem/wsman/1/windows/shell

Another point to be aware of is that WS-Man URIs require that forward slashes be used. Using a backslash will result in an error. With an understanding of how to address a resource, let's return to our original task of retrieving the `Win32_OperatingSystem` resource.

Getting the Win32_OperatingSystem resource

The WMI path for the class you're targeting is \\root\cimv2\Win32_OperatingSystem, so the WS-Man URI you'll use is wmicimv2/Win32_OperatingSystem, which is equivalent to

```
http://schemas.microsoft.com/wbem/wsman/1/wmi/root/cimv2
```

Now you're ready to run the command, which produces the following results:

```
PS (4) > Get-WSManInstance `
>>   -ResourceURI wmicimv2/Win32_OperatingSystem |
>>     Format-List $properties
>>
Caption           : Microsoftr Windows VistaT Home Premium
OSArchitecture    : 64-bit
Version           : 6.0.6002
WindowsDirectory : C:\Windows
```

From the output, it appears the results are identical to what you got from the WMI command. When you dig in a bit further, you'll see that that isn't exactly true.

Let's see the object types returned by the cmdlets as well as the methods defined on those objects. Rerun the two commands, piping the output into `Get-Member`. First, the WMI command:

```
PS (5) > Get-WmiObject -Namespace root\cimv2 `
>>   -Class Win32_OperatingSystem |
>>     Get-Member -MemberType method
>>
   TypeName: System.Management.ManagementObject#root\cimv2\Win32_Oper
atingSystem

Name                  MemberType Definition
----                  ---------- ----------
Reboot                Method     System.Management.ManagementBaseOb...
SetDateTime           Method     System.Management.ManagementBaseOb...
Shutdown              Method     System.Management.ManagementBaseOb...
Win32Shutdown         Method     System.Management.ManagementBaseOb...
Win32ShutdownTracker Method     System.Management.ManagementBaseOb...
```

And then the WS-Man command:

```
PS (6) > Get-WSManInstance `
>>   -ResourceURI wmicimv2/Win32_OperatingSystem |
>>     Get-Member -MemberType method
>>

   TypeName: System.Xml.XmlElement#http://schemas.microsoft.com/wbem/
wsman/1/wmi/root/cimv2/Win32_OperatingSystem#Win32_OperatingSystem

Name                  MemberType Definition
----                  ---------- ----------
AppendChild           Method     System.Xml.XmlNode AppendChild(Sys...
Clone                 Method     System.Xml.XmlNode Clone()
CloneNode             Method     System.Xml.XmlNode CloneNode(bool ...
CreateNavigator       Method     System.Xml.XPath.XPathNavigator Cr...
Equals                Method     bool Equals(System.Object obj)
:
```

In the WMI case, you get back a "live" `ManagementObject`, which has methods that can be used to manipulate that object. In the WS-Man case, what you get back is a "dead" XML document that contains a representation of that data. This is conceptually similar to the way PowerShell remoting returns "dead" `PSObjects`; however, the actual XML representations are completely different. The first part of the returned XML (which is in the `OuterXML` property) looks like this:

```
<p:Win32_OperatingSystem xmlns:xsi = "http://www.w3.org/2001/XMLSchem
a-instance" xmlns:p = "http://schemas.microsoft.com/wbem/wsman/1/wmi/
root/cimv2/Win32_OperatingSystem" xmlns:cim = "http://schemas.dmtf.or
g/wbem/wscim/1/common" xsi:type = "p:Win32_OperatingSystem_Type" xml:
lang = "en-US" >
  <p:BootDevice>
    \Device\HarddiskVolume1
  </p:BootDevice>
```

```
  <p:BuildNumber>
    6002
  </p:BuildNumber>
  <p:BuildType>
    Multiprocessor Free
  </p:BuildType>
  <p:Caption>
    Microsoftr Windows VistaT Home Premium
  </p:Caption>
  <p:CodeSet>
    1252
  </p:CodeSet>
  <p:CountryCode>
    1
  </p:CountryCode>
:
```

Given that you only get back data, you'll have to use the `Invoke-WSManAction` to call methods on the object. We'll get to that in a minute. First, let's talk about getting enumeration compared to getting an instance.

Singleton resources vs. enumerations

For classes like `Win32_OperatingSystem` that are singletons (i.e., there's only ever a single instance), enumeration versus instance doesn't matter. There's only a single object to retrieve; hence, it's called a singleton. There are, however, many classes that have a collection of instances like `Win32_Process`. If you try to access this class the way you did `Win32_OperatingSystem`, you'll get an error:

```
PS (7) > Get-WSManInstance -ResourceURI wmicimv2/Win32_Process
Get-WSManInstance : <f:WSManFault xmlns:f="http://schemas.microsoft.com/
            wbem/wsman/1/wsmanfault" Code="2150859002"
            Machine="localhost"><f:Message><f:ProviderFault provider="WMI
            Provider"
            path="%systemroot%\system32\WsmWmiPl.dll"><f:WSManFault
            xmlns:f="http://schemas.microsoft.com/wbem/wsman/1/wsmanfault"
            Code="2150859002" Machine="brucepayquad"><f:Message>The WinRM
            client cannot process the request. The resource URI is not
            valid: it does not contain keys, but the class selected is not
            a singleton. To access an instance which is not a singleton,
            keys must be provided. Use the following command to get more
            information in how to construct a resource URI: "winrm help
            uris". </f:Message></f:WSManFault></f:ProviderFault></
            f:Message></f:WSManFault>
At line:1 char:18
+ Get-WSManInstance <<<<  -ResourceURI wmicimv2/Win32_Process
    + CategoryInfo          : InvalidOperation: (wmicimv2/
            Win32_Process:Uri) [Get-WSManInstance],
            InvalidOperationException
    + FullyQualifiedErrorId : WsManError,Microsoft.WSMan.Management.
   GetWSManInstanceCommand
```

This (rather long) error message is an XML document that has a number of significant pieces of information. Let's use the `Format-XmlDocument` function from section 16.4.3 to make it a bit more readable:

```
PS (8) > Format-XmlDocument -string ($error[0].Exception.Message)
<f:WSManFault xmlns:f = "http://schemas.microsoft.com/wbem/wsman/1/ws
manfault" Code = "2150859002" Machine = "localhost" >
  <f:Message>
    <f:ProviderFault provider = "WMI Provider" path = "%systemroot%\s
ystem32\WsmWmiPl.dll" >
      <f:WSManFault xmlns:f = "http://schemas.microsoft.com/wbem/wsma
n/1/wsmanfault" Code = "2150859002" Machine = "brucepayquad" >
        <f:Message>
          The WinRM client cannot process the request. The resource U
RI is not valid: it does not contain keys, but the class selected is
not a singleton. To access an instance which is not a singleton, keys
 must be provided. Use the following command to get more information
in how to construct a resource URI: "winrm help uris".
        </f:Message>
      </f:WSManFault>
    </f:ProviderFault>
  </f:Message>
</f:WSManFault>
```

First, it lets you know that the class isn't a singleton. It then mentions using *keys* to get a singleton instance. It also mentions using the command `winrm help uris` to get help on specifying URIs. It doesn't, however, mention using the `-Enumerate` parameter, but you'll cleverly intuit that this is what you need to do. Add that parameter to the command and try again, filtering the output for brevity's sake:

```
PS (8) > Get-WSManInstance -Enumerate `
>>   -ResourceURI wmicimv2/Win32_Process |
>>     select -First 5  |
>>       Format-Table -AutoSize ProcessID,ParentProcessId,Name
>>

ProcessId ParentProcessId Name
--------- --------------- ----
0         0               System Idle Process
4         0               System
496       4               smss.exe
572       560             csrss.exe
632       624             csrss.exe
```

Note that this more closely matches our experience with the WMI commands, which enumerate by default.

Filtering enumeration results

As was the case with collections in WMI, you can filter WS-Man enumerations with the `-Filter` parameter. This parameter allows you to specify a WQL predicate to subset the data that's returned. Let's add a filter to the command that retrieves `Win32_Process` instances. The command using WMI looks like this:

```
Get-WmiObject -Class Win32_Process -Filter "Name = 'powershell.exe'"
```

The corresponding command with `Get-WSmanInstance` is

```
PS (9) > Get-WSManInstance -Enumerate -ResourceURI wmicimv2/* -Filter @"
>>   select Name,Handle, ParentProcessId from win32_process
>>     where name = 'powershell.exe'
>> "@  | Format-Table -AutoSize Name, Handle, ParentProcessId
>>

Name           Handle ParentProcessId
----           ------ ---------------
powershell.exe 6452   2148
powershell.exe 7632   2148
powershell.exe 6768   2148
```

There are a number of differences between the two commands. First, `-Filter` on the `Get-WSManInstance` is more closely equivalent to the `-Query` parameter on `Get-WmiObject`:

```
PS (10) > Get-WmiObject -Query @"
>>   select Name,Handle, ParentProcessId from win32_process
>>     where name = 'powershell.exe'
>> "@ | Format-Table -AutoSize Name, Handle, ParentProcessId
>>

Name           Handle ParentProcessId
----           ------ ---------------
powershell.exe 6452              2148
powershell.exe 7632              2148
powershell.exe 6768              2148
```

But unlike the `Get-WmiObject` case, the `-ResourceURI` is mandatory. But just to make things difficult, you can't have the class name in the resource URI; it has to be * instead. Unfortunately, this means you can't just add a filter to an enumeration request. The resource URI also has to be changed. Now let's switch our focus back to getting singleton instances.

Selecting instances

To select a singleton instance from an enumeration, you use the `-SelectorSet` parameter to specify the key properties for the target instance. This parameter takes a hashtable containing the keys and values needed to identify the object you want to get.

> **NOTE** The properties in the selector set are equivalent to the key properties you saw in WMI object paths. There's one significant difference: in WMI paths, the case of the key property names doesn't matter, whereas the selector names in WS-Man are case sensitive.

In the case of processes, as you saw with `Invoke-WmiMethod`, this key is the `Handle` property. Let's try this. First, launch `calc.exe`, and then use a filter to get its process handle:

```
PS (1) > calc
PS (2) > $o = Get-WSManInstance -Enumerate `
>>   -ResourceURI wmicimv2/* -Filter @"
>>       select Name,Handle from win32_process
>>       where name = 'calc.exe'
>> "@
>>
PS (3) > $o | Format-Table -AutoSize Name, Handle

Name     Handle
----     ------
calc.exe 10640
```

Now you know that the handle you want is available in `$o.Handle`. Next, get the corresponding instance using the selector set:

```
PS (4) > $target = @{
>>   ResourceURI = "wmicimv2/Win32_Process";
>>   SelectorSet = @{ Handle = $o.Handle }
>> }
>>
PS (5) > Get-WSManInstance @target | Format-Table -AutoSize Name,
Handle

Name     Handle
----     ------
calc.exe 10640
```

This is a rather awkward way to target a specific object. You can make it easier by taking advantage of *splatting* (see section 5.8.4). You'll construct a hashtable of properties that will target the specific instance:

```
PS (4) > $target = @{
>>   ResourceURI = "wmicimv2/Win32_Process";
>>   SelectorSet = @{ Handle = $o.Handle }
>> }
>>
```

You can use this hashtable to target the instance you want:

```
PS (5) > Get-WSManInstance @target |
>> Format-Table -AutoSize Name, Handle

Name     Handle
----     ------
calc.exe 10640
```

With the ability to identify an instance, you can move on to the next section, where you'll see how to update an object's properties through WS-Man.

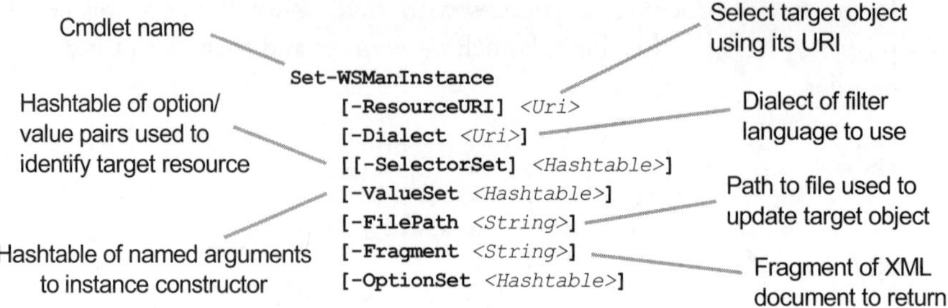

Figure 19.9 The `Get-WSManInstance` cmdlet is used to invoke a method on the target management resource or object. If the target object isn't a singleton, a set of selectors must be provided to identify the target resource.

19.4.3 Updating resources using Set-WSManInstance

Another consequence of the fact that `Get-WSManInstance` returns dead objects is that you can't simply update the object and call `Put()` as you did with the WMI type accelerators. The pattern for updating a resource using a WS-Man mirrors how you used `Set-WmiInstance` to update WMI objects in that you use the `Set-WSManInstance` cmdlet. The syntax for this cmdlet is shown in figure 19.9.

We'll recast the WMI example in section 19.3.3 where you used the `VolumeName` property on the `Win32_LogicalDisk` class to change the volume name of the C: drive. To do so, you need to be able to target the object by key property, which, for this class, is `DeviceID`. First, you'll list all of the hard drives on the target machine to see what their device IDs and current volume names are. You'll use `Get-WSManInstance -Enumerate`, filtering on the `DriveType` property (which you happen to know from earlier is `3`). Here's the command:

```
PS (1) > Get-WSManInstance `
>>   -Enumerate wmicimv2/* -Filter `
>>   "select * from Win32_LogicalDisk where DriveType = '3'" |
>>     Format-Table DeviceID, DriveType, VolumeName
>>

DeviceID                DriveType               VolumeName
--------                ---------               ----------
C:                      3                       c_drive
D:                      3                       FACTORY_IMAGE
L:                      3
M:                      3                       backup
```

You can see that, on this particular computer, four drives are available. The C: drive, not surprisingly, has C: as the drive ID and its current volume label is c_drive. To target this specific object, use `Get-WSManInstance` with the `-SelectorSet` parameter to pick that drive:

```
PS (2) > Get-WSManInstance wmicimv2/Win32_LogicalDisk `
>>   -SelectorSet @{ DeviceID = "C:" } |
>>     Format-Table DeviceID,  DriveType, VolumeName
```

```
>>
DeviceID                 DriveType                VolumeName
--------                 ---------                ----------
C:                       3                        c_drive
```

You can use the same selector set to target the call to `Set-WSManInstance`. You specify the new values for the properties in the hashtable passed to the `-ValueSet` parameter:

```
PS (3) > Set-WSManInstance wmicimv2/Win32_LogicalDisk `
>>   -SelectorSet @{ DeviceID = "C:" } `
>>   -ValueSet @{ VolumeName = "New Name" }|
>>     Format-Table DeviceID,  DriveType, VolumeName
>>

DeviceID                 DriveType                VolumeName
--------                 ---------                ----------
C:                       3                        New Name
```

The `Set-WSManInstance` cmdlet emits the updated object to the output stream, verifying that the property has been updated. You can also rerun the `Get` command to double-check that the update has occurred:

```
PS (4) >  Get-WSManInstance wmicimv2/Win32_LogicalDisk `
>>   -SelectorSet @{ DeviceID = "C:" } |
>>     Format-Table DeviceID,  DriveType, VolumeName
>>

DeviceID                 DriveType                VolumeName
--------                 ---------                ----------
C:                       3                        New Name
```

The `Get` and `Set-WSManInstance` cmdlets give you the ability to view and update objects using WS-Man. The last piece we need to consider is how to invoke methods.

19.4.4 Invoking methods with Invoke-WSManAction

In this section, you'll learn how to invoke WS-Man actions using the `Invoke-WSManAction` cmdlet. The signature for this cmdlet is shown in figure 19.10.

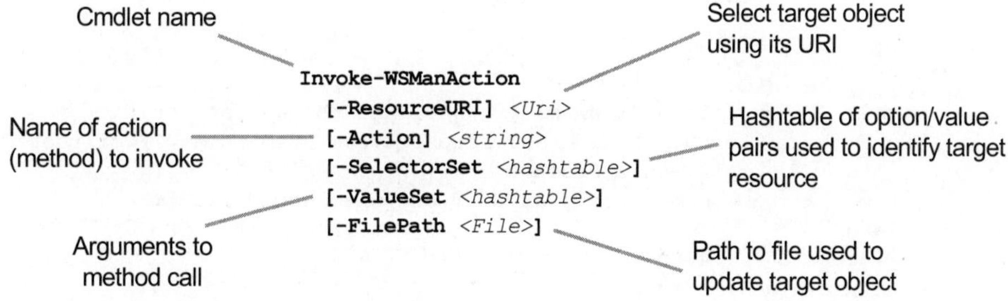

Figure 19.10 The `Invoke-WSManAction` cmdlet is used to invoke a method on the target management resource or object. If the target object isn't a singleton, a set of selectors must be provided to identify the target resource.

Let's use this cmdlet to terminate the calc process you started in the last section. At the time you created a hashtable that you splatted to retrieve the singleton process object. You can use that same table to target the resource you want to apply the action to. Let's try it out and terminate that calc process:

```
PS (6) > $result = Invoke-WSManAction @target terminate
```

Now, assuming that the instance of the process was still around, it should have been terminated. Let's look at the result that was returned. If the `Terminate()` method was successful, the return value should be 0:

```
PS (7) > $result.ReturnValue
0
```

And it is. But what about the larger result object? In keeping with the design of WS-Man, the object returned is an XML document. You'll use the document formatting function from section 16.4.3 to display the complete document returned from the action invocation:

```
PS (8) > Format-XmlDocument -string $result.OuterXml
<p:terminate_OUTPUT xmlns:xsi = "http://www.w3.org/2001/XMLSchema-instance"
            xmlns:p = "http://schemas.microsoft.com/wbem/wsman/1/wmi/root/
            cimv2/Win32_Process" xmlns:cim = "http://schemas.dmtf.org/
            wbem/wscim/1/common" xml:lang = "en-US" >
  <p:ReturnValue>
    0
  </p:ReturnValue>
</p:terminate_OUTPUT>
```

The resulting XML shows you that this is the output from invoking the `Terminate()` method on the `Win32_Process` class as defined by the referenced XML schema.

This covers instance methods, so let's move on to static or class methods. As an example, you'll use the static `Create()` method on the `Win32_Process` class to start a new calc process. Here's the command to do so:

```
PS (10) > Invoke-WSManAction -ResourceURI wmicimv2/win32_process `
>>    -Action Create -ValueSet @{
>>      CommandLine = 'calc'
>>      CurrentDirectory = 'c:\'
>>    }
>>

xsi         : http://www.w3.org/2001/XMLSchema-instance
p           : http://schemas.microsoft.com/wbem/wsman/1/wmi/root/cimv
              2/Win32_Process
cim         : http://schemas.dmtf.org/wbem/wscim/1/common
lang        : en-US
ProcessId   : 4780
ReturnValue : 0
```

As was the case in the previous example, the resource URI targets the class, and the `-Action` parameter names the method. But this time, you'll use the `-ValueSet` parameter to pass arguments to the method call. This hashtable defines named parameters for the target method.

From the invocation's resulting document, you can see that the `ReturnValue` field is 0, meaning that process creation was successful. But even though the process creation was successful, you won't see a calculator window displayed. That's because the WinRM service that handled the process creation request doesn't create the process in an interactive session. As was the case with PowerShell remoting, it's not possible to use WS-Man remoting to start an interactive GUI application. This doesn't mean that the applications fail to launch—you just can't see them on the desktop. What you can do is verify that the process was created by trying to retrieve the `Win32_Process` instance that corresponds to the `ProcessId` property in the result document. (The handle and process ID in this class have the same value.) You run the required `Get-WSManInstance` command:

```
PS (13) > Get-WSManInstance -ResourceURI wmicimv2/win32_process `
>>   -SelectorSet @{ Handle = 8524 } |
>>     Format-Table Name,Handle
>>

Name                                Handle
----                                ------
calc.exe                            8524
```

And you do, in fact, get your instance. Now, let's terminate that instance using the instance method:

```
PS (14) > Invoke-WSManAction wmicimv2/win32_process Terminate `
>>   -SelectorSet @{Handle = 8524 }
>>
xsi         : http://www.w3.org/2001/XMLSchema-instance
p           : http://schemas.microsoft.com/wbem/wsman/1/wmi/root/cimv
              2/Win32_Process
cim         : http://schemas.dmtf.org/wbem/wscim/1/common
lang        : en-US
ReturnValue : 0
```

Then, rerun the `Get-WSmanInstance` command to confirm that the process was terminated:

```
PS (16) > Get-WSManInstance -ResourceURI wmicimv2/win32_process `
>>   -SelectorSet @{ Handle = 8524 } |
>>     Format-Table Name,Handle
>>
Get-WSManInstance : <f:WSManFault xmlns:f="http://schemas.microsoft.com/
             wbem/wsman/1/wsmanfault" Code="2150858752"
             Machine="localhost"><f:Message>
<f:ProviderFault provider="WMI Provider"
             path="%systemroot%\system32\WsmWmiPl.dll"><f:WSManFault
             xmlns:f="http://schemas.microsoft.com/wbem/wsman/1/wsmanfault"
             Code="2150858752" Machine="brucepayquad"><f:Message>The WS-
             Management service cannot process the request. The service
```

```
            cannot find the resource identified by the resource URI and
            selectors. </f:Message></
            f:WSManFault><f:ExtendedError><p:__ExtendedStatus
            xmlns:xsi="http://www.w3.org/2001/XMLSchema-instance"
            xmlns:p="http://schemas.microsoft.com/wbem/wsman/1/wmi/root/
            cimv2/__ExtendedStatus" xmlns:cim="http://schemas.dmtf.org/
            wbem/wscim/1/common"
            xsi:type="p:__ExtendedStatus_Type"><p:Description
            xsi:nil="true" /><p:Operation>GetObject</
            p:Operation><p:ParameterInfo>Win32_Process.Handle="8524"</
            p:ParameterInfo><p:ProviderName>CIMWin32</
            p:ProviderName><p:StatusCode xsi:nil="true" /></
            p:__ExtendedStatus></f:ExtendedError></f:ProviderFault></
            f:Message></f:WSManFault>
At line:1 char:18
+ Get-WSManInstance <<<<  -ResourceURI wmicimv2/win32_process `
    + CategoryInfo          : InvalidOperation: (wmicimv2/win32_proc
   ess:Uri) [Get-WSManInstance], InvalidOperationException
    + FullyQualifiedErrorId : WsManError,Microsoft.WSMan.Management.
   GetWSManInstanceCommand
```

Again, you need to reformat the error message for it to be readable. Here's what the reformatted result XML looks like:

```
PS (17) > Format-XmlDocument -string ($error[0].Exception.Message)
<f:WSManFault xmlns:f = "http://schemas.microsoft.com/wbem/wsman/1/
             wsmanfault" Code = "2150858752" Machine = "localhost" >
  <f:Message>
    <f:ProviderFault provider = "WMI Provider" path =
      "%systemroot%\system32\WsmWmiPl.dll" >
       <f:WSManFault xmlns:f = "http://schemas.microsoft.com/wbem/wsman/1/
          wsmanfault" Code = "2150858752" Machine = "brucepayquad" >
        <f:Message>The WS-Management service cannot process the request.
           The service cannot find the resource identified by the resource
           URI and selectors.
        </f:Message>
       </f:WSManFault>
      <f:ExtendedError>
        <p:__ExtendedStatus xmlns:xsi = "http://www.w3.org/2001/XMLSchema-
             instance" xmlns:p = "http://schemas.microsoft.com/wbem/wsman
            /1/wmi/root/cimv2/__ExtendedStatus" xmlns:cim = "http://
           schemas.dmtf.org/wbem/wscim/1/common" xsi:type =
          "p:__ExtendedStatus_Type" >
        <p:Description xsi:nil = "true" />
          <p:Operation>
            GetObject
          </p:Operation>
          <p:ParameterInfo>
            Win32_Process.Handle="8524"
          </p:ParameterInfo>
          <p:ProviderName>
            CIMWin32
          </p:ProviderName>
          <p:StatusCode xsi:nil = "true" />
```

```
      </p:__ExtendedStatus>
    </f:ExtendedError>
  </f:ProviderFault>
</f:Message>
</f:WSManFault>
```

This output is still not great. But you can see that the operation you were trying to execute was `GetObject` and that the targeted object instance was `Win32_Process.Handle="8524"`.

19.5 SUMMARY

This chapter introduced the industry standard Common Information Model defined by the DTMF, Microsoft's implementation of this model (WMI), and how to use the model from PowerShell. We covered the following:

- We explored the basic concepts behind CIM and WMI, which are to provide a distributed, platform-agnostic mechanism for modeling management elements. CIM is distinct from other object systems like .NET and COM in that it was designed from the ground up to be a systems management framework instead of a general-purpose programming framework. CIM is a discoverable system, which means that it provides mechanisms that allow the user to find out what's available by querying the system itself.
- We covered the cmdlets that PowerShell provides for exploring and applying these models to perform management tasks: `Get-WmiObject`, `Set-WmiInstance`, `Invoke-WmiMethod`, and `Remove-WmiObject`.
- You learned how to use `Get-WmiObject` to leverage the discoverable nature of CIM. You saw how to list available classes with `-List` and explore namespaces using the `__NAMESPACE` class.
- Once you knew what you wanted to retrieve, we showed you how to use `Get-WmiObject` to get object instances on both local and remote computers.
- We explained how to use WQL queries with the `-Query` and `-Filter` parameters on `Get-WmiObject` to select specific instances to be returned from the target computer.
- We covered using `Set-WmiInstance` to update objects identified either from standard input or through a WMI path, including instance paths.
- You learned how to invoke both static and dynamic methods on WMI classes and objects with `Invoke-WmiMethod` and how to remove instances using `Remove-WmiInstance`.
- We covered the WMI object adapter and what it does as well as how to use the type accelerators `[WMI]`, `[WMICLASS]`, and `[WMISEARCHER]` to query and manipulate objects. This section also explained the requirement to use the `Put()` method to cause the updates to an object to be committed on the remote system.

The second section in this chapter built on what you've learned about the WMI object framework by introducing WS-Man, which provides a way to use standard internet protocols (e.g., web services and HTTP) to execute CIM operations. We introduced the corresponding WS-Man cmdlets and explored how they compare to their WMI equivalents. In the process, we discussed some of the advantages (standard protocols, cross-platform support) and some of the disadvantages (dead objects sent as XML documents).

At this point, we've covered three object models: .NET, COM, and CIM/WMI. All of these models have common traits: instances and classes, properties, and methods. But there's another common aspect to these objects that we've been avoiding up until now: *events* and *eventing*. Events are operations where the system calls you instead of the other way around. They require a rather different way of thinking about scripting—sufficiently so that events are covered in their own chapter. In chapter 20, we'll look at events in detail—how to use them, how to apply them, and some of the complexities that the eventing model has. Despite all these warnings, eventing is extremely powerful and should be in the toolkit of every advanced IT professional.

CHAPTER 20

Responding in real time with eventing

Exit, pursued by a bear

—Stage directions from *The Winter's Tale*,
by William Shakespeare

Over the last 19 chapters, we've covered an enormous amount of material. We've covered cmdlets, functions, scripts, and modules. We've looked at the major elements of the CLR and the .NET Framework, including assemblies, types, instances, and generics. We've also explored the COM and WMI object models and WSMan management web services. But there's still one area we haven't formally addressed: *eventing*. In chapter 17, we used one type of event, called a *synchronous event,* in our GUI programming. In this chapter, we'll spend more time working with synchronous events but the majority of the material will focus on *asynchronous events.* Asynchronous event handling allows scripts to respond to real-world events in a timely manner. Although this is a somewhat advanced topic, knowing how to use eventing can be a huge asset when you're managing a distributed datacenter environment. In this chapter, we'll explore the basic concepts of *event-driven* scripting, the PowerShell eventing model and infrastructure, and how to apply this feature.

20.1 FOUNDATIONS OF EVENT HANDLING

There are three major categories, or *sources*, of events supported by PowerShell: .NET object events, WMI events, and engine events (that is, events generated by PowerShell itself). But before we go into specific discussions on any of these topics, you need a common understanding of the concepts and terminology used in event-based programming.

In the .NET Framework (and therefore in PowerShell), events are a "first-class" concept just like methods and properties. By first class, we mean that they're tangible objects represented using classes. When you look at any class in the .NET Framework, you'll see that, along with methods and properties, each class also exposes some events. It's these event members that are the focus of our discussion of .NET eventing.

Now let's talk about what an event is and what makes event-based scripting different from traditional procedural scripting. The key difference with event-based scripting is that, instead of an activity being executed as a result of an action in the *script*, a script (or at least a portion of it) is executed as a result of an action by the *system*. This pattern is sometimes called inversion of control, but it can be expressed more colorfully as "Don't call me, I'll call you."

> **NOTE** This way of characterizing event-based programming captures the essence of the model perfectly. Crispin Cowan (Linux Security and now Windows Security Guru Extraordinaire) suggested this definition as we were hiking through the Cougar Mountains in Washington. Clearly, inspiration can arrive anywhere.

The traditional and event-driven flow control patterns are shown in figure 20.1.

Take a look at the traditional flow of control illustrated in the figure. In the traditional model, the flow of control always belongs to the mainline of the program. If an action is required, the mainline program directly invokes that action. In contrast, with the eventing pattern, rather than directly initiating actions, the mainline program registers the set of actions with an event source and then goes to sleep. It never initiates any actions on its own. Instead, the event source is responsible for initiating actions as required. In this scenario, you are, in effect, turning control over to the event service.

Sometimes this event service is a library routine that the mainline calls and allows this library to handle dispatching events to the callbacks. This model is frequently used in GUI programming. We'll cover this model in detail in section 20.2.

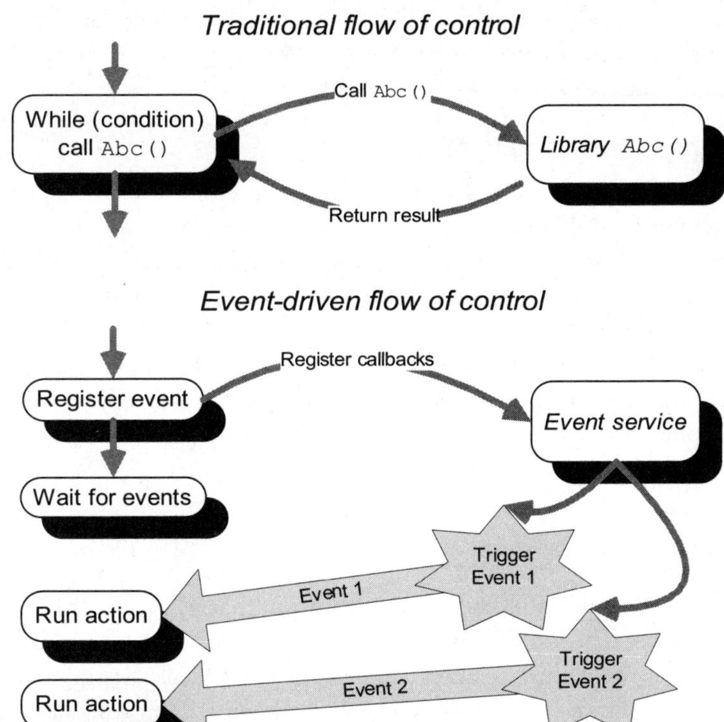

Figure 20.1 The normal flow of control in a script is compared to the flow in an event-based script. In the normal flow of control, the main thread of execution always retains control, calling library routines as needed. In event-based programming, the mainline registers a set of callback actions that will be executed when the specified event occurs. The event service then controls the flow of execution.

> **NOTE** In practice, we've been using this callback pattern all along, not just in GUIs. This is how the `ForEach-Object` and `Where-Object` cmdlets work: you pass action scriptblocks to the cmdlets and the cmdlets take care of calling your code when it's needed.

In other situations, the event service may be an active entity like another thread or process. In practice, real programs rarely restrict themselves to a single model but instead use different models at different times as appropriate. Starting in section 20.3, we'll explore these models in more detail and you'll see how to apply them in PowerShell. But before we get to that, let's examine synchronous event handling.

20.2 SYNCHRONOUS EVENTS

In this section, we're going to look at the synchronous eventing pattern in detail. The defining characteristic of synchronous eventing is that there's never more than one action occurring at any given time. All of the event-driven actions are *synchronized* and no action is ever interrupted. This is the event-handling pattern used in most GUI frameworks like Windows Forms (section 17.3.1) or Windows Presentation Foundation (section 17.3.3).

20.2.1 Synchronous eventing in GUIs

In synchronous GUI frameworks, you create a collection of GUI elements and then register actions with these elements so that when the user does something like click a button, your actions will be executed. Once you're done creating the GUI and registering the event actions, you hand control over to the framework, which will call the actions you defined when it needs to.

In PowerShell, for defining synchronous event handlers, you can usually just attach a scriptblock directly to the event member on the object. In fact, you've already applied this pattern many times as in the following, familiar example:

```
$button = New-Object Windows.Forms.Button
$button.text="Push Me!"
$button.Dock="fill"
$button.add_Click({$form.close()})
```

By now, you know that this code creates a button that will close its containing form when it's clicked. The last line of this example is where the event handler is attached, or "bound," to the control. The `Button` object has a Click event, which fires when the button is clicked. To add the Click event handler, you call the `add_Click()` method, passing in the scriptblock to execute. Because the `add_Click()` method requires an argument of type `System.EventHandler`, PowerShell automatically wraps the scriptblock with a generated subclass of `System.EventHandler`. This is a simple scenario and worked in PowerShell v1 because it was essentially hardcoded into the PowerShell runtime. The `System.EventHandler` class is an example of what is called a *delegate* in .NET terminology.

20.2.2 Delegates and delegation

In the GUI examples you saw in section 17.3, you set up control actions in the GUI by attaching event handlers to the controls in the UI. When you set up event handlers like this, you are, in effect, delegating the execution of that code to the UI and depending on it to call the code at the right time. Because this involves delegated actions, a logical name for these event handlers would be delegates—which is what they're called in .NET.

Earlier in this chapter (section 20.1) we said that events in .NET are a first-class concept. You've seen that events are represented as members on a class. The delegate values that you assign to event members are also first-class concepts and, like everything else in .NET, are represented by types that derive from a common base type. In this case, the common base type is `System.Delegate`. Depending on the argument type for the target event member, the required event handler argument will be a specific subclass of `Delegate`. In the PowerShell world, the role of the delegate is always played by scriptblocks. But because scriptblocks don't derive from `System.Delegate`, the PowerShell runtime has to synthesize `Delegate` *wrapper classes* for the scriptblock that match the argument type required by the event member. Let's see how this works in a non-GUI example.

> **NOTE** PowerShell v1 only supported the single subclass of delegate, `System.EventHandler`, due to time restrictions. This type was chosen because it's widely used in the framework, especially by the GUI frameworks. This meant that there were a lot of useful things you could do even though you only had the one type. In v2, the delegate wrapping support was generalized to cover all types of delegates so you no longer have to deal with the limitations of only one delegate type.

A non-GUI synchronous event example

Although the use of `System.EventHandler` is very common in .NET, there are additional synchronous delegate types in the .NET Framework that don't follow the `System.EventHandler` pattern. In PowerShell v1, working with these other delegate types required writing some complicated code that manually generated a scriptblock wrapper for the target type. This wasn't practical for most PowerShell users, so in PowerShell v2, Microsoft greatly improved the support for delegate types and the PowerShell runtime can automatically generate wrappers for any type of delegate.

> **NOTE** You can generate a wrapper for any event type, but you can't always automatically infer what type to generate in all scenarios. For those cases, the use of an explicit cast is required to disambiguate things. When you cast a scriptblock to the target type, the correct wrapper can be synthesized.

In this example, we'll look at how PowerShell's enhanced delegate handling works. You're going to use a scriptblock as the `MatchEvaluator` in a call to the static `Replace()` method on the [regex] class. The overload of `Replace()` you're interested in uses a delegate to do custom transformations during the replace operation. The signature for this method is

```
static string Replace(
string input,
string pattern,
System.Text.RegularExpressions.MatchEvaluator evaluator)
```

The first two arguments are the string to act on and the pattern to search for. The final argument is a delegate of type

```
[System.Text.RegularExpressions.MatchEvaluator]
```

Now, examine this type:

```
PS (1) > [System.Text.RegularExpressions.MatchEvaluator] |
>> Format-List Name,FullName,BaseType
>>

Name     : MatchEvaluator
FullName : System.Text.RegularExpressions.MatchEvaluator
BaseType : System.MulticastDelegate
```

You can see that it derives from `System.MulticastDelegate`. Because delegates are invoked using the `Invoke()` method, by looking at this method's signature you can see what parameters your scriptblock requires. Let's see what this method looks like for the `MatchEvaluator` delegate (note the leading space in the `' Invoke'` pattern, which reduces the set of matched members):

```
PS (2) > [System.Text.RegularExpressions.MatchEvaluator] |
>>   foreach {
>>     [string] ($_.GetMembers() -match ' Invoke')
>>   }
>>
System.String Invoke(System.Text.RegularExpressions.Match)
```

You see that the delegate takes a single parameter representing the matched text so the scriptblock will look like

```
{param($match) ... }
```

Note that in this scriptblock definition, we've omitted the type attribute for simplicity and in practice they aren't needed. The delegate signature guarantees that the scriptblock will never be called with the wrong argument types.

And now that you have the signature figured out, let's find out what this method actually does. Looking up the `MatchEvaluator` class on MSDN (Microsoft Developer's Network), you see the following:

> *You can use a* `MatchEvaluator` *delegate method to perform a custom verification or manipulation operation for each match found by a replacement method such as* `Regex.Replace(String, MatchEvaluator)`. *For each matched string, the* `Replace` *method calls the* `MatchEvaluator` *delegate method with a* `Match` *object that represents the match. The delegate method performs whatever processing you prefer and returns a string that the* `Replace` *method substitutes for the matched string.*

For our purposes, this means that whatever the scriptblock returns will replace the matched substring. Let's try this out. Write an expression that will replace all the characters in a string with their corresponding hex representation:

```
PS (4) > $inputString = "abcd"
PS (5) > [regex]::replace($inputString, ".",
>>     [System.Text.RegularExpressions.MatchEvaluator] {
>>         param($match)
```

```
>>            "{0:x4}" -f [int] [char]$match.value })
>>
0061006200630064
PS (6) >
```

Inside the scriptblock, you take each argument character and then use the format operator to turn it into a set of four hexadecimal digits.

By now, you should be comfortable with synchronous events. It's a pattern you've worked with at length over the course of this book. Asynchronous events, on the other hand, haven't been covered at all thus far. Asynchronous events introduce a number of considerations that make handling them more complicated. But because asynchronous events are a much more realistic way to model the world, the ability to handle them in PowerShell is important in scenarios such as responding to alerts. Beginning with the next section, you'll spend quite a bit of time mastering these event patterns and learning how to apply them to solve real problems.

20.3 ASYNCHRONOUS EVENTS

Asynchronous events are much trickier to deal with than their synchronous cousins. A synchronous event effectively runs on the same thread of execution as everything else. By analogy, this is like attending a formal lecture where the speaker conducts the main thread of conversation but periodically takes questions from the audience. By following this synchronous question-and-answer policy, at no point are there ever two actions (that is, two conversations) occurring at the same. This makes following the flow of conversation much easier. Everything happens deterministically, eliminating any collisions or consistency/coherency issues. Unfortunately that model doesn't match the way much of the real world works. Real-world events don't occur in a strict deterministic order—they happen when they happen, interrupting whatever else might be going on at that time. In the lecture analogy, this is like the audience spontaneously yelling out questions, interrupting the speaker and possibly confusing everyone. This type of concurrent operation makes life difficult for scripters because it means that things may possibly get changed out of order or in unanticipated ways, resulting in inconsistencies and errors.

In PowerShell v1, there was no support for the asynchronous pattern, which made it pretty much impossible to handle asynchronous events. In fact, out of concern over the possibility that things might happen out of order, PowerShell actively checks to see if you're trying to perform asynchronous actions and shuts down (that is, calls the `FailFast()` API, causing a crash) if it detects them.

> **NOTE** The rationale behind this behavior was, essentially, that it's better to be absolutely useless than to be possibly wrong. This is a somewhat extreme view and not everyone agrees with this line of reasoning. On the other hand, crashing and thereby halting an operation rather than, say, possibly launching a rocket at the wrong target does make a certain amount of sense. You can't un-launch a rocket, and saying "Sorry, my bad" after blowing up a city just doesn't cover it.

To allow for robust handling of asynchronous events, PowerShell v2 added an eventing subsystem that uses a centralized event manager to ensure that this occurs in a rational sequence. This subsystem takes care of all the bookkeeping and synchronization needed to ensure a stable and consistent system without a lot of work on the part of the script author. In the next section, we'll introduce the model PowerShell uses for doing this.

20.3.1 Subscriptions, registrations, and actions

The scripting model PowerShell uses for handling asynchronous events involves a few core concepts. The first concept is the idea of an *event subscription*, where you select the type of events you want to know about and then subscribe to be notified when they occur. These subscriptions are registered with a source identifier, which allows you to give a friendly name to each subscription. Once registered, the event subscription will be notified about relevant events as soon as they occur and will continue to receive notifications until the subscription is cancelled by explicitly unregistering it. Each event subscription may optionally specify an action to be taken. With these concepts in mind, we'll look at the eventing cmdlets in the next section.

20.3.2 The eventing cmdlets

The PowerShell eventing cmdlets are shown in table 20.1. These cmdlets allow you to register and unregister event subscriptions and list the existing subscriptions. You can also list pending *events* (as opposed to subscriptions) and handle or remove them as desired. There is also a cmdlet that allow scripts to generate their own events.

Table 20.1 The PowerShell eventing cmdlets

Cmdlet name	Description
`Register-ObjectEvent`	This cmdlet registers an event subscription for events generated by .NET objects.
`Register-WmiEvent`	Registers an event subscription for events generated by WMI objects (see chapter 18).
`Register-EngineEvent`	Registers an event subscription for events generated by PowerShell itself.
`Get-EventSubscriber`	Gets a list of the registered event subscriptions in the session.
`Unregister-Event`	Removes one or more of the registered event subscriptions.
`Wait-Event`	Waits for an event to occur. This cmdlet can wait for a specific event or any event. It also allows a timeout to be specified limiting how long it will wait for the event. The default is to wait forever.
`Get-Event`	Gets pending unhandled events from the event queue.
`Remove-Event`	Removes a pending event from the event queue.
`New-Event`	This cmdlet is called in a script to allow the script to add its own events to the event queue.

When handling events, you need to be able to register actions in response to these events. You do so using cmdlets, but because there are several types or sources of events, there are also several event registration cmdlets, as you saw in the table. The three event subscription registration cmdlets are `Register-EngineEvent`, `Register-ObjectEvent`, and `Register-WmiEvent`. PowerShell-specific events are handled using the `Register-EngineEvent` cmdlet, asynchronous events on .NET objects are handled using `Register-ObjectEvent`, and WMI events are addressed with `Register-WmiEvent`. (WMI events are covered in section 20.7 and engine events are covered in section 20.8.)

In the next section, we'll focus on .NET events—the so-called object events. In the process of doing this, we'll also cover most of the core eventing concepts that apply when working with any of the event sources.

20.4 WORKING WITH ASYNCHRONOUS .NET EVENTS

You use the `Register-ObjectEvent` cmdlet to create subscriptions for asynchronous events on .NET objects. The signature for this cmdlet is shown in figure 20.2.

Let's see how these parameters are used. First you need to identify the event you're interested in. For .NET events, this means that you need an object and the name of the event member on that object to bind. This is the same pattern you've already seen with Windows Forms and WPF, where, for example, a `Button` object has a `Click` event accessed through the `add_Click()` member.

Once you've decided on the event to handle, you need to specify what to do with the event. The `-Action` parameter on the cmdlet allows you to provide a scriptblock to execute when an event fires. This scriptblock will receive a lot of information about the event when it's run, but there may be some additional, custom data that you want to pass to the event handler. You can do this with the `-MessageData` parameter.

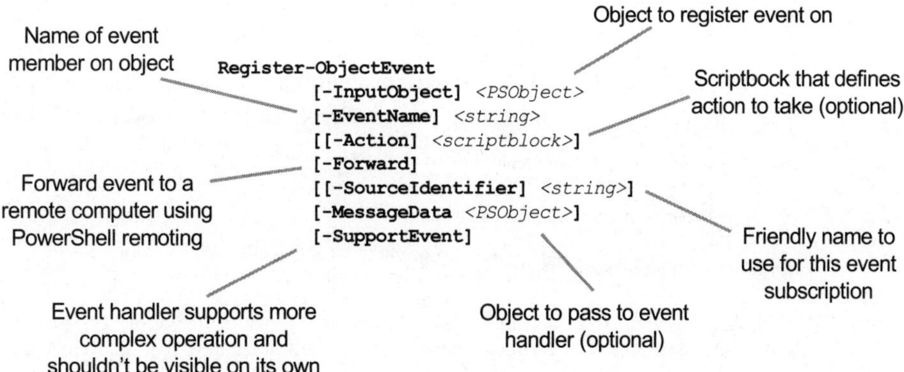

Figure 20.2 The signature of the `Register-ObjectEvent` cmdlet. This cmdlet is used to set up event handling for asynchronous events generated by .NET objects.

Finally, when you have a number of events that you're working with, the ability to attach a friendly name to the subscription will make things easier to manage. This is what `-SourceIdentifier` is for: it allows you to name the event registration or *event source*.

There's one last parameter that we haven't discussed yet: `-SupportEvent`. In larger event-driven scripts, there may be a number of event registrations that only exist to support higher-level constructs within the application. In these scenarios, it's useful to be able to hide these supporting events much like the rationale behind the way you hide supporting functions in modules. This event-handler hiding is accomplished using the `-SupportEvent` switch. As was the case with modules, if you do want to see the hidden events, you can specify the `-Force` switch on `Get-EventSubscriber`.

20.4.1 Writing a timer event handler

Okay, enough talk—let's start doing something with .NET events. One of the most obvious examples of an asynchronous event is a timer. A timer event fires at regular intervals regardless of what else is going on. Let's see how you can set up a subscription events generated by the .NET `System.Timers.Timer` class.

> **NOTE** These cmdlets can *only* be used for asynchronous .NET events. It's not possible to set up event handlers for synchronous events using the PowerShell eventing cmdlets. This is because synchronous events all execute on the same thread and the cmdlets expect (require) that the events will happen on another thread. Without the second thread, the PowerShell engine will simply block the main thread and nothing will ever get executed.

Creating the Timer object

The first thing you need for our example is a `Timer` object. You use `New-Object` to create it:

```
PS (1) > $timer = New-Object System.Timers.Timer
```

Because events are first-class and exist as members on a class, you can use `Get-Member`, filtering the results on the `Event` member type, to see what events this object exposes:

```
PS (2) > $timer | Get-Member -MemberType Event

   TypeName: System.Timers.Timer

Name     MemberType Definition
----     ---------- ----------
Disposed Event      System.EventHandler Disposed(System.Objec...
Elapsed  Event      System.Timers.ElapsedEventHandler Elapsed...
```

From this output, you can see that the `Elapsed` event is what you're looking for—it fires when the timer period has elapsed.

Setting the timer event parameters

But you need to know more about this object than just the events—you need to know how to set the timer interval, and start and stop the timer. Again you can use `Get-Member` to find this information. (Note that the output shown here has been trimmed to the interesting members for brevity's sake.)

```
PS (3) > $timer | Get-Member

   TypeName: System.Timers.Timer

Name                      MemberType Definition
----                      ---------- ----------
Disposed                  Event      System.EventHandler Disp...
Elapsed                   Event      System.Timers.ElapsedEve...
Close                     Method     System.Void Close()
Start                     Method     System.Void Start()
Stop                      Method     System.Void Stop()
ToString                  Method     string ToString()
AutoReset                 Property   System.Boolean AutoReset...
Enabled                   Property   System.Boolean Enabled {...
Interval                  Property   System.Double Interval {...
```

When you look at the output, the way to start and stop the timer is obvious. The `AutoReset` property determines if the timer only fires once (`AutoReset = $false`) or fires repeatedly every interval (`AutoReset = $true`). Finally, the `Interval` property controls the firing interval. Because the value is a double, you can guess that it's specified in milliseconds.

> **NOTE** Yes, you could've gone to the MSDN documentation. But, really, why bother? With `Get-Member` and a reasonably decent understanding of .NET, `Get-Member` is frequently all you need. This makes PowerShell a useful tool for developers as well as IT professionals. Even in Visual Studio, sometimes we'll still flip over to a PowerShell window to search for information about a type. Simple text and typing is still faster sometimes.

Binding the event action

lLet's register for an event on this object, which you do with the following command:

```
PS (4) > Register-ObjectEvent -InputObject $timer `
>> -EventName Elapsed -Action { Write-Host "<TIMER>" }

Id              Name            State       HasMoreData     Locat
                                                            ion
--              ----            -----       -----------     -----
2               605793a1-1af... NotStarted False
```

This command attaches a scriptblock to the event that will write out the phrase "<TIMER>" when it fires. You have to use Write-Host in this scriptblock because the output from a triggered event action is simply discarded.

> **Using Register-ObjectEvent**
>
> As a handy way to remember how to use the Register-ObjectEvent cmdlet, think of assigning the scriptblock to the event member. If PowerShell supported this, it'd look something like this: `$timer.Elapsed = { Write-Host "<TIMER>" }`.
>
> The Register-ObjectEvent command allows positional parameters in the same order, so the command would look like
>
> ```
> Register-ObjectEvent $timer Elapsed { Write-Host "<TIMER2>" }
> ```
>
> where the order of the elements is the same: object/member/action.

Now you'll wait a minute...and...nothing happens. This is because you haven't done all of the other things to the Timer object to make it start firing (though obviously, binding the event handler beforehand is usually a good idea).

Enabling the event

Let's complete the remaining steps needed to start the timer triggering. Set the interval to 500 milliseconds so the timer will fire in half a second:

```
PS (5) > $timer.Interval = 500
```

You want to fire repeatedly, so set the AutoReset property to $true:

```
PS (6) > $timer.AutoReset = $true
```

Next you enable the timer by setting the Enabled property to $true (or by calling the Start() method which also sets Enabled to $true):

```
PS (7) > $timer.Enabled = $true
<TIMER>
<TIMER>
<TIMER>
<TIMER>
```

The timer starts running and you see the output you expected. Next comes the hard part: getting it to stop. The command is easy; just type $timer.Stop() and press Enter. But in the console shell, the timer is writing to the screen at the same time you're typing. This results in scrambled output, looking something like this:

```
<TIMER>
<TIMER>
<TIMER>
<TIMER>
$timer.Stop()<TIMER>
<TIMER>
```

(Here's another place where the ISE just works better—the timer output doesn't interfere with the ability to run commands.) Once you've stopped the timer, you can restart it by calling the `Start()` method a second time:

```
PS (9) > $timer.Start()
PS (10) > <TIMER>
<TIMER>
<TIMER>
<TIMER>
$timer.Stop()<TIMER>

PS (12) >
```

Now that you know how to register a basic event subscription, we'll look at how to manage these subscriptions.

20.4.2 Managing event subscriptions

In this section, you'll see how to find your event subscriptions and how to remove them when you're done with them. Being able to remove them is important because event subscriptions persist in the session until explicitly removed.

Listing event subscriptions

Of course, before you can remove a subscription, you have to find it. PowerShell provides the `Get-EventSubscriber` to do this. Let's use it to look at the subscription you registered in the previous section:

```
PS (1) > Get-EventSubscriber

SubscriptionId   : 1
SourceObject     : System.Timers.Timer
EventName        : Elapsed
SourceIdentifier : fca4b869-8d5a-4f11-8d45-e84af30845f1
Action           : System.Management.Automation.PSEventJob
HandlerDelegate  :
SupportEvent     : False
ForwardEvent     : False
```

The `Get-EventSubscriber` cmdlet returns `PSEventSubscriber` objects, which have complete information about the registration: the object generating the event, the action to execute, and so on. There are a couple of interesting properties to note in this output. Because you didn't give the subscription a friendly name using `-SourceIdentifier` when you created it, the `Register-ObjectEvent` generated one for you. This autogenerated name is the string representation of a GUID, so you know it's unique (but not very friendly). The other thing to notice is that the action shows up as a PowerShell `Job` object (see section 12.5). Because the relationship between events and jobs is a somewhat longer discussion, we'll defer it to section 20.10.

Removing event subscriptions

Now that you can list the event subscriptions, you can set about removing them. The cmdlet to do this is *not* `Unsubscribe-Event` because unsubscribe isn't on the approved verbs list and it's not what you want to do anyway. You registered event subscriptions with `Register-ObjectEvent`, so what you need to do is *unregister* the subscription, which you'll do with `Unregister-Event`. The cmdlet noun in this case is `Event`, not `ObjectEvent`, because you can use a common mechanism to unregister any kind of event. It's only the registration part that varies. The rest of the eventing cmdlets remain the same.

When you're unregistering an event subscription, there are two ways of identifying the event to unregister: by the `SubscriptionId` property or by the `SourceIdentifier`. The subscription ID is simply an integer that's incremented each time an event subscription is created. Because you didn't give your event registration a friendly name, you'll use the `SubscriptionId` to unregister it:

```
PS (4) > Unregister-Event -SubscriptionId 1 -Verbose
VERBOSE: Performing operation "Unsubscribe" on Target "Event
subscription 'timertest2'".
PS (5) >
```

Note that you included the `-Verbose` flag in this command so that you could see something happening. Let's try running the command again

```
PS (5) > Unregister-Event -SubscriptionId 1
Unregister-Event : Event subscription with identifier '1' does not
exist.
At line:1 char:17
+ Unregister-Event <<<<  -SubscriptionId 1
    + CategoryInfo          : InvalidArgument: (:) [Unregister-Event
   ], ArgumentException
    + FullyQualifiedErrorId : INVALID_SUBSCRIPTION_IDENTIFIER,
   Microsoft.PowerShell.Commands.UnregisterEventCommand
```

and it results in an error. The `Unregister-Event` cmdlet is silent as long as nothing goes wrong. If something does go wrong, you get an error.

We've covered the basics of creating and managing event subscriptions. But before the handlers for these events can do much useful work, they'll need access to additional information. In the next section, you'll write more sophisticated handlers and see how they can use the automatic variables provided by the eventing subsystem.

20.5 ASYNCHRONOUS EVENT HANDLING WITH SCRIPTBLOCKS

In this section, we'll look at the automatic variables and other features that PowerShell provides to allow scriptblocks to be used as effective event handlers.

20.5.1 Automatic variables in the event handler

In PowerShell eventing, the scriptblock that handles the event action has access to a number of variables that provide information about the event being handled: `$event`, `$eventSubscriber`, `$sender`, `$sourceEventArgs`, and `$sourceArgs`. These variables are described in table 20.2.

Table 20.2 The automatic variables available in the event handler scriptblock

Variable	Description
`$event`	This variable contains an object of type `System.Management.Automation.PSEventArgs` that represents the event that's being handled. It allows you to access a wide variety of information about the event, as you'll see in an example. The value of this variable is the same object that the `Get-Event` cmdlet returns.
`$eventSubscriber`	This variable contains the `PSEventSubscriber` object that represents the event subscriber of the event that's being handled. The value of this variable is the same object that the `Get-EventSubscriber` cmdlet returns.
`$sender`	The value in this variable is the object that generated the event. This variable is a shortcut for `$EventArgs.Sender`.
`$sourceEventArgs`	Contains objects that represent the arguments of the event that's being processed. This variable is a shortcut for `$Event.SourceArgs`.
`$sourceArgs`	Contains the values from `$Event.SourceArgs`. Like any other scriptblock, if there is a `param` statement, the parameters defined by that statement will be populated and `$args` will only contain leftover values for which there were no parameters.

Let's write a quick test event handler to see what's in the object in `$Event`. You'll use the timer event again:

```
PS (1) > $timer = New-Object System.Timers.Timer -Property @{
>>   Interval = 1000; Enabled = $true; AutoReset = $false }
>>
```

In the event subscription action, you'll display the contents of the event object:

```
PS (2) > Register-ObjectEvent $timer Elapsed -Action {
>>     $Event | Out-Host
>> }
>>

Id              Name            State      HasMoreData     Locat
                                                           ion
--              ----            -----      -----------     -----
4               9e3586c3-534... NotStarted False
```

You'll start the timer to generate the event:

```
PS (3) > $timer.Start()
PS (4) >

ComputerName     :
RunspaceId       : 373d0ee9-47a5-4ceb-89e5-61e6389d6838
EventIdentifier  : 7
Sender           : System.Timers.Timer
SourceEventArgs  : System.Timers.ElapsedEventArgs
SourceArgs       : {System.Timers.Timer, System.Timers.ElapsedEv
                   entArgs}
SourceIdentifier : 9e3586c3-534b-465a-84b3-7404110a0f12
```

```
TimeGenerated     : 8/10/2010 12:17:40 PM
MessageData       :
```

In this output, you see the properties on the PSEvent object that correspond to the variables listed in table 20.2. The Timer object that generated the event is available through the Sender property on the object and the $sender variable in the scriptblock. The PSEvent object also includes context data about the event, including the time the event occurred, the event identifier, and the RunspaceId this event is associated with. (Runspaces were discussed briefly in section 15.2.1.) The ComputerName property is blank because this is a local event; but in the case of a remote event, it would contain the name of the computer where the event occurred. (Section 20.9 covers remote events.)

20.5.2 Dynamic modules and event handler state

Because an event can fire at any time, you could never know what variables were in scope and this, in turn, could make it hard to know what state will exist when the action is executed. Instead, you want to be able to run the event handlers in a well-defined, isolated environment. This objective aligns with the design goals for PowerShell modules, so you can leverage this feature by creating a *dynamic module* (section 11.4) for the action scriptblock. The eventing subsystem does this by calling the NewBoundScriptBlockScriptblock() method to attach a dynamic module to the handler scriptblock (section 11.4.2).

Beyond ensuring a coherent runtime environment for your event handler scriptblock, the module also allows it to have private state. This ability can be quite useful when you're monitoring a system's behavior over a period of time. The information can be accumulated privately and then processed once enough samples have been gathered. Let's look at an example that illustrates how this state isolation works. The following is a trivial example where you maintain a count of the number of timer events fired. Once you reach a predetermined limit, the timer will be stopped. Let's walk through the example. First, you create the Timer object:

```
PS (1) > $timer = New-Object System.Timers.Timer -Property @{
>>   Interval = 500; AutoReset = $true}
>>
```

As usual, subscribe to the Elapsed event on the timer:

```
PS (2) > Register-ObjectEvent -InputObject $timer `
>>    -MessageData 5 `
>>   -SourceIdentifier Stateful -EventName Elapsed -Action {
>>     $script:counter += 1
>>     Write-Host "Event counter is $counter"
>>     if ($counter -ge $Event.MessageData)
>>     {
>>        Write-Host "Stopping timer"
>>        $timer.Stop()
>>     }
>>   } > $null
>>
```

In the handler scriptblock for this event, you're updating a script-scoped variable `$script:counter`, which holds the number of times the event has fired. This variable will only be visible within the dynamic module associated with the event, thus preventing your `$counter` from colliding with any other users of a variable called `$counter`. After the variable is incremented, you print the event count and then check to see if the limit has been reached. Notice that you're making use of the `-MessageData` parameter to pass the limit to the event handler, which it retrieves from the `MessageData` property on the `Event` object. Now start the timer running to see it in action:

```
PS (3) > $timer.Start()
PS (4) >
PS (5) > Event counter is 1
Event counter is 2
Event counter is 3
Event counter is 4
Event counter is 5
Stopping timer

PS (6) >
```

As intended, the timer message is displayed five times and then the timer is stopped. This example can easily be modified to, for example, monitor CPU usage or process working sets over a period of time.

Setting up action scriptblocks for asynchronous events allows you to efficiently handle events in the background. This, in turn, lets the main thread of your script continue execution in the foreground or, in interactive sessions, allows you to continue entering commands at the shell prompt. There are, however, many monitoring scenarios where there's no main thread and all you want to do is wait for events to happen. For example, if a service process crashes or faults, you want to be notified so you can take action to restart it. Otherwise, you simply wait for the next event to arrive. This "wait for an event" pattern is addressed using the `Wait-Event` cmdlet.

20.6 QUEUED EVENTS AND THE WAIT-EVENT CMDLET

As an alternative to setting up a lot of individual event handler actions, you can use the `Wait-Event` cmdlet to process events in a loop. This cmdlet allows you to block, waiting until an event or events happen. When the event arrives, you can take whatever action is required, then loop and wait for the next event. This event loop pattern is very common, especially in GUI programming. The syntax for the `Wait-Event` command is simple:

```
Wait-Event [[-SourceIdentifier] <string>] [-Timeout <int>]
```

By using the `-SourceIdentifier` parameter you can wait for a specific named event. If you don't use it, then any unhandled event will unblock you. By using the `-Timeout` parameter, you can limit the length of time you'll wait for the event. This allows you to take remedial actions if the event you're waiting for failed to occur in the prescribed time.

> **NOTE** You can either register an action for an event or wait for an event but you can't do both. If an action has been registered, when the event fires the event object will be removed from the queue and passed to the action scriptblock for processing. As a result, any `Wait-Event` calls listening for this event will never receive it and will block forever.

Let's experiment with this cmdlet using something other than the timer event. In this example, you'll work with the file system watcher class: `System.IO.FileSystemWatcher`. This class is used to generate events when changes are made to monitored portions of the file system. Let's look at the events exposed by this type:

```
PS (1) > [System.IO.FileSystemWatcher].GetEvents() |
>>   Select-String .
>>

System.IO.FileSystemEventHandler Changed
System.IO.FileSystemEventHandler Created
System.IO.FileSystemEventHandler Deleted
System.IO.ErrorEventHandler Error
System.IO.RenamedEventHandler Renamed
System.EventHandler Disposed
```

Using this class, you can register for notifications when a file or directory is created, changed, deleted, or renamed. You can create a `FileSystemWatcher` object that will monitor changes to your desktop. First, you need to get the resolved path to the desktop folder:

```
PS (2) > $path = (Resolve-Path ~/desktop).Path
```

You have to do this because, as discussed previously, when you use PowerShell paths as arguments to .NET methods (including constructors) you must pass in a fully resolved path because .NET doesn't understand PowerShell's enhanced notion of paths. Now, construct the file watcher object for the target path:

```
PS (3) > $fsw = [System.IO.FileSystemWatcher] $path
```

Set up an event subscription for the `Created` and `Changed` events:

```
PS (4) > Register-ObjectEvent -InputObject $fsw -EventName Created `
>> -SourceIdentifier fsw1
PS (5) > Register-ObjectEvent -InputObject $fsw -EventName Changed `
>> -SourceIdentifier fsw2
```

Finally, enable event generation by the object:

```
PS (6) > $fsw.EnableRaisingEvents = $true
```

At this point when you call `Get-Event`, you should see nothing:

```
PS (7) > Get-Event
```

This assumes that no other process is writing to the desktop while you're doing this. Let's perform an operation that will trigger the event. Create a new file on the desktop:

```
PS (8) > Get-Date > ~/desktop/date.txt
```

You didn't set up an action for either of the event registrations, so you won't see anything happen immediately. The events, however, haven't been lost. Unhandled events are added to the session *event queue* where they can be retrieved later. Let's see what's in the queue at this point:

```
PS (9) > Get-Event | select SourceIdentifier

SourceIdentifier
----------------
fsw1
fsw2
```

In the output, you see that two events have been added: one for the creation of the date.txt file and a second indicating that a change to the containing directory has occurred. Note that simply reading the events doesn't remove them from the queue. You need to use the `Remove-Event` cmdlet to do this; otherwise, you'll keep rereading the same event objects. The `Remove-Event` cmdlet allows events to be removed either by `SourceIdentifier` or by `EventIdentifier`. To discard all the events in the queue, pipe `Get-Event` into `Remove-Event`:

```
PS (10) > Get-Event | Remove-Event
```

The queue is now empty, so you can call `Wait-Event` and the session will block until a new event is generated (or you press Ctrl-C):

```
PS (11) > Wait-Event
```

To trigger an event, from another PowerShell session update the date.txt file by using this:

```
Get-Date > ~/desktop/date.txt
```

This code will cause an event to be added to the queue, terminating the `Wait-Event`, which will write the terminating event object to the output stream:

```
PS (11) > Wait-Event

ComputerName     :
RunspaceId       : 9c3c1728-7704-4e05-bba1-50ccc16d651f
EventIdentifier  : 3
Sender           : System.IO.FileSystemWatcher
SourceEventArgs  : System.IO.FileSystemEventArgs
SourceArgs       : {System.IO.FileSystemWatcher, date.txt}
SourceIdentifier : fsw2
TimeGenerated    : 8/9/2010 3:57:13 PM
MessageData      :
```

Although you're unblocked, the event hasn't technically been handled, so it still exists in the queue and you still have to manually remove it from the queue:

```
PS (12) > Get-Event | Remove-Event
```

Let's call `Wait-Event` again but with a 2-second timeout and let the timeout expire:

```
PS (13) > Wait-Event -Timeout 2
PS (14) >
```

In this case, you were unblocked but no object was written. This makes it easy to distinguish between a timeout and an actual event.

Now let's move on to the second type of events that can be handled by the PowerShell eventing infrastructure: WMI events.

20.7 WORKING WITH WMI EVENTS

In this section, we're going to cover how to work with WMI events in PowerShell. As was the case with .NET events, you handle WMI events using a cmdlet to register actions associated with the events: the `Register-WmiEvent` cmdlet syntax is shown in figure 20.3.

All the other eventing cmdlets remain the same as you saw for object events. (You'll see that this is also the case for engine events [section 20.8] and would also be the same for any new object sources that might be added in the future.)

20.7.1 WMI event basics

WMI events are, in some ways, considerably more sophisticated than .NET events. First, WMI events are represented as WMI objects and so, like all WMI objects, can be retrieved from either a local or remote computer in a transparent way. Second, because WMI event subscriptions can take the form of a WQL query, event filtering

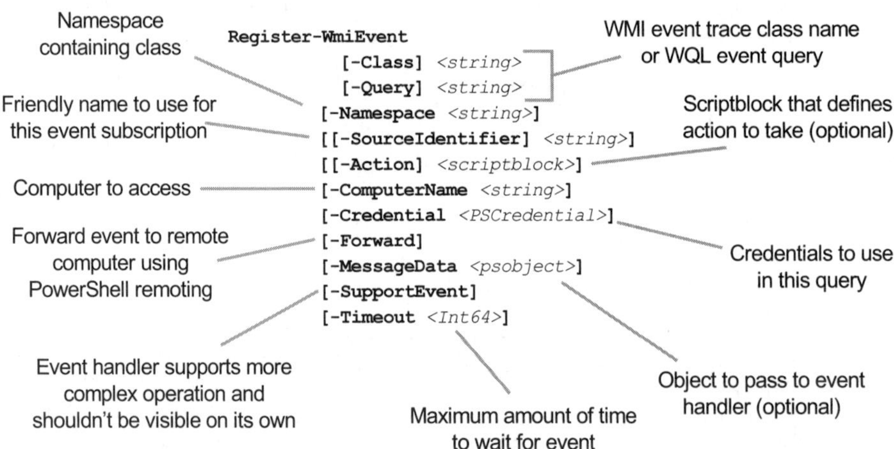

Figure 20.3 The signature of the `Register-WmiEvent` cmdlet. This cmdlet is used to set up event handling for asynchronous WMI events.

can take place at the event source instead of transmitting all events to the receiver, who is forced to do all the filtering. This is important if you're monitoring a small set of events on a large number of computers. By doing the filtering at the source (remote) end, far less data is transmitted to the receiver and much less processing needs to be done by the receiver, allowing for the overall monitoring task to scale to far more computers than would otherwise be possible.

> **NOTE** On the other hand, unlike object events, there's no notion of synchronous WMI events so all event handling must go through the eventing subsystem.

We'll begin our exploration of WMI events by looking at the `Win32_*Trace` classes, which are much simpler to deal with than the full query-based event subscriptions.

20.7.2 Class-based WMI event registration

Before jumping into the full complexity of query-based event subscriptions, we'll look at some predefined WMI event classes. These classes hide a lot of the complexity required by query-based event registration, making them easier to use. You can use the following command to get a list of these classes. You'll also display their superclasses to see the relationships between the classes:

```
PS (1) > Get-WmiObject -List Win32_*trace |
>>   Format-List Name,__SUPERCLASS
>>

Name         : Win32_SystemTrace
__SUPERCLASS : __ExtrinsicEvent

Name         : Win32_ProcessTrace
__SUPERCLASS : Win32_SystemTrace

Name         : Win32_ProcessStartTrace
__SUPERCLASS : Win32_ProcessTrace

Name         : Win32_ProcessStopTrace
__SUPERCLASS : Win32_ProcessTrace

Name         : Win32_ThreadTrace
__SUPERCLASS : Win32_SystemTrace

Name         : Win32_ThreadStartTrace
__SUPERCLASS : Win32_ThreadTrace

Name         : Win32_ThreadStopTrace
__SUPERCLASS : Win32_ThreadTrace

Name         : Win32_ModuleTrace
__SUPERCLASS : Win32_SystemTrace

Name         : Win32_ModuleLoadTrace
__SUPERCLASS : Win32_ModuleTrace
```

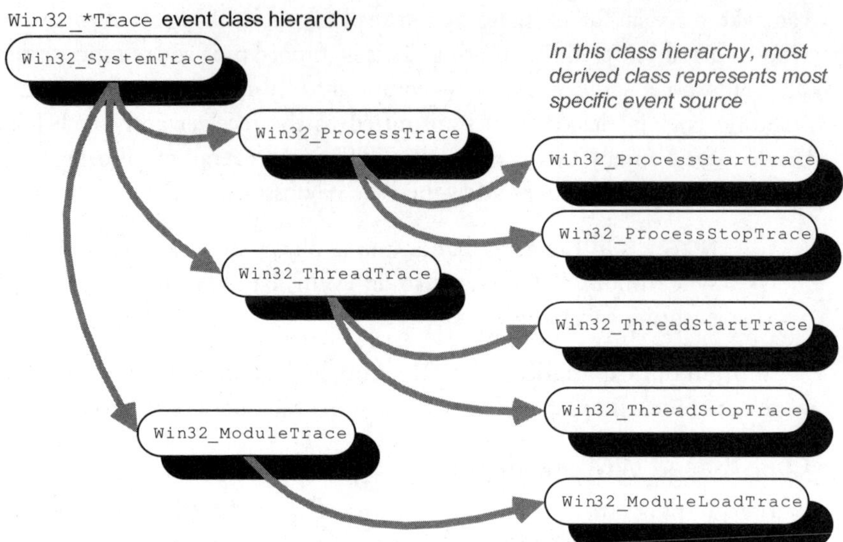

Figure 20.4 This figure shows the hierarchy of classes representing simplified WMI event sources. The most derived class matches the most specific event. `Win32_ProcessStartTrace` will only fire for process starts whereas `Win32_ProcessTrace` will fire for both process starts and process stops.

By inspecting the class/superclass relationships, you can see that these classes form a hierarchy of event sources, where the further you go from the root, the more specific the event becomes. This hierarchy is illustrated in figure 20.4.

Let's work through an example that shows how this works.

> **NOTE** Because these event sources fire for *any* process event, regardless of who starts them, these commands must be run from an elevated shell on Windows Vista, Window 7, Windows Server 2008, and Windows Server 2008 R2. Also be aware that, because you're recording all process events in the first set of examples, you may see additional output from other processes starting and stopping.

Using the Win32_ProcessTrace events

You'll use the `Win32_Process*Trace` classes in this experiment. First you'll set up an event subscription to the `Win32_ProcessStartTrace`, which will fire every time a process starts:

```
PS (2) > Register-WmiEvent -Class Win32_ProcessStartTrace `
>>   -Action {
>>     "Process Start: " +
>>       $event.SourceEventArgs.NewEvent.ProcessName |
>>         Out-Host
>>   }
>>
```

```
Id              Name              State      HasMoreData     Location
--              ----              -----      -----------     -----
18              d999e74a-57c... NotStarted False
```

You can assign an action scriptblock to these event subscriptions, just as you did with object events. In the body of the scriptblock, you'll write a message indicating what type of event was fired along with the process name. You'll set up similar event handlers for the Win32_ProcessStopTrace and Win32_ProcessTrace events, again displaying the type of the event and the process name:

```
PS (3) > Register-WmiEvent -Class Win32_ProcessStopTrace `
>>   -Action {
>>     "Process Stop: " +
>>       $event.SourceEventArgs.NewEvent.ProcessName |
>>         Out-Host
>>   }
>>
Id              Name              State      HasMoreData     Location
--              ----              -----      -----------     -----
19              c4b4bf9d-368... NotStarted False
PS (4) > Register-WmiEvent -Class  Win32_ProcessTrace `
>>   -Action {
>>     "Process Any: " +
>>       $event.SourceEventArgs.NewEvent.ProcessName |
>>         Out-Host
>>   }
>>
Id              Name              State      HasMoreData     Location
--              ----              -----      -----------     -----
20              e4a5ad65-d35... NotStarted False
```

From the hierarchy (and the names of the events), you know that Win32_ProcessStartTrace fires when a process starts, Win32_ProcessStopTrace fires when a process is terminated, and Win32_ProcessTrace fires on either kind of process event. To test these subscriptions, run the following command, which will start and stop an instance of the calc process a number of times:

```
PS (5) > & {
>> $p = Start-Process calc -PassThru
>> Start-Sleep 3
>> $p | Stop-Process
>> Start-Sleep 3
>> $p = Start-Process calc -PassThru
>> Start-Sleep 3
>> $p | Stop-Process
>> Start-Sleep 3
>> }
>>
```

In this command you're using Start-Process to start the calc process with -PassThru to capture the process object and save it in a variable. Then, after three seconds, you pass the captured object to Stop-Process to terminate the calc instance. This pattern is repeated three times and the whole thing is wrapped in a scriptblock to cause it to be executed as a single command. (This way, you avoid having your commands mixed in with the output and cluttering things up. Alternatively, you could've used the PowerShell ISE instead of the console shell; see section 15.1.1.) Here's the output produced by this command:

```
Process Start: calc.exe
Process Any: calc.exe
Process Any: calc.exe
Process Stop: calc.exe
Process Start: calc.exe
Process Any: calc.exe
Process Any: calc.exe
Process Stop: calc.exe
```

The first two records were generated by the first `calc` process starting. You get both `Win32_ProcessStartTrace` and `Win32_ProcessTrace` firing but not `Win32_ProcessStopTrace`. The `calc` process is then stopped, resulting in two more records, and this is repeated one more time for a total of eight records. (The order in which the specific and general events are fired is nondeterministic, so the exact order will change with different runs of the start/stop command.)

Verifying that the events fired

To verify that the events fire for all process creations, let's start and stop the Telnet service. This will cause the service manager to start the `TlntSvr` process, which should, in turn, trigger an event:

```
PS (6) > Start-Service TlntSvr; Stop-Service TlntSvr
Process Any: tlntsvr.exe
Process Start: tlntsvr.exe
PS (7) > Process Stop: tlntsvr.exe
Process Any: tlntsvr.exe
```

This is confirmed by the output, indicating that the service process was started and stopped.

The final step in this experiment is to clean up the event subscriptions you created. Here's the easiest way to do this:

```
PS (7) > Get-EventSubscriber | Unregister-Event
PS (8) >
```

Note that this code removes all event subscriptions for this session. This is fine for experimentation but you should be careful doing this in a production environment and be selective about what is removed.

This completes the easy part of WMI event handling. Although setting up event handlers this way was easy, it was also very limited. In chapter 19, when you retrieved WMI object instances using `Get-WmiObject`, you were able to do sophisticated filtering and could be precise about the objects you retrieved. You can be just as precise with events, but doing so requires the use of WQL queries. We'll cover this in the next section.

20.7.3 Query-based WMI event registrations

In chapter 19 (section 19.2.2) you used the WMI Query Language (WQL) to select and filter WMI objects. The format of those instance-based WQL queries was

```
SELECT <propertyList> FROM <ObjectClass> WHERE <predicateExpression>
```

With a little bit of additional syntax, WQL can also be used to select and filter WMI events.

> **NOTE** In CIM parlance, what you actually filter is called a *notification,* not an event. CIM defines an event as something that happens at a particular point in time like a process starting or a user logging on. Notifications are the object representation (or model) for these event occurrences. For simplicity, we're going to stick to using *event* for both cases in the rest this chapter.

The core syntax for event queries is the same as for instance queries but with some additional features. We'll look at these features in the next couple of sections.

The WITHIN keyword

The first of the additional keywords we'll discuss is `WITHIN`. This keyword is used in a query as follows:

```
SELECT <propertyList> FROM <EventClass> WITHIN <Seconds> WHERE
            <predicateExpression>
```

The `WITHIN` keyword is used to specify the *polling interval* that the WMI service should use to monitor and relay event data. The polling interval is the frequency with which the monitored resource is checked. The smaller the polling interval, the more often the monitored resource will be checked. This results in faster and more accurate event notifications, but it also places more burden on the monitored system. The argument to the `WITHIN` keyword is a floating-point number. This means you could theoretically specify polling intervals of less than one second. However, specifying a value that's too small (like 0.001 seconds) could cause the WMI service to reject a query as not valid due to the resource-intensive nature of polling. The polling interval should be chosen based on the type of event being monitored. If the event doesn't require instant action, it's generally recommended that the polling interval be greater than 300 seconds (that is, 5 minutes).

The WMI intrinsic event classes

The objects you query for are also a bit different. With object events, you create an instance of an object and then subscribe to an event on that object. With WMI event queries, you subscribe to the type of event and then specify the event-generating class you're interested in. Some of the most useful of these intrinsic event classes are `_InstanceCreationEvent`, `__InstanceDeletionEvent`, and

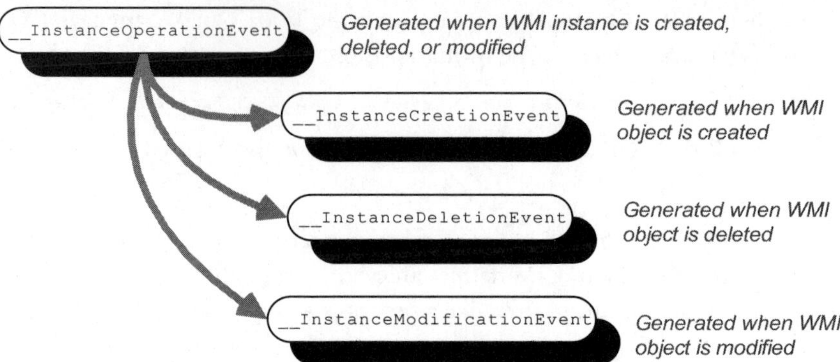

Figure 20.5 The class hierarchy for the WMI instance operation event class. These events are generated when a WMI is object is created, deleted, or modified. The base event class is triggered for all three.

`_InstanceModificationEvent`, which are all derived from `_InstanceOperationEvent`. These classes and their relationships are shown in figure 20.5.

These classes mirror the pattern you saw in the previous section where `Win32_ProcessTrace` was the root event with `Win32_ProcessStartTrace` and `Win32_ProcessStopTrace` as derived events. The difference here is that there's no class like Win32_Process mentioned in these events. They are general-purpose events generated by all objects. So, when you want to register an event subscription for one of these events, you use the ISA operator to select which class you're interested in receiving instance notifications from. Let's see what a query using the `WITHIN` keyword and these instance notifications events looks like:

```
SELECT * FROM __InstanceOperationEvent WITHIN 1
WHERE TargetInstance ISA 'Win32_Service'
  AND TargetInstance.Name='TlntSvr'
```

This query says to retrieve all events from `InstanceOperationEvent` with a polling interval of one second (this is an experiment so you'll use a small value) where the object generating the event is an instance of the `Win32_Service` class and the `Name` property on the instance is `TlntSvr`. In other words, you want to generate an event anytime something happens to the Telnet service.

> **NOTE** This example assumes that you have the Telnet service installed on the target computer. Because the Telnet service is an optional install, you may have to install it. To do so, from an elevated PowerShell instance, run `appwiz.cpl` to launch the Programs And Features control panel applet. In this applet, select "Turn Windows Features on or off," locate Telnet service in the list, and click the check box beside it. (This process might vary slightly depending on which version of Windows you're running.) Click OK and the Telnet service will be installed.

Let's try this out. Assign the query to a variable:

```
PS (1) > $svcQuery = @"
>> Select * From __InstanceOperationEvent Within 1
>> Where TargetInstance Isa 'Win32_Service'
>>   and
>>     TargetInstance.Name='TlntSvr'
>> "@
>>
```

Now use the `Register-WmiEvent` to subscribe to this event. In the action field, display a message indicating the source of the event and then print out the contents of the `$event` variable:

```
PS (2) > Register-WmiEvent -Query $svcQuery -Action {
>>     Write-Host "Got instance operation event on Win32_Service"
>>     $Event | Format-List * | Out-Host
>> }
>>

Id              Name            State      HasMoreData     Location
--              ----            -----      -----------     -----
2               ecd3a80c-a70... NotStarted False
PS (3) >
```

With the event subscription set up, trigger the event by starting the Telnet service:

```
PS (4) > Start-Service TlntSvr
Got specific instance operation event on Win32_Service
ComputerName       :
RunspaceId         : e4ac72a7-0868-488b-af17-4aeb9a1b04d1
EventIdentifier    : 5
Sender             : System.Management.ManagementEventWatcher
SourceEventArgs    : System.Management.EventArrivedEventArgs
SourceArgs         : {System.Management.ManagementEventWatcher, Sy
                     stem.Management.EventArrivedEventArgs}
SourceIdentifier   : ecd3a80c-a70c-4e21-a420-3038be93aade
TimeGenerated      : 9/12/2010 9:36:31 PM
MessageData        :
```

And, after a second or so, you see the message printed out by the action scriptblock. Stop the service:

```
PS (6) > Stop-Service TlntSvr
PS (7) > Got specific instance operation event on Win32_Service

ComputerName       :
RunspaceId         : e4ac72a7-0868-488b-af17-4aeb9a1b04d1
EventIdentifier    : 6
Sender             : System.Management.ManagementEventWatcher
SourceEventArgs    : System.Management.EventArrivedEventArgs
SourceArgs         : {System.Management.ManagementEventWatcher, Sy
                     stem.Management.EventArrivedEventArgs}
SourceIdentifier   : ecd3a80c-a70c-4e21-a420-3038be93aade
TimeGenerated      : 9/12/2010 9:36:36 PM
MessageData        :
```

And you get a second message because the event you've subscribed to fires for any change.

In the next section, we'll look at additional features for improving the network behavior of the system by grouping events instead of sending them one at a time.

Aggregating events with GROUP

The next keyword we'll cover is `GROUP`. The `GROUP` clause is used to *aggregate* the events based on certain criteria. This means that instead of generating one notification per event, the WMI service will group them together with a count and a representative instance. This is another way to reduce the load on the client and the network:

```
SELECT * FROM EventClass [WHERE property = value]
    GROUP WITHIN interval [BY property_list]
    [HAVING NumberOfEvents operator integer]
```

You create a query-based WMI event registration using the `-Query` parameter set on `Register-WmiEvent`:

```
Select * From __InstanceOperationEvent Within .5
Where TargetInstance Isa 'Win32_Service'
and TargetInstance.Name='TlntSvr'
Group Within 20
```

Let's set up this new event subscription. First save your query in a string and set up a counter that will record the total number of events:

```
PS (1) > $GroupQuery = @"
>> Select * From __InstanceOperationEvent Within .5
>> Where TargetInstance Isa 'Win32_Service'
>> and TargetInstance.Name='TlntSvr'
>> Group Within 20
>> "@
>>
PS (2) > $global:TotalEvents = 0
```

Now register this event subscription:

```
PS (3) > Register-WmiEvent -Query $GroupQuery -Action {
>>     Write-Host "Got grouped event"
>>     $ne = $Event.SourceEventArgs.NewEvent
>>     $ti = $ne.Representative.TargetInstance
>>     $global:TotalEvents += $ne.NumberOfEvents
>>     $msg = "Type: " + $ne.__CLASS +
>>       " Num Evnts: " + $ne.NumberOfEvents +
>>         " Name: " + $ti.Name +
>>           " (" + $ti.DisplayName + ')' |
>>             Out-Host
>> }
>>

Id              Name            State       HasMoreData     Location
--              ----            -----       -----------     --------
3               d251cd26-2e2... NotStarted False
```

In the body of the event action scriptblock, you'll format a string containing some of the more interesting fields (at least for the purpose of this experiment). You'll show the type of the event class, the number of events that have been aggregated, and then the `Name` and `DisplayName` for the matched service. You'll generate a series of events using a `foreach` loop to cause the event aggregation to fire:

```
PS (4) > foreach ($i in 1..3)
>> {
>>   Start-Service TlntSvr
>>   Start-Sleep 2
>>   Stop-Service TlntSvr
>>   Start-Sleep 2
>> }
>>
```

These events will all be accumulated in the event group and, when the group interval expires, you should get an event notification. Use the `Start-Sleep` command to wait for the timeout to expire:

```
PS (5) > Start-Sleep 10
Got grouped event
Type: __AggregateEvent Num Evnts: 6 Name: TlntSvr (Telnet)
```

The event count shows your total:

```
PS (6) > "Total events: $TotalEvents"
Total events: 6
PS (7) >
```

Now that you have your event, let's clean up the event subscription:

```
PS (8) > Get-EventSubscriber | Unregister-Event
```

In this example, you've seen how you can use the `GROUP` keyword to further reduce the number of events that need to be sent to the monitoring script.

This completes our look at WMI eventing so let's move on to something a bit different. Up until now, we've only been talking about how to respond to events. In the next section, you'll see how to generate some events of your own.

20.8 ENGINE EVENTS

The last category of events we're going to look at is called *engine events*. With engine events, the notifications are generated by the PowerShell engine itself, either through one of the predefined engine events or by explicitly generating an event in a script.

20.8.1 Predefined engine events

In the released version of PowerShell v2, there's currently only one predefined engine event identified by the string `"PowerShell.Exiting"`. This string can also be retrieved using a static method as follows:

```
PS (1) > `
>> [System.Management.Automation.PsEngineEvent]::Exiting
```

```
>>
PowerShell.Exiting
```

This event is triggered when the PowerShell engine is shutting down and allows you to perform actions before the session exits. Here's an example event registration:

```
Register-EngineEvent `
  -SourceIdentifier PowerShell.Exiting `
  -Action {
    "@{Directory='$PWD'}" > ~/pshState.ps1
  }
```

This command registers an action to take when the PowerShell session ends. This action writes a hashtable to the file pshState.ps1 in the user's directory. The hashtable captures the user's current directory at the time the session was exited. Let's use this in an example. You'll create a child `PowerShell.exe` process to run your script so you don't have to exit the current process. PowerShell recognizes when a scriptblock is passed to the `PowerShell.exe` command and makes sure that everything gets passed to the command correctly. Let's run the command:

```
PS (1) > powershell {
>>     Register-EngineEvent `
>>       -SourceIdentifier PowerShell.Exiting `
>>       -Action {
>>         "@{Directory='$PWD'}" > ~/pshState.ps1
>>         } | Format-List Id,Name
>>      cd ~/desktop
>>      exit
>>   }
>>

Id   : 1
Name : PowerShell.Exiting
```

Now look at the content of the file:

```
PS (2) > Get-Content ~/pshState.ps1
@{Directory='C:\Users\brucepay.REDMOND\desktop'}
```

And you see that the file contains a hashtable with the current directory recorded in it. This example can easily be expanded to include things like the user's history or the contents of the function: drive, but adding those extensions is left as an exercise for the reader.

The other class of engine events is script-generated events. We'll look at those next.

20.8.2 Generating events in functions and scripts

The last of the core eventing cmdlets to look at is the `New-Event` cmdlet. This cmdlet allows a script to generate its own events. Let's use this cmdlet in an example to see how it works. First you create the timer object:

```
PS (1) > $timer = New-Object System.Timers.Timer -Property @{
>>   Interval = 5000; Enabled = $true; AutoReset = $false }
>>
```

And register the event subscription:

```
PS (2) > Register-ObjectEvent $timer Elapsed -Action {
>>   Write-Host '<TIMER>'
>>     New-Event -SourceIdentifier generatedEvent -Sender 3.14
>> } > $null
>>
```

In the handler scriptblock, as well as writing out a message, you're also calling `New-Event` to generate a new event in the event queue. Finally, start the timer

```
PS (3) > $timer.Start() > $null
PS (4) >
```

and wait for the event. Pipe the object returned from `Wait-Event` into the `foreach` cmdlet for processing:

```
PS (5) > Wait-Event -SourceIdentifier generatedEvent |
>>   foreach {
>>     "Received generated event"
>>     $_ |
>>       Format-Table -AutoSize SourceIdentifier, EventIdentifier
, Sender
>>     $_ | Remove-Event
>>   }
>>
<TIMER>
Received generated event

SourceIdentifier EventIdentifier Sender
---------------- --------------- ------
generatedEvent                12   3.14
```

In the output, you first see the `<TIMER>` message indicating that the timer event has triggered. Then you see the output from `Wait-Event`. In the `foreach` block, you display the source identifier of the event generated by `New-Event`, and the `Sender` field shows the number you passed to the cmdlet. When you're done with this example, you'll remove the event subscription:

```
PS (6) > Get-EventSubscriber | Unregister-Event
```

This pretty much completes the local event handling story. But with PowerShell v2 adding remoting capabilities, obviously our eventing infrastructure needs to work in a distributed environment as well. In the next section you'll see how to work with events in remote scenario.

20.9 REMOTING AND EVENT FORWARDING

Being able to set up local event handlers is useful, but you also need to be able to process events generated on remote computers to manage distributed datacenters. The PowerShell eventing subsystem, by building on top of PowerShell remoting, makes this surprisingly easy. In figures 20.1 and 20.2 you saw the `-Forward` parameter. This

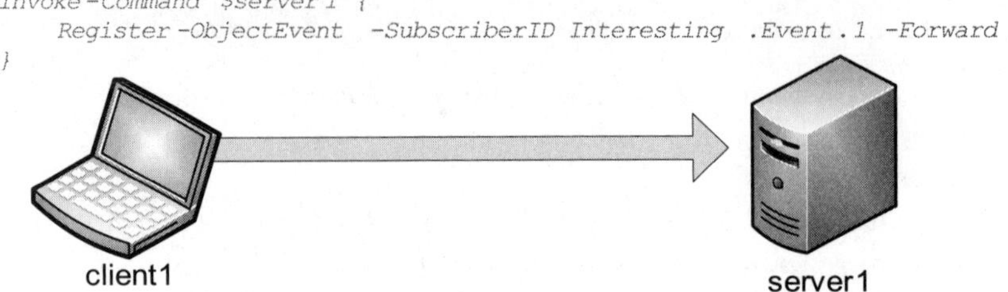

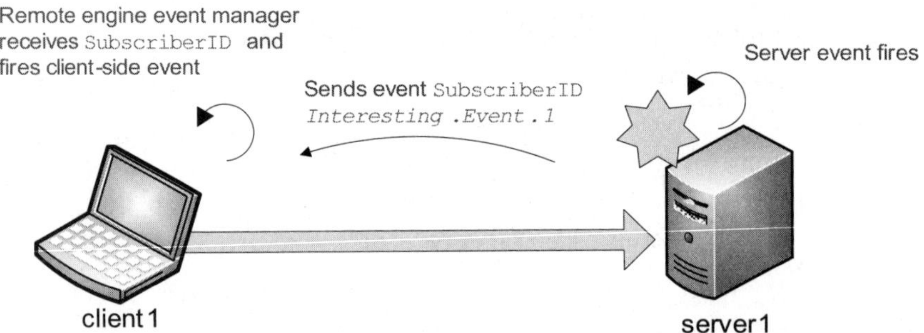

Figure 20.6 The second-hop authentication changes when credential delegation is used. Without delegation, the second hop from server 1 to server 2 authenticates as the user that the service is running under. With credential forwarding enabled, server 1 can use the client credentials to authenticate to server 2 as the client user.

parameter does exactly what you might expect: it forwards the subscribed event to a remote session. This is where the `-SourceIdentifier` parameter becomes critical. The source identifier name that's specified at the event source end becomes the name of the event to process on the receiving end. This process is illustrated in figure 20.6.

Here's where the engine events come into play. The forwarded events are handled using engine event processing. The cmdlet for subscribing to this type of event is shown in figure 20.7. (The events generated by `New-Event` in the previous section are also engine events.)

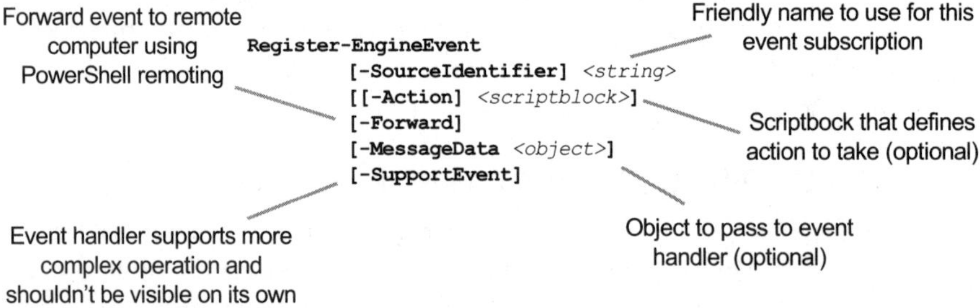

Figure 20.7 The signature of the `Register-EngineEvent` cmdlet. This cmdlet is used to set up event handling for events generated by the PowerShell engine.

This cmdlet lets you register subscriptions that trigger the event handler based on the subscription identifier sent from the remote end. In the next section, we'll look at a detailed example where you forward an event from one machine for processing on another.

20.9.1 Handling remote EventLog events

In this section, you're going to apply what you've learned. Your goal is to be notified locally every time an event is written into the event log on a remote computer. The .NET `EventLog` class exposes just such an event: `EntryWritten`. To set this up, you must establish event forwarding on the remote machine and then register a load event handler. You'll also need to maintain a connection to the remote end using the duration of time you want to get events because the events are being forwarded over this channel.

The first thing you need to do is to establish a connection to the target computer. You do so with the `New-PSSession` cmdlet, passing credentials if needed (see section 12.3.2 for more information on `New-PSSession`):

```
PS (1) > $s = New-PSSession -ComputerName brucepayquad
```

This is the session you'll use to set up the event forwarding and then to transfer the forwarded events. Next you'll use `Invoke-Command` to set up the event forwarding registration. The code to do this looks like this:

```
PS (2) > Invoke-Command $s {
>>     $myLog = New-Object System.Diagnostics.EventLog application
>>     Register-ObjectEvent `
>>         -InputObject $myLog  `
>>         -SourceIdentifier EventWatcher1 `
>>         -EventName EntryWritten `
>>         -Forward
>>
>>     $myLog.EnableRaisingEvents = $true
>> }
>>
```

Inside the scriptblock passed to `Invoke-Command`, you're creating an `EventLog` object associated with the `Application` event log. Then you use `Register-ObjectEvent` to set up event forwarding for events that occur on the `EntryWritten` event. You'll use the source identifier name `EventWatcher1`. Finally, you enable raising events on the event log object.

With the remote end configured, now it's time to set up the local end. This task is much simpler. You register an engine event handler that will trigger on the source ID matching the remote end:

```
PS (3) > Register-EngineEvent -SourceIdentifier EventWatcher1 -Action {
>>    param($sender, $event)
>>
>>    Write-Host "Got an event: $($event.entry.message)"
>> }
>>
```

And you're done. Now whenever an entry is added to the Application event log on the remote computer, you'll see the entry message displayed on your console. Of course, if you're impatient, you can trigger an event yourself. Use the .NET `FailFast()` API to cause a "Watson" event to be generated by crashing a PowerShell process:

```
PS (4) > powershell "[System.Environment]::FailFast('An event')"
PS (5) >
```

After a short time, you'll see something like the following displayed on the console:

```
PS (6) > Got an event:
```

Well, this sort of worked: the event did trigger the event handler and you got the part of the event you wrote. Unfortunately, the most interesting piece—the message in the event itself—is mysteriously absent. You'll see what happened in the next section.

20.9.2 Serialization issues with remote events

The serialization mechanism used by remoting can sometimes cause problems when using remote events. Because the event is being sent over the remoting channel, it has to be serialized by the PowerShell serializer. By default, the serialization depth is only one. This means you get the top-level properties but not the second-level properties. So to preserve the message content in `$event.Entry.Message`, you need to change the serialization depth for this type of object to 2. Back in section 11.7.3, we covered the types.ps1xml files and how they can be used to add metadata to a type. In section 12.6.5, we also talked about how those files can be used to change the serialization depth for a type. So you need an XML document that you can pass to `Update-TypeData` to change the serialization depth for `System.Diagnostics.EntryWrittenEventArgs` to 2. Save this XML in a variable as a string for now:

```
PS (7) > $typeSpec = @'
>>     <Types>
>>        <Type>
>>            <Name>System.Diagnostics.EntryWrittenEventArgs</Name>
>>             <Members>
>>                 <MemberSet>
>>                     <Name>PSStandardMembers</Name>
>>                     <Members>
>>                         <NoteProperty>
>>                             <Name>SerializationDepth</Name>
>>                             <Value>2</Value>
>>                         </NoteProperty>
>>                     </Members>
>>                 </MemberSet>
>>             </Members>
>>        </Type>
>>     </Types>
>> '@
>>
```

Now before you use this to set up new events, you should remove the existing event registrations on both the local and remote ends of the connection:

```
PS (8) > Invoke-Command $s { Unregister-Event EventWatcher1 }
PS (9) > Unregister-Event EventWatcher1
```

You have the XML in a local variable but you need to update the type metadata on the remote end. You need to get the content of the `$typeSpec` variable over to the remote machine, which you'll do by passing it as an argument to the `Invoke-Command` scriptblock:

```
PS (10) > Invoke-Command -ArgumentList $typeSpec -Session $s {
>>     param ($typeSpec)
>>
>>     $tempFile = [System.IO.Path]::GetTempFileName()
>>     $tempFile = $tempFile -replace '\.tmp$', '.ps1xml'
>>     $typeSpec > $tempFile
>>     try
>>     {
>>         Update-TypeData $tempFile
>>     }
>>     finally
>>     {
>>         Remove-Item $tempFile
>>     }
>> }
>>
```

Let's go over what's happening in this scriptblock. First you're using the .NET `GetTempFileName()` method to get a temporary filename to use to store the data. Because the default extension on the filename that's returned is .tmp and you need it to be .ps1xml, you used the `-replace` operator to change the extension. Then you write `$typeSpec` to the file in `$tempFile` using redirection, call `Update-TypeData` to load the file, and finally clean up by removing the temp file. You're using the `try/finally` statement to make sure that the file gets cleaned up even if there's a problem updating.

With the type metadata updated, you can set up the remote event registration, just like before:

```
PS (11) > Invoke-Command $s {
>>     $myLog = New-Object System.Diagnostics.EventLog application
>>     Register-ObjectEvent `
>>         -InputObject $myLog `
>>         -SourceIdentifier EventWatcher1 `
>>         -EventName EntryWritten `
>>         -Forward
>>
>>     $myLog.EnableRaisingEvents = $true
>> }
>>
```

Then the local event subscription:

```
PS (12) > Register-EngineEvent -SourceIdentifier EventWatcher1 -Action
 {
>>     param($sender, $event)
>>
>>     Write-Host "Got an event: $($event.entry.message)"
>> }
>>

Id              Name            State      HasMoreData     Location
--              ----            -----      -----------     --------
2               EventWatcher1   NotStarted False
```

And finally, you're ready to try your event trigger again:

```
PS (13) > powershell "[System.Environment]::FailFast('An event')"
PS (14) >
PS (15) > Got an event: .NET Runtime version 2.0.50727.4200 - An event
PS (16) >
```

This time, when you see the event message, it includes the text from the call to `FailFast()` as written into the event log on the remote system.

Congratulations! We've pretty much reached the end of our eventing discussion and you're still with us. Event processing is an advanced topic, even for full-time programmers. Trying to understand how multiple actions are going to interoperate can be mind-boggling. PowerShell's approach to eventing is designed to make this as simple as possible, but understanding how it works under the hood can go a long way to helping you figure things out. Let's take a peek.

20.10 How eventing works

The eventing infrastructure relies on two other components of PowerShell introduced in PowerShell v2: modules (for isolation, as discussed earlier) and jobs (for managing subscriptions). When you registered an event subscription, you saw that an object was returned. This object is in fact a job object, with the same base class as the object you get back from `Start-Job` or the `-AsJob` parameter on `Invoke-Command`. Once an event subscription is created, it will show up in the `Job` table, which means that you can use the `Get-Job` cmdlet as another way to find this subscription. Let's go back to our timer event subscription (see 20.4.1) and see what this looks like:

```
PS (6) > Get-Job | Format-List

Module        : __DynamicModule_3fd88733-cbcb-4c0b-b489-1e1305782970
StatusMessage :
HasMoreData   : False
Location      :
Command       :  Write-Host "<TIMER>"
JobStateInfo  : NotStarted
Finished      : System.Threading.ManualResetEvent
InstanceId    : d3f41e39-776d-4fe8-9bd2-db82a7e1311c
```

```
Id          : 1
Name        : fca4b869-8d5a-4f11-8d45-e84af30845f1
ChildJobs   : {}
Output      : {}
Error       : {}
Progress    : {}
Verbose     : {}
Debug       : {}
Warning     : {}
State       : NotStarted
```

Let's start the timer running again, setting the interval to something large so you can still type:

```
PS (21) > $timer.Interval = 60000
PS (22) > $timer.Start()
```

Now when you run `Get-Job`

```
PS (29) > Get-Job | Format-Table State,Command -AutoSize

  State Command
  ----- -------
Running  Write-Host "<TIMER>"
```

you see that the job state has been changed to `Running`. The other thing you should be able to do if it's a `Job` is to stop it by calling `Stop-Job`. Let's try it:

```
PS (33) > Stop-Job
PS (33) > Get-Job | Format-Table State,Command -AutoSize

  State Command
  ----- -------
Stopped  Write-Host "<TIMER>"
```

It works. But this code has done more than just stop the job—it's also removed the event subscription:

```
PS (35) > Get-EventSubscriber
PS (36) >
```

Because event handlers are effectively running in the background, it seems logical to manage an active subscription as a `Job`. You should note that, although the executing event handler is represented as a `Job`, it wasn't started using `Start-Job` and, unlike PowerShell jobs, still runs in process with the session that set up the subscription.

At the beginning of our discussion on events, we talked about the issues involved in dealing with asynchronous events. Because these events can occur in any order, great care is required to make sure that the integrity of shared data structures is maintained. To maintain this integrity, you have to make sure that programs synchronize access to the shared objects, and doing so turns out to be difficult. In fact, this is one of the most common reasons that a program stops responding and appears to be hung. If two actions are trying to update a synchronized object at the same time, they can end up blocking each other, each trying to get exclusive access to the resource. This type of contention is called a *deadlock*.

PowerShell deals with this problem by imposing a strict order on the actions instead of on individual data objects. When an asynchronous event occurs, the eventing subsystem adds that event object to the event queue. Then, at various points in the PowerShell runtime, the engine checks to see if there are any events posted to the event queue. If there are, the engine suspends the mainline activity, pulls an event off the queue, switches to the module context for that event handler, and then executes the event scriptblock. Going back to the lecture analogy I used at the beginning of the chapter, this operates like an online "Live Meeting" where the participants use instant messaging to submit their questions. These questions get added to the queue without interrupting the speaker. The audience can message at any time, but the speaker will only address a question when it's a suitable time to do so. This queuing mechanism is illustrated in figure 20.8.

Events are added to the queue as they arrive and then are pulled off the queue by the engine and processed when a convenient spot is reached.

To make sure events get processed in a timely manner, the engine needs to check the queue fairly often. On the other hand, if it checks too often, it would substantially slow down the interpreter. As implemented in PowerShell v2, the engine checks for events in all calls that write objects, including between each stage in a pipeline. It also checks between each statement in a script and anywhere the engine might loop

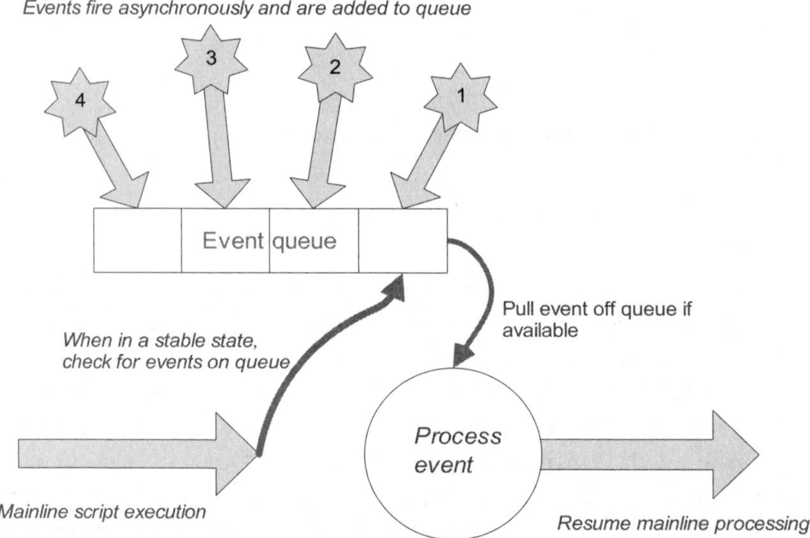

Figure 20.8 How asynchronous event processing is handled in PowerShell. As events occur, they are added to the queue asynchronously. At various stable points, the engine checks the queue and pulls events off to execute. Once the event execution is complete, normal processing resumes.

for a long time. This provides a good tradeoff between event latency and overall performance. In the case where there are multiple events pending on the queue at the time of the check, the engine will use a throttling policy to decide how many of the pending events will be processed before returning to the mainline so that the foreground activity isn't "starved." (As an aside, the places where the event queue is checked are the same places that the engine checks to see if it has been requested to stop executing, such as when the user presses Ctrl-C.)

If the event has an action block associated with it, that scriptblock executes until it's completed. Once the event action is finished, the mainline activity is resumed. Because the engine only processes events when it knows that the system state is stable, problems related to inconsistent system state don't arise and all activity is effectively synchronous.

> **NOTE** An event action runs until it's complete. As long as it's running, no other events are processed and the mainline activity is suspended. This means that event handlers shouldn't be written to execute for a long time. The same consideration exists when writing GUIs. If a control's event handler runs on the UI thread for a long time, the UI will be blocked, unable to respond to events, causing it to appear to hang.

This architecture isn't as efficient as the more fine-grained techniques so it's not appropriate for programs that are very performance sensitive. It is however simple, effective, and completely sufficient for PowerShell scripting. It makes asynchronous event handling in PowerShell a reasonable, if somewhat advanced, proposition.

This completes our coverage of eventing. We started with the basic synchronous event handling mechanisms carried over from PowerShell v1. Then we moved on to asynchronous processing, introducing the eventing cmdlets. We looked at a couple of different event sources and how you can use them. You saw how eventing and remoting work together and explored how the eventing infrastructure works.

20.11 SUMMARY

In this chapter, we introduced an advanced but useful topic: *eventing.* This feature allows you to write scripts that can respond to real-world events in a timely manner.

The chapter began by introducing key concepts used in eventing and described how event-driven scripts operate with the "don't-call-me-I'll-call-you" principle. We explored the idea that there are two fundamental event types: *synchronous* and *asynchronous.*

In synchronous events, all activities are synchronized so that no activity is ever interrupted. This model has been used all along in PowerShell for things like the `ForEach-Object` and `Where-Object` cmdlets and in the kind of GUI scripting you saw in section 17.3. Digging further into synchronous events, we looked at how

.NET represents events using the System.Delegate type. We also looked at a subclass of System.Delegate: the System.EventHandler type. In PowerShell v1, only the System.EventHandler type was directly supported by PowerShell.

In section 20.3, we introduced asynchronous events, which execute in a nondeterministic order. To deal with these asynchronous events, PowerShell includes an *eventing subsystem* that takes care of synchronizing all operations. The core model for eventing in PowerShell is built around the idea of *event subscriptions*. There are three cmdlets for creating these subscriptions: Get-ObjectEvent, Get-WmiEvent, and Get-EngineEvent for .NET, WMI, and PowerShell engine events respectively.

As part of the event subscription, an *action scriptblock* may be specified that will be executed when the event is triggered. Context information for the event is made available to the scriptblock through the $Event automatic variable. Some of the properties on the object in $Event are also directly available through additional automatic variables (see table 20.2).

Events may also be processed by calling Wait-Event to block for an event and then process them as they arrive. Event subscripts can be listed with Get-EventSubscription and unregistered using Unregister-Event.

Handling events that come from .NET objects involves setting up an event subscription on the event member of the class or object of interest. For WMI events, a small number of events may be subscribed to by using specific WMI classes, but creating arbitrary event subscriptions requires the use of the eventing extensions to the WMI Query Language. As opposed to normal instance queries (section 19.2.2), event queries require the use of the WITHIN keyword to specify the polling interval for the event being monitored. Queries are written using the intrinsic event classes (such as __InstanceModified) to specify the event to subscribe to. Because the intrinsic events apply to a large number of classes, the WHERE clause should be used to select a specific target class by doing something like:

```
Where TargetInstance Isa 'Win32_Service'
```

Additional instance filter criteria can also be specified in the WHERE clause if needed.

To *aggregate* or group together related sets of WMI events, the GROUP keyword can be added to the query. By grouping events, you reduce the network and processing overhead on the client that would be incurred if each event was sent individually. This can be important when writing a scalable application.

The final event source was engine events. These are PowerShell-specific events that are subscribed to by name using the Register-EngineEvent cmdlet with the -SourceIdentifier parameter. Engine events may be generated by the PowerShell engine itself (though only one event is currently defined: Engine.Exiting). Scripts can also generate their own engine events with the New-Event cmdlet. Finally, *event forwarding* allows remote event subscriptions to act as a source of engine events. When using PowerShell remoting, an event subscription can be created on a remote computer, which, instead of executing a taking local action, *forwards* the events over the remoting connection to the client for processing. The source identifier defined for the event on the remote computer becomes a subscribable engine event on the client side.

Wrapping things up, in this chapter we introduced some advanced features that have traditionally only been used by programmers. The PowerShell eventing subsystem makes these powerful techniques accessible to the nonprogrammer and IT professional as well. Mastering these features gives you the ability to create more responsive, efficient, and reliable scripts.

And now, in the last chapter of this book, we're going to shift from doing things to *not* doing things, or more specifically, to keeping *unauthorized* users from doing things to our systems. Chapter 21 looks at security, the role PowerShell plays in securing a computing environment, and the security features included in PowerShell. With an environment as powerful as PowerShell, a good understanding of the security topics involving PowerShell is critical. Remember: security is only boring until you've been hacked.

CHAPTER 21

Security, security, security

Oh brave new world, that has such people in it!

—Miranda in William Shakespeare's *The Tempest*

In this chapter, we'll explore the topics of security and secure programming to see how they impact PowerShell. In contrast to the previous chapters where our focus has been on what people can *do* with PowerShell, with security our focus is on how to *prevent* people (or at least the wrong people) from doing things. This switch is radical but it's the essence of security.

We'll begin the chapter by introducing security-modeling concepts, and then look at the security features in PowerShell. We'll also show you how to write secure scripts in PowerShell. Boring, you say. Do you need to know this stuff? Yes, you do. In a connected world, security is incredibly important. A small mistake can have huge consequences. People will talk about a "zone of influence"—the idea that something that happens far away can't impact you. This idea is meaningless in a connected world. Anyone, anywhere can attack your system just as if they were next door. You also have to consider cascading consequences: a useful script that someone posts on her blog may get copied thousands of times. If there's a security flaw in that script, it will propagate along with the script, get copied into new scripts, and so on. A small flaw in the original script may be replicated around the world. Now that we're all appropriately terrified, let us proceed.

When discussing security and PowerShell, there's only one thing you should keep in mind: PowerShell executes code. That's what it does—that's all it does. As a consequence, you need to consider how having PowerShell on your system might introduce security risks. Of course, this isn't specific to PowerShell. It's true of anything that runs code—Perl, Python, even `cmd.exe`. Making sure that a system with PowerShell installed is secure is the topic of the first part of this chapter. Once you have PowerShell installed, you're going to want to write, deploy, and execute scripts. The latter portion of the chapter covers some approaches to writing secure PowerShell scripts.

21.1 INTRODUCTION TO SECURITY

We'll begin our security discussion with some basic definitions. In this section, we'll look at what security is and what that means. We'll also talk about what it isn't, which can be just as important.

21.1.1 What security is and what it isn't

Computer security is the field devoted to the creation of techniques and technologies that allow computers to be used in a secure manner. Obvious perhaps, but there are two parts to the story. Secure means that the computer is protected against external danger or loss of valuables (financial, personal, or otherwise). The flip side is that the system has to remain useful. (There's a joke in the security industry that the only way to make a computer completely secure is to turn it off, disconnect all the cables, seal it in concrete, and dump it into the middle of the ocean. This makes for a very *secure* computer, but it's not a very *useful* one.)

In approaching security, you must balance security requirements with utility. If the techniques needed to secure a system are too hard to use, users won't use them, and the system will be unsecured. If they interfere with the basic tasks that need to be performed, they'll be disabled or bypassed and the system will be unsecured. Are you getting the picture?

Now let's look at what security isn't. Security isn't just cryptography. This fact is oddly surprising to many people. Security uses cryptography—it's one of the main tools used to secure an environment. They are, however, separate fields. The corollary is that unless you're a cryptographer, you shouldn't write your own cryptography code. It's very hard. And even the experts don't always get it right. Even if it's right today, it may be wrong tomorrow.

> **NOTE** An example of this is the MD5 hash algorithm, which had been considered the gold standard for secure hashes for a long time before it was found to be vulnerable.

The PowerShell environment, through .NET and the Windows platform, has access to a variety of cryptographic tools for building secure systems. You should use these tools instead of trying to roll your own. We'll spend a considerable amount of time on some of these tools later in this chapter.

21.1.2 Security: perception and reality

One last thing: Regardless of what computer security is or isn't, sometimes it's the *perception* of security that matters most. Let's take a look at a couple of stories that illustrate this.

The Danom virus

As we've discussed, PowerShell can be used to write scripts. It can be used to create, copy, and modify files. This means that, like any scripting or programming language, it can be used to write viruses, worms, and other malware.

> **NOTE** The term *malware* is short for malicious software and is used to generally describe all forms of software (spyware, viruses, and so on) designed to cause damage in a computing environment. This may be the only definition in the security vocabulary that everybody agrees on. Or maybe not.

The fact that PowerShell could be used for this purpose didn't go unnoticed in the malware community. In August 2005, a virus author created a proof-of-concept virus called Danom (Monad backwards). This virus script was essentially a port of existing virus code to the PowerShell language. The same virus code had previously been written in a variety of other scripting languages. It didn't take advantage of any vulnerability in either the operating system or the language interpreter. It required explicit and significant user action to execute the virus code. In fact, all it did was demonstrate that PowerShell was a decent scripting language. There wasn't even a delivery vehicle. In other words, there was no way to distribute the malicious code. And with no mechanism to distribute the virus code, the threat was purely hypothetical.

This coding exercise was noticed by a security researcher, who then issued a bulletin about it. This bulletin was picked up, first by the blogs and later by members of the popular press, without investigating the details of the situation.

Because of the work that was going on with the next generation of Windows at the time (the rather ill-fated Vista release), the press called this the first Vista virus. The Microsoft security response team members responded by saying that it wasn't a Vista virus because PowerShell wasn't in the official list of features for Vista at that time. The press immediately turned this into "PowerShell cancelled due to virus threat." None of this was true, of course, but it made a good headline and lots of people, even inside Microsoft, believed the story.

Out of all of this, one thing that was gratifying was how the community responded to all this coverage. They reviewed the virus code and the security measures that the PowerShell team had designed into the product and saw that Danom presented no significant threat. With the help of the community and some aggressive blogging, the tide was turned and people realized that there was no threat. All returned to normal, at least for a while.

The MSH/Cibyz worm

Almost exactly one year later, in August 2006, the MSH/Cibyz worm was released. This was essentially the Danom code with some updates and bug fixes.

> **NOTE** Between the first and second releases, the malware dictionary had been revised, so the second time around, the same code was reclassified as a worm instead of a virus. It's like being at a ball game listening to the guy handing out today's program: "Programs! Programs! Get your programs! You can't tell a worm from a virus without a program!"

This time, there was a delivery vehicle using one of the peer-to-peer networks. The story was picked up by the blogging community initially, but eventually a large security software vendor issued a press release with an inflammatory title. The body of the release, essentially said, "There's nothing to see here. These aren't the droids you're looking for. Please move along." But it still generated discussion and rumors for about a week.

The moral of the story is that it pays to investigate security alerts rather than just react to headlines. Without being properly informed, it's impossible to plan appropriate action, and planning is the key to establishing a secure environment. Because one of the best tools for planning is security modeling, we'll spend the next couple of sections discussing these techniques.

21.2 SECURITY MODELING

In this section, we'll briefly review some of the theories and concepts that have been developed to help build secure systems. We'll review the concepts of threats, vulnerabilities, and attacks. We'll also cover the basics of threat modeling and why it's important. Note that this topic is an active and rapidly changing area of research. Theories and approaches are postulated, applied, and refuted over very short periods of time. The theoretical material we present in this section may even be obsolete by the time you read this book. Still, having an awareness of the approaches that are being developed for building secure systems is always beneficial.

21.2.1 Introduction to threat modeling

Threat modeling is a systematic approach to identifying and categorizing threats to a system. So what does that mean? A model is a simplified representation of a system with unnecessary or unimportant details left out. By building a model, you can focus on the details that matter and ignore the ones that don't. Modern computer systems are too complex to address every detail. You have to focus your attention on what matters most.

Let's look at some more definitions. A *threat* to a system is a potential event that will have unpleasant or undesirable consequences. A *vulnerability* is a weakness in the design or implementation of a system that an attacker may exploit to cause one of these undesirable events. An *attack* is when someone takes advantage of these vulnerabilities to gain some advantage that they aren't otherwise permitted to have.

Back to modeling. The point of a model is to have a formal approach for looking at threats and vulnerabilities with the idea of defeating attacks. This is important because you can quite literally spend the rest of eternity trying to guard a system against things that don't matter. If you don't have a way of focusing your efforts, the result will be a solution that will be useless at best.

21.2.2 Classifying threats using the STRIDE model

STRIDE is a well-known threat classification model. STRIDE is an acronym for Spoofing, Tampering, Repudiation, Information Disclosure, Denial of Service, and Elevation of Privilege. It's a way to categorize all the significant threats to a system. Remember—a threat is something the attacker wants to happen, which means it's something you don't want. The idea is that if you model all of the STRIDE threat classifications, you have a decent chance of covering the most important areas. Table 21.1 explains each of the components of STRIDE.

Table 21.1 The threat classifications in the STRIDE model

Threat classification	Explanation
Spoofing identity	Spoofing refers to various ways of assuming the identity of another user for the duration of a task.
Tampering with data	Tampering means changing data. Note that this doesn't imply information disclosure—simple corruption may be all that's achieved.
Repudiation	From an attacker's perspective, repudiation essentially means covering your tracks. A particular act can't be traced or attributed to the source of the act.
Information disclosure	Information disclosure is allowing unauthorized persons access to sensitive information such as credit card numbers and passwords.
Denial of service	A denial-of-service (DoS) attack involves some form of resource exhaustion. It could be network bandwidth, CPU cycles, or disk space. The problem with DoS attacks is that they're easy to launch anonymously and sometimes it's difficult to tell if it's actually an attack or that $2.99 special that you just announced on your website that's causing a sudden burst of network traffic.
Elevation of privilege	In elevation of privilege attacks, an unprivileged user or process gains privileged access.

For more information on STRIDE, see *Writing Secure Code, Second Edition*, by Michael Howard and David LeBlanc (Microsoft Press, 2004).

Now that you have a system for understanding and classifying threats, let's look at the remaining pieces you need to build the threat model.

21.2.3 Security basics: threats, assets, and mitigations

There are three parts to building a security model: threats, assets, and mitigations. We talked about threats in the previous section. Assets are things that motivate the attacker to launch an attack. These assets may be things that are of direct value, such as credit card numbers or other financial information. They may also be of indirect value, such as code execution. This is an asset because once you have the ability to execute code on a machine, you can use these resources to do things such as send spam or execute distributed DoS attacks against other targets.

Mitigation is what you're doing to mitigate those threats. The standard definition of mitigation is to cause something to become less harsh or severe. I use this term instead of *prevent* because it may well be that the activity you're mitigating is necessary; for example, the ability to execute code in PowerShell can't be prevented, because that's its purpose. But you want to allow only authorized users to be able to execute approved scripts. The threat of unauthorized script execution is mitigated through a variety of approaches we'll describe later in this chapter. Let's look at a few things you should keep in mind when securing a system.

Avoid lawn gnome mitigation

There's a tendency, when trying to mitigate problems or otherwise reduce the attack surface of a system, to focus on reducing attacks in a particular area instead of looking at the system as a whole. This approach can add complexity to the system without increasing security. This approach is known as *lawn gnome mitigation*. The story goes like this. You hire a security consultant to secure your home. He drives up to your house, parks, gets out, and stands on the sidewalk looking at the house. After a while, he says that he sees where the vulnerability lies. He goes to the trunk of his car, takes out a ceramic lawn gnome (as illustrated in figure 21.1), and places it on the lawn between himself and the front door of the house. "I've mitigated the threat," he says. "That will be $2,000 please."

Figure 21.1 A brave and noble lawn gnome protecting a home in Kitchener, Ontario, Canada. Hopefully it didn't cost the owner $2,000.

Has your high-priced security consultant mitigated a threat? As a matter of fact, he has. A burglar trying to break into the house, who crosses the lawn at that exact spot, will now trip over a lawn gnome. Of course, the burglar could go around it, or come at the house from a different direction. In fact, your house isn't any safer, and you have an ugly ceramic statue in the middle of your lawn that you have to mow around.

> **NOTE** There's a variation of this approach that's considered legitimate, sometimes called "picket-fence" mitigation. A picket fence has holes in it, so you put another one behind it. And if there are still holes then you keep adding fences until there are no more holes. This is equivalent to dumping truckloads of lawn gnomes on your property until the house is surrounded by a 30-foot-high wall of ceramic gnomes. It'll work, but it's not very attractive.

The moral of this story is that, when securing a system, don't add unnecessary or inappropriate checks. You have to look at the system as a whole. This is particularly true when writing code. The more lawn gnomes you add, the more code you add to the system. Each new line of code introduces new possibilities for errors, and these errors can, in turn, become additional vulnerabilities.

Blacklisting/whitelisting

Short and sweet—blacklisting is saying who's bad and whitelisting is saying who's good. In general, whitelisting is preferred. Assume that the world is bad and you only trust people you know. This method is inherently the most secure approach to use with PowerShell. The number of people you trust to give you scripts to run is much smaller than the number of people you don't trust to run scripts. PowerShell supports the use of script signing to verify the identity of a script publisher and also validate the integrity of a published script. (Signing is discussed at length in section 21.4.)

Whitelisting is also an approach that should be used when constructing constrained remoting sessions, as discussed in chapter 13, section 13.2.5. A constrained session should only expose the commands that are needed and all others should be marked private by default.

Authentication, authorization, and roles

Authentication is verifying the identity of the user. *Authorization* is determining whether the user is authorized to perform an action. *Roles* are groupings of activities for which authorization can be granted. Grouping multiple activities into a role makes it easier to manage authorization. When users are assigned a particular role, they're automatically authorized to perform all the activities associated with that role. PowerShell depends on the operating system for authentication and authorization (see section 13.1.4). For role-based access control (RBAC) in PowerShell v2, through remoting and constrained sessions it's possible to implement role-based mechanisms, though there are some significant limitations. A PowerShell script operates with the capabilities associated with the security token of the user who's running the script. This means that the remoting mechanism can't grant the user any more privileges than they'd normally have. It can only restrict the set of operations they can perform.

Input validation

The rule is that you must validate any input received from outside your script. In scripting, this is the second most important rule for writing secure scripts. (The most important rule is "Don't run unknown or untrusted scripts.")

Most scripting environments have the ability to dynamically compile and execute code (this is one of the things that makes them dynamic languages). It's tempting to use this capability to simplify your code. Say the user needs to do some arithmetic calculations in a script. In PowerShell, you could just pass this code directly to the `Invoke-Expression` cmdlet and let it evaluate the expression:

```
PS (1) > $userInput = "2+2"
```

Now use `Invoke-Expression` to execute the command:

```
PS (2) > Invoke-Expression $userInput
4
```

Wasn't that easy? But what if the user types the following?

```
PS (3) > $userInput = "2+2; 'Hi there'"
PS (4) > Invoke-Expression $userInput
4
Hi there
```

It still executed the calculation, but it also executed the code after the semicolon. In this example, it was a harmless statement. But it might have been something like

```
$userInput = "2+2; del -rec -force c:\"
```

If this statement were executed, it'd try to delete everything on your C: drive…which would be bad.

There are other places where you need to do input validation. If the user is supplying a path, you should make sure that it's a path that the user should have access to. For example:

```
$userInput = "mydata.txt"
Get-Content $userInput
```

This fragment of script will return the contents of the file mydata.txt from the current directory. This is what the script author intended. But because the script isn't doing any path checking, the user could have specified a path like

```
$userInput = "..\bob_dobbs\mydata.txt"
```

in which case they might get the contents of another user's file. Suppose instead, the script were written as

```
PS (1) > $userinput = "..\bob_dobbs\mydata.txt"
PS (2) > $safePath = Join-Path . `
```

```
>> (Split-Path -Leaf $userInput)
>>
PS (3) > $safePath
.\mydata.txt
```

Then, despite providing a relative path, users can still only get their own data. Alternatively, you may wish to generate an error message explaining that it's an invalid filename:

```
PS (5) > if (Split-Path -Parent $userInput) {
>> "Invalid file name: $userInput"
>> }
>>
Invalid file name: ..\bob_dobbs\mydata.txt
```

But you need to be careful with this; you may inadvertently leak information about the system through the error message.

> **NOTE** People sometimes find it hard to understand why this is an issue. Let's look at an example. Say you're logging into a system. If you enter a username and password and the system responds with "invalid account" if the username is wrong and "invalid password" if the password is wrong, the attacker now has a way of finding out whether an account name is valid. In a sense, they've won half the battle.

You need to balance being friendly to the user with maintaining a secure system. So even in quite simple systems, it's tricky to get this kind of thing right.

Code injection

Code injection is closely related to the input validation. In fact, the first couple of examples that we looked at in the input validation section are code injection attacks. When you're writing PowerShell code, any use of `Invoke-Expression` is suspect. There are usually other ways of doing the same thing that don't require using `Invoke-Expression`. But there are other ways of injecting code into a PowerShell session. Scripts are the most obvious one. Every time a script is called, the script is loaded, parsed, and executed. Not only must you not execute scripts from unknown sources, you must make sure that no one can tamper with your own scripts. In the next section, we'll go over the features in PowerShell for doing exactly that.

Because PowerShell exists in mixed-language environments, you also need to be careful with other types of code injection attacks. The most common example is SQL injection attacks. This is the classic attack in the web application world. The basic attack mechanism is the same—nonvalidated user input is used to construct a SQL query. This query is then passed to the database and bad things happen. The query is being executed on behalf of the user, so there may be an information disclosure attack. The query may delete data from the database, in which case you're looking at a DoS attack.

Even more common in the PowerShell environment is the use of languages such as VBScript and/or `cmd.exe` batch scripts. All these file types represent opportunities for code injection.

At this point, we've covered the basic principles for creating a secure computing environment. Let's take a look at the features in PowerShell that were designed to support these principles.

21.3 SECURING THE POWERSHELL ENVIRONMENT

The whole point of PowerShell is to execute scripts that automate system management tasks. As a consequence, there's no such thing as an inherently safe PowerShell script. PowerShell has no concept of sandboxing; that is, executing in a safe restricted environment. You must treat all PowerShell scripts as if they were executables. Because of this, when PowerShell is installed, it does a number of things to be secure by default. In this section, we'll go over these features.

21.3.1 Secure by default

First, we'll go over the elements of the PowerShell installation process that are intended to meet the requirement that it be secure by default. Secure by default means that simply installing PowerShell on a system shouldn't introduce any security issues.

Notepad, the default file association for PowerShell

File association is the way Windows figures out what application to launch as the default handler for files having a particular extension. For many scripting languages, the default association launches the interpreter for that language. This has led to many virus outbreaks. With PowerShell, the default file association for the .ps1 extension launches an editor: `notepad.exe` in version 1 and `powershell_ise.exe` in version 2. This means that if an attacker does manage to get a script onto your computer and you accidentally double-click on this script, instead of executing the script it will open in Notepad, at which point you can review the hacker's code, or just delete the script.

Remoting is disabled by default

PowerShell remoting is disabled by default. Explicit action by a privileged user is required to enable remoting, and even after it has been enabled, the default remoting configurations are set up so that only members of the local Administrators group can access the configuration.

No execution of scripts by default

PowerShell is installed in such a way that it won't run scripts by default and can only be used as an interactive command interpreter.

Before scripts can be run, the user has to take explicit action to change the execution policy for PowerShell to allow script execution. In the default configuration, the only way to execute code is if the user manually starts PowerShell and types commands in at the prompt.

So PowerShell is secure by default because it doesn't do much of anything. Now let's see how to make it useful by enabling script execution. But before you do that, you should know where the scripts we're running are coming from. Like most shells, PowerShell uses the `$ENV:PATH` environment variable to find commands. The use of this variable has security implications, so we'll review those first before we talk about how to enable scripting.

Managing the command path

A common local attack vector involves the `$ENV:PATH` and `$ENV:PATHEXT` environment variables. These variables control where commands are found and which files are considered to be executable. The `$ENV:PATHEXT` variable lists the extensions of all of the file types that PowerShell will try to execute directly through the `CreateProcess()` API. The `$ENV:PATH` variable controls what directories PowerShell will look in when it searches for external commands. If an attacker can compromise these variables or any of the files or directories that they reference, the attacker can use a "Trojan Horse" attack—making something dangerous appear harmless.

> **NOTE** Okay, who thinks a 20-foot-high wooden horse looks harmless? If you saw a 20-foot wooden horse appear in your driveway, would you say "Oh, look dear, let's bring this giant wooden horse that we've never seen before into our house. Perhaps it will be our pet. I've always wanted a giant wooden horse as a pet! What could possibly go wrong?"

The most important mitigation for this type of attack is to not include the current directory in your command search path. This is the default behavior in PowerShell. Omitting the current directory in your search path guards against the situation where you `cd` into an untrusted user's directory and then execute what you think is a trusted system command such as `ipconfig`. If you execute commands out of the current directory and the user had placed a Trojan `ipconfig` command in this directory, their command would execute with all the privileges you have as a user. Not a good thing. In general, it's best to leave the current path out of `$ENV:PATH`.

There's one other thing you should consider in this situation. The `cmd.exe` interpreter does execute out of the current directory, so if you run a `cmd` script from PowerShell in an untrusted directory, there's a risk that the batch file could be compromised by Trojan programs.

21.3.2 Enabling scripting with execution policy

When PowerShell is installed, script execution is disabled by default. Script execution is controlled by the PowerShell *execution policy* setting. It's important to understand what the execution policy is intended to do. It isn't intended to prevent people from using PowerShell—even in restricted mode it's still possible to use PowerShell interactively. The goal of the execution policy mechanism is to reduce the ways that PowerShell can be exploited by an attacker, allowing a user to operate more securely. It does so by preventing unintended execution of unknown and potentially malicious scripts. We'll look at the various modes you can set execution policy to in the next section.

NOTE When reviewing this chapter, I stumbled across a question on a technical help site. The poster was asking for help converting a PowerShell script to VBScript. This was being done for "security reasons." When someone asked what the security issue was, the poster responded that they felt that it was necessary to keep their execution policy set to a very restrictive mode for fear of remote code execution attacks. The perception was that VBScript was somehow safer because it *couldn't be restricted.* In essence, because there was a knob for PowerShell but not VBScript, VBScript had to be less dangerous. Although there might be a grain of truth to this (VBScript has been around longer so, in theory, the ecosystem is more attuned to its potential security issues) in practice, they're pretty much equally dangerous. PowerShell is just less easy to exploit by default.

Choosing an execution policy setting

PowerShell v1 defined four execution policies: `Restricted`, `AllSigned`, `RemoteSigned`, and `Unrestricted`. PowerShell v2 introduced two new policy settings: `Bypass` and `Undefined`. The details of these policies are shown in table 21.2.

Table 21.2 Descriptions of the various execution policies

Policy	Description
`Restricted`	This is the default execution policy upon installation. When this policy is in effect, script execution is disabled. This includes script modules, profile files and types, and format files. PowerShell itself isn't disabled and may still be used as an interactive command interpreter. Although this is the most secure policy, it severely impacts your ability to use PowerShell for automation.
`AllSigned`	When the execution policy is `AllSigned`, scripts can be executed but they must be Authenticode-signed before they'll run. When running a signed script, you'll be asked if you want to trust the signer of the script. Section 21.4 covers the details of script signing. `AllSigned` is still a secure policy setting, but it makes script development difficult. In an environment where scripts will be deployed rather than created, this is the best policy.
`RemoteSigned`	`RemoteSigned` requires that all scripts that are downloaded from a remote location be Authenticode-signed before they can be executed. Note that this depends on whether the application doing the download marks the script as coming from a remote location. Not all applications do this. Anything downloaded by Internet Explorer 6.0 or above, Outlook, or Outlook Express will be properly marked. `RemoteSigned` is the minimum recommended execution policy setting. It's the best policy setting for script development.

Table 21.2 **Descriptions of the various execution policies *(continued)***

Policy	Description
`Unrestricted`	When the execution policy is `Unrestricted`, PowerShell will run any script. It will still prompt the user when it encounters a script that has been downloaded. `Unrestricted` is the least secure setting. We don't recommend that you use this setting, but it may be necessary in some developer scenarios where `RemoteSigned` is still too restrictive.
`Bypass` (v2 only)	Nothing is blocked and there are no warnings or prompts. This execution policy is designed for configurations in which PowerShell scripts are part of a larger application that has its own security model. The Windows Diagnostics feature in Windows 7 is a good example of this type of application.
`Undefined` (v2 only)	Removes the currently assigned execution policy from the current scope. This parameter won't remove an execution policy that's set in a Group Policy scope (User scope or Machine scope).

In version 1, execution policy could only be controlled by a Registry key, which was set using the `Set-ExecutionPolicy` cmdlet. This approach had two major problems. First, setting this key required elevated privileges, making it awkward for non-admin users. Second, this single Registry key was much too broadly scoped for many scenarios. In the next section, we'll look at how these problems were addressed in version 2.

Controlling and scoping execution policy

In this section, we'll look at how execution policy is set and scoped. By scope, we mean the set of users and processes that are affected by a particular setting.

In PowerShell v1, setting the execution policy required changing Registry keys and this in turn meant that the operation required administrator privileges. Because the settings were always done in the Registry, they were persistent and affected all instances of PowerShell. Version 2 changed this practice in a couple of ways. First, the `Set-ExecutionPolicy` cmdlet was enhanced to have some additional scope

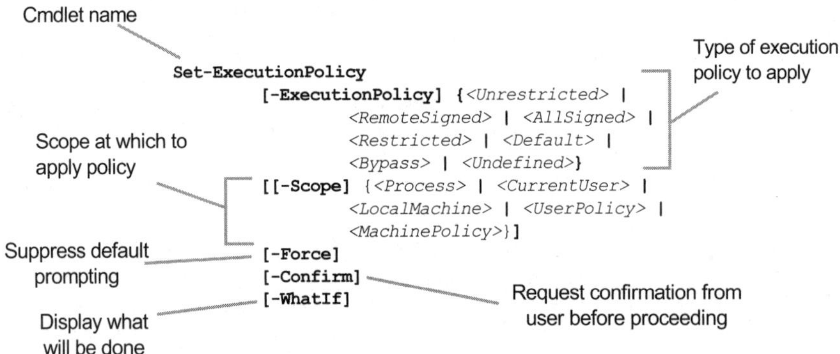

Figure 21.2 The `Set-ExecutionPolicy` cmdlet parameters. This cmdlet allows you to control what scripts can be run using scoped policy settings.

settings. The syntax for the PowerShell v2 `Set-ExecutionPolicy` cmdlet is shown in figure 21.2.

Table 21.3 lists the scopes and their meanings. The major change is the addition of a process-level execution policy scope.

Table 21.3 PowerShell execution policy scope settings

Setting	Description	Version
MachinePolicy	Group policy setting for the machine.	v1 and v2
UserPolicy	Group policy setting for the user.	v1 and v2
LocalMachine	This policy setting applies to all users on the system.	v1 and v2
LocalUser	The policy setting only applies to the current user. Other users on this machine aren't affected.	v1 and v2
Process	The policy setting only applies to the current process and will be discarded when the process exits. In this case, the execution policy is saved in the `PSExecutionPolicyPreference` environment variable (`$ENV:PSExecutionPolicyPreference`) instead of in the Registry.	v2 only

PowerShell examines these settings in the following order, where the first policy setting found is applied:

1 The Group Policy setting for the machine level or Computer Configuration, which applies to all users of this machine
2 The Group Policy setting for the user level or User Configuration, which applies to all users, independent of the computer they're using in a domain environment
3 The process-level policy
4 The execution policy for a user as specified in the Registry settings for that user
5 The execution policy for the machine as specified in the machine Registry

This policy processing order means the Group Policy settings override the process-level policy, which overrides the user-level policy, with the local machine policy being last. Be aware that on x64 systems there are policy settings in the Registry for both 64- and 32-bit versions of PowerShell.

Because the process-level policy is transient (it only lasts until the process exists), you need a way to set it for a process. This brings us to another important improvement: the addition of the `-ExecutionPolicy` parameter to `powershell.exe`. This parameter allows the user to run PowerShell with different policies without requiring a persistent change to a Registry setting. It also means that you can establish a shortcut to run a script even when the machine policy is set to, for example, Restricted. The following example shows how to start the shell in `Bypass` mode:

```
powershell.exe -ExecutionPolicy bypass
```

It's also possible to change the execution policy setting for a process that's already running by using the Set-ExecutionPolicy cmdlet within that process. For example, you can get the current execution policy setting using Get-ExecutionPolicy:

```
PS (1) > Get-ExecutionPolicy
RemoteSigned
```

Here you see that the policy is set to RemoteSigned. Now run the command to change it to Bypass. As was the case when you enabled PowerShell remoting in section 12.1.3, you're prompted to confirm making this change because the change has security implications:

```
PS (2) > Set-ExecutionPolicy -Scope Process -ExecutionPolicy
 Bypass

Execution Policy Change
The execution policy helps protect you from scripts that
you do not trust. Changing the execution policy might
expose you to the security risks described in the
about_Execution_Policies help topic. Do you want to change
the execution policy?
[Y] Yes  [N] No  [S] Suspend  [?] Help (default is "Y"): y
```

You respond with Y and then verify that the policy has changed:

```
PS (3) > Get-ExecutionPolicy
Bypass
```

If you want to suppress the prompt, as was the case with Enable-PSRemoting, you use the -Force switch:

```
PS (4) > Set-ExecutionPolicy -Scope process -ExecutionPolicy
 remotesigned -Force
```

And again, verify that the policy has been changed:

```
PS (5) > Get-ExecutionPolicy
RemoteSigned
PS (6) >
```

> **NOTE** This particular feature of execution policy allows you to work around a problem with implicit remoting (see section 12.4). Implicit remoting generates a temporary module to contain the command proxies it generates. This temporary module is then loaded; but modules, like scripts, are subject to the current execution policy setting. This means you can't use implicit remoting if the execution policy is set to Restricted or AllSigned, because you won't be able to load the temporary module. To work around this problem, you can set the process-local execution policy to something less restrictive, call Import-PSSession, and then restore the old policy. You can even create a proxy function for Import-PSSession that hides the details of this workaround.

The final way to set the execution policy for a process is by setting the `$env:PS-ExecutionPolicyPreference` environment. You'll examine the variable's value and then change it:

```
PS (6) > $ENV:PSExecutionPolicyPreference
RemoteSigned
PS (7) > $ENV:PSExecutionPolicyPreference = "allsigned"
```

To verify that the environment variable has affected the current process, you run `Get-ExecutionPolicy`:

```
PS (8) > Get-ExecutionPolicy
AllSigned
```

You can see that it has. Now let's start a new instance of `powershell.exe`:

```
PS (9) > powershell.exe Get-ExecutionPolicy
File C:\Users\brucepay\Documents\WindowsPowerShell\profile.
ps1 cannot be loaded. The file C:\Users\brucepay\Documents\
WindowsPowerShell\profile.ps1 isn't digitally signed. The
script will not execute on the system. Please see "get-help
 about_signing" for more details..
At line:1 char:2
+ . <<<<  'C:\Users\brucepay\Documents\WindowsPowerShell\pr
ofile.ps1'
    + CategoryInfo          : NotSpecified: (:) [], PSSecu
   rityException
    + FullyQualifiedErrorId : RuntimeException

AllSigned
```

Because environment variables are automatically inherited by the child process, you see an error saying that the profile couldn't be run because the execution policy isn't All-Signed, which is confirmed by the output from the `Get-ExecutionPolicy` command.

> **NOTE** When Microsoft introduced these changes, some people were concerned that they had weakened the security model for PowerShell because now users could override the execution policy setting in the Registry. But remember that this feature isn't intended to prevent a user from doing something bad *deliberately*. (If they wanted to run a script, they could read the script file into a variable and use `Invoke-Expression`.) Its purpose is to help the user avoid making mistakes and running malicious script code *accidentally*. This is similar to the User Access Control (UAC) feature. In both cases, the user is prompted to confirm actions that may have significant consequences. If you really feel the need to restrict access to PowerShell for a user, then something like `AppLocker` in Windows 7/Server 2008 R2 is much more appropriate.

A couple of the execution policy settings (`RemoteSigned` and `AllSigned`) depend on being able to sign your scripts. In the next section, we'll review the overall script-signing architecture in Windows and look at how to sign scripts in PowerShell.

21.4 SIGNING SCRIPTS

Signing a script is the process of adding extra information to a script file that identifies the publisher of the script in a secure way. By *secure way*, we mean that it's done in such a way that you can reliably and mechanically verify that:

- The script really was signed by the correct person
- The contents of the script haven't been changed in any way since it was signed

In the next section, we'll look at the basic technologies that are used to accomplish these goals.

21.4.1 How public key encryption and one-way hashing work

Script signing is accomplished using two technologies: public key encryption and one-way hashes. Public key encryption is important because it uses two keys: a private key for encrypting information and a second public key for decrypting the data encrypted with the private key. The other technology you need is a one-way hash function. This is a type of function where it's easy to calculate the output for any input but is very hard to recover the input if you have only the output. These hash functions also need to be collision resistant. In other words, it should be highly unlikely that two inputs produce the same output. Here's how these technologies are used to verify the authenticity and integrity of the script:

1. The script author (or publisher) calculates a one-way hash of the contents of the script using a secure hashing algorithm.
2. This hash is then encrypted with the publisher's private key and attached to the script in the form of a comment block.
3. The script is then delivered to the consumer who is going to run the script.
4. Before the script is run, PowerShell removes the signature block, and then calculates its own one-way hash of the document using the same algorithm as the publisher.
5. Using the publisher's public decryption key, PowerShell decrypts the hash contained in the signature comment block.
6. It compares the hash it calculated against the one that was recovered from the signature block. If they match, the script was created by the owner of the private key and hasn't been tampered with. If they don't match, the script is rejected. It's either not legitimately signed by the publisher or it has been tampered with.

There's one small thing that we've skipped in this discussion. How do you get the right public key to decrypt the signature in the first place? Calling up the publisher on the telephone every time you run the script isn't going to work. This is where signing authorities and certificates come in. First we'll look at the role of a signing authority in creating certificates. Then we'll talk about how you can create your own self-signed certificates. This is a two-stage process: first you create a local signing authority and then use that authority to issue a certificate.

21.4.2 Signing authorities and certificates

Making all of this signing stuff work requires a way of getting the public key associated with a signer's identity. This is done using the signing certificate. A certificate is a piece of data that uses a digital signature to bind together a public key and an identity. But wait! If it's signed then aren't you back where you started? Now you need to get a public key to verify who you should get the public key from. Yikes. Here's where signing authorities come in. These are well-known, trusted, third-party organizations from which authors can purchase signing certificates. When someone wants to be able to sign scripts, they contact a signing authority to purchase a certificate. The signing authority then verifies the identity of the party requesting the certificate. Once this is done, the signer receives the private key and can then start signing documents. Part of the signature includes the user's identity, which will be verified using the public key of the certificate that you look up at the signing authority. This is called the *chain of trust*.

All of this machinery is part of what's called a Public Key Infrastructure (PKI). There are a number of additional pieces necessary to make it all work. One of these pieces is the local certificate store. This store is used as a local cache for certificates. If you had to establish a network connection to the signing authority every time you wanted to do something, it wouldn't work very well. Also, you wouldn't be able to work when you weren't connected to a network. By caching the certificates locally, you can avoid these problems. (There are other intermediate tiers in the trust chain, and some other details such as expiry and revocation that we're not going to cover here because they are well documented elsewhere. MSDN has a good discussion of this material, for example.)

So do you need to contact a signing authority before you can safely run scripts? This is the topic of the next section on self-signed certificates.

21.4.3 Self-signed certificates

What does the average person do if you want to sign scripts but don't want to invest time and money getting a certificate from a signing authority? The answer is that you can use self-signed certificates. This certificate is one you create for yourself where the computer becomes the signing authority. Obtaining this type of certificate doesn't have the issues associated with a public signing authority. It's free and easy to get, but other computers won't trust your computer as a valid authority and so won't run scripts that you sign with this certificate.

> **NOTE** If you create a self-signed certificate, be sure to enable strong private-key protection on your certificate. Doing so will prevent other programs from signing scripts on your behalf. You'll see how to do this later in the chapter.

This approach sounds somewhat less than useful, but it allows you to control what scripts can be run on your computer. In the next section, we'll see how to create a self-signed certificate.

Creating a self-signed certificate

To create a self-signed certificate, we'll use the `MakeCert.exe` program. This utility is included as part of the Microsoft .NET Framework SDK and the Microsoft Platform SDK. These can be freely downloaded from Microsoft if you don't already have them. Even if they're installed on the computer, you may have to modify the setting of `$ENV:PATH` so it includes the directory that contains these commands. You can use `Get-Command` to see whether `MakeCert.exe` is installed and where it's located:

```
PS (1) > Get-Command makecert.exe | fl

Name             : makecert.exe
CommandType      : Application
Definition       : C:\Program Files\Microsoft Visual Studio 8\SDK
                   \v2.0\Bin\makecert.exe
Extension        : .exe
Path             : C:\Program Files\Microsoft Visual Studio 8\SDK
                   \v2.0\Bin\makecert.exe
FileVersionInfo : File:             C:\Program Files\Microsoft V
                   isual Studio 8\SDK\v2.0\Bin\makecert.exe
                   InternalName:     MAKECERT.EXE
                   OriginalFilename: MAKECERT.EXE
                   FileVersion:      5.131.3790.0 (srv03_rtm.0303
                   24-2048)
                   FileDescription:  ECM MakeCert
                   Product:          Microsoftr Windowsr Operatin
                   g System
                   ProductVersion:   5.131.3790.0
                   Debug:            False
                   Patched:          False
                   PreRelease:       False
                   PrivateBuild:     False
                   SpecialBuild:     False
                   Language:         English (United States)
```

You can see that it's installed in the Visual Studio SDK directory. (This doesn't mean you have to run out and buy Visual Studio, by the way. The free SDK is all you need.) This command is fairly complex with a lot of options. You're going to get set up for signing in two steps—creating a local certificate authority and using that authority to create a signing certificate.

Creating a local certificate authority

First, run the following command to create a local certificate authority for your computer:

```
PS (2) > makecert -n "CN=PowerShell Local Certificate Root" `
>> -a sha1 -eku 1.3.6.1.5.5.7.3.3 -r -sv root.pvk root.cer `
>> -ss Root -sr localMachine
```

Figure 21.3 What you see when you run `makecert` to create the self-signing authority

```
>>
Succeeded
```

When you run this command, a dialog box will appear, asking you to establish your identity by entering a password for this signing authority (see figure 21.3).

So what did this command actually do? You've instructed the command to create a self-signed certificate that will be used for code-signing purposes. You want this certificate placed in the root certificate store on the local machine. You've also said that you want to use SHA-1 (Secure Hash Algorithm, version 1) for hashing files. Table 21.4 has further explanation for each of the parameters you specified to the command.

Table 21.4 `MakeCert` parameters used to create a self-signing authority

`MakeCert` parameter	Description
`-r`	Instruct the utility to create a self-signed certificate.
`-n "CN=PowerShell Local Certificate Root"`	This allows you to specify the X.500 name to use for the certificate subject. You're going to use `CN=PowerShell Local Certificate Root`.
`-a sha1`	This selects the algorithm used to generate the signature hash. The value can be either `md5` or `sha1`. The default is `md5`, but this is no longer considered robust so choose `sha1` instead.
`-eku 1.3.6.1.5.5.7.3.3`	Inserts a set of comma-separated Enhanced Key Usage (`eku`) object identifiers (or OIDs) into the certificate. In our case, the enhanced use you want is for code signing. That is, you want to create a key for the particular purpose of signing executable files.
`-sv root.pvk`	Specify the name of the file where the private key is to be written. In this example, a file called root.pvk will be created in the current directory.
`-ss Root`	Subject's certificate store name that stores the output certificate.
`-sr localMachine`	Specify whether the certificate is to be created in the current user's store or the local machine's store. The default is `CurrentUser`, but you want this certificate to be machine-wide so you specify `LocalMachine`.

Creating the signing certificate

Now that you've created a signing authority, you need to give yourself a signing certificate. Again, you can do this with `MakeCert.exe` by running the following command:

```
PS (3) > makecert -pe -n "CN=PowerShell User" -ss MY -a sha1 `
>> -eku 1.3.6.1.5.5.7.3.3 -iv root.pvk -ic root.cer
>>
Succeeded
PS (4) >
```

This code creates a certificate file in root.cer using the private key stored in the root.pvk file. Table 21.5 explains the options you're using in this command.

Table 21.5 `MakeCert` parameters used to create a code-signing certificate

`MakeCert` parameter	Description
`-pe`	Marks the generated private key as exportable. This allows the private key to be included in the certificate.
`-n "CN=PowerShell User"`	Specifies the X.500 name for the signer.
`-ss MY`	Specifies the subject's certificate store name that stores the output certificate.
`-a sha1`	Specifies the hash algorithm to use.
`-eku 1.3.6.1.5.5.7.3.3`	Specifies that you want code-signing certificates.
`-iv root.pvk`	Specifies where the certificate issuer's PVK private key file is. (You created this file in the previous step with the `-sv` parameter.)
`-ic root.cer`	Specifies the location where the issuer's certificate file should be written.

Let's check out what you've created. Let's look for files named "root" in the current directory:

```
PS (10) > dir root.*

    Directory: Microsoft.PowerShell.Core\FileSystem::C:\working\

Mode                LastWriteTime     Length Name
----                -------------     ------ ----
-a---         8/12/2006   6:32 PM        591 root.cer
-a---         8/12/2006   6:32 PM        636 root.pvk
```

In the first step, you create the file root.pvk—the private key—for your signing authority. In the second step, you create the certificate file root.cer that you need for signing. But the more important question is whether or not you created the certificate in the certificate store. You can verify this using the Certificate snap-in in MMC. Figure 21.4 shows what this looks like.

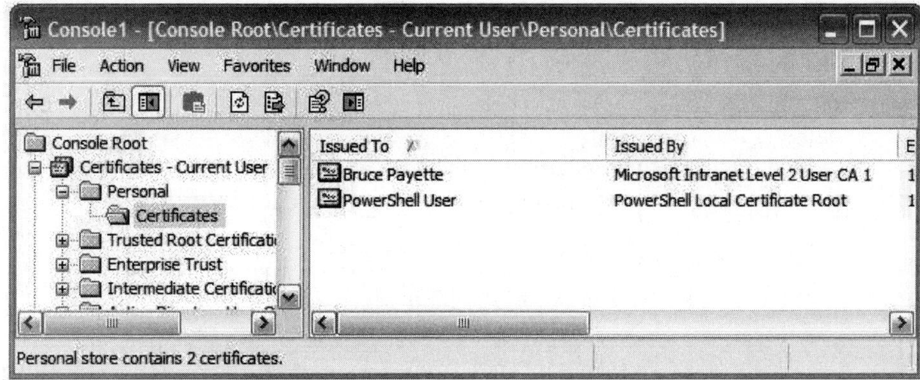

Figure 21.4 Verifying that the certificates have been created from the Certificates snap-in

Of course, this is PowerShell, so there must be a way to verify from the command line. You can do so using the PowerShell certificate provider by typing the following command:

```
PS (13) > dir cert:\CurrentUser\My -CodeSigningCert | fl

Subject      : CN=PowerShell User
Issuer       : CN=PowerShell Local Certificate Root
Thumbprint   : 145F9E3BF835CDA7DC21BD07BDB26B7FCFEA0687
FriendlyName :
NotBefore    : 8/12/2006 6:34:31 PM
NotAfter     : 12/31/2039 3:59:59 PM
Extensions   : {System.Security.Cryptography.Oid, System.
                Security.Cryptography.Oid}
```

If the certificate was created, the output shows you the thumbprint of the certificate, which contains authentication data for "PowerShell User." You have everything set up! You've established a signing authority and issued yourself a certificate. Let's move on and sign some scripts.

21.4.4 Using a certificate to sign a script

Now that you have a self-signed certificate, you can sign scripts. In this section, we'll go through the steps to do so. We'll also show you how to change the script execution policy to verify that your scripts are signed properly.

Setting up a test script

First, create an unsigned script that you can use for testing purposes:

```
PS (16) > '"Hello there"' > test-script.ps1
```

Assuming that your execution policy is currently set to something like `Remote-Signed` that lets you run local scripts, let's run `test-script.ps1`:

```
PS (17) > ./test-script.ps1
Hello there
```

Now change the execution policy to `AllSigned` and verify that you can't run unsigned scripts any longer. You'll use `Set-ExecutionPolicy`:

```
PS (18) > Set-ExecutionPolicy AllSigned
```

When you try to run the script, it will fail:

```
PS (19) > ./test-script.ps1
File C:\Temp\test-script.ps1 cannot be loaded. The file C:\Temp\
test-script.ps1 isn't digitally signed. The script will not
execute on the system. Please see "get-help about_signing" for more
 details..
At line:1 char:17
+ ./test-script.ps1 <<<<
```

The error message tells you that the script isn't signed and suggests a help topic that will explain what's going on. Next, let's sign the script.

Signing the test script

First you need to get a certificate object to use to sign the script. You use the PowerShell certificate provider to do this:

```
PS (20) > $cert = @(Get-ChildItem cert:\CurrentUser\My `
>> -codesigning)[0]
>>
PS (21) > $cert

    Directory: Microsoft.PowerShell.Security\Certificate::Curren
    tUser\My

Thumbprint                                Subject
----------                                -------
145F9E3BF835CDA7DC21BD07BDB26B7FCFEA0687  CN=PowerShell User
```

This shows that you have a certificate object in `$cert`. Use the `Set-Authenticode-Signature` cmdlet (remember, tab completion works on cmdlet names) to sign this file:

```
PS (22) > Set-AuthenticodeSignature test-script.ps1 $cert

    Directory: C:\Temp

SignerCertificate                         Status       Path
-----------------                         ------       ----
145F9E3BF835CDA7DC21BD07BDB26B7FCFEA0687  Valid        test-sc...
```

This cmdlet returns the signature information for the signed file. Now try to run it:

```
PS (23) > ./test-script

Do you want to run software from this untrusted publisher?
File C:\Temp\test-script.ps1 is published by CN=PowerShell User
and isn't trusted on your system. Only run scripts from trusted
 publishers.
[V] Never run  [D] Do not run  [R] Run once  [A] Always run
[?] Help(default is "D"): a
Hello there
```

Notice that you're prompted to confirm that this signing authority should be trusted. Assuming you trust yourself, you answer that you should always trust the signing authority you created. Now let's run this script again:

```
PS (24) > ./test-script
Hello there
```

This time, you didn't get prompted, because you've told the system that this certificate should always be trusted.

So what exactly happened to the script? It used to be one line long. Let's look at the beginning of the script. Use the `Select-Object` cmdlet to get the first 10 lines of the file:

```
PS (25) > Get-Content Test-Script.ps1 | Select-Object -First 10
"Hello there"

# SIG # Begin signature block
# MIIEMwYJKoZIhvcNAQcCoIIEJDCCBCACAQExCzAJBgUrDgMCGgUAMGkGCisGAQQB
# gjcCAQSgWzBZMDQGCisGAQQBgjcCAR4wJgIDAQABBAfzDtgWUsITrck0sYpfvNR
# AgEAAgEAAgEAAgEAAgEAMCEwCQYFKw4DAhoFAAQU0O2MiFZBx/X1iLwTml3Dg6o3
# iOygggI9MIICOTCCAaagAwIBAgIQ0QlVf5hB+oZM3DApkhHZMTAJBgUrDgMCHQUA
# MCwxKjAoBgNVBAMTIVBvd2VyU2hlbGwgTG9jYWwgQ2VydGlmaWNhdGUgUm9vdDAe
# Fw0wNjA4MTMwMTM0MzFaFw0zOTEyMzEyMzU5NTlaMBoxGDAWBgNVBAMTD1Bvd2Vy
# U2hlbGwgVXNlcjCBnzANBgkqhkiG9w0BAQEFAAOBjQAwgYkCgYEAtB75pWZTD5Jo
```

How long is the file? Let's check:

```
PS (26) > (Get-Content Test-Script.ps1).count
27
```

Signing the file increased the size from 1 line to 27. As you can see, signing a file adds a lot of ugly comments to the end of the file. You can use `Get-Authenticode-Signature` to retrieve the signature information from the file:

```
PS (28) > Get-AuthenticodeSignature test-script.ps1 | Format-List

SignerCertificate      : [Subject]
                           CN=PowerShell User

                         [Issuer]
                           CN=PowerShell Local Certificate Root
```

```
                                        [Serial Number]
                                          D109557F9841FA864CDC30299211D931

                                        [Not Before]
                                          8/12/2006 6:34:31 PM

                                        [Not After]
                                          12/31/2039 3:59:59 PM

                                        [Thumbprint]
                                          145F9E3BF835CDA7DC21BD07BDB26B7FCFEA0
                                        687

TimeStamperCertificate :
Status                 : Valid
StatusMessage          : Signature verified.
Path                   : C:\Temp\test-script.ps1
```

Among other things, this code shows you who signed the file (PowerShell User) and who issued the certificate (PowerShell Local Certificate Root), both of which you've just created. Now let's see what happens if you tamper with this file.

Testing the integrity of the script

Let's use an editor and duplicate the "Hello there" line in the script:

```
PS (29) > notepad test-script.ps1
```

So the file looks like

```
PS (30) > Get-Content test-script.ps1 | Select-Object -first 10
"Hello there"
"Hello there"

# SIG # Begin signature block
# MIIEMwYJKoZIhvcNAQcCoIIEJDCCBCACAQExCzAJBgUrDgMCGgUAMGkGCisGAQQB
# gjcCAQSgWzBZMDQGCisGAQQBgjcCAR4wJgIDAQAABBAfzDtgWUsITrck0sYpfvNR
# AgEAAgEAAgEAAgEAAgEAMCEwCQYFKw4DAhoFAAQU0O2MiFZBx/X1iLwTml3Dg6o3
# iOygggI9MIICOTCCAaagAwIBAgIQ0QlVf5hB+oZM3DApkhHZMTAJBgUrDgMCHQUA
# MCwxKjAoBgNVBAMTIVBvd2VyU2hlbGwgTG9jYWwgQ2VydGlmaWNhdGUgUm9vdDAe
# Fw0wNjA4MTMwMTM0MzFaFw0zOTEyMzEyMzU5NTlaMBoxGDAWBgNVBAMTD1Bvd2Vy
```

Try to run the modified file:

```
PS (31) > ./test-script
File C:\Temp\test-script.ps1 cannot be loaded. The contents of file
            C:\Temp\test-script.ps1 may have been tampered because the
            hash of the file does not match the hash stored in the digital
            signature. The script will not execute on the system. Please
            see "get-help about_signing" for more details..
At line:1 char:13
+ ./test-script <<<<
```

It fails with an error telling you that the file has been tampered with. This shows how signing is used to verify the integrity of the script. Let's look at the last topic we're going to cover on signing scripts.

21.4.5 Enabling strong private key protection

When you create a private certificate on your computer, it's possible that malicious programs might be able to access the certificate and sign scripts on your behalf. The malicious program could then create Trojan scripts that appear to be legitimately signed.

To address this vulnerability, you'll use the Certificate Manager tool (`Certmgr.exe`), another utility included in the .NET SDK and the Microsoft Platform SDK. It's also included with Internet Explorer 5 and later.

The Certificate Manager enables you to export the signing certificate to a PFX file. Once you have the PFX available, you can use it to sign a document, but you'll have to interactively provide a password as part of the signing process. This interactive step prevents a malicious program from quietly signing scripts. A user has to provide the password.

In this section, we'll go over the steps necessary to export a certificate, and then you'll use the exported file to re-sign the file you tampered with in section 21.4.3.

Exporting the certificate

Exporting a certificate using the Certificate Manager is a straightforward task. You'll take the certificate you created in the previous sections and export it to a file called mycert.pfx.

Step 1: Start Certmgr.exe and select the certificate to export

First you start the Certificate Manager (which is a graphical tool). A window opens on your desktop that looks something like figure 21.5.

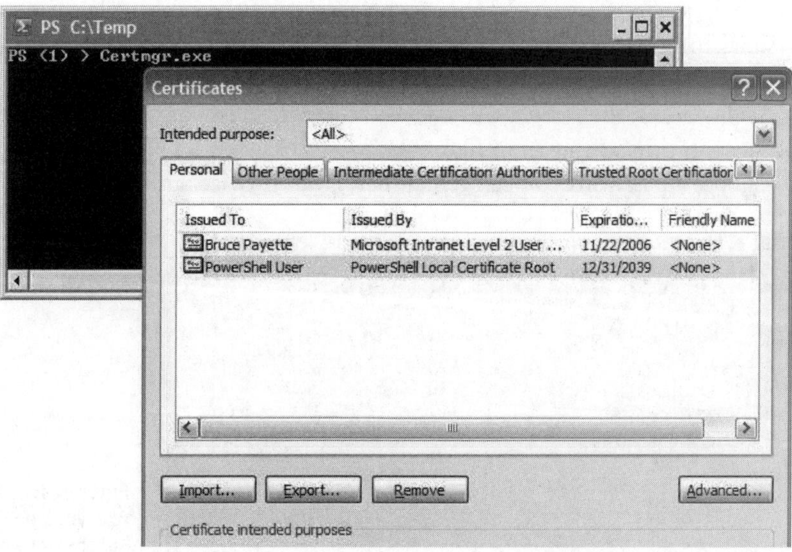

Figure 21.5 Launching the Certificate Manager tool

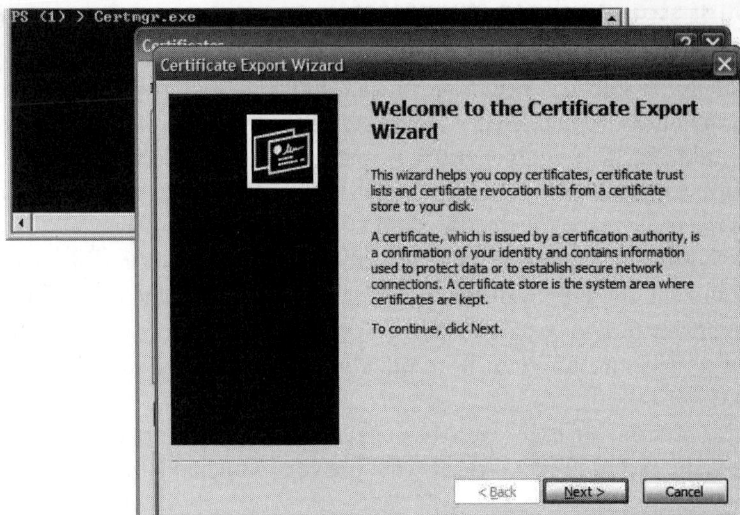

Figure 21.6 Launching the Certificate Export Wizard

The Certificate Manager window will display one or more certificates. Select the certificate you created in section 21.4.2. This will be the one issued by the PowerShell Local Certificate Root. When you've selected the certificate, click Export to start the Certificate Export Wizard. Now you should see something that looks like figure 21.6.

Click Next. This will take you to a dialog with two option buttons. Select the "Yes, export the private key" option and click Next.

Step 2: Specify the file format and password

The next step in the wizard will ask you to specify the export file format. Select the Personal Information Exchange option. If it's visible, be sure that the Enable Strong Protection check box is selected (this should be the default).

At this point, the system will ask you to enter a password to use to protect the key you're exporting, as shown in figure 21.7.

Choose a password you can remember, enter it twice, and click Next.

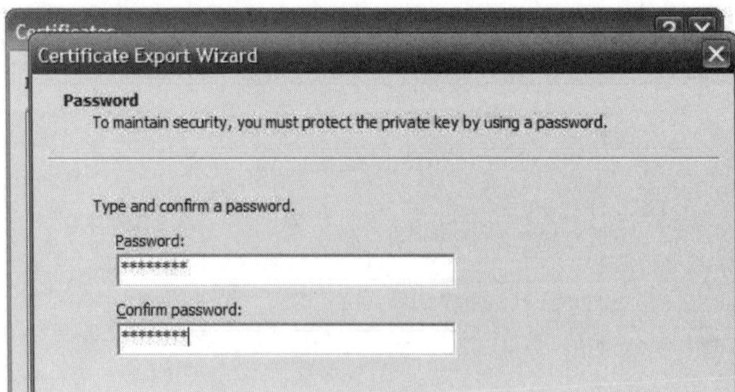

Figure 21.7 In this figure, you see the dialog to set the password used to secure the private key.

Step 3: Specify the name for the PFX file

Now you enter the name of the file you want to create with a .pfx extension. Call it mycert.pfx. Click Next, verify the information, and click Finish. The export is done.

Step 4: Verify that the PFX file was created

Verify that the file was created by entering the following command:

```
PS (1) > Certmgr.exe
CertMgr Succeeded
PS (2) > dir *.pfx

    Directory: Microsoft.PowerShell.Core\FileSystem::C:\Temp

Mode                LastWriteTime     Length Name
----                -------------     ------ ----
-a---          8/13/2006   5:38 PM      1768 mycert.pfx
```

And there it is: mycert.pfx as requested.

21.4.6 Using the PFX file to sign a file

You can use this file to get a signing certificate by using the `Get-PfxCertificate` cmdlet:

```
PS (3) > $cert = Get-PfxCertificate mycert.pfx
Enter password: ********

PS (4) > $cert

Thumbprint                                Subject
----------                                -------
145F9E3BF835CDA7DC21BD07BDB26B7FCFEA0687  CN=PowerShell User
```

Let's use this certificate object to re-sign the file you tampered with earlier:

```
PS (5) > Set-AuthenticodeSignature test-script.ps1 $cert

    Directory: C:\Temp

SignerCertificate                         Status       Path
-----------------                         ------       ----
145F9E3BF835CDA7DC21BD07BDB26B7FCFEA0687  Valid        test-sc...
```

Next, make sure that the execution policy is set to `AllSigned`, and then run the script:

```
PS (6) > Set-ExecutionPolicy allsigned
PS (7) > ./test-script.ps1
Hello there
Hello there
PS (8) >
```

The script runs properly. There's no prompt because you've already told the system that you trust this signing authority.

We've concluded our discussion of signing as well as our discussion on securing PowerShell installations. In the next (and final) part of this chapter, we're going to shift our focus away from securing PowerShell and over to writing secure PowerShell scripts.

21.5 WRITING SECURE SCRIPTS

As you've seen, the PowerShell team has been careful in designing the various security features in the PowerShell runtime. In the end, though, the whole point of PowerShell is to allow people to create and run scripts that will automate system administration tasks. As a consequence, vulnerable or badly written scripts could inadvertently lead to substantial damage to the system. All the security features in the world can't defend you from badly written scripts, so we're going to look at some of the techniques you can use to make your code more secure.

In fact, we (the PowerShell team) have been described as obsessive in our security focus. Here's a quote from Microsoft security guru Michael Howard:

> *I want folks to realize that the PowerShell guys are very, VERY savvy when it comes to security. In fact, they are borderline anal. Actually, they're not borderline at all.*

21.6 USING THE SECURESTRING CLASS

At some point, you'll want to write a script that acquires passwords or other sensitive data such as credit card numbers. PowerShell, through .NET, provides a number of features for dealing with sensitive data in a secure way. In this section, we're going to discuss how to use those features to write scripts that can deal with sensitive information.

Most of the sensitive data you'll be dealing with will be in the form of strings. When a string is created in .NET, the runtime retains that string in memory so it can efficiently reuse it. Even after you're done with the data, the string will remain in memory until it's finally cleaned up by the garbage collector process from the .NET Framework. So what's the big deal—if an attacker can access the process's memory, we're already compromised, right? That's true if the information only stays in memory, but there are a number of ways that it could end up being persisted to the disk. For one thing, Windows uses virtual memory. This means that blocks of memory are periodically paged to disk. Once it's on the disk, it potentially becomes available to applications that can do raw accesses to the disk. Now, this may require the attacker to steal your hard disk and use forensic tools to analyze it, but it's possible and has happened before. Similarly, using Hibernate on a laptop will write an image of memory to the disk. Finally, the string could wind up on the disk due to a crash dump, where an image of the computer's memory is dumped to the disk during a system crash.

How can you avoid these problems? When writing .NET programs, the way to safely work with strings containing sensitive data is to use the `System.Security.SecureString` class. This type is a container for text data that the .NET runtime stores in memory in an encrypted form. The most common way to get secure strings is using the Get-Credential cmdlet or the [System.Management.Automation.PSCredential] type. This type also forms the basis for writing secure scripts in PowerShell using the SecureString cmdlets, which we'll look at next.

21.6.1 Creating a SecureString object

When you write a script or function that requires sensitive data such as passwords, the best practice is to designate that password parameter as a SecureString object in order to help keep passwords confidential. Let's look at a how you can create a secure string. The simplest way is to use the -AsSecureString parameter on the Read-Host cmdlet:

```
PS (1) > Read-Host -AsSecureString -Prompt "Password"
Password: ********
System.Security.SecureString
```

Let's take a look at the members on the SecureString object using the Get-Member cmdlet:

```
PS (2) > $ss = Read-Host -AsSecureString -Prompt "Password"
Password: ********
PS (3) > $ss | Get-Member

   TypeName: System.Security.SecureString

Name          MemberType Definition
----          ---------- ----------
AppendChar    Method     System.Void AppendChar(Char c)
Clear         Method     System.Void Clear()
Copy          Method     System.Security.SecureString Copy()
Dispose       Method     System.Void Dispose()
Equals        Method     System.Boolean Equals(Object obj)
get_Length    Method     System.Int32 get_Length()
GetHashCode   Method     System.Int32 GetHashCode()
GetType       Method     System.Type GetType()
InsertAt      Method     System.Void InsertAt(Int32 index, Cha...
IsReadOnly    Method     System.Boolean IsReadOnly()
MakeReadOnly  Method     System.Void MakeReadOnly()
RemoveAt      Method     System.Void RemoveAt(Int32 index)
SetAt         Method     System.Void SetAt(Int32 index, Char c)
ToString      Method     System.String ToString()
Length        Property   System.Int32 Length {get;}
```

The only way you can convert an existing string to a secure string is by appending one character at a time to the secure string. Let's append another character to the string:

```
PS (4) > $ss.AppendChar("1")
```

Here's a way to make a secure string out of a normal one. First, you create an instance of the secure string class:

```
PS (9) > $ss = New-Object System.Security.SecureString
```

Then you send each character to the foreach cmdlet and append it to that secure string. Normally strings in PowerShell don't stream by default, but if you explicitly get an enumerator, it's possible to stream a string one character at a time:

```
PS (10) > "Hello there".GetEnumerator() | foreach {$ss.AppendChar($_)}
```

Now let's look at the results:

```
PS (11) > $ss
System.Security.SecureString
```

Not very interesting, is it? But that's the point. It's secure—there's no easy way to get the data back. Let's take one final precaution. You don't want your secure string tampered with, so make it read-only:

```
PS (12) > $ss.MakeReadOnly()
PS (13) > $ss.IsReadOnly()
True
```

If you try to modify it, you'll get an error:

```
PS (14) > $ss.AppendChar('!')
Exception calling "AppendChar" with "1" argument(s): "Instance i
s read-only."
At line:1 char:15
+ $ss.AppendChar( <<<< '!')
```

Marking a secure string read-only once it's complete is generally considered to be a best practice. Doing it all by hand is a bit painful, so PowerShell includes some cmdlets to make this process much easier.

21.6.2 The SecureString cmdlets

Manually building secure strings is a bit tedious, so PowerShell has two cmdlets for working with secure strings: ConvertTo-SecureString and ConvertFrom-SecureString. These cmdlets allow you to write data to disk in a reasonably secure fashion.

By default, the SecureString cmdlets use the Windows Data Protection API (DPAPI) when they convert your SecureString to and from a plain-text representation. The DPAPI is the standard way on the Microsoft Windows platform for programs to protect sensitive data. The encryption key that the DPAPI uses is based on Windows logon credentials. This means that you don't have to specify a key to encrypt or decrypt data—the system will generate one for you automatically based on your logon credentials. This means that you can only decrypt your own data using this mechanism. If you have to export or share encrypted data across multiple machines or with additional users, then you have to create and manage a key for those purposes.

There are many instances when you may want to automatically provide the SecureString input to a cmdlet, rather than have the host prompt you for it. In these situations, the ideal solution is to import a previously exported SecureString

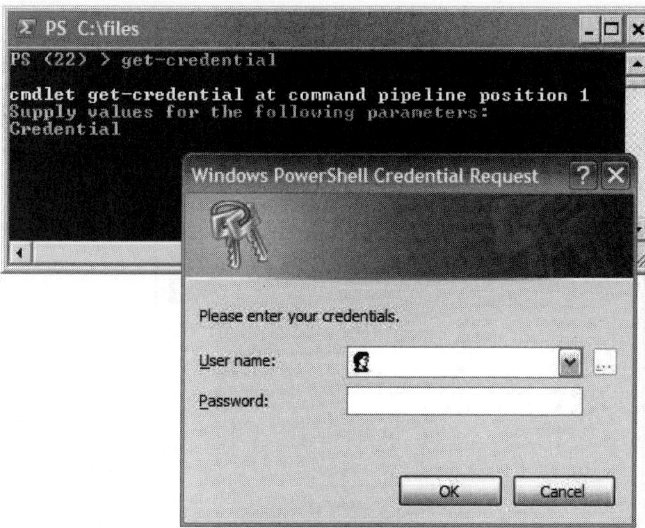

Figure 21.8 When you use the `Get-Credential` cmdlet, it will open a dialog box that looks like this.

from disk (using `ConvertTo-SecureString`). This approach retains the confidentiality of your data and still allows you to automate the input.

If the data is highly dynamic (for example, coming from a CSV file), then the best approach is to use something like this:

```
$secureString = ConvertTo-SecureString "Kinda Secret" `
    -AsPlainText -Force
```

The cmdlet requires the `-Force` parameter to ensure you acknowledge the fact that PowerShell can't protect plain-text data, even after you've put it in a `SecureString`.

One of the areas where secure strings are particularly important is in credential management. Credentials include passwords, and you want to minimize the amount of time passwords are exposed in a readable form.

21.6.3 Working with credentials

To do any sort of administrative work on a computer, at some point you're going to need to get the credentials of the user account authorized to do the work. Obviously, it's bad practice to put passwords in scripts, so you should always prompt for passwords or credentials. In PowerShell, you do so using the `Get-Credential` cmdlet, as shown in figure 21.8.

Running the `Get-Credential` cmdlet returns a credential object that you can then use for operations that require a password. To do this, you need to store the credential object in a variable as shown:

```
PS (2) > $cred = Get-Credential

cmdlet Get-Credential at command pipeline position 1
Supply values for the following parameters:
Credential
```

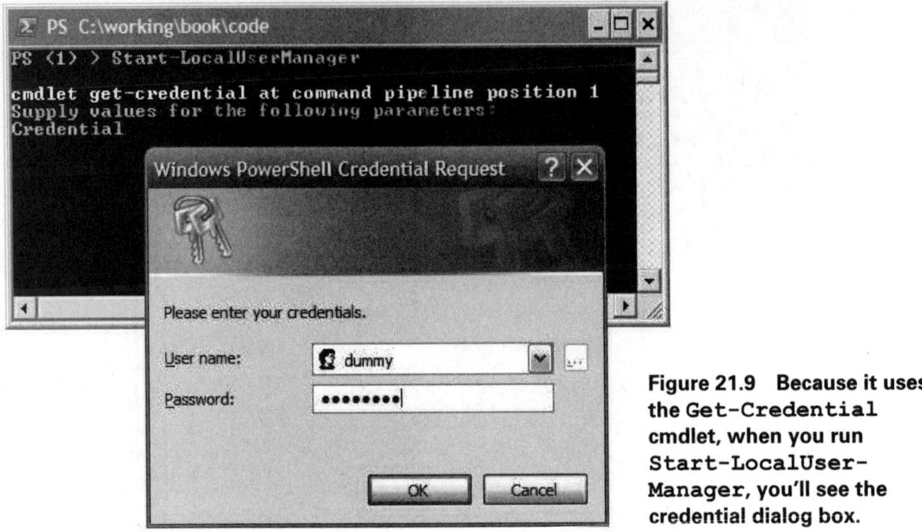

Figure 21.9 Because it uses the `Get-Credential` cmdlet, when you run `Start-LocalUser-Manager`, you'll see the credential dialog box.

Now let's display this credential object:

```
PS (3) > $cred

UserName                                              Password
--------                                              --------
mymachine\myuserid                    System.Security.SecureString
```

The domain and username are stored as a regular string, but the password has been stored as an instance of the type `System.Security.SecureString`. As discussed previously, this allows the credential object to remain in memory without presenting a significant security risk.

Let's look at an example where you want to use the credential object. Let's write a function called `Start-LocalUserManager` that will start a process using different credentials. This works approximately like the `runas.exe` command. You'll use this function to launch the Local User Administration dialog box. When you run the script, you'll see something that resembles figure 21.9.

In this example, enter the username and password for a user who hasn't logged in yet, so you'll get an error:

```
PS (1) > Start-LocalUserManager

cmdlet Get-Credential at command pipeline position 1
Supply values for the following parameters:
Credential
Exception calling "Start" with "1" argument(s): "The user's pass
word must be changed before logging on the first time"
At line:12 char:36
+ [System.Diagnostics.Process]::Start( <<<< $StartInfo)
PS (2) >
```

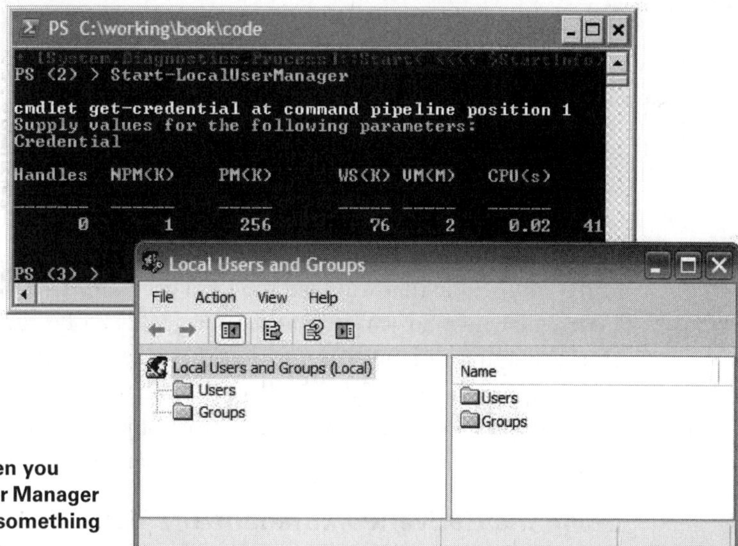

Figure 21.10 When you start the Local User Manager snap-in, you'll see something that looks like this.

Now try it again but with a valid user account. This time you see the Local User and Groups management console appear, as shown in figure 21.10.

Let's see how this `Start-LocalUserManager` function is implemented. The source for this function is shown in listing 21.1.

> **NOTE** This listing shows how the function would have to be implemented in PowerShell v1. In PowerShell v2, it simply becomes a call to the `Start-Process` cmdlet where most of the laborious construction of the `ProcessStartInfo` object is handled by the cmdlet. The actual conversion to the `Start-Process` implementation is left as an exercise for the reader.

Listing 21.1 The `Start-LocalUserManager` function

```
function Start-LocalUserManager
{
    $cred = Get-Credential
    $StartInfo = New-Object System.Diagnostics.ProcessStartInfo
    $StartInfo.UserName = $cred.Username
    $StartInfo.Password = $cred.Password
    $StartInfo.FileName = "$env:windir\system32\mmc.exe"
    $StartInfo.Arguments = "$env:windir\system32\lusrmgr.msc"
    $StartInfo.WorkingDirectory = "$env:windir\system32"
    $StartInfo.LoadUserProfile = $true
    $StartInfo.UseShellExecute = $false
    [System.Diagnostics.Process]::Start($StartInfo)
}
```

Because the function will prompt for credentials, you don't need to give it any arguments. The first thing you do is call `Get-Credential` to get the credential information that you want the process to run with. Then you create a `ProcessStartInfo` object that you'll use to set the various properties you want the process to have when it starts. The most important of these in this example are the `UserName` and `Password` properties. The `Process` object will safely decrypt the password `SecureString` using the DPAPI when creating the process. Next you set the program you want to run—the Microsoft Management Console (`mmc.exe`)—and give it the path to the MMC console file that will load the local user admin MMC snap-in. You're running as a particular user, so you want the user profile to be run and you don't want to use `ShellExecute` to launch the process because then you wouldn't be able to pass the credentials to the underlying `CreateProcess()` call. Once you've finished setting all the properties on the `ProcessStartInfo` object, you call the static `Start()` method on `[System.Diagnostics.Process]` to start the process running.

Using the GetNetworkCredential() Method

Using secure strings to store passwords in the `PSCredential` object works well when you're calling an API that can handle passwords stored in secure strings. Unfortunately, this isn't always the case and sometimes you need to use the password in clear text. You encountered this situation in section 18.6.4 while working with the Task Scheduler COM API. As you saw in that example, the `PSCredential` object includes a `GetNetworkCredential()` method that will return the username and password in clear text. Let's quickly review how this works. First you call `Get-Credential` to get the credential object:

```
PS (1) > $cred = Get-Credential

cmdlet Get-Credential at command pipeline position 1
Supply values for the following parameters:
Credential
```

When you display this object, you can see the username and domain but not the password:

```
PS (2) > $cred

UserName                                              Password
--------                                              --------
smith\john                        System.Security.SecureString
```

Now let's call the `GetNetworkCredential()` method and see what it shows:

```
PS (3) > $cred.GetNetworkCredential()

UserName                Password                Domain
--------                --------                ------
john                    Its_a_secret            smith
```

You can see everything in clear text, including the password. At this point, some people might wonder why you bother with secure strings at all if it's so easy to get the data back. The thing to remember is that *you* typed in the password in the first place so it isn't telling you anything you don't already know. As discussed in section 21.5.1, the intent is to minimize the amount of time the password is exposed as clear text, thereby minimizing the amount of time it might be captured during a crash dump or hibernate.

You now have a good working knowledge of secure strings and credentials, but these technologies by themselves don't guarantee security. If an exploitable vulnerability exists in the script itself, all your careful credential management will be useless. Let's look at some things you need to be particularly aware of when trying to write secure scripts.

21.6.4 Avoiding Invoke-Expression

At the beginning of this chapter, we talked about the risks of using the `Invoke-Expression` cmdlet and code injection attacks in general. If you can avoid using this cmdlet, it's a good idea for two reasons: first, not using it makes your code less vulnerable, and second, `Invoke-Expression` has performance consequences because it requires that the expression be recompiled every time it gets called. In most circumstances, it's possible to rewrite your code using scriptblocks instead of `Invoke-Expression`.

> **WARNING** If you use the features described in section 13.2.5, `Invoke-Expression` is one cmdlet that should always be omitted from that session configuration. You should also be careful with any code in a constrained session that uses `Invoke-Expression` and make sure that a thorough security review of that code is done.

In this section, we'll work through a real example where you take a piece of script code using `Invoke-Expression` and rewrite it to use scriptblocks.

The original wheres script

The idea behind this script was to come up with a version of the `Where-Object` cmdlet that had a simpler syntax. The function was created by one of the developers on the PowerShell team. Instead of typing a command line that looked like this

```
PS (3) > dir | where {$_.extension -eq ".ps1"}

    Directory: Microsoft.PowerShell.Core\FileSystem::C:\Temp

Mode                LastWriteTime     Length Name
----                -------------     ------ ----
-a---         8/13/2006   5:44 PM       3250 test-script.ps1
```

he wanted to simply type

```
PS (1) > dir | wheres extension eq .ps1

    Directory: Microsoft.PowerShell.Core\FileSystem::C:\Temp

Mode                LastWriteTime     Length Name
----                -------------     ------ ----
-a---         8/13/2006   5:44 PM       3250 test-script.ps1
```

There's certainly a lot less punctuation in the second command line, so it seems a worthy goal. The original version of the command is shown in the following listing.

Listing 21.2 The original `wheres` function

```
function wheres($property, $operator, $matchText)
{
   begin {
$expression = "`$_.$property -$operator `"$matchText`""
   }
   process {
       if( Invoke-Expression $expression)
       {
           $_
       }
    }
}
```

This function takes three parameters—the property on the inbound pipeline object to check, the operation to perform, and the value to check against. In the `begin` clause of the function, you precalculate as much of the expression as possible, expanding the property name and the operator into `$expression`. This gets rid of the string expansion step that would otherwise be performed for each pipeline object. Finally, in the `process` clause of the function, `Invoke-Expression` is used to evaluate the expression for the current pipeline object and emit the object if it matches.

This is a straightforward implementation of the function, but there's one worrisome aspect. Executing a command such as the following is fine

```
dir | wheres mode match d
```

but something like this

```
dir | wheres extension eq '.ps1"; Write-Host hi; "'
```

will both interfere with the results you expect and execute the extra code `Write-Host hi`. If the extra code were something like `del -Force -Recurse c:\`, then it'd be more than merely annoying.

Of course, the author of this script would never do anything like this. But someone else who's just using the script might think it's safe to pass untrusted arguments to it. After all, looking at it from the outside, there are no obvious code injection vulnerabilities. It appears to accept a simple operator, nothing more. This is why you need to be cautious with this kind of script—because of the cascading consequences problem we discussed at the beginning of the chapter. This script appears on a blog, gets copied into someone else's application, which gets copied into a third individual's web application, and now this script that was never intended to be used with untrusted input is being used for exactly that in a network-facing application. Not a good situation. Let's see what you can do to make the script more robust and also run faster at the same time.

A safer, faster wheres script

The problem with the old script was that it used `Invoke-Expression` to evaluate an expression at runtime. You want to use scriptblocks to be a bit more static in your approach. The solution is shown here.

Listing 21.3 The safe `wheres` function

```
function wheres
{
    begin {
        if ($args.count -ne 3)                          ❶ Validate arguments
        {
            throw "wheres: syntax <prop> <op> <val>"
        }
        $prop,$op,$y= $args
        $op_fn = $(
            switch ($op)
            {
                eq      {{$x.$prop -eq $y}; break}              ❷ Implement EQ
                ne      {{$x.$prop -ne $y}; break}
                gt      {{$x.$prop -gt $y}; break}
                ge      {{$x.$prop -ge $y}; break}
                lt      {{$x.$prop -lt $y}; break}
                le      {{$x.$prop -le $y}; break}
                like    {{$x.$prop -like $y}; break}
                notlike {{$x.$prop -notlike $y}; break}
                match   {{$x.$prop -match $y}; break}          ❸ Throw error
                notmatch {{$x.$prop -notmatch $y}; break}        on unknown
                default {                                        operator
                    throw "wh: operator '$op' isn't defined"
                }
            }
        )
    }                                                   ❹ Invoke operator
    process { $x=$_; if( . $op_fn) { $x }}                function
}
```

In this version of the function, you begin by validating the number of arguments ❶ and reporting an error if there aren't three arguments. You want to place a scriptblock in the variable `$op_fn`, which you'll use to implement the processing for that operator. You use a `switch` statement to select the right scriptblock to return. There's one scriptblock for each operator; for example, the `eq` operator is shown in ❷. If the operator isn't one of the ones you've chosen to implement, you'll throw an error ❸.

Once you've selected the scriptblock, you'll invoke it ❹ once for each inbound pipeline object. Notice that you don't pass any arguments to the scriptblock. Dynamic scoping allows the scriptblock to pick up the arguments from the enclosing scope.

This second implementation is clearly more complex, but it does more error checking, is more robust in general, and has no code injection vulnerabilities. It's also significantly faster than the `Invoke-Expression` version. (It also makes a good illustration of the use of scriptblocks.)

There are many more examples where you can replace `Invoke-Expression` with scriptblocks, but in the end, the approach is basically the same—decide whether you really need to generate code at runtime or whether you can just select from a set of precompiled alternatives. If the set of alternatives is large, you may want to use a hashtable instead of a `switch` statement, but the principle remains the same.

This brings us to the end of our discussion of security and PowerShell. Securing systems and writing secure code can be a subtle, twisty, and arcane topic. It can also be alternately completely fascinating or as dull as toast.

21.7 SUMMARY

Let's review what we covered in this chapter. We began with a rant (sorry—discussion) on security and threat modeling. We discussed:

- What security is—mechanisms for operating a computer without the risk of danger or loss
- That security isn't equivalent to cryptography and its related technologies (although these tools are used to build a secure system)
- Basic threat modeling and the STRIDE approach
- Definitions for the elements of a threat model: vulnerability, threat, asset, and mitigation

In the next section, we covered securing the PowerShell installation itself. This included discussions of how PowerShell is secure by default. As installed, PowerShell limits its attack surface by

- Having no default file association; this prevents use of attachment invocation or point-and-click social engineering attacks.
- Exposing no remote access endpoints, forcing a hopeful attacker to depend on other tools.
- Having a default execution policy of `Restricted`, which prevents any scripts from running.
- Not including the current directory in the command search path, preventing working directory exploits.

- Additional issues around managing the execution path.
- Execution policy—what it is and how you can examine the current execution policy using `Get-ExecutionPolicy`. To allow signed scripts to run, use `Set-ExecutionPolicy AllSigned`, and to allow any local scripts to run—the loosest reasonable policy—use `Set-ExecutionPolicy RemoteSigned`.
- Script signing—how it works and how to set up certificates, keys, and so on.

The final part of the chapter explored technologies and techniques you can use for making your scripts more robust. The topics included

- The fact that you should always store sensitive information in memory using the .NET `SecureString` class and that you can read data as a secure string from the keyboard using the `Read-Host` cmdlet
- Working with credentials and using the `Get-Credential` cmdlet
- Approaches for avoiding the use of `Invoke-Expression` in scripts

Computer security is a complex, evolving field. It's obviously important to keep abreast of the latest tools and techniques, as well as monitor the current crop of threats and exploits. Thinking through a problem can be facilitated by tools and models, but in the end, there's no replacement for common sense.

You're done with your journey through the PowerShell world. It's been a rather long journey—the scope and range of what can be done with PowerShell can be both dazzling and daunting at times. But always remember that PowerShell is a tool created for you, the user. Don't be afraid to experiment with it, play with it, and then apply it. To quote Jeffrey Snover, the inventor of PowerShell:

> *All you need to do is to learn what you need to accomplish the task at hand...and a bit more. Then do it again. And again. And again. Have fun with it and push the envelope.*

index

Symbols

Numerics

A

B

C

D

E

F

G

H

I

J

M

O

P

Q

R

S

T

U

V

W

X

Z